Professional C#

Third Edition

Professional C#

Third Edition

Simon Robinson
Christian Nagel
Jay Glynn
Morgan Skinner
Karli Watson
Bill Evjen

WILEY
Wiley Publishing, Inc.

Professional C#, Third Edition
Published by
Wiley Publishing, Inc.
10475 Crosspoint Boulevard
Indianapolis, IN 46256
www.wiley.com

Library of Congress Control Number: 2004103177

ISBN: 0-7645-5759-9

Printed in the United States of America

10 9 8 7 6 5 4 3 2 1

About the Authors

Simon Robinson

Simon Robinson is the editor-in-chief of ASP Today, one of the leading sites related to Web programming on the Windows platform.

Simon's first experience of commercial computer programming was in the early 1980s, when a computer project he was working on at college became the school's student timetabling program, running on the BBC Micro. Later he studied for a Ph.D. in physics and subsequently spent a couple of years working as a university physics researcher. From there he moved on to working as a computer programmer, then writing books about programming, and finally on to his present job at ASP Today.

He has an extremely broad experience of programming on Windows. These days his core specialty is .NET programming. He is comfortable coding in C++, C#, VB, and IL, and has skills ranging from graphics and Windows Forms to ASP.NET to directories and data access to Windows services and the native Windows API.

Simon lives in Lancaster, UK. His outside interests include theater, dance, performing arts, and politics. You can visit Simon's Web site, http://www.SimonRobinson.com.

Christian Nagel

Christian Nagel is an independent software architect and developer who offers training and consulting on how to design and develop Microsoft .NET solutions. He looks back to more than 15 years' experience as a developer and software architect. Christian started his computing career with PDP 11 and VAX/VMS platforms, covering a variety of languages and platforms. Since the year 2000—when .NET was just a technology preview—he has been working with various .NET technologies to build distributed solutions. With his profound knowledge of Microsoft technologies, he has also written numerous .NET books; is certified as Microsoft Certified Trainer (MCT), Solution Developer (MCSD), and Systems Engineer (MCSE); and is the Microsoft Regional Director for Austria. Christian is a speaker at international conferences (TechED, DevDays, VCDC) and is the regional manager of INETA Europe (International .NET User Group Association) supporting .NET user groups. You can contact Christian via his Web site, http://www.christiannagel.com.

Jay Glynn

Jay Glynn started writing software nearly 20 years ago, writing applications for the PICK operating system using PICK basic. Since then, he has created software using Paradox PAL and Object PAL, Delphi, VBA, Visual Basic, C, C++, Java, and of course C#. He is currently a Project coordinator and Architect for a large financial services company in Nashville, Tennessee, working on software for the TabletPC platform. He can be contacted at jlsglynn@hotmail.com.

Morgan Skinner

Morgan Skinner began his computing career at a tender age on a Sinclair ZX80 at school, where he was underwhelmed by some code a teacher had written and so began programming in assembly language. After getting hooked on Z80 (which he believes is far better than those paltry 3 registers on the 6502), he graduated through the school's ZX81s to his own ZX Spectrum.

Since then he's used all sorts of languages and platforms, including VAX Macro Assembler, Pascal, Modula2, Smalltalk, X86 assembly language, PowerBuilder, C/C++, VB, and currently C#. He's been programming in .NET since the PDC release in 2000, and liked it so much, he joined Microsoft in 2001. He now works in Premier Support for Developers and spends most of his time assisting customers with C#.

You can reach Morgan at `http://www.morganskinner.com`.

Karli Watson

Karli Watson is a freelance author and the technical director of 3form Ltd (`http://www.3form.net`). Despite starting out by studying nanoscale physics, the lure of cold, hard cash proved too much and dragged Karli into the world of computing. He has since written numerous books on .NET and related technologies, SQL, mobile computing, and a novel that has yet to see the light of day (but that doesn't have any computers in it). Karli is also known for his multicolored clothing, is a snowboarding enthusiast, and still wishes he had a cat.

Bill Evjen

Bill Evjen is an active proponent of the .NET technologies and community-based learning initiatives for .NET. He has been actively involved with .NET since the first bits were released in 2000 and has since become president of the St. Louis .NET User Group (`http://www.stlusergroups.org`). Bill is also the founder and executive director of the International .NET ssociation (`http://www.ineta.org`), which represents more than 125,000 members worldwide. Based in St. Louis, Missouri, USA, Bill is an acclaimed author and speaker on ASP.NET and XML Web services. He has written *XML Web Services for ASP.NET*, *Web Services Enhancements: Understanding the WSE for Enterprise Applications*, *Visual Basic .NET Bible*, and *ASP.NET Professional Secrets* (all published by Wiley). Bill is a Technical Director for Reuters, the international news and financial services company. He graduated from Western Washington University in Bellingham, Washington, with a Russian language degree. You can reach Bill at `evjen@yahoo.com`.

Contributor

Allen Jones

Allen Jones has a career spanning 15 years that covers a broad range of IT disciplines, including enterprise management, solution and enterprise architecture, and project management. But software development has always been Allen's passion. Allen has architected and developed Microsoft Windows–based solutions since 1990, including a variety of e-commerce, trading, and security systems.

Allen has co-authored four popular .NET books including the *C# Programmer's Cookbook* (Microsoft Press) and *Programming .NET Security* (O'Reilly), and he is actively involved in the development of courseware for Microsoft Learning covering emerging .NET technologies.

Credits

Vice President and Executive Group Publisher
Richard Swadley

Vice President and Executive Publisher
Bob Ipsen

Vice President and Publisher
Joseph B. Wikert

Executive Editorial Director
Mary Bednarek

Acquisitions Editors
Sharon Cox
Katie Mohr

Editorial Manager
Kathryn A. Malm

Development Editor
Sharon Nash

Production Editor
Eric Newman

Text Design & Composition
Wiley Indianapolis Composition Services

Contents

Contents

Contents

Contents

Contents

Contents

Contents

Contents

Contents

Introduction

If we were to describe the C# language and its associated environment, the .NET Framework, as the most important new technology for developers for many years, we would not be exaggerating. .NET is designed to provide a new environment within which you can develop almost any application to run on Windows, while C# is a new programming language that has been designed specifically to work with .NET. Using C# you can, for example, write a dynamic Web page, an XML Web service, a component of a distributed application, a database access component, or a classic Windows desktop application. This book covers the .NET Framework 1.1, the second release of the framework, though most of this book also applies to .NET Framework 1.0. If you are coding using version 1.0, then you might have to make some changes, which we try to note throughout the book.

Don't be fooled by the .NET label. The NET bit in the name is there to emphasize Microsoft's belief that distributed applications, in which the processing is distributed between client and server, are the way forward, but C# is not just a language for writing Internet or network-aware applications. It provides a means for you to code up almost any type of software or component that you might need to write for the Windows platform. Between them, C# and .NET are set both to revolutionize the way that you write programs, and to make programming on Windows much easier than it has ever been.

That's quite a substantial claim, and it needs to be justified. After all, we all know how quickly computer technology changes. Every year Microsoft brings out new software, programming tools, or versions of Windows, with the claim that these will be hugely beneficial to developers. So what's different about .NET and C#?

The Significance of .NET and C#

In order to understand the significance of .NET, it is useful to remind ourselves of the nature of many of the Windows technologies that have appeared in the past ten years or so. Although they may look quite different on the surface, all of the Windows operating systems from Windows 3.1 (introduced in 1992) through Windows Server 2003 have the same familiar Windows API at their core. As we've progressed through new versions of Windows, huge numbers of new functions have been added to the API, but this has been a process of evolving and extending the API rather than replacing it.

The same can be said for many of the technologies and frameworks that we've used to develop software for Windows. For example, **COM (Component Object Model)** originated as **OLE (Object Linking and Embedding)**. At the time, it was, to a large extent, simply a means by which different types of Office documents could be linked, so that for example you could place a small Excel spreadsheet in your Word document. From that it evolved into COM, **DCOM (Distributed COM)**, and eventually COM+—a sophisticated technology that formed the basis of the way almost all components communicated, as well as implementing transactions, messaging services, and object pooling.

Microsoft chose this evolutionary approach to software for the obvious reason that it is concerned about backward compatibility. Over the years a huge base of third-party software has been written for Windows, and Windows wouldn't have enjoyed the success it has had if every time Microsoft introduced a new technology it broke the existing code base!

While backward compatibility has been a crucial feature of Windows technologies and one of the strengths of the Windows platform, it does have a big disadvantage. Every time some technology evolves and adds new features, it ends up a bit more complicated than it was before.

It was clear that something had to change. Microsoft couldn't go on forever extending the same development tools and languages, always making them more and more complex in order to satisfy the conflicting demands of keeping up with the newest hardware and maintaining backward compatibility with what was around when Windows first became popular in the early 1990s. There comes a point where you have to start with a clean slate if you want a simple yet sophisticated set of languages, environments, and developer tools, which make it easy for developers to write state-of-the-art software.

This fresh start is what C# and .NET are all about. Roughly speaking, .NET is a new framework—a new API—for programming on the Windows platform. Along with the .NET Framework, C# is a new language that has been designed from scratch to work with .NET, as well as to take advantage of all the progress in developer environments and in our understanding of object-oriented programming principles that have taken place over the past 20 years.

Before we continue, we should make it clear that backward compatibility has not been lost in the process. Existing programs will continue to work, and .NET was designed with the ability to work with existing software. Communication between software components on Windows presently almost entirely takes place using COM. Taking account of this, .NET does have the ability to provide wrappers around existing COM components so that .NET components can talk to them.

It is true that you don't need to learn C# in order to write code for .NET. Microsoft has extended C++, provided another new language called J#, and made substantial changes to Visual Basic to turn it into the more powerful language Visual Basic .NET, in order to allow code written in either of these languages to target the .NET environment. These other languages, however, are hampered by the legacy of having evolved over the years rather than having been written from the start with today's technology in mind.

This book will equip you to program in C#, while at the same time provide the necessary background in how the .NET architecture works. We will not only cover the fundamentals of the C# language but also go on to give examples of applications that use a variety of related technologies, including database access, dynamic Web pages, advanced graphics, and directory access. The only requirement is that you be familiar with at least one other high-level language used on Windows—either C++, Visual Basic, or J++.

Advantages of .NET

We've talked in general terms about how great .NET is, but we haven't said much about how it helps to make your life as a developer easier. In this section, we'll discuss some of the improved features of .NET in brief.

❑ **Object-Oriented Programming**—both the .NET Framework and C# are entirely based on object-oriented principles right from the start.

❑ **Good Design**—a base class library, which is designed from the ground up in a highly intuitive way.

❏ **Language Independence**—with .NET, all of the languages Visual Basic .NET, C#, J#, and managed C++ compile to a common **Intermediate Language**. This means that languages are interoperable in a way that has not been seen before.

❏ **Better Support for Dynamic Web Pages**—while ASP offered a lot of flexibility, it was also inefficient because of its use of interpreted scripting languages, and the lack of object-oriented design often resulted in messy ASP code. .NET offers an integrated support for Web pages, using a new technology—ASP.NET. With ASP.NET, code in your pages is compiled, and may be written in a .NET-aware high-level language such as C#, J#, or Visual Basic .NET.

❏ **Efficient Data Access**—a set of .NET components, collectively known as ADO.NET, provides efficient access to relational databases and a variety of data sources. Components are also available to allow access to the file system, and to directories. In particular, XML support is built into .NET, allowing you to manipulate data, which may be imported from or exported to non-Windows platforms.

❏ **Code Sharing**—.NET has completely revamped the way that code is shared between applications, introducing the concept of the **assembly**, which replaces the traditional DLL. Assemblies have formal facilities for versioning, and different versions of assemblies can exist side by side.

❏ **Improved Security**—each assembly can also contain built-in security information that can indicate precisely who or what category of user or process is allowed to call which methods on which classes. This gives you a very fine degree of control over how the assemblies that you deploy can be used.

❏ **Zero Impact Installation**—there are two types of assembly: shared and private. Shared assemblies are common libraries available to all software, while private assemblies are intended only for use with particular software. A private assembly is entirely self-contained, so the process of installing it is simple. There are no registry entries; the appropriate files are simply placed in the appropriate folder in the file system.

❏ **Support for Web Services**—.NET has fully integrated support for developing Web services as easily as you'd develop any other type of application.

❏ **Visual Studio .NET 2003**—.NET comes with a developer environment, Visual Studio .NET, which can cope equally well with C++, C#, J#, and Visual Basic .NET, as well as with ASP.NET code. Visual Studio .NET integrates all the best features of the respective language-specific environments of Visual Studio 6.

❏ **C#**—C# is a new object-oriented language intended for use with .NET.

We will be looking more closely at the benefits of the .NET architecture in Chapter 1.

What's New in the .NET Framework 1.1

The first version of the .NET Framework (1.0) was released in 2002 to much enthusiasm. The latest version, the .NET Framework 1.1, was introduced in 2003 and is considered a minor release of the framework. Even though this is considered a minor release of the framework, there are some pretty outstanding new changes and additions to this new version and it definitely deserves some attention.

With all the changes made to version 1.1 of the framework, Microsoft tried to ensure that there were minimal breaking changes to code developed in using version 1.0. Even though the effort was there,

there are some breaking changes between the versions. A lot of these breaking changes were made in order to improve security. You will find a comprehensive list of breaking changes on Microsoft's GotDotNet Web site at http://www.gotdotnet.com.

> **Make sure that you create a staging server to completely test the upgrade of your applications to the .NET Framework 1.1 as opposed to just upgrading a live application.**

The following details some of the changes that are new to the .NET Framework 1.1 as well as new additions to Visual Studio .NET 2003—the development environment for the .NET Framework 1.1.

Mobility

When using the .NET Framework 1.0 and Visual Studio .NET 2002, to be able to build mobile applications you had to go out and download the Microsoft Mobile Internet Toolkit (MMIT). Now, with the .NET Framework 1.1 and Visual Studio .NET 2003, this is built right in and therefore no separate download is required.

This is all quite evident when you create a new project using Visual Studio .NET 2003. For instance, when you look at the list of available C# project types you can create, you will find ASP.NET Mobile Web Application and Smart Device Application. You would use the ASP.NET Mobile Web Application project type to build Web-based mobile applications (as the name describes). Building a Smart Device Application allows you to create applications for the Pocket PC or any other Windows CE device. The thick-client applications built for a Windows CE device utilize the Compact Framework, a trimmed-down version of the .NET Framework.

Opening one of these mobile project types, you will then be presented with a list of available mobile server controls in the Visual Studio .NET Toolbox that you can then use to build your applications.

New Data Providers

Another big area of change in the framework is to ADO.NET. ADO.NET, the .NET way of accessing and working with data, now has two new data providers—one for ODBC and another for Oracle.

An ODBC data provider was available when working with the .NET Framework 1.0, but this required a separate download. Also, once downloaded, the namespace for this data provider was Microsoft.Data.Odbc.

With the .NET Framework 1.1, the ODBC data provider is built right in, and no separate download is required. You will now be able to work with ODBC data sources through the System.Data.Odbc namespace. This also gives you access to ODBC data connection, data adapter, and data reader objects.

The other new data provider is for working with Oracle databases. This database is quite popular in the enterprise space, and the lack of an Oracle data provider often times was a big barrier for .NET to enter this space. To work with this new data provider, you will need to make a reference to the System.Data.OracleClient namespace in your project.

A New Language: Visual J#

When you install Visual Studio .NET 2003, you will notice that a new language is available to you for building .NET applications—J#. Prior to this, when using Visual Studio .NET 2002, you were forced to install the language as a separate download.

Visual J#, or simply J# (pronounced *J-sharp*), is the next version of the Visual J++ language. You will find that it is very similar to the Java language. The hope with this language is that Java developers will find it an easy transition to .NET. A J# developer will use the .NET class libraries in place of the Java runtime libraries.

J# developers will have access to much of the same capabilities as a C# developer on the .NET platform. Using J#, it is just as possible to build .NET classes, Windows Forms applications, ASP.NET Web applications, and XML Web services. In addition, you can use J# in the same cross-language ways that you can use other .NET-compliant languages. For instance, you can build a J# class and use this class in your C# application or vice versa.

Also like the other languages, there is a built-in compiler for J# now in the .NET Framework. To find any of the compilers, you will see them at `C:\Windows\Microsoft.NET\Framework\v1.1.xxxx`. The C# compiler is `csc.exe`, the Visual Basic .NET compiler is `vbc.exe`, and the J# compiler is `vjc.exe`.

Side-by-Side Execution

Side-by-side execution is the ability to run multiple versions of an application on the same server where different application versions target different runtime versions. This was always promised to us as developers, but it was always hard to visualize as only one version of the framework was available. With the release of a second version of the framework (.NET Framework 1.1), we can actually see that it is possible to have this capability. Therefore, you can build new versions of your .NET applications that target this latest .NET Framework version release, but at the same time you can allow the older versions of your application that target the .NET Framework 1.0 to continue to work just as they always have.

Support for Internet Protocol Version 6 (IPv6)

Presently, much of the Internet runs using IP version 4, also referred to as IPv4. IPv4 gives us IP addresses such as `255.255.255.255`. The .NET Framework 1.1 now supports IPv6, which was created in 1995 to address many of the problems that the world was facing with IPv4. Most of the problems deal with the fact that by the world's continual use of IPv4, we are rapidly running out of available IP addresses.

IPv6 is supported in the .NET Framework 1.1 through the `System.Net` namespace as well as in ASP.NET and XML Web services.

Visual Studio .NET 2003 Enhancements

Along with the upgrade to the .NET Framework, Visual Studio .NET itself has also undergone an upgrade. You will notice that there are some new graphics on the Start Page available and that things on this page are organized a little differently. Besides that, the biggest thing to notice with this new IDE is that once installed, it does not simply upgrade Visual Studio .NET 2002 to Visual Studio .NET 2003.

Instead, it installs a completely new version of the IDE, and if you already have VS.NET 2002 on your machine, then you will have two complete VS.NET IDEs on your box. The reason for this is so that if you want to build and work with applications that target the .NET Framework version 1.0, then you will use VS.NET 2002, and if you want to build and work with applications that target the .NET Framework version 1.1 then you will use VS.NET 2003.

You should also be aware that when you open a project that was built using VS.NET 2002, you will be asked if you want to upgrade the project to be a VS.NET 2003 project. Doing this will then cause the project to be re-targeted at the .NET Framework 1.1. Be careful about doing this as it is an irreversible process.

Besides these big changes, you will find that VS.NET 2003 is a better IDE with smarter Intellisense and code completion. This version of the IDE is the IDE that is used throughout the examples of this book.

Where C# Fits In

In one sense, C# can be seen as being the same thing to programming languages as .NET is to the Windows environment. Just as Microsoft has been adding more and more features to Windows and the Windows API over the past decade, Visual Basic and C++ have undergone expansion. Although Visual Basic and C++ have ended up as hugely powerful languages as a result of this, both languages also suffer from problems due to the legacies of how they have evolved.

In the case of Visual Basic 6 and earlier, the main strength of the language was the fact that it was simple to understand and didn't make many programming tasks easy, largely hiding the details of the Windows API and the COM component infrastructure from the developer. The downside to this was that Visual Basic was never truly object-oriented, so that large applications quickly become disorganized and hard to maintain. As well as this, because Visual Basic's syntax was inherited from early versions of BASIC (which, in turn, was designed to be intuitively simple for beginning programmers to understand, rather than to write large commercial applications), it didn't really lend itself to well-structured or object-oriented programs.

C++, on the other hand, has its roots in the ANSI C++ language definition. It isn't completely ANSI-compliant for the simple reason that Microsoft first wrote its C++ compiler before the ANSI definition had become official, but it comes close. Unfortunately, this has led to two problems. First, ANSI C++ has its roots in a decade-old state of technology, and this shows up in a lack of support for modern concepts (such as Unicode strings and generating XML documentation), and in some archaic syntax structures designed for the compilers of yesteryear (such as the separation of declaration from definition of member functions). Second, Microsoft has been simultaneously trying to evolve C++ into a language that is designed for high-performance tasks on Windows, and in order to achieve that they've been forced to add a huge number of Microsoft-specific keywords as well as various libraries to the language. The result is that on Windows, the language has become a complete mess. Just ask C++ developers how many definitions for a string they can think of: `char*`, `LPTSTR`, `string`, `CString` (MFC version), `CString` (WTL version), `wchar_t*`, `OLECHAR*`, and so on.

Now enter .NET—a completely new environment that is going to involve new extensions to both languages. Microsoft has gotten around this by adding yet more Microsoft-specific keywords to C++, and by completely revamping Visual Basic into Visual Basic .NET, a language that retains some of the basic VB syntax but that is so different in design that we can consider it to be, for all practical purposes, a new language.

It's in this context that Microsoft has decided to give developers an alternative—a language designed specifically for .NET, and designed with a clean slate. Visual C# .NET is the result. Officially, Microsoft describes C# as a "simple, modern, object-oriented, and type-safe programming language derived from C and C++." Most independent observers would probably change that to "derived from C, C++, and Java." Such descriptions are technically accurate but do little to convey the beauty or elegance of the language. Syntactically, C# is very similar to both C++ and Java, to such an extent that many keywords are the same, and C# also shares the same block structure with braces ({}) to mark blocks of code, and semicolons to separate statements. The first impression of a piece of C# code is that it looks quite like C++ or Java code. Behind that initial similarity, however, C# is a lot easier to learn than C++, and of comparable difficulty to Java. Its design is more in tune with modern developer tools than both of those other languages, and it has been designed to give us, simultaneously, the ease of use of Visual Basic, and the high-performance, low-level memory access of C++ if required. Some of the features of C# are:

❑   Full support for classes and object-oriented programming, including both interface and implementation inheritance, virtual functions, and operator overloading.

❑   A consistent and well-defined set of basic types.

❑   Built-in support for automatic generation of XML documentation.

❑   Automatic cleanup of dynamically allocated memory.

❑   The facility to mark classes or methods with user-defined attributes. This can be useful for documentation and can have some effects on compilation (for example, marking methods to be compiled only in debug builds).

❑   Full access to the .NET base class library, as well as easy access to the Windows API (if you really need it, which won't be all that often).

❑   Pointers and direct memory access are available if required, but the language has been designed in such a way that you can work without them in almost all cases.

❑   Support for properties and events in the style of Visual Basic.

❑   Just by changing the compiler options, you can compile either to an executable or to a library of .NET components that can be called up by other code in the same way as ActiveX controls (COM components).

❑   C# can be used to write ASP.NET dynamic Web pages and XML Web services.

Most of the above statements, it should be pointed out, do also apply to Visual Basic .NET and Managed C++. The fact that C# is designed from the start to work with .NET, however, means that its support for the features of .NET is both more complete, and offered within the context of a more suitable syntax than for those other languages. While the C# language itself is very similar to Java, there are some improvements: in particular, Java is not designed to work with the .NET environment.

Before we leave the subject, we should point out a couple of limitations of C#. The one area the language is not designed for is time-critical or extremely high performance code—the kind where you really are worried about whether a loop takes 1,000 or 1,050 machine cycles to run through, and you need to clean up your resources the millisecond they are no longer needed. C++ is likely to continue to reign supreme among low-level languages in this area. C# lacks certain key facilities needed for extremely high performance apps, including the ability to specify inline functions and destructors that are guaranteed to run at particular points in the code. However, the proportions of applications that fall into this category are very low.

What You Need to Write and Run C# Code

.NET will run on Windows 98, 2000, XP, and 2003. In order to write code using .NET, you will need to install the .NET SDK unless you are using Windows Server 2003, which comes with the .NET Framework 1.0 and 1.1 already installed. Unless you are intending to write your C# code using a text editor or some other third party developer environment, you will almost certainly also want Visual Studio .NET 2003. The full SDK isn't needed to run managed code, but the .NET runtime is needed. You may find you need to distribute the .NET runtime with your code for the benefit of those clients who do not have it already installed.

What This Book Covers

In this book, we start by reviewing the overall architecture of .NET in the next chapter in order to give us the background we need to be able to write managed code. After that the book is divided into a number of sections that cover both the C# language and its application in a variety of areas.

Part I: The C# Language

This section gives us a good grounding in the C# language itself. This section doesn't presume knowledge of any particular language, although it does assume you are an experienced programmer. We start by looking at C#'s basic syntax and datatypes, and then discuss the object-oriented features of C# before moving on to look at more advanced C# programming topics.

Part II: The .NET Environment

In this section, we look at the principles of programming in the .NET environment. In particular, we look at Visual Studio .NET, security, threading deployment of .NET applications, and how to generate your own libraries as assemblies.

Part III: Windows Forms

This section focuses on building classic Windows applications, which are called Windows Forms in .NET. Windows Forms are the thick-client version of applications, and using .NET to build these types of applications is a quick and easy way of accomplishing this task. In addition to looking at Windows Forms, we will take a look at GDI+, which is the technology we will use for building applications that include advanced graphics.

Part IV: Data

Here we look at accessing databases with ADO.NET, and at interacting with directories and Active Directory. We also extensively cover support in .NET for XML and on the Windows operating system side.

Part V: Web Programming

In this section, we cover writing components that will run on Web sites, serving up Web pages. This covers both ASP.NET and the writing of XML Web services.

Part VI: Interop

Backward compatibility with COM is an important part of .NET. Not only that, but COM+ is not strictly legacy—it will still be responsible for transactions, object pooling, and message queuing. In this section we'll look at the support .NET offers for working with COM and COM+, as well as discussing how to write C# code that interacts with these technologies.

Part VII: Windows Base Services

This section, the concluding part of the main body of the book, covers accessing the file and registry, accessing the Internet through your applications, and working with Windows Services.

Part VIII: Appendices (Web Site Only)

This section includes several appendices detailing the principles of object-oriented programming as well as programming language–specific information about C#. These appendices are available as PDFs on the Web site accompanying this book (http://www.wrox.com).

Conventions

We have used a number of different styles of text and layout in the book to help differentiate between the different kinds of information. Here are examples of the styles we use and an explanation of what they mean:

Bullets appear indented, with each new bullet marked as follows:

❑ **Important Words** are in a bold type font.

❑ Words that appear on the screen in menus like the File or Window are in a similar font to the one that you see on screen.

❑ Keys that you press on the keyboard, like *Ctrl* and *Enter*, are in italics.

Code appears in a number of different ways. If it's a word that we're talking about in the text—for example, when discussing the `if...else` loop—it's in `this font`. If it's a block of code that you can type in as a program and run, then it's also in a gray box:

```
public static void Main()
{
    AFunc(1,2,"abc");
}
```

Sometimes you'll see code in a mixture of styles, like this:

```
// If we haven't reached the end, return true, otherwise
// set the position to invalid, and return false.
pos++;
if (pos < 4)
    return true;
```

```
else {
    pos = -1;
    return false;
}
```

The code with a white background is code we've already looked at and that we don't wish to examine further.

Advice, hints, and background information come in an italicized, indented font like this.

Important pieces of information come in boxes like this.

We demonstrate the syntactical usage of methods, properties (and so on) using the following format:

```
Regsvcs BookDistributor.dll [COM+AppName] [TypeLibrary.tbl]
```

Here, italicized parts indicate object references, variables, or parameter values to be inserted; the square braces indicate optional parameters.

Source Code

As you work through the examples in this book, you may choose either to type in all the code manually or to use the source code files that accompany the book. All of the source code used in this book is available for download at http://www.wrox.com. Once at the site, simply locate the book's title (either by using the Search box or by using one of the title lists) and click the Download Code link on the book's detail page to obtain all the source code for the book.

Because many books have similar titles, you may find it easiest to search by ISBN; this book's ISBN is 0-7645-5759-9.

Once you download the code, just decompress it with your favorite compression tool. Alternately, you can go to the main Wrox code download page at http://www.wrox.com/dynamic/books/download.aspx to see the code available for this book and all other Wrox books.

Errata

We make every effort to ensure that there are no errors in the text or in the code. However, no one is perfect, and mistakes do occur. If you find an error in one of our books, like a spelling mistake or faulty piece of code, we would be very grateful for your feedback. By sending in errata you may save another reader hours of frustration, and at the same time you will be helping us provide even higher quality information.

To find the errata page for this book, go to http://www.wrox.com and locate the title using the Search box or one of the title lists. Then, on the book details page, click the Book Errata link. On this page you can view all errata that have been submitted for this book and posted by Wrox editors. A complete book list including links to each book's errata is also available at http://www.wrox.com/misc-pages/booklist.shtml.

If you don't spot "your" error already on the Book Errata page, go to http://www.wrox.com/contact/techsupport.shtml and complete the form there to send us the error you have found. We'll check the information and, if appropriate, post a message to the book's errata page and fix the problem in subsequent editions of the book.

p2p.wrox.com

For author and peer discussion, join the P2P forums at p2p.wrox.com. The forums are a Web-based system for you to post messages relating to Wrox books and related technologies and to interact with other readers and technology users. The forums offer a subscription feature to e-mail you topics of interest of your choosing when new posts are made to the forums. Wrox authors, editors, other industry experts, and your fellow readers are present on these forums.

At http://p2p.wrox.com you will find a number of different forums that will help you not only as you read this book, but also as you develop your own applications. To join the forums, just follow these steps:

1. Go to p2p.wrox.com and click the Register link.
2. Read the terms of use and click Agree.
3. Supply the required information to join as well as any optional information you wish to provide and click Submit.

You will receive an e-mail with information describing how to verify your account and complete the joining process.

You can read messages in the forums without joining P2P, but you must join in order to post your own messages.

Once you join, you can post new messages and respond to other users' posts. You can read messages at any time on the Web. If you would like to have new messages from a particular forum e-mailed to you, click the Subscribe to this Forum icon by the forum name in the forum listing.

For more information about how to use the Wrox P2P, be sure to read the P2P FAQs for answers to questions about how the forum software works as well as many common questions specific to P2P and Wrox books. To read the FAQs, click the FAQ link on any P2P page.

Part I: The C# Language

Chapter 1: .NET Architecture

Chapter 2: C# Basics

Chapter 3: Objects and Types

Chapter 4: Inheritance

Chapter 5: Operators and Casts

Chapter 6: Delegates and Events

Chapter 7: Memory Management and Pointers

Chapter 8: Strings and Regular Expressions

Chapter 9: Collections

Chapter 10: Reflection

Chapter 11: Errors and Exceptions

1

.NET Architecture

You'll find that we emphasize throughout this book that the C# language cannot be viewed in isolation, but must be considered in parallel with the .NET Framework. The C# compiler specifically targets .NET, which means that all code written in C# will always run within the .NET Framework. This has two important consequences for the C# language:

❑   The architecture and methodologies of C# reflect the underlying methodologies of .NET.

❑   In many cases, specific language features of C# actually depend upon features of .NET, or of the .NET base classes.

Because of this dependence, it is important to gain some understanding of the architecture and methodology of .NET before we begin C# programming. That is the purpose of this chapter.

We will begin by going over what happens when all code (including C#) that targets .NET is compiled and run. Once we have this broad overview, we will take a more detailed look at the *Microsoft Intermediate Language* (MSIL or simply IL), the assembly language which all compiled code ends up in on .NET. In particular, we will see how IL, in partnership with the *Common Type System* (CTS) and *Common Language Specification* (CLS) works to give us interoperability between languages that target .NET. We'll also discuss where common languages (including Visual Basic and C++) fit into .NET.

Once we've done that, we will move on to examine some of the other features of .NET, including assemblies, namespaces, and the .NET base classes. We'll finish the chapter with a brief look at the kinds of applications we can create as C# developers.

The Relationship of C# to .NET

C# is a relatively new programming language, and is significant in two respects:

❑   It is specifically designed and targeted for use with Microsoft's .NET Framework (a feature-rich platform for the development, deployment, and execution of distributed applications).

❑   It is a language based on the modern object-oriented design methodology, and when designing it Microsoft has been able to learn from the experience of all the other similar languages that have been around since object-oriented principles came to prominence some 20 years ago.

One important thing to make clear is that C# is a language in its own right. Although it is designed to generate code that targets the .NET environment, it is not itself part of .NET. There are some features that are supported by .NET but not by C#, and you might be surprised to learn that there are actually features of the C# language that are not supported by .NET (for example, some instances of operator overloading)!

However, since the C# language is intended for use with .NET, it is important for us to have an understanding of this Framework if we want to develop applications in C# effectively. So, in this chapter we're going to take some time to peek underneath the surface of .NET. Let's get started.

The Common Language Runtime

Central to the .NET Framework is its runtime execution environment, known as the *Common Language Runtime* (CLR) or the *.NET runtime*. Code running under the control of the CLR is often termed *managed code*.

However, before it can be executed by the CLR, any source code that we develop (in C# or some other language) needs to be compiled. Compilation occurs in two steps in .NET:

1.   Compilation of source code to IL

2.   Compilation of IL to platform-specific code by the CLR

This two-stage compilation process is very important, because the existence of the IL (managed code) is the key to providing many of the benefits of .NET. Let's see why.

Advantages of Managed Code

Microsoft intermediate language shares with Java byte code the idea that it is a low-level language with a simple syntax (based on numeric codes rather than text), which can be very quickly translated into native machine code. Having this well-defined universal syntax for code has significant advantages.

Platform independence

First, it means that the same file containing byte code instructions can be placed on any platform; at runtime the final stage of compilation can then be easily accomplished so that the code will run on that particular platform. In other words, by compiling to IL we obtain platform independence for .NET, in much the same way as compiling to Java byte code gives Java platform independence.

You should note that the platform independence of .NET is only theoretical at present because, at the time of writing, a complete implementation of .NET is only available for Windows. However, there is a partial implementation available (see for example the Mono project, an effort to create an open source implementation of .NET, at www.go-mono.com/).

Performance improvement

Although we previously made comparisons with Java, IL is actually a bit more ambitious than Java byte code. IL is always *Just-In-Time* compiled (known as JIT compilation), whereas Java byte code was often interpreted. One of the disadvantages of Java was that, on execution, the process of translating from Java byte code to native executable resulted in a loss of performance (with the exception of more recent cases, where Java is JIT compiled on certain platforms).

Instead of compiling the entire application in one go (which could lead to a slow start-up time), the JIT compiler simply compiles each portion of code as it is called (just-in-time). When code has been compiled once, the resultant native executable is stored until the application exits, so that it does not need to be recompiled the next time that portion of code is run. Microsoft argues that this process is more efficient than compiling the entire application code at the start, because of the likelihood that large portions of any application code will not actually be executed in any given run. Using the JIT compiler, such code will never be compiled.

This explains why we can expect that execution of managed IL code will be almost as fast as executing native machine code. What it doesn't explain is why Microsoft expects that we will get a performance *improvement*. The reason given for this is that, since the final stage of compilation takes place at runtime, the JIT compiler will know exactly what processor type the program will run on. This means that it can optimize the final executable code to take advantage of any features or particular machine code instructions offered by that particular processor.

Traditional compilers will optimize the code, but they can only perform optimizations that are independent of the particular processor that the code will run on. This is because traditional compilers compile to native executable before the software is shipped. This means that the compiler doesn't know what type of processor the code will run on beyond basic generalities, such as that it will be an x86-compatible processor or an Alpha processor. Visual Studio 6, for example, optimizes for a generic Pentium machine, so the code that it generates cannot take advantage of hardware features of Pentium III processors. On the other hand, the JIT compiler can do all the optimizations that Visual Studio 6 can, and in addition it will optimize for the particular processor the code is running on.

Language interoperability

The use of IL not only enables platform independence; it also facilitates *language interoperability*. Simply put, you can compile to IL from one language, and this compiled code should then be interoperable with code that has been compiled to IL from another language.

You're probably now wondering which languages aside from C# are interoperable with .NET, so let's briefly discuss how some of the other common languages fit into .NET.

Visual Basic .NET

Visual Basic .NET has undergone a complete revamp from Visual Basic 6 to bring it up-to-date with .NET. The way that Visual Basic has evolved over the last few years means that in its previous version, Visual Basic 6, it was not a suitable language for running .NET programs. For example, it is heavily integrated into COM and works by exposing only event handlers as source code to the developer—most of the background code is not available as source code. Not only that, it does not support implementation inheritance, and the standard data types Visual Basic 6 uses are incompatible with .NET.

Visual Basic 6 was upgraded to Visual Basic .NET, and the changes that were made to the language are so extensive you might as well regard Visual Basic .NET as a new language. Existing Visual Basic 6 code does not compile as Visual Basic .NET code. Converting a Visual Basic 6 program to Visual Basic .NET requires extensive changes to the code. However, Visual Studio .NET (the upgrade of VS for use with .NET) can do most of the changes for you. If you attempt to read a Visual Basic 6 project into Visual Studio .NET, it will upgrade the project for you, which means that it will rewrite the Visual Basic 6 source code into Visual Basic .NET source code. Although this means that the work involved for you is heavily cut down, you will need to check through the new Visual Basic .NET code to make sure that the project still works as intended because the conversion might not be perfect.

One side effect of this language upgrade is that it is no longer possible to compile Visual Basic .NET to native executable code. Visual Basic .NET compiles only to IL, just as C# does. If you need to continue coding in Visual Basic 6, you may do so, but the executable code produced will completely ignore the .NET Framework, and you'll need to keep Visual Studio 6 installed if you want to continue to work in this developer environment.

Visual C++ .NET

Visual C++ 6 already had a large number of Microsoft-specific extensions on Windows. With Visual C++ .NET, extensions have been added to support the .NET Framework. This means that existing C++ source code will continue to compile to native executable code without modification. It also means, however, that it will run independently of the .NET runtime. If you want your C++ code to run within the .NET Framework, then you can simply add the following line to the beginning of your code:

```
#using <mscorlib.dll>
```

You can also pass the flag `/clr` to the compiler, which then assumes that you want to compile to managed code, and will hence emit IL instead of native machine code. The interesting thing about C++ is that when you compile to managed code, the compiler can emit IL that contains an embedded native executable. This means that you can mix managed types and unmanaged types in your C++ code. Thus the managed C++ code:

```
class MyClass
{
```

defines a plain C++ class, whereas the code:

```
__gc class MyClass
{
```

will give you a managed class, just as if you'd written the class in C# or Visual Basic .NET. The advantage of using managed C++ over C# code is that we can call unmanaged C++ classes from managed C++ code without having to resort to COM interop.

The compiler raises an error if you attempt to use features that are not supported by .NET on managed types (for example, templates or multiple inheritance of classes). You will also find that you will need to use nonstandard C++ features (such as the __gc keyword shown in the previous code) when using managed classes.

Because of the freedom that C++ allows in terms of low-level pointer manipulation and so on, the C++ compiler is not able to generate code that will pass the CLR's memory type safety tests. If it's important that your code is recognized by the CLR as memory type safe, then you'll need to write your source code in some other language (such as C# or Visual Basic .NET).

Visual J# .NET

The latest language to be added to the mix is Visual J# .NET. Prior to .NET Framework 1.1, users were able to use J# only after making a separate download. Now the J# language is built into the .NET Framework. Because of this, J# users are able to take advantage of all the usual features of Visual Studio .NET. Microsoft expects that most J++ users will find it easiest to use J# if they want to work with .NET. Instead of being targeted at the Java runtime libraries, J# uses the same base class libraries that the rest of the .NET compliant languages use. This means that you can use J# for building ASP.NET Web applications, Windows Forms, XML Web services, and everything else that is possible—just as C# and Visual Basic .NET can.

Scripting languages

Scripting languages are still around, although, in general, their importance is likely to decline with the advent of .NET. JScript, on the other hand, has been upgraded to JScript .NET. We can now write ASP.NET pages in JScript .NET, run JScript .NET as a compiled rather than an interpreted language, and write strongly typed JScript .NET code. With ASP.NET there is no reason to use scripting languages in server-side Web pages. VBA is, however, still used as a language for Microsoft Office and Visual Studio macros.

COM and COM+

Technically speaking, COM and COM+ aren't technologies targeted at .NET, because components based on them cannot be compiled into IL (although it's possible to do so to some degree using managed C++, if the original COM component was written in C++). However, COM+ remains an important tool, because its features are not duplicated in .NET. Also, COM components will still work—and .NET incorporates COM interoperability features that make it possible for managed code to call up COM components and vice versa (this is discussed in Chapter 29). In general, however, you will probably find it more convenient for most purposes to code new components as .NET components, so that you can take advantage of the .NET base classes as well as the other benefits of running as managed code.

A Closer Look at Intermediate Language

From what we learned in the previous section, Microsoft intermediate language obviously plays a fundamental role in the .NET Framework. As C# developers, we now understand that our C# code will be compiled into IL before it is executed (indeed, the C# compiler *only* compiles to managed code). It makes sense, then, that we should now take a closer look at the main characteristics of IL, since any language that targets .NET would logically need to support the main characteristics of IL too.

Here are the important features of IL:

- ❑ Object-orientation and use of interfaces
- ❑ Strong distinction between value and reference types
- ❑ Strong data typing
- ❑ Error handling through the use of exceptions
- ❑ Use of attributes

Let's now take a closer look at each of these characteristics.

Support for Object Orientation and Interfaces

The language independence of .NET does have some practical limitations. IL is inevitably going to implement some particular programming methodology, which means that languages targeting it are going to have to be compatible with that methodology. The particular route that Microsoft has chosen to follow for IL is that of classic object-oriented programming, with single implementation inheritance of classes.

Those readers unfamiliar with the concepts of object orientation should refer to Appendix A for more information. Appendix A is posted at www.wrox.com.

Besides classic object-oriented programming, IL also brings in the idea of interfaces, which saw their first implementation under Windows with COM. .NET interfaces are not the same as COM interfaces; they do not need to support any of the COM infrastructure (for example, they are not derived from IUnknown, and they do not have associated GUIDs). However, they do share with COM interfaces the idea that they provide a contract, and classes that implement a given interface must provide implementations of the methods and properties specified by that interface.

Object orientation and language interoperability

We have now seen that working with .NET means compiling to IL, and that in turn means that you will need to use traditional object-oriented methodologies. However, that alone is not sufficient to give us language interoperability. After all, C++ and Java both use the same object-oriented paradigms, but they are still not regarded as interoperable. We need to look a little more closely at the concept of language interoperability.

To start with, we need to consider exactly what we mean by language interoperability. After all, COM allowed components written in different languages to work together in the sense of calling each other's methods. What was inadequate about that? COM, by virtue of being a binary standard, did allow components to instantiate other components and call methods or properties against them, without worrying about the language the respective components were written in. In order to achieve this, however, each object had to be instantiated through the COM runtime, and accessed through an interface. Depending on the threading models of the relative components, there may have been large performance losses associated with marshaling data between apartments or running components or both on different threads. In the extreme case of components that are hosted as an executable rather than DLL files, separate processes would need to be created in order to run them. The emphasis was very much that components could talk to each other, but only via the COM runtime. In no way with COM did components written in different languages directly communicate with each other, or instantiate instances of each other—it was always done with COM as an intermediary. Not only that, but the COM architecture did not permit implementation inheritance, which meant that it lost many of the advantages of object-oriented programming.

An associated problem was that, when debugging, you would still have to debug components written in different languages independently. It was not possible to step between languages in the debugger. So what we *really* mean by language interoperability is that classes written in one language should be able to talk directly to classes written in another language. In particular:

- ❑ A class written in one language can inherit from a class written in another language.
- ❑ The class can contain an instance of another class, no matter what the languages of the two classes are.
- ❑ An object can directly call methods against another object written in another language.
- ❑ Objects (or references to objects) can be passed around between methods.
- ❑ When calling methods between languages we can step between the method calls in the debugger, even when this means stepping between source code written in different languages.

This is all quite an ambitious aim, but amazingly, .NET and IL have achieved it. In the case of stepping between methods in the debugger, this facility is really offered by the Visual Studio .NET IDE rather than by the CLR itself.

Distinct Value and Reference Types

As with any programming language, IL provides a number of predefined primitive data types. One characteristic of IL, however, is that it makes a strong distinction between value and reference types. *Value types* are those for which a variable directly stores its data, while *reference types* are those for which a variable simply stores the address at which the corresponding data can be found.

In C++ terms, reference types can be considered to be similar to accessing a variable through a pointer, while for Visual Basic, the best analogy for reference types are objects, which in Visual Basic 6 are always accessed through references. IL also lays down specifications about data storage: instances of reference types are always stored in an area of memory known as the *managed heap*, while value types are normally stored on the *stack* (although if value types are declared as fields within reference types, then they will be stored inline on the heap). We will discuss the stack and the heap and how they work in Chapter 3.

Strong Data Typing

One very important aspect of IL is that it is based on exceptionally *strong data typing*. What we mean by that is that all variables are clearly marked as being of a particular, specific data type (there is no room in IL, for example, for the `Variant` data type recognized by Visual Basic and scripting languages). In particular, IL does not normally permit any operations that result in ambiguous data types.

For instance, Visual Basic 6 developers are used to being able to pass variables around without worrying too much about their types, because Visual Basic 6 automatically performs type conversion. C++ developers are used to routinely casting pointers between different types. Being able to perform this kind of operation can be great for performance, but it breaks type safety. Hence, it is permitted only under certain circumstances in some of the languages that compile to managed code. Indeed, pointers (as opposed to references) are only permitted in marked blocks of code in C#, and not at all in Visual Basic (although they are allowed in managed C++). Using pointers in your code causes it to fail the memory type safety checks performed by the CLR.

You should note that some languages compatible with .NET, such as Visual Basic .NET, still allow some laxity in typing, but that is only possible because the compilers behind the scenes ensure the type safety is enforced in the emitted IL.

Although enforcing type safety might initially appear to hurt performance, in many cases the benefits gained from the services provided by .NET that rely on type safety far outweigh this performance loss. Such services include:

- ❏   Language interoperability
- ❏   Garbage collection
- ❏   Security
- ❏   Application domains

Let's take a closer look at why strong data typing is particularly important for these features of .NET.

The Importance of strong data typing for language interoperability

If a class is to derive from or contains instances of other classes, it needs to know about all the data types used by the other classes. This is why strong data typing is so important. Indeed, it is the absence of any agreed system for specifying this information in the past that has always been the real barrier to inheritance and interoperability across languages. This kind of information is simply not present in a standard executable file or DLL.

Suppose that one of the methods of a Visual Basic .NET class is defined to return an Integer—one of the standard data types available in Visual Basic .NET. C# simply does not have any data type of that name. Clearly, we will only be able to derive from the class, use this method, and use the return type from C# code, if the compiler knows how to map Visual Basic .NET's Integer type to some known type that is defined in C#. So how is this problem circumvented in .NET?

Common Type System

This data type problem is solved in .NET through the use of the *Common Type System* (CTS). The CTS defines the predefined data types that are available in IL, so that all languages that target the .NET Framework will produce compiled code that is ultimately based on these types.

For the example that we were considering before, Visual Basic .NET's Integer is actually a 32-bit signed integer, which maps exactly to the IL type known as Int32. This will therefore be the data type specified in the IL code. Because the C# compiler is aware of this type, there is no problem. At source code level, C# refers to Int32 with the keyword int, so the compiler will simply treat the Visual Basic .NET method as if it returned an int.

The CTS doesn't merely specify primitive data types, but a rich hierarchy of types, which includes well-defined points in the hierarchy at which code is permitted to define its own types. The hierarchical structure of the Common Type System reflects the single-inheritance object-oriented methodology of IL, and resembles Figure 1-1.

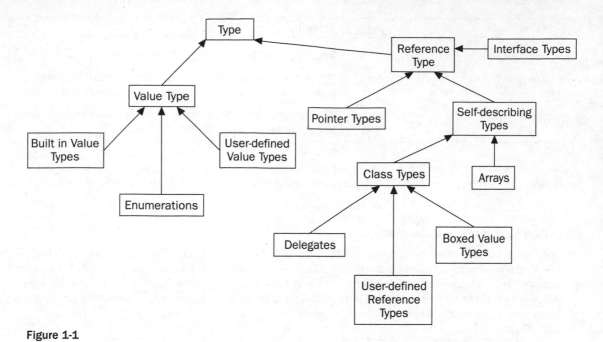

Figure 1-1

The following table explains the types shown in Figure 1-1.

Type	Meaning
Type	Base class that represents any type.
Value Type	Base class that represents any value type.
Reference Types	Any data types that are accessed through a reference and stored on the heap.
Built-in Value Types	Includes most of the standard primitive types, which represent numbers, Boolean values, or characters.
Enumerations	Sets of enumerated values.
User-defined Value Types	Types that have been defined in source code and are stored as value types. In C# terms, this means any struct.
Interface Types	Interfaces.
Pointer Types	Pointers.
Self-describing Types	Data types that provide information about themselves for the benefit of the garbage collector (see the next section).
Arrays	Any type that contains an array of objects.
Class Types	Types that are self-describing but are not arrays.

Table continued on following page

Type	Meaning
Delegates	Types that are designed to hold references to methods.
User-defined Reference Types	Types that have been defined in source code and are stored as reference types. In C# terms, this means any class.
Boxed Value Types	A value type that is temporarily wrapped in a reference so that it can be stored on the heap.

We won't list all of the built-in value types here, because they are covered in detail in Chapter 2. In C#, each predefined type recognized by the compiler maps onto one of the IL built-in types. The same is true in Visual Basic .NET.

Common Language Specification

The Common Language Specification (CLS) works with the CTS to ensure language interoperability. The CLS is a set of minimum standards that all compilers targeting .NET must support. Since IL is a very rich language, writers of most compilers will prefer to restrict the capabilities of a given compiler to only support a subset of the facilities offered by IL and the CTS. That is fine, as long as the compiler supports everything that is defined in the CLS.

> **It is perfectly acceptable to write non–CLS-compliant code. However, if you do, the compiled IL code isn't guaranteed to be fully language interoperable.**

For example, let's look at case sensitivity. IL is case-sensitive. Developers who work with case-sensitive languages regularly take advantage of the flexibility this case sensitivity gives them when selecting variable names. Visual Basic .NET, however, is not case sensitive. The CLS works around this by indicating that CLS-compliant code should not expose any two names that differ only in their case. Therefore, Visual Basic .NET code can work with CLS-compliant code.

This example shows that the CLS works in two ways. First, it means that individual compilers do not have to be powerful enough to support the full features of .NET—this should encourage the development of compilers for other programming languages that target .NET. Second, it provides a guarantee that, if you restrict your classes to only exposing CLS-compliant features, then it is guaranteed that code written in any other compliant language can use your classes.

The beauty of this idea is that the restriction to using CLS-compliant features only applies to public and protected members of classes and public classes. Within the private implementations of your classes, you can write whatever non-CLS code you want, because code in other assemblies (units of managed code, see later in this chapter) cannot access this part of your code anyway.

We won't go into the details of the CLS specifications here. In general, the CLS won't affect your C# code very much, because there are very few non–CLS-compliant features of C# anyway.

Garbage collection

The *garbage collector* is .NET's answer to memory management, and in particular to the question of what to do about reclaiming memory that running applications ask for. Up until now there have been two techniques used on the Windows platform for de-allocating memory that processes have dynamically requested from the system:

❑   Make the application code do it all manually.

❑   Make objects maintain reference counts.

Having the application code responsible for de-allocating memory is the technique used by lower-level, high-performance languages such as C++. It is efficient, and it has the advantage that (in general) resources are never occupied for longer than unnecessary. The big disadvantage, however, is the frequency of bugs. Code that requests memory also should explicitly inform the system when it no longer requires that memory. However, it is easy to overlook this, resulting in memory leaks.

Although modern developer environments do provide tools to assist in detecting memory leaks, they remain difficult bugs to track down, because they have no effect until so much memory has been leaked that Windows refuses to grant any more to the process. By this point, the entire computer may have appreciably slowed down due to the memory demands being made on it.

Maintaining reference counts is favored in COM. The idea is that each COM component maintains a count of how many clients are currently maintaining references to it. When this count falls to zero, the component can destroy itself and free up associated memory and resources. The problem with this is that it still relies on the good behavior of clients to notify the component that they have finished with it. It only takes one client not to do so, and the object sits in memory. In some ways, this is a potentially more serious problem than a simple C++-style memory leak, because the COM object may exist in its own process, which means that it will never be removed by the system (at least with C++ memory leaks, the system can reclaim all memory when the process terminates).

The .NET runtime relies on the garbage collector instead. This is a program whose purpose is to clean up memory. The idea is that all dynamically requested memory is allocated on the heap (that is true for all languages, although in the case of .NET, the CLR maintains its own managed heap for .NET applications to use). Every so often, when .NET detects that the managed heap for a given process is becoming full and therefore needs tidying up, it calls the garbage collector. The garbage collector runs through variables currently in scope in your code, examining references to objects stored on the heap to identify which ones are accessible from your code—that is to say which objects have references that refer to them. Any objects that are not referred to are deemed to be no longer accessible from your code and can therefore be removed. Java uses a similar system of garbage collection to this.

Garbage collection works in .NET because IL has been designed to facilitate the process. The principle requires that you cannot get references to existing objects other than by copying existing references and that IL is type safe. In this context, what we mean is that if any reference to an object exists, then there is sufficient information in the reference to exactly determine the type of the object.

It would not be possible to use the garbage collection mechanism with a language such as unmanaged C++, for example, because C++ allows pointers to be freely cast between types.

One important aspect of garbage collection is that it is not deterministic. In other words, you cannot guarantee when the garbage collector will be called; it will be called when the CLR decides that it is needed (unless you explicitly call the collector). Though it is also possible to override this process and call up the garbage collector in your code.

Security

.NET can really excel in terms of complementing the security mechanisms provided by Windows because it can offer code-based security, whereas Windows only really offers role-based security.

Role-based security is based on the identity of the account under which the process is running, in other words, who owns and is running the process. Code-based security on the other hand is based on what the code actually does and on how much the code is trusted. Thanks to the strong type safety of IL, the CLR is able to inspect code before running it in order to determine required security permissions. .NET also offers a mechanism by which code can indicate in advance what security permissions it will require to run.

The importance of *code-based security* is that it reduces the risks associated with running code of dubious origin (such as code that you've downloaded from the Internet). For example, even if code is running under the administrator account, it is possible to use code-based security to indicate that that code should still not be permitted to perform certain types of operation that the administrator account would normally be allowed to do, such as read or write to environment variables, read or write to the registry, or to access the .NET reflection features.

Security issues are covered in more depth in Chapter 14.

Application domains

Application domains are an important innovation in .NET and are designed to ease the overhead involved when running applications that need to be isolated from each other, but which also need to be able to communicate with each other. The classic example of this is a Web server application, which may be simultaneously responding to a number of browser requests. It will, therefore, probably have a number of instances of the component responsible for servicing those requests running simultaneously.

In pre-.NET days, the choice would be between allowing those instances to share a process, with the resultant risk of a problem in one running instance bringing the whole Web site down, or isolating those instances in separate processes, with the associated performance overhead.

Up until now, the only means of isolating code has been through processes. When you start a new application, it runs within the context of a process. Windows isolates processes from each other through address spaces. The idea is that each process has available 4GB of virtual memory in which to store its data and executable code (4GB is for 32-bit systems; 64-bit systems use more memory). Windows imposes an extra level of indirection by which this virtual memory maps into a particular area of actual physical memory or disk space. Each process gets a different mapping, with no overlap between the actual physical memories that the blocks of virtual address space map to (see Figure 1-2).

In general, any process is only able to access memory by specifying an address in virtual memory— processes do not have direct access to physical memory. Hence it is simply impossible for one process to access the memory allocated to another process. This provides an excellent guarantee that any badly behaved code will not be able to damage anything outside its own address space. (Note that on Windows 95/98, these safeguards are not quite as thorough as they are on Windows NT/2000/XP/2003, so the theoretical possibility exists of applications crashing Windows by writing to inappropriate memory.)

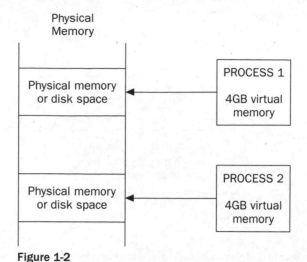

Figure 1-2

Processes don't just serve as a way to isolate instances of running code from each other. On Windows NT/2000/XP/2003 systems, they also form the unit to which security privileges and permissions are assigned. Each process has its own security token, which indicates to Windows precisely what operations that process is permitted to do.

While processes are great for security reasons, their big disadvantage is in the area of performance. Often a number of processes will actually be working together, and therefore need to communicate with each other. The obvious example of this is where a process calls up a COM component, which is an executable, and therefore is required to run in its own process. The same thing happens in COM when surrogates are used. Since processes cannot share any memory, a complex marshaling process has to be used to copy data between the processes. This results in a very significant performance hit. If you need components to work together and don't want that performance hit, then you have to use DLL-based components and have everything running in the same address space—with the associated risk that a badly behaved component will bring everything else down.

Application domains are designed as a way of separating components without resulting in the performance problems associated with passing data between processes. The idea is that any one process is divided into a number of application domains. Each application domain roughly corresponds to a single application, and each thread of execution will be running in a particular application domain (see Figure 1-3).

If different executables are running in the same process space, then they are clearly able to easily share data, because theoretically they can directly see each other's data. However, although this is possible in principle, the CLR makes sure that this does not happen in practice by inspecting the code for each running application, to ensure that the code cannot stray outside its own data areas. This sounds at first sight like an almost impossible trick to pull off—after all how can you tell what the program is going to do without actually running it?

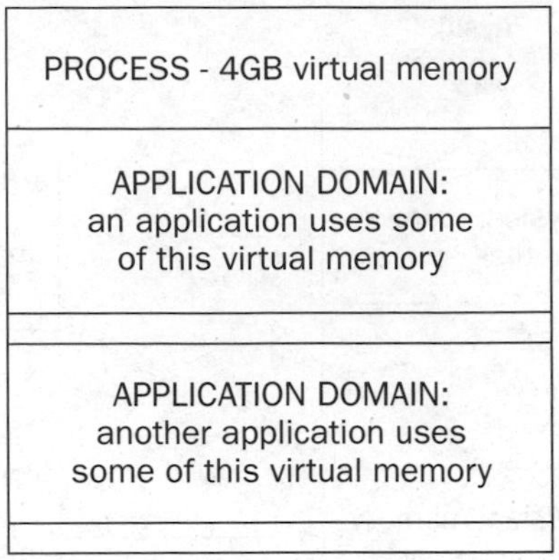

Figure 1-3

In fact, it is usually possible to do this because of the strong type safety of the IL. In most cases, unless code is using unsafe features such as pointers, the data types it is using will ensure that memory is not accessed inappropriately. For example, .NET array types perform bounds checking to ensure that no out-of-bounds array operations are permitted. If a running application does need to communicate or share data with other applications running in different application domains, then it must do so by calling on .NET's remoting services.

Code that has been verified to check that it cannot access data outside its application domain (other than through the explicit remoting mechanism) is said to be *memory type-safe*. Such code can safely be run alongside other type-safe code in different application domains within the same process.

Error Handling with Exceptions

The .NET Framework is designed to facilitate handling of error conditions using the same mechanism, based on exceptions, that is employed by Java and C++. C++ developers should note that because of IL's stronger typing system, there is no performance penalty associated with the use of exceptions with IL in the way that there is in C++. Also, the `finally` block, which has long been on many C++ developers' wish list, is supported by .NET and by C#.

We will cover exceptions in detail in Chapter 11. Briefly, the idea is that certain areas of code are designated as exception handler routines, with each one able to deal with a particular error condition (for example, a file not being found, or being denied permission to perform some operation). These conditions can be defined as narrowly or as widely as you wish. The exception architecture ensures that when an error condition occurs, execution can immediately jump to the exception handler routine that is most specifically geared to handle the exception condition in question.

The architecture of exception handling also provides a convenient means to pass an object containing precise details of the exception condition to an exception handling routine. This object might include an appropriate message for the user and details of exactly where in the code the exception was detected.

Most exception handling architecture, including the control of program flow when an exception occurs, is handled by the high-level languages (C#, Visual Basic .NET, C++), and is not supported by any special

IL commands. C#, for example, handles exceptions using `try{}`, `catch{}`, and `finally{}` blocks of code. (For more details, see Chapter 11.)

What .NET does do, however, is provide the infrastructure to allow compilers that target .NET to support exception handling. In particular, it provides a set of .NET classes that can represent the exceptions, and the language interoperability to allow the thrown exception objects to be interpreted by the exception handling code, irrespective of what language the exception handling code is written in. This language independence is absent from both the C++ and Java implementations of exception handling, although it is present to a limited extent in the COM mechanism for handling errors, which involves returning error codes from methods and passing error objects around. The fact that exceptions are handled consistently in different languages is a crucial aspect of facilitating multi-language development.

Use of Attributes

Attributes are a feature that is familiar to developers who use C++ to write COM components (through their use in Microsoft's COM Interface Definition Language [IDL]). The initial idea of an attribute was that it provided extra information concerning some item in the program that could be used by the compiler.

Attributes are supported in .NET—and hence now by C++, C#, and Visual Basic .NET. What is, however, particularly innovative about attributes in .NET is that a mechanism exists whereby you can define your own custom attributes in your source code. These user-defined attributes will be placed with the metadata for the corresponding data types or methods. This can be useful for documentation purposes, where they can be used in conjunction with reflection technology in order to perform programming tasks based on attributes. Also, in common with the .NET philosophy of language independence, attributes can be defined in source code in one language, and read by code that is written in another language.

Attributes are covered in Chapter 10.

Assemblies

An *assembly* is the logical unit that contains compiled code targeted at the .NET Framework. We are not going to cover assemblies in great detail in this chapter, because they are covered in detail in Chapter 13, but we will summarize the main points here.

An assembly is completely self-describing, and is a logical rather than a physical unit, which means that it can be stored across more than one file (indeed dynamic assemblies are stored in memory, not on file at all). If an assembly is stored in more than one file, then there will be one main file that contains the entry point and describes the other files in the assembly.

Note that the same assembly structure is used for both executable code and library code. The only real difference is that an executable assembly contains a main program entry point, whereas a library assembly doesn't.

An important characteristic of assemblies is that they contain metadata that describes the types and methods defined in the corresponding code. An assembly, however, also contains assembly metadata that describes the assembly itself. This assembly metadata, contained in an area known as the *manifest*, allows checks to be made on the version of the assembly, and on its integrity.

ildasm, a Windows-based utility, can be used to inspect the contents of an assembly, including the manifest and metadata. We discuss ildasm in Chapter 13.

The fact that an assembly contains program metadata means that applications or other assemblies that call up code in a given assembly do not need to refer to the registry, or to any other data source, in order to find out how to use that assembly. This is a significant break from the old COM way of doing things, in which the GUIDs of the components and interfaces had to be obtained from the registry, and in some cases, the details of the methods and properties exposed would need to be read from a type library.

Having data spread out in up to three different locations meant there was the obvious risk of something getting out of synchronization, which would prevent other software from being able to use the component successfully. With assemblies, there is no risk of this happening, because all the metadata is stored with the program executable instructions. Note that even though assemblies are stored across several files, there are still no problems with data going out of synchronization. This is because the file that contains the assembly entry point also stores details of, and a hash of, the contents of the other files, which means that if one of the files gets replaced, or in any way tampered with, this will almost certainly be detected and the assembly will refuse to load.

Assemblies come in two types: *shared* and *private* assemblies.

Private Assemblies

Private assemblies are the simplest type. They normally ship with software and are intended to be used only with that software. The usual scenario in which you will ship private assemblies is when you are supplying an application in the form of an executable and a number of libraries, where the libraries contain code that should only be used with that application.

The system guarantees that private assemblies will not be used by other software, because an application may only load private assemblies that are located in the same folder that the main executable is loaded in, or in a subfolder of it.

Because we would normally expect that commercial software would always be installed in its own directory, this means that there is no risk of one software package overwriting, modifying, or accidentally loading private assemblies intended for another package. As private assemblies can only be used by the software package that they are intended for, this means that you have much more control over what software uses them. There is, therefore, less need to take security precautions, since there is no risk, for example, of some other commercial software overwriting one of your assemblies with some new version of it (apart from the case where software is designed specifically to perform malicious damage). There are also no problems with name collisions. If classes in your private assembly happen to have the same name as classes in someone else's private assembly that doesn't matter, because any given application will only be able to see the one set of private assemblies.

Because a private assembly is entirely self-contained, the process of deploying it is simple. You simply place the appropriate file(s) in the appropriate folder in the file system (there are no registry entries that need to be made). This process is known as *zero impact (xcopy) installation.*

Shared Assemblies

Shared assemblies are intended to be common libraries that any other application can use. Because any other software can access a shared assembly, more precautions need to be taken against the following risks:

❑ Name collisions, where another company's shared assembly implements types that have the same names as those in your shared assembly. Because client code can theoretically have access to both assemblies simultaneously, this could be a serious problem.

❑ The risk of an assembly being overwritten by a different version of the same assembly—the new version being incompatible with some existing client code.

The solution to these problems involves placing shared assemblies in a special directory subtree in the file system, known as the *global assembly cache* (GAC). Unlike with private assemblies, this cannot be done by simply copying the assembly into the appropriate folder—it needs to be specifically installed into the cache. This process can be performed by a number of .NET utilities and involves carrying out certain checks on the assembly, as well as setting up a small folder hierarchy within the assembly cache that is used to ensure assembly integrity.

In order to avoid the risk of name collisions, shared assemblies are given a name that is based on private key cryptography (private assemblies are simply given the same name as their main file name). This name is known as a *strong name*, is guaranteed to be unique, and must be quoted by applications that reference a shared assembly.

Problems associated with the risk of overwriting an assembly are addressed by specifying version information in the assembly manifest, and by allowing side-by-side installations.

Reflection

Since assemblies store metadata, including details of all the types and members of these types that are defined in the assembly, it is possible to access this metadata programmatically. Full details of this can be found in Chapter 10. This technique, known as *reflection*, raises interesting possibilities, since it means that managed code can actually examine other managed code, or can even examine itself, to determine information about that code. This is most commonly used to obtain the details of attributes, although you can also use reflection, among other purposes, as an indirect way of instantiating classes or calling methods, given the names of those classes on methods as strings. In this way you could select classes to instantiate methods to call at runtime, rather than compile time, based on user input (dynamic binding).

.NET Framework Classes

Perhaps one of the biggest benefits of writing managed code, at least from a developer's point of view, is that you get to use the .NET *base class library*.

The .NET base classes are a massive collection of managed code classes that allow you to do almost any of the tasks that were previously available through the Windows API. These classes follow the same object model IL uses, based on single inheritance. This means that you can either instantiate objects of whichever .NET base class is appropriate, or you can derive your own classes from them.

The great thing about the .NET base classes is that they have been designed to be very intuitive and easy to use. For example, to start a thread, you call the `Start()` method of the `Thread` class. To disable a `TextBox`, you set the `Enabled` property of a `TextBox` object to `false`. This approach—while familiar to Visual Basic and Java developers, whose respective libraries are just as easy to use—will be a welcome relief to C++ developers, who for years have had to cope with such API functions as `GetDIBits()`, `RegisterWndClassEx()`, and `IsEqualIID()`, as well as a whole plethora of functions that required Windows handles to be passed around.

On the other hand, C++ developers always had easy access to the entire Windows API, whereas Visual Basic 6 and Java developers were more restricted in terms of the basic operating system functionality that they have access to from their respective languages. What is new about the .NET base classes is that they combine the ease of use that was typical of the Visual Basic and Java libraries with the relatively comprehensive coverage of the Windows API functions. There are still many features of Windows that are not available through the base classes, and for which you will need to call into the API functions, but in general, these are now confined to the more exotic features. For everyday use, you will probably find the base classes adequate. And if you do need to call into an API function, .NET offers a so-called *platform-invoke* which ensures data types are correctly converted, so the task is no harder than calling the function directly from C++ code would have been—regardless of whether you are coding in C#, C++, or Visual Basic .NET.

> *WinCV, a Windows-based utility, can be used to browse the classes, structs, interfaces, and enums in the base class library. We discuss WinCV in Chapter 12.*

Although Chapter 3 is nominally dedicated to the subject of base classes, in reality, once we have completed our coverage of the syntax of the C# language, most of the rest of this book shows you how to use various classes within the .NET base class library. That is how comprehensive base classes are. As a rough guide, the areas covered by the .NET base classes include:

❑ Core features provided by IL (including, the primitive data types in the CTS discussed in Chapter 3)

❑ Windows GUI support and controls (see Chapter 19)

❑ Web Forms (ASP.NET, discussed in Chapters 25 through 27)

❑ Data Access (ADO.NET, see Chapters 21 and 22)

❑ Directory Access (see Chapter 24)

❑ File system and registry access (see Chapter 30)

❑ Networking and Web browsing (see Chapter 31)

❑ .NET attributes and reflection (see Chapter 10)

❑ Access to aspects of the Windows OS (environment variables and so on; see Chapter 14)

❑ COM interoperability (see Chapters 28 and 29)

Incidentally, according to Microsoft sources, a large proportion of the .NET base classes have actually been written in C#!

Namespaces

Namespaces are the way that .NET avoids name clashes between classes. They are designed to avoid the situation in which you define a class to represent a customer, name your class `Customer`, and then someone else does the same thing (a likely scenario—the proportion of businesses that have customers seems to be quite high).

A namespace is no more than a grouping of data types, but it has the effect that the names of all data types within a namespace automatically get prefixed with the name of the namespace. It is also possible to nest namespaces within each other. For example, most of the general-purpose .NET base classes are in a namespace called `System`. The base class `Array` is in this namespace, so its full name is `System.Array`.

.NET requires all types to be defined in a namespace, so for example you could place your `Customer` class in a namespace called `YourCompanyName`. This class would have the full name `YourCompanyName.Customer`.

> *If a namespace is not explicitly supplied, then the type will be added to a nameless global namespace.*

Microsoft recommends that for most purposes you supply at least two nested namespace names: the first one refers to the name of your company, the second one refers to the name of the technology or software package that the class is a member of, such as `YourCompanyName.SalesServices.Customer`. This protects, in most situations, the classes in your application from possible name clashes with classes written by other organizations.

We will look more closely at namespaces in Chapter 2.

Creating .NET Applications Using C#

C# can also be used to create console applications: text-only applications that run in a DOS window. You'll probably use console applications when unit testing class libraries, and for creating Unix or Linux daemon processes. However, more often you'll use C# to create applications that use many of the technologies associated with .NET. In this section, we'll give you an overview of the different types of application that you can write in C#.

Creating ASP.NET Applications

Active Server Pages (ASP) is a Microsoft technology for creating Web pages with dynamic content. An ASP page is basically an HTML file with embedded chunks of server-side VBScript or JavaScript. When a client browser requests an ASP page, the Web server delivers the HTML portions of the page, processing the server-side scripts as it comes to them. Often these scripts query a database for data, and mark up that data in HTML. ASP is an easy way for clients to build browser-based applications.

However, ASP is not without its shortcomings. First, ASP pages sometimes render slowly because the server-side code is interpreted instead of compiled. Second, ASP files can be difficult to maintain because they were unstructured; the server-side ASP code and plain HTML are all jumbled up together. Third, ASP sometimes make development difficult because there is little support for error handling and type-checking.

Specifically, if you are using VBScript and want to implement error handling in your pages, you have to use the `On Error Resume Next` statement, and follow every component call with a check to `Err.Number` to make sure that the call had gone well.

ASP.NET is a complete revision of ASP that fixes many of its problems. It does not replace ASP; rather, ASP.NET pages can live side by side on the same server with legacy ASP applications. Of course, you can also program ASP.NET with C#!

The following section explores the key features of ASP.NET. For more details, refer to Chapters 25 through 27.

Features of ASP.NET

First, and perhaps most importantly, ASP.NET pages are *structured*. That is, each page is effectively a class that inherits from the .NET `System.Web.UI.Page` *class*, and can override a set of methods that are evoked during the `Page` object's lifetime. (You can think of these events as page-specific cousins of the `OnApplication_Start` and `OnSession_Start` events that went in the `global.asa` files of plain old ASP.) Because you can factor a page's functionality into event handlers with explicit meanings, ASP.NET pages are easier to understand.

Another nice thing about ASP.NET pages is that you can create them in Visual Studio .NET, the same environment in which you create the business logic and data access components that those ASP.NET pages use. A Visual Studio .NET project, or *solution*, contains all of the files associated with an application. Moreover, you can debug your classic ASP pages in the editor as well; in the old days of Visual InterDev, it was often a vexing challenge to configure InterDev and the project's Web server to turn debugging on.

For maximum clarity, the ASP.NET `code-behind` feature lets you take the structured approach even further. ASP.NET allows you to isolate the server-side functionality of a page to a class, compile that class into a DLL, and place that DLL into a directory below the HTML portion. A `code-behind` directive at the top of the page associates the file with its DLL. When a browser requests the page, the Web server fires the events in the class in the page's `code-behind` DLL.

Last but not least, ASP.NET is remarkable for its increased performance. Whereas classic ASP pages are interpreted with each page request, the Web server caches ASP.NET pages after compilation. This means that subsequent requests of an ASP.NET page execute more quickly than the first.

ASP.NET also makes it easy to write pages that cause forms to be displayed by the browser, which you might use in an intranet environment. The traditional wisdom is that form-based applications offer a richer user interface, but are harder to maintain because they run on so many different machines. For this reason, people have relied on form-based applications when rich user interfaces were a necessity and extensive support could be provided to the users.

With the advent of Internet Explorer 5 and the lackluster performance of Navigator 6, however, the advantages of form-based applications are clouded. IE 5's consistent and robust support for DHTML allows the programmer to create Web-based applications that are every bit as pretty as their fat client equivalents. Of course, such applications necessitate standardizing on IE and not supporting Navigator. In many industrial situations, this standardization is now common.

Web Forms

To make Web page construction even easier, Visual Studio .NET supplies *Web Forms*. They allow you to build ASP.NET pages graphically in the same way that Visual Basic 6 or C++ Builder windows are created; in other words, by dragging controls from a toolbox onto a form, then flipping over to the code aspect of that form, and writing event handlers for the controls. When you use C# to create a Web Form, you are creating a C# class that inherits from the `Page` base class, and an ASP.NET page that designates that class as its code-behind. Of course, you don't have to use C# to create a Web Form; you can use Visual Basic .NET or another .NET language just as well.

In the past, the difficulty of Web development has discouraged some teams from attempting it. To succeed in Web development, you had to know so many different technologies, such as VBScript, ASP, DHTML, JavaScript, and so on. By applying the Form concepts to Web pages, Web Forms have made Web development considerably easier.

Web controls

The controls used to populate a Web Form are not controls in the same sense as ActiveX controls. Rather, they are XML tags in the ASP.NET namespace that the Web browser dynamically transforms into HTML and client-side script when a page is requested. Amazingly, the Web server is able to render the same server-side control in different ways, producing a transformation that is appropriate to the requestor's particular Web browser. This means that it is now easy to write fairly sophisticated user interfaces for Web pages, without having to worry about how to ensure that your page will run on any of the available browsers—because Web Forms will take care of that for you.

You can use C# or Visual Basic .NET to expand the Web Form toolbox. Creating a new server-side control is simply a matter of implementing .NET's `System.Web.UI.WebControls.WebControl` class.

XML Web services

Today, HTML pages account for most of the traffic on the World Wide Web. With XML, however, computers have a device-independent format to use for communicating with each other on the Web. In the future, computers may use the Web and XML to communicate information rather than dedicated lines and proprietary formats such as *Electronic Data Interchange* (EDI). XML Web services are designed for a service-oriented Web, in which remote computers provide each other with dynamic information that can be analyzed and re-formatted, before final presentation to a user. An XML Web service is an easy way for a computer to expose information to other computers on the Web in the form of XML.

In technical terms, an XML Web service on .NET is an ASP.NET page that returns XML instead of HTML to requesting clients. Such pages have a `code-behind` DLL containing a class that derives from the `WebService` class. The Visual Studio .NET IDE provides an engine that facilitates Web Service development.

There are two main reasons that an organization might choose to use XML Web services. The first reason is that they rely on HTTP; XML Web services can use existing networks (HTTP) as a medium for conveying information. The other is that because XML Web services use XML, the data format is self-describing, non-proprietary, and platform-independent.

Creating Windows Forms

Although C# and .NET are particularly suited to Web development, they still offer splendid support for so-called *fat-client* or *thick-client* apps, applications that have to be installed on the end-user's machine where most of the processing takes place. This support is from *Windows Forms*.

A Windows Form is the .NET answer to a Visual Basic 6 Form. To design a graphical window interface, you just drag controls from a toolbox onto a Windows Form. To determine the window's behavior, you write event-handling routines for the form's controls. A Windows Form project compiles to an executable that must be installed alongside the .NET runtime on the end user's computer. Like other .NET project types, Windows Form projects are supported by both Visual Basic .NET and C#. We examine Windows Forms more closely in Chapter 19.

Windows Controls

Although Web Forms and Windows Forms are developed in much the same way, you use different kinds of controls to populate them. Web Forms use Web Controls, and Windows Forms use *Windows Controls*.

A Windows Control is a lot like an ActiveX control. After a Windows control is implemented, it compiles to a DLL that must be installed on the client's machine. In fact, the .NET SDK provides a utility that creates a wrapper for ActiveX controls, so that they can be placed on Windows Forms. As is the case with Web Controls, Windows Control creation involves deriving from a particular class, `System.Windows.Forms.Control`.

Windows Services

A Windows Service (originally called an NT Service) is a program that is designed to run in the background in Windows NT/2000/XP/2003 (but not Windows 9x). Services are useful where you want a program to be running continuously and ready to respond to events without having been explicitly started by the user. A good example would be the World Wide Web Service on Web servers, which listens out for Web requests from clients.

It is very easy to write services in C#. There are .NET Framework base classes available in the `System.ServiceProcess` namespace that handle many of the boilerplate tasks associated with services, and in addition, Visual Studio .NET allows you to create a C# Windows Service project, which uses C# source code for a basic Windows service. We'll explore how to write C# Windows Services in Chapter 32.

The Role of C# in the .NET Enterprise Architecture

C# requires the presence of the .NET runtime, and it will probably be a few years before most clients—particularly most home computers—have .NET installed. In the meantime, installing a C# application is likely to mean also installing the .NET redistributable components. Because of that, it is likely that we will see many C# applications first in the enterprise environment. Indeed, C# arguably presents an outstanding opportunity for organizations that are interested in building robust, n-tiered client-server applications.

When combined with ADO.NET, C# has the ability to access quickly and generically data stores like SQL Server and Oracle databases. The returned datasets can easily be manipulated using the ADO.NET object model, and automatically render as XML for transport across an office intranet.

Once a database schema has been established for a new project, C# presents an excellent medium for implementing a layer of data access objects, each of which could provide insertion, updates, and deletion access to a different database table.

Because it's the first component-based C language, C# is a great language for implementing a business object tier, too. It encapsulates the messy plumbing for inter-component communication, leaving developers free to focus on gluing their data access objects together in methods that accurately enforce their organizations' business rules. Moreover, with attributes, C# business objects can be outfitted for method-level security checks, object pooling, and JIT activation supplied by COM+ Services. Furthermore, .NET ships with utility programs that allows your new .NET business objects to interface with legacy COM components.

To create an enterprise application with C#, you create a Class Library project for the data access objects and another for the business objects. While developing, you can use Console projects to test the methods on your classes. Fans of extreme programming can build Console projects that can be executed automatically from batch files to unit test that working code has not been broken.

On a related note, C# and .NET will probably influence the way you physically package your reusable classes. In the past, many developers crammed a multitude of classes into a single physical component because this arrangement made deployment a lot easier; if there was a versioning problem, you knew just where to look. Because deploying .NET enterprise components simply involves copying files into directories, developers can now package their classes into more logical, discrete components without encountering "DLL Hell."

Last but not least, ASP.NET pages coded in C# constitute an excellent medium for user interfaces. Because ASP.NET pages compile, they execute quickly. Because they can be debugged in the Visual Studio .NET IDE, they are robust. Because they support full-scale language features like early binding, inheritance, and modularization, ASP.NET pages coded in C# are tidy and easily maintained.

Seasoned developers acquire a healthy skepticism about strongly hyped new technologies and languages and are reluctant to utilize new platforms simply because they are urged to. If you're an enterprise developer in an IT department, though, or if you provide application services across the World Wide Web, let us assure you that C# and .NET offer at least four solid benefits, even if some of the more exotic features like XML Web services and server-side controls don't pan out:

❑   Component conflicts will become infrequent and deployment is easier, because different versions of the same component can run side by side on the same machine without conflicting.

❑   Your ASP.NET code won't look like spaghetti code.

❑   You can leverage a lot of the functionality in the .NET base classes.

❑   For applications requiring a Windows Forms user interface, C# makes it very easy to write this kind of application.

Windows Forms have to some extent been downplayed in the last year due to the advent of Web Forms and Internet-based applications. However, if you or your colleagues lack expertise in JavaScript, ASP, or related technologies, then Windows Forms are still a viable option for creating a user interface with speed and ease. Just remember to factor your code so that the user interface logic is separate from the business logic and the data access code. Doing so will allow you to migrate your application to the browser at some point in the future if you need to do so. Also, it is likely that Windows Forms will remain the dominant user interface for applications for use in homes and small businesses for a long time to come.

Summary

We've covered a lot of ground in this chapter, briefly reviewing important aspects of the .NET Framework and C#'s relationship to it. We started by discussing how all languages that target .NET are compiled into Microsoft intermediate language (IL) before this is compiled and executed by the Common Language Runtime (CLR). We also discussed the roles of the following features of .NET in the compilation and execution process:

❑ Assemblies and .NET base classes

❑ COM components

❑ JIT compilation

❑ Application domains

❑ Garbage Collection

Figure 1-4 provides an overview of how these features come into play during compilation and execution.

We also discussed the characteristics of IL, particularly its strong data typing and object-orientation. We noted how these characteristics influence the languages that target .NET, including C#. We also noted how the strongly typed nature of IL enables language interoperability, as well as CLR services such as garbage collection and security.

Finally, we talked about how C# can be used as the basis for applications that are built upon several .NET technologies, including ASP.NET.

The following chapter discusses how to write code in C#.

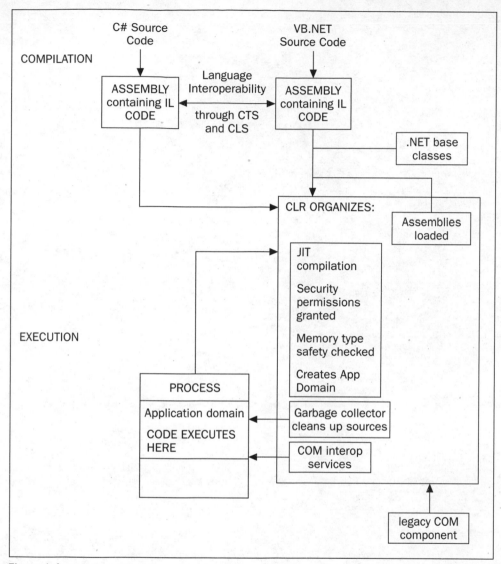

Figure 1-4

2

C# Basics

Now that you understand a little more about what C# can do, you will want to learn how to use it. This chapter on the basics of C# will give you a good start in that direction by providing you with a basic knowledge of the fundamentals of C# programming, which we will build on in subsequent chapters. The main topics we will be covering are:

- ❑ Declaring variables
- ❑ Initialization and scope of variables
- ❑ Predefined C# data types
- ❑ Dictating the flow of execution within a C# program using loops and conditional statements
- ❑ Enumerations
- ❑ Namespaces
- ❑ The `Main()` method
- ❑ Basic command line C# compiler options
- ❑ Using `System.Console` to perform console I/O
- ❑ Using documentation features in C# and Visual Studio .NET
- ❑ C# identifiers and keywords
- ❑ Recommended guidelines and conventions for good programming in C#.

By the end of this chapter you will know enough C# to write simple programs, though without using inheritance or other object-oriented features, which are covered in the following chapters.

Before We Start

As we have already mentioned, C# is an object-oriented language. As we get you up to speed in the fundamentals of the C# language, we will be assuming that you have a good grasp of the concepts behind object-oriented (OO) programming. In other words, we will expect you to understand what we mean by *classes*, *objects*, *interfaces*, and *inheritance*. If you have programmed in C++ or Java before, you should have a pretty good grounding in object-oriented programming (OOP). However, if you do not have a background in OOP, there are plenty of good sources of information on this subject. You can start with Appendix A, which presents a detailed introduction to OOP concepts and is posted at www.wrox.com. We also recommend Beginning Visual C#, the revised edition of *Beginning C# for .NET v1.0* (ISBN 0-7645-4382-2) which teaches both object-oriented programming and C# from scratch.

If you are an experienced developer in Visual Basic 6, C++, or Java, you should note that we will make many comparisons between C#, C++, Java, and Visual Basic 6 as we walk you through the basics of C#. However, you might prefer to learn C# initially by reading a comparison between C# and your selected language. If so, we have also made available separate documents for download on the Wrox Press Web site (www.wrox.com) that give introductions to C# from the point of view of each of those languages.

Our First C# Program

Let's start in the traditional way by compiling and running the simplest possible C# program—a simple class consisting of a console application that writes a message to the screen.

The Code

Type the following into a text editor (such as Notepad), and save it with a .cs extension (for example, First.cs):

```csharp
using System;

namespace Wrox.ProCSharp.Basics
{
    class MyFirstCSharpClass
    {
        static void Main()
        {
            Console.WriteLine("This isn't at all like Java!");
            Console.ReadLine();
            return;
        }
    }
}
```

The following chapters present a number of code samples. The most common technique for writing C# programs is to use Visual Studio .NET to generate a basic project and add your own code to it. However, since the aim of these early chapters is to teach the C# language, we are going to keep things simple and avoid relying on Visual Studio .NET until Chapter 12. Instead, we will present the code as simple files that you can type in using any text editor and compile from the command line.

Compiling and Running the Program

You can compile this program by simply running the C# command line compiler (csc.exe) against the source file, like this:

csc First.cs

If you want to compile code from the command line using the csc command, you should be aware that the .NET command line tools, including csc, are only available if certain environment variables have been set up. Depending on how you installed .NET (and Visual Studio .NET), this may or may not be the case on your machine.

> *If you do not have the environment variables set up, you have the following two options. The first is to run the batch file %Microsoft Visual Studio.NET%\Vc7\bin\vcvars32.bat from the command prompt before running csc, where %Microsoft Visual Studio .NET is the folder to which Visual Studio .NET has been installed. The second (easier) way is to use the Visual Studio .NET command prompt instead of the usual command prompt window. You will find the Visual Studio .NET command prompt in the Start Menu, under Programs, Microsoft Visual Studio.NET 2003, Microsoft Visual Studio .NET Tools. It is simply a command prompt window that automatically runs vcvars32.bat when it opens.*

Compiling the code produces an executable file named First.exe, which we can run from the command line or from Windows Explorer like any other executable. Give it a try:

csc First.cs

```
Microsoft (R) Visual C# .NET Compiler version 7.10.3052.4
for Microsoft (R) .NET Framework version 1.1.4322
Copyright (C) Microsoft Corporation 2001-2002. All rights reserved.
```

First

```
This isn't at all like Java!
```

Well, maybe that message isn't quite true! There are some fairly fundamental similarities to Java in this program, although there are one or two points (such as the capitalized Main() function) to catch out the unwary Java or C++ developer. Let's look a little more closely at what's going on in the code.

A Closer Look

First, a few general comments about C# syntax. In C#, as in other C-style languages, every statement must end in a semicolon (;) and can continue over multiple lines without needing a continuation character (such as the underscore in Visual Basic). Statements can be joined into blocks using curly braces ({}). Single-line comments begin with two forward slash characters (//), and multi-line comments begin with a slash and an asterisk (/*) and end with the same combination reversed (*/). In these aspects, C# is identical to C++ and Java, but different from Visual Basic. It is the semicolons and curly braces that give C# code such a different visual appearance to Visual Basic code. If your background is predominantly Visual Basic, then take extra care to remember the semicolon at the end of every statement.

Omitting this is usually the biggest single cause of compilation errors among developers new to C-style languages.

The first couple of lines in the previous code example have to do with *namespaces* (mentioned in Chapter 1), which are a way to group together associated classes. This concept will be familiar to Java and C++ developers but may be new to Visual Basic 6 developers. C# namespaces are basically the same as C++ namespaces or, equivalently, Java packages, but there is no comparable concept in Visual Basic 6. The `namespace` keyword declares the namespace our class should be associated with. All code within the following braces is regarded as being within that namespace. The `using` statement specifies a namespace that the compiler should look at to find any classes that are referenced in your code but which aren't defined in the current namespace. This performs the same purpose as the `import` statement in Java and the `using namespace` statement in C++.

```
using System;

namespace Wrox.ProCSharp.Basics
{
```

The reason for the presence of the `using` statement in the First.cs file is that we are going to use a library class, `System.Console`. The `using System` statement allows us to refer to this class simply as `Console` (and similarly for any other classes in the `System` namespace). The standard `System` namespace is where the most commonly used .NET types reside. It is important to realize that everything we do in C# depends on the .NET base classes; in this case, we are using the `Console` class within the `System` namespace in order to write to the console window.

> Since almost *every* C# program uses classes in the System namespace, we will assume that a `using System;` statement is present in the file for all code snippets in this chapter.

Note that C# has no built-in keywords of its own for input or output; it is completely reliant on the .NET classes.

Next, we declare a class ostensibly called `MyFirstClass`. However, because it has been placed in a namespace called `Wrox.ProCSharp.Basics` the fully qualified name of this class is `Wrox.ProCSharp.Basics.MyFirstCSharpClass`.

```
class MyFirstCSharpClass
{
```

As in Java, all C# code must be contained within a class. Classes in C# are similar to classes in Java and C++, and very roughly comparable to class modules in Visual Basic 6. The class declaration consists of the `class` keyword, followed by the class name and a pair of curly braces. All code associated with the class should be placed between these braces.

Next we declare a method called `Main()`. Every C# executable (such as console applications, Windows applications, and Windows services) must have an entry point—the `Main()` method (note the capital `M`):

```
static void Main()
{
```

The method is called when the program is started, like the `main()` function in C++ or Java, or `Sub Main()` in a Visual Basic 6 module. This method must return either nothing (`void`) or an integer (`int`). A C# method corresponds to a method in C++ and Java (sometimes referred to in C++ as a member function). It also corresponds to either a Visual Basic `Function` or a Visual Basic `Sub`, depending on whether the method returns anything (unlike Visual Basic, C# makes no conceptual distinction between functions and subroutines).

Note the format of method definitions in C#:

```
[modifiers] return_type MethodName([parameters])
{
    // Method body. NB. This code block is pseudo-code
}
```

Here, the first square brackets represent certain optional keywords. Modifiers are used to specify certain features of the method we are defining, such as where the method can be called from. In our case, we have two modifiers: `public` and `static`. The `public` modifier means that the method can be accessed from anywhere, so it can be called from outside our class. This is the same meaning as `public` in C++ and Java, and `Public` in Visual Basic. The `static` modifier indicates that the method does not operate on a specific instance of our class and therefore is called without first instantiating the class. This is important since we are creating an executable rather than a class library. Once again, this has the same meaning as the `static` keyword in C++ and Java, though in this case there is no Visual Basic equivalent (the `Static` keyword in Visual Basic has a different meaning). We set the return type to `void`, and in our example, we don't include any parameters.

Finally we come to the code statements themselves:

```
Console.WriteLine("This isn't at all like Java!");
Console.ReadLine();
return;
```

In this case, we simply call the `WriteLine()` method of the `System.Console` class to write a line of text to the console window. `WriteLine()` is a `static` method, so we don't need to instantiate a `Console` object before calling it.

`Console.ReadLine()` reads user input. Adding this line forces the application to wait for the carriage return key to be hit before the application exits, and, in the case of Visual Studio .NET, the console window disappears.

We then call `return` to exit from the method (and, since this is the `Main()` method, the program). We specified `void` in our method header, so we don't return any parameters. The `return` statement is equivalent to `return` in C++ and Java, and `Exit Sub` or `Exit Function` in Visual Basic.

Now that we have given you a taste of basic C# syntax, we are ready to go into more detail with the various aspects of C#. Since it is virtually impossible to write any non-trivial program without *variables*, we will start by looking at variables in C#.

Variables

We declare variables in C# using the following syntax:

```
datatype identifier;
```

for example:

```
int i;
```

This statement declares an `int` named `i`. The compiler won't actually let us use this variable until we have initialized it with a value, but the declaration allocates four bytes on the stack to hold the value.

Once it has been declared, we can assign a value to the variable using the assignment operator, =:

```
i = 10;
```

We can also declare the variable and initialize its value at the same time:

```
int i = 10;
```

This syntax is identical to C++ and Java syntax, but very different from Visual Basic syntax for declaring variables. If you are coming from Visual Basic 6, you should also be aware that C# doesn't distinguish between objects and simple types, so there is no need for anything like the `Set` keyword, even if we want our variable to refer to an object. The C# syntax for declaring variables is the same no matter what the data type of the variable.

If we declare and initialize more than one variable in a single statement, all of the variables will be of the same data type:

```
int x = 10, y =20;    // x and y are both ints
```

To declare variables of different types, you need to use separate statements. Don't assign different data types within a multiple variable declaration:

```
int x = 10;
bool y = true;            // Creates a variable that stores true or false
int x = 10, bool y = true;   // This won't compile!
```

Initialization of Variables

Variable initialization demonstrates another example of C#'s emphasis on safety. Briefly, the C# compiler requires that any variable be initialized with some starting value before we refer to that variable in an operation. Most modern compilers will flag violations of this as a warning, but the ever-vigilant C# compiler treats such violations as errors. This prevents us from unintentionally retrieving junk values from memory that is left over from other programs.

C# has two methods for ensuring that variables are initialized before use:

❑ Variables that are fields in a class or struct, if not initialized explicitly, are by default zeroed out when they are created.

❑ Variables that are local to a method must be explicitly initialized in your code prior to any statements in which their values are used. In this case, the initialization doesn't have to happen when the variable is declared, but the compiler will check all possible paths through the method and will flag an error if it detects any possibility of the value of a local variable being used before it is initialized.

C#'s approach contrasts with that of C++, in which the compiler leaves it up to the programmer to make sure that variables are initialized before use, and that of Visual Basic, in which all variables are zeroed out automatically.

For example, we can't do the following in C#:

```
public static int Main()
{
   int d;
   Console.WriteLine(d);    // Can't do this! Need to initialize d before use
   return 0;
}
```

Notice that for this code snippet we have demonstrated defining `Main()` so it returns an `int` instead of `void`.

When we attempt to compile these lines, we will receive this kind of error message:

```
Use of unassigned local variable 'd'
```

The same rules apply to reference types as well. Consider the following statement:

```
Something objSomething;
```

In C++, this line would create an instance of the `Something` class on the stack. In C#, this same line of code would only create a *reference* for a `Something` object, but this reference does not yet actually refer to any object. Any attempt to call a method or property against this variable would result in an error.

Instantiating a reference object in C# requires use of the `new` keyword. We create a reference as shown in the previous example and then point the reference at an object allocated on the heap using the `new` keyword:

```
objSomething = new Something();    // This creates a Something on the heap
```

Variable Scope

The *scope* of a variable is the region of code from which the variable can be accessed. In general, the scope is determined by the following rules:

❑ A *field* (also known as a member variable) of a class is in scope for as long as its containing class is in scope (this is the same as for C++, Java, and VB).

❑ *local variable* is in scope until a closing brace indicates the end of the block statement or method in which it was declared.

❑ A local variable that is declared in a `for`, `while`, or similar statement is in scope in the body of that loop. (C++ developers will note that this is the same behavior as the ANSI standard for C++. Early versions of the Microsoft C++ compiler did not comply with this standard, but scoped such variables to remain in scope after the loop terminated.)

Scope clashes for local variables

It's common in a large program to use the same variable name for different variables in different parts of the program. This is fine as long as the variables are scoped to completely different parts of the program so there is no possibility for ambiguity. However bear in mind that local variables with the same name can't be declared twice in the same scope, so we can't do this:

```
int x = 20;
// some more code
int x = 30;
```

Consider the following code sample:

```
using System;

namespace Wrox.ProCSharp.Basics
{
   public class ScopeTest
   {
      public static int Main()
      {
         for (int i = 0; i < 10; i++)
         {
            Console.WriteLine(i);
         }   // i goes out of scope here

         // We can declare a variable named i again, because
         // there's no other variable with that name in scope
         for (int i = 9; i >= 0; i--)
         {
            Console.WriteLine(i);
         }   // i goes out of scope here
         return 0;
      }
   }
}
```

This code simply prints out the numbers from 0 to 9, and then back again from 9 to 0, using a `for` loop. The important thing to note is that we declare the variable `i` twice in this code, within the same method. The reason that we can do this is that `i` is declared in two separate loops, so each `i` variable is local to its own loop.

Let's have a look at another example:

```
      public static int Main()
      {
         int j = 20;
```

```
        for (int i = 0; i < 10; i++)
        {
            int j = 30;   // Can't do this - j is still in scope
            Console.WriteLine(j + i);
        }
        return 0;
    }
```

If we try to compile this, we'll get an error:

```
ScopeTest.cs(12,14): error CS0136: A local variable named 'j' cannot be declared in
this scope because it would give a different meaning to 'j', which is already used
in a 'parent or current' scope to denote something else
```

This is because the variable j, which we defined before the start of the for loop, is still in scope within the for loop, and won't go out of scope until the Main() method has finished executing. Although the second j (the illegal one) is in the loop's scope, that scope is nested within the Main() method's scope. The compiler has no way to distinguish between these two variables, so it won't allow the second one to be declared. This is again different from C++ where variable hiding is permitted.

Scope clashes for fields and local variables

In certain circumstances, however, we can distinguish between two identifiers with the same name (although not the same fully qualified name) and the same scope, and in this case the compiler will allow us to declare the second variable. The reason is that C# makes a fundamental distinction between variables that are declared at the type level (fields) and variables declared within methods (local variables):

Consider the following code snippet:

```
using System;

namespace Wrox.ProCSharp.Basics
{
    class ScopeTest2
    {
        static int j = 20;

        public static void Main()
        {
            int j = 30;
            Console.WriteLine(j);
            return;
        }
    }
}
```

This code will compile, even though we have two variables named j in scope within the Main() method: the j that was defined at the class level, and doesn't go out of scope until the class is destroyed (when the Main() method terminates, and the program ends), and the j defined in Main(). In this case, the new variable named j that we declare in the Main() method *hides* the class-level variable with the same name, so when we run this code, the number 30 will be displayed.

However, what if we want to refer to the class-level variable? We can actually refer to fields of a class or struct from outside the object, using the syntax object.fieldname. In the previous example, we are accessing a static field (we will look at what this means in the next section) from a static method, so we can't use an instance of the class; we just use the name of the class itself:

```
...
public static void Main()
{
    int j = 30;
    Console.WriteLine(ScopeTest2.j);
}
...
```

If we were accessing an instance field (a field that belongs to a specific instance of the class), we would need to use the this keyword instead. This keyword performs the same role as this in C++ and Java, and Me in Visual Basic.

Constants

Prefixing a variable with the const keyword when it is declared and initialized designates that variable as a constant. As the name implies, a constant is a variable whose value cannot be changed throughout its lifetime:

```
const int a = 100;    // This value cannot be changed
```

Constants will be familiar to Visual Basic and C++ developers. C++ developers should, however, note that C# does not permit all the subtleties of C++ constants. In C++, not only could variables be declared as constant, but depending on the declaration, you could have constant pointers, variable pointers to constants, constant methods (that don't change the contents of the containing object), constant parameters to methods, and so on. These subtleties have been discarded in C#, and all you can do is declare local variables and fields to be constant.

Constants have the following characteristics:

- ❑ They must be initialized when they are declared, and once a value has been assigned, it can never be overwritten.

- ❑ The value of a constant must be computable at compile time. Therefore, we can't initialize a constant with a value taken from a variable. If you need to do this, you will need to use a read-only field (which we explain in Chapter 3).

- ❑ Constants are always implicitly static. However, notice that we don't have to (and, in fact, are not permitted to) include the static modifier in the constant declaration.

There are at least three advantages to using constants in your programs:

- ❑ Constants make your programs easier to read by replacing magic numbers and strings with readable names whose values are easy to understand.

- ❑ Constants make your programs easier to modify. For example, let's assume that you have a SalesTax constant in one of your C# programs, and that constant is assigned a value of

6 percent. If the sales tax rate changes at a later point in time, you can modify the behavior of all tax calculations simply by assigning a new value to the constant; you don't have to hunt throughout your code for the value .06 and change each one, hoping that you've found all of them.

❑ Constants make it easier to avoid mistakes in your programs. If you attempt to assign another value to a constant somewhere in your program other than at the point where the constant is declared, the compiler will flag the error.

Predefined Data Types

Now that we have seen how to declare variables and constants, we shall take a closer look at the data types available in C#. As we will see, C# is a lot fussier about the types available and their definitions than some other languages are.

Value Types and Reference Types

Before examining the data types in C#, it is important to understand that C# distinguishes between two categories of data type:

❑ Value types

❑ Reference types

We will look in detail at the syntax for value and reference types over the next few sections. Conceptually, the difference is that a *value type* stores its value directly, while a *reference type* stores a reference to the value. Compared to other languages, value types in C# are basically the same thing as simple types (integer, float, but not pointers or references) in Visual Basic or C++. Reference types are the same as reference types in Visual Basic, or are similar to types accessed through pointers in C++.

These types are stored in different places in memory; value types in an area known as the *stack*, while reference types are stored in an area known as the *managed heap*. It is important to be aware of whether a type is a value type or a reference type because of the different effect that assignment has. For example, int is a value type, which means that the following statement will result in two locations in memory storing the value 20:

```
// i and j are both of type int
i = 20;
j = i;
```

However, consider the following code. For this code, we will assume we have defined a class called Vector. We assume that Vector is a reference type and has an int member variable called Value:

```
Vector x, y;
x = new Vector();
x.Value = 30;    // Value is a field defined in Vector class
y = x;
Console.WriteLine(y.Value);
y.Value = 50;
Console.WriteLine(x.Value);
```

The crucial point to understand is that after executing this code, there is only one Vector object around. x and y both point to the memory location that contains this object. Since x and y are variables of a reference type, declaring each variable simply reserves a reference—it doesn't instantiate an object of the given type. This is the same as declaring a pointer in C++ or an object reference in Visual Basic. In neither case does an object actually get created. In order to create an object we have to use the new keyword, as shown. Since x and y refer to the same object, changes made to x will affect y and vice versa. Hence the previous code will display 30 then 50.

> C++ developers should note that this syntax is like a reference, not a pointer. We use the . notation, not
> ->, to access object members. Syntactically, C# references look more like C++ reference variables.
> However, behind the superficial syntax, the real similarity is with C++ pointers.

If a variable is a reference, it is possible to indicate that it does not refer to any object by setting its value to null:

```
y = null;
```

This is just the same as setting a reference to null in Java, a pointer to NULL in C++, or an object reference in Visual Basic to Nothing. If a reference is set to null, then clearly it is not possible to call any non-static member functions or fields against it; doing so would cause an exception to be thrown at runtime.

In languages like C++, the developer could choose whether a given value was to be accessed directly or via a pointer. Visual Basic was more restrictive, taking the view that COM objects were reference types and simple types were always value types. C# is similar to Visual Basic in this regard: whether a variable is a value or reference is determined solely by its data type, so int for example is always a value type. It is not possible to declare an int variable as a reference (although in Chapter 5 when we cover *boxing*, we will see it is possible to wrap value types in references of type object).

In C#, basic data types like bool and long are value types. This means that if we declare a bool variable and assign it the value of another bool variable, we will have two separate bool values in memory. Later, if we change the value of the original bool variable, the value of the second bool variable does not change. These types are copied by value.

In contrast, most of the more complex C# data types, including classes that we ourselves declare, are reference types. They are allocated upon the heap, have lifetimes that can span multiple function calls, and can be accessed through one or several aliases. The Common Language Runtime (CLR) implements an elaborate algorithm to track which reference variables are still reachable, and which have been orphaned. Periodically, the CLR will destroy orphaned objects and return the memory that they once occupied back to the operating system. This is done by the garbage collector.

C# has been designed this way because high performance is best served by keeping primitive types (like int and bool) as value types, while having larger types that contain many fields (as is usually the case with classes) as reference types. If you want to define your own type as a value type, you should declare it as a struct.

CTS Types

As we pointed out in Chapter 1, the basic predefined types recognized by C# are not intrinsic to the language but part of the .NET Framework. For example, when you declare an int in C#, what you are actually declaring is an instance of a .NET struct, System.Int32. This may sound like an esoteric point, but it has a profound significance: it means that you are able to treat all the primitive data types syntactically as if they were classes that supported certain methods. For example, to convert an int i to a string you can write:

```
string s = i.ToString();
```

It should be emphasized that, behind this syntactical convenience, the types really are stored as primitive types, so there is absolutely no performance cost associated with the idea that the primitive types are notionally represented by .NET structs.

Let's now review the types that are recognized as built-in types in C#. We will list each type, along with its definition and the name of the corresponding .NET type (CTS type). C# has 15 predefined types, 13 value types, and 2 (string and object) reference types.

Predefined Value Types

The built-in value types represent primitives, such as integer and floating-point numbers, character, and Boolean types.

Integer types

C# supports eight predefined integer types:

Name	CTS Type	Description	Range (min:max)
sbyte	System.SByte	8-bit signed integer	-128:127 (-2^7:2^7-1)
short	System.Int16	16-bit signed integer	-32,768:32,767 (-2^{15}:2^{15}-1)
int	System.Int32	32-bit signed integer	-2,147,483,648:2,147,483,647 (-2^{31}:2^{31}-1)
long	System.Int64	64-bit signed integer	-9,223,372,036,854,775,808: 9,223,372,036,854,775,807 (-2^{63}:2^{63}-1)
byte	System.Byte	8-bit unsigned integer	0:255 (0:2^8-1)
ushort	System.UInt16	16-bit unsigned integer	0:65,535 (0:2^{16}-1)
uint	System.UInt32	32-bit unsigned integer	0:4,294,967,295 (0:2^{32}-1)
ulong	System.UInt64	64-bit unsigned integer	0:18,446,744,073,709,551,615 (0:2^{64}-1)

Future versions of Windows will target 64-bit processors, which can move bits into and out of memory in larger chunks to achieve faster processing times. Consequently, C# supports a rich palette of signed and unsigned integer types ranging in size from 8 to 64 bits.

Many of these type names will be new to Visual Basic. C++ and Java developers should be careful; some of the names of C# types are the same as C++ and Java types, but the types have different definitions.

For example, in C#, an `int` is always a 32-bit signed integer. In C++ an `int` is a signed integer, but the number of bits is platform-dependent (32 bits on Windows). In C#, all data types have been defined in a platform-independent manner in order to allow for the possible future porting of C# and .NET to other platforms.

A `byte` is the standard 8-bit type for values in the range 0 to 255 inclusive. Be aware that, in keeping with its emphasis on type safety, C# regards the `byte` type and the `char` type as completely distinct, and any programmatic conversions between the two must be explicitly requested. Also be aware that unlike the other types in the integer family, a `byte` type is by default unsigned. Its signed version bears the special name `sbyte`.

With .NET, a `short` is no longer quite so short; it is now 16 bits long. The `int` type is 32 bits long. The `long` type reserves 64 bits for values. All integer-type variables can be assigned values in decimal or in hex notation. The latter require the `0x` prefix:

```
long x = 0x12ab;
```

If there is any ambiguity about whether an integer is `int`, `uint`, `long`, or `ulong`, it will default to an `int`. In order to specify which of the other integer types the value should take, you can append one of the following characters to the number:

```
uint ui = 1234U;
long l = 1234L;
ulong ul = 1234UL;
```

We can also use lowercase `u` and `l`, although the latter could be confused with the integer `1` (one).

Floating point types

Although C# provides a plethora of integer data types, it supports floating-point types as well. They will be familiar to C and C++ programmers:

Name	CTS Type	Description	Significant Figures	Range (approximate)
float	System.Single	32-bit single-precision floating point	7	$\pm1.5 \_ 10^{-45}$ to $\pm3.4 \_ 10^{38}$
double	System.Double	64-bit double-precision floating point	15/16	$\pm5.0 \_ 10^{-324}$ to $\pm1.7 \_ 10^{308}$

The `float` data type is for smaller floating-point values, for which less precision is required. The `double` data type is bulkier than the `float` data type, but offers twice the precision (15 digits).

If you hard-code in a non-integer number (such as 12.3) in your code, the compiler will normally assume you want the number interpreted as a double. If we want to specify that the value is a `float`, we append the character F (or f) to it:

```
float f = 12.3F;
```

The decimal type

In addition, there is a `decimal` type representing higher precision floating-point numbers:

Name	CTS Type	Description	Significant Figures	Range (approximate)
decimal	System.Decimal	128-bit high precision decimal notation	28	$\pm1.0 \_ 10^{-28}$ to $\pm7.9 \_ 10^{28}$

One of the great things about the CTS and C# is the provision of a dedicated `decimal` type for financial calculations. How you use the 28 digits that the decimal type provides is up to you. In other words, you can track smaller dollar amounts with greater accuracy for cents, or larger dollar amounts with more rounding in the fractional area. You should bear in mind, however, that `decimal` is not implemented under the hood as a primitive type, so using `decimal` will have a performance impact on your calculations.

To specify that our number is of a `decimal` type rather than a `double`, `float`, or an integer, we can append the `M` (or `m`) character to the value as shown in the following example:

```
decimal d = 12.30M;
```

The Boolean type

The C# `bool` type is used to contain Boolean values of either `true` or `false`:

Name	CTS Type	Values
bool	System.Boolean	true or false

We cannot implicitly convert `bool` values to and from integer values. If a variable (or a function return type) is declared as a `bool`, then we can only use values of `true` and `false`. We will get an error if we try to use zero for `false` and a non-zero value for `true`.

The character type

For storing the value of a single character, C# supports the `char` data type:

Name	CTS Type	Values
char	System.Char	Represents a single 16-bit (Unicode) character

Although this data type has a superficial resemblance to the `char` type provided by C and C++, there is a significant difference. C++ char represents an 8-bit character, whereas a C# char contains 16 bits. This is part of the reason that implicit conversions between the `char` type and the 8-bit `byte` type are not permitted.

Although 8 bits may be enough to encode every character in the English language and the digits 0-9, they aren't enough to encode every character in more expansive symbol systems (such as Chinese). In a gesture toward universality, the computer industry is moving away from the 8-bit character set and toward the 16-bit Unicode scheme, of which the ASCII encoding is a subset.

Literals of type char are signified by being enclosed in single quotes, for example 'A'. If we try to enclose a character in double quotes, the compiler will treat this as a string and throw an error.

As well as representing chars as character literals, we can represent them with 4-digit hex Unicode values (for example '\u0041'), as integer values with a cast (for example, (char) 65), or as hexadecimal values ('\x0041'). They can also be represented by an escape sequence:

Escape Sequence	Character
\'	Single quote
\"	Double quote
\\	Backslash
\0	Null
\a	Alert
\b	Backspace
\f	Form feed
\n	Newline
\r	Carriage return
\t	Tab character
\v	Vertical tab

C++ developers should note that because C# has a native string type, we don't need to represent strings as arrays of chars.

Predefined Reference Types

C# supports two predefined reference types:

Name	CTS Type	Description
object	System.Object	The root type, from which all other types in the CTS derive (including value types)
string	System.String	Unicode character string

The object type

Many programming languages and class hierarchies provide a root type, from which all other objects in the hierarchy derive. C# and .NET are no exception. In C#, the object type is the ultimate parent type from which all other intrinsic and user-defined types derive. This is a key feature of C#, which distinguishes it from both Visual Basic and C++, although its behavior here is very similar to Java. All types implicitly derive ultimately from the System.Object class. This means that we can use the object type for two purposes.

❑ We can use an object reference to bind to an object of any particular sub-type. For example, in Chapter 5 we'll see how we can use the object type to box a value object on the stack to move it to the heap. object references are also useful in reflection, when code must manipulate objects whose specific types are unknown. This is similar to the role played by a void pointer in C++ or by a Variant data type in VB.

❑ The object type implements a number of basic, general-purpose methods, which include Equals(), GetHashCode(), GetType(), and ToString(). Responsible user-defined classes may need to provide replacement implementations of some of these methods using an object-oriented technique known as *overriding*, which we will discuss in Chapter 4. When we override ToString(), for example, we equip our class with a method for intelligently providing a string representation of itself. If we don't provide our own implementations for these methods in our classes, the compiler will pick up the implementations in object, which may or may not be correct or sensible in the context of our classes.

We'll examine the object type in more detail in subsequent chapters.

The string type

Veterans of C and C++ probably have battle scars from wrestling with C-style strings. A C or C++ string was nothing more than an array of characters, so the client programmer had to do a lot of work just to copy one string to another or to concatenate two strings. In fact, for a generation of C++ programmers, implementing a string class that wrapped up the messy details of these operations was a rite of passage requiring many hours of teeth gnashing and head scratching. Visual Basic programmers had a somewhat easier life, with a string type, while Java people had it even better, with a String class that is in many ways very similar to C# string.

C# recognizes the string keyword, which under the hood is translated to the .NET class, System.String. With it, operations like string concatenation and string copying are a snap:

```
string str1 = "Hello ";
string str2 = "World";
string str3 = str1 + str2; // string concatenation
```

Despite this style of assignment, string is a reference type. Behind the scenes, a string object is allocated on the heap, not the stack, and when we assign one string variable to another string, we get two references to the same string in memory. However, with string there are some differences from the usual behavior for reference types. For example, should we then make changes to one of these strings, note that this will create an entirely new string object, leaving the other string unchanged. Consider the following code:

```
using System;

class StringExample
{
    public static int Main()
    {
        string s1 = "a string";
```

```
        string s2 = s1;
        Console.WriteLine("s1 is " + s1);
        Console.WriteLine("s2 is " + s2);
        s1 = "another string";
        Console.WriteLine("s1 is now " + s1);
        Console.WriteLine("s2 is now " + s2);
        return 0;
    }
}
```

The output from this is:

```
s1 is a string
s2 is a string
s1 is now another string
s2 is now a string
```

In other words, changing the value of s1 had no effect on s2, contrary to what we'd expect with a reference type! What's happening here is that when s1 is initialized with the value a string, a new string object is allocated on the heap. When s2 is initialized, the reference points to this same object, so s2 also has the value a string. However, when we now change the value of s1, instead of replacing the original value, a new object will be allocated on the heap for the new value. Our s2 variable will still point to the original object, so its value is unchanged. Under the hood, this happens as a result of operator overloading, a topic that we will explore in Chapter 5. In general, the string class has been implemented so that its semantics follow what you would normally intuitively expect for a string.

String literals are enclosed in double quotes (" . . . "); if we attempt to enclose a string in single quotes, the compiler will take the value as a char, and throw an error. C# strings can contain the same Unicode and hexadecimal escape sequences as chars. Since these escape sequences start with a backslash, we can't use this character unescaped in a string. Instead, we need to escape it with two backslashes (\\):

```
string filepath = "C:\\ProCSharp\\First.cs";
```

Even if you are confident you can remember to do this all the time, it can prove annoying typing all those double backslashes. Fortunately, C# gives us an alternative. We can prefix a string literal with the at character (@) and all the characters in it will be treated at face value; they won't be interpreted as escape sequences:

```
string filepath = @"C:\ProCSharp\First.cs";
```

This even allows us to include line breaks in our string literals:

```
string jabberwocky = @"'Twas brillig and the slithy toves
Did gyre and gimble in the wabe.";
```

Then the value of jabberwocky would be this:

```
'Twas brillig and the slithy toves
Did gyre and gimble in the wabe.
```

Flow Control

In this section, we will look at the real nuts and bolts of the language: the statements that allow us to control the *flow* of our program rather than executing every line of code in the order it appears in the program.

Conditional Statements

Conditional statements allow us to branch our code depending on whether certain conditions are met or on the value of an expression. C# has two constructs for branching code—the `if` statement, which allows us to test whether a specific condition is met, and the `switch` statement, which allows us to compare an expression with a number of different values.

The if statement

For conditional branching, C# inherits the C and C++ `if...else` construct. The syntax should be fairly intuitive for anyone who has done any programming with a procedural language:

```
if (condition)
    statement(s)
else
    statement(s)
```

If more than one statement is to be executed as part of either condition, these statements will need to be joined together into a block using curly braces (`{ ... }`) (this also applies to other C# constructs where statements can be joined into a block, such as the `for` and `while` loops):

```
bool isZero;
if (i == 0)
{
   isZero = true;
   Console.WriteLine("i is Zero");
}
else
{
   isZero = false;
   Console.WriteLine("i is Non-zero");
}
```

The syntax here is similar to C++ and Java but once again different from Visual Basic. Visual Basic developers should note that C# does not have any statement corresponding to Visual Basic's `EndIf`. Instead, the rule is that each clause of an `if` contains just one statement. If you need more than one statement, as in the above example, you should enclose the statements in braces, which will cause the whole group of statements to be treated as a single block statement.

If we want to, we can use an `if` statement without a final `else` statement. We can also combine `else if` clauses to test for multiple conditions.

```
using System;

namespace Wrox.ProCSharp.Basics
{
```

```
class MainEntryPoint
{
   static void Main(string[] args)
   {
      Console.WriteLine("Type in a string");
      string input;
      input = Console.ReadLine();
      if (input == "")
      {
         Console.WriteLine("You typed in an empty string");
      }
      else if (input.Length < 5)
      {
         Console.WriteLine("The string had less than 5 characters");
      }
      else if (input.Length < 10)
      {
         Console.WriteLine("The string had at least 5 but less than 10
            characters");
      }
      Console.WriteLine("The string was " + input);
   }
}
```

There is no limit to how many `else if`'s we can add to an `if` clause.

You'll notice that in the previous example, we declare a string variable called `input`, get the user to enter text at the command line, feed this into `input`, and then test the length of this string variable. The code also shows us how easy string manipulation can be in C#. To find the length of `input`, for example, use `input.Length`.

One point to note about `if` is that we don't need to use the braces if there's only one statement in the conditional branch:

```
if (i == 0)
   Console.WriteLine("i is Zero");        // This will only execute if i == 0
Console.WriteLine("i can be anything");   // Will execute whatever the
                                          // value of i
```

However, for consistency, many programmers prefer to use curly braces whenever they use an `if` statement.

The `if` statements we have presented also illustrate some of the C# operators that compare values. Note in particular that, like C++ and Java, C# uses == to compare variables for equality. Do not use = for this purpose. A single = is used to assign values.

In C#, the expression in the `if` clause must evaluate to a Boolean. C++ programmers should be particularly aware of this; unlike C++, it is not possible to test an integer (returned from a function, say) directly. In C#, we have to convert the integer that is returned to a Boolean `true` or `false`, for example by comparing the value with zero or with `null`:

```
if (DoSomething() != 0)
{
    // Non-zero value returned
}
else
{
    // Returned zero
}
```

This restriction is there in order to prevent some common types of run-time bugs that occur in C++. In particular, in C++ it was common to mistype = when == was intended, resulting in unintentional assignments. In C# this will normally result in a compile-time error, since unless you are working with bool values, = will not return a bool.

The switch statement

The switch...case statement is good for selecting one branch of execution from a set of mutually exclusive ones. It will be familiar to C++ and Java programmers and is similar to the Select Case statement in Visual Basic.

It takes the form of a switch argument followed by a series of case clauses. When the expression in the switch argument evaluates to one of the values beside a case clause, the code immediately following the case clause executes. This is one example where we don't need to use curly braces to join statements into blocks; instead, we mark the end of the code for each case using the break statement. We can also include a default case in the switch statement, which will execute if the expression evaluates to none of the other cases. The following switch statement tests the value of the integerA variable:

```
switch (integerA)
{
    case 1:
        Console.WriteLine("integerA =1");
        break;
    case 2:
        Console.WriteLine("integerA =2");
        break;
    case 3:
        Console.WriteLine("integerA =3");
        break;
    default:
        Console.WriteLine("integerA is not 1,2, or 3");
        break;
}
```

Note that the case values must be constant expressions; variables are not permitted.

Though the switch...case statement should be familiar to C and C++ programmers, C#'s switch... case is a bit safer than its C++ equivalent. Specifically, it prohibits fall-through conditions in almost all cases. This means that if a case clause is fired early on in the block, later clauses cannot be fired unless you use a goto statement to mark that you want them fired too. The compiler enforces this restriction by flagging every case clause that is not equipped with a break statement as an error similar to this:

```
Control cannot fall through from one case label ('case 2:') to another
```

While it is true that fall-through behavior is desirable in a limited number of situations, in the vast majority of cases it is unintended and results in a logical error that's hard to spot. Isn't it better to code for the norm rather than for the exception?

By getting creative with `goto` statements (which C# does support) however, you can duplicate fall-through functionality in your `switch...cases`. However, if you find yourself really wanting to, you probably should re-consider your approach. The following code illustrates both how to use `goto` to simulate fall-through, and how messy the resultant code can get.

```
// assume country and language are of type string
switch(country)
{
   case "America":
      CallAmericanOnlyMethod();
      goto case "Britain";
   case "France":
      language = "French";
      break;
   case "Britain":
      language = "English";
      break;
}
```

There is one exception to the no–fall-through rule however, in that we can fall through from one case to the next if that case is empty. This allows us to treat two or more cases in an identical way (without the need for `goto` statements):

```
switch(country)
{
   case "au":
   case "uk":
   case "us":
      language = "English";
      break;
   case "at":
   case "de":
      language = "German";
      break;
}
```

One intriguing point about the `switch` statement in C# is that the order of the cases doesn't matter—we can even put the `default` case first! As a result, no two cases can be the same. This includes different constants that have the same value, so we can't, for example, do this:

```
// assume country is of type string
const string england = "uk";
const string britain = "uk";
switch(country)
{
   case england:
   case britain:      // this will cause a compilation error
      language = "English";
      break;
}
```

The previous code also shows another way in which the switch statement is different in C# from C++: In C#, you are allowed to use a string as the variable being tested.

Loops

C# provides four different loops (for, while, do...while, and foreach) that allow us to execute a block of code repeatedly until a certain condition is met. The for, while, and do...while loops are essentially identical to those encountered in C++. The for loop is the first that we shall examine.

The for loop

C# for loops provide a mechanism for iterating through a loop where we test whether a particular condition holds before we perform another iteration. The syntax is:

```
for (initializer; condition; iterator)
    statement(s)
```

where:

❑   The initializer is the expression evaluated before the first loop is executed (usually initializing a local variable as a loop counter).

❑   The condition is the expression that is checked before each new iteration of the loop (this must evaluate to true for another iteration to be performed).

❑   The iterator is an expression that will be evaluated after each iteration (usually incrementing the loop counter). The iterations end when the condition evaluates to false.

The for loop is a so-called pre-test loop, because the loop condition is evaluated before the loop statements are executed, and so the contents of the loop won't be executed at all if the loop condition is false.

The for loop is excellent for repeating a statement or a block of statements for a predetermined number of times. The following example is typical of the use of a for loop. The following code will write out all the integers from 0 to 99:

```
for (int i = 0; i < 100; i = i+1)    // this is equivalent to
                                     // For i = 0 To 99 in VB.
{
    Console.WriteLine(i);
}
```

Here, we declare an int called i and initialize it to zero. This will be used as the loop counter. We then immediately test whether it is less than 100. Since this condition evaluates to true, we execute the code in the loop, displaying the value 0. We then increment the counter by one, and walk through the process again. Looping ends when i reaches 100.

Actually, the way we have written the above loop isn't quite how you would normally write it. C# has a shorthand for adding 1 to a variable, so instead of i = i + 1, we can simply write i++:

```
for (int i = 0; i < 100; i++)
{
    // etc.
```

C# `for` loop syntax is far more powerful than the Visual Basic `For...Next` loop, since the iterator can be any statement. In Visual Basic, all you can do is add or subtract some number from the loop control variable. In C# you can do anything; for example, you can multiply the loop control variable by 2.

It's not unusual to nest `for` loops so that an inner loop executes once completely for each iteration of an outer loop. This scheme is typically employed to loop through every element in a rectangular multidimensional array. The outermost loop loops through every row, and the inner loop loops through every column in a particular row. The following code is available as the `NumberTable` sample, and displays rows of numbers. It also uses another `Console` method, `Console.Write()`, which does the same as `Console.WriteLine()` but doesn't send a carriage return to the output.

```
using System;

namespace Wrox.ProCSharp.Basics
{
    class MainEntryPoint
    {
        static void Main(string[] args)
        {
            // This loop iterates through rows...
            for (int i = 0; i < 100; i+=10)
            {
                // This loop iterates through columns...
                for (int j = i; j < i + 10; j++)
                {
                    Console.Write("  " + j);
                }
                Console.WriteLine();
            }
        }
    }
}
```

Although `j` is an integer, it will be automatically converted to a string so that the concatenation can take place. C++ developers will note that this is far easier than string handling ever was in C++; for Visual Basic developers this is familiar ground.

C programmers should take note of one particular feature of the example above. The counter variable in the innermost loop is effectively re-declared with each successive iteration of the outer loop. This syntax is legal not only in C#, but in C++ as well.

The above sample results in this output:

csc NumberTable.cs

```
Microsoft (R) Visual C# .NET Compiler version 7.10.3052.4
for Microsoft (R) .NET Framework version 1.0.4322
Copyright (C) Microsoft Corporation 2001-2002. All rights reserved.

  0  1  2  3  4  5  6  7  8  9
 10 11 12 13 14 15 16 17 18 19
 20 21 22 23 24 25 26 27 28 29
 30 31 32 33 34 35 36 37 38 39
```

```
40  41  42  43  44  45  46  47  48  49
50  51  52  53  54  55  56  57  58  59
60  61  62  63  64  65  66  67  68  69
70  71  72  73  74  75  76  77  78  79
80  81  82  83  84  85  86  87  88  89
90  91  92  93  94  95  96  97  98  99
```

Although it is technically possible to evaluate something other than a counter variable in a `for` loop's test condition, it is certainly not typical. It is also possible to omit one (or even all) of the expressions in the `for` loop. In such situations, however, you should consider using the `while` loop.

The while loop

The `while` loop is identical to the `while` loop in C++ and Java, and the `While...Wend` loop in Visual Basic. Like the `for` loop, `while` is a pre-test loop. The syntax is similar, but `while` loops take only one expression:

```
while(condition)
    statement(s);
```

Unlike the `for` loop, the `while` loop is most often used to repeat a statement or a block of statements for a number of times that is not known before the loop begins. Usually, a statement inside the `while` loop's body will set a Boolean flag to `false` on a certain iteration, triggering the end of the loop, as in the following example:

```
bool condition = false;
while (!condition)
{
    // This loop spins until the condition is true
    DoSomeWork();
    condition = CheckCondition();   // assume CheckCondition() returns a bool
}
```

All of C#'s looping mechanisms, including the `while` loop, can forego the curly braces that follow them if they intend to repeat just a single statement and not a block of statements. Again, many programmers consider it good practice to use braces all of the time.

The do...while loop

The `do...while` loop is the post-test version of the `while` loop. It does the same thing with the same syntax as `do...while` in C++ and Java, and the same thing as `Loop...While` in Visual Basic. This means that the loop's test condition is evaluated after the body of the loop has been executed. Consequently, `do...while` loops are useful for situations in which a block of statements must be executed at least one time, as in this example:

```
bool condition;
do
{
    // this loop will at least execute once, even if Condition is false
    MustBeCalledAtLeastOnce();
    condition = CheckCondition();
} while (condition);
```

The foreach loop

The foreach loop is the final C# looping mechanism that we will discuss. While the other looping mechanisms were present in the earliest versions of C and C++, the foreach statement is a new addition (borrowed from Visual Basic), and a very welcome one at that.

The foreach loop allows us to iterate through each item in a collection. For the time being we won't worry about exactly what a collection is—we'll explain fully in Chapter 9. For now, we will just say that it is an object that contains other objects. Technically, to count as a collection, it must support an interface called IEnumerable. Examples of collections include C# arrays, the collection classes in the System.Collection namespaces, and user-defined collection classes. We can get an idea of the syntax of foreach from the following code, if we assume that arrayOfInts is (unsurprisingly) an array if ints:

```
foreach (int temp in arrayOfInts)
{
    Console.WriteLine(temp);
}
```

Here, foreach steps through the array one element at a time. With each element, it places the value of the element in the int variable called temp, and then performs an iteration of the loop.

An important point to note with foreach is that we can't change the value of the item in the collection (temp above), so code such as the following will not compile:

```
foreach (int temp in arrayOfInts)
{
    temp++;
    Console.WriteLine(temp);
}
```

If you need to iterate through the items in a collection and change their values, you will need to use a for loop instead.

Jump Statements

C# provides a number of statements that allow us to jump immediately to another line in the program. The first of these is, of course, the notorious goto statement.

The goto statement

The goto statement allows us to jump directly to another specified line in the program, indicated by a *label* (this is just an identifier followed by a colon):

```
goto Label1;
    Console.WriteLine("This won't be executed");
Label1:
    Console.WriteLine("Continuing execution from here");
```

There are a couple of restrictions involved with goto. We can't jump into a block of code such as a for loop, we can't jump out of a class, and we can't exit a finally block after try...catch blocks (we will look at exception handling with try...catch...finally in Chapter 11).

The reputation of the `goto` statement probably precedes it, and in most circumstances, its use is sternly frowned upon. In general, it certainly doesn't conform to good object-oriented programming practice. However, there is one place where it is quite handy: jumping between cases in a `switch` statement, particularly since C#'s `switch` is so strict on fall-through. We saw the syntax for this earlier in this chapter.

The break statement

We have already met the `break` statement briefly—when we used it to exit from a case in a `switch` statement. In fact, `break` can also be used to exit from `for`, `foreach`, `while`, or `do...while` loops too. Control will switch to the statement immediately after the end of the loop.

If the statement occurs in a nested loop, control will switch to the end of the innermost loop. If the break occurs outside of a `switch` statement or a loop, a compile-time error will occur.

The continue statement

The `continue` statement is similar to `break`, and must also be used within a `for`, `foreach`, `while`, or `do...while` loop. However, it exits only from the current iteration of the loop, meaning execution will restart at the beginning of the next iteration of the loop, rather than outside the loop altogether.

The return statement

The `return` statement is used to exit a method of a class, returning control to the caller of the method. If the method has a return type, `return` must return a value of this type; otherwise if the method returns `void`, then you should use `return` without an expression.

Enumerations

An *enumeration* is a user-defined integer type. When we declare an enumeration, we specify a set of acceptable values that instances of that enumeration can contain. Not only that, but we can give the values user-friendly names. If, somewhere in our code, we attempt to assign a value that is not in the acceptable set of values to an instance of that enumeration, the compiler will flag an error. This concept may be new to Visual Basic programmers. C++ does support enumerations (or enums), but C# enumerations are far more powerful than their C++ counterparts.

Creating an enumeration can end up saving you lots of time and headaches in the long run. There are at least three benefits to using enumerations instead of plain integers:

❑ As mentioned, enumerations make your code easier to maintain by helping to ensure that your variables are assigned only legitimate, anticipated values.

❑ Enumerations make your code clearer by allowing you to refer to integer values by descriptive names rather than by obscure "magic" numbers.

❑ Enumerations make your code easier to type, too. When you go to assign a value to an instance of an enumerated type, the Visual Studio .NET IDE will, through IntelliSense, pop up a list box of acceptable values in order to save you some keystrokes and to remind you of what the possible options are.

We can define an enumeration as follows:

```
public enum TimeOfDay
{
   Morning = 0,
   Afternoon = 1,
   Evening = 2
}
```

In this case, we use an integer value to represent each period of the day in the enumeration. We can now access these values as members of the enumeration. For example, `TimeOfDay.Morning` will return the value `0`. We will typically use this enumeration to pass an appropriate value into a method, and iterate through the possible values in a `switch` statement:

```
class EnumExample
{
   public static int Main()
   {
      WriteGreeting(TimeOfDay.Morning);
      return 0;
   }

   static void WriteGreeting(TimeOfDay timeOfDay)
   {
      switch(timeOfDay)
      {
         case TimeOfDay.Morning:
            Console.WriteLine("Good morning!");
            break;
         case TimeOfDay.Afternoon:
            Console.WriteLine("Good afternoon!");
            break;
         case TimeOfDay.Evening:
            Console.WriteLine("Good evening!");
            break;
         default:
            Console.WriteLine("Hello!");
            break;
      }
   }
}
```

The real power of enums in C# is that behind the scenes they are instantiated as structs derived from the base class, `System.Enum`. This means it is possible to call methods against them to perform some useful tasks. Note that because of the way the .NET Framework is implemented there is no performance loss associated with treating the enums syntactically as structs. In practice, once your code is compiled, enums will exist as primitive types, just like `int` and `float`.

You can retrieve the string representation of an enum as in the following example, using our earlier `TimeOfDay` enum:

```
TimeOfDay time = TimeOfDay.Afternoon;
Console.WriteLine(time.ToString());
```

This will return the string `Afternoon`.

Alternatively you can obtain an enum value from a string.

```
TimeOfDay time2 = (TimeOfDay) Enum.Parse(typeof(TimeOfDay), "afternoon", true);
Console.WriteLine((int)time2);
```

This code snippet illustrates both obtaining an enum value from a string and converting to an integer. To convert from a string, we need to use the static `Enum.Parse()` method, which as shown here takes three parameters. The first is the type of enum we wish to consider. The syntax is the keyword `typeof` followed by the name of the enum class in brackets. We will explore the `typeof` operator in more detail in Chapter 5. The second parameter is the string to be converted, and the third parameter is a `bool` indicating whether or not we should ignore case when doing the conversion. Finally, note that `Enum.Parse()` actually returns an object reference — we need to explicitly convert this to the required enum type (this is an example of an unboxing operation). For the above code, this returns the value 1 as an object, corresponding to the enum value of `TimeOfDay.Afternoon`. On converting explicitly to an `int`, this produces the value 1 again.

There are other methods on `System.Enum` to do things like return the number of values in an enum definition or to list the names of the values. Full details are in the MSDN documentation.

Arrays

We won't say too much about arrays in this chapter, because we cover arrays and collections in detail in Chapter 9. However we'll give you just enough syntax here that you can code 1-dimensional arrays. Arrays in C# are declared by fixing a set of square brackets to the end of the variable type of the individual elements (note that all the elements in an array must be of the same data type).

> *A note to Visual Basic users: arrays in C# use square brackets, not parentheses. C++ users will be familiar with the square brackets, but should check the code we present here carefully because C# syntax for actually declaring array variables is not the same as C++ syntax.*

For example, while `int` represents a single integer, `int[]` represents an array of integers:

```
int[] integers;
```

To initialize the array with specific dimensions, we can use the `new` keyword, giving the size in the square brackets after the type name:

```
// Create a new array of 32 ints
int[] integers = new int[32];
```

All arrays are reference types and follow reference semantics. Hence, in this code, even though the individual elements are primitive value types, the `integers` array is a reference type. Hence if we later write

```
int [] copy = integers;
```

this will simply assign the variable `copy` to refer to the same array—it won't create a new array.

To access an individual element within the array, we use the usual syntax, placing the index of the element in square brackets after the name of the array. All C# arrays use zero-based indexing, so we can reference the first variable with the index zero:

```
integers[0] = 35;
```

Similarly, we reference the 32 element value with an index value of 31:

```
integers[31] = 432;
```

C#'s array syntax is flexible. In fact, C# allows us to declare arrays without initializing them, so that the array can be dynamically sized later in the program. With this technique, we are basically creating a null reference, and later pointing that reference at a dynamically allocated stretch of memory locations requested with the new keyword:

```
int[] integers;
integers = new int[32];
```

You can find out how many elements are in any array by using this syntax:

```
int numElements = integers.Length;     // integers is any reference to an array.
```

Namespaces

As we have seen earlier, namespaces provide a way of organizing related classes and other types. Unlike a file or a component, a namespace is a logical, rather than a physical grouping. When we define a class in a C# file, we can include it within a namespace definition. Later, when we define another class that performs related work in another file, we can include it within the same namespace, creating a logical grouping that gives an indication to other developers using the classes how they are related and used:

```
namespace CustomerPhoneBookApp
{
    using System;

    public struct Subscriber
    {
        // Code for struct here...
    }
}
```

Placing a type in a namespace effectively gives that type a long name, consisting of the type's namespace as a series of names separated with periods (.), terminating with the name of the class. In the example above, the full name of the Subscriber struct is CustomerPhoneBookApp.Subscriber. This allows distinct classes with the same short name to be used within the same program without ambiguity.

We can also nest namespaces within other namespaces, creating a hierarchical structure for our types:

```
namespace Wrox
{
    namespace ProCSharp
    {
        namespace Basics
        {
            class NamespaceExample
            {
                // Code for the class here...
            }
        }
    }
}
```

Each namespace name is composed of the names of the namespaces it resides within, separated with periods, starting with the outermost namespace and ending with its own short name. So the full name for the ProCSharp namespace is Wrox.ProCSharp, and the full name of our NamespaceExample class is Wrox.ProCSharp.Basics.NamespaceExample.

We can use this syntax to organize the namespaces in our namespace definitions too, so the previous code could also be written:

```
namespace Wrox.ProCSharp.Basics
{
    class NamespaceExample
    {
        // Code for the class here...
    }
}
```

Note that we are not permitted to declare a multi-part namespace nested within another namespace.

Namespaces are not related to assemblies. It is perfectly acceptable to have different namespaces in the same assembly, or define types in the same namespace in different assemblies.

The using Statement

Obviously, namespaces can grow rather long and tiresome to type, and the ability to indicate a particular class with such specificity may not always be necessary. Fortunately, as we noted at the beginning of the chapter, C# allows us to abbreviate a class's full name. To do this, we list the class's namespace at the top of the file, prefixed with the using keyword. Throughout the rest of the file, we can refer to the types in the namespace simply by their type names.

```
using System;
using Wrox.ProCSharp;
```

As remarked earlier, virtually all C# source code will start with the statement using System; simply because so many useful classes supplied by Microsoft are contained in the System namespace.

If two namespaces referenced by using statements contain a type of the same name, then we will have to use the full (or at least, a longer) form of the name to ensure that the compiler knows which type is to be accessed. For example, say classes called NamespaceExample exist both in the Wrox.ProCSharp.Basics and Wrox.ProCSharp.OOP namespaces. If we then create a class called Test in the Wrox.ProCSharp namespace, and instantiate one of the NamespaceExample classes in this class, we need to specify which of these two classes we're talking about:

```
using Wrox.ProCSharp;

class Test
{
   public static int Main()
   {
      Basics.NamespaceExample nSEx = new Basics.NamespaceExample();
    // do something with the nSEx variable
      return 0;
   }
}
```

Since using statements occur at the top of C# files, in the same place that C and C++ list #include statements, it's easy for programmers moving from C++ to C# to confuse namespaces with C++-style header files. Don't make this mistake. The using statement does no physical linking between files, and C# has no equivalent to C++ header files.

Your organization will probably want to spend some time developing a namespace schema so that its developers can quickly locate functionality that they need and so that the names of the organization's homegrown classes won't conflict with those in off-the-shelf class libraries. We will discuss guidelines on establishing your own namespace scheme along with other naming recommendations later in this chapter.

Namespace Aliases

Another use of the using keyword is to assign aliases to classes and namespaces. If we have a very long namespace name that we want to refer to several times in our code, but don't want to include in a simple using statement (for example, to avoid type name conflicts), we can assign an alias to the namespace. The syntax for this is:

```
using alias = NamespaceName;
```

The following example (a modified version of the previous example) assigns the alias Introduction to the Wrox.ProCSharp.Basics namespace, and uses this to instantiate a NamespaceExample object, which is defined in this namespace. This object has one method, GetNamespace(), which uses the GetType() method exposed by every class to access a Type object representing the class's type. We use this object to return a name of the class's namespace:

```
using System;
using Introduction = Wrox.ProCSharp.Basics;

class Test
{
```

```
    public static int Main()
    {
        Introduction.NamespaceExample NSEx =
            new Introduction.NamespaceExample();

        Console.WriteLine(NSEx.GetNamespace());

        return 0;
    }
}
```

```
namespace Wrox.ProCSharp.Basics
{
    class NamespaceExample
    {
        public string GetNamespace()
        {
            return this.GetType().Namespace;
        }
    }
}
```

The Main() Method

We saw at the start of this chapter that C# programs start execution at a method named `Main()`. As we saw earlier, this must be a static method of a class (or struct), and must have a return type of either `int` or `void`.

Although it is common to specify the `public` modifier explicitly, since by definition the method must be called from outside the program, it doesn't actually matter what accessibility level we assign to the entry point method—it will run even if we mark the method as `private`.

Multiple Main() Methods

When a C# console or Windows application is compiled, by default the compiler looks for exactly one `Main()` method in any class matching the signature listed above and makes that class method the entry point for the program. If there is more than one `Main()` method, the compiler will return an error message. For example, consider the following code called MainExample.cs:

```
using System;

namespace Wrox.ProCSharp.Basics
{
    class Client
    {
        public static int Main()
        {
            MathExample.Main();
```

```
            return 0;
        }
    }

    class MathExample
    {
        static int Add(int x, int y)
        {
            return x + y;
        }

        public static int Main()
        {
            int i = Add(5,10);
            Console.WriteLine(i);
            return 0;
        }
    }
}
```

This contains two classes, both of which have a `Main()` method. If we try to compile this code in the usual way we will get the following errors:

csc MainExample.cs

```
Microsoft (R) Visual C# .NET Compiler version 7.10.3052.4
for Microsoft (R) .NET Framework version 1.1.4322
Copyright (C) Microsoft Corporation 2001-2002. All rights reserved.

MainExample.cs(7,25): error CS0017: Program 'MainExample.exe' has more than one
entry point defined: 'Wrox.ProCSharp.Basics.Client.Main()'
MainExample.cs(21,25): error CS0017: Program 'MainExample.exe' has more than one
entry point defined: 'Wrox.ProCSharp.Basics.MathExample.Main()'
```

However, we can explicitly tell the compiler which of these methods to use as the entry point for the program using the /main switch, together with the full name (including namespace) of the class to which the `Main()` method belongs:

csc MainExample.cs /main:Wrox.ProCSharp.Basics.MathExample

Passing Arguments to Main()

In our examples so far, we have only shown the `Main()` method without any parameters. However, when the program is invoked, we can get the CLR to pass any command line arguments to the program by including a parameter. This parameter is a string array, traditionally called `args` (although C# will accept any name). The program can use this array to access any options passed through the command line when the program is started.

The following sample, ArgsExample.cs, loops through the string array passed in to the `Main()` method and writes the value of each option to the console window:

```
using System;

namespace Wrox.ProCSharp.Basics
{
    class ArgsExample
    {
        public static int Main(string[] args)
        {
            for (int i = 0; i < args.Length; i++)
            {
                Console.WriteLine(args[i]);
            }
            return 0;
        }
    }
}
```

We can compile this as usual using command line. When we run the compiled executable, we can pass in arguments after the name of the program, for example:

ArgsExample /a /b /c

```
/a
/b
/c
```

More on Compiling C# Files

So far, we have seen how to compile console applications using csc.exe, but what about other types of application? What if we want to reference a class library? The full set of compilation options for the C# compiler is of course detailed in the MSDN documentation, but we list here the most important options.

To answer the first question, we can specify what type of file we want to create using the /target switch, often abbreviated to /t. This can be one of the following:

Option	Output
/t:exe	A console application (the default)
/t:library	A class library with a manifest
/t:module	A component without a manifest
/t:winexe	A Windows application (without a console window)

If we want a non-executable file (such as a DLL) to be loadable by the .NET runtime, we must compile it as a library. If we compile a C# file as a module, no assembly will be created. Although modules cannot be loaded by the runtime, they can be compiled into another manifest using the /addmodule switch.

Another option we need to mention is /out. This allows us to specify the name of the output file produced by the compiler. If the /out option isn't specified, the compiler will base the name of the output file on the name of the input C# file, adding an extension according to the target type (for example, exe for a Windows or console application, or dll for a class library). Note that the /out and /t, or /target, options must precede the name of the file we want to compile.

If we want to reference types in assemblies that aren't referenced by default, we can use the /reference or /r switch, together with the path and filename of the assembly. The following example demonstrates how we can compile a class library and then reference that library in another assembly. It consists of two files:

❑   The class library

❑   A console application, which will call a class in the library.

The first file is called MathLibrary.cs and contains the code for our DLL. To keep things simple, it contains just one (public) class, MathLib, with a single method that adds two ints:

```
namespace Wrox.ProCSharp.Basics
{
   public class MathLib
   {
      public int Add(int x, int y)
      {
         return x + y;
      }
   }
}
```

We can compile this C# file into a .NET DLL using the following command:

csc /t:library MathLibrary.cs

The console application, MathClient.cs, will simply instantiate this object and call its Add() method, displaying the result in the console window:

```
using System;

namespace Wrox.ProCSharp.Basics
{
   class Client
   {
      public static void Main()
      {
         MathLib mathObj = new MathLib();
         Console.WriteLine(mathObj.Add(7,8));
      }
   }
}
```

We can compile this code using the /r switch to point at or reference our newly compiled DLL:

csc MathClient.cs /r:MathLibrary.dll

We can then run it as normal just by entering **MathClient** at the command prompt. This displays the number 15—the result of our addition.

Console I/O

By this point, you should have a basic familiarity with C#'s data types, as well as some knowledge of how the thread-of-control moves through a program that manipulates those data types. During this chapter we have also used several of the Console class's static methods used for reading and writing data. Since these methods are so useful when writing basic C# programs, we will quickly go over them in a little more detail.

To read a line of text from the console window, we use the Console.ReadLine() method. This will read an input stream (terminated when the user presses the Return key) from the console window and return the input string. There are also two corresponding methods for writing to the console, which we have already used extensively:

❑ Console.Write()—Writes the specified value to the console window.

❑ Console.WriteLine()—Which does the same, but adds a new line character at the end of the output.

There are various forms (overloads) of these methods for all of the predefined types (including object), so in most cases we don't have to convert values to strings before we display them.

For example, the following code lets the user input a line of text, and displays that text:

```
string s = Console.ReadLine();
Console.WriteLine(s);
```

Console.WriteLine() also allows us to display formatted output in a way comparable to C's printf() function. To use WriteLine() in this way, we pass in a number of parameters. The first is a string containing markers in curly braces where the subsequent parameters will be inserted into the text. Each marker contains a zero-based index for the number of the parameter in the following list. For example, {0} represents the first parameter in the list. Consider the following code:

```
int i = 10;
int j = 20;
Console.WriteLine("{0} plus {1} equals {2}", i, j, i + j);
```

This code displays:

```
10 plus 20 equals 30
```

We can also specify a width for the value, and justify the text within that width, using positive values for right justification and negative values for left justification. To do this, we use the format {n, w}, where n is the parameter index and w is the width value:

```
int i = 940;
int j = 73;
Console.WriteLine(" {0,4}\n+{1,4}\n ----\n {2,4}", i, j, i + j);
```

The result of this is:

```
 940
+  73
 ----
 1013
```

Finally, we can also add a format string, together with an optional precision value. It is not possible to give a complete list of possible format strings, since, as we will see in Chapter 8, it is possible to define your own format strings. However, the main ones in use for the predefined types are:

String	Description
C	Local currency format.
D	Decimal format. Converts an integer to base 10, and pads with leading zeros if a precision specifier is given.
E	Scientific (exponential) format. The precision specifier sets the number of decimal places (6 by default). The case of the format string (e or E) determines the case of the exponential symbol.
F	Fixed-point format; the precision specifier controls the number of decimal places. Zero is acceptable.
G	General format. Uses E or F formatting, depending on which is the most compact.
N	Number format. Formats the number with commas as thousands separators, for example 32,767.44.
P	Percent format.
X	Hexadecimal format. The precision specifier can be used to pad with leading zeros.

Note that the format strings are normally case-insensitive, except for e/E.

If you want to use a format string, you should place it immediately after the marker that gives the parameter number and field width, and separated from it by a colon. For example, to format a decimal value as currency for the computer's locale, with precision to two decimal places, we would use C2:

```
decimal i = 940.23m;
decimal j = 73.7m;
Console.WriteLine(" {0,9:C2}\n+{1,9:C2}\n ---------\n {2,9:C2}", i, j, i + j);
```

The output of this in the United States is:

```
    $940.23
+    $73.70
  ---------
  $1,013.93
```

As a final trick, we can also use placeholder characters instead of these format strings to map out formatting. For example:

```
double d = 0.234;
Console.WriteLine("{0:#.00}", d);
```

This displays as `.23`, because the # symbol (#) is ignored if there is no character in that place, and zeros will either be replaced by the character in that position if there is one or else printed as a zero.

Using Comments

The next topic we will look at looks very simple on the surface—adding comments to our code.

Internal Comments Within the Source Files

As we noted earlier in this chapter, C# uses the traditional C-type single-line (`//` ...) and multi-line (`/*` ... `*/`) comments:

```
// This is a single-line comment
/* This comment
   spans multiple lines */
```

Everything in a single-line comment, from the `//` to the end of the line, will be ignored by the compiler, and everything from an opening `/*` to the next `*/` in a multi-line comment combination will be ignored. Obviously we can't include the combination `*/` in any multi-line comments, as this will be treated as the end of the comment.

It is actually possible to put multi-line comments within a line of code:

```
Console.WriteLine(/* Here's a comment! */ "This will compile");
```

Inline comments like this should be used with care as they can make code hard to read. However, they can be useful when debugging if, say, you temporarily want to try running the code with a different value somewhere:

```
DoSomething(Width, /*Height*/ 100);
```

Comment characters included in string literals are of course treated like normal characters:

```
string s = "/* This is just a normal string */";
```

XML Documentation

In addition to the C-type comments, illustrated above, C# has a very neat feature that we can't omit from this chapter: the ability to produce documentation in XML format automatically from special comments. These comments are single-line comments, but begin with three slashes (///), instead of the usual two. Within these comments, we can place XML tags containing documentation of the types and type members in our code.

The following tags are recognized by the compiler:

Tag	Description
`<c>`	Marks up text within a line as code, for example: `<c>int i = 10;</c>`
`<code>`	Marks multiple lines as code.
`<example>`	Marks up a code example.
`<exception>`	Documents an exception class. (Syntax verified by the compiler.)
`<include>`	Includes comments from another documentation file. (Syntax verified by the compiler.)
`<list>`	Inserts a list into the documentation.
`<param>`	Marks up a method parameter. (Syntax verified by the compiler.)
`<paramref>`	Indicates that a word is a method parameter. (Syntax verified by the compiler.)
`<permission>`	Documents access to a member. (Syntax verified by the compiler.)
`<remarks>`	Adds a description for a member.
`<returns>`	Documents the return value for a method.
`<see>`	Provides a cross-reference to another parameter. (Syntax verified by the compiler.)
`<seealso>`	Provides a "see also" section in a description. (Syntax verified by the compiler.)
`<summary>`	Provides a short summary of a type or member.
`<value>`	Describes a property.

To see how this works, let's add some XML comments to the MathLibrary.cs file from an earlier section, and call it Math.cs. We will add a `<summary>` element for the class and for its `Add()` method, and also a `<returns>` element and two `<param>` elements for the `Add()` method:

```
// Math.cs
namespace Wrox.ProCSharp.Basics
{
```

```
///<summary>
///    Wrox.ProCSharp.Basics.Math class.
///    Provides a method to add two integers.
///</summary>
public class Math
{
    ///<summary>
    ///    The Add method allows us to add two integers
    ///</summary>
    ///<returns>Result of the addition (int)</returns>
    ///<param name="x">First number to add</param>
    ///<param name="y">Second number to add</param>
    public int Add(int x, int y)
    {
        return x + y;
    }
}
}
```

The C# compiler can extract the XML elements from the special comments and use them to generate an XML file. To get the compiler to generate the XML documentation for an assembly, we specify the /doc option when we compile, together with the name of the file we want to be created:

csc /t:library /doc:Math.xml Math.cs

The compiler will throw an error if the XML comments do not result in a well-formed XML document.

This will generate an XML file named Math.xml, which looks like this:

```
<?xml version="1.0"?>
<doc>
    <assembly>
        <name>Math</name>
    </assembly>
    <members>
        <member name="T:Wrox.ProCSharp.Basics.Math">
            <summary>
                Wrox.ProCSharp.Basics.Math class.
                Provides a method to add two integers.
            </summary>
        </member>
        <member name=
            "M:Wrox.ProCSharp.Basics.Math.Add(System.Int32,System.Int32)">
            <summary>
                The Add method allows us to add two integers
            </summary>
            <returns>Result of the addition (int)</returns>
            <param name="x">First number to add</param>
            <param name="y">Second number to add</param>
        </member>
    </members>
</doc>
```

Notice how the compiler has actually done some work for us; it has created an `<assembly>` element and also added a `<member>` element for each type or member of a type in the file. Each `<member>` element has a `name` attribute with the full name of the member as its value, prefixed by a letter that indicates whether this is a type (`T:`), field (`F:`), or member (`M:`).

The C# Preprocessor Directives

Besides the usual keywords, most of which we have now encountered, C# also includes a number of commands that are known as *preprocessor directives*. These commands never actually get translated to any commands in your executable code, but instead they affect aspects of the compilation process. For example, you can use preprocessor directives to prevent the compiler from compiling certain portions of your code. You might do this if you are planning to release two versions of the code, a basic version, and an enterprise version that will have more features. You could use preprocessor directives to prevent the compiler from compiling code related to the additional features when you are compiling the basic version of the software. Another scenario is that you might have written bits of code that are intended to provide you with debugging information. You probably don't want those portions of code compiled when you actually ship the software.

The preprocessor directives are all distinguished by beginning with the # symbol.

> C++ developers will recognize the preprocessor directives as something that plays an important part in C and C++. However, there aren't as many preprocessor directives in C#, and they are not used as often. C# provides other mechanisms, such as custom attributes, that achieve some of the same effects as C++ directives. Also, note that C# doesn't actually have a separate preprocessor in the way that C++ does. The so-called preprocessor directives are actually handled by the compiler. Nevertheless, C# retains the name preprocessor directive because these commands give the impression of a preprocessor.

We will briefly cover the purposes of the preprocessor directives here.

#define and #undef

`#define` is used like this:

```
#define DEBUG
```

What this does is tell the compiler that a symbol with the given name (in this case DEBUG) exists. It is a little bit like declaring a variable, except that this variable doesn't really have a value—it just exists. And this symbol isn't part of your actual code; it only exists for the benefit of the compiler, while the compiler is compiling the code, and has no meaning within the C# code itself.

`#undef` does the opposite, and removes the definition of a symbol:

```
#undef DEBUG
```

If the symbol doesn't exist in the first place, then `#undef` has no effect. Similarly, `#define` has no effect if a symbol already exists.

You need to place any `#define` and `#undef` directives at the beginning of the C# source file, before any code that declares any objects to be compiled.

`#define` isn't much use on its own, but when combined with other preprocessor directives, especially `#if`, it becomes very powerful.

Incidentally, you might notice some changes from the usual C# syntax. Preprocessor directives are not terminated by semicolons, and normally constitute the only command on a line. That's because for the preprocessor directives, C# abandons its usual practice of requiring commands to be separated by semicolons. If it sees a preprocessor directive, it assumes the next command is on the next line.

#if, #elif, #else, and #endif

These directives inform the compiler whether or not to compile a block of code. Consider this method:

```
int DoSomeWork(double x)
{
    // do something
    #if DEBUG
        Console.WriteLine("x is " + x);
    #endif
}
```

This code will compile as normal, except for the `Console.WriteLine()` method call that is contained inside the `#if` clause. This line will only be executed if the symbol `DEBUG` has been defined by a previous `#define` directive. When the compiler finds the `#if` directive, it checks to see if the symbol concerned exists, and only compiles the code inside the `#if` clause if the symbol does exist. Otherwise, the compiler simply ignores all the code until it reaches the matching `#endif` directive. Typical practice is to define the symbol `DEBUG` while you are debugging, and have various bits of debugging-related code inside `#if` clauses. Then, when you are close to shipping, you simply comment out the `#define` directive, and all the debugging code miraculously disappears, the size of the executable file gets smaller, and your end users don't get confused by being shown debugging information. (Obviously, you would do more testing to make sure your code still works without `DEBUG` defined). This technique is very common in C and C++ programming and is known as *conditional compilation*.

The `#elif` (=else if) and `#else` directives can be used in `#if` blocks and have the intuitively obvious meanings. It is also possible to nest `#if` blocks:

```
#define ENTERPRISE
#define W2K

// further on in the file

#if ENTERPRISE
    // do something
    #if W2K
        // some code that is only relevant to enterprise
        // edition running on W2K
    #endif
#elif PROFESSIONAL
    // do something else
#else
    // code for the leaner version
#endif
```

Note that, unlike the situation in C++, using #if is not the only way to compile code conditionally. C# provides an alternative mechanism through the Conditional attribute, which we will explore in Chapter 10.

#if and #elif support a limited range of logical operators too, using the operators !, ==, !=, and ||. A symbol is considered to be true if it exists and false if it doesn't. For example:

```
#if W2K && (ENTERPRISE==false)    // if W2K is defined but ENTERPRISE isn't
```

#warning and #error

Two other very useful preprocessor directives are #warning and #error. These will respectively cause a warning or an error to be raised when the compiler encounters them. If the compiler sees a #warning directive, then it will display whatever text appears after the #warning to the user, after which compilation continues. If it encounters a #error directive, it will display the subsequent text to the user as if it were a compilation error message, and then immediately abandon the compilation, so no IL code will be generated.

You can use these directives as checks that you haven't done anything silly with your #define statements; you can also use the #warning statements to remind yourself to do something:

```
#if DEBUG && RELEASE
    #error "You've defined DEBUG and RELEASE simultaneously!"
#endif

#warning "Don't forget to remove this line before the boss tests the code!"
    Console.WriteLine("*I hate this job*");
```

#region and #endregion

The #region and #endregion directives are used to indicate that a certain block of code is to be treated as a single block with a given name, like this:

```
#region Member Field Declarations
    int x;
    double d;
    Currency balance;
#endregion
```

This doesn't look that useful by itself; it doesn't affect the compilation process in any way. However, the real advantage is that these directives are recognized by some editors, including the Visual Studio .NET editor. These editors can use these directives to lay out your code better on the screen. We will see how this works in Chapter 12, when we look at Visual Studio. NET.

#line

The #line directive can be used to alter the file name and line number information that is output by the compiler in warnings and error messages. You probably won't want to use this directive that often. Its main use occurs if you are coding in conjunction with some other package that alters the code you are typing in before sending it to the compiler, since this will mean line numbers, or perhaps the file names reported by the compiler, won't match up to the line numbers in the files or the file names you are editing. The #line directive can be used to restore the match. You can also use the syntax #line default to restore the line to the default line numbering:

```
#line 164 "Core.cs"    // we happen to know this is line 164 in the file
                       // Core.cs, before the intermediate
                       // package mangles it.

// later on

#line default          // restores default line numbering
```

C# Programming Guidelines

In this final section of the chapter we're going to look at the guidelines you need to bear in mind when writing C# programs.

Rules for Identifiers

In this section we examine the rules governing what names we can use for variables, classes, methods, and so on. Note that the rules presented in this section are not merely guidelines: They are enforced by the C# compiler.

Identifiers are the names we give to variables, to user-defined types such as classes and structs, and to members of these types. Identifiers are case-sensitive, so for example variables named interestRate and InterestRate would be recognized as different variables. There are a couple of rules determining what identifiers we can use in C#:

❑ They must begin with a letter or underscore, although they can contain numeric characters.

❑ We can't use C# keywords as identifiers.

C# has the following reserved keywords:

abstract	do	Implicit	params	switch
as	double	In	private	this
base	else	Int	protected	throw
bool	enum	Interface	public	true
break	event	Internal	readonly	try
byte	explicit	Is	ref	typeof
case	extern	lock	return	uint
catch	false	long	sbyte	ulong

Table continued on following page

char	finally	namespace	sealed	unchecked
checked	fixed	new	short	unsafe
class	float	null	sizeof	ushort
const	for	object	stackalloc	using
continue	foreach	operator	static	virtual
decimal	goto	out	string	volatile
default	if	override	struct	void
delegate				while

If we do need to use one of these words as an identifier (for example, if we are accessing a class written in a different language), we can prefix the identifier with the @ symbol to indicate to the compiler that what follows is to be treated as an identifier, not as a C# keyword (so abstract is not a valid identifier, but @abstract is).

Finally, identifiers can also contain Unicode characters, specified using the syntax \uXXXX, where XXXX is the four-digit hex code for the Unicode character. The following are some examples of valid identifiers:

❑   Name

❑   überfluß

❑   _Identifier

❑   \u005fIdentifier

The last two items in this list are identical and interchangeable (because 005f is the Unicode code for the underscore character), so obviously these identifiers couldn't both be declared in the same scope. Note that although syntactically you are allowed to use the underscore character in identifiers, this isn't recommended in most situations because it doesn't follow the guidelines for naming variables that Microsoft has written in order to ensure that developers use the same conventions, making it easier to read each other's code.

Usage Conventions

In any development language there usually arise certain traditional programming styles. The styles are not part of the language itself but are conventions concerning, for example, how variables are named or how certain classes, methods, or functions are used. If most developers using that language follow the same conventions, it makes it easier for different developers to understand each other's code—which in turn generally helps program maintainability. For example, a common (though not universal) convention in Visual Basic 6 was that variables that represents strings have names beginning with lowercase s or lowercase str, as in the Visual Basic 6 statements Dim sResult As String or Dim strMessage As String. Conventions do, however, depend on the language and the environment. For example, C++ developers programming on the Windows platform have traditionally used the prefixes psz or lpsz to indicate strings: char *pszResult; char *lpszMessage;, but on Unix machines it's more common not to use any such prefixes: char *Result; char *Message;.

You'll notice from the sample code in this book that the convention in C# is to name variables without prefixes: `string Result; string Message;`.

> *The convention by which variable names are prefixed with letters that represent the data type is known as Hungarian notation. It means that other developers reading the code can immediately tell from the variable name what data type the variable represents. Hungarian notation is widely regarded as redundant in these days of smart editors and intellisense.*

Whereas, with many languages, usage conventions simply evolved as the language was used, with C# and the whole of the .NET Framework Microsoft has written very comprehensive usage guidelines, which are detailed in the .NET/C# MSDN documentation. This should mean that, right from the start, .NET programs will have a high degree of interoperability in terms of developers being able to understand code. The guidelines have also been developed with the benefit of some twenty years hindsight in object-oriented programming, and as a result have been carefully thought out and appear to have been well received in the developer community to judge by the relevant newsgroups. Hence the guidelines are well worth following.

It should be noted, however, that the guidelines are not the same as language specifications. You should try to follow the guidelines when you can. Nevertheless, you won't run into problems if you do have a good reason for not doing so—for example, you won't get a compilation error because you don't follow these guidelines. The general rule is that if you don't follow the usage guidelines you must have a convincing reason. Departing from the guidelines should be a positive decision rather than simply not bothering. Also, if you compare the guidelines with the samples in the remainder of this book, you'll notice that in numerous examples in this book, we have chosen not to follow the conventions. That's usually because the conventions are designed for much larger programs than our samples, and while they are great if you are writing a complete software package, they are not really so suitable for small 20-line standalone programs. In many cases following the conventions would have made our samples harder rather than easier to follow.

The full guidelines for good programming style are quite extensive. Here we will confine ourselves to describing some of the more important guidelines, as well as the ones most likely to surprise you. If you want to make absolutely certain your code follows the usage guidelines completely, then you will need to refer to the MSDN documentation.

Naming conventions

One important aspect to making your programs understandable is how you choose to name your items—and that includes naming variables, methods, classes, enumerations, and namespaces.

It is intuitively obvious that your names should reflect the purpose of the item and should be designed not to clash with other names. The general philosophy in the .NET Framework is also that the name of a variable should reflect the purpose of that variable instance and not the data type. For example, `height` is a good name for a variable, while `integerValue` isn't. However, you will probably feel that that principle is an ideal that is hard to achieve. Particularly when you are dealing with controls, in most cases, you'll probably feel happier sticking with variable names like `confirmationDialog` and `chooseEmployeeListBox`, which do indicate the data type in the name.

Let's look at some of the things you need to think about when choosing names.

Casing of names

In many cases you should use *Pascal casing* for names. Pascal casing means that the first letter of each word in a name is capitalized: `EmployeeSalary`, `ConfirmationDialog`, `PlainTextEncoding`. You will notice that essentially all of the names of namespaces, classes, and members in the base classes follow Pascal casing. In particular, the convention of joining words using the underscore character is discouraged. So you should try not to use names like `employee_salary`. It has also been common in other languages to use all-capitals for names of constants. This is not advised in C#, since such names are harder to read—the convention is to use Pascal casing throughout:

```
const int MaximumLength;
```

The only other casing scheme that you are advised to use is *camel casing*. Camel casing is similar to Pascal casing, except that the first letter of the first word in the name is not capitalized: `employeeSalary`, `confirmationDialog`, `plainTextEncoding`. There are three situations in which you are advised to use camel casing:

❑   For names of all private member fields in types:

```
public int subscriberID;
```

Note however that often it is conventional to prefix names of member fields with an underscore:

```
public int subscriberID;
```

❑   For names of all parameters passed to methods:

```
public void RecordSale(string salesmanName, int quantity);
```

❑   To distinguish items that would otherwise have the same name. A common example is when a property wraps around a field:

```
private string employeeName;

public string EmployeeName

{

    get

    {

        return employeeName;

    }

}
```

If you are doing this, you should always use camel casing for the private member and Pascal casing for the public or protected member, so that other classes that use your code see only names in Pascal case (except for parameter names).

You should also be wary about case sensitivity. C# is case sensitive, so it is syntactically correct for names in C# to differ only by the case, as in the previous examples. However, you should bear in mind that your assemblies might at some point be called from Visual Basic .NET applications—and *Visual Basic .NET is not case-sensitive*. Hence, if you do use names that differ only by a case, it is important to do so only in situations in which both names will never be seen outside your assembly. (The pervious example qualifies as okay because camel case is used with the name that is attached to a `private` variable.) Otherwise you may prevent other code written in Visual Basic .NET from being able to use your assembly correctly.

Name styles

You should try to be consistent about your style of names. For example, if one of the methods in a class is called `ShowConfirmationDialog()`, then you should not give another method a name like `ShowDialogWarning()`, or `WarningDialogShow()`. The other method should be called `ShowWarningDialog()`. Get the idea?

Namespace names

Namespace names are particularly important to design carefully in order to avoid risk of ending up with the same name for one of your namespaces as someone else uses. Remember, namespace names are the *only* way that .NET distinguishes names of objects in shared assemblies. So if you use the same namespace name for your software package as another package, and both packages get installed on the same computer, there are going to be problems. Because of this, it's almost always a good idea to create a top-level namespace with the name of your company, and then nest successive namespaces that narrow down the technology, group, or department you are working in or the name of the package your classes are intended for. Microsoft recommends namespace names that begin with `<CompanyName>`.`<TechnologyName>` as in these two examples:

```
WeaponsOfDestructionCorp.RayGunControllers
WeaponsOfDestructionCorp.Viruses
```

Names and keywords

It is important that the names do not clash with any keywords. In fact, if you attempt to name an item in your code with a word that happens to be a C# keyword, you'll almost certainly get a syntax error because the compiler will assume the name refers to a statement. However, because of the possibility that your classes will be accessed by code written in other languages, it is important that you also don't use names that are keywords in other .NET languages. Generally speaking, C++ keywords are similar to C# keywords, so confusion with C++ is unlikely, and those commonly encountered keywords that are unique to Visual C++ tend to start with two underscore characters. Like C#, C++ keywords are spelled in lowercase, so if you hold to the convention of naming your public classes and members with Pascal-style names, then they will always have at least one uppercase letter in their names, and there will be no risk of clashes with C++ keywords. On the other hand, you are more likely to have problems with Visual Basic .NET, which has many more keywords than C# does, and being non–case-sensitive means you cannot rely on Pascal-style names for your classes and methods.

The following table lists the keywords and standard function calls in Visual Basic .NET, which should if possible be avoided, in whatever case combination, for your public C# classes.

Abs	Do	Loc	RGB
Add	Double	Local	Right
AddHandler	Each	Lock	RmDir
AddressOf	Else	LOF	Rnd
Alias	ElseIf	Log	RTrim
And	Empty	Long	SaveSettings
Ansi	End	Loop	Second
AppActivate	Enum	LTrim	Seek
Append	EOF	Me	Select
As	Erase	Mid	SetAttr
Asc	Err	Minute	SetException
Assembly	Error	MIRR	Shared
Atan	Event	MkDir	Shell
Auto	Exit	Module	Short
Beep	Exp	Month	Sign
Binary	Explicit	MustInherit	Sin
BitAnd	ExternalSource	MustOverride	Single
BitNot	False	MyBase	SLN
BitOr	FileAttr	MyClass	Space
BitXor	FileCopy	Namespace	Spc
Boolean	FileDateTime	New	Split
ByRef	FileLen	Next	Sqrt
Byte	Filter	Not	Static
ByVal	Finally	Nothing	Step
Call	Fix	NotInheritable	Stop
Case	For	NotOverridable	Str
Catch	Format	Now	StrComp
CBool	FreeFile	NPer	StrConv
CByte	Friend	NPV	Strict
CDate	Function	Null	String
CDbl	FV	Object	Structure
CDec	Get	Oct	Sub
ChDir	GetAllSettings	Off	Switch

ChDrive	GetAttr	On	SYD
Choose	GetException	Open	SyncLock
Chr	GetObject	Option	Tab
CInt	GetSetting	Optional	Tan
Class	GetType	Or	Text
Clear	GoTo	Overloads	Then
CLng	Handles	Overridable	Throw
Close	Hex	Overrides	TimeOfDay
Collection	Hour	ParamArray	Timer
Command	If	Pmt	TimeSerial
Compare	Iif	PPmt	TimeValue
Const	Implements	Preserve	To
Cos	Imports	Print	Today
CreateObject	In	Private	Trim
CShort	Inherits	Property	Try
CSng	Input	Public	TypeName
CStr	InStr	Put	TypeOf
CurDir	Int	PV	UBound
Date	Integer	QBColor	UCase
DateAdd	Interface	Raise	Unicode
DateDiff	Ipmt	RaiseEvent	Unlock
DatePart	IRR	Randomize	Until
DateSerial	Is	Rate	Val
DateValue	IsArray	Read	Weekday
Day	IsDate	ReadOnly	While
DDB	IsDbNull	ReDim	Width
Decimal	IsNumeric	Remove	With
Declare	Item	RemoveHandler	WithEvents
Default	Kill	Rename	Write
Delegate	Lcase	Replace	WriteOnly
DeleteSetting	Left	Reset	Xor
Dim	Lib	Resume	Year
Dir	Line	Return	

Use of properties and methods

One area that can cause confusion in a class is whether a particular quantity should be represented by a property or a method. The rules here are not hard and fast, but in general, you ought to use a property if something really should look and feel like a variable. (If you're not sure what a property is, we'll be covering properties in Chapter 3.) This means, among other things, that:

❑ Client code should be able to read its value. Write-only properties are not recommended, so for example use a `SetPassword()` method, not a write-only `Password` property.

❑ Reading the value should not take too long. The fact that something is a property usually suggests that reading it will be relatively quick.

❑ Reading the value should not have any observable and unexpected side effect. Further, setting the value of a property should not have any side effect that is not directly related to the property. Setting the width of a dialog box has the obvious effect of changing the appearance of the dialog box on the screen. That's fine, as that's obviously related to the property in question.

❑ It should be possible to set properties in any order. In particular, it is not good practice when setting a property to throw an exception because another related property has not yet been set. For example, if in order to use a class that accesses a database you need to set `ConnectionString`, `UserName`, and `Password`, then the author of the class should make sure the class is implemented so the user really can set them in any order.

❑ Successive reads of a property should give the same result. If the value of a property is likely to change unpredictably, then you should code it up as a method instead. `Speed`, in a class that monitors the motion of an automobile, is not a good candidate for a property. Use a `GetSpeed()` method here; on the other hand, `Weight` and `EngineSize` are good candidates for properties as they will not change for a given object.

If the item you are coding satisfies all of the above criteria, then it is probably a good candidate for a property. Otherwise you should use a method.

Use of fields

The guidelines are pretty simple here. Fields should almost always be private, except that in some cases it may be acceptable for constant or read-only fields to be public. The reason is that if you make a field public, you may hinder your ability to extend or modify the class in the future.

The above guidelines should give you a rough idea of good practices, and you should also use them in conjunction with good object-oriented programming style.

It's also worth bearing in mind that Microsoft has been fairly careful about being consistent and has followed its own guidelines when writing the .NET base classes. So a very good way to get an intuitive feel for the conventions to follow when writing .NET code is to simply look at the base classes—see how classes, members, and namespaces are named, and how the class hierarchy works. If you try to write your code in the same style as the base classes, then you shouldn't go wrong.

Summary

In this chapter, we have examined some of the basic syntax of C#, covering the areas needed to write simple C# programs. We have covered a lot of ground, but much of it will be instantly recognizable to developers who are familiar with any C-style language (or even JavaScript). Some of the topics we have covered include:

❑ Variable scope and access levels

❑ Declaring variables of various data types

❑ Controlling the flow of execution within a C# program

❑ Comments and Xml documentation

❑ Preprocessor directives

❑ Usage guidelines and naming conventions, the guidelines that you should adhere to when writing C# code, so that your code follows normal .NET practice and can be easily understood by others

We have seen that C# syntax is similar to C++ and Java syntax, although there are many minor differences. We have also seen that in many areas this syntax is combined with facilities to write code very quickly, for example high-quality string handling facilities. C# also has a strongly defined type system, based on a distinction between value and reference types. In the following two chapters we cover the C# object-oriented programming features.

3

Objects and Types

So far, we've been introduced to some of the main building blocks that make up the C# language, including declaring variables, data types, and program flow statements, and we have seen a couple of very short complete programs containing little more than the `Main()` method. What we haven't really seen is how we can put all these together to form a longer complete program. The key to this lies in working with classes—the subject of this chapter. In particular, we will cover:

❑   The differences between classes and structs

❑   Fields, properties, and methods

❑   Passing values by value and reference

❑   Method overloading

❑   Constructors and static constructors

❑   Read-only fields

❑   The `Object` class, from which all other types are derived

We discuss inheritance and features related to inheritance in Chapter 4.

> In this chapter, we will introduce the basic syntax associated with classes. However, we will assume that you are already familiar with the underlying principles of using classes—for example, that you know what a constructor or a property is, and we will largely confine ourselves to seeing how to apply those principles in C# code. If you are not familiar with the concept of the class, then you might want to take a look at Appendix A, which is available with the code downloads for the book on the Web at www.wrox.com.

We will introduce and explain those concepts that are not necessarily supported by most object-oriented languages. For example, although object constructors are a widely used concept that you should be familiar with, static constructors are something new to C#, so we will explain how static constructors work.

Classes and Structs

Classes and structs are essentially templates from which we can create objects. Each object contains data and has methods to manipulate and access that data. The class defines what data and functionality each particular object (called an *instance*) of that class can contain. For example, if we have a class that represents a customer, it might define fields such as CustomerID, FirstName, LastName, and Address, which we will use to hold information about a particular customer. It might also define functionality that acts upon the data stored in these fields. We can then instantiate an object of this class to represent one specific customer, set the field values for that instance, and use its functionality.

```
class PhoneCustomer
{
    public const string DayOfSendingBill = "Monday";
    public int CustomerID;
    public string FirstName;
    public string LastName;
}
```

Structs differ from classes in the way that they are stored in memory and accessed (classes are reference types stored in the heap, structs are value types stored on the stack), and in some of the features (for example, structs don't support inheritance). You will tend to use structs for smaller data types for performance reasons. In terms of syntax, however, structs look very similar to classes; the main difference is that we use the keyword struct instead of class to declare them. For example, if we wanted all PhoneCustomer instances to be allocated on the stack instead of the managed heap, we could write:

```
struct PhoneCustomerStruct

{
    public const string DayOfSendingBill = "Monday";
    public int CustomerID;
    public string FirstName;
    public string LastName;
}
```

For both classes and structs, you use the keyword new to declare an instance: This keyword creates the object and initializes it; in the following example, the default behavior is to zero out its fields.

```
PhoneCustomer myCustomer = new PhoneCustomer();         // works for a class
PhoneCustomerStruct myCustomer2 = new PhoneCustomerStruct(); // works for a struct
```

In most cases you'll find you use classes much more often than structs. For this reason, we discuss classes first, then we point out the differences between classes and structs and the specific reasons why you might choose to use a struct instead of a class. Unless otherwise stated, however, you can assume that code we present for a class will work equally well for a struct.

Class Members

The data and functions within a class are known as the class's *members*. Microsoft's official terminology distinguishes between data members and function members. As well as these members, classes can also contain nested types (such as other classes). All members of a class can be declared as `public` (in which case they are directly accessible from outside the class) or as `private` (in which case they are only visible to other code within the class), just as in Visual Basic, C++, and Java. C# also has variants on this theme, such as `protected` (which indicates a member is visible only to the class in question and to any derived classes). We provide a comprehensive list of the different accessibilities in Chapter 4.

Data Members

Data members are those members that contain the data for the class—fields, constants, and events. Data members can be either static (associated with the class as a whole) or instance (each instance of the class has its own copy of the data). As usual for object-oriented languages, a class member is always an instance member unless it is explicitly declared as `static`.

Fields are any variables associated with the class. We have already seen fields being used in the `PhoneCustomer` class in the previous example.

Once we have instantiated a `PhoneCustomer` object, we can then access these fields using the `Object.FieldName` syntax as shown in this example:

```
PhoneCustomer Customer1 = new PhoneCustomer();
Customer1.FirstName = "Simon";
```

Constants can be associated with classes in the same way as variables. We declare a constant using the `const` keyword. Once again, if it is declared as `public`, it will be accessible from outside the class.

```
class PhoneCustomer
{
   public const string DayOfSendingBill = "Monday";
   public int CustomerID;
   public string FirstName;
   public string LastName;
}
```

Events are class members that allow an object to notify a caller whenever something noteworthy happens, such as a field or property of the class changing, or some form of user interaction occurring. The client can have code known as an event handler that reacts to the event. We look at events in detail in Chapter 6.

Function Members

Function members are those members that provide some functionality for manipulating the data in the class. They include methods, properties, constructors, finalizers, operators, and indexers.

Methods are functions that are associated with a particular class. They can be either instance methods, which work on a particular instance of a class, or static methods, which provide more generic functionality that doesn't require us to instantiate a class (like the `Console.WriteLine()` method). We discuss methods in the next section.

Properties are sets of functions that can be accessed from the client in a similar way to the public fields of the class. C# provides a specific syntax for implementing read and write properties on our classes, so we don't have to jury-rig methods whose names have the words `Get` or `Set` embedded in them. Since there's a dedicated syntax for properties that is distinct from that for normal functions, the illusion of objects as actual things is strengthened for client code.

Constructors are special functions that are called automatically when an object is instantiated. They must have the same name as the class to which they belong, and cannot have a return type. Constructors are useful for initializing the values of fields.

Finalizers are similar to constructors, but are called when the CLR detects that an object is no longer needed. They have the same name as the class, preceded by a tilde (~). C++ programmers should note that finalizers are used much less frequently than their nearest C++ equivalent, destructors, because the CLR handles garbage collection automatically. Also, it is impossible to predict precisely when a finalizer will be called. We discuss finalizers in Chapter 7.

Operators are at their simplest are actions like + or -. When you add two integers you are, strictly speaking, using the + operator for integers. However, C# also allows us to specify how existing operators will work with our own classes (*operator overloading*). We look at operators in detail in Chapter 5.

Indexers allow our objects to be indexed in the same way as an array or collection. This topic is also covered in Chapter 5.

Methods

In Visual Basic, C, and C++, we could define global functions that were not associated with a particular class. This is not the case in C#. As noted earlier, in C# every function must be associated with a class or struct.

Note that official C# terminology does in fact make a distinction between functions and methods. In this terminology, the term function member includes not only methods, but also other non-data members of a class or struct. This includes indexers, operators, constructors, destructors, and also—perhaps somewhat surprisingly—properties. These are contrasted with data members: fields, constants, and events. In this chapter, we confine ourselves to looking at methods.

Declaring methods

The syntax for defining a method in C# is just what you'd expect from a C-style language, and is virtually identical to the syntax in C++ and Java. The main syntactical difference from C++ is that, in C#, each method is separately declared as public or private. It is not possible to use `public:` blocks to group several method definitions. Also, all C# methods are declared and defined in the class definition. There is no facility in C# to separate the method implementation as in C++.

In C#, the definition of a method consists of any method modifiers (such as the method's accessibility), the type of the return value, followed by the name of the method, followed by a list of input arguments enclosed in parentheses, followed by the body of the method enclosed in curly braces:

```
[modifiers] return_type MethodName([parameters])
{
    // Method body
}
```

Each parameter consists of the name of the type of the parameter, and the name by which it can be referenced in the body of the method. Also, if the method returns a value, a return statement must be used with the return value to indicate the exit point. For example:

```
public bool IsSquare(Rectangle rect)
{
    return (rect.Height == rect.Width);
}
```

This code uses one of the .NET base classes, `System.Drawing.Rectangle`, which represents a rectangle.

If the method doesn't return anything, we specify a return type of void, because we can't omit the return type altogether; and if it takes no arguments, we still need to include an empty set of parentheses after the method name (as with the `Main()` method). In this case, including a return statement is optional—the method returns automatically when the closing curly brace is reached. You should note that a method can contain as many return statements as required:

```
public bool IsPositive(int value)
{
    if (value < 0)
        return false;
    return true;
}
```

Invoking methods

The syntax for invoking a method is exactly the same in C# as it is in C++ and Java, and the only difference between C# and Visual Basic is that round brackets must always be used when invoking the method in C#—this is actually simpler than the Visual Basic 6 set of rules whereby brackets were sometimes necessary and at other times not allowed.

The following sample, MathTest, illustrates the syntax for definition of and instantiation of classes, and definition and invocation of methods. Besides the class that contains the `Main()` method, it defines a class named `MathTest`, which contains a couple of methods and a field.

```
using System;

namespace Wrox.ProCSharp.MathTestSample
{
    class MainEntryPoint
    {
        static void Main()
```

```
        {
            // Try calling some static functions
            Console.WriteLine("Pi is " + MathTest.GetPi());
            int x = MathTest.GetSquareOf(5);
            Console.WriteLine("Square of 5 is " + x);

            // Instantiate at MathTest object
            MathTest math = new MathTest();   // this is C#'s way of
                                              // instantiating a reference type

            // Call non-static methods
            math.value = 30;
            Console.WriteLine(
                "Value field of math variable contains " + math.value);
            Console.WriteLine("Square of 30 is " + math.GetSquare());
        }
    }

    // Define a class named MathTest on which we will call a method
    class MathTest
    {
        public int value;

        public int GetSquare()
        {
            return value*value;
        }

        public static int GetSquareOf(int x)
        {
            return x*x;
        }

        public static double GetPi()
        {
            return 3.14159;
        }
    }
}
```

Running the MathTest sample produces these results:

csc MathTest.cs

```
Microsoft (R) Visual C# .NET Compiler version 7.10.3052.4
for Microsoft (R) .NET Framework version 1.1.4322
Copyright (C) Microsoft Corporation 2001-2002. All rights reserved.


MathTest
Pi is 3.14159
Square of 5 is 25
Value field of math variable contains 30
Square of 30 is 900
```

As you can see from the code, the `MathTest` class contains a field that contains a number, as well as a method to find the square of this number. It also contains two static methods, to return the value of pi, and to find the square of the number passed in as a parameter.

There are some features of this class that are not really good examples of C# program design. For example, `GetPi()` would usually be implemented as a `const` field, but following good design here would mean using some concepts than we have not yet introduced.

Most of the syntax in the previous sample should be familiar to C++ and Java developers. If your background is in Visual Basic, then just think of the `MathTest` class as being like a Visual Basic class module that implements fields and methods. There are a couple of points to watch out for though, whatever your language.

Passing parameters to methods

Arguments can in general be passed into methods by reference, or by value. When a variable is passed by reference, the called method gets the actual variable—so any changes made to the variable inside the method persist when the method exits. On the other hand, if a variable is passed by value, then the called method gets an identical copy of the variable—which means any changes made are lost when the method exits. For complex data types, passing by reference is more efficient because of the large amount of data that must be copied when passing by value.

In C#, all parameters are passed by value unless we specifically say otherwise. This is the same behavior as in C++, but the opposite to Visual Basic. However, we need to be careful in understanding the implications of this for reference types. Since reference type variables only hold a reference to an object, it is this reference that will be copied, not the object itself. Hence changes made to the underlying object will persist. Value type variables, in contrast, hold the actual data, so a copy of the data itself will be passed into the method. An `int`, for instance, is passed by value to a method, and any changes that the method makes to the value of that `int` do not change the value of the original `int` object. Conversely, if an array or any other reference type, such as a class, is passed into a method, and the method uses the reference to change a value in that array, the new value is reflected in the original array object.

Here is an example, ParameterTest.cs, that demonstrates this:

```csharp
using System;

namespace Wrox.ProCSharp.ParameterTestSample
{
   class ParameterTest
   {
      static void SomeFunction(int[] ints, int i)
      {
         ints[0] = 100;
         i = 100;
      }

      public static int Main()
      {
         int i = 0;
         int[] ints = { 0, 1, 2, 4, 8 };
         // Display the original values
         Console.WriteLine("i = " + i);
```

```
            Console.WriteLine("ints[0] = " + ints[0]);
            Console.WriteLine("Calling SomeFunction...");

            // After this method returns, ints will be changed,
            // but i will not
            SomeFunction(ints, i);
            Console.WriteLine("i = " + i);
            Console.WriteLine("ints[0] = " + ints[0]);
            return 0;
        }
    }
}
```

The output of this is:

csc ParameterTest.cs

```
Microsoft (R) Visual C# .NET Compiler version 7.10.3052.4
for Microsoft (R) .NET Framework version 1.1.4322
Copyright (C) Microsoft Corporation 2001-2002. All rights reserved.


ParameterTest
i = 0
ints[0] = 0
Calling SomeFunction...
i = 0
ints[0] = 100
```

Notice how the value of `i` remains unchanged, but the value we changed in `ints` is also changed in the original array.

The behavior of strings is different again. This is because strings are immutable (if we alter a string's value, we create an entirely new string), so strings don't display the typical reference-type behavior. Any changes made to a string within a method call won't affect the original string. This point is discussed in more detail in Chapter 8.

ref parameters

Passing variables by value is the default. We can, however, force value parameters to be passed by reference. To do so, we use the `ref` keyword. If a parameter is passed to a method, and if the input argument for that method is prefixed with the `ref` keyword, then any changes that the method makes to the variable will affect the value of the original object:

```
static void SomeFunction(int[] ints, ref int i)
{
    ints[0] = 100;
    i = 100;      // the change to i will persist after SomeFunction() exits
}
```

We will also need to add the `ref` keyword when we invoke the method:

```
SomeFunction(ints, ref i);
```

Adding the `ref` keyword in C# serves the same purpose as using the `&` syntax in C++ to specify passing by reference. However, C# makes the behavior more explicit (thus hopefully preventing bugs) by requiring the use of the `ref` keyword when invoking the method.

Finally, it is also important to understand that C# continues to apply initialization requirements to parameters passed to methods. Any variable must be initialized before it is passed into a method, whether it is passed in by value or reference.

out parameters

In C-style languages, it is common for functions to be able to output more than one value from a single routine. This is accomplished using output parameters, by assigning the output values to variables that have been passed to the method by reference. Often, the starting values of the variables that are passed by reference are unimportant. Those values will be overwritten by the function, which may never even look at any previous value.

It would be convenient if we could use the same convention in C#. However, C# requires that variables be initialized with a starting value before they are referenced. Although we could initialize our input variables with meaningless values before passing them into a function that will fill them with real, meaningful ones, this practice seems at best needless and at worst confusing. However, there is a way to short-circuit the C# compiler's insistence on initial values for input arguments.

This is achieved with the `out` keyword. When a method's input argument is prefixed with `out`, that method can be passed a variable that has not been initialized. The variable is passed by reference, so any changes that the method makes to the variable will persist when control returns from the called method. Again, we also need to use the `out` keyword when we call the method, as well as when we define it:

```
static void SomeFunction(out int i)
{
   i = 100;
}

public static int Main()
{
   int i; // note how i is declared but not initialized
   SomeFunction(out i);
   Console.WriteLine(i);
   return 0;
}
```

The `out` keyword is an example of something new in C# that has no analogy in either Visual Basic or C++, and which has been introduced to make C# more secure against bugs. If an `out` parameter isn't assigned a value within the body of the function, the method won't compile.

Method overloading

C# supports method overloading—several versions of the method that have different signatures (that is, the name, number of parameters, and parameter types). However, C# does not support default parameters in the way that, say, C++ or Visual Basic do. In order to overload methods, you simply declare the methods with the same name but different numbers or types of parameters:

```
class ResultDisplayer
{
    void DisplayResult(string result)
    {
        // implementation
    }

    void DisplayResult(int result)
    {
        // implementation
    }
}
```

Because C# does not support optional parameters, you will need to use method overloading to achieve the same effect:

```
class MyClass
{
    int DoSomething(int x)    // want 2nd parameter with default value 10
    {
        DoSomething(x, 10);
    }

    int DoSomething(int x, int y)
    {
        // implementation
    }
}
```

As in any language, method overloading carries with it the potential for subtle runtime bugs if the wrong overload is called. In Chapter 4 we discuss how to code defensively against these problems. For now, we'll point out that C# does place some minimum differences on the parameters of overloaded methods.

❑   It is not sufficient for two methods to differ only in their return type.

❑   It is not sufficient for two methods to differ only by virtue of a parameter having been declared as ref or out.

Properties

Properties are unusual in that they represent an idea that C# has taken from Visual Basic, not from C++/Java. The idea of a property is that it is a method or pair of methods that are dressed to look like a field as far as any client code is concerned. A good example of this is the Height property of a Windows Form. Suppose you have the following code:

```
// mainForm is of type System.Windows.Forms
mainForm.Height = 400;
```

On executing this code, the height of the window will be set to 400 and you will see the window resize on the screen. Syntactically, the above code looks like we're setting a field, but in fact we are calling a property accessor that contains code to resize the form.

To define a property in C#, we use the following syntax.

```csharp
public string SomeProperty
{
   get
   {
      return "This is the property value";
   }
   set
   {
      // do whatever needs to be done to set the property
   }
}
```

The `get` accessor takes no parameters and must return the same type as the declared property. You should not specify any explicit parameters for the set accessor either, but the compiler assumes it takes one parameter, which is of the same type again, and which is referred to as `value`. As an example, the following code contains a property called `ForeName`, which sets a field called `foreName`, and which applies a length limit.

```csharp
private string foreName;

public string ForeName
{
   get
   {
      return foreName;
   }
   set
   {
      if (value.Length > 20)
         // code here to take error recovery action
         // (eg. throw an exception)
      else
         foreName = value;
   }
}
```

Note the naming convention used here. We take advantage of C#'s case sensitivity by using the same name, Pascal-cased for the public property and camel-cased for the equivalent private field if there is one. This is standard practice. Some developers prefer to use field names that are prefixed by an underscore: _foreName; this provides an extremely convenient way of identifying fields.

Visual Basic 6 programmers should remember that C# does not distinguish between Visual Basic 6 `Set` and Visual Basic 6 `Let`: In C#, the write accessor is always identified with the keyword, `set`.

Read-only and write-only properties

It is possible to create a read-only property by simply omitting the set accessor from the property definition. Thus, to make `ForeName` read-only in the previous example:

```
private string foreName;

public string ForeName
{
   get
   {
      return foreName;
   }
}
```

It is similarly possible to create a write-only property by omitting the `get` accessor. However, this is regarded as poor programming practice because it could be confusing to authors of client code. In general, it is recommended that if you are tempted to do this, you should use a method instead.

Access modifiers for properties

C# does not permit setting different access modifiers to the `get` and `set` accessor of a property. This may cause you some headaches if you have a property that wraps a private field, where you need public access for reading, but you want to confine write access to derived classes. It's tempting in this case to make the underlying field protected rather than private, but this is generally regarded as poor coding practice. In this situation, the most common workaround, is to declare a public read-only property and a protected or private `Set()` function.

```
public string ForeName
{
   get
   {
      return foreName;
   }
}

protected void SetForeName(string value)
{
   if (value.Length > 20)
      // code here to take error recovery action
      // (eg. throw an exception)
   else
      foreName = value;
}
```

A note about inlining

Some developers may worry that, in the previous sections, we have presented a number of situations in which standard C# coding practices have led to very small functions—for example, accessing a field via a property instead of directly. Is this going to hurt performance because of the overhead of the extra function call? The answer is that there is no need to worry about performance loss from these kinds of programming methodologies in C#. Recall that C# code is compiled to IL then JIT compiled at runtime to native executable code. The JIT compiler is designed to generate highly optimized code, and will ruthlessly inline code as appropriate (in other words, replace function calls by inline code). A method or property whose implementation simply calls another method or returns a field will almost certainly be inlined. Note however that the decision of where to inline is made entirely by the CLR. There is no way for you to control which methods are inlined, by using, for example, some keyword similar to the `inline` keyword of C++.

Constructors

The syntax for declaring basic constructors in C# is the same as in Java and C++. We declare a method that has the same name as the containing class, and which does not have any return type:

```
public class MyClass
{
   public MyClass()
   {
   }
   // rest of class definition
```

As in C++ and Java, it's not necessary to provide a constructor for your class. We haven't supplied one for any of our examples so far in the book. In general, if you don't supply any constructor, the compiler will just make up a default one for you behind the scenes. It'll be a very basic constructor that just initializes all the member fields by zeroing them out (null reference for reference types, zero for numeric data types, and false for bools). Often, that will be adequate; if not, you'll need to write your own constructor.

> **For C++ programmers: Because primitive fields in C# are by default initialized by being zeroed out, whereas primitive fields in C++ are by default uninitialized, you may find you don't need to write constructors in C# as often as you would in C++.**

Constructors follow the same rules for overloading as other methods. In other words, you can provide as many overloads to the constructor as you want, provided they are clearly different in signature:

```
public MyClass()    // zero-parameter constructor
{
   // construction code
}
public MyClass(int number)    // another overload
{
   // construction code
}
```

Note, however, that if you supply any constructors that take parameters, then the compiler will not automatically supply a default one. This is only done if you have not defined any constructors at all. In the following example, because we have defined a one-parameter constructor, the compiler assumes that this is the only constructor we want to be available, and so will not implicitly supply any others:

```
public class MyNumber
{
   private int number;
   public MyNumber(int number)
   {
      this.number = number;
   }
}
```

The previous code also illustrates typical use of the `this` keyword to distinguish member fields from parameters of the same name. If we now try instantiating a `MyNumber` object using a no-parameter constructor, we will get a compilation error:

```
MyNumber numb = new MyNumber();   // causes compilation error
```

We should mention that it is possible to define constructors as private or protected, so that they are invisible to code in unrelated classes too:

```
public class MyNumber
{
   private int number;
   private MyNumber(int number)    // another overload
   {
      this.number = number;
   }
}
```

In this example we haven't actually defined any public or even any protected constructors for MyNumber. This would actually make it impossible for MyNumber to be instantiated by outside code using the new operator (though you might write a public static property or method in MyNumber that can instantiate the class). This is useful in two situations:

❑   If your class serves only as a container for some static members or properties, and therefore should never be instantiated

❑   If you want the class to only ever be instantiated by calling some static member function (this is the so-called class factory approach to object instantiation)

Static constructors

One novel feature of C# is that it is also possible to write a static no-parameter constructor for a class. Such a constructor will only be executed once, as opposed to the constructors we've written so far, which are instance constructors, and are executed whenever an object of that class is created. There is no equivalent to the static constructor in C++ or Visual Basic 6.

```
class MyClass
{
   static MyClass()
   {
      // initialization code
   }
   // rest of class definition
}
```

One reason for writing a static constructor would be if your class has some static fields or properties that need to be initialized from an external source before the class is first used.

The .NET runtime makes no guarantees about when a static constructor will be executed, so you should not place any code in it that relies on it being executed at a particular time (for example, when an assembly is loaded). Nor is it possible to predict in what order static constructors of different classes will execute. However, what is guaranteed is that the static constructor will run at most once, and that it will be invoked before your code makes any reference to the class. In C#, the static constructor usually seems to be executed immediately before the first call to any member of the class.

Notice that the static constructor does not have any access modifiers. It's never called by any other C# code, but always by the .NET runtime when the class is loaded, so any access modifier like `public` or `private` would be meaningless. For this same reason, the static constructor cannot ever take any parameters, and there can only be one static constructor for a class. It should also be obvious that a static constructor can only access static members, not instance members, of the class.

Note that it is possible to have a static constructor and a zero-parameter instance constructor defined in the same class. Although the parameter lists are identical, there is no conflict because the static constructor is executed when the class is loaded, but the instance constructor is executed whenever an instance is created —so there won't be any confusion about which constructor gets executed when.

Note that if you have more than one class that has a static constructor, the static constructor that will be executed first is undefined. This means that you should not put any code in a static constructor that depends on other static constructors having been or not having been executed. On the other hand, if any static fields have been given default values, these will be allocated before the static constructor is called.

We'll now present a sample that illustrates the use of a static constructor. The sample is imaginatively called StaticConstructor and is based on the idea of a program that has user preferences (which are presumably stored in some configuration file). To keep things simple, we'll assume just one user preference— a quantity called `BackColor`, which might represent the background color to be used in an application. And since we don't want to get into the details of writing code to read data from an external source here, we'll make the assumption that the preference is to have a background color of red on weekdays and green at weekends. All the program will do is display the preference in a console window—but this is enough to see a static constructor at work.

```
namespace Wrox.ProCSharp.StaticConstructorSample
{
   public class UserPreferences
   {
      public static readonly Color BackColor;

      static UserPreferences()
      {
         DateTime now = DateTime.Now;
         if (now.DayOfWeek == DayOfWeek.Saturday
            || now.DayOfWeek == DayOfWeek.Sunday)
            BackColor = Color.Green;
         else
            BackColor = Color.Red;
      }

      private UserPreferences()
      {
      }
   }
}
```

This code shows how the color preference is stored in a static variable, which is initialized in the static constructor. We have declared this field as read-only, which means that its value can only be set in a constructor. We'll look at read-only fields in more detail later in this chapter. The code makes use of a couple of useful structs that have been supplied by Microsoft as part of the framework class library,

`System.DateTime.` and `System.Drawing.Color`. `DateTime` implements a static property, `Now`, which returns the current time, and an instance property, `DayOfWeek`, which works out what day of the week a date-time represents. `Color` (which is discussed in Chapter 20) is used to store colors. It implements various static properties, such as `Red` and `Green` as used in this example, which return commonly used colors. In order to use `Color`, we need to reference the `System.Drawing.dll` assembly when compiling, and we must add a `using` statement for the `System.Drawing` namespace.

```
using System;
using System.Drawing;
```

We test the static constructor with this code:

```
class MainEntryPoint
{
   static void Main(string[] args)
   {
      Console.WriteLine("User-preferences: BackColor is: " +
                        UserPreferences.BackColor.ToString());
   }
}
```

Compiling and running this code results in this output:

C:> StaticConstructor

```
User-preferences: BackColor is: Color [Red]
```

Calling constructors from other constructors

You may sometimes find yourself in the situation where you have several constructors in a class, perhaps to accommodate some optional parameters, for which the constructors have some code in common. For example, consider this:

```
class Car
{
   private string description;
   private uint nWheels;
   public Car(string model, uint nWheels)
   {
      this.description = description;
      this.nWheels = nWheels;
   }

   public Car(string model)
   {
      this.description = description;
      this.nWheels = 4;
   }
// etc.
```

Both constructors initialize the same fields. It would clearly be neater to place all the code in one place, and C# has a special syntax, known as a constructor initializer, to allow this.

```
class Car
{
   private string description;
   private uint nWheels;

   public Car(string model, uint nWheels)
   {
      this.description = description;
      this.nWheels = nWheels;
   }

   public Car(string model) : this(model, 4)
   {
   }
   // etc
```

In this context, the this keyword simply causes the constructor with the nearest matching parameters to be called. Note that any constructor initializer is executed before the body of the constructor. Say the following code is run:

```
Car myCar = new Car("Proton Persona");
```

In this example, the two-parameter constructor executes before any code in the body of the one-parameter constructor (though in this particular case, since there is no code in the body of the one-parameter constructor, it makes no difference).

A C# constructor initializer may contain either one call to another constructor in the same class (using the syntax just presented) or one call to a constructor in the immediate base class (using the same syntax, but using the keyword base instead of this). It is not possible to put more than one call in the initializer.

The syntax for constructor initializers in C# is similar to that for constructor initialization lists in C++, but C++ developers should beware. Behind the similarity in syntax, C# initializers follow very different rules for what can be placed in them. Whereas you can use a C++ initialization list to indicate initial values of any member variables or to call a base constructor, the only thing you can put in a C# initializer is one call to one other constructor. This forces C# classes to follow a strict sequence for how they get constructed, where C++ allows some laxity. We study this issue more in Chapter 4, where we will see that the sequence enforced by C# arguably amounts to no more than good programming practice anyway.

readonly Fields

The concept of a constant, as a variable that contains a value that cannot be changed, is something that C# shares with most programming languages. However, constants don't necessarily meet all requirements. On occasion, you may have some variable whose value shouldn't be changed, but where the value is not known until runtime. C# provides another type of variable that is useful in this scenario: the readonly field.

The readonly keyword gives a bit more flexibility than const, allowing for the case in which you might want a field to be constant but also need to carry out some calculations to determine its initial value. The rule is that you can assign values to a readonly field inside a constructor, but not anywhere else. It's also possible for a readonly field to be an instance rather than a static field, having a different value for each instance of a class. This means that, unlike a `const` field, if you want a `readonly` field to be static, you have to declare it as such.

Suppose we have an MDI program that edits documents, but that for licensing reasons we want to restrict the number of documents that can be opened simultaneously. Now assume that we are selling different versions of the software, and it's possible that customers can upgrade their licenses to open more documents simultaneously. Clearly this means we can't hard-code the maximum number in the source code. We'd probably need a field to represent this maximum number. This field will have to be read in—perhaps from a registry key or some other file storage—each time the program is launched. So our code might look something like this:

```
public class DocumentEditor
{
    public static readonly uint MaxDocuments;

    static DocumentEditor()
    {
        MaxDocuments = DoSomethingToFindOutMaxNumber();
    }
}
```

In this case, the field is static, since the maximum number of documents only needs to be stored once per running instance of the program. This is why it is initialized in the static constructor. If we had an instance `readonly` field then we would initialize it in the instance constructor(s). For example, presumably each document we edit has a creation date, which you wouldn't want to allow the user to change (because that would be rewriting the past!). Note that the field is also public—we don't normally need to make `readonly` fields private, because by definition they cannot be modified externally (the same principle also applies to constants).

As noted earlier, date is represented by the class `System.DateTime`. In the following code we use a `System.DateTime` constructor that takes three parameters (the year, month, and day of the month—you can find details of this and other `DateTime` constructors in the MSDN documentation):

```
public class Document
{
    public readonly DateTime CreationDate;

    public Document()
    {
        // read in creation date from file. Assume result is 1 Jan 2002
        // but in general this can be different for different instances
        // of the class
        CreationDate = new DateTime(2002, 1, 1);
    }
}
```

`CreationDate` and `MaxDocuments` in the previous code snippet are treated like any other field, except that because they are read-only, it cannot be assigned to outside the constructors.

```
void SomeMethod()
{
    MaxDocuments = 10;     // compilation error here. MaxDocuments is readonly
}
```

It's also worth noting that you don't have to assign a value to a `readonly` field in a constructor. If you don't do so, it will be left with the default value for its particular data type or whatever value you initialized it to at its declaration. That applies to both static and instance `readonly` fields.

Structs

So far, we have seen how classes offer a great way of encapsulating objects in your program. We have also seen how they are stored on the heap in a way that gives you much more flexibility in data lifetime, but with a slight cost in performance. This performance cost is small thanks to the optimizations of managed heaps. However, there are some situations when all you really need is a small data structure. In this case, a class provides more functionality than you need, and for performance reasons you will probably prefer to use a struct. Look at this example:

```
class Dimensions
{
   public double Length;
   public double Width;
}
```

We've defined a class called `Dimensions`, which simply stores the length and width of some item. Perhaps we're writing a furniture-arranging program to let people experiment with rearranging their furniture on the computer and we want to store the dimensions of each item of furniture. It looks like we're breaking the rules of good program design by making the fields public, but the point is that we don't really need all the facilities of a class for this at all. All we have is two numbers, which we find convenient to treat as a pair rather than individually. There is no need for lots of methods, or for us to be able to inherit from the class, and we certainly don't want to have the .NET runtime go to the trouble of bringing in the heap with all the performance implications, just to store two doubles.

As mentioned earlier in this chapter, the only thing we need to change in the code to define a type as a struct instead of a class is to replace the keyword `class` with `struct`:

```
struct Dimensions
{
   public double Length;
   public double Width;
}
```

Defining functions for structs is also exactly the same as defining them for classes. The following code demonstrates a constructor and a property for a struct:

```
struct Dimensions
{
   public double Length;
   public double Width;

   Dimensions(double length, double width)
   { Length=length; Width=width; }

   public int Diagonal
```

```
    {
        {
            get
            {
                return Math.Sqrt(Length*Length + Width*Width);
            }
        }
    }
}
```

In many ways you can think of structs in C# as being like scaled-down classes. They are basically the same as classes, but designed more for cases where you simply want to group some data together. They differ from classes in the following ways:

❏ Structs are value types, not reference types. This means they are stored either in the stack or inline (if they are part of another object that is stored on the heap) and have the same lifetime restrictions as the simple data types.

❏ Structs do not support inheritance.

❏ There are some differences in the way constructors work for structs. In particular, the compiler always supplies a default no-parameter constructor, which you are not permitted to replace.

❏ With a struct, you can specify how the fields are to be laid out in memory (we will examine this in Chapter 10 when we cover attributes).

Because structs are really intended to group data items together, you'll sometimes find that most or all of their fields are declared as public. This is strictly speaking contrary to the guidelines for writing .NET code—according to Microsoft, fields (other than const fields) should always be private and wrapped by public properties. However, for simple structs, many developers would nevertheless consider public fields to be acceptable programming practice.

C++ developers beware; structs in C# are very different from classes in their implementation. This is very different to the situation in C++, for which classes and structs are virtually the same thing.

Let's look at some of these differences in more detail.

Structs Are Value Types

Although structs are value types, you can often treat them syntactically in the same way as classes. For example, with our definition of the Dimensions class in the previous section, we could write:

```
Dimensions point = new Dimensions();
point.Length = 3;
point.Width = 6;
```

Note that because structs are value types, the new operator does not work in the same way as it does for classes and other reference types. Instead of allocating memory on the heap, the new operator simply calls the appropriate constructor, according to the parameters passed to it, initializing all fields. Indeed, for structs it is perfectly legal to write:

```
Dimensions point;
point.Length = 3;
point.Width = 6;
```

If `Dimensions` was a class, this would produce a compilation error, because point would contain an uninitialized reference—an address that points nowhere, so we could not start setting values to its fields. For a struct however, the variable declaration actually allocates space on the stack for the entire struct, so it's ready to assign values to. Note, however, that the following code would cause a compilation error, with the compiler complaining that you are using an uninitialized variable:

```
Dimensions point;
Double D = point.Length;
```

Structs follow the same rules as any other data type: everything must be initialized before use. A struct is considered fully initialized either when the new operator has been called against it, or when values have been individually assigned to all its fields. And of course, a struct defined as a member field of a class is initialized by being zeroed-out automatically when the containing object is initialized.

The fact that structs are value types will affect performance, though depending on how you use your struct, this can be good or bad. On the positive side, allocating memory for structs is very fast because this takes place inline or on the stack. The same goes for removing structs when they go out of scope. On the other hand, whenever you pass a struct as a parameter or assign a struct to another struct (as in A=B, where A and B are structs), the full contents of the struct are copied, whereas for a class only the reference is copied. This will result in a performance loss that depends on the size of the struct—this should emphasize the fact that structs are really intended for small data structures. Note, however, that when passing a struct as a parameter to a method, you can avoid this performance loss by passing it as a `ref` parameter—in this case only the address in memory of the struct will be passed in, which is just as fast as passing in a class. On the other hand, if you do this, you'll have to be aware that it means the called method can in principle change the value of the struct.

Structs and Inheritance

Structs are not designed for inheritance. This means that it is not possible to inherit from a struct. The only exception to this is that structs, in common with every other type in C#, derive ultimately from the class `System.Object`. Hence, structs also have access to the methods of `System.Object`, and it is even possible to override them in structs—an obvious example would be overriding the `ToString()` method. The actual inheritance chain for structs is that each struct derives from a class, `System.ValueType`, which in turn derives from `System.Object`. `ValueType` does not add any new members to `Object`, but provides implementations of some of them that are more suitable for structs. Note that you cannot supply a different base class for a struct: Every struct is derived from `ValueType`.

Constructors for Structs

You can define constructors for structs in exactly the same way that you can for classes, except that you are not permitted to define a constructor that takes no parameters. This may seem nonsensical, and the reason is buried in the implementation of the .NET runtime. There are some rare circumstances in which the .NET runtime would not be able to call a custom zero-parameter constructor that you have supplied. Microsoft has therefore taken the easy way out and banned zero-parameter constructors for structs in C#.

That said, the default constructor, which initializes all fields to zero values, is always present implicitly, even if you supply other constructors that take parameters. It's also impossible to circumvent the default constructor by supplying initial values for fields. The following code will cause a compile-time error:

```
struct Dimensions
{
    public double Length = 1;      // error. Initial values not allowed
    public double Width = 2;       // error. Initial values not allowed
```

Of course, if `Dimensions` had been declared as a class, this code would have compiled without any problems.

Incidentally, you can supply a `Close()` or `Dispose()` method for a struct in the same way you do for a class.

The Object Class

We indicated earlier that all .NET classes are ultimately derived from `System.Object`. In fact, if you don't specify a base class when you define a class, the compiler will automatically assume that it derives from `Object`. Since we have not used inheritance in this chapter, that means that every class we have shown here is actually derived from `System.Object`. (As noted earlier, for structs this derivation is indirect: A struct is always derived from `System.ValueType`, which in turn derives from `System.Object`.)

The practical significance of this is that, besides the methods and properties and so on that you define, you also have access to a number of public and protected member methods that have been defined for the `Object` class. These methods are available in all other classes that you define.

System.Object Methods

The methods defined in `Object` are as shown in the following table.

Method	Access Modifiers	Purpose
string ToString()	public virtual	Returns a string representation of the object
int GetHashTable()	public virtual	Used if implementing dictionaries (hash tables)
bool Equals(object obj)	public virtual	Compares instances of the object for equality
bool Equals(object objA, object objB)	public static	Compares instances of the object for equality
bool ReferenceEquals (object objA, object objB)	public static	Compares whether two references refer to the same object
Type GetType()	Public	Returns details of the type of the object.
object MemberwiseClone()	Protected	Makes a shallow copy of the object
void Finalize()	protected virtual	This is the .NET version of a destructor

We haven't yet covered enough of the C# language to be able to understand how to use all these methods. For the time being, we will simply summarize the purpose of each method, with the exception of `ToString()`, which we examine in more detail.

❑ `ToString()`—This is intended as a fairly basic, quick-and-easy string representation; use it when you just want a quick idea of the contents of an object, perhaps for debugging purposes. It provides very little choice of how to format the data: For example, dates can in principle be expressed in a huge variety of different formats, but `DateTime.ToString()` does not offer you any choice in this regard. If you need a more sophisticated string representation that, for example, takes account of your formatting preferences or of the culture (the locale), then you should implement the `IFormattable` interface (see Chapter 8).

❑ `GetHashCode()`—This is used if objects are placed in a data structure known as a map (also known as a hash table or dictionary). It is used by classes that manipulate these structures in order to determine where to place an object in the structure. If you intend your class to be used as key for a dictionary, then you will need to override `GetHashCode()`. There are some fairly strict requirements for how you implement your overload, and we deal with those when we examine dictionaries in Chapter 9.

❑ `Equals()` (both versions) and `ReferenceEquals()`—As you'll gather by the existence of three different methods aimed at comparing the equality of objects, The .NET Framework has quite a sophisticated scheme for measuring equality. There are subtle differences between how these three methods, along with the comparison operator, `==`, are intended to be used. Not only that but there are also restrictions on how you should override the virtual, one parameter version of `Equals()` if you choose to do so, because certain base classes in the `System.Collections` namespace call the method and expect it to behave in certain ways. We explore the use of these methods in Chapter 5 when we examine operators.

❑ `Finalize()`—We cover this method in Chapter 7. It is intended as the nearest that C# has to C++-style destructors, and is called when a reference object is garbage collected to clean up resources. The `Object` implementation of `Finalize()` actually does nothing and is ignored by the garbage collector. You will normally override `Finalize()` if an object owns references to unmanaged resources which need to be removed when the object is deleted. The garbage collector cannot do this directly as it only knows about managed resources, so it relies on any finalizers that you supply.

❑ `GetType()`—This method returns an instance of a class derived from `System.Type`. This object can provide an extensive range of information about the class of which your object is a member, including base type, methods, properties, and so on. `System.Type` also provides the entry point into .NET's reflection technology. We will examine this topic in Chapter 10.

❑ `MemberwiseClone()`—This is the only member of `System.Object` that we don't examine in detail anywhere in the book. There is no need to, since it is fairly simple in concept. It simply makes a copy of the object and returns a reference (or in the case of a value type, a boxed reference) to the copy. Note that the copy made is a shallow copy—this means that it copies all the value types in the class. If the class contains any embedded references, then only the references will be copied, not the objects referred to. This method is protected and so cannot be called to copy external objects. It is also not virtual, so you cannot override its implementation.

The ToString() Method

We have already encountered `ToString()` in Chapter 2. It provides the most convenient way to get a quick string representation of an object.

For example:

```
int i = -50;
string str = i.ToString();   // returns "-50"
```

Here's another example:

```
enum Colors {Red, Orange, Yellow};
// later on in code...
Colors favoriteColor = Colors.Orange;
string str = favoriteColor.ToString();          // returns "Orange"
```

Object.ToString() is actually declared as virtual, and in all these examples, we are taking advantage of the fact that its implementation in the C# predefined data types has been overridden for us in order to return correct string representations of those types. You might not think that our Colors enum counts as a predefined data type. It actually gets implemented as a struct derived from System.Enum, and System.Enum has a rather clever override of ToString() that deals with all the enums you define.

If you don't override ToString() in classes that you define, then your classes will simply inherit the System.Object implementation—which displays the name of the class. If you want ToString() to return a string that contains information about the value of objects of your class, then you will need to override it. We illustrate this with a sample, Money, which defines a very simple class, also called Money, which represent U.S. currency amounts. Money simply acts as a wrapper for the decimal class but supplies a ToString() method. Note that this method must be declared as override because it is replacing (overriding) the ToString() method supplied by Object. We discuss overriding in more detail in Chapter 4. The complete code for the sample is as follows. Note that it also illustrates use of properties to wrap fields:

```
using System;

namespace Wrox.ProCSharp.OOCSharp
{
    class MainEntryPoint
    {
        static void Main(string[] args)
        {
            Money cash1 = new Money();
            cash1.Amount = 40M;
            Console.WriteLine("cash1.ToString() returns: " + cash1.ToString());
            Console.ReadLine();
        }
    }
    class Money
    {
        private decimal amount;

        public decimal Amount
        {
            get
            {
                return amount;
            }
```

```
        set
        {
            amount = value;
        }
    }
    public override string ToString()
    {
        return "$" + Amount.ToString();
    }
}

}
```

You'll realize that this sample is there just to illustrate syntactical features of C#. C# already has a predefined type to represent currency amounts, decimal, so in real life, you wouldn't write a class to duplicate this functionality unless you wanted to add various other methods to it. And in many cases due to formatting requirements, you'd probably use the String.Format() method (which we cover in Chapter 8) rather than ToString() to display a currency string.

In the Main() method we instantiate first a Money object, then a BetterMoney object. In both cases we call ToString(). For the Money object, we'll pick up the Object version of this method that displays class information. For the BetterMoney object, we'll pick up our own override. Running this code gives the following results:

```
StringRepresentations
cash1.ToString() returns: $40
```

Summary

In this chapter we've examined C# syntax for declaring and manipulating objects. We have seen how to declare static and instance fields, properties, methods, and constructors. We have also seen that C# adds some new features not present in the OOP model of some other languages: Static constructors provide a means of initializing static fields, while structs allow you to define high-performance types, albeit with a more restricted feature set, which do not require the use of the managed heap. We have also seen how all types in C# derive ultimately from the type System.Object, which means that all types start with a basic set of useful methods, including ToString().

In Chapter 4 we examine implementation and interface inheritance in C#.

Inheritance

In Chapter 3, we examined how to use individual classes in C#. The focus in that chapter was on how to define methods, constructors, properties, and other members of a single class (or a single struct). Although we did point out the fact that all classes ultimately derive from the class System.Object, we did not examine how to create a hierarchy of inherited classes. Inheritance is the subject of this chapter. We will briefly discuss the scope of C#'s support for inheritance, before examining in detail how to code first implementation inheritance then interface inheritance in C#. Note that this chapter presumes familiarity with the basic concepts of inheritance, including virtual functions and overriding. We will concentrate on the syntax used to provide inheritance and inheritance-related topics, such as virtual functions, and on those aspects of the C# inheritance model that are particular to C# and not necessarily shared by other object-oriented languages.

Types of Inheritance

We're going to start off by reviewing exactly what C# does and does not support as far as inheritance is concerned.

Implementation Versus Interface Inheritance

Gurus of object-oriented programming will know that there are two distinct types of inheritance: implementation inheritance and interface inheritance.

❑ **Implementation inheritance** means that a type derives from a base type, taking all the base type's member fields and functions. With implementation inheritance, a derived type adopts the base type's implementation of each function, unless it is indicated in the definition of the derived type that a function implementation is to be overridden. This type of inheritance is most useful when you need to add functionality to an existing type, or where a number of related types share a significant amount of common functionality. A good example of this comes in the Windows Forms classes, which we discuss in Chapter

19. (Chapter 19 also looks at the base class System.Windows.Forms.Control, which provides a very sophisticated implementation of a generic Windows control, and numerous other classes such as System.Windows.Forms.TextBox and System.Windows.Forms.ListBox that derive from Control and override functions or provide new functions to implement specific types of control.)

❑ **Interface inheritance** means that a type inherits only the signatures of the functions, but does not inherit any implementations. This type of inheritance is most useful when you want to specify that a type makes certain features available. For example, certain types can indicate that they provide a resource cleanup method called Dispose() by deriving from an interface, System.IDisposable (see Chapter 7). Since the way that one type cleans up resources is likely to be very different from the way that another type cleans up resources, there is no point defining any common implmentation, so interface inheritance is appropriate here. Interface inheritance is often regarded as providing a contract: By deriving from an interface, a type is guaranteed to provide certain functionality to clients.

Traditionally, languages such as C++ have been very strong on implementation inheritance: Indeed, implementation inheritance has been at the core of the C++ programming model. On the other hand, Visual Basic 6 did not support any implementation inheritance of classes but did support interface inheritance thanks to its underlying COM foundations.

In C#, we have both implementation and interface inheritance. There is arguably no preference, as both types of inheritance are fully built into the language from the ground up. This makes it easy for you to choose the best architecture for your solution.

Multiple Inheritance

Some languages such as C++ support what is known as *multiple inheritance*, which a class derives from more than one other class. The benefits of using of multiple inheritance are debatable: On the one hand, there is no doubt that it is possible to use multiple inheritance to write extremely sophisticated, yet compact, code, as demonstrated by the C++ ATL library. On the other hand, code that uses multiple implementation inheritance is often difficult to understand and debug (a point that is equally well demonstrated by the C++ ATL library). As we mentioned, making it easy to write robust code was one of the crucial design goals behind the development of C#. Accordingly, C# does not support multiple implementation inheritance. On the other hand, it does allow types to derive from multiple interfaces. This means that a C# class can derive from one other class, and any number of interfaces. Indeed, we can be more precise: Thanks to the presence of System.Object as a common base type, every C# class (except for Object) has exactly one base class, and may additionally have any number of base interfaces.

Structs and Classes

In Chapter 3 we distinguish between structs (value types) and classes (reference types). One restriction of using a struct is that structs do not support inheritance, beyond the fact that every struct is automatically derived from System.ValueType. In fact we should be more careful. It's true that it is not possible to code a type hierarchy of structs; however, it is possible for structs to implement interfaces: In other words, structs don't really support implementation inheritance, but they do support interface inheritance. Indeed, we can summarize the situation for any types that you define as follows:

❑ **Structs** are always derived from `System.ValueType`. They can also derive from any number of interfaces.

❑ **Classes** are always derived from one other class of your choosing. They can also derive from any number of interfaces.

Implementation Inheritance

If you want to declare that a class derives from another class, use the following syntax:

```
class MyDerivedClass : MyBaseClass
{
    // functions and data members here
}
```

This syntax is very similar to C++ and Java syntax. However, C++ programmers, who will be used to the concepts of public and private inheritance, should note that C# does not support private inheritance, hence the absence of a public or private qualifier on the base class name. Supporting private inheritance would have complicated the language for very little gain: In practice private inheritance is used extremely rarely in C++ anyway.

If a class (or a struct) also derives from interfaces, then the list of base class and interfaces is separated by commas:

```
public class MyDerivedClass : MyBaseClass, IInterface1, IInterface2
{
        // etc.
```

For a struct, the syntax is as follows:

```
public struct MyDerivedStruct : IInterface1, IInterface2
{
        // etc.
```

If you do not specify a base class in a class definition, the C# compiler will assume that `System.Object` is the base class. Hence the following two pieces of code yield the same result:

```
class MyClass : Object  // derives from System.Object
{
    // etc.
}
```

and

```
class MyClass    // derives from System.Object
{
    // etc.
}
```

For the sake of simplicity, the second form is more common.

Since C# supports the `object` keyword, which serves as a pseudonym for the `System.Object` class, you can also write:

```
class MyClass : object    // derives from System.Object
{
   // etc.
}
```

If you want to reference the `Object` class, use the `object` keyword, which is recognized by intelligent editors such as Visual Studio .NET and thus facilitates editing your code.

Virtual Methods

By declaring a base class function as `virtual`, we allow the function to be overridden in any derived classes:

```
class MyBaseClass
{
   public virtual string VirtualMethod()
   {
      return "This method is virtual and defined in MyBaseClass";
   }
}
```

It is also permitted to declare a property as `virtual`. For a virtual or overridden property, the syntax is the same as for a non-virtual property with the exception of the keyword `virtual`, which is added to the definition. The syntax looks like this:

```
public virtual string ForeName
{
   get { return foreName;}
   set { foreName = value;}
}
private string foreName;
```

For simplicity, the following discussion focuses mainly on methods, but it applies equally well to properties.

The concepts behind virtual functions in C# are identical to standard OOP concepts: We can override a virtual function in a derived class, and when the method is called, the appropriate method for the type of object is invoked. In C#, functions are not virtual by default, but (aside from constructors) can be explicitly declared as `virtual`. This follows the C++ methodology: for performance reasons, functions are not virtual unless indicated. In Java, by contrast, all functions are virtual. C# differs from C++ syntax, however, because it requires you to declare when a derived class's function overrides another function, using the `override` keyword:

```
class MyDerivedClass : MyBaseClass
{
   public override string VirtualMethod()
   {
      return "This method is an override defined in MyDerivedClass";
   }
}
```

This syntax for method overriding removes potential runtime bugs that can easily occur in C++, when a method signature in a derived class unintentionally differs slightly from the base version, resulting in the method failing to override the base version. In C# this is picked up as a compile-time error, since the compiler would see a function marked as `override`, but no base method for it to override.

Neither member fields nor static functions can be declared as virtual. The concept simply wouldn't make sense for any class member other than an instance function member.

Hiding Methods

If a method with the same signature is declared in both base and derived classes, but the methods are not declared as `virtual` and `override` respectively, then the derived class version is said to *hide* the base class version. The result is that which version of a method gets called depends on the type of the variable used to reference the instance, not the type of the instance itself.

In most cases you would want to override methods rather than hide them; by hiding them you risk calling the "wrong" method for a given class instance. However, as we will show in the following example, C# syntax is designed to ensure that the developer is warned at compile time about this potential problem, thus making it safer to hide methods if that is your intention. This also has versioning benefits for developers of class libraries.

Suppose you have a class called `HisBaseClass`:

```
class HisBaseClass
{
    // various members
}
```

At some point in the future you write a derived class that adds some functionality to `HisBaseClass`. In particular, you add a method called `MyGroovyMethod()`, which is not present in the base class:

```
class MyDerivedClass: HisBaseClass
{
    public int MyGroovyMethod()
    {
        // some groovy implementation
        return 0;
    }
}
```

Now one year later, you decide to extend the functionality of the base class. By coincidence, you add a method that is also called `MyGroovyMethod()` and has the same name and signature as yours, but probably doesn't do the same thing. When you compile your code using the new version of the base class, you have a potential clash because your program won't know which method to call. It's all perfectly legal C#, but since your `MyGroovyMethod()` is not intended to be related in any way to the base class `MyGroovyMethod()` the result of running this code does not yield the result you want. Fortunately C# has been designed in such a way that it copes very well when conflicts of this type arise.

In these situations, C# generates a compilation warning. That reminds us to use the new keyword to declare that we intend to hide a method, like this:

```
class MyDerivedClass : HisBaseClass
{
    public new int MyGroovyMethod()
    {
        // some groovy implementation
        return 0;
    }
}
```

However, because your version of `MyGroovyMethod()` is not declared as `new`, the compiler will pick up on the fact that it's hiding a base class method without being instructed to do so and generate a warning (this applies whether or not you declared `MyGroovyMethod()` as `virtual`). If you want, you can rename your version of the method. This is the recommended course of action, since it will eliminate future confusion. However, if you decide not to rename your method for whatever reason (for example, you've published your software as a library for other companies, so you can't change the names of methods), all your existing client code will still run correctly, picking up your version of `MyGroovyMethod()`. That's because any existing code that accesses this method must be doing so through a reference to `MyDerivedClass` (or a further derived class).

Your existing code cannot access this method through a reference to `HisBaseClass`; it would generate a compilation error when compiled against the earlier version of `HisBaseClass`. The problem can only happen in client code you have yet to write. C# arranges things so that you get a warning that a potential problem might occur in future code—and you will need to pay attention to this warning, and take care not to attempt to call your version of `MyGroovyMethod()` through any reference to `HisBaseClass` in any future code you add. However, all your existing code will still work fine. It may be a subtle point, but it's quite an impressive example of how C# is able to cope with different versions of classes.

Calling Base Versions of Functions

C# has a special syntax for calling base versions of a method from a derived class: `base.<MethodName>()`. For example, if you want a method in a derived class to return 90 percent of the value returned by the base class method, you can use the following syntax:

```
class CustomerAccount
{
    public virtual decimal CalculatePrice()
    {
        // implementation
        return 0.0M;
    }
}
class GoldAccount : CustomerAccount
{
    public override decimal CalculatePrice()
    {
        return base.CalculatePrice() * 0.9M;
    }
}
```

Java uses a similar syntax, with the exception that Java uses the keyword `super` rather than `base`. C++ has no similar keyword but instead requires specification of the class name (`CustomerAccount:` `:CalculatePrice()`). Any equivalent to `base` in C++ would have been ambiguous since C++ supports multiple inheritance.

Note that you can use the `base.<MethodName>()` syntax to call any method in the base class—you don't have to call it from inside an override of the same method.

Abstract Classes and Functions

C# allows both classes and functions to be declared as abstract. An abstract class cannot be instantiated, while an abstract function does not have an implementation, and must be overridden in any non-abstract derived class. Obviously, an abstract function is automatically virtual (although you don't need to supply the `virtual` keyword; doing so results in a syntax error). If any class contains any abstract functions, then that class is also abstract and must be declared as such.

```
abstract class Building
{
   public abstract decimal CalculateHeatingCost();   // abstract method
}
```

C++ developers will notice some syntactical differences in C# here. C# does not support the =0 syntax to declare abstract functions. In C#, this syntax would be misleading, since =<value> is allowed in member fields in class declarations to supply initial values:

```
abstract class Building
{
   private bool damaged = false;   // field
   public abstract decimal CalculateHeatingCost();   // abstract method
}
```

C++ developers should also note the slightly different terminology: In C++, abstract functions are often described as pure virtual; in the C# world, the only correct term to use is abstract.

Sealed Classes and Methods

C# allows classes and methods to be declared as `sealed`. In the case of a class, this means that you can't inherit from that class. In the case of a method, this means that you can't override that method.

```
sealed class FinalClass
{
   // etc
}
class DerivedClass : FinalClass        // wrong. Will give compilation error
{
   // etc
}
```

Java developers will recognize sealed as the C# equivalent of Java's final.

The most likely situation when you'll mark a class or method as `sealed` will be if the class or method is internal to the operation of the library, class, or other classes that you are writing, so you are sure that any attempt to override some of its functionality will cause problems. You might also mark a class or method as `sealed` for commercial reasons, in order to prevent a third party from extending your classes in a manner that is contrary to the licensing agreements. In general, however, you should be careful about marking a class or member as `sealed`, since by doing so you are severely restricting how it can be used. Even if you don't think it would be useful to inherit from a class or override a particular member of it, it's still possible that at some point in the future someone will encounter a situation you hadn't anticipated in which it is useful to do so. The .NET base class library frequently uses sealed classes in order to make these classes inaccessible to third-party developers who might want to derive their own classes from them. For example, string is a sealed class.

Declaring a method as `sealed` serves a similar purpose as for a class, although you rarely will want to declare a method as `sealed`.

```
class MyClass
{
   public sealed override void FinalMethod()
   {
      // etc.
   }
}
class DerivedClass : MyClass
{
   public override void FinalMethod()        // wrong. Will give compilation error
   {
   }
}
```

It does not make sense to use the `sealed` keyword on a method unless that method is itself an override of another method in some base class. If you are defining a new method and you don't want anyone else to override it, then you would not declare it as `virtual` in the first place. If, however, you have overridden a base class method then the sealed keyword provides a way of ensuring that the override you supply to a method is a "final" override in the sense that no one else can override it again.

Constructors of Derived Classes

In Chapter 3 we discuss how constructors can be applied to individual classes. An interesting question arises as to what happens when you start defining your own constructors for classes that are part of a hierarchy, inherited from other classes that may also have custom constructors?

Let's assume you have not defined any explicit constructors for any of your classes. This means that the compiler supplies default zeroing-out constructors for all your classes. There is actually quite a lot going on under the hood when that happens, but the compiler is able to arrange it so that things work out nicely throughout the class hierarchy and every field in every class gets initialized to whatever its default value is. When you add a constructor of your own, however, you are effectively taking control of construction. This has implications right down through the hierarchy of derived classes, and you have to make sure that you don't inadvertently do anything to prevent construction through the hierarchy from taking place smoothly.

You might be wondering why there is any special problem with derived classes. The reason is that when you create an instance of a derived class, there is actually more than one constructor at work. The constructor of the class you instantiate isn't by itself sufficient to initialize the class—the constructors of the base classes must also be called. That's why we've been talking about construction through the hierarchy.

To see why base class constructors must be called, we're going to develop an example based on a cell phone company called MortimerPhones. The example contains an abstract base class, GenericCustomer, which represents any customer. There is also a (non-abstract) class, Nevermore60Customer, that represents any customer on a particular rate called the Nevermore60 rate. All customers have a name, represented by a private field. Under the Nevermore60 rate, the first few minutes of the customer's call time are charged at a higher rate, necessitating the need for the field highCostMinutesUsed, which details how many of these higher cost minutes each customer has used up. The class definitions look like this:

```
abstract class GenericCustomer
{
    private string name;
    // lots of other methods etc.
}
class Nevermore60Customer : GenericCustomer
{
    private uint highCostMinutesUsed;
    // other methods etc.
}
```

We won't worry about what other methods might be implemented in these classes, as we are concentrating solely on the construction process here. And if you download the sample code for this chapter, you'll find that the class definitions include only the constructors.

Let's look at what happens when you use the new operator to instantiate a Nevermore60Customer.

```
GenericCustomer customer = new Nevermore60Customer();
```

Clearly both of the member fields name and highCostMinutesUsed must be initialized when customer is instantiated. If we don't supply constructors of our own, but rely simply on the default constructors, then we'd expect name to be initialized to the null reference, and highCostMinutesUsed to zero. Let's look in a bit more detail at how this actually happens.

The highCostMinutesUsed field presents no problem: the default Nevermore60Customer constructor supplied by the compiler will initialize this field to zero.

What about name? Looking at the class definitions, it's clear that the Nevermore60Customer constructor can't initialize this value. This field is declared as private, which means that derived classes don't have access to it. So the default Nevermore60Customer constructor simply won't even know that this field exists. The only code items that have that knowledge are other members of GenericCustomer. This means that if name is going to be initialized, that'll have to be done by some constructor in GenericCustomer. No matter how big your class hierarchy is, this same reasoning applies right down to the ultimate base class, System.Object.

Now that we have an understanding of the issues involved, we can look at what actually happens whenever a derived class is instantiated. Assuming default constructors are used throughout, the compiler first grabs the constructor of the class it is trying to instantiate, in this case `Nevermore60Customer`. The first thing that the default `Nevermore60Customer` constructor does is attempt to run the default constructor for the immediate base class, `GenericCustomer`. Then the `GenericCustomer` constructor attempts to run the constructor for its immediate base, `System.Object`. `System.Object` doesn't have any base classes, so its constructor just executes and returns control to the `GenericCustomer` constructor. That constructor now executes, initializing `name` to `null`, before returning control to the `Nevermore60Customer` constructor. That constructor in turn executes, initializing `highCostMinutesUsed` to zero, and exits. At this point, the `Nevermore60Customer` instance has been successfully constructed and initialized.

The net result of all this is that the constructors are called in order of `System.Object` first, then progressing down the hierarchy until the compiler reaches the class being instantiated. Notice also that in this process, each constructor handles initialization of the fields in its own class. That's how it should normally work, and when you start adding your own constructors you should try to stick to that principle.

Notice the order in which this happens. It's always the base class constructors that get called first. This means that there are no problems with a constructor for a derived class invoking any base class methods, properties, and any other members that it has access to, because it can be confident that the base class has already been constructed and its fields initialized. It also means that if the derived class doesn't like the way that the base class has been initialized, it can change the initial values of the data, provided it has access to do so. However, good programming practice almost invariably means you'll try to prevent that situation from occurring if you can, and you will trust the base class constructor to deal with its own fields.

Now that you know how the process of construction works, you can start fiddling with it by adding your own constructors.

Adding a No-Parameter Constructor in a Hierarchy

We'll take the simplest case first and see what happens if we simply replace the default constructor somewhere in the hierarchy with another constructor that takes no parameters. Suppose that we decide that we want everyone's name to be initially set to the string, `"<no name>"` instead of to the `null` reference. We'd modify the code in `GenericCustomer` like this:

```
public abstract class GenericCustomer
{
    private string name;
    public GenericCustomer()
        : base()  // we could omit this line without affecting the compiled code
    {
        name = "<no name>";
    }
}
```

Adding this code will work fine. `Nevermore60Customer` still has its default constructor, so the sequence of events described above will proceed as before, except that the compiler will use our custom `GenericCustomer` constructor instead of generating a default one, so the `name` field will always be initialized to `"<no name>"` as required.

Notice that in our constructor, we've added a call to the base class constructor before the GenericCustomer constructor is executed, using a syntax similar to what we were using earlier when we discussed how to get different overloads of constructors to call each other. The only difference is that this time we use the base keyword instead of this, to indicate it's a constructor to the base class rather than a constructor to the current class we want to call. There are no parameters in the brackets after the base keyword—that's important because it means we are not passing any parameters to the base constructor, so the compiler will have to look for a parameterless constructor to call. The result of all this is that the compiler will inject code to call the System.Object constructor, just as would happen by default anyway.

In fact, we can omit that line of code, and write the following (as we've done for most of the constructors so far in the chapter):

```
public GenericCustomer()
{
    name = "<no name>";
}
```

If the compiler doesn't see any reference to another constructor before the opening curly brace, it assumes that we intended to call the base class constructor; this fits in with the way default constructors work.

The base and this keywords are the only keywords allowed in the line which calls another constructor. Anything else causes a compilation error. Also note that only one other constructor can be specified.

So far this code works fine. One good way to mess up the progression through the hierarchy of constructors, however, is to declare a constructor as private:

```
private GenericCustomer()
{
    name = "<no name>";
}
```

If you try this, you'll find you get an interesting compilation error, which could really throw you if you don't understand how construction down a hierarchy works:

```
'Wrox.ProCSharp.GenericCustomer()' is inaccessible due to its protection level
```

The interesting thing is that the error occurs not in the GenericCustomer class, but in the derived class, Nevermore60Customer. What's happened is that the compiler has tried to generate a default constructor for Nevermore60Customer, but not been able to because the default constructor is supposed to invoke the no-parameter GenericCustomer constructor. By declaring that constructor as private, we've made it inaccessible to the derived class. A similar error occurs if we supply a constructor to GenericCustomer, which takes parameters, but at the same time we fail to supply a no-parameter constructor. In this case the compiler will not generate a default constructor for GenericCustomer, so when it tries to generate the default constructors for any derived class, it'll again find that it can't because a no-parameter base class constructor is not available. A workaround would be to add your own constructors to the derived classes, even if you don't actually need to do anything in these constructors, so that the compiler doesn't try to generate any default constructor for them.

Now that you have all the theoretical background you need, you're ready to move on to an example of how you can neatly add constructors to a hierarchy of classes. In the next section we'll start adding constructors that take parameters to the MortimerPhones example.

Adding Constructors with Parameters to a Hierarchy

We're going to start with a one-parameter constructor for GenericCustomer which controls that customers can be instantiated only when they supply their names.

```
abstract class GenericCustomer
{
   private string name;
   public GenericCustomer(string name)
   {
      this.name = name;
   }
}
```

So far, so good. However, as mentioned previously, this will cause a compilation error when the compiler tries to create a default constructor for any derived classes, because the default compiler-generated constructors for Nevermore60Customer will try to call a no-parameter GenericCustomer constructor and GenericCustomer does not possess such a constructor. Therefore, we'll need to supply our own constructors to the derived classes to avoid a compilation error.

```
class Nevermore60Customer : GenericCustomer
{
   private uint highCostMinutesUsed;
   public Nevermore60Customer(string name)
      :  base(name)
   {
   }
}
```

Now instantiation of Nevermore60Customer objects can only take place when a string containing the customer's name is supplied, which is what we want anyway. The interesting thing is what our Nevermore60Customer constructor does with this string. Remember that it can't initialize the name field itself, because it has no access to private fields in its base class. Instead, it passes the name through to the base class for the GenericCustomer constructor to handle. It does this by specifying that the base class constructor to be executed first is the one that takes the name as a parameter. Other than that, it doesn't take any action of its own.

Next we're going to investigate what happens if you have different overloads of the constructor as well as a class hierarchy to deal with. To this end we're going to assume that Nevermore60 customers may have been referred to MortimerPhones by a friend as part of one of these sign-up-a-friend-and-get-a-discount offers. This means that when we construct a Nevermore60Customer, we may need to pass in the referrer's name as well. In real life the constructor would have to do something complicated with the name, like process the discount, but here we'll just store the referrer's name in another field.

The Nevermore60Customer definition will now look like this:

```
class Nevermore60Customer : GenericCustomer
{
   public Nevermore60Customer(string name, string referrerName)
      : base(name)
```

```
    {
        this.referrerName = referrerName;
    }

    private string referrerName;
    private uint highCostMinutesUsed;
```

The constructor takes the name and passes it to the `GenericCustomer` constructor for processing. `referrerName` is the variable that is our responsibility here, so the constructor deals with that parameter in its main body.

However, not all `Nevermore60Customers` will have a referrer, so we still need a constructor that doesn't require this parameter (or a constructor that gives us a default value for it). In fact we will specify that if there is no referrer, then the `referrerName` field should be set to `"<None>"`, using the following one-parameter constructor:

```
        public Nevermore60Customer(string name)
            : this(name, "<None>")
        {
        }
```

We've now got all our constructors set up correctly. It's instructive to examine the chain of events that now occurs when we execute a line like this:

```
        GenericCustomer customer = new Nevermore60Customer("Arabel Jones");
```

The compiler sees that it needs a one-parameter constructor that takes one string, so the constructor it'll identify is the last one that we've defined:

```
        public Nevermore60Customer(string Name)
            : this(Name, "<None>")
```

When we instantiate `customer`, this constructor will be called. It immediately transfers control to the corresponding `Nevermore60Customer` 2-parameter constructor, passing it the values `"Arabel Jones"`, and `"<None>"`. Looking at the code for this constructor, we see that it in turn immediately passes control to the one-parameter `GenericCustomer` constructor, giving it the string `"Arabel Jones"`, and in turn that constructor passes control to the `System.Object` default constructor. Only now do the constructors execute. First, the `System.Object` constructor executes. Next comes the `GenericCustomer` constructor, which initializes the `name` field. Then the `Nevermore60Customer` 2-parameter constructor gets control back, and sorts out initializing the `referrerName` to `"<None>"`. Finally, the `Nevermore60Customer` one-parameter constructor gets to execute; this constructor doesn't do anything else.

As you can see, this is a very neat and well-designed process. Each constructor handles initialization of the variables that are obviously its responsibility, and in the process our class has been correctly instantiated and prepared for use. If you follow the same principles when you write your own constructors for your classes, you should find that even the most complex classes get initialized smoothly and without any problems.

Modifiers

We have already encountered quite a number of so-called modifiers—keywords that can be applied to a type or to a member. Modifiers can indicate the visibility of a method, such as `public` or `private`, or the nature of an item, such as whether a method is `virtual` or `abstract`. C# has a number of modifiers, and at this point it's worth taking a minute to provide the complete list.

Visibility Modifiers

These modifiers indicate which other code items can view an item.

Modifier	Applies To	Description
public	Any types or members	The item is visible to any other code.
protected	Any member of a type, also any nested type	The item is visible only to any derived type.
internal	Any member of a type, also any nested type	The item is visible only within its containing assembly.
private	Any types or members	The item is visible only inside the type to which it belongs.
protected internal	Any member of a type, also any nested type	The item is visible to any code within its containing assembly and also to any code inside a derived type.

Note that type definitions can be public or private, depending on whether you want the type to be visible outside its containing assembly.

```
public class MyClass
{
    // etc.
```

You cannot define types as protected, internal, or protected internal, as these visibility levels would be meaningless for a type contained in a namespace. Hence these visibilities can only be applied to members. However, you can define nested types (that is, types contained within other types) with these visibilities, since in this case the type also has the status of a member. Hence the following code is correct:

```
public class OuterClass
{
    protected class InnerClass
    {
        // etc.
    }
    // etc.
}
```

If you have a nested type, the inner type is always able to see all members of the outer type. Hence with the above code, any code inside `InnerClass` always has access to all members of `OuterClass`, even where those members are private.

Other Modifiers

These modifiers can be applied to members of types, and have various uses. A few of these modifiers also make sense when applied to types.

Modifier	Applies To	Description
new	Function members	The member hides an inherited member with the same signature.
static	All members	The member does not operate on a specific instance of the class.
virtual	Classes and function members only	The member can be overridden by a derived class.
abstract	Function members only	A virtual member that defines the signature of the member, but doesn't provide an implementation.
override	Function members only	The member overrides an inherited virtual or abstract member.
sealed	Classes	The member overrides an inherited virtual member, but cannot be overridden by any classes that inherit from this class. Must be used in conjunction with override.
extern	static [DllImport] methods only.	The member is implemented externally, in a different language.

Of these, `internal` and `protected internal` are the ones that are new to C# and the .NET Framework. `internal` acts in much the same way as `public`, but access is confined to other code in the same assembly—in other words, code that is being compiled at the same time in the same program. You can use `internal` to ensure all the other classes that you are writing have access to a particular member, while at the same time hiding it from other code written by other organizations. `protected internal` combines protected and internal, but in an OR sense, not an AND sense. A protected internal member can be seen by any code in the same assembly. It can also be seen by any derived classes, even those in other assemblies.

Interfaces

As we mentioned earlier, by deriving from an interface a class is declaring that it implements certain functions. Because not all object-oriented languages support interfaces, we will examine C#'s implementation of interfaces in detail in this section.

Developers familiar with COM should be aware that, although conceptually C# interfaces are similar to COM interfaces, they are not the same thing. The underlying architecture is different. For example, C# interfaces do not derive from IUnknown. A C# interface provides a contract stated in terms of .NET functions. Unlike a COM interface, a C# interface does not represent any kind of binary standard.

We will illustrate interfaces by presenting the complete definition of one of the interfaces that has been predefined by Microsoft, `System.IDisposable`. `IDisposable` contains one method, `Dispose()`, which is intended to be implemented by classes to clean up code.

```
public interface IDisposable
{
   void Dispose();
}
```

This code shows that declaring an interface works syntactically in pretty much the same way as declaring an abstract class. You should be aware, however, that it is not permitted to supply implementations of any of the members of an interface. In general, an interface can only contain declarations of methods, properties, indexers, and events.

You can never instantiate an interface; it only contains the signatures of its members. An interface has neither constructors (how can you construct something that you can't instantiate?) nor fields (because that would imply some internal implementation). An interface definition is also not allowed to contain operator overloads, though that's not because there is any problem in principle with declaring them— there isn't; it is because interfaces are usually intended to be public contracts, and having operator overloads would cause some incompatibility problems with other .NET languages, such as Visual Basic .NET, which do not support operator overloading.

It is also not permitted to declare modifiers on the members in an interface definition. Interface members are always implicitly `public`, and cannot be declared as `virtual` or `static`. That's up to implementing classes to decide on. It is therefore fine for implementing classes to declare access modifiers, as we do in the example in this section.

Take for example `IDisposable`. If a class wants to declare publicly that it implements the `Dispose()` method, then it must implement `IDisposable`—which in C# terms means that the class derives from `IDisposable`.

```
class SomeClass : IDisposable
{
   // this class MUST contain an implementation of the
   // IDisposable.Dispose() method, otherwise
   // you get a compilation error
   public void Dispose()
   {
      // implementation of Dispose() method
   }
   // rest of class
}
```

In this example, if `SomeClass` derives from `IDisposable` but doesn't contain a `Dispose()` implementation with the exact same signature as defined in `IDisposable`, then you get a compilation error, because the class would be breaking its agreed contract to implement `IDisposable`. Of course, there's no problem for the compiler about a class having a `Dispose()` method but not deriving from

`IDisposable`. The problem then would be that other code would have no way of recognizing that `SomeClass` has agreed to support the `IDisposable` features.

> *`IDisposable` is a relatively simple interface, since it defines only one method. Most interfaces will contain more members.*

Another good example of an interface is provided by the `foreach` loop in C#. In principle, the `foreach` loop works internally by querying the object to find out whether it implements an interface called `System.Collections.IEnumerable`. If it does, then the C# compiler will inject IL code, which uses the methods on this interface to iterate through the members of the collection. If it doesn't, then `foreach` will raise an exception. We will examine the `IEnumerable` interface in more detail in Chapter 9. It's worth pointing out that both `IEnumerable` and `IDisposable` are somewhat special interfaces to the extent that they are actually recognized by the C# compiler, which takes account of these interfaces in the code that it generates. Obviously, any interfaces that you define yourself won't be so privileged!

Defining and Implementing Interfaces

We're going to illustrate how to define and use interfaces by developing a short program that follows the interface inheritance paradigm. The example is based on bank accounts. We assume we are writing code that will ultimately allow computerized transfers between bank accounts. And we'll assume for our example that there are many companies that may implement bank accounts, but they have all mutually agreed that any classes that represent bank accounts will implement an interface, `IBankAccount`, which exposes methods to deposit or withdraw money, and a property to return the balance. It is this interface that will allow outside code to recognize the various bank account classes implemented by different bank accounts. Although our aim is to allow the bank accounts to talk to each other to allow transfers of funds between accounts, we won't introduce that feature just yet.

To keep things simple, we will keep all the code for our sample in the same source file. Of course if something like our example were used in real life, we could surmise that the different bank account classes would not only be compiled to different assemblies but would be hosted on different machines owned by the different banks. (We explore how .NET assemblies hosted on different machines can communicate in Chapter 16 when we cover remoting.) That's all much too complicated for our purposes here. However, to maintain some attempt at realism, we will define different namespaces for the different companies.

To begin, we need to define the `IBank` interface:

```
namespace Wrox.ProCSharp
{
   public interface IBankAccount
   {
      void PayIn(decimal amount);
      bool Withdraw(decimal amount);
      decimal Balance
      {
         get;
      }
   }
}
```

Notice the name of the interface, IBankAccount. It's a convention that an interface name traditionally starts with the letter I, so that we know that it's an interface.

> *We pointed out in Chapter 2 that, in most cases, .NET usage guidelines discourage the so-called Hungarian notation in which names are preceded by a letter that indicates the type of object being defined. Interfaces are one of the few exceptions in which Hungarian notation is recommended.*

The idea is that we can now write classes that represent bank accounts. These classes don't have to be related to each other in any way, they can be completely different classes. They will, however, all declare that they represent bank accounts by the mere fact that they implement the IBankAccount interface.

Let's start off with the first class, a saver account run by the Royal Bank of Venus:

```
namespace Wrox.ProCSharp.VenusBank
{
    public class SaverAccount : IBankAccount
    {
        private decimal balance;
        public void PayIn(decimal amount)
        {
            balance += amount;
        }
        public bool Withdraw(decimal amount)
        {
            if (balance >= amount)
            {
                balance -= amount;
                return true;
            }
            Console.WriteLine("Withdrawal attempt failed.");
            return false;
        }
        public decimal Balance
        {
            get
            {
                return balance;
            }
        }
        public override string ToString()
        {
            return String.Format("Venus Bank Saver: Balance = {0,6:C}", balance);
        }
    }
}
```

It should be pretty obvious what the implementation of this class does. We maintain a private field, balance, and adjust this amount when money is deposited or withdrawn. We display an error message if an attempt to withdraw money fails because there is insufficient money in the account. Notice also that, because we want to keep the code as simple as possible, we are not implementing extra properties, such as the account holder's name! In real life that would be pretty essential information, but for this example it's unnecessarily complicated.

The only really interesting line in this code is the class declaration:

```
public class SaverAccount : IBankAccount
```

We've declared that `SaverAccount` derives from one interface, `IBankAccount`, and we have not explicitly indicated any other base classes (which of course means that `SaverAccount` derives directly from `System.Object`). By the way, derivation from interfaces acts completely independently from derivation from classes.

Being derived from `IBankAccount` means that `SaverAccount` gets all the members of `IBankAccount`. But since an interface doesn't actually implement any of its methods, `SaverAccount` must provide its own implementations of all of them. If any implementations are missing, you can rest assured that the compiler will complain. Recall also that the interface just indicates the presence of its members. It's up to the class to decide if it wants any of them to be `virtual` or `abstract` (though `abstract` functions are of course only allowed if the class itself is `abstract`). For our particular example, we don't have any reason to make any of the interface functions virtual.

To illustrate how different classes can implement the same interface, we will assume the Planetary Bank of Jupiter also implements a class to represent one of its bank accounts—a Gold Account.

```
namespace Wrox.ProCSharp.JupiterBank
{
    public class GoldAccount : IBankAccount
    {
        // etc
    }
}
```

We won't present details of the `GoldAccount` class here because in the sample code it's basically identical to the implementation of `SaverAccount`. We stress that `GoldAccount` has no connection with `VenusAccount`, other than that they happen to implement the same interface.

Now that we have our classes, we can test them out. We first need a couple of `using` statements:

```
using System;
using Wrox.ProCSharp;
using Wrox.ProCSharp.VenusBank;
using Wrox.ProCSharp.JupiterBank;
```

Now we need a `Main()` method:

```
namespace Wrox.ProCSharp
{
    class MainEntryPoint
    {
        static void Main()
        {
            IBankAccount venusAccount = new SaverAccount();
            IBankAccount jupiterAccount = new GoldAccount();
            venusAccount.PayIn(200);
            venusAccount.Withdraw(100);
            Console.WriteLine(venusAccount.ToString());
            jupiterAccount.PayIn(500);
```

```
        jupiterAccount.Withdraw(600);
        jupiterAccount.Withdraw(100);
        Console.WriteLine(jupiterAccount.ToString());
    }
  }
}
```

This code (which if you download the sample, you can find in the file BankAccounts.cs) produces this output:

```
C:> BankAccounts
Venus Bank Saver: Balance = £100.00
Withdrawal attempt failed.
Jupiter Bank Saver: Balance = £400.00
```

The main point to notice about this code is the way that we have declared both our reference variables as IBankAccount references. This means that they can point to any instance of any class that implements this interface. It does, however, mean that we can only call methods that are part of this interface through these references—if we want to call any methods implemented by a class that are not part of the interface, then we need to cast the reference to the appropriate type. In our code, we were able to call ToString() (not implemented by IBankAccount) without any explicit cast, purely because ToString() is a System.Object method, so the C# compiler knows that it will be supported by any class (put differently: the cast from any interface to System.Object is implicit). We cover the syntax for how to perform casts in Chapter 5.

Interface references can in all respects be treated like class references—but the power of an interface reference is that it can refer to any class that implements that interface. For example, this allows us to form arrays of interfaces, where each element of the array is a different class:

```
IBankAccount[] accounts = new IBankAccount[2];
accounts[0] = new SaverAccount();
accounts[1] = new GoldAccount();
Note, however, that we'd get a compiler error if we tried something like this
accounts[1] = new SomeOtherClass();    // SomeOtherClass does NOT implement
                                       // IBankAccount: WRONG!!
```

This causes a compilation error similar to this:

```
Cannot implicitly convert type 'Wrox.ProCSharp. SomeOtherClass' to
'Wrox.ProCSharp.IBankAccount'
```

Derived Interfaces

It's possible for interfaces to inherit from each other in the same way that classes do. We'll illustrate this concept by defining a new interface, ITransferBankAccount, which has the same features as IBankAccount, but also defines a method to transfer money directly to a different account:

```
namespace Wrox.ProCSharp
{
   public interface ITransferBankAccount : IBankAccount
   {
      bool TransferTo(IBankAccount destination, decimal amount);
   }
}
```

Because `ITransferBankAccount` derives from `IBankAccount`, it gets all the members of `IBankAccount` as well as its own. That means that any class that implements (derives from) `ITransferBankAccount` must implement all the methods of `IBankAccount`, as well as the new `TransferTo()` method defined in `ITransferBankAccount`. Failure to implement all of these methods will result in a compilation error.

Note that `TransferTo()` method uses an `IBankAccount` interface reference for the destination account. This illustrates the usefulness of interfaces: When implementing and then invoking this method, we don't need to know anything about what type of object we are transferring money to—all we need to know is that this object implements `IBankAccount`.

We'll illustrate `ITransferBankAccount` by assuming that the Planetary Bank of Jupiter also offers a current account. Most of the implementation of the `CurrentAccount` class is identical to the implementations of `SaverAccount` and `GoldAccount` (again this is just in order to keep this sample simple—that won't normally be the case), so in the following code we've just highlighted the differences:

```
public class CurrentAccount : ITransferBankAccount
{
    private decimal balance;
    public void PayIn(decimal amount)
    {
        balance += amount;
    }
    public bool Withdraw(decimal amount)
    {
        if (balance >= amount)
        {
            balance -= amount;
            return true;
        }
        Console.WriteLine("Withdrawal attempt failed.");
        return false;
    }
    public decimal Balance
    {
        get
        {
            return balance;
        }
    }
    public bool TransferTo(IBankAccount destination, decimal amount)
    {
        bool result;
        if ((result = Withdraw(amount)) == true)
            destination.PayIn(amount);
        return result;
    }
    public override string ToString()
    {
        return String.Format("Jupiter Bank Current Account: Balance = {0,6:C}",
                                                        balance);
    }
}
```

We can demonstrate the class with this code:

```
static void Main()
{
    IBankAccount venusAccount = new SaverAccount();
    ITransferBankAccount jupiterAccount = new CurrentAccount();
    venusAccount.PayIn(200);
    jupiterAccount.PayIn(500);
    jupiterAccount.TransferTo(venusAccount, 100);
    Console.WriteLine(venusAccount.ToString());
    Console.WriteLine(jupiterAccount.ToString());
}
```

This code (CurrentAccount.cs) produces the following output, which as you can verify shows the correct amounts have been transferred:

```
C:> CurrentAccount
Venus Bank Saver: Balance = £300.00
Jupiter Bank Current Account: Balance = £400.00
```

Summary

In this chapter we have examined how to code inheritance in C#. We have seen that C# offers rich support for both multiple interface and single implementation inheritance, as well as provides a number of useful syntactical constructs designed to assist in making code more robust, such as the override keyword, which indicates when a function should override a base function; the new keyword, which indicates when a function hides a base function; and the rigid rules for constructor initializers that are designed to ensure that constructors are designed to interoperate in a robust manner.

In the next chapter we will examine C#'s support for operators, operator overloads, and casting between types.

5

Operators and Casts

In the preceding chapters, we have covered most of what you need to start writing useful programs using C#. In this chapter, we complete our discussion of the essential language elements and go on to discuss powerful aspects of C# that allow you to extend the capabilities of the C# language. Specifically in this chapter we discuss:

- ❑ The operators available in C#
- ❑ The idea of equality when dealing with reference and value types
- ❑ Data conversion between the primitive data types
- ❑ Converting value types to reference types using boxing
- ❑ Converting between reference types by casting
- ❑ Overloading the standard operators to support operations on the custom types you define
- ❑ Adding cast operators to the custom types you define to support seamless data type conversions

Operators

Although most of C#'s operators should be familiar to C and C++ developers, we will discuss the most important ones here for the benefit of new programmers and Visual Basic converts, and to shed light on some of the changes introduced with C#.

C# supports the operators listed in the following table, although four (`sizeof`, `*`, `->`, and `&`) are only available in unsafe code (code that bypasses C#'s type safety checking), which we will look at in Chapter 7:

Category	Operator
Arithmetic	`+ - * / %`
Logical	`&	^ ~ && || !`
String concatenation	`+`
Increment and decrement	`++ --`
Bit shifting	`<< >>`
Comparison	`== != < > <= >=`
Assignment	`= += -= *= /= %= &= |= ^= <<= >>=`
Member access (for objects and structs)	`.`
Indexing (for arrays and indexers)	`[]`
Cast	`()`
Conditional (the Ternary Operator)	`?:`
Object Creation	`new`
Type information	`sizeof` (unsafe code only) `is typeof as`
Overflow exception control	`checked unchecked`
Indirection and Address	`* -> &` (unsafe code only) `[]`

One of the biggest pitfalls to watch out for when using C# operators is that, like other C-style languages, C# uses different operators for assignment =, and comparison ==. For instance, the following statement means *let x equal three*:

```
x = 3;
```

If we now want to compare x to a value, we need to use the double equals sign ==:

```
if (x == 3)
```

Fortunately, C#'s strict type safety rules prevent the very common C error where assignment is performed instead of comparison in logical statements. This means that in C# the following statement will generate a compiler error:

```
if (x = 3)
```

Visual Basic programmers who are used to using the ampersand (&) character to concatenate strings will have to make an adjustment. In C#, the plus sign (+) is used instead, while & denotes a bit-wise AND between two different integer values. | allows you to perform a bit-wise OR between two integers. Visual Basic programmers also might not recognize the modulus (%) arithmetic operator. This returns the remainder after division, so for example x % 5 returns 2 if x is equal to 7.

You will use few pointers in C#, and so, you will use few indirection operators ->. Specifically, the only place you will use them is within blocks of unsafe code, because that's the only place in C# where pointers are allowed.

Operator Shortcuts

The following table shows the full list of shortcut assignment operators available in C#:

Shortcut Operator	Equivalent To
x++, ++x	x = x + 1
x--, --x	x = x - 1
x += y	x = x + y
x -= y	x = x - y
x *= y	x = x * y
x /= y	x = x / y
x %= y	x = x % y
x >>= y	x = x >> y
x <<= y	x = x << y
x &= y	x = x & y
x |= y	x = x | y
x ^= y	x = x ^ y

You may be wondering why there are two examples each for the ++ increment and the – decrement operators. Placing the operator *before* the expression is known as a *prefix*, and placing the operator *after* the expression is known as a *postfix*. The expressions x++ and ++x are both equivalent to x = x + 1, but there is a difference in the way they behave.

The increment and decrement operators can act both as whole expressions and within expressions. As lines on their own, they are identical and correspond to the statement x = x + 1. When used within expressions, the prefix operator will increment the value of x *before* the expression is evaluated; in other words, x is incremented and the new value is used in the expression. In contrast, the postfix operator increments the value of x *after* the expression is evaluated—the expression is evaluated using the original value. The following example shows the difference between the two operators:

```
int x = 5;
if (++x == 6)
{
   Console.WriteLine("This will execute");
}
if (x++ == 7)
{
   Console.WriteLine("This won't");
}
```

The first `if` condition evaluates to `true`, because `x` is incremented from 5 to 6 before the expression is evaluated. The condition in the second `if` statement is `false`, however, because `x` is only incremented to 7 after the entire expression has been evaluated.

The prefix and postfix operators –x and x– behave in the same way, but decrement rather than increment the operand.

The other shortcut operators, such as += and -=, require two operands, and are used to modify the value of the first operand by performing an arithmetic, logical, or bit-wise operation on it. For example, the next two lines are equivalent:

```
x += 5;
x = x + 5;
```

The Ternary Operator

The ternary operator (`?:`) is a shorthand form of the `if...else` construction. It gets its name from the fact that it involves three operands. It allows us to evaluate a condition, returning one value if that condition is true, or another value if it is false. The syntax is:

condition `?` *true_value* `:` *false_value*

Here, *condition* is the Boolean expression to be evaluated, *true_value* is the value that will be returned if *condition* is true, and *false_value* is the value that will be returned otherwise.

When used sparingly, the ternary operator can add a dash of terseness to your programs. It is especially handy for providing one of a couple of arguments to a function that is being invoked. You can use it to quickly convert a Boolean value to a string value of `true` or `false`. It is also handy for displaying the correct singular or plural form of a word, for example:

```
int x = 1;
string s = x.ToString() + " ";
s += (x == 1 ? "man" : "men");
Console.WriteLine(s);
```

This code displays `1 man` if `x` is equal to one, but will display the correct plural form for any other number. Note, however, that if your output needs to be localized to different languages then you will have to write more sophisticated routines to take account of the different grammatical rules of different languages.

The checked and unchecked Operators

Consider the following code:

```
byte b = 255;
b++;
Console.WriteLine(b.ToString());
```

The `byte` data type can only hold values in the range zero to 255, so incrementing the value of b causes an overflow. How the CLR handles this depends on a number of issues, including compiler options, so whenever there's a risk of an unintentional overflow, we need some way of making sure that we get the result we want.

To do this, C# provides the `checked` and `unchecked` operators. If we mark a block of code as `checked`, the CLR will enforce overflow checking, and throw an exception if an overflow occurs. Let's change our code to include the `checked` operator:

```
byte b = 255;
```

```
checked
{
    b++;
}
```

```
Console.WriteLine(b.ToString());
```

When we try to run this code, we will get an error message like this:

```
Unhandled Exception: System.OverflowException: Arithmetic operation resulted in an
overflow.
   at Wrox.ProCSharp.Basics.OverflowTest.Main(String[] args)
```

We can enforce overflow checking for all unmarked code in our program by compiling with the /checked option.

If we want to suppress overflow checking, we can mark the code as `unchecked`:

```
byte b = 255;
```

```
unchecked
{
    b++;
}
```

```
Console.WriteLine(b.ToString());
```

In this case, no exception will be raised, but we will lose data—since the `byte` type can't hold a value of 256, the overflowing bits will be discarded, and our b variable will hold a value of zero.

Note that `unchecked` is the default behavior. The only time where you are likely to need to explicitly use the `unchecked` keyword is if you need a few unchecked lines of code inside a larger block that you have explicitly marked as `checked`.

The is Operator

The `is` operator allows us to check whether an object is compatible with a specific type. For example, to check whether a variable is compatible with the `object` type:

By the phrase is compatible, we mean that an object is either of that type or is derived from that type.

```
int i = 10;
if (i is object)
{
    Console.WriteLine("i is an object");
}
```

int, like all C# data types, inherits from object, therefore the expression i is object will evaluate to true, and the message will be displayed.

The as Operator

The as operator is used to perform explicit type conversions of reference types. If the type being converted is compatible with the specified type, conversion is performed successfully. However, if the types are incompatible, then the as operator returns the value null. As shown in the following code, attempting to convert an object reference to a string will return null if the object reference does not actually refer to a string instance:

```
object o1 = "Some String";
object o2 = 5;

string s1 = o1 as string;    // s1 = "Some String"
string s2 = o2 as string;    // s2 = null
```

The as operator allows you to perform a safe type conversion in a single step without the need to first test the type using the is operator and then perform the conversion.

The sizeof Operator

We can determine the size (in bytes) required on the stack by a value type using the sizeof operator:

```
string s = "A string";
unsafe
{
    Console.WriteLine(sizeof(int));
}
```

This will display the number 4, as an int is four bytes long.

Notice that we can only use the sizeof operator in unsafe code. We will look at unsafe code in more detail in Chapter 7.

The typeof Operator

The typeof operator returns a System.Type object representing a specified type. For example, typeof(string) will return a Type object representing the System.String type. This is useful when we want to use reflection to find out information about an object dynamically. We will look at reflection in Chapter 10.

Operator Precedence

The following table shows the order of precedence of the C# operators. The operators at the top of the table are those with the highest precedence (that is, the ones which are evaluated first in an expression containing multiple operators):

Group	Operators
Primary	`() . [] x++ x— new typeof sizeof checked unchecked`
Unary	`+ - ! ~ ++x –x` and casts
Multiplication/Division	`* / %`
Addition/Subtraction	`+ -`
Bitwise shift operators	`<< >>`
Relational	`< > <= >= is as`
Comparison	`== !=`
Bitwise AND	`&`
Bitwise XOR	`^`
Bitwise OR	`|`
Boolean AND	`&&`
Boolean OR	`||`
Ternary operator	`?:`
Assignment	`= += -= *= /= %= &= |= ^= <<= >>= >>>=`

In complex expressions, you should avoid relying on operator precedence to produce the correct result. Using parentheses to specify the order in which you want operators applied clarifies your code and avoids potential confusion.

Type Safety

In Chapter 1 we noted that the Intermediate Language (IL) enforces strong type safety upon its code. We noted that strong typing enables many of the services provided by .NET, including security and language interoperability. As we would expect from a language that is compiled into IL, C# is also strongly typed. Among other things, this means that data types are not always seamlessly interchangeable. In this section, we will look at conversions between primitive types.

C# also supports conversions between different reference types and allows you to define how data types that you create behave when converted to and from other types. We will look at both these topics later in this chapter.

Type Conversions

We often need to convert data from one type to another. Consider the following code:

```
byte value1 = 10;
byte value2 = 23;
byte total;
total = value1 + value2;
Console.WriteLine(total);
```

When we attempt to compile these lines, we get the error message:

```
Cannot implicitly convert type 'int' to 'byte'
```

The problem here is that when we add two bytes together, the result will be returned as an `int`, not as another `byte`. This is because a `byte` can only contain eight bits of data, so adding two bytes together could very easily result in a value that can't be stored in a single `byte`. If we do want to store this result in a `byte` variable, then we're going to have to convert it back to a `byte`. There are two ways this can happen, either *implicitly* or *explicitly*.

Implicit conversions

Conversion between types can normally be achieved automatically (implicitly) only if we can guarantee that the value is not changed in any way. This is why our previous code failed; by attempting a conversion from an `int` to a `byte`, we were potentially losing three bytes of data. The compiler isn't going to let us do that unless we explicitly tell it that that's what we want to do. If we store the result in a `long` instead of a `byte` however, we'll have no problems:

```
byte value1 = 10;
byte value2 = 23;

long total;                 // this will compile fine

total = value1 + value2;
Console.WriteLine(total);
```

This is because a `long` holds more bytes of data than an `int`, so there is no risk of data being lost. In these circumstances, the compiler is happy to make the conversion for us, without us needing to ask for it explicitly.

The following table shows the implicit type conversions that are supported in C#:

From	To
sbyte	short, int, long, float, double, decimal
byte	short, ushort, int, uint, long, ulong, float, double, decimal
short	int, long, float, double, decimal
ushort	int, uint, long, ulong, float, double, decimal

From	To
int	long, float, double, decimal
uint	long, ulong, float, double, decimal
long, ulong	float, double, decimal
float	double
char	ushort, int, uint, long, ulong, float, double, decimal

As you would expect, we can only perform implicit conversions from a smaller integer type to a larger one, not from larger to smaller. We can also convert between integers and floating-point values; however, the rules are slightly different here. Though we can convert between types of the same size, such as int/uint to float and long/ulong to double, we can also convert from long/ulong back to float. We might lose four bytes of data doing this, but this only means that the value of the float we receive will be less precise than if we had used a double; this is regarded by the compiler as an acceptable possible error because the magnitude of the value is not affected.

We can also assign an unsigned variable to a signed variable so long as the limits of value of the unsigned type fit between the limits of the signed variable.

Explicit conversions

There are many conversions that cannot be implicitly made between types and the compiler will give an error if any are attempted. These are some of the conversions that cannot be made implicitly:

❑ int to short—May lose data

❑ int to uint—May lose data

❑ uint to int—May lose data

❑ float to int—Will lose everything after the decimal point

❑ Any numeric type to char—Will lose data

❑ decimal to any numeric type—Since the decimal type is internally structured differently from both integers and floating-point numbers

However, we can explicitly carry out such conversions using *casts*. When we cast one type to another, we deliberately force the compiler to make the conversion. A cast looks like this:

```
long val = 30000;
int i = (int)val;    // A valid cast. The maximum int is 2147483647
```

We indicate the type to which we're casting by placing its name in parentheses before the value to be converted. For programmers familiar with C, this is the typical syntax for casts. For those familiar with the C++ special cast keywords such as static_cast, these do not exist in C# and you have to use the older C-type syntax.

Casting can be a dangerous operation to undertake. Even a simple cast from a `long` to an `int` can cause problems if the value of the original `long` is greater than the maximum value of an `int`:

```
long val = 3000000000;
int i = (int)val;          // An invalid cast. The maximum int is 2147483647
```

In this case, you will not get an error, but you also will not get the result you expect. If you run the code above and output the value stored in `i`, this is what you get:

```
-1294967296
```

It is good practice to assume that an explicit cast will not give the results you expect. As we saw earlier, C# provides a `checked` operator that we can use to test whether an operation causes an arithmetic overflow. We can use the `checked` operator to check that a cast is safe and to force the runtime to throw an overflow exception if it isn't:

```
long val = 3000000000;
```

```
int i = checked ((int)val);
```

Bearing in mind that all explicit casts are potentially unsafe, you should take care to include code in your application to deal with possible failures of the casts. We will introduce structured exception handling using the `try` and `catch` statements in Chapter 11.

Using casts, we can convert most primitive data types from one type to another, for example:

```
double price = 25.30;
int approximatePrice = (int)(price + 0.5);
```

This will give the price rounded to the nearest dollar. However, in this conversion, data is lost—namely everything after the decimal point. Therefore, such a conversion should never be used if you want to go on to do more calculations using this modified price value. However, it is useful if you want to output the approximate value of a completed or partially completed calculation—if you do not want to bother the user with lots of figures after the decimal point.

This example shows what happens if you convert an unsigned integer into a `char`:

```
ushort c = 43;
char symbol = (char)c;
Console.WriteLine(symbol);
```

The output is the character that has an ASCII number of 43, the + sign. You can try out any kind of conversion you want between the numeric types (including `char`), and it will work, such as converting a `decimal` into a `char`, or vice versa.

Converting between value types is not just restricted to isolated variables, as we have shown. We can convert an array element of type `double` to a struct member variable of type `int`:

```
struct ItemDetails
{
   public string Description;
   public int ApproxPrice;
```

```
    }

    //...

    double[] Prices = { 25.30, 26.20, 27.40, 30.00 };

    ItemDetails id;
    id.Description = "Whatever";
    id.ApproxPrice = (int)(Prices[0] + 0.5);
```

Using explicit casts and a bit of care and attention, you can convert any instance of a simple value type to almost any other. However there are limitations on what we can do with explicit type conversions—as far as value types are concerned, we can only convert to and from the numeric and char types and enum types. We can't directly cast Booleans to any other type or vice versa.

If we need to convert between numeric and string, there are methods provided in the .NET class library. The Object class implements a ToString() method, which has been overridden in all the .NET predefined types and which returns a string representation of the object:

```
    int i = 10;
    string s = i.ToString();
```

Similarly, if we need to parse a string to retrieve a numeric or Boolean value, we can use the Parse() method supported by all the predefined value types:

```
    string s = "100";
    int i = int.Parse(s);
    Console.WriteLine(i + 50);    // Add 50 to prove it is really an int
```

Note that Parse() will register an error by throwing an exception if it is unable to convert the string (for example, if you try to convert the string Hello to an integer). We cover exceptions in Chapter 11.

Boxing and Unboxing

We noted in Chapter 2 that all types, both the simple predefined types such as int and char, and the complex types such as classes and structs, derive from the object type. This means that we can treat even literal values as though they were objects:

```
    string s = 10.ToString();
```

However, we also saw that C# data types are divided into value types, which are allocated on the stack, and reference types, which are allocated on the heap. How does this square with the ability to call methods on an int, if the int is nothing more than a four-byte value on the stack?

The way C# achieves this is through a bit of magic called *boxing*. Boxing and its counterpart, *unboxing*, allow us to convert value types to reference types and then back to value types. This has been included in the section on casting as this is essentially what we are doing—we are casting our value to the object type. Boxing is the term used to describe the transformation of a value type to a reference type. Basically, the runtime creates a temporary reference-type box for the object on the heap.

This conversion can occur implicitly, as in the example above, but we can also perform it manually:

```
int i = 20;
object o = i;
```

Unboxing is the term used to describe the reverse process, where the value of a previously boxed value type is cast back to a value type. We use the term *cast* here, as this has to be done explicitly. The syntax is similar to explicit type conversions already described:

```
int i = 20;
object o = i;       // Box the int
int j = (int)o;     // Unbox it back into an int
```

We can only unbox a variable that has previously been boxed. If we executed the last line when o is not a boxed int, we will get an exception thrown at runtime.

One word of warning. When unboxing, we have to be careful that the receiving value variable has enough room to store all the bytes in the value being unboxed. C#'s ints, for example, are only 32 bits long, so unboxing a long value (64 bits) into an int as shown below will result in an InvalidCastException:

```
long a = 333333423;
object b = (object)a;
int c = (int)b;
```

Comparing Objects for Equality

After discussing operators and briefly touching on the equality operator, it is worth considering for a moment what equality means when dealing with instances of classes and structs. Understanding the mechanics of object equality is essential for programming logical expressions and is important when implementing operator overloads and casts, which is the topic of the rest of this chapter.

The mechanism of object equality are different depending on whether you are comparing reference types (instances of classes), or value types (the primitive data types, instances of structs or enums). We'll look at the equality of reference and value types independently.

Comparing Reference Types for Equality

One aspect of System.Object that can look surprising at first sight is the fact that it defines three different methods for comparing objects for equality: ReferenceEquals() and two version of Equals(). Add to this the comparison operator (==), and we actually have four ways of comparing for equality. There are some subtle differences between the different methods, which we will now examine.

The ReferenceEquals() Method

ReferenceEquals() is a static method that tests whether two references refer to the same instance of a class: specifically whether the two references contain the same address in memory. As a static method, it is not possible to override, so the System.Object implementation is what you always have.

ReferenceEquals() will always return true if supplied with two references that refer to the same object instance, and false otherwise. It does, however, consider null to be equal to null:

```
SomeClass x, y;
x = new SomeClass();
y = new SomeClass();
bool B1 = ReferenceEquals(null, null);    // returns true
bool B2 = ReferenceEquals(null,x);        // returns false
bool B3 = ReferenceEquals(x, y);          // returns false because x and y
                                          // point to different objects
```

The virtual Equals() Method

The System.Object implementation of the virtual version of Equals() also works by comparing references. However, because this method is virtual, you can override it in your own classes in order to compare objects by value. In particular, if you intend instances of your class to be used as keys in a dictionary, then you will need to override this method to compare values. Otherwise, depending on how you override Object.GetHashCode(), the dictionary class that contains your objects will either not work at all, or will work very inefficiently. One point you should note when overriding Equals() is that your override should never throw exceptions. Once again, this is because doing so could cause problems for dictionary classes and possibly certain other .NET base classes that internally call this method.

The static Equals() Method

The static version of Equals() actually does the same thing as the virtual instance version. The difference is that the static version takes two parameters and compares them for equality. This method is able to cope when either of the objects is null, and therefore, provides an extra safeguard against throwing exceptions if there is a risk that an object might be null. The static overload first checks whether the references it has been passed are null. If they are both null, then it returns true (since null is considered to be equal to null). If just one of them is null, then it returns false. If both references actually refer to something, then it calls the virtual instance version of Equals(). This means that when you override the instance version of Equals(), the effect is as if you were overriding the static version as well.

Comparison Operator (==)

The comparison operator can be best seen as an intermediate option between strict value comparison and strict reference comparison. In most cases, writing:

```
bool b = (x == y);   // x, y object references
```

means that you are comparing references. However, it is accepted that there are some classes whose meanings are more intuitive if they are treated as values. In those cases, it is better to override the comparison operator to perform a value comparison. We talk about overriding operators next, but the obvious example of this is the System.String class for which Microsoft has overridden this operator to compare the contents of the strings rather than their references.

Comparing Value Types for Equality

When comparing value types for equality, the same principles hold as for reference types: ReferenceEquals() is used to compare references, Equals() is intended for value comparisons, and

143

the comparison operator is viewed as an intermediate case. However the big difference is that value types need to be boxed in order to convert them to references so that methods can be executed on them. In addition, Microsoft has already overloaded the instance `Equals()` method in the `System.ValueType` class in order to test equality appropriate to value types. If you call `sA.Equals(sB)` where `sA` and `sB` are instances of some struct, then the return value will be `true` or `false` according to whether `sA` and `sB` contain the same values in all their fields. On the other hand, no overload of `==` is available by default for your own structs. Writing `(sA == sB)` in any expression will result in a compilation error unless you have provided an overload of `==` in your code for the struct in question.

Another point is that `ReferenceEquals()` always returns `false` when applied to value types, because in order to call this method, the value types will need to be boxed into objects. Even if you write:

```
bool b = ReferenceEquals(v,v);    // v is a variable of some value type
```

you will still get the answer of `false` because v will be boxed separately when converting each parameter, which means you get different references. Calling `ReferenceEquals()` to compare value types doesn't really make much sense.

Although the default override of `Equals()` supplied by `System.ValueType` will almost certainly be adequate for the vast majority of structs that you define, you might want to override it again for your own structs in order to improve performance. Also, if a value type contains reference types as fields, you might want to override `Equals()` to provide appropriate semantics for these fields, as the default override of `Equals()` will simply compare their addresses.

Operator Overloading

In this section, we're going to look at another type of member that you can define for a class or a struct: the *operator overload*.

Operator overloading is something that will be familiar to C++ developers. However, since the concept will be new to both Java and Visual Basic developers, we'll explain it here. C++ developers will probably prefer to skip ahead to the main example.

The point of operator overloading is that you don't always just want to call methods or properties on class instances. Often you need to do things like adding quantities together, multiplying them, or performing logical operations such as comparing objects. Suppose for example you had defined a class that represents a mathematical matrix. Now in the world of math, matrices can be added together and multiplied, just like numbers. So it's quite plausible that you'd want to write code like this:

```
Matrix a, b, c;
// assume a, b and c have been initialized
Matrix d = c * (a + b);
```

By overloading the operators, you can tell the compiler what + and * do when used in conjunction with a `Matrix`, allowing you to write code like that above. If we were coding in a language that didn't support operator overloading, we would have to define methods to perform those operations. The result would certainly be less intuitive, and would probably look something like this:

```
Matrix d = c.Multiply(a.Add(b));
```

With what you've learned so far, operators like + and * have been strictly for use with the predefined data types, and for good reason: the compiler knows what all the common operators mean for those data types. For example, it knows how to add two `long`s or how to divide one `double` by another `double`, and can generate the appropriate intermediate language code. When we define our own classes or structs, however, we have to tell the compiler everything: what methods are available to call, what fields to store with each instance, and so on. Similarly, if we want to use operators with our own types, we'll have to tell the compiler what the relevant operators mean in the context of that class. The way we do that is by defining overloads for the operators.

The other thing we should stress is that overloading isn't just concerned with arithmetic operators. We also need to consider the comparison operators, ==, <, >, !=, >=, and <=. Take the statement if (a==b). For classes, this statement will, by default, compare the references a and b—it tests to see if the references point to the same location in memory, rather than checking to see if the instances actually contain the same data. For the `string` class, this behavior is overridden so that comparing strings really does compare the contents of each string. You might want to do the same for your own classes. For structs, the == operator doesn't do anything at all by default. Trying to compare two structs to see if they are equal produces a compilation error unless you explicitly overload == to tell the compiler how to perform the comparison.

There are a large number of situations in which being able to overload operators will allow us to generate more readable and intuitive code, including:

❑ Almost any mathematical object such as coordinates, vectors, matrices, tensors, functions, and so on. If you are writing a program that does some mathematical or physical modeling, you will almost certainly use classes representing these objects.

❑ Graphics programs that use mathematical or coordinate-related objects when calculating positions on screen.

❑ A class that represents an amount of money (for example, in a financial program).

❑ A word processing or text analysis program that uses classes representing sentences, clauses and so on; you might want to use operators to combine sentences (a more sophisticated version of concatenation for strings).

However, there are also many types for which operator overloading would not be relevant. Using operator overloading inappropriately will make code that uses your types far more difficult to understand. For example, multiplying two `DateTime` objects just doesn't make any sense conceptually.

How Operators Work

In order to understand how to overload operators, it's quite useful to think about what happens when the compiler encounters an operator. Using the addition operator (+) as an example, suppose the compiler processes the following lines of code:

```
int a = 3;
uint b = 2;
double d = 4.0;
long l = a + b;
double x = d + a;
```

What happens when the compiler encounters the following line?

```
long l = a + b;
```

The compiler identifies that it needs to add two integers and assign the result to a `long`. However, the expression `a + b` is really just an intuitive and convenient syntax for calling a method that adds two numbers together .The method takes two parameters, a and b, and returns their sum. Therefore, the compiler does the same thing as it does for any method call—it looks for the best matching overload of the addition operator based on the parameter types. In this case, one that takes two integers. As with normal overloaded methods, the desired return type does not influence the compiler's choice as to which version of a method it calls. As it happens, the overload called in the example takes two `int` parameters and returns an `int`; this return value is subsequently converted to a `long`.

The next line causes the compiler to use a different overload of the addition operator:

```
double x = d + a;
```

In this instance, the parameters are a `double` and an `int`, but as it happens there isn't an overload of the addition operator that takes this combination of parameters. Instead, the compiler identifies the best matching overload of the addition operator as being the version that takes two doubles as its parameters, and implicitly casts the `int` to a `double`. Adding together two doubles requires a different process than adding two integers. Floating-point numbers are stored as a mantissa and an exponent. Adding them involves bit-shifting the mantissa of one of the `double`s so that the two exponents have the same value, adding the mantissas, then shifting the mantissa of the result and adjusting its exponent to maintain the highest possible accuracy in the answer.

Now, we're in a position to see what happens if the compiler finds something like this:

```
Vector vect1, vect2, vect3;
// initialise vect1 and vect2
vect3 = vect1 + vect2;
vect1 = vect1*2;
```

Here `Vector` is the struct that we shall define shortly. The compiler will see that it needs to add two `Vector`s, `vect1` and `vect2` together. It'll look for an overload of the addition operator, which takes two `Vector`s as its parameters.

If the compiler finds an appropriate overload, it'll call up the implementation of that operator. If it can't find one, it'll look to see if there is any other overload for + that it can use as a best match—perhaps something that has two parameters of other data types that can be implicitly converted to `Vector` instances. If the compiler can't find a suitable overload, it'll raise a compilation error, just as it would if it couldn't find an appropriate overload for any other method call.

Operator Overloading Example: The Vector Struct

In this section we're going to demonstrate operator overloading by developing a struct named `Vector` that represents a 3-dimensional mathematical vector. Don't worry if mathematics is not your strong point—we'll keep the vector example very simple. As far as we are concerned, a 3D-vector is just a set of three numbers (doubles) that tell you how far something is moving. The variables representing the numbers are called x, y, and z: x tells you how far something moves East, y tells you how far it moves North, and z tells you how far it moves upwards (in height). Combine the three numbers together and you get the total movement. For example, if x=3.0, y=3.0, and z=1.0, (which we'd normally write as (3.0, 3.0, 1.0) then you're moving 3 units East, 3 units North, and rising upwards by 1 unit.

You can add or multiply vectors by other vectors or by numbers. Incidentally, in this context we'll use the term *scalar*, which is math-speak for a simple number—in C# terms that's just a double. The significance of addition should be clear. If you move first by the vector (3.0, 3.0, 1.0) then you move by the vector (2.0, -4.0, -4.0), the total amount you have moved can be worked out by adding the two vectors. Adding vectors means adding each component individually, so you get (5.0, -1.0, -3.0). In this context, mathematicians write c=a+b, where a and b are the vectors and c is the resulting vector. We want to be able to use our Vector struct the same way.

> *The fact that our example will be developed as a struct rather than a class is not significant. Operator overloading works in the same way for both structs and classes.*

The following is the definition for Vector—containing the member fields, constructors, and a ToString() override so we can easily view the contents of a Vector, and finally that operator overload:

```
namespace Wrox.ProCSharp.OOCSharp
{
    struct Vector
    {
        public double x, y, z;

        public Vector(double x, double y, double z)
        {
            this.x = x;
            this.y = y;
            this.z = z;
        }

        public Vector(Vector rhs)
        {
            x = rhs.x;
            y = rhs.y;
            z = rhs.z;
        }

        public override string ToString()
        {
            return "( " + x + " , " + y + " , " + z + " )";
        }
    }
```

We've supplied two constructors that require the initial value of the vector to be specified, either by passing in the values of each component or by supplying another Vector whose value can be copied. Constructors like our second one that takes single Vector argument are often termed *copy constructors*, since they effectively allow you to initialize a class or struct instance by copying another instance. Note that in order to keep things simple we've left the fields as public. We could have made them private and written corresponding properties to access them, but it wouldn't have made any difference to the example, other than to make the code longer.

Here is the interesting part of the Vector struct—the operator overload that provides support for the addition operator.

```
        public static Vector operator + (Vector lhs, Vector rhs)
        {
            Vector result = new Vector(lhs);
            result.x += rhs.x;
            result.y += rhs.y;
            result.z += rhs.z;
            return result;
        }
    }
}
```

The operator overload is declared in much the same way as a method, except the operator keyword tells the compiler it's actually an operator overload we're defining. The operator keyword is followed by the actual symbol for the relevant operator, in this case the addition operator (+). The return type is whatever type you get when you use this operator. Adding two vectors results in a vector, so the return type is Vector. For this particular override of the addition operator, the return type is the same as the containing class, but that's not necessarily the case as we'll see later in this example. The two parameters are the things you're operating on. For binary operators (those that take two parameters), like the addition and subtraction operators, the first parameter is the value on the left of the operator, and the second parameter is the value on the right.

C# requires that all operator overloads are declared as public and static, which means that they are associated with their class or struct, not with a particular instance. Because of this, the body of the operator overload has no access to non-static class members and has no access to the this identifier. This is fine because the parameters provide all the input data the operator needs to know to perform its task.

Now that we've dealt with the syntax for the addition operator declaration, we can look at what happens inside the operator:

```
        {
            Vector result = new Vector(lhs);
            result.x += rhs.x;
            result.y += rhs.y;
            result.z += rhs.z;
            return result;
        }
```

This part of the code is exactly the same as if we were declaring a method, and you should easily be able to convince yourself that this really will return a vector containing the sum of lhs and rhs as defined above. We simply add the members x, y, and z together individually.

Now all we need to do is write some simple code to test our Vector struct. Here it is:

```
    static void Main()
    {
        Vector vect1, vect2, vect3;
        vect1 = new Vector(3.0, 3.0, 1.0);
        vect2 = new Vector(2.0, -4.0, -4.0);
        vect3 = vect1 + vect2;
        Console.WriteLine("vect1 = " + vect1.ToString());
        Console.WriteLine("vect2 = " + vect2.ToString());
        Console.WriteLine("vect3 = " + vect3.ToString());
    }
```

Saving this code as Vectors.cs, and compiling and running it returns this result:

Vectors

```
vect1 = ( 3 , 3 , 1 )
vect2 = ( 2 , -4 , -4 )
vect3 = ( 5 , -1 , -3 )
```

Adding more overloads

In addition to adding vectors, you can also multiply and subtract them, and compare their values. In this section we'll develop the Vector example further by adding a few more operator overloads. We won't develop the complete set that you'd probably need for a real and fully functional Vector type, but enough to demonstrate some other aspects of operator overloading. First, we'll overload the multiplication operator to support multiplying vectors by a scalar and multiplying vectors by another vector.

Multiplying a vector by a scalar simply means multiplying each component individually by the scalar: for example, 2 * (1.0, 2.5, 2.0) returns (2.0, 5.0, 4.0). The relevant operator overload looks like this:

```
public static Vector operator * (double lhs, Vector rhs)
{
    return new Vector(lhs * rhs.x, lhs * rhs.y, lhs * rhs.z);
}
```

This by itself, however, is not sufficient. If a and b are declared as type Vector, it will allow us to write code like this:

```
b = 2 * a;
```

The compiler will implicitly convert the integer 2 to a double in order to match the operator overload signature. However, code like the following will not compile:

```
b = a * 2;
```

The thing is that the compiler treats operator overloads exactly like method overloads. It examines all the available overloads of a given operator to find the best match. The above statement requires the first parameter to be a Vector and the second parameter to be an integer, or something that an integer can be implicitly converted to. We have not provided such an overload. The compiler can't start swapping the order of parameters so the fact that we've provided an overload that takes a double followed by a Vector is not sufficient. We need to explicitly define an overload that takes a Vector followed by a double as well. There are two possible ways of implementing this. The first way involves breaking down the vector multiplication operation in the same way that we've done for all operators so far:

```
public static Vector operator * (Vector lhs, double rhs)
{
    return new Vector(rhs * lhs.x, rhs * lhs.y, rhs *lhs.z);
}
```

Given that we've already written code to implement essentially the same operation, however, you might prefer to reuse that code by writing:

```
        public static Vector operator * (Vector lhs, double rhs)
        {
            return rhs * lhs;
        }
```

This code works by effectively telling the compiler that if it sees a multiplication of a `Vector` by a `double`, it can simply reverse the parameters and call the other operator overload. Which you prefer is to some extent a matter of preference. In the sample code for this chapter we've gone for the second version, because it looks neater and because we want to illustrate the idea in action. This version also makes for more maintainable code, since it saves duplicating the code to perform the multiplication in two separate overloads.

Next we need to overload the multiplication operator to support vector multiplication. In mathematics there are a couple of ways of multiplying vectors together, but the one we are interested in here is known as the *dot product* or *inner product*, and it actually gives a scalar as a result. That's the reason we're introducing that example, so that we can demonstrate that arithmetic operators don't have to return the same type as the class in which they are defined.

In mathematical terms, if you have two vectors (x, y, z) and (X, Y, Z), then the inner product is defined to be the value of $x*X + y*Y + z*Z$. That might look like a strange way to multiply two things together, but it's actually very useful, since it can be used to calculate various other quantities. Certainly, if you ever end up writing code that displays complex 3D graphics, for example using Direct3D or DirectDraw, you'll almost certainly find your code needs to work out inner products of vectors quite often as an intermediate step in calculating where to place objects on the screen. What concerns us here is that we want people to be able to write `double X = a*b` where a and b are `Vector` objects and what they intend is for the dot product to be calculated. The relevant overload looks like this:

```
        public static double operator * (Vector lhs, Vector rhs)
        {
            return lhs.x * rhs.x + lhs.y * rhs.y + lhs.z * rhs.z;
        }
```

Now, we've defined the arithmetic operators, we can check that they work using a simple test method:

```
    static void Main()
    {
        // stuff to demonstrate arithmetic operations
        Vector vect1, vect2, vect3;
        vect1 = new Vector(1.0, 1.5, 2.0);
        vect2 = new Vector(0.0, 0.0, -10.0);
        vect3 = vect1 + vect2;
        Console.WriteLine("vect1 = " + vect1);
        Console.WriteLine("vect2 = " + vect2);
        Console.WriteLine("vect3 = vect1 + vect2 = " + vect3);
        Console.WriteLine("2*vect3 = " + 2*vect3);
        vect3 += vect2;
        Console.WriteLine("vect3+=vect2 gives " + vect3);
        vect3 = vect1*2;
        Console.WriteLine("Setting vect3=vect1*2 gives " + vect3);
        double dot = vect1*vect3;
        Console.WriteLine("vect1*vect3 = " + dot);
    }
```

Running this code (Vectors2.cs) produces this result:

Vectors2

```
vect1 = ( 1 , 1.5 , 2 )
vect2 = ( 0 , 0 , -10 )
vect3 = vect1 + vect2 = ( 1 , 1.5 , -8 )
2*vect3 = ( 2 , 3 , -16 )
vect3+=vect2 gives ( 1 , 1.5 , -18 )
Setting vect3=vect1*2 gives ( 2 , 3 , 4 )
vect1*vect3 = 14.5
```

This shows that the operator overloads have given us the correct results, but if you look at the test code closely, you might be surprised to notice that we've actually used an operator that we hadn't overloaded—the addition assignment operator "+=":

```
vect3 += vect2;
Console.WriteLine("vect3 += vect2 gives " + vect3);
```

Although += normally counts as a single operator, it can be broken down into two steps: the addition and the assignment. Unlike C++, C# won't actually allow you to overload the = operator, but if you overload +, the compiler will automatically use your overload of + to work out how to carry out a += operation. The same principle works for the all of the assignment operators like -=, *=, /=, &=, and so on.

Overloading the comparison operators

There are six comparison operators in C#, and they come in three pairs:

❑   == and !=

❑   > and <

❑   >= and <=

C# requires that you overload these operators in pairs. That is, if you overload "==", then you must overload "!=" too, otherwise you get a compiler error. In addition, the comparison operators must return a bool. This is the fundamental difference between these operators and the arithmetic operators. The result of adding or subtracting two quantities, for example, can theoretically be any type depending on the quantities. We've already seen that multiplying two Vector objects can be implemented to give a scalar. Another example involves the .NET base class System.DateTime. It's possible to subtract two DateTime instances, but the result is not a DateTime, instead it is a System.TimeSpan instance. By contrast, it doesn't really make much sense for a comparison to return anything other than a bool.

> *If you overload == and !=, you must also override the Equals() and GetHashCode() methods inherited from System.Object, otherwise you'll get a compiler warning. The reasoning is that the Equals() method should implement the same kind of equality logic as the == operator.*

Apart from these differences, overloading the comparison operators follows the same principles as overloading the arithmetic operators. However, comparing quantities isn't always as simple as you'd think. For example, if you simply compare two object references, you will compare the memory address where the objects are stored. This is rarely the desired behavior of a comparison operator, and so you must code the operator to compare the value of the objects and return the appropriate Boolean response. We're going to override the == and != operators for our `Vector` struct. Here's our implementation of ==:

```
public static bool operator == (Vector lhs, Vector rhs)
{
    if (lhs.x == rhs.x && lhs.y == rhs.y && lhs.z == rhs.z)
       return true;
    else
       return false;
}
```

This approach simply compares two `Vector` objects for equality based on the values of their components. For most structs, that is probably what you will want to do, though in some cases you may need to think carefully about what you mean by equality. For example, if there are embedded classes, should you simply compare whether the references point to the same object (*shallow comparison*) or whether the values of the objects are the same (*deep comparison*)?

> *Don't be tempted to overload the comparison operator by calling the instance version of the* `Equals()` *method inherited from* `System.Object`. *If you do and then attempt is made to evaluate* (`objA == objB`) *when* `objA` *happens to be* `null`, *you will get an exception as the .NET runtime tries to evaluate* `null.Equals(objB)`. *Working the other way round (overriding* `Equals()` *to call the comparison operator) should be safe.*

We also need to override the != operator. The simple way to do it is like this:

```
public static bool operator != (Vector lhs, Vector rhs)
{
 return ! (lhs == rhs);
}
```

As usual, we'll quickly check that our override works with some test code. This time we'll define three `Vector` *objects and compare them:*

```
static void Main()
{
    Vector vect1, vect2, vect3;
    vect1 = new Vector(3.0, 3.0, -10.0);
    vect2 = new Vector(3.0, 3.0, -10.0);
    vect3 = new Vector(2.0, 3.0, 6.0);
    Console.WriteLine("vect1==vect2 returns   " + (vect1==vect2));
    Console.WriteLine("vect1==vect3 returns   " + (vect1==vect3));
    Console.WriteLine("vect2==vect3 returns   " + (vect2==vect3));
    Console.WriteLine();
    Console.WriteLine("vect1!=vect2 returns   " + (vect1!=vect2));
    Console.WriteLine("vect1!=vect3 returns   " + (vect1!=vect3));
    Console.WriteLine("vect2!=vect3 returns   " + (vect2!=vect3));
}
```

Compiling this code (the `Vectors3.cs` sample in the code download), generates this compiler warning because we haven't overridden `Equals()` for our `Vector`. For our purposes here, that doesn't matter and we will ignore it.

csc Vectors3.cs

```
Microsoft (R) Visual C# .NET Compiler version 7.00.9466
for Microsoft (R) .NET Framework version 1.0.3705
Copyright (C) Microsoft Corporation 2001. All rights reserved.

Vectors3.cs(5,11): warning CS0660: 'Wrox.ProCSharp.OOCSharp.Vector' defines
        operator == or operator != but does not override Object.Equals(object o)
Vectors3.cs(5,11): warning CS0661: 'Wrox.ProCSharp.OOCSharp.Vector' defines
        operator == or operator != but does not override Object.GetHashCode()
```

Running the example produces these results at the command line:

Vectors3

```
vect1==vect2 returns  True
vect1==vect3 returns  False
vect2==vect3 returns  False

vect1!=vect2 returns  False
vect1!=vect3 returns  True
vect2!=vect3 returns  True
```

Which Operators Can You Overload?

It is not possible to overload all of the available operators. The operators that you can overload are:

Category	Operators	Restrictions
Arithmetic binary	+, *, /, -, %	None.
Arithmetic unary	+, -, ++, —	None.
Bitwise binary	&, |, ^, <<, >>	None.
Bitwise unary	!, ~ true, false	The true and false operators must be overloaded as a pair.
Comparison	==, != >=, <= >, <	They must be overloaded in pairs.
Assignment	+=, -=, *=, /=, >>=, <<=, %=, &=, |=, ^=	You cannot explicitly overload these operators; they are overridden implicitly when you override the individual operators such as +, -, %, and so on.
Index	[]	You cannot overload the index operator directly. The indexer member type, discussed in Chapter 2, allows you to support the index operator on your classes and structs.
Cast	()	You cannot overload the cast operator directly. User-defined casts (discussed in the second part of this chapter) allow you to define custom cast behavior.

User-Defined Casts

Earlier in this chapter, we examined how you can convert values between predefined data types. We saw that this is done through a process of *casting*. We also saw that C# allows two different types of casts: implicit and explicit casts.

For an explicit cast, you *explicitly* mark the cast in your code by writing the destination data type inside parentheses:

```
int I = 3;
long l = I;             // implicit
short s = (short)I;     // explicit
```

For the predefined data types, explicit casts are required where there is a risk that the cast might fail or some data might be lost, examples include:

❑   When converting from an int to a short, because the short might not be large enough to hold the value of the int.

❑   When converting from signed to unsigned data types will return incorrect results if the signed variable holds a negative value,

❑   When converting from floating-point to integer data types, the fractional part of the number will be lost.

The idea is that by making the cast explicit in your code, C# forces you to affirm that you understand there is a risk of data loss, and therefore presumably you have written your code to take this into account.

Since C# allows you to define your own data types (structs and classes), it follows that you will need the facility to support casts to and from your data types. The mechanism is that you can define a cast as a member operator of one of the relevant classes. Your cast operator must be marked as either implicit or explicit to indicate how you are intending it to be used. The expectation is that you follow the same guidelines as for the predefined casts: if you know the cast is always safe whatever the value held by the source variable, then you define it as implicit. If on the other hand you know there is a risk of something going wrong for certain values—perhaps some loss of data or an exception being thrown—then you should define the cast as explicit.

> **You should define any custom casts you write as explicit if there are any source data values for which the cast will fail, or if there is any risk of an exception being thrown.**

The syntax for defining a cast is similar to that for overloading operators discussed in the first half of this chapter. This is not a coincidence, since a cast is regarded as an operator whose effect is to convert from the source type to the destination type. To illustrate the syntax, the following is taken from an example struct named Currency, which we will introduce later in this section:

```
public static implicit operator float (Currency value)
{
   // processing
}
```

The return type of the operator defines the target type of the cast operation, and the single parameter is the source object for the conversion. The cast defined here allows us to implicitly convert the value of a Currency into a float. Note that if a conversion has been declared as implicit, then the compiler will permit its use either implicitly or explicitly. If it had been declared as explicit, the compiler will only permit it to be used explicitly. In common with other operator overloads, casts must be declared as both public and static.

C++ developers will notice that this is different from C++, in which casts are instance members of classes.

Implementing User-Defined Casts

In this section, we will illustrate the use of implicit and explicit user-defined casts in an example called SimpleCurrency (which, as usual, is found in the code download). In this example, we will define a struct, Currency, that holds a positive USD ($) monetary value. C# provides the decimal type for this purpose, but it is possible you might still want to write your own struct or class to represent monetary values if you want to perform sophisticated financial processing, and therefore, want to implement specific methods on such a class.

The syntax for casting is the same for structs and classes. Our example happens to be for a struct, but would work just as well if we declared Currency as a class.

Initially, the definition of the Currency struct is as follows:

```
struct Currency
{
    public uint Dollars;
    public ushort Cents;

    public Currency(uint dollars, ushort cents)
    {
        this.Dollars = dollars;
        this.Cents = cents;
    }

    public override string ToString()
    {
        return string.Format("${0}.{1,-2:00}", Dollars,Cents);
    }
}
```

The use of unsigned data types for the Dollar and Cents fields ensures that a Currency instance can only hold positive values. We are restricting it this way so that we can illustrate some points about explicit casts later on. You might want to use a class like this to hold, for example, salary information for employees of a company (people's salaries tend not to be negative!). In order to keep the class simple, we are making our fields public, but usually, you would make them private and define corresponding properties for the dollars and cents.

Let's start off by assuming that we want to be able to convert Currency instances to float values, where the integer part of the float represents the dollars. In other words we would like to be able to write code like this:

```
Currency balance = new Currency(10,50);
float f = balance; // We want f to be set to 10.5
```

To be able to do this, we need to define a cast. Hence we add the following to our `Currency` definition:

```
public static implicit operator float (Currency value)
{
    return value.Dollars + (value.Cents/100.0f);
}
```

This cast is implicit. This is a sensible choice in this case, because, as should be clear from the definition of `Currency`, any value that can be stored in the currency can also be stored in a `float`. There's no way that anything should ever go wrong in this cast.

> *There is a slight cheat here—in fact, when converting a* uint *to a* float, *there can be a loss in precision, but Microsoft has deemed this error sufficiently marginal to count the uint-to-float cast as implicit anyway.*

However, if we have a `float` that we would like to be converted to a `Currency`, the conversion is not guaranteed to work; a `float` can store negative values, which `Currency` instances can't; and a `float` can store numbers of a far higher magnitude than can be stored in the (`uint`) `Dollar` field of `Currency`. So if a `float` contains an inappropriate value, converting it to a `Currency` could give unpredictable results. As a result of this risk, the conversion from `float` to `Currency` should be defined as explicit. Here is our first attempt, which we will say now won't give quite the correct results, but it is instructive to examine why:

```
public static explicit operator Currency (float value)
{
    uint dollars = (uint)value;
    ushort cents = (ushort)((value-dollars)*100);
    return new Currency(dollars, cents);
}
```

The following code will now successfully compile:

```
float amount = 45.63f;
Currency amount2 = (Currency)amount;
```

However, the following code, if we tried it, would generate a compilation error, because it attempts to use an explicit cast implicitly:

```
float amount = 45.63f;
Currency amount2 = amount;    // wrong
```

By making the cast explicit, you warn the developer to be careful because data loss might occur. However, as we will see soon, this isn't how we want our `Currency` struct to behave. We will try writing a test harness and running the sample. Here is the `Main()` method, which instantiates a `Currency` struct and attempts a few conversions. At the start of this code, we write out the value of balance in two different ways (because we will need to use this to illustrate something later on in the example):

```
static void Main()
{
    try
    {
```

```
      Currency balance = new Currency(50,35);
      Console.WriteLine(balance);
      Console.WriteLine("balance is " + balance);
      Console.WriteLine("balance is (using ToString()) " +
         balance.ToString());
      float balance2= balance;
      Console.WriteLine("After converting to float, = " + balance2);
      balance = (Currency) balance2;
      Console.WriteLine("After converting back to Currency, = " + balance);

      Console.WriteLine("Now attempt to convert out of range value of " +
                        "-$100.00 to a Currency:");
      checked
      {
         balance = (Currency) (-50.5);
         Console.WriteLine("Result is " + balance.ToString());
      }
   }
   catch(Exception e)
   {
      Console.WriteLine("Exception occurred: " + e.Message);
   }
}
```

Notice that we have placed the entire code in a `try` block to catch any exceptions that occur during our casts. Also, we have placed the lines that test converting an out-of-range value to `Currency` in a `checked` block in an attempt to trap negative values. Running this code gives this output:

SimpleCurrency

```
50.35
Balance is $50.35
Balance is (using ToString()) $50.35
After converting to float, = 50.35
After converting back to Currency, = $50.34
Now attempt to convert out of range value of -$100.00 to a Currency:
Result is $4294967246.60486
```

This output shows that the code didn't quite work as we expected. First, converting back from `float` to `Currency` gave a wrong result of $50.34 instead of $50.35. Second, no exception was generated when we tried to convert an obviously out-of-range value.

The first problem is caused by rounding errors. If a cast is used to convert from a `float` to a `uint`, the computer will *truncate* the number rather than *rounding* it. The computer stores numbers in binary rather than decimal, and the fraction 0.35 cannot be exactly represented as a binary fraction (just like 1/3 cannot be represented exactly as a decimal fraction; it comes out as 0.3333 recurring). So, the computer ends up storing a value very slightly lower than 0.35, and which can be represented exactly in binary format. Multiply by 100 and you get a number fractionally less than 35, which gets truncated to 34 cents. Clearly in our situation, such errors caused by truncation are serious, and the way to avoid them is to ensure that some intelligent rounding is performed in numerical conversions instead. Luckily, Microsoft has written a class that will do this, `System.Convert`. `System.Convert` contains a large number of static methods to perform various numerical conversions, and the one that we want is `Convert.ToUInt16()`. Note that the extra care taken by the `System.Convert` methods does come at a performance cost, so you should only use them when you need them.

Now let's examine why the expected overflow exception didn't get thrown. The problem here is this: the place where the overflow really occurs isn't actually in the Main() routine at all—it is inside the code for the cast operator, which is called from the Main() method. And we didn't mark that code as checked.

The solution here is to ensure that the cast itself is computed in a checked context too. With both of these changes, the revised code for the conversion looks like this:

```
public static explicit operator Currency (float value)
{
    checked
    {
        uint dollars = (uint)value;
        ushort cents = Convert.ToUInt16((value-dollars)*100);
        return new Currency(dollars, cents);
    }
}
```

Note that we use Convert.ToUInt16() to calculate the cents, as described above, but we do not use it for calculating the dollar part of the amount. System.Convert is not needed when working out the dollar amount because truncating the float value is what we want there.

> It is worth noting that the System.Convert methods also carry out their own overflow checking. Hence, for the particular case we are considering, there is no need to place the call to Convert.ToUInt16() inside the checked context. The checked context is still required, however, for the explicit casting of value to dollars.

We won't show a new set of results with this new checked cast just yet, because we have some more modifications to make to the SimpleCurrency example later in this section.

> If you are defining a cast that will be used very often, and for which performance is at an absolute premium, you may prefer not to do any error checking. That's also a legitimate solution, provided the behavior of your cast and the lack of error checking are very clearly documented.

Casts between classes

Our Currency example involves only classes that convert to or from float—one of the predefined data types. However, it is not necessary to involve any of the simple data types. It is perfectly legitimate to define casts to convert between instances of different structs or classes that you have defined. There are a couple of restrictions to be aware of, however. These are:

❑   You cannot define a cast if one of the classes is derived from the other (these types of cast already exist, as we will see).

❑   The cast must be defined inside the definition of either the source or destination data type.

To illustrate these requirements, suppose you have the class hierarchy shown in Figure 5-1.

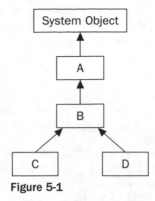

Figure 5-1

In other words, classes C and D are indirectly derived from A. In this case, the only legitimate user-defined cast between A, B, C, or D would be to convert between classes C and D, because these classes are not derived from each other. The code to do so might look like this (assuming you want the casts to be explicit, which is usually the case when defining casts between user-defined casts):

```
public static explicit operator D(C value)
{
    // and so on
}
public static explicit operator C(D value)
{
    // and so on
}
```

For each of these casts, you have a choice of where you place the definitions — inside the class definition of C, or inside the class definition of D, but not anywhere else. C# requires you to put the definition of a cast inside either the source class (or struct) or the destination class (or struct). A side effect of this is that you can't define a cast between two classes unless you have access to edit the source code for at least one of them. This is sensible because it prevents third parties from introducing casts into your classes.

Once you have defined a cast inside one of the classes, you also can't define the same cast inside the other class. Obviously, there should only be one cast for each conversion—otherwise the compiler wouldn't know which one to pick.

Casts between base and derived classes

To see how these casts work, let's start by considering the case where the source and destination are both reference types, and consider two classes, MyBase and MyDerived, where MyDerived is derived directly or indirectly from MyBase.

Firstly from MyDerived to MyBase; it is always possible (assuming the constructors are available) to write:

```
MyDerived derivedObject = new MyDerived();
MyBase baseCopy = derivedObject;
```

In this case, we are casting implicitly from MyDerived to MyBase. This works because of the rule that any reference to a type MyBase is allowed to refer to objects of class MyBase or to objects of anything derived from MyBase. In OO programming, instances of a derived class are, in a real sense, instances of the base class, plus something extra. All the functions and fields defined on the base class are defined in the derived class too.

Alternatively, we can also write:

```
MyBase derivedObject = new MyDerived();
MyBase baseObject = new MyBase();
MyDerived derivedCopy1 = (MyDerived) derivedObject;    // OK
MyDerived derivedCopy2 = (MyDerived) baseObject;       // Throws exception
```

This code is perfectly legal C# (in a syntactic sense, that is), and illustrates casting from a base class to a derived class. However, the final statement will throw an exception when executed. What happens when we perform the cast is that the object being referred to is examined. Since a base class reference can in principle refer to a derived class instance, it is possible that this object is actually an instance of the derived class that we are attempting to cast to. If that's the case, then the cast succeeds, and the derived reference is set to refer to the object. If, however, the object in question is not an instance of the derived class (or of any class derived from it) then the cast fails and an exception is thrown.

Notice the casts that the compiler has supplied, which convert between base and derived class do not actually do any data conversion on the object in question. All they do is set the new reference to refer to the object if it is legal for that conversion to occur. To that extent, these casts are very different in nature from the ones that you will normally define yourself. For example, in our SimpleCurrency sample earlier, we defined casts that convert between a Currency struct and a float. In the float-to-Currency cast, we actually instantiated a new Currency struct and initialized it with the required values. The predefined casts between base and derived classes do not do this. If you actually want to convert a MyBase instance into a real MyDerived object with values based on the contents of the MyBase instance, you would not be able to use the cast syntax to do this. The most sensible option is usually to define a derived class constructor that takes a base class instance as a parameter, and have this constructor perform the relevant initializations:

```
class DerivedClass : BaseClass
{
    public DerivedClass(BaseClass rhs)
    {
        // initialize object from the Base instance
    }
    // etc.
```

Boxing and unboxing casts

The previous discussion focused on casting between base and derived classes where both were reference types. Similar principles apply when casting value types, although in this case it is not possible to simply copy references —some copying of data must take place.

It is not, of course, possible to derive from structs or primitive value types. So, casting between base and derived structs invariably means casting between a primitive type or a struct and System.Object (theoretically, it is possible to cast between a struct and System.ValueType, though it is hard to see why you would want to do this).

The cast from any struct (or primitive type) to `object` is always available as an implicit cast—since it is a cast from derived to base type—and is just the familiar process of boxing that we have encountered briefly in Chapter 2. For example, with our `Currency` struct:

```
Currency balance = new Currency(40,0);
object baseCopy = balance;
```

When this implicit cast is executed, the contents of `balance` are copied onto the heap into a boxed object, and the `baseCopy` object reference set to this object. What actually happens behind the scenes is this: when we originally defined the `Currency` struct, the .NET Framework implicitly supplied another (hidden) class, a boxed `Currency` class, which contains all the same fields as the `Currency` struct, but is a reference type, stored on the heap. This happens whenever we define a value type—whether it is a `struct` or `enum`, and similar boxed reference types exist corresponding to all the primitive value types of `int`, `double`, `uint`, and so on. It is not possible, nor necessary, to gain direct programmatic access to any of these boxed classes in source code, but they are the objects that are working behind the scenes whenever a value type is cast to `object`. When we implicitly cast `Currency` to `object`, a boxed `Currency` instance gets instantiated, and initialized with all the data from the `Currency` struct. In the above code, it is this boxed `Currency` instance that `baseCopy` will refer to. By these means, it is possible for casting from derived to base type to work syntactically in the same way for value types as for reference types.

Casting the other way is known as *unboxing*. Just as for casting between a base reference type and a derived reference type, it is an explicit cast, since an exception will be thrown if the object being cast is not of the correct type:

```
object derivedObject = new Currency(40,0);
object baseObject = new object();
Currency derivedCopy1 = (Currency)derivedObject;   // OK
Currency derivedCopy2 = (Currency)baseObject;      // Exception thrown
```

The previous code works analogously to the similar code presented earlier for reference types. Casting `derivedObject` to `Currency` works fine because `derivedObject` actually refers to a boxed `Currency` instance—the cast will be performed by copying the fields out of the boxed `Currency` object into a new `Currency` struct. The second cast fails because `baseObject` does not refer to a boxed `Currency` object.

When using boxing and unboxing, it is important to understand both processes actually copy the data into the new boxed or unboxed object. Hence, manipulations on the boxed object for example will not affect the contents of the original value type.

Multiple Casting

One thing you will have to watch for when you are defining casts is if the C# compiler is presented with a situation in which no direct cast is available to perform a requested conversion, it will attempt to find a way of combining casts to do the conversion. For example, with our `Currency` struct, suppose the compiler encounters a couple of lines of code like this:

```
Currency balance = new Currency(10,50);
long amount - (long)balance;
double amountD = balance;
```

We first initialize a `Currency` instance, and then we attempt to convert it to a `long`. The trouble is that we haven't defined the cast to do that. However, this code will still compile successfully. What will happen is that the compiler will realize that you have defined an implicit cast to get from `Currency` to `float`, and the compiler already knows how to explicitly cast a `float` to a `long`. Hence, it will compile that line of code into IL code that converts balance first to a `float`, and then converts that result to a `long`. The same thing happens in the final line of the above code, when we convert `balance` to a double. However, since the cast from `Currency` to `float` and the predefined cast from `float` to `double` are both implicit, we can write this conversion in our code as an implicit cast. If we'd preferred, we could have specified the casting route explicitly:

```
Currency balance = new Currency(10,50);
long amount = (long)(float)balance;
double amountD = (double)(float)balance;
```

However, in most cases, this would be seen as needlessly complicating your code. The following code by contrast would produce a compilation error:

```
Currency balance = new Currency(10,50);
long amount = balance;
```

The reason is the best match for the conversion that the compiler can find is still to convert first to `float` then to `long`. The conversion from `float` to `long` needs to be specified explicitly, though.

All this by itself shouldn't give you too much trouble. The rules are, after all, fairly intuitive and designed to prevent any data loss from occurring without the developer knowing about it. However, the problem is that if you are not careful when you define your casts, it is possible for the compiler to figure out a path that leads to unexpected results. For example, suppose it occurs to someone else in the group writing the `Currency` struct, that it would be useful to be able to convert a `uint` containing the total number of cents in an amount into a `Currency` (cents not dollars because the idea is not to lose the fractions of a dollar). So, this cast might be written to try to achieve this:

```
public static implicit operator Currency (uint value)
{
    return new Currency(value/100u, (ushort)(value%100));
} // Don't do this!
```

Note the `u` after the first 100 in this code to ensure that `value/100u` is interpreted as a `uint`. If we'd written `value/100` then the compiler would have interpreted this as an `int`, not a `uint`.

We have clearly commented `Don't do this` in this code, and here's why. Look at the following code snippet; all we do in it is convert a `uint` containing `350` into a `Currency` and back again. What do you think `bal2` will contain after executing this?

```
uint bal = 350;
Currency balance = bal;
uint bal2 = (uint)balance;
```

The answer is not `350`, but `3`! And it all follows logically. We convert `350` implicitly to a `Currency`, giving the result `Balance.Dollars=3`, `Balance.Cents=50`. Then the compiler does its usual figuring out of best path for the conversion back. Balance ends up getting implicitly converted to a `float` (value `3.5`), and this gets converted explicitly to a `uint` with value `3`.

Of course, other instances exist in which converting to another data type and back again causes data loss. For example, converting a `float` containing `5.8` to an `int` and back to a `float` again will lose the fractional part, giving a result of `5`, but there is a slight difference in principle between losing the fractional part of a number and dividing an integer by more than 100! `Currency` has suddenly become a rather dangerous class that does strange things to integers!

The problem is that there is a conflict between how our casts interpret integers. Our casts between `Currency` and `float` interpret an integer value of `1` as corresponding to one dollar, but our latest `uint`-to-`Currency` cast interprets this value as one cent. This is an example of very poor design. If you want your classes to be easy to use, then you should make sure all your casts behave in a way that is mutually compatible, in the sense that they intuitively give the same results. In this case, the solution is obviously to rewrite our `uint`-to-`Currency` cast so that it interprets an integer value of `1` as one dollar:

```
public static implicit operator Currency (uint value)
{
   return new Currency(value, 0);
}
```

Incidentally, you might wonder whether this new cast is necessary at all. The answer is that it could be useful. Without this cast, the only way for the compiler to carry out a `uint`-to-`Currency` conversion would be via a `float`. Converting directly is a lot more efficient in this case, so having this extra cast gives performance benefits, but we need to make sure it gives the same result as we would get going via a `float`, which we have now done. In other situations, you may also find that separately defining casts for different predefined data types allows more conversions to be implicit rather than explicit, though that's not the case here.

A good test of whether your casts are compatible is to ask whether a conversion will give the same results (other than perhaps a loss of accuracy as in `float`-to-`int` conversions), irrespective of which path it takes. Our `Currency` class provides a good example of this. Look at this code:

```
Currency balance = new Currency(50, 35);
ulong bal = (ulong) balance;
```

At present, there is only one way that the compiler can achieve this conversion: by converting the `Currency` to a `float` implicitly, then to a `ulong` explicitly. The `float`-to-`ulong` conversion requires an explicit conversion, but that's fine because we have specified one here.

Suppose, however, that we then added another cast, to convert implicitly from a `Currency` to a `uint`. We will actually do this by modifying the `Currency` struct by adding the casts both to and from `uint`. This code is available as the `SimpleCurrency2` example:

```
public static implicit operator Currency (uint value)
{
    return new Currency(value, 0);
}
```

```
public static implicit operator uint (Currency value)
{
    return value.Dollars;
}
```

Now the compiler has another possible route to convert from `Currency` to `ulong`: to convert from `Currency` to `uint` implicitly then to `ulong` implicitly. Which of these two routes will it take? C# does have some precise rules (which we won't detail in this book; if you are interested, details are in the MSDN documentation) to say how the compiler decides which is the best route if there are several possibilities. The best answer is that you should design your casts so that all routes give the same answer (other than possible loss of precision), in which case it doesn't really matter which one the compiler picks. (As it happens in this case, the compiler picks the `Currency-to-uint-to-ulong` route in preference to `Currency-to-float-to-ulong`.)

To test the `SimpleCurrency2` sample, we will add this code to the test code for `SimpleCurrency`:

```
try
{
    Currency balance = new Currency(50,35);
    Console.WriteLine(balance);
    Console.WriteLine("balance is " + balance);
    Console.WriteLine("balance is (using ToString()) " + balance.ToString());

    uint balance3 = (uint) balance;
    Console.WriteLine("Converting to uint gives " + balance3);
```

Running the sample now gives these results:

SimpleCurrency2

```
50
balance is $50.35
balance is (using ToString()) $50.35
Converting to uint gives 50
After converting to float, = 50.35
After converting back to Currency, = $50.34
Now attempt to convert out of range value of -$100.00 to a Currency:
Exception occurred: Arithmetic operation resulted in an overflow.
```

The output shows that the conversion to `uint` has been successful, though as expected, we have lost the cents part of the `Currency` in making this conversion. Casting a negative `float` to `Currency` has also produced the expected overflow exception now that the `float-to-Currency` cast itself defines a `checked` context.

However, the output also demonstrates one last potential problem that you need to be aware of when working with casts. The very first line of output has not displayed the balance correctly, displaying `50` instead of `$50.35`. Consider these lines:

```
Console.WriteLine(balance);
Console.WriteLine("balance is " + balance);
Console.WriteLine("balance is (using ToString()) " + balance.ToString());
```

Only the last two lines correctly display the `Currency` as a string. So what's going on? The problem here is that when you combine casts with method overloads, you get another source of unpredictability. We will look at these lines in reverse order.

The third `Console.WriteLine()` statement explicitly calls the `Currency.ToString()` method ensuring the `Currency` is displayed as a string. The second does not do so. However, the string literal `"balance is"` passed to `Console.WriteLine()` makes it clear to the compiler that the parameter is to be interpreted as a string. Hence the `Currency.ToString()` method will be called implicitly.

The very first `Console.WriteLine()` method, however, simply passes a raw `Currency` struct to `Console.WriteLine()`. Now, `Console.WriteLine()` has many overloads, but none of them takes a `Currency` struct. So the compiler will start fishing around to see what it can cast the `Currency` to in order to make it match up with one of the overloads of `Console.WriteLine()`. As it happens, one of the `Console.WriteLine()` overloads is designed to display `uint`s quickly and efficiently, and it takes a `uint` as a parameter, and we have now supplied a cast that converts `Currency` implicitly to `uint`.

In fact, `Console.WriteLine()` has another overload that takes a `double` as a parameter and displays the value of that `double`. If you look closely at the output from the first `SimpleCurrency` example, you will find the very first line of output displayed `Currency` as a `double`, using this overload. In that example, there wasn't a direct cast from `Currency` to `uint`, so the compiler picked `Currency`-to-`float`-to-`double` as its preferred way of matching up the available casts to the available `Console.WriteLine()` overloads. However, now that there is a direct cast to `uint` available in `SimpleCurrency2`, the compiler has opted for this route.

The upshot of this is that if you have a method call that takes several overloads, and you attempt to pass it a parameter whose data type doesn't match any of the overloads exactly, then you are forcing the compiler to decide not only what casts to use to perform the data conversion, but which overload, and hence which data conversion, to pick. The compiler always works logically and according to strict rules, but the results may not be what you expected. If there is any doubt, you are probably better off specifying which cast to use explicitly.

Summary

In this chapter we've looked at the standard operators provided by C#, described the mechanics of object equality, and examined how the compiler converts the standard data types from one to another. We have also demonstrated how you can implement custom operator support on your data types using operator overloads. Finally, we looked at a special type of operator overload, the cast operator, which allows you to specify how instances of your types are converted to other data types.

In the following chapter, we focus on two closely related member types that you can implement in your types to support very clean event-based object models: delegates and events.

6

Delegates and Events

Callback functions are an important part of programming in Windows. If you have a background in C or C++ programming you have seen callbacks used in many of the Windows APIs. With the addition of the AddressOf keyword, Visual Basic developers are now able to take advantage of the API that once was off limits. Callback functions are really a pointer to a method call. Also known as function pointers, they are a very powerful programming feature. .NET has implemented the concept of a function pointer in the form of delegates. What makes them special is that unlike the C function pointer the .NET delegate is type-safe. What this means is that a function pointer in C is nothing but a pointer to a memory location. You have no idea what that pointer is really pointing to. Things like parameters and return types are not known. As you will see in this chapter, .NET has made delegates a type-safe operation. Later in the chapter you will see how .NET uses delegates as the means of implementing events.

Delegates

Delegates can best be seen as a new type of object in C#, which has some similarities to classes. They exist for situations in which you want to pass methods around to other methods. To see what we mean by that, consider this line of code:

```
int i = int.Parse("99");
```

We are so used to passing data to methods as parameters, as in the previous example, we don't consciously think about it; and for this reason the idea of passing methods around instead of data might sound a little strange. However, there are cases in which you have a method that does something, and rather than operating on data, the method might need to do something that involves invoking another method. To complicate things further, you do not know at compile-time what this second method is. That information is only available at runtime and hence will need to be passed in as a parameter to the first method. That might sound confusing, but should be clearer with a couple of examples:

❑ **Starting Threads**—It is possible in C# to tell the computer to start some new sequence of execution in parallel with what it is currently doing. Such a sequence is known as a thread, and starting one up is done using the `Start()` method on an instance of one of the base classes, `System.Threading.Thread`. If you are going to tell the computer to start a new sequence of execution, you have got to tell it where to start that sequence. You have to supply it with the details of a method in which execution can start. In other words, the `Thread.Start()` method has to take a parameter that defines the method to be invoked by the thread.

❑ **Generic Library Classes**—There are of course many libraries that contain code to perform various standard tasks. It is usually possible for these libraries to be self-contained, in the sense that you know when you write to the library exactly how the task must be performed. However, sometimes the task contains some subtask, which only the individual client code that uses the library knows how to perform. For example, say we want to write a class that takes an array of objects and sorts them into ascending order. Part of the sorting process involves repeatedly taking two of the objects in the array and comparing them in order to see which one should come first. If we want to make the class capable of sorting arrays of any object, there is no way that it can tell in advance how to do this comparison. The client code that hands our class the array of objects will also have to tell our class how to do this comparison for the particular objects it wants sorted. In other words, the client code will have to pass our class details of an appropriate method that can be called and does the comparison.

❑ **Events**—The general idea here is that often, you have code that needs to be informed when some event takes place. GUI programming is full of situations like this. When the event is raised, the runtime will need to know what method should be executed. This is done by passing the method that handles the event as a parameter to a delegate. This will be discussed later in the chapter.

So, we have established the principle that sometimes, methods need to take details of other methods as parameters. Next, we need to figure out how we can do that. The simplest way would appear to be to just pass in the name of a method as a parameter. To take our example from threading, suppose we are going to start a new thread, and we have a method called `EntryPoint()`, which is where we want our thread to start running:

```
void EntryPoint()
{
   // do whatever the new thread needs to do
}
```

Alternatively you can also start the new thread off with some code like this:

```
Thread NewThread = new Thread();
Thread.Start(EntryPoint);                  // WRONG
```

In fact, this is the simple way of doing it, and it is what some languages, such as C and C++, do in this kind of situation (in C and C++, the parameter `EntryPoint` is the function pointer).

Unfortunately, this direct approach causes some problems with type safety, and it also neglects the fact that when we are doing object-oriented programming, methods rarely exist in isolation, but usually need to be associated with a class instance before they can be called. As a result of these problems, the .NET Framework does not syntactically permit this direct approach. Instead, if you want to pass methods around, you have to wrap up the details of the method in a new kind of object, a delegate. Delegates quite simply are a special type of object—special in the sense that, whereas all the objects we have defined up to now contain data, a delegate just contains the details of a method.

Using Delegates in C#

When we want to use a class in C#, there are two stages. First, we need to define the class—that is, we need to tell the compiler what fields and methods make up the class. Then (unless we are using only static methods), we instantiate an object of that class. With delegates it is the same thing. We have to start off by defining the delegates we want to use. In the case of delegates, defining it means telling the compiler what kind of method a delegate of that type will represent. Then, we have to create one or more instances of that delegate.

The syntax for defining delegates looks like this:

```
delegate void VoidOperation(uint x);
```

In this case, we have defined a delegate called VoidOperation, and we have indicated that each instance of this delegate can hold a reference to a method that takes one uint parameter and returns void. The crucial point to understand about delegates is that they are very type-safe. When you define the delegate, you have to give full details of the signature of the method that it is going to represent.

> **One good way of understanding delegates is by thinking of a delegate as something that gives a name to a method signature.**

Suppose we wanted to define a delegate called TwoLongsOp that will represent a function that takes two longs as its parameters and returns a double. We could do it like this:

```
delegate double TwoLongsOp(long first, long second);
```

Or, to define a delegate that will represent a method that takes no parameters and returns a string, we might write this:

```
delegate string GetAString();
```

The syntax is similar to that for a method definition, except that there is no method body, and the definition is prefixed with the keyword delegate. Since what we are doing here is basically defining a new class, we can define a delegate in any of the same places that we would define a class—that is to say either inside another class or outside of any class and in a namespace as a top-level object. Depending on how visible we want our definition to be, we can apply any of the normal access modifiers to delegate definitions—public, private, protected, and so on:

```
public delegate string GetAString();
```

We really mean what we say when we describe defining a delegate as defining a new class. Delegates are implemented as classes derived from the class System.MulticastDelegate which is derived from the base class, System.Delegate. The C# compiler is aware of this class and uses its delegate syntax to shield us from the details of the operation of this class. This is another good example of how C# works in conjunction with the base classes to make programming as easy as practicable.

After we have defined a delegate, we can create an instance of it so that we can use it to store details of a particular method.

> *There is an unfortunate problem with terminology here. With classes there are two distinct terms—class, which indicates the broader definition, and object, which means an instance of the class. Unfortunately, with delegates there is only the one term. When you create an instance of a delegate, what you have created is also referred to as a delegate. You need to be aware of the context to know which meaning we are using when we talk about delegates.*

The following code snippet demonstrates the use of a delegate. It is a rather long-winded way of calling the `ToString()` method on an `int`:

```
private delegate string GetAString();

static void Main(string[] args)
{
    int x = 40;
    GetAString firstStringMethod = new GetAString(x.ToString);
    Console.WriteLine("String is" + firstStringMethod());
    // With firstStringMethod initialized to x.ToString(),
    // the above statement is equivalent to saying
    // Console.WriteLine("String is" + x.ToString());
```

In this code, we instantiate a delegate of type `GetAString`, and we initialize it so that it refers to the `ToString()` method of the integer variable x. Delegates in C# always syntactically take a one-parameter constructor, the parameter being the method to which the delegate will refer. This method must match the signature with which we originally defined the delegate. So in this case, we would get a compilation error if we tried to initialize `firstStringMethod` with any method that did not take parameters and return a string. Notice that since `int.ToString()` is an instance method (as opposed to a static one) we need to specify the instance (x) as well as the name of the method to initialize the delegate properly.

The next line actually uses the delegate to display the string. In any code, supplying the name of a delegate instance, followed by brackets containing any parameters, has exactly the same effect as calling the method wrapped by the delegate. Hence, in the previous code snippet, the `Console.WriteLine()` statement is completely equivalent to the commented-out line.

One feature of delegates is that they are type-safe to the extent that they ensure the signature of the method being called is correct. However, interestingly, they do not care what type of object the method is being called against, or even whether the method is a static method or an instance method.

> **An instance of a given delegate can refer to any instance or static method on any object of any type, provided that the signature of the method matches the signature of the delegate.**

To demonstrate this, we will expand the previous code snippet so that it uses the `firstStringMethod` delegate to call a couple of other methods on another object—an instance method and a static method. For this, we will use the `Currency` struct that is defined as follows:

```
struct Currency
{
  public uint Dollars;
  public ushort Cents;

  public Currency(uint dollars, ushort cents)
  {
     this.Dollars = dollars;
     this.Cents = cents;
  }

  public override string ToString()
  {
     return string.Format("${0}.{1,-2:00}", Dollars,Cents);
  }

  public static explicit operator Currency (float value)
  {
     checked
     {
       uint dollars = (uint)value;
       ushort cents = (ushort)((value-dollars)*100);
       return new Currency(dollars, cents);
     }
  }

  public static implicit operator float (Currency value)
  {
     return value.Dollars + (value.Cents/100.0f);
  }

  public static implicit operator Currency (uint value)
  {
     return new Currency(value, 0);
  }

  public static implicit operator uint (Currency value)
  {
     return value.Dollars;
  }
}
```

Notice that the Currency struct has its own overload of ToString(). In order to demonstrate using delegates with static methods, we will also add a static method with the same signature to Currency:

```
struct Currency
{
   public static string GetCurrencyUnit()
   {
      return "Dollar";
   }
```

Now we can use our `GetAString` instance as follows:

```
    private delegate string GetAString();

    static void Main(string[] args)
    {
        int x = 40;
        GetAString firstStringMethod = new GetAString(x.ToString);
        Console.WriteLine("String is " + firstStringMethod());
        Currency balance = new Currency(34, 50);
        firstStringMethod = new GetAString(balance.ToString);
        Console.WriteLine("String is " + firstStringMethod());
        firstStringMethod = new GetAString(Currency.GetCurrencyUnit);
        Console.WriteLine("String is " + firstStringMethod());
```

This code shows how you can call a method via a delegate, and subsequently reassign the delegate to refer to different methods on different instances of classes, even static methods or methods against instances of different types of class, provided that the signature of each method matches the delegate definition.

However, we still haven't demonstrated the process of actually passing a delegate to another method. Nor have we actually achieved anything particularly useful yet. It is possible to call the `ToString()` method of `int` and `Currency` objects in a much more straightforward way than using delegates! Unfortunately, it is in the nature of delegates that we need a fairly complex example before we can really appreciate their usefulness. We are now going to present two delegate examples. The first one simply uses delegates to call a couple of different operations. It illustrates how to pass delegates to methods, and how you can use arrays of delegates—although arguably it still doesn't do much that you couldn't do a lot more simply without delegates. Then, we will present a second, much more complex example of a `BubbleSorter` class, which implements a method to sort out arrays of objects into increasing order. This class would be difficult to write without delegates.

SimpleDelegate Example

For this example, we will define a `MathsOperations` class that has a couple of static methods to perform two operations on doubles. Then, we will use delegates to call up these methods. The math class looks like this:

```
class MathsOperations
{
  public static double MultiplyByTwo(double value)
  {
    return value*2;
  }

  public static double Square(double value)
  {
    return value*value;
  }
}
```

We call up these methods like this:

```csharp
using System;

namespace SimpleDelegate
{
   delegate double DoubleOp(double x);

   class MainEntryPoint
   {
      static void Main()
      {
         DoubleOp [] operations =
            {
               new DoubleOp(MathsOperations.MultiplyByTwo),
               new DoubleOp(MathsOperations.Square)
            };

         for (int i=0 ; i<operations.Length ; i++)
         {
            Console.WriteLine("Using operations[{0}]:", i);
            ProcessAndDisplayNumber(operations[i], 2.0);
            ProcessAndDisplayNumber(operations[i], 7.94);
            ProcessAndDisplayNumber(operations[i], 1.414);
            Console.WriteLine();
         }
      }

      static void ProcessAndDisplayNumber(DoubleOp action, double value)
      {
         double result = action(value);
         Console.WriteLine(
            "Value is {0}, result of operation is {1}", value, result);
      }
```

In this code, we instantiate an array of `DoubleOp` delegates (remember that once we have defined a delegate class, we can basically instantiate instances just like we can with normal classes, so putting some into an array is no problem). Each element of the array gets initialized to refer to a different operation implemented by the `MathOperations` class. Then, we loop through the array, applying each operation to three different values. This illustrates one way of using delegates—that you can group methods together into an array using them, so that you can call several methods in a loop.

The key lines in this code are the ones in which we actually pass each delegate to the `ProcessAndDisplayNumber()` method, for example:

```csharp
ProcessAndDisplayNumber(operations[i], 2.0);
```

Here, we are passing in the name of a delegate, but without any parameters. Given that `operations[i]` is a delegate, syntactically:

- ❑   `operations[i]` means *the delegate*, in other words the method represented by the delegate.

- ❑   `operations[i](2.0)` means *actually call this method, passing in the value in parentheses*.

The `ProcessAndDisplayNumber()` method is defined to take a delegate as its first parameter:

```
static void ProcessAndDisplayNumber(DoubleOp action, double value)
```

Then, when in this method, we call:

```
double result = action(value);
```

This actually causes the method that is wrapped up by the `action` delegate instance to be called and its return result stored in `Result`.

Running this sample gives the following:

```
SimpleDelegate
Using operations[0]:
Value is 2, result of operation is 4
Value is 7.94, result of operation is 15.88
Value is 1.414, result of operation is 2.828

Using operations[1]:
Value is 2, result of operation is 4
Value is 7.94, result of operation is 63.0436
Value is 1.414, result of operation is 1.999396
```

BubbleSorter Example

We are now ready for an example that will show delegates working in a situation in which they are very useful. We are going to write a class called `BubbleSorter`. This class implements a static method, `Sort()`, which takes as its first parameter an array of objects, and rearranges this array into ascending order. In other words, suppose we were to pass it this array of ints: `{0, 5, 6, 2, 1}`. It would rearrange this array into `{0, 1, 2, 5, 6}`.

The bubble-sorting algorithm is a well-known and very simple way of sorting numbers. It is best suited to small sets of numbers, since for larger sets of numbers (more than about 10) there are far more efficient algorithms available). It works by repeatedly looping through the array, comparing each pair of numbers and, if necessary, swapping them, so that the largest numbers progressively move to the end of the array. For sorting ints, a method to do a bubble sort might look like this:

```
// Note that this isn't part of the sample
for (int i = 0; i < sortArray.Length; i++)
{
   for (int j = i + 1; j < sortArray.Length; j++)
   {
      if (sortArray[j] < sortArray[i])   // problem with this test
      {
         int temp = sortArray[i];   // swap ith and jth entries
         sortArray[i] = sortArray[j];
         sortArray[j] = temp;
      }
   }
}
```

This is all very well for `ints`, but we want our `Sort()` method to be able to sort any object. In other words, if some client code hands us an array of `Currency` structs or any other class or struct that it may have defined, we need to be able to sort the array. This gives us a problem with the line `if(sortArray[j] < sortArray[i])` in the above code, since that requires us to compare two objects on the array to see which one is greater. We can do that for `ints`, but how are we to do it for some new class that is unknown or undecided until runtime? The answer is the client code that knows about the class will have to pass in a delegate wrapping a method that will do the comparison.

We define the delegate like this:

```
delegate bool CompareOp(object lhs, object rhs);
```

And we give our `Sort` method this signature:

```
static public void Sort(object [] sortArray, CompareOp gtMethod)
```

The documentation for this method states that `gtMethod` must refer to a static method that takes two arguments, and returns `true` if the value of the second argument is *greater than* (in other words should come later in the array than) the first one.

> *Although we are using delegates here, it is possible to solve this problem alternatively, by using interfaces. .NET in fact makes the `IComparer` interface available for that purpose. However, we will use delegates here since this is still the kind of problem that lends itself to delegates.*

Now we are all set. Here is the definition for the `BubbleSorter` class:

```
class BubbleSorter
{
    static public void Sort(object [] sortArray, CompareOp gtMethod)
    {
        for (int i=0 ; i<sortArray.Length ; i++)
        {
            for (int j=i+1 ; j<sortArray.Length ; j++)
            {
                if (gtMethod(sortArray[j], sortArray[i]))
                {
                    object temp = sortArray[i];
                    sortArray[i] = sortArray[j];
                    sortArray[j] = temp;
                }
            }
        }
    }
}
```

In order to use this class, we need to define some other class, which we can use to set up an array that needs sorting. For this example, we will assume that our Mortimer Phones mobile phone company has a list of employees and wants them sorted according to salary. The employees are each represented by an instance of a class, `Employee`, which looks like this:

```
class Employee
{
    private string name;
    private decimal salary;

    public Employee(string name, decimal salary)
    {
        this.name = name;
        this.salary = salary;
    }

    public override string ToString()
    {
        return string.Format(name + ", {0:C}", salary);
    }

    public static bool RhsIsGreater(object lhs, object rhs)
    {
        Employee empLhs = (Employee) lhs;
        Employee empRhs = (Employee) rhs;
        return (empRhs.salary > empLhs.salary) ? true : false;
    }
}
```

Notice that in order to match the signature of the `CompareOp` delegate, we have had to define `RhsIsGreater` in this class as taking two object references, rather than `Employee` references as parameters. This means that we have had to cast the parameters into `Employee` references in order to perform the comparison.

Now we are ready to write some client code to request a sort:

```
using System;

namespace Wrox.ProCSharp.AdvancedCSharp
{
    delegate bool CompareOp(object lhs, object rhs);

    class MainEntryPoint
    {
        static void Main()
        {
            Employee [] employees =
                {
                    new Employee("Bugs Bunny", 20000),
                    new Employee("Elmer Fudd", 10000),
                    new Employee("Daffy Duck", 25000),
                    new Employee("Wiley Coyote", (decimal)1000000.38),
                    new Employee("Foghorn Leghorn", 23000),
                    new Employee("RoadRunner'", 50000)};
            CompareOp employeeCompareOp = new CompareOp(Employee.RhsIsGreater);
```

```
                    BubbleSorter.Sort(employees, employeeCompareOp);

                    for (int i=0 ; i<employees.Length ; i++)
                        Console.WriteLine(employees[i].ToString());
            }
        }
```

Running this code shows that the `Employees` are correctly sorted according to salary:

BubbleSorter
```
Elmer Fudd, $10,000.00
Bugs Bunny, $20,000.00
Foghorn Leghorn, $23,000.00
Daffy Duck, $25,000.00
RoadRunner, $50,000.00
Wiley Coyote, $1,000,000.38
```

Multicast Delegates

So far, each of the delegates we have used wraps just one single method call. Calling the delegate amounts to calling that method. If we want to call more than one method, we need to make an explicit call through a delegate more than once. However, it is possible for a delegate to wrap more than one method. Such a delegate is known as a *multicast delegate*. If a multicast delegate is called, it will successively call each method in order. For this to make sense, the delegate signature must return a `void` (otherwise, where would all the return values go?), and in fact, if the compiler sees a delegate that returns a `void`, it automatically assumes you mean a multicast delegate. Consider this code, which is adapted from the `SimpleDelegate` example. Although the syntax is the same as before, it is actually a multicast delegate, `Operations`, that gets instantiated:

```
        delegate void DoubleOp(double value);
//      delegate double DoubleOp(double value);    // can't do this now

        class MainEntryPoint
        {
            static void Main()
            {
                DoubleOp operations = new DoubleOp(MathOperations.MultiplyByTwo);
                operations += new DoubleOp(MathOperations.Square);
```

In our earlier example, we wanted to store references to two methods so we instantiated an array of delegates. Here, we simply add both operations into the same multicast delegate. Multicast delegates recognize the operators + and +=. Alternatively, we can also expand the last two lines of the previous code as in this snippet:

```
        DoubleOp operation1 = new DoubleOp(MathOperations.MultiplyByTwo);
        DoubleOp operation2 = new DoubleOp(MathOperations.Square);
        DoubleOp operations = operation1 + operation2;
```

Multicast delegates also recognize the operators − and −= to remove method calls from the delegate.

177

In terms of what's going on under the hood, a multicast delegate is a class derived from
`System.MulticastDelegate`, *which in turn is derived from* `System.Delegate`.
`System.MulticastDelegate` *has additional members to allow chaining of method calls together
into a list.*

To illustrate the use of multicast delegates, we have recast the `SimpleDelegate` sample into a new sample, `MulticastDelegate`. Since we now need the delegate to refer to methods that return `void`, we have to rewrite the methods in the `MathOperations` class, so they display their results instead of returning them:

```
class MathOperations
{
    public static void MultiplyByTwo(double value)
    {
        double result = value*2;
        Console.WriteLine(
            "Multiplying by 2: {0} gives {1}", value, result);
    }

    public static void Square(double value)
    {
        double result = value*value;
        Console.WriteLine("Squaring: {0} gives {1}", value, result);
    }
}
```

To accommodate this change, we also have to rewrite `ProcessAndDisplayNumber`:

```
static void ProcessAndDisplayNumber(DoubleOp action, double value)
{
    Console.WriteLine("\nProcessAndDisplayNumber called with value = " +
                      value);
    action(value);
}
```

Now we can try out our multicast delegate like this:

```
static void Main()
{
    DoubleOp operations = new DoubleOp(MathOperations.MultiplyByTwo);
    operations += new DoubleOp(MathOperations.Square);

    ProcessAndDisplayNumber(operations, 2.0);
    ProcessAndDisplayNumber(operations, 7.94);
    ProcessAndDisplayNumber(operations, 1.414);
    Console.WriteLine();
}
```

Now, each time that `ProcessAndDisplayNumber` is called, it will display a message to say that it has been called. Then the following statement will cause each of the method calls in the `action` delegate instance to be called in succession:

```
action(value);
```

Running this code gives this result:

```
MulticastDelegate

ProcessAndDisplayNumber called with value = 2
Multiplying by 2: 2 gives 4
Squaring: 2 gives 4

ProcessAndDisplayNumber called with value = 7.94
Multiplying by 2: 7.94 gives 15.88
Squaring: 7.94 gives 63.0436

ProcessAndDisplayNumber called with value = 1.414
Multiplying by 2: 1.414 gives 2.828
Squaring: 1.414 gives 1.999396
```

If you are using multicast delegates, you should be aware that the order in which methods chained to the same delegate will be called is formally undefined. You should, therefore, avoid writing code that relies on such methods being called in any particular order.

Events

Windows-based applications are message based. What this means is that the application is communicating with Windows and Windows is communicating with the application by using predefined messages. These messages are structures that contain various pieces of information that the application and Windows will use to determine what to do next. Prior to libraries such as MFC or to development environments such as Visual Basic, the developer would have to handle the message that Windows sends to the application. Visual Basic and now .NET wrap some of these incoming messages as something called events. If you need to react to a specific incoming message, then you would handle the corresponding event. A common example of this is when the user clicks a button on a form. Windows is sending a WM_MOUSECLICK message to the buttons message handler (sometimes referred to as the Windows Procedure or WndProc). To the .NET developer this is exposed as the OnClick event of the button.

In developing object-based applications another form of communication between objects is required. When something of interest happens in one of your objects, chances are that other objects will want to be informed. Again events come to the rescue. Just as the .NET Framework wraps up Windows messages in events you can also utilize events as the communications medium between your objects.

Delegates are used as the means of wiring the event up when the message is received by the application.

Believe it or not, in the preceding section on delegates, we learned just about everything we needed to know to understand how events work. However, one of the great things about how Microsoft has designed C# events is that you don't actually need to understand anything about the underlying delegates in order to use them. So, we are going to start off with a short discussion of events from the point of view of the client software. We will focus on what code you need to write in order to receive notifications of events, without worrying too much about what is happening behind the scenes—just so we can show how easy handling events really is. After we have done that, we will write a sample that generates events, and as we do so, we should see how the relationship between events and delegates work.

The discussion in this section will be of most use to C++ developers since C++ does not have any concept similar to events. C# events on the other hand are quite similar in concept to Visual Basic events, although the syntax and the underlying implementation are different in C#.

In this context, we are using the term event in two different senses. Firstly, as something interesting that happens; and secondly, as a precisely defined object in the C# language—the object that handles the notification process. When we mean the latter, we will usually refer to it either as a C# event, or, when the meaning is obvious from the context, simply as an event.

The Receiver's View of Events

The event receiver is any application, object, or component that wants to be notified when something happens. To go along with the receiver there will of course be the event sender. The sender's job will be to raise the event. The sender can be either another object or assembly in your application, or in the case of system events such as mouse clicks or keyboard entry the sender will be the .NET runtime. It is important to note that the sender of the event will not have any knowledge of who or what the receiver is. This is what makes events so useful.

Now, somewhere inside the event receiver there will be a method that is responsible for handling the event. This event handler will be executed each time the event that it is registered to is raised. This is where the delegate comes in. Since the sender has no idea who the receiver(s) will be, there cannot be any type of reference set between the two. So the delegate is used as the intermediary. The sender defines the delegate that will be used by the receiver. The receiver registers the event handler with the event. The process of hooking up the event handler is known as wiring up an event. A simple example of wiring up the Click event will help illustrate this process.

First create a simple Windows Forms application. Drag over a button control from the toolbox and place it on the form. In the properties window rename the button to btnOne. In the code editor add the following line of code in the Form1 constructor:

```
btnOne.Click += new EventHandler(Button_Click);
```

Now in Visual Studio you should have noticed that after you typed in the += operator all you had to do was press the Tab key a couple of times and the editor will do the rest of the work for you. In most cases this is fine. However, in this example the default handler name is not being used, so you should just enter the text yourself.

What is happening is that you are telling the runtime that when the Click event of btnOne is raised that Button_Click method should be executed. EventHandler is the delegate that the event uses to assign the handler (Button_Click) to the event (Click). Notice that you used the += operator to add this new method to the delegate list. This is just like the multicast example that you looked at earlier in this chapter. This means that you can add more then one handler for any event. Since this is a multicast delegate all of the rules about adding multiple methods apply; however, there is no guarantee as to the order that the methods are called. Go ahead and drag another button onto the form and rename it to btnTwo. Now connect the btnTwo Click event to the same Button_Click method, as shown in this example:

```
btnOne.Click += new EventHandler(Button_Click);
btnTwo.Click += new EventHandler(Button_Click);
```

The EventHandler delegate is defined for you in the framework. It is in the System namespace and all of the events that are defined in the framework use it. As we discussed earlier, a delegate requires that all of the methods that are added to the delegate list must have the same signature. This obviously holds true for event delegates as well. Here is the Button_Click method defined:

```
private void Button_Click(object sender, EventArgs e)
{

}
```

There are a few things that are important about this method. First, it always returns void. Event handlers cannot return a value. Next are the parameters. As long as you use the EventHandler delegate, your parameters will be object and EventArgs. The first parameter is the object that raised the event. In this example it is either btnOne or btnTwo, depending on which button is clicked. By sending a reference to the object that raised the event you can assign the same event handler to more then one object. For example, you can define one button click handler for several buttons and then determine which button was clicked by asking the sender parameter.

The second parameter, EventArgs, is an object that contains other potentially useful information about the event. This parameter could actually be any type as long as it is derived from EventArgs. The MouseDown event uses the MouseDownEventArgs. It contains properties for which button was used, the X and Y coordinates of the pointer, and other info related to the event. Notice the naming pattern of ending the type with EventArgs. Later in the chapter you will see how to create and use a custom EventArgs-based object.

The name of the method should also be mentioned. As a convention any event handlers follow a naming convention of object_event. Object is the object that is raising the event and event is the event being raised. There is a convention and for readability's sake it should be followed.

The last thing to do in this example is to add some code to actually do something in the handler. Now remember that there are two buttons using the same handler. So first you have to determine which button raises the event, then you can call the action that should be performed. In this example, you can just output some text to a label control on the form. Drag a label control from the toolbox onto the form and name it lblInfo. Then write the following code on the Button_Click method:

```
if(((Button)sender).Name == "btnOne")
   lblInfo.Text = "Button One was pressed";
else
   lblInfo.Text = "Button Two was pressed";
```

Notice that since the sender parameter is sent as object, you will have to cast it to whatever object is raising the event, in this case Button. In this example, we use the Name property to determine what button raised the event; however, you can also use another property. The Tag property is handy to use in this scenario, because it can contain anything that you want to place in it. To see how the multicast capability of the event delegate works, add another method to the btnTwo Click event. Use the default method name. The constructor of the form should look something like this now:

```
btnOne.Click += new EventHandler(Button_Click);
btnTwo.Click += new EventHandler(Button_Click);
btnTwo.Click += new EventHandler(btnTwo_Click);
```

If you let Visual Studio create the stub for you, you will have the following method at the end of the source file. However, you have to add the call to the Messagebox function.

```
private void btnTwo_Click(object sender, EventArgs e)
{
    MessageBox.Show("This only happens in Button 2 click event");
}
```

When you run this example, clicking btnOne will change the text in the label. Clicking btnTwo will not only change the text but also display the MessageBox. Again the important thing to remember is that there is no guarantee that the label text changes before the MessageBox appears, so be careful not to write dependent code in the handlers.

You might have had to learn a lot of concepts to get this far, but the amount of coding you need to do in the receiver is fairly trivial. Also bear in mind that you will find yourself writing event receivers a lot more often than you write event senders. At least in the field of the Windows user interface, Microsoft has already written all the event senders you are likely to need (these are in the .NET base classes, in the Windows.Forms namespace).

Generating Events

Receiving events and responding to them is only one side of the story. In order to be really useful you need the ability to generate events and raise them in your code. This example looks at creating, raising, receiving, and optionally cancelling an event.

The example has a form raise an event that will be listened to by another class. When the event is raised the receiving object will determine if the process should execute and then cancel the event if the process cannot continue. The goal in this case is to determine whether the number of seconds of the current time is greater than or less than 30. If the number of seconds is less than 30 then a property is set with a string that represents the current time; if the number of seconds is greater then 30, then the event is cancelled and the time string is set to an empty string.

The form used to generate the event has a button and a label on it. The code in the example download has the button named btnRaise and the label is lblInfo; however, you can use any name you want for your labels. After you have created the form and added the two controls you will be able to create the event and the corresponding delegate. Add the following code in the class declaration section of the form class:

```
public delegate void ActionEventHandler(object sender, ActionCancelEventArgs ev);
public static event ActionEventHandler Action;
```

So what exactly is going on with these two lines of code? First you are declaring a new delegate type of ActionEventHandler. The reason that you have to create a new one and not use one of the predefined delegates in the framework is that there will be a custom EventArgs class used. Remember the method signature must match the delegate. So you now have a delegate to use, the next line actually defines the event. In this case the Action event is defined, and the syntax for defining the event requires that you specify the delegate that will be associated with the event. You can also use a delegate that is defined in the framework. There are nearly 100 classes that are derived from the EventArgs class, so you might find one that works for you. Again since a custom EventArgs class is used in this example, a new delegate type has to be created that matches it.

The new EventArgs-based class, ActionCancelEventArgs is actually derived from CancelEventArgs which is derived from EventArgs. CancelEventArgs adds the Cancel property. Cancel is a Boolean that informs the sender object that the receiver wants to cancel or stop the event processing. In the ActionCancelEventArgs class a Message property has been added. This is a string property that will contain textual information on the processing state of the event. Here is the code for the ActionCancelEventArgs class:

```
public class ActionCancelEventArgs : System.ComponentModel.CancelEventArgs
{

  string _msg = "";

  public ActionCancelEventArgs()  : base()  {}

  public ActionCancelEventArgs(bool cancel) : base(cancel)  {}

  public ActionCancelEventArgs(bool cancel, string message) : base(cancel)
  {
    _msg = message;
  }

  public string Message
  {
    get {return _msg;}
    set {_msg = value;}
  }
}
```

You can see that all an EventArgs-based class does is carry information about an event to and from the sender and receiver. Most times the information used from the EventArgs class will be used by the receiver object in the event handler. However, sometimes the event handler can add information into the EventArgs class and it will be available to the sender. This is how the example will be using the EventArgs class. Notice that there are a couple of constructors available in the EventArgs class. This extra flexibility adds to the usability of the class by others.

At this point, an event has been declared, the delegate has been defined and the EventArgs class has been created. The next thing that has to happen is that the event needs to be raised. The only thing that really needs to be done is to make a call to the event with the proper parameters as shown in this example:

```
ActionCancelEventArgs ev = new CancelEventArgs();
Action(this, ev);
```

Simple enough. Create the new ActionCancelEventArgs class and pass it in as one of the parameters to the event. However, there is one small problem. What if the event hasn't been used anywhere yet. What if an event handler has not yet been defined for the event. The Action event would actually be null. If you tried to raise the event, you would get a null reference exception. If you wanted to derive a new form class and use the form that has the Action event defined as the base, you would have to do something else whenever the Action event is raised. Currently you would have to enable another event handler in the derived form in order to get access to it. In order to make this process a little easier and to catch the null reference error you have to create a method with the name OnEventName where

EventName is the name of the event. In the example there is a method named OnAction. Here is the complete code for the OnAction method.

```
protected void OnAction(object sender, ActionCancelEventArgs ev)
{
  if(Action != null)
    Action(sender, ev);
}
```

Not much to it but it does accomplish what is needed. By making the method protected then only derived classes have access to it. You can also see that the event is tested against null before it is raised. If you were to derive a new class that contains this method and event, you would have to override the OnAction method and then you would be hooked into the event. To do this, you would have to call base.OnAction() in the override. Otherwise the event would not be raised. This naming convention is used throughout the .NET Framework and is documented in the .NET SDK documentation.

Notice the two parameters that are passed into the OnAction method. They should look familiar to you since they are the same parameters that will need to be passed to the event. If the event would need to be raised from another object other than the one that the method is defined in, then you would need to make the accessor internal or public and not protected. Sometimes it makes sense to have a class that consists of nothing but event declarations and that these events are called from other classes. You would still want to create the OnEventName methods. However, in that case they might be static methods.

So now that the event has been raised, something needs to handle it. Create a new class in the project. In this sample we called it BusEntity. Remember that the goal of this project is to check the seconds property of the current time, and if it is less than 30, set a string value to the time and if it is greater than 30 set the string to : : and cancel the event. Here is the code:

```
using System;
using System.IO;
using System.ComponentModel;

namespace SimpleEvent
{
  public class BusEntity
  {

    string _time = "";

    public BusEntity()
    {
      Form1.Action += new Form1.ActionEventHandler(Form1_Action);
    }

    private void Form1_Action(object sender, ActionCancelEventArgs ev)
    {
      ev.Cancel = !DoActions();
      if(ev.Cancel)
        ev.Message = "Wasn't the right time.";
    }

    private bool DoActions()
    {
```

```
          bool retVal = false;
          DateTime tm = DateTime.Now;

          if(tm.Second < 30)
          {
            _time = "The time is " + DateTime.Now.ToLongTimeString();
            retVal = true;
          }
          else
            _time = "";

          return retVal;

        }

      public string TimeString
      {
        get {return _time;}
      }

    }
  }
```

In the constructor the handler for the `Form1.Action` event is declared. Notice the syntax is very similar to the Click event that we registered earlier. Since we used the same pattern for declaring the event the usage syntax stays consistent as well. Something else that is worth mentioning at this point is how you were able to get a reference to the Action event without having a reference to Form1 in the BusEntity class. Remember in the Form1 class the Action event is declared static. This isn't a requirement, but it does make it easier to create the handler. You could have declared the event public, but then an instance of Form1 would need to be referenced.

When we coded the event in the constructor, we called the method that was added to the delegate list Form1_Action, in keeping with the naming standards. In the handler a decision on whether or not to cancel the event needs to be done. The `DoActions` method returns a Boolean value based on the time criteria that we described earlier. DoAction also sets the _time string to the proper value.

After the `DoActions` return value is set to the `ActionCancelEventArgs Cancel` property. Remember that `EventArg` classes generally do not do anything other then carry values to and from the event senders and receivers. If the event is cancelled (`ev.Cancel = true`), the Message property is also set with a string value that describes why the event was cancelled.

Now if you look at the code in the btnRaise_Click event handler again you will be able to see how the Cancel property is used.

```
private void btnRaise_Click(object sender, EventArgs e)
{
  ActionCancelEventArgs cancelEvent = new ActionCancelEventArgs();
  OnAction(this, cancelEvent);
  if(cancelEvent.Cancel)
    lblInfo.Text = cancelEvent.Message;
  else
    lblInfo.Text = _busEntity.TimeString;
}
```

Note that the `ActionCancelEventArgs` object is created. Next the event Action is raised, passing in the newly created `ActionCancelEventArgs` object. When the `OnAction` method is called and the event is raised, the code in the Action event handler in the BusEntity object is executed. If there were other objects that had registered for the Action event, they too would execute. Something to keep in mind is that if there were other objects handling this event, they would all see the same `ActionCancelEventArgs` object. If you needed to keep up with which object canceled the event and if more than one object canceled the event, then you would need some type of list-based data structure in the `ActionCancelEventArgs` class.

After the handlers that have been registered with the event delegate have been executed, you can query the `ActionCancelEventArgs` object to see if it has been canceled. If it has been cancelled, then lblInfo will contain the Message property value. If the event has not been canceled, the lblInfo will show the current time.

This should give you the basic idea of how you can utilize events and the `EventArgs`-based object in the event to pass information around in your applications.

Summary

This chapter gave you the basics of delegates and events. We explained how to declare a delegate and add methods to the delegate list. We also explained the process of declaring event handlers to respond to an event, as well as how to create a custom event and use the patterns for raising the vent.

As a .NET developer, you will be using delegates and events extensively,, especially when developing Windows Forms applications. Events are the means that the .NET developer has to monitor the various Windows messages that occur while the application is executing. Otherwise you would have to monitor the WndProc and catch the WM_MOUSEDOWN message instead of getting the mouse Click event for a button.

The use of delegates and events in the design of a large application can reduce dependencies and the coupling of layers. This allows you to develop components that have a higher reusability factor.

7

Memory Management and Pointers

In this chapter we look at various aspects of memory management and memory access. Although the runtime takes much of the responsibility for memory management away from the programmer, you must still understand how memory management works and know what to do when working with unmanaged resources.

If you have a good understanding of memory management and knowledge of the pointer capabilities provided by C#, you are also better positioned to integrate C# code with legacy code and perform highly efficient memory manipulation in performance-critical systems.

Specifically, this chapter discusses:

❑ How the runtime allocates space on the stack and the heap

❑ How garbage collection works

❑ How to use destructors and the `System.IDisposable` interface to ensure unmanaged resources are released correctly

❑ The syntax for using pointers in C#

❑ How to use pointers to implement high-performance stack-based arrays

Memory Management under the Hood

One of the advantages of C# programming is that the programmer doesn't need to worry about detailed memory management; in particular the garbage collector deals with the problem of memory cleanup on your behalf. The result is that you get something that approximates the efficiency of languages like C++ without the complexity of having to handle memory management yourself as you do in C++. However, although you don't have to manage memory manually, if you need to write efficient code, it still pays to understand what is going on behind the scenes. In this section we will take a look at what happens in the computer's memory when you allocate variables.

The precise details of much of the content of this section are undocumented. You should interpret this section as a simplified guide to the general processes rather than as a statement of exact implementation.

Value Data Types

Windows uses a system known as *virtual addressing*, in which the mapping from the memory address seen by your program to the actual location in hardware memory is entirely managed by Windows. The result of this is that each process on a 32-bit processor sees 4GB of available memory, irrespective of how much hardware memory you actually have in your computer (on 64-bit processors this number will be greater). This 4GB of memory contains everything that is part of the program, including the executable code, any DLLs loaded by the code, and the contents of all variables used when the program runs. This 4GB of memory is known as the *virtual address space* or *virtual memory*. For convenience we will continue referring to it simply as *memory*.

Each memory location in the available 4GB is numbered starting from zero. To access a value stored at a particular location in memory, you need to supply the number that represents that memory location. In any compiled high-level language, including C#, Visual Basic, C++, and Java, the compiler converts human-readable variable names into memory addresses that the processor understands.

Somewhere inside a process' virtual memory is an area known as the *stack*. The stack stores value data types that are not members of objects. In addition, when you call a method, the stack is used to hold a copy of any parameters passed to the method. In order to understand how the stack works, we need to understand the importance of variable scope in C#. It is *always* the case that if a variable a goes into scope before variable b, then b will go out of scope first. Look at this code:

```
{
    int a;
    // do something
    {
        int b;
        // do something else
    }
}
```

First, a gets declared. Then, inside the inner code block, b gets declared. Then the inner code block terminates and b goes out of scope, then a goes out of scope. So, the lifetime of b is entirely contained within the lifetime of a. This idea that you always deallocate variables in the reverse order to how you allocate them is crucial to the way that the stack works.

We don't know exactly where in the address space the stack is—we don't need to know for C# development. A *stack pointer* (a variable maintained by the operating system) identifies the next free location on the stack. When your program first starts running, the stack pointer will point to just past the end of the block of memory that is reserved for the stack. The stack actually fills downward, from high memory addresses to low addresses. As data is put on the stack, the stack pointer is adjusted accordingly, so it always points to just past the next free location. This illustrated in Figure 7-1, which shows a stack pointer with a value of 800000 (0xC3500 in hex) and the next free location is the address 799999.

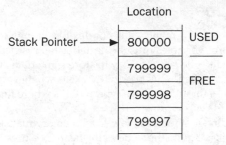

Figure 7-1

In the following code we have instructed the compiler that we need space in memory to store an integer and a double, and that these memory locations are to be referred to as nRacingCars and engineSize. The line that declares each variable indicates the point at which we will start requiring access to this variable, and the closing curly brace of the block in which the variables are declared identifies the point at which both variables go out of scope.

```
{
    int nRacingCars = 10;
    double engineSize = 3000.0;
    // do calculations;
}
```

Assuming we use the stack shown in Figure 7-1, when the variable nRacingCars comes into scope and is assigned the value 10, the value 10 is placed in locations 799996 through 799999, the four bytes just below the location pointed to by the stack pointer. (Four bytes because that's how much memory is needed to store an int.) To accommodate this, 4 is subtracted from the value of the stack pointer, so it now points to the location 799996, just after the new first free location (799995).

The next line of code declares the variable engineSize (a double) and initializes it to the value 3000.0. A double occupies 8 bytes, so the value 3000.0 will be placed in locations 799988 through 799995 on the stack, and the stack pointer is decremented by 8, so that once again, it points just after the next free location on the stack.

When engineSize goes out of scope, the computer knows that it is no longer needed. Due to the way variable lifetimes are always nested, we can guarantee that, whatever else has happened while engineSize was in scope, the stack pointer is now pointing to the location where engineSize is stored. To remove engineSize from the stack, the stack pointer is incremented by 8, so that it now points to the location immediately after the end of engineSize. At this point in our code, we are at the closing curly brace and so nRacingCars also goes out of scope. The stack pointer gets incremented by 4. When another variable comes into scope after engineSize and nRacingCars have been removed from the stack, it would overwrite the memory descending from location 799999, where nRacingCars used to be stored.

If the compiler hits a line like int i, j, the order of coming into scope looks indeterminate. Both variables are declared at the same time and go out of scope at the same time. In this situation, it doesn't matter to us in what order the two variables are removed from memory. The compiler internally always ensures that the one that was put in memory first is removed last, thus preserving our rule about no crossover of variable lifetimes.

Reference Data Types

While the stack gives very high performance, it is not flexible enough to be used for all variables. The requirement that the lifetimes of variables must be nested is too restrictive for many purposes. Often, you will want to use a method to allocate memory to store some data and be able to keep that data available long after that method has exited. This possibility exists whenever storage space is requested with the new operator—as is the case for all reference types. That's where the *managed heap* comes in.

If you have done any C++ coding that required low-level memory management, you will be familiar with the heap. The managed heap is not quite the same as the heap C++ uses; the managed heap works under the control of the garbage collector and provides significant benefits when compared to traditional heaps.

The managed heap (or heap for short) is just another area of memory from the process's available 4GB. The following code demonstrates how the heap works and how memory is allocated for reference data types:

```
void DoWork()
{
    Customer arabel;
    arabel = new Customer();
    Customer mrJones = new Nevermore60Customer();
}
```

In this code, we have assumed the existence of two classes, Customer and Nevermore60Customer. These classes are in fact taken from the Mortimer Phones examples in Appendix A (which is posted at www.wrox.com).

First, we declare a Customer reference called arabel. The space for this will be allocated on the stack, but remember that this is only a reference, not an actual Customer object. The arabel reference takes up 4 bytes, enough space to hold the address at which a Customer object will be stored. (We need 4 bytes to represent a memory address as an integer value between 0 and 4GB.)

Then we get to the next line:

```
arabel = new Customer();
```

This line of code does several things. First, it allocates memory on the heap to store a Customer object (a real object, not just an address). Then, it sets the value of the variable arabel to the address of the memory it has allocated to the new Customer object. (It also calls the appropriate Customer() constructor to initialize the fields in the class instance, but we won't worry about that here.)

The Customer instance is not placed on the stack—it is placed on the heap. In this example, we don't know precisely how many bytes a Customer object occupies, but let's say for the sake of argument it is 32. These 32 bytes contain the instance fields of Customer as well as some information that .NET uses to identify and manage its class instances.

To find a storage location on the heap for the new Customer object, the .NET runtime will look through the heap and grab the first contiguous, unused block of 32 bytes. For the sake of argument, we will say that this happens to be at address 200000, and that the arabel reference occupied locations 799996 through 799999 on the stack. This means that before instantiating the arabel object, the memory contents will look similar to Figure 7-2.

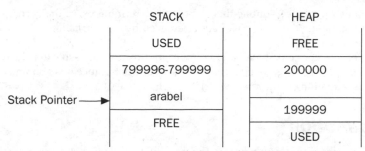

Figure 7-2

After allocating the new `Customer` object, the contents of memory will look like Figure 7-3. Note that unlike the stack, memory in the heap is allocated upwards, so the free space can be found above the used space.

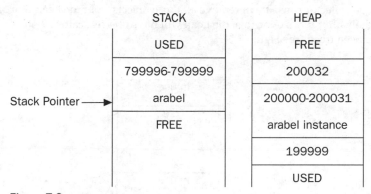

Figure 7-3

The next line of code both declares a `Customer` reference and instantiates a `Customer` object. In this instance, space on the stack for the `mrJones` reference is allocated at the same time as the space for `mrJones` object is allocated on the heap:

```
Customer mrJones = new Nevermore60Customer();
```

This line allocates 4 bytes on the stack to hold the `mrJones` reference, stored at locations `799992` through `799995` The `mrJones` object is allocated starting at location `200032`.

It is clear from the example that the process of setting up a reference variable is more complex than that for setting up a value variable, and there is a performance overhead. In fact we have somewhat oversimplified the process, since the .NET runtime needs to maintain information about the state of the heap, and this information needs to be updated whenever new data is added to the heap. Despite these overheads, we now have a mechanism for allocating variables that is not constrained by the limitations of the stack. By assigning the value of one reference variable to another of the same type, you have two variables that reference the same object in memory. When a reference variable goes out of scope, it is removed from the stack as we described in the previous section, but the data for a referenced object is still sitting on the heap.

The data will remain on the heap until either the program terminates, or the garbage collector removes it, which will only happen when it is no longer referenced by any variables.

That's the power of reference data types, and you will see this feature used extensively in C# code. It means that we have a high degree of control over the lifetime of our data, since it is guaranteed to exist in the heap as long as we are maintaining some reference to it.

Garbage Collection

The previous discussion and diagrams show the managed heap working very much like the stack, to the extent that successive objects are placed next to each other in memory. This means that we can work out where to place the next object by using a heap pointer that indicates the next free memory location, and which gets adjusted as we add more objects to the heap. However, things are complicated because the lives of the heap-based objects are not coupled to the scope of the individual stack-based variables that reference them.

When the garbage collector runs, it will remove all those objects from the heap that are no longer referenced. Immediately after it has done this, the heap will have objects scattered on it, mixed up with memory that has just been freed (see Figure 7-4).

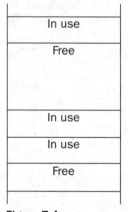

Figure 7-4

If the managed heap stayed like this, allocating space for new objects would be an awkward process, with the runtime having to search through the heap for a block of memory big enough to store each new object. However, the garbage collector doesn't leave the heap in this state. As soon as the garbage collector has freed up all the objects it can, it compacts the heap by moving all remaining objects to form one contiguous block of memory. This means that the heap can continue working just like the stack as far as locating where to store new objects is concerned. Of course, when the objects are moved about, all the references to those objects need to be updated with the correct new addresses, but the garbage collector handles that too.

This action of compacting by the garbage collector is where the managed heap really works differently from old unmanaged heaps. With the managed heap, it is just a question of reading the value of the heap pointer, rather than iterating through a linked list of addresses to find somewhere to put the new data. For this reason, instantiating an object under .NET is much faster. Interestingly, accessing objects tends to be faster too, since the objects are compacted towards the same area of memory on the heap, resulting in less page swapping. Microsoft believes that these performance gains more than compensate for the performance penalty that we get whenever the garbage collector needs to do some work to compact the heap and change all those references to objects it has moved.

Generally, the garbage collector runs when the .NET runtime determines that a garbage collection is required. You can force the garbage collector to run at a certain point in your code by calling `System` `.GC.Collect()`*. The* `System.GC` *class is a .NET class that represents the garbage collector, and the* `Collect()` *method initiates a garbage collection. The* `GC` *class is intended for rare situations in which you know that it's a good time to call the garbage collector; for example, if you have just dereferenced a large number of objects in your code. However, the logic of the garbage collector does not guarantee that all unreferenced objects will be removed form the heap in a single garbage collection pass.*

Freeing Unmanaged Resources

The presence of the garbage collector means that you will usually not worry about objects that you no longer need; you will simply allow all references to those objects to go out of scope and allow the garbage collector to free memory as required. However, the garbage collector does not know how to free unmanaged resources (such as file handles, network connections, and database connections). When managed classes encapsulate direct or indirect references to unmanaged resources, you need to make special provision to ensure the unmanaged resources are released when an instance of the class is garbage collected.

When defining a class, there are two mechanisms you can use to automate the freeing of unmanaged resources. These mechanisms are often implemented together as each provides a slightly different approach to the solution of the problem. The mechanisms are:

❑   Declaring a destructor (or finalizer) as a member of your class

❑   Implementing the `System.IDisposable` interface in your class

We will discuss each of these mechanisms in turn, and then look at how to implement them together for best effect.

Destructors

We've seen that constructors allow you to specify actions that must take place whenever an instance of a class is created. Conversely, destructors are called before an object is destroyed by the garbage collector. Given this behavior, a destructor would initially seem like a great place to put code to free unmanaged resources and perform a general cleanup. Unfortunately, things are not so straightforward.

Although we talk about destructors in C#, in the underlying .NET architecture, these are known as finalizers. When you define a destructor in C#, what is emitted into the assembly by the compiler is actually a method called `Finalize()`*. That's something that doesn't affect any of your source code, but you'll need to be aware of the fact if you need to examine the contents of an assembly.*

The syntax for a destructor will be familiar to C++ developers. It looks like a method, with the same name as the containing class, but prefixed with a tilde (~). It has no return type, and takes no parameters and no access modifiers. Here is an example:

```
class MyClass
{
   ~MyClass()
   {
      // implementation
   }
}
```

When the C# compiler compiles a destructor, it implicitly translates the destructor code to the equivalent of a `Finalize()` method that ensures the `Finalize()` method of the parent class is executed. The following example shows the C# code equivalent to the IL that the compiler would generate for the ~MyClass destructor:

```
protected override void Finalize()
{
   try
   {
      // implementation
   }
   finally
   {
      base.Finalize();
   }
}
```

As shown, the code implemented in the ~MyClass destructor is wrapped in a `try` block contained in the `Finalize()` method. A call to the parent's `Finalize()` method is ensured by placing the call in a `finally` block. We discuss `try` and `finally` blocks in Chapter 11.

Experienced C++ developers make extensive use of destructors, and sometimes not only to clean up resources, but also to provide debugging information or perform other tasks. C# destructors are used far less than their C++ equivalents. The problem with C# destructors when compared with their C++ counterparts is that they are non deterministic. When a C++ object is destroyed, its destructor runs immediately. However, because of the way the garbage collector works, there is no way to know when an object's destructor will actually execute. Hence, you cannot place any code in the destructor that relies on being run at a certain time, and you shouldn't rely on the destructor being called for different class instances in any particular order. When your object is holding scarce and critical resources need to be freed as soon as possible, you don't want to wait for garbage collection.

Another problem is that the implementation of a destructor delays the final removal of an object from memory. Objects that do not have a destructor get removed from memory in one pass of the garbage collector, but objects that have destructors require two passes to be destroyed: the first one calls the destructor without removing the object, the second actually deletes the object. In addition, the runtime uses a single thread to execute the `Finalize()` methods of all objects. If you use destructors frequently, and use them to execute lengthy cleanup tasks, the impact on performance can be noticeable.

The IDisposable Interface

The recommended alternative to using a destructor is using the `System.IDisposable` interface. The `IDisposable` interface defines a pattern (with language-level support) that provides a deterministic mechanism for freeing unmanaged resources and avoids the garbage collector–related problems inherent with destructors. The `IDisposable` interface declares a single method named `Dispose()`, which takes no parameters and returns `void`. Here is an implementation for `MyClass`:

```
class MyClass : IDisposable
{
   public void Dispose()
   {
      // implementation
   }
}
```

The implementation of `Dispose()` should explicitly free all unmanaged resources used directly by an object and call `Dispose()` on any encapsulated objects that also implement the `IDisposable` interface. In this way, the `Dispose()` method provides precise control over when unmanaged resources are freed.

Suppose we have a class named `ResourceGobbler`, which relies on the use of some external resource and implements `IDisposable`. If we want to instantiate an instance of this class, use it, and then dispose of it, we could do it like this:

```
ResourceGobbler theInstance = new ResourceGobbler();

// do your processing

theInstance.Dispose();
```

Unfortunately, this code fails to free the resources consumed by `theInstance` if an exception occurs during processing, and so we should write the code as follows using a `try` block (which we discuss fully in Chapter 11):

```
ResourceGobbler theInstance = null;

try
{
   theInstance = new ResourceGobbler();

   // do your processing
}
finally
{
   if (theInstance != null) theInstance.Dispose();
}
```

This version ensures that `Dispose()` is always called on `theInstance` and that any resources consumed by it are always freed, even if an exception occurs during processing. However, it would make for confusing code if you always had to repeat such a construct. C# offers a syntax that you can use to guarantee that `Dispose()` will automatically be called against an object that implements `IDisposable` when its reference goes out of scope. The syntax to do this involves the `using` keyword—though now in a very different context, which has nothing to do with namespaces. The following code generates IL code equivalent to the `try` block just shown:

```
using (ResourceGobbler theInstance = new ResourceGobbler())
{
   // do your processing
}
```

The `using` statement, followed in brackets by a reference variable declaration and instantiation, will cause that variable to be scoped to the accompanying statement block. In addition, when that variable goes out of scope, its `Dispose()` method will be called automatically, even if exceptions occur. If you are already using `try` blocks to catch other exceptions, it is cleaner and avoids additional code indentation if you avoid the `using` statement and simply call `Dispose()` in the `Finally` clause of the existing `try` block.

*For some classes, the notion of a **Close()** method is more logical than **Dispose()**; for example, when dealing with files or database connections. In these cases it is common to implement the **IDisposable** interface and then implement a separate **Close()** method that simply calls **Dispose()**. This approach provides clarity in the use of your classes, but also supports the **using** statement provided by C#.*

Implementing IDisposable and a Destructor

In the previous sections we discussed two alternatives for freeing unmanaged resources used by the classes you create:

❑　The execution of a destructor is enforced by the runtime but is nondeterministic and places an unacceptable overhead on the runtime because of the way garbage collection works.

❑　The `IDisposable` interface provides a mechanism that allows users of a class to control when resources are freed, but requires discipline to ensure that `Dispose()` is called.

In general, the best approach is to implement both mechanisms in order to gain the benefits of both while overcoming their limitations. You implement `IDisposable` on the assumption that most programmers will call `Dispose()` correctly, but implement a destructor as a safety mechanism in case `Dispose()` is not called. Here is an example of a dual implementation:

```
public class ResourceHolder : IDisposable
{

   private bool isDisposed = false;

   public void Dispose()
   {
      Dispose(true);
      GC.SuppressFinalize(this);
   }

   protected virtual void Dispose(bool disposing)
   {
      if (!isDisposed)
      {
         if (disposing)
{
```

```
            // Cleanup managed objects by calling their
            // Dispose() methods.
        }
        // Cleanup unmanaged objects
    }
    isDisposed = true;
}

~ResourceHolder()
{
    Dispose (false);
}
}
```

You can see from this code that there is a second `protected` overload of `Dispose()`, which takes one `bool` parameter—and this is the method that does all cleaning up. `Dispose(bool)` is called by both the destructor and by `IDisposable.Dispose()`. The point of this approach is to ensure that all cleanup code is in one place.

The parameter passed to `Dispose(bool)` indicates whether `Dispose(bool)` has been invoked by the destructor or by `IDisposable.Dispose()`—`Dispose(bool)` should not be invoked from anywhere else in your code. The idea is this:

❑   If a consumer calls `IDisposable.Dispose()`, then that consumer is indicating that all managed and unmanaged resources associated with that object should be cleaned up.

❑   If a destructor has been invoked, then all resources still need to be cleaned up. However, in this case, we know that the destructor must have been called by the garbage collector and we should not attempt to access other managed objects because we can no longer be certain of their state. In this situation, the best we can do is clean up the known unmanaged resources, and hope that any referenced managed objects also have destructors that will perform their own cleaning up.

The `isDisposed` member variable indicates whether the object has already been disposed and allows us to ensure we do not try to dispose of member variables more than once. This simplistic approach is not thread-safe and depends on the caller ensuring only one thread is calling the method concurrently. Requiring a consumer to enforce synchronization is a reasonable assumption and one that is used repeatedly throughout the .NET class libraries (in the Collection classes for example). We discuss threading and synchronization in Chapter 15.

Finally, `IDisposable.Dispose()` contains a call to the method `System.GC.SuppressFinalize()`. `GC` is the class that represents the garbage collector, and the `SuppressFinalize()` method tells the garbage collector that a class no longer needs to have its destructor called. Since our implementation of `Dispose()` has already done all the cleanup required, there's nothing left for the destructor to do. Calling `Suppress Finalize()` means that the garbage collector will treat that object as if it doesn't have a destructor at all.

Unsafe Code

As we have just seen, C# is very good at hiding much of the basic memory management from the developer, thanks to the garbage collector and the use of references. However, there are cases in which you will want direct access to memory. For example, you might want to access a function in an external (non-.NET)

DLL that requires a pointer to be passed as a parameter (as many Windows API functions do), or possibly for performance reasons. In this section, we will examine C#'s facilities that provide direct access to the contents of memory.

Pointers

Although we are introducing *pointers* as if they are a new topic, in reality pointers are not new to us at all. We have been using references freely in our code, and a reference is simply a type-safe pointer. We have already seen how variables that represent objects and arrays actually store the address in memory of where the corresponding data (the *referent*) is stored. A pointer is simply a variable that stores the address of something else in the same way as a reference. The difference is that C# does not allow you direct access to the address contained in a reference variable. With a reference, the variable is treated syntactically as if it stores the actual contents of the referent.

C# references are designed to make the language simpler to use, and to prevent you from inadvertently doing something that corrupts the contents of memory. With a pointer, on the other hand, the actual memory address is available to you. This gives you a lot of power to perform new kinds of operations. For example, you can add 4 bytes to the address, so that you can examine or even modify whatever data happens to be stored 4 bytes further on.

There are two main reasons for using pointers:

❑ **Backwards compatibility**—Despite all of the facilities provided by the .NET runtime, it is still possible to call native Windows API functions, and for some operations, this may be the only way to accomplish your task. These API functions are generally written in C and often require pointers as parameters. However, in many cases it is possible to write the DllImport declaration in a way that avoids use of pointers, for example, by using the System.IntPtr class.

❑ **Performance**—On those occasions where speed is of the utmost importance, pointers can provide a route to optimized performance. Provided you know what you are doing, you can ensure that data is accessed or manipulated in the most efficient way. However, be aware that more often than not, there are other areas of your code where you can make the necessary performance improvements without resorting to using pointers. Try using a code profiler to look for the bottlenecks in your code—one comes with Visual Studio .NET.

Low-level memory access comes at a price. The syntax for using pointers is more complex than that for reference types and pointers are unquestionably more difficult to use correctly. You need good programming skills and an excellent ability to think carefully and logically about what your code is doing in order to use pointers successfully. If you are not careful, it is very easy to introduce subtle, difficult to find bugs into your program using pointers. For example, it is easy to overwrite other variables, cause stack overflows, access areas of memory that don't store any variables, or even overwrite information about your code that is needed by the .NET runtime, thereby crashing your program.

In addition, if you use pointers your code must be granted a high level of trust by the code access security mechanism or it will not be allowed to execute. Under the default code access security policy, this is only possible if your code is running on the local machine. If your code must be run from a remote location, such as the Internet, users must grant your code additional permissions for it to work. Unless the user trusts you and your code, they are unlikely to grant these permissions. We discuss code access security more in Chapter 14.

Despite these issues, pointers remain a very powerful and flexible tool in the writing of efficient code and are worth learning about.

We strongly advise against using pointers unnecessarily because your code will not only be harder to write and debug, but it will also fail the memory type-safety checks imposed by the CLR, which we discussed in Chapter 1.

Writing unsafe code

Due to the risks associated with pointers, C# only allows the use of pointers in blocks of code that you have specifically marked for this purpose. The keyword to do this is unsafe. You can mark an individual method as being unsafe like this:

```
unsafe int GetSomeNumber()
{
    // code that can use pointers
}
```

Any method can be marked as unsafe, irrespective of what other modifiers have been applied to it (for example, static methods, or virtual methods). In the case of methods, the unsafe modifier applies to the method's parameters, allowing you to use pointers as parameters. You can also mark an entire class or struct as unsafe, which means that all of its members are assumed to be unsafe:

```
unsafe class MyClass
{
    // any method in this class can now use pointers
}
```

Similarly, you can mark a member as unsafe:

```
class MyClass
{
    unsafe int *pX;   // declaration of a pointer field in a class
}
```

Or you can mark a block of code within a method as unsafe:

```
void MyMethod()
{
    // code that doesn't use pointers
    unsafe
    {
        // unsafe code that uses pointers here
    }
    // more 'safe' code that doesn't use pointers
}
```

Note, however, that you cannot mark a local variable by itself as unsafe:

```
int MyMethod()
{
    unsafe int *pX;   // WRONG
}
```

If you want to use an unsafe local variable, you will need to declare and use it inside a method or block that is unsafe. There is one more step before you can use pointers. The C# compiler rejects unsafe code unless you tell it that your code includes unsafe blocks. The flag to do this is `unsafe`. Hence, to compile a file named `MySource.cs` that contains unsafe blocks (assuming no other compiler options), the command is:

csc /unsafe MySource.cs

or:

csc –unsafe MySource.cs

If you are using Visual Studio .NET, you will find the option to compile unsafe code in the project properties. For the Visual Studio .NET versions of the downloadable samples in this section, you will find that we have already set the unsafe compilation option.

Pointer syntax

Once you have marked a block of code as `unsafe`, you can declare a pointer using this syntax:

```
int* pWidth, pHeight;
double* pResult;
byte*[] pFlags;
```

This code declares four variables: `pWidth` and `pHeight` are pointers to integers, `pResult` is a pointer to a `double`, and `pFlags` is an array of pointers to bytes. It is common practice to use the prefix p in front of names of pointer variables to indicate that they are pointers. When used in a variable declaration, the symbol * indicates that you are declaring a pointer, in other words, something that stores the address of a variable of the specified type.

*C++ developers should be aware of the syntax difference between C++ and C#. The C# statement `int* pX, pY;` corresponds to the C++ statement `int *pX, *pY;`. In C#, the * symbol is associated with the type rather than the variable name.*

Once you have declared variables of pointer types, you can use them in the same way as normal variables, but first you need to learn two more operators:

❑ & means *take the address of*, and converts a value data type to a pointer, for example `int` to `*int`. This operator is known as the *address operator*.

❑ * means *get the contents of this address*, and converts a pointer to a value data type (for example, `*float` to `float`). This operator is known as the *indirection operator* (or sometimes as the *dereference operator*).

You will see from these definitions that & and * have the opposite effect to one another.

*You might be wondering how it is possible to use the symbols & and * in this manner, since these symbols also refer to the operators of bitwise AND (&) and multiplication (*). Actually, it is always possible for both you and the compiler to know what is meant in each case, because with the new pointer meanings, these symbols always appear as unary operators—they only act on one variable and appear in front of that variable in your code. On the other hand, bitwise AND and multiplication are binary operators— they require two operands.*

The following code shows examples of how to use these operators:

```
int x = 10;
int* pX, pY;
pX = &x;
pY = pX;
*pY = 20;
```

We start off by declaring an integer, x, followed by two pointers to integers, pX and pY. We then set pX to point to x (in other words, we set the contents of pX to be the address of x). Then we assign the value of pX to pY, so that pY also points to x. Finally, in the statement *pY = 20, we assign the value 20 as the contents of the location pointed to by pY—in effect changing x to 20 since pY happens to point to x. Note that there is no particular connection between the variables pY and x. It's just that at the present time, pY happens to point to the memory location at which x is held.

To get a better understanding of what is going on, consider that the integer x is stored at memory locations 0x12F8C4 through 0x12F8C7 (1243332 to 1243335 in decimal) on the stack (there are 4 locations because an int occupies 4 bytes). Since the stack allocates memory downward, this means that the variables pX will be stored at locations 0x12F8C0 to 0x12F8C3, and pY will end up at locations 0x12F8BC to 0x12F8BF. Note that pX and pY also occupy 4 bytes each. That is not because an int occupies 4 bytes. It's because on a 32-bit processor you need 4 bytes to store an address. With these addresses, after executing the previous code, the stack will look like Figure 7-5.

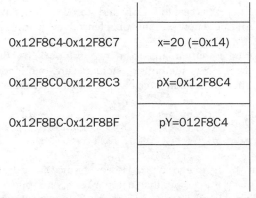

0x12F8C4-0x12F8C7	x=20 (=0x14)
0x12F8C0-0x12F8C3	pX=0x12F8C4
0x12F8BC-0x12F8BF	pY=012F8C4

Figure 7-5

Although we have illustrated this process with integers, which will be stored consecutively on the stack on a 32-bit processor, this doesn't happen for all data types. The reason is that 32-bit processors work best retrieving data from memory in 4-byte chunks. Memory on such machines tends to be divided into 4-byte blocks, and each block is sometimes known under Windows as a DWORD because this was the name of a 32-bit unsigned int in pre-.NET days. It is most efficient to grab DWORDs from memory— storing data across DWORD boundaries normally gives a hardware performance hit. For this reason, the .NET runtime normally pads out data types so that the memory they occupy is a multiple of 4. For example, a short occupies 2 bytes, but if a short is placed on the stack, the stack pointer will still be decremented by 4, not 2, so that the next variable to go on the stack will still start at a DWORD boundary.

You can declare a pointer to any value type, in other words, any of the predefined types uint, int, byte, and so on, or to a struct. However, it is not possible to declare a pointer to a class or array; this is because doing so could cause problems for the garbage collector. In order to work properly, the garbage collector needs to know exactly what class instances have been created on the heap, and where they are, but if your code started manipulating classes using pointers, you could very easily corrupt the information on the heap concerning classes that the .NET runtime maintains for the garbage collector. In this context, any data type that the garbage collector can access is known as a *managed type*. Pointers can only be declared as *unmanaged types* since the garbage collector cannot deal with them.

Casting pointers to integer types

Since a pointer really stores an integer that represents an address, you won't be surprised to know that the address in any pointer can be converted to or from any integer type. Pointer-to-integer-type conversions must be explicit. Implicit conversions are not available for such conversions. For example, it is perfectly legitimate to write the following:

```
int x = 10;
int* pX, pY;
pX = &x;
pY = pX;
*pY = 20;
uint y = (uint)pX;
int* pD = (int*)y;
```

The address held in the pointer pX is cast to a uint and stored in the variable y. We have then cast y back to an int* and stored it in the new variable pD. Hence, now pD also points to the value of x.

The primary reason for casting a pointer value to an integer type is in order to display it. The Console.Write() and Console.WriteLine() methods do not have any overloads that can take pointers, but will accept and display pointer values that have been cast to integer types:

```
Console.WriteLine("Address is " + pX);    // wrong -- will give a
                                           // compilation error
Console.WriteLine("Address is " + (uint)pX);   // OK
```

You can cast a pointer to any of the integer types. However, since an address occupies 4 bytes on 32-bit systems, casting a pointer to anything other than a uint, long, or ulong is almost certain to lead to overflow errors. (An int causes problems because its range is from roughly -2 billion to 2 billion, whereas an address runs from zero to about 4 billion.) When C# is released for 64-bit processors, an address will occupy 8 bytes. Hence, on such systems, casting a pointer to anything other than ulong is likely to lead to overflow errors. It is also important to be aware that the checked keyword does not apply to conversions involving pointers. For such conversions, exceptions will not be raised when overflows occur, even in a checked context. The .NET runtime assumes that if you are using pointers you know what you are doing and not worried about possible overflows.

Casting between pointer types

You can also explicitly convert between pointers pointing to different types. For example:

```
byte aByte = 8;
byte* pByte= &aByte;
double* pDouble = (double*)pByte;
```

This is perfectly legal code, though again, if you try something like this, be careful. In the previous example, if we look up the `double` pointed to by `pDouble`, we will actually be looking up some memory that contains a byte, combined with some other memory, and treating it as if this area of memory contained a double, which won't give a meaningful value. However, you might want to convert between types in order to implement a union, or you might want to cast pointers to other types into pointers to `sbyte` in order to examine individual bytes of memory.

void pointers

If you want to maintain a pointer, but do not want to specify what type of data it points to, you can declare it as a pointer to a `void`:

```
int* pointerToInt;
void* pointerToVoid;
pointerToVoid = (void*)pointerToInt;
```

The main use of this is if you need to call an API function that requires `void*` parameters. Within the C# language, there isn't a great deal that you can do using `void` pointers. In particular, the compiler will flag an error if you attempt to dereference a `void` pointer using the `*` operator.

Pointer arithmetic

It is possible to add or subtract integers to and from pointers. However, the compiler is quite clever about how it arranges for this to be done. For example, suppose you have a pointer to an `int`, and you try to add 1 to its value. The compiler will assume you actually mean you want to look at the memory location following the `int`, and hence will increase the value by 4 bytes—the size of an `int`. If it is a pointer to a `double`, adding 1 will actually increase the value of the pointer by 8 bytes, the size of a `double`. Only if the pointer points to a `byte` or `sbyte` (1 byte each) will adding 1 to the value of the pointer actually change its value by 1.

You can use the operators +, -, +=, -=, ++, and – with pointers, with the variable on the right-hand side of these operators being a `long` or `ulong`.

> *It is not permitted to carry out arithmetic operations on void pointers.*

For example, let's assume these definitions:

```
uint u = 3;
byte b = 8;
double d = 10.0;
uint* pUint= &u;          // size of a uint is 4
byte* pByte = &b;         // size of a byte is 1
double* pDouble = &d;     // size of a double is 8
```

Next, let's assume the addresses to which these pointers point are:

❑   pUint: 1243332

❑   pByte: 1243328

❑   pDouble: 1243320

Then execute this code:

```
++pUint;                // adds (1*4) = 4 bytes to pUint
pByte -= 3;             // subtracts (3*1) = 3 bytes from pByte
double* pDouble2 = pDouble + 4; // pDouble2 = pDouble + 32 bytes (4*8 bytes)
```

The pointers now contain:

❑   pUint: 1243336

❑   pByte: 1243325

❑   pDouble2: 1243352

> **The general rule is that adding a number X to a pointer to type T with value P gives the result P + X*(sizeof(T)).**

You need to be aware of the previous rule. If successive values of a given type are stored in successive memory locations, then pointer addition works very well to allow you to move pointers between memory locations. If you are dealing with types such as byte or char though, whose sizes are not multiples of 4, successive values will not by default be stored in successive memory locations.

You can also subtract one pointer from another pointer, provided both pointers point to the same data type. In this case, the result is a long whose value is given by the difference between the pointer values divided by the size of the type that they represent:

```
double* pD1 = (double*)1243324;   // note that it is perfectly valid to
                                  // initialize a pointer like this.
double* pD2 = (double*)1243300;
long L = pD1-pD2;                 // gives the result 3 (=24/sizeof(double))
```

The sizeof operator

Throughout this section, we have been referring to the sizes of various data types. If you need to use the size of a type in your code, you can use the sizeof operator, which takes the name of a data type as a parameter, and returns the number of bytes occupied by that type. For example:

```
int x = sizeof(double);
```

This will set x to the value 8.

The advantage of using sizeof is that you don't have to hardcode data type sizes in your code, making your code more portable. For the predefined data types, sizeof returns the following values:

sizeof(sbyte) = 1;	sizeof(byte) = 1;
sizeof(short) = 2;	sizeof(ushort) = 2;
sizeof(int) = 4;	sizeof(uint) = 4;

```
sizeof(long) = 8;              sizeof(ulong) = 8;

sizeof(char) = 2;              sizeof(float) = 4;

sizeof(double) = 8;            sizeof(bool) = 1;
```

You can also use `sizeof` for structs that you define yourself, though in that case, the result depends on what fields are in the struct. You cannot use `sizeof` for classes, and it can only be used in an `unsafe` code block.

Pointers to structs: The pointer member access operator

Pointers to structs work in exactly the same way as pointers to the predefined value types. There is, however, one condition—the struct must not contain any reference types. This is due to the restriction we mentioned earlier that pointers cannot point to any reference types. To avoid this, the compiler will flag an error if you create a pointer to any struct that contains any reference types.

Suppose we had a struct defined like this:

```
struct MyStruct
{
    public long X;
    public float F;
}
```

We could define a pointer to it like this:

```
MyStruct* pStruct;
```

Then we could initialize it like this:

```
MyStruct Struct = new MyStruct();
pStruct = &Struct;
```

It is also possible to access member values of a struct through the pointer:

```
(*pStruct).X = 4;
(*pStruct).F = 3.4f;
```

However, this syntax is a bit complex. For this reason, C# defines another operator that allows you to access members of structs through pointers using a simpler syntax. It is known as the *pointer member access operator*, and the symbol is a dash followed by a greater than sign, so it looks like an arrow: ->.

C++ developers will recognize the pointer member access operator, since C++ uses the same symbol for the same purpose.

Using the pointer member access operator, the previous code can be rewritten:

```
pStruct->X = 4;
pStruct->F = 3.4f;
```

You can also directly set up pointers of the appropriate type to point to fields within a struct:

```
long* pL = &(Struct.X);
float* pF = &(Struct.F);
```

or, equivalently:

```
long* pL = &(pStruct->X);
float* pF = &(pStruct->F);
```

Pointers to class members

We have indicated that it is not possible to create pointers to classes. That's because the garbage collector does not maintain any information about pointers, only about references, so creating pointers to classes could cause garbage collection to not work properly.

However, most classes do contain value type members, and you might wish to create pointers to them. This is possible, but requires a special syntax. For example, suppose we rewrite our struct from our previous example as a class:

```
class MyClass
{
   public long X;
   public float F;
}
```

Then you might want to create pointers to its fields, X and F, in the same way as we did earlier. Unfortunately, doing so will produce a compilation error:

```
MyClass myObject = new MyClass();
long* pL = &(myObject.X);   // wrong -- compilation error
float* pF = &(myObject.F);  // wrong -- compilation error
```

Although X and F are unmanaged types, they are embedded in an object, which sits on the heap. During garbage collection, the garbage collector might move MyObject to a new location, which would leave pL and pF pointing to the wrong memory addresses. Because of this the compiler will not let you assign addresses of members of managed types to pointers in this manner.

The solution is to use the `fixed` keyword, which tells the garbage collector that there may be pointers referencing members of certain objects, and so those objects must not be moved. The syntax for using `fixed` looks like this if we just want to declare one pointer:

```
MyClass myObject = new MyClass();
```

```
fixed (long* pObject = &(myObject.X))
{
   // do something
}
```

We define and initialize the pointer variable in the brackets following the keyword `fixed`. This pointer variable (`pObject` in the example) is scoped to the `fixed` block identified by the curly braces. In doing this, the garbage collector knows not to move the `myObject` object while the code inside the `fixed` block is executing.

If you want to declare more than one pointer, you can place multiple `fixed` statements before the same code block:

```
MyClass myObject = new MyClass();

fixed (long* pX = &(myObject.X))
fixed (float* pF = &(myObject.F))
{
    // do something
}
```

You can nest entire `fixed` blocks if you want to fix several pointers for different periods:

```
MyClass myObject = new MyClass();

fixed (long* pX = &(myObject.X))
{
    // do something with pX
    fixed (float* pF = &(myObject.F))
    {
        // do something else with pF
    }
}
```

You can also initialize several variables within the same `fixed` block, provided they are of the same type:

```
MyClass myObject = new MyClass();
MyClass myObject2 = new MyClass();
fixed (long* pX = &(myObject.X), pX2 = &(myObject2.X))
{
    // etc.
```

In all these cases, it is immaterial whether the various pointers you are declaring point to fields in the same or different objects or to static fields not associated with any class instance.

Pointer Example: PointerPlayaround

We are now ready to present an example that uses pointers. The following code is a sample named Pointer-Playaround. It does some simple pointer manipulation and displays the results, allowing us to see what is happening in memory and where variables are stored:

```
using System;

namespace Wrox.ProCSharp.Chapter07
{
    class MainEntryPoint
    {
        static unsafe void Main()
        {
            int x=10;
            short y = -1;
            byte y2 = 4;
```

```
               double z = 1.5;
               int* pX = &x;
               short* pY = &y;
               double* pZ = &z;

               Console.WriteLine(
                  "Address of x is 0x{0:X}, size is {1}, value is {2}",
                  (uint)&x, sizeof(int), x);
               Console.WriteLine(
                  "Address of y is 0x{0:X}, size is {1}, value is {2}",
                  (uint)&y, sizeof(short), y);
               Console.WriteLine(
                  "Address of y2 is 0x{0:X}, size is {1}, value is {2}",
                  (uint)&y2, sizeof(byte), y2);
               Console.WriteLine(
                  "Address of z is 0x{0:X}, size is {1}, value is {2}",
                  (uint)&z, sizeof(double), z);
               Console.WriteLine(
                  "Address of pX=&x is 0x{0:X}, size is {1}, value is 0x{2:X}",
                  (uint)&pX, sizeof(int*), (uint)pX);
               Console.WriteLine(
                  "Address of pY=&y is 0x{0:X}, size is {1}, value is 0x{2:X}",
                  (uint)&pY, sizeof(short*), (uint)pY);
               Console.WriteLine(
                  "Address of pZ=&z is 0x{0:X}, size is {1}, value is 0x{2:X}",
                  (uint)&pZ, sizeof(double*), (uint)pZ);

               *pX = 20;
               Console.WriteLine("After setting *pX, x = {0}", x);
               Console.WriteLine("*pX = {0}", *pX);

               pZ = (double*)pX;
               Console.WriteLine("x treated as a double = {0}", *pZ);

               Console.ReadLine();
            }
        }
    }
```

This code declares three value variables:

❑   An int x

❑   A short y

❑   A double z

It also declares pointers to these values: pX, pY, and pZ.

Next, we display the values of these variables as well as their sizes and addresses. Note that in taking the address of pX, pY, and pZ, we are effectively looking at a pointer *to* a pointer—an address of an address of a value. Notice that, in accordance with the usual practice when displaying addresses, we have used the {0:X} format specifier in the Console.WriteLine() commands to ensure that memory addresses are displayed in hexadecimal format.

Finally, we use the pointer pX to change the value of x to 20 and do some pointer casting to see what happens if we try to treat the content of x as if it were a double.

Compiling and running this code results in this output. In this screen output we have demonstrated the effects of attempting to compile both with and without the /unsafe flag:

```
csc PointerPlayaround.cs
Microsoft (R) Visual C# .NET Compiler version 7.10.3052.4
for Microsoft (R) .NET Framework version 1.1.4322
Copyright (C) Microsoft Corporation 2001-2002. All rights reserved.

PointerPlayaround.cs(7,26): error CS0227: Unsafe code may only appear if
        compiling with /unsafe

csc /unsafe PointerPlayaround.cs
Microsoft (R) Visual C# .NET Compiler version 7.10.3052.4
for Microsoft (R) .NET Framework version 1.1.4322
Copyright (C) Microsoft Corporation 2001-2002. All rights reserved.

PointerPlayaround
Address of x is 0x12F8C4, size is 4, value is 10
Address of y is 0x12F8C0, size is 2, value is -1
Address of y2 is 0x12F8BC, size is 1, value is 4
Address of z is 0x12F8B4, size is 8, value is 1.5
Address of pX=&x is 0x12F8B0, size is 4, value is 0x12F8C4
Address of pY=&y is 0x12F8AC, size is 4, value is 0x12F8C0
Address of pZ=&z is 0x12F8A8, size is 4, value is 0x12F8B4
After setting *pX, x = 20
*pX = 20
x treated as a double = 2.63837073472194E-308
```

Checking through these results confirms our description of how the stack operates, which we gave in the *Memory Management under the Hood* section, earlier in this chapter. It allocates successive variables moving downward in memory. Notice how it also confirms that blocks of memory on the stack are always allocated in multiples of 4 bytes. For example, y is a short (of size 2), and has the address 1243328, indicating that the memory locations reserved for it are locations 1243328 through 1243331. If the .NET runtime had been strictly packing variables up next to each other, then Y would have occupied just two locations, 1243328 and 1243329.

Adding classes and structs to our example

In this section, we will illustrate pointer arithmetic, as well as pointers to structs and class members, using a second example, which we will call PointerPlayaround2. To start off, we will define a struct named CurrencyStruct, which represents a currency value as dollars and cents. We also define an equivalent class named CurrencyClass:

```
struct CurrencyStruct
{
    public long Dollars;
    public byte Cents;

    public override string ToString()
    {
```

```
        return "$" + Dollars + "." + Cents;
    }
}

class CurrencyClass
{
    public long Dollars;
    public byte Cents;

    public override string ToString()
    {
        return "$" + Dollars + "." + Cents;
    }
}
```

Now that we have our struct and class defined, we can apply some pointers to them. Here is the code for the new example. Since the code is fairly long, we will go through it in detail. We start off by displaying the size of `CurrencyStruct`, creating a couple of `CurrencyStruct` instances and creating some `Currency Struct` pointers. We use the `pAmount` pointer to initialize the members of the `amount1` `CurrencyStruct`, and then display the addresses of our variables:

```
public static unsafe void Main()
{
    Console.WriteLine(
        "Size of CurrencyStruct struct is " + sizeof(CurrencyStruct));
    CurrencyStruct amount1, amount2;
    CurrencyStruct* pAmount = &amount1;
    long* pDollars = &(pAmount->Dollars);
    byte* pCents = &(pAmount->Cents);

    Console.WriteLine("Address of amount1 is 0x{0:X}", (uint)&amount1);
    Console.WriteLine("Address of amount2 is 0x{0:X}", (uint)&amount2);
    Console.WriteLine("Address of pAmount is 0x{0:X}", (uint)&pAmount);
    Console.WriteLine("Address of pDollars is 0x{0:X}", (uint)&pDollars);
    Console.WriteLine("Address of pCents is 0x{0:X}", (uint)&pCents);
    pAmount->Dollars = 20;
    *pCents = 50;
    Console.WriteLine("amount1 contains " + amount1);
```

Now we do some pointer manipulation that relies on our knowledge of how the stack works. Due to the order in which the variables were declared, we know that `amount2` will be stored at an address immediately below `amount1`. The `sizeof(CurrencyStruct)` operator returns 16 (as demonstrated in the screen output coming up), so `CurrencyStruct` occupies a multiple of 4 bytes. Therefore, after we decrement our currency pointer, it will point to `amount2`:

```
    --pAmount;    // this should get it to point to amount2
    Console.WriteLine("amount2 has address 0x{0:X} and contains {1}",
        (uint)pAmount, *pAmount);
```

Notice that when we call `Console.WriteLine()` we display the contents of `amount2` but we haven't yet initialized it. What gets displayed will be random garbage—whatever happened to be stored at that location in memory before execution of the sample. There is an important point here: normally, the C# compiler would prevent us from using an uninitialized variable, but when you start using pointers, it is very easy to circumvent many of the usual compilation checks. In this case we have done so because the compiler has no way of knowing that we are actually displaying the contents of amount2. Only we know that, because our knowledge of the stack means we can tell what the effect of decrementing pAmount will be. Once you start doing pointer arithmetic, you find you can access all sorts of variables and memory locations that the compiler would usually stop you from accessing, hence the description of pointer arithmetic as unsafe.

Next we do some pointer arithmetic on our pCents pointer. pCents currently points to amount1.Cents, but our aim here is to get it to point to amount2.Cents, again using pointer operations instead of directly telling the compiler that's what we want to do. To do this we need to decrement the address pCents contains by sizeof(Currency):

```
// do some clever casting to get pCents to point to cents
// inside amount2
CurrencyStruct* pTempCurrency = (CurrencyStruct*)pCents;
pCents = (byte*) ( --pTempCurrency );
Console.WriteLine("Address of pCents is now 0x{0:X}", (uint)&pCents);
```

Finally, we use the fixed keyword to create some pointers that point to the fields in a class instance, and use these pointers to set the value of this instance. Notice that this is also the first time that we have been able to look at the address of an item that is stored on the heap rather than the stack:

```
Console.WriteLine("\nNow with classes");
// now try it out with classes
CurrencyClass amount3 = new CurrencyClass();

fixed(long* pDollars2 = &(amount3.Dollars))
fixed(byte* pCents2 = &(amount3.Cents))
{
    Console.WriteLine(
        "amount3.Dollars has address 0x{0:X}", (uint)pDollars2);
    Console.WriteLine(
        "amount3.Cents has address 0x{0:X}", (uint) pCents2);
    *pDollars2 = -100;
    Console.WriteLine("amount3 contains " + amount3);
}
```

Compiling and running this code gives output similar to this:

```
csc /unsafe PointerPlayaround2.cs
Microsoft (R) Visual C# .NET Compiler version 7.10.3052.4
for Microsoft (R) .NET Framework version 1.1.4322
Copyright (C) Microsoft Corporation 2001-2002. All rights reserved.


PointerPlayaround2
Size of CurrencyStruct struct is 16
Address of amount1 is 0x12F698
Address of amount2 is 0x12F688
Address of pAmount is 0x12F684
Address of pDollars is 0x12F680
Address of pCents is 0x12F67C
amount1 contains $20.50
```

```
amount2 has address 0x12F688 and contains $0.236
Address of pCents is now 0x12F67C

Now with classes
amount3.Dollars has address 0x4B8850C
amount3.Cents has address 0x4B88514
amount3 contains $-100.0
```

These results were obtained using the .NET Framework version 1.1. You might find that the actual addresses displayed are different if you run the sample on a different version of .NET.

Notice in this output the uninitialized value of `amount2` that we display, and that the size of the `Currency Struct` struct is `16`—somewhat larger than we would expect given the sizes of its fields (a `long` and a `byte` should total 9 bytes). This is the effect of word alignment that we discussed earlier.

Using Pointers to Optimize Performance

Until now, all of our examples have been designed to demonstrate the various things that you can do with pointers. We have played around with memory in a way that is probably interesting only to people who like to know what's happening under the hood, but doesn't really help us to write better code. Here we're going to apply our understanding of pointers and demonstrate an example in which judicious use of pointers will have a significant performance benefit.

Creating stack-based arrays

In this section, we are going to look at one of the main areas in which pointers can be useful; creating high-performance, low overhead arrays on the stack. As discussed in Chapter 2, C# includes rich support for handling arrays. Although C# makes it very easy to use both one-dimensional and rectangular or jagged multidimensional arrays, it suffers from the disadvantage that these arrays are actually objects; they are instances of `System.Array`. This means that the arrays are stored on the heap with all of the overhead that this involves. There may be occasions when you need to create a short-lived high-performance array and don't want the overhead of reference objects. You can do this using pointers, although as we will show in this section, this is only easy for one-dimensional arrays.

In order to create a high-performance array we need to use a new keyword: `stackalloc`. The `stackalloc` command instructs the .NET runtime to allocate an amount of memory on the stack. When you call `stackalloc`, you need to supply it with two pieces of information:

❑   The type of data you want to store

❑   How many of these data items you need to store

For example, to allocate enough memory to store 10 `decimal` data items, you can write:

```
decimal* pDecimals = stackalloc decimal[10];
```

This command simply allocates the stack memory; it doesn't attempt to initialize the memory to any default value. This is fine for our purposes because we are creating a high-performance array, and initializing values unnecessarily would hurt performance.

Similarly, to store 20 double data items you write:

```
double* pDoubles = stackalloc double[20];
```

Although this line of code specifies the number of variables to store as a constant, this can equally be a quantity evaluated at runtime. So you can write the previous example like this:

```
int size;
size = 20;   // or some other value calculated at run-time
double* pDoubles = stackalloc double[size];
```

You will see from these code snippets that the syntax of stackalloc is slightly unusual. It is followed immediately by the name of the data type you want to store (and this must be a value type), and then by the number of items you need space for in square brackets. The number of bytes allocated will be this number multiplied by sizeof (*data type*). The use of square brackets in the above code sample suggests an array, which isn't too surprising. If you have allocated space for 20 doubles, then what you have is an array of 20 doubles. The simplest type of array that you can have is a block of memory that stores one element after another (see Figure 7-6).

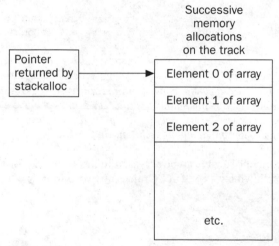

Figure 7-6

In this diagram, we have also shown the pointer returned by stackalloc, which is always a pointer to the allocated data type that points to the top of the newly allocated memory block. To use the memory block you simply dereference the returned pointer. For example, to allocate space for 20 doubles and then set the first element (element 0 of the array) to the value 3.0, write this:

```
double* pDoubles = stackalloc double [20];
*pDoubles = 3.0;
```

To access the next element of the array, you use pointer arithmetic. As described earlier, if you add 1 to a pointer, its value will be increased by the size of whatever data type it points to. In this case, this will be just enough to take us to the next free memory location in the block that we have allocated. So, we can set the second element of the array (element number 1) to the value 8.4 like this:

```
double* pDoubles = stackalloc double [20];
*pDoubles = 3.0;
*(pDoubles+1) = 8.4;
```

By the same reasoning, you can access the element with index X of the array with the expression *(pDoubles+X).

Effectively, we have a means by which we can access elements of our array, but for general purpose use this syntax is too complex. Fortunately, C# defines an alternative syntax using square brackets. C# gives a very precise meaning to square brackets when they are applied to pointers; if the variable p is any pointer type and X is an integer, then the expression p[X] is always interpreted by the compiler as meaning *(p+X). This is true for all pointers, not only those initialized using stackalloc. With this shorthand notation, we now have a very convenient syntax for accessing our array. In fact, it means that we have exactly the same syntax for accessing one-dimensional stack-based arrays as we do for accessing heap-based arrays that are represented by the System.Array class:

```
double* pDoubles = stackalloc double [20];
pDoubles[0] = 3.0;   // pDoubles[0] is the same as *pDoubles
pDoubles[1] = 8.4;   // pDoubles[1] is the same as *(pDoubles+1)
```

This idea of applying array syntax to pointers isn't new. It has been a fundamental part of both the C and the C++ languages ever since those languages were invented. Indeed, C++ developers will recognize the stack-based arrays we can obtain using stackalloc as being essentially identical to classic stack-based C and C++ arrays. It is this syntax and the way it links pointers and arrays which was one of the reasons why the C language became popular in the 1970s, and the main reason why the use of pointers became such a popular programming technique in C and C++.

Although our high-performance array can be accessed in the same way as a normal C# array, a word of caution is in order. The following C# code in C# raises an exception:

```
double[] myDoubleArray = new double [20];
myDoubleArray[50] = 3.0;
```

The exception occurs because we are trying to access an array using an index that is out of bounds; the index is 50, whereas the maximum allowed value is 19. However, if you declare the equivalent array using stackalloc, there is no object wrapped around the array that can perform bounds checking. Hence, the following code will *not* raise an exception:

```
double* pDoubles = stackalloc double [20];
pDoubles[50] = 3.0;
```

In this code, we allocate enough memory to hold 20 doubles. Then we set sizeof(double) memory locations starting at the location given by the start of this memory + 50*sizeof(double) to hold the double value 3.0. Unfortunately, that memory location is way outside the area of memory that we have allocated for the doubles. There is no knowing what data might be stored at that address. At best, we may have used some currently unused memory, but it is equally possible that we may have just overwritten some locations in the stack that were being used to store other variables or even the return address from the method currently being executed. Once again, we see that the high performance to be gained from pointers comes at a cost; you need to be certain you know what you are doing, or you will get some very strange runtime bugs.

QuickArray example

We will end our discussion of pointers with a `stackalloc` example called `QuickArray`. In this example, the program simply asks the user how many elements they want to be allocated for an array. The code then uses `stackalloc` to allocate an array of `longs` that size. The elements of this array are populated with the squares of the integers starting with `0` and the results displayed on the console:

```csharp
using System;

namespace Wrox.ProCSharp.Chapter07
{
   class MainEntryPoint
   {
      static unsafe void Main()
      {
         Console.Write("How big an array do you want? \n> ");
         string userInput = Console.ReadLine();
         uint size = uint.Parse(userInput);

         long* pArray = stackalloc long [(int)size];
         for (int i=0 ; i<size ; i++)
            pArray[i] = i*i;

         for (int i=0 ; i<size ; i++)
            Console.WriteLine("Element {0} = {1}", i, *(pArray+i));
      }
   }
}
```

Here is the output for the `QuickArray` sample:

```
QuickArray
How big an array do you want?
> 15
Element 0 = 0
Element 1 = 1
Element 2 = 4
Element 3 = 9
Element 4 = 16
Element 5 = 25
Element 6 = 36
Element 7 = 49
Element 8 = 64
Element 9 = 81
Element 10 = 100
Element 11 = 121
Element 12 = 144
Element 13 = 169
Element 14 = 196
```

Summary

Remember, to become a truly proficient C# programmer, you must have a solid understanding of how memory allocation and garbage collection works. In this chapter, we've provided a description of how the CLR manages and allocates memory on the heap and the stack. We've also discussed how to write classes that free unmanaged resources correctly, and how to use pointers in C#. These are both advanced topics that are poorly understood and often implemented incorrectly by novice programmers.

In the next chapter, we discuss strings and a powerful mechanism for string manipulation: regular expressions.

Strings and Regular Expressions

In the beginning part of this book, we have been almost constantly using strings, and have taken for granted the stated mapping that the `string` keyword in C# actually refers to the .NET base class `System.String`. `System.String` is a very powerful and versatile class, but it is not by any means the only string-related class in the .NET armory. In this chapter, we start off by reviewing the features of `System.String`, and then we look at some quite nifty things you can do with strings using some of the other .NET classes—in particular those in the `System.Text` and `System.Text.RegularExpressions` namespaces. We will cover the following areas:

❑ *Building strings*—If you're performing repeated modifications on a string, for example in order to build up a lengthy string prior to displaying it or passing it to some other method or application, the `String` class can be very inefficient. For this kind of situation, another class, `System.Text.StringBuilder` is more suitable, since it has been designed exactly for this situation.

❑ *Formatting expressions*—We will also take a closer look at those formatting expressions that we have been using in the `Console.WriteLine()` method throughout these last few chapters. These formatting expressions are processed using a couple of useful interfaces, `IFormatProvider` and `IFormattable`, and by implementing these interfaces on your own classes, you can actually define your own formatting sequences so that `Console.WriteLine()` and similar classes will display the values of your classes in whatever way you specify.

❑ *Regular expressions*—.NET also offers some very sophisticated classes that deal with the situation in which you need to identify or extract substrings that satisfy certain fairly sophisticated criteria; for example, finding all occurrences within a string where a character or set of characters is repeated, or finding all words that begin with s and contain at least one n, or strings that adhere to employee ID or social security number constructions. Although you can write methods to perform this kind of processing using the `String` class, such methods are cumbersome to write. Instead, you can use some classes from `System.Text.RegularExpressions`, which are designed specifically to perform this kind of processing.

System.String

Before we examine the other string classes, we will quickly review some of the available methods on the `String` class.

`System.String` is a class that is specifically designed to store a string, and allow a large number of operations on the string. Also, because of the importance of this data type, C# has its own keyword and associated syntax to make it particularly easy to manipulate strings using this class.

You can concatenate strings using operator overloads:

```
string message1 = "Hello";  // returns "Hello"
message1 += ", There"; // returns "Hello, There"
string message2 = message1 + "!"; // returns "Hello, There!"
```

C# also allows extraction of a particular character using an indexer-like syntax:

```
char char4 = message[4];   // returns 'a'. Note the char is zero-indexed
```

This enables us to perform such common tasks as replacing characters, removing whitespace, and capitalization. The following table introduces the key methods.

Method	Purpose
Compare	Compares the contents of strings, taking into account the culture (locale) in assessing equivalence between certain characters
CompareOrdinal	As `Compare`, but doesn't take culture into account
Format	Formats a string containing various values and specifiers for how each value should be formatted
IndexOf	Locates the first occurrence of a given substring or character in the string
IndexOfAny	Locates the first occurrence of any one of a set of characters in the string
LastIndexOf	As for `IndexOf`, but finds the last occurrence
LastIndexOfAny	As for `IndexOfAny`, but finds the last occurrence
PadLeft	Pads out the string by adding a specified repeated character to the beginning of it
PadRight	Pads out the string by adding a specified repeated character to the end of it
Replace	Replaces occurrences of a given character or substring in the string with another character or substring
Split	Splits the string into an array of substrings, the breaks occurring wherever a given character occurs
Substring	Retrieves the substring starting at a specified position in the string
ToLower	Converts string to lowercase

Method	Purpose
ToUpper	Converts string to uppercase
Trim	Removes leading and trailing whitespace

Please note that this table is not comprehensive, but is intended to give you an idea of the features offered by strings.

Building Strings

As we have seen, `String` is an extremely powerful class that implements a large number of very useful methods. However, the `String` class has a shortcoming that makes it very inefficient for making repeated modifications to a given string—it is actually an *immutable* data type, which is to say that once you initialize a string object, that string object can never change. The methods and operators that appear to modify the contents of a string actually create new strings, copying the contents of the old string if necessary. For example, look at the following code:

```
string greetingText = "Hello from all the guys at Wrox Press. ";
greetingText += "We do hope you enjoy this book as much as we enjoyed writing it.";
```

What happens when this code executes is this: first, an object of type `System.String` is created and initialized to hold the text "`Hello from all the guys at Wrox Press. `" Note the space *after* the full stop. When this happens, the .NET runtime allocates just enough memory in the string to hold this text (39 chars), and we set the variable `greetingText` to refer to this string instance.

In the next line, syntactically it looks like we're adding some more text onto the string—we are not. Instead, we create a new string instance, with just enough memory allocated to store the combined text—that's 103 characters in total. The original text, "`Hello from all the people at Wrox Press. `", is copied into this new string along with the extra text, "`We do hope you enjoy this book as much as we enjoyed writing it.`" Then, the address stored in the variable `greetingText` is updated, so the variable correctly points to the new `String` object. The old `String` object is now unreferenced—there are no variables that refer to it—and so will be removed the next time the garbage collector comes along to clean out any unused objects in your application.

By itself, that doesn't look too bad, but suppose we wanted to encode that string by replacing each letter (not the punctuation) with the character which has an ASCII code further on in the alphabet, as part of some extremely simple encryption scheme. This would turn the string to "`Ifmmp gspn bmm uif hvst bu Xspy Qsftt. Xf ep ipqf zpv fokpz uijt cppl bt nvdi bt xf fokpzfe xsjujoh ju.`" There are several ways of doing this, but the simplest and (if you are restricting yourself to using the `String` class) almost certainly the most efficient way is to use the `String.Replace()` method, which replaces all occurrences of a given substring in a string with another substring. Using `Replace()`, the code to encode the text looks like this:

```
string greetingText = "Hello from all the guys at Wrox Press. ";
greetingText += "We do hope you enjoy this book as much as we enjoyed writing it.";

for(int i = (int)'z'; i>=(int)'a' ; i--)
{
    char old1 = (char)i;
```

```
    char new1 = (char)(i+1);
    greetingText = greetingText.Replace(old1, new1);
}

for(int i = (int)'Z'; i>=(int)'A' ; i--)
{
    char old1 = (char)i;
    char new1 = (char)(i+1);
    greetingText = greetingText.Replace(old1, new1);
}
Console.WriteLine("Encoded:\n" + greetingText);
```

For simplicity, this code doesn't wrap Z to A or z to a. These letters get encoded to [and {, respectively.

Replace() works in a fairly intelligent way, to the extent that it won't actually create a new string unless it does actually make some changes to the old string. Our original string contained 23 different lowercase characters and 3 different uppercase ones. Replace() will therefore have allocated a new string 26 times in total, each new string storing 103 characters. That means that as a result of our encryption process there will be string objects capable of storing a combined total of 2,678 characters now sitting on the heap waiting to be garbage-collected! Clearly, if you use strings to do text processing extensively, your applications will run into severe performance problems.

In order to address this kind of issue, Microsoft has supplied the System.Text.StringBuilder class. StringBuilder isn't as powerful as String in terms of the number of methods it supports. The processing you can do on a StringBuilder is limited to substitutions and appending or removing text from strings. However, it works in a much more efficient way.

When you construct a string, just enough memory gets allocated to hold the string. The StringBuilder, however, normally allocates more memory than needed. You have the option to indicate how much memory to allocate, but if you don't, then the amount will default to some value that depends on the size of the string that StringBuilder is initialized with. The StringBuilder class has two main properties:

❑ Length, which indicates the length of the string that it actually contains

❑ Capacity, which indicates the maximum length of the string in the memory allocation

Any modifications to the string take place within the block of memory assigned to the StringBuilder instance, which makes appending substrings and replacing individual characters within strings very efficient. Removing or inserting substrings is inevitably still inefficient, because it means that the following part of the string has to be moved. Only if you perform some operation that exceeds the capacity of the string is it necessary to allocate new memory and possibly move the entire contained string. At the time of writing, Microsoft has not documented how much extra capacity will be added; based on our experiments the StringBuilder appears to double its capacity if it detects the capacity has been exceeded and no new value for the capacity has been set.

For example, if we use a StringBuilder object to construct our original greeting string, we might write this code:

```
StringBuilder greetingBuilder =
    new StringBuilder("Hello from all the guys at Wrox Press. ", 150);
greetingBuilder.Append("We do hope you enjoy this book as much as we enjoyed
                        writing it");
```

In order to use the `StringBuilder` class, you will need a `System.Text` reference in your code.

In this code, we have set an initial capacity of 150 for the `StringBuilder`. It is always a good idea to set some capacity that covers the likely maximum length of a string, to ensure the `StringBuilder` doesn't need to relocate because its capacity was exceeded. Theoretically, you can set as large a number as you can pass in an `int`, although the system will probably complain that it doesn't have enough memory if you actually try to allocate the maximum of 2 billion characters (this is the theoretical maximum that a `StringBuilder` instance is in principle allowed to contain).

When the above code is executed, we first create a `StringBuilder` object that looks like Figure 8-1.

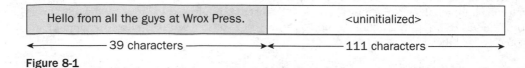

Hello from all the guys at Wrox Press.	<uninitialized>
←————— 39 characters —————→	←————— 111 characters —————→

Figure 8-1

Then, on calling the `Append()` method, the remaining text is placed in the empty space, without the need for more memory allocation. However, the real efficiency gain from using a `StringBuilder` comes when we are making repeated text substitutions. For example, if we try to encrypt the text in the same way as before, then we can perform the entire encryption without allocating any more memory whatsoever:

```
StringBuilder greetingBuilder =
    new StringBuilder("Hello from all the guys at Wrox Press. ", 150);
greetingBuilder.Append("We do hope you enjoy this book as much as we enjoyed
                        writing it");
```

```
for(int i = (int)'z'; i>=(int)'a' ; i--)
{
   char old1 = (char)i;
   char new1 = (char)(i+1);
   greetingBuilder = greetingBuilder.Replace(old1, new1);
}

for(int i = (int)'Z'; i>=(int)'A' ; i--)
{
   char old1 = (char)i;
   char new1 = (char)(i+1);
   greetingBuilder = greetingBuilder.Replace(old1, new1);
}
Console.WriteLine("Encoded:\n" + greetingBuilder.ToString());
```

This code uses the `StringBuilder.Replace()` method, which does the same thing as `String.Replace()`, but without copying the string in the process. The total memory allocated to hold strings in the above code is 150 for the `StringBuilder` instance, as well as the memory allocated during the string operations performed internally in the final `Console.WriteLine()` statement.

Normally, you will want to use `StringBuilder` to perform any manipulation of strings, and `String` to store or display the final result.

StringBuilder members

We have demonstrated one constructor of `StringBuilder`, which takes an initial string and capacity as its parameters. There are others. For example, you can supply only a string:

```
StringBuilder sb = new StringBuilder("Hello");
```

Or you can create an empty `StringBuilder` with a given capacity:

```
StringBuilder sb = new StringBuilder(20);
```

Apart from the `Length` and `Capacity` properties, there is a read-only `MaxCapacity` property that indicates the limit to which a given `StringBuilder` instance is allowed to grow. By default, this is given by `int.MaxValue` (roughly 2 billion, as noted earlier), but you can set this value to something lower when you construct the `StringBuilder` object:

```
// This will both set initial capacity to 100, but the max will be 500.
// Hence, these StringBuilder can never grow to more than 500 characters,
// otherwise it will raise exception if you try to do that.
StringBuilder sb = new StringBuilder(100, 500);
```

You can also explicitly set the capacity at any time, though an exception will be raised if you set it to a value less than the current length of the string, or a value that exceeds the maximum capacity:

```
StringBuilder sb = new StringBuilder("Hello");
sb.Capacity = 100;
```

The following table lists the main `StringBuilder` methods.

Method	Purpose
Append()	Appends a string to the current string
AppendFormat()	Appends a string that has been worked out from a format specifier
Insert()	Inserts a substring into the current string
Remove()	Removes characters from the current string
Replace()	Replaces all occurrences of a character by another character or a substring with another substring in the current string
ToString()	Returns the current string cast to a System.String object (overridden from System.Object)

There are several overloads of many of these methods.

> `AppendFormat()` is actually the method that is ultimately called when you call `Console`
> `.WriteLine()`, which has responsibility for working out what all the format expressions like `{0:D}`
> should be replaced with. We will examine this method in the next section.

There is no cast (either implicit or explicit) from `StringBuilder` to `String`. If you want to output the contents of a `StringBuilder` as a `String`, you must use the `ToString()` method.

Format Strings

So far, we have written a large number of classes and structs for the code samples presented in this book, and we have normally implemented a `ToString()` method for each of these in order to be able to display the contents of a given variable. However, quite often users might want the contents of a variable to be displayed in different, often culture- and locale-dependent, ways. The .NET base class, `System.DateTime`, provides the most obvious example of this. For example, you might want to display the same date as 14 February 2002, 14 Feb 2002, 2/14/02 (USA), 14/2/02 (UK), or 14. Februar 2002 (Germany).

Similarly, for our `Vector` struct that we wrote in Chapter 3, we implemented the `Vector.ToString()` method to display the vector in the format `(4, 56, 8)`. There is, however, another very common way of writing vectors, in which this vector would appear as `4i + 56j + 8k`. If we want the classes that we write to be user-friendly, then they need to support the facility to display their string representations in any of the formats that users are likely to want to use. The .NET runtime defines a standard way that this should be done, the `IFormattable` interface. Showing how to add this important feature to your classes and structs is the subject of this section.

As you probably know, you need to specify the format in which you want a variable displayed when you call `Console.WriteLine()`. Therefore, we are going to use this method as an example, although most of our discussion applies to any situation in which you want to format a string. For example, if you want to display the value of a variable in a list box or text box, you will normally use the `String.Format()` method to obtain the appropriate string representation of the variable. However, the actual format specifiers you use to request a particular format are identical to those passed to `Console.WriteLine()`. Hence, we will focus on `Console.WriteLine()` as an example. We start by examining what actually happens when you supply a format string to a primitive type, and from this we will see how we can plug in format specifiers for our own classes and structs into the process.

In Chapter 2 we use format strings in `Console.Write()` and `Console.WriteLine()` like this:

```
double d = 13.45;
int i = 45;
Console.WriteLine("The double is {0,10:E} and the int contains {1}", d, i);
```

The format string itself consists mostly of the text to be displayed, but wherever there is a variable to be formatted, its index in the parameter list appears in braces. You might also include other information inside the brackets concerning the format of that item. For example, you can include:

❑   The number of characters to be occupied by the representation of the item, prefixed by a comma. A negative number indicates that the item should be left-justified, while a positive number indicates that it should be right-justified. If the item actually occupies more characters than have been requested, it will still appear in full.

❑   A format specifier, preceded by a colon. This indicates how we want the item to be formatted. For example, we can indicate whether we want a number to be formatted as a currency or displayed in scientific notation.

The following table lists the common format specifiers for the numeric types, which we briefly discussed in Chapter 2.

Specifier	Applies To	Meaning	Example
C	Numeric types	Locale-specific monetary value	$4834.50 (USA) £4834.50 (UK)
D	Integer types only	General integer	4834
E	Numeric types	Scientific notation	4.834E+003
F	Numeric types	Fixed point decimal	4384.50
G	Numeric types	General number	4384.5
N	Numeric types	Common locale-specific format for numbers	4,384.50 (UK/USA) 4 384,50 (continental Europe)
P	Numeric types	Percentage notation	432,000.00%
X	Integer types only	Hexadecimal format	1120 (If you want to display 0x1120, you will have to write out the 0x separately)

If you want an integer to be padded with zeros, you can use the format specifier 0 (zero) repeated as many times as the number length is required. For example, the format specifier 0000 will cause 3 to be displayed as 0003, and 99 to be displayed as 0099, and so on.

It is not possible to give a complete list, because other data types can add their own specifiers. Showing how to define our own specifiers for our own classes is the aim of this section.

How the string is formatted

As an example of how strings are formatted, we will execute the following statement:

```
Console.WriteLine("The double is {0,10:E} and the int contains {1}", d, i);
```

Console.WriteLine() just passes the entire set of parameters to the static method, String.Format(). This is the same method that you would call if you wanted to format these values for use in a string to be displayed in a textbox, for example. The implementation of the 3-parameter overload of WriteLine() basically does this:

```
// Likely implementation of Console.WriteLine()

public void WriteLine(string format, object arg0, object arg1)
{
    Console.WriteLine(string.Format(format, arg0, arg1));
}
```

The one-parameter overload of this method, which is in turn getting called in the previous code sample, simply writes out the contents of the string it has been passed, without doing any further formatting on it.

`String.Format()` now needs to construct the final string by replacing each format specifier by a suitable string representation of the corresponding object. However, as we saw earlier, for this process of building up a string we need a `StringBuilder` instance rather than a `string` instance. In this example, a `String Builder` instance is created and initialized with the first known portion of the string, the text "The double is ". Next, the `StringBuilder.AppendFormat()` method is called, passing in the first format specifier, `{0,10:E}`, as well as the associated object, `double`, in order to add the string representation of this object to the string object being constructed, and this process continues with `StringBuilder.Append()` and `StringBuilder.AppendFormat()` being called repeatedly until the entire formatted string has been obtained.

Now comes the interesting part; `StringBuilder.AppendFormat()` has to figure out how to format the object. First thing it probes the object to find out whether it implements an interface in the `System` namespace called `IFormattable`. You can find this out quite simply by trying to cast an object to this interface and seeing whether the cast succeeds, or by using the C# `is` keyword. If this test fails, then `AppendFormat()` calls the object's `ToString()` method, which all objects either inherit from `System.Object` or override. This is exactly what happens here, since none of the classes we have written so far have implemented this interface. That is why our overrides of `Object.ToString()` have been sufficient to allow our structs and classes from earlier chapters such as `Vector` to get displayed in `Console.WriteLine()` statements.

However, all of the predefined primitive numeric types do implement this interface, which means that for those types, and in particular for `double` and `int` in our example, the basic `ToString()` method inherited from `System.Object` will not be called. To understand what happens instead, we need to examine the `IFormattable` interface.

`IFormattable` defines just one method, which is also called `ToString()`. However, this method takes two parameters as opposed to the `System.Object` version, which doesn't take any parameters. The following code shows the definition of `IFormattable`:

```
interface IFormattable
{
    string ToString(string format, IFormatProvider formatProvider);
}
```

The first parameter that this overload of `ToString()` expects is a string that specifies the requested format. In other words, it is the specifier portion of the string that appears inside the braces (`{}`) in the string originally passed to `Console.WriteLine()` or `String.Format()`. For example, in our example the original statement was:

```
Console.WriteLine("The double is {0,10:E} and the int contains {1}", d, i);
```

Hence, when evaluating the first specifier, `{0,10:E}`, this overload will be called against the `double` variable, `d`, and the first parameter passed to it will be `E`. `StringBuilder.AppendFormat()` will pass in here the text that appears after the colon in the appropriate format specifier from the original string.

We won't worry about the second `ToString()` parameter in this book. It is a reference to an object that implements the `IFormatProvider` interface. This interface gives further information that `ToString()` might need to consider when formatting the object such as culture-specific details (a .NET culture is similar to a Windows locale; if you are formatting currencies or dates then you need this information). If you are calling this ToString() overload directly from your source code, you might want to supply such an object. However, StringBuilder.AppendFormat() passes in null for this parameter. If format Provider is null, then ToString() is expected to use the culture specified in the system settings.

Let's get back to our example. The first item we want to format is a double, for which we are requesting exponential notation, with the format specifier E. The StringBuilder.AppendFormat() method establishes that the double does implement IFormattable, and will therefore call the two-parameter ToString() overload, passing it the string E for the first parameter and null for the second parameter. It is now up to the double's implementation of this method to return the string representation of the double in the appropriate format, taking into account the requested format and the current culture. StringBuilder.AppendFormat() will then sort out padding the returned string with spaces, if necessary, in order to fill the 10 characters the format string specified.

The next object to be formatted is an int, for which we are not requesting any particular format (the format specifier was simply {1}). With no format requested, StringBuilder.AppendFormat() passes in a null reference for the format string. The two-parameter overload of int.ToString() is expected to respond appropriately. No format has been specifically requested, therefore it will call the no-parameter ToString() method.

This entire string formatting process is summarized in Figure 8-2.

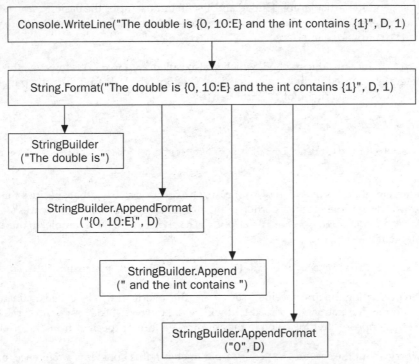

Figure 8-2

The FormattableVector example

Now that we have established how format strings are constructed, we are going to extend the `Vector` example from earlier in the book, so that we can format vectors in a variety of ways. You can download the code for this example from www.wrox.com. Now that you understand the principles involved, you will discover the actual coding is quite simple. All you need to do is implement `IFormattable` and supply an implementation of the `ToString()` overload defined by that interface.

The format specifiers we are going to support are:

❑ `N`—Should be interpreted as a request to supply a quantity known as the `Norm` of the `Vector`. This is just the sum of squares of its components, which for mathematics buffs happens to be equal to the square of the length of the `Vector`, and is usually displayed between double vertical bars, like this: `||34.5||`.

❑ `VE`—Should be interpreted as a request to display each component in scientific format, just as the specifier `E` applied to a double indicates (`2.3E+01, 4.5E+02, 1.0E+00`).

❑ `IJK`—Should be interpreted as a request to display the vector in the form `23i + 450j + 1k`.

❑ Anything else should simply return the default representation of the `Vector` (`23, 450, 1.0`).

To keep things simple, we are not going to implement any option to display the vector in combined `IJK` and scientific format. We will, however, make sure we test the specifier in a case-insensitive way, so that we allow `ijk` instead of `IJK`. Note that it is entirely up to us which strings we use to indicate the format specifiers.

To achieve this, we first modify the declaration of `Vector` so it implements `IFormattable`:

```
struct Vector : IFormattable
{
    public double x, y, z;
```

Now we add our implementation of the two-parameter `ToString()` overload:

```
public string ToString(string format, IFormatProvider formatProvider)
{
    if (format == null)
        return ToString();
    string formatUpper = format.ToUpper();
    switch (formatUpper)
    {
        case "N":
            return "|| " + Norm().ToString() + " ||";
        case "VE":
            return String.Format("( {0:E}, {1:E}, {2:E} )", x, y, z);
        case "IJK":
            StringBuilder sb = new StringBuilder(x.ToString(), 30);
            sb.Append(" i + ");
            sb.Append(y.ToString());
            sb.Append(" j + ");
            sb.Append(z.ToString());
            sb.Append(" k");
            return sb.ToString();
```

```
        default:
            return ToString();
    }
}
```

That is all we have to do! Notice how we take the precaution of checking whether format is `null` before we call any methods against this parameter—we want this method to be as robust as reasonably possible. The format specifiers for all the primitive types are case-insensitive, so that's the behavior that other developers are going to expect from our class too. For the format specifier VE, we need each component to be formatted in scientific notation, so we just use `String.Format()` again to achieve this. The fields x, y, and z are all doubles. For the case of the IJK format specifier, there are quite a few substrings to be added to the string, so we use a `StringBuilder` object to improve performance.

For completeness, we will also reproduce the no-parameter `ToString()` overload that we developed earlier:

```
public override string ToString()
{
    return "( " + x + " , " + y + " , " + z + " )";
}
```

Finally, we need to add a `Norm()` method that computes the square (norm) of the vector, since we didn't actually supply this method when we developed the `Vector` struct:

```
public double Norm()
{
    return x*x + y*y + z*z;
}
```

Now we can try out our formattable vector with some suitable test code:

```
static void Main()
{
    Vector v1 = new Vector(1,32,5);
    Vector v2 = new Vector(845.4, 54.3, -7.8);
    Console.WriteLine("\nIn IJK format,\nv1 is {0,30:IJK}\nv2 is {1,30:IJK}",
                       v1, v2);
    Console.WriteLine("\nIn default format,\nv1 is {0,30}\nv2 is {1,30}", v1,
                       v2);
    Console.WriteLine("\nIn VE format\nv1 is {0,30:VE}\nv2 is {1,30:VE}", v1,
                       v2);
    Console.WriteLine("\nNorms are:\nv1 is {0,20:N}\nv2 is {1,20:N}", v1,
                       v2);
}
```

The result of running this sample is this:

```
FormattableVector
In IJK format,
v1 is               1 i + 32 j + 5 k
v2 is        845.4 i + 54.3 j + -7.8 k
```

```
In default format,
v1 is                 ( 1 , 32 , 5 )
v2 is           ( 845.4 , 54.3 , -7.8 )

In VE format
v1 is ( 1.000000E+000, 3.200000E+001, 5.000000E+000 )
v2 is ( 8.454000E+002, 5.430000E+001, -7.800000E+000 )

Norms are:
v1 is                 || 1050 ||
v2 is         || 717710.49 ||
```

This shows that our custom specifiers are being picked up correctly.

Regular Expressions

Regular expressions are part of those small technology areas that is incredibly useful in a wide range of programs, yet rarely used among developers. One can think of regular expressions as a mini-programming language with one specific purpose: to locate substrings within a large string expression. It is not a new technology; it originated in the UNIX environment and is commonly used with the Perl language. Microsoft ported it onto Windows, where up until now it has been used mostly with scripting languages. Regular expressions are, however, supported by a number of .NET classes in the namespace System. Text.RegularExpressions.

Many readers will not be familiar with the regular expressions language, so we will use this section as a very basic introduction to both regular expressions and their related .NET classes. If you are already familiar with regular expressions then you'll probably want to just skim through this section to pick out the references to the .NET base classes. You might like to know that the .NET regular expression engine is designed to be mostly compatible with Perl 5 regular expressions, though it has a few extra features.

Introduction to Regular Expressions

The regular expressions language is a language designed specifically for string processing. It contains two features:

❑   A set of *escape codes* for identifying specific types of characters. You will be familiar with the use of the * character to represent any substring in DOS expressions. (For example, the DOS command Dir Re* lists the names of files with names beginning with Re.) Regular expressions use many sequences like this to represent items such as *any one character, a word break, one optional character*, and so on.

❑   A system for grouping parts of substrings and intermediate results during a search operation.

With regular expressions, you can perform quite sophisticated and high-level operations on strings. For example, you can:

❑   Identify (and perhaps either flag or remove) all repeated words in a string (for example, "The computer books books" to "The computer books")

❑   Convert all words to title case (for example, "this is a Title" to "This Is A Title")

❑ Convert all words longer than three characters long to title case (for example, "this is a Title" to "This is a Title")

❑ Ensure that sentences are properly capitalized

❑ Separate the various elements of a URI (for example, given `http://www.wrox.com`, extract the protocol, computer name, file name, and so on)

These are all of course, tasks that can be performed in C# using the various methods on `System.String` and `System.Text.StringBuilder`. However, in some cases, this would involve writing a fair amount of C# code. If you use regular expressions, this code can normally be compressed to just a couple of lines. Essentially, you instantiate a `System.Text.RegularExpressions.RegEx` object (or, even simpler, invoke a static `RegEx()` method), pass it the string to be processed, and pass in a regular expression (a string containing the instructions in the regular expressions language), and you're done.

A regular expression string looks at first sight rather like a regular string, but interspersed with escape sequences and other characters that have a special meaning. For example, the sequence `\b` indicates the beginning or end of a word (a word boundary), so if we wanted to indicate we were looking for the characters `th` at the beginning of a word, we would search for the regular expression, `\bth` (that is, the sequence word boundary-t-h). If we wanted to search for all occurrences of `th` at the end of a word, we would write `th\b` (the sequence t-h-word boundary). However, regular expressions are much more sophisticated than that, and include, for example, facilities to store portions of text that are found in a search operation. In this section, we will merely scratch the surface of the power of regular expressions.

Suppose your application needed to convert U.S. phone numbers to an international format. In the United States, the phone numbers have this format: 314-123-1234, which is often written as (314) 123-1234. When converting this national format to an international format you have to +1 (the country code of the United States) and add brackets around the area code: +1 (314) 123-1234. As find-and-replace operations go, that's not too complicated, but would still require some coding effort if you were going to use the `String` class for this purpose (which would mean that you would have to write your code using the methods available on `System.String`).The regular expressions language allows us to construct a short string that achieves the same result.

This section is intended only as a very simple example, so we will concentrate on searching strings to identify certain substrings, not on modifying them.

The RegularExpressionsPlayaround Example

For the rest of this section, we will develop a short example that illustrates some of the features of regular expressions and how to use the .NET regular expressions engine in C# by performing and displaying the results of some searches. The text we are going to use as our sample document the Web page introduction to a Wrox Press book on ASP.NET (Professional ASP.NET 1.1, ISBN 0-7645-5890-0):

```
string Text =
@"This comprehensive compendium provides a broad and thorough investigation of all
aspects of programming with ASP.NET. Entirely revised and updated for the 1.1
Release of .NET, this book will give you the information you need to master ASP.NET
and build a dynamic, successful, enterprise Web application.";
```

The previous code is valid C# code, despite all the line breaks. It nicely illustrates the utility of verbatim strings that are prefixed by the @ symbol.

We will refer to this text as the *input string*. To get our bearings and get used to the regular expressions .NET classes, we will start with a basic plain text search that doesn't feature any escape sequences or regular expression commands. Suppose that we want to find all occurrences of the string `ion`. We will refer to this search string as the *pattern*. Using regular expressions and the `Text` variable declared above, we can write this:

```
string Pattern = "ion";
MatchCollection Matches = Regex.Matches(Text, Pattern,
                              RegexOptions.IgnoreCase |
                              RegexOptions.ExplicitCapture);
foreach (Match NextMatch in Matches)
{
    Console.WriteLine(NextMatch.Index);
}
```

In this code, we have used the static method `Matches()` of the `Regex` class in the `System.Text.Regular Expressions` namespace. This method takes as parameters some input text, a pattern, and a set of optional flags taken from the `RegexOptions` enumeration. In this case, we have specified that all searching should be case-insensitive. The other flag, `ExplicitCapture`, modifies the way that the match is collected in a way that, for our purposes, makes the search a bit more efficient—we will see why this is later (although it does have other uses that we won't explore here). `Matches()` returns a reference to a `MatchCollection` object. A *match* is the technical term for the results of finding an instance of the pattern in the expression. It is represented by the class `System.Text.RegularExpressions.Match`. Therefore, we return a `MatchCollection` that contains all the matches, each represented by a `Match` object. In the previous code, we simply iterate over the collection, and use the `Index` property of the `Match` class, which returns the index in the input text of where the match was found. Running this code results in three matches.

So far, there is not really anything new here apart from some new .NET base classes. However, the power of regular collections really comes from that pattern string. The reason is that the pattern string doesn't only have to contain plain text. As hinted at earlier, it can also contain what are known as *meta-characters*, which are special characters that give commands, as well as escape sequences, which work in much the same way as C# escape sequences. They are characters preceded by a backslash (\) and have special meanings.

For example, suppose we wanted to find words beginning with n. We could use the escape sequence \b, which indicates a word boundary (a word boundary is just a point where an alphanumeric character precedes or follows a whitespace character or punctuation symbol). We would write this:

```
string Pattern = @"\bn";
MatchCollection Matches = Regex.Matches(Text, Pattern,
                              RegexOptions.IgnoreCase |
                              RegexOptions.ExplicitCapture);
```

Notice the @ character in front of the string. We want the \b to be passed to the .NET regular expressions engine at runtime—we don't want the backslash intercepted by a well-meaning C# compiler that thinks it's an escape sequence intended for itself! If we want to find words ending with the sequence `ion`, then we write this:

```
string Pattern = @"ion\b";
```

If we want to find all words beginning with the letter a and ending with the sequence ion (which has as its only match the word *application* in our example), we will have to put a bit more though into our code. We clearly need a pattern that begins with \ba and ends with ion\b, but what goes in the middle? We need to somehow tell the application that between the n and the ion there can be any number of characters as long as none of them are whitespace. In fact, the correct pattern looks like this:

```
string Pattern = @"\ba\S*ion\b";
```

Eventually you will get used to seeing weird sequences of characters like this when working with regular expressions. It actually works quite logically. The escape sequence \S indicates any character that is not a whitespace character. The * is called a *quantifier*. It means that the preceding character can be repeated any number of times, including zero times. The sequence \S* means *any number of characters as long as they are not whitespace characters*. The previous pattern will, therefore, match any single word that begins with a and ends with ion.

The following table lists some of the main special characters or escape sequences that you can use. It is not comprehensive, but a fuller list is available in the MSDN documentation.

Symbol	Meaning	Example	Matches
^	Beginning of input text	^B	B, but only if first character in text
$	End of input text	X$	X, but only if last character in text
.	Any single character except the newline character (\n)	i.ation	isation, ization
*	Preceding character may be repeated 0 or more times	ra*t	rt, rat, raat, raaat, and so on
+	Preceding character may be repeated 1 or more times	ra+t	rat, raat, raaat and so on, (but not rt)
?	Preceding character may be repeated 0 or 1 times	ra?t	rt and rat only
\s	Any whitespace character	\sa	[space]a, \ta, \na (\t and \n have the same meanings as in C#)
\S	Any character that isn't a whitespace	\SF	aF, rF, cF, but not \tf
\b	Word boundary	ion\b	Any word ending in ion
\B	Any position that isn't a word boundary	\BX\B	Any X in the middle of a word

If you want to search for one of the meta-characters, you can do so by escaping the corresponding character with a backslash. For example, . (a single period) means any single character other than the newline character, while \. means a dot.

You can request a match that contains alternative characters by enclosing them in square brackets. For example [1|c] means one character that can be either 1 or c. If you wanted to search for any occurrence of the words map or man, you would use the sequence ma[n|p]. Within the square brackets, you can also indicate a range, for example [a-z] to indicate any single lowercase letter, [A-E] to indicate any uppercase letter between A and E, or [0-9] to represent a single digit. If you want to search for an integer (that is, a sequence that contains only the characters 0 through 9), you could write [0-9]+ (note the use of the + character to indicate there must be at least one such digit, but there may be more than one—so this would match 9, 83, 854, and so on).

Displaying Results

In this section we will code our RegularExpressionsPlayaround example, so you can get a feel for how the regular expressions work.

The core of the example is a method called WriteMatches(), which writes out all the matches from a MatchCollection in a more detailed format. For each match, it displays the index of where the match was found in the input string, the string of the match, and a slightly longer string, which consists of the match plus up to ten surrounding characters from the input text—up to 5 characters before the match and up to 5 afterwards (it is less than 5 characters if the match occurred within 5 characters of the beginning or end of the input text). In other words, a match on the word messaging that occurs near the end of the input text quoted earlier would display and messaging of d (five characters before and after the match), but a match on the final word data would display g of data. (only one character after the match), because after that we get to the end of the string. This longer string lets you see more clearly where the regular expression locates the match:

```
static void WriteMatches(string text, MatchCollection matches)
{
   Console.WriteLine("Original text was: \n\n" + text + "\n");
   Console.WriteLine("No. of matches: " + matches.Count);
   foreach (Match nextMatch in matches)
   {
      int Index = nextMatch.Index;
      string result = nextMatch.ToString();
      int charsBefore = (Index < 5) ? Index : 5;
      int fromEnd = text.Length - Index - result.Length;
      int charsAfter = (fromEnd < 5) ? fromEnd : 5;
      int charsToDisplay = charsBefore + charsAfter + result.Length;

      Console.WriteLine("Index: {0}, \tString: {1}, \t{2}",
         Index, result,
         text.Substring(Index - charsBefore, charsToDisplay));

   }
}
```

The bulk of the processing in this method is devoted to the logic of figuring out how many characters in the longer substring it can display without overrunning the beginning or end of the input text. Note that we use another property on the Match object, Value, which contains the string identified for the match. Other than that, RegularExpressionsPlayaround simply contains a number of methods with names like `Find1`, `Find2`, and so on, which perform some of the searches based on the examples in this section. For example, `Find2` looks for any string that contains a at the beginning of a word:

```
static void Find2()
{
    string text = @"This comprehensive compendium provides a broad and thorough
        investigation of all aspects of programming with ASP.NET. Entirely revised and
        updated for the 1.0 Release of .NET, this book will give you the information
        you need to master ASP.NET and build a dynamic, successful, enterprise Web
        application.";
    string pattern = @"\ba";
    MatchCollection matches = Regex.Matches(text, pattern,
        RegexOptions.IgnoreCase);
    WriteMatches(text, matches);
}
```

Along with this comes a simple `Main()` method that you can edit to select one of the `Find<n>()` methods:

```
static void Main()
{
    Find1();
    Console.ReadLine();
}
```

The code also makes use of the `RegularExpressions` namespace:

```
using System;
using System.Text.RegularExpressions;
```

Running the example with the `Find1()` method as above gives these results:

RegularExpressionsPlayaround
```
Original text was:

This comprehensive compendium provides a broad and thorough investigation of all
aspects of programming with ASP.NET. Entirely revised and updated for the 1.1
Release of .NET, this book will give you the information you need to master ASP.NET
and build a dynamic, successful, enterprise Web application.

No. of matches: 1
Index: 291,    String: application,    Web application.
```

Matches, Groups, and Captures

One nice feature of regular expressions is that you can group characters. It works the same way as compound statements in C#. In C# you can group any number of statements by putting them in braces, and the result is treated as one compound statement. In regular expression patterns, you can group any characters (including meta-characters and escape sequences), and the result is treated as a single character. The only difference is you use parentheses instead of braces. The resultant sequence is known as a *group*.

For example, the pattern `(an)+` locates any recurrences of the sequence an. The + quantifier applies only to the previous character, but because we have grouped the characters together, it now applies to repeats of an treated as a unit. This means that if we apply `(an)+` to the input text, `bananas came to Europe late in the annals of history`, the `anan` from `bananas` is identified. On the other hand, if we write `an+`, the program selects the `ann` from `annals`, as well as two separate sequences of `an` from `bananas`. The expression `(an)+` identifies occurrences of `an`, `anan`, `ananan`, and so on, while the expression `an+` identifies occurrences of `an`, `ann`, `annn`, and so on.

> *You might wonder why with the previous example, `(an)+`, picks out anan from the word banana, but doesn't identify either of the two occurrences of an from the same word. The rule is that matches must not overlap. If there are a couple of possibilities that would overlap, then by default the longest possible sequence will be matched.*

However, groups are actually more powerful than that. By default, when you form part of the pattern into a group, you are also asking the regular expression engine to remember any matches against just that group, as well as any matches against the entire pattern. In other words you are treating that group as a pattern to be matched and returned in its own right. This can actually be extremely useful if you want to break up strings into component parts.

For example, URIs have the format: *<protocol>*`://`*<address>*`:`*<port>*, where the port is optional. An example of this is `http://www.wrox.com:4355`. Suppose you want to extract the protocol, the address, and the port from a URI, where you know that there may or may not be whitespace, (but no punctuation) immediately following the URI. You could do so using this expression:

```
\b(\S+)://(\S+)(?::(\S+))?\b
```

Here is how this expression works: First, the leading and trailing `\b` sequences ensure that we only consider portions of text that are entire words. Within that, the first group, `(\S+)://` identifies one or more characters that don't count as whitespace, and which are followed by `://`—the `http://` at the start of an HTTP URI. The brackets cause the `http` to be stored as a group. The subsequent `(\S+)` identifies the string `www.wrox.com` in the URI. This group will end either when it encounters the end of the word (the closing `\b`) or a colon (`:`) as marked by the next group.

The next group identifies the port (`:4355`). The following `?` indicates that this group is optional in the match—if there is no `:xxxx` then this won't prevent a match from being marked. This very important, because the port number is not always specified in a URI—in fact it is absent most of the time. However, things are a bit more complicated than that. We want to indicate that the colon might or might not appear too, but we don't want to store this colon in the group. We've achieved this by having two nested groups. The inner `(\S+)` identifies anything that follows the colon (for example, `4355`). The outer group contains the inner group preceded by the colon, and this group in turn is preceded by the sequence `?:`. This sequence indicates that the group in question should not be saved (we only want to save `4355`; we don't need `:4355` as well!). Don't get confused by the two colons following each other—the first colon is part of the `?:` sequence that says "don't save this group," and the second is text to be searched for.

If you run this pattern on the following string, you'll get one match: `http://www.wrox.com`.

```
Hey I've just found this amazing URI at http:// what was it -- oh yes
http://www.wrox.com
```

Within this match, you will find the three groups just mentioned as well as a fourth group, which represents the match itself. Theoretically, it is possible that each group itself might return no, one, or more than one match. Each of these individual matches is known as a *capture*. So, the first group, `(\S+)`, has one capture, `http`. The second group also has one capture (`www.wrox.com`). The third group, however, has no captures, since there is no port number on this URI.

Notice that the string contains a second `http://`. Although this does match up to our first group, it will not be captured by the search because the entire search expression does not match this part of the text.

We don't have space to show any examples of C# code that uses groups and captures, but we will mention that the .NET `RegularExpressions` classes support groups and captures, through classes known as `Group` and `Capture`. There are also the `GroupCollection` and `CaptureCollection` classes, which represent collections of groups and captures. The `Match` class exposes the `Groups()` method, which returns the corresponding `GroupCollection` object. The `Group` class correspondingly implements the `Captures()` method, which returns a `CaptureCollection`. The relationship between the objects is as shown in Figure 8-3.

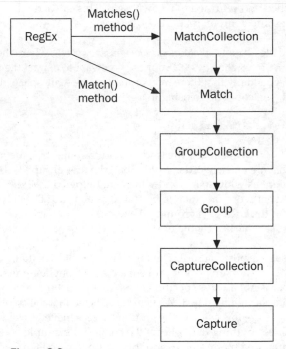

Figure 8-3

You might not want to return a `Group` object every time you just want to group some characters. There's a fair amount of overhead involved in instantiating the object, which is not necessary if all you want is to group some characters as part of your search pattern. You can disable this by starting the group with the character sequence `?:` for an individual group, as we did for our URI example, or for all groups by specifying the `RegExOptions.ExplicitCaptures` flag on the `RegEx.Matches()` method, as we did in the earlier examples.

Summary

You have quite a number of available data types at your disposal when working with the .NET Framework. One of the most used types in your applications (especially apps that focus on the submission and retrieval of data) is the `String` data type. The `string`, being as important as it is, was the reason that this book has a complete chapter focused on how to use the `string` data type and manipulate it in your applications.

When working with strings in the past, it was quite common just to slice and dice the strings as needed using concatenation. With the .NET Framework, you can use the new `StringBuilder` class to accomplish a lot of this task with better performance than before.

Last, but hardly least, advanced string manipulation using regular expressions are an excellent tool to search through and validate your strings.

9

Collections

There are situations when it is necessary to hold more than a single item in your data collection. There are moments where you are going to want to hold a group or collection of data that is related in some fashion in a larger construct. The C# language and the .NET Framework provide you with a number of opportunities for performing this type of value sorting in your code.

This chapter shows you how to work with groups of objects. We will take a close look at array lists, dictionaries, and collections as well as how to use them properly in your C# code for the best possible performance.

Examining Groups of Objects

Let's start by looking at how the .NET base classes support data structures that consist of a group of similar objects. Chapter 3 introduces the ordinary array, the simplest data structure of this kind. The ordinary array is an instance of the class `System.Array` namespace, but C# wraps its own syntax around this class. `System.Array` has two advantages: it is relatively efficient for accessing an individual element given its index, and it has its own C# syntax, which obviously makes using it more intuitive. However, it also has a huge disadvantage: You must specify its size when you instantiate it. There is no facility for adding, inserting, or removing elements later on. You also have to have a numeric index in order to be able to access an element. This is not particularly useful if, for example, you are dealing with a set of employee records and need to look up a given record from the name of the employee.

.NET has quite extensive support for a number of other data structures that are useful in different circumstances. Not only that, but there are also a number of interfaces that classes can implement in order to declare that they support all the functionality of a particular type of data structure. In this chapter, we are going to survey three of these structures:

- ❑ Array lists
- ❑ Collections
- ❑ Dictionaries (also sometimes known as maps)

With the exception of the basic `System.Array`, all the data structure classes are located in the `System.Collections` namespace.

> *The name `System.Collections` reflects another of those terminology ambiguities that plague computing. Collection is often used informally to denote any data structure. However, it also has the more specific meaning of a class that implements `IEnumerable` or `ICollection`—a particular type of data structure that we will investigate later in this chapter. In this chapter, we will always use the term* collection *to refer to the more specific meaning, except where .NET base class names force us to use it in the general sense.*

Array Lists

An *array list* is very similar to an array, except that it has the ability to grow. It is represented by the class `System.Collections.ArrayList`.

The `ArrayList` class also has some similarities with the `StringBuilder` class. Just as a `StringBuilder` allocates enough space in memory to store a certain number of characters, and allows you to manipulate characters within the space, the `ArrayList` allocates enough memory to store a certain number of object references. You can then efficiently manipulate these object references . If you try to add more objects to the `ArrayList` than permitted, then it will automatically increase its capacity by allocating a new area of memory big enough to hold twice as many elements as the current capacity, and relocate the objects to this new location.

You can instantiate an array list by indicating the initial capacity you want. For this example, we will assume we are creating a list of `Vector`s:

```
ArrayList vectors = new ArrayList(20);
```

If you don't specify the initial size, it defaults to 16:

```
ArrayList vectors = new ArrayList();    // capacity of 16
```

You can then add elements using the `Add()` method:

```
vectors.Add(new Vector(2,2,2));
vectors.Add(new Vector(3,5,6));
```

The `ArrayList` treats all its elements as object references. That means you can store whatever objects you like in an `ArrayList`, but when accessing the objects, you will need to cast them back to the appropriate data type:

```
Vector element1 = (Vector)vectors[1];
```

This example also shows that `ArrayList` defines an indexer, so that you can access its elements with an array-like syntax. You can also insert elements into the `ArrayList`:

```
vectors.Insert(1, new Vector(3,2,2));    // inserts at position 1
```

There is also a useful override of `Insert` that allows you to insert all the elements of a collection into an `ArrayList`, given an `ICollection` interface reference.

You can remove elements:

```
vvectors.RemoveAt(1);    // removes object at position 1
```

You can also supply an object reference to another method, `Remove()`. However, this takes longer since it will cause the `ArrayList` to make a linear search through the array to find the object.

Note that adding or removing an element causes all subsequent elements to have to be correspondingly shifted in memory, even if no reallocation of the entire `ArrayList` is needed.

You can modify or read the capacity with the `Capacity` property:

```
vectors.Capacity = 30;
```

Note, however, that changing the capacity causes the entire `ArrayList` to be reallocated to a new block of memory with the required capacity.

The number of elements in the `ArrayList` can be obtained with the `Count` property:

```
int nVectors = vectors.Count;
```

An array list can be really useful if you need to build up an array of objects but you do not know in advance how big the array is going to be. In that case, you can construct the array in an `ArrayList`, and then copy the `ArrayList` back to a plain old array when you have finished, provided that you actually need the data as an array (this would be the case, for example, if the array is to be passed to a method that expects an array as a parameter). The relationship between `ArrayList` and `Array` is in many ways similar to that between `StringBuilder` and `String`.

Unfortunately, unlike the `StringBuilder` class, there is no single method to do this conversion from an array list to an array. You have to use a loop to manually copy back references. Note, however, that you are only copying the references not the objects, so this should not result in much of a performance hit:

```
// vectors is an ArrayList instance being used to store Vector instances
Vector [] vectorsArray = new Vector[vectors.Count];
for (int i=0 ; i< vectors.Count ; i++)
   vectorsArray[i] = (Vector)vectors [i];
```

Collections

The idea of a *collection* is that it represents a set of objects that you can access by stepping through each element in turn. In particular, it is the set of objects that you access using a `foreach` loop. In other words, when you write something like the following code, you are assuming that the variable `messageSet` is a collection.

```
foreach (string nextMessage in messageSet)
{
   DoSomething(nextMessage);
}
```

The ability to use a `foreach` loop is the main purpose of collections. They offer little in the way of additional features.

Over the next couple of pages, we are going to look in more detail at what a collection is and implement our own collection by converting our `Vector` example. The broad concepts behind collections are actually not new to the .NET Framework. Collections have been a part of COM for years and have also been used in Visual Basic 6 with the convenient `For...Each` syntax. Java also has a `foreach` loop, and in both cases the underlying architecture is very similar to that for .NET collections.

What is a collection?

Internally, an object is a collection if it is able to supply a reference to a related object, known as an *enumerator*, which is able to step through the items in the collection. More specifically, a collection must implement the interface `System.Collections.IEnumerable`. `IEnumerable` defines just one method and looks like this:

```
interface IEnumerable
{
    IEnumerator GetEnumerator();
}
```

The purpose of `GetEnumerator()` is to return the enumerator object. As you can gather from the previous code, the enumerator object is expected to implement an interface, `System.Collections.IEnumerator`.

There is an additional collections interface, `ICollection`, which is derived from `IEnumerable`. More sophisticated collections will implement this interface as well. Besides `GetEnumerator()`, it implements a property that returns the number of elements in the collection. It also features support for copying the collection to an array and can supply information indicating if it is thread-safe. However, here we will only consider the simpler collection interface, `IEnumerable`.

`IEnumerator` looks like this:

```
interface IEnumerator
{
    object Current { get; }
    bool MoveNext();
    void Reset();
}
```

`IEnumerator` is intended to work like this: the object that implements it should be associated with one particular collection. When this object is first initialized, it does not yet refer to any elements in the collection, and you must call `MoveNext()`, which moves the enumerator so that it refers to the first element in the collection. You can then retrieve this element with the `Current` property. `Current` returns an object reference, so you will have to cast it to the type of object you are expecting to find in the collection. You can do whatever you want with that object then move to the next item in the collection by calling `MoveNext()` again. You repeat this process until there are no more items in the collection—you will know this has happened when the `Current` property returns `null`. You can return to the start of the collection by calling the `Reset()` method at any time. Note that `Reset()` actually returns to just before the start of the collection so if you call this method, you must call `MoveNext()` again to get to the first element.

You can see from this example that the point of the collection is simply to provide a way of stepping through all the elements when you don't want to supply an index, and you are happy to rely on the collection itself to choose the order in which the elements are returned to you. This usually means that you are not bothered about the order in which the elements are retrieved, as long as you get to see all of them, although in some cases a particular collection might be instructed to return the elements in a certain order. In one sense, a collection is a very basic type of group of objects, because it does not allow you to add or remove items from the group. All you can do is retrieve the items in an order determined by the collection, and examine them. It is not even possible to replace or modify items in the collection, because the `Current` property is read-only. The most frequent use of the collection is to give you the syntactical convenience of the `foreach` loop.

Arrays are also collections, as should be obvious because the `foreach` command works successfully with arrays. For the particular case of arrays, the enumerator supplied by the `System.Array` class steps through the elements in increasing order of index from zero upwards.

In fact, the previous `foreach` loop in C# is just a syntactical shortcut for writing the following code:

```
{
    IEnumerator enumerator = MessageSet.GetEnumerator();
    string nextMessage;
    enumerator.MoveNext();
    while ( (nextMessage = enumerator.Current) != null)
    {
        DoSomething(nextMessage);    // NB. We only have read access
                                     // toNextMessage
        enumerator.MoveNext();
    }
}
```

Note the enclosing curly braces framing the previous code snippet. We have supplied them in order to ensure that this code has exactly the same effect as the earlier `foreach` loop. If we hadn't included them, then this code would have differed to the extent that the `nextMessage` and `enumerator` variables would have remained in scope after the loop had finished being executed.

One important aspect of collections is that the enumerator is returned as a separate object. It should not be the same object as the collection itself. The reason is to allow for the possibility that more than one enumerator might be applied simultaneously to the same collection.

Adding collection support to the Vector struct

Our `Vector` struct that we started in Chapter 3 is about to get another extension with collection support.

So far our `Vector` struct contains a `Vector` instance with three components, x, y, and z, and because we defined an indexer in Chapter 3, it is possible to treat a `Vector` instance as an array, so that we can access the x-component by writing `SomeVector[0]`, the y-component by writing `SomeVector[1]`, and the z-component by writing `SomeVector[2]`.

We will now extend the `Vector` struct into a new code sample, the `VectorAsCollection` project, in which it is also possible to iterate through the components of a `Vector` by writing code like this:

```
foreach (double component in someVector)
    Console.WriteLine("Component is " + component);
```

Our first task is to mark `Vector` as a collection by having it implement the `IEnumerable` interface. We start by modifying the declaration of the `Vector` struct:

```
struct Vector : IFormattable, IEnumerable
{
    public double x, y, z;
```

Note that the `IFormattable` interface is present because we added support for string format specifiers earlier. Now we need to implement the `IEnumerable` interface:

```
        public IEnumerator GetEnumerator()
        {
            return new VectorEnumerator(this);
        }
```

The implementation of `GetEnumerator()` could hardly be simpler, but it depends on the existence of a new class, `VectorEnumerator`, which we need to define. Since `VectorEnumerator` is not a class that any outside code has to see directly, we declare it as a private class inside the `Vector` struct. Its definition looks like this:

```
private class VectorEnumerator : IEnumerator
{
    Vector theVector;       // Vector object that this enumerator refers to
    int location;   // which element of theVector the enumerator is
                    // currently referring to

    public VectorEnumerator(Vector theVector)
    {
        this.theVector = theVector;
        location = -1;
    }

    public bool MoveNext()
    {
        ++location;
        return (location > 2) ? false : true;
    }

    public object Current
    {
        get
        {
            if (location < 0 || location > 2)
                throw new InvalidOperationException(
                    "The enumerator is either before the first element or " +
                    "after the last element of the Vector");
            return theVector[(uint)location];
        }
    }

    public void Reset()
```

```
private class VectorEnumerator : IEnumerator
    {
        location = -1;
    }
}
```

As required for an enumerator, `VectorEnumerator` implements the `IEnumerator` interface. It also contains two member fields, `theVector`, which is a reference to the `Vector` (the collection) that this enumerator is to be associated with, and `location`, an `int` that indicates the enumerator's reference point in the collection—put differently, whether the `Current` property should retrieve the x, y, or z component of the vector.

The way we will work in this case is by treating `location` as an index and internally implementing the enumerator to access `Vector` as an array. When accessing `Vector` as an array, the valid indices are 0, 1, and 2—we will extend this by using -1 as the value that indicates where the enumerator is before the start of the collection, and 3 to indicate that it is beyond the end of the collection. Hence, the initialization of this field to -1 in the `VectorEnumerator` constructor:

```
public VectorEnumerator(Vector theVector)
{
    this.theVector = theVector;
    location = -1;
}
```

Notice the constructor also takes a reference to the `Vector` instance that we are to enumerate—this was supplied in the `Vector.GetEnumerator()` method:

```
public IEnumerator GetEnumerator()
{
    return new VectorEnumerator(this);
}
```

Dictionaries

Dictionaries represent a very sophisticated data structure that allows you to access an element based on some key, which can be of any data type you want. They are also known as *maps* or *hash tables*. Dictionaries are great if you want to store objects as if they were an array, but where you want to use some other data type rather than a numeric type to index into the structure. They also allow you to add and remove items freely, a bit like an `ArrayList`, but without the performance overhead of having to shift subsequent items in memory.

We will illustrate the kinds of situations in which dictionaries can be useful using the example that we will develop later in this section, the `MortimerPhonesEmployees` example. This example assumes that Mortimer Phones (the mobile phone company that we first introduced in Chapter 3) has some software that processes details of its employees. To that end, we need a data structure—something like an array—that contains data for employees. We assume that each Mortimer Phones employee is identified by an employee ID, which is a set of characters such as B342 or W435, and is stored as an `EmployeeID` object. Each employee's details are stored as an `EmployeeData` object; for our example, this just contains the employee's ID, name, and salary.

Suppose we have this EmployeeID:

```
EmployeeID id = new EmployeeID("W435");
```

and a variable called employees, which we can treat syntactically as an array of EmployeeData objects. In actuality, this is not an array; it is a dictionary, and because it is a dictionary, we can get the details of an employee with the previously declared ID like this:

```
EmployeeData theEmployee = employees[id];
    // Note that id is NOT a numeric type - it is an EmployeeID instance
```

That's the power of dictionaries. They look like arrays (but are more powerful than that; they are more like ArrayLists since you can dynamically set their capacity, and add and remove elements), but you don't have to use an integer to index into them; you can use any data type you want. For a dictionary, this is called a *key* rather than an index. Roughly speaking, what happens is that the dictionary takes the key supplied when you access an element (in the previous example this is the ID object) and it does some processing on the value of this key. This processing returns an integer that depends on the value of the key, and is used to work out where in the array the entry should be stored or retrieved from. Here is a short list of other examples where you might want to use a dictionary to store objects:

❑   If you want to store details of employees or other people, indexed by their social security numbers. Although the social security number is basically an integer, you cannot use an array with social security numbers as the index because a U.S. social security number theoretically can go up to the value of 999999999. On a 32-bit system you'd never fit an array that big in a program's address space! Most of the array would be empty anyway. Using a dictionary, you can have a social security number to index an employee, but still keep the dictionary size small.

❑   If you want to store addresses, indexed by zip code. In the United States, zip codes are just numbers, but in Canada and the United Kingdom they use letters and numbers together.

❑   If you want to store any data for objects or people, indexed by the name of the object or person.

Although the effect of a dictionary is that it looks to client code much like a dynamic array with a very flexible means of indexing into it, there is a lot of work that goes on behind the scenes to bring this about. In principle you can use an object of any class as an index key for dictionaries. However, you must implement certain features on a class before it can be used as a key. This also pertains to the GetHashCode() method that all classes and structs inherit from System.Object. In this section, we will take a closer look under the hood at what a dictionary is, how it works, and how GetHashCode() is involved. Then, we will move on to our MortimerPhonesEmployees example, which demonstrates how to use a dictionary and how to set up a class so that it can be used as a key.

Dictionaries in real life

The term *dictionary* is used because the structure is very similar to a real-life dictionary's. In a real dictionary you will normally want to look up the meaning of a word (or in the case of a foreign dictionary, the details of how to translate a word). The couple of lines of text that give the meaning (or the translation) are the data you are really interested in. The fact that a large dictionary will have tens of thousands of data items in it is no problem when you want to look up a meaning, because you just look for the word in alphabetical order. In a sense, the word you are looking up is equivalent to the key that you use to get at the data you are really interested in. It is not really the word itself you are interested in so much as the data associated with it. The word just provides the means to locate the entry in the dictionary. This means that there are really three things here that you need to build a dictionary:

❏ The data you want to look up

❏ The key

❏ The algorithm that allows you to find where the data is in the dictionary

The algorithm is a crucial part of the dictionary. Just knowing what the key is is not sufficient—you also need a way that you can use the key to find out the location of the item in the data structure. In real-life dictionaries, this algorithm is provided by arranging words in alphabetical order.

Dictionaries in .NET

In .NET, the basic dictionary is represented by the class `Hashtable`, which works on the same principles as a real-life dictionary, except that it assumes that the key and item are both of type `Object`. This means that a `Hashtable` can store whatever data structure you want. By contrast, a real-life dictionary uses strings as the keys.

Although `Hashtable` represents the generic will-store-anything dictionary, it is permissible to define your own more specialized dictionary classes. Microsoft has provided an abstract base class, `DictionaryBase`, which provides basic dictionary functionality, and from which you can derive your classes. There is also a ready-made .NET base class, `System.Collections.Specialized.StringDictionary`, which you should use in place of `Hashtable` if your keys are strings.

When you create a `Hashtable` object, you can indicate its initial capacity, just as you would for `String Builder` and `ArrayList`:

```
Hashtable employees = new Hashtable(53);
```

As usual there are many other constructors, but this is the one you will probably use most often. Notice the unusual size of the initial capacity that we've chosen: 53. There is a good reason for this. Due to the internal algorithms used in dictionaries, they work most efficiently if their capacity is a prime number.

Adding an object to the `Hashtable` is done with the `Add()` method, but `Hashtable.Add()` takes two parameters, both of them are object references. The first is a reference to the key; the second is a reference to the data. Carrying on with the `EmployeeID` and `EmployeeData` classes from the example that we will develop soon:

```
EmployeeID id;
EmployeeData data;

// initialize id and data to refer to some employee
// assume employees is a Hashtable instance
//that contains EmployeeData references

employees.Add(id, data);
```

In order to retrieve the data for an item, you need to supply the key. `Hashtable` implements an indexer so that you can retrieve data—this is how we get the array syntax we discussed earlier:

```
EmployeeData data = employees[id];
```

You can also remove items from the dictionary by supplying the key of the object to be removed:

```
employees.Remove(id);
```

You can also find out how many items are in the hash table using the `Count` property:

```
int nEmployees = employees.Count;
```

Notice, however, that there is no `Insert()` method. We have not yet looked at how a dictionary works internally, but there is no difference between adding and inserting data. Unlike an array or an `ArrayList`, you don't find one big block of data at the beginning of the structure and an empty block at the end. Instead, the situation looks more like the diagram in Figure 9-1, in which any unmarked parts of the dictionary are empty.

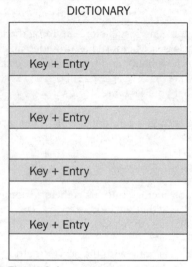

Figure 9-1

When you add an entry, it will actually be placed at some location that could be anywhere in the dictionary. How the location is worked out from the key is something that you don't need to know about when you are using the dictionary. The important point is that the algorithm used to work out the location of an item is reliable. As long as you remember what the key is, you can just hand it to the `Hashtable` object, and it will be able to use the key to quickly work out where the item is and retrieve it for you. We will examine how the algorithm works later in this section. Hint: It relies on the key's `GetHashCode()` method.

Note that the above diagram is simplified. Each key/entry pair is not actually stored inside the dictionary structure—as is common for reference types, what is stored are the object references that indicate where on the heap the objects themselves are located.

How the dictionary works

So far, we've seen that dictionaries (hash tables) are extremely convenient to use, but there is a snag: `Hashtable` (and indeed any other dictionary class) uses some sort of algorithm to work out where to place each object based on the key, and that algorithm isn't entirely provided by the Hashtable class. It has two stages, and the code for one of these stages must be provided by the key class. If you are using a class that Microsoft has written, and which can be used as a key (such as String), then there's no problem (Microsoft will have written all the code already). However, if the key class is one that you have written yourself, then you will have to write this part of the algorithm yourself.

In computer parlance, the part of the algorithm implemented by the key class is known as a *hash* (hence the term *hash table*), and the Hashtable class looks in a very particular place for the hash algorithm. It looks in your object's GetHashCode() method, which it inherits from System.Object. Whenever a dictionary class needs to work out where an item should be located, it simply calls the key object's GetHashCode() method. This is why we emphasized when we were discussing System.Object() that if you override GetHashCode(), there are fairly stringent requirements on how you do it, because your implementation needs to behave in certain ways for dictionary classes to work correctly. (If you don't intend your class to ever be used as a key in a dictionary, there's no need to override GetHashCode().)

The way it works is that GetHashCode() returns an int, and it somehow uses the value of the key to generate this int. Hashtable will take this int and do some other processing on it that involves some sophisticated mathematical calculations, and which returns the index of where in the dictionary an item with the given hash should be stored. We won't go into this part of the algorithm—that part has already been coded by Microsoft, so we don't need to know about it. What you should know is that it involves prime numbers and is the reason why the hash table capacity should be a prime number.

For this to work properly, there are some fairly strict requirements for the GetHashCode() override, which we will look at here. These requirements are going to sound quite abstract and daunting, but don't worry too much. As our MortimerPhonesEmployees example demonstrates, it is not at all difficult to code a key class that satisfies these requirements:

- ❑ It should be fast (because placing or retrieving entries in a dictionary is supposed to be fast).

- ❑ It must be consistent; if you regard two keys as representing the same value, then they must give the same value for the hash.

- ❑ It should ideally give values that are likely to be evenly distributed across the entire range of numbers that an int can store.

The reason for this last condition is because of a potential problem; what happens if you get two entries in the dictionary whose hashes both give the same index?

If this happens, the dictionary class will have to start fiddling about looking for the nearest available free location to store the second item—and will have to do some searching in order to retrieve this item later on. This is obviously going to hurt performance, and clearly, if lots of your keys are tending to give the same indexes for where they should be stored, this kind of clash becomes more likely. However, because of the way Microsoft's part of the algorithm works, this risk is minimized when the calculated hash values are evenly distributed between int.MinValue and int.MaxValue.

The risk of clashes between keys also increases as the dictionary gets fuller, so it's normally a good idea to make sure the capacity of the dictionary is substantially greater than the number of elements actually in it. For this reason, Hashtable will automatically relocate in order to increase its capacity well before it actually becomes full. The proportion of the table that is full is termed the *load*, and you can set the maximum value that you want the load to reach before `Hashtable` relocates in another of the `Hashtable` constructors:

```
// capacity =50, Max Load = 0.5

Hashtable employees = new Hashtable(50, 0.5);
```

The smaller the maximum load, the more efficiently your hash table works and the more memory it occupies. Incidentally, when a hash table relocates in order to increase its capacity, it always chooses a prime number as its new capacity.

Another important point we mentioned earlier is that the hashing algorithm must be consistent. If two objects contain what you regard as the same data, then they must give the same hash value, and this is where we come to the important restrictions on how you override the `Equals()` and `GetHashCode()` methods of `System.Object`. You see, the way that the `Hashtable` determines whether two keys A and B are equal is that it calls `A.Equals(B)`. This means you must ensure that the following is always true:

> If **A.Equals(B)** is true, then **A.GetHashCode()** and **B.GetHashCode()** must always return the same hash code.

This probably seems a fairly subtle point, but it is crucial. If you contrived some way of overriding these methods so that the previous statement is not always true, then a hash table that uses instances of this class as its keys will simply not work properly. Instead, you'll find funny things happening. For example, you might place an object in the hash table and then discover that you can never retrieve it, or you might try to retrieve an entry and get the wrong entry returned.

For this reason, the C# compiler will display a compilation warning if you supply an override for Equals() but don't supply an override for GetHashCode().

For `System.Object` this condition is true, because `Equals()` simply compares references, and `GetHashCode()` actually returns a hash that is based solely on the address of the object. This means that hash tables based on a key that doesn't override these methods will work correctly. However, the problem with this way of doing things is that keys are regarded as equal only if they are the same object. That means that when you place an object in the dictionary, you then have to hang on to the reference to the key. You can't simply instantiate another key object later that has the same value, because the same value is defined as meaning the very same instance. This means that if you don't override the `Object` versions of `Equals()` and `GetHashCode()`, your class won't be very convenient to use in a hash table. It makes more sense to implement `GetHashCode()` to generate a hash based on the value of the key rather than its address in memory. This is why you will invariably need to override `GetHashCode()` and `Equals()` for any class that you want to be used as a key.

Incidentally, `System.String` has had these methods overloaded appropriately. `Equals()` has been overloaded to provide value comparison, and `GetHashCode()` has also been correspondingly overloaded to return a hash based on the value of the string. For this reason it is convenient to use strings as keys in a dictionary.

The MortimerPhonesEmployees example

The `MortimerPhonesEmployees` example is a program that sets up a dictionary of employees. As mentioned earlier, the dictionary is indexed using `EmployeeID` objects, and each item stored in the dictionary is an `EmployeeData` object that stores details of an employee. The program simply instantiates a dictionary, adds a couple of employees to it, and then invites the user to type in employee IDs. For each ID the user types in, the program attempts to use the ID to index a dictionary and retrieve the employee's details. The process iterates until the user types in X. The example, when run, looks like this:

```
MortimerPhonesEmployees
Enter employee ID (format:A999, X to exit)> B001
Employee: B001: Mortimer          $100,000.00

Enter employee ID (format:A999, X to exit)> W234
Employee: W234: Arabel Jones      $10,000.00

Enter employee ID (format:A999, X to exit)> X
```

This example contains a number of classes. In particular, we need the `EmployeeID` class, which is the key used to identify employees, and the `EmployeeData` class that stores employee data. We will examine the `EmployeeID` class first, since this is the one where all the action happens in terms of preparing it to be used as a dictionary key. The definition of this class is as follows:

```csharp
class EmployeeID
{
   private readonly char prefix;
   private readonly int number;


   public EmployeeID(string id)
   {
      prefix = (id.ToUpper())[0];
      number = int.Parse(id.Substring(1,3));
   }

   public override string ToString()
   {
      return prefix.ToString() + string.Format("{0,3:000}", number);
   }

   public override int GetHashCode()
   {
      return ToString().GetHashCode();
   }

   public override bool Equals(object obj)
   {
      EmployeeID rhs = obj as EmployeeID;
      if (rhs == null)
         return false;
      if (prefix == rhs.prefix && number == rhs.number)
         return true;
      return false;
   }
}
```

The first part of the class definition simply stores the actual ID. Remember that the ID takes a format such as B001 or W234. In other words, it consists of a single letter prefix, followed by three numeric characters. We store this as a char for the prefix and an int for the remainder of the code.

The constructor simply takes a string and breaks it up to form these fields. Note that to keep the example simple, no error checking is performed. We will just assume the string passed into the constructor is in the correct format. The ToString() method simply returns the ID as a string:

```
return prefix.ToString() + string.Format("{0,3:000}", number);
```

Note the format specifier (3:000) that ensures the int containing the number is padded with zeros, so we get for example B001, and not B1.

Now we come to the two method overrides that we need for the dictionary. First, we have overridden Equals() so that it compares the values of EmployeeID instances:

```
public override bool Equals(object obj)
{
    EmployeeID rhs = obj as EmployeeID;
    if (rhs == null)
        return false;
    if (prefix == rhs.prefix && number == rhs.number)
        return true;
    return false;
}
```

This is the first time we have seen an example of an override of Equals(). Notice that our first task is to check whether the object passed as a parameter is actually an EmployeeID instance. If it isn't, then it obviously isn't going to equal this object, so we return false. We test the type by attempting to cast it to EmployeeID using C#'s as keyword. Once we have established that we have an EmployeeID object, we just compare the values of the fields to see if they contain the same values as this object.

Next, we look at GetHashCode(). The implementation of this is shorter, though at first sight it is perhaps harder to understand what's going on:

```
public override int GetHashCode()
{
    string str = this.ToString();
    return str.GetHashCode();
}
```

Earlier, we listed some strict requirements that the calculated hash code had to satisfy. Of course, there are all sorts of ways to devise simple and efficient hashing algorithms. Generally, taking the fields, multiplying them by large prime numbers, and adding the results together is a good way to do this. However, for our convenience, Microsoft has already implemented a sophisticated, yet efficient hashing algorithm for the String class, so we may as well take advantage of that. String.GetHashCode() produces well-distributed numbers based on the contents of the string. It satisfies all the requirements of a hash code.

The only disadvantage of leveraging this method is that there is some performance loss associated with converting our EmployeeID class to a string in the first place. If you are concerned about that and need the last ounce of performance in your hashing algorithms, you will need to design your own hash. Designing hashing algorithms is a complex topic that we cannot discuss in depth in this book. However, we will suggest one simple approach to the problem, which is to multiply numbers based on the component fields of the class by different prime numbers (for mathematical reasons, multiplying by different prime numbers helps to prevent different combinations of values of the fields from giving the same hash code). The following snippet shows a suitable implementation of GetHashCode():

```
public override int GetHashCode()     // alternative implementation
{
   return (int)prefix*13 + (int)number*53;
}
```

This particular example, will work more quickly than the ToString()-based algorithm that we use in the example, but has the disadvantage that the hash codes generated by different EmployeeIDs are less likely to be evenly spread across the range of int. Incidentally, the primitive numeric types do have GetHashCode() methods defined, but these methods simply return the value of the variable, and are hence not particularly useful. The primitive types aren't really intended to be used as keys.

Notice that our GetHashCode() and Equals() implementations do between them satisfy the requirements for equality that we mentioned earlier. With our override of Equals(), two EmployeeID objects will be considered equal if, and only if they have the same values of prefix and number. However, in that case ToString() provides the same value for both of them, and so they will give the same hash code. That's the crucial test that must be satisfied.

Next, we can look at the class that contains the employee data. The definition of this class is fairly basic and intuitive:

```
class EmployeeData
{
   private string name;
   private decimal salary;
   private EmployeeID id;

   public EmployeeData(EmployeeID id, string name, decimal salary)
   {
      this.id = id;
      this.name = name;
      this.salary = salary;
   }

   public override string ToString()
   {
      StringBuilder sb = new StringBuilder(id.ToString(), 100);
      sb.Append(": ");
      sb.Append(string.Format("{0,-20}", name));
      sb.Append(" ");
      sb.Append(string.Format("{0:C}", salary));
      return sb.ToString();
   }
}
```

Notice how once again for performance reasons, we use a `StringBuilder` object to generate the string representation of an `EmployeeData` object. Finally, we create the test harness. This is defined in the `TestHarness` class:

```
class TestHarness
{

    Hashtable employees = new Hashtable(31);

    public void Run()
    {
        EmployeeID idMortimer = new EmployeeID("B001");
        EmployeeData mortimer = new EmployeeData(idMortimer, "Mortimer",
                                                 100000.00M);
        EmployeeID idArabel = new EmployeeID("W234");
        EmployeeData arabel= new EmployeeData(idArabel, "Arabel Jones",
                                              10000.00M);

        employees.Add(idMortimer, mortimer);
        employees.Add(idArabel, arabel);

        while (true)
        {
            try
            {
                Console.Write("Enter employee ID (format:A999, X to exit)> ");
                string userInput = Console.ReadLine();
                userInput = userInput.ToUpper();
                if (userInput == "X")
                    return;
                EmployeeID id = new EmployeeID(userInput);
                DisplayData(id);
            }
            catch (Exception e)
            {
                Console.WriteLine("Exception occurred. Did you use the correct
                                  format for the employee ID?");
                Console.WriteLine(e.Message);
                Console.WriteLine();
            }

            Console.WriteLine();
        }
    }

    private void DisplayData(EmployeeID id)
    {
        object empobj = employees[id];
        if (empobj != null)
        {
            EmployeeData employee = (EmployeeData)empobj;
            Console.WriteLine("Employee: " + employee.ToString());
        }
        else
```

```
            Console.WriteLine("Employee not found: ID = " + id);
    }
}
```

TestHarness contains the member field, which actually is the dictionary.

As usual for a dictionary, we have set the initial capacity to a prime number; in this case, 31. The guts of the test harness are in the Run() method. This method first sets up details for two employees—mortimer and arabel—and adds their details to the dictionary:

```
employees.Add(idMortimer, mortimer);

employees.Add(idArabel, arabel);
```

Next, we enter the while loop that repeatedly asks the user to input an employeeID. There is a try block inside the while loop, which is just there to trap any problems caused by the user typing in something that's not the correct format for an EmployeeID, which would cause the EmployeeID constructor to throw an exception when it tries to construct an ID from the string:

```
string userInput = Console.ReadLine();
userInput = userInput.ToUpper();
if (userInput == "X")
    return;
EmployeeID id = new EmployeeID(userInput);
```

If the EmployeeID was constructed correctly, we display the associated employee by calling a method, DisplayData(). This is the method in which we finally get to access the dictionary with array syntax. Indeed, retrieving the employee data for the employee with this ID is the first thing we do in this method:

```
private void DisplayData(EmployeeID id)
{
```

```
    object empobj = employees[id];
```

If there is no employee with that ID in the dictionary, then employees[id] will return null, which is why we check for a null reference and display an appropriate error message if we find one. Otherwise, we simply cast our returned empobj reference to an EmployeeData. (Remember that Hashtable is a very generic dictionary class; it is storing objects, so retrieving an element from it will return an object reference, which we need to cast back to the type that we originally placed in the dictionary.) Once we have our EmployeeID reference, we can simply display the employee data using the EmployeeData.ToString() method:

```
        EmployeeData employee = (EmployeeData)empobj;
        Console.WriteLine("Employee: " + employee.ToString());
```

We have one final part of the code—the Main() method that kicks the whole sample off. This simply instantiates a TestHarness object and runs it:

```
static void Main()
{
    TestHarness harness = new TestHarness();
    harness.Run();
}
```

Summary

This chapter took a look at working with different sorts of collections in your code. We discussed array lists, dictionaries, and collections. In addition to these types of collections, if you look in the SDK documentation of all the collections that implement the `ICollection` or `IEnumerable` interfaces, you will actually find a long list of available classes at your disposal. Included in this list of classes, you will find a collection that should satisfy your needs. For example, in addition to the `ArrayList` and `Hashtable` classes, you will find other great collection objects such as the `SortedList`, `Queue`, and `Stack` classes. When implementing a collection in your code, think through the size, type, and performance that your collection requires and consider all your options. The .NET Framework provides a tremendous amount of possibilities for this type of work.

10

Reflection

Reflection is a generic term that describes the ability to inspect and manipulate program elements at runtime. For example, reflection allows you to:

- ❑ Enumerate the members of a type
- ❑ Instantiate a new object
- ❑ Execute the members of an object
- ❑ Find out information about a type
- ❑ Find out information about an assembly
- ❑ Inspect the custom attributes applied to a type
- ❑ Create and compile a new assembly

This list represents a great deal of functionality and encompasses some of the most powerful and complex capabilities provided by the .NET Framework class library. Unfortunately, we do not have the space to cover all the capabilities of reflection in this chapter and so we will focus on those elements you will use most frequently.

We begin with a discussion of custom attributes, a mechanism that allows you to associate custom metadata with program elements. This metadata is created at compile time and embedded in an assembly. You can then inspect the metadata at runtime using some of the capabilities of reflection.

After looking at custom attributes we look at some of the fundamental classes that enable reflection, including the `System.Type` and `System.Reflection.Assembly` classes, which provide the access points for much of what you can do with reflection.

To demonstrate custom attributes and reflection, we will develop an example based on a company that regularly ships upgrades to its software, and wants to have details of these upgrades documented automatically. In the example, we will define custom attributes that indicate the date when program elements where last modified, and what changes were made. We will then use reflection to develop an application that looks for these attributes in an assembly, and can automatically display all the details about what upgrades that have been made to the software since a given date.

Another example we will discuss considers an application that reads from or writes to a database and uses custom attributes as a way of marking which classes and properties correspond to which database tables and columns. By reading these attributes from the assembly at runtime, the program is able to automatically retrieve or write data to the appropriate location in the database, without requiring specific logic for each table or column.

Custom Attributes

We've discussed how you can define attributes on various items within your program. These attributes have been defined by Microsoft as part of the .NET Framework class library, many of which receive special support by the C# compiler. This means that for those particular attributes, the compiler could customize the compilation process in specific ways; for example, laying out a struct in memory according to the details in the StructLayout attributes.

The .Net Framework also allows you to define your own attributes. Clearly, these attributes will not have any effect on the compilation process, because the compiler has no intrinsic awareness of them. However, these attributes will be emitted as metadata in the compiled assembly when they are applied to program elements. By itself, this metadata might be useful for documentation purposes, but what makes attributes really powerful is that using reflection, your code can read this metadata and use it to make decisions at runtime. This means that the custom attributes that you define can have a direct effect on how your code runs.

Writing Custom Attributes

In order to understand how to write custom attributes, it is useful to know what the compiler does when it encounters an element in your code that has a custom attribute applied to it. To take our database example, suppose you have a C# property declaration that looks like this:

```
[FieldName("SocialSecurityNumber")]
public string SocialSecurityNumber
{
    get {
        // etc.
```

When the C# compiler recognizes that this property has an attribute applied to it (FieldName), it will start by appending the string Attribute to this name, forming the combined name FieldNameAttribute. The compiler will then search all the namespaces in its search path (those namespaces that have been mentioned in a using statement) for a class with the specified name. Note that if you mark an item with an attribute whose name already ends in the string Attribute, then the compiler won't add the string to the name a second time, leaving the attribute name unchanged. Therefore, the previous code is equivalent to this:

```
[FieldNameAttribute("SocialSecurityNumber")]
public string SocialSecurityNumber
{
   get {
   // etc.
```

The compiler expects to find a class with this name and it expects this class to be derived from `System.Attribute`. The compiler also expects that this class contains information that governs the use of the attribute. In particular, the attribute class needs to specify:

❑ The types of program elements to which the attribute can be applied (classes, structs, properties, methods, and so on).

❑ Whether it is legal for the attribute to be applied more than once to the same program element.

❑ Whether the attribute, when applied to a class or interface, is inherited by derived classes and interfaces.

❑ The compulsory and optional parameters the attribute takes.

If the compiler cannot find a corresponding attribute class or it finds one, but the way that you have used that attribute doesn't match the information in the attribute class, then the compiler will raise a compilation error. For example, if the attribute class indicates that the attribute can only be applied to classes, but you have applied it to a struct definition, a compilation error will occur.

To continue with our example, let's assume we have defined the `FieldName` attribute like this:

```
[AttributeUsage(AttributeTargets.Property,
   AllowMultiple=false,
   Inherited=false)]
public class FieldNameAttribute : Attribute
{
   private string name;
   public FieldNameAttribute(string name)
   {
      this.name = name;
   }
}
```

We will discuss each element of this definition in the following sections.

AttributeUsage attribute

The first thing to note is that our attribute class itself is marked with an attribute—the `System.AttributeUsage` attribute. This is an attribute defined by Microsoft for which the C# compiler provides special support. (You could argue that `AttributeUsage` isn't an attribute at all; it is more like a meta-attribute, because it applies to other attributes, not simply to any class.) The primary purpose of `AttributeUsage` is to indicate which types of program elements your custom attribute can be applied to. This information is given by the first parameter of the `AttributeUsage` attribute—this parameter is mandatory, and is of an enumerated type, AttributeTargets. In the previous example, we have indicated that the FieldName attribute can be applied only to properties, which is fine, because that is exactly what we have applied it to in our earlier code fragment. The members of the AttributeTargets enumeration are:

```
public enum AttributeTargets
{
   All = 0x00003FFF,
   Assembly = 0x00000001,
   Class = 0x00000004,
   Constructor = 0x00000020,
   Delegate = 0x00001000,
   Enum = 0x00000010,
   Event = 0x00000200,
   Field = 0x00000100,
   Interface = 0x00000400,
   Method = 0x00000040,
   Module = 0x00000002,
   Parameter = 0x00000800,
   Property = 0x00000080,
   ReturnValue = 0x00002000,
   Struct = 0x00000008
}
```

This list identifies all of the program elements to which you can apply attributes. Note that when applying the attribute to a program element, we place the attribute in square brackets immediately before the element. However, there are two values in the above list that do not correspond to any program element: Assembly and Module. An attribute can be applied to an assembly or module as a whole instead of to an element in your code; in this case the attribute can be placed anywhere in your source code, but needs to be prefixed with the Assembly or Module keyword:

```
[assembly:SomeAssemblyAttribute(Parameters)]
[module:SomeAssemblyAttribute(Parameters)]
```

When indicating the valid target elements of a custom attribute, you can combine these values using the bitwise OR operator. For example, if we wanted to indicate that our FieldName attribute could be applied to both a properties and fields, we could write:

```
[AttributeUsage(AttributeTargets.Property | AttributeTargets.Field,

   AllowMultiple=false,
   Inherited=false)]
public class FieldNameAttribute : Attribute
```

You can also use AttributeTargets.All to indicate that your attribute can be applied to all types of program elements. The AttributeUsage attribute also contains two other parameters, AllowMultiple and Inherited. These are specified using the syntax of <ParameterName>=<ParameterValue>, instead of simply giving the values for these parameters. These parameters are optional parameters—you can omit them if you want.

The AllowMultiple parameter indicates whether an attribute can be applied more than once to the same item. The fact that it is set to false here indicates that the compiler should raise an error if it sees something like this:

```
[FieldName("SocialSecurityNumber")]
[FieldName("NationalInsuranceNumber")]
public string SocialSecurityNumber
{

    // etc.
```

If the `Inherited` parameter is set to `true`, an attribute that is applied to a class or interface will also automatically be applied to all derived classes or interfaces. If the attribute is applied to a method or property, then it will automatically apply to any overrides of that method or property, and so on.

Specifying attribute parameters

Now let's examine how we can specify the parameters that our custom attribute takes. The way it works is that when the compiler encounters a statement such as

```
[FieldName("SocialSecurityNumber")]
public string SocialSecurityNumber
{

    // etc.
```

it examines the parameters passed into the attribute—in this case a string—and looks for a constructor for the attribute that takes exactly those parameters. If the compiler finds an appropriate constructor, the compiler will emit the specified metadata to the assembly. If the compiler doesn't find an appropriate constructor, a compilation error occurs. As we discuss later in this chapter, reflection involves reading metadata (attributes) from assemblies and instantiating the attribute classes they represent. Because of this, the compiler must ensure an appropriate constructor exists that will allow the runtime instantiation of the specified attribute.

In our case, we have supplied just one constructor for `FieldNameAttribute`, and this constructor takes one string parameter. Therefore, when applying the `FieldName` attribute to a property, we must supply one string as a parameter, as we have done in the previous sample code.

If you want to allow a choice of what types of parameters should be supplied with an attribute, you can provide different constructor overloads, although normal practice is to supply just one constructor, and use properties to define any other optional parameters, as we explain next.

Specifying optional attribute parameters

We demonstrated with reference to the `AttributeUsage` attribute, there is an alternative syntax by which optional parameters can be added to an attribute. This syntax involves specifying the names and values of the optional parameters. It works through `public` properties or fields in the attribute class. For example, suppose we modified our definition of the `SocialSecurityNumber` property as follows:

```
[FieldName("SocialSecurityNumber", Comment="This is the primary key field")]
public string SocialSecurityNumber
{

    // etc.
```

In this case, the compiler recognizes the <ParameterName>= <ParameterValue> syntax of the second parameter, and does not attempt to match this parameter to a FieldNameAttribute constructor. Instead, it looks for a public property or field (although public fields are not considered good programming practice, so normally you will work with properties) of that name that it can use to set the value of this parameter. If we want the above code to work, we have to add some code to FieldNameAttribute:

```
[AttributeUsage(AttributeTargets.Property,
    AllowMultiple=false,
    Inherited=false)]
public class FieldNameAttribute : Attribute
{
    private string comment;
    public string Comment
    {
        get
        {
            return comment;
        }
        set
        {
            comment = value;
        }
    }

        // etc.
```

Custom Attribute Example: WhatsNewAttributes

In this section, we will start developing the WhatsNewAttributes example described earlier, which provides for an attribute that indicates when a program element was last modified. This is a rather more ambitious code sample than many of the others we use in that it consists of three separate assemblies:

❑   The WhatsNewAttributes assembly, which contains the definitions of the attributes.

❑   The VectorClass assembly, which contains the code to which the attributes have been applied. (This is similar to the Vector sample that we have used in other chapters.)

❑   The LookUpWhatsNew assembly, which contains the project that displays details of items that have changed.

Of these, only LookUpWhatsNew is a console application of the type that we have used up until now. The remaining two assemblies are libraries—they each contain class definitions, but no program entry point. For the VectorClass assembly, this means that we have taken the VectorAsCollection sample and removed the entry point and test harness class, leaving only the Vector class.

Managing three related assemblies by compiling at the command line is tricky; and although we provide the commands for compiling all these source files separately, you might prefer to edit the code sample (which you can download from the Wrox Web site at www.wrox.com) as a combined Visual Studio .NET solution as discussed in Chapter 12. The download includes the required Visual Studio .NET solution files.

The WhatsNewAttributes library assembly

We will start off with the core `WhatsNewAttributes` assembly. The source code is contained in the file WhatsNewAttributes.cs. The syntax for doing this is quite simple. At the command line we supply the flag `target:library` to the compiler. To compile `WhatsNewAttributes`, type in:

```
csc /target:library WhatsNewAttributes.cs
```

The WhatsNewAttributes.cs file defines two attribute classes, `LastModifiedAttribute` and `Supports WhatsNewAttribute`. `LastModifiedAttribute` is the attribute that we can use to mark when an item was last modified. It takes two mandatory parameters (parameters that are passed to the constructor): the date of the modification, and a string containing a description of the changes. There is also one optional parameter named `issues` (for which a `public` property exists), which can be used to describe any outstanding issues for the item.

In real life you would probably want this attribute to apply to anything. In order to keep our code simple, we are going to limit its usage here to classes and methods. We will allow it to be applied more than once to the same item, however, (`AllowMultiple=true`) since an item might be modified more than once, and each modification will have to be marked with a separate attribute instance.

`SupportsWhatsNew` is a smaller class representing an attribute that doesn't take any parameters. The idea of this attribute is that it's an assembly attribute that is used to mark an assembly for which we are maintaining documentation via the `LastModifiedAttribute`. This way, the program that will examine this assembly later on knows that the assembly it is reading is one on which we are actually using our automated documentation process. Here is the complete source code for this part of the example:

```csharp
using System;

namespace Wrox.ProCSharp.WhatsNewAttributes
{
   [AttributeUsage(
      AttributeTargets.Class | AttributeTargets.Method,
      AllowMultiple=true, Inherited=false)]
   public class LastModifiedAttribute : Attribute
   {
      private DateTime dateModified;
      private string changes;
      private string issues;

      public LastModifiedAttribute(string dateModified, string changes)
      {
         this.dateModified = DateTime.Parse(dateModified);
         this.changes = changes;
      }

      public DateTime DateModified
      {
         get
         {
            return dateModified;
         }
      }
```

```
      public string Changes
      {
         get
         {
            return changes;
         }
      }

      public string Issues
      {
         get
         {
            return issues;
         }
         set
         {
            issues = value;
         }
      }
   }

   [AttributeUsage(AttributeTargets.Assembly)]
   public class SupportsWhatsNewAttribute : Attribute
   {
   }
}
```

This code should be clear with reference to our previous descriptions. Notice, however, that we have not bothered to supply set accessors to the Changes and DateModified properties. There is no need for these accessors, since we are requiring these parameters to be set in the constructor as compulsory parameters. (In case you're wondering why we need the get accessors, we use them so we can read the values of these attributes if necessary.)

The VectorClass assembly

Next, we need to use these attributes. To this end, we use a modified version of the earlier VectorAs Collection sample. Note that we need to reference the WhatsNewAttributes library that we have just created. We also need to indicate the corresponding namespace with a using statement so the compiler can recognize the attributes:

```
using System;
using Wrox.ProCSharp.WhatsNewAttributes;
using System.Collections;
using System.Text;
[assembly: SupportsWhatsNew]
```

In this code, we have also added the line that will mark the assembly itself with the SupportsWhatsNew attribute.

Now for the code for the Vector class. We are not making any major changes to this class; we only add a couple of LastModified attributes to mark out the work that we have done on this class in this chapter, and we define Vector as a class instead of a struct to simplify the code (of the next iteration of our sample) that displays the attributes. (In the `VectorAsCollection` sample, `Vector` is a struct, but its enumerator is a class. This means the next iteration of our sample would have had to pick out both classes and structs when looking at the assembly, which would have made the example less straightforward.)

```
namespace Wrox.ProCSharp.VectorClass
{
    [LastModified("14 Feb 2002", "IEnumerable interface implemented " +
        "So Vector can now be treated as a collection")]
    [LastModified("10 Feb 2002", "IFormattable interface implemented " +
        "So Vector now responds to format specifiers N and VE")]
    class Vector : IFormattable, IEnumerable
    {
        public double x, y, z;

        public Vector(double x, double y, double z)
        {
            this.x = x;
            this.y = y;
            this.z = z;
        }

        [LastModified("10 Feb 2002",
                     "Method added in order to provide formatting support")]
        public string ToString(string format, IFormatProvider formatProvider)
        {
            if (format == null)
                return ToString();
```

We also mark the contained `VectorEnumerator` class as new:

```
        [LastModified("14 Feb 2002",
                     "Class created as part of collection support for Vector")]
        private class VectorEnumerator : IEnumerator
        {
```

That's as far as we can get with this sample for now. We can't run anything yet, because all we have are two libraries. We will develop the final part of the example, in which we look up and display these attributes, as soon as we've had a look at how reflection works.

In order to compile this code from the command line you should type the following:

csc /target:library /reference:WhatsNewAttributes.dll VectorClass.cs

Reflection

In this section, we take a closer look at the `System.Type` class, which lets you access information concerning the definition of any given data type. We will then discuss the `System.Reflection.Assembly` class, which you can use to access information about an assembly, or to load that assembly into your program. Finally, we will combine the code in this section with the code of the previous section to complete the `WhatsNewAttributes` sample.

The System.Type Class

So far we have used the `Type` class only to hold the reference to a type as follows:

```
Type t = typeof(double);
```

Although we have previously referred to `Type` as a class, it is an abstract base class. Whenever you instantiate a `Type` object, you are actually instantiating a class derived from `Type`. `Type` has one derived class corresponding to each actual data type, though in general the derived classes simply provide different overloads of the various `Type` methods and properties that return the correct data for the corresponding data type. They do not generally add new methods or properties. In general, there are three common ways of obtaining a `Type` reference that refers to any given type:

❑ You can use the C# `typeof` operator as in the previous code. This operator takes the name of the type (not in quote marks however) as a parameter.

❑ You can use the `GetType()` method, which all classes inherit from `System.Object`:

```
double d = 10;
Type t = d.GetType();
```

`GetType()` is called against a variable, rather than taking the name of a type. Note, however, that the `Type` object returned is still associated with only that data type. It does not contain any information that relates to that instance of the type. The `GetType()` method can be useful if you have a reference to an object, but are not sure what class that object is actually an instance of.

❑ You can call the `static` method of the `Type` class, `GetType()`:

```
Type t = Type.GetType("System.Double");
```

`Type` is really the gateway to much of the reflection technology. It implements a huge number of methods and properties—far too many to provide a comprehensive list here. However, the following sub-sections should give you some idea of the kind of things you can do with the `Type` class. Note that the available properties are all read-only; you use `Type` to find out about the data type—you can't use it to make any modifications to the type!

Type properties

You can split the properties implemented by `Type` into three categories:

❑ There are a number of properties that retrieve the strings containing various names associated with the class:

Property	Returns
Name	The name of the data type
FullName	The fully qualified name of the data type (including the namespace name)
Namespace	The name of the namespace in which the data type is defined

❏ It is also possible to retrieve references to further type objects that represent related classes:

Property	Returns Type Reference Corresponding To
BaseType	Immediate base type of this type
UnderlyingSystemType	The type that this type maps to in the .NET runtime (recall that certain .NET base types actually map to specific predefined types recognized by IL)

❏ There are a number of Boolean properties that indicate whether or not this type is, for example, a class, an enum, and so on. These properties include IsAbstract, IsArray, IsClass, IsEnum, IsInterface, IsPointer, IsPrimitive (one of the predefined primitive data types), IsPublic, IsSealed, and IsValueType.

For example, using a primitive data type:

```
Type intType = typeof(int);
Console.WriteLine(intType.IsAbstract);    // writes false
Console.WriteLine(intType.IsClass);       // writes false
Console.WriteLine(intType.IsEnum);        // writes false
Console.WriteLine(intType.IsPrimitive);   // writes true
Console.WriteLine(intType.IsValueType);   // writes true
```

Or using our Vector class:

```
Type intType = typeof(Vector);
Console.WriteLine(intType.IsAbstract);    // writes false
Console.WriteLine(intType.IsClass);       // writes true
Console.WriteLine(intType.IsEnum);        // writes false
Console.WriteLine(intType.IsPrimitive);   // writes false
Console.WriteLine(intType.IsValueType);   // writes false
```

You can also retrieve a reference to the assembly that the type is defined in. This is returned as a reference to an instance of the System.Reflection.Assembly class, which we will examine shortly:

```
Type t = typeof (Vector);
Assembly containingAssembly = new Assembly(t);
```

Methods

Most of the methods of System.Type are used to obtain details of the members of the corresponding data type—the constructors, properties, methods, events, and so on. There are quite a large number of methods, but they all follow the same pattern. For example, there are two methods that retrieve details of the methods of the data type: GetMethod() and GetMethods(). GetMethod() returns a reference to a System.Reflection.MethodInfo object, which contains details of a method. GetMethods() returns an array of such references. The difference is that GetMethods() returns details of all the methods, while GetMethod() returns details of just one method with a specified parameter list. Both methods have overloads that take an extra parameter, a BindingFlags enumerated value that indicates which members should be returned—for example, whether to return public members, instance members, static members, and so on.

So for example, the simplest overload of GetMethods() takes no parameters and returns details of all the public methods of the data type:

```
Type t = typeof(double);
MethodInfo [] methods = t.GetMethods();
foreach (MethodInfo nextMethod in methods)
{

   // etc.
```

Following the same pattern are the following member methods of Type:

Type of Object Returned	Methods (The Method with the Plural Name Returns an Array)
ConstructorInfo	GetConstructor(), GetConstructors()
EventInfo	GetEvent(), GetEvents()
FieldInfo	GetField(), GetFields()
InterfaceInfo	GetInterface(), GetInterfaces()
MemberInfo	GetMember(), GetMembers()
MethodInfo	GetMethod(), GetMethods()
PropertyInfo	GetProperty(), GetProperties()

The GetMember() and GetMembers() methods return details of any or all members of the data type, irrespective of whether these members are constructors, properties, methods, and so on. Finally, note that it is possible to invoke members either by calling the InvokeMember() method of Type, or by calling the Invoke() method of the MethodInfo, PropertyInfo, and the other classes.

The TypeView Example

We will now demonstrate some of the features of the Type class by writing a short example, TypeView, which we can use to list the members of a data type. We will demonstrate how to use TypeView for a double; however, we can swap this type with any other data type just by changing one line of the code for the sample. TypeView displays far more information than can be displayed in a console window, so we're going to take a break from our normal practice and display the output in a message box. Running TypeView for a double produces the results shown in Figure 10-1.

The message box displays the name, full name, and namespace of the data type as well as the name of the underlying type and the base type. Next, it simply iterates through all the public instance members of the data type, displaying for each member the declaring type, the type of member (method, field, and so on) and the name of the member. The *declaring type* is the name of the class that actually declares the type member (in other words, System.Double if it is defined or overridden in System.Double, or the name of the relevant base type if the member is simply inherited from some base class).

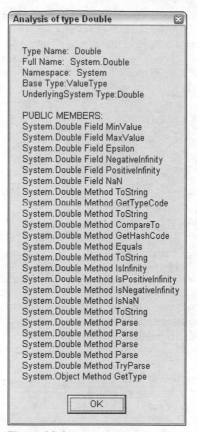

Figure 10-1

`TypeView` does not display signatures of methods because we are retrieving details of all public instance members through `MemberInfo` objects, and information about parameters is not available through a `MemberInfo` object. In order to retrieve that information, we would need references to `MethodInfo` and other more specific objects, which means we would need to obtain details of each type of member separately.

`TypeView` does display details of all public instance members, but it happens that for doubles, the only ones defined are fields and methods. We will compile `TypeView` as a console application—there is no problem with displaying a message box from a console application. However, the fact that we are using a message box means that we need to reference the base class assembly `System.Windows.Forms.dll`, which contains the classes in the `System.Windows.Forms` namespace in which the `MessageBox` class that we will need is defined. The code for `TypeView` is as follows; to begin, we need to add a couple of `using` statements:

```
using System;
using System.Text;
using System.Windows.Forms;
using System.Reflection;
```

We need `System.Text` because we will be using a `StringBuilder` object to build up the text to be displayed in the message box, and `System.Windows.Forms` for the message box itself. The entire code is in one class, `MainClass`, which has a couple of `static` methods, and one `static` field, a `StringBuilder` instance called `OutputText`, which will be used to build up the text to be displayed in the message box. The main method and class declaration look like this:

```
class MainClass
{
   static void Main()
   {
      // modify this line to retrieve details of any
      // other data type
      Type t = typeof(double);

      AnalyzeType(t);
      MessageBox.Show(OutputText.ToString(), "Analysis of type "
                                        + t.Name);

      Console.ReadLine();
   }
```

The `Main()` method implementation starts by declaring a `Type` object to represent our chosen data type. We then call a method, `AnalyzeType()`, which extracts the information from the `Type` object and uses it to build up the output text. Finally, we show the output in a message box. Using it is fairly intuitive. We just call its `static` `Show()` method, passing it two strings, which will, respectively, be the text in the box and the caption. `AnalyzeType()` is where the bulk of the work is done:

```
   static void AnalyzeType(Type t)
   {
      AddToOutput("Type Name:   " + t.Name);
      AddToOutput("Full Name:   " + t.FullName);
      AddToOutput("Namespace:   " + t.Namespace);
      Type tBase = t.BaseType;
      if (tBase != null)
         AddToOutput("Base Type:" + tBase.Name);
      Type tUnderlyingSystem = t.UnderlyingSystemType;
      if (tUnderlyingSystem != null)
         AddToOutput("UnderlyingSystem Type:" + tUnderlyingSystem.Name);

      AddToOutput("\nPUBLIC MEMBERS:");
      MemberInfo [] Members = t.GetMembers();
      foreach (MemberInfo NextMember in Members)
      {
         AddToOutput(NextMember.DeclaringType + " " +
         NextMember.MemberType + " " + NextMember.Name);
      }
   }
```

We implement this method by calling various properties of the `Type` object to get the information we need concerning the names, then call the `GetMembers()` method to get an array of `MemberInfo` objects that we can use to display the details of each method. Note that we use a helper method, `AddToOutput()`, to build up the text to be displayed in the message box:

```
static void AddToOutput(string Text)
{
    OutputText.Append("\n" + Text);
}
```

Compile the `TypeView` assembly using this command:

csc /reference:System.Windows.Forms.dll TypeView.cs

The Assembly Class

The `Assembly` class is defined in the `System.Reflection` namespace, and allows you access to the metadata for a given assembly. It also contains methods to allow you to load and even execute an assembly, assuming the assembly is an executable. Like the `Type` class, `Assembly` contains a large number of methods and properties—too many for us to cover here. Instead, we will confine ourselves to covering those methods and properties that you need to get started, and which we will use to complete the `WhatsNewAttributes` sample.

Before you can do anything with an `Assembly` instance, you need to load the corresponding assembly into the running process. You can do this with either the `static` members `Assembly.Load()` or `Assembly.LoadFrom()`. The difference between these methods is that `Load()` takes the name of the assembly, and the runtime searches in a variety of locations in an attempt to locate the assembly. These locations include the local directory and the global assembly cache. `LoadFrom()` takes the full path name of an assembly and does not attempt to find the assembly in any other location:

```
Assembly assembly1 = Assembly.Load("SomeAssembly");
Assembly assembly2 = Assembly.LoadFrom
    (@"C:\My Projects\Software\SomeOtherAssembly");
```

There are a number of other overloads of both methods, which supply additional security information. Once you have loaded an assembly, you can use various properties on it to find out, for example, its full name:

```
string name = assembly1.FullName;
```

Finding out about types defined in an assembly

One nice feature of the `Assembly` class is that it allows you to obtain details of all the types that are defined in the corresponding assembly. You simply call the `Assembly.GetTypes()` method, which returns an array of `System.Type` references containing details of all the types. You can then manipulate these `Type` references just as you would with a `Type` object obtained from the C# `typeof` operator, or from `Object.GetType()`:

```
Type[] types = theAssembly.GetTypes();
foreach(Type definedType in types)
{
    DoSomethingWith(definedType);
}
```

Finding out about custom attributes

The methods you use to find out which custom attributes are defined on an assembly or type depend on what type of object the attribute is attached to. If you want to find out what custom attributes are attached to an assembly as a whole, you need to call a static method of the `Attribute` class, `GetCustom Attributes()`, passing in a reference to the assembly:

```
Attribute[] definedAttributes =
           Attribute.GetCustomAttributes(assembly1);
           // assembly1 is an Assembly object
```

This is actually quite significant. You may have wondered why, when we defined custom attributes, we had to go to all the trouble of actually writing classes for them, and why Microsoft hadn't come up with some simpler syntax. Well, the answer is here. The custom attributes do genuinely exist as objects, and when an assembly is loaded you can read in these attribute objects, examine their properties, and call their methods.

`GetCustomAttributes()`, used to get assembly attributes, has a couple of overloads. If you call it without specifying any parameters other than an assembly reference, then it will simply return all the custom attributes defined for that assembly. You can also call `GetCustomAttributes()` specifying a second parameter, which is a `Type` object that indicates the attribute class in which you are interested. In this case `GetCustomAttributes()` returns an array consisting of all the attributes present that are of that type.

Note that all attributes are retrieved as plain `Attribute` references. If you want to call any of the methods or properties you defined for your custom attributes, then you will need to cast these references explicitly to the relevant custom attribute classes. You can obtain details of custom attributes that are attached to a given data type by calling another overload of `Assembly.GetCustomAttributes()`, this time passing a `Type` reference that describes the type for which you want to retrieve any attached attributes. On the other hand, if you want to obtain attributes that are attached to methods, constructors, fields, and so on, then you will need to call a `GetCustomAttributes()` method that is a member of one of the classes `MethodInfo`, `ConstructorInfo`, `FieldInfo`, and so on.

If you only expect a single attribute of a given type, you can call the `GetCustomAttribute()` method instead, which returns a single `Attribute` object. We will use `GetCustomAttribute()` in the `Whats NewAttributes` example in order to find out whether the `SupportsWhatsNew` attribute is present in the assembly. To do this, we call `GetCustomAttribute()`, passing in a reference to the `WhatsNewAttributes` assembly, and the type of the `SupportWhatsNewAttribute` attribute. If this attribute is present, we get an `Attribute` instance. If there are no instances of it defined in the assembly, then we get `null`. And if there are two or more instances found, `GetCustomAttribute()` throws a `System.Reflection.AmbiguousMatchException`:

```
Attribute supportsAttribute =
           Attribute.GetCustomAttributes(assembly1,
           typeof(SupportsWhatsNewAttribute));
```

Completing the WhatsNewAttributes Sample

We now have enough information to complete the `WhatsNewAttributes` sample by writing the source code for the final assembly in the sample, the `LookUpWhatsNew` assembly. This part of the application is a console application. However, it needs to reference the other assemblies of `WhatsNewAttributes` and

`VectorClass`. Although this is going to be a command-line application, we will follow the previous `TypeView` sample in actually displaying our results in a message box, since there is a lot of text output—too much to show in a console window screenshot.

The file is called `LookUpWhatsNew.cs`, and the command to compile it is:

csc /reference:WhatsNewAttributes.dll /reference:VectorClass.dll LookUpWhatsNew.cs

In the source code of this file, we first indicate the namespaces we want to infer. `System.Text` is there because we need to use a `StringBuilder` object again:

```
using System;
using System.Reflection;
using System.Windows.Forms;
using System.Text;
using Wrox.ProCSharp.VectorClass;
using Wrox.ProCSharp.WhatsNewAttributes;

namespace Wrox.ProCSharp.LookUpWhatsNew
{
```

The class that contains the main program entry point as well as the other methods is `WhatsNewChecker`. All the methods we define are in this class, which also has two static fields: `outputText`, which contains the text as we build it up in preparation for writing it to the message box, and `backDateTo`, which stores the date we have selected. All modifications made since this date will be displayed. Normally, we would display a dialog box inviting the user to pick this date, but we don't want to get sidetracked into that kind of code. For this reason, `backDateTo` is hard-coded to a value of 1 Feb 2002. You can easily change this date if you want when you download the code:

```
class WhatsNewChecker
{
    static StringBuilder outputText = new StringBuilder(1000);
    static DateTime backDateTo = new DateTime(2002, 2, 1);

    static void Main()
    {
        Assembly theAssembly = Assembly.Load("VectorClass");
        Attribute supportsAttribute =
            Attribute.GetCustomAttribute(
                theAssembly, typeof(SupportsWhatsNewAttribute));
        string Name = theAssembly.FullName;

        AddToMessage("Assembly: " + Name);
        if (supportsAttribute == null)
        {
            AddToMessage(
                "This assembly does not support WhatsNew attributes");
            return;
        }
        else
            AddToMessage("Defined Types:");
```

```
                  Type[] types = theAssembly.GetTypes();
               foreach(Type definedType in types)
                  DisplayTypeInfo(theAssembly, definedType);

               MessageBox.Show(outputText.ToString(),
                  "What\'s New since " + backDateTo.ToLongDateString());
               Console.ReadLine();
            }
```

The `Main()` method first loads the `VectorClass` assembly, and verifies that it is indeed marked with the `SupportsWhatsNew` attribute. We know `VectorClass` has the `SupportsWhatsNew` attribute applied to it because we have only recently compiled it, but this is a check that would be worth making if the user was given a choice of what assembly to check.

Assuming all is well, we use the `Assembly.GetTypes()` method to get an array of all the types defined in this assembly, and then loop through them. For each one, we call a method that we have written, `Display TypeInfo()`, which will add the relevant text, including details of any instances of `LastModified Attribute`, to the `outputText` field. Finally, we show the message box with the complete text. The `DisplayTypeInfo()` method looks like this:

```
         static void DisplayTypeInfo(Assembly theAssembly, Type type)
         {
            // make sure we only pick out classes
            if (!(type.IsClass))
               return;
            AddToMessage("\nclass " + type.Name);

            Attribute [] attribs = Attribute.GetCustomAttributes(type);
            if (attribs.Length == 0)
               AddToMessage("No changes to this class\n");
            else
               foreach (Attribute attrib in attribs)
                  WriteAttributeInfo(attrib);

            MethodInfo [] methods = type.GetMethods();
            AddToMessage("CHANGES TO METHODS OF THIS CLASS:");
            foreach (MethodInfo nextMethod in methods)
            {
               object [] attribs2 =
                  nextMethod.GetCustomAttributes(
                     typeof(LastModifiedAttribute), false);
               if (attribs2 != null)
               {
                  AddToMessage(
                     nextMethod.ReturnType + " " + nextMethod.Name + "()");
                  foreach (Attribute nextAttrib in attribs2)
                     WriteAttributeInfo(nextAttrib);
               }
            }
         }
```

Notice that the first thing we do in this method is check whether the `Type` reference we have been passed actually represents a class. Since, in order to keep things simple, we have specified that the

LastModified attribute can only be applied to classes or member methods, we would be wasting our time doing any processing if the item is not a class (it could be a class, delegate, or enum).

Next, we use the Attribute.GetCustomAttributes() method to find out if this class does have any LastModifiedAttribute instances attached to it. If it does, we add their details to the output text, using a helper method, WriteAttributeInfo().

Finally, we use the Type.GetMethods() method to iterate through all the member methods of this data type, and then do the same with each method as we did for the class—check if it has any LastModified Attribute instances attached to it and, if so, display them using WriteAttributeInfo().

The next bit of code shows the WriteAttributeInfo() method, which is responsible for working out what text to display for a given LastModifiedAttribute instance. Note that this method is passed an Attribute reference, so it needs to cast this to a LastModifiedAttribute reference first. After it has done that, it uses the properties that we originally defined for this attribute to retrieve its parameters. It checks that the date of the attribute is sufficiently recent before actually adding it to the text for display:

```
static void WriteAttributeInfo(Attribute attrib)
{

    LastModifiedAttribute lastModifiedAttrib =
        attrib as LastModifiedAttribute;
    if (lastModifiedAttrib == null)
        return;

    // check that date is in range
    DateTime modifiedDate = lastModifiedAttrib.DateModified;
    if (modifiedDate < backDateTo)
        return;

    AddToMessage("  MODIFIED: " +
        modifiedDate.ToLongDateString() + ":");
    AddToMessage("      " + lastModifiedAttrib.Changes);
    if (lastModifiedAttrib.Issues != null)
        AddToMessage("      Outstanding issues:" +
            lastModifiedAttrib.Issues);
}
```

Finally, here is the helper AddToMessage() method:

```
static void AddToMessage(string message)
{
    outputText.Append("\n" + message);
}
```

Running this code produces these results shown in Figure 10-2.

Notice that when we list the types defined in the VectorClass assembly, we actually pick up two classes: Vector, and the embedded VectorEnumerator class. Also notice that since the backDateTo date of 1 Feb is hard-coded in this example, we actually pick up the attributes that are dated 14 Feb (when we added the collection stuff), but not those dated 14 Jan (when we added the IFormattable interface).

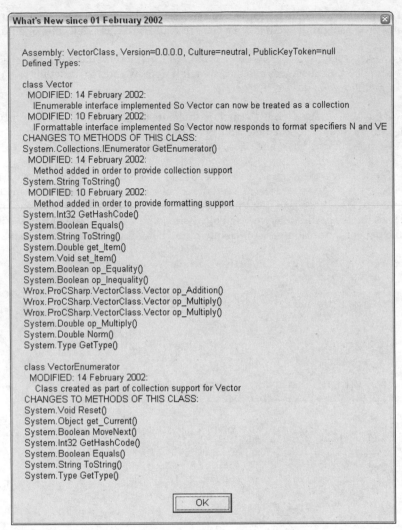

What's New since 01 February 2002

Assembly: VectorClass, Version=0.0.0.0, Culture=neutral, PublicKeyToken=null
Defined Types:

class Vector
  MODIFIED: 14 February 2002:
    IEnumerable interface implemented So Vector can now be treated as a collection
  MODIFIED: 10 February 2002:
    IFormattable interface implemented So Vector now responds to format specifiers N and VE
CHANGES TO METHODS OF THIS CLASS:
System.Collections.IEnumerator GetEnumerator()
  MODIFIED: 14 February 2002:
    Method added in order to provide collection support
System.String ToString()
  MODIFIED: 10 February 2002:
    Method added in order to provide formatting support
System.Int32 GetHashCode()
System.Boolean Equals()
System.String ToString()
System.Double get_Item()
System.Void set_Item()
System.Boolean op_Equality()
System.Boolean op_Inequality()
Wrox.ProCSharp.VectorClass.Vector op_Addition()
Wrox.ProCSharp.VectorClass.Vector op_Multiply()
Wrox.ProCSharp.VectorClass.Vector op_Multiply()
System.Double op_Multiply()
System.Double Norm()
System.Type GetType()

class VectorEnumerator
  MODIFIED: 14 February 2002:
    Class created as part of collection support for Vector
CHANGES TO METHODS OF THIS CLASS:
System.Void Reset()
System.Object get_Current()
System.Boolean MoveNext()
System.Int32 GetHashCode()
System.Boolean Equals()
System.String ToString()
System.Type GetType()

[OK]

Figure 10-2

Summary

In this chapter, we did not attempt to cover the entire topic of reflection. Reflection is an extensive subject worthy of a book of its own. Instead, we looked at the Type and Assembly classes, which are the primary entry points through which you can access the extensive capabilities provided by reflection.

In addition, we demonstrated a specific aspect of reflection that you are likely to use more often than any other—the inspection of custom attributes. We showed you how to define and apply your own custom attributes, and how to retrieve information about custom attributes at runtime.

In the next chapter, we look at exceptions and structured exception handing.

Errors and Exceptions

Errors happen, and it isn't always because of the person who coded the application. Sometimes your application will generate an error because of an action that was initiated by the end user of your application. In any case, you should anticipate errors occurring in your applications and code accordingly.

The .NET Framework has enhanced the ways in which you deal with errors. C#'s mechanism for handling error conditions allows us to provide custom handling for each type of error condition as well as to separate code that identifies errors from the code that handles them.

The main topics covered in this chapter include:

❑ Looking at the exception classes

❑ Using `try` – `catch` – `finally` to capture exceptions

❑ Creating user-defined exceptions

By the end of the chapter, you will have a good handle on advanced exception handling in your C# applications.

Looking into Errors and Exception Handling

No matter how good your coding is, your programs will always have to be able to handle possible errors. For example, in the middle of some complex processing your code may discover that it doesn't have permission to read a file, or while it is sending network requests the network may go down. In such exceptional situations, it is not enough for a method to simply return an appropriate error code—there might be 15 or 20 nested method calls, so what you really want the program to do is jump back up through all those 15 or 20 calls in order to exit the task completely and take the appropriate counter actions. The C# language has very good facilities to handle this kind of situation, through the mechanism known as *exception handling*.

> *Error-handling facilities in Visual Basic 6 are very restricted and essentially limited to the* On Error GoTo *statement. If you are coming from a Visual Basic 6 background, you will find C# exceptions open up a whole new world of error handling in your programs. On the other hand, Java and C++ developers will be familiar with the principle of exceptions since these languages also handle errors in a similar way to C#. Developers using C++ are sometimes wary of exceptions because of possible C++ performance implications, but this is not the case in C#. Using exceptions in C# code in general does not adversely affect performance. Visual Basic .NET developers will find that working with exceptions in C# is very similar using exceptions in Visual Basic .NET (except for the syntax differences).*

Exception Classes

In C#, an exception is an object created (or *thrown*) when a particular exceptional error condition occurs. This object contains information that should help track down the problem. Although we can create our own exception classes (and we will be doing so later), .NET provides us with many predefined exception classes.

Base class exception classes

In this section, we will provide a quick survey of some of the exceptions that are available in the base classes. Microsoft has provided a large number of exception classes in .NET—too many to provide a comprehensive list here. This class hierarchy diagram in Figure 11-1 shows but a few of these classes, to give you a sense of the general pattern.

All the classes in Figure 11-1 are part of the System namespace, with the exception of IOException and the classes derived from IOException, which are part of the namespace System.IO. The System.IO namespace deals with reading and writing data to files. In general, there is no specific namespace for exceptions; exception classes should be placed in whatever namespace is appropriate to the classes that can generate them—hence IO-related exceptions are in the System.IO namespace, and you will find exception classes in quite a few of the base class namespaces.

The generic exception class, System.Exception is derived from System.Object, as we would expect for a .NET class. In general, you should not throw generic System.Exception objects in your code, because they provide no specifics of the error condition.

There are two important classes in the hierarchy that are derived from System.Exception:

❑   System.SystemException—This class is for exceptions that are usually thrown by the .NET runtime, or which are considered to be of a generic nature and might be thrown by almost any application. For example, StackOverflowException will be thrown by the .NET runtime if it detects the stack is full. On the other hand, you might choose to throw ArgumentException or its subclasses in your own code, if you detect that a method has been called with inappropriate arguments. Subclasses of System.SystemException include classes that represent both fatal and non-fatal errors.

❑   System.ApplicationException—This class is important, because it is the intended base for any class of exception defined by third parties. Hence, if you define any exceptions covering error conditions unique to your application, you should derive these directly or indirectly from System.ApplicationException.

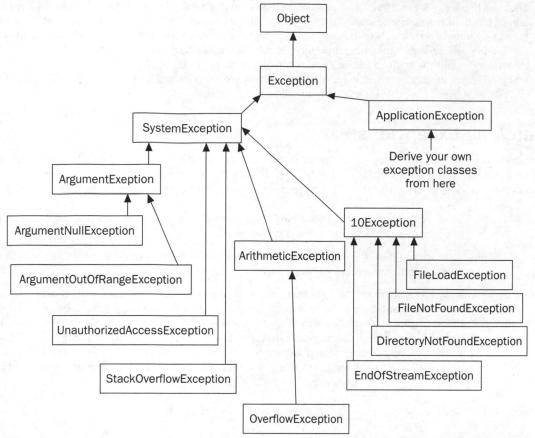

Figure 11-1

Other exception classes that might come in handy include the following:

❑ StackOverflowException—This exception is thrown when the area of memory allocated to the stack is full. A stack overflow can occur if a method continuously calls itself recursively. This is generally a fatal error, since it prevents your application from doing anything apart from terminating (in which case it is unlikely that even the `finally` block will execute). Trying to handle errors like this yourself is usually pointless.

❑ EndOfStreamException— The usual cause of an EndOfStreamException is an attempt to read past the end of a file. A *stream* represents a flow of data between data sources. We cover streams in detail in Chapter 31.

❑ OverflowException—An OverflowException is what happens if you attempt to cast an `int` containing a value of `-40` to a `uint` in a `checked` context.

We are not going to discuss all of the other exception classes shown in Figure 11-1; you should be able to guess their purposes by looking at their names.

The class hierarchy for exceptions is somewhat unusual in that most of these classes do not add any functionality to their respective base classes. However, in the case of exception handling, the common reason for adding inherited classes is to indicate more specific error conditions, and there is often no need to override methods or add any new ones (although it is not uncommon to add extra properties that carry extra information about the error condition). For example, you might have a base ArgumentException class intended for method calls where inappropriate values are passed in, and an ArgumentNullException class derived from it, which is intended to handle a null argument if passed.

Catching Exceptions

Given that .NET includes a spade of predefined base class exception objects, how do you use them in your code to trap error conditions? In order to deal with possible error conditions in C# code, you will normally divide the relevant part of your program into blocks of three different types:

❑　try blocks contain code that forms part of the normal operation of your program, but which might encounter some serious error conditions.

❑　catch blocks contain the code that deals with the various error conditions for the errors that your code might encounter by working through the code in the try block.

❑　finally blocks contain the code that cleans up any resources or takes any other action that you will normally want done at the end of a try or catch block. It is important to understand that the finally block is executed whether or not an exception is thrown. Since the aim is that the finally block contains cleanup code that should always be executed, the compiler will flag an error if you place a return statement inside a finally block. For example you might close any connections that were opened in the try block within the finally block. The finally block is optional.

So how do these blocks fit together to trap error conditions? Here's how:

1.　The execution flow enters a try block.

2.　If no errors occur, execution proceeds normally through the try block, and when the end of the try block is reached, the flow of execution jumps to the finally block (Step 5). However, if an error occurs within the try block, execution jumps to a catch block (next step).

3.　The error condition is handled in the catch block.

4.　At the end of the catch block, execution automatically transfers to the finally block.

5.　The finally block is executed.

The C# syntax used to bring all this about looks roughly like this:

```
try
{
   // code for normal execution
}
catch
{
   // error handling
}
finally
```

```
{
    // clean up
}
```

Actually, there are a few variations on this theme:

❑   You can omit the `finally` block since it is optional.

❑   You can also supply as many `catch` blocks as you want to handle specific types of errors.

❑   You can omit the `catch` blocks altogether, in which case the syntax serves not to identify exceptions, but as a way of guaranteeing that code in the `finally` block will be executed when execution leaves the `try` block. This is useful if the `try` block contains several exit points.

So far so good, but the question that has yet to be answered is this: If the code is running in the `try` block, how does it know when to switch to the `catch` block if an error has occurred? If an error is detected, the code does something that is known as *throwing an exception*. In other words, it instantiates an exception object class and throws it:

```
throw new OverflowException();
```

Here we have instantiated an exception object of the `OverflowException` class. As soon as the computer encounters a `throw` statement inside a `try` block, it immediately looks for the `catch` block associated with that `try` block. If there is more than one `catch` block associated with the `try` block, it identifies the correct `catch` block by checking which exception class the `catch` block is associated with. For example, when the `OverflowException` object is thrown, execution jumps to the following `catch` block:

```
catch (OverflowException e)
{
```

In other words, the computer looks for the `catch` block that indicates a matching exception class instance of the same class (or of a base class).

With this extra information, we can expand the `try` block we have just demonstrated. Let's assume, for the sake of argument, that there are two possible serious errors that can occur in the `try` block: an overflow and an array out of bounds. We will assume that our code contains two Boolean variables, `Overflow` and `OutOfBounds`, which indicate whether these conditions exist. We have already seen that a predefined exception class exists to indicate overflow (`OverflowException`); similarly, an `IndexOutOfRangeException` class exists to handle an array out-of-bounds.

Now our `try` block looks like this:

```
try
{
    // code for normal execution

    if (Overflow == true)
        throw new OverflowException();

    // more processing

    if (OutOfBounds == true)
```

```
       throw new IndexOutOfRangeException();

    // otherwise continue normal execution
}
catch (OverflowException e)
{
    // error handling for the overflow error condition
}
catch (IndexOutOfRangeException e)
{
    // error handling for the index out of range error condition
}
finally
{
    // clean up
}
```

So far, this might not look that much different from what we could have done with the Visual Basic 6 On Error GoTo statement (with the exception perhaps that the different parts in the code are separated). C#, however, provides a far more powerful and flexible mechanism for error handling.

This is because we can have throw statements that are nested in several method calls inside the try block, but the same try block continues to apply even as execution flow enters these other methods. If the computer encounters a throw statement, it immediately goes back up through all the method calls on the stack, looking for the end of the containing try block and the start of the appropriate catch block. During this process, all the local variables in the intermediate method calls will correctly go out of scope. This makes the try...catch architecture well suited to the situation we described at the beginning of this section, where the error occurs inside a method call that is nested inside 15 or 20 method calls, and processing has to stop immediately.

As you can probably gather from the previous discussion, try blocks can play a very significant part in controlling the flow of execution of your code. However, it is important to understand that exceptions are intended for exceptional conditions, hence their name. You wouldn't want to use them as a way of controlling when to exit a do...while loop.

Implementing multiple catch blocks

The easiest way to see how try...catch...finally blocks work in practice is with a couple of examples. Our first example is called SimpleExceptions. It repeatedly asks the user to type in a number and then displays it. However, for the sake of this example, we will imagine that the number has to be between 0 and 5, otherwise the program won't be able to process the number properly. Therefore we will throw an exception if the user types in anything outside this range.

The program will then continue to ask for more numbers for processing until the user simply presses the Enter key without entering anything.

> *You should note that this code does not provide a good example of when to use exception handling. As we have already indicated, the idea of exceptions is that they are provided for exceptional circumstances. Users are always typing in silly things, so this situation doesn't really count. Normally, your program will handle incorrect user input by performing an instant check and asking the user to retype the input if there is a problem. However, generating exceptional situations is difficult in a small sample that you can read through in a few minutes! So, we will tolerate this bad practice for now in order to demonstrate how exceptions work. The examples that follow present more realistic situations.*

The code for `SimpleExceptions` looks like this:

```
using System;

namespace Wrox.ProCSharp.AdvancedCSharp
{
    public class MainEntryPoint
    {
        public static void Main()
        {
            string userInput;
            while ( true )
            {
                try
                {
                    Console.Write("Input a number between 0 and 5 " +
                        "(or just hit return to exit)> ");
                    userInput = Console.ReadLine();
                    if (userInput == "")
                        break;
                    int index = Convert.ToInt32(userInput);
                    if (index < 0 || index > 5)
                        throw new IndexOutOfRangeException(
                            "You typed in " + userInput);
                    Console.WriteLine("Your number was " + index);
                }
                catch (IndexOutOfRangeException e)
                {
                    Console.WriteLine("Exception: " +
                        "Number should be between 0 and 5. " + e.Message);
                }
                catch (Exception e)
                {
                    Console.WriteLine(
                        "An exception was thrown. Message was: " + e.Message);
                }
                catch
                {
                    Console.WriteLine("Some other exception has occurred");
                }
                finally
                {
                    Console.WriteLine("Thank you");
                }
            }
        }
    }
}
```

The core of this code is a `while` loop, which continually uses `Console.ReadLine()` to ask for user input. `ReadLine()` returns a string, so our first task is to convert it to an `int` using the `System.Convert.ToInt32()` method. The `System.Convert` class contains various useful methods to perform data conversions and provides an alternative to the `int.Parse()` method. In general, `System.Convert` contains methods to perform various type conversions. Recall that the C# compiler resolves `int` to instances of the `System.Int32` base class.

It is also worth pointing out that the parameter passed to the catch block is scoped to that catch block—which is why we are able to use the same parameter name, e, in successive catch blocks in the previous code.

In the previous example, we also check for an empty string, since this is our condition for exiting the `while` loop. Notice how the `break` statement actually breaks right out of the enclosing `try` block as well as the `while` loop—this is valid. Of course, as execution breaks out of the `try` block, the `Console.WriteLine()` statement in the `finally` block is executed. Although we just display a greeting here, more commonly, you will be doing tasks like closing file handles and calling the `Dispose()` method of various objects in order to perform any cleaning up. Once the computer leaves the `finally` block, it simply carries on executing unto the next statement that it would have executed, had the `finally` block not been present. In this case, we iterate back to the start of the `while` loop, and enter the `try` block again (unless the `finally` block was entered as a result of executing the `break` statement in the `while` loop, in which case we simply exit the `while` loop).

Next, we check for our exception condition:

```
if (index < 0 || index > 5)
    throw new IndexOutOfRangeException("You typed in " + userInput);
```

When throwing an exception, we need to choose what type of exception to throw. Although the class `System.Exception` is available, it is only intended as a base class; it is considered bad programming practice to throw an instance of this class as an exception, because it conveys no information about the nature of the error condition. Instead, the .NET Framework contains many other exception classes that are derived from `System.Exception`. Each of these matches a particular type of exception condition, and you are free to define your own ones as well. The idea is that you give as much information as possible about the particular exception condition by throwing an instance of a class that matches the particular error condition. In this case we have picked `System.IndexOutOfRangeException` as the best choice in the circumstances. `IndexOutOfRangeException` has several constructor overloads. The one we have chosen takes a string, which describes the error. Alternatively, we might choose to derive our own custom `Exception` object that describes the error condition in the context of our application.

Suppose the user then types in a number that is not between 0 and 5. This will be picked up by the `if` statement and an `IndexOutOfRangeException` object will be instantiated and thrown. At this point the computer will immediately exit the `try` block and hunt for a `catch` block that handles `IndexOutOfRangeException`. The first `catch` block it encounters is this:

```
catch (IndexOutOfRangeException e)
{
    Console.WriteLine(
        "Exception: Number should be between 0 and 5." + e.Message);
}
```

Since this `catch` block takes a parameter of the appropriate class, the `catch` block will be passed the exception instance and executed. In this case, we display an error message and the `Exception.Message` property (which corresponds to the string we passed to `IndexOutOfRange`'s constructor). After executing this `catch` block, control switches to the `finally` block, just as if no exception had occurred.

Notice that we have also provided another `catch` block:

```
catch (Exception e)
{
    Console.WriteLine("An exception was thrown. Message was: " + e.Message);
}
```

This `catch` block would also be capable of handling an `IndexOutOfRangeException` if it weren't for the fact that such exceptions will already have been caught by the previous `catch` block@@a reference to a base class can also refer to any instances of classes derived from it, and all exceptions are derived from `System.Exception`. So why doesn't this `catch` block get executed? The answer is that the computer executes only the first suitable `catch` block it finds. So why is this second `catch` block here? Well, it is not only our code that is covered by the `try` block; inside the block, we actually make three separate calls to methods in the `System` namespace (`Console.ReadLine()`, `Console.Write()`, and `Convert.ToInt32()`), and any of these methods might throw an exception.

If we type in something that's not a number—say `a` or `hello`—then the `Convert.ToInt32()` method will throw an exception of the class `System.FormatException` to indicate that the string passed into `ToInt32()` is not in a format that can be converted to an `int`. When this happens, the computer will trace back through the method calls, looking for a handler that can handle this exception. Our first `catch` block (the one that takes an `IndexOutOfRangeException`) won't do. The computer then looks at the second `catch` block. This one will do because `FormatException` is derived from `Exception`, so a `FormatException` instance can be passed in as a parameter here.

The structure of our example is actually fairly typical of a situation with multiple `catch` blocks. We start off with `catch` blocks that are designed to trap very specific error conditions. Then, we finish with more general blocks that will cover any errors for which we have not written specific error handlers. Indeed, the order of the `catch` blocks is important. If we had written the previous two blocks in the opposite order, the code would not have compiled, because the second `catch` block is unreachable (the `Exception` `catch` block would catch all exceptions). Therefore, the uppermost `catch` blocks should be the most granular options available and ending with the most general options.

However, in the previous example, we have a third `catch` block listed in the code:

```
catch
{
    Console.WriteLine("Some other exception has occurred");
}
```

This is the most general `catch` block of all—it doesn't take any parameter. The reason this `catch` block is here is to catch exceptions thrown by other code that isn't written in C#, or isn't even managed code at all. You see, it is a requirement of the C# language that only instances of classes that are derived from `System.Exception` can be thrown as exceptions, but other languages might not have this restriction—C++, for example, allows any variable whatsoever to be thrown as an exception. If your code calls into libraries or assemblies that have been written in other languages, then it might find an exception has been thrown that is not derived from `System.Exception`, although in many cases, the .NET `PInvoke` mechanism will trap these exceptions and convert them into .NET `Exception` objects. However, there is not that much that this `catch` block can do, because we have no idea what class the exception might represent.

For our particular example, there is no point in adding this catch-all catch handler. Doing this is useful if you are calling into some other libraries that are not .NET-aware and which might throw exceptions. However, we have included it in our example to illustrate the principle.

Now that we have analyzed the code for our example, we can run it. The following output illustrates what happens with different inputs and demonstrates both the IndexOutOfRangeException and the FormatException being thrown:

```
SimpleExceptions
Input a number between 0 and 5 (or just hit return to exit)> 4
Your number was 4
Thank you
Input a number between 0 and 5 (or just hit return to exit)> 0
Your number was 0
Thank you
Input a number between 0 and 5 (or just hit return to exit)> 10
Exception: Number should be between 0 and 5. You typed in 10
Thank you
Input a number between 0 and 5 (or just hit return to exit)> hello
An exception was thrown. Message was: Input string was not in a correct format.
Thank you
Input a number between 0 and 5 (or just hit return to exit)>
Thank you
```

Catching exceptions from other code

In our previous example, we have demonstrated the handling of two exceptions. One of them, IndexOutOfRangeException, was thrown by our own code. The other, FormatException, was thrown from inside one of the base classes. It is very common for code in a library to throw an exception if it detects that some problem has occurred, or if one of the methods has been called inappropriately by being passed the wrong parameters. However, library code rarely attempts to catch exceptions; this is regarded as the responsibility of the client code.

Often, you will find that exceptions get thrown from the base class libraries while you are debugging. The process of debugging to some extent involves determining why exceptions have been thrown and removing the causes. Your aim should be to ensure that by the time the code is actually shipped, exceptions do occur only in very exceptional circumstances, and if at all possible, are handled in some appropriate way in your code.

System.Exception properties

In our example, we have only illustrated the use of the Message property of the exception object. However, a number of other properties are available in System.Exception:

Property	Description
HelpLink	This is a link to a help file that provides more information about the exception.
Message	This is text that describes the error condition.
Source	This is the name of the application or object that caused the exception.

Property	Description
StackTrace	This provides details of the method calls on the stack (to help track down the method that threw the exception).
TargetSite	This is a .NET reflection object that describes the method that threw the exception.
InnerException	If this exception was thrown inside a catch block, it contains the exception object that sent the code into that catch block.

Of these properties, StackTrace and TargetSite are supplied automatically by the .NET runtime if a stack trace is available. Source will always be filled in by the .NET runtime as the name of the assembly in which the exception was raised (though you might want to modify the property in your code to give more specific information), while Message, HelpLink, and InnerException must be filled in by the code that threw the exception, by setting these properties immediately before throwing the exception. For example, the code to throw an exception might look something like this:

```
if (ErrorCondition == true)
{
    Exception myException = new ClassmyException("Help!!!!");
    myException.Source = "My Application Name";
    myException.HelpLink = "MyHelpFile.txt";
    throw myException;
}
```

Here, ClassMyException is the name of the particular exception class you are throwing. Note that it is common practice for the names of all exception classes to end with Exception.

What happens if an exception isn't handled?

Sometimes an exception might be thrown, but there might not be a catch block in your code that is able to handle that kind of exception. Our SimpleExceptions example can serve to illustrate this. Suppose, for example, we omitted the FormatException and catch-all catch blocks, and only supplied the block that traps an IndexOutOfRangeException. In that event, what would happen if a FormatException got thrown?

The answer is that the .NET runtime would catch it. Later in this section we explain how you can nest try blocks, and in fact, there is already a nested try block behind the scenes in the sample. The .NET runtime has effectively placed our entire program inside another huge try block—it does this for every .NET program. This try block has a catch handler that can catch any type of exception. If an exception occurs that your code doesn't handle, then the execution flow will simply pass right out of your program and get trapped by this catch block in the .NET runtime. However, the results probably won't be what you wanted. It means execution of your code will be terminated promptly and the user will see a dialog box that complains that your code hasn't handled the exception, as well as any details about the exception the .NET runtime was able to retrieve. At least the exception will have been caught though! This is what actually happened earlier in Chapter 2 in the Vector example when our program threw an exception.

In general, if you are writing an executable, you should try to catch as many exceptions as you reasonably can, and handle them in a sensible way. If you are writing a library, it is normally best not to handle exceptions (unless a particular exception represents something wrong in your code that you can handle), but to assume instead that the calling code will handle them. However, you may nevertheless want to catch any Microsoft-defined exceptions, so that you can throw your own exception objects that give more specific information to the client code.

Nested try blocks

One nice feature of exceptions is that you can nest try blocks inside each other, like this:

```
try
{
    // Point A
    try
    {
        // Point B
    }
    catch
    {
        // Point C
    }
    finally
    {
        // clean up
    }
    // Point D
}
catch
{
    // error handling
}
finally
{
    // clean up
}
```

Although each try block is only accompanied by one catch block in the example above, we could string several catch blocks together too. Let's take a closer look at how nested try blocks work.

If an exception is thrown inside the outer try block but outside the inner try block (points A and D), then the situation is no different to any of the scenarios we have seen before: either the exception is caught by the outer catch block and the outer finally block is executed, or the finally block is executed and the .NET runtime handles the exception.

If an exception is thrown in the inner try block (point B), and there is a suitable inner catch block to handle the exception, then again we are in familiar territory: the exception is handled there, and the inner finally block is executed before execution resumes inside the outer try block (at point D).

Now suppose an exception occurs in the inner try block but there *isn't* a suitable inner catch block to handle it. This time, the inner finally block is executed as usual, but then the .NET runtime will have no choice but to leave the entire inner try block in order to search for a suitable exception handler. The next obvious place to look is in the outer `catch` block. If the system finds one here, then that handler will be executed and then the outer `finally` block. If there is no suitable handler here, then the search for one will go on. In this case it means the outer `finally` block will be executed, and then, since there are no more `catch` blocks, control will transfer to the .NET runtime. Note that at no point is the code beyond point D in the outer `try` block executed.

An even more interesting thing happens if an exception is thrown at point C. If the program is at point C then it must be already processing an exception that was thrown at point B. It is in fact quite legitimate to throw another exception from inside a `catch` block. In this case, the exception is treated as if it had been thrown by the outer `try` block, so flow of execution will immediately leave the inner `catch` block, and execute the inner `finally` block, before the system searches the outer `catch` block for a handler. Similarly, if an exception is thrown in the inner `finally` block, control will immediately transfer to the best appropriate handler, with the search starting at the outer `catch` block.

> **It is perfectly legitimate to throw exceptions from `catch` and `finally` blocks.**

Although we have shown the situation with just two `try` blocks, the same principles hold no matter how many `try` blocks you nest inside each other. At each stage, the .NET runtime will smoothly transfer control up through the `try` blocks, looking for an appropriate handler. At each stage, as control leaves a `catch` block, any cleanup code in the corresponding `finally` block will be executed, but no code outside any `finally` block will be run until the correct `catch` handler has been found and run.

We have now shown how having nested `try` blocks can work. The obvious next question is why would you want to do that? There are two reasons:

❑ To modify the type of exception thrown

❑ To enable different types of exception to be handled in different places in your code

Modifying the type of exception

Modifying the type of the exception can be useful when the original exception thrown does not adequately describe the problem. What typically happens is that something—possibly the .NET runtime—throws a fairly low level exception that says something like an overflow occurred (`OverflowException`) or an argument passed to a method was incorrect (a class derived from `ArgumentException`). However, because of the context in which the exception occurred, you will know that this reveals some other underlying problem (for example, an overflow can only have happened at that point in your code because a file you have just read contained incorrect data). In that case, the most appropriate thing that your handler for the first exception can do is throw another exception that more accurately describes the problem, so that another `catch` block further along can deal with it more appropriately. In this case, it can also forward the original exception through a property implemented by `System.Exception` called `InnerException`. `InnerException` simply contains a reference to any other related exception that was thrown—in case the ultimate handler routine will need this extra information.

Of course there is also the situation where an exception occurs inside a `catch` block. For example, you might normally read in some configuration file that contains detailed instructions for handling the error, and it might turn out that this file is not there.

Handling different exceptions in different laces

The second reason for having nested `try` blocks is so that different types of exceptions can be handled at different locations in your code. A good example of this is if you have a loop where various exception conditions can occur. Some of these might be serious enough that you need to abandon the entire loop, while others might be less serious and simply require that you abandon that iteration and move on to the next iteration around the loop. You could achieve this by having one `try` block inside the loop, which handles the less serious error conditions, and an outer `try` block outside the loop, which handles the more serious error conditions. We will see how this works in the exceptions example that we are going to unveil next.

User-Defined Exception Classes

We are now ready to look at a second example that illustrates exceptions. This example, called `MortimerColdCall`, contains two nested `try` blocks and also illustrates the practice of defining our own custom exception classes, and throwing another exception from inside a `try` block.

For this example, we are going to return to the Mortimer Phones mobile phone company that we used in Chapter 4. We are going to assume that Mortimer Phones wants to have additional customers. Its sales team is going to ring up a list of people in order to invite them to become customers, a practice known in sales jargon as cold-calling people. To this end, we have a text file available that contains the names of the people to be cold-called. The file should be in a well-defined format in which the first line contains the number of people in the file and each subsequent line contains the name of the next person. In other words a correctly formatted file of names might look like this:

```
4
George Washington
Zbigniew Harlequin
John Adams
Thomas Jefferson
```

Since this is only an example, we are not really going to cold-call these people! Our version of cold-calling is designed to display the name of the person on the screen (perhaps for the sales guy to read). That's why we only put names, and not phone numbers in the file.

Our program will ask the user for the name of the file, and will then simply read it in and display the names of people.

That sounds like a simple task, but even so there are a couple of things that can go wrong and require us to abandon the entire procedure:

❑   The user might type in the name of a file that doesn't exist. This will be caught as a `FileNotFound` exception.

❑   The file might not be in the correct format. There are two possible problems here. Firstly, the first line of the file might not be an integer. Secondly, there might not be as many names in the file as the first line of the file indicates. In both cases, we want to trap this oddity as a custom exception that we have written specially for this purpose, `ColdCallFileFormatException`.

There is also something else that could go wrong which won't cause us to abandon the entire process but will mean we need to abandon that person and move on to the next person in the file (and hence this will need to be trapped by an inner `try` block). Some people are spies working for rival land-line telephone companies, and obviously, we wouldn't want to let these people know what we are up to by accidentally phoning one of them. Our research has indicated that we can identify who the land-line spies are because their names begin with Z. Such people should have been screened out when the data file was first prepared, but just in case any have slipped through, we will need to check each name in the file and throw a `LandLineSpyFoundException` if we detect a land-line spy. This, of course, is another custom exception object.

Finally, we will implement this sample by coding a class, `ColdCallFileReader`, which maintains the connection to the cold-call file and retrieves data from it. We will code this class in a very safe way, which means its methods will all throw exceptions if they are called inappropriately; for example, if a method that will read a file is called before the file has even been opened. For this purpose, we will write another exception class, `UnexpectedException`.

Catching the user-defined exceptions

Let's start with the `Main()` method of the `MortimerColdCall` sample, which catches our user-defined exceptions. Note that we will need to call up file-handling classes in the `System.IO` namespace as well as the `System` namespace.

```
using System;
using System.IO;

namespace Wrox.ProCSharp.AdvancedCSharp
{
   class MainEntryPoint
   {
      static void Main()
      {
         string fileName;
         Console.Write("Please type in the name of the file " +
            "containing the names of the people to be cold-called > ");
         fileName = Console.ReadLine();
         ColdCallFileReader peopleToRing = new ColdCallFileReader();

         try
         {
            peopleToRing.Open(fileName);
            for (int i=0 ; i<peopleToRing.NPeopleToRing; i++)
            {
               peopleToRing.ProcessNextPerson();
            }
            Console.WriteLine("All callers processed correctly");
         }
         catch(FileNotFoundException e)
         {
            Console.WriteLine("The file {0} does not exist", fileName);
         }
         catch(ColdCallFileFormatException e)
         {
            Console.WriteLine(
            "The file {0} appears to have been corrupted", fileName);
            Console.WriteLine("Details of problem are: {0}", e.Message);
            if (e.InnerException != null)
```

```
            Console.WriteLine(
                "Inner exception was: {0}", e.InnerException.Message);
        }
        catch(Exception e)
        {
            Console.WriteLine("Exception occurred:\n" + e.Message);
        }
        finally
        {
            peopleToRing.Dispose();
        }
        Console.ReadLine();
    }
}
```

This code is basically little more than a loop to process people from the file. We start off by asking the user for the name of the file. Then we instantiate an object of a class called `ColdCallFileReader` that we will define later. This is the class that handles the file reading. Notice that we do this outside the initial `try` block—that's because the variables that we instantiate here need to be available in the subsequent `catch` and `finally` blocks, and if we declared them inside the `try` block they'd go out of scope at the closing curly brace of the `try` block.

In the `try` block we open the file (using the `ColdCallFileReader.Open()` method) and loop over all the people in it. The `ColdCallFileReader.ProcessNextPerson()` method reads in and displays the name of the next person in the file, while the `ColdCallFileReader.NPeopleToRing` property tells us how many people should be in the file (obtained by reading the first line of the file).

There are three `catch` blocks, one for `FileNotFoundException`, one for `ColdCallFileFormatException`, and one to trap any other .NET exceptions.

In the case of a `FileNotFoundException`, we display a message to that effect. Notice that in this `catch` block, we don't actually use the exception instance at all. The reason is that I decided to use this `catch` block to illustrate the user-friendliness of our application. Exception objects generally contain technical information that is useful for developers, but not the sort of stuff you want to show to your end users. So in this case, we create a simpler message of our own.

For the `ColdCallFileFormatException` handler, we have done the opposite, and illustrated how to give fuller technical information, including details of the inner exception, if one is present.

Finally, if we catch any other generic exceptions, we display a user-friendly message, instead of letting any such exceptions fall through to the .NET runtime. Note that we have chosen not to handle any other exceptions not derived from `System.Exception`, since we are not calling directly into non-.NET code.

The `finally` block is there to clean up resources. In this case, this means closing any open file—performed by the `ColdCallFileReader.Dispose()` method.

Throwing the user-defined exceptions

Now let's have a look at the definition of the class that handles the file reading and (potentially) throws our user-defined exceptions: `ColdCallFileReader`. Since this class maintains an external file connection, we will need to make sure it gets disposed of correctly in accordance with the principles we laid down for the disposing of objects in Chapter 4. Hence we derive this class from `IDisposable`.

First, we declare some variables:

```
class ColdCallFileReader :IDisposable
{
    FileStream fs;
    StreamReader sr;
    uint nPeopleToRing;
    bool isDisposed = false;
    bool isOpen = false;
```

FileStream and StreamReader, both in the System.IO namespace, are the base classes that we will use to read the file. FileStream allows us to connect to the file in the first place, while StreamReader is specially geared up to reading text files, and implements a method, StreamReader(), which reads a line of text from a file. We will look at StreamReader more closely in Chapter 31 when we discuss file handling in depth.

The isDisposed field indicates whether the Dispose() method has been called. We have chosen to implement ColdCallFileReader so that once Dispose() has been called, it is not permitted to reopen connections and reuse the object. isOpen is also used for error checking—in this case, checking whether the StreamReader actually connects to an open file.

The process of opening the file and reading in that first line—the one that tells us how many people are in the file—is handled by the Open() method:

```
public void Open(string fileName)
{
    if (isDisposed)
        throw new ObjectDisposedException("peopleToRing");
    fs = new FileStream(fileName, FileMode.Open);
    sr = new StreamReader(fs);
    try
    {
        string firstLine = sr.ReadLine();
        nPeopleToRing = uint.Parse(firstLine);
        isOpen = true;
    }
    catch (FormatException e)
    {
        throw new ColdCallFileFormatException(
            "First line isn\'t an integer", e);
    }
}
```

The first thing we do in this method (as with all other ColdCallFileReader methods) is check whether the client code has inappropriately called it after the object has been disposed of, and throw a predefined ObjectDisposedException object if that has occurred. The Open() method checks the isDisposed field to see whether Dispose() has already been called. Since calling Dispose() implies the caller has now finished with this object, we regard it as an error to attempt to open a new file connection if Dispose() has been called.

Next, the method contains the first of two inner try blocks. The purpose of this one is to catch any errors resulting from the first line of the file not containing an integer. If that problem arises, the .NET runtime will throw a FormatException, which we trap and convert to a more meaningful exception that indicates there is actually a problem with the format of the cold-call file. Note that `System.FormatException` is there to indicate format problems with basic data types, not with files, and so is not a particularly useful exception to pass back to the calling routine in this case. The new exception thrown will be trapped by the outermost `try` block. Since there is no cleanup needed here, there is no need for a `finally` block.

If everything is fine, we set the `isOpen` field to `true` to indicate that there is now a valid file connection from which data can be read.

The `ProcessNextPerson()` method also contains an inner `try` block:

```
public void ProcessNextPerson()
{
   if (isDisposed)
      throw new ObjectDisposedException("peopleToRing");
   if (!isOpen)
      throw new UnexpectedException(
         "Attempt to access cold call file that is not open");
   try
   {
      string name;
      name = sr.ReadLine();
      if (name == null)
         throw new ColdCallFileFormatException("Not enough names");
      if (name[0] == 'Z')
      {
         throw new LandLineSpyFoundException(name);
      }
      Console.WriteLine(name);
   }
   catch(LandLineSpyFoundException e)
   {
      Console.WriteLine(e.Message);
   }

   finally
   {
   }
}
```

There are two possible problems with the file here (assuming there actually is an open file connection; the `ProcessNextPerson()` method checks this first). First, we might read in the next name and discover that it is a land-line spy. If that condition occurs, the exception is trapped by the first of the `catch` blocks in this method. Since that exception has been caught here, inside the loop, it means that execution can subsequently continue in the `Main()` method of the program, and the subsequent names in the file will continue to be processed.

A problem might also occur if we try to read the next name and discover that we have already reached the end of the file. The way that the `StreamReader`'s `ReadLine()` method works, is if it has gone past the end of the file, it doesn't throw an exception, but simply returns `null`. So if we find a null string, we know that the format of the file was incorrect because the number in the first line of the file indicated a larger number of names than were actually present in the file. If that happens, we throw a `ColdCallFileFormatException`, which will be caught by the outer exception handler (which will cause execution to terminate).

Once again, we don't need a `finally` block here since there is no cleanup to do; however, this time we have put an empty one in, just to show that you can do so, if you want.

We have nearly finished the example. We have just two more members of `ColdCallFileReader` to look at: the `NPeopleToRing` property, which returns the number of people supposed to be in the file, and the `Dispose()` method, which closes an open file. Notice that the `Dispose()` method just returns if it has already been called—this is the recommended way of implementing it. It also checks that there actually is a file stream to close before closing it. This example is here to illustrate defensive coding techniques, so that's what we are doing!

```
public uint NPeopleToRing
{
   get
   {
      if (isDisposed)
         throw new ObjectDisposedException("peopleToRing");
      if (!isOpen)
         throw new UnexpectedException(
            "Attempt to access cold call file that is not open");
      return nPeopleToRing;
   }
}

public void Dispose()
{
   if (isDisposed)
      return;

   isDisposed = true;
   isOpen = false;
   if (fs != null)
   {
      fs.Close();
      fs = null;
   }
}
```

Defining the exception classes

Finally, we need to define our own three exception classes. Defining our own exception is quite easy, since there are rarely any extra methods to add. It is just a case of implementing a constructor to ensure that the base class constructor is called correctly. Here is the full implementation of `LandLineSpyFoundException`:

```
class LandLineSpyFoundException : ApplicationException
{
   public LandLineSpyFoundException(string spyName)
      :   base("LandLine spy found, with name " + spyName)
   {
   }

   public LandLineSpyFoundException(
      string spyName, Exception innerException)
```

```
           :    base(
                "LandLine spy found with name " + spyName, innerException)
       {
       }
   }
```

Notice we've derived it from `ApplicationException`, as you would expect for a custom exception. In fact, if we'd been going about this even more formally, we would probably have put in an intermediate class, something like `ColdCallFileException`, derived from `ApplicationException`, and derived both of our exception classes from this class, just to make sure that the handling code has that extra fine degree of control over which exception handler handles which exception. However, to keep the example simple, we won't do that.

We have done one bit of processing in `LandLineSpyFoundException`. We have assumed the message passed into its constructor is just the name of the spy found, and so we turn this string into a more meaningful error message. We have also provided two constructors, one that simply takes a message, and one that also takes an inner exception as a parameter. When defining your own exception classes, it is best to include as a minimum, at least these two constructors (although we won't actually be using the second `LandLineSpyFoundException` constructor in this example).

Now for the `ColdCallFileFormatException`. This follows the same principles as the previous exception, except that we don't do any processing on the message:

```
class ColdCallFileFormatException : ApplicationException
{
    public ColdCallFileFormatException(string message)
        :   base(message)
    {
    }

    public ColdCallFileFormatException(
        string message, Exception innerException)
        :   base(message, innerException)
    {
    }
}
```

And finally, `UnexpectedException`, which looks much the same as `ColdCallFileFormatException`:

```
class UnexpectedException : ApplicationException
{
    public UnexpectedException(string message)
        :   base(message)
    {
    }

    public UnexpectedException(string message, Exception innerException)
        :   base(message, innerException)
    {
    }
}
```

Now we are ready to test the program. First, we try the `people.txt` file whose contents we displayed earlier. This has four names (which match the number given in the first line of the file) including one spy. Then, we will try the following `people2.txt` file, which has an obvious formatting error:

```
49
George Washington
Zbigniew Harlequin
John Adams
Thomas Jefferson
```

Finally, we will try the example but specify the name of a file that does not exist, `people3.txt`, say. Running the program three times for the three filenames gives these results:

```
MortimerColdCall
Please type in the name of the file containing the names of the people to be cold-
called > people.txt
George Washington
LandLine spy found, with name Zbigniew Harlequin
John Adams
Thomas Jefferson
All callers processed correctly
```

```
MortimerColdCall
Please type in the name of the file containing the names of the people to be cold-
called > people2.txt
George Washington
LandLine spy found, with name Zbigniew Harlequin
John Adams
Thomas Jefferson
The file people2.txt appears to have been corrupted
Details of the problem are: Not enough names
```

```
MortimerColdCall
Please type in the name of the file containing the names of the people to be cold-
called > people3.txt
The file people3.txt does not exist
```

In the end, this little application shows you a number of different ways in which you can handle the errors and exceptions that you might find in your own applications.

Summary

This chapter took a close look at the rich mechanism C# has for dealing with error conditions through exceptions. You are not limited to the generic error codes that could be output from your code, but you have the ability to go in and uniquely handle the most granular of error conditions. Sometimes these error conditions are provided to you through the .NET Framework itself, but at other times, you might want to go in and code your own error conditions as was shown here in this chapter. In either case, you have a lot of ways of protecting the workflow of your applications from unnecessary and dangerous faults.

In the next chapter, we will take a look at the main integrated development environment (IDE) for working in the .NET world—Visual Studio .NET 2003. This new IDE allows you to build any type of C# application at your disposal including Windows Forms, Web Forms, Classes, XML Web services, and more.

Part II: The .NET Environment

12

Visual Studio .NET

At this point we've familiarized ourselves with the C# language itself and are almost ready to move on to the applied sections of the book, in which we will look at how to use C# to program a variety of applications. Before we do that, however, we need to examine how we can use Visual Studio .NET and some of the features provided by the .NET environment to get the best from our programs.

In this chapter we look at what programming in the .NET environment means in practice. We cover Visual Studio .NET, the main development environment in which you will write, compile, debug, and optimize your C# programs, and provide guidelines for writing good applications. Visual Studio .NET is the main. For more details on Windows Forms and how to write user interface code see Chapter 19.

Working with Visual Studio .NET 2003

Visual Studio .NET 2003 is a fully integrated development environment. It is designed to make the process of writing your code, debugging it, and compiling it to an assembly to be shipped, as easy as possible. What this means in practice is that Visual Studio .NET gives you a very sophisticated multiple-document-interface application in which you can do just about everything related to developing your code. It offers these features:

❑ **Text editor.** Using this editor you can write your C# (as well as Visual Basic .NET, J#, and C++) code. This text editor is quite sophisticated. For example, as you type, it automatically lays out your code by indenting lines, matching start and end brackets of code blocks, and color-coding keywords. It also performs some syntax checks as you type and underlines code that causes compilation errors, also known as design-time debugging. In addition it features IntelliSense, which automatically displays the names of classes, fields, or methods as you begin to type them. As you start typing parameters to methods, it will also show you the parameter lists for the available overloads. Figure 12-1 shows the IntelliSense feature in action with one of the .NET base classes, `ListBox`.

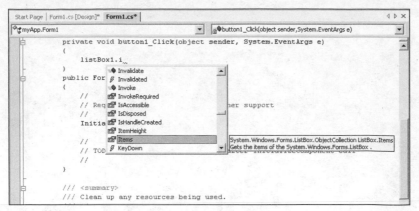

Figure 12-1

A useful shortcut to remember is that by pressing CTRL+SPACE, you can bring back the IntelliSense list box if you need it and for any reason it's not visible.

❑ Design view editor. This editor enables you to place user-interface and data-access controls in your project; Visual Studio .NET automatically adds the necessary C# code to your source files to instantiate these controls in your project. (This is possible because all .NET controls are instances of particular base classes.)

❑ Supporting windows. These windows allow you to view and modify aspects of your project, such as the classes in your source code as well as the available properties (and their startup values) for Windows Forms and Web Forms classes. You can also use these windows to specify compilation options, such as which assemblies your code needs to reference.

❑ The ability to compile from within the environment. Instead of having to run the C# compiler from the command line, you can simply select a menu option to compile the project and Visual Studio .NET will call the compiler for you and pass all the relevant command-line parameters to the compiler, detailing such things as which assemblies to reference and what type of assembly you want to be emitted (executable or library .dll, for example). If you want, it can also run the compiled executable for you so you can see whether it runs satisfactorily. You can even choose between different build configurations, for example, a release or debug build.

❑ Integrated debugger. It's in the nature of programming that your code won't run correctly the first time you try it. Or the second time. Or the third time. Visual Studio .NET seamlessly links up to a debugger for you, allowing you to set breakpoints and watches on variables from within the environment.

❑ Integrated MSDN help. Visual Studio .NET enables you to access the MSDN documentation from within the IDE. For example, if you're not sure of the meaning of a keyword while using the text editor, simply select the keyword and press the F1 key, and Visual Studio .NET accesses MSDN to show you related topics. Similarly, if you're not sure what a certain compilation error means, you can bring up the documentation for that error by selecting the error message and pressing F1.

❑ Access to other programs. Visual Studio .NET can also access a number of other utilities that allow you to examine and modify aspects of your computer or network, without you having to leave the developer environment. Among the tools available, you can check running services and database connections, look directly into your SQL Server tables, and even browse the Web using an Internet Explorer window.

If you've developed previously using C++ or Visual Basic, you will already be familiar with the relevant Visual Studio 6 version of the IDE and many of the previous features will not be new to you. What is new in Visual Studio .NET is that it combines all the features that were previously available across all Visual Studio 6 development environments. This means that whatever language you used in Visual Studio 6, you'll find some new features in Visual Studio .NET. For example, in the older Visual Basic environment, you could not compile separate debug and release builds. On the other hand, if you are coming to C# from a background of C++, much of the support for data access and the ability to drop controls into your application with a click of the mouse, which has long been part of the Visual Basic developers experience, will be new to you. In the C++ development environment drag-and-drop support is limited to the most common user-interface controls.

> *C++ developers will miss two Visual Studio 6 features in Visual Studio .NET: edit-and-continue debugging and an integrated profiler. Visual Studio .NET also does not include a full profiler application. Instead, you will find a number of .NET classes that assist with profiling in the* System.Diagnostics *namespace. The perfmon profiling tool is available from the command line (just type perfmon) and has a number of new .NET-related performance monitors.*

Whatever your background, you will find the overall look of the Visual Studio .NET 2002 and 2003 developer environment has changed since days of Visual Studio 6 to accommodate the new features, the single cross-language IDE, and the integration with .NET. There are new menu and toolbar options, and many of the existing ones from Visual Studio 6 have been renamed. So you'll have to spend some time familiarizing yourself with the layout and commands available in Visual Studio .NET.

The differences between Visual Studio .NET 2002 and Visual Studio .NET 2003 are limited to a few nice additions that facilitate working in Visual Studio .NET 2003Visual Studio .NET. The biggest changes in Visual Studio .NET 2003 include the ability to build smart device applications using the .NET Compact Framework as well as ASP.NET Mobile Device applications which used to require a separate Microsoft Mobile Internet Toolkit. Other new items include the addition of the J# language, a Java-like language that has been put on par with the likes of C# and Visual Basic .NET, enabling Visual Studio .NET 2003 developers can use the J# language to build Web applications, Windows Forms, and XML Web services just as you can with the other core .NET languages.

One of the biggest items to notice with your installation of Visual Studio .NET 2003 is that this new IDE works with the .NET Framework 1.1. In fact, when you install Visual Studio .NET 2003, you will also be installing the .NET Framework 1.1 if it isn't already installed. Visual Studio .NET 2003 is not built to work with version 1.0 of the .NET Framework, which means that if you still want to develop 1.0 applications, then you will want to keep Visual Studio .NET 2002 installed on your machine. Installing Visual Studio .NET 2003 installs a complete and new copy of Visual Studio .NET and does not upgrade the previous Visual Studio .NET 2002 IDE. The two copies of Visual Studio .NET will then run side-by-side.

Note that if you attempt to open your Visual Studio .NET 2002 projects using Visual Studio .NET 2003, the IDE will warn you that your solution will be upgraded to Visual Studio .NET 2003 if you continue (see Figure 12-2).

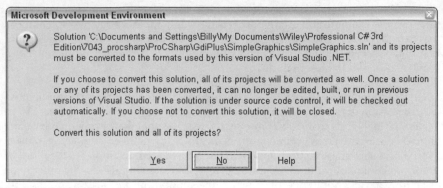

Figure 12-2

Be careful when upgrading your solutions from Visual Studio .NET 2002 to Visual Studio .NET 2003—you will not be able to revert to the previous version. Don't upgrade production solutions without testing your programs first in a staging environment to ensure your application will not be affected by the changes between versions 1.0 and 1.1 of the .NET Framework.

Since this is a professional-level book, we are not going to look in detail at every feature or menu option available in Visual Studio .NET 2003. Surely you will be able to find your way around the IDE. The real aim of our Visual Studio .NET coverage is to ensure that you are sufficiently familiar with the concepts involved when building and debugging a C# application, so you can make the most of working with Visual Studio .NET 2003. Figure 12-3 shows what your screen might look like when working in Visual Studio .NET 2003. (Note that since the appearance of Visual Studio .NET is highly customizable, the windows might not be in the same locations or different windows might be visible when you launch this development environment.)

In the following sections we are going to go through the process of creating, coding, and debugging a project, seeing what Visual Studio .NET can do to help you at each stage.

Creating a Project

Once you have installed Visual Studio .NET 2003, you will want to start your first project. With Visual Studio .NET, you rarely start with a blank file and then add C# code, in the way that we've been doing in the previous chapters in this book. (Of course, the option of asking for an empty application project is there if you really do want to start writing your code from scratch.) Instead, the idea is that you tell Visual Studio .NET roughly what type of project you want to create, and then Visual Studio .NET generates the files and C# code that provides a framework for the type of project you want to create. You then work by adding your code to this outline. For example, if you want to build a Windows GUI-interface-based application (or, in .NET terminology, a Windows Form), Visual Studio .NET will start you off with a file containing C# source code that creates a basic form. This form is capable of talking to Windows and receiving events. It can be maximized, minimized, or resized; all you have to do is add the controls and functionality you want. If your application is intended to be a command-line utility (a console application) then Visual Studio .NET will give you a basic namespace, class, and `Main()` method to start you off.

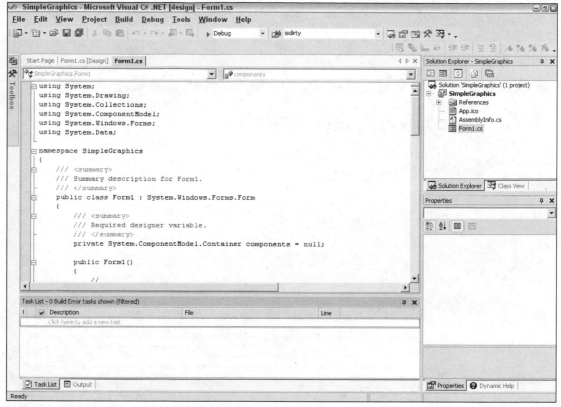

Figure 12-3

Last, but hardly least, when you create your project Visual Studio .NET also sets up the compilation options that you are likely to supply to the C# compiler—whether it is to compile to a command-line application, a library, or a Windows application. It will also tell the compiler which base class libraries you will need to reference (a Windows GUI application will need to reference many of the Windows.Forms-related libraries; a console application probably won't). You can of course modify all these settings as you are editing, if you need to.

The first time you start Visual Studio .NET, you will be presented with what is known as the Start Page (see Figure 12-4). The Start Page is an HTML page that contains various links to useful Web sites and enables you to set the appearance and configuration of Visual Studio .NET (the My Profile tab), open existing projects, or start a new project.

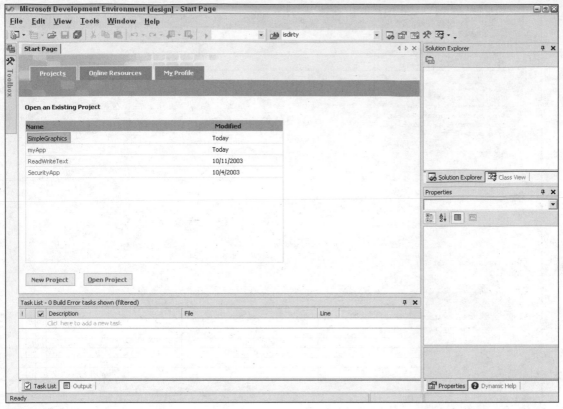

Figure 12-4

Figure 12-4 shows the type of Start Page you get after you've used Visual Studio .NET; it includes a list of the most recently edited projects. You can just click on one of these projects to open it again.

Under the My Profile option, you can even change the appearance of Visual Studio .NET to match what you might have been used to in your previous developer environment. For example you can set up Visual Studio .NET so its user interface looks a bit like the older Visual Basic or C++ IDEs. Note, however, that this option only really changes where the various windows are positioned on the screen. You'll still find that most of the menu and toolbar options, as well as the detailed features of each window, are new.

Selecting a project type

You can create a new project either by clicking the New Project button on the start page or by selecting New⇨Project from the File menu. Either way, you will get the New Project dialog box (see Figure 12-5)—and your first inkling of the variety of different projects you can create.

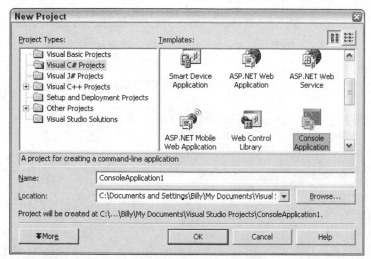

Figure 12-5

Using this dialog box, you effectively select the initial framework files and code you want Visual Studio .NET to generate for you, the type of compilation options you want, and the compiler you want to compile your code with—the C#, Visual Basic .NET, J#, or Visual C++ .NET compiler. You can immediately see the language integration that Microsoft has promised for .NET at work here! For this particular example, we've opted for a C# console application.

> *We don't have space to cover all the various options for different types of projects here. On the C++ side, all the old C++ project types are there—MFC application, ATL project, and so on. On the Visual Basic .NET side, the options have changed somewhat. For example, you can create a Visual Basic .NET command-line application (Console Application), a .NET component (Class Library), or a .NET control (Windows Control Library). However, you can not create an old-style COM-based control (the .NET control is intended to replace such ActiveX controls).*

The following table lists all the options that are available to you under Visual C# Projects as well as the chapters in which these options are discussed in detail. Note that there are some other more specialized C# template projects available under the Other Projects option.

If you choose . . .	You get the C# code and compilation options to generate . . .	See chapter
Windows Application	A basic empty form that responds to events.	19
Class Library	A .NET class that can be called up by other code.	13
Windows Control Library	A .NET class that can be called up by other code and which has a user interface. (Like an old-style ActiveX control.)	19
Smart Device Application	An application type for building smart device applications that utilize the .NET Compact Framework.	

Table continued on following page

If you choose . . .	You get the C# code and compilation options to generate . . .	See chapter
ASP.NET Web Application	An ASP.NET-based Web site: ASP.NET pages and C# classes that generate the HTML response sent to browsers from those pages.	25
ASP.NET Web Service	A C# class that acts as a fully operational Web service.	27
ASP.NET Mobile Web Application	An application type that allows you to build ASP.NET pages that target mobile devices.	27
Web Control Library	A control that can be called up by ASP.NET pages, to generate the HTML code that gives the appearance of a control when displayed on a browser.	26
Console Application	An application that runs at the command-line prompt, or in a console window.	12
Windows Service	A service that runs in the background on Windows NT and Windows 2000.	32
Empty Project	Installs nothing. You have to write all your code from scratch; but you still get the benefit of all the Visual Studio .NET facilities when you are writing.	—
Empty Web Project	The same as Empty Project, but the compilation settings are set to instruct the compiler to generate code for ASP.NET pages.	—
New Project In Existing Folder	New project files for an empty project. Use this option if you have some straight C# source code (for example typed in a text editor) and want to turn it into a Visual Studio .NET project.	—

The newly created console project

When we click OK after selecting the Console Application option, Visual Studio .NET gives us a number of files, including a source code file, Class1.cs, which contains the initial framework code.

Figure 12-6 shows what code Visual Studio .NET has written for us.

As you can see, we have here a C# program that doesn't do anything yet, but which contains the basic items required in any C# executable program: a namespace and a class that contains the Main() method, which is the program's entry point. (Strictly speaking, the namespace isn't necessary, but it would be very bad programming practice not to declare one.) This code is all ready to compile and run, which you can do immediately by pressing the F5 key or by selecting the Debug menu and choosing Start. However, before we do that we'll add one line of code—to make our application actually do something!

```
static void Main(string[] args)
{
    //
    // TODO: Add code to start application here
    //
    Console.WriteLine("Hello from all the editors at Wrox Press");
}
```

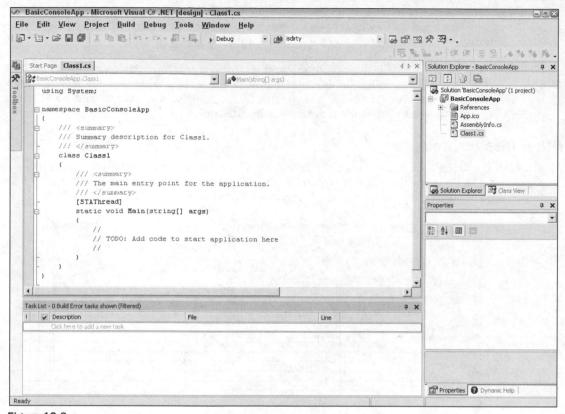

Figure 12-6

If you compile and run the project, you'll see a console window that stays barely long enough onscreen so you have time to read the message. The reason this happens is that Visual Studio .NET, remembering the settings you specified when you created the project, arranged for it to be compiled and run as a console application. Windows then realizes that it has to run a console application but doesn't have a console window to run it from. So Windows creates a console window and runs the program. As soon as the program exits, Windows recognizes that it doesn't need the console window any more and promptly removes it. That's all very logical but doesn't help you very much if you actually want to look at the output from your project!

A good way to avoid this problem is to insert the following line just before the `Main()` method returns in your code.

```
static void Main(string[] args)
{
    //
    // TODO: Add code to start application here
    //
    Console.WriteLine("Hello from all the editors at Wrox Press");
    Console.ReadLine();
}
```

That way, your code will run, display its output, and then it will come across the `Console.ReadLine()` statement, at which point it will wait for you to press the Return (or Enter) key before the program exits. This means that the console window will hang around until you press Return.

Note that all this is only an issue for console applications that you test-run from Visual Studio .NET—if you are writing a Windows application then the window displayed by the application will automatically remain on screen until you exit it. Similarly, if you run a console application from the command line prompt, you won't have any problems about the window disappearing.

Other files created

The Class1.cs source code file isn't the only file that Visual Studio .NET has created for you. If you have a look in the folder in which you asked Visual Studio .NET to create your project, you will see not just the C# file, but a complete directory structure that looks like what is shown here in Figure 12-7:

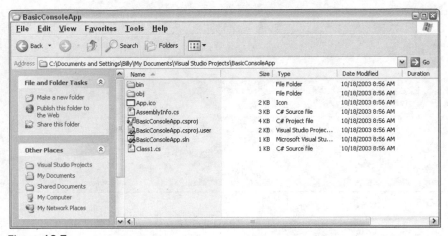

Figure 12-7

The two folders, bin and obj, store compiled and intermediate files. Subfolders of obj hold various temporary or intermediate files; subfolders of bin hold the compiled assemblies.

> *Traditionally, Visual Basic developers would simply write the code then run it. Before shipping, the code would then have to be compiled into an executable; Visual Basic tended to hide the process of compilation when debugging. In C#, it's more explicit: to run the code, you have to compile (or build) it first, which means an assembly must be created somewhere.*

The remaining files in the project's main folder, `BasicConsoleApp`, are there for Visual Studio .NET's benefit. They contain information about the project (for example, the files it contains) so that Visual Studio .NET knows how to have the project compiled, and how to read it in the next time you open the project.

Solutions and Projects

One important distinction you must understand is that between a project and a solution.

- ❑   A project is a set of all the source code files and resources that will compile into a single assembly (or in some cases, a single module). For example, a project might be a class library, or a Windows GUI application.

- ❑   A solution is the set of all the projects that make up a particular software package (application).

To understand this distinction look at what happens when you ship a project—the project consists of more than one assembly. For example, you might have a user interface, custom controls, and other components that ship as libraries of the parts of the application. You might even have a different user interface for administrators. Each of these parts of the application might be contained in a separate assembly, and hence, they are regarded by Visual Studio .NET as a separate project. However, it is quite likely that you will be coding these projects in parallel and in conjunction with each other. Thus it is quite useful to be able to edit them all as one single unit in Visual Studio .NET. Visual Studio .NET allows this by regarding all the projects as forming one solution, and treats the solution as the unit that it reads in and allows you to work on.

Up until now we have been loosely talking about creating a console project. In fact, in the example we are working on, Visual Studio .NET has actually created a solution for us—though this particular solution contains just one project. We can see the situation in a window in Visual Studio .NET known as the Solution Explorer (see Figure 12-8), which contains a tree structure that defines your solution.

Figure 12-8

Figure 12-2 shows that the project contains our source file, Class1.cs, as well as another C# source file, AssemblyInfo.cs, which allows us to provide information that describes the assembly as well as the ability to specify versioning information. (We'll look at this file in detail in Chapter 13.) The Solution Explorer also indicates the assemblies that our project references according to namespace. You can see this by expanding the References folder in the Solution Explorer.

If you haven't changed any of the default settings in Visual Studio .NET you will probably find the Solution Explorer in the top-right corner of your screen. If you can't see it, just go to the View menu and select Solution Explorer.

The solution is described by a file with the extension .sln—in the case of our example, it's
`BasicConsoleApp.sln`. The project is described by various other files in the project's main folder.
If you attempt to edit these files using Notepad, you'll find that they are mostly plain text files; and, in
accordance with the principle that .NET and .NET tools rely on open standards wherever possible, they
are mostly in XML format.

> *C++ developers will recognize that a Visual Studio .NET solution corresponds to an old Visual C++
> project workspace (stored in a .dsw file) and a Visual Studio .NET project corresponds to an old C++
> project (.dsp file). By contrast, Visual Basic developers will recognize that a solution corresponds to an
> old Visual Basic project group (.vbg file), and the .NET project corresponds to an old Visual Basic pro-
> ject (.vbp file). Visual Studio .NET differs from the old Visual Basic IDE in that it always creates a solu-
> tion for you automatically. In Visual Studio 6, Visual Basic developers would get a project; however,
> they would have to request a project group from the IDE separately.*

Adding another project to the solution

As we work through the following sections we will demonstrate how Visual Studio .NET works with
Windows applications as well as console ones. To that end, we will create a Windows project called
BasicForm that we will add to our current solution, BasicConsoleApp.

> *This means we'll end up with a solution containing a Windows application and a console application. That's
> not a very common scenario—you're more likely to have one application and a number of libraries—but it
> allows us to demonstrate more code! You might, however, create a solution like ours if, for example, you are
> writing a utility that you want to run either as a Windows application or as a command-line utility.*

There are two ways of creating the new project. You can select New⇨Project from the File menu (as
we've done already) or you can right-click the name of the solution in the Solution Explorer and select
Add – New Project from the context menu. Either option brings up the familiar New Project dialog box;
this time, however, you'll notice two radio buttons near the bottom of the dialog box (see Figure 12-9).
These buttons allow us to specify whether we want to create a new solution for this project or add it to
the existing solution.

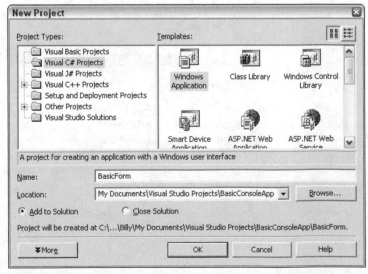

Figure 12-9

If we select Add to Solution, we will get a new project so that the BasicConsoleApp solution now contains a console application and a Windows application.

In accordance with the language-independence of Visual Studio .NET, the new project doesn't have to be a C# project. It's perfectly acceptable to put a C# project, a Visual Basic .NET project and a C++ project in the same solution. But we'll stick with C# here since this is a C# book!

Of course, this means that BasicConsoleApp isn't really an appropriate name for the solution any more! To change the name, we can right-click on the name of the solution and select Rename from the context menu. We'll call the new solution DemoSolution. The Solution Explorer window now looks like Figure 12-10.

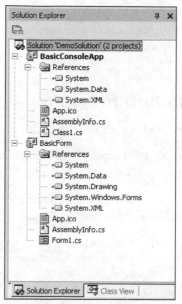

Figure 12-10

We can see from this that Visual Studio .NET has made our newly added Windows project automatically reference some of the extra base classes that are important for Windows Forms functionality.

You'll notice if you look in Windows Explorer that the name of the solution file has changed to DemoSolution.sln. In general, if you want to rename any files, the Solution Explorer window is the best place to do so, because Visual Studio .NET will then automatically update any references to that file in the other project files. If you just rename files using Windows Explorer, you might find you break the solution because Visual Studio .NET won't be able to locate all the files it needs to read in. You will then have to manually edit the project and solution files to update the file references.

Setting the startup project

One thing you'll need to bear in mind if you have multiple projects in a solution is that only one of them can be run at a time! When you compile the solution, all the projects in it will be compiled. However, you have to specify which one is the one you want Visual Studio .NET to start running when you press F5 or select Start. If you have one executable and several libraries that it calls, then this will clearly be the executable. In our case, where we have two independent executables in the project, we'd simply have to debug each in turn.

You can tell Visual Studio .NET which project to run by right-clicking on that project in the Solution Explorer window and selecting Set as Startup Project from the context menu. You can tell which one is the current startup project—it is the one that appears in bold in the Solution Explorer window (BasicConsoleApp in Figure 12-10).

Windows Application Code

A Windows application contains a lot more code right from the start than a console application when Visual Studio .NET first creates it. That's because creating a window is an intrinsically more complex process. We discuss the code for a Windows application in detail in Chapter 19; for now, take a look at the code in the Form1 class in the BasicForm project to see for yourself how much is auto-generated.

Reading in Visual Studio 6 Projects

If you are coding in C#, then you won't need to read in any old Visual Studio 6 projects, since C# doesn't exist in Visual Studio 6. However, language interoperability is a key part of the .NET Framework, so you might want your C# code to work alongside code written in Visual Basic or in C++. In that situation you might have to edit projects that were created with Visual Studio 6.

Visual Studio .NET has no problems reading in and upgrading Visual Studio 6 projects and workspaces. The situation is different for C++, Visual Basic, and J++ projects.

❑   In Visual C++, no change to the source code is needed. All your old Visual C++ code still works fine with the new C++ compiler. Obviously it is not managed code, but it will still compile to code that runs outside the .NET runtime; if you want your code to integrate with the .NET Framework, then you will need to edit it. If you get Visual Studio .NET to read in an old Visual C++ project, it will simply add a new solution file and updated project files. It will leave the old .dsw and .dsp files unchanged so that the project can still be edited by Visual Studio 6, if necessary.

❑   In the case of Visual Basic, things are a bit more complicated. As we mentioned in Chapter 1, although Visual Basic .NET has been designed very much around Visual Basic and shares much of the same syntax, it is in many ways a new language. In Visual Basic, the source code largely consisted of the event handlers for the controls. In Visual basic, the code that actually instantiates the main window and many of its controls is not part of Visual Basic, but is instead hidden behind the scenes as part of the configuration of your project. In contrast, Visual Basic .NET works in the same way as C#, by putting the entire program out in the open as source code, so all the code that displays the main window and all the controls on it needs to be in the source file. Also, like C#, Visual Basic .NET requires everything to be object-oriented and part of a class, whereas VB didn't even recognize the concept of classes in the .NET sense. If you try to read a Visual Basic project with Visual Studio .NET, it will have to upgrade the entire source code to Visual Basic .NET before it can handle it—and this involves making a lot of changes to the Visual Basic code. Visual Studio .NET can, to a large extent, make these changes automatically and will then create a new Visual Basic .NET solution for you. You will find that the source code it gives you looks very different from the corresponding Visual Basic code, and you will still need to check carefully through the generated code to make sure the project still works correctly. You might even find areas of code where Visual Studio .NET has left comments to the effect that it can't figure out exactly what you wanted the code to do, and you might have to edit the code manually.

- As far as Microsoft is concerned, J++ is now an obsolete language and is not directly supported in .NET. However, in order that existing J++ code can continue to operate, separate tools are available to allow J++ code to work with .NET. Visual Studio .NET 2003 includes the J# development environment and will work with J++ code. There is also a utility that can convert legacy J++ code to C# code—similar to the Visual Basic 6 to Visual Basic .NET upgrade facility. These tools are grouped under the name JUMP (Java User Migration Path) and at the time of writing are neither bundled with .NET nor Visual Studio .NET; you can download them instead as at `http://msdn.microsoft.com/visualj/jump/default.asp`.

Exploring and Coding a Project

In this section we will look at the features that Visual Studio .NET provides to help us add code to our project.

The folding editor

One really exciting feature of Visual Studio .NET is its use of a folding editor as its default code editor (see Figure 12-11).

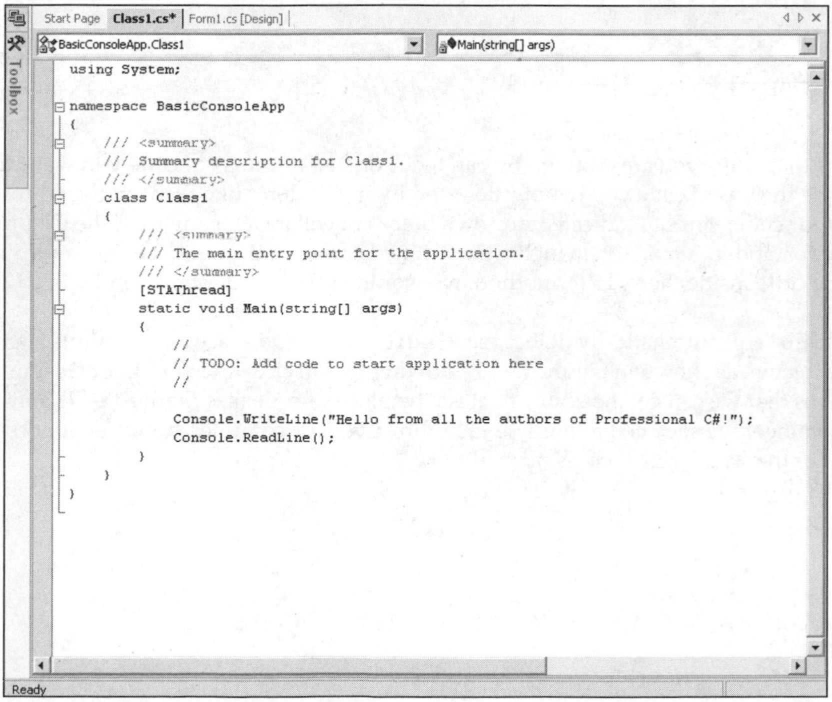
Start Page
Class1.cs*
Form1.cs [Design]
Toolbox
BasicConsoleApp.Class1
Main(string[] args)
using System;
namespace BasicConsoleApp
{
/// <summary>
/// Summary description for Class1.
/// </summary>
class Class1
{
/// <summary>
/// The main entry point for the application.
/// </summary>
[STAThread]
static void Main(string[] args)
{
//
// TODO: Add code to start application here
//
Console.WriteLine("Hello from all the authors of Professional C#!");
Console.ReadLine();
}
}
}
Ready

Figure 12-11

Figure 12-11 shows the code for the console application that we generated earlier. Notice those little minus signs on the left-hand side of the window. These signs mark the points where the editor assumes a new block of code (or documentation comment) begins. You can click on these icons to close up the view of the corresponding block of code just as you would close a node in a tree control (see Figure 12-12).

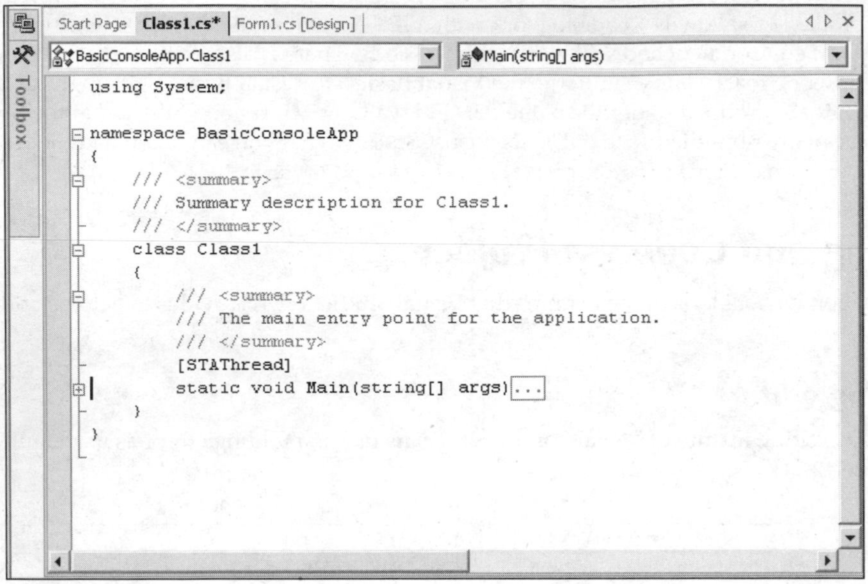

Figure 12-12

This means that while you are editing you can focus on just the areas of code you want to look at, and you can hide the bits of code you're not interested in. If you don't like the way the editor has chosen to block off your code, you can indicate your own blocks of collapsing code with the C# preprocessor directives, `#region` and `#endregion`, which we examined earlier in the book. For example, if we wanted to collapse the code inside the `Main()` method, we would add the code shown in Figure 12-13.

The code editor will automatically detect the `#region` block and place a new minus sign by the `#region` directive as shown in Figure 12-13, allowing you to close the region. Enclosing this code in a region means that we can get the editor to close the block of code (see Figure 12-14), marking the area with the comment we specified in the `#region` directive. The compiler, however, ignores the directives and compiles the `Main()` method as normal.

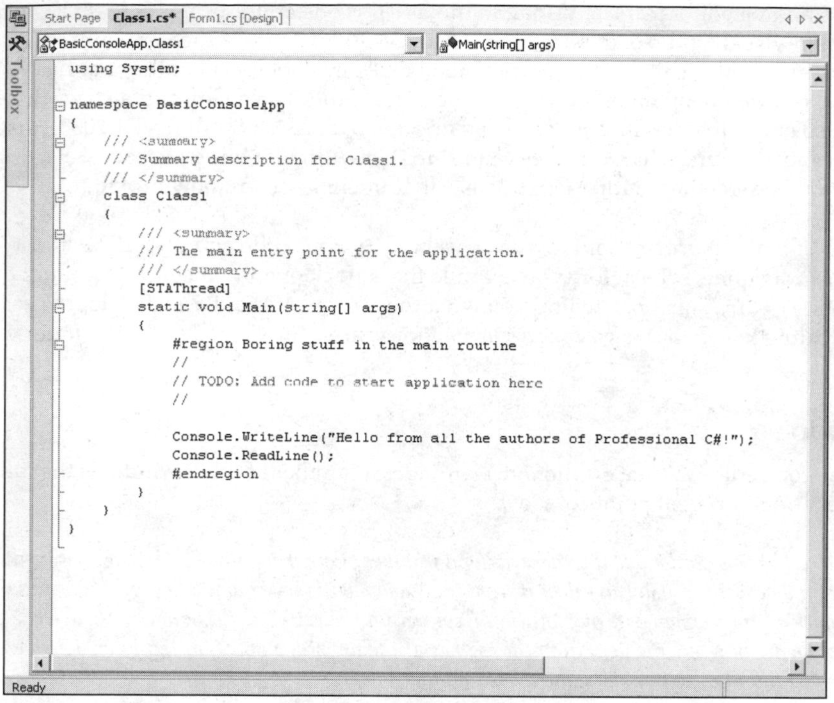

Figure 12-13

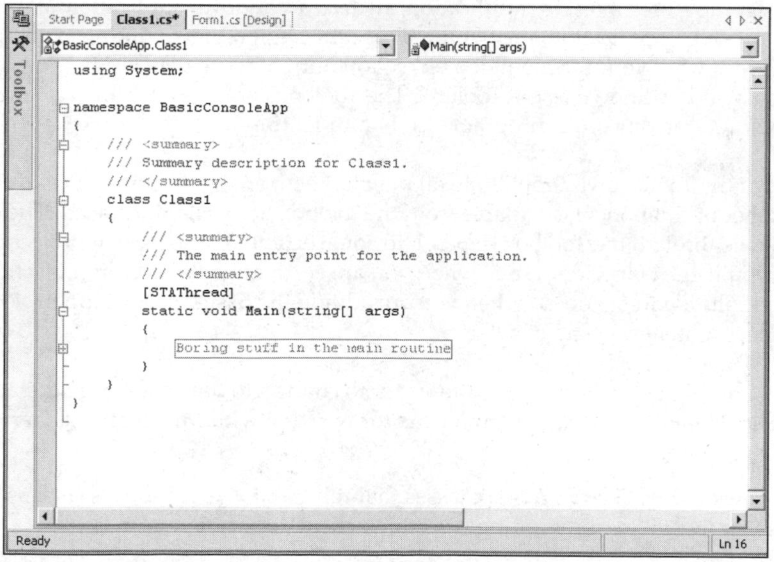

Figure 12-14

Besides the folding editor feature, Visual Studio .NET's code editor brings across all the familiar functionality from Visual Studio 6. In particular it features IntelliSense, which not only saves you typing, but also ensures that you use the correct parameters. C++ developers will notice that the Visual Studio .NET IntelliSense feature is a bit more robust than the Visual Studio 6 version and also works more quickly. You will also notice that IntelliSense has been improved in Visual Studio .NET 2003. It is now smarter in that it remembers your preferred choices and starts off with this choice instead of starting directly at the beginning of the sometimes rather lengthy lists that IntelliSense can now provide.

The code editor also performs some syntax checking on your code and underlines most syntax errors with a short wavy line, even before you compile the code. Hovering the mouse pointer over the underlined text brings up a small box telling you what the error is. Visual Basic developers have been familiar with this feature known as *design-time debugging* for years; now C# and C++ developers can benefit from it as well.

Other windows

Besides the code editor, Visual Studio .NET provides a number of other windows that allow you to view your project from different points of view.

For the rest of this section we'll be describing a number of other windows. If one of these windows is not visible on your screen, you can select it from the View menu. To show the Design View and Code Editor, right-click on the file name in the Solution Explorer and select View Designer or View Code from the context menu, or select the item from the toolbar at the top of the Solution Explorer. The Design View and Code Editor both share the same tabbed window.

The Design View window

If you are designing a user interface application, such as a Windows application, Windows control library, or an ASP.NET application, then you will use the Design View window. This window presents a visual overview of what your form will look like. You normally use the Design View window in conjunction with a window known as the Toolbox. The Toolbox contains a large number of .NET components that you can drag onto your program (see Figure 12-15).

The principle of the Toolbox was applied in all development environments in Visual Studio 6, but with .NET the number of components available from the toolbox has vastly increased. The categories of components available through the Toolbox depend, to some extent, on the type of project you are editing—for example, you'll get a far wider range when you are editing the BasicForm project in the DemoSolution solution than you do when you are editing the BasicConsoleApp project. The most important ranges of items available include:

❑　**Data Components.** Classes that allow you to connect to data sources and manage the data they contain. Here you will find components for working with Microsoft SQL Server, Oracle, and any OleDb data source.

❑　**Windows Forms Components.** Classes that represent visual controls such as text boxes, list boxes, or tree views for working with thick-client applications.

❑　**Web Forms Components.** Classes that basically do the same thing as Windows controls, but which work in the context of Web browsers, and which work by sending HTML output to simulate the controls to the browser.

❑　**Components.** Miscellaneous .NET classes that perform various useful tasks on your machine, such as connecting to directory services or to the event log.

Figure 12-15

You can also add your own custom categories to the Toolbox by right-clicking on any category and selecting Add Tab from the context menu. You can also place other tools in the Toolbox by selecting Customize Toolbox from the same context menu—this is particularly useful for adding your favorite COM components and ActiveX controls, which are not present in the Toolbox by default. If you add a COM control, you can still click to place it in your project just as you would with a .NET control. Visual Studio .NET automatically adds all the required COM interoperability code to allow your project to call up the control. In this case, what is actually added to your project is a .NET control that Visual Studio .NET creates behind the scenes, and which acts as a wrapper for your COM control.

> *C++ developers will recognize the Toolbox as Visual Studio .NET's (much enhanced) version of the resource editor. Visual Basic developers might not be that impressed at first; after all, Visual Studio 6 also has a Toolbox. However, the Toolbox in Visual Studio .NET has a dramatically different effect on your source code than its precursor.*

To see how the Toolbox works, we place a text box in our basic form project. We simply click on the TextBox control contained within the Toolbox and then click again to place it in the form in the design view (or if you prefer, you can simply drag and drop the control directly onto the design surface). Now the design view looks like Figure 12-16, showing roughly what BasicForm will look like if we compile and run it.

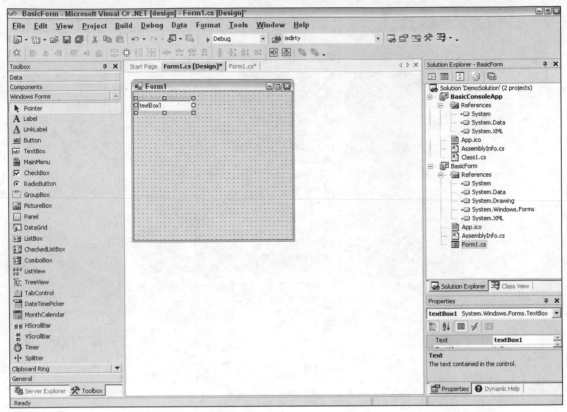

Figure 12-16

If we look at the code view of our form, we see that Visual Studio .NET has added the code that instantiates a `TextBox` object to go on the form. There's a new member variable in the `Form1` class:

```
public class Form1 : System.Windows.Forms.Form
{
    private System.Windows.Forms.TextBox textBox1;
```

There is also some code to initialize it in the method, `InitializeComponent()`, which is called from the `Form1` constructor:

```
/// <summary>
/// Required method for Designer support - do not modify
/// the contents of this method with the code editor.
/// </summary>
private void InitializeComponent()
{
```

```
        this.textBox1 = new System.Windows.Forms.TextBox();
        this.SuspendLayout();
        //
        // textBox1
        //
        this.textBox1.Location = new System.Drawing.Point(8, 8);
        this.textBox1.Name = "textBox1";
        this.textBox1.TabIndex = 0;
        this.textBox1.Text = "textBox1";

        //
        // Form1
        //
        this.AutoScaleBaseSize = new System.Drawing.Size(5, 13);
        this.ClientSize = new System.Drawing.Size(292, 268);
        this.Controls.AddRange(new System.Windows.Forms.Control[] {
                                                this.textBox1});
```

In one sense there is no difference between the code editor and the design view: they simply present different views of the same code. What actually happened when we clicked to add the TextBox into the design view is that the editor has placed the above extra code in our C# source file for us. The design view simply reflects this change because Visual Studio .NET is able to read our source code and determine from it what controls should be around when the application starts up. This is a fundamental shift from the old Visual Basic way of looking at things, in which everything was based around the visual design. Now, your C# source code is what fundamentally controls your application, and the design view is just a different way of viewing the source code. Incidentally, if you do write any Visual Basic .NET code with Visual Studio .NET, you'll find the same principles at work.

If we'd wanted to, we could have worked the other way round: if we manually added the same code as above to our C# source files, then Visual Studio .NET would have automatically detected from the code that our application contained a TextBox control, and would have shown it in the design view at the designated position. It is best to add these controls visually, and let Visual Studio handle the initial code generation—it's a lot quicker and less error-prone to click the mouse button a couple of times than to type a few lines of code!

Another reason for adding these controls visually is that, in order to recognize that they are there, Visual Studio .NET does need the relevant code to conform to certain criteria—and code that you write by hand might not do so. In particular, you'll notice that the InitializeComponent() method that contains the code to initialize the TextBox is commented to warn you against modifying it. That's because this is the method that Visual Studio .NET looks at in order to determine what controls are around when your application starts up. If you create and define a control somewhere else in your code, Visual Studio .NET won't be aware of it and you won't be able to edit it in the design view or certain other useful windows.

In fact, despite the warnings, you can modify the code in InitializeComponent(), provided you are careful. There's generally no harm in changing the values of some of the properties, for example, so that a control displays different text or so that it is a different size. In practice, the developer studio is pretty robust when it comes to working around any other code you place in this method. Just be aware that if you make too many changes to InitializeComponent(), you do run the risk that Visual Studio .NET won't recognize some of your controls. We should stress that this won't affect your application whatsoever when it is compiled, but it might disable some of the editing features of Visual Studio .NET for those controls. Hence, if you want to add any other substantial initialization, it's probably better to do so in the Form1 constructor or in some other method.

The Properties window

This is another window that has its origins in the old Visual Basic IDE. We know from the first part of the book that .NET classes can implement properties. In fact, as we'll discover when building Windows Forms (see Chapter 19), the .NET base classes that represent forms and controls have a lot of properties that define their action or appearance—properties such as `Width`, `Height`, `Enabled` (whether the user can type input to the control), and `Text` (the text displayed by the control)—and Visual Studio .NET knows about many of these properties. The Properties window, shown in Figure 12-17, displays and allows you to edit the initial values of most of these properties for the controls that Visual Studio .NET has been able to detect by reading your source code.

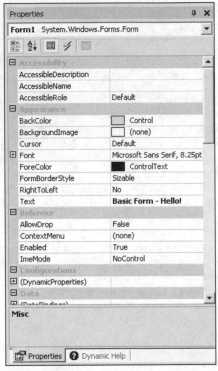

Figure 12-17

The Properties window can also show events. You can view events for what you are focused on in the IDE or selected in the drop-down list box directly in the Properties window by clicking the icon that looks like a lightning flash at the top of the window.

At the top of the Properties window is a list box that allows you to select which control you want to view. We've selected `Form1`, the main form class for our BasicForm project, and have edited the text to "Basic Form—Hello!" If we now check the source code we can see that what we have actually done is edit the source code—using a more friendly user interface:

```
        this.AutoScaleBaseSize = new System.Drawing.Size(5, 13);
        this.ClientSize = new System.Drawing.Size(292, 268);
        this.Controls.AddRange(new System.Windows.Forms.Control[]
{this.textBox1});
        this.Name = "Form1";
        this.Text = "Basic Form - Hello!";
```

Not all the properties shown in the Properties window are explicitly mentioned in our source code. For those that aren't, Visual Studio .NET will display the default values that were set when the form was created and which are set when the form is actually initialized. Obviously, if you change a value for one of these properties in the Properties window, a statement explicitly setting that property will magically appear in your source code—and vice versa. It is interesting to note that if a property is changed from its original value, this property will then appear in bold type within the list box of the Properties window. Sometimes double-clicking the property in the Property window returns the value back to its original value.

The Properties window provides a convenient way to get a broad overview of the appearance and properties of a particular control or window.

> It is interesting to note that the Properties window is implemented as a `System.Windows.Forms`
> `.PropertyGrid` instance, which will internally use the reflection technology we described in Chapter
> 10 to identify the properties and property values to display.

The Class View window

Unlike the Properties window, the Class View window, shown in Figure 12-18, owes its origins to the C++ (and J++) developer environments. This window will be new to Visual Basic developers since Visual Basic 6 did not even support the concept of the class, other than in the sense of a COM component. The Class View is not actually treated by Visual Studio .NET as a window in its own right—rather it is an additional tab to the Solution Explorer window. The Class View shows the hierarchy of the namespaces and classes in your code. It gives you a tree view that you can expand out to see what namespaces contain what classes and what classes contain what members.

A nice feature of the Class View is that if you right-click on the name of any item for which you have access to the source code, the context menu features the Go To Definition option, which takes you to the definition of the item in the code editor. Alternatively, you can do this by double-clicking the item in Class View (or, indeed, by right-clicking the item you want in the source code editor and choosing the same option from the resulting context menu). The context menu also gives you the option to add a field, method, property, or indexer to a class. This means that you specify the details of the relevant member in a dialog box, and the code gets added for you. This might not be that useful in the case of fields or methods, which can be quickly added to your code; however, you might find this feature helpful in the case of properties and indexers, where it can save you quite a bit of typing.

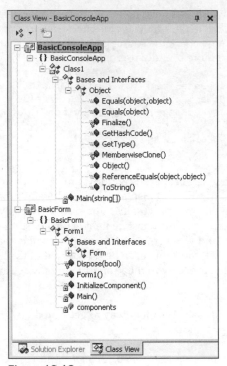

Figure 12-18

The Object Browser window

One important aspect of programming in the .NET environment is being able to find out what methods and other code items are available in the base classes and any other libraries that you are referencing from your assembly. This feature is available through a window called the Object Browser. You can access this window by selecting Object Browser from the View menu in Visual Studio .NET 2003.

The Object Browser window is quite similar to the Class View window in that it displays a tree view that gives the class structure of your application, allowing you to inspect the members of each class. The user interface is slightly different in that it displays class members in a separate pane rather than in the tree view itself. The real difference is that it lets you look at not just the namespaces and classes in your project, but also the ones in all the assemblies that are referenced by the project. Figure 12-19 shows the Object Browser viewing the SystemException class from the .NET base classes.

The only point you have to watch with the Object Browser is that it groups classes by the assembly in which they are located first and by namespace second. Unfortunately, since namespaces for the base classes are often spread across several assemblies, this means you might have trouble locating a particular class unless you know what assembly it is in.

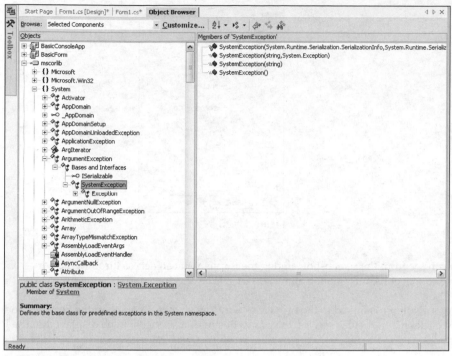

Figure 12-19

The Object Browser is there to view .NET objects. If for any reason you want to investigate installed COM objects, you'll find that the OLEView tool previously used in the C++ IDE is still available—it's located in the Tools menu (the OLE/COM Object Viewer menu item), along with several other similar utilities.

> *Visual Basic developers should not confuse the .NET Object Browser with the Object Browser of the Visual Basic 6 IDE. The .NET Object Viewer is there to view .NET classes, whereas the tool of that name in Visual Basic 6 is used to view COM components. If you want the functionality of the old Object Browser, you should now use the OLEView tool.*

The Server Explorer window

You can use the Server Explorer window, shown in Figure 12-20, to find out about aspects of the computers in your network while coding.

Figure 12-20

As you can see from the screenshot, among the things you can access through the Server Explorer are database connections, information about services, Web Services, and running processes.

The Server Explorer is linked to the Properties window so that if you open the Services node, for example, and click on a particular service, the properties of that service will be displayed in the Properties window.

Pin buttons

While exploring Visual Studio .NET you might have noticed that many of the windows we are describing have some interesting functionality more reminiscent of toolbars. In particular, apart from the code editor, they can all be docked. Another, very new, feature of them is that when they are docked, they have an extra icon that looks like a pin next to the minimize button in the top-right corner of each window. This icon really does act like a pin—it can be used to pin the windows open. When they are pinned (the pin is displayed vertically), they behave just like the regular windows that you are used to. When they are unpinned, however, (the pin is displayed horizontally), they only remain open as long as they have the focus. As soon as they lose the focus (because you clicked or moved your mouse somewhere else) they smoothly retreat into the main border around the entire Visual Studio .NET application. (You can also feel the speed of your computer by how fast or slow they open and close).

Pinning and unpinning windows provides another way of making the best use of the limited space on your screen. It's not really been seen a great deal in Windows before, though a few third-party applications such as PaintShop Pro have used similar concepts. Pinned windows have, however, been around on many Unix-based systems for quite a while.

Building a Project

In this section, we'll examine the options that Visual Studio .NET gives you for building your project.

Building, compiling, and making

Before we examine the various build options, we want to clarify some terminology. You'll often see three different terms used in connection with the process of getting from your source code to some sort of executable code: compiling, building, and making. The origin of these various terms comes from the fact that until recently, the process of getting from source code to executable code involved more than one step (and this is still the case in C++). This was due in large part to the number of source files in a program. In C++, for example, each source file needs to be compiled individually. This leads to what are known as object files, each containing something like executable code, but where each object file relates to only one source file. In order to generate an executable, these object files need to be linked together, a process that is officially known as linking. The combined process was usually referred to—at least on the Windows platform—as building your code. However, in C# terms the compiler is more sophisticated and is able to read in and treat all your source files as one block. Hence there isn't really a separate linking stage, so in the context of C# the terms *compile* and *build* are used interchangeably.

In addition to this, the term *make* basically means the same as *build*, though it's not really used in the context of C#. The term originated on old mainframe systems on which, when a project was composed of many source files, a separate file would be written that contained instructions to the compiler on how to build a project—which files to include and what libraries to link to and so on. This file was generally known as a make file and is still quite standard on Unix systems. Make files are not normally needed on Windows though you can still write them (or get Visual Studio .NET to generate them) if you need to.

Debug and release builds

The idea of having separate builds is very familiar to C++ developers and less so to those with a Visual Basic background. The point here is that when you are debugging you typically want your executable to behave differently than it does when you are ready to ship the software. When you are ready to ship your ware, you want the size of the executable to be as small as possible and the executable itself to be as fast as possible. Unfortunately, these requirements aren't really compatible with your needs when you are debugging code, as we will explain in the following sections.

Optimization

High performance is achieved partly by the compiler doing a lot of optimizations on the code. This means that the compiler actively looks at your source code as it's compiling in order to identify places where it can modify the precise details of what you're doing in a way that doesn't change the overall effect, but which makes things more efficient. For example, if the compiler encountered the following source code:

```
double InchesToCm(double Ins)
{
    return Ins*2.54;
}

// later on in the code

Y = InchesToCm(X);
```

it might replace it with this:

```
Y = X * 2.54;
```

Or it might replace this code:

```
{
    string Message = "Hi";
    Console.WriteLine(Message);
}
```

with this:

```
Console.WriteLine("Hi");
```

By doing so, it bypasses having to declare an unnecessary object reference in the process.

It's not possible to exactly pin down what optimizations the C# compiler does—nor whether the two previous examples actually would occur with any particular example, because those kinds of details are not documented (chances are that for managed languages such as C#, the above optimizations would occur at JIT compilation time, not when the C# compiler compiles source code to assembly). For obvious commercial reasons, companies that write compilers are usually quite reluctant to give too many details about the tricks that their compilers use. We should stress that optimizations do not affect your source code—they affect only the contents of the executable code. However, the previous examples should give you a good idea of what to expect from optimizations.

The problem is that while optimizations like the previous ones help a great deal in making your code run faster, they aren't that helpful for debugging. Suppose with the first example, that you want to set a breakpoint inside the InchesToCm() method to see what's going on in there. How can you possibly do that if the executable code doesn't actually have an InchesToCm() method because the compiler has removed it? And how can you set a watch on the Message variable when that doesn't exist in the compiled code either?

Debugger symbols

When you're debugging, you often have to look at values of variables, and you will specify them by their source code names. The trouble is that executable code generally doesn't contain those names—the compiler replaces the names with memory addresses. .NET has modified this situation somewhat, to the extent that certain items in assemblies are stored with their names, but this is only true of a small minority of items—such as public classes and methods—and those names will still be removed when the assembly is JIT-compiled. Asking the debugger to tell you what the value is in the variable called HeightInInches isn't going to get you very far if, when the debugger examines the executable code, it sees only addresses and no reference to the name HeightInInches anywhere. So, in order to debug properly, you need to have extra debugging information made available in the executable. This information includes, among other things, names of variables and line information that allows the debugger to match up which executable machine assembly language instructions correspond to those of your original source code instructions. You won't, however, want that information in a release build, both for commercial reasons (debugging information makes it a lot easier for other people to disassemble your code) and because it increases the size of the executable.

Extra source code debugging commands

A related issue is that quite often while you are debugging there will be extra lines in your code to display crucial debugging-related information. Obviously you want the relevant commands removed entirely from the executable before you ship the software. You could do this manually but wouldn't it be so much easier if you could simply mark those statements in some way so that the compiler ignores them when it is compiling your code to be shipped. We've already seen in the first part of the book how this can be done in C# by defining a suitable processor symbol, and possibly using this in conjunction with the `Conditional` attribute, giving you what is known as *conditional compilation*.

What all these factors add up to is that you need to compile almost all commercial software in a slightly different way when debugging, compared to the final product that is shipped. Visual Studio .NET is able to take this into account because, as we have already seen, it stores details of all the options that it is supposed to pass to the compiler when it has your code compiled. All that Visual Studio has to do in order to support different types of build is to store more than one set of such details. The different sets of build information are referred to as configurations. When you create a project Visual Studio .NET automatically gives you two configurations, called Debug and Release.

❏ The Debug configuration commonly specifies that no optimizations are to take place, extra debugging information is to be present in the executable, and the compiler is to assume that the debug preprocessor symbol `Debug` is present unless it is explicitly `#undefined` in the source code

❏ The Release configuration specifies that the compiler should optimize, that there should be no extra debugging information in the executable, and that the compiler should not assume that any particular preprocessor symbol is present

You can define your own configurations as well. You might want to do this, for example if you want to set up professional-level builds and enterprise-level builds so you can ship two versions of the software. In the past, because of issues concerning the Unicode character encodings being supported on Windows NT but not on Windows 95, it was common for C++ projects to feature a Unicode configuration and an MBCS (multibyte character set) configuration.

Selecting a configuration

One obvious question is that, since Visual Studio .NET stores details of more than one configuration, how does it determine which one to use when arranging for a project to be built? The answer is that there is always an active configuration, which is the configuration that will be used when you ask Visual Studio .NET to build a project. (Note that configurations are set for each project rather than for each solution.)

By default, when you create a project, the debug configuration is the active configuration. You can change which configuration is the active one by clicking on the Build menu option and selecting the item Configuration Manager. It is also available through a dropdown menu in the main Visual Studio .NET toolbar.

Editing configurations

Besides choosing the active configuration you can also examine and edit the configurations. To do this, you select the relevant project in the Solution Explorer, and then select the Properties from the Project menu. This brings up a very sophisticated dialog box. (Alternatively, you can access the same dialog box by right-clicking the name of the project in the Solution Explorer, and then selecting Properties from the context menu.)

This dialog contains a tree view, which allows you to select quite a lot of different general areas to examine or edit. We don't have space to show all of these areas but we will show a couple of the most important ones.

Figure 12-21 shows the tree view with two top-level nodes, Common Properties and Configuration Properties. Common properties are those properties that are common across all the configurations; configuration properties are specific to a particular configuration.For this screenshot we are showing the general cross-configuration compiler options for the BasicConsoleApp project that we created earlier in the chapter.

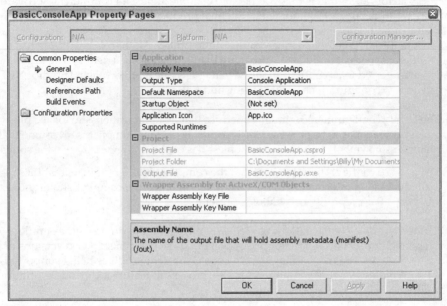

Figure 12-21

Among the points to note are that we can select the name of the assembly, as well as the type of assembly to be generated. The options here are Console Application, Windows Application, and Class Library. You can, of course, change the assembly type if you want. (Though arguably, if you want, you might wonder why you didn't pick the correct project type at the time that you asked Visual Studio .NET to generate the project for you in the first place!)

Figure 12-22 shows the build configuration properties. You'll notice that a list box near the top of the dialog box allows you to specify which configuration you want to look at. In this case we can see—in the case of the Debug configuration —that the compiler assumes that the DEBUG and TRACE preprocessor symbols have been defined. Also, the code is not optimized and extra debugging information is generated.

In general, it's not that often that you'll have to adjust the configuration settings. However, if you ever do need to use them, you now know the difference between the available configuration properties.

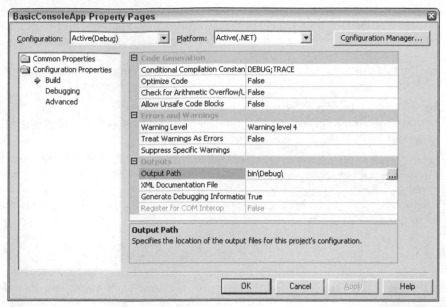

Figure 12-22

Debugging

After the long discussion about building and build configurations, you might be surprised to learn that we're not going to spend a great deal of time discussing debugging itself. The reason for that is that the principles and the process of debugging—setting breakpoints and examining the values of variables—isn't really significantly different in Visual Studio .NET from in any of the various Visual Studio 6 IDEs. Instead we will briefly review the features offered by Visual Studio .NET, focusing on those areas that might be new to some developers. We will also discuss how to deal with exceptions, since these can cause problems during debugging.

In C#, as in pre-.NET languages, the main technique involved in debugging is simply setting breakpoints and using them to examine what is going on in your code at a certain point in its execution.

Breakpoints

You can set breakpoints from Visual Studio .NET on any line of your code that is actually executed. The simplest way is to click the line in the code editor, within the shaded area towards the far left of the document window (or press the F9 key when the appropriate line is selected). This sets up a breakpoint on that particular line, which causes execution to break and control to be transferred to the debugger as soon as that line is reached in the execution process. As in previous versions of Visual Studio, a breakpoint is indicated by a large circle to the left of the line in the code editor. Visual Studio .NET also highlights the line by displaying the text and background in a different color. Clicking the circle again removes the breakpoint.

If breaking every time at a particular line isn't adequate for your particular problem, you can also set conditional breakpoints. To do this, select Debug⇨Windows⇨Breakpoints. This brings up a dialog box asking you for details of the breakpoint you wish to set. Among the options available you can:

❑ Specify that execution should break only after the breakpoint has been passed a certain number of times.

❑ Specify that the breakpoint should come into effect only every so-many times that the line is reached, for example every twentieth time that a line is executed. (This is useful when debugging large loops.)

❑ Set the breakpoints relative to a variable rather than to an instruction. In this case, the value of the variable will be monitored and the breakpoints will be triggered whenever the value of this variable changes. You might find, however, that using this option slows your code down considerably. Checking whether the value of a variable has changed after every instruction adds a lot of processor time.

Watches

After a breakpoint has been hit you will usually want to investigate the values of variables. The simplest way to do this is to simply hover the mouse cursor over the name of the variable in the code editor. This causes a little box that shows the value of that variable to pop up. However, you might also prefer to use the Watch window to examine the contents of variables. The Watch window (shown in Figure 12-23) is a tabbed window that appears only when the program is running under the debugger.

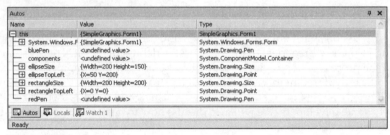

Figure 12-23

Variables that are classes or structs are shown with a + icon next to them, which you can click to expand the variable and see the values of its fields.

The three tabs to this window are each designed to monitor different variables:

❑ **Autos** monitors the last few variables that have been accessed as the program was executing.

❑ **Locals** monitors variables that are accessible in the method currently being executed.

❑ **Watch** monitors any variables that you have explicitly specified by typing their names into the Watch window.

Exceptions

Exceptions are great when you ship your application and making sure that error conditions are handled in an appropriate way within your application. Used well, they can ensure that your application copes with difficulties well and the user never gets presented with a technical dialog box. Unfortunately, exceptions are not so great when you're trying to debug your application. The problem is twofold.

❑   If an exception occurs when you're debugging, then you often don't want it to be handled automatically—especially if automatically handling it means retiring gracefully and terminating execution! Rather, you want the debugger to help you find out why the exception has occurred. Of course the trouble is that if you have written good, robust, defensive code, then your program will automatically handle almost anything—including the bugs that you want to detect!

❑   If an exception occurs that you haven't written a handler for, the .NET runtime will still go off looking for a handler. But by the time it discovers that there isn't one, it will have terminated your program. There won't be a call stack left and you won't be able to look at the values of any of your variables, because they will all have gone out of scope.

Of course, you can set breakpoints in your catch blocks, but that often doesn't help very much because when the `catch` block is reached, flow of execution will, by definition, have exited the corresponding `try` block. That means that the variables you probably wanted to examine the values of in order to find out what's gone wrong will have gone out of scope. You won't even be able to look at the stack trace to find out what method was being executed when the `throw` statement occurred—because control will have left that method. Setting the breakpoints at the `throw` statement will of course solve this, except that if you are coding defensively there will be a lot of `throw` statements in your code. How can you tell which one is the one that threw the exception?

In fact, Visual Studio provides a very neat answer to all of this. If you look into the main Debug menu, you'll find a menu item called Exceptions. This item opens the Exceptions dialog box (see Figure 12-24), which allows you to specify what happens when an exception is thrown. You can choose to continue execution or to stop and start debugging—in which case execution stops and the debugger steps in at the `throw` statement itself.

What makes this a really powerful tool is that you can customize the behavior according to which class of exception is thrown. For example, in Figure 12-24, we've told Visual Studio .NET to break into the debugger whenever it encounters any exception thrown by a .NET base class, but not to break into the debugger if the exception is an `AppDomainUnloadedException`.

Visual Studio .NET knows about all the exception classes available in the .NET base classes, and also about quite a few exceptions that can be thrown outside the .NET environment. Visual Studio .NET isn't automatically aware of your own custom exception classes that you write, but you can manually add your exception classes to the list and thereby specify which of your exceptions should cause execution to stop immediately. To do this you just click the Add button (which is enabled when you have selected a top-level node from the tree) and type in the name of your exception class.

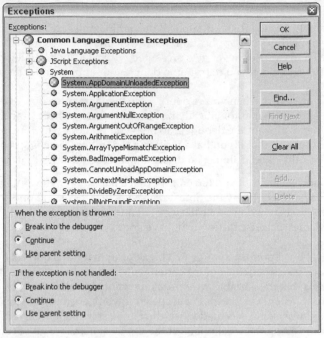

Figure 12-24

Other .NET Tools

We've spent a lot of time exploring Visual Studio .NET, because you will be spending a lot of your development time using it. However, there are a number of other tools available to assist with your programming.

The ASP.NET Web Matrix Project

Besides Visual Studio .NET, Microsoft has provided another IDE for building .NET applications called the ASP.NET Web Matrix Project (see Figure 12-25). You can download this lightweight IDE for free at http://www.asp.net. Microsoft created this IDE because it provides hobbyist developers a quick-and-easy way of learning and working with .NET.

The Web Matrix does not do everything that Visual Studio .NET does. The Web Matrix does not allow you to build Windows Forms; however, it does allow you to build XML Web services and Web Forms. The other big downer of the Web Matrix is that it does not support Intellisense, so you need to know what you are typing because you cannot depend on the IDE to complete your code for you. But you can't beat the price!

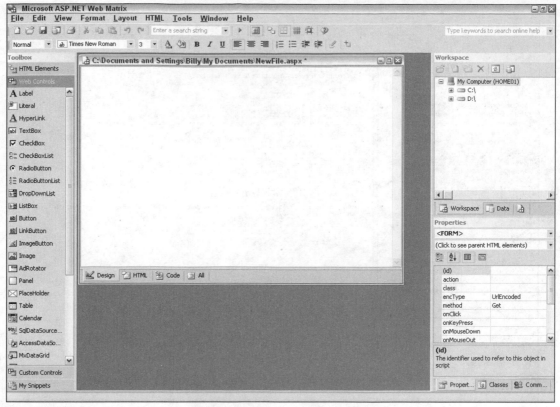

Figure 12-25

For Web Forms development, you will find three new controls included in the Web Matrix—the MxDataGrid control, the SqlDataSourceControl and the AccessDataSourceControl. The MxDataGrid control is a super-smart datagrid that allows you to apply sorting and paging easily to your tables just by simply setting a property of the control. The SqlDataSourceControl and the AccessDataSourceControl allow you to easily connect to and pull data from Microsoft SQL Server or Access with little effort involved.

WinCV

You can use the WinCV utility (see Figure 12-26), which Microsoft has provided, to explore the base classes and see what methods are available. It is very similar to the Visual Studio .NET object browser, except that it is an independent application, and it will show you all the base classes, whereas the object browser shows only those in the assemblies that are referenced by your project.

Figure 12-26

`WinCV` is quite easy to use. You run it from the Visual Studio .NET command line prompt by typing in `wincv`. Then, when it is running, you simply type in some text in the list box near the top of the `wincv` window. As you type, `wincv` will search through the base classes and pick out all the classes whose name includes the word you have typed in. These classes are displayed in the left-hand list box. If you click on a particular class, its members are displayed, roughly in a format that corresponds to C# syntax, on the right.

You'll find the Visual Studio .NET command prompt under Microsoft Visual Studio .NET in the Start menu. It is an ordinary command prompt, but with a couple of extra environment variables defined to allow you to use various .NET tools. You won't be able to run wincv (or other .NET tools) from the usual command prompt.

Summary

In this chapter we've looked at one of the most important programming tools in the .NET environment—Visual Studio .NET 2003. We spent the bulk of the chapter examining how this tool facilitates writing code in C# (and C++ and Visual Basic .NET). We also briefly covered the Web Matrix, which you can use when working with Web Forms and XML Web services, as well as wincv, a useful utility that allows you to examine the base classes.

In the next chapter, we will take a look at assemblies in detail.

13

Assemblies

In this chapter we discuss *assemblies*. An assembly is the .NET term for a deployment and configuration unit. We'll discuss exactly what they are, how they can be used, and why they are such a useful feature. In particular, we will cover:

❑ The innovations offered by assemblies over previous technologies

❑ How to create and view assemblies

❑ What the Common Language Specification means, and how cross-language support is made possible

❑ How to share assemblies

Let's begin this chapter with an overview of assemblies:

What Are Assemblies?

Before the .NET platform was introduced you had to deal with the predecessors of assemblies: normal DLLs exporting global functions, and COM DLLs exporting COM classes. Microsoft itself introduced the phrase "DLL Hell" to describe traditional problems with DLLs—problems that are known all too well.

Often applications break because a newly installed application overwrites a DLL that has also been used by another application. Sometimes it happens that the installation replaces a new DLL with an old one, because the installation program does not correctly check the versions, or the versions are not correctly set. More often, an old DLL is replaced by a new version. Normally this shouldn't be a problem—the new DLL should be backwardly compatible with the old version; however, often that is not the case.

Windows 2000 introduced the *side-by-side* feature that allows the installation of DLLs in the application's directory. With side-by-side, you can install a different version of an already installed, shared DLL to the directory of the application. The `LoadLibrary()` Win32 API call was rewritten so that it first checks for a `.local` file in the application directory. If it is found, the API first checks if a DLL was in the same directory of the application, before the other mechanisms are used to find a shared DLL. This also modifies the fixed path that is in the registry for COM DLLs. Side-by-side is an afterthought, and doesn't solve all of the issues, and even introduces some new problems with COM DLLs. Another feature of Windows 2000 or later Windows operating systems that deals with DLL Hell is file protection: system DLLs are protected from being overwritten by unauthorized parties. All of these features deal with the symptoms and not with the causes.

The versioning problems of DLLs exist because it's not clear which version of a specific DLL each application needs. Dependencies are not tracked or enforced with the traditional DLL architecture. COM DLLs seem to solve a lot of the DLL problems because of a better separation of the implementation and the interface. The interface is a contract between the client and the component, which, according to COM rules, should never be changed, and thus can't break. However, even with COM, changes of implementations can break existing applications.

Side-by-side also supports COM DLLs. If you have ever tried side-by-side with COM DLLs, you have seen that it's just a hack. New problems arise when using side-by-side COM DLLs. If we're installing the same DLL over the old one (without uninstalling the old DLL), what happens when two versions of the same component use different threading configurations? The configuration information is taken from the last installed version. This problem exists because the configuration of a COM component is not stored in the component DLL itself, but in the Registry.

The Answer to DLL Hell

The .NET platform's answer to DLL Hell and to all of its problems is *assemblies*. Assemblies are self-describing installation units, consisting of one or more files. One assembly could be a single DLL or EXE that includes metadata, or it can be made of different files, for example, resource files, metadata, DLLs, and an EXE. Installation of an assembly can be as simple as copying all of its files. An *xcopy* installation can be done. Another big feature of assemblies is that they can be *private* or *shared*. With COM this differentiation doesn't exist, since practically all COM components are shared. If you search for a COM component in the Registry or use `OleView`, you have to walk through hundreds and hundreds of components. Only a small number of these components were ever meant to be used from more than one application; however, every component must have a global unique identifier (GUID).

There's a big difference between private and shared assemblies. Many developers will be happy with just private assemblies. No special management, registration, versioning, and so on needs to be done with private assemblies. The only application that could have version problems with private assemblies is your own application. The private components you use within your application are installed at the same time as the application itself. Local application directories are used for the assemblies of the components, so you shouldn't have any versioning problems. No other application will ever overwrite your private assemblies. Of course it is still a good idea to use version numbers for private assemblies too. This helps a lot with code changes, but this is not a requirement of .NET.

With private assemblies you can still have versioning problems during development time. Let's see an example: if a component you use in your application references version 1 of assembly X, and you use version 2 of assembly X in your application, which version of the assembly is copied to your application directory?

The answer to this question depends on what assembly you have referenced first—this versioning problem must be solved during development time. On the installed system, a hot fix can be easily applied to an application by simply replacing a private assembly with a new version. The only application that could have problems with the new version is the one where this fix is applied, as no other applications can be influenced.

When using shared assemblies, several applications can use this assembly and have a dependency on it. With shared assemblies, many rules must be fulfilled. A shared assembly must have a special version number, a unique name, and usually it's installed in the *global assembly cache*.

Features of Assemblies

The features of assemblies can be summarized as follows:

❑ Assemblies are *self-describing*. It's no longer necessary to pay attention to Registry keys for apartments, to get the type library from some other place, and so on. Assemblies include metadata that describes the assembly. The metadata includes the types exported from the assembly and a manifest; we'll look at exactly what a manifest is in the next section.

❑ *Version dependencies* are recorded inside an assembly manifest. By storing the version of any referenced assemblies in the manifest of the assembly, we are able to know exactly the version number of the referenced assembly that was used during development. The version of the referenced assembly that will be used can be configured by the developer and the system administrator. In a later section of this chapter, we will look at which version policies are available, and how they work.

❑ Assemblies can be loaded *side-by-side*. Using Windows 2000 we already have a side-by-side feature where different versions of the same DLL can be used on a system. .NET extends this functionality of Windows 2000, allowing different versions of the same assembly to be used inside a single process! Maybe you're asking where this could be useful? If assembly A references version 1 of the shared assembly Shared, and assembly B uses version 2 of the shared assembly Shared, and you are using both assembly A and B, you need both versions of the shared assembly Shared in your application—and with .NET both versions are loaded and used.

❑ Application isolation is ensured using *application domains*. With application domains a number of applications can run independently inside a single process. Faults in one application cannot directly affect other applications inside the same process.

❑ Installation can be as easy as copying the files that belong to an assembly. An xcopy can be enough. This feature is named *no-touch deployment*. However, there are cases when no-touch deployment cannot be applied, and a normal Windows installation is required. We discuss deployment of applications in Chapter 18.

Application Domains and Assemblies

Before .NET, processes were used as isolation boundaries, with every process having its private virtual memory; an application running in one process cannot write to the memory of another application and thereby crash the other application. The process is used as an isolation and security boundary between applications. With the .NET architecture we have a new boundary for applications: *application domains*. With managed IL code the runtime can ensure that access to the memory of another application inside a single process can't happen. Multiple applications can run in a single process within multiple application domains (see Figure 13-1).

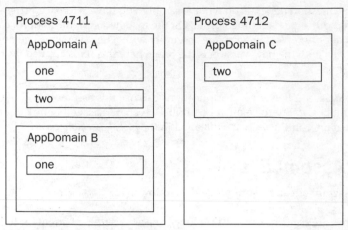

Figure 13-1

An assembly is loaded into an application domain. In Figure 13-1 you can see process *4711* with two application domains. In application domain A, the objects one and two are instantiated, one in assembly One, and two in assembly Two. The second application domain in process 4711 has an instance one. To minimize memory consumption, the code of assemblies is only loaded once into an application domain. Instance and static members are not shared between application domains. It's not possible to directly access objects within another application domain; a proxy is needed instead. So in Figure 13-1, the object one in application domain B cannot directly access the objects one or two in application domain A without a proxy.

You can read more about proxies and communication across application domains in Chapter 16.

The AppDomain class is used to create and terminate application domains, load and unload assemblies and types, and to enumerate assemblies and threads in a domain. Let's program a small example to see application domains in action.

First, create a C# Console Application AssemblyA. In the Main() method add a Console.WriteLine() so that you can see when this method gets called. In addition, add a constructor with two int values as arguments, which will be used to create instances with the AppDomain class. The AssemblyA.exe assembly will be loaded from the second application that will be created.

```csharp
using System;

namespace Wrox.ProCSharp.Assemblies.AppDomains
{
    class Class1
    {
        public Class1(int val1, int val2)
        {
            Console.WriteLine("Constructor with the values {0}, {1}" +
                        " in domain {2} called", val1, val2,
                        AppDomain.CurrentDomain.FriendlyName);
        }
```

```
    [STAThread]
    static void Main(string[] args)
    {
        Console.WriteLine("Main in domain {0} called",
                          AppDomain.CurrentDomain.FriendlyName);
    }
  }
}
```

The second project created is again a C# Console Application: DomainTest. First, display the name of the current domain using the property `FriendlyName` of the `AppDomain` class. With the `CreateDomain()` method, a new application domain with the friendly name `New AppDomain` is created. Then load the assembly `AssemblyA` into the new domain and call the `Main()` method by calling `ExecuteAssembly()`:

```
using System;
namespace Wrox.ProCSharp.Assemblies.AppDomains
{
    class Test
    {
        [STAThread]
        static void Main(string[] args)
        {
            AppDomain currentDomain = AppDomain.CurrentDomain;
            Console.WriteLine(currentDomain.FriendlyName);
            AppDomain secondDomain =
                            AppDomain.CreateDomain("New AppDomain");
            secondDomain.ExecuteAssembly("AssemblyA.exe");
        }
    }
}
```

Before starting the program DomainTest.exe, copy the assembly AssemblyA.exe to the directory of DomainTest.exe so that the assembly can be found. It's not possible to add a reference to AssemblyA.exe, because Visual Studio .NET only supports adding references to assemblies stored in DLL formats, and not EXE formats. However, this is possible from the command line. If the assembly cannot be found, a `System.IO.FileNotFoundException` exception is thrown.

When DomainTest.exe is run, you get the console output shown in Figure 13-2. DomainTest.exe is the friendly name of the first application domain. The second line is the output of the newly loaded assembly in the New AppDomain. With a process viewer you will not see the process AssemblyA.exe executing because there's no new process created. AssemblyA is loaded into the process DomainTest.exe.

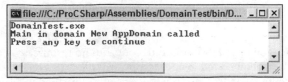

Figure 13-2

343

Instead of calling the `Main()` method in the newly loaded assembly, you can also create a new instance. In the following example replace the `ExecuteAssembly()` method with a `CreateInstance()`. The first argument is the name of the assembly, `AssemblyA`. The second argument defines the type that should be instantiated: `Wrox.ProCSharp.Assemblies.AppDomains.Class1`. The third argument, `true`, means that case is ignored. `System.Reflection.BindingFlags.CreateInstance` is a binding flag enumeration value to specify that the constructor should be called:

```
AppDomain secondDomain =
    AppDomain.CreateDomain("New AppDomain");
// secondDomain.ExecuteAssembly("AssemblyA.exe");
secondDomain.CreateInstance("AssemblyA",
    "Wrox.ProCSharp.Assemblies.AppDomains.Class1", true,
    System.Reflection.BindingFlags.CreateInstance,
    null, new object[] {7, 3}, null, null, null);
```

Figure 13-3 shows the result of a successful run of the application.

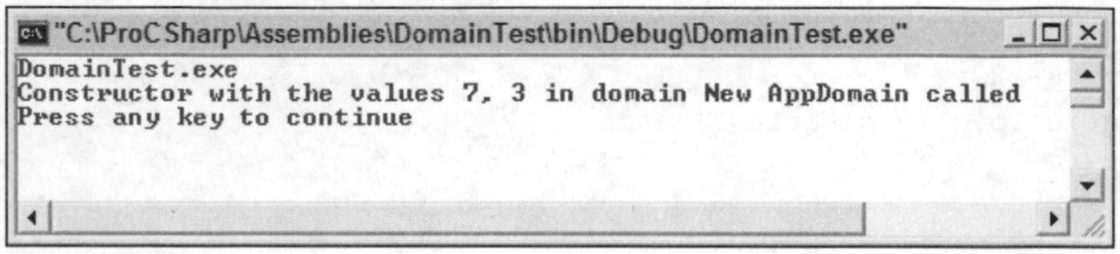

Figure 13-3

Now you have seen how to create and call application domains. In runtime hosts, application domains are created automatically. ASP.NET creates an application domain for each Web application that runs on a Web server. Internet Explorer creates application domains in which managed controls will run. For applications, it can be useful to create application domains if you want to unload an assembly. Unloading assemblies can only be done by terminating an application domain.

Assembly Structure

An assembly consists of assembly metadata describing the complete assembly, type metadata describing the exported types and methods, MSIL code, and resources. All these parts can be inside of one file or spread across several files.

In this example (see Figure 13-4), the assembly metadata, type metadata, MSIL Code, and resources are all in one file—Component.dll. The assembly consists of a single file.

The second example shows a single assembly spread across three files (see Figure 13-5). Component.dll has assembly metadata, type metadata, and MSIL code, but no resources. The assembly uses a picture from picture.jpeg that is not embedded inside Component.dll, but is referenced from within the assembly metadata. The assembly metadata also references a module called `util.netmodule`, which itself includes only type metadata and MSIL code for a class. A module has no assembly metadata. Thus the module itself has no version information; it also cannot be installed separately. All three files in this example make up a single assembly. The assembly is the installation unit. It would also be possible to put the manifest in a different file.

Component.dll

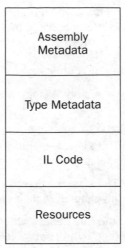

Figure 13-4

Component.dll

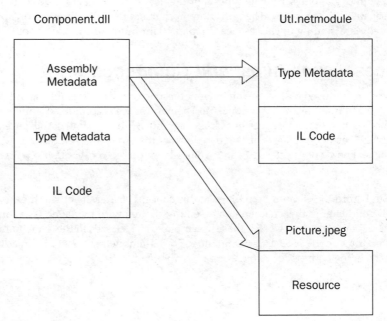

Figure 13-5

Assembly Manifests

An important part of an assembly is a *manifest*, which is part of the metadata. It describes the assembly with all the information that's needed to reference it and lists all its dependencies. The parts of the manifest are:

❑   **Identity** (name, version, culture, and public key)

❑   **A list of files** belonging to this assembly. A single assembly must have at least one file, but may contain a number of files.

❑   **A list of referenced assemblies**. Documented inside the manifest are all assemblies that are used from the assembly, including the version number, and the public key. The public key is used to uniquely identify assemblies. We will discuss the public key later.

❑   **A set of permission requests**. These are the permissions needed to run this assembly. We will not talk about permissions in this chapter. More information can be found in Chapter 14.

❑   **Exported types**, provided that they are defined within a module, and the module is referenced from the assembly. Otherwise they are not part of the manifest. A module is a unit of reuse. The type description is stored as metadata inside the assembly. We can get the structures and classes with the properties and methods from the metadata. This replaces the type library that was used with COM to describe the types. For the use of COM clients it's easy to generate a type library out of the manifest. The reflection mechanism uses the information about the exported types for late binding to classes. See Chapter 10 for more information about reflection.

Namespaces, Assemblies, and Components

Maybe you're now confused by the meanings of namespaces, types, assemblies, and components. How does a namespace fit into the assembly concept? The namespace is completely independent of an assembly. You can have different namespaces in a single assembly, but the same namespace can be spread across assemblies. The namespace is just an extension of the type name—it belongs to the name of the type. Thus, the real name of the class `Class1` we used before is `Wrox.ProCSharp.Assemblies.AppDomains.Class1`.

The diagram in Figure 13-6 should help to make this concept clearer. It shows three assemblies, which we will build later in this chapter—an assembly written with managed C++, one with Visual Basic .NET, and one with C#. All these assemblies have classes in the same namespace: `Wrox.ProCSharp.Assemblies.CrossLanguage`. The assembly `HelloCSharp` in addition, has a class `Math` that's in the namespace `Wrox.Utils`.

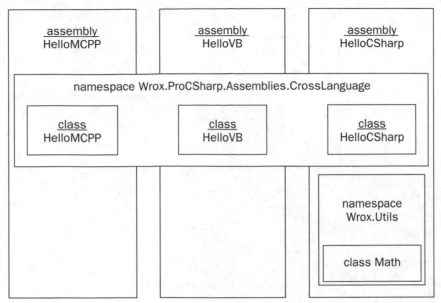

Figure 13-6

Private and Shared Assemblies

Assemblies can be shared or private. A *private assembly* is found either in the same directory as the application, or within one of its subdirectories. With a private assembly, it's not necessary to think about naming conflicts with other classes or versioning problems. The assemblies that are referenced during the build process are copied to the application directory. Private assemblies are the normal way to build assemblies, especially when applications and components are built within the same company.

When using *shared assemblies*, you have to be aware of some rules. The assembly must be unique, and therefore have a unique name called a *strong name*. Part of the strong name is a mandatory version number. Shared assemblies will mostly be used when a vendor, different from that of the application, builds the component, or where a large application is split into subprojects.

Viewing Assemblies

Assemblies can be viewed using the command line utility ildasm, the MSIL disassembler. An assembly can be opened by starting ildasm from the command line, with the assembly as argument or by selecting the menu File⇨Open.

Figure 13-7 shows ildasm opening the example that we are about to build, HelloCSharp.exe. ildasm shows the manifest and the `HelloCSharp` type in the `Wrox.ProCSharp.Assemblies.CrossLanguage` namespace. Opening the manifest, you can see the version number, and the assembly attributes as well as the referenced assemblies and their versions. Opening the methods of the class, you can see the MSIL code.

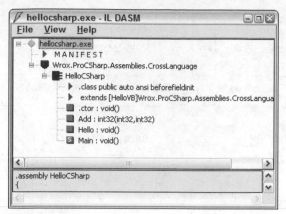

Figure 13-7

ildasm symbols

The following table lists the symbols that are used with ildasm.

Symbol	Description
	Represents a namespace.
	Represents a reference type, a class. Similar symbols are used by value types (structs) that have a light color, delegates that are real classes with the MSIL code, interfaces that have an "I" in the graphic, and enumerations with an "E."
	Represents a method and get and set accessors of a property; an "S" in the graphic means that this method is static.
	Represents a field.
	Represents an event.
	Represents a property.
	This means that more information is available, for example manifest information or information about a class declaration.

Building Assemblies

You have learned what assemblies are, now it is time to build some. Of course, you have already built assemblies in previous chapters, because a .NET executable counts as an assembly. Now, however, we take a look at special options for assemblies.

Creating modules and assemblies

All C# project types in Visual Studio .NET create an assembly. Whether you choose a DLL or EXE project type, an assembly is always created. With the command line C# compiler *csc*, it's also possible to create modules. A module is a DLL without assembly attributes (so it's not an assembly, but it can be added to assemblies at a later time). The command

```
csc /target:module hello.cs
```

creates a module hello.netmodule. You can view this module using ildasm.

A module also has a manifest, but there is no `.assembly` entry inside the manifest (except for the external assemblies that are referenced), since a module has no assembly attributes. It's not possible to configure versions or permissions with modules; that can only be done at the assembly scope. In the manifest of the module, references to assemblies can be found. With the /addmodule option of csc, it's possible to add modules to existing assemblies.

To compare modules to assemblies, create a simple class A and compile it by using:

```
csc /target:module A.cs
```

The compiler generates the file A.netmodule, which doesn't include assembly information (as you can see using ildasm looking at the manifest information). The manifest of the module shows the referenced assembly mscorlib and the `.module` entry in Figure 13-8.

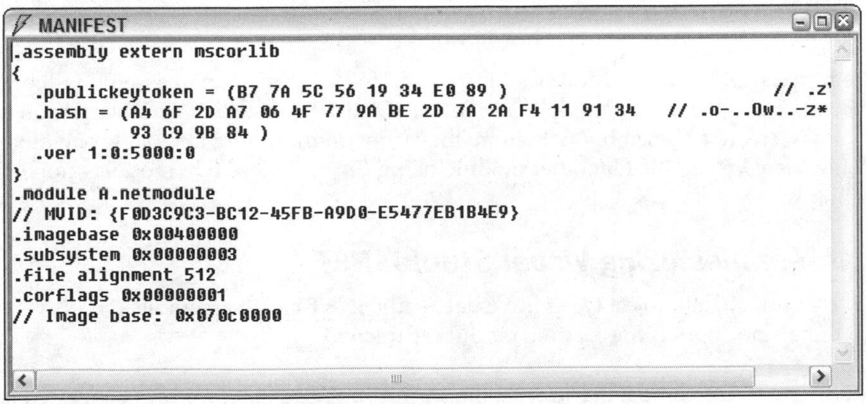

```
MANIFEST
.assembly extern mscorlib
{
  .publickeytoken = (B7 7A 5C 56 19 34 E0 89 )                        // .z'
  .hash = (A4 6F 2D A7 06 4F 77 9A BE 2D 7A 2A F4 11 91 34    // .o-..0w..-z*
           93 C9 9B 84 )
  .ver 1:0:5000:0
}
.module A.netmodule
// MVID: {F0D3C9C3-BC12-45FB-A9D0-E5477EB1B4E9}
.imagebase 0x00400000
.subsystem 0x00000003
.file alignment 512
.corflags 0x00000001
// Image base: 0x070c0000
```

Figure 13-8

Next, create an assembly B that includes the module A.netmodule. It's not necessary to have a source file to generate this assembly. The command to build the assembly is:

```
csc /target:library /addmodule:A.netmodule /out:B.dll
```

When looking at the assembly using ildasm, you can only find a manifest. In the manifest, the assembly mscorlib is referenced. Next we see the assembly section with a hash algorithm and the version. The number of the algorithm defines the type of the algorithm that was used to create the hash code of the assembly. When creating an assembly programmatically it is possible to select the algorithm. Part of the manifest is a list of all modules belonging to the assembly. In Figure 13-9 we see `.module` A.netmodule that belongs to the assembly. Classes exported from modules are part of the assembly manifest; classes exported from the assembly itself are not.

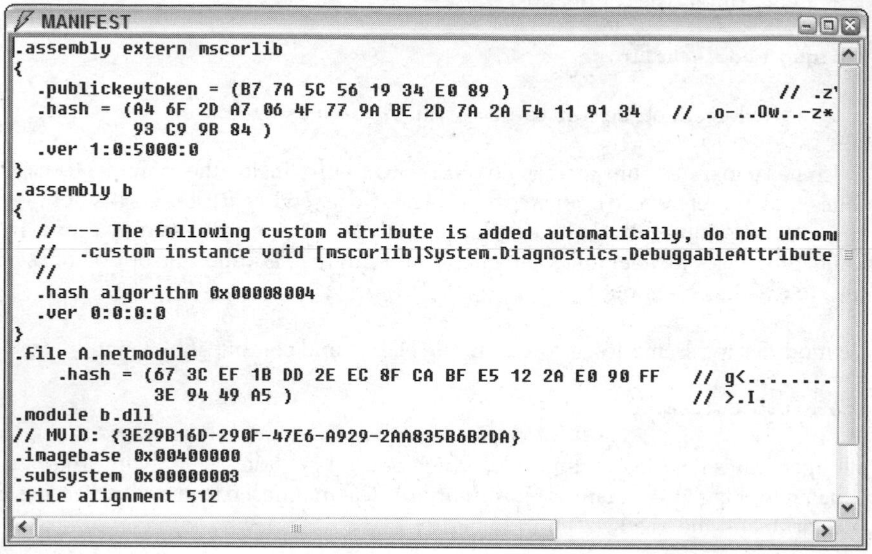

```
// MANIFEST                                                        _ □ X
.assembly extern mscorlib
{
  .publickeytoken = (B7 7A 5C 56 19 34 E0 89 )                    // .z'
  .hash = (A4 6F 2D A7 06 4F 77 9A BE 2D 7A 2A F4 11 91 34    // .o-..Ow..-z*
           93 C9 9B 84 )
  .ver 1:0:5000:0
}
.assembly b
{
  // --- The following custom attribute is added automatically, do not uncom
  //   .custom instance void [mscorlib]System.Diagnostics.DebuggableAttribute
  //
  .hash algorithm 0x00008004
  .ver 0:0:0:0
}
.file A.netmodule
    .hash = (67 3C EF 1B DD 2E EC 8F CA BF E5 12 2A E0 90 FF    // g<........
             3E 94 49 A5 )                                       // >.I.
.module b.dll
// MVID: {3E29B16D-290F-47E6-A929-2AA835B6B2DA}
.imagebase 0x00400000
.subsystem 0x00000003
.file alignment 512
```

Figure 13-9

What's the purpose of modules? Modules can be used for faster startup of assemblies because not all types are inside a single file. The modules are only loaded when needed. Another reason to use modules is if you want to create an assembly with more than one programming language; one module could be written using Visual Basic .NET, another module using C#, and these two modules can be included in a single assembly.

Creating assemblies using Visual Studio .NET

As already mentioned, all project types in Visual Studio .NET create assemblies. With Visual Studio .NET 2003 there's no support for creating modules directly.

When creating a Visual Studio .NET project, the source file AssemblyInfo.cs is generated automatically. You can use the normal source code editor to configure the assembly attributes in this file. This is the file generated from the wizard:

```
using System.Reflection;
using System.Runtime.CompilerServices;
//
// General Information about an assembly is controlled through the
// following set of attributes. Change these attribute values to modify
// the information associated with an assembly.
//
[assembly: AssemblyTitle("")]
```

```
[assembly: AssemblyDescription("")]
[assembly: AssemblyConfiguration("")]
[assembly: AssemblyCompany("")]
[assembly: AssemblyProduct("")]
[assembly: AssemblyCopyright("")]
[assembly: AssemblyTrademark("")]
[assembly: AssemblyCulture("")]
//
// Version information for an assembly consists of the following four
// values:
//
//      Major Version
//      Minor Version
//      Build Number
//      Revision
//
// You can specify all the values or you can default the Revision and
// Build Numbers by using the '*' as shown below:
[assembly: AssemblyVersion("1.0.*")]
//
// In order to sign your assembly you must specify a key to use. Refer to the
// Microsoft .NET Framework documentation for more information on assembly signing.
//
// Use the attributes below to control which key is used for signing.
//
// Notes:
//   (*) If no key is specified - the assembly cannot be signed.
//   (*) KeyName refers to a key that has been installed in the Crypto
//       Service Provider (CSP) on your machine.
//   (*) If the key file and a key name attributes are both specified,
//       the following processing occurs:
//       (1) If the KeyName can be found in the CSP - that key is used.
//       (2) If the KeyName does not exist and the KeyFile does exist,
//           the key in the file is installed into the CSP and used.
//   (*) Delay Signing is an advanced option - see the Microsoft .NET
//       Framework documentation for more information on this.
//
[assembly: AssemblyDelaySign(false)]
[assembly: AssemblyKeyFile("")]
[assembly: AssemblyKeyName("")]
```

This file is used for configuration of the assembly manifest. The compiler reads the assembly attributes to inject the specific information into the manifest.

[assembly], and [module] are assembly level attributes. Assembly level attributes are, in contrast to the other attributes, not attached to a specific language element. The arguments that can be used for the assembly attribute are classes of the namespaces System.Reflection, System.Runtime.CompilerServices, and System.Runtime.InteropServices.

In Chapter 10 you can read more about attributes and how to create and use custom attributes.

Here's a list of assembly attributes that are defined within the `System.Reflection` namespace.

Assembly Attribute	Description
`AssemblyCompany`	Specifies the company name.
`AssemblyConfiguration`	Specifies build information such as retail or debugging information.
`AssemblyCopyright` and `AssemblyTrademark`	Hold the copyright and trademark information.
`AssemblyDefaultAlias`	Can be used if the assembly name is not easily readable (such as a GUID when the assembly name is created dynamically). With this attribute an alias name can be specified.
`AssemblyDescription`	Describes the assembly or the product. Looking at the properties of the executable file this value shows up as Comments.
`AssemblyProduct`	Specifies the name of the product where the assembly belongs.
`AssemblyInformational Version`	This attribute isn't used for version checking when assemblies are referenced, it is for information only. It is very useful to specify the version of an application that uses multiple assemblies. Opening the properties of the executable we can see this value as the Product Version.
`AssemblyTitle`	Used to give the assembly a friendly name. The friendly name can include spaces. With the file properties we can see this value as Description.

Here's an example of how these attributes might be configured:

```
[assembly: AssemblyTitle("Professional C#")]
[assembly: AssemblyDescription("")]
[assembly: AssemblyConfiguration("Retail version")]
[assembly: AssemblyCompany("Wrox Press")]
[assembly: AssemblyProduct("Wrox Professional Series")]
[assembly: AssemblyCopyright("Copyright (C) Wrox Press 2003")]
[assembly: AssemblyTrademark("Wrox is a registered trademark of John Wiley & Sons,
Inc.")]
[assembly: AssemblyCulture("en-US")]
```

The following attributes correspond to classes in the `System.Runtime.CompilerServices` namespace:

❑ `AssemblyCulture` tells about the culture of the assembly. Cultures are discussed in Chapter 17.

❑ `AssemblyDelaySign`, `AssemblyKeyFile`, and `AssemblyKeyName` are used to create strong names for shared assemblies.

❑ `AssemblyVersion` specifies the version number of the assembly. Versioning plays an important part for shared assemblies.

*Additional COM interoperability attributes within the **System.Runtime.InteropServices** namespace can be used to make .NET types visible to COM, to specify application IDs for example. COM interoperability is the subject of Chapter 28.*

Cross-Language Support

One of the best features of COM is its support for multiple languages. It's possible to create a COM component with Visual Basic and to make use of it from within a scripting client such as JScript. On the other hand, it's also possible to create a COM component using C++ that a Visual Basic program can't make use of. A scripting client has different requirements than a Visual Basic client, and a C++ client is able to use many more COM features than any other client language.

When writing COM components it's always necessary to have the client programming language in mind. The server must be developed for a specific client language, or for a group of client languages. If designing a COM component for a scripting client, this component can also be used from within C++, but then the C++ client has some disadvantages. Many rules must be followed when different clients should be supported, and the compiler can't help with COM; the COM developer has to know the requirements of the client language and has to create the interfaces accordingly.

How does this compare with the .NET platform? With the *Common Type System* (CTS), .NET defines how value types and reference types can be defined from a .NET language, the memory layout of such types. But the CTS does not guarantee that a type which is defined from any language can be used from any other language. This is the role of the *Common Language Specification* (CLS). The CLS defines the minimum requirement of types that must be supported by a .NET language.

We briefly mention the CTS and CLS in Chapter 2. In this section, we shall go deeper and explore:

- ❑ Both CTS and CLS.

- ❑ Language independence in action by creating a C++, Visual Basic .NET and a C# class that derive from each other. We look at the MSIL code that's generated from these compilers.

- ❑ The requirements of the CLS.

The CTS and the CLS

All types are declared with the guidance of the CTS. The CTS defines a set of rules that language compilers must follow to define, reference, use, and store reference and value types. Therefore, by following the CTS, objects written in different languages can interact with each other.

However, not all types are available to all programming languages. To build components that are accessible from all .NET languages use the CLS. With the CLS the compiler can check for valid code according to the CLS specification.

Any language that supports .NET isn't just restricted to the common subset of features that is defined with the CLS; even with .NET it's still possible to create components that can't be used from different languages. Supporting all languages is much easier with .NET than it was with COM. If you do restrict yourself to the CLS, it's *guaranteed* that this component can be used from all languages. It is most likely that libraries written by third parties will restrict themselves to the CLS to make the library available to all languages.

The .NET Framework was designed from the ground up to support multiple languages. During the design phase of .NET, Microsoft invited many compiler vendors to build their own .NET languages. Microsoft itself delivers Visual Basic .NET, managed C++, C#, J#, and JScript .NET. In addition, more than 40 languages from different vendors, such as COBOL, Smalltalk, Perl, and Eiffel are available. Each of these languages has its specific advantages and many different features. The compilers of all these languages have been extended to support .NET.

> **The CLS is the minimum specification of requirements that a language must support. This means that if we restrict our public methods to the CLS, all languages supporting .NET can use our classes!**

Most, but not all, of the classes in the .NET Framework are CLS compliant. The non-compliant classes and methods are specially marked as not compliant in the MSDN documentation. One example is the UInt32 structure in the System namespace. UInt32 represents a 32-bit unsigned integer. Not all languages (including Visual Basic .NET or J#) support unsigned data types; such data types are not CLS compliant.

Figure 13-10 shows the relation of the CLS to the CTS, and how types of programming languages relate.

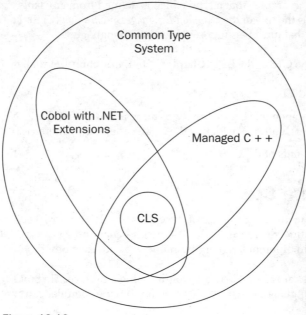

Figure 13-10

Language Independence in Action

Let's see CLS in action. The first assembly created includes a base class with Visual C++. The second assembly has a Visual Basic .NET class that inherits from the C++ class. The third assembly is a C# console application with a class deriving from the Visual Basic .NET code, and a Main function that's using the C# class. The implementation should just show how the languages make use of .NET classes, and how they handle numbers, so all these classes have a simple Hello() method where the System.Console class is used, and an Add() method where two numbers are added. Figure 13-11 shows the UML class diagram with these classes and methods.

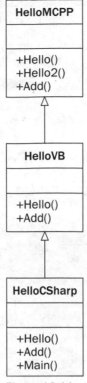

Figure 13-11

Writing the managed C++ class

The first project type you can create for this sample is a .NET Class Library, which is created from the Visual C++ Projects project type of Visual Studio .NET, and given the name HelloMCPP (see Figure 13-12).

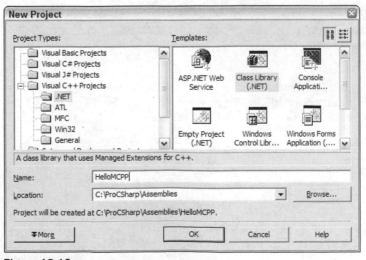

Figure 13-12

With Visual Studio .NET 2003 you can create pure managed code with C++. In this example we will mix native and managed code inside one file, so some project properties needs to be changed.

- ❑ The C Runtime Library must be added to the linker. This is done by adding msvcrt.lib to additional dependencies with the Linker⇨Input configuration.

- ❑ From the same configuration nochkclr.obj must be removed. This is a security check if the C Runtime Library is not used.

- ❑ Using C functions an entry point is needed. Add __DllMainCRTStartup@12 to Force Symbol References.

- ❑ The necessary configuration changes can be seen in Figure 13-13.

Visual Studio .NET 2003 enables you to create purely managed code with C++. This was not possible with Visual Studio .NET 2002, where the configuration changes are not needed.

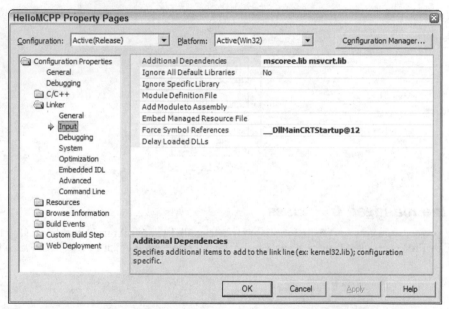

Figure 13-13

The application wizard generates a class HelloMCPP that is marked with __gc to make the class a managed type. Without a special attribute, the class would be a normal unmanaged C++ class generating native code. This class is in the file HelloMCPP.h:

```
// HelloMCPP.h
#pragma once
using namespace System;
namespace HelloMCPP
{
   public __gc class Class1
   {
      // TODO: Add your methods for this class here.
```

```
    };
}
```

For demonstration purposes, change the namespace and class name, and add three methods to the class. The virtual method Hello2() uses a C runtime function printf() that demonstrates the use of native code within a managed class. To make this method available the header file stdio.h must be included. Within the Hello() method we are using the Console managed class from the System namespace. The C++ using namespace statement is similar to the C# using statement. using namespace System opens the System namespace, so we don't have to write System::Console::WriteLine(). Mark the method Hello() with the virtual keyword, so that it can be overridden. Hello() will be overridden in the Visual Basic and C# classes. Similar to C#, C++ member functions are not virtual by default. Add a third method, Add(), which returns the sum of two int arguments, to the class so that we can compare the generated MSIL to the different languages to see how they handle numbers. All three examples use the same namespace Wrox.ProCSharp.Assemblies.CrossLanguage.

```cpp
// HelloMCPP.h
#pragma once
```

```cpp
#include <stdio.h>
using namespace System;
namespace Wrox
{
   namespace ProCSharp
   {
      namespace Assemblies
      {
         namespace CrossLanguage
         {
            public __gc class HelloMCPP
            {
            public:
               virtual void Hello()
               {
                  Console::WriteLine(S"Hello, Managed C++");
               }
               virtual void Hello2()
               {
                  printf("Hello, calling native code\n");
               }
               int Add(int val1, int val2)
               {
                  return val1 + val2;
               }
            };
         }
      }
   }
}
```

To compare the programs with running code we are using the release build instead of the debug configuration. With debug configurations you can see some non-optimized IL code. Looking at the generated DLL using ildasm (see Figure 13-14), besides the class HelloMCPP with its members we see one static method printf(). This method calls a native unmanaged function using pinvoke. The private field $ArrayType$0xf2eda509 holds our native string "Hello, calling native code\n".

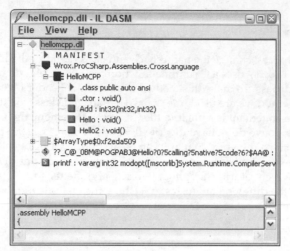

Figure 13-14

The Hello2() method (see Figure 13-15) pushes the address of the field $ArrayType$0xf2eda509, that keeps the string on the stack. In line IL_0005 a call to the static printf() method can be seen where a pointer to the string "Hello, calling native code" is passed.

```
 HelloMCPP::Hello2 : void()

.method public newslot virtual instance void
        Hello2() cil managed
{
  // Code size       12 (0xc)
  .maxstack  1
  IL_0000:  ldsflda     valuetype $ArrayType$0xf2eda509 modopt([Microsoft.Visu
  IL_0005:  call        vararg int32 modopt([mscorlib]System.Runtime.Compiler!
  IL_000a:  pop
  IL_000b:  ret
} // end of method HelloMCPP::Hello2
```

Figure 13-15

printf() itself is called via the *platform invoke* mechanism (see Figure 13-16). With the platform invoke, you can call all native functions like the C runtime and Win32 API calls.

```
 Global Functions::printf : vararg int32 modopt([mscorlib]System.Runtime.CompilerServ...

.method public static pinvokeimpl(/* No map */)
        vararg int32 modopt([mscorlib]System.Runtime.CompilerServices.CallCor
        printf(int8 modopt([Microsoft.VisualC]Microsoft.VisualC.NoSignSpecif:
{
  .custom instance void [mscorlib]System.Security.SuppressUnmanagedCodeSecur:
  // Embedded native code
  //  Disassembly of native methods is not supported.
  //  Managed TargetRVA = 0x16a4
} // end of method 'Global Functions'::printf
```

Figure 13-16

The Hello() method (see Figure 13-17) is completely made up of MSIL code; there's no native code. Because the string was prefixed with an "S", a managed string is written into the assembly and it is put onto the stack with ldstr. In line IL_0005 we are calling the WriteLine() method of the System.Console class using the string from the stack:

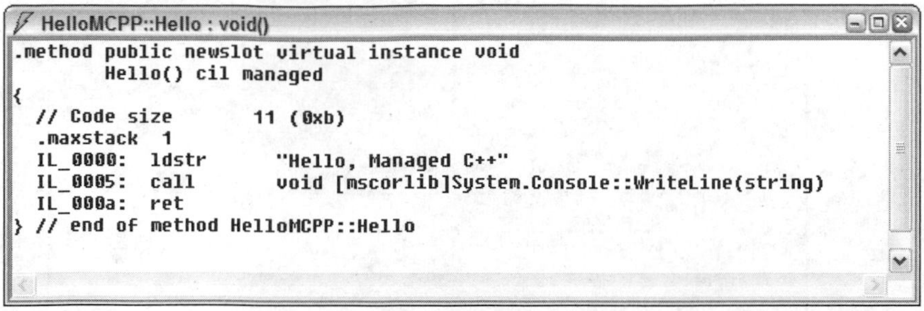

```
HelloMCPP::Hello : void()
.method public newslot virtual instance void
        Hello() cil managed
{
  // Code size       11 (0xb)
  .maxstack  1
  IL_0000: ldstr      "Hello, Managed C++"
  IL_0005: call       void [mscorlib]System.Console::WriteLine(string)
  IL_000a: ret
} // end of method HelloMCPP::Hello
```

Figure 13-17

To demonstrate how numbers are used within Managed C++, we're now going to take a look at the MSIL code of the Add() method (see Figure 13-18). The passed arguments are put on the stack with ldarg.1 and ldarg.2, add adds the stack values and puts the result on the stack, and in line IL_0003 the result is returned.

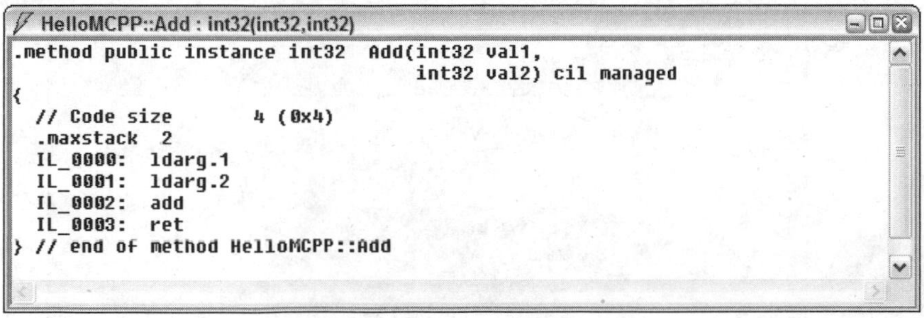

```
HelloMCPP::Add : int32(int32,int32)
.method public instance int32  Add(int32 val1,
                                   int32 val2) cil managed
{
  // Code size       4 (0x4)
  .maxstack  2
  IL_0000: ldarg.1
  IL_0001: ldarg.2
  IL_0002: add
  IL_0003: ret
} // end of method HelloMCPP::Add
```

Figure 13-18

What's the advantage of using managed C++ compared to C# and other languages of the .NET framework? Managed C++ makes it easier to make traditional C++ code available to .NET. MSIL code and native code can be mixed easily.

Writing the Visual Basic .NET class

Now we're going to use Visual Basic .NET to create a class. Again, use the Class Library wizard, and name the project HelloVB (see Figure 13-19).

Change the namespace of the class to Wrox.ProCSharp.Assemblies.CrossLanguage. In a Visual Basic .NET project this can be done by changing the root namespace of the project in the project properties as can be seen in Figure 13-20.

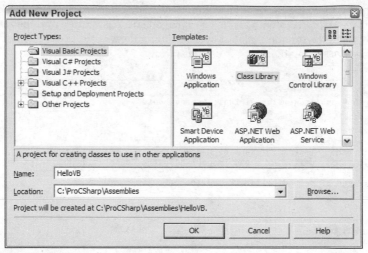

Figure 13-19

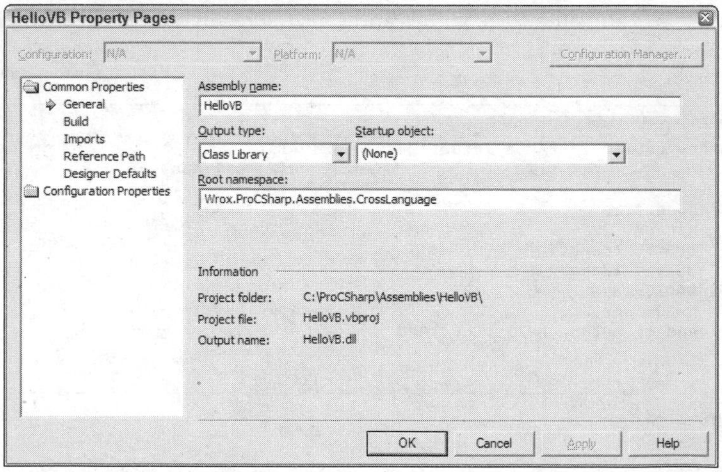

Figure 13-20

To make it possible to derive the class from `HelloMCPP` a reference to HelloMCPP.dll is needed. Add the reference to the C++ project by selecting Project⇨Add Reference. When building the assembly the reference can be seen inside the manifest: `.assembly extern HelloMCPP`. Adding the reference to the project copies the referenced assembly to the output directory of the Visual Basic .NET project, so that we are independent of later changes made to the original referenced assembly.

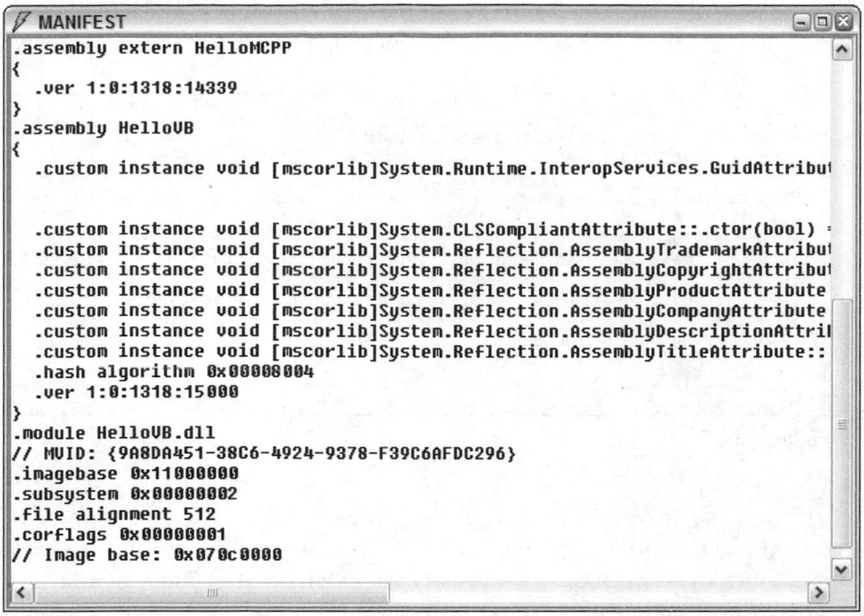

```
MANIFEST                                                        [_][□][x]
.assembly extern HelloMCPP
{
  .ver 1:0:1318:14339
}
.assembly HelloVB
{
  .custom instance void [mscorlib]System.Runtime.InteropServices.GuidAttribut

  .custom instance void [mscorlib]System.CLSCompliantAttribute::.ctor(bool)
  .custom instance void [mscorlib]System.Reflection.AssemblyTrademarkAttribut
  .custom instance void [mscorlib]System.Reflection.AssemblyCopyrightAttribut
  .custom instance void [mscorlib]System.Reflection.AssemblyProductAttribute
  .custom instance void [mscorlib]System.Reflection.AssemblyCompanyAttribute
  .custom instance void [mscorlib]System.Reflection.AssemblyDescriptionAttri
  .custom instance void [mscorlib]System.Reflection.AssemblyTitleAttribute::
  .hash algorithm 0x00008004
  .ver 1:0:1318:15000
}
.module HelloVB.dll
// MVID: {9A8DA451-38C6-4924-9378-F39C6AFDC296}
.imagebase 0x11000000
.subsystem 0x00000002
.file alignment 512
.corflags 0x00000001
// Image base: 0x070c0000
```

Figure 13-21

Create the class `HelloVB` using the following code. The class `HelloVB` inherits from `HelloMCPP`. Visual Basic .NET uses the keyword `Inherits` to derive from a base class. `Inherits` must be in the line after the `Class` statement. Override the `Hello()` method in the base class. The Visual Basic .NET `Overrides` keyword does the same thing as the C# `override` keyword. In the implementation of the `Hello()` method, the `Hello()` method of the base class is called using the Visual Basic .NET keyword `MyBase`. The `MyBase` keyword is the same as `base` in C#. The method `Add()` is implemented so that we can examine the generated MSIL code to see how Visual Basic .NET works with numbers. The `Add()` method from the base class is not virtual, so it can't be overridden. Visual Basic .NET uses the keyword `Shadows` to hide a method of a base class. `Shadows` is similar to C#'s `new` modifier. The C# `new` modifier is introduced in Chapter 4.

```
Public Class HelloVB
    Inherits HelloMCPP

    Public Overrides Sub Hello()
        MyBase.Hello()
        Console.WriteLine("Hello, VB.NET")
    End Sub

    Public Shadows Function Add(ByVal val1 As Integer, _
                               ByVal val2 As Integer) As Integer
        Return val1 + val2
    End Function
End Class
```

Let's look at the MSIL code that is generated from the Visual Basic .NET compiler.

The `HelloVB.Hello()` method (see Figure 13-22) first calls the `Hello()` method of the base class `HelloMCPP`. In line `IL_0006`, a string stored in the metadata is pushed on the stack using `ldstr`.

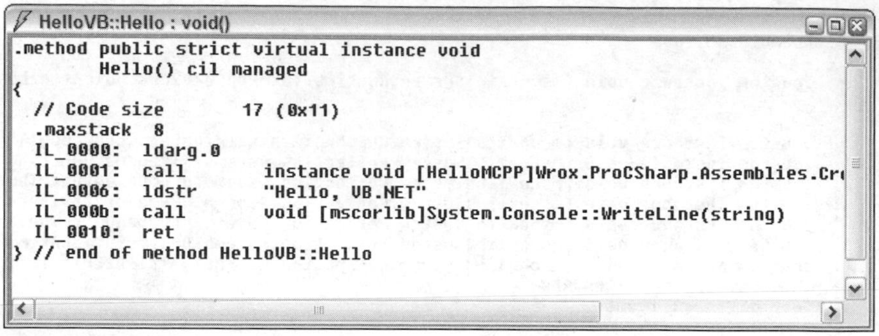

```
HelloVB::Hello : void()                                    _ □ ☒
.method public strict virtual instance void
        Hello() cil managed
{
  // Code size        17 (0x11)
  .maxstack  8
  IL_0000:  ldarg.0
  IL_0001:  call       instance void [HelloMCPP]Wrox.ProCSharp.Assemblies.Cr
  IL_0006:  ldstr      "Hello, VB.NET"
  IL_000b:  call       void [mscorlib]System.Console::WriteLine(string)
  IL_0010:  ret
} // end of method HelloVB::Hello
```

Figure 13-22

The other method (see Figure 13-23) we are looking at is `Add()`. Visual Basic .NET uses `add.ovf` instead of the `add` method that was used in the managed C++–generated MSIL code. This is just a single MSIL statement that's different between C++ and Visual Basic .NET, but the statement `add.ovf` generates more lines of native code, as `add.ovf` performs overflow checking. If the result of the addition of the two arguments is too large to be represented in the target type, `add.ovf` generates an exception of type `OverflowException`. In contrast, `add` just performs an addition of the two values, whether or not the target fits. In the case where the target is not big enough, the true value of the summation is lost, and the result is a wrong number. So, `add` is faster, but `add.ovf` is safer.

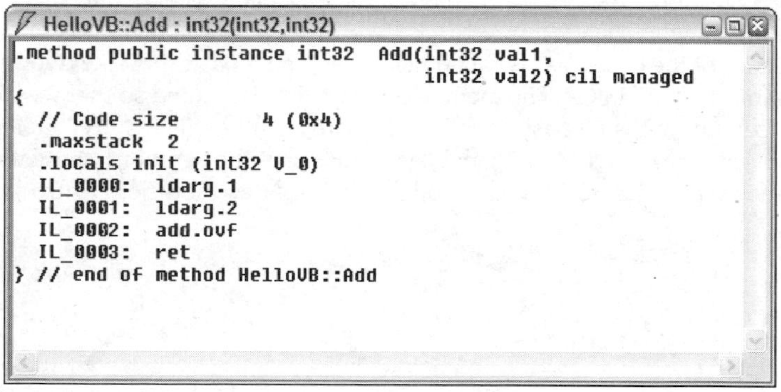

```
HelloVB::Add : int32(int32,int32)                          _ □ ☒
.method public instance int32  Add(int32 val1,
                                   int32 val2) cil managed
{
  // Code size        4 (0x4)
  .maxstack  2
  .locals init (int32 V_0)
  IL_0000:  ldarg.1
  IL_0001:  ldarg.2
  IL_0002:  add.ovf
  IL_0003:  ret
} // end of method HelloVB::Add
```

Figure 13-23

Writing the C# class

The third class is created using C#, which is the language this book is written about. For this project, create a C# Console Application HelloCSharp. Add a reference to the HelloVB and the HelloMCPP assembly, because the C# class will derive from the Visual Basic .NET class.

Create the class `HelloCSharp` according to the code below. The methods implemented in the C# class are similar to the managed C++ and the Visual Basic .NET classes. `Hello()` is an overridden method of the base class; `Add()` is a new method:

```csharp
using System;

namespace Wrox.ProCSharp.Assemblies.CrossLanguage
{
    public class HelloCSharp : HelloVB
    {
        public HelloCSharp()
        {
        }
        public override void Hello()
        {
            base.Hello();
            Console.WriteLine("Hello, C#");
        }
        public new int Add(int val1, int val2)
        {
            return val1 + val2;
        }
        [STAThread]
        public static void Main()
        {
            HelloCSharp hello = new HelloCSharp();
            hello.Hello();
        }
    }
}
```

As you can see in Figure 13-24, the generated MSIL code for the `Hello()` method is the same as the MSIL code from the Visual Basic .NET compiler.

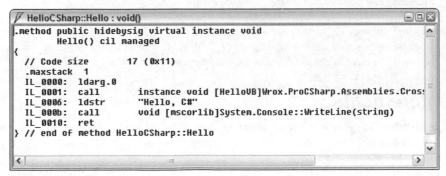

Figure 13-24

The `Add()` method (see Figure 13-25) differs, and yet is similar to the MC++ code. When doing calculations, the C# compiler doesn't use the methods with overflow; checking with the default compiler settings in a Visual Studio .NET project. The faster MSIL method `add` is used instead of `add.ovf`; but it's possible to change this option by using the configuration properties of C# and Visual Basic .NET projects. By setting Check for overflow underflow to true in a C# project, the MSIL code that the C# compiler generates for our example will be the same as that generated by the Visual Basic .NET compiler. Unlike Visual Basic .NET, with C# it's also possible to choose this option on an expression-by-expression basis with the `checked` and `unchecked` operators. We discuss the `checked` and `unchecked` operators in Chapter 5.

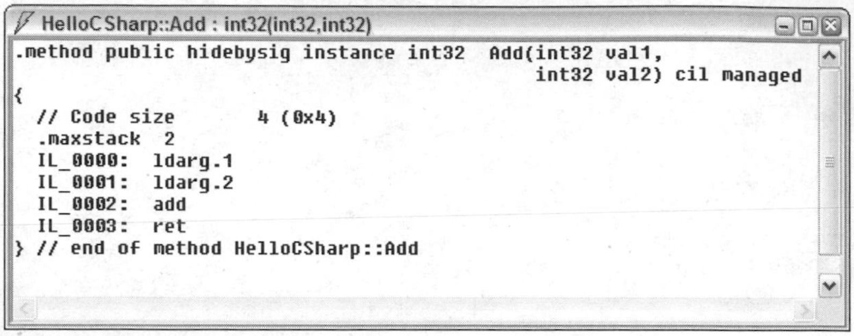

```
HelloCSharp::Add : int32(int32,int32)                              _ □ ⊠
.method public hidebysig instance int32   Add(int32 val1,
                                              int32 val2) cil managed
{
  // Code size        4 (0x4)
  .maxstack  2
  IL_0000:  ldarg.1
  IL_0001:  ldarg.2
  IL_0002:  add
  IL_0003:  ret
} // end of method HelloCSharp::Add
```

Figure 13-25

Finally, in Figure 13-26 you can see the console application output.

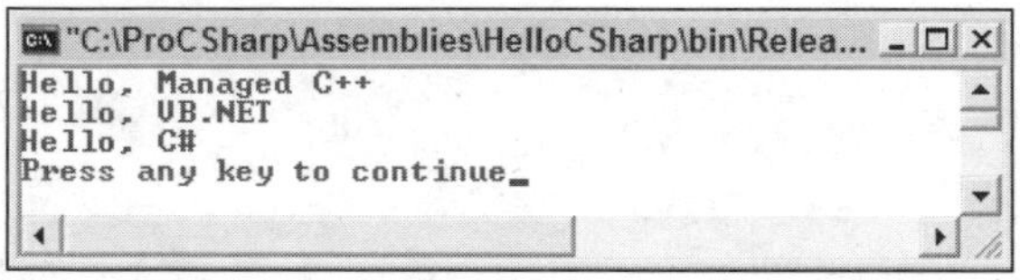

```
"C:\ProCSharp\Assemblies\HelloCSharp\bin\Relea...  _ □ ×
Hello, Managed C++
Hello, UB.NET
Hello, C#
Press any key to continue_
```

Figure 13-26

Because all the .NET languages generate MSIL code and all the languages make use of the classes in the .NET Framework, it's often said that there is no difference regarding performance. As you can see, however, small differences are still there. First, depending on the language, some languages support different data types from others. Second, the generated MSIL code can still be different. One example that we've seen is that the number calculations are implemented differently: while the default configuration of Visual Basic .NET is for safety, the default for C# is for speed. C# is also more flexible.

CLS Requirements

We've just seen the CLS in action when we looked at cross-language inheritance between managed C++, Visual Basic .NET, and C#. Until now we didn't pay any attention to the CLS requirements when building our project. We were lucky—the methods we defined in the base classes were callable from the derived classes. If a method had the `System.UInt32` data type as one of its arguments, we wouldn't be able to use it from Visual Basic .NET. Unsigned data types are not CLS-compliant; for a .NET language, it's not necessary to support this data type.

The CLS exactly defines the requirements to make a component CLS compliant, which enables it to be used with different .NET languages. With COM we had to pay attention to language-specific requirements when designing a component. JScript had different requirements from Visual Basic 6, and the requirements of Visual J++ were different again. That's no longer the case with .NET. When designing a component that should be used from other languages, we just have to make it CLS compliant; it's guaranteed that this component can be used from all .NET languages. If we mark a class as CLS compliant, the compiler can warn us about non-compliant methods.

All .NET languages must support the CLS. When talking about .NET languages we have to differentiate between *.NET consumer* and *.NET extender* tools.

A .NET consumer language just uses classes from the .NET Framework—it can't create .NET classes that can be used from other languages. A consumer tool can use any CLS-compliant class. A .NET extender tool has the requirements of a consumer and can in addition inherit any CLS-compliant .NET class and define new CLS-compliant classes that can be used by consumers. C++, Visual Basic .NET, and C# all are extender tools. With these languages, it's possible to create CLS-compliant classes.

The CLSCompliant attribute

With the CLSCompliant attribute, we can mark our assembly to be CLS compliant. Doing this guarantees that the classes in this assembly can be used from all .NET consumer tools. The compiler issues warnings when we are using non-CLS compliant data types in public and protected methods. The data types we use in the private implementation don't matter—when using other languages outside of the class, we don't have direct access to private methods anyway.

To get compiler warnings when a data type is not compliant in public and protected methods, we set the attribute CLSCompliant in the assembly by adding this attribute to the file AssemblyInfo.cs:

```
[assembly: System.CLSCompliant(true)]
```

This way, all the defined types and public methods inside the assembly must be compliant. Using a non-compliant uint type as argument type, we get this error from the compiler:

error CS3001: Argument type uint is not CLS-compliant

When we mark an assembly as compliant, it's still possible to define methods that are not compliant. This can be useful if you want to override some method to make it available with both compliant and non-compliant argument data types. The methods that are not compliant must be marked, within the class, by the CLSCompliant attribute with a value of false. The CLSCompliant attribute can be applied to types, methods, properties, fields, and events:

```
[CLSCompliant(false)]
void Method(uint i)
{
    //...
```

CLS rules

The requirements for an assembly to be CLS compliant are the following:

❑   All types appearing in a method prototype must be CLS compliant.

❑   Array elements must have a CLS-compliant element type. Arrays must also be 0-indexed.

❑   A CLS-compliant class must inherit from a CLS-compliant class. System.Object is CLS compliant.

❑ Although method names in CLS-compliant classes are not case-sensitive, method names may not only be different in their case.

❑ Enumerations must be of type `Int16`, `Int32`, or `Int64`. Enumerations of other types are not compliant.

All the listed requirements only apply to public and protected members. The private implementation itself doesn't matter—non-compliant types can be used there, and the assembly is still compliant.

Besides these requirements, there are the more general naming guidelines discussed in Chapter 12. These guidelines do not define that classes should be CLS compliant, but they make life much easier.

In addition to these naming guidelines to support multiple languages, it's necessary to pay attention to method names where the type is part of the name. Data type names are language-specific, for example, the C# `int`, `long`, and `float` types are equivalent to the Visual Basic .NET `Integer`, `Long`, and `Single` types. When a data type name is used in a name of a method, the universal type names—`Int32`, `Int64`, and `Single`—and not the language-specific type names should be used:

```
int ReadInt32();
long ReadInt64();
float ReadSingle();
```

As you can see when complying with the CLS specs and guidelines, it's easy to create components that can be used from multiple languages. It's not necessary to test the component by using all .NET consumer languages.

Global Assembly Cache

The *global assembly cache* is, as the name implies, a cache for globally available assemblies. Most shared assemblies are installed inside this cache, but some private assemblies can also be found here. If a private assembly is compiled to native code using the native image generator, the compiled native code goes into this cache, too!

In this section, we explore:

❑ Creating native images at installation time

❑ Viewing shared assemblies with the Global Assembly Cache Viewer and the Global Assembly Cache Utility

Native Image Generator

With the native image generator Ngen.exe we can compile the IL code to native code at installation time. This way the program can start faster because the compilation during runtime is no longer necessary. The ngen utility installs the native image in the native image cache, which is part of the global assembly cache.

> Creating native images with ngen only makes sense if native images are created for all assemblies used by the application. Otherwise the JIT compiler would have to be started anyway.

With ngen myassembly, we can compile the MSIL code to native code and install it into the native image cache. This should be done from an installation program if we would like to put the assembly in the native image cache.

> After compiling the assembly to native code you cannot delete the original assembly with the MSIL code because the native code assembly doesn't include metadata with .NET 1.1, and metadata is still needed. If the security changes on the system, the native code needs to be rebuilt.

With ngen we can also display all assemblies from the native image cache with the option /show. If we add an assembly name to the /show option we get the information about all installed versions of this assembly as can be seen in Figure 13-27.

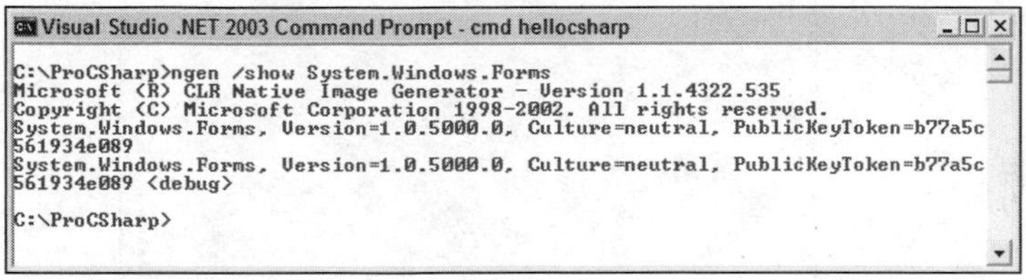

Figure 13-27

Global Assembly Cache Viewer

The global assembly cache can be displayed using shfusion.dll, which is a Windows shell extension to view and manipulate the contents of the cache. A Windows shell extension is a COM DLL that integrates with the Windows explorer. You just have to start the explorer and go to the <windir>/assembly directory.

Figure 13-28 shows the Assembly Cache Viewer.

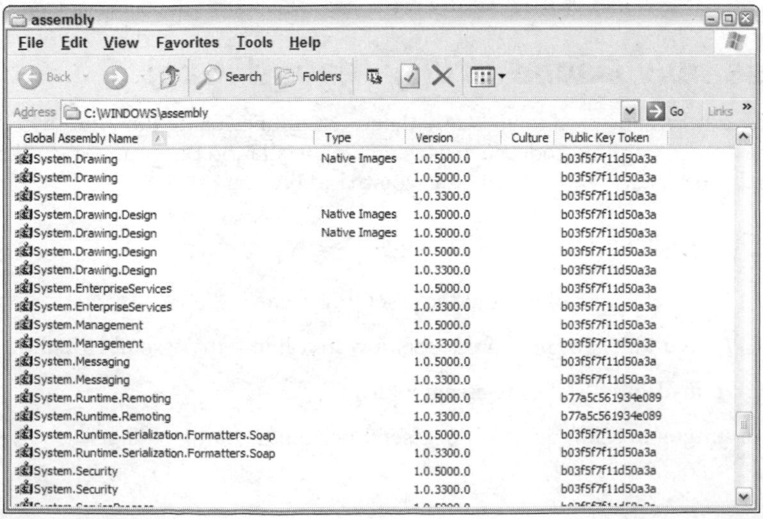

Figure 13-28

367

With the Assembly Cache Viewer, the Global Assembly Name, Type, Version, Culture, and the Public Key Token can be seen. With the Type we can see if the assembly was installed using the native image generator. Using the context menu when selecting an assembly, it's possible to delete an assembly and to view the properties (see Figure 13-29).

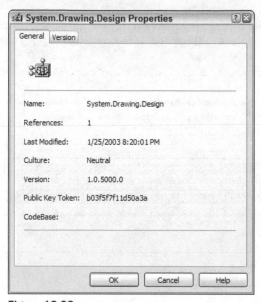

Figure 13-29

The real files and directories behind the assembly cache can be seen by viewing the directory from the command line. Inside the <windir>\assembly directory there's a GAC and NativeImages_<runtime version> directory. GAC is the directory for shared assemblies, and in NativeImages_<runtime version> you can find the assemblies compiled to native code. If you go deeper in the directory structure you will find directory names that are similar to the assembly names, and below that a version directory and the assemblies themselves. This makes it possible that different versions of the same assembly can be installed.

Global Assembly Cache Utility (gacutil.exe)

The assembly viewer can be used to view and delete assemblies using the Windows explorer, but it's not possible to use it from scripting code, such as to create installation programs. gacutil.exe is a utility to install, uninstall, and list assemblies using the command line.

The following list explains some of the gacutil options:

❑ **gacutil /l** lists all assemblies from the assembly cache

❑ **gacutil /i mydll** installs the shared assembly mydll into the assembly cache

❑ **gacutil /u mydll** uninstalls the assembly mydll

❑ **gacutil /ungen mydll** uninstalls the assembly from the native image cache

Creating Shared Assemblies

Assemblies can be isolated for use by a single application—not sharing an assembly is the default. When using private assemblies it's not necessary to pay attention to any requirements that are necessary for sharing.

In this section, we explore:

❑   Strong names as a requirement for shared assemblies

❑   Creating shared assemblies

❑   Installing shared assemblies in the global assembly cache

❑   Delayed signing of shared assemblies

Shared Assembly Names

The goal of a shared assembly name is that it must be globally unique, and it must be possible to protect the name. At no time may any other person create an assembly using the same name.

COM solved only the first problem by using a globally unique identifier (GUID). The second problem, however, still existed as anyone could steal the GUID and create a different object with the same identifier. Both problems are solved with *strong names* of .NET assemblies.

A strong name is made of these items:

❑   The *name* of the assembly itself.

❑   A *version number*. This makes it possible to use different versions of the same assembly at the same time. Different versions can also work side-by-side and can be loaded concurrently inside the same process.

❑   A *public key* guarantees that the strong name is unique. It also guarantees that a referenced assembly can't be replaced from a different source.

❑   A *culture*. Cultures are discussed in Chapter 17.

> **A shared assembly must have a strong name to uniquely identify the assembly.**

A strong (shared) name is a simple text name accompanied by a version number, a public key, and a culture. You wouldn't create a new public key with every assembly, but you'd have one in the company, so the key uniquely identifies your company's assemblies.

However, this key cannot be used as a trust key. Assemblies can carry Authenticode signatures to build up a trust. The key for the Authenticode signature can be a different one from the key used for the strong name.

For development purposes a different public key can be used and later exchanged easily with the real key. We discuss this feature later in this chapter, in the Delayed Signing of Assemblies section.

To uniquely identify the assemblies in your companies, a useful namespace hierarchy should be used to name your classes. Here is a simple example showing how to organize namespaces: Wrox Press can use the major namespace `Wrox` for its classes and namespaces. In the hierarchy below the namespace, the namespaces must be organized so that all classes are unique. Every chapter of this book uses a different namespace of the form `Wrox.ProCSharp.<Chapter>`; this chapter uses `Wrox.ProCSharp.Assemblies`. So if there is a class `Hello` in two different chapters there's no conflict because of different namespaces. Utility classes that are used across different books can go into the namespace `Wrox.Utilities`.

A company name that is commonly used as the first part of the namespace is not necessarily unique, so something more must be used to build a strong name. For this the public key is used. Because of the public/private key principle in strong names, no one without access to your private key can destructively create an assembly that could be unintentionally called by the client.

Public key cryptography

If you already know about public key cryptography, you can skip this section. For the rest of you, this is a simple introduction to keys. For encryption we have to differentiate between *symmetric* encryption and *public/private key* encryption.

With a symmetric key, the same key can be used for encryption and decryption, but this is not the case with a public/private key pair. If something is encrypted using a public key, it can be decrypted by using the corresponding private key, but it is not possible with the public key. This also works the other way around: if something is encrypted using a private key, it can be decrypted by using the corresponding public key, but not the private key.

Public and private keys are always created as a pair. The public key can be made available to everybody, and it can even be put on a Web site, but the private key must be safely locked away. Let's look at some examples where these public and private keys are used.

If Sarah sends a mail to Julian, and Sarah wants to make sure that no one else but Julian can read the mail, she uses Julian's public key. The message is encrypted using Julian's public key. Julian opens the mail and can decrypt it using his secretly stored private key. This guarantees that no one else except Julian can read Sarah's mail.

There's one problem left: Julian can't be sure that the mail comes from Sarah. Anyone could use Julian's public key to encrypt mails sent to Julian. We can extend this principle. Let's start again with Sarah sending a mail to Julian. Before Sarah encrypts the mail using Julian's public key, she adds her signature and encrypts the signature using her own private key. Then she encrypts the mail using Julian's public key. Therefore, it is guaranteed that no one else but Julian can read the mail. When Julian decrypts the mail, he detects an encrypted signature. The signature can be decrypted using Sarah's public key. For Julian it's not a problem to access Sarah's public key, because this key is public. After decrypting the signature, Julian can be sure that Sarah has sent the mail.

Next we will look at how this public/private key principle is used with assemblies.

Integrity using strong names

When creating a shared component, a public/private key pair must be used. The compiler writes the public key to the manifest, creates a hash of all files that belong to the assembly, and signs the hash with the private key. The private key is not stored within the assembly. This way it is guaranteed that no one can change your assembly. The signature can be verified with the public key.

During development, the client assembly must reference the shared assembly. The compiler writes the public key of the referenced assembly to the manifest of the client assembly. To reduce storage, it is not the public key that is written to the manifest of the client assembly, but a public key token. The public key token is the last eight bytes of a hash of the public key, and that is unique.

At runtime, during loading of the shared assembly (or at install-time if the client is installed using the native image generator), the hash of the shared component assembly can be verified by using the public key stored inside the client assembly. Only the owner of the private key can change the shared component assembly. There is no way a component Math that was created by vendor A and referenced from a client can be replaced by a component from a hacker. Only the owner of the private key can replace the shared component with a new version. Integrity is guaranteed in so far as the shared assembly is from the expected publisher.

Figure 13-30 shows a shared component with a public key that is referenced by a client assembly that has a public key token of the shared assembly inside the manifest.

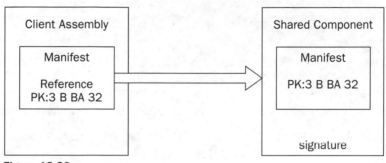

Figure 13-30

Creating a Shared Assembly

In the next example you will create a shared assembly and a client that uses it.

If you want to create a shared assembly, there are not a lot of differences to creating private assemblies. Create a simple Visual C# Class Library project with the name SharedDemo. Change the namespace to Wrox.ProCSharp.Assemblies.Sharing, and the class name to SharedDemo. Enter the following code. In the constructor of the class all lines of a file are read into a StringCollection. The name of the file is passed as an argument to the constructor. The method GetQuoteOfTheDay() just returns a random string of the collection.

```
using System;
using System.Collections.Specialized;
using System.IO;

namespace Wrox.ProCSharp.Assemblies.Sharing
{
    public class SharedDemo
    {
        private StringCollection quotes;
        private Random random;
```

```
    public SharedDemo(string filename)
    {
        quotes = new StringCollection();
        Stream stream = File.OpenRead(filename);
        StreamReader streamReader = new StreamReader(stream);
        string quote;
        while ((quote = streamReader.ReadLine()) != null)
        {
            quotes.Add(quote);
        }
        streamReader.Close();
        stream.Close();
        random = new Random();
    }

    public string GetQuoteOfTheDay()
    {
        int index = random.Next(1, quotes.Count);
        return quotes[index];
    }
  }
}
```

Create a strong name

To share this assembly a strong name is needed. You can create such a name with the *strong name utility* (sn):

```
sn -k mykey.snk
```

The strong name utility generates and writes a public/private key pair, and writes this pair to a file; here the file is mykey.snk. Now we can set the `AssemblyKeyFile` attribute in the wizard-generated file Assemblyinfo.cs. The attribute must be either set to an absolute path to the key file, or the key file must be addressed relatively from the %ProjectDirectory%\obj\<configuration> directory, so ../../mykey.snk references a key in the project directory. When starting a build of the project, the key is installed in the *Crypto Service Provider* (CSP). As soon as the key is installed in the CSP, it's possible to use the `AssemblyKeyName` attribute instead.

Here are the changes to AssemblyInfo.cs. The attribute `AssemblyKeyFile` is set to the file mykey.snk:

```
[assembly: AssemblyDelaySign(false)]
[assembly: AssemblyKeyFile("../../mykey.snk")]
[assembly: AssemblyKeyName("")]
```

After rebuilding, the public key can be found inside the manifest. You can verify this using ildasm as can be seen in Figure 13-31.

```
⌐Ø MANIFEST                                                        _ □ X
  .custom instance void [mscorlib]System.Reflection.AssemblyTitleAttribute::  ▲
  // --- The following custom attribute is added automatically, do not uncom
  //   .custom instance void [mscorlib]System.Diagnostics.DebuggableAttribute
  //
  .publickey = (00 24 00 00 04 80 00 00 94 00 00 00 06 02 00 00   // .$.....
                00 24 00 00 52 53 41 31 00 04 00 00 01 00 01 00   // .$..RSA
                AD 54 3C AB C7 B3 62 0F 66 68 77 AF C1 D6 1C 07   // .T<...b
                39 DE B7 C5 07 35 84 16 1C 0B 1C E8 01 A5 F1 35   // 9....5.
                45 83 B8 B8 31 F5 5C 9B D7 7E 99 5B 4A BC E9 07   // E...1.\
                19 8B 87 50 9F 09 C0 51 10 42 DC 4D 72 C4 34 FE   // ...P...
                71 72 73 EA 87 C2 08 FA ED 9B 97 37 55 07 90 26   // qrs....
                72 DC 3E 93 15 84 C2 92 FA 50 8D 3E 53 6A EC 25   // r.>....
                81 BB CD 6F 42 B6 1D 4A 47 A9 18 C0 2B D0 A3 36   // ...oB...
                ED 5D 85 34 3D 2A 34 E2 FC 70 4B 3B C0 72 0B C2 ) // .].4=*4
  .hash algorithm 0x00008004
  .ver 1:0:1318:27763
}
.module SharedDemo.dll
// MVID: {22D05FBA-AFB5-4F39-B1CB-35AE2BFAC7DB}
.imagebase 0x11000000
.subsystem 0x00000003
.file alignment 4096
◄                        IIII                                      ►
```

Figure 13-31

Install the shared assembly

With a public key in the assembly, you can now install it in the global assembly cache using the global assembly cache tool *gacutil* with the /i option:

```
gacutil /i SharedDemo.dll
```

Then you can use the Global Assembly Cache Viewer to check the version of the shared assembly, and check if it is successfully installed.

Using the shared assembly

To use the shared assembly create a C# Console Application called *Client*. Instead of adding the new project to the previous solution, create a new solution so that the shared assembly doesn't get rebuilt when rebuilding the client. Change the name of the namespace to Wrox.ProCSharp.Assemblies.Sharing, and the name of the class to Client.

Reference the assembly SimpleShared in the same way as private assemblies are referenced: select Project⇨Add Reference, or use the context menu in Solution Explorer. Then click the Browse button to find the assembly SimpleShared, and add it to the references.

> **With shared assemblies the reference property CopyLocal can be set to False. This way the assembly is not copied to the directory of the output files but will be loaded from the global assembly cache instead.**

Here's the code for the client application:

```
using System;
namespace Wrox.ProCSharp.Assemblies.Sharing
{
    class Client
```

```
        {
            [STAThread]
            static void Main(string[] args)
            {
                SharedDemo quotes =
                    new SharedDemo(@"C:\ProCSharp\Assemblies\Quotes.txt");
                for (int i=0; i < 3; i++)
                {
                    Console.WriteLine(quotes.GetQuoteOfTheDay());
                    Console.WriteLine();
                }
            }
        }
    }
```

When viewing the manifest in the client assembly using ildasm (see Figure 13-32) we can see the reference to the shared assembly SharedDemo: .assembly extern SharedDemo. Part of this referenced information is the version number we will talk about next, and the token of the public key.

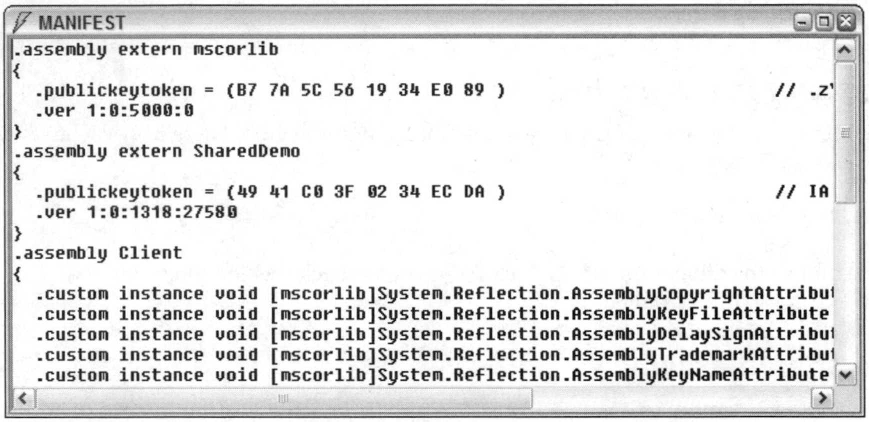

Figure 13-32

The token of the public key can also be seen within the shared assembly using the strong name utility: sn –T shows the token of the public key in the assembly, sn –Tp shows the token, and the public key. Pay attention to the use of the uppercase T!

The result of our program with a sample quotes file is shown in Figure 13-33.

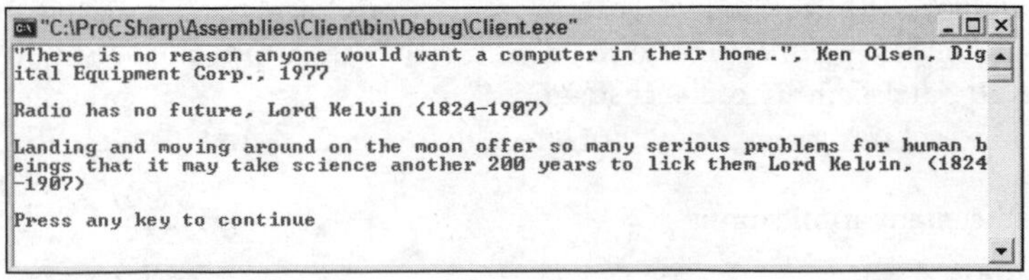

Figure 13-33

Delayed signing of assemblies

The private key of a company should be safely stored. Most companies don't give all developers access to the private key; just a few security people have access to it. That's why the signature of an assembly can be added at a later date, such as before distribution. When the global assembly attribute `AssemblyDelaySign` is set to `true`, no signature is stored in the assembly, but enough free space is reserved so that it can be added later. However, without using a key, we can't test the assembly and install it in the global assembly cache; but we can use a temporary key for testing purposes, and replace this key with the real company key later.

The following steps are required to delay signing of assemblies:

1. Create a public/private key pair with the strong name utility sn. The generated file mykey.snk includes both the public and private key.

    `sn -k mykey.snk`

2. Extract the public key to make it available to developers. The option –p extracts the public key of the keyfile. The file mykeypub.snk only holds the public key.

    `sn -p mykey.snk mykeypub.snk`

    All developers in the company can use this keyfile mykeypub.snk and set the `AssemblyDelaySign` and `AssemblyKeyFile` attributes in the file AssemblyInfo.cs:

    ```
    [assembly: AssemblyDelaySign(true)]
    [assembly: AssemblyKeyFile("../../mykeypub.snk")]
    ```

3. Turn off the verification of the signature, because the assembly doesn't have a signature.

    `sn -Vr SharedDemo.dll`

4. Before distribution the assembly can be re-signed with the sn utility. Use the –R option to re-sign previously signed or delayed signed assemblies.

    `sn -R MyAssembly.dll mykey.snk`

> **The signature verification should only be turned off during the development process. Never distribute an assembly without verification, as it would be possible that this assembly is replaced by a malicious one.**

References

The Properties dialog box (see Figure 13-29) also lists a reference count. This reference count is responsible for the fact that a cached assembly cannot be deleted if it is still needed by an application. For example, if a shared assembly is installed by a Microsoft installer package (MSI file), it can only be deleted by uninstalling the application, but not by deleting it from the global assembly cache. Trying to delete the assembly from the global assembly cache results in the error message "Assembly *<name>* could not be uninstalled because it is required by other applications."

A reference to the assembly can be set using the gacutil utility with the option /r. The option /r requires a reference type, a reference id, and a description. The type of the reference can be one of three options: UNINSTALL_KEY, FILEPATH, or OPAQUE. UNINSTALL_KEY is used by MSI where a registry key is defined that is also needed with the uninstallation. With FILEPATH a directory can be specified. A useful directory would be the one of the application. The OPAQUE reference type allows you to set any type of reference.

The command line

```
gacutil /i shareddemo.dll /r FILEPATH c:\ProCSharp\Assemblies\Client "Shared Demo"
```

installs the assembly shareddemo in the global assembly cache with a reference to the directory of the client application. Another installation of the same assembly can happen with a different path, or an OPAQUE id like in this command line:

```
gacutil /i shareddemo.dll OPAQUE 4711 "Opaque installation"
```

Now the assembly is only once in the global assembly cache, but it has two references. To delete the assembly from the global assembly cache, both references must be removed:

```
gacutil /u shareddemo OPAQUE 4711 "Opaque installation"
```

```
gacutil /u shareddemo FILEPATH c:\ProCSharp\Assemblies\Client "Shared Demo"
```

In Chapter 18 we deal with deployment of assemblies, where the reference count is being dealt with in an MSI package.

Configuration

COM components used the registry to configure components. Configuration of .NET applications is done by using configuration files. With registry configurations, an xcopy-deployment is not possible. The configuration files use XML syntax to specify startup and runtime settings for applications.

In this section, we explore:

❑ What you can configure using the XML base configuration files

❑ How you can redirect a strong named referenced assembly to a different version

❑ How you can specify the directory of assemblies to find private assemblies in subdirectories and shared assemblies in common directories or on a server

Configuration Categories

We can group the configuration into these categories:

❑ **Startup settings** enable us to specify the version of the required runtime. It's possible that different versions of the runtime could be installed on the same system. With the <startup> element, the version of the runtime can be specified.

❑ **Runtime settings** enable us to specify how garbage collection is performed by the runtime, and how the binding to assemblies works. We can also specify the version policy and the code base with these settings. We will take a more detailed look into the runtime settings later in this chapter.

❑ **Remoting settings** are used to configure applications using .NET Remoting. We deal with these configurations in Chapter 16.

❑ **Security settings** are introduced in Chapter 14, and configuration for cryptography and permissions is done there.

These settings can be provided in three types of configuration files:

❑ **Application configuration files** include specific settings for an application, such as binding information to assemblies, configuration for remote objects, and so on. Such a configuration file is placed into the same directory as the executable; it has the same name as the executable with a .config extension appended. ASP.NET configuration files are named web.config.

❑ **Machine configuration files** are used for system-wide configurations. We can also specify assembly binding and remoting configurations here. During a binding process, the machine configuration file is consulted before the application configuration file. The application configuration can override settings from the machine configuration. The application configuration file should be the preferred place for application-specific settings so that the machine configuration file stays smaller and manageable. A machine configuration file is located in %runtime _install_path%\config\Machine.config.

❑ **Publisher policy files** can be used by a component creator to specify that a shared assembly is compatible with older versions. If a new assembly version just fixes a bug of a shared component, it is not necessary to put application configuration files in every application directory that uses this component; the publisher can mark it as compatible by adding a publisher policy file instead. In case that the component doesn't work with all applications it is possible to override the publisher policy setting in an application configuration file. In contrast to the other configuration files, publisher policy files are stored in the global assembly cache.

How are these configuration files used? How a client finds an assembly (also called *binding*) depends on whether the assembly is private or shared. Private assemblies must be in the directory of the application or in a subdirectory thereof. A process called *probing* is used to find such an assembly. For probing, the version number is not used, but the culture is an important aspect.

Shared assemblies can be installed in the global assembly cache, placed in a directory, a network share, or on a Web site. We specify such a directory with the configuration of the codeBase, as we discuss shortly. The public key, version, and culture are all important aspects when binding to a shared assembly. The reference of the required assembly is recorded in the manifest of the client assembly, including the name, the version, and the public key token. All configuration files are checked to apply the correct version policy. The global assembly cache and code bases specified in the configuration files are checked, followed by the application directories, and probing rules are then applied.

Versioning

For private assemblies, versioning is not important because the referenced assemblies are copied with the client. The client uses the assembly it has in its private directories.

This is, however, different for shared assemblies. Let's look at the traditional problems that can occur with sharing. Using shared components, more than one client application can use the same component. The new version can break existing clients when updating a shared component with a newer version. We can't stop shipping new versions because new features are requested and introduced with new versions of existing components. We can try to program carefully to be backward compatible, but that's not always possible.

A solution to this dilemma could be an architecture that allows installation of different versions of shared components, with clients using the version that they referenced during the build process. This solves a lot of problems, but not all of them. What happens if we detect a bug in a component that's referenced from the client? We would like to update this component and make sure that the client uses the new version instead of the version that was referenced during the build process.

Therefore, depending on the type in the fix of the new version, sometimes we want to use a newer version, and sometimes we want to use the older referenced version. All this is possible with the .NET architecture.

In .NET, the original referenced assembly is used by default. We can redirect the reference to a different version using configuration files. Versioning plays a key role in the binding architecture—how the client gets the right assembly where the components live.

Version numbers

Assemblies have a four-part version number, for example, 1.0.479.36320. The parts are:

```
<Major>.<Minor>.<Build>.<Revision>
```

How these numbers are used depends on your application configuration.

A good policy would be that you change the major or minor number on changes incompatible with the previous version, but just the build or revision number with compatible changes. This way we can assume that redirecting an assembly to a new version where just the build and revision changed is safe.

The version number is specified in the assembly with the assembly attribute AssemblyVersion. In Visual Studio .NET projects this attribute is in the file AssemblyInfo.cs:

```
[assembly: AssemblyVersion("1.0.*")]
```

The first two numbers specify the major and minor version, and the asterisk (*) means that the build and revision numbers are auto-generated. The build number is the number of days since January 1, 2000, and the revision is the number of two seconds since midnight. Of course, you can also specify four values, but then you have to be sure to change the version number when rebuilding the assembly manually.

This version is stored in the .assembly section of the manifest.

Referencing the assembly in the client application stores the version of the referenced assembly in the manifest of the client application.

Getting the version programmatically

To make it possible to check the version of the assembly that is used from our client application, add the method GetAssemblyFullName() to the SharedDemo class created earlier to return the strong name of the assembly. For easy use of the Assembly class, you have to add the System.Reflection namespace:

```
public string GetAssemblyFullName()
{
    Assembly assembly = Assembly.GetExecutingAssembly();
    return assembly.FullName;
}
```

The FullName property of the Assembly class holds the name of the class, the version, the locality, and the public key token as you see in the following output, when calling GetAssemblyFullName() in our client application.

In the client application, just add a call to GetAssemblyFullName() in the Main() method after creating the shared component:

```
static void Main(string[] args)
{
    SharedDemo quotes = new
        SharedDemo(@"C:\ProCSharp\Assemblies\Quotes.txt");

    Console.WriteLine(quotes.GetAssemblyFullName());
```

Be sure to register the new version of the shared assembly SharedDemo again in the global assembly cache using gacutil. If the referenced version cannot be found, you will get a System.IO .FileLoadException, because the binding to the correct assembly failed.

With a successful run, you can see the full name of the referenced assembly similar to Figure 13-34.

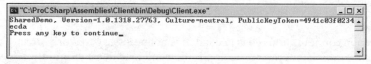

Figure 13-34

This client program can now be used to test different configurations of this shared component.

Application configuration files

With a configuration file you can specify that the binding should happen to a different version of a shared assembly. Let's say you create a new version of the shared assembly SharedDemo with major and minor versions 1.1. Maybe you don't want to rebuild the client, but instead just the new version of the assembly should be used with the existing client. This is useful in cases where either a bug is fixed with the shared assembly, or you just want to get rid of the old version because the new version is compatible.

Figure 13-35 shows the global assembly cache viewer, where the versions 1.0.1318.24054, 1.0.1330.27544, and 1.1.1330.27636 are installed for the SharedDemo assembly.

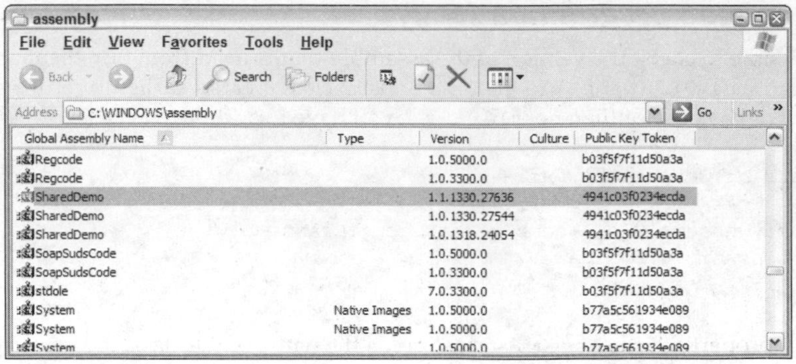

Figure 13-35

Figure 13-36 shows the manifest of the client application where the client references version 1.0.1318.27763 of the assembly SharedDemo.

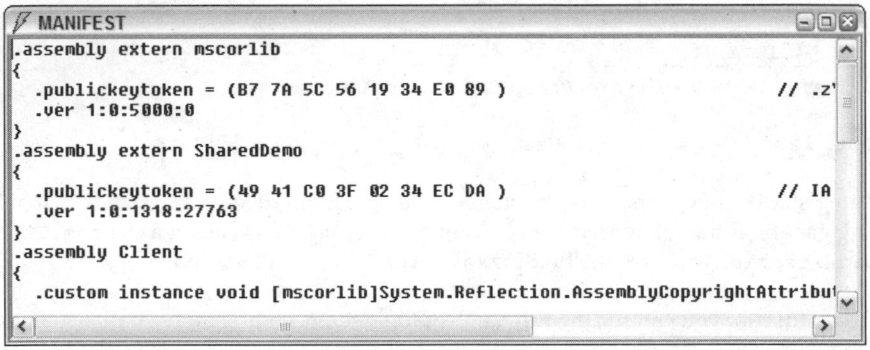

Figure 13-36

Now an application configuration file is needed. It is not necessary to work directly with XML; the .NET Framework Configuration tool can create application and machine configuration files. Figure 13-37 shows the .NET Framework Configuration tool that is an MMC Snap-in. You can start this tool from the Administrative Tools in the Control Panel.

When you select Applications on the left side, and then select Action⇨Add, you'll get a list that shows all .NET applications that have been previously started on this computer. Select the application Client.exe to create an application configuration file for this application. After adding the client application to the .NET Admin tool, the assembly dependencies can be listed as is shown in Figure 13-38.

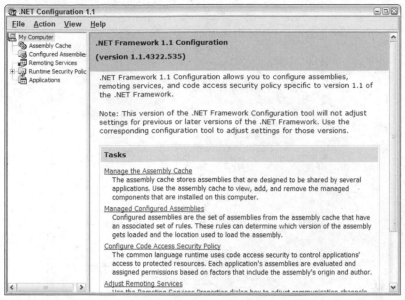

Figure 13-37

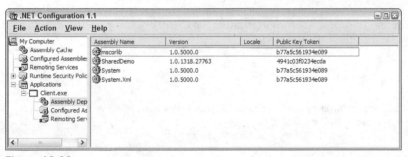

Figure 13-38

Selecting *Configured Assemblies* and the menu *Action | Add...* configure the dependency of the assembly *SharedDemo* from the dependency list as is shown in Figure 13-39.

For the Requested Version, specify the version that's referenced in the manifest of the client assembly. New Version specifies the new version of the shared assembly. In Figure 13-39 it is defined that the version 1.1.1330.27636 should be used instead of any version in the range of 1.0.0.0 to 1.0.999.99999.

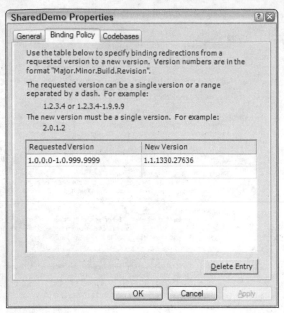

Figure 13-39

Now you can find the application configuration file Client.exe.config in the directory of the Client.exe application that includes this XML code:

```xml
<?xml version="1.0"?>
<configuration>
    <runtime>
        <assemblyBinding xmlns="urn:schemas-microsoft-com:asm.v1">
            <dependentAssembly>
                <assemblyIdentity name="SharedDemo"
                                  publicKeyToken="be9f9ce7b9a0a62f" />
                <bindingRedirect oldVersion="1.0.0.0-1.0.999.99999"
                                 newVersion="1.1.1330.27636" />
            </dependentAssembly>
        </assemblyBinding>
    </runtime>
</configuration>
```

With the `<runtime>` element, runtime settings can be configured. The subelement of `<runtime>` is `<assemblyBinding>`, which in turn has a subelement `<dependentAssembly>`. `<dependentAssembly>` has a required subelement `<assemblyIdentity>`. We specify the name of the referenced assembly with `<assemblyIdentity>`. `name` is the only mandatory attribute for `<assemblyIdentity>`. The optional attributes are `publicKeyToken` and `culture`. The other subelement of `<dependentAssembly>` that's needed for version redirection is `<bindingRedirect>`. With this element the old and the new version of the dependent assembly is specified.

Starting the client with this configuration file, you will get the new version of the referenced shared assembly.

Publisher policy files

Using assemblies that are shared in the global assembly cache you can also use publisher policies to override versioning issues. Let's assume that we have a shared assembly that is used by some applications. What if a bug is found in the shared assembly? We have seen that it is not necessary to rebuild all the applications that use this shared assembly as we can use configuration files to redirect to the new version of this shared assembly. Maybe we don't know all the applications that use this shared assembly, but we want to get the bug fix to all of them. In that case we can create publisher policy files to redirect all applications to the new version of the shared assembly.

> **Publisher policy files only apply to shared assemblies installed into the global assembly cache.**

To set up publisher policies we have to:

- ❑ Create a publisher policy file.
- ❑ Create a publisher policy assembly.
- ❑ Add the publisher policy assembly to the global assembly cache.

Create a Publisher Policy File

A publisher policy file is an XML file that redirects an existing version or version range to a new version. The syntax used is the same as for application configuration files, so we can use the same file we created earlier to redirect the old versions 1.0.0.0 through 1.0.999.99999 to the new version 1.1.1330.27636.

Rename the previously created file to mypolicy.config to use it as a publisher policy file.

```
<?xml version="1.0"?>
<configuration>
   <runtime>
      <assemblyBinding xmlns="urn:schemas-microsoft-com:asm.v1">
         <dependentAssembly>
            <assemblyIdentity name="SharedDemo"
                              publicKeyToken="be9f9ce7b9a0a62f" />
            <bindingRedirect oldVersion="1.0.0.0-1.0.999.99999"
                             newVersion="1.1.1330.27636" />
         </dependentAssembly>
      </assemblyBinding>
   </runtime>
</configuration>
```

Create a Publisher Policy Assembly

To associate the publisher policy file with the shared assembly it is necessary to create a publisher policy assembly, and put it into the global assembly cache. The tool that can be used to create such files is the assembly linker al. The option /linkresource adds the publisher policy file to the generated assembly. The name of the generated assembly must start with policy, followed by the major and minor version number of the assembly that should be redirected, and the filename of the shared assembly. In our case the publisher policy assembly must be named policy.1.0.SharedDemo.dll to redirect the assemblies SharedDemo with the major version 1, and minor version 0. The key that must be added to this publisher key with the option /keyfile is the same key that was used to sign the shared assembly SharedDemo to guarantee that the version redirection is from the same publisher.

```
al /linkresource:mypolicy.config /out:policy.1.0.SharedDemo.dll
/keyfile:..\..\mykey.snk
```

Add the Publisher Policy Assembly to the Global Assembly Cache

The publisher policy assembly can now be added to the global assembly cache with the utility gacutil.

```
gacutil -i policy.1.0.SharedDemo.dll
```

Now remove the application configuration file that was placed in the directory of the client application, and start the client application. Although the client assembly references 1.0.1318.24054 we use the new version 1.1.1330.27636 of the shared assembly because of the publisher policy.

Overriding Publisher Policies

With a publisher policy, the publisher of the shared assembly guarantees that a new version of the assembly is compatible with the old version. As we know from changes of traditional DLLs, such guarantees don't always hold. Maybe all but one application is working with the new shared assembly. To fix the one application that has a problem with the new release, the publisher policy can be overridden by using an application configuration file.

With the .NET Framework configuration tool you can override the publisher policy by deselecting the check box Enable Publisher Policy as shown in Figure 13-40.

Figure 13-40

Disabling the publisher policy with the .NET Framework Configuration results in a configuration file with the XML element `<publisherPolicy>` and the attribute `apply="no"`.

```xml
<?xml version="1.0"?>
<configuration>
  <runtime>
    <assemblyBinding xmlns="urn:schemas-microsoft-com:asm.v1">
      <dependentAssembly>
        <assemblyIdentity name="SharedDemo" publicKeyToken="be9f9ce7b9a0a62f" />

        <publisherPolicy apply="no" />

      </dependentAssembly>
    </assemblyBinding>
  </runtime>
</configuration>
```

Disabling the publisher policy we can configure different version redirection in the application configuration file.

Fixing an application

If an application doesn't run because a configuration is wrong or because newly installed assemblies let it fail, the .NET Framework Configuration has an option to fix .NET applications. Clicking the Fix an Application hyperlink lists all .NET applications that were running previously and it allows you to restore the last version of the application configuration file (see Figure 13-41), or select any previous configuration. Selecting the Application SafeMode disables publisher policies.

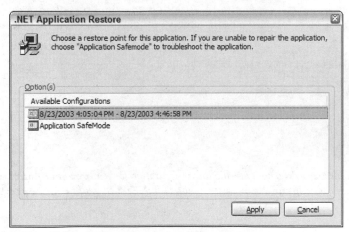

Figure 13-41

Runtime version

Installing and using multiple versions is not only possible with assemblies, but also with the .NET runtime. Both versions 1.0 and 1.1 (and future versions) of the .NET runtime can be installed on the same operating system side by side. Visual Studio .NET 2003 by default targets applications running on .NET 1.1. However, this can be changed by modifying the values in the application configuration file.

An application that was built using .NET 1.0 may run without changes on .NET 1.1. If an operating system has both versions of the runtime installed, the application will use the version with which it was built. However, if only version 1.1 is installed with the operating system, and the application was built with version 1.0, it tries to run with the newer version. The registry key HKEY_LOCAL_MACHINE \Software\Microsoft\.NETFramework\policy lists the ranges of the versions that will be used for a specific runtime.

If an application was built using .NET 1.1, it may run without changes on .NET 1.0, in case no classes or methods are used that are only available with .NET 1.1. To make this possible, an application configuration file is needed.

In an application configuration file, it's not only possible to redirect versions of referenced assemblies; we can also define the required version of the runtime. Different .NET runtime versions can be installed on a single machine. We can specify the version that's required for the application in an application configuration file. The element <supportedVersion> marks the runtime versions that are supported by the application.

```xml
<?xml version="1.0"?>
<configuration>
   <startup>
      <supportedRuntime version="v1.1.4322" />
      <supportedRuntime version="v1.0.3512" />
   </startup>
</configuration>
```

However, with .NET 1.0 instead of the element <supportedVersion> the element <requiredRuntime> was used to specify the needed runtime. Configuring the .NET Framework versions in the project properties (see Figure 13-42) adds both <supportedRuntime> and <requiredRuntime> elements as well as assembly binding information we discussed earlier.

```xml
<?xml version="1.0"?>
<configuration>
   <startup>
 <supportedRuntime version="v1.1.4322"/>
 <supportedRuntime version="v1.0.3705"/>
      <requiredRuntime version="v1.0.3512" safeMode="true" />
   </startup>
</configuration>
```

<requiredRuntime> does not overrule the configuration for <supportedRuntime> as it may look like, because <requiredRuntime> is used only with .NET 1.0, while <supportedRuntime> is used by .NET 1.1 and later versions.

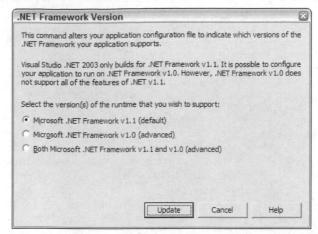

Figure 13-42

Configuring Directories

We've already seen how to redirect referenced assemblies to a different version so that we can locate our assemblies, but there are more options to configure! For example, it's not necessary to install a shared assembly in the global assembly cache. It's also possible that shared assemblies can be found with the help of specific directory settings in configuration files. This feature can be used if you want to make the shared components available on a server. Another possible scenario is if you want to share an assembly between your applications, but you don't want to make it publicly available in the global assembly cache, so you put it into a shared directory instead.

There are two ways to find the correct directory for an assembly: the codeBase element in an XML configuration file, or through probing. The codeBase configuration is only available for shared assemblies, and probing is done for private assemblies.

<codeBase>

The <codeBase> can also be configured using the .NET Admin Tool. Codebases can be configured by selecting the properties of the configured application, SimpleShared, inside the Configured Assemblies in the Applications tree. Similar to the Binding Policy, we can configure lists of versions with the Codebases tab. In the following screen we have configured that the version 1.0 should be loaded from the Web server http://www.christiannagel.com/WroxUtils:

Figure 13-43

The .NET Admin tool creates this application configuration file:

```xml
<?xml version="1.0"?>
<configuration>
  <runtime>
    <assemblyBinding xmlns="urn:schemas-microsoft-com:asm.v1">
      <dependentAssembly xmlns="">
        <assemblyIdentity name="SimpleShared"
                          publicKeyToken="6ca9587197f6f8c2" />
        <codeBase version="1.0" href="http://www.christiannagel.com/WroxUtils" />
      </dependentAssembly>
    </assemblyBinding>
  </runtime>
</configuration>
```

The `<dependentAssembly>` element is the same used previously for the version redirection. The `<codeBase>` element has the attributes `version` and `href`. With `version`, the original referenced version of the assembly must be specified. With `href`, we can define the directory from where the assembly should be loaded. In our example, a path using the HTTP protocol is used. A directory on a local system or a share is specified using `href="file:C:/WroxUtils"`.

When using that assembly loaded from the network a System.Security.Permissions exception occurs. You must configure the required permissions for assemblies loaded from the network. In Chapter 14 we show how to configure security for assemblies.

<probing>

When the `<codeBase>` is not configured and the assembly is not stored in the global assembly cache, the runtime tries to find an assembly with probing. The .NET runtime tries to find an assembly with either a .dll or an .exe file extension in the application directory, or in one of its subdirectories, that has the same name as the assembly searched for. If the assembly is not found here, the search continues. You can configure search directories with the `<probing>` element in the `<runtime>` section of application configuration files. This XML configuration can also be done easily by selecting the properties of the application with the .NET Framework Configuration tool. You can configure the directories where the probing should occur by using the search path in the .NET Framework configuration (see Figure 13-44).

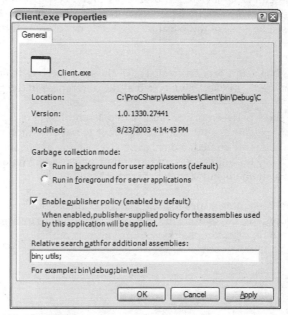

Figure 13-44

The XML file produced has these entries:

```xml
<?xml version="1.0"?>
<configuration>
   <runtime>
      <gcConcurrent enabled="enabled" />
      <assemblyBinding xmlns="urn:schemas-microsoft-com:asm.v1">
         <probing privatePath="bin;utils;" xmlns="" />
      </assemblyBinding>
   </runtime>
</configuration>
```

The `<probing>` element has just a single required attribute: `privatePath`. This application configuration file tells the runtime that assemblies should be searched for in the base directory of the application, followed by the `bin` and the `util` directory. Both directories are subdirectories of the application base directory. It's not possible to reference a private assembly outside the application base directory or a subdirectory thereof. An assembly outside of the application base directory must have a shared name and can be referenced using the <codeBase> element as we've done before.

Summary

Assemblies are the new installation unit for the .NET platform. Microsoft learned from problems with previous architectures and did a complete redesign to avoid the old problems. In this chapter we discussed the features of assemblies: they are self-describing and no type library and registry information is needed. Version dependencies are exactly recorded so that with assemblies, the DLL Hell we had with old DLLs no longer exists. Because of these features, not only development but also deployment and administration have become a lot easier.

We discussed cross-language support and created a C# class that derives from a Visual Basic .NET class that makes use of a managed C++ class, and looked at the differences in the generated MSIL code.

We discussed the differences between private and shared assemblies and explained how shared assemblies can be created. With private assemblies we don't have to pay attention to uniqueness and versioning issues as these assemblies are copied and only used by a single application. Sharing assemblies has the requirement to use a key for uniqueness, and to define the version. We looked at the global assembly cache that can be used as an intelligent store for shared assemblies.

We looked at overriding versioning issues to use a version of an assembly different from the one that was used during development; this is done through publisher policies and application configuration files. Finally we discussed how probing works with private assemblies.

14

.NET Security

You're sitting at your machine and you click a button on an application you're using. Behind the scenes, your application responds to the fact that you are attempting to use a feature for which it does not have the relevant module. It connects to the Internet, downloads the module into the Download Assembly Cache, and begins executing—all without prompting you.

This kind of behind-the-scenes upgrade functionality is already used with many .NET applications, but clearly there is a concern here over the security implications relating to what we call *mobile code*. In clear terms, what evidence do you actually have that you can trust the code your computer is downloading? How do you know that the module you requested is, in fact, the one that you are receiving? What does the CLR do behind the scenes to ensure, for example, that a control on a Web site is not reading your private e-mails?

.NET enforces a security policy around assemblies. It uses the evidence it has about assemblies, such as where they are from or who publishes them, to split the assemblies into groups with similar characteristics. For example, the runtime places all code from the local intranet into a specific group. It then uses the security policy (normally defined by a system administrator using the Code Access Security Policy Tool [caspol.exe] command line utility, or the Microsoft Management Console) to decide what permissions the code should be granted at a very granular level. What do you have to do to enable security on a machine or for a specific application? Nothing—all code automatically runs within the security context of the CLR, although you can turn off security if necessary.

In addition to high levels of confidence that the code we are executing can be trusted, it is also important to permit the application users access to the features they need, but no more. By virtue of its role-based security, .NET facilitates effective management of users and roles.

In this chapter we look through the features available in .NET to help us manage security, including how .NET protects us from malicious code, how to administer security policies, and how to access the security subsystem programmatically. We also take a look at deploying .NET applications securely and see a number of short example applications to solidify the concepts in this chapter for you.

Code Access Security

Code access security is a feature of .NET that manages code, dependent on our level of trust. If the CLR trusts the code enough to allow it to run, it will begin executing the code. Depending on the permissions provided to the assembly, however, it might run within a restricted environment. If the code is not trusted enough to run, or if it runs but then attempts to perform an action, for which it does not have the relevant permissions, a security exception (of type `SecurityException`, or a subclass of it) is thrown. The code access security system means that we can stop malicious code running, but we can also allow code to run within a protected environment where we are confident that it cannot do any damage.

For example, if a user attempted to run an application that attempted to execute code downloaded from the Internet, the default security policy would raise an exception and the application would fail to start. In a similar way, if the user ran an application from a network drive it would begin executing, but if the application then attempted to access a file on the local drive, the runtime would raise an exception and, depending on the error handling in the application, would either gracefully degrade or exit.

For most applications, .NET's code access security is a significant benefit, but one that sits at the back of the room quietly helping out. It provides high levels of protection from malicious code, but generally, you do not need to get involved. However, one area you will be involved in is the management of security policy, and this is especially true when configuring desktops to trust code from the locations of software suppliers who are delivering applications to you.

Another area where code access security is a very important aspect is when you are building an application that includes an element whose security you want to control closely. For example, if there is a database within your organization containing extremely sensitive data, you would use code access security to state what code is allowed to access that database, and what code must not access it.

It is important to realize how code access security is about protecting resources (local drive, network, user interface) from malicious code; it is not primarily a tool for protecting software from users. For security in relation to users, you will generally use the built-in Windows 2000 user security subsystem, or make use of .NET role-based security, which we discuss later in this chapter.

Code access security is based on two high-level concepts: *code groups* and *permissions*. Let's look at these before we start since they form the foundations of the following:

❑ **Code groups** bring together code with similar characteristics, although the most important property is usually where the code came from. Two examples for code groups are Internet and Intranet. The group Internet defines code that is sourced from the Internet, the group Intranet defines code sourced from the LAN. The information used to place assemblies into code groups is called *evidence*. Other evidence is collected by the CLR, including the publisher of the code, the strong name, and (where applicable) the URI from which it was downloaded. Code groups are arranged in a hierarchy, and assemblies are nearly always matched to several code groups. The code group at the root of the hierarchy is called All Code and contains all other code groups. The hierarchy is used for deciding which code groups an assembly belongs to; if an assembly does not provide evidence that matches it to a group in the tree, no attempt is made to match it to code groups below.

❑ **Permissions** are the actions we allow each code group to perform. For example, permissions include "able to access the user interface" and "able to access local storage." The system administrator usually manages the permissions at the enterprise, machine, and user levels.

The Virtual Execution System within the CLR loads and runs programs. It provides the functionality required to execute managed code and uses assembly metadata to connect modules together at run time. When the VES loads an assembly, the VES matches the assembly to one or more of a number of code groups. Each code group is assigned to one or more permissions that specify what actions assemblies can do in that code group. For example, if the MyComputer code group is assigned the permission FileIOPermission, this means that assemblies from the local machine can read and write to the local file system.

Code Groups

Code groups have an entry requirement called *membership condition*. For an assembly to be filed into a code group, it must match the group's membership condition. Membership conditions include "the assembly is from the site www.microsoft.com" or "the publisher of this software is Microsoft Corporation."

Each code group has one, and only one, membership condition. The following list provides the types of code group membership conditions available in .NET:

- ❑ **Zone**—The region from which the code originated.

- ❑ **Site**—The Web site from which the code originated.

- ❑ **Strong name**—A unique, verifiable name for the code. Strong names are discussed in Chapter 13.

- ❑ **Publisher**—The publisher of the code.

- ❑ **URL**—The specific location from which the code originated.

- ❑ **Hash value**—The hash value for the assembly.

- ❑ **Skip verification**—This condition requests that it bypasses code verification checks. Code verification ensures the code accesses types in a well-defined and acceptable way. The runtime cannot enforce security on code that is not type safe.

- ❑ **Application directory** —The location of the assembly within the application.

- ❑ **All code**—All code fulfills this condition.

- ❑ **Custom**—A user-specified condition.

The first, and most commonly used, type of membership condition in the list is the *Zone* condition. A zone is the region of origin of a piece of code and refers to one of the following: MyComputer, Internet, Intranet, Trusted, or Untrusted. These zones can be managed by using the security options in Internet Explorer. We discuss zones in more detail later in this chapter, when we look at how to manage the security policy. Although the settings are managed within Internet Explorer, they apply to the entire machine. Clearly, these configuration options are not available in non-Microsoft browsers and, in fact, in-page controls written using the .NET Framework will not work in browsers other than Internet Explorer.

Code groups are arranged hierarchically with the All Code membership condition at the root (see Figure 14-1). You can see that each code group has a single membership condition and specifies the permissions that the code group has been granted. Note that if an assembly does not match the membership condition in a code group, the CLR does not attempt to match code groups below it.

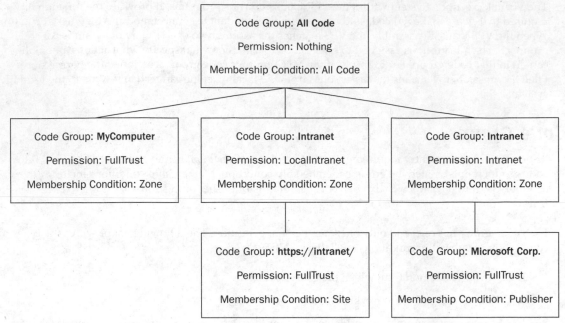

Figure 14-1

caspol.exe—The Code Access Security Policy tool

We'll spend a good deal of time in this chapter looking at the command line Code Access Security Policy tool. To get a list of options for the tool, just type the following at the command prompt:

```
caspol.exe -?
```

To send the output to a text file use:

```
caspol.exe > caspol.txt
```

.NET also includes a snap-in for the Microsoft Management Console to manage code access security. However, we will restrict ourselves to the command line utility, because the examples are easier to follow, and you'll also be in a position to create scripts to alter the security policy, which is very useful when applying policies to large numbers of machines.

Let's look at the code groups on a machine using caspol.exe. The output of the command lists the hierarchical structure of the code groups on the machine, and next to each group is a description of the code group. Type this command:

```
caspol.exe -listdescription
```

Alternatively, the -listdescription parameter has a shortcut: -ld. You will see something like this:

```
Microsoft (R) .NET Framework CasPol 1.1.4322.535
Copyright (C) Microsoft Corporation 1998-2002. All rights reserved.
```

```
Security is ON
Execution checking is ON
Policy change prompt is ON

Level = Machine

Full Trust Assemblies:

1. All_Code: Code group grants no permissions and forms the root of the code
group tree.
    1.1. My_Computer_Zone: Code group grants full trust to all code originating
         on the local computer
        1.1.1. Microsoft_Strong_Name: Code group grants full trust to code signed
               with the Microsoft strong name.
        1.1.2. ECMA_Strong_Name: Code group grants full trust to code signed with
               the ECMA strong name.
    1.2. LocalIntranet_Zone: Code group grants the intranet permission set to
         code from the intranet zone. This permission set grants intranet code
         the right to use isolated storage, full UI access, some capability to do
         reflection, and limited access to environment variables.
        1.2.1. Intranet_Same_Site_Access: All intranet code gets the right to
               connect back to the site of its origin.
        1.2.2. Intranet_Same_Directory_Access: All intranet code gets the right to
               read from its install directory.
    1.3. Internet_Zone: Code group grants code from the Internet zone the
         Internet permission set. This permission set grants Internet code the right
         to use isolated storage and limited UI access.
        1.3.1. Internet_Same_Site_Access: All Internet code gets the right to
               connect back to the site of its origin.
    1.4. Restricted_Zone: Code coming from a restricted zone does not receive any
         permissions.
    1.5. Trusted_Zone: Code from a trusted zone is granted the Internet
         permission set. This permission set grants the right to use isolated
         storage and limited UI access.
        1.5.1. Trusted_Same_Site_Access: All Trusted Code gets the right to
               connect back to the site of its origin.
Success
```

The .NET security subsystem ensures that code from each code group is allowed to do only certain things. For example, code from the Internet zone will, by default, have much stricter limits than code from the local drive. Code from the local drive is normally granted access to data stored on the local drive, but assemblies from the Internet are not granted this permission by default.

Using caspol, and its equivalent in the Microsoft Management Console, you can specify what level of trust you have for each code access group, as well as managing code groups and permissions in a more granular fashion.

Let's take another look at the code access groups, but this time in a slightly more compact view. Make sure you're logged in as a local administrator, go to a command prompt, and type this command:

```
caspol.exe -listgroups
```

You will see something like this:

```
Microsoft (R) .NET Framework CasPol 1.1.4322.535
Copyright (C) Microsoft Corporation 1998-2002. All rights reserved.

Security is ON
Execution checking is ON
Policy change prompt is ON

Level = Machine

Code Groups:

1.  All code: Nothing
    1.1.  Zone - MyComputer: FullTrust
       1.1.1.  StrongName - 00240000004800000094000000060200000024000052534131300040
0000100010007D1FA57C4AED9F0A32E84AA0FAEFD0DE9E8FD6AEC8F87FB03766C834C99921EB23BE
79AD9D5DCC1DD9AD236132102900B723CF980957FC4E177108FC607774F29E8320E92EA05ECE4E82
1C0A5EFE8F1645C4C0C93C1AB99285D622CAA652C1DFAD63D745D6F2DE5F17E5EAF0FC4963D261C8
A12436518206DC093344D5AD293: FullTrust
       1.1.2.  StrongName - 0000000000000000000400000000000000: FullTrust
    1.2.  Zone - Intranet: LocalIntranet
    1.2.1.  All code: Same site Web.
    1.2.2.  All code: Same directory FileIO - Read, PathDiscovery
    1.3.  Zone - Internet: Internet
    1.3.1.  All code: Same site Web.
    1.4.  Zone - Untrusted: Nothing
    1.5.  Zone - Trusted: Internet
       1.5.1.  All code: Same site Web.
Success
```

You'll notice that near the start of the output it says, Security is ON. Later in the chapter, you will see that it can be turned off and then turned on again.

The Execution Checking setting is on by default, which means all assemblies must be granted the permission to execute before they can run. If execution checking is turned off using caspol (caspol.exe –execution on | off), assemblies that do not have the permission to run can execute, although they might cause security exceptions if they attempt to act contrary to the security policy later in their execution.

The Policy change prompt option specifies whether you see an "Are you sure" warning message when you attempt to alter the security policy.

As code is broken down into these groups, you can manage security at a more granular level, and apply full trust to a much smaller percentage of code. Note that each group has a label (for example, 1.2). These labels are auto-generated by .NET, and can differ between machines. Generally security is not managed for each assembly; it is managed using a code group instead.

When a machine has several side-by-side installations of .NET, the copy of caspol.exe that you run will only alter the security policy for the installation of .NET with which it is associated. To keep security policy management simpler, you might want to remove previous copies of .NET as you install successive versions.

Viewing an assembly's code groups

Assemblies are matched to code groups dependent on the membership conditions they match. If we go back to our example code groups and load an assembly from the `https://intranet/` Web site, it would match the code groups shown in Figure 14-2. The assembly is a member of the root code group (All Code); since it came from the local network it is also a member of the Intranet code group. However, because it was loaded from the specific site `https://intranet`, it is also granted *FullTrust*, which means it can run unrestrictedly.

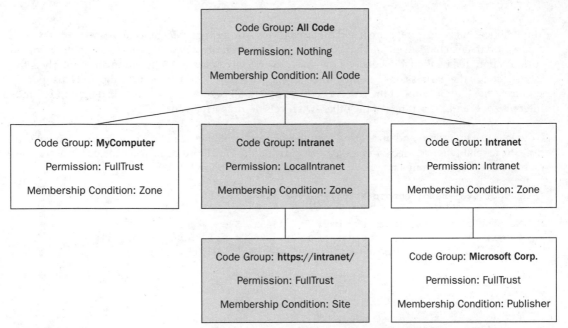

Figure 14-2

You can easily view the code groups that an assembly is a member of using this command:

```
caspol.exe -resolvegroup assembly.dll
```

Running this command on an assembly on the local drive produces this output:

```
Microsoft (R) .NET Framework CasPol 1.1.4322.535
Copyright (C) Microsoft Corporation 1998-2002. All rights reserved.

Level = Enterprise

Code Groups:

1.  All code: FullTrust

Level = Machine

Code Groups:
```

```
1.  All code: Nothing
   1.1.  Zone - MyComputer: FullTrust

Level = User

Code Groups:

1.  All code: FullTrust

Success
```

You'll notice that code groups are listed on three levels—Enterprise, Machine, and User. For now, stay focused on the machine level. We'll look at the other two in more detail later in this chapter. If you are curious about the relationship between the three, the effective permission given to an assembly is the intersection of the permissions from the three levels. For example, if you remove the FullTrust permission from the Internet zone at the enterprise-level policy, all permissions are revoked for code from the Internet zone, and the settings of the other two levels become irrelevant.

Now let's use this command once more with the same assembly to read the code groups. However, this time the assembly is accessed from a Web server using the HTTP protocol. You can see the assembly is a member of different groups that have much more restrictive permissions:

caspol.exe –resolvegroup http://server/assembly.dll

```
Microsoft (R) .NET Framework CasPol 1.1.4322.535
Copyright (C) Microsoft Corporation 1998-2002. All rights reserved.


Level = Enterprise

Code Groups:

1.  All code: FullTrust
Level = Machine

Code Groups:

1.  All code: Nothing
   1.1.  Zone - Internet: Internet
      1.1.1.  All code: Same site Web.


Level = User

Code Groups:

1.  All code: FullTrust

Success
```

The assembly grants the Internet and the Same Site Web permissions. The intersection of the permissions allows the code limited UI access. It also permits it to establish connections to the site it originated from.

Let's take a closer look at permissions.

Code Access Permissions and Permissions Sets

Imagine yourself administering security policy on a network of desktop machines in a large enterprise scenario. In this environment it's immensely useful for the CLR to collect evidence information on code before it executes it. Likewise, you as the administrator must have the opportunity to control what code is allowed to do on the several hundred machines you manage once the CLR has identified its origin. This is where permissions come in.

After an assembly has been matched to code groups, the CLR looks at the security policy to calculate the permissions it grants to an assembly. When managing permissions in Windows you generally don't want to apply permissions to users, but instead you apply permissions to user groups. The same is true with assemblies; permissions are applied to code groups rather than to individual assemblies, which makes the management of security policy in .NET a much easier task.

The security policy specifies what actions assemblies are permitted to perform in a code group. The following list summarizes the code access permissions provided by the CLR; as you can see, you have quite a bit of control over what code is and is not permitted to do:

❑ **DirectoryServicesPermission** controls the ability to access Active Directory through the `System.DirectoryServices` classes.

❑ **DnsPermission** controls the ability to use the TCP/IP Domain Name System (DNS).

❑ **EnvironmentPermission** controls the ability to read and to write environment variables.

❑ **EventLogPermission** controls the ability to read and to write to the event log.

❑ **FileDialogPermission** controls the ability to access files that have been selected by the user in the Open dialog box. This permission is commonly used when `FileIOPermission` is not granted to allow limited access to files.

❑ **FileIOPermission** controls the ability to work with files (reading, writing, and appending to file, as well as creating and altering folders and accessing).

❑ **IsolatedStorageFilePermission** controls the ability to access private virtual file systems.

❑ **IsolatedStoragePermission** controls the ability to access isolated storage; storage that is associated with an individual user and with some aspect of the code's identity, such as its Web site, signature, or publisher.

❑ **MessageQueuePermission** controls the ability to use message queues through the Microsoft Message Queue.

❑ **OleDbPermission** controls the ability to access databases with OLE DB providers.

❑ **PerformanceCounterPermission** controls the ability to make use of performance counters.

❑ **PrintingPermission** controls the ability to print.

❑ **ReflectionPermission** controls the ability to discover information about a type at runtime using `System.Reflection`.

❑ **RegistryPermission** controls the ability to read, write, create, or delete registry keys and values.

❑ **SecurityPermission** controls the ability to execute, assert permissions, call into unmanaged code, skip verification, and other rights.

❑ **ServiceControllerPermission** controls the ability to control Windows services.

❑ **SocketPermission** controls the ability to make or accept TCP/IP connections on a network transport address.

❑ **SQLClientPermission** controls the ability to access SQL Server databases with the .NET data provider for SQL Server.

❑ **UIPermission** controls the ability to access the user interface.

❑ **WebPermission** controls the ability to make or accept connections to or from the Web.

With each of these permission classes, often it is possible to specify an even deeper level of granularity. For example, later in this chapter you'll see an example of requesting not just file access but a specific level of file access.

In terms of best practice, you are well advised to ensure any attempts to make use of the resources relating to the permissions in this list are enclosed within `try...catch` error handling blocks, so that your application degrades gracefully should it be running under restricted permissions. The design of your application should specify how your application should act under these circumstances. Do not assume that it will be running under the same security policy under which you develop it. For example, if your application cannot access the local drive, should it exit or operate in an alternative fashion?

An assembly is associated with several code groups; the effective permission of an assembly within the security policy is the union of all permissions from all the code groups to which it belongs. That is, each code group that an assembly matches extends what it is allowed to do. Note that code groups further down the tree are often assigned more relaxed permissions than those higher up.

There is another set of permissions that are assigned by the CLR on the basis of the identity of the code, which cannot be granted. These permissions relate to the evidence the CLR has collated about the assembly and are called *Identity Permissions*. Here are the names of the classes for the identity permissions:

❑ **PublisherIdentityPermission** refers to the software publisher's digital signature.

❑ **SiteIdentityPermission** refers to the name of the Web site from which the code originated.

❑ **StrongNameIdentityPermission** refers to the assembly's strong name.

❑ **URLIdentityPermission** refers to the URL from which the code came (including the protocol, for example, `https://`).

❑ **ZoneIdentityPermission** refers to the zone from which the assembly originates.

Usually, the permissions are applied in blocks, which is why .NET has the concept of permission sets. These are lists of code access permissions grouped into a named set. The following list explains the named permission sets we get out of the box:

❑ **FullTrust** means no permission restrictions.

❑ **Execution** grants the ability to run, but not to access any protected resources.

❑ **Nothing** grants no permissions and prevents the code from executing.

❑ **LocalIntranet** specifies the default policy for the local intranet, a subset of the full set of permissions. For example, file IO is restricted to read access on the share where the assembly originates.

❑ **Internet** specifies the default policy for code of unknown origin. This is the most restrictive policy listed. For example, code executing in this permission set has no file IO capability, cannot read or write event logs, and cannot read or write environment variables.

❑ **Everything** grants all the permissions that are listed under this set, except the permission to skip code verification. The administrator can alter any of the permissions in this permission set. This is useful where the default policy needs to be tighter.

Note that of these you can only change the definitions of the Everything permission set— the other sets are fixed and cannot be changed.

Identity permissions cannot be included in permission sets because the CLR is the only body able to grant identity permissions to code. For example, if a piece of code is from a specific publisher, it would make little sense for the administrator to give it the identity permissions associated with another publisher. The CLR grants identity permissions where necessary, and if you want you can use them.

Viewing an assembly's permissions

Imagine you're using a Microsoft application, and you attempt to use a feature that you have not used before. The application does not have a copy of the code stored locally, so it requests it and the code is then downloaded into the Download Assembly Cache. Figure 14-3 illustrates what an assembly's code group membership might look like with code from the Internet published by a named organization that has signed the assembly with a certificate.

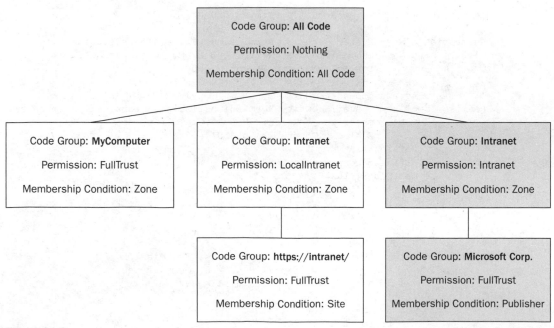

Figure 14-3

According to our policy in this example, although the All Code and Internet code groups bring only limited permissions, membership of the code group in the bottom right-hand corner grants the assembly the FullTrust permission. The overall effective permission is the *union* of permissions across the matching code groups. When the permissions are merged in this way, the effective permission is that of the highest permissions granted. That is, each code group to which an assembly belongs brings additional permissions.

Just as it can be checked at what code groups an assembly belongs to, it is also possible to look at the permissions assigned to the code groups to which it belongs. Doing this you'll see not only the code access permissions (what the code is allowed to do) but also the code identity permissions that will give us access to the evidence the code presented to the runtime. To see the permissions for an assembly's code groups, use a command like this:

```
caspol.exe -resolveperm assembly.dll
```

Let's try this on an assembly and look at the code access and identity permissions it is granted when we access it over a local intranet. If you type the following command you will see the code access permissions and then the three identity permissions at the end:

```
caspol.exe -resolveperm http://intranet/assembly.dll
```

```
Microsoft (R) .NET Framework CasPol 1.1.4322.535
Copyright (C) Microsoft Corporation 1998-2002. All rights reserved.

Resolving permissions for level = Enterprise
Resolving permissions for level = Machine
Resolving permissions for level = User
Grant =
<PermissionSet class="System.Security.PermissionSet"
                version="1">
   <IPermission class="System.Security.Permissions.FileDialogPermission,
                    mscorlib, Version=1.0.5000.0, Culture=neutral,
                    PublicKeyToken=b77a5c561934e089"
                version="1"
                Access="Open"/>
   <IPermission class="System.Security.Permissions.IsolatedStorageFilePermission,
                    mscorlib, Version=1.0.5000.0, Culture=neutral,
                    PublicKeyToken=b77a5c561934e089"
                version="1"
                Allowed="DomainIsolationByUser"
                UserQuota="10240"/>
   <IPermission class="System.Security.Permissions.SecurityPermission,
                    mscorlib, Version=1.0.5000.0, Culture=neutral,
                    PublicKeyToken=b77a5c561934e089"
                version="1"
                Flags="Execution"/>
   <IPermission class="System.Security.Permissions.UIPermission,
                    mscorlib, Version=1.0.5000.0, Culture=neutral,
                    PublicKeyToken=b77a5c561934e089"
                version="1"
                Window="SafeTopLevelWindows"
                Clipboard="OwnClipboard"/>
   <IPermission class="System.Net.WebPermission,
```

```
                        System, Version=1.0.5000.0, Culture=neutral,
                        PublicKeyToken=b77a5c561934e089"
                version="1">
        <ConnectAccess>
          <URI uri="(https|http)://some\.host\.com/.*"/>
        </ConnectAccess>
    </IPermission>
    <IPermission class="System.Drawing.Printing.PrintingPermission,
                        System.Drawing, Version=1.0.5000.0, Culture=neutral,
                        PublicKeyToken=b03f5f7f11d50a3a"
                version="1"
                Level="SafePrinting"/>
    <IPermission class="System.Security.Permissions.SiteIdentityPermission,
                        mscorlib, Version=1.0.5000.0, Culture=neutral,
                        PublicKeyToken=b77a5c561934e089"
                version="1"
                Site="some.host.com"/>
    <IPermission class="System.Security.Permissions.UrlIdentityPermission,
                        mscorlib, Version=1.0.5000.0, Culture=neutral,
                        PublicKeyToken=b77a5c561934e089"
                version="1"
                Url="http://some.host.com/dev/testdll.dll"/>
    <IPermission class="System.Security.Permissions.ZoneIdentityPermission,
                        mscorlib, Version=1.0.5000.0, Culture=neutral,
                        PublicKeyToken=b77a5c561934e089"
                version="1"
                Zone="Internet"/>
</PermissionSet>

Success
```

The output shows each of the permissions in XML, including the class defining the permission, the assembly containing the class, the permission version, and an encryption token. The output suggests that it is possible for us to create our own permissions, and you'll learn more about that later in this chapter. We can also see that each of the identity permissions includes more detailed information on, for example, the `UrlIdentityPermission` class, which provides access to the URL from which the code originated.

Note how at the start of the output, caspol.exe resolved the permissions at the enterprise, machine, and user levels and then listed the effective granted permissions. Let's look at these now.

Policy Levels: Machine, User, and Enterprise

Up to now we have looked at security in the context of a single machine. It's often necessary to specify security policies for specific users or for an entire organization, and that is why .NET provides not one, but three levels of code groups:

❑   Machine

❑   Enterprise

❑   User

The code group levels are independently managed and exist in parallel:

Figure 14-4

If there are three security policies, how do we know which one applies? The effective permission is the *intersection* of the permissions from the three levels. Each of the three levels has the ability to veto the permissions allowed by another—this is really good news for administrators as their settings will override user settings.

To work with code groups and permissions on the user or enterprise levels using caspol.exe, add either the –enterprise or -user argument to change the command's mode. caspol.exe works at the Machine level by default and that's how we've been using it up to now. Let's see the code groups listing at the User level:

```
caspol.exe -user -listgroups
```

The output of the command on a default installation looks like this:

```
Security is ON
Execution checking is ON
Policy change prompt is ON

Level = User

Code Groups:

1.  All code: FullTrust
Success
```

Now let's run the same command, but this time to see the code groups at the enterprise level:

```
caspol.exe -enterprise -listgroups
```

The output of the command looks like this:

```
Security is ON
Execution checking is ON
Policy change prompt is ON

Level = Enterprise

Code Groups:

1.  All code: FullTrust
Success
```

As you can see, by default, both the user level and the enterprise level are configured to allow FullTrust for the single code group All Code. The result of this is that the default setting for .NET security places no restrictions at the Enterprise or User levels, and the enforced policy is dictated solely by the machine-level policy. For example, if we were to assign a more restrictive permission or permission set to either the enterprise or user levels than FullTrust, those restrictions would restrict the overall permissions, and probably override permissions at the Machine level. The effective permissions are intersected, so, for example, if you want to apply FullTrust to a code group, this permission must be assigned to the code group on each of the three policy levels.

When we run caspol.exe as an administrator, it defaults to the Machine level, but if we log out and log back in as a user who is not in the Administrator user group, caspol.exe will instead default to the User level. In addition, caspol.exe will not allow us to alter the security policy in a way that renders the caspol.exe utility itself inoperable.

We've had a high-level look at the security architecture in .NET; let's now look at how we can access its features programmatically.

Support for Security in the Framework

For .NET security to work, programmers must trust the CLR to enforce the security policy. When a call is made to a method that demands specific permissions (for example, accessing a file on the local drive), the CLR walks up the stack to ensure that every caller in the call chain has the permissions being demanded.

At this point the term *performance* is probably ringing in your mind, and clearly that is a concern, but to gain the benefits of a managed environment like .NET it is the price we pay. The alternative is that assemblies which are not fully trusted could make calls to trusted assemblies and our system is open to attack.

For reference, the parts of the .NET Framework library namespace most applicable to this chapter are:

❏ System.Security.Permissions

❏ System.Security.Policy

❏ System.Security.Principal

Note that evidence-based code access security works in tandem with Windows logon security. If you attempt to run a .NET desktop application, the relevant .NET code access security permissions must be granted, but you as the logged-in user must also be using a Windows account that has the relevant permissions to execute the code. With desktop applications, this means the current user must have been granted the relevant rights to access the relevant assembly files on the drive. For Internet applications, the account under which Internet Information Server is running must have access to the assembly files.

Demanding Permissions

To see how demanding permissions work, create a Windows Forms application that just contains a button. When clicked, this performs an action that accesses the drive. If the application does not have the relevant permission to access the local drive (FileIOPermission), the button will be marked as unavailable (dimmed).

If you import the namespace System.Security.Permissions, you can change the constructor of the class Form1 to check for permissions by creating a FileIOPermission object, calling its Demand() method, and then acting on the result:

```
public Form1()
{
    InitializeComponent();

    try
    {
        FileIOPermission fileioperm = new
            FileIOPermission(FileIOPermissionAccess.AllAccess,@"c:\");
        fileioperm.Demand();
    }
    catch
    {
        button1.Enabled = false;
    }
}
```

FileIOPermission is contained within the System.Security.Permissions namespace, which is the home to the full set of permissions, and also provides classes for declarative permission attributes and enumerations for the parameters that are used to create permissions objects (for example, when creating a FileIOPermission specifying whether we need full access, or read-only).

If you run the application from the local drive where the default security policy allows access to local storage, you will see a dialog box that resembles the one in Figure 14-5.

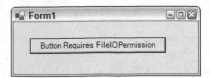

Figure 14-5

However, if you copy the executable to a network share and run it again, you are operating within the `LocalIntranet` permission sets, which blocks access to local storage, and the button will be dimmed as is shown in Figure 14-6.

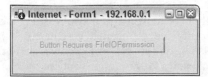

Figure 14-6

If the functionality to make the button access the disk when clicking it is implemented, you will not have to write any security code, because the relevant class in the .NET Framework demands the file permissions, and the CLR ensures that each caller up the stack has those permissions before proceeding. If you run the application from the intranet, and it attempts to open a file on the local disk, you will see an exception unless the security policy has been altered to grant access to the local drive.

If you want to catch exceptions thrown by the CLR when code attempts to act contrary to its granted permissions, you can catch the exception of the type `SecurityException`, which provides access to a number of useful pieces of information, including a human-readable stack trace (`SecurityException` `.StackTrace`) and a reference to the method that threw the exception (`SecurityException.TargetSite`). `SecurityException` even provides you with the `SecurityException.PermissionType` property, which returns the type of `Permission` object that caused the security exception to occur. If you're having problems to diagnose security exceptions, this should be one of your first ports of call. Simply remove the `try` and `catch` blocks from the previous code to see the security exception.

Requesting Permissions

As we discussed in the previous section, demanding permissions is where you state clearly what you need at runtime; however, you can configure an assembly so it makes a softer request for permissions right at the start of execution where it states what it requires before it begins executing.

You can request permissions in three ways:

❑ **Minimum** permissions specifies to the permissions your code must run.

❑ **Optional** permissions specifies the permissions your code can use but is able to run effectively without.

❑ **Refused** permissions specifies the permissions that you want to ensure are not granted to your code.

Why would you want to request permissions when your assembly starts? There are several reasons:

❑ If your assembly needs certain permissions to run, it makes sense to state this at the start of execution rather than during execution to ensure the user does not experience a road block after beginning to work in your program.

❑ You will only be granted the permissions you request and no more. Without explicitly requesting permissions your assembly might be granted more permissions than it needs to execute. This increases the risk of your assembly being used for malicious purposes by other code.

❑ If you only request a minimum set of permissions, you are increasing the probability that your assembly will run, since you cannot predict the security policies that are in effect at an end user's location.

Requesting permissions is likely to be most useful if you're doing more complex deployment, and there is a higher risk that your application will be installed on a machine that does not grant the requisite permissions. It's usually preferable for the application to know right at the start of execution, if it will not be granted permissions, rather than halfway through execution.

To successfully request the permissions your assembly needs, you must keep track of exactly what permissions your assembly is using. In particular, you must be aware of the permission requirements of the calls your assembly is making into other class libraries, including the .NET Framework.

Let's look at three examples from an AssemblyInfo.cs file that demonstrate using attributes to request permissions. If you are following this with the code download, these examples can be found in the SecurityApp2 project. The first attribute requests that the assembly have UIPermission granted, which will allow the application access to the user interface. The request is for the minimum permissions, so if this permission is not granted, the assembly will fail to start:

```
using System.Security.Permissions;
[assembly:UIPermissionAttribute(SecurityAction.RequestMinimum, Unrestricted=true)]
```

Next, there is a request that the assembly is refused access to the C:\ drive. This attribute's setting means the entire assembly will be blocked from accessing this drive:

```
[assembly:FileIOPermissionAttribute(SecurityAction.RequestRefuse, Read="C:\\")]
```

Finally, here's an attribute that requests our assembly be optionally granted the permission to access unmanaged code:

```
[assembly:SecurityPermissionAttribute(SecurityAction.RequestOptional,
                        Flags = SecurityPermissionFlag.UnmanagedCode)]
```

In this scenario you will want to add this attribute to an application that accesses unmanaged code in at least one place. In this case, it is specified that this permission is optional, which means that the application can run without the permission to access unmanaged code. If the assembly is not granted permission to access unmanaged code, and attempts to do so, a SecurityException will be raised, which the application should expect and handle accordingly. The following table shows the full list of available SecurityAction enumeration values; some of these values are covered in more detail later in this chapter.

Security Action	Description
Assert	Allows code to access resources not available to the caller.
Demand	Requires all callers in the call stack to have the specified permission.
Deny	Denies a permission by forcing any subsequent demand for the permission to fail.
InheritanceDemand	Requires derived classes to have the specified permission granted.
LinkDemand	Requires the immediate caller to have the specified permission.
PermitOnly	Similar to deny, subsequent demands for resources not explicitly listed by PermitOnly are refused.
RequestMinimum	Applied at assembly scope; this contains a permission required for an assembly to operate correctly.
RequestOptional	Applied at assembly scope; this asks for permissions the assembly can use, if available, to provide additional features and functionality.
RequestRefuse	Applied at assembly scope when there is a permission you do not want your assembly to have.

When you consider the permission requirements of our application, you have to decide between one of two options:

❑ Request all the permissions you need at the start of execution, and degrade gracefully or exit if those permissions are not granted.

❑ Avoid requesting permissions at the start of execution, but be prepared to handle security exceptions throughout our application.

After an assembly has been configured using permission attributes in this way, you can use the permview.exe utility to view the permissions by aiming it at the assembly file that contains the assembly manifest:

```
>permview.exe <path>\SecurityApp2\bin\Debug\SecurityApp2.exe
```

The output for an application using the three previously discussed attributes looks like this:

```
Microsoft (R) .NET Framework Permission Request Viewer.  Version 1.1.4322.573
Copyright (C) Microsoft Corporation 1998-2002. All rights reserved.

minimal permission set:
<PermissionSet class="System.Security.PermissionSet"
                    version="1">
   <IPermission class="System.Security.Permissions.UIPermission, mscorlib,
                    Version=1.0.5000.0, Culture=neutral,
                    PublicKeyToken=b77a5c561934e089"
                    version="1"
                    Unrestricted="true"/>
   </PermissionSet>
```

```
optional permission set:
<PermissionSet class="System.Security.PermissionSet" version="1">
   <IPermission class="System.Security.Permissions.SecurityPermission, mscorlib,
                      Version=1.0.5000.0, Culture=neutral,
                      PublicKeyToken=b77a5c561934e089"
                      version="1"
                      Flags="UnmanagedCode"/>
</PermissionSet>

refused permission set:
<PermissionSet class="System.Security.PermissionSet"
                      version="1">
   <IPermission class="System.Security.Permissions.FileIOPermission, mscorlib,
                      Version=1.0.5500.0, Culture=neutral,
                      PublicKeyToken=b77a5c561934e089"
                      version="1"
                      Read="c:\"/>
</PermissionSet>
```

In addition to requesting permissions, you can also request permissions sets; the advantage is that you can request a whole set of permissions all at once. Since the Everything permission set can be altered through the security policy while an assembly is running, it cannot be requested. For example, if an assembly requests at runtime that it must be granted all permissions in the Everything permission set to execute, and the administrator then tightens the Everything permission set while the application is running, he might be unaware that the permission set is still operating with a wider set of permissions than the policy dictates.

Here's an example, of how to request a built-in permission set:

```
[assembly:PermissionSetAttribute(SecurityAction.RequestMinimum,
                             Name = "FullTrust")]
```

In this example the assembly requests that as a minimum it needs the FullTrust built-in permission set granted. If this set of permissions is not granted, the assembly will throw a security exception at runtime.

Implicit Permission

When permissions are granted, there is often an implicit statement that we are also granted other permissions. For example, if you assign the FileIOPermission for C:\ there is an implicit assumption that there is also access to its subdirectories (Windows account security allowing).

If you want to check whether a granted permission implicitly brings another permission as a subset, you can do this:

```
// Example from SecurityApp3

   class SecurityApp3
   {
      static void Main(string[] args)
      {
```

```
        CodeAccessPermission permissionA =
            new FileIOPermission(FileIOPermissionAccess.AllAccess, @"C:\");
        CodeAccessPermission permissionB =
            new FileIOPermission(FileIOPermissionAccess.Read, @"C:\temp");
        if (permissionB.IsSubsetOf(permissionA))
        {
            Console.WriteLine("PermissionB is a subset of PermissionA");
        }
        else
        {
            Console.WriteLine("PermissionB is NOT a subset of PermissionA");
        }
    }
}
```

The output looks like this:

```
PermissionB is a subset of PermissionA
```

Denying Permissions

Under certain circumstances you might want to perform an action and be absolutely sure that the method that is called is acting within a protected environment where it cannot do anything untoward. For example, let's say you want to make a call to a third-party class in a way that it will not access the local disk.

To do that, create an instance of the permission you want to ensure the method is not granted, and then call its `Deny()` method before making the call to the class:

```
using System;
using System.IO;
using System.Security;
using System.Security.Permissions;
namespace Wrox.ProCSharp.Security
{
    class SecurityApp4
    {
        static void Main(string[] args)
        {
            CodeAccessPermission permission =
                new FileIOPermission(FileIOPermissionAccess.AllAccess,@"C:\");
            permission.Deny();
            UntrustworthyClass.Method();
            CodeAccessPermission.RevertDeny();
        }
    }
    class UntrustworthyClass
    {
        public static void Method()
        {
            try
            {
```

```
                    StreamReader din = File.OpenText(@"C:\textfile.txt");
                }
                catch
                {
                    Console.WriteLine("Failed to open file");
                }
            }
        }
    }
```

If you build this code the output will state *Failed to open file*, as the untrustworthy class does not have access to the local disk.

Note that the `Deny()` call is made on an instance of the `permission` object, whereas the `RevertDeny()` call is made statically. The reason for this is that the `RevertDeny()` call reverts all deny requests within the current stack frame; this means if you have made several calls to `Deny()` you only need to make one follow-up call to `RevertDeny()`.

Asserting Permissions

Imagine that there is an assembly that has been installed with full trust on a user's system. Within that assembly there is a method that saves auditing information to a text file on the local disk. If later an application is installed that wants to make use of the auditing feature, it will be necessary for the application to have the relevant FileIOPermission permissions to save the data to disk.

This seems excessive, however, because all we really want to do is perform a highly restricted action on the local disk. In these situations, it would be useful if assemblies with limiting permissions could make calls to more trusted assemblies that can temporarily increase the scope of the permissions on the stack, and perform operations on behalf of the caller that it does not have the permissions to do itself.

To achieve this, assemblies with high enough levels of trust can assert permissions that they require. If the assembly has the permissions it needs to assert additional permissions, it removes the need for callers up the stack to have such wide-ranging permissions.

The code that follows contains a class called `AuditClass` that implements a method called `Save()`, which takes a string and saves audit data to C:\audit.txt. The `AuditClass` method asserts the permissions it needs to add the audit lines to the file. To test it out, the `Main()` method for the application explicitly denies the file permission that the `Audit` method needs:

```csharp
using System;
using System.IO;
using System.Security;
using System.Security.Permissions;
namespace Wrox.ProCSharp.Security
{
    class SecurityApp5
    {
        static void Main(string[] args)
        {
            CodeAccessPermission permission =
```

```
                    new FileIOPermission(FileIOPermissionAccess.Append,
                                    @"C:\audit.txt");
            permission.Deny();
            AuditClass.Save("some data to audit");
            CodeAccessPermission.RevertDeny();
        }
    }
    class AuditClass
    {
        public static void Save(string value)
        {
            try
            {
                FileIOPermission permission =
                    new FileIOPermission(FileIOPermissionAccess.Append,
                                    @"C:\audit.txt");
                permission.Assert();
                FileStream stream = new FileStream(@"C:\audit.txt",
                    FileMode.Append, FileAccess.Write);

                // code to write to audit file here...
                CodeAccessPermission.RevertAssert();
                Console.WriteLine("Data written to audit file");
            }
            catch
            {
                Console.WriteLine("Failed to write data to audit file");
            }
        }
    }
}
```

When this code is executed, you'll find that the call to the `AuditClass` method does not cause a security exception, even though when it was called it did not have the required permissions to carry out the disk access.

Like `RevertDeny()`, `RevertAssert()` is a static method, and it reverts all assertions within the current frame.

It's important to be very careful when using assertions. We are explicitly assigning permissions to a method that has been called by code that might not have those permissions, and this could open a security hole. For example, in the auditing example, even if the security policy dictated that an installed application cannot write to the local disk, our assembly would be able to write to the disk when the auditing assembly asserts `FileIOPermissions` for writing. To perform the assertion the auditing assembly must have been installed with permission for `FileIOAccess` and `SecurityPermission`. The `SecurityPermission` allows an assembly to perform an assert, and the assembly will need both the `SecurityPermission` and the permission being asserted to complete successfully.

Creating Code Access Permissions

The .NET Framework implements code access security permissions that provide protection for the resources that it exposes. However, there might be occasions when you want to create your own permissions. You can do so by subclassing CodeAccessPermission. Deriving a custom permission class from the class CodeAccessPermission gives you the benefits of the .NET code access security system, including stack walking and policy management.

Here are two examples of cases where you might want to roll your own code access permissions:

❑ **Protecting a resource not already protected by the Framework.** For example, you have developed a .NET application for home automation that is implemented by using an onboard hardware device. Creating your own code access permissions, you have a highly granular level of control over the access given to the home automation hardware.

❑ **Providing a finer degree of management than existing permissions.** For example, although the .NET Framework provides permissions that allow granular control over access to the local file system, you might have an application where you want to control access to a specific file or folder much more tightly. In this scenario, you might find it useful to create a code access permission that relates specifically to that file or folder; without that permission no managed code can access that area of the disk.

Declarative Security

You can deny, demand, and assert permissions by calling classes in the .NET Framework. However, you can also use attributes and specify permission requirements declaratively.

The main benefit of using declarative security is that the settings are accessible through reflection. This can be of enormous benefit to system administrators, who often will want to view the security requirements of applications.

For example, we can specify that a method must have permission to read from C:\ to execute:

```
using System;
using System.Security.Permissions;
namespace Wrox.ProCSharp.Security
{
    class SecurityApp6
    {
        static void Main(string[] args)
        {
            MyClass.Method();
        }
    }

    [FileIOPermission(SecurityAction.Assert, Read="C:\\")]
    class MyClass
    {
        public static void Method()
        {
```

```
        // implementation goes here

    }
  }
}
```

Be aware that if you use attributes to assert or demand permissions, you cannot catch any exceptions that are raised if the action fails, because there is no imperative code around in which you can place a `try-catch-finally` clause.

Role-Based Security

As you have seen, code access security gives the CLR the ability to make intelligent decisions behind the scenes as to whether code should run and with what permissions based on the evidence it presents. In addition, .NET provides role-based security that specifies whether code can perform actions on the basis of evidence about the user and their role, rather than just the code. You'll probably be glad to hear that it does this without walking the stack!

Role-based security is especially useful in situations where access to resources is an issue; a primary example is the finance industry, where employees' roles define what information they can access and what actions they can perform.

Role-based security is also ideal for use in conjunction with Windows accounts, Microsoft Passport, or a custom user directory to manage access to Web-based resources. For example, a Web site could restrict access to its content until a user registers with the site, and then additionally provide access to special content only, if the user is a paying subscriber. In many ways, ASP.NET makes role-based security easier because much of the code is based on the server.

For example, if you want to implement a Web service that requires authentication, you could use the account subsystem of Windows and write the Web method in such a way that it ensures the user is a member of a specific Windows user group before allowing access to the method's functionality.

The Principal

.NET gives the current thread easy access to the application user, which it refers to as a principal. The principal is at the core of the role-based security that .NET provides, and through it, we can access the user's identity, which will usually map to a user account of one of these types:

❑   Windows account

❑   Passport account

❑   ASP.NET cookie-authenticated user

As an added bonus, the role-based security in .NET has been designed so that you can create your own principals by implementing the `IPrincipal` interface. If you are not relying on Windows authentication, Passport, or simple cookie authentication, you should look at creating your own using a custom principal class.

With access to the principal you can make security decisions based on the principal's identity and roles. A role is a collection of users who have the same security permissions, and is the unit of administration for users. For example, if you're using Windows authentication to authenticate our users, you will use the `WindowsIdentity` type as our choice of identity. You can use that type to find out whether the user is a member of a specific Windows user account group. You can then use that information to decide whether to grant or deny access to code and resources.

You'll generally find that it's much easier to manage security if you allow access to resources and functionality on the basis of roles rather than individual users. Imagine a scenario where you have three methods and each provides access to a feature over which you need tight control to ensure only authorized personnel can access it. If the application had, say, four users, we could quite easily specify within each method which users can and which users cannot access the method. However, imagine a time in the future where the number of features has extended to nine; to allow access to an additional user potentially requires changing every one of the nine methods even though this is an administrative task! Even worse, as users move between roles in the company you would have to change the code each time that happens. If you had instead implemented the system using roles, you could then simply add users to and remove users from roles, rather than adding and removing individual users to and from the application. This simplifies the application, as for each method you simply request that the user be a member of a specific role. It also simplifies the management of roles, as the administrator can do it rather than the application developer. The developer should be concerned with ensuring that, for example, managers but not secretaries can access a method.

.NET's role-based security builds on an idea that has been provided in MTS and COM+, and offers a flexible framework that can be used to build fences around sections of the application that have to be protected. If COM+ is installed on a machine, its role-based security will interoperate with .NET; however, COM is not required for .NET's role-based security to function.

Windows Principal

In the following example we create a console application that gives access to the principal in an application that, in turn, enables us to access the underlying Windows account. You need to import the `System.Security.Principal` and `System.Threading` namespaces. First of all, you must specify that .NET automatically hooks up the principal with the underlying Windows account, as .NET does not automatically populate the thread's `CurrentPrincipal` property for security reasons. You can do that like this:

```
using System;
using System.Security.Principal;
using System.Security.Permissions;
using System.Threading;

namespace Wrox.ProCSharp.Security
{
    class SecurityApp7
    {
        static void Main(string[] args)
        {
            AppDomain.CurrentDomain.SetPrincipalPolicy(
                PrincipalPolicy.WindowsPrincipal);
```

It's possible to use WindowsIdentity.GetCurrent() to access the Windows account details; however, that method is best used when you're only going to look at the principal once. If you want to access the principal a number of times it is more efficient to set the policy so that the current thread provides access to the principal for you. Using the SetPrincipalPolicy method it is specified that the principal in the current thread should hold a WindowsIdentity object. All identity classes, like WindowsIdentity, implement the IIdentity interface. The interface contains three properties (AuthenticationType, IsAuthenticated, and Name) for all derived identity classes to implement.

Let's add some code to access the principal's properties from the Thread object:

```
        WindowsPrincipal principal =
            (WindowsPrincipal)Thread.CurrentPrincipal;
        WindowsIdentity identity = (WindowsIdentity)principal.Identity;
        Console.WriteLine("IdentityType:" + identity.ToString());
        Console.WriteLine("Name:" + identity.Name);
        Console.WriteLine("'Users'?:" + principal.IsInRole("BUILTIN\\Users"));
        Console.WriteLine("'Administrators'?:" +
            principal.IsInRole(WindowsBuiltInRole.Administrator));
        Console.WriteLine("Authenticated:" + identity.IsAuthenticated);
        Console.WriteLine("AuthType:" + identity.AuthenticationType);
        Console.WriteLine("Anonymous?:" + identity.IsAnonymous);
        Console.WriteLine("Token:" + identity.Token);
    }
  }
}
```

The output from this console application looks similar to the following lines, depending on your machine configuration and the roles associated with the account under which you're signed in:

```
IdentityType:System.Security.Principal.WindowsIdentity
Name:MACHINE\alaric
'Users'?:True
'Administrators'?:True
Authenticated:True
AuthType:NTLM
Anonymous?:False
Token:256
```

It is enormously beneficial to be able to access details about the current user and their roles so easily. With this information we can make decisions about what actions to permit and to deny. The ability to make use of roles and Windows user groups provides the added benefit that administration can be done by using standard user administration tools, and you can usually avoid altering the code when user roles change. Let's look at roles in more detail.

Roles

Imagine a scenario with an intranet application that relies on Windows accounts. The system has a group called Manager and one called Assistant; users are assigned to these groups dependent on their role within the organization. Let's say the application contains a feature that displays information about employees that should only be accessed by users in the Managers group. You can easily use code that checks whether the current user is a member of the Managers group and permit or deny access based on this.

417

However, if you decide later to rearrange the account groups and to introduce a group called `Personnel` that also has access to employee details, you will have a problem. This way you have to go through all the code and update it in order to include rules for this new group.

A better solution would be to create a permission called something like `ReadEmployeeDetails` and to assign it to groups where necessary. If the code applies a check for the `ReadEmployeeDetails` permission, in order to update the application to allow those in the `Personnel` group access to employee details is simply a matter of creating the group, placing the users in it, and assigning the `ReadEmployeeDetails` permission.

Declarative Role-Based Security

Just as with code access security, you can implement role-based security requests ("the user must be in the Administrators group") using imperative requests (as you saw in the preceding section), or using attributes. You can state permission requirements declaratively at the class level like this:

```csharp
using System;
using System.Security;
using System.Security.Principal;
using System.Security.Permissions;

namespace Wrox.ProCSharp.Security
{
    class SecurityApp8
    {
        static void Main(string[] args)
        {
            AppDomain.CurrentDomain.SetPrincipalPolicy(
                PrincipalPolicy.WindowsPrincipal);
            try
            {
                ShowMessage();
            }
            catch (SecurityException exception)
            {
                Console.WriteLine("Security exception caught (" +
                                exception.Message + ")");
                Console.WriteLine("The current principal must be in the local"
                                + "Users group");
            }
        }

        [PrincipalPermissionAttribute(SecurityAction.Demand,
                                Role = "BUILTIN\\Users")]
        static void ShowMessage()
        {
            Console.WriteLine("The current principal is logged in locally ");
            Console.WriteLine("(they are a member of the local Users group)");
        }
    }
}
```

The `ShowMessage()` method will throw an exception unless you execute the application in the context of a user in the Windows local Users group. For a Web application, the account under which the ASP.NET code is running must be in the group, although in a real-world example you would certainly avoid adding this account to the administrators group!

If you run the previous code using an account in the local Users group, the output will look like this:

```
The current principal is logged in locally
(they are a member of the local Users group)
```

For more information on role-based security in .NET, your first stop should be the MSDN documentation for the `System.Security.Principal` namespace.

Managing Security Policy

Although .NET's security features are wide ranging and far in advance of anything seen before on Windows, there are some limitations that we should be aware of:

❑ .NET security policy does not enforce security on unmanaged code (although it provides some protection against calls to unmanaged code).

❑ If a user copies an assembly to a local machine, the assembly has FullTrust and security policy is effectively bypassed. To work around this, you can limit the permissions granted to local code.

❑ .NET security policy provides very little help in dealing with script-based viruses and malicious Win32 .exe files, which Microsoft is dealing with in different ways. For example, recent versions of Outlook block executable files from e-mails.

However, .NET helps enormously in assisting the operating system in making intelligent decisions about how much trust to give to code, whether it originates from an intranet application, a control on a Web page, or a Windows Forms application downloaded from a software supplier on the Internet.

The Security Configuration File

As you've already seen, the glue that connects code groups, permissions, and permission sets consists of our three levels of security policy (enterprise, machine, and user). Security configuration information in .NET is stored in XML configuration files that are protected by Windows security. For example, the machine-level security policy is only writable to users in the Administrator, Power User, and SYSTEM Windows groups.

The files that store the security policy are located in the following paths:

❑ Enterprise policy configuration: *<windir>\Microsoft.NET\Framework\v1.0.xxxx\Config\ enterprise.config*

❑ Machine policy configuration: *<windir>\Microsoft.NET\Framework\v1.0.xxxx\Config\ security.config*

❑ User policy configuration: *%USERPROFILE%\application data\Microsoft\ CLR security config\vxx.xx\security.config*

The version number marked with multiple *x*s varies depending on the version of the .NET Framework you have on your machine. If necessary, it's possible to edit these configuration files manually, for example, if an administrator needs to configure policy for a user without logging into his account. However, in general it's recommended to use caspol.exe or the Runtime Security Policy node in the .NET Framework Configuration MMC snap-in to manage security policy.

A simple example

Given everything you've read so far, create a simple application that accesses the local drive, the kind of behavior we're likely to want to manage carefully. The application is a C# Windows Forms application with a list box and a button (see Figure 14-7). If you click the button, the list box is populated from a file called *animals.txt* in the root of the C:\ drive.

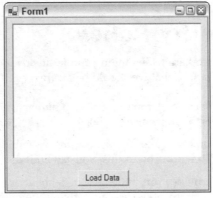

Figure 14-7

The application was created by using Visual Studio .NET and the only changes were to add the list box and Load Data button to the form and to add an event to the button that looks like this:

```
// Example from SecurityApp9

private void button1_Click(object sender, System.EventArgs e)
{
    StreamReader stream = File.OpenText(@"C:\animals.txt");
    String str;
    while ((str=stream.ReadLine()) != null)
    {
        listBox1.Items.Add(str);
    }
}
```

It opens a simple text file from the root of the C:\ drive, which contains a list of animals on separate lines, and loads each line into a string, which it then uses to create each item in the list box.

If you run the application from our local machine and click the button, you'll see the data loaded from the root of the C:\ drive and displayed in the list box (see Figure 14-8). Behind the scenes the runtime has granted the assembly the permission it needs to execute, access the user interface, and read data from the local disk.

Figure 14-8

As mentioned earlier, the permissions on the intranet zone code group are more restrictive than on the local machine; in particular, they do not allow access to the local disk. If you run the application again, but this time from a network share, it will run just as before because it is granted the permissions to execute and access the user interface; however, if you now click the *Load Data* button on the form, a security exception is thrown (see Figure 14-9). You'll see in the exception message text that it mentions the `System.Security.Permissions.FileIOPermission` object; this is the permission that the application was not granted and that was demanded by the class in the Framework which was used to load the data from the file on the local disk.

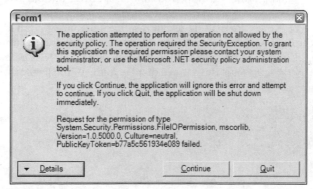

Figure 14-9

By default, the Intranet code group is granted the LocalIntranet permission set; let's change the permission set to FullTrust so any code from the intranet zone can run completely unrestricted.

First, you need to get the numeric label of the LocalIntranet code group. You can do this with the following command.

```
>caspol.exe -listgroups
```

This will output something like this:

```
Code Groups:

1.  All code: Nothing
    1.1.  Zone - MyComputer: FullTrust
        1.1.1.  StrongName -
002400000480000009400000006020000002400005253413100040000010001007D1FA57C4AED9F0A32
E84AA0FAEFD0DE9E8FD6AEC8F87FB03766C834C99921EB23BE79AD9D5DCC1DD9AD236132102900B723C
F980957FC4E177108FC607774F29E8320E92EA05ECE4E821C0A5EFE8F1645C4C0C93C1AB99285D622CA
A652C1DFAD63D745D6F2DE5F17E5EAF0FC4963D261C8A12436518206DC093344D5AD293: FullTrust
        1.1.2.  StrongName - 0000000000000000400000000000000: FullTrust
    1.2.  Zone - Intranet: LocalIntranet
        1.2.1.  All code: Same site Web.
        1.2.2.  All code: Same directory FileIO - Read, PathDiscovery
    1.3.  Zone - Internet: Internet
        1.3.1.  All code: Same site Web.
    1.4.  Zone - Untrusted: Nothing
    1.5.  Zone - Trusted: Internet
        1.5.1.  All code: Same site Web.
```

Notice the LocalIntranet group is listed as 1.2. You can use the following command to apply full trust:

```
>caspol.exe -chggroup 1.2 FullTrust
```

If you run the application from the network share again and click the button, you'll see that the list box is populated with the content of the file in the root of the C:\ drive and no exception occurs.

In scenarios like these where you're making use of resources that are governed by permissions, it is advisable to extend the code so that security exceptions are caught, and the application can degrade gracefully. For example, in the sample application you can add a try-catch block around the file access code and if a SecurityException is thrown we display a line in the list box saying, *Permission denied accessing file*:

```
// Code from SecurityApp9

private void button1_Click(object sender, System.EventArgs e)
{
    try
    {
        StreamReader din = File.OpenText(@"C:\animals.txt");
        String str;
        while ((str=din.ReadLine()) != null)
        {
            listBox1.Items.Add(str);
        }
    }
    catch (SecurityException exception)
    {
        listBox1.Items.Add("Permission denied accessing file");
    }
}
```

In reality, if you wanted to run a specific application from a network share, you'd most likely opt for a solution that didn't open up the client machine to all code on the intranet. Instead, code groups and membership conditions can be used to tightly control the requirements of the application—perhaps using its location on the intranet, a strong name, or a certificate proving the identity of the publisher.

Managing Code Groups and Permissions

Managing security on .NET, if you find that an assembly is failing with a security exception, you usually have three choices:

- ❏ Ease the policy permissions
- ❏ Move the assembly
- ❏ Apply a strong name to the assembly

When making these kinds of decisions you must ensure that you have to take into account your level of trust of the assembly.

Turning Security On and Off

By default .NET security is enabled. If, for any reason, you need to turn it off, you can do it like this:

```
>caspol.exe -security off
```

To turn security back on, use this:

```
>caspol.exe -security on
```

Generally, the security risks are too high when you turn off security. We recommend you only do this for testing and debugging purposes.

Something you should be aware of is that the previous command does not need administrative privileges; this means any user (or a virus) could turn off .NET security. You are well advised to alter the Windows file security on the caspol utility to guard against malicious or misinformed usage.

Resetting Security Policy

If you need to return the security configuration to its original state, you can type this command:

```
>caspol.exe -reset
```

This command resets the security policy to the installation default.

Creating a Code Group

You can create your own code groups and then apply specific permissions to them. For example, you could specify that we want to trust all code from the Web site www.wrox.com and to give it full access to the system (without trusting code from any other Web site).

Earlier it was already shown running caspol to display a list with the available group and number assignments. The zone Internet is labeled 1.3, so now type this command:

```
>caspol.exe -addgroup 1.3 -site www.wrox.com FullTrust
```

Note that this command will ask for confirmation, because this is an attempt to alter the security policy on the machine. If the command caspol.exe –listgroups is now run again, you'll see the new code group has been added and assigned FullTrust:

```
...
1.2.   Zone - Intranet: LocalIntranet
    1.2.1.  All code: Same site Web.
    1.2.2.  All code: Same directory FileIO - Read, PathDiscovery
  1.3.   Zone - Internet: Internet
    1.3.1.  All code: Same site Web.
    1.3.2.  Site - www.wrox.com: FullTrust
  1.4.   Zone - Untrusted: Nothing
  1.5.   Zone - Trusted: Internet
    1.5.1.  All code: Same site Web.
```

Let's look at another example. Let's say we want to create a code group under the Intranet code group *(1.2)* that grants FullTrust to all applications running from a specific network share:

```
>caspol.exe -addgroup 1.2 -url file:///\\intranetserver/sharename/* FullTrust
```

Deleting a Code Group

To remove a code group that has been created, you can type a command like this:

```
>caspol.exe -remgroup 1.3.2
```

It will ask for confirmation that you want to alter the security policy, and if you give positive confirmation it will state that the group has been removed.

> **Be aware that although you cannot delete the code group All Code, you can delete code groups at the level below, including the Internet, MyComputer, and LocalIntranet groups.**

Changing a Code Group's Permissions

To ease or restrict the permissions assigned to a code group, caspol.exe will be used again. Let's say we want to apply FullTrust to the Intranet zone, first we need to get the label that represents the Intranet code group:

```
>caspol.exe -listgroups
```

The output shows the Intranet code group:

```
Code Groups:

1.  All code: Nothing
    1.1.   Zone - MyComputer: FullTrust
       1.1.1.   StrongName -
0024000004800000940000000602000000240000525341310004000001000100007D1FA57C4AED9F0A32
E84AA0FAEFD0DE9E8FD6AEC8F87FB03766C834C99921EB23BE79AD9D5DCC1DD9AD236132102900B72
3CF980957FC4E177108FC607774F29E8320E92EA05ECE4E821C0A5EFE8F1645C4C0C93C1AB99285D622
CAA652C1DFAD63D745D6F2DE5F17E5EAF0FC4963D261C8A12436518206DC093344D5AD293:
FullTrust
       1.1.2.   StrongName - 00000000000000000400000000000000: FullTrust
    1.2.   Zone - Intranet: LocalIntranet
       1.2.1.   All code: Same site Web.
       1.2.2.   All code: Same directory FileIO - Read, PathDiscovery
    1.3.   Zone - Internet: Internet
       1.3.1.   All code: Same site Web.
    1.4.   Zone - Untrusted: Nothing
    1.5.   Zone - Trusted: Internet
       1.5.1.   All code: Same site Web.
```

Once you have the Intranet code group's label, 1.2, you can enter a second command to alter the code group's permissions:

```
>caspol.exe -chggroup 1.2 FullTrust
```

The command asks to confirm the change to the security policy, and if you run the caspol.exe –listgroups command again, you can see the permission on the end of the Intranet line has changed to FullTrust:

```
Code Groups:

1.  All code: Nothing
    1.1.   Zone - MyComputer: FullTrust
       1.1.1.   StrongName -
0024000004800000940000000602000000240000525341310004000001000100007D1FA57C4AED9F0A32
E84AA0FAEFD0DE9E8FD6AEC8F87FB03766C834C99921EB23BE79AD9D5DCC1DD9AD236132102900B723C
F980957FC4E177108FC607774F29E8320E92EA05ECE4E821C0A5EFE8F1645C4C0C93C1AB99285D622CA
A652C1DFAD63D745D6F2DE5F17E5EAF0FC4963D261C8A12436518206DC093344D5AD293: FullTrust
       1.1.2.   StrongName - 00000000000000000400000000000000: FullTrust
    1.2.   Zone - Intranet: FullTrust
       1.2.1.   All code: Same site Web.
       1.2.2.   All code: Same directory FileIO - Read, PathDiscovery
    1.3.   Zone - Internet: Internet
       1.3.1.   All code: Same site Web.
    1.4.   Zone - Untrusted: Nothing
    1.5.   Zone - Trusted: Internet
       1.5.1.   All code: Same site Web.
```

Creating and Applying Permissions Sets

You can create new permission sets using a command like this:

```
>caspol.exe -addpset MyCustomPermissionSet permissionset.xml
```

425

This command specifies that we are creating a new permissions set called MyCustomPermissionSet, and basing it on the contents of the specified XML file. The XML file must contain a standard format that specifies a `PermissionSet`. For reference, here's the permission set file for the Everything permission set, which you can trim down to the permission set you want to create:

```xml
<PermissionSet class="System.Security.NamedPermissionSet"
            version="1"
            Name="Everything"
            Description="Allows unrestricted access to all
                resources covered by built-in permissions">
    <IPermission class="System.Security.Permissions.EnvironmentPermission,
        mscorlib, Version=1.0.5000.0, Culture=neutral,
        PublicKeyToken=b77a5c561934e089"
      version="1" Unrestricted="true"/>
    <IPermission class="System.Security.Permissions.FileDialogPermission,
        mscorlib, Version=1.0.5000.0, Culture=neutral,
        PublicKeyToken=b77a5c561934e089"
      version="1" Unrestricted="true"/>
    <IPermission class="System.Security.Permissions.FileIOPermission,
        mscorlib, Version=1.0.5000.0, Culture=neutral,
        PublicKeyToken=b77a5c561934e089"
      version="1" Unrestricted="true"/>
    <IPermission class="System.Security.Permissions.IsolatedStorageFilePermission,
        mscorlib, Version=1.0.5000.0, Culture=neutral,
        PublicKeyToken=b77a5c561934e089"
      version="1" Unrestricted="true"/>
    <IPermission class="System.Security.Permissions.ReflectionPermission,
        mscorlib, Version=1.0.5000.0, Culture=neutral,
        PublicKeyToken=b77a5c561934e089"
      version="1" Unrestricted="true"/>
    <IPermission class="System.Security.Permissions.RegistryPermission,
        mscorlib, Version=1.0.5000.0, Culture=neutral,
        PublicKeyToken=b77a5c561934e089"
      version="1" Unrestricted="true"/>
    <IPermission class="System.Security.Permissions.SecurityPermission,
        mscorlib, Version=1.0.5000.0, Culture=neutral,
        PublicKeyToken=b77a5c561934e089"
      version="1"
      Flags="Assertion, UnmanagedCode, Execution, ControlThread, ControlEvidence,
            ControlPolicy, SerializationFormatter, ControlDomainPolicy,
            ControlPrincipal, ControlAppDomain, RemotingConfiguration,
            Infrastructure"/>
    <IPermission class="System.Security.Permissions.UIPermission,
        mscorlib, Version=1.0.5000.0, Culture=neutral,
        PublicKeyToken=b77a5c561934e089"
      version="1" Unrestricted="true"/>
    <IPermission class="System.Net.DnsPermission, System, Version=1.0.3300.0,
        Culture=neutral, PublicKeyToken=b77a5c561934e089"
      version="1" Unrestricted="true"/>
    <IPermission class="System.Drawing.Printing.PrintingPermission,
        System.Drawing, Version=1.0.5000.0, Culture=neutral,
        PublicKeyToken=b03f5f7f11d50a3a"
      version="1" Unrestricted="true"/>
    <IPermission class="System.Diagnostics.EventLogPermission, System,
```

```
                    Version=1.0.5000.0, Culture=neutral,
                    PublicKeyToken=b77a5c561934e089"
            version="1" Unrestricted="true"/>
    <IPermission class="System.Net.SocketPermission, System, Version=1.0.5000.0,
            Culture=neutral, PublicKeyToken=b77a5c561934e089"
            version="1" Unrestricted="true"/>
    <IPermission class="System.Net.WebPermission, System, Version=1.0.5000.0,
            Culture=neutral, PublicKeyToken=b77a5c561934e089"
            version="1" Unrestricted="true"/>
    <IPermission class="System.Diagnostics.PerformanceCounterPermission, System,
            Version=1.0.5000.0, Culture=neutral,
            PublicKeyToken=b77a5c561934e089"
            version="1" Unrestricted="true"/>
    <IPermission class="System.DirectoryServices.DirectoryServicesPermission,
            System.DirectoryServices, Version=1.0.5000.0,
            Culture=neutral, PublicKeyToken=b03f5f7f11d50a3a"
            version="1" Unrestricted="true"/>
    <IPermission class="System.Messaging.MessageQueuePermission, System.Messaging,
            Version=1.0.5000.0, Culture=neutral,
            PublicKeyToken=b03f5f7f11d50a3a"
            version="1" Unrestricted="true"/>
    <IPermission class="System.ServiceProcess.ServiceControllerPermission,
            System.ServiceProcess, Version=1.0.5000.0, Culture=neutral,
            PublicKeyToken=b03f5f7f11d50a3a"
            version="1" Unrestricted="true"/>
    <IPermission class="System.Data.OleDb.OleDbPermission, System.Data,
            Version=1.0.5000.0, Culture=neutral,
            PublicKeyToken=b77a5c561934e089"
            version="1" AllowBlankPassword="False" Unrestricted="true"/>
    <IPermission class="System.Data.SqlClient.SqlClientPermission, System.Data,
            Version=1.0.5000.0, Culture=neutral,
            PublicKeyToken=b77a5c561934e089"
            version="1" AllowBlankPassword="False" Unrestricted="true"/>
</PermissionSet>
```

To view all permission sets in XML format, you can use this command:

```
>caspol.exe -listpset
```

If you want to give a new definition to an existing permission set by applying an XML PermissionSet configuration file, you can use this command:

```
>caspol.exe -chgpset permissionset.xml MyCustomPermissionSet
```

Distributing Code Using a Strong Name

.NET provides the ability to match an assembly to a code group when the assembly's identity and integrity have been confirmed using a strong name. This scenario is very common when assemblies are being deployed across networks, for example, distributing software over the Internet.

If you are a software company, and you want to provide code to your customers via the Internet, you build an assembly and give it a strong name. The strong name ensures that the assembly can be uniquely identified, and also provides protection against tampering. Your customers can incorporate this strong name into their code access security policy; an assembly that matches this unique strong name can then be assigned permissions explicitly. As we discussed in Chapter 13, the strong name includes checksums for hashes of all the files within an assembly, so we have strong evidence that the assembly has not been altered since the publisher created the strong name.

Note that, if your application uses an installer, the installer will install assemblies that have already been given a strong name. The strong name is generated once for each distribution before being sent to customers; the installer does not run these commands. The reason for this is that the strong name provides an assurance that the assembly has not been modified since it left your company; a common way to achieve this is to give your customer not only the application code, but also, separately, a copy of the strong name for the assembly. You might find it beneficial to pass the strong name to your customer using a secure form (perhaps fax or encrypted e-mail) to guard against the assembly being tampered with in the process.

Let's look at an example where an assembly with a strong name is created to distribute it in such a way that the recipient of the assembly can use the strong name to grant the FullTrust permission to the assembly.

First, a key pair is needed, because strong names make use of public key encryption. The public and private keys are stored in the file we specify and are used to sign the strong name. To create a key pair, use the Strong Name utility (sn.exe), which in addition to helping us create key pairs can also be used to manage keys and strong names. Create a key file by typing the following command:

```
>sn.exe -k key.snk
```

Then place the key file key.snk in the project folder and add the key to the code using an assembly attribute. After you have added this attribute to the file AssemblyInfo.cs, you have to rebuild the assembly. The recompilation ensures the hash is recalculated and the assembly is protected against malicious modifications.

```
[assembly: AssemblyKeyFileAttribute("../../key.snk")]
```

The assembly has now been compiled and signed; it has a unique identifying strong name. Now you can create a new code group on the machine where we want the assembly to execute, which has a membership condition that requires a match for the strong name of the assembly.

The following command states that a new code group is created using the strong name from the specified assembly manifest file, that the code group is independent of the version number of the assembly, and that the code group has granted the FullTrust permissions:

```
>caspol.exe -addgroup 1 -strong -file \bin\debug\SecurityApp10.exe -noname -
noversion FullTrust
```

In this example the application will now run from any zone, even the Internet zone, because the strong name provides powerful evidence that the assembly can be trusted. If we look at our code groups using caspol.exe -listgroups, you'll see the new code group (1.6 and its associated public key in hexadecimal):

```
Code Groups:

1.  All code: Nothing
```

```
   1.1.   Zone - MyComputer: FullTrust
      1.1.1.  StrongName -
0024000004800000940000000602000000240000525341310004000001000100007D1FA57C4AED9F0A32
E84AA0FAEFD0DE9E8FD6AEC8F87FB03766C834C99921EB23BE79AD9D5DCC1DD9AD236132102900B723C
F980957FC4E177108FC607774F29E8320E92EA05ECE4E821C0A5EFE8F1645C4C0C93C1AB99285D622CA
A652C1DFAD63D745D6F2DE5F17E5EAF0FC4963D261C8A12436518206DC093344D5AD293: FullTrust
      1.1.2.  StrongName - 00000000000000000400000000000000: FullTrust
   1.2.   Zone - Intranet: LocalIntranet
      1.2.1.  All code: Same site Web.
      1.2.2.  All code: Same directory FileIO - Read, PathDiscovery
   1.3.   Zone - Internet: Internet
      1.3.1.  All code: Same site Web.
   1.4.   Zone - Untrusted: Nothing
   1.5.   Zone - Trusted: Internet
      1.5.1.  All code: Same site Web.
   1.6.   StrongName -
0024000004800000940000000602000000240000525341310004000001000100D51335D1B5B64BE976A
D8B08030F8E36A0DBBC3EEB5F8A18D0E30E8951DA059B440281997D760FFF61A6252A284061C1D714EF
EE5B329F410983A01DB324FA85BCE6C4E6384A2F3BC1FFA01E2586816B23888CFADD38D5AA5DF041ACE
2F81D9E8B591556852E83C473017A1785203B12F56B6D9DC23A8C9F691A0BC525D7B7EA: FullTrust
Success
```

If you want to access the strong name in an assembly you can use the secutil.exe tool against the assembly manifest file. Let's use secutil.exe to view the strong name information for our assembly. Using the -hex option, the public key is shown in hexadecimal (like caspol.exe); the argument -strongname specifies that the strong name should be shown. Type this command, and you'll see a listing containing the strong name public key, the assembly name, and the assembly version:

```
>secutil.exe -hex -strongname securityapp10.exe
Microsoft (R) .NET Framework SecUtil 1.1.4322.573
Copyright (C) Microsoft Corporation 1998-2002. All rights reserved.

Public Key =
0x0024000004800000940000000602000000240000525341310004000001000100D51335D1B5B64BE97
6AD8B08030F8E36A0DBBC3EEB5F8A18D0E30E8951DA059B440281997D760FFF61A6252A284061C1D714
EFEE5B329F410983A01DB324FA85BCE6C4E6384A2F3BC1FFA01E2586816B23888CFADD38D5AA5DF041A
CE2F81D9E8B591556852E83C473017A1785203B12F56B6D9DC23A8C9F691A0BC525D7B7EA
Name =
SecurityApp10
Version =
1.0.1372.39648
Success
```

The curious among you might be wondering what the two strong name code groups installed by default refer to. One is a strong name key for Microsoft code; the other strong name key is for the parts of .NET that have been submitted to the ECMA for standardization, which Microsoft will have much less control over.

Distributing Code Using Certificates

In the last section it was discussed how a strong name can be applied to an assembly so system administrators can explicitly grant permissions to assemblies that match that strong name using a code access group. Although this method of security policy management can be very effective, it's sometimes necessary to work at a higher level, where the administrator of the security policy grants permissions on the basis of the publisher of the software, rather than each individual software component. You'll probably have seen a similar method used before when you have downloaded executables from the Internet that have been Authenticode signed.

To provide information about the software publisher, you can make use of digital certificates and sign assemblies so that consumers of the software can verify the identity of the software publisher. In a commercial environment you would obtain a certificate from a company such as Verisign or Thawte.

The benefit of purchasing a certificate from a supplier such as this, rather than creating your own, is that it provides high levels of trust in its authenticity; the supplier acts as a trusted third-party. For test purposes however .NET includes a command line utility we can use to create a test certificate. The process of creating certificates and using them to publish software is complex, but to give you a picture of what's involved we'll walk through an example without going into too much detail; if we did this chapter would be twice as long!

The sample will be made for the fictive company called ABC Corporation. With this company the software product "ABC Suite" should be trusted. First off, create a test certificate by typing the following command:

```
>makecert -sk ABC -n "CN=ABC Corporation" abccorptest.cer
```

The command creates a test certificate under the name "ABC Corporation" and saves it to a file called abccorptest.cer. The -sk ABC argument creates a key container location, which is used by the public key cryptography.

To sign the assembly with the certificate, use the signcode.exe utility on the assembly file containing the assembly manifest. Often the easiest way to sign an assembly is to use the signcode.exe in its wizard mode; to start the wizard, just type signcode.exe with no parameters.

When you click Next, The program asks you to specify where the file is that should be signed. For an assembly, select the file containing the manifest, for example SecurityApp11.exe, and click the Next button. With the Signing Options page you have to select the Custom option to define the previously created certificate file.

In the next dialog box you are asked to specify the certificate that should be used to sign the assembly. Click Select from File and browse to the file abccorptest.cer. You will now see the confirmation screen shown in Figure 14-10.

The following screen that appears asks you for our private key. This key file was created by the makecert utility, so you can select the options as shown in Figure 14-11. The cryptographic service provider is an application that implements the cryptographic standards (see Chapter 13).

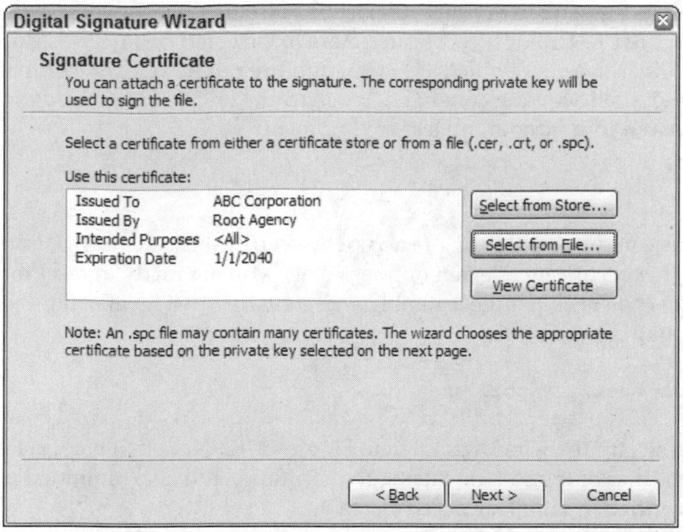

Figure 14-10

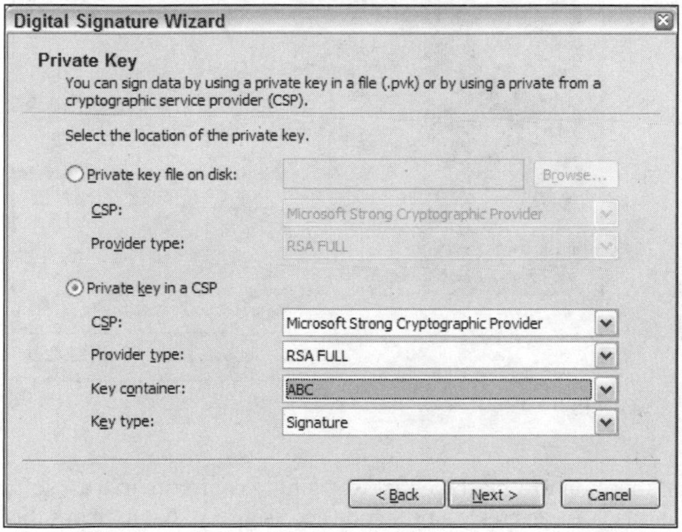

Figure 14-11

Next you're asked a series of questions about the encryption algorithm that should be used for signing the assembly (md5 or sha1), the name and URL of the application, and a final confirmation dialog.

As the executable is now signed with the certificate, a recipient of the assembly has access to strong evidence as to who published the software; the runtime can examine the certificate and match the publisher of the assembly to a code group with high levels of confidence as to the identity of the code, because the trusted third-party certifies the publisher's identity.

Let's look at the signed assembly in a bit more detail. Although a test certificate is used, you can temporarily configure .NET to treat test certificates more like trusted certificates issued by a trusted third-party using the utility setreg.exe, which lets you configure public key and certificate settings in the Registry. If you enter the following command, the machine will be configured to trust the test root certificate, which gives a more meaningful test environment:

```
>setreg.exe 1 true
```

The utility setreg.exe allows configuring to accept test certificates, enable or disable expiration dates on certificates, and other certificate relevant options. When you are ready to reset the value, pass false as the last parameter. You can check out the assembly and verify its trust level using the Certification Verification Tool chktrust.exe utility:

```
>chktrust.exe securityapp11.exe
```

This command brings up the window shown in Figure 14-12. Note that chktrust.exe has successfully confirmed the publisher of the software using the certificate, but also reminded us that, although the certificate has been verified, it is still a test certificate.

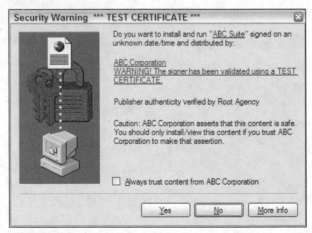

Figure 14-12

Let's now turn our attention to a machine that we want to configure to trust software from the ABC Corporation. To do this you can create a new code access group that matches this software from ABC Corporation. You just have to grab a hexadecimal representation of the certificate from the assembly using the secutil.exe tool:

```
>secutil.exe -hex -x securityapp11.exe
```

This command results in the following output:

```
Microsoft (R) .NET Framework SecUtil 1.1.4322.573
Copyright (c) Microsoft Corp 1999-2002. All rights reserved.

X.509 Certificate =
```

```
0x308201BF30820169A00302010202104A1AF74BCB3F54BC4D1E30685397B68C300D06092A864886F70
D0101040500301631143012060355040313 0B526F6F74204167656E6379301E170D3033313030353039
313730305A170D3339313233313233353935395A301A3118301606035504031 30F41424320436F7270
6F726174696F6E30819F300D06092A864886F70D010101050003818D0030818902818100E537F563C230
4ECDA2DBEC892DED389C3C17E36500F381BD96E1C76185420F4EEA46051AD6972139AC7F0BCE3A473F7
B9E1DA0DB5F19CCB0A1774C7065DF9E56E4EC6E1F301FEEA899BD7D37A66F8150A987CD105059B402DE
641FB635A7E122F70A1F766D4A2B5030B32BA5189E1C918B0EF9E87151DACA49EB0160B051815902030
10001A34B304930470603551D010440303E801012E4092D061D1D4F008D6121DC166463A11830163114
30120603550403130B526F6F74204167656E6379821006376C00AA00648A11CFB8D4AA5C35F4300D060
92A864886F70D010104050003410076FB204253DCA01C5B992DDCCC3CD26F0910E8EDA1C19552491492
8C1916FCD67E6093238152C50EDEBA9476983A9E660DD4849EFE3CFF3A5D2C09B7D4B9585E
Success
```

Let's now create the new code group and apply the FullTrust permission to assemblies published by the ABC Corporation using this (rather long) command:

```
>caspol -addgroup 1 -pub -hex 0x308201BF30820169A00302010202104A1AF74BCB3F54BC4D1E
30685397B68C300D06092A864886F70D0101040500301631143012060355040313 0B526F6F74204167 6
56E6379301E170D3033313030353039313730305A170D3339313233313233353935395A301A31183016
0603550403130F41424320436F72706F726174696F6E30819F300D06092A864886F70D0101010500038
18D0030818902818100E537F563C2304ECDA2DBEC892DED389C3C17E36500F381BD96E1C76185420F4E
EA46051AD6972139AC7F0BCE3A473F7B9E1DA0DB5F19CCB0A1774C7065DF9E56E4EC6E1F301FEEA899B
D7D37A66F8150A987CD105059B402DE641FB635A7E122F70A1F766D4A2B5030B32BA5189E1C918B0EF9
E87151DACA49EB0160B051815902030100 01A34B304930470603551D010440303E801012E4092D061D1
D4F008D6121DC166463A118301631143012060355040313 0B526F6F74204167656E6379821006376C00
AA00648A11CFB8D4AA5C35F4300D06092A864886F70D010104050003410076FB204253DCA01C5B992DD
CCC3CD26F0910E8EDA1C195524914928C1916FCD67E6093238152C50EDEBA9476983A9E660DD4849EFE
3CFF3A5D2C09B7D4B9585E FullTrust
```

The parameters specify that the code group should be added at the top level (1.), and that the code group membership condition is of the type Publisher, and the last parameter specifies the permission set to grant (FullTrust). The command will ask for confirmation:

```
Microsoft (R) .NET Framework CasPol 1.1.4322.535
Copyright (C) Microsoft Corporation 1998-2002. All rights reserved.

The operation you are performing will alter security policy.
Are you sure you want to perform this operation? (yes/no)
y
Added union code group with "-pub" membership condition to the Machine level.
Success
```

The machine is now configured to trust fully all assemblies that have been signed with the certificate from ABC Corporation. To confirm that, you can run a caspol.exe –lg command, which lists the new code access group (1.7):

```
Security is ON
Execution checking is ON
Policy change prompt is ON

Level = Machine

Code Groups:
```

```
1.  All code: Nothing
   1.1.   Zone - MyComputer: FullTrust
      1.1.1.   StrongName -
0024000004800000940000000602000000240000525341310004000001000100070D1FA57C4AED9F0A32
E84AA0FAEFD0DE9E8FD6AEC8F87FB03766C834C99921EB23BE79AD9D5DCC1DD9AD236132102900B723C
F980957FC4E177108FC607774F29E8320E92EA05ECE4E821C0A5EFE8F1645C4C0C93C1AB99285D622CA
A652C1DFAD63D745D6F2DE5F17E5EAF0FC4963D261C8A12436518206DC093344D5AD293: FullTrust
      1.1.2.   StrongName - 0000000000000000000400000000000000: FullTrust
   1.2.   Zone - Intranet: LocalIntranet
      1.2.1.   All code: Same site Web.
      1.2.2.   All code: Same directory FileIO - Read, PathDiscovery
   1.3.   Zone - Internet: Internet
      1.3.1.   All code: Same site Web.
   1.4.   Zone - Untrusted: Nothing
   1.5.   Zone - Trusted: Internet
      1.5.1.   All code: Same site Web.
   1.6.   StrongName -
0024000004800000940000000602000000240000525341310004000001000100D51335D1B5B64BE976A
D8B08030F8E36A0DBBC3EEB5F8A18D0E30E8951DA059B440281997D760FFF61A6252A284061C1D714EF
EE5B329F410983A01DB324FA85BCE6C4E6384A2F3BC1FFA01E2586816B23888CFADD38D5AA5DF041ACE
2F81D9E8B591556852E83C473017A1785203B12F56B6D9DC23A8C9F691A0BC525D7B7EA: FullTrust
   1.7.   Publisher -
30818902818100E537F563C2304ECDA2DBEC892DED389C3C17E36500F381BD96E1C76185420F4EEA460
51AD6972139AC7F0BCE3A473F7B9E1DA0DB5F19CCB0A1774C7065DF9E56E4EC6E1F301FEEA899BD7D37
A66F8150A987CD105059B402DE641FB635A7E122F70A1F766D4A2B5030B32BA5189E1C918B0EF9E8715
1DACA49EB0160B05181590203010001: FullTrust: FullTrust
Success
```

As another check, let's ask caspol.exe to tell us what code groups our assembly matches:

```
>caspol.exe -resolvegroup securityapp11.exe
Level = Enterprise

Code Groups:

1.  All code: FullTrust


Level = Machine

Code Groups:
1.  All code: Nothing
   1.1.   Zone - MyComputer: FullTrust
   1.2.   Publisher -
30818902818100E537F563C2304ECDA2DBEC892DED389C3C17E36500F381BD96E1C76185420F4EEA460
51AD6972139AC7F0BCE3A473F7B9E1DA0DB5F19CCB0A1774C7065DF9E56E4EC6E1F301FEEA899BD7D37
A66F8150A987CD105059B402DE641FB635A7E122F70A1F766D4A2B5030B32BA5189E1C918B0EF9E8715
1DACA49EB0160B05181590203010001: FullTrust

Level = User

Code Groups:

1.  All code: FullTrust

Success
```

In the center of the results we can see that the assembly has been successfully matched to our new code group and granted the FullTrust permission set.

Managing Zones

Earlier we talked about the zones that Windows provides and that we manage using Internet Explorer's security tools. The four zones that can be managed in this way are:

❑ Internet specifies all Web sites that you haven't placed in other zones.

❑ Intranet specifies all Web sites that are on your organization's intranet.

❑ Trusted Sites specifies Web sites that you trust not to damage your data.

❑ Restricted Sites specifies Web sites that could potentially damage your computer.

These settings are managed from within Internet Explorer because they apply to sites visited using the browsers that access .NET code (whether downloaded, or in page controls). If you are using a non-Microsoft browser, it will most likely not support .NET code, and so there will be no options to manage the associated zones.

Any user on a machine can alter the zone settings; however, the security settings for the zones that they specify only apply to their account. That is, it is not possible for one user to alter another user's zone settings. That said, there is a risk, because users might alter the zone settings without understanding what they are doing and inadvertently open their machines up to attack.

To alter the settings associated with each zone, open Internet Explorer and open the Internet Options dialogue box from the Tools menu. In the Options box, move to the Security tab (see Figure 14-13).

Figure 14-13

At the top you can see the four zones. When you select one of the zones, you can use the Sites button to specify sites that you want included in that zone. For example, if you want to configure the Local intranet zone, use the dialog box that is shown in Figure 14-14. The options here give you enough scope to accurately define what constitutes the intranet in your organization. In addition, the Advanced button gives you access to a dialog box where you can specify URIs for particular sites you want to include in the Local intranet zone (see Figure 14-15).

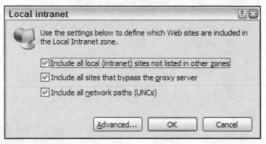

Figure 14-14

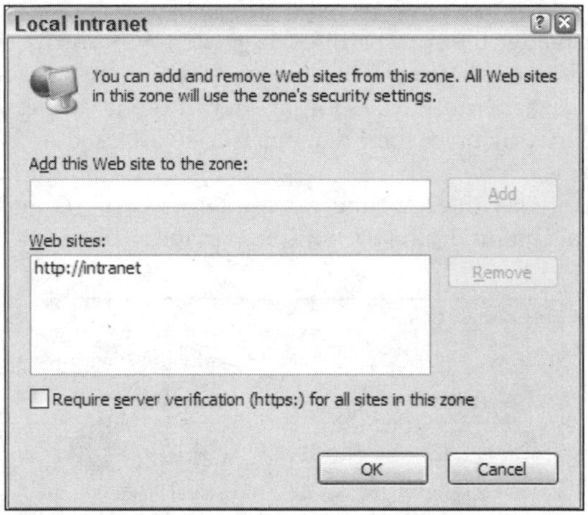

Figure 14-15

Note the option at the bottom of this dialogue box, which is provided for each of the zones except the Internet zone. It allows you to specify that you only trust sites in this zone when they are accessed over secure HTTP using Secure Sockets Layer (SSL) encryption. If you trust a site that is accessed over an unencrypted connection, you are potentially risking an attack because your traffic might be intercepted. If you want to verify that a site is held within a specific zone, visit the site and look at the bottom right-hand corner of the Internet Explorer window, which displays the name of the zone for the Web address you are currently viewing.

In addition to specifying the scope of the zone by detailing sites you trust or do not trust, you can also specify what actions are permitted within each zone using the security-level settings. These settings enable you to specify whether a prompt should be given for ActiveX controls, and whether cookies are accepted.

Summary

In this chapter, we've covered how assemblies are matched to code groups, and how those code groups are assigned permissions by the security policy at the user, enterprise, and machine levels, and we've seen how we can use tools to manage this policy. We've also seen how, for an assembly to execute, it must have the relevant permissions at the three policy levels, as well as the correct role-based permissions and the relevant Windows account permissions. We've also looked at the options available to us in distributing code using strong names and digital certificates.

Clearly, there are more security checks in place with .NET than we have seen before on Windows, and much of the security comes "for free" as we do not need to do much to make use of it at the basic level. However, when we do want to extend it, we are provided with the classes and frameworks to do that.

Security is an ongoing challenge, and although Microsoft has not solved all the problems, the managed security environment provided by .NET is a significant step in the right direction because it provides a framework within which code is challenged before it executes. It's no coincidence that these developments are occurring at a time when Microsoft is moving toward distributing its products over the Web.

15

Threading

In this chapter, we look at the support that C# and the .NET base classes offer for developing applications that employ the use of multiple threads. We briefly examine the Thread class, through which much of the threading support takes place, and develop a couple of examples that illustrate threading principles. Then we examine some of the issues that arise when we consider thread synchronization. Due to the complexity of the subject, the emphasis is solely on understanding some of the basic principles involved through some simple sample applications. This chapter focuses on:

- ❑   How to start a thread
- ❑   Providing thread priorities
- ❑   Controlling access to objects through synchronization

By the end of the chapter, you will feel quite comfortable in working with threads in your code. Let's start by running through the basics of threading.

Threading

A *thread* is a sequence of execution in a program. All our C# programs up to this point have one entry point—the Main() method. Execution starts with the first statement in the Main() method and continues until that method returns.

This program structure is all very well for programs in which there is one identifiable sequence of tasks, but often a program actually needs to be doing more than one thing at the same time; for example, when you start up Internet Explorer and get increasingly frustrated with the time it takes a page to load. Eventually, you get so fed up (if you're like me, after about 2 seconds!) that you click the Back button or type in some other URL. For this to work, Internet Explorer must be doing at least three things:

❑ Grabbing the data for the page as it is returned from the Internet, along with any accompanying files

❑ Rendering the page

❑ Watching for any user input that might indicate the user wants Internet Explorer to do something else instead (for example, watching for button clicks)

The same situation applies to any case where a program is performing some task while at the same time displaying a dialog box that gives you the chance to cancel the task at any time.

Let's look at the example with Internet Explorer in more detail. We will simplify the problem by ignoring the task of storing the data as it arrives from the Internet, and assume that Internet Explorer is simply faced with two tasks:

❑ Displaying the page

❑ Watching for user input

We will assume that this is a Web page that takes a long time to display; it might have some processor-intensive JavaScript in it, or it might contain a marquee element in it that needs to be updated continually. One way that you can approach this situation is to write a method that does a little bit of work in rendering the page. After a short time, let us say a twentieth of a second, the method checks to see if there has been any user input. If so, the input is processed (which may mean canceling the rendering task). Otherwise, the method carries on rendering the page for another twentieth of the second.

This approach works, but it is going to be a very complicated method to implement. Also, it totally ignores the event-based architecture of Windows. Recall from our coverage of events from earlier in the book that if any user input arrives, the system will want to notify the application by raising an event. Let's modify our method to allow Windows to use events:

❑ We will write an event handler that responds to user input. The response may include setting some flag to indicate that rendering should stop.

❑ We will write a method that handles the rendering. This method is designed to be executed whenever we are not doing anything else.

This solution is better, because it works with the Windows event architecture. However, look at what it has to do. For starters, it will have to time itself carefully. While this method is running, the computer cannot respond to any user input. That means this method will have to make a note of the time that it gets called, continue monitoring the time as it works, and return as soon as a fairly suitable period of time has elapsed (the absolute maximum to retain user responsiveness would be a bit less than a tenth of a second). Furthermore, before this method returns, it will need to store the exact state it was at when it was interrupted, so that the next time it is called it can carry on. It is certainly possible to write a method that would do that, and in the days of Windows 3.1, that's exactly what you would have had to do to handle this sort of situation. Luckily, NT 3.1 and then Windows 95 brought multithreaded processes, which provide a far more convenient solution to this type of problem.

Applications with Multiple Threads

The previous example illustrates the situation in which an application needs to do more than one thing, so the obvious solution is to give the application more than one thread of execution. As we mentioned, a thread represents the sequence of instructions that the computer executes. There is no reason why an application should only have one such sequence. In fact, it can have as many as you want. All that is required is that each time you create a new thread of execution, you indicate a method at which execution should start. The first thread in an application always starts at the Main() method because the first thread is started by the .NET runtime, and Main() is the method that the .NET runtime selects. Subsequent threads will be started internally by your application, which means that your application chooses where those threads starts.

How Does This Work?

So far, we have spoken rather loosely about threads happening at the same time. In fact, one processor can do only one thing at a time. If you have a multiprocessor system, then it is theoretically possible for more than one instruction to be executed simultaneously—one on each processor. However, for the majority of us who work on single-processor computers, things just don't happen simultaneously. What actually happens is that the Windows operating system gives the appearance of many processes taking place at the same time by a procedure known as *pre-emptive multitasking*.

Pre-emptive multitasking means that Windows picks a thread in some process and allows that thread to run for a short period of time. Microsoft has not documented the duration of this period, because it is one of those internal operating system parameters that it wants to be free to tweak as Windows evolves in order to maintain optimum performance. In any case, it is not the kind of information you need to know to run the Windows applications. In human terms, this time is very short—certainly no more than milliseconds. It is known as the thread's *time slice*. When the time slice is finished, Windows takes control back and selects another thread, which will then be allocated a time slice. These time slices are so short that we get the illusion of lots of things happening simultaneously.

Even when your application only has one thread, this process of pre-emptive multitasking is going on because there are many other processes running on the system, and each process needs to be given time slices for each of its threads. That's how, when you have lots of windows on your screen, each one representing a different process, you can still click on any of them and have it appear to respond straight away. The response isn't instantaneous—it happens the next time that the thread in the relevant process that is responsible for handling user input from that window gets a time slice. However, unless the system is very busy, the wait before that happens is so short that you don't notice it.

Manipulating Threads

Threads are manipulated using the class Thread, which can be found in the System.Threading namespace. An instance of Thread represents one thread, or one sequence of execution. You can create another thread by simply instantiating another instance of the thread object.

Starting a Thread

To make the following code snippets more concrete, let's suppose you are writing a graphics image editor, and the user requests to change the color depth of the image. For a large image this can take a while. It's the type of situation where you'd probably create a separate thread to do the processing so that you don't tie up the user interface while the color depth change is happening. To start up a thread, you first need to instantiate a thread object:

```
// entryPoint has been declared previously as a delegate
// of type ThreadStart
Thread depthChangeThread = new Thread(entryPoint);
```

Here we have given the variable the name depthChangeThread.

Additional threads that are created within an application in order to perform some task are often known as worker threads.

The previous code shows that the Thread constructor requires one parameter, which is used to indicate the entry point of the thread—that is, the method at which the thread starts executing. Since we are passing in the details of a method, this is a situation that calls for the use of delegates. In fact, a delegate has already been defined in the System.Threading class. It is called ThreadStart, and its signature looks like this:

```
public delegate void ThreadStart();
```

The parameter we pass to the constructor must be a delegate of this type.

After doing this, however, the new thread isn't actually doing anything so far. It is simply sitting there waiting to be started. We start a thread by calling the Thread.Start() method.

Suppose we have a method, ChangeColorDepth(), which does this processing:

```
void ChangeColorDepth()
{
    // processing to change color depth of image
}
```

You would arrange for this processing to be performed with this code:

```
ThreadStart entryPoint = new ThreadStart(ChangeColorDepth);
Thread depthChangeThread = new Thread(entryPoint);
depthChangeThread.Name = "Depth Change Thread";
depthChangeThread.Start();
```

After this point, both threads will run simultaneously.

In this code, we have also assigned a user-friendly name to the thread using the Thread.Name property (see Figure 15-1). It's not necessary to do this, but it can be useful.

Note that because the thread entry point (ChangeColorDepth() in this example) cannot take any parameters, you will have to find some other means of passing in any information that the method needs. The most obvious way would be to use member fields of the class this method is a member of. Also, the method can not return anything. (Where would any return value be returned to? As soon as this method returns a value, the thread that is running it will terminate, so there is nothing around to receive any return value and we can hardly return it to the thread that invoked this thread, since that thread will presumably be busy doing something else.)

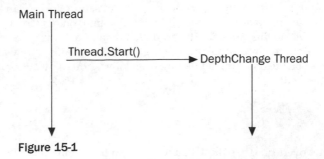

Figure 15-1

Once you have started a thread, you can also suspend, resume, or abort it. Suspending a thread means pausing the thread or putting it to sleep—the thread will simply not run for a period, which also means it will not take up any processor time while it waits. It can later be resumed, which means it will simply carry on from the point at which it was suspended. If a thread is aborted, then it will stop running altogether. Windows will permanently destroy all data that it maintains relating to that thread, so the thread subsequently can not be restarted after it is aborted.

Continuing with the image editor example, we will assume that for some reason the user interface thread displays a dialog giving the user a chance to suspend temporarily the conversion process (it is not usual for a user to want to do this, but it is only an example; a more realistic example might be the user pausing the playing of a sound or video file). We code the response like this in the main thread:

```
depthChangeThread.Suspend();
```

If the user subsequently asks for the processing to resume, use this method:

```
depthChangeThread.Resume();
```

Finally, if the user (more realistically) decides against the conversion after all and chooses to cancel it, use this method:

```
depthChangeThread.Abort();
```

Note that the Suspend() and Abort() methods do not necessarily work instantly. In the case of Suspend(), .NET might allow the thread being suspended to execute a few more instructions in order to reach a point at which .NET regards the thread as safely suspendable. This is for technical reasons—to ensure the correct operation of the garbage collector (for details see the SDK documentation). In the case of aborting a thread, the Abort() method actually works by throwing a ThreadAbortException in the affected thread. ThreadAbortException is a special exception class that is never handled. This ensures that any associated finally blocks are executed before the thread that is currently executing code inside try blocks is killed. Furthermore, this ensures that any appropriate cleaning up of resources can be done and also gives the thread a chance to make sure that any data it was manipulating (for example, fields of a class instance that will remain around after the thread has been killed) is left in a valid state.

Prior to .NET, aborting a thread in this way was not recommended except in extreme cases because the affected thread simply was killed immediately, which meant that any data it was manipulating could be left in an invalid state, and any resources the thread was using would be left open. The exception mechanism used by .NET in this situation means that aborting threads is safer.

Although this exception mechanism makes aborting a thread safe, it does mean that aborting a thread might actually take some time, since theoretically there is no limit on how long code in a `finally` block could take to execute. Due to this, after aborting a thread, you might want to wait until the thread has actually been killed before continuing any processing. You would really only wait if any of your subsequent processing relies on the other thread having been killed. You can wait for a thread to terminate by calling the `Join()` method:

```
depthChangeThread.Abort();
depthChangeThread.Join();
```

`Join()` also has other overloads that allow you to specify a time limit on how long you are prepared to wait. If the time limit is reached, then execution will continue anyway. If no time limit is specified, then the thread that is waiting will wait for as long as it has to.

The previous code snippets will result in one thread performing actions on another thread (or at least in the case of `Join()`, waiting for another thread). However, what happens if the main thread wants to perform some actions on itself? In order to do this it needs a reference to a thread object that represents its own thread. It can get such a reference using a static property, `CurrentThread`, of the `Thread` class:

```
Thread myOwnThread = Thread.CurrentThread;
```

`Thread` is actually a slightly unusual class to manipulate because there is always one thread present even before you instantiate any others—the thread that you are currently executing. This means that there are two ways that you can manipulate the class:

❑   You can instantiate a thread object, which will then represent a running thread, and whose instance members apply to that running thread.

❑   You can call any of a number of static methods. These generally apply to the thread you are actually calling the method from.

One static method you might want to call is `Sleep()`. This method puts the running thread to sleep for a set period of time, after which it will continue.

The ThreadPlayaround Sample

To illustrate how to use threads, we will build a small sample program called `ThreadPlayaround`. The aim of this example is to give us a feel for how manipulating threads works, so it is not intended to illustrate any realistic programming situations.

The core of the `ThreadPlayaround` sample is a short method, `DisplayNumbers()`, that counts up to a large number, displaying every so often it's current count. `DisplayNumbers()` starts by displaying the name and culture of the thread that it is being run on:

```
static void DisplayNumbers()
{
    Thread thisThread = Thread.CurrentThread;
    string name = thisThread.Name;
    Console.WriteLine("Starting thread: " + name);
    Console.WriteLine(name + ": Current Culture = " +
```

```
                                    thisThread.CurrentCulture);
        for (int i=1 ; i<= 8*interval ; i++)
        {
           if (i%interval == 0)
               Console.WriteLine(name + ": count has reached " + i);
        }
    }
```

The limit of the count depends on `interval`, which is a field whose value is typed in by the user. If the user types in `100`, then we will count up to 800, displaying the values `100`, `200`, `300`, `400`, `500`, `600`, `700`, and `800`. If the user types in `1000` then we will count up to 8000, displaying the values `1000`, `2000`, `3000`, `4000`, `5000`, `6000`, `7000`, and `8000` along the way, and so on. This might all seem like a pointless exercise, but the purpose of it is to tie up the processor for a period while allowing us to see how far the processor is progressing with its task.

`ThreadPlayaround` starts a second worker thread, which will run `DisplayNumbers()`, but immediately after starting the worker thread, the main thread begins executing the same method. This means that we should see both counts happening at the same time.

The `Main()` method for `ThreadPlayaround` and its containing class looks like this:

```
class EntryPoint
{
   static int interval;

   static void Main()
   {
       Console.Write("Interval to display results at?> ");
       interval = int.Parse(Console.ReadLine());

       Thread thisThread = Thread.CurrentThread;
       thisThread.Name = "Main Thread";

       ThreadStart workerStart = new ThreadStart(StartMethod);
       Thread workerThread = new Thread(workerStart);
       workerThread.Name = "Worker";
       workerThread.Start();

       DisplayNumbers();
       Console.WriteLine("Main Thread Finished");

       Console.ReadLine();
   }
}
```

We have shown the start of the class declaration here so that we can see that `interval` is a static field of this class. In the `Main()` method, we first ask the user for the interval. Then, we retrieve a reference to the thread object that represents the main thread—this is done so that we can give this thread a name so that we can see what's going on in the output.

Next, we create the worker thread, set its name, and start it off by passing it a delegate that indicates that the method it must start in is a method called workerStart. Finally, we call the DisplayNumbers() method to start counting. The entry point for the worker thread is this:

```
static void StartMethod()
{
   DisplayNumbers();
   Console.WriteLine("Worker Thread Finished");
}
```

Note that all these methods are static methods in the same class, EntryPoint. Note also that the two counts take place entirely separately, since the variable i in the DisplayNumbers() method that is used to do the counting is a local variable. Local variables are not only scoped to the method they are defined in, but are also visible only to the thread that is executing that method. If another thread starts executing the same method, than that thread will get its own copy of the local variables. We will start by running the code, and selecting a relatively small value of 100 for the interval:

```
ThreadPlayaround
Interval to display results at?> 100
Starting thread: Main Thread
Main Thread: Current Culture = en-US
Main Thread: count has reached 100
Main Thread: count has reached 200
Main Thread: count has reached 300
Main Thread: count has reached 400
Main Thread: count has reached 500
Main Thread: count has reached 600
Main Thread: count has reached 700
Main Thread: count has reached 800
Main Thread Finished
Starting thread: Worker
Worker: Current Culture = en-US
Worker: count has reached 100
Worker: count has reached 200
Worker: count has reached 300
Worker: count has reached 400
Worker: count has reached 500
Worker: count has reached 600
Worker: count has reached 700
Worker: count has reached 800
Worker Thread Finished
```

As far as threads working in parallel are concerned, this doesn't immediately look like it's working too well! We see that the main thread starts, counts up to 800, and then claims to finish. The worker thread then starts and runs through separately.

The problem here is actually that starting a thread is a major process. After instantiating the new thread, the main thread comes across this line of code:

```
workerThread.Start();
```

This call to `Thread.Start()` informs Windows that the new thread is to be started, then immediately returns. While we are counting up to 800, Windows is busily making the arrangements for the thread to be started. This internally means, among other things, allocating various resources for the thread, and performing various security checks. By the time the new thread is actually starting up, the main thread has already finished its work!

We can solve this problem by choosing a larger interval, so that both threads spend longer in the `DisplayNumbers()` method. We'll try `1000000` this time:

```
ThreadPlayaround
Interval to display results at?> 1000000
Starting thread: Main Thread
Main Thread: Current Culture = en-US
Main Thread: count has reached 1000000
Starting thread: Worker
Worker: Current Culture = en-US
Main Thread: count has reached 2000000
Worker: count has reached 1000000
Main Thread: count has reached 3000000
Worker: count has reached 2000000
Main Thread: count has reached 4000000
Worker: count has reached 3000000
Main Thread: count has reached 5000000
Main Thread: count has reached 6000000
Worker: count has reached 4000000
Main Thread: count has reached 7000000
Worker: count has reached 5000000
Main Thread: count has reached 8000000
Main Thread Finished
Worker: count has reached 6000000
Worker: count has reached 7000000
Worker: count has reached 8000000
Worker Thread Finished
```

Now we can see the threads really working in parallel. The main thread starts and counts up to one million. At some point, while the main thread is counting the next million numbers, the worker thread starts off, and from then on, the two threads progress at the same rate until they both finish.

It is important to understand that unless you are running a multi-processor computer, using two threads in a CPU-intensive task will not have saved any time. On a single-processor machine, having both threads count up to 8 million will have taken just as long as having one thread count up to 16 million. Arguably, it will take slightly longer, since with the extra thread around, the operating system has to do a little bit more thread switching, but this difference will be negligible. The advantage of using more than one thread is two-fold. First, you gain responsiveness, in that one of the threads could be dealing with user input while the other thread does some work behind the scenes. Second, you will save time if at least one thread is doing something that doesn't involve CPU time, such as waiting for data to be retrieved from the Internet, because the other threads can carry out their processing while the inactive thread(s) are waiting.

Thread Priorities

What happens if you are going to have multiple threads running in your application, but some threads are more important than others? For this, it is possible to assign different priorities to different threads within a process. In general, a thread will not be allocated any time slices if there are any higher priority threads working. The advantage of this is that you can guarantee user responsiveness by assigning a slightly higher priority to a thread that handles receiving user input. For most of the time, such a thread will have nothing to do, and the other threads can carry on their work. However, if the user does anything, this thread will immediately take priority over other threads in your application for the short time that it spends handling the event.

High priority threads can completely block threads of lower priority, so you should be careful when changing thread priorities. The thread priorities are defined as values of the `ThreadPriority` enumeration. The possible values are `Highest`, `AboveNormal`, `Normal`, `BelowNormal`, `Lowest`.

You should note that each process has a base priority, and that these values are relative to the priority of your process. Giving a thread a higher priority might ensure that it gets priority over other threads in that process, but there might still be other processes running on the system whose threads get an even higher priority. Windows tends to give a higher priority to its own operating system threads.

We can see the effect of changing a thread priority by making the following change to the `Main()` method in the `ThreadPlayaround` sample:

```
ThreadStart workerStart = new ThreadStart(StartMethod);
Thread workerThread = new Thread(workerStart);
workerThread.Name = "Worker";

workerThread.Priority = ThreadPriority.AboveNormal;

workerThread.Start();
```

What we have done is indicate that the worker thread should have a slightly higher priority than the main thread. The result is dramatic:

```
ThreadPlayaroundWithPriorities
Interval to display results at?> 1000000
Starting thread: Main Thread
Main Thread: Current Culture = en-US
Starting thread: Worker
Worker: Current Culture = en-US
Main Thread: count has reached 1000000
Worker: count has reached 1000000
Worker: count has reached 2000000
Worker: count has reached 3000000
Worker: count has reached 4000000
Worker: count has reached 5000000
Worker: count has reached 6000000
Worker: count has reached 7000000
Worker: count has reached 8000000
Worker Thread Finished
Main Thread: count has reached 2000000
Main Thread: count has reached 3000000
```

```
Main Thread: count has reached 4000000
Main Thread: count has reached 5000000
Main Thread: count has reached 6000000
Main Thread: count has reached 7000000
Main Thread: count has reached 8000000
Main Thread Finished
```

This shows that when the worker thread has an `AboveNormal` priority, the main thread scarcely gets a look-in once the worker thread has started.

Synchronization

One crucial aspect of working with threads is the *synchronization* of access to any variables which more than one thread has access to. Synchronization means that only one thread should be able to access the variable at any one time. If we do not ensure that access to variables is synchronized, then subtle bugs can result. In this section, we will briefly review some of the main issues involved.

What is synchronization?

The issue of synchronization arises because what looks like a single statement in your C# source code in most cases will translate into many statements in the final compiled assembly language machine code. Take, for example, the following statement:

```
message += ", there";   // message is a string that contains "Hello"
```

This statement looks syntactically in C# like one statement, but it actually involves a large number of operations when the code is being executed. Memory will need to be allocated to store the new longer string; the variable `message` will need to be set to refer to the new memory; the actual text will need to be copied, and so on.

Obviously, we've exaggerated the case here by selecting a string—one of the more complex data types—as our example, but even when performing arithmetic operations on primitive numeric types, there is quite often more going on behind the scenes than you would imagine from looking at the C# code. In particular, many operations cannot be carried out directly on variables stored in memory locations, and their values have to be separately copied into special locations in the processor known as *registers*.

In a situation where a single C# statement translates into more than one native machine code command, it is quite possible that the thread's time slice might end in the middle of executing that statement process. If this happens, then another thread in the same process might be given a time slice, and, if access to variables involved with that statement (here: `message`) is not synchronized, this other thread might attempt to read or write to the same variables. In our example, was the other thread intended to see the new value of message or the old value?

The problems can get even worse than this. The statement we use in our example is relatively simple, but in a more complicated statement, some variable might have an undefined value for a brief period, while the statement is being executed. If another thread attempts to read that value in that instant, then it might simply read garbage. More seriously, if two threads simultaneously try to write data to the same variable, then it is almost certain that that variable will contain an incorrect value afterward.

Synchronization is not an issue that affects the ThreadPlayAround sample, because both threads use mostly local variables. The only variable that both threads have access to is the Interval field, but this field is initialized by the main thread before any other thread starts, and subsequently only reads from either thread, so there is still not a problem. Synchronization issues only arise if at least one thread is writing to a variable while other threads are either reading or writing to it.

Fortunately, C# provides an extremely easy way of synchronizing access to variables, and the C# language keyword that does it is lock. You use lock like this:

```
lock (x)
{
    DoSomething();
}
```

What the lock statement does is wrap an object known as a *mutual exclusion lock*, or *mutex*, around the variable in the round brackets. The mutex will remain in place while the compound statement attached to the lock keyword is executed. While the mutex is wrapped around a variable, no other thread is permitted access to that variable. We can see this with the above code; the compound statement will execute, and eventually this thread will lose its time slice. If the next thread to gain the time slice attempts to access the variable x, access to the variable will be denied. Instead, Windows will simply put the thread to sleep until the mutex has been released.

The mutex is the simplest of a number of mechanisms that can be used to control access to variables. We don't have the space to go into the others here, but we will mention that they are all controlled through the .NET base class System.Threading.Monitor. In fact, the C# lock statement is simply a C# syntax wrapper around a couple of method calls to this class.

In general, you should synchronize variables wherever there is a risk that any thread might try writing to a variable at the same time as other threads are trying to read from or write to the same variable. We don't have space here to cover the details of thread synchronization, but we will point out that it is a fairly big topic in its own right. Here, we will simply confine ourselves to pointing out a couple of the potential pitfalls.

Synchronization issues

Synchronizing threads is vital in multithreaded applications. However, it's an area in which it is important to proceed carefully because a number of subtle and hard-to-detect bugs can easily arise, in particular *deadlocks* and *race conditions*.

Don't Overuse Synchronization

While thread synchronization is important, it is important to use it only where it is necessary, because it can impact performance for two reasons: First, there is some overhead associated with actually putting a lock on an object and taking it off, though this is admittedly minimal. Second, and more importantly, the more thread synchronization you have, the more threads can get held up waiting for objects to be released. Remember that if one thread holds a lock on any object, any other thread that needs to access that object will simply halt execution until the lock is released. It is important, therefore, that you place as little code inside lock blocks as you can without causing thread synchronization bugs. In this sense, you can think of lock statements as temporarily disabling the multithreading ability of an application, and therefore temporarily removing all the benefits of multithreading.

However, the dangers of using synchronization too often (performance and responsiveness go down) are not as great as the dangers associated with not using synchronization when you need it (subtle run-time bugs that are very hard to track down).

Deadlocks

A *deadlock* (or a deadly embrace) is a bug that can occur when two threads have to access resources that are locked by the other. Suppose one thread is running the following code, where a and b are two object references that both threads have access to:

```
lock (a)
{
    // do something

    lock (b)
    {
        // do something
    }
}
```

At the same time another thread is running this code:

```
lock (b)
{
    // do something

    lock (a)
    {
        // do something
    }
}
```

Depending on the times that the threads come across the various statements, the following scenario is quite possible: the first thread acquires a lock on a, while at about the same time the second thread acquires a lock on b. A short time later, thread A comes across the lock(b) statement, and immediately goes to sleep, waiting for the lock on b to be released. Soon afterward, the second thread comes across its lock(a) statement and also puts itself to sleep, ready for Windows to wake it up the instant the lock on a gets released. Unfortunately, the lock on a is never going to be released because the first thread, which owns this lock, is sleeping and won't wake up until the lock on b gets released, which won't happen until the second thread wakes up. The result is deadlock. Both threads just permanently sit there doing nothing, each waiting for the other thread to release its lock. This kind of problem can cause an entire application to just hang, so that you have no choice but to using the Task Manager to terminate the entire process.

> *In this situation, it is not possible for another thread to release the locks; a mutual exclusion lock can only be released by the thread that claims the lock in the first place.*

Deadlocks can usually be avoided by having both threads claim locks on objects in the same order. In the previous example, if the second thread claimed the locks in the same order as the first thread, a first, then b, then whichever thread has the lock on a first would completely finish its task, then the other thread would start. This way, no deadlock can occur.

You might think that it is easy to avoid coding deadlocks—after all, in the previous example, it looks fairly obvious that a deadlock could occur so you probably wouldn't write that code in the first place. However, remember that different locks can occur in different method calls. With this example, the first thread might actually be executing this code:

```
lock (a)
{
    // do bits of processing

    CallSomeMethod()
}
```

Here, `CallSomeMethod()` might call other methods, and so on, and buried in there somewhere is a `lock(b)` statement. In this situation, it might not be nearly so obvious when you write your code that you are allowing a possible deadlock.

Race Conditions

A *race condition* is somewhat subtler than a deadlock. It rarely halts execution of a process, but it can lead to data corruption. It is hard to give a precise definition of a race, but it generally occurs when several threads attempt to access the same data, and do not adequately take account of what the other threads are doing. Race conditions are best understood using an example.

Suppose we have an array of objects, where each element in the array needs to be processed somehow, and we have a number of threads that are between them doing this processing. We might have an object, let's call it `ArrayController`, which contains the array of objects as well as an `int` that indicates how many of them have been processed, and therefore, which one should be processed next. `ArrayController` might implement this method:

```
public int GetObject(int index)
{

    // returns the object at the given index.

}
```

It also implements this read/write property:

```
public int ObjectsProcessed
{

    // indicates how many of the objects have been processed.

}
```

Now, each thread that is helping to process the objects might execute some code that looks like this:

```
lock(ArrayController)
{
    int nextIndex = ArrayController.ObjectsProcessed;
    Console.WriteLine("Object to be processed next is " + nextIndex);
    ++ArrayController.ObjectsProcessed;
```

```
        object next = ArrayController.GetObject(nextIndex);
    }
    ProcessObject(next);
```

This by itself should work, but suppose that in an attempt to avoid tying up resources for longer than necessary, we decide not to hold the lock on `ArrayController` while we're displaying the user message. Therefore, we rewrite the previous code like this:

```
    lock(ArrayController)
    {
        int nextIndex = ArrayController.ObjectsProcessed;
    }
    Console.WriteLine("Object to be processed next is " + nextIndex);
    lock(ArrayController)
    {
        ++ArrayController.ObjectsProcessed;
        object next = ArrayController.GetObject(nextIndex);
    }
    ProcessObject(next);
```

Here, we have a possible problem. What could happen is that one thread gets an object (say the 11th object in the array), and displays the message saying that it is about to process this object. Meanwhile, a second thread also starts executing the same code, calls `ObjectsProcessed`, and determines that the next object to be processed is the 11th object, because the first thread hasn't yet updated `Array Controller.ObjectsProcessed`. While the second thread is happily writing to the console that it will now process the 11th object, the first thread acquires another lock on the `ArrayController` and inside this lock increments `ObjectsProcessed`. Unfortunately, it is too late. Both threads are now committed to processing the same object— a text book example of a race condition.

For both deadlocks and race conditions, it is not often obvious when the condition can occur; and when it does, it is hard to identify the bug. In general, this is an area where you largely learn from experience. However, it is important to consider very carefully all the parts of the code where you need synchronization when you are writing multithreaded applications to check whether there is any possibility of deadlocks or race conditions arising. Keep in mind that you can not predict the exact times that different threads will encounter different instructions.

Summary

In this chapter, we took a quick look at how to code applications that utilize multiple threads using the `System.Threading` namespace. Using multithreading in your applications takes careful planning. Too many threads can cause resource issues and not enough threads can cause your applications to seem sluggish and to perform rather poorly.

The `System.Threading` namespace in the .NET Framework does allow you to manipulate threads; however, this does not mean that the .NET Framework handles all the difficult tasks of multithreading for you. You have to consider thread priority and synchronization issues. This chapter discussed these issues and how to code for them in your C# applications. We also took a look at the problems associated with deadlocks and race conditions.

Just remember, if you are going to use multithreading in your C# applications, that careful planning should be a big part of your efforts.

16

Distributed Applications with .NET Remoting

In this chapter we explore .NET Remoting. .NET Remoting can be used for accessing objects in another application domain, for example on another server. .NET Remoting also offers calling objects using the SOAP protocol. Last, but hardly least, .NET Remoting provides a faster format for communication between .NET applications on the client and on the server side.

In this chapter we develop .NET Remoting objects, clients, and servers using the HTTP and TCP channel with the SOAP and binary formatter. First, we define the channel and formatter programmatically before we change the application to use configuration files instead, where only a few .NET Remoting methods are required. We also write small programs to use .NET Remoting asynchronously, and calling event handlers in the client application.

The .NET Remoting classes can be found in the namespace `System.Runtime.Remoting` and its sub-namespaces. Many of these classes can be found in the core assembly `mscorlib`, and some that are needed only for cross-network communication are available in the assembly `System.Runtime.Remoting`.

The .NET Remoting topics we look at in this chapter include:

❑   An overview of .NET Remoting

❑   Contexts, which are used to group objects with similar execution requirements

❑   Implementing a simple remote object, client, and server

❑   The .NET Remoting architecture

❑   .NET Remoting configuration files

❑   Hosting .NET Remoting objects in ASP.NET

❑   Using Soapsuds to access the metadata of remote objects

❑   Calling .NET Remoting methods asynchronously

❑   Calling methods in the client with the help of events

❑   Using the `CallContext` to automatically pass data to the server

Let's begin with finding out what .NET Remoting is.

> Be aware that you have to turn the local Windows XP firewall off if you are using
> Windows XP to start both client and server applications from this chapter. You can
> do that in the Control Panel using the Network Connections item. Open the item,
> select the Advanced option in the Properties of the Local Area Network or Dial Up
> Connection panels or any other network type for which your system is configured
> and on which you intend to run these applications.

What Is .NET Remoting?

Many applications are not standalone applications that are running on a single system, but they use some network communication technologies to invoke methods on a remote server. This is what .NET Remoting is good for.

For communication with a client and a server application, different technologies can be used. You can program your application by using sockets, or you can use some helper classes from the `System.Net` namespace that make it easier to deal with protocols, IP addresses, and port numbers (see Chapter 31 for details). Using this technology you always have to send data across the network. The data you send can be your own custom protocol where the packet is interpreted by the server, so that the server knows what methods should be invoked. You do not only have to deal with the data that is sent, it is also necessary to create threads yourself.

Instead of sending data, you can invoke methods across the network in a server application. This is what XML Web services and .NET Remoting offer. While XML Web services make use of the SOAP protocol to ensure interoperability between different platforms, .NET Remoting has different goals.

The goals of .NET Remoting can be described with the application types and protocols that are supported, and by looking at the term CLR Object Remoting.

Application Types and Protocols

Some of the main features that can be assigned to .NET Remoting are that .NET Remoting can be used in *any application type* over *any transport*, using *any payload encoding*. .NET Remoting is an extremely flexible architecture.

Using SOAP and HTTP together is just one way to call remote objects. The transport channel is pluggable and can be replaced. With .NET 1.1 you get HTTP and TCP channels represented by the classes `HttpChannel` and `TcpChannel`. You can build transport channels to use UDP, IPX, SMTP, a shared memory mechanism, or message queuing—the choice is entirely yours.

The term pluggable is often used with .NET Remoting. Pluggable means that a specific part is designed so that it can be replaced by a custom implementation.

The payload is used to transport the parameters of a method call. This payload encoding can also be replaced. Microsoft delivers SOAP and binary encoding mechanisms. You can use either the SOAP formatter with the HTTP channel or HTTP with the binary formatter. Of course, both of these formatters can also be used with the TCP channel.

Although SOAP is used with .NET Remoting—be aware that .NET Remoting only supports the SOAP RPC style, while ASP.NET Web services supports both the DOC style (default) and the RPC style.

.NET Remoting not only enables you to use server functionality in every .NET application. You can use .NET Remoting anywhere—regardless of whether you are building a console or a Windows application, a Windows Service, or a COM+ component. .NET Remoting is also a good technology for peer-to-peer communication.

CLR Object Remoting

CLR Object Remoting is an importing aspect of .NET Remoting. All of the language constructs, such as constructors, delegates, interfaces, methods, properties, and fields can be used with remote objects. .NET Remoting extends the CLR object functionality across the network. CLR Object Remoting deals with activation, distributed identities, lifetimes, and call contexts.

This is a major difference to XML Web services. With XML Web services, the objects are abstracted, and the client doesn't need to know the object types of the server. Unlike .NET Remoting, XML Web services are platform independent.

.NET Remoting Overview

.NET Remoting can be used for accessing objects in another application domain. .NET Remoting can always be used whether the two objects live inside a single process, in separate processes, or on separate systems.

Remote assemblies can be configured to work locally in the application domain or as part of a remote application. If the assembly is part of the remote application, then the client receives a proxy to talk to instead of the real object. The proxy is a representative of the remote object in the client process, used by the client application to call methods. When the client calls a method in the proxy, the proxy sends a message into the channel that is passed on to the remote object.

.NET applications work within an application domain. An application domain can be seen as a subprocess within a process. Traditionally, processes were used as an isolation boundary. An application running in one process cannot access and destroy memory in another process. For applications to communicate with each other, cross-process communication is needed. With .NET, the application domain is the new safety boundary inside a process, because the MSIL code is type-safe and verifiable. As we discussed in Chapter 13, different applications can run inside the same process but within different application domains. Objects inside the same application domain can interact directly; a proxy is needed in order to access objects in a different application domain.

The following list provides an overview of the key elements of the architecture:

❑ A *remote object* is an object that's running on the server. The client doesn't call methods on this object directly, but uses a proxy instead. With .NET it's easy to distinguish remote objects from local objects: every class that's derived from `MarshalByRefObject` never leaves its application domain. The client can call methods of the remote object via a proxy.

❑ A *channel* is used for communication between the client and the server. There are client and server parts of the channel. .NET Framework 1.1 offers two channel types that communicate via TCP or HTTP. You can also create a custom channel that communicates by using a different protocol.

❑ *Messages* are sent into the channel. Messages are created for communication between the client and the server. These messages hold the information about the remote object, the method name called, and all of the arguments.

❑ The *formatter* defines how messages are transferred into the channel. With .NET Framework 1.1, we have SOAP and binary formatters. The SOAP formatter can be used to communicate with Web services that are not based on.NET Framework. Binary formatters are much faster and can be used efficiently in an intranet environment. Of course, you also have the possibility to create a custom formatter.

❑ A *formatter provider* is used to associate a formatter with a channel. By creating a channel, you can specify what formatter provider to use, and this in turn defines the formatter that is used to transfer the data into the channel.

❑ The client calls methods on a *proxy* instead of the remote object. There are two types of proxies: the *transparent proxy* and the *real proxy*. To the client, the transparent proxy looks like the remote object. On the transparent proxy, the client can call the methods implemented by the remote objects. In turn, the transparent proxy calls the `Invoke()` method on the real proxy. The `Invoke()` method uses the message sink to pass the message to the channel.

❑ A *message sink*, or *sink* for short, is an interceptor object. Interceptors are used on both the client and the server. A sink is associated with the channel. The real proxy uses the message sink to pass the message into the channel, so the sink can do some interception before the message goes into the channel. Depending on where the sink is used, it is known as an envoy sink, a server context sink, an object context sink, and so on.

❑ The client can use an *activator* to create a remote object on the server or to get a proxy of a server-activated object.

❑ `RemotingConfiguration` is a utility class to configure remote servers and clients. This class can be used either to read configuration files, or to configure remote objects dynamically.

❑ `ChannelServices` is a utility class to register channels and then to dispatch messages to them.

Figure 16-1 shows a conceptual picture of how these pieces fit together.

When the client calls methods on a remote object, it actually calls methods on a transparent proxy instead. The transparent proxy looks like the real object—it implements the public methods of the real object. The transparent proxy knows about the public methods of the real object by using the reflection mechanism to read the metadata from the assembly.

Application Domain

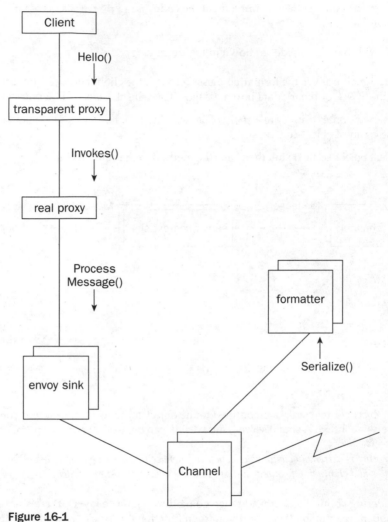

Figure 16-1

In turn, the transparent proxy calls the real proxy. The real proxy is responsible for sending the message to the channel. The real proxy is pluggable; you can replace it with a custom implementation. A custom implementation can be used to write a log, or to use another way to find a channel, and so on. The default implementation of the real proxy locates the collection (or chain) of envoy sinks and passes the message to the first envoy sink. An envoy sink can intercept and change the message. Examples of such sinks are debugging sinks, security sinks, and synchronization sinks.

The last envoy sink sends the message into the channel. How the messages are sent over the wire depends on the formatter. As previously stated, SOAP and binary formatters are available with .NET

Framework 1.1. The formatter, however, is also pluggable. The channel is responsible for either connecting to a listening socket on the server or sending the formatted data. With a custom channel you can do something different; you just have to implement the code and to do what's necessary to transfer the data to the other side.

Let's continue with the server side as shown in Figure 16-2.

❏   The channel receives the formatted messages from the client and uses the formatter to unmarshal the SOAP or binary data into messages. Then the channel calls server-context sinks.

❏   The server-context sinks are a chain of sinks, where the last sink in the chain continues the call to the chain of object-context sinks.

❏   The last object-context sink then calls the method in the remote object.

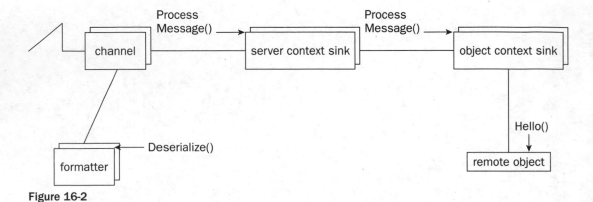

Figure 16-2

Note that the object context sinks are confined to the object context, and the server context sinks are confined to the server context. A single server context sink can be used to access a number of object sinks.

> *.NET Remoting is extremely customizable: you can replace the real proxy, add sink objects, or replace the formatter and channel. Of course, you can also use what's already provided.*

If you're wondering about the overhead when going through these layers, there's not much overhead if nothing is happening in there. If you add your own functionality, the overhead will depend on that.

Contexts

Before we look at using .NET Remoting to build servers and clients that communicate across a network, let's look at the cases where a channel is needed inside an application domain: calling objects across contexts.

If you've previously written COM+ components, you already know about COM+ contexts. Contexts in .NET are very similar. A context is a boundary containing a collection of objects. Likewise, with a COM+ context, the objects in such a collection require the same usage rules that are defined by the context attributes.

As you already know, a single process can have multiple application domains. An application domain is something like a subprocess with security boundaries. We discuss application domains in Chapter 13.

An application domain can have different contexts. A context is used to group objects with similar execution requirements. Contexts are composed from a set of properties and are used for interception: when a *context-bound object* is accessed by a different context, an *interceptor* can do some work before the call reaches the object. Examples where this can be used are for thread synchronization, transactions, and security management.

A class that is derived from `MarshalByRefObject` is bound to the application domain. Outside the application domain a proxy is needed to access the object. A class derived from `ContextBoundObject` that is derived from `MarshalByRefObject` is bound to a context. Outside the context, a proxy is needed to access the object.

Context-bound objects can have *context attributes*. A context-bound object without context attributes is created in the context of the creator. A context-bound object with context attributes is created in a new context or in the creator's context if the attributes are compatible.

To further understand contexts you must familiarize yourself with these terms:

❑ Creating an application domain creates the *default context* in this application domain. If a new object is instantiated that needs different context properties a new context is created.

❑ *Context attributes* can be assigned to classes derived from `ContextBoundObject`. You can create a custom attribute class by implementing the interface `IContextAttribute`. The .NET Framework has one context attribute class in the namespace `System.Runtime.Remoting` `.Contexts: SynchronizationAttribute`.

❑ Context attributes define *context properties* that are needed for an object. A context property class implements the interface `IContextProperty`. Active properties contribute message sinks to the call chain. The class `ContextAttribute` implements both `IContextProperty` and `IContextAttribute`, and can be used as a base class for custom attributes.

❑ A *message sink* is an interceptor for a method call. With a message sink method calls can be intercepted. Properties can contribute to message sinks.

Activation

A new context is created if an instance of a class that's created needs a context different from the calling context. The attribute classes that are associated with the target class are asked if all the properties of the current context are acceptable. If any of these properties are unacceptable, the runtime asks for all property classes associated with the attribute class and creates a new context. The runtime then asks the property classes for the sinks they want to install. A property class can implement one of the `IContributeXXXSink` interfaces to contribute sink objects. There are several of these interfaces to go with the variety of sinks.

Attributes and Properties

With context attributes the properties of a context are defined. A context attribute class primarily is an attribute. You will find more about attributes in Chapter 10. Context attribute classes must implement the interface `IContextAttribute`. A custom context attribute class can derive from the class `ContextAttribute`, because this class already has a default implementation of this interface.

With .NET Framework 1.1 there is one context attribute class: `System.Runtime.Remoting.Contexts.SynchronizationAttribute`. The `Synchronization` attribute defines synchronization requirements; it specifies the synchronization property that is needed by the object. With this attribute you can specify that multiple threads cannot access the object concurrently, but the thread accessing the object can change.

With the constructor of this attribute you can set one of four values:

- `NOT_SUPPORTED` defines that the class should not be instantiated in a context where the synchronization is set.
- `REQUIRED` specifies that a synchronization context is required.
- With `REQUIRES_NEW` always a new context is created.
- `SUPPORTED` means that it doesn't matter what context we get, the object can live in it.

Communication between Contexts

How does the communication between contexts happen? The client uses a proxy instead of the real object. The proxy creates a message that is transferred to a channel, and sinks can do interception. Does this sound familiar? It ought to. The same mechanism is used for communication across different application domains or different systems. A TCP or HTTP channel is not required for the communication across contexts, but a channel is used here too. `CrossContextChannel` can use the same virtual memory in both the client and server sides of the channel, and formatters are not required for crossing contexts.

Remote Objects, Clients, and Servers

Before we step into the details of the .NET Remoting architecture, let's look briefly at a remote object and a very small, simple client-server application that uses this remote object. After that the required steps and options are discussed in more detail.

Figure 16-3 shows the major classes of the classes in the client and server application. The remote object that will be implemented is called `Hello`. `HelloServer` is the main class of the application on the server, and `HelloClient` is for the client.

Remote Objects

Remote objects are needed for distributed computing. An object that should be called remotely from a different system must be derived from `System.MarshalByRefObject`. `MarshalByRefObject` objects are *confined to the application domain* in which they were created. This means that they are never passed across application domains; instead a proxy object is used to access the remote object from another application domain. The other application domain can live inside the same process, in another process, or on another system.

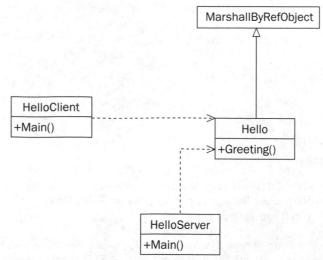

Figure 16-3

A remote object has *distributed identity*. Because of this, a reference to the object can be passed to other clients, and they will still access the same object. The proxy knows about the identity of the remote object.

The MarshalByRefObject class has, in addition to the inherited methods from the Object class, methods to initialize and to get the lifetime services. The lifetime services define how long the remote object lives. Lifetime services and leasing features will be dealt with later in this chapter.

To see .NET Remoting in action, create a Class Library for the remote object. The class Hello derives from System.MarshalByRefObject. In the constructor and destructor, a message is written to the console that provides information about the object's lifetime. In addition, add the method Greeting() that will be called from the client.

In order to distinguish easily between the assembly and the class in the following sections, give them different names in the arguments of the method calls used. The name of the assembly is RemoteHello, and the class is named Hello.

```csharp
using System;

namespace Wrox.ProCSharp.Remoting
{

    public class Hello : System.MarshalByRefObject
    {
        public Hello()
        {
            Console.WriteLine("Constructor called");
        }
        ~Hello()
        {
            Console.WriteLine("Destructor called");
```

```
        }

        public string Greeting(string name)
        {
            Console.WriteLine("Greeting called");
            return "Hello, " + name;
        }
    }
}
```

A Simple Server

For the server create a new C# console application `HelloServer`. To use the `TcpServerChannel` class, you have to reference the System.Runtime.Remoting assembly. It's also required that you reference the RemoteHello assembly that was created earlier.

In the `Main()` method a object of type `System.Runtime.Remoting.Channels.Tcp` `.TcpServerChannel` is created with the port number `8086`. This channel is registered with the `System.Runtime.Remoting.Channels.ChannelServices` class to make it available for remote objects. The remote object type is registered using `System.Runtime.Remoting.RemotingConfiguration` `.RegisterWellKnownServiceType`. In the sample the type of the remote object class, the URI that is used by the client, and a mode is specified. The mode `WellKnownObject.SingleCall` means that a new instance is created for every method call; in the sample application no state is held in the remote object.

> *.NET Remoting allows creating stateless and stateful remote objects. In the first example well-known single-call objects that don't hold state are used. The other object type is called client-activated. Client-activated objects hold state. Later in this chapter, when looking at the object activation sequence, we discuss more details about these differences and show how these object types can be used.*

After registration of the remote object, it is necessary to keep the server running until a key is pressed:

```
using System;
using System.Runtime.Remoting;
using System.Runtime.Remoting.Channels;
using System.Runtime.Remoting.Channels.Tcp;

namespace Wrox.ProCSharp.Remoting
{
    public class HelloServer
    {
        public static void Main(string[] args)
        {
            TcpServerChannel channel = new TcpServerChannel(8086);
            ChannelServices.RegisterChannel(channel);
            RemotingConfiguration.RegisterWellKnownServiceType(
                    typeof(Hello), "Hi", WellKnownObjectMode.SingleCall);
            System.Console.WriteLine("press return to exit");
            System.Console.ReadLine();
        }
    }
}
```

A Simple Client

The client is again a C# console application: HelloClient. With this project you also have to reference the System.Runtime. Remoting assembly so that the `TcpClientChannel` class can be used. In addition, you also have to reference the RemoteHello assembly. Although the object will be created on the remote server, the assembly is needed on the client for the proxy to read the type information during runtime.

In the client program create a `TcpClientChannel` object that's registered in `ChannelServices`. For the `TcpChannel` you can use the default constructor, so a free port is selected. Next the `Activator` class is used to return a proxy to the remote object. The proxy is of type `System.Runtime.Remoting.Proxies` `.__TransparentProxy`. This object looks like the real object as it offers the same methods. The transparent proxy uses the real proxy to send messages to the channel:

```
using System;
using System.Runtime.Remoting.Channels;
using System.Runtime.Remoting.Channels.Tcp;

namespace Wrox.ProCSharp.Remoting
{
   public class HelloClient
   {
      public static void Main(string[] args)
      {
         ChannelServices.RegisterChannel(new TcpClientChannel());
         Hello obj = (Hello)Activator.GetObject(
                                   typeof(Hello), "tcp://localhost:8086/Hi");
         if (obj == null)
         {
            Console.WriteLine("could not locate server");
            return;
         }
         for (int i=0; i< 5; i++)
         {
            Console.WriteLine(obj.Greeting("Christian"));
         }
      }
   }
}
```

When you start the server and the client program `Hello, Christian` appears five times in the client console. With your server console window you can see the output shown in Figure 16-4. As you can see, for every method call a new instance gets created because the `WellKnownObjectMode.SingleCall` activation mode was selected. Depending on timing and resources needed, you might also see some calls to the destructor. If you start the client a few times you are sure to see some destructor calls.

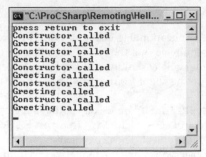

Figure 16-4

.NET Remoting Architecture

After a simple client and server in action is shown, we are going to discuss an overview of the .NET architecture before we step into the details. Based on the previously created program we will look at the details of the architecture and you will see mechanisms for extensibility.

In this section, we explore all the topics in this list:

❑ The functionality of a channel and how a channel can be configured

❑ Formatters and how they are used

❑ The utility classes ChannelServices and RemotingConfiguration

❑ Different ways to activate remote objects, and how stateless and stateful objects can be used with .NET Remoting

❑ Functionality of message sinks

❑ How to pass objects by value and by reference

❑ Lifetime management of stateful objects with .NET Remoting leasing mechanisms

Channels

A channel is used to communicate between a .NET client and a server. .NET Framework 1.1 ships with channel classes that communicate using TCP or HTTP. You can create custom channels for other protocols.

The *HTTP channel* is used by most Web services. It uses the HTTP protocol for communication. Because firewalls usually have port 80 opened so that the clients can access Web servers, .NET Remoting Web services can listen to port 80 so that they can easily be used by these clients.

It's also possible to use the *TCP channel* on the Internet, but here the firewalls must be configured so that clients can access a specified port that's used by the TCP channel. The TCP channel can be used to communicate more efficiently in an intranet environment compared to the HTTP channel.

When performing a method call on the remote object, the client channel object sends a message to the remote channel object.

Both the server and the client application must create a channel. This code shows how a `TcpServerChannel` can be created on the server side:

```
using System.Runtime.Remoting.Channels.Tcp;
   ...
TcpServerChannel channel = new TcpServerChannel(8086);
```

The port on which the TCP socket is listening is specified in the constructor argument. The server channel must specify a well-known port, and the client must use this port when accessing the server. For creating a `TcpClientChannel` on the client, however, it isn't necessary to specify a well-known port. The default constructor of `TcpClientChannel` chooses an available port, which is passed to the server at connection-time so that the server can return data back to the client.

Creating a new channel instance immediately switches the socket to the listening state, which can be verified by typing **netstat –a** at the command line.

The HTTP channels can be used similarly to the TCP channels. We can specify the port where the server can create the listening socket.

A server can listen to multiple channels. Here we are creating both an HTTP and a TCP channel in the file HelloServer.cs:

```
using System;
using System.Runtime.Remoting;
using System.Runtime.Remoting.Channels;
using System.Runtime.Remoting.Channels.Tcp;
using System.Runtime.Remoting.Channels.Http;

namespace Wrox.ProCSharp.Remoting
{

   public class HelloServer
   {
      public static void Main(string[] args)
      {
         TcpServerChannel tcpChannel = new TcpServerChannel(8086);
         HttpServerChannel httpChannel = new HttpServerChannel(8085);

         // register the channels
         ChannelServices.RegisterChannel(tcpChannel);
         ChannelServices.RegisterChannel(httpChannel);
         //...
      }
```

A channel class must implement the `IChannel` interface. The `IChannel` interface has these two properties:

❑   `ChannelName` is a read-only property that returns the name of the channel. The name of the channel depends on the type; for example, the HTTP channel is named HTTP.

❑ ChannelPriority is a read-only property. More than one channel can be used for communication between a client and a server. The priority defines the order of the channel. On the client, the channel with the higher priority is chosen first to connect to the server. The bigger the priority value, the higher the priority. The default value is 1, but negative values are allowed to create lower priorities.

Additional interfaces are implemented depending on whether the channel is a client channel or a server channel. The server versions of the channels implement the IChannelReceiver interface, the client versions implement the IChannelSender interface.

The HttpChannel and TcpChannel classes can be used for both the client and the server. They implement IChannelSender and IChannelReceiver. These interfaces derive from IChannel.

The client-side IChannelSender has, in addition to IChannel, a single method called CreateMessageSink(), which returns an object that implements IMessageSink. The IMessageSink interface can be used for putting synchronous as well as asynchronous messages into the channel. With the server-side interface IChannelReceiver, the channel can be put into listening mode using StartListening(), and stopped again with StopListening(). The property ChannelData can be used to access the received data.

You can get information about the configuration of the channels using properties of the channel classes. For both channels, the properties ChannelName, a ChannelPriority, and a ChannelData are offered. The ChannelData property can be used to get information about the URIs that are stored in the ChannelDataStore class. With the HttpChannel there's also a Scheme property. The following code shows a helper method, ShowChannelProperties(), in our file HelloServer.cs that displays this information:

```
protected static void ShowChannelProperties(IChannelReceiver channel)
{
    Console.WriteLine("Name: " + channel.ChannelName);
    Console.WriteLine("Priority: " + channel.ChannelPriority);
    if (channel is HttpChannel)
    {
        HttpChannel httpChannel = channel as HttpChannel;
        Console.WriteLine("Scheme: " + httpChannel.ChannelScheme);
    }
    ChannelDataStore data = (ChannelDataStore)channel.ChannelData;
    foreach (string uri in data.ChannelUris)
    {
        Console.WriteLine("URI: " + uri);
    }
    Console.WriteLine();
}
```

The method ShowChannelProperties() is called after creating the channels in our Main() method. Starting the server you will get the console output that is shown in Figure 16-5. As you can see here, the default name for the TcpServerChannel is *tcp*, and the HTTP channel is called *http*. Both channels have a default priority of 1. The ports that have been set with the constructors are seen in the URI. The URI of the channels shows the protocol, IP address, and port number.

```
TcpServerChannel tcpChannel = new TcpServerChannel(8086);
ShowChannelProperties(tcpChannel);
HttpServerChannel httpChannel = new HttpServerChannel(8085);
ShowChannelProperties(httpChannel);
```

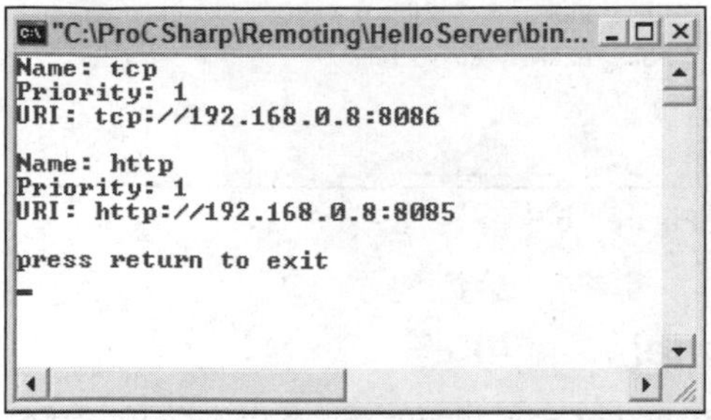

Figure 16-5

Setting channel properties

You can set all the properties of a channel in a list using the constructor
`TcpServerChannel(IDictionary, IServerChannelSinkProvider)`. The `Hashtable` class implements `IDictionary`, so you can set the `Name`, `Priority`, and `Port` property with help of this class. In
order to use the `Hashtable` class you have to declare the use of the `System.Collections` namespace.

With the constructor of the class `TcpServerChannel`, you can pass a object that implements the interface `IServerChannelSinkProvider` in addition to the `IDictionary` parameter. In the sample a
`SoapServerFormatterSinkProvider` is set instead of the `BinaryServerFormatterSinkProvider`,
which is the default of the `TcpServerChannel`. The default implementation of the
`SoapServerFormatterSinkProvider` class associates a `SoapServerFormatterSink` class with the
channel that uses a `SoapFormatter` object to convert the data for the transfer:

```
IDictionary properties = new Hashtable();
properties["name"] = "TCP Channel with a SOAP Formatter";
properties["priority"] = "20";
properties["port"] = "8086";
SoapServerFormatterSinkProvider sinkProvider =
                    new SoapServerFormatterSinkProvider();
TcpServerChannel tcpChannel =
                    new TcpServerChannel(properties, sinkProvider);
ShowChannelProperties(tcpChannel);
```

The new output from the server console shows the new properties of the TCP channel (see Figure 16-6).

Depending on the channel types, different properties can be specified. Both the TCP and the HTTP channel support the `name` and `priority` channel property that we used in our example. These channels also
support other properties such as `bindTo`, which specifies an IP address for binding that can be used if
the computer has multiple IP addresses configured. `rejectRemoteRequests` is supported by the TCP
server channel to allow client connections only from the local computer.

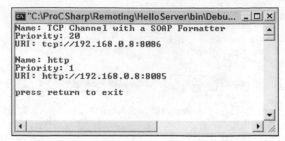

Figure 16-6

Pluggability of a channel

A custom channel can be created to send the messages using a transport protocol other than HTTP or TCP, or you can extend the existing channels:

❑ The sending part must implement the `IchannelSender` interface. The most important part is the `CreateMessageSink()` method, which the client sends a URL, and with this a connection to the server can be instantiated. Here a message sink must be created, which is then used by the proxy to send messages to the channel.

❑ The receiving part must implement the `IchannelReceiver` interface. You have to start the listening in the `ChannelData get` property. Then you can wait in a separate thread to receive data from the client. After unmarshaling the message, you can use `ChannelServices.SyncDispatchMessage()` to dispatch the message to the object.

Formatters

The .NET Framework delivers two formatter classes:

❑ `System.Runtime.Serialization.Formatters.Binary.BinaryFormatter`

❑ `System.Runtime.Serialization.Formatters.Soap.SoapFormatter`

Formatters are associated with channels through formatter sink objects and formatter sink providers.

Both of these formatter classes implement the interface `System.Runtime.Remoting.Messaging.IRemotingFormatter`, which defines the methods `Serialize()` and `Deserialize()` to transfer the data to and from the channel.

The formatter is also pluggable. When you're writing a custom formatter class, an instance must be associated with the channel you want to use. This is done by using a formatter sink and a formatter sink provider. The formatter sink provider, for example, `SoapServerFormatterSinkProvider`, can be passed as an argument when creating a channel as we saw earlier. A formatter sink provider implements the interface `IServerChannelSinkProvider` for the server, and `IClientChannelSinkProvider` for the client. Both of these interfaces define a `CreateSink()` method where a formatter sink must be returned. The `SoapServerFormatterSinkProvider` returns an instance of the class `SoapServerFormatterSink`.

On the client side the `SoapClientFormatterSink` class uses the `SyncProcessMessage()` and `AsyncProcessMessage()` methods of the `SoapFormatter` class to serialize the message. The `SoapServerFormatterSink` class deserializes the message, again using the `SoapFormatter` class.

All these sink and provider classes can be extended and replaced with custom implementations.

ChannelServices and RemotingConfiguration

The `ChannelServices` utility class is used to register channels into the .NET Remoting runtime. With this class you can also access all registered channels. This is extremely useful if configuration files are used to configure the channel, because here the channel is created implicitly, as we will see later.

A channel is registered using the static method `ChannelServices.RegisterChannel()`.

You can see here the server code to register our HTTP and TCP channels:

```
TcpChannel tcpChannel = new TcpChannel(8086);
HttpChannel httpChannel = new HttpChannel(8085);
ChannelServices.RegisterChannel(tcpChannel);
ChannelServices.RegisterChannel(httpChannel);
```

The `ChannelServices` utility class can now be used to dispatch synchronous and asynchronous messages, and to unregister specific channels. The `RegisteredChannels` property returns an `IChannel` array of all the channels we registered. You can also use the `GetChannel()` method to get to a specific channel by its name. With the help of `ChannelServices` you can write a custom administration utility that manages our channels. Here is a small example that shows how the server channel can be stopped from listening to incoming requests:

```
HttpServerChannel channel =(HttpServerChannel)ChannelServices.GetChannel("http");
channel.StopListening(null);
```

The `RemotingConfiguration` class is another .NET Remoting utility class. On the server side it's used to register remote object types for server-activated objects, and to marshal remote objects to a marshaled object reference class `ObjRef`. `ObjRef` is a serializable representation of an object that's sent over the wire. On the client side, `RemotingServices` is used to unmarshal a remote object in order to create a proxy from the object reference.

Here is the server-side code to register a well-known remote object type to the `RemotingServices`:

```
RemotingConfiguration.RegisterWellKnownServiceType(
                          typeof(Hello),                    // Type
                          "Hi",                             // URI
                          WellKnownObjectMode.SingleCall); // Mode
```

The first argument of `RegisterWellKnownServiceType()`, `typeof(Hello)`, specifies the type of the remote object. The second argument, `"Hi"`, is the uniform resource identifier of the remote object that the client uses to access the remote object. The last argument is the mode of the remote object. The mode can be a value of the `WellKnownObjectMode` enumeration: `SingleCall` or `Singleton`.

❑ *SingleCall* means that the object holds no state. With every call to the remote object a new instance is created. A single-call object is created from the server with the `RemotingConfiguration.RegisterWellKnownServiceType()` method, and a `WellKnownObjectMode.SingleCall` argument. This is very efficient on the server because it means that we don't need to hold any resources for maybe thousands of clients.

❑ With a *Singleton t*he object is shared for all clients of the server; typically, such object types can be used if you want to share some data between all clients. This shouldn't be a problem for read-only data, but with read-write data you have to be aware of locking issues and scalability. A singleton object is created by the server with the `RemotingConfiguration.Register WellKnownServiceType()` method and a `WellKnownObjectMode.Singleton` argument. You have to pay attention to locking of resources held by the singleton object; you have to make sure that data can't be corrupted when clients are accessing the singleton object concurrently, but you also have to check that the locking is done efficiently enough so that the required scalability is reached.

Server for client-activated objects

If a remote object should hold state for a specific client, you can use client-activated objects. In the next section we will look at how to call server-activated or client-activated objects on the client side. On the server side client-activated objects must be registered in a different way from server-activated objects.

Instead of calling `RemotingConfiguration.RegisterWellKnownType()`, you have to call `RemotingConfiguration.RegisterActivatedServiceType()`. With this method, only the type is specified, and not the URI. The reason for this is that for client-activated objects, the clients can instantiate different object types with the same URI. The URI for all client-activated objects must be defined using `RemotingConfiguration.ApplicationName`:

```
RemotingConfiguration.ApplicationName = "HelloServer";
RemotingConfiguration.RegisterActivatedServiceType(typeof(Hello));
```

Object Activation

Clients can use and create remote `Activator` class. You can get a proxy to a server-activated or well-known remote object using the `GetObject()` method. The `CreateInstance()` method returns a proxy to a client-activated remote object.

Instead of using the `Activator` class, the `new` operator can also be used to activate remote objects. To make this possible, the remote object must also be configured within the client using the `RemotingConfiguration` class.

Application URL

In all activation scenarios, you have to specify a URL to the remote object. This URL is the same one you'd use when browsing with a Web browser. The first part specifies the protocol followed by the server name or IP address, the port number, and a URI that was specified when registering the remote object on the server in this form:

```
protocol://server:port/URI
```

In the code samples two URL examples are used continuously in the code. With the URL, the protocol is specified with `http` and `tcp`, the server name is `localhost`, the port numbers are 8085 and 8086, and the URI is `Hi`, as follows:

```
http://localhost:8085/Hi
tcp://localhost:8086/Hi
```

Activating well-known objects

In the previous, simple client example well-known objects have been activated. Now we are going to take a more detailed look at the activation sequence.

```
using System;
using System.Runtime.Remoting;
using System.Runtime.Remoting.Channels;
using System.Runtime.Remoting.Channels.Tcp;

// ...
TcpClientChannel channel = new TcpClientChannel();
ChannelServices.RegisterChannel(channel);
```

```
Hello obj = (Hello)Activator.GetObject(typeof(Hello),
                              "tcp://localhost:8086/Hi");
```

`GetObject()` is a static method of the class `System.Activator` that calls `RemotingServices` `.Connect()` to return a proxy object to the remote object. The first argument of this method specifies the type of the remote object. The proxy implements all public and protected methods and properties, so that the client can call these methods as it would on the real object. The second argument is the URL to the remote object. Here the string `tcp://localhost:8086/Hi` is used. `tcp` is the protocol, `localhost:8086` is the hostname and the port number, and finally `Hi` is the URI of the object that is specified using `RemotingConfiguration.RegisterWellKnownServiceType()`.

Instead of using `Activator.GetObject()`, you can also use `RemotingServices.Connect()` directly:

```
Hello obj = (Hello)RemotingServices.Connect(typeof(Hello),
                                  "tcp://localhost:8086/Hi");
```

If you prefer to use the `new` operator to activate well-known remote objects, the remote object can be registered on the client using `RemotingConfiguration.RegisterWellKnownClientType()`. The arguments needed here are similar: the type of the remote object and the URI. `new` doesn't really create a new remote object, it returns a proxy similar to `Activator.GetObject()` instead. If the remote object is registered with a flag `WellKnownObjectMode.SingleCall`, the rule always stays the same—the remote object is created with every method call:

```
RemotingConfiguration.RegisterWellKnownClientType(typeof(Hello),
                                        "tcp://localhost:8086/Hi");
Hello obj = new Hello();
```

Activating client-activated objects

Remote objects can hold state for a client. `Activator.CreateInstance()` creates a client-activated remote object. Using the `Activator.GetObject()` method, the remote object is created on a method call, and is destroyed when the method is finished. The object doesn't hold state on the server. The situation is different with `Activator.CreateInstance()`. With the static `CreateInstance()` method an activation sequence is started to create the remote object. This object lives until the lease time is expired and a garbage collection occurs. We discuss the leasing mechanism later in this chapter.

Some of the overloaded `Activator.CreateInstance()` methods can only be used to create local objects. To create remote objects a method is needed where it's possible to pass activation attributes. One of these overloaded methods is used in the example. This method accepts two string parameters, the first is the name of the assembly and the second is the type, and a third parameter, an array of objects. The channel and the object name are specified in the object array with the help of a `UrlAttribute`. To use the `UrlAttribute` class the namespace `System.Runtime.Remoting.Activation` must be specified.

```
object[] attrs = {new UrlAttribute("tcp://localhost:8086/HelloServer") };
ObjectHandle handle = Activator.CreateInstance(
              "RemoteHello", "Wrox.ProCSharp.Remoting.Hello", attrs);
if (handle == null)
{
   Console.WriteLine("could not locate server");
    return;
}
Hello obj = (Hello)handle.Unwrap();
Console.WriteLine(obj.Greeting("Christian"));
```

Of course, for client-activated objects it's again possible to use the new operator instead of the `Activator` class. By doing this you have to register the client-activated object using `RemotingConfiguration.RegisterActivatedClientType()`. In the architecture of client-activated objects the new operator not only returns a proxy but also creates the remote object:

```
RemotingConfiguration.RegisterActivatedClientType(typeof(Hello),
                                  "tcp://localhost:8086/HelloServer");
Hello obj = new Hello();
```

Proxy objects

The `Activator.GetObject()` and `Activator.CreateInstance()` methods return a proxy to the client. Actually, two proxies are used: the transparent proxy and the real proxy. The transparent proxy looks like the remote object—it implements all public methods of the remote object. These methods just call the `Invoke()` method of the `RealProxy`, where a message containing the method to call is passed. The real proxy sends the message to the channel with the help of message sinks.

With `RemotingServices.IsTransparentProxy()`, you can check if our object is really a transparent proxy. You can also get to the real proxy using `RemotingServices.GetRealProxy()`. Using the Visual Studio .NET debugger, it's now easy to see all the properties of the real proxy:

```
ChannelServices.RegisterChannel(new TCPChannel());
Hello obj = (Hello)Activator.GetObject(typeof(Hello),
                                  "tcp://localhost:8086/Hi");
if (obj == null)
{
   Console.WriteLine("could not locate server");
   return;
```

```
}
if (RemotingServices.IsTransparentProxy(obj))
{
    Console.WriteLine("Using a transparent proxy");
    RealProxy proxy = RemotingServices.GetRealProxy(obj);

    // proxy.Invoke(message);
}
```

Pluggability of a proxy

The real proxy can be replaced with a custom proxy. A custom proxy can extend the base class System.Runtime.Remoting.Proxies.RealProxy. The type of the remote object is received in the constructor of the custom proxy. Calling the constructor of the RealProxy creates a transparent proxy in addition to the real proxy. In the constructor, the registered channels can be accessed with the help of the ChannelServices class to create a message sink IChannelSender.CreateMessageSink(). Besides implementing the constructor, a custom channel has to override the Invoke() method. In Invoke() a message is received that can be analyzed and sent to the message sink.

Messages

The proxy sends a message into the channel. On the server side, a method call can be made after analyzing the message, so let's look at messages.

.NET Framework has some message classes for method calls, responses, return messages, and so on. What all the message classes have in common is that they implement the IMessage interface. This interface has a single property: Properties. This property represents a dictionary with the IDictionary interface which packages the URI to the object, MethodName, MethodSignature, TypeName, Args, and CallContext.

Figure 16-7 shows the hierarchy of the message classes and interfaces. The message that is sent to the real proxy is an object of type MethodCall. With the interfaces IMethodCallMessage and IMethodMessage you can have easier access to the properties of the message than through the IMessage interface. Instead of having to use the IDictionary interface, you have direct access to the method name, the URI, the arguments, and so on. The real proxy returns a ReturnMessage to the transparent proxy.

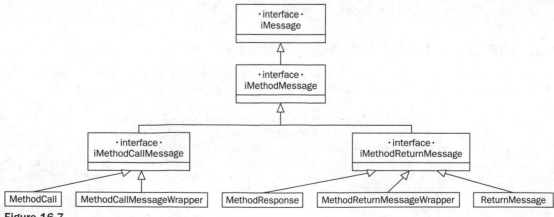

Figure 16-7

Message Sinks

The `Activator.GetObject()` method calls `RemotingServices.Connect()` to connect to a well-known object. In the `Connect()` method, an `Unmarshal()` happens where not only the proxy, but also envoy sinks, are created. The proxy uses a chain of envoy sinks to pass the message to the channel. All the sinks are interceptors that can change the messages and perform some additional actions such as creating a lock, writing an event, performing security checking, and so on.

All message sinks implement the interface `IMessageSink`. This interface defines one property and two methods:

❑ The property `NextSink` is used by a sink to get to the next sink and pass the message along.

❑ For synchronous messages, `SyncProcessMessage()` is invoked by a previous sink or by the remoting infrastructure. It has an `IMessage` parameter to send a message and to return a message.

❑ For asynchronous messages, `AsyncProcessMessage()` is invoked by a previous sink in the chain, or by the remoting infrastructure. `AsyncProcessMessage()` has two parameters: a message and a message sink that receives the reply.

Let's take a look at the three different message sinks available for use.

Envoy sink

You can get to the chain of envoy sinks using the `IEnvoyInfo` interface. The marshaled object reference `ObjRef` has the `EnvoyInfo` property which returns the `IEnvoyInfo` interface. The envoy list is created from the server context, so the server can inject functionality into the client. Envoys can collect identity information about the client and pass that information to the server.

Server context sink

When the message is received on the server side of the channel, it is passed to the server context sinks. The last of the server context sinks routes the message to the object sink chain.

Object sink

The object sink is associated with a particular object. If the object class defines particular context attributes, context sinks are created for the object.

Passing Objects in Remote Methods

The parameter types of remote method calls aren't just limited to basic data types, but can also be classes that we define ourselves. For remoting three types of classes must be differentiated:

❑ **Marshal-by-value classes**—These classes are serialized through the channel. Classes that should be marshaled must be marked with the `[Serializable]` attribute. Objects of these classes don't have a remote identity, because the complete object is marshaled through the channel, and the object that is serialized to the client is independent of the server object (or the other way around). Marshal-by-value classes are also called *unbound classes* because they don't have data that depends on the application domain.

❑ **Marshal-by-reference classes**—These classes do have a remote identity. The objects are not passed across the wire, but a proxy is returned instead. A class that is marshaled by reference must derive from MarshalByRefObject. MarshalByRefObjects are known as *application domain–bound objects*. A specialized version of MarshalByRefObject is ContextBoundObject: the abstract class ContextBoundObject is derived from MarshalByRefObject. If a class is derived from ContextBoundObject, a proxy is needed even in the same application domain when context boundaries are crossed. Such objects are called *context-bound objects*, and they are only valid in the creation context.

❑ **Not-remotable classes**—These are classes that are not serializable and don't derive from MarshalByRefObject. Classes of these types cannot be used as parameters in a remote object's public methods. These classes are bound to the application domain where they are created. Non-remotable classes should be used if the class has a data member that is only valid in the application domain, such as a Win32 file handle.

To see marshaling in action, change the remote object in order to send two objects to the client: the class MySerialized will be sent marshal-by-value, the class MyRemote marshal-by-reference. In the methods a message is written to the console so that you can verify if the call was made on the client or on the server. In addition, the Hello class is extended to return a MySerialized and a MyRemote instance:

```csharp
using System;

namespace Wrox.ProCSharp.Remoting
{
    [Serializable]
    public class MySerialized
    {
        public MySerialized(int val)
        {
            a = val;
        }
        public void Foo()
        {
            Console.WriteLine("MySerialized.Foo called");
        }
        public int A
        {
            get
            {
                Console.WriteLine("MySerialized.A called");
                return a;
            }
            set
            {
                a = value;
            }
        }
        protected int a;
    }
    public class MyRemote : System.MarshalByRefObject
    {
        public MyRemote(int val)
```

```
        {
            a = val;
        }
        public void Foo()
        {
            Console.WriteLine("MyRemote.Foo called");
        }
        public int A
        {
            get
            {
                Console.WriteLine("MyRemote.A called");
                return a;
            }
            set
            {
                a = value;
            }
        }
        protected int a;
    }

public class Hello : System.MarshalByRefObject
{
    public Hello()
    {
        Console.WriteLine("Constructor called");
    }
    ~Hello()
    {
        Console.WriteLine("Destructor called");
    }
    public string Greeting(string name)
    {
        Console.WriteLine("Greeting called");
        return "Hello, " + name;
    }
    public MySerialized GetMySerialized()
    {
        return new MySerialized(4711);
    }
    public MyRemote GetMyRemote()
    {
        return new MyRemote(4712);
    }
}
}
```

The client application also needs to be changed to see the effects when using marshaled-by-value and marshaled-by-reference objects. Invoke the methods GetMySerialized() and GetMyRemote() to retrieve the new objects. Also make use of the method RemotingServices.IsTransparentProxy() to check if the returned object is a proxy or not.

```
ChannelServices.RegisterChannel(new TcpChannel());
Hello obj = (Hello)Activator.GetObject(typeof(Hello),
                                       "tcp://localhost:8086/Hi");

if (obj == null)
{
    Console.WriteLine("could not locate server");
    return;
}
MySerialized ser = obj.GetMySerialized();
if (!RemotingServices.IsTransparentProxy(ser))
{
    Console.WriteLine("ser is not a transparent proxy");
}
ser.Foo();
MyRemote rem = obj.GetMyRemote();
if (RemotingServices.IsTransparentProxy(rem))
{
    Console.WriteLine("rem is a transparent proxy");
}
rem.Foo();
```

In the client console window (see Figure 16-8), you can see that the `ser` object is called on the client. This object is not a transparent proxy because it's serialized to the client. In contrast, the `rem` object on the client is a transparent proxy. Methods called on this object are transferred to the server.

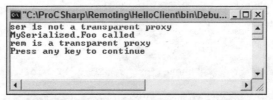

Figure 16-8

The server output (see Figure 16-9) reveals that the `Foo()` method is called with the remote object `MyRemote`.

Figure 16-9

Security and serialized objects

One important difference with .NET Remoting and ASP.NET Web services is how objects are marshaled. With ASP.NET Web services, only the public fields and properties are transferred across the wire. .NET Remoting uses a different serialization mechanism to serialize all data, including all private data. Malicious clients could use the serialization and deserialization phases to harm the application.

To take this problem into account, .NET 1.1 changed the behavior passing objects across .NET Remoting boundaries to define two automatic deserialization levels: low and full.

By default, low-level deserialization is used. With low-level deserialization it is not possible to pass ObjRef objects, and objects that implement the ISponsor interface. To make this possible, you can change the deserialization level to full. You can do this programmatically by creating a formatter sink provider, and assign the property TypeFilterLevel. For the binary formatter, the provider class is BinaryServerFormatterSinkProvider, whereas for the SOAP formatter the provider class is SoapServerFormatterSinkProvider.

The following code shows how you can create a TCP channel with full serialization support.

```
BinaryServerFormatterSinkProvider serverProvider =
    new BinaryServerFormatterSinkProvider();
serverProvider.TypeFilterLevel = TypeFilterLevel.Full;

BinaryClientFormatterSinkProvider clientProvider =
    new BinaryClientFormatterSinkProvider();

IDictionary props = new Hashtable();
props["port"] = 6789;

TcpChannel channel = new TcpChannel(props, clientProvider, serverProvider);
```

At first, a BinaryServerFormatterSinkProvider is created where the property TypeFilterLevel is set to TypeFilterLevel.Full. The enumeration TypeFilterLevel is defined in the namespace System.Runtime.Serialization.Formatters, so you have to declare this namespace. For the client side of the channel, a BinaryClientFormatterSinkProvider is created. Both the client-side and the server-side formatter sink provider instances are passed to the constructor of the TcpChannel, as well as the IDictionary properties that define the attributes of the channel.

Directional attributes

Remote objects are never transferred over the wire, whereas value types and serializable classes are transferred. Sometimes the data should be sent only in one direction. This can be especially important when the data is transferred over the network. For example, if you want to send data in a collection to the server for the server to perform some calculation on this data and return a simple value to the client, it would not be very efficient to send the collection back to the client. With COM it was possible to declare directional attributes [in], [out], and [in, out] to the arguments if the data should be sent to the server, to the client, or in both directions.

C# has similar attributes as part of the language: ref and out method parameters. The ref and out method parameters can be used for value types and for reference types that are serializable. Using the ref parameter, the argument is marshaled in both directions, out goes from the server to the client, and using no parameter sends the data to the server.

You can read more about the **out** *and* **ref** *keywords in Chapter 3.*

Lifetime Management

How do a client and a server detect if the other side is not available anymore, and what are the problems we might get into?

For a client, the answer can be simple. As soon as the client does a call to a method on the remote object you get an exception of type System.Runtime.Remoting.RemotingException. You just have to handle this exception and do what's necessary, for example, perform a retry, write to a log, inform the user, and so on.

What about the server? When does the server detect if the client is not around anymore, meaning that the server can go ahead and clean up any resources it's holding for the client? You could wait until the next method call from the client—but maybe it will never arrive. In the COM realm, the DCOM protocol used a ping mechanism. The client sent a ping to the server with the information about the object referenced. A client can have hundreds of objects referenced on the server, and so the information in the ping can be very large. To make this mechanism more efficient, DCOM didn't send all the information about all objects, but just the difference from the previous ping.

This ping mechanism was efficient on a LAN, but it is not suitable for scalable solutions—imagine thousands of clients sending ping information to the server! .NET Remoting has a much more scalable solution for lifetime management: the *Leasing Distributed Garbage Collector* (LDGC).

This lifetime management is only active for *client-activated objects* and well-known singleton objects. Single-call objects can be destroyed after every method call because they don't hold state. Client-activated objects do have state and we should be aware of the resources used. For client-activated objects that are referenced outside the application domain a lease is created. A lease has a lease time. When the lease time reaches zero the lease expires and the remote object is disconnected and, finally, it is garbage-collected.

Lease renewals

If the client calls a method on the object when the lease has expired, an exception is thrown. If you have a client where the remote object could be needed for more than 300 seconds (the default value for lease times), you have three ways to renew a lease:

❏ **Implicit renewal**—This renewal of the lease is automatically done when the client calls a method on the remote object. If the current lease time is less than the RenewOnCallTime value, the lease is set to RenewOnCallTime.

❏ **Explicit renewal**—With this renewal the client can specify the new lease time. This is done with the Renew() method of the ILease interface. You can get to the ILease interface by calling the GetLifetimeService() method of the transparent proxy.

❏ **Sponsoring renewal**—In the case of this renewal the client can create a sponsor that implements the ISponsor interface and registers the sponsor in the leasing services using the Register() method of the ILease interface. The sponsor defines the lease extension time. When a lease expires the sponsor is asked for an extension of the lease. The sponsoring mechanism can be used if you want long-lived remote objects on the server.

Leasing configuration values

Let's look at the values that can be configured:

❏ LeaseTime defines the time until a lease expires.

❏ RenewOnCallTime is the time the lease is set on a method call if the current lease time has a lower value.

❏ If a sponsor is not available within the SponsorshipTimeout, the remoting infrastructure looks for the next sponsor. If there are no more sponsors, the lease expires.

❏ The LeaseManagerPollTime defines the time interval at which the lease manager checks for expired objects.

The default values are listed in the following table.

Lease Configuration	Default Value (seconds)
LeaseTime	300
RenewOnCallTime	120
SponsorshipTimeout	120
LeaseManagerPollTime	10

Classes used for lifetime management

The ClientSponsor class implements the ISponsor interface. It can be used on the client side for lease extension. With the ILease interface you can get all information about the lease, all the lease properties, and the current lease time and state. The state is specified with the LeaseState enumeration. With the LifetimeServices utility class you can get and set the properties for the lease of all remote objects in the application domain.

Getting lease information example

In this small code example the lease information is accessed by calling the GetLifetimeService() method of the transparent proxy. For the ILease interface you have to declare the namespace System. Runtime.Remoting.Lifetime.

The leasing mechanism can only be used with stateful (client-activated and singleton) objects. Single-call objects are instantiated with every method call anyway, so the leasing mechanism doesn't apply. To offer client-activated objects with the server you can change the remoting configuration to a call to RegisterActivatedServiceType() in the file HelloServer.cs:

```
RemotingConfiguration.ApplicationName = "Hello";
RemotingConfiguration.RegisterActivatedServiceType(typeof(Hello));
```

In the client application the instantiation of the remote object must be changed, too. Instead of using the method `Activator.GetObject()`, `Activator.CreateInstance()` is used to invoke client-activated objects:

```
ChannelServices.RegisterChannel(new TcpChannel());
```

```
object[] attrs = {new UrlAttribute("tcp://localhost:8086/Hello") };
Hello obj = (Hello)Activator.CreateInstance(typeof(Hello), null, attrs);
```

To show the leasing time you can use the `ILease` interface that is returned by calling `GetLifetimeService()` from the proxy object:

```
ILease lease = (ILease)obj.GetLifetimeService();
if (lease != null)
{
    Console.WriteLine("Lease Configuration:");
    Console.WriteLine("InitialLeaseTime: " +
                        lease.InitialLeaseTime);
    Console.WriteLine("RenewOnCallTime: " +
                        lease.RenewOnCallTime);
    Console.WriteLine("SponsorshipTimeout: " +
                        lease.SponsorshipTimeout);
    Console.WriteLine(lease.CurrentLeaseTime);
}
```

Figure 16-10 shows the output you will see in the client console window.

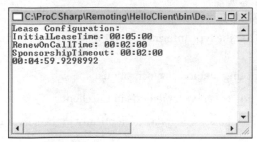

Figure 16-10

Changing default lease configurations

The server itself can change the default lease configuration for all remote objects of the server using the `System.Runtime.Remoting.Lifetime.LifetimeServices` utility class:

```
LifetimeServices.LeaseTime = TimeSpan.FromMinutes(10);
LifetimeServices.RenewOnCallTime = TimeSpan.FromMinutes(2);
```

If you want different default lifetimes depending on the type of the remote object, you can change the lease configuration of the remote object by overriding the `InitializeLifetimeService()` method of the base class `MarshalByRefObject`:

```
public class Hello : System.MarshalByRefObject
{
   public Hello()
   {
      Console.WriteLine("Constructor called");
   }
   ~Hello()
   {
      Console.WriteLine("Destructor called");
   }
   public override Object InitializeLifetimeService()
   {
      ILease lease = (ILease)base.InitializeLifetimeService();
      lease.InitialLeaseTime = TimeSpan.FromMinutes(10);
      lease.RenewOnCallTime = TimeSpan.FromSeconds(40);
      return lease;
   }
}
```

The lifetime services configuration can also be done by using a configuration file as will be discussed next.

Miscellaneous .NET Remoting Features

In the final section of this chapter we explore the following .NET Remoting features:

❑   How application configuration files can be used to define remoting channels

❑   Hosting .NET Remoting Servers in a IIS Server by using the ASP.NET runtime

❑   Different ways to get the type information of the server for building the client with the utility SOAPSuds

❑   Calling .NET Remoting methods asynchronously

❑   Implementing events to callback methods in the client

❑   Using call contexts to pass some data automatically to the server behind the scenes

Configuration Files

Instead of writing the channel and object configuration in the source code, you can use configuration files. This way the channel can be reconfigured, additional channels can be added, and so on, without changing the source code. Like all the other configuration files on the .NET platform, XML is used. The same application and configuration files that you read about in Chapter 13 and in Chapter 14 are used here, too. For .NET Remoting, there are some more XML elements and attributes to configure the channel and the remote objects. What's different with the remoting configuration file is that this configuration doesn't need to be in the application configuration file itself; the file can have any name. For ease of use in this chapter, we will write the Remoting configuration inside the application configuration files that are named with a .config file extension after the filename of the executable.

The code download (from www.wrox.xom) contains the following example configuration files in the root directory of the client and the server examples: clientactivated.config and wellknown.config. With the client example you will also find the file wellknownhttp.config that specifies an HTTP channel to a well-known remote object. To use these configurations, the files must be renamed as above and placed in the directory containing the executable file.

Here is just one example of what such a configuration file might look like:

```
<configuration>
   <system.runtime.remoting>
      <application name="Hello">
         <service>
            <wellknown mode="SingleCall"
               type="Wrox.ProCSharp.Remoting.Hello, RemoteHello"
                  objectUri="Hi" />
         </service>
         <channels>
            <channel ref="tcp" port="6791" />
            <channel ref="http" port="6792" />
         </channels>
      </application>
   </system.runtime.remoting>
</configuration>
```

<configuration> is the XML root element for all .NET configuration files. All the remoting configurations can be found in the subelement <system.runtime.remoting>. <application> is a subelement of <system.runtime.remoting>.

Let's look at the main elements and attributes of the parts within <system.runtime.remoting>:

❑ With the <application> element you can specify the name of the application using the attribute name. On the server side, this is the name of the server, and on the client side it's the name of the client application. As an example for a server configuration, <application name="Hello"> defines the remote application name Hello, which is used as part of the URL by the client to access the remote object.

❑ On the server, the element <service> is used to specify a collection of remote objects. It can have <wellknown> and <activated> subelements to specify the type of the remote object as well-known or client-activated.

❑ The client part of the <service> element is <client>. Like the <service> element, it can have <wellknown> and <activated> subelements to specify the type of the remote object. Unlike the <service> counterpart, <client> has a url attribute to specify the URL to the remote object.

❑ <wellknown> is a element that's used on the server and the client to specify well-known remote objects. The server part could look like this:

```
<wellknown mode="SingleCall"
   type="Wrox.ProCSharp.Remoting.Hello, RemoteHello"
      objectURI="Hi" />
```

While the `mode` attribute `SingleCall` or `Singleton` can be specified, the type is the type of the remote class, including the namespace `Wrox.ProCSharp.Remoting.Hello`, followed by the assembly name RemoteHello. `objectURI` is the name of the remote object that's registered in the channel.

On the client, the `type` attribute is the same as it is for the server version. `mode` and `objectURI` are not needed, but instead the `url` attribute is used to define the path to the remote object: protocol, hostname, port number, application name, and the object URI:

```
<wellknown type="Wrox.ProCSharp.Remoting.Hello, RemoteHello"
           url="tcp://localhost:6791/Hello/Hi" />
```

❑   The `<activated>` element is used for client-activated objects. With the `type` attribute the type and the assembly must be defined for both the client and the server application:

```
<activated type="Wrox.ProCSharp.Remoting.Hello, RemoteHello" />
```

❑   To specify the channel, the `<channel>` element is used. It's a subelement of `<channels>` so that a collection of channels can be configured for a single application. Its use is similar for clients and servers. With the XML attribute `ref` we reference a channel name that is configured in the configuration file machine.config. We will look into this file next. For the server channel you have to set the port number with the XML attribute `port`. The XML attribute `displayName` is used to specify a name for the channel that is used from the .NET Framework Configuration tool, as we will discuss later in this chapter.

```
<channels>
    <channel ref="tcp" port="6791" displayName="TCP Channel" />
    <channel ref="http" port="6792" displayName="HTTP Channel" />
</channels>
```

Predefined channels in machine.config

Predefined channels can be found in the machine.config configuration file that you can find in the directory <windir>\Microsoft.NET\Framework\<version>\CONFIG. You can use these predefined channels in your application, or you can specify your own channel class.

In the XML file below you can see an extract of the machine.config file showing the predefined channels. The `<channel>` element is used as a subelement of `<channels>` to define channels. Here the attribute `id` specifies a name of a channel that can be referenced with the `ref` attribute. With the `type` attribute the class of the channel is specified followed by the assembly; for example, the channel class `System.Runtime.Remoting.Channels.Http.HttpChannel` can be found in the assembly `System.Runtime.Remoting`. Because the `System.Runtime.Remoting` assembly is shared, the strong name of the assembly must be specified with `Version`, `Culture`, and `PublicKeyToken`.

```
<system.runtime.remoting>
  <!-- ... -->
    <channels>
      <channel id="http" type="System.Runtime.Remoting.Channels.Http.HttpChannel,
        System.Runtime.Remoting, Version=1.0.5000.0, Culture=neutral,
        PublicKeyToken=b77a5c561934e089"/>
      <channel id="http client"
        type="System.Runtime.Remoting.Channels.Http.HttpClientChannel,
        System.Runtime.Remoting, Version=1.0.5000.0, Culture=neutral,
```

```
            PublicKeyToken=b77a5c561934e089"/>
        <channel id="http server"
          type="System.Runtime.Remoting.Channels.Http.HttpServerChannel,
          System.Runtime.Remoting, Version=1.0.5000.0, Culture=neutral,
          PublicKeyToken=b77a5c561934e089"/>
        <channel id="tcp" type="System.Runtime.Remoting.Channels.Tcp.TcpChannel,
          System.Runtime.Remoting, Version=1.0.5000.0, Culture=neutral,
          PublicKeyToken=b77a5c561934e089"/>
        <channel id="tcp client"
          type="System.Runtime.Remoting.Channels.Tcp.TcpClientChannel,
          System.Runtime.Remoting, Version=1.0.5000.0, Culture=neutral,
          PublicKeyToken=b77a5c561934e089"/>
        <channel id="tcp server"
          type="System.Runtime.Remoting.Channels.Tcp.TcpServerChannel,
          System.Runtime.Remoting, Version=1.0.5000.0, Culture=neutral,
          PublicKeyToken=b77a5c561934e089"/>
      </channels>
    <!-- ... -->
  <system.runtime.remoting>
```

Server configuration for well-known objects

This example file, Wellknown_Server.config, has the value Hello for the name property. In the configuration file below the TCP channel is set to listen on port 6791, and the HTTP channel to listen on port 6792. The remote object class is Wrox.ProCSharp.Remoting.Hello in the assembly RemoteHello, the object is called Hi in the channel, and the object mode SingleCall:

```
<configuration>
   <system.runtime.remoting>
      <application name="Hello">
         <service>
            <wellknown mode="SingleCall"
                       type="Wrox.ProCSharp.Remoting.Hello, RemoteHello"
                       objectUri="Hi" />
         </service>
         <channels>
            <channel ref="tcp" port="6791"
               displayName="TCP Channel (HelloServer)" />
            <channel ref="http" port="6792"
               displayName="HTTP Channel (HelloServer)" />
         </channels>
      </application>
   </system.runtime.remoting>
</configuration>
```

Client configuration for well-known objects

For well-known objects, you have to specify the assembly and the channel in the client configuration file Wellknown_Client.config. The types for the remote object can be found in the RemoteHello assembly, Hi is the name of the object in the channel, and the URI for the remote type Wrox.ProCSharp.Remoting. Hello is tcp://localhost:6791/Hi. In the client a TCP channel is used as well, but no port is specified, so a free port is selected:

```
<configuration>
   <system.runtime.remoting>
      <application name="Client">
         <client displayName="Hello client for well-known objects">
            <wellknown type = "Wrox.ProCSharp.Remoting.Hello, RemoteHello"
                             url="tcp://localhost:6791/Hello/Hi" />
         </client>
         <channels>
            <channel ref="tcp" displayName="TCP Channel (HelloClient)" />
         </channels>
      </application>
   </system.runtime.remoting>
</configuration>
```

A small change in the configuration file, and you're using the HTTP channel (as can be seen in WellknownHttp_Client.config):

```
<client>
   <wellknown type="Wrox.ProCSharp.Remoting.Hello, RemoteHello"
                   url="http://localhost:6792/Hello/Hi" />
</client>
<channels>
   <channel ref="http" displayName="HTTP Channel (HelloClient)" />
</channels>
```

Server configuration for client-activated objects

By changing only the configuration file (which is located in ClientActivated_Server.config), you can change the server configuration from server-activated to client-activated objects. Here the `<activated>` subelement of the `<service>` element is specified. With the `<activated>` element for the server configuration, just the `type` attribute must be specified. The `name` attribute of the `application` element defines the URI:

```
<configuration>
   <system.runtime.remoting>
      <application name="HelloServer">
         <service>
            <activated type="Wrox.ProCSharp.Remoting.Hello, RemoteHello" />
         </service>
         <channels>
            <channel ref="http" port="6788"
                     displayName="HTTP Channel (HelloServer)" />
            <channel ref="tcp" port="6789"
                displayName="TCP Channel (HelloServer)" />
         </channels>
      </application>
   </system.runtime.remoting>
</configuration>
```

Client configuration for client-activated objects

The ClientActivated_Client.config file defines the client-activated remote object using the `url` attribute of the `<client>` element and the `type` attribute of the `<activated>` element:

```
<configuration>
    <system.runtime.remoting>
        <application>
            <client url="http://localhost:6788/HelloServer"
                    displayName="Hello client for client-activated objects">
                <activated type="Wrox.ProCSharp.Remoting.Hello, RemoteHello" />
            </client>
            <channels>
                <channel ref="http" displayName="HTTP Channel (HelloClient)" />
                <channel ref="tcp" displayName="TCP Channel (HelloClient)" />
            </channels>
        </application>
    </system.runtime.remoting>
</configuration>
```

Server code using configuration files

In the server code you have to configure remoting using the static method `Configure()` from the `RemotingConfiguration` class. Here all the channels that are defined are built up and instantiated. Maybe we also want to know about the channel configurations from the server application—that's why I've created the static methods `ShowActivatedServiceTypes()` and `ShowWellKnownServiceTypes()`; they are called after loading and starting the remoting configuration:

```
public static void Main(string[] args)
{
    RemotingConfiguration.Configure("HelloServer.exe.config");
    Console.WriteLine("Application: " + RemotingConfiguration.ApplicationName);
    ShowActivatedServiceTypes();
    ShowWellKnownServiceTypes();
    System.Console.WriteLine("press return to exit");
    System.Console.ReadLine();
    return;
}
```

These two functions show configuration information of well-known and client-activated types:

```
public static void ShowWellKnownServiceTypes()
{
    WellKnownServiceTypeEntry[] entries =
    RemotingConfiguration.GetRegisteredWellKnownServiceTypes();
    foreach (WellKnownServiceTypeEntry entry in entries)
    {
        Console.WriteLine("Assembly: " + entry.AssemblyName);
        Console.WriteLine("Mode: " + entry.Mode);
        Console.WriteLine("URI: " + entry.ObjectUri);
        Console.WriteLine("Type: " + entry.TypeName);
    }
}
public static void ShowActivatedServiceTypes()
{
    ActivatedServiceTypeEntry[] entries =
    RemotingConfiguration.GetRegisteredActivatedServiceTypes();
    foreach (ActivatedServiceTypeEntry entry in entries)
```

```
    {
        Console.WriteLine("Assembly: " + entry.AssemblyName);
        Console.WriteLine("Type: " + entry.TypeName);
    }
}
```

Client code using configuration files

In the client code, it is only necessary to configure the remoting services using the configuration file client.exe.config. After that, you can use the new operator to create new instances of the remote class Hello, no matter whether you work with server-activated or client-activated remote objects. However, there's a small difference—with client-activated objects it's now possible to use *non-default constructors* with the new operator. This isn't possible for server-activated objects: single-call objects can have no state because they are destroyed with every call; singleton objects are created just once. Calling non-default constructors is only useful for client-activated objects because it is only for this kind of objects that the new operator really calls the constructor in the remote object.

In the Main() method of the file HelloClient.cs you can now change the remoting code to use the configuration file with RemotingConfiguration.Configure(), and you create the remote object with the new operator:

```
RemotingConfiguration.Configure("HelloClient.exe.config");
Hello obj = new Hello();
if (obj == null)
{
    Console.WriteLine("could not locate server");
    return;
}
for (int i=0; i < 5; i++)
{
    Console.WriteLine(obj.Greeting("Christian"));
}
```

Delayed loading of client channels

With the configuration file machine.config, two channels are configured that can be used automatically if the client doesn't configure a channel.

```
<system.runtime.remoting>
    <application>
        <channels>
            <channel ref="http client" displayName="http client (delay loaded)"
                    delayLoadAsClientChannel="true"/>
            <channel ref="tcp client" displayName="tcp client (delay loaded)"
                    delayLoadAsClientChannel="true"/>
        </channels>
    </application>
</system.runtime.remoting>
```

The XML attribute delayLoadAsClientChannel with a value true defines that the channel should be used from a client that doesn't configure a channel. The runtime tries to connect to the server using the delay-loaded channels. So it is not necessary to configure a channel in the client configuration file, and a client configuration file for the well-known object we have used earlier can look as simple as this:

```
<configuration>
   <system.runtime.remoting>
      <application name="Client">
         <client url="tcp:/localhost:6791/Hello">
            <wellknown type = "Wrox.ProCSharp.Remoting.Hello, RemoteHello"
                       url="tcp://localhost:6791/Hello/Hi" />
         </client>
      </application>
   </system.runtime.remoting>
</configuration>
```

Lifetime services in configuration files

Leasing configuration for remote servers can also be done with the application configuration files. The `<lifetime>` element has the attributes `leaseTime`, `sponsorshipTimeOut`, `renewOnCallTime`, and `pollTime` as shown in this example:

```
<configuration>
   <system.runtime.remoting>
      <application>
         <lifetime leaseTime = "15M" sponsorshipTimeOut = "4M"
                   renewOnCallTime = "3M" pollTime = "30s"/>
      </application>
   </system.runtime.remoting>
</configuration>
```

Using configuration files, it is possible to change the remoting configuration by editing files instead of working with source code. We can easily change the channel to use HTTP instead of TCP, change a port, the name of the channel, and so on. With the addition of a single line the server can listen to two channels instead of one.

Formatter providers

Earlier in this chapter a major change with .NET 1.1 has already been discussed where properties of the formatter provider needs to be changed to support marshaling all objects across the network. Instead of doing this programmatically as it was done earlier, you can also configure the properties of a formatter provider in a configuration file.

The following server configuration file is changed within the `<channel>` element, in that `<serverProviders>` and `<clientProviders>` are defined as child elements. With the `<serverProviders>`, the built-in providers wsdl, soap, and binary are referenced, and with the soap and binary providers the property `typeFilterLevel` is set to `Full`.

```
<configuration>
   <system.runtime.remoting>
      <application name="HelloServer">
         <service>
            <activated type="Wrox.ProCSharp.Remoting.Hello, RemoteHello" />
         </service>
         <channels>
```

```
            <channel ref="tcp" port="6789"
                     displayName="TCP Channel (HelloServer)">
              <serverProviders>
                <provider ref="wsdl" />
                <provider ref="soap" typeFilterLevel="Full" />
                <provider ref="binary" typeFilterLevel="Full" />
              </serverProviders>
              <clientProviders>
                <provider ref="binary" />
              </clientProviders>
            </channel>
          </channels>
        </application>
      </system.runtime.remoting>
    </configuration>
```

.NET Framework configuration tool

The System Administrator can use the .NET Framework Configuration tool (see Figure 16-11) to reconfigure existing configuration files. This tool is part of the Administrative Tools, which you can access using the Control Panel.

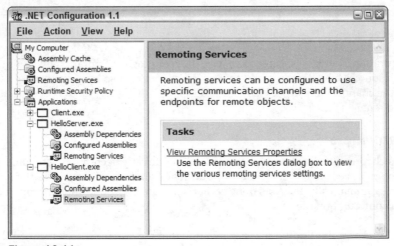

Figure 16-11

Adding the application HelloClient.exe where we used the client configuration file to the configured applications in this tool, we can configure the URL of the remote object by selecting the hyperlink View Remoting Services Properties.

As shown in Figure 16-12, for the client application you can see the value of the displayName attribute in the combo box. This combo box allows selecting the remote application so you can change the URL of the remote object.

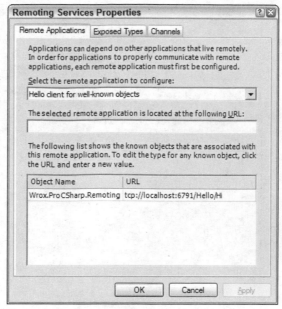

Figure 16-12

Adding the server application to this tool you can change the configuration of the remote object and the channels as shown in Figures 16-13 and 16-14.

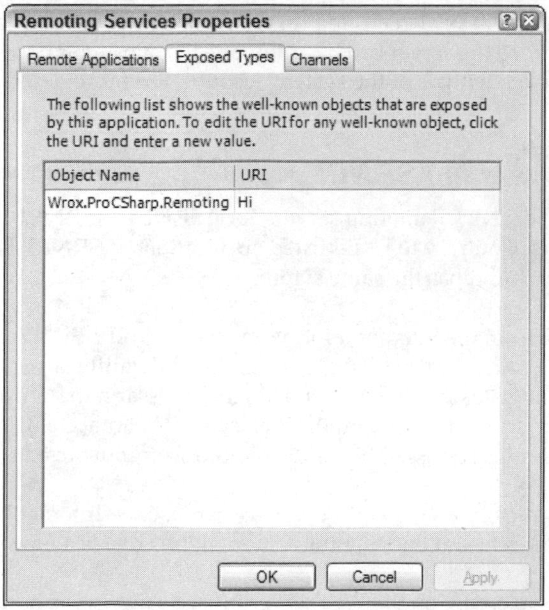

Figure 16-13

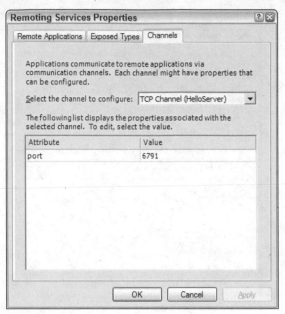

Figure 16-14

Hosting Applications

Up to this point all our sample servers were running in self-hosted .NET servers. A self-hosted server must be launched manually. A .NET remoting server can also be started in a lot of other application types. In a Windows Service the server can be automatically started at boot-time, and in addition the process can run with the credentials of the system account. For more details on Windows Services see Chapter 32.

Hosting remote servers in ASP.NET

There's special support for .NET Remoting servers for ASP.NET. ASP.NET can be used for the automatic startup of remote servers. Contrary to EXE-hosted applications, ASP.NET-hosted Remoting uses a different file for configuration, but it has the same syntax.

To use the infrastructure from the Internet Information Server and ASP.NET, you have to create a class that derives from `System.MarshalByRefObject` and has a default constructor. The code used earlier for our server to create and register the channel is no longer necessary; that's done by the ASP.NET runtime. You just have to create a virtual directory on the Web server that maps a directory into which we put the configuration file web.config. The assembly of the remote class must reside in the bin subdirectory.

To configure a virtual directory on the Web server we can use the Internet Information Services MMC. Selecting the Default Web site and opening the Action menu creates a new Virtual Directory.

The configuration file web.config on the Web server must be put in the home directory of the virtual Web site. With the default IIS configuration, the channel that will be used listens to port 80:

```
<configuration>
   <system.runtime.remoting>
      <application>
         <service>
            <wellknown mode="SingleCall"
                  type="Wrox.ProCSharp.Remoting.Hello, RemoteHello"
                  objectUri="HelloService.soap" />
         </service>
      </application>
   </system.runtime.remoting>
</configuration>
```

> If the remoting object is hosted within IIS, the name of the remote object must end either with .soap, or .bin, depending on the type of formatter that is used (SOAP or the binary).

The client can now connect to the remote object using the following configuration file. The URL that must be specified for the remote object here is the Web server localhost, followed by the Web application name RemoteHello (specified when creating the virtual Web site), and the URI of the remote object HelloService.soap that is defined in the file web.config. It's not necessary to specify the port number 80, because that's the default port for the HTTP protocol. Not specifying a <channels> section means that the delay loaded HTTP channel from the configuration file machine.config is used:

```
<configuration>
   <system.runtime.remoting>
      <application>
         <client url="http:/localhost/RemoteHello">
            <wellknown type="Wrox.ProCSharp.Remoting.Hello, RemoteHello"
                     url="http://localhost/RemoteHello/HelloService.soap" />
         </client>
      </application>
   </system.runtime.remoting>
</configuration>
```

> Hosting remote objects in ASP.NET only supports well-known objects.

Classes, Interfaces, and SoapSuds

In the .NET Remoting samples that have been done up until now, you have always copied the assembly of the remote object not only to the server, but also to the client application. This way the MSIL code of the remote object is on both the client and the server system, although in the client application only the metadata is needed. However, copying the remoting object assembly means that it's not possible for the client and the server to be programmed independently. A much better way to use just the metadata is to use interfaces or the **SoapSuds.exe** utility instead.

Interfaces

You get a cleaner separation of the client and server code by using interfaces. An interface simply defines the methods without implementation. This way the contract (the interface) is separated from the implementation, and just the contract is needed on the client system. Here are the necessary steps for using an interface:

1. Define an interface that will be placed in a separate assembly.

2. Implement the interface in the remote object class. To do this, the assembly of the interface must be referenced.

3. On the server side no more changes are required. The server can be programmed and configured in the usual ways.

4. On the client side, reference the assembly of the interface instead of the assembly of the remote class.

5. The client can now use the interface of the remote object rather than the remote object class. The object can be created using the `Activator` class as it was done earlier. You can't use the `new` operator in this way, because the interface itself cannot be instantiated.

The interface defines the contract between the client and server. The two applications can now be developed independently of each other. If you also stick to the old COM rules about interfaces (that interfaces should never be changed), you will not have any versioning problems.

Soapsuds

You can also use the Soapsuds utility to get the metadata from an assembly if an HTTP channel and the SOAP formatter are used. Soapsuds can convert assemblies to XML Schemas, XML Schemas to wrapper classes, and also works in the other directions.

The following command converts the type `Hello` from the assembly RemoteHello to the assembly HelloWrapper where a transparent proxy is generated that calls the remote object:

```
soapsuds -types:Wrox.ProCSharp.Remoting.Hello,RemoteHello -oa:HelloWrapper.dll
```

With Soapsuds you can also get the type information directly from a running server, if the HTTP channel and the SOAP formatter are used:

```
soapsuds -url:http://localhost:6792/hello/hi?wsdl -oa:HelloWrapper.dll
```

In the client you can now reference the generated assembly instead of the original one. Some of the soapsuds options are listed in the following table.

Option	Description
-url	Retrieve schema from the specified URL
-proxyurl	If a proxy server is required to access the server, specify the proxy with this option
-types	Specify a type and assembly to read the schema information from it

Option	Description
-is	Input schema file
-ia	Input assembly file
-os	Output schema file
-oa	Output assembly file

Generating a WSDL Document with .NET Remoting

We discuss WSDL in more detail in Chapter 26, in the context of ASP.NET Web services WSDL is used to describe Web services. WSDL is also supported by .NET Remoting when an HTTP channel and the SOAP formatter are used. You can test this easily by using a browser to access a remote object. Adding ?wsdl to the URI of the remote object returns a WSDL document (see Figure 16-15) that shows the output from accessing our remote server we have created earlier.

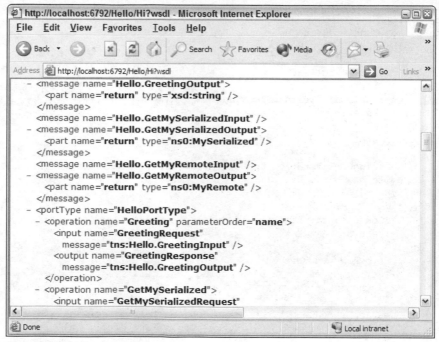

Figure 16-15

.NET Remoting uses the RPC style of WSDL documents, unlike ASP.NET Web services, which uses the Document style by default.

You can access the WSDL document across the network only if you use a well-known remote object type. For client-activated objects the URI is created dynamically. With client activated objects you can use the assembly with the -ia option of soapsuds to get the metadata.

Asynchronous Remoting

If server methods take a while to complete and the client needs to do some different work at the same time, it isn't necessary to start a separate thread to do the remote call. By doing an asynchronous call, the method starts but returns immediately to the client. Asynchronous calls can be made on a remote object as they are made on a local object with the help of a delegate. With methods that don't return a value you can also use the OneWay attribute.

Using delegates with .NET remoting

To make an asynchronous method, you create a delegate, GreetingDelegate, with the same argument and return value as the Greeting() method of the remote object. With the delegate keyword a new class GreetingDelegate that derives from MulticastDelegate is created. You can verify this by using ildasm and checking the assembly. The argument of the constructor of this delegate class is a reference to the Greeting() method. You start the Greeting() call using the BeginInvoke() method of the delegate class. The second argument of BeginInvoke() is an AsyncCallback instance that defines the method HelloClient.Callback(), which is called when the remote method is finished. In the Callback() method the remote call is finished using EndInvoke():

```
using System;
using System.Runtime.Remoting;
namespace Wrox.ProCSharp.Remoting
{
    public class HelloClient
    {
        private delegate String GreetingDelegate(String name);
        private static string greeting;

        public static void Main(string[] args)
        {
            RemotingConfiguration.Configure("HelloClient.exe.config");
            Hello obj = new Hello();
            if (obj == null)
            {
                Console.WriteLine("could not locate server");
                return;
            }
            // synchronous version
            // string greeting = obj.Greeting("Christian");
            // asynchronous version

            GreetingDelegate d = new GreetingDelegate(obj.Greeting);
            IAsyncResult ar = d.BeginInvoke("Christian", null, null);

            // do some work and then wait
            ar.AsyncWaitHandle.WaitOne();
            if (ar.IsCompleted)
            {
                greeting = d.EndInvoke(ar);
            }

            Console.WriteLine(greeting);
```

```
        }
    }
}
```

You can read more about delegates and events in Chapter 6.

OneWay attribute

A method that has a void return and only input parameters can be marked with the OneWay attribute. The OneWay attribute (defined within the namespace System.Runtime.Remoting.Messaging) makes a method automatically asynchronous, regardless of how the client calls it. Adding the method TakeAWhile() to our remote object class RemoteHello creates a fire-and-forget method. If the client calls it by the proxy, the proxy immediately returns to the client. On the server, the method finishes some time later:

```
[OneWay]
public void TakeAWhile(int ms)
{
    Console.WriteLine("TakeAWhile started");
    System.Threading.Thread.Sleep(ms);
    Console.WriteLine("TakeAWhile finished");
}
```

Remoting and Events

Not only can the client invoke methods on the remote object across the network, but the server can do the same: invoking methods in the client. For this, a mechanism that we already know from the basic language features is used: *delegates and events*.

In principle, the architecture is simple. The server has a remotable object that the client can call, and the client has a remotable object that the server can call:

❑   The remote object in the server must declare an external function (a delegate) with the signature of the method that the client will implement in a handler.

❑   The arguments that are passed with the handler function to the client must be marshalable, so all the data sent to the client must be serializable.

❑   The remote object must also declare an instance of the delegate function modified with the event keyword; the client will use this to register a handler.

❑   The client must create a sink object with a handler method that has the same signature as the delegate defined, and it has to register the sink object with the event in the remote object.

To help explain this, let's take a look at an example. To see all the parts of event handling with .NET Remoting, create five classes: Server, Client, RemoteObject, EventSink, and StatusEventArgs. The dependencies of these classes are shown in Figure 16-16.

The Server class is a remoting server such as the one you already are familiar with. The Server class will create a channel based on information from a configuration file and register the remote object that's implemented in the RemoteObject class in the remoting runtime. The remote object declares the arguments of a delegate and fires events in the registered handler functions. The argument that's passed to the handler function is of type StatusEventArgs. The class StatusEventArgs must be serializable so it can be marshaled to the client.

The Client class represents the client application. This class creates an instance of the EventSink class and registers the StatusHandler() method of this class as a handler for the delegate in the remote object. EventSink must be remotable like the RemoteObject class, because this class will also be called across the network:

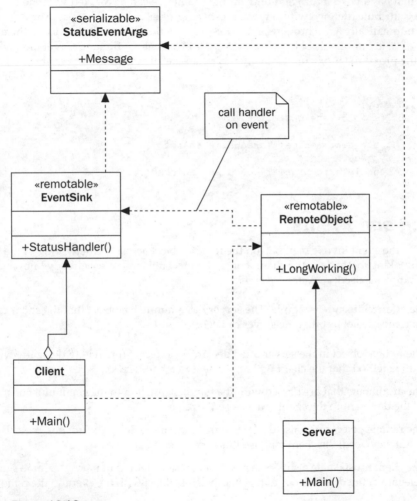

Figure 16-16

Remote object

The remote object class is implemented in the file RemoteObject.cs. The remote object class must be derived from MarshalByRefObject, as you already know from our previous examples. To make it possible that the client can register an event handler that can be called from within the remote object, you have to declare an external function with the delegate keyword. Declare the delegate StatusEvent()

with two arguments: the sender (so the client knows about the object that fired the event) and a variable of type StatusEventArgs. Into the argument class you can put all the additional information that you want to send to the client.

The method that will be implemented in the client has some strict requirements. It can only have input parameters—return types, ref, and out parameters are not allowed—and the argument types must be either [Serializable] or remotable (derived from MarshalByRefObject). These requirements are fulfilled by the parameters that are defined with this StatusEvent delegate:

```
public delegate void StatusEvent(object sender, StatusEventArgs e);

public class RemoteObject : MarshalByRefObject
{
```

Within the RemoteObject class, declare an event name Status of type StatusEvent, which is the delegate. The client must add an event handler to the Status event to receive status information from the remote object:

```
public class RemoteObject : MarshalByRefObject
{
    public RemoteObject()
    {
        Console.WriteLine("RemoteObject constructor called");
    }
    public event StatusEvent Status;
```

In the LongWorking() method it is checked if an event handler is registered before the event is fired by calling Status(this, e). To verify that the event is fired asynchronously, fire an event at the start of the method before doing the Thread.Sleep(), and after the sleep:

```
public void LongWorking(int ms)
{
    Console.WriteLine("RemoteObject: LongWorking() Started");
    StatusEventArgs e = new StatusEventArgs(
                        "Message for Client: LongWorking() Started");
    // fire event
    if (Status != null)
    {
        Console.WriteLine("RemoteObject: Firing Starting Event");
        Status(this, e);
    }
    System.Threading.Thread.Sleep(ms);
    e.Message = "Message for Client: LongWorking() Ending";
    // fire ending event
    if (Status != null)
    {
        Console.WriteLine("RemoteObject: Firing Ending Event");
        Status(this, e);
    }
    Console.WriteLine("RemoteObject: LongWorking() Ending");
}
```

Event arguments

As you've seen in the `RemoteObject` class, the class `StatusEventArgs` is used as an argument for the delegate. With the `[Serializable]` attribute an instance of this class can be transferred from the server to the client. Here is a simple property of type `string` to send a message to the client:

```
[Serializable]
public class StatusEventArgs
{
    public StatusEventArgs(string m)
    {
        message = m;
    }
    public string Message
    {
        get
        {
            return message;
        }
        set
        {
            message = value;
        }
    }
    private string message;
}
```

Server

The server is implemented within a console application. You only have to wait for a user to end the server after reading the configuration file, setting up the channel, and the remote object:

```
using System;
using System.Runtime.Remoting;
namespace Wrox.ProCSharp.Remoting
{
    class Server
    {
        static void Main(string[] args)
        {
            RemotingConfiguration.Configure("Server.exe.config");
            Console.WriteLine("press return to exit");
            Console.ReadLine();
        }
    }
}
```

Server configuration file

The server configuration file, Server.exe.config, is also created as already discussed. There is just one important point: because the client at first registers the event handler and calls the remote method afterward, the remote object must keep state for the client. You can not use single-call objects with events, so the `RemoteObject` class is configured as a client-activated type. Also, to support delegates, you have to enable full serialization by specifying the `typeFilterLevel` attribute with the `<provider>` element.

```
<configuration>
   <system.runtime.remoting>
      <application name="CallbackSample">
         <service>
            <activated type="Wrox.ProCSharp.Remoting.RemoteObject,
                             RemoteObject" />
         </service>
         <channels>
            <channel ref="http" port="6791">
               <serverProviders>
                  <provider ref="binary" typeFilterLevel="Full" />
               </serverProviders>
            </channel>
         </channels>
      </application>
   </system.runtime.remoting>
</configuration>
```

Event sink

An event sink library is required for use by the client, and to be invoked by the server. The event sink implements the handler `StatusHandler()` that's defined with the delegate. As previously noted, the method can only have input parameters, and only a void return. `EventSink` class must also inherit from the class `MarshalByRefObject` to make it remotable because it will be called remotely from the server:

```
using System;
using System.Runtime.Remoting.Messaging;
namespace Wrox.ProCSharp.Remoting
{
   public class EventSink : MarshalByRefObject
   {
      public EventSink()
      {
      }
      public void StatusHandler(object sender, StatusEventArgs e)
      {
         Console.WriteLine("EventSink: Event occurred: " + e.Message);
      }
   }
}
```

Client

The client reads the client configuration file with the `RemotingConfiguration` class, which is not different from the clients that have been discussed so far. The client creates an instance of the remotable sink class `EventSink` locally. The method that should be called from the remote object on the server is passed to the remote object:

```
using System;
using System.Runtime.Remoting;
namespace Wrox.ProCSharp.Remoting
{
   class Client
```

```
    {
        static void Main(string[] args)
        {
            RemotingConfiguration.Configure("Client.exe.config");
```

The differences start here. We have to create an instance of the remotable sink class `EventSink` locally. Since this class will not be configured with the `<client>` element, it's instantiated locally. Next, the remote object class `RemoteObject` is instantiated. This class is configured in the `<client>` element, so it's instantiated on the remote server:

```
            EventSink sink = new EventSink();
            RemoteObject obj = new RemoteObject();
```

Now you can register the handler method of the `EventSink` object in the remote object. `StatusEvent` is the name of the delegate that was defined in the server. The `StatusHandler()` method has the same arguments as defined in the `StatusEvent`.

By calling the `LongWorking()` method, the server will call back into the method `StatusHandler()` at the beginning and at the end of the method:

```
            // register client sink in server - subscribe to event

            obj.Status += new StatusEvent(sink.StatusHandler);
            obj.LongWorking(5000);
```

Now we are no longer interested in receiving events from the server and unsubscribe from the event. The next time we call `LongWorking()` no events will be received:

```
            // unsubscribe from event

            obj.Status -= new StatusEvent(sink.StatusHandler);
            obj.LongWorking(5000);
            Console.WriteLine("press return to exit");
            Console.ReadLine();
        }
    }
}
```

Client configuration file

The configuration file for the client, client.exe.config, is nearly the same configuration file for client-activated objects that we've already seen. The difference can be found in defining a port number for the channel. Since the server must reach the client with a known port, we have to define the port number for the channel as an attribute of the `<channel>` element. It isn't necessary to define a `<service>` section for our `EventSink` class, because this class will be instantiated from the client with the `new` operator locally. The server does not access this object by its name; it will receive a marshaled reference to the instance instead:

```
<configuration>
    <system.runtime.remoting>
        <application name="Client">
```

```
            <client url="http://localhost:6791/CallbackSample">
                <activated type="Wrox.ProCSharp.Remoting.RemoteObject,
                               RemoteObject" />
            </client>
            <channels>
                <channel ref="http" port="0">
                    <serverProviders>
                        <provider ref="binary" typeFilterLevel="Full" />
                    </serverProviders>
                </channel>
            </channels>
        </application>
    </system.runtime.remoting>
</configuration>
```

Running programs

Figure 16-17 shows the resulting output of the server. The constructor of the remote object is called once because we have a client-activated object. Next, you can see the call to LongWorking() has started and an event is fired to the client. The next start of the LongWorking() method doesn't fire events, because the client has already unregistered its interest in the event.

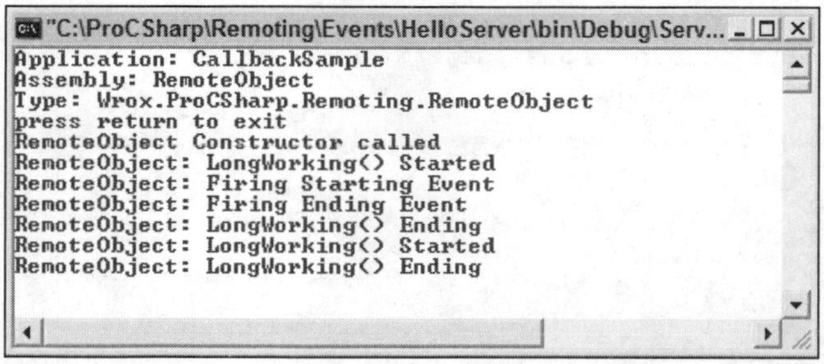

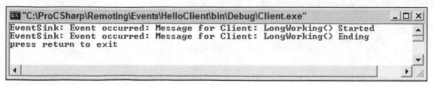

```
"C:\ProCSharp\Remoting\Events\HelloServer\bin\Debug\Serv... _ □ ×
Application: CallbackSample
Assembly: RemoteObject
Type: Wrox.ProCSharp.Remoting.RemoteObject
press return to exit
RemoteObject Constructor called
RemoteObject: LongWorking() Started
RemoteObject: Firing Starting Event
RemoteObject: Firing Ending Event
RemoteObject: LongWorking() Ending
RemoteObject: LongWorking() Started
RemoteObject: LongWorking() Ending
```

Figure 16-17

Figure 16-18 shows the client output of the events that made it across the network.

```
"C:\ProCSharp\Remoting\Events\HelloClient\bin\Debug\Client.exe"    _ □ ×
EventSink: Event occurred: Message for Client: LongWorking() Started
EventSink: Event occurred: Message for Client: LongWorking() Ending
press return to exit
```

Figure 16-18

Call Contexts

Client-activated objects can hold state for a specific client. With client-activated objects, the server allocates resources for every client. With server-activated SingleCall objects, a new instance is created for every instance call, and no resources are held on the server; these objects can't hold state for a client. For state management you can keep state on the client side; the state information is sent with every method call to the server. To implement such a state management it is not necessary to change all method signatures to include an additional parameter that passes the state to the server, this is automatically done by the *call context*.

A call context flows with a logical thread and is passed with every method call. A *logical thread* is started from the calling thread and flows through all method calls that are started from the calling thread, passing through different contexts, different application domains, and different processes.

You can assign data to the call context using `CallContext.SetData()`. The class of the object that's used as data for the `SetData()` method must implement the interface `ILogicalThreadAffinative`. You can get this data again in the same logical thread (but possibly a different physical thread) using `CallContext.GetData()`.

For the data of the call context create a new C# Class Library with the class `CallContextData`. This class will be used to pass some data from the client to the server with every method call. The class that's passed with the call context must implement the `System.Runtime.Remoting.Messaging.ILogicalThreadAffinative` interface. This interface doesn't have a method; it's just a markup for the runtime to define that instances of this class should flow with a logical thread. The `CallContextData` class must also be marked with the `Serializable` attribute so it can be transferred through the channel:

```
using System;
using System.Runtime.Remoting.Messaging;
namespace Wrox.ProCSharp.Remoting
{
    [Serializable]
    public class CallContextData : ILogicalThreadAffinative
    {
        public CallContextData()
        {
        }
        public string Data
        {
            get
            {
                return data;
            }
            set
            {
                data = value;
            }
        }
        protected string data;
    }
}
```

In the remote object class `Hello`, change the `Greeting()` method to access the call context. For the use of the `CallContextData` class you have to reference the previously created assembly `CallContextData` in the file CallContextData.dll. To work with the `CallContext` class, the namespace `System.Runtime.Remoting.Messaging` must be opened. The variable cookie holds the data that is sent from the client to the server. The name cookie is chosen because the context works similar to a browser-based cookie, where the client automatically sends data to the Web server.

```
public string Greeting(string name)
{
    Console.WriteLine("Greeting started");
    CallContextData cookie =
        (CallContextData)CallContext.GetData("mycookie");
    if (cookie != null)
    {
        Console.WriteLine("Cookie: " + cookie.Data);
    }
    Console.WriteLine("Greeting finished");
    return "Hello, " + name;
}
```

In the client code the call context information is set by calling `CallContext.SetData()`. With this method an instance of the class `CallContextData` is assigned to be passed to the server. Now every time the method `Greeting()` is called in the `for` loop, the context data is automatically passed to the server.

```
CallContextData cookie = new CallContextData();
cookie.Data = "information for the server";
CallContext.SetData("mycookie", cookie);
for (int i=0; i < 5; i++)
{
    Console.WriteLine(obj.Greeting("Christian"));
}
```

You can use such a call context to send information about the user, the name of the client system, or simply a unique identifier that's used on the server side to get some state information from a database.

Summary

In this chapter we've seen that .NET Remoting facilitates the task of invoking methods across the network: A remote object has to inherit form `MarshalByRefObject`. In the server application only a single method is needed to load the configuration file so that the channels and remote objects are both set up and running. Within the client, we load the configuration file and can use the `new` operator to instantiate the remote object.

We also used .NET Remoting without the help of configuration files. On the server, we simply created a channel and registered a remote object. On the client, we created a channel and used the remote object.

Furthermore, we've also discussed that the .NET Remoting architecture is flexible and can be extended. All parts of this technology such as channels, proxies, formatters, message sinks, and so on are pluggable and can be replaced with custom implementations.

We used HTTP and TCP channels for the communication across the network, and SOAP and binary formatters to format the parameters before sending them.

We discussed the use of stateless and stateful object types that are used by well-known and client-activated objects. With client-activated objects we have seen how the leasing mechanism is used to specify the lifetime of remote objects.

We have also seen that .NET Remoting is very well integrated in other parts of .NET Framework, such as calling asynchronous methods, performing callbacks using the delegate and event keywords, among others.

17

Localization

NASA's Mars Climate Orbiter was lost on September 23, 1999 at a cost of $125 million because one engineering team used metric units, while another one used inches for a key spacecraft operation. When writing applications for international distribution, different cultures and regions must be kept in mind.

Different cultures have diverging calendars and use different number and date formats, and also the sort order with the letters A-Z may lead to various results. To make applications fit for global markets you have to globalize and localize them.

Globalization is about internationalizing applications: preparing applications for international markets. With globalization, the application supports number and date formats depending on the culture, different calendars, and so on. *Localization* is about translating applications for specific cultures. For translations of strings, you can use resources.

.NET supports globalization and localization of Windows and Web applications. To globalize an application you can use classes from the namespace System.Globalization; to localize an application you can use resources that are supported by the namespace System.Resources.

This chapter covers the globalization and localization of .NET applications; more specifically, we discuss:

❑ Using classes that represent cultures and regions

❑ Internationalization of applications

❑ Localization of applications

Namespace System.Globalization

The System.Globalization namespace holds all culture and region classes to support different date formats, different number formats, and even different calendars that are represented in classes such as GregorianCalendar, HebrewCalendar, JapaneseCalendar, and so on. Using these classes you can display different representations depending on the user's locale.

Using the namespace System.Globalization we will look at these issues and considerations:

- ❏ Unicode issues
- ❏ Cultures and regions
- ❏ An example showing all cultures and their characteristics
- ❏ Sorting

Unicode Issues

A Unicode character has 16 bits, so there is room for 65,536 characters. Is this enough for all languages that are currently used in information technology? In the case of the Chinese language, for example, more than 80,000 characters are needed. However, Unicode has been designed to deal with this issue. With Unicode you have to differentiate between base characters and combining characters. You can add multiple combining characters to a base character to build up a single display character or a text element.

Take, for example, the Icelandic character Ogonek. Ogonek can be combined by using the base character 0x006F (latin small letter o) and the combining characters 0x0328 (combining Ogonek) and 0x0304 (combining Macron) as shown in Figure 17-1. Combining characters are defined within ranges from 0x0300 to 0x0345. For American and European markets, predefined characters exist to facilitate dealing with the characters. The character Ogoneck is also defined with the predefined character 0x01ED.

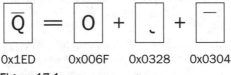

0x1ED   0x006F   0x0328   0x0304

Figure 17-1

For Asian markets where more than 80,000 characters are necessary for Chinese alone, such predefined characters do not exist. In the case of Asian languages, you always have to deal with combining characters. The problem with this issue is getting the right number of display characters or text elements, getting to the base characters instead of the combined characters. The namespace System.Globalization offers the class StringInfo that you can use to deal with this issue.

The following table lists the static methods of the class StringInfo that help dealing with combined characters.

Method	Description
GetNextTextElement	Returns the first text element (base character and all combining characters) of a specified string.
GetTextElementEnumerator	Returns a `TextElementEnumerator` object that allows iterating all text elements of a string.
ParseCombiningCharacters	Returns an integer array referencing all base characters of a string.

> A single display character can contain multiple Unicode characters. For adhering with this issue, if you write applications that support international markets don't use the data type char, but use string instead. A string can hold a text element that contains both base characters and combining characters, while a char cannot.

Cultures and Regions

The world is divided into multiple cultures and regions, and applications have to be aware of these cultural and regional differences. A culture is a set of preferences based on a user's language and cultural habits. RFC 1766 defines culture names that are used worldwide depending on a language and a country or region. Some examples are en-AU, en-CA, en-GB, and en-US for the English language in Australia, Canada, United Kingdom, and the United States.

Possibly the most important class in the `System.Globalization` namespace is the class `CultureInfo`. `CultureInfo` represents a culture and defines calendars, formatting of numbers and dates, and sorting strings that are used with the culture.

The class `RegionInfo` represents regional settings (such as the currency) and shows if the region is using the metric system. In the same region, you can use multiple languages. One example is the region of Spain with its Basque (eu-ES), Catalan (ca-ES), Spanish (es-ES), Galician (gl-ES) cultures. While one region has multiple languages, one language can be spoken in different regions; for example, Spanish is spoken in Mexico, Spain, Guatemala, Argentina, and Peru, to name but a few.

Later in this chapter we will present a sample application that demonstrates these characteristics of cultures and regions.

Specific, neutral, and invariant cultures

With the use of cultures in .NET Framework, you have to differentiate between three types: *specific*, *neutral*, and *invariant* cultures.

A specific culture is associated with a real, existing culture that is defined with RFC 1766 as we have seen in the last section. A specific culture can be mapped to a neutral culture. For example, de is the neutral culture of the specific cultures de-AT, de-DE, de-CH, and others. de is the shorthand for the language German; AT, DE, CH are shorthands for the countries Austria, Germany and Switzerland.

When translating applications, it is typically not necessary to do translations for every region; there is not much difference between the German language in the countries Austria and Germany. Instead of using specific cultures, you can use a neutral culture for localizing applications.

The invariant culture is independent of a real culture. Storing formatted numbers or dates into files, or sending them across a network to a server, using a culture that is independent of any user settings is the best option.

Figure 17-2 shows how the culture types relate to each other.

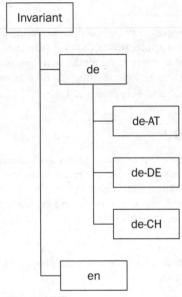

Figure 17-2

CurrentCulture and CurrentUICulture

Setting cultures, you have to differentiate between a culture for the user interface and a culture for the number and date formats. Cultures are associated with a thread, and with these two culture types, two culture settings can be applied to a thread. Setting the culture with the thread, the `Thread` class has the properties `CurrentCulture` and `CurrentUICulture`. The property `CurrentCulture` is for setting the culture that is used with formatting and sort options, whereas the property `CurrentUICulture` is used for the language of the user interface.

Users can change the default setting of the `CurrentCulture` using the Regional and Language options in the Windows Control Panel (see Figure 17-3). With this configuration, it is also possible to change the default number, the time, and the date format for the culture.

The `CurrentUICulture` does not depend on this configuration. The `CurrentUICulture` setting depends on the language of the operating system. There is one exception: if a multi-language user interface (MUI) is installed with Windows XP or Windows 2000, it is possible to change the language of the user interface with the regional configuration, and this influences the property `CurrentUICulture`.

Figure 17-3

These settings make a very good default, and in many cases, there is no need for changing the default behavior. If the culture should be changed, that can easily be done by changing both cultures of the thread to the Spanish culture as shown in this code snippet:

```
System.Globalization.CultureInfo ci = new
    System.Globalization.CultureInfo("es-ES");
System.Threading.Thread.CurrentThread.CurrentCulture = ci;
System.Threading.Thread.CurrentThread.CurrentUICulture = ci;
```

Having learned about setting the culture, we are going to discuss number and date formatting as is influenced by the CurrentCulture setting.

Number formatting

The number structures Int16, Int32, Int64, and so on, in the System namespace have an overloaded ToString() method. This method can be used to create a different representation of the number depending on the locale. For the Int32 structure, ToString() is overloaded with these four versions:

```
public string ToString();
public string ToString(IFormatProvider);
public string ToString(string);
public string ToString(string, IFormatProvider);
```

ToString() without arguments returns a string without format options. We can also pass a string and a class that implements IFormatProvider.

The string specifies the format of the representation. The format can be a standard numeric formatting string or a picture numeric formatting string. For standard numeric formatting, strings are predefined where C specifies the currency notation, D creates a decimal output, E scientific output, F fixed-point output, G general output, N number output, and X hexadecimal output. With a picture numeric format string, it is possible to specify the number of digits, section and group separators, percent notation, and so on. The picture numeric format string ###,### means two 3-digit blocks separated by a group separator.

The IFormatProvider interface is implemented by the NumberFormatInfo, DateTimeFormatInfo, and CultureInfo classes. This interface defines a single method GetFormat() that returns a format object.

NumberFormatInfo can be used to define custom formats for numbers. With the default constructor of NumberFormatInfo, a culture-independent or invariant object is created. Using the properties of NumberFormatInfo it is possible to change all the formatting options like a positive sign, a percent symbol, a number group separator, a currency symbol, and a lot more. A read-only culture-independent NumberFormatInfo object is returned from the static property InvariantInfo. A NumberFormatInfo object where the format values are based on the CultureInfo of the current thread is returned from the static property CurrentInfo.

To create the next example you can start with a simple Console Project. In this code, the first example shows a number displayed in the format of the culture of the thread (here: English-US, the setting of the operating system). The second example uses the ToString() method with the IFormatProvider argument. CultureInfo implements IFormatProvider, so create a CultureInfo object using the French culture. The third example changes the culture of the thread. Using the property CurrentCulture of the Thread instance, the culture is changed to German:

```csharp
using System;
using System.Globalization;
using System.Threading;

namespace Wrox.ProCSharp.Localization
{
    class Class1
    {
        static void Main(string[] args)
        {
            int val = 1234567890;

            // culture of the current thread
            Console.WriteLine(val.ToString("N"));

            // use IFormatProvider
            Console.WriteLine(val.ToString("N",
                            new CultureInfo("fr-FR")));

            // change the culture of the thread
            Thread.CurrentThread.CurrentCulture =
```

```
                        new CultureInfo("de-DE");
          Console.WriteLine(val.ToString("N"));
        }
      }
    }
```

The output is shown in Figure 17-4. You can compare the outputs with the previously listed differences for U.S. English, French, and German.

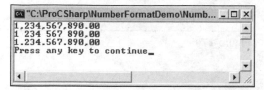

Figure 17-4

Date formatting

The same support for numbers is here for dates. The `DateTime` structure has some methods for date-to-string conversions. The public instance methods `ToLongDateString()`, `ToLongTimeString()`, `ToShortDateString()`, `ToShortTimeString()` create string representations using the current culture. Using the `ToString()` method you can assign a different culture:

```
public string ToString();
public string ToString(IFormatProvider);
public string ToString(string);
public string ToString(string, IFormatProvider);
```

With the string argument of the `ToString()` method, you can specify a predefined format character or a custom format string for converting the date to a string. The class `DateTimeFormatInfo` specifies the possible values. With the `IFormatProvider` argument, you can specify the culture. Using an overloaded method without the `IFormatProvider` argument implies that the culture of the current thread is used:

```
DateTime d = new DateTime(2003, 08, 09);

// current culture
Console.WriteLine(d.ToLongDateString());

// use IFormatProvider
Console.WriteLine(d.ToString("D", new CultureInfo("fr-FR")));

// use culture of thread
CultureInfo ci = Thread.CurrentThread.CurrentCulture;
Console.WriteLine(ci.ToString() + ": " + d.ToString("D"));

ci = new CultureInfo("es-ES");
Thread.CurrentThread.CurrentCulture = ci;
Console.WriteLine(ci.ToString() + ": " + d.ToString("D"));
```

The output of our example program shows ToLongDateString() with the current culture of the thread, a French version where a CultureInfo instance is passed to the ToString() method, and a Spanish version where the CurrentCulture property of the thread is changed to es-ES (see Figure 17-5).

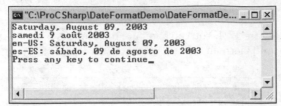

```
"C:\ProCSharp\DateFormatDemo\DateFormatDe..."
Saturday, August 09, 2003
samedi 9 août 2003
en-US: Saturday, August 09, 2003
es-ES: sábado, 09 de agosto de 2003
Press any key to continue_
```

Figure 17-5

Cultures in Action

To see all cultures in action, we use a sample Windows Forms application that lists all cultures and demonstrates different characteristics of culture properties. Figure 17-6 shows the user interface of the application in the Visual Studio .NET Forms Designer.

```
Culture Demo

  Culture Name:        [        ]   □ Is Neutral
  English Name:        [          ]
  Native Name:         [          ]
  Default Calendar:    [          ]
  Optional Calendars:  [ listCalendars      ]

  ┌─ Samples ──────────────────────┐
  │  Number:    [          ]        │
  │  Full Date: [          ]        │
  │  Time:      [          ]        │
  └────────────────────────────────┘

  ┌─ Region Information ───────────┐
  │  Region:    [          ]        │
  │  Currency:  [      ] [      ]    │
  │             □ Is Metric          │
  └────────────────────────────────┘
```

Figure 17- 6

Let us look into the code. During initialization of the application, all available cultures are added to the tree view control that is placed on the left side of the application. This initialization happens in the method AddCulturesToTree() that is called in the constructor of the form class CultureDemoForm:

```
public CultureDemoForm()
{
    //
    // Required for Windows Form Designer support
    //
    InitializeComponent();

    AddCulturesToTree();
}
```

In the method AddCulturesToTree() you get all cultures from the static method CultureInfo. GetCultures(). Passing CultureTypes.AllCultures to this method returns an array of all available cultures. In the foreach loop every single culture is added to the tree view. For every single culture a TreeNode object is created, because the TreeView class uses TreeNode objects for display. The Tag property of the TreeNode object is set to the CultureInfo object, so that you can access the CultureInfo object at a later time from within the tree.

Where the TreeNode is added inside the tree depends on the culture type. If the culture is a neutral culture or an invariant culture, it is added to the root nodes of the tree. TreeNodes that represent specific cultures are added to their parent neutral culture node.

```
// add all cultures to the tree view
public void AddCulturesToTree()
{
    // get all cultures
    CultureInfo[] cultures =
        CultureInfo.GetCultures(CultureTypes.AllCultures);
    TreeNode[] nodes = new TreeNode[cultures.Length];

    int i = 0;
    TreeNode parent = null;
    foreach (CultureInfo ci in cultures)
    {
        nodes[i] = new TreeNode();
        nodes[i].Text = ci.DisplayName;
        nodes[i].Tag = ci;

        if (ci.IsNeutralCulture)
        {
            // rembember neutral cultures as parent of the
            // following cultures
            parent = nodes[i];
            treeCultures.Nodes.Add(nodes[i]);
        }
        else if (ci.ThreeLetterISOLanguageName ==
            CultureInfo.InvariantCulture.ThreeLetterISOLanguageName)
        {
            // invariant cultures don't have a parent
            treeCultures.Nodes.Add(nodes[i]);
        }
        else
        {
```

```
            // specific cultures are added to the neutral parent
            parent.Nodes.Add(nodes[i]);
        }
        i++;
    }
}
```

When the user selects a node inside the tree, the handler of the AfterSelect event of the TreeView will be called. Here the handler is implemented in the method OnSelectCulture(). Within this method all fields are cleared by calling the method ClearTextFields(), before we get the CultureInfo object from the tree by selecting the Tag property of the TreeNode. Then some text fields are set using the properties Name, NativeName, and EnglishName of the CultureInfo object. If the CultureInfo is a neutral culture that can be queried with the IsNeutralCulture property, the corresponding check box will be set.

```
private void OnSelectCulture(object sender,
                System.Windows.Forms.TreeViewEventArgs e)
{
    ClearTextFields();

    // get CultureInfo object from tree
    CultureInfo ci = (CultureInfo)e.Node.Tag;

    textName.Text = ci.Name;
    textNativeName.Text = ci.NativeName;
    textEnglishName.Text = ci.EnglishName;

    checkIsNeutral.Checked = ci.IsNeutralCulture;
```

Then we get the calendar information about the culture. The Calendar property of the CultureInfo class returns the default Calendar object for the specific culture. Because the Calender class doesn't have a property to tell its name, use the ToString() method of the base class to get the name of the class, and remove the namespace of this string to display it in the text field textCalendar.

Because a single culture might support multiple calendars, the OptionalCalendars property returns an array of additional supported Calendar objects. These optional calendars are displayed in the list box listCalendars. The GregorianCalendar class that derives from Calendar has an additional property CalendarType that lists the type of the Gregorian calendar. This type can be a value of the enumeration GregorianCalendarTypes: Arabic, MiddleEastFrench, TransliteratedFrench, USEnglish, or Localized depending on the culture. With Gregorian calendars, the type is also displayed in the list box.

```
    // default calendar
    textCalendar.Text = ci.Calendar.ToString().Remove(0, 21);

    // fill optional calendars
    listCalendars.Items.Clear();
    foreach (Calendar optCal in ci.OptionalCalendars)
    {
        string calName = optCal.ToString().Remove(0, 21);

        // for GregorianCalendar add type information
```

```
            if (optCal is System.Globalization.GregorianCalendar)
            {
                GregorianCalendar gregCal = optCal as GregorianCalendar;
                calName += " " + gregCal.CalendarType.ToString();
            }
            listCalendars.Items.Add(calName);
        }
```

Next check if the culture is a specific culture (not a neutral culture) by using !ci.IsNeutralCulture in an if statement. Use the method ShowSamples() to display number and date samples. This method will be implemented next. Use the method ShowRegionInformation() to display some information about the region. With the invariant culture, you can only display number and date samples, but no region information. The invariant culture is not related to any real language, and so it is not associated with a region.

```
        // display number and date samples
        if (!ci.IsNeutralCulture)
        {
            groupSamples.Enabled = true;
            ShowSamples(ci);

            // invariant culture doesn't have a region
            if (ci.ThreeLetterISOLanguageName == "IVL")
            {
                groupRegionInformation.Enabled = false;
            }
            else
            {
                groupRegionInformation.Enabled = true;
                ShowRegionInformation(ci.LCID);
            }
        }
        else // neutral culture: no region, no number/date formatting
        {
            groupSamples.Enabled = false;
            groupRegionInformation.Enabled = false;
        }
    }
```

To show some localized sample numbers and dates, the selected object of type CultureInfo is passed with the IFomatProvider argument of the ToString() method.

```
    private void ShowSamples(CultureInfo ci)
    {
        double number = 9876543.21;
        textSampleNumber.Text = number.ToString("N", ci);

        DateTime today = DateTime.Today;
        textSampleDate.Text = today.ToString("D", ci);

        DateTime now = DateTime.Now;
        textSampleTime.Text = now.ToString("T", ci);
    }
```

To display the information that is associated with a `RegionInfo` object, in the method `ShowRegion Information()` a `RegionInfo` object is constructed passing the selected culture identifier. Then access the properties `DisplayName`, `CurrencySymbol`, `ISOCurrencySymbol`, and `IsMetric` properties to display this information.

```
private void ShowRegionInformation(int culture)
{
    RegionInfo ri = new RegionInfo(culture);
    textRegionName.Text = ri.DisplayName;
    textCurrency.Text = ri.CurrencySymbol;
    textCurrencyName.Text = ri.ISOCurrencySymbol;
    checkIsMetric.Checked = ri.IsMetric;
}
```

Starting the application you can see all available cultures in the tree view, and selecting a culture lists the cultural characteristics as shown in Figure 17-7.

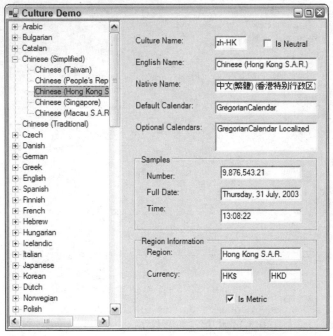

Figure 17-7

Sorting

Sorting strings is dependent on the culture. Some cultures have different sorting orders. One example is Finnish where the characters V and W are treated the same. The algorithms that compare strings for sorting by default use a culture-sensitive sort where the sort is dependent on the culture.

To demonstrate this behavior of a Finnish sort I have created a small sample Console application where some U.S. states are stored unsorted inside an array. We are going to use classes from the namespaces `System.Collections`, `System.Threading`, and `System.Globalization`, so these namespaces must be declared. The method `DisplayNames()` shown below is used to display all elements of an array or of a collection on the console:

```
static void DisplayNames(IEnumerable e)
{
    foreach (string s in e)
      Console.Write(s + " - ");
    Console.WriteLine();
}
```

In the `Main()` method, after creating the array with some of the U.S. states, the thread property `CurrentCulture` is set to the Finnish culture, so that the following `Array.Sort()` uses the Finnish sort order. Calling the method `DisplayNames()` displays all the states on the console.

```
static void Main(string[] args)
{
    string[] names = {"Alabama", "Texas", "Washington",
                      "Virginia", "Wisconsin", "Wyoming",
                      "Kentucky", "Missouri", "Utah", "Hawaii",
                      "Kansas", "Lousiana", "Alaska", "Arizona"};

    Thread.CurrentThread.CurrentCulture =
      new CultureInfo("fi-FI");

    Array.Sort(names);
    Console.WriteLine("\nsorted...");
    DisplayNames(names);
```

After the first display of some U.S. states in the Finnish sort order, the array is sorted once again. If we want to have a sort that is independent of the users' culture, which would be useful when the sorted array is sent to a server or stored somewhere, we can use the invariant culture.

We can do this by passing a second argument to `Array.Sort()`. The `Sort()` method expects an object implementing `IComparer` with the second argument. The `Comparer` class from the `System.Collections` namespace implements `IComparer`. `Comparer.DefaultInvariant` returns a `Comparer` object that uses the invariant culture for comparing the array values for a culture-independent sort.

```
    // sort using the invariant culture
    Array.Sort(names, Comparer.DefaultInvariant);
    Console.WriteLine("\nsorted with invariant culture...");
    DisplayNames(names);
}
```

Figure 17-8 shows the output of this program: a sort with the Finnish culture and a culture-independent sort are shown in. As you can see in this sort, Washington is listed before Virginia.

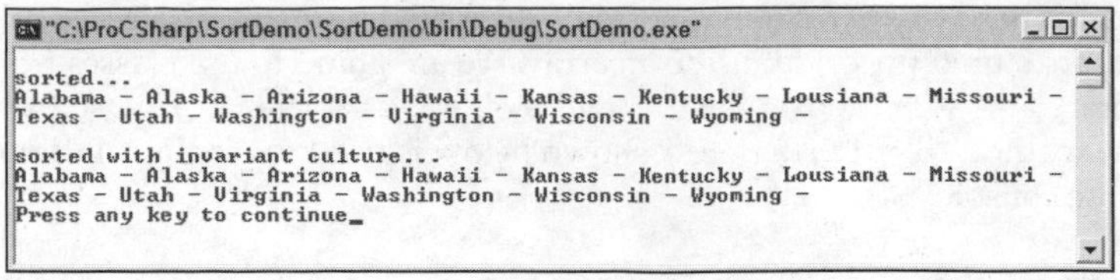

Figure 17-8

> If sorting a collection should be independent of a culture the collection must be
> sorted with the invariant culture. This can particularly be useful when sending the
> sort result to a server or storing it inside a file.

In addition to a locale-dependent formatting and measurement system, depending on the culture strings
also have different values or locale-dependent pictures. This is where resources come into play.

Resources

Resources such as pictures or string tables can be put into resource files or satellite assemblies. Such
resources can be very helpful when localizing applications, and .NET has built-in support to search for
localized resources.

Before we show you how to use resources to localize applications, we discuss how resources can be created and read without looking at language aspects.

Creating Resource Files

Resource files can contain such things as pictures and string tables. A resource file is created by using
either a normal text file or a .resX file that utilizes XML. We will start with a simple text file.

A resource that embeds a string table can be created by using a normal text file. The text file just assigns
strings to keys. The key is the name that can be used from a program to get the value. Spaces are allowed
in both keys and values.

This example shows a simple string table in the file strings.txt:

```
Title = Professional C#
Chapter = Localization
Author = Christian Nagel
Publisher = Wrox Press
```

ResGen

The resgen.exe utility can be used to create a resource file out of strings.txt. Typing

```
resgen strings.txt
```

will create the file strings.resources. The resulting resource file can be added to an assembly either as an external file or embedded into the DLL or EXE. Resgen also supports the creation of XML-based .resX resource files. One easy way to build an XML file is by using ResGen itself:

```
resgen strings.txt strings.resX
```

This command creates the XML resource file strings.resX. We will look at how to work with XML resource files when we look at localization later in this chapter.

The resgen utility does not support adding pictures. With the .NET Framework SDK samples, you will get a ResXGen sample with the tutorials. With ResXGen it is possible to add pictures to a .resX file. Adding pictures can also be done programmatically by using the `ResourceWriter` class, as you will see next.

ResourceWriter

Instead of using the resgen utility to build resource files, a simple program can be written. `ResourceWriter` is a class in the `System.Resources` namespace that also supports pictures and any other object that is serializable.

In the following code example, we will create a `ResourceWriter` object, rw, using a constructor with the filename Demo.resources. After creating an instance, you can add a number of resources of up to 2GB in total size using the `AddResource()` method of the `ResourceWriter` class. The first argument of `AddResource()` specifies the name of the resource and the second argument specifies the value. A picture resource can be added using an instance of the `Image` class. To use the `Image` class, you have to reference the assembly `System.Drawing`. Also add the `using` directive to open the namespace `System.Drawing`.

Create an `Image` object by opening the file logo.gif. You will have to copy the picture to the directory of the executable, or specify the full path to the picture in the method argument of `Image.ToFile()`. The `using` statement specifies that the image resource should automatically be disposed at the end of the using block. Additional simple string resources are added to the `ResourceWriter` object. The `Close()` method of the `ResourceWriter` class automatically calls `ResourceWriter.Generate()` to finally write the resources to the file Demo.resources.

```csharp
using System;
using System.Resources;
using System.Drawing;

class Class1
{
    static void Main()
    {
        ResourceWriter rw = new ResourceWriter("Demo.resources");
```

```
        using (Image image = Image.FromFile("logo.gif"))
        {
            rw.AddResource("WroxLogo", image);
            rw.AddResource("Title", "Professional C#");
            rw.AddResource("Chapter", "Localization");
            rw.AddResource("Author", "Christian Nagel");
            rw.AddResource("Publisher", "Wrox Press");
            rw.Close();
        }
    }
}
```

Starting this small program creates the resource file Demo.resources. The resources will now be used in a Windows application.

Using Resource Files

You can add resource files to assemblies with the assembly generation tool al.exe, using the /embed option, or the C# compiler csc.exe using the /resource option, or directly with Visual Studio .NET. To see how resource files can be used with Visual Studio .NET, create a C# Windows application and name it *ResourceDemo*.

Use the context menu of the Solution Explorer (Add⇨Add Existing Item) to add the previously created resource file Demo.resources to this project. By default, BuildAction of this resource is set to Embedded Resource so that this resource is embedded into the output assembly (see Figure 17-9).

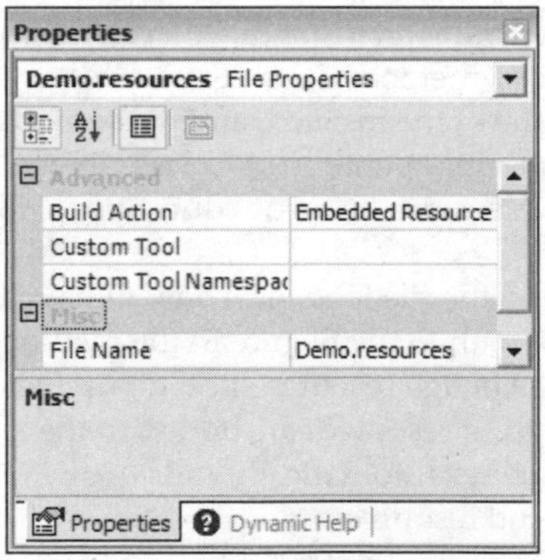

Figure 17-9

After building the project, you can check the generated assembly with ildasm to see the attribute .mresource in the manifest (see Figure 17-10). .mresource declares the name for the resource in the assembly. If .mresource is declared public (as in our example), the resource is exported from the assembly and can be used from classes in other assemblies. .mresource private means that the resource is not exported and only available within the assembly.

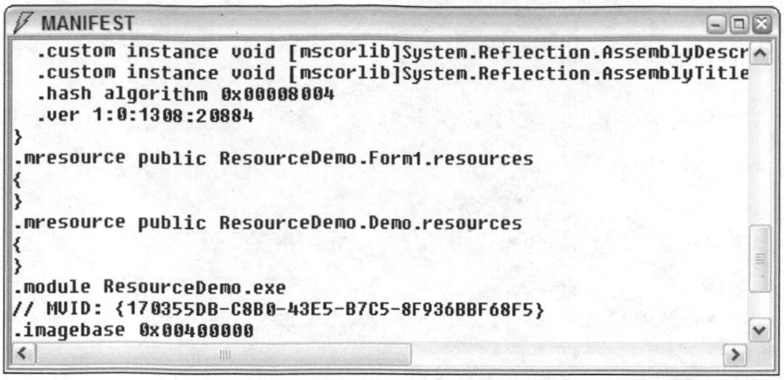

```
MANIFEST                                                        _ □ ☒
  .custom instance void [mscorlib]System.Reflection.AssemblyDescr ▲
  .custom instance void [mscorlib]System.Reflection.AssemblyTitle
  .hash algorithm 0x00008004
  .ver 1:0:1308:20884
}
.mresource public ResourceDemo.Form1.resources
{
}
.mresource public ResourceDemo.Demo.resources
{
}
.module ResourceDemo.exe
// MVID: {170355DB-C8B0-43E5-B7C5-8F936BBF68F5}
.imagebase 0x00400000                                              ▼
◄                           ▥                                  ►
```

Figure 17-10

When adding resources to the assembly using Visual Studio .NET, the resource is always public as shown in Figure 17-10. If the assembly generation tool is used to create assemblies, we can use command line options to differentiate between adding public and private resources. The option /embed:demo.resources,Y adds the resource as public, while /embed:demo.resources,N adds the resource as private.

> If the assembly was generated using Visual Studio .NET, you can change the visibility of the resources later. Use ilasm and select FileÍDump to open the assembly and generate an MSIL source file. You can change the MSIL code with a text editor. Using the text editor, you can change .mresource public to .mresource private. Using the tool ilasm, you can then regenerate the assembly with the MSIL source code: ilasm /exe ResourceDemo.il.

In our Windows application, we add some text boxes and a picture by dropping Windows Forms elements from the Toolbox to the designer. The values from the resources will be displayed in these Windows Forms elements. Change the Text and Name properties of the text boxes and the labels to the values that you can see in the following code. The name property of the PictureBox control is changed to logo. Figure 17-11 shows the final form in the Forms Designer. The PictureBox control is shown as a rectangle without grid in the upper left-hand corner.

To access the embedded resource, use the ResourceManager class from the System.Resources namespace. You can pass the assembly that has the resources as an argument to the constructor of the Resource Manager class. In this example the resources are embedded in the executing assembly, so pass the result of Assembly.GetExecutingAssembly() as the second argument. The first argument is the root name of the resources. The root name consists of the namespace, with the name of the resource file but without the resources extension. As you have seen earlier, ildasm shows the name. All you have to do is remove the file extension resources from the name shown. You can also get the name programmatically using the GetManifestResourceNames() method of the System.Reflection.Assembly class.

Figure 17-11

```
using System.Reflection;
using System.Resources;

//...

    public class Form1 : System.Windows.Forms.Form
    {
        //...
        private System.Resources.ResourceManager rm;

        public Form1()
        {
            //
            // Required for Windows Form Designer support
            //
            InitializeComponent();

            Assembly assembly = Assembly.GetExecutingAssembly();

            rm = new ResourceManager("ResourceDemo.Demo", assembly);
```

Using the `ResourceManager` instance `rm` you can get all the resources by specifying the key to the methods `GetObject()` and `GetString()`:

```
            logo.Image = (Image)rm.GetObject("WroxLogo");
            textTitle.Text = rm.GetString("Title");
            textChapter.Text = rm.GetString("Chapter");
            textAuthor.Text = rm.GetString("Author");
            textPublisher.Text = rm.GetString("Publisher");
        }
```

When you run the code, you can see the string and picture resources (see Figure 17-12).

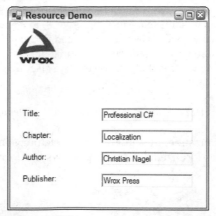

Figure 17-12

Now we will move on to look at localization and the use of resource files with localization.

The System.Resources Namespace

Before we move on to the next example, we conclude this section with a review of the classes contained in the System.Resources namespace that deal with resources:

❑ The ResourceManager class can be used to get resources for the current culture from assemblies or resource files. Using the ResourceManager, you can also get a ResourceSet for a particular culture.

❑ A ResourceSet represents the resources for a particular culture. When a ResourceSet instance is created it enumerates over a class, implementing the interface IResourceReader, and stores all resources in a Hashtable.

❑ The interface IResourceReader is used from the ResourceSet to enumerate resources. The class ResourceReader implements this interface.

❑ The class ResourceWriter is used to create a resource file. ResourceWriter implements the interface IResourceWriter.

❑ ResXResourceSet, ResXResourceReader, and ResXResourceWriter are similar to ResourceSet, ResourceReader, and ResourceWriter; however, they are used to create a XML-based resource file .resX instead of a binary file. You can use ResXFileRef to make a link to a resource instead of embedding it inside an XML file.

Localization Example Using Visual Studio .NET

For this section, we create a simple Windows application to show you how to use Visual Studio .NET for localization. This application will not use complex Windows Forms and does not have any real inner functionality, because the key feature we want to demonstrate here is localization. In the automatically generated source code change the namespace to `Wrox.ProCSharp.Localization`, and the class name to `BookOfTheDayForm`. The namespace is not only changed in the source file BookOfTheDayForm.cs, but also in the project settings, so that all generated resource files will get this namespace, too. You can change the namespace for all new items that are created by selecting Common Properties of Project⇨Properties.

Windows Forms applications will be covered more detailed in the Chapters 19 through 21.

To show some issues with localization, this program has a picture, some text, a date, and a number. The picture shows a flag that is also localized. Figure 17-13 shows this form of the application as seen in the Windows Forms Designer.

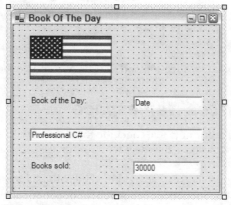

Figure 17-13

The following table lists the values for the Name and Text properties of the Windows Forms elements.

Name	Text
labelBookOfTheDay	Book of the day
labelItemsSold	Books sold
textDate	Date
textTitle	Professional C#
textItemsSold	30000
pictureFlag	

In addition to this form, you might want a message box that displays a welcome message; this message might change depending on the current time of day. This example will demonstrate that the localization for dynamically created dialogs must be done differently. In the method `WelcomeMessage()`, display a message box using `MessageBox.Show()`. Call the method `WelcomeMessage()` in the constructor of the form class `BookOfTheDayForm`, before the call to `InitializeComponent()`.

Here is the code for the method WelcomeMessage():

```
public void WelcomeMessage()
{
   DateTime now = DateTime.Now;
   string message;
   if (now.Hour <= 12)
   {
      message = "Good Morning";
   }
   else if (now.Hour <= 19)
   {
      message = "Good Afternoon";
   }
   else
   {
      message = "Good Evening";
   }
   MessageBox.Show(message + "\nThis is a localization sample");
}
```

The number and date in the form should be set by using formatting options. Add a new method SetDateAndNumber() to set the values with the format option. In a real application, these values could be received from a Web Service or a database, but in this example we are just concentrating on localization. The date is formatted using the D option (to display the long date name). The number is displayed using the picture number format string ###,###,### where # represents a digit and "," is the group separator:

```
public void SetDateAndNumber()
{
   DateTime today = DateTime.Today;
   textDate.Text = today.ToString("D");
   int itemsSold = 327444;
   textItemsSold.Text = itemsSold.ToString("###,###,###");
}
```

In the constructor of the BookOfTheDayForm class both the WelcomeMessage() and SetDateAndNumber() methods are called.

```
public BookOfTheDayForm()
{
   WelcomeMessage();

   //
   // Required for Windows Form Designer support
   //
   InitializeComponent();

   SetDateAndNumber();
}
```

A magic feature of the Windows Forms designer is started when we set the `Localizable` property of the form from `false` to `true`: this results in the creation of an XML-based resource file for the dialog box that stores all resource strings, properties (including the location and size of Windows Forms elements), embedded pictures, and so on. In addition, the implementation of the `InitializeComponent()` method is changed; an instance of the class `System.Resources.ResourceManager` is created, and to get to the values and positions of the text fields and pictures, the `GetObject()` method is used instead of writing the values directly into the code. `GetObject()` uses the `CurrentUICulture` property of the current thread for finding the correct localization of the resources.

Here is part of `InitializeComponent()` before the `Localizable` property is set to true, where all properties of `textboxTitle` are set:

```
private void InitializeComponent()
{
    //...
    this.textTitle = new System.Windows.Forms.TextBox();
    //...
    //
    // textTitle
    //
    this.textTitle.Location = new System.Drawing.Point(24, 152);
    this.textTitle.Name = "textTitle";
    this.textTitle.Size = new System.Drawing.Size(256, 20);
    this.textTitle.TabIndex = 2;
    this.textTitle.Text = "Professional C#";
```

This is automatically changed code for `IntializeComponent()` with the `Localizable` property set to `true`:

```
private void InitializeComponent()
{
    System.Resources.ResourceManager resources = new
        System.Resources.ResourceManager(typeof(BookOfTheDayForm));
    //...
    this.textTitle = new System.Windows.Forms.TextBox();
    //...
    //
    // textTitle
    //
    this.textTitle.AccessibleDescription =
        resources.GetString("textTitle.AccessibleDescription");
    this.textTitle.AccessibleName =
        resources.GetString("textTitle.AccessibleName");
    this.textTitle.Anchor = ((System.Windows.Forms.AnchorStyles)
        (resources.GetObject("textTitle.Anchor")));
    this.textTitle.AutoSize =
        ((bool)(resources.GetObject("textTitle.AutoSize")));
    this.textTitle.BackgroundImage = ((System.Drawing.Image)
        (resources.GetObject("textTitle.BackgroundImage")));
    this.textTitle.Dock = ((System.Windows.Forms.DockStyle)
```

```
                      (resources.GetObject("textTitle.Dock")));
         this.textTitle.Enabled = ((bool)
                      (resources.GetObject("textTitle.Enabled")));
         this.textTitle.Font = ((System.Drawing.Font)
                      (resources.GetObject("textTitle.Font")));
         this.textTitle.ImeMode = ((System.Windows.Forms.ImeMode)
                      (resources.GetObject("textTitle.ImeMode")));
         this.textTitle.Location = ((System.Drawing.Point)
                      (resources.GetObject("textTitle.Location")));
         this.textTitle.MaxLength = ((int)
                      (resources.GetObject("textTitle.MaxLength")));
         this.textTitle.Multiline = ((bool)
                      (resources.GetObject("textTitle.Multiline")));
         this.textTitle.Name = "textTitle";
         this.textTitle.PasswordChar = ((char)
                      (resources.GetObject("textTitle.PasswordChar")));
         this.textTitle.RightToLeft =
              ((System.Windows.Forms.RightToLeft)
                      (resources.GetObject("textTitle.RightToLeft")));
         this.textTitle.ScrollBars =
              ((System.Windows.Forms.ScrollBars)
                      (resources.GetObject("textTitle.ScrollBars")));
         this.textTitle.Size = ((System.Drawing.Size)
                      (resources.GetObject("textTitle.Size")));
         this.textTitle.TabIndex = ((int)
                      (resources.GetObject("textTitle.TabIndex")));
         this.textTitle.Text = resources.GetString("textTitle.Text");
         this.textTitle.TextAlign =
              ((System.Windows.Forms.HorizontalAlignment)
                      (resources.GetObject("textTitle.TextAlign")));
         this.textTitle.Visible = ((bool)
                      (resources.GetObject("textTitle.Visible")));
         this.textTitle.WordWrap = ((bool)
                      (resources.GetObject("textTitle.WordWrap")));
```

Where does the resource manager get the data from? When the `Localizable` property is set to `true`, the resource file *BookOfTheDay.resX* is generated. In this file, you can find the scheme of the XML resource, followed by all elements in the form: `Type`, `Text`, `Location`, `TabIndex`, and so on.

The following XML segment shows a few of the properties of `textBoxTitle`: the `Location` property has a value of `24, 152`, the `TabIndex` property has a value of `2`, the `Text` property is set to `Professional C#`, and so on. For every value, the type of the value is stored as well. For example, the `Location` property is of type `System.Drawing.Point`, and this class can be found in the assembly `System.Drawing`.

Why are the locations and sizes stored in this XML file? With translations, many strings will have completely different sizes and do not any longer fit in to the original positions. When the locations and sizes are all stored inside the resource file, everything that is needed for localizations is stored in these files, separate from the C# code:

```
    <data name="textTitle.Location" type="System.Drawing.Point, System.Drawing,
Version=1.0.5000.0, Culture=neutral, PublicKeyToken=b03f5f7f11d50a3a">
        <value>24, 152</value>
    </data>
    <data name="textTitle.RightToLeft" type="System.Windows.Forms.RightToLeft,
System.Windows.Forms, Version=1.0.5000.0, Culture=neutral,
PublicKeyToken=b77a5c561934e089">
        <value>Inherit</value>
    </data>
    <data name="textTitle.Size" type="System.Drawing.Size, System.Drawing,
Version=1.0.5000.0, Culture=neutral, PublicKeyToken=b03f5f7f11d50a3a">
        <value>256, 20</value>
    </data>
    <data name="textTitle.TabIndex" type="System.Int32, mscorlib,
Version=1.0.5000.0, Culture=neutral, PublicKeyToken=b77a5c561934e089">
        <value>2</value>
    </data>
    <data name="textTitle.Text">
        <value>Professional C#</value>
    </data>
    <data name="textTitle.TextAlign" type="System.Windows.Forms.HorizontalAlignment,
System.Windows.Forms, Version=1.0.5000.0, Culture=neutral,
PublicKeyToken=b77a5c561934e089">
        <value>Left</value>
    </data>
    <data name="textTitle.Visible" type="System.Boolean, mscorlib,
Version=1.0.5000.0, Culture=neutral, PublicKeyToken=b77a5c561934e089">
        <value>True</value>
    </data>
```

When changing some of these resource values, it is not necessary to work directly with the XML code. You can change these resources directly in the Visual Studio designer. Whenever you change the Language property of the form and the properties of some form elements, a new resource file is generated for the specified language. Create a German version of the form by setting the Language property to German, and a French version by setting the Language property to French. For every language, you get a resource file with the changed properties: BookOfTheDayForm.de.resX and BookOfTheDayForm.fr.resX.

The following table shows the changes needed for the German version.

German Name	Value
$this.Text (title of the form)	Buch des Tages
labelItemsSold.Text	Bücher verkauft:
labelBookOfTheDay.Text	Buch des Tages

The following table lists the changes for the French version. For both languages, we also change the flag representing the country.

French Name	Value
$this.Text (title of the form)	Le livre du jour
labelItemsSold.Text	Des livres vendus
labelBookOfTheDay.Text	Le livre du jour

Compiling the project now creates a *satellite assembly* for each language. Inside the debug directory (or the release, depending on your active configuration), language subdirectories like de and fr are created. In such a subdirectory, you will find the file LocalizationDemo.resources.dll. Such a file is a satellite assembly that only includes localized resources. Opening this assembly with ildasm (see Figure 17-14), we see a manifest with the embedded resources and a defined locale. The assembly has the locale de in the assembly attributes, and so it can be found in the de subdirectory. You can also see the name of the resource with .mresource; it is prefixed with the namespace name Wrox.ProCSharp.Localization, followed by the class name BookOfTheDayForm and the language code de.

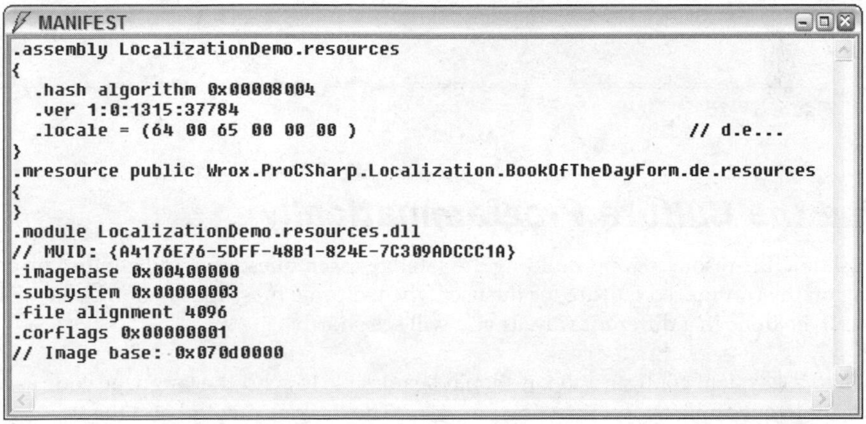

```
MANIFEST                                                                    _ □ X
.assembly LocalizationDemo.resources
{
  .hash algorithm 0x00008004
  .ver 1:0:1315:37784
  .locale = (64 00 65 00 00 00 )                              // d.e...
}
.mresource public Wrox.ProCSharp.Localization.BookOfTheDayForm.de.resources
{
}
.module LocalizationDemo.resources.dll
// MVID: {A4176E76-5DFF-48B1-824E-7C309ADCCC1A}
.imagebase 0x00400000
.subsystem 0x00000003
.file alignment 4096
.corflags 0x00000001
// Image base: 0x070d0000
```

Figure 17-14

Outsourcing Translations

It is an easy task to outsource translations using resource files. When translating resource files it is not necessary to install Visual Studio .NET; a simple XML editor will suffice. The disadvantage of using an XML editor is that there is no real chance to rearrange Windows Forms elements and change the sizes if the translated text does not fit into the original borders of a label or button. Using a Windows Forms designer to do translations is a natural choice.

Microsoft provides a tool as part of the .NET Framework SDK that fulfills all these requirements: the Windows Resource Localization Editor winres.exe (see Figure 17-15). Users working with this tool do not need access to the C# source files; only binary or XML-based resource files are needed for translations. After these translations are completed, we can import the resource files to the Visual Studio .NET project to build satellite assemblies.

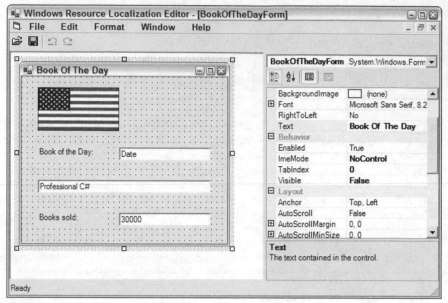

Figure 17-15

Changing the Culture Programmatically

After translating the resources and building the satellite assemblies, you will get the correct translations depending on the configured culture for the user. The welcome message is not translated at this time. This needs to be done in a different way, as you will see shortly.

In addition to the system configuration, it should be possible to send the language code as a command-line argument to our application for testing purposes. The Main() method and the BookOfTheDayForm constructor are changed to support command-line arguments. In the Main() method we pass the culture string to the BookOfTheDayForm constructor. In the constructor, we have to concern ourselves with something else: a CultureInfo instance is created to pass it to the CurrentCulture and CurrentUICulture properties of the current thread. Remember that the CurrentCulture is used for formatting, while the CurrentUICulture is used for loading of resources.

```
[STAThread]
static void Main(string[] args)
{
    string culture = "";
    if (args.Length == 1)
    {
        culture = args[0];
    }
    Application.Run(new BookOfTheDayForm(culture));
}

public BookOfTheDayForm(string culture)
{
```

```
        if (culture != "")
        {
            CultureInfo ci = new CultureInfo(culture);
            // set culture for formatting
            Thread.CurrentThread.CurrentCulture = ci;
            // set culture for resources
            Thread.CurrentThread.CurrentUICulture = ci;
        }

    WelcomeMessage();
    //
    // Required for Windows Form Designer support
    //
    InitializeComponent();
    SetDateAndNumber();
}
```

Now we can start the application by using command-line options. With the running application you can see that the formatting options and the resources that were generated from the Windows Forms designer show up. Figures 17-16 and 17-17 show two localizations where the application is started with the command-line options fr-fr and the de-de.

Figure 17-16

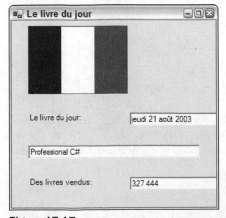

Figure 17-17

There is still a problem with our welcome message box: the strings are hard-coded inside the program. Since these strings are not properties of elements inside the form, the Forms Designer does not extract XML resources as it does from the properties inside the `InitializeComponent()` method when we change the `Localizable` property of the form. You have to create resources ourselves. In the next two sections doing localization will be shown with binary and XML-based resource files.

Using Binary Resource Files

For the welcome message, you have to translate the hard-coded strings. The following table shows the translations for German and French.

English	German	French
Good Morning	Guten Morgen	Bonjour
Good Afternoon	Guten Tag	Bonjour
Good Evening	Guten Abend	Bonsoir
This is a localization sample.	Das ist ein Beispiel mit Lokalisierung.	C'est un exemple avec la localisation.

To support this we are creating a simple text file (Welcome.txt), representing the default as well as German and French versions.

Default version, welcome.txt:

```
Good Morning = Good Morning
Good Afternoon = Good Afternoon
Good Evening = Good Evening
Description =This is a localization sample.
```

German version, welcome.de.txt:

```
Good Morning = Guten Morgen
Good Afternoon = Guten Tag
Good Evening = Guten Abend
Description = Das ist ein Beispiel mit Lokalisierung.
```

French version, welcome.fr.txt

```
Good Morning = Bonjour
Good Afternoon = Bonjour
Good Evening = Bonsoir
Description = C'est un exemple avec la localization.
```

We can use resgen to create the binary resource files Welcome.resources, Welcome.de.resources, and Welcome.fr.resources; for example, resgen Welcome.de.txt creates Welcome.de.resources. You can add these files to the solution by selecting Add⇨Add Existing Item in Solution Explorer. With all these resource files the BuildAction is set automatically to Embedded Resource, otherwise the satellite assembly will not be created. The name of the resources can be found using ildasm, as usual. The resources from the file Welcome.de.resources are named Wrox.ProCSharp.Localization.Welcome.de (the name of the namespace followed by the file name). Instead of using binary resource files, you can also add XML-based resource files to Visual Studio .NET projects, as you will learn next.

Using XML Resource Files

With the resgen command, we create XML resources out of the text-based resource files:

```
resgen welcome.txt welcome.resx
resgen welcome.de.txt welcome.de.resx
resgen welcome.fr.txt welcome.fr.resx
```

The generated XML-based resource files are then added to the project by selecting Add⇨Add Existing Item in the Solution Explorer. Similar to binary resource files, the BuildAction for .resx files is set to Embedded Resource. When building the project, the resources are added to the satellite assemblies.

Now there are two .mresource entries in the satellite assembly as can be seen in Figure 17-18—the resource Wrox.ProCSharp.Localization.BookOfTheDayForm.de was originally created with the Windows Forms designer, and Wrox.ProCSharp.Localization.Welcome.de is the resource from the new Welcome.de.resx resource file.

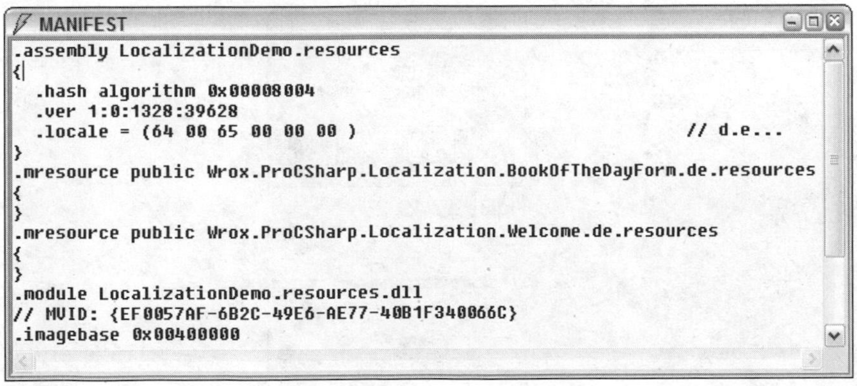

```
MANIFEST

.assembly LocalizationDemo.resources
{
  .hash algorithm 0x00008004
  .ver 1:0:1328:39628
  .locale = (64 00 65 00 00 00 )                          // d.e...
}
.mresource public Wrox.ProCSharp.Localization.BookOfTheDayForm.de.resources
{
}
.mresource public Wrox.ProCSharp.Localization.Welcome.de.resources
{
}
.module LocalizationDemo.resources.dll
// MVID: {EF0057AF-6B2C-49E6-AE77-40B1F340066C}
.imagebase 0x00400000
```

Figure 17-18

Of course, the source code of the method WelcomeMessage() must also be changed to use the resources. A ResourceManager instance is created to get the resource named Wrox.ProCSharp.Assemblies .Localization.Welcome from the current assembly. With this resource manager, you get the resources we created previously in the resource files using GetString() methods.

For the ResourceManager class, you have to declare the use of the System.Resources namespace; the Assembly class is in the System.Reflection namespace.

```
public void WelcomeMessage()
{
    ResourceManager resource =
        new ResourceManager("Wrox.ProCSharp.Localization.Welcome",
                            Assembly.GetExecutingAssembly());
    DateTime now = DateTime.Now;
    string message;
    if (now.Hour <= 12)
    {
        message = resource.GetString("Good Morning");
    }
    else if (now.Hour <= 19)
    {
        message = resource.GetString("Good Afternoon");
    }
    else
    {
        message = resource.GetString("Good Evening");
    }
    MessageBox.Show(message + "\nThis is a localization sample");
}
```

When the program is started using English, German, or French you will get the message boxes shown in Figures 17-19, 17-20 and 17-21.

Figure 17-19

Figure 17-20

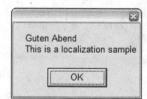

Figure 17-21

Automatic Fallback for Resources

For the French and German versions, in the sample all the resources are inside the satellite assemblies. If not all the values of labels or text boxes are changed, this is not a problem at all. You only must have the values that will change in the satellite assembly; the other values will be taken from the parent assembly. For example, for de-at (Austria) you could change the value for the *Good Afternoon* resource to *Grüß Gott* while leaving the other values intact. During runtime, when looking for the value of the resource *Good Morning* that is not located in the de-at satellite assembly, the parent assembly would be searched. The parent for de-at is de. In cases where the de assembly does not have this resource either, the value would be searched for in the parent assembly of de, the neutral assembly. The neutral assembly does not have a culture code.

Keep in mind, the culture code of the main assembly should be blank!

Globalization and Localization with ASP.NET

With ASP.NET applications, localization happens in a similar way to Windows applications. In Chapter 25, we discuss the functionality of ASP.NET applications as this is done in; in this section, we discuss the localization issues of ASP.NET applications. Visual Studio .NET 2003 does not provide the same support for ASP.NET as it does for Windows Forms applications. However, adapting globalization and localization is not rocket science.

With .ASPX files you can assign cultural settings to complete Web sites or to specific pages. Configuring the cultural setting of the Web site in the configuration file web.config makes it independent of the installed operating system. The culture can be configured with the `<globalization>` element as can be seen in the XML section below. The XML attribute `culture` defines the current culture of the thread that is used for formatting, while `uiCulture` defines the culture used by the resource manager:

```
<configuration>
   <system.web>
      <globalization culture="en-US" uiCulture="en-US" />
   </system.web>
</configuration>
```

If different pages should be accessed from users within different cultures, you can configure the cultural formatting and language output with the page directive that is in the first line of an ASPX file.

```
<%Page Language="C#" Culture="en-US" UICulture="en-US" %>
```

If you want the cultural setting for a Web page to be dependent on the user's browser settings, you can specify the cultural setting of the thread programmatically with the `CurrentCulture` and `CurrentUICulture` properties of the `Thread` class. The best place to do this is in the file global.asax where the method `Application_BeginRequest()` is invoked with every request of a page. When this method is invoked, the thread that handles the user request is known, and this thread will flow through all pages to fulfill the user request. `Request.UserLanguages` returns an array of language strings the user has configured with the browser. Here we use the first language of the list, and pass it to the static method `CultureInfo.CreateSpecificCulture()`. Internet Explorer sends the string de if the configured culture is German (Germany). Because the string de represents a neutral culture instead of a specific culture, we have to create a specific culture with this method, because it is not allowed to set neutral cultures with the culture of the thread. `CreateSpecificCulture()` returns the default specific culture if a neutral culture is passed. The default specific culture for `de` is `de-DE`. Using the browser, you can also configure a custom language string. If we get a string that is not supported as a culture, we deal with in the exception-handling block by creating a default culture `en-US`.

```
protected void Application_BeginRequest(Object sender,
                                        EventArgs e)
{
   CultureInfo ci = null;
   try
   {
      ci = CultureInfo.CreateSpecificCulture(
                        Request.UserLanguages[0]);
   }
   catch
   {
      // default for bad user setting
      ci = new CultureInfo("en-US");
   }
   Thread.CurrentThread.CurrentCulture = ci;
   Thread.CurrentThread.CurrentUICulture = ci;
}
```

Other than these issues, ASP.NET applications are no different from Windows applications when it comes to localization. You can use formatting and satellite assemblies as resources in the same way as you have done it earlier in this chapter.

A Custom Resource Reader

With the resource readers that are part of .NET Framework 1.1, you can read resources from resource files and satellite assemblies. If you want to put the resources into a different store (such as a database), you can create a custom resource reader.

For using a custom resource reader, it is also necessary to create a custom resource set and a custom resource manager. However, doing this is not a hard task, because you can derive the custom classes from existing classes.

For the sample application, you have to create a simple database with just one table for storing messages that has one column for every supported language. The following table lists the columns and their corresponding values.

Key	Default	de	es	fr	it
Welcome	Welcome	Willkommen	Recepción	Bienvenue	Benvenuto
Good Morning	Good Morning	Guten Morgen	Buonas díaz	Bonjour	Buona Mattina
Good Evening	Good Evening	Guten Abend	Buonas noches	Bonsoir	Buona sera

Key	Default	de	es	fr	it
Thank you	Thank you	Danke	Gracias	Merci	Grazie
Goodbye	Goodbye	Auf Wiedersehen	Adiós	Au revoir	Arrivederci

For the custom resource reader create a component library with three classes. The classes are `DatabaseResourceReader`, `DatabaseResourceSet`, and `DatabaseResourceManager`.

Creating a DatabaseResourceReader

With the class `DatabaseResourceReader` define two fields, the data source name `dsn` that is needed to access the database, and the language that should be returned by the reader. These fields are filled inside the constructor of this class. The field `language` is set to the name of the culture that is passed with the `CultureInfo` object to the constructor.

```
public class DatabaseResourceReader : IResourceReader
{
   private string dsn;
   private string language;

   public DatabaseResourceReader(string dsn, CultureInfo culture)
   {
      this.dsn = dsn;
      this.language = culture.Name;
   }
}
```

A resource reader has to implement the interface `IResourceReader`. This interface defines the methods `Close()` and `GetEnumerator()` to return an `IDictionaryEnumerator` that returns keys and values for the resources. In the implementation of `GetEnumerator()` create a `Hashtable` where all keys and values for a specific language are stored. Next, you can use the `SqlConnection` class in the namespace `System.Data.SqlClient` to access the database in SQL Server. `Connection.CreateCommand()` creates a `SqlCommand()` object that we use to specify the SQL SELECT statement to access the data in the database. If the language is set to de, the SELECT statement is `SELECT [key], [de] FROM Messages`. Then you use a `SqlDataReader` object to read all values from the database, and put it into a `Hashtable`. Finally, the enumerator of the `Hashtable` is returned.

For more information about accessing data with ADO.NET see Chapter 21.

```
public System.Collections.IDictionaryEnumerator GetEnumerator()
{
   Hashtable dict = new Hashtable();

   SqlConnection connection = new SqlConnection(dsn);
   SqlCommand command = connection.CreateCommand();
   if (language == "")
      language = "Default";

   command.CommandText = "SELECT [key], [" + language + "] " +
                         "FROM Messages";
```

```
        try
        {
            connection.Open();

            SqlDataReader reader = command.ExecuteReader();
            while (reader.Read())
            {
                if (reader.GetValue(1) != System.DBNull.Value)
                dict.Add(reader.GetString(0), reader.GetString(1));
            }

            reader.Close();
        }
        catch   // ignore missing columns in the database
        {
        }
        finally
        {
            connection.Close();
        }
        return dict.GetEnumerator();
    }

    public void Close()
    {
    }
```

Because the interface `IResourceReader` derives from `IEnumerable` and `IDisposable`, the methods `GetEnumerator()` returning an `IEnumerator` interface and `Dispose()` must be implemented, too.

```
    IEnumerator IEnumerable.GetEnumerator()
    {
        return this.GetEnumerator();
    }

    void IDisposable.Dispose()
    {
    }
}
```

Creating a DatabaseResourceSet

The class `DatabaseResourceSet` can use nearly all implementation of the base class `ResourceSet`. You just need a different constructor that initializes the base class with our own resource reader `DatabaseResourceReader`. The constructor of `ResourceSet` allows passing an object implementing `IResourceReader`; this requirement is fulfilled by `DatabaseResourceReader`.

```
    public class DatabaseResourceSet : ResourceSet
    {
        internal DatabaseResourceSet(string dsn, CultureInfo culture)
            : base(new DatabaseResourceReader(dsn, culture))
        {
```

```
    }

    public override Type GetDefaultReader()
    {
        return typeof(DatabaseResourceReader);
    }
}
```

Creating a DatabaseResourceManager

The third class you have to create is the custom resource manager. DatabaseResourceManager derives from the class ResourceManager, and you only have to implement a new constructor and override the method InternalGetResourceSet().

In the constructor, create a new Hashtable to store all queried resource sets and set it into the field ResourceSets that is defined by the base class.

```
public class DatabaseResourceManager : ResourceManager
{
    private string dsn;

    public DatabaseResourceManager(string dsn)
    {
        this.dsn = dsn;
        ResourceSets = new Hashtable();
    }
```

The methods of the ResourceManager class that you can use to access resources (such as GetString() and GetObject()), invoke the method InternalGetResourceSet() to access a resource set where the appropriate values can be returned.

In the implementation of InternalGetResourceSet(), check first if the resource set for the culture queried for a resource is already in the hash table; if it already exists, return it to the caller. If the resource set is not available, create a new object DatabaseResourceSet with the queried culture, add it to the hash table, and return it to the caller.

```
    protected override ResourceSet InternalGetResourceSet(
        CultureInfo culture, bool createIfNotExists, bool tryParents)
    {
        DatabaseResourceSet rs = null;

        if (ResourceSets.Contains(culture.Name))
        {
            rs = ResourceSets[culture.Name] as DatabaseResourceSet;
        }
        else
        {
            rs = new DatabaseResourceSet(dsn, culture);
            ResourceSets.Add(culture.Name, rs);
        }
        return rs;
    }
}
```

Client Application for DatabaseResourceReader

How the class ResourceManager is used from the client application here does not differ a lot to the use of the ResourceManager class earlier. The only difference is that the custom class DatabaseResourceManager is used instead of the class ResourceManager. The code snippet demonstrates how you can use your own resource manager.

A new `DatabaseResourceManager` object is created by passing the database connection string to the constructor. Then you can invoke the `GetString()` method that is implemented in the base class as we have done earlier, passing the key and an optional object of type `CultureInfo` to specify a culture. In turn, you get a resource value from the database, because this resource manager is using the classes `DatabaeResourceSet` and `DatabaseResourceReader`.

```
    DatabaseResourceManager rm = new DatabaseResourceManager(
 "server=localhost;database=LocalizationDemo;trusted_connection=true");

    string spanishWelcome = rm.GetString("Welcome",
                                        new CultureInfo("es-ES"));
    string italianThankyou = rm.GetString("Thank you",
                                        new CultureInfo("it"));
    string threadDefaultGoodMorning = rm.GetString("Good Morning");
```

Summary

In this chapter, we have discussed the globalization and localization of .NET applications.

In the context of globalization of applications, we discussed the namespace `System.Globalization` to format culture-dependent numbers and dates. Furthermore, we discussed that sorting strings by default depends on the culture. We used the invariant culture for a culture-independent sort.

Localization of applications is accomplished by using resources. Resources can be packed into files, satellite assemblies, or in a custom store such as a database. The classes used with localization are in the namespace `System.Resources`.

18

Deployment

The development process does not end when the source code is compiled and testing is complete. At that stage, the job of getting the application into the user's hands begins. Whether it's an ASP.NET application, a smart client application, or an application built using the Compact Framework, the software must be deployed to a target environment. .NET Framework has made deployment much easier then it was in the past. The pains of registering COM components and writing new hives to the registry are all gone.

This chapter looks at the options that are available for application deployment, both from an ASP.NET perspective and from the smart client perspective.

Designing for Deployment

Deployment often is an afterthought in the development process that can lead to nasty, if not costly, surprises. To avoid grief in deployment scenarios, the deployment process should be planned out during the initial design stage. Any special deployment considerations—such as server capacity, desktop security, or where assemblies will be loaded from—should be built into the design from the start, resulting in a much smoother deployment process.

Another issue that must be addressed early in the development process is the environment in which to test the deployment. While unit testing of application code and of deployment options can be done on the developer's system, the deployment must be tested in an environment that resembles the target system. This is important to eliminate the dependencies that don't exist on a targeted computer. An example of this might be a third-party library that has been installed on the developer's computer early in the project. The target computer might not have this library on it. It can be easy to forget to include it in the deployment package. Testing on the developer's system would not uncover the error since the library already exists. Documenting dependencies can help in eliminating this potential problem.

Deployment processes can be very complex for a large application. Planning ahead for the deployment can save time and effort when the deployment process is implemented.

Deployment Options

This section provides an overview of the deployment options that are available to .NET developers. Most of these options are discussed in greater detail later in this chapter.

Xcopy

The xcopy utility enables you to copy an assembly or group of assemblies to an application folder, cutting down on your development time. Since assemblies are self-discovering, that is the metadata that describes the assembly is included in the assembly, there is no need to register anything in the registry. Each assembly keeps track of what other assemblies it requires to execute. By default the assembly looks in the current application folder for the dependencies. The process of moving (or probing) assemblies to other folders is discussed later in this chapter.

Copy Project

If you are developing a Web project, using the Copy Project option on the Project menu will deploy the components needed to run the application to the server. It creates a new Web application on the server, but does not change any of the IIS directory options.

Deployment Projects

Visual Studio .NET has the capability to create setup programs for an application. There are three options based on Microsoft Windows Installer technology: creating merge modules, creating a setup for client applications, and creating a setup for Web applications. The ability to create cab files is also available. Deployment projects offer a great deal of flexibility and customization for the setup process. One of these deployment options will be useful for larger applications.

Deployment Requirements

It is instructive to look at the runtime requirements of a .NET-based application. The CLR does have certain requirements on the target platform before any managed application can execute.

The first requirement that must be met is the operating system. Currently the following operating systems can run .NET-based applications:

- Windows 98
- Windows 98 Second Edition (SE)
- Windows Millennium Edition (ME)
- Windows NT 4.0 (Service Pack 6a)
- Windows 2000
- Windows XP Home
- Windows XP Professional
- Windows XP Professional TabletPC Edition

The following server platforms are supported:

- ❑   Windows 2000 Server and Advanced Server
- ❑   Windows 2003 Server Family

Other requirements are Windows Internet Explorer version 5.01 or later, MDAC version 2.6 or later (if the application is designed to access data), and Internet Information Services (IIS) for ASP.NET applications.

You also must consider hardware requirements when deploying .NET applications. The minimum requirements for hardware are:

- ❑   Client: Pentium 90 MHz and 32MB RAM
- ❑   Server: Pentium 133 MHz and 128MB RAM

For best performance, increase the amount of RAM—the more RAM the better your .NET application runs. This is especially true for server applications.

Simple Deployment

If deployment is part of an application's original design considerations, then deployment can be as simple as copying a set of files to the target computer. For a Web application, it can be a simple menu choice in Visual Studio .NET. This section discusses these simple deployment scenarios.

In order to see how the various deployment options are set up, you must have an application to deploy. The sample download at www.wrox.com contains three projects: SampleClientApp, SampleWebApp, and AppSupport. SampleClientApp is a smart client application. SampleWebApp is a simple Web app. AppSupport is a class library that contains one simple class that returns a string with the current date and time. SampleClientApp and SampleWebApp use AppSupport to fill a label with the output of AppSupport. In order to use the examples, first load and build AppSupport. Then in each of the other applications set a reference to the newly built AppSupport dll.

Here is the code for the AppSupport assembly:

```
using System;

namespace AppSupport
  {
  /// <summary>
  /// Simple assembly to return date and time string.
  /// </summary>
  public class Support
  {
    private Support()
    {
    }

    public static string GetDateTimeInfo()
    {
      DateTime dt = DateTime.Now;
```

```
        return string.Concat(dt.ToLongDateString(), " ", dt.ToLongTimeString());
    }
  }
}
```

This simple assembly suffices to demonstrate the deployment options available to you.

Xcopy

Xcopy deployment is a term used for the process of copying a set of files to a folder on the target machine and then executing the application on the client. The term comes from the DOS command xcopy.exe Regardless of the number of assemblies, if the files are copied into the same folder, the application will execute—rendering the task of editing the configuration settings or registry obsolete.

To see how an xcopy deployment works, open the SampleClientApp solution (SampleClientApp.sln) that is part of the sample download file. Change the target to Release and do a full compile. Next, use either My Computer or File Explorer to navigate to the project folder\SampleClientApp\ bin\Release and double-click SampleClientApp.exe to run the application. Now click the button to open another dialog. This verifies that the application functions properly. Of course this folder is where Visual Studio placed the output, so you would expect the application to work.

Create a new folder and call it ClientAppTest. Copy the two files from the release folder to this new folder and then delete the release folder. Again, double-click the SampleClientApp.exe file to verify it's working.

That's all there is to it; xcopy deployment provides the ability to deploy a fully functional application simply by copying the assemblies to the target machine. Just because the example that is used here is simple does not mean that this process can not work for more complex applications. There really is no limit to the size or number of assemblies that can be deployed using this method. The reason that you might not want to use xcopy deployment is the ability to place assemblies in the Global Assembly Cache (GAC), or the ability to add icons to the Start Menu. Also if your application still relies on a COM library of some type, then you will not be able to register the COM components easily.

Xcopy and Web Applications

Xcopy deployment can also work with Web applications with exception of the folder structure. You must establish the virtual directory of your Web application and configure the proper user rights. This process is generally accomplished with the IIS administration tool. After the virtual directory is set up, the Web application files can be copied to the virtual directory. Copying a Web application's files can be a bit tricky. There are a couple of configuration files that need to be as accounted for as well as the images that the pages might be using. There is a way to determine what files you must include. When you open the C# or Visual Basic .NET project file (*.csproj or *.vbproj), you can look at the <Files> element. This element lists the files that make up the project. The BuildAction attribute has one of four values: None, Content, Compile, and Embedded Resource. Any file element that has the BuildAction of Compile or Embedded Resource will be compiled into the aspx or dlls of the application. The Content elements should be copied. The RelPath attribute indicates the relative path to which the file should be copied. Here is the <Files> element from the SampleWebApp.

```
<Files>
    <Include>
        <File
            RelPath = "AssemblyInfo.cs"
            SubType = "Code"
            BuildAction = "Compile"
        />
        <File
            RelPath = "Global.asax"
            SubType = "Component"
            BuildAction = "Content"
        />
        <File
            RelPath = "Global.asax.cs"
            DependentUpon = "Global.asax"
            SubType = "Code"
            BuildAction = "Compile"
        />
        <File
            RelPath = "Global.asax.resx"
            DependentUpon = "Global.asax.cs"
            BuildAction = "EmbeddedResource"
        />
        <File
            RelPath = "SampleWebForm.aspx"
            SubType = "Form"
            BuildAction = "Content"
        />
        <File
            RelPath = "SampleWebForm.aspx.cs"
            DependentUpon = "SampleWebForm.aspx"
            SubType = "ASPXCodeBehind"
            BuildAction = "Compile"
        />
        <File
            RelPath = "SampleWebForm.aspx.resx"
            DependentUpon = "SampleWebForm.aspx.cs"
            BuildAction = "EmbeddedResource"
        />
        <File
            RelPath = "Web.config"
            BuildAction = "Content"
        />
    </Include>
</Files>
```

If you look closely you can see that the files AssemblyInfo.cs, Global.asax.cs, Global.asax.resx, SampleWebForm.aspx, and SampleWebForm.aspx.resx have the build action set to Compile. You don't have to worry about copying these files, because they will be compiled into the output of the project. Web.config and SampleWebForm.aspx have the `BuildAction` attribute value of `Content`, so these files must be copied. Keep in mind that you will have to do this with each project that makes up the solution of the application.

Copy Project

Instead of going through all of those steps in the previous section, the easier way would be to select the Copy Project command from the Project menu to open the Copy Project dialog box (see Figure 18-1).

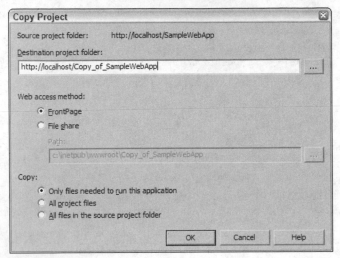

Figure 18-1

In this dialog box, you must specify the destination folder or virtual directory in which the application will run; the Web Access method (you can choose between FrontPage or File Share); and Copy, which enables you to specify the files that are copied to the server.

If the virtual directory does not exist, Copy Project will create it. However, to alter the folder permissions you must use the admin tool. Copy Project provides an xcopy style of deployment. Unlike xcopy, however, it enables you to specify the files that need to be copied and where these files should be deployed. If you select the first option under Copy in the Copy Project dialog box, only the set of files that are required to run the application are copied. This includes all files with BuildAction set to Content and the build outputs (dlls and so on). The second option sends both the source files and the project files. For a production deployment, choose the first option.

Using xcopy deployment or Copy Project has a couple of advantages. First the deployment process itself is very easy. It can be done with simple scripts to automate the process. Updates are copied to the target machine as well. By implementing simple probing you can even incorporate simple versioning scenarios. Shared assemblies can also be copied as long as they don't exist in the GAC. (Refer to Chapter 13 for more on probing and shared assemblies.) The drawback of xcopy and Copy Project deployment is that you don't get the benefits of Windows Installer. These benefits include rollback, uninstall, and repair functionality. It is more difficult to install assemblies into the GAC or handle any type of conditional deployment issues. Also if you are using COM or deploying a COM component with the application, making sure the component is registered properly can be a hassle.

Installer Projects

Xcopy deployment can be easy to use, but there are times when the lack of functionality becomes an issue. To overcome this shortcoming, Visual Studio .NET has five installer project types. Four of these options are based on the Windows Installer technology. The following table lists the project types.

Project Type	Description
Setup Project	Used for the installation of client applications, middle-tier applications, and applications that run as Windows Service.
Web Setup Project	Used for the installation of Web-based applications.
Merge Module Project	Creates merge modules that can be used with other Windows Installer–based setup applications.
Cab Project	Creates cab files for distribution through older deployment technologies.
Setup Wizard	Aids in the creation of a deployment project.

Setup and Web Setup Projects are very similar. The key difference is that with Web Setup the project is deployed to a virtual directory on a Web server, whereas with Setup Project it is deployed to a folder structure. Both project types are based on Windows Installer and have all of the features of a Windows Installer–based setup program. Merge Module Project is generally used when you have created a component or library of functionality that is included in a number of deployment projects. By creating a merge module you can set any configuration items specific to the component and without having to worry about them in the creation of the main deployment project. The Cab Project type simply creates cab files for the application. Cab files are used by older installation technologies as well as some Web-based installation processes. The Setup Wizard project type steps through the process of creating a deployment project, asking specific questions along the way. The following sections discuss how to create each of these deployment projects, what settings and properties can be changed, and what customization you can add.

What Is Windows Installer?

Windows Installer is a service that manages the installation, update, repair, and removal of applications on most Windows operating systems. It is part of Windows ME, Windows 2000, and Windows XP and is available for Windows 95, Windows 98, and Windows NT 4.0. The current version of Windows Installer is 2.0.

Windows Installer tracks the installation of applications in a database. When an application has to be uninstalled, one can easily track and remove the registry settings that were added, the files that were copied to the hard drive, and the desktop and Start Menu icons that were added. If a particular file is still referenced by another application, the installer will leave it on the hard drive so that the other application doesn't break. The database also makes it possible to perform repairs. If a registry setting or a dll associated with an application becomes corrupt or is accidentally deleted, you can repair the installation. During a repair, the installer reads the database from the last install and replicates that installation.

The deployment projects in Visual Studio .NET give you the ability to create a Windows Installation package. The deployment projects give you access to most of what you will need to do in order to install a given application. However, if you need even more control, check out the Windows Installer SDK, which is part of the Platform SDK—it contains documentation on creating custom installation packages for your application. The following sections deal with creating these installation packages using the Visual Studio .NET deployment projects.

Creating Installers

Creating installation packages for client applications or for Web applications is not that difficult. One of the first tasks is to identify all of the external resources your application requires, including configuration files, COM components, third-party libraries, and controls and images. Earlier we mentioned about including a list of dependencies in the project documentation. This is where having that documentation can prove to be very useful. Visual Studio .NET can do a reasonable job of interrogating an assembly and retrieving the dependencies for it, but you still have to audit the findings to make sure nothing is missing.

Another concern might be when in the overall process is the install package is created. If you have an automated build process set up, then you can include the building of the installation package upon a successful build of the project. Automating the process greatly reduces the chance for errors in what can be a time-consuming and complicated process for large projects. What you can do is to include the deployment project with the project solution. The Solution Property Pages dialog box has a setting for Configuration Properties. You can use this setting to select the projects that will be included for your various build configurations. If you select the Build check box under Release builds only, the installation package will only be created when you are creating a release build. This is the process we use in the following examples. Figure 18-2 shows the Solution Property pages dialog box of the SampleClientApp solution.

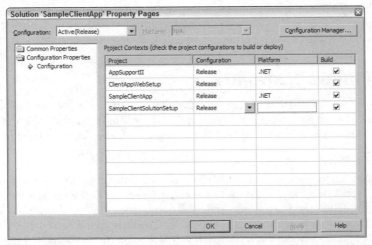

Figure 18-2

Simple Client Application

In the following example, we create an installer for the SimpleClientApp solution (which is included in the sample download, together with the completed installer projects).

For the SimpleClientApp we create two deployment projects. One is done as a separate solution, the other is done in the same solution. This enables you to see the pros and cons of choosing either option.

For the first example we show you how to create the deployment project in a separate solution. Before you get started on creating the deployment project make sure that you have a release build of the application that will be deployed. Next, create a new project in Visual Studio .NET. In the New Project dialog box select Setup and Deployment Projects on the left. On the right select Setup Project and assign it a name of your choice (for example, SampleClientStandaloneSetup). At this point, what you see on your screen resembles Figure 18-3.

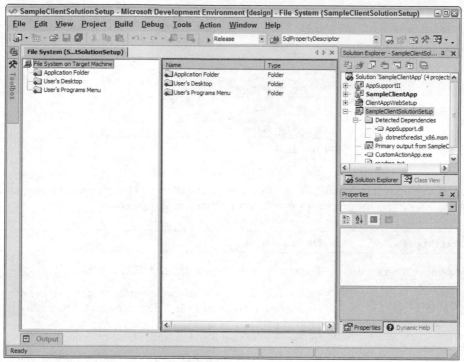

Figure 18-3

In the Solution Explorer window click the project and then the Properties window. You will see a list of properties (see Figure 18-4). These properties will be displayed during the setup of your application. Some of these properties are also displayed in the Add Remove Programs control panel applet. Since most of these properties are visible to the user during the installation process (or when they are looking at your installation in Add Remove Programs), setting them correctly will add a professional touch to your application.

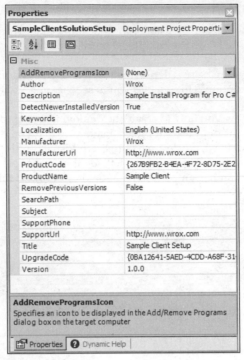

Figure 18-4

The list of properties is important, especially if your application will be deployed commercially. The following table describes the properties and the values that you should enter.

Project Property	Description
AddRemoveProgramsIcon	The icon that appears in the Add/Remove dialog box.
Author	The author of the application. Generally this property setting is the same as the manufacturer. It is displayed on the Summary page of the Properties dialog of the msi package, as well as the Contact field of the SupportInfo page on the Add/Remove dialog box.
Description	A freeform text field that describes the application or component that is being installed. This information is displayed on the Summary page of the Properties dialog of the msi package, as well as the Contact field of the SupportInfo page on the Add/Remove dialog box.
DetectNewerInstalled-Version	A Boolean value that, when set to true, will check to see if a newer version of the application is already installed. If so, the installation process will stop.
Keywords	Keywords that can be used to search for the msi file on the target computer. This information is displayed on the Summary page of the Properties dialog of the msi package.

Project Property	Description
Localization	The locale used for string resources and registry settings. This affects the user interface of the installer.
Manufacturer	Name of the company that manufactured the application of component. Typically this is the same information as specified in the Author property. This information is displayed on the Summary page of the Properties dialog box of the msi package as well as the Publisher field of the SupportInfo page in the Add/Remove dialog box. It is used as part of the default installation path of the application.
ManufacturerURL	The URL for a Web site that relates to the application or component being installed.
ProductCode	A string GUID that is unique to this application or component. Windows Installer uses this property to identify the application for subsequent upgrades or installs.
ProductName	A name that describes the application. Used as the description of an application in the Add/Remove dialog box as well as part of the default install path: C:\Program Files\Manufacturer\ProductName.
RemovePreviousVersions	Boolean value that, if set to true, will check for a previous version of the application. If yes, the uninstall function of the previous version is called before installation continues. This property uses ProductCode and UpgradeCode to determine if uninstall should occur. UpgradeCode should be the same; ProductCode should be different.
SearchPath	A string that represents the search path for dependant assemblies, files, or merge modules. Used when the installer package is built on the development machine.
Subject	Additional information regarding the application. This information is displayed on the Summary page of the Properties dialog box of the msi package.
SupportPhone	A phone number for support of the application or component. This information is displayed in the Support Information field of the SupportInfo page on the Add/Remove dialog box.
SupportURL	A URL for support of the application or component. This information is displayed in the Support Information field of the SupportInfo page in the Add/Remove dialog box.
Title	The title of the installer. This is displayed on the Summary page of the Properties dialog box of the msi package.
UpgradeCode	A string GUID that represents a shared identifier of different versions of the same application. The UpgradeCode should not change for different versions or different language version of the application. Used by the DetectNewerInstalledVersion and RemovePreviousVersion.
Version	The version number of the installer, cab file or merge module. Note that this is not the version of the application being installed.

After you have set the properties, you can start to add assemblies. In this example the only assembly you have to add is the main executable (SampleClientApp.exe). To do this you can either right-click on the project in the Solution Explorer and select Add from the Project menu. You have four options:

- ❑ **Project Output**. We explore this option in the next example.

- ❑ **File**. This is used for adding a readme text file or any other file that is not part of the build process.

- ❑ **Merge Module**. A merge module that was created separately.

- ❑ **Assembly**. Use this option to select an assembly that is part of the installation.

Choose Assembly for this example. You will be presented with the Component Selector dialog box, which resembles the dialog box you use for adding references to a project. Browse to the \bin\release folder of your application. Select SampleClientApp.exe and then click OK in the Component Selector dialog box. You can now see SampleClientApp.exe listed in the Solution Explorer of the deployment project. In the Detected Dependancies section you can see that Visual Studio interrogated SampleClientApp.exe to find the assemblies on which it depends; in this case AppSupport.dll is included automatically. You would continue this process until all of the assemblies in your application are accounted for in the Solution Explorer of the deployment project.

Next you have to determine where the assemblies will be deployed. By default the File System editor is displayed in Visual Studio .NET. The File System editor is split into two panes: The left pane shows the hierarchical structure of the file system on the target machine; the right pane provides a detail view of the selected folder. The folder names might not be what you expect to see, but keep in mind that these are for the target machine; for example, the folder labeled User's Programs Menu maps to the C:\ Documents and Settings\User Name\Start Menu\Programs folder on the target client.

You can add other folders at this point, either special folders or a custom folder. To add a special folder make sure that File System on Target Machine is highlighted in the left pane, then select Action menu on the main menu. The Add Special Folder menu choice provides a list of folders that can be added. For example, if you want to add a folder under the Application folder, you can select the Application Folder folder in the left pane of the editor and then select the Action menu. This time there will be an Add menu that enables you to create the new folder. Rename the new folder and it will be created for you on the target machine.

One of the special folders that you might want to add is a folder for the GAC. AppSupport.dll can be installed to the GAC if it is used by several different applications. In order to add an assembly to the GAC it does have to have a strong name. The process for adding the assembly to the GAC is to add the GAC from the Special Folder menu as described previously and then drag the assembly that you want in the GAC from the current folder to the Global Assembly Cache Folder. If you try and do this with an assembly that is not strongly named, the deployment project will not compile.

If you select Application Folder you will see on the right pane that the assemblies that you added are automatically added to the Application Folder. You can move the assemblies to other folders, but keep in mind that the assemblies have to be able to find each other. (For more details on probing, see Chapter 13.)

If you want to add a shortcut to the application on the user's desktop or to the Start Menu, then drag the items to the appropriate folders. To create a desktop shortcut go to the Application Folder. On the right side of the editor select the application. Go to the Action menu and select the Create Shortcut item to create a shortcut to the application. After the shortcut is created, drag it to the User's Desktop folder. Now when the application is installed, the shortcut will appear on the desktop. Typically, it is up to the user to decide if he or she wants a desktop shortcut to your application. The process of asking the user for input and taking conditional steps is explored later in this chapter. The same process can be followed to create an item in the Start Menu. Also if you look at the properties for the shortcut that you just created, you will see that you can configure the basic shortcut properties such as Arguments and what icon to use. The application icon is the default icon.

Before you build the deployment project you might have to check some project properties. If you select Project menu then SampleClientStandaloneSetup Properties you will see the project Property Pages dialog box. These are properties that are specific to a current configuration. After selecting the configuration in the Configuration drop down, you can change the properties listed in the following table.

Property	Description
Output file name	The name of the msi or msm file that is generated when the project is compiled.
Package files	This property enables you to specify how the files are packaged. Your options are:
	As loose uncompressed files. All of the deployment files are stored in the same directory as the .msi file.
	In setup file. Files are packaged in the .msi file (default setting).
	In cabinet file(s). Files are in one or more cab files in the same directory. When this is selected the CAB file size option becomes available.
Bootstrapper	This enables you to specify whether a bootstrapper is included in the setup. The bootstrapper provides Windows Installer version 2.0. The options are:
	None. No bootstrapper is included.
	Windows Installer Bootstrapper. Bootstrapper to install application son the client pc will be included (default setting).
	Web Bootstrapper. Bootstrapper for downloading from the Web. When this is selected a dialog box appears asking for the installation and optionally the upgrade URL.
Compression	This specifies the compression style for the files included. Your options are:
	Optimized for speed. Larger files but faster installation time (default setting).
	Optimized for size. Smaller files but slower installation time.
	None. No compression applied.
CAB size	This is enabled when the Package file setting is set to In cabinet files. Unlimited creates one single cabinet file; custom allows you to set the maximum size for each cab file.
Authenticode signature	When this is checked the deployment project output is signed using Authenticode; the default setting is unchecked.
Certificate file	The certificate used for signing.
Private key file	The private key that contains the digital encryption key for the signed files.
Timestamp server URL	URL for timestamp server.

After you have set the project properties you should be able to build the deployment project and create the setup for the SampleClientApp application. After you build the project you can test the installation by right-clicking on the project name in the Solution Explorer. This enables you to access an Install and Uninstall choice in the context menu. If you have done everything correctly, you should be able to install and uninstall SampleClientApp successfully.

Same Solution Project

The previous example works well for creating a deployment package but it does have a couple of downsides. For example, what happens when a new assembly is added to the original application. The deployment project will not automatically recognize any changes; you will have to add the new assemblies and verify that any new dependencies are covered. In smaller applications (like our example) this isn't that big of a deal. However, when you're dealing with an application that contains dozens or maybe hundreds of assemblies this can become quite tedious to maintain. Visual Studio .NET has a simple way of resolving this potential headache. Include the deployment project in your applications solution. You can then capture the output of the main project as your deployment assemblies. We can look at the SimpleClientApp as an example.

Open SimpleClientApp solution in Visual Studio .NET. Add a new project using Solution Explorer. Select Deployment and Setup Projects and then select Setup Project, following the steps outlined in the previous section. You can name this project SimpleAppSolutionSetup. In the previous example, you added the assemblies by selecting Add⇨Assemblies from the Project menu. This time, select Add⇨Project Output from Project menu. This opens the Add Project Output Group dialog box (see Figure 18-5).

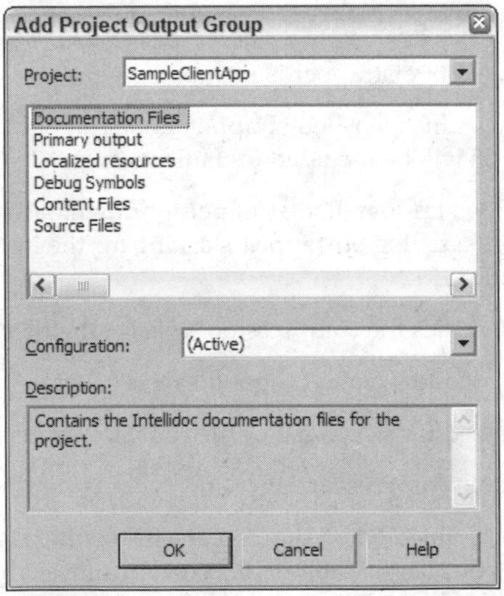

Figure 18-5

The top part of the dialog box has a drop-down list box that shows all projects in the current solution. Select the main startup project. Then select the items you want to include in your project from the list below. Your options are Documentation, Primary Output, Localized Resources, Debug Symbols, Content Files, and Source Files. First select Primary Output. This includes the output and all dependencies when the application is built. There is another drop-down list box that lists the valid configurations: Debug and Release plus any custom configurations you might have added. This also determines what outputs are picked up. For deployment you will most likely want to use the Release configuration.

After you make these selections, a new item is added to your deployment project in Solution Explorer. The name of the item is Primary output form SampleClientApp (Release .NET). You will also see the file AppSupport.dll listed under the dependencies. As before, no need to search for the dependant assemblies.

At this point all of the various project properties that we discuss in the previous section still apply. You can change the Name, Manufacturer, cab file size and other properties. After setting the properties, do a Release build of the solution and test the installation. Everything should work as expected.

To see the advantage of adding the deployment package to the applications solution, add a new project to the solution. In the example it is called AppSupportII. In it is a simple test method that returns the string Hello World. Set a reference in SampleTestApp to the newly added project, and do another Release build of the solution. You should see that the deployment project picked up the new assembly without you having to do anything. If you go back and open up the standalone deployment project from the previous example, unless you specifically add the assembly it will not be picked up.

Simple Web application

Creating an installation package for a Web application is not that different then creating a client install package. The download examples include a SimpleWebApp that also utilizes the AppSupport.dll assembly. You can create the deployment project the same way that the client deployment projects are created, either standalone or in the same solution. In this example, the deployment project is built in the same solution.

Start the SimpleWebApp solution and add a new Deployment and Setup Project. This time be sure to choose Web Setup Project in the Templates window. If you look at the properties view for the project you will see that all of the same properties exist for Web applications as did for client applications. The only addition is RestartWWWService. This is a Boolean value that will restart IIS during the install. If you're using ASP.NET components and not replacing any ATL or ISAPI dlls you shouldn't have to do this.

If you look at the File System editor you will notice that there is only one folder. The Web Application folder is what will be your virtual directory. By default the name of the directory is the name of the deployment project, and it is located below the Web root directory. The following table explains the properties that can be set from the installer. The properties that we discuss in the previous section are not included.

Property	Description
AllowDirectoryBrowsing	Boolean value that, if true, allows an HTML listing of the files and sub-folders of the virtual directory. Maps to the Directory browsing property of IIS.
AllowReadAccess	Boolean value that, if true, allows users to read or download files. Maps to the Read property of IIS.
AllowScriptSourceAccess	Boolean value that, if true, allows users to access source code, including scripts. Maps to Script source access in IIS.
AllowWriteAccess	Boolean value that, if true, allows users to change content in write-enabled files. Maps to Write property of IIS.

Table continued on following page

Property	Description
ApplicationProtection	Determines the protection level of applications that are run on the server. The valid values are:
	Low. Applications run in the same process as Web Services.
	Medium. Applications run in same process, but not the same as Web services.
	High. Application runs in its own process.
	Maps to the Application Protection property in IIS. Has no effect if the IsApplication property is false.
AppMappings	A list of application names and document or data files that are associated with the applications. Maps to the Application Mappings property of IIS.
DefaultDocument	The default or startup document when the user first browses to the site.
ExecutePermissions	The level of permissions that a user has to execute applications. The valid values are:
	None. Only static content can be accessed.
	ScriptsOnly. Only scripts can be accessed. Includes ASP.
	ScriptsAndExecutables. Any files can be accessed.
	Maps to Execute Permissions.in IIS.
Index	Boolean value that, if true, would allow indexing of the content for Microsoft Indexing Service.
	Maps to the Index this resource property of IIS.
IsApplication	Boolean value that, if true, instructs IIS to create the application root for the folder.
LogVisits	Boolean value that, if true, logs visits to the Web site in a log file. Maps to the Log visits property of IIS.
Port	The port that the Web server uses. Default is 80.
VirtualDirectory	The virtual directory for the application. This is relative to the Web server.

You might notice that most of these properties are properties of IIS and can be set in the IIS administrator tool. So the logical assumption is that in order to set these properties in the installer, the installer will need to run with administrator privileges. The settings that are made here can potentially compromise security, so the changes should be well documented.

Other then these properties the process of creating the deployment package is very similar to the previous client example. The main difference between the two projects is the ability to modify IIS from the installation process. As you can see, you have a great deal of control over the IIS environment.

Client from Web server

Another installation scenario is either running the install program from a Web site or actually running the application from a Web site. Both of these are attractive options if you must deploy an application to a large number of users. By deploying from a Web site you eliminate the need for a distribution medium such as CD-ROM, DVD, or even floppy disks. By running the application from a Web site or even a network share you eliminate the need to distribute a setup program at all.

Running an installer from a Web site is fairly simple. You use the Web Bootstrapper project compile option discussed earlier in this chapter. You will be asked to provide the URL of the setup folder. This is the folder in which the setup program is going to look for the msi and other files necessary for the setup to work. After you set this option and compile the deployment package you can copy it to the Web site that you specify in the Setup folder URL property. At this point when the user navigates to the folder, she will be able to either run the setup or download it and then run it. In both instances, the user must be able to connect to the same site to finish the installation.

No Touch Deployment

You can also run the application from a Web site or network share. This process becomes a little more involved and is a prime reason that you should design the application with deployment in mind. This is sometimes referred to as *No Touch Deployment* (NTD).

In order to make this process work the application code must be written in a way to support it. There are a couple of ways to architect the application to take advantage of NTD. One way is to write the majority of the application code into dll assemblies. The dlls will live on a Web server or file share on the network. Then you create a smaller application exe that will be deployed to the client pcs. This stub program will start the application by calling into one of the dll assemblies using the LoadFrom method. The only thing that the stub program will see is the main entry point in the dll. Once the dll assembly has been loaded, the application will continue loading other assemblies from the same URL or network share. Remember that an assembly first looks for dependant assemblies in the application directory; that is the URL that was used to start the application. Here is the code that is used in the stub application on the user's client. This example calls the AppSupportII dll assembly and puts the output of the TestMethod call in label1.

```
Assembly testAssembly =
                Assembly.LoadFrom("http://localhost/AppSupport/AppSupportII.dll");
Type type = testAssembly.GetType("AppSupportII.TestClass");
object testObject = Activator.CreateInstance(type);
label1.Text = (string)type.GetMethod("TestMethod").Invoke(testObject,null);
```

This process uses Reflection to first load the assembly from the Web server. In this example the Web site is a folder on the local machine (localhost). Next, the type of the class is retrieved (here: TestClass). Now that we have type information the object can be created using the Activator.CreateInstance method. The last step is to get a MethodInfo object (the output of GetMethod) and call the Invoke method. In a more complex application this is the main entry point of the application. From this point on, the stub is not needed anymore.

Alternatively, you can also deploy the entire application to a Web site. For this method, create a simple Web page that contains a link to the application's setup executable or perhaps a shortcut on the users desktop that has the Web site link. When the link is clicked, the application will be downloaded to the users' assembly download cache, which is located in the Global Assembly Cache. The application will run from the download cache. Each time a new assembly is requested, it will go to the download cache first to see if it exists; if not it will go to the URL that the main application came from.

The advantage to deploying the application in this way is that when an update is made available for the application, it has to be deployed in only one place. You place the new assemblies in the Web folder and when the user starts the application, the runtime will actually look at the assemblies in the URL and the assemblies in the download cache to compare versions. If a new version is found at the URL, it is then downloaded to replace the current one in the download cache. This way, the user always has access to the most current version of the application.

The biggest issue with deploying applications this way is to get the security right. Since the code is being downloaded from what is considered by default an untrusted area, the code will not have permissions to do certain things. For more details on how code access security and permissions work see the Chapter 14 on .NET security.

For internal corporate applications, this can be a great way to deploy applications. The security issues are much easier to deal with when you can administer the client computers. The proper policies can be set, allowing the proper level of trust to the URL.

Advanced Options

The installation processes that we have discussed so far are very powerful and can do quite a bit. But there is much more that you can control in the installation process. For example, you can use the various editors in Visual Studio .NET to build conditional installations, or add registry keys and custom dialog boxes. The SampleClientSetupSolution example has all of these advanced options enabled.

File System Editor

The File System editor enables you to specify where in the target the various files and assemblies that make up the application will be deployed. By default a standard set of deployment folders is displayed. You can add any number of custom and special folders with the editor. This is also where you would add desktop and Start Menu shortcuts to the application. Any file that must be part of the deployment must be referenced in the File System editor.

Registry Editor

The Registry Editor allows you to add keys and data to the registry. When the editor is first displayed, a standard set of main keys is displayed (see Figure 18-6):

❑ HKEY_CLASSES_ROOT

❑ HKEY_CURRENT_USER

❑ HKEY_LOCAL_MACHINE

❑ HKEY_USERS

HKEY_CURRENT_USER and HKEY_LOCAL_MACHINE contains additional entries in the Software/ [Manufacturer] key where Manufacturer is the information you entered in the Manufacturer property of the deployment project.

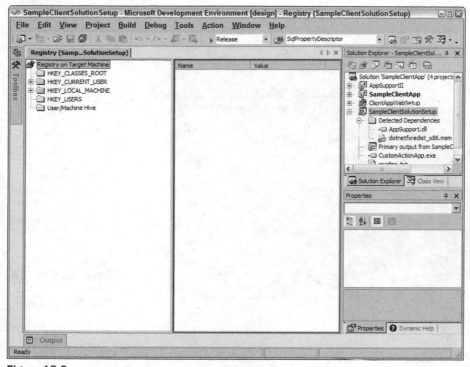

Figure 18-6

To add additional keys and values highlight one of the main keys on the left side of the editor. Select Action from the main menu and then select New. Select the key or the value type that you want to add. Repeat this step until you have all of the registry settings that you want. If you select the Registry on target Machine item on the left pane and then select the Action menu you will see an Import option, which enables you to import an already defined *.reg file.

To create a default value for a key you must first enter value for the key. Then select the value name in the right or value pane. Select Rename from the File menu and delete the name. Press Enter, and the value name is replaced with (Default).

You can also set some properties for the subkeys and values in the editor. The only one that hasn't been discussed already is the DeleteAtUninstall property. A well-designed application should remove all keys that have been added by the application at uninstall time. The default setting is not to delete the keys.

One thing to keep in mind is that the preferred method for maintaining application settings is to use XML-based configuration files. These files offer a great deal more flexibility and are much easier to restore and backup than registry entries.

File Types Editor

The File Types Editor is used to establish associations between files and applications. For example, when you double-click a file with the .doc extension, the file is opened in Word. You can create these same associations for your application. Figure 18-7 shows the File Types Editor.

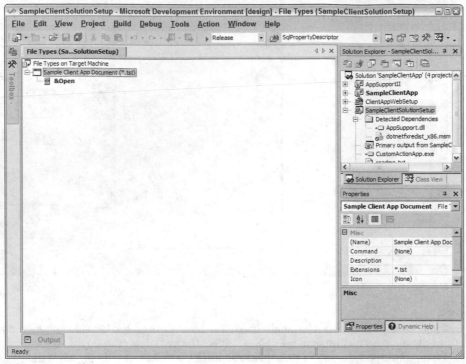

Figure 18-7

In order to add an association, select File Types on Target Machine from the Action menu. Then select Add File Type. In the properties window you can now set the name of the association. In the Extension property add the file extension that should be associated with the application. Do not enter the periods; you can separate multiple extensions with a semicolon like this **ex1;ex2**. In the Command property select the ellipse button. Now select the file (typically an executable) that you want to associate with the specified file types. Keep in mind that any one extension should be associated with only one application.

By default the editor shows &Open as the Document Action. You can add others. The order in which the actions appear in the editor is the order in which they will appear in the context menu when the user right-clicks the file type. Keep in mind that the first item is always the default action. You can set the Arguments property for the actions. This is the command line argument that is used to start the application.

User Interface Editor

Sometimes you might want to ask the user for more information during the installation process. The User Interface Editor is used to specify properties for a set of predefined dialog boxes. The editor is separated into two sections, Install and Admin. One is for the standard installation and the other is used for an administrator's installation. Each section is broken up into three subsections: Start, Progress, and End. These subsections represent the three basic stages of the installation process (see Figure 18-8).

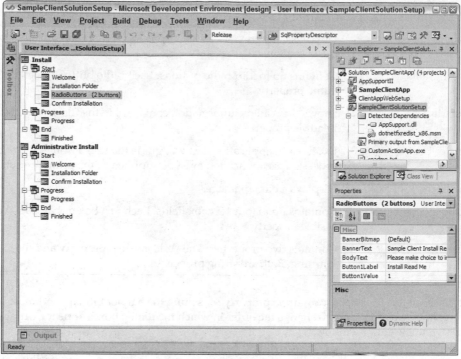

Figure 18-8

The following table lists the types of dialog boxes that you can add to the project.

Dialog Box	Description
Checkboxes	Contains up to four check boxes. Each check box has a Label, Value, and Visible property.
Confirm Installation	Gives the user the ability to confirm the various settings before installation takes place.
Customer Information	Has edit fields for the collection name, organization name, and serial number. Organization name and serial number are optional.
Finished	Displayed at the end of the setup process.
Installation Address	For Web applications, displays a dialog box so users can choose an alternate installation URL.
Installation Folder	For client applications, displays a dialog box so users can select an alternate installation folder.
License Agreement	Displays the license agreement that is located in a file specified by the LicenseFile property.

Table continued on following page

Dialog Box	Description
Progress	Displays a progress indicator during the installation process that shows the current installation status.
RadioButtons	Contains up to four radio buttons. Each radio button has a Label and Value property.
Read Me	Shows the read me information contained in the file specified by the ReadMe property.
Register User	Executes an application that will guide the user through the registration process. This application must be supplied in the setup project.
Splash	Displays a bitmap image.
TextBoxes	Contains up to four text box fields. Each text box has a Label, Value, and Visible property.
Welcome	Contains two properties. The WelcomeText property and the Copyright-Warning. Both are string properties.

Each of these dialog boxes also contains a property for setting the banner bitmap, and most have a property for banner text. You can also change the order in which the dialog boxes appear by dragging them up or down in the editor window.

Now that you can capture some of this information, the question is, how do you make use of it. This is where the Condition property that appears on most of the objects in the project comes in. The Condition property must evaluate to true for the installation step to proceed. For example, say the installation comes with three optional installation components. In this case, you would add a dialog box with three check boxes. The dialog should be somewhere after the Welcome and before the Confirm Installation dialog box. Change the Label property of each check box to describe the action. The first action could be "Install Component A," the second could be "Install Component B," and so on. In the File System Editor select the file that represents Component A. Assuming that the name of the check box on the dialog box is CHECKBOXA1, then the Condition property of the file would be CHECKBOXA1=Checked—, that is, if CHECKBOXA1 is checked, then install the file; otherwise don't install it.

Custom Actions Editor

The Custom Actions Editor allows you to define custom steps that will take place during certain phases of the installation. Custom actions are created beforehand and consist of a DLL, EXE, script or Installer class. The action would contains special steps to perform that can't be defined in the standard deployment project. The actions will be performed at 4 specific points in the deployment. When the editor is first started, you will see the four points in the project (see Figure 18-9):

❑ **Install.** Actions will be executed at the end of the installation phase.

❑ **Commit.** Actions will be executed after the installation has finished and no errors have been recorded.

❑ **Rollback.** Actions occur after the rollback phase has completed.

❑ **Uninstall.** Actions occur after uninstall has completed.

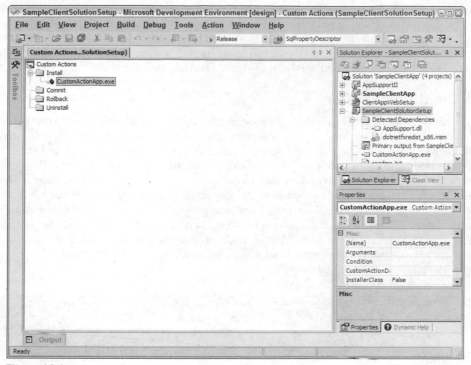

Figure 18-9

To add an action you first select the phase of the installation in which you want the action to occur. Select the Add Custom Action menu selection from the Action menu to open the file system dialog box. This means that the component that contains the action must be part of the deployment project. Since it will be executing on the target machine it has to be deployed, therefore it should be listed in the File System editor.

After you have added the action, you can select one or more of the properties listed in the following table.

Arguments	Command Line Arguments
Condition	A Windows Installer condition that must be evaluated and result in true for the action to execute.
CustomDataAction	Custom data that will be available to the action.
EntryPoint	The entry point for the custom DLL that contains the action. If the Action is contained in an executable, then this property does not apply.
InstallerClass	A Boolean value that, if true, specifies that the action is a .NET `ProjectInstaller` class.
Name	Name of the action. Defaults to the file name of the action.
SourcePath	The path to action on the development machine.

Since the action is code that you develop outside of the deployment project, you have the freedom to add just about anything that adds a professional touch to your application. . The thing to remember is that these actions happen after the phase it is associated with is complete. If you select the Install phase, the action will not execute until after the install phase has completed. If you want to make determinations before the process, then you will want to create a launch condition.

Launch Conditions Editor

The Launch Conditions Editor allows you to specify that certain conditions must be met before installation can continue. Launch conditions are organized into types of conditions. The basic launch conditions are File Search, Registry Search, and Windows Installer Search. When the editor is first started you see two groups (see Figure 18-10): Search Target Machine and Launch Conditions. Typically what happens is that a search is conducted, and based on the success or failure of that search a condition is executed. This happens by setting the `Property` property of the search. The `Property` property can be accessed by the installation process. It can be checked in the Condition property of other actions, for example. You can also add a Launch Condition in the editor. In this condition you set the `Condition` property to the value of the `Property` property in the search. In the condition you can specify a URL that will download the file, registry key, or installer component that was being search for. Notice in Figure 18-10 that a .NET Framework condition is added by default.

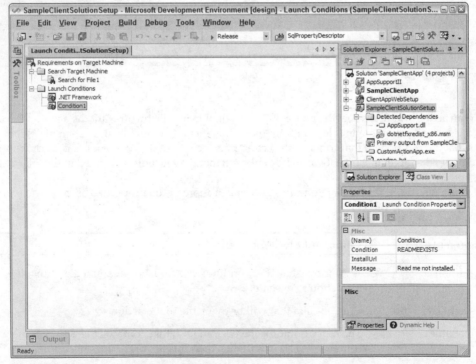

Figure 18-10

File Search will search for a file or type of file. You can set many different file-related properties that determine how files are searched, including file name, folder location, various date values, version information, and size. You can also set the number of subfolders that are searched.

The Registry Search allows you to search for keys and values. It also allows you to set the root key for searching.

The Windows Installer Search looks for the specified Installer component. The search is conducted by GUID.

The Launch Conditions Editor provides two pre-packaged launch conditions: The .NET Framework Launch Condition, which allows you to search for a specific version of the runtime, and a search for a specific version of MDAC, which uses the registry search to find the relevant MDAC registry entries.

Summary

In this chapter we explored the deployment capabilities of Visual Studio .NET. After reading this chapter, you should be able to create a deployment package that solves almost any deployment issue that you might have. Deployment options exist for installing client- and Web-based applications. Client applications can be deployed locally or via the Internet or intranet. You can also use a feature of the .NET runtime known as No Touch Deployment. Using deployment projects to install Web applications can make the process of configuring IIS much easier as well.

Part III: Windows Forms

19

Windows Forms

Web-based applications have become very popular over the past several years. The ability to have all of your application logic reside on a centralized server is very appealing from an administrator's viewpoint. Deploying client-based software can be very difficult, especially COM-based client software. The downside of Web-based applications is that they cannot provide that rich user experience. .NET Framework has given developers the ability to create rich, smart client applications and eliminate the deployment problems and "DLL hell" that existed before. The new deployment services that .NET provides, coupled with the `System.Windows.Forms` and `System.Windows.Forms.Design` namespaces that make up Windows Forms, promise to make client applications popular again.

Windows Forms has already made an impact on Windows development. Now when an application is in the initial design phase, the decision between building a Web-based application or a client application has become a little more difficult. Windows client applications can be developed quickly and efficiently, and they can provide users with the rich experience that they expect.

Windows Forms will seem somewhat familiar to Visual Basic developers. You create new forms (also known as windows or dialogs) in the same fashion of dragging and dropping controls from a toolbox onto the form designer. However, if your background is in the classic C style of windows programming where you create the message pump and monitor messages, or if you're an MFC programmer you will find that you're able to get to the lower-level internals if you need to. You can override the wndproc and catch those messages but you might be surprised that you really won't need to very often.

In this chapter we are going to look at the following aspects of Windows Forms:

- ❑ The form class
- ❑ The class hierarchy of Windows Forms
- ❑ The controls and components that are part of the `System.Windows.Forms` namespace
- ❑ Menus and toolbars
- ❑ Creating controls
- ❑ Creating user controls

Creating a Windows Form Application

The first thing we need to do is create a Windows Form application. For the following example create a blank form and show it on the screen. We will not use Visual Studio .NET for this example. This example has been entered in a text editor and compiled using the command line compiler. Here is the code listing:

```
using System;
using System.Windows.Forms;
namespace NotepadForms
{

  public class MyForm : System.Windows.Forms.Form
  {
    public MyForm()
    {
    }

    [STAThread]
    static void Main()
    {
      Application.Run(new MyForm());
    }
  }
}
```

When you compile and run this example you will get a small blank form without caption. Not real functional, but it is a Windows Form.

Looking at the code there are two items that deserve attention. The first is the fact that we have used inheritance to create the MyForm class. The following line declares that MyForm is derived from System .Windows.Forms.

```
public class MyForm : System.Windows.Forms.Form
```

The Form class is one of the main classes in the System.Windows.Forms namespace. The other section of code that we want to look at is

```
[STAThread]
static void Main()
{
  Application.Run(new MyForm());
}
```

Main is the default entry point into any C# client application. Typically in larger applications, the Main() method would not be in a form, but in a class that is responsible for any startup processing that needs to be done. In this case, you would set the start-up class name in the project properties dialog box. Notice the attribute [STAThread]. This sets the COM threading model to single-threaded apartment (STA).

The Application.Run() method is responsible for starting the standard application message loop. ApplicationRun() has three overloads: The first takes no parameter; the second takes an Application-Context object as a parameter; and the one you see in the example takes a form object as a parameter.

In the example, the `MyForm` object will become the main form of the application. This means that when this form is closed, the application ends. By using the `ApplicationContext` class, you can gain a little more control over when the main message loop ends and the application exits.

The `Application` class contains some very useful functionality. It provides a handful of static methods and properties for controlling the applications starting and stopping process and to gain access to the Windows messages that are being processed by the application. The following table lists some of the more useful of these methods and properties.

Method / Property	Description
CommonAppDataPath	The path for the data that is common for all users of the application. Typically this is BasePath\Company Name\Product Name\ Version where BasePath is C:\Documents and Settings\username\ ApplicationData. If it does not exist, the path will be created.
ExecutablePath	This is the path and file name of the executable file that starts the application.
LocalUserAppDataPath	Similar to `CommonAppDataPath` with the exception that this property supports roaming.
MessageLoop	True or false if a message loop exists on the current thread.
StartupPath	Similar to `ExecutablePath`, except the file name is not returned.
AddMessageFilter	Used to pre-process messages. By implementing an IMessagerFilter-based object the messages can be filtered from the message loop or special processing can take place prior to the message being passed to the loop.
DoEvents	Similar to the Visual Basic `DoEvents` statement. Allows messages in the queue to be processed.
EnableVisualStyles	Enables XP visual styles for the various visual elements of the application. The `FlatStyle` property should be set to `Flat Style.System`.
Exit and ExitThread	`Exit` ends all currently running message loops and exits the application. `ExitThread` ends the message loop on the current thread.

Now what does this sample application look like when it is generated in Visual Studio .NET? Check out the following code:

```
using System;
using System.Drawing;
using System.Collections;
using System.ComponentModel;
using System.Windows.Forms;
using System.Data;

namespace VSNETForm
{
```

```csharp
/// <summary>
/// Summary description for Form1.
/// </summary>
public class Form1 : System.Windows.Forms.Form
{
  /// <summary>
  /// Required designer variable.
  /// </summary>
  private System.ComponentModel.Container components = null;

  public Form1()
  {
    //
    // Required for Windows Form Designer support
    //
    InitializeComponent();

    //
    // TODO: Add any constructor code after InitializeComponent call
    //
  }

  /// <summary>
  /// Clean up any resources being used.
  /// </summary>
  protected override void Dispose( bool disposing )
  {
    if( disposing )
    {
      if (components != null)
      {
        components.Dispose();
      }
    }
    base.Dispose( disposing );
  }

  #region Windows Form Designer generated code
  /// <summary>
  /// Required method for Designer support - do not modify
  /// the contents of this method with the code editor.
  /// </summary>
  private void InitializeComponent()
  {
    this.components = new System.ComponentModel.Container();
    this.Size = new System.Drawing.Size(300,300);
    this.Text = "Form1";
  }
  #endregion

  /// <summary>
  /// The main entry point for the application.
  /// </summary>
  [STAThread]
```

```
    static void Main()
    {
      Application.Run(new Form1());
    }
  }
}
```

First off, the code for this sample application is much longer. There are several using statements at the start of the class, most are not necessary for this example. There is not a penalty for keeping them there. The class Form1 is derived from System.Windows.Forms just like the earlier notepad example, but things start to get different at this point. First there is this line:

```
private System.ComponentModel.Container components = null;
```

In our example, this line of code doesn't really do anything. It only comes into play when you add a component to your form. When you add a component to a form you can also add it to the components object, which is a container. The reason for adding to this container has to do with disposing of the form. The form class supports the IDisposable interface since it is implemented in the Component class. When a component is added to the components container, the container will make sure that the components are tracked properly and disposed of when the form is disposed of. You can see this if you look at the Dispose method in the code:

```
    protected override void Dispose( bool disposing )
    {
      if( disposing )
      {
        if (components != null)
        {
          components.Dispose();
        }
      }
      base.Dispose( disposing );
    }
```

Here you can see that when the Dispose method is called, the Dispose method of the components object is also called and since the component object contains the other components, they are also disposed.

The constructor of the Form1 class looks like:

```
public Form1()
{
  //
  // Required for Windows Form Designer support
  //
  InitializeComponent();

  //
  // TODO: Add any constructor code after InitializeComponent call
  //
}
```

Notice the call to `InitializeComponent()` and the comment about it being required for the designer. `InitializeComponent()` does pretty much what it describes and that is to initialize any controls that might have been added to the form. It also initializes the form properties. This is what `Initialize-Component()` looks like for this simple example:

```
private void InitializeComponent()
{
  this.components = new System.ComponentModel.Container();
  this.Size = new System.Drawing.Size(300,300);
  this.Text = "Form1";
}
```

As you can see it is basic initialization code. The thing about this method is that it is tied to the Forms Designer. When you make changes to the form by using the designer, the changes are reflected in `InitializeComponent()`. If you make any type of code change in `InitializeComponent()`, the next time you make a change in the designer, your changes will most likely be lost. `InitializeComponent()` gets regenerated after each change in the designer. If you need to add additional initialization code for the form or controls and components on the form, be sure to add it after `InitializeComponent()` is called. `InitializeComponent()` is also responsible for instantiating the controls so any call that references a control prior to `InitializeComponent()` will fail with a null reference exception.

To add a control or component to the form press Ctrl-Alt-X or select Toolbox from the View menu in Visual Studio .NET. `Form1` should be in design mode. Right-click Form1.cs in Solution Explorer and select View Designer from the context menu. Select the Button control and drag it to the form in the designer. You can also double-click the control and it will be added to the form. Do the same with the TextBox control.

Now that you have added a TextBox control and a Button control to the form, `InitializeComponent()` expands to include the following code:

```
private void InitializeComponent()
{
  this.button1 = new System.Windows.Forms.Button();
  this.textBox1 = new System.Windows.Forms.TextBox();
  this.SuspendLayout();
  //
  // button1
  //
  this.button1.Location = new System.Drawing.Point(96, 56);
  this.button1.Name = "button1";
  this.button1.TabIndex = 0;
  this.button1.Text = "button1";
  //
  // textBox1
  //
  this.textBox1.Location = new System.Drawing.Point(88, 104);
  this.textBox1.Name = "textBox1";
  this.textBox1.TabIndex = 1;
  this.textBox1.Text = "textBox1";
  //
  // Form1
  //
  this.AutoScaleBaseSize = new System.Drawing.Size(5, 13);
```

```
        this.ClientSize = new System.Drawing.Size(292, 271);
     this.Controls.Add(this.textBox1);
        this.Controls.Add(this.button1);
        this.Name = "Form1";
        this.Text = "Form1";
        this.ResumeLayout(false);

    }
```

If you look at the first three lines of code in the method you can see the Button and Textbox controls are instantiated. Notice the names given to the controls, `textBox1` and `button1`. By default the designer uses the name of the control and adds an integer value to the name. When you add another button, the designer adds the name `button2`, and so on. The next line is part of the `SuspendLayout` and `ResumeLayout` pair. `SuspendLayout()` temporarily suspends the layout events that take place when a control is first initialized. At the end of the method the `ResumeLayout()` method is called to set things back to normal. In a complex form with many controls, the `InitializeComponent()` method can get quite large.

To change a property value of a control, either press F4 or select Properties Window from the View menu. The Properties Window enables you to modify most of the properties for a control or component. By making a change in the Property Window, the `InitializeComponent()` method will be rewritten to reflect the new property value. For example, if the Text property is changed to My Button in the Property Window, `InitializeComponent()` will contain this code:

```
//
// button1
//
this.button1.Location = new System.Drawing.Point(96, 56);
this.button1.Name = "button1";
this.button1.TabIndex = 0;
this.button1.Text = "button1";
this.button1.Text = "My Button";
```

If you are using an editor other than Visual Studio .NET, you will want to include an `InitializeComponent()` type function in your designs. Keeping all of this initialization code in one spot will help keep the constructor cleaner, not to mention that if you have multiple constructors you can make sure the initialization code is called from each constructor.

Control Class

The `System.Windows.Forms` namespace has one particular class that is the base class for virtually every control and form that is created. This class is the `System.Windows.Forms.Control` class. The `Control` class implements the core functionality to create the display that the user sees. The Control class is derived from the `System.ComponentModel.Component` class. The `Component` class provides the Control class with the necessary infrastructure required to be dropped on a design surface and to be contained by another object. The Control class provides a large list of functionality to the classes that are derived from it. The list is too long to itemize here, so we will look at the more important items that are provided by the Control class. Later in the chapter when we look at the specific controls that are based on the Control class we will see the properties and methods in some example code. The following subsections group the methods and properties by functionality, so related items can be looked at together.

Size and Location

The size and location of a control are determined by the properties Height, Width, Top, Bottom, Left, and Right along with the complimentary properties Size and Location. The difference is that Height, Width, Top, Bottom, Left, and Right all take single integers as their value. Size takes a Size structure and Location takes a Point structure as their values. The Size and Point structures are a contained version of XY coordinates. Point generally relates to a location and Size is the height and width of an object. Size and Point are in the `System.Drawing` namespace. Both are very similar in that they provide an XY coordinate pair, but also have overridden operators for easy comparison and conversion. You can, for example, add two Size structures together. In the case of the Point structure the Addition operator is overridden so that you can add a Size structure to a Point and get a new Point in return.

The Bounds property returns a Rectangle object that represents the area of a control. This area includes scroll bars and title bars. Rectangle is also part of the `System.Drawing` namespace. The ClientSize property is a Size structure that represents the client area of the control, minus the scrollbars and title bar.

The `PointToClient` and `PointToScreen` methods are handy conversion methods that take a Point and return a Point. The `PointToClient` takes a Point that represents screen coordinates and translates them to coordinates based on the current client object. This is handy for drag-and-drop actions. The `PointToScreen` does just the opposite—it takes coordinates of a client object and translates them to screen coordinates. There are also the `RectangleToScreen` and `ScreenToRectangle` methods that perform the same functionality with Rectangle structures instead of Points.

The Dock property determines which edge of the parent control the control will be docked to. A DockStyle enumeration value is used as the properties values. This value can be Top, Bottom, Right, Left, Fill, and None. Fill would set the control's size to match the client area of the parent control.

The Anchor property anchors an edge of the control to the edge of the parent control. This is different from docking in that it does not set the edge to the parent control, but sets the current distance from the edge to be constant. For example, if you anchor the right edge of the control to the right edge of the parent, and the parent is resized, the right edge of the control will maintain the same distance from the parent's right edge. The Anchor property takes a value of the AnchorStyles enumeration. The values are Top, Bottom, Left, Right, and None. By setting the values you can make control resize dynamically with the parent as the parent is resized. This way buttons and text boxes will not be cut off or hidden as the form is resized by the user.

Appearance

Properties that relate to the appearance of the control are BackColor and ForeColor which take a `System.Drawing.Color` object as a value. The BackGroundImage property takes an Image-based object as a value. The `System.Drawing.Image` class is an abstract class that is used as the base for the `Bitmap` and `Metafile` classes.

The Font and Text property deal with displaying the written word. In order to change the Font you will need to create a `Font` object. When you create the `Font` object you specify the font name, size, and style.

User Interaction

User interaction is best described as the various events that a control creates and responds to. Some of the more common events are Click, DoubleClick, KeyDown, KeyPress, Validating, and Paint.

The Mouse events—Click, DoubleClick, MouseDown, MouseUp, MouseEneter, MouseLeave, and MouseHover—deal with the interaction of the mouse and the control. If you are handling both the Click and the DoubleClick events, every time you catch a DoubleClick event the Click event is raised as well. This can result in undesired results if not handled properly. Also the Click and DoubleClick receive an EventArgs as an argument, while the MouseDown and MouseUp events receive a MouseEventArgs. The MouseEventArgs contain several pieces of useful information such as the button that was clicked, the number of times the button was clicked, the number of mouse wheel detents (notches in the mouse wheel) and the current X and Y coordinates of the mouse. If you have access to any of this information, then you will have to handle either the MouseDown or MouseUp events and not the Click or DoubleClick events.

The keyboard events work in a similar fashion: the amount of information that is needed determines the event that is handled. For simple situations the KeyPress event receives a `KeyPressEventArgs`. This contains the KeyChar, which is a char value that represents the key pressed. The Handled property is used to determine if the event was handled or not. By setting the Handled property to true, the event is not passed on for default handling by the operating system. If you need more information about the key that was pressed, then the KeyDown or KeyUp event is more appropriate to handle. They both receive a KeyEvent Args. Properties in KeyEventArgs include whether the Ctrl, Alt, or Shift key was pressed. The KeyCode property returns a Keys enumeration value that identifies the key that was pressed. Unlike the KeyPress EventArgs.KeyChar property, the KeyCode property tells you about every key on the keyboard, not just the alphanumeric keys. The KeyData property returns a Keys value and will also set the modifier. The modifiers are ORd with the value. This tells you that the Shift key or the Ctrl key was pressed as well. The KeyValue property is the int value of the Keys enumeration. The Modifiers property contains a Keys value that represents the modifier keys that were pressed. If more then one has been selected, the values are ORs together. The key events are raised in the following order:

1. KeyDown
2. KeyPress
3. KeyUp

The Validating, Validated, Enter, Leave, GotFocus, and LostFocus events all deal with a control gaining focus (or becoming active) or losing focus. This happens when the user tabs into a control or selects the control with the mouse. Enter, Leave, GotFocus and LostFocus seem to be very similar in what they do. The GotFocus and LostFocus events are lower-level events that are tied to the `WM_SETFOCUS` and the `WM_KILLFOCUS` Windows messages. Generally you should use the Enter and Leave events if possible. The Validating and Validated events are raised when the control is validating. These events receive a CancelEventArgs. With this you can cancel the following events by setting the Cancel property to true. If you have custom validation code, and validation fails, you can set Cancel to true and the control will not lose focus. Validating occurs during validation, Validated occurs after validation. The order in which these events are raised is as follows:

1. Enter
2. GotFocus
3. Leave
4. Validating
5. Validated
6. LostFocus

Understanding the order of these events is important so that you don't inadvertently create a recursive situation. For example, trying to set the focus of a control from the control's LostFocus event creates a message deadlock and the application stops responding.

Windows Functionality

The `System.Windows.Forms` namespace is one of the few namespaces that relies on Windows functionality. The Control class is a good example of that. If you were to do a disassembly of the System.Windows.Forms.dll, you would see a list of references to the `UnsafeNativeMethods` class. .NET Framework uses this class to wrap all of the standard Win32 API calls. By using interop to the Win32 API, the look and feel of a standard Windows application can still be achieved with the `System.Windows.Forms` namespace.

Functionality that supports the interaction with Windows includes the Handle and IsHandleCreated properties. Handle returns an IntPtr that contains the HWND (Windows handle) for the control. The window handle is an HWND that uniquely identifies the window. A control can be considered a window, so it has a corresponding HWND. You can use the Handle property to call any number of Win32 API calls.

In order to gain access to the windows messages you can override the WndProc method. The WindProc takes a Message object as a parameter. The Message object is a simple wrapper for a windows message. It contains the HWnd, LParam, WParam, Msg, and Result properties. If you want to have the message processed by the system, then you must make sure that you pass the message to the base.WndProc(msg) method. If you want to handle the message then you don't want to pass the message on.

Miscellaneous Functionality

Some items that are a little more difficult to classify are the data-binding capabilities. The BindingContext property returns a `BindingManagerBase` object. The DataBindings collection maintains a ControlBindings-Collection, which is a collection of binding objects for the control. Data-binding is discussed in Chapter 21.

The CompanyName, ProductName, and Product version provide data on the origination of the control and its current version.

The Invalidate method allows you to invalidate a region of the control for repainting. You can invalidate the entire control or specify a region or rectangle to invalidate. This causes a paint message to be sent to the controls WindProc. You also have the option to invalidate any child controls at the same time.

There are dozens of other properties, methods, and events that make up the Control class. This list represents some of the more commonly used ones and is meant to give you an idea of the functionality that is available.

Class Hierarchy

In the beginning of this section it was stated that the Control class is the base class for most of the classes in the `System.Windows.Forms` namespace. There are other classes that add functionality to the Control class that is needed by some controls. One of these classes is the `System.Windows.Forms.ScrollableControl` class. As the name implies, ScrollableControl adds auto-scrolling behavior. The class adds properties such as AutoScroll, which if set to true will automatically add scroll bars if the control contains other controls that are out of the visible bounds. HScroll and VScroll are both Boolean values that determine if a horizontal or vertical scroll bar is present and visible.

The ContainerControl class is derived from ScrollableControl class. Controls based on this class can be containers of other controls. The Form class is derived from the ContainerControl class. So is the UserControl class. We will be looking at these two classes in detail later in the chapter.

Figure 19-1 shows the class hierarchy of the Control class and its super- and subclasses.

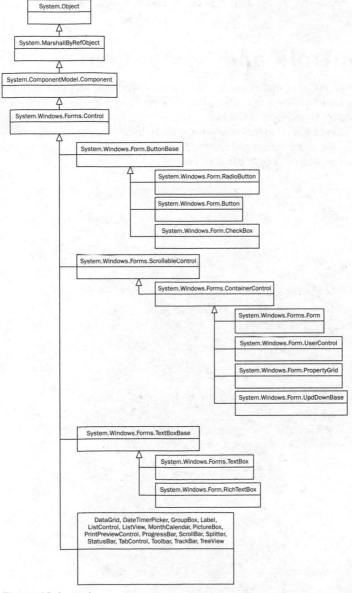

Figure 19-1

The importance of understanding the hierarchy becomes apparent during the design and construction of custom controls. If your custom control is a derivative of a current control, for example a text box with some added properties and methods, then you will want to inherit form the text box control and then override and add the properties and methods to suit your needs. However, if you are creating a control that doesn't match up to any of the controls included with the .NET Framework, then you will have to inherit form one of the three base control classes—Control or ScrollableControl if you need autoscrolling capabilities, and ContainerControl if your control needs to be a container of other controls.

Standard Controls and Components

The previous section covers some of the common methods and properties for controls. In this section we are going to look at the various controls that ship with .NET Framework, and explain what each of them offers in added functionality. The sample download (www.wrox.com) includes a sample application called ControlExample. This application includes a form that contains many controls with basic functionality enabled. Some of the example code in the following section is included in the ControlExample project. Figure 19-2 shows what this example looks like.

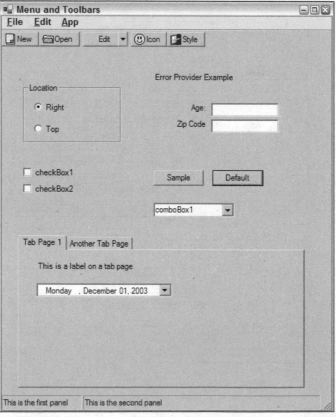

Figure 19-2

Button

The `Button` class represents the simple command button and is derived from `ButtonBase` class. The most common thing to do is to write code to handle the Click event of the button. The following code snippet implements an event handler for the Click event. When the button is clicked, a message box pops up that displays the button's name.

```
private void btnTest_Click(object sender, System.EventArgs e)
{
    MessageBox.Show(((Button)sender).Name + " was clicked.");
}
```

With the `PerformClick` method you can simulate the Click event on a button without the user actually clicking the button. The `NotifyDefault` method takes a Boolean value as a parameter and tells the button to draw itself as the default button. Typically the default button on a form has a slightly thicker border. To identify the button as default, you set the AcceptButton property on the form to the button. Then, when the user presses the Enter key, the button click event for the default button is raised. Figure 19-3 shows that the button with the caption Default is the default button (notice the dark border).

Figure 19-3

Buttons can have images as well as text. Images are supplied by way of an `ImageList` object. `ImageList` objects are explained later in this chapter. Both Text and Image have an `Align` property to align the text or image on the Button.

CheckBox

The CheckBox control is used to accept a two-state or three-state response from the user. If you set the ThreeState property to true, then the CheckBox's CheckState property can be one of the three CheckState enum values,

Checked	The CheckBox has a check mark
Unchecked	The CheckBox does not have a check mark
Indeterminate	In this state the checkbox becomes gray.

The Indeterminate value can be set only in code and not by a user. You can also check the Checked property if you want a Boolean value.

The CheckedChanged and CheckStateChanged events might also be useful. These events occur when the CheckState or Checked properties change. Catching these events can be useful for setting other values based on the new state of the CheckBox.

ComboBox and ListBox

ComboBox and ListBox are both derived from the `ListControl` class. This class provides some of the basic list management functionality. SelectedIndex returns an integer value that corresponds to the index of the currently selected item. Getting a value from the list can be a little trickier. When you add items to a list control, you are not limited to adding string values. You can add any type of object you want to the list. If you add something other then a string, then you must set two other properties. The first is the DisplayMember property. This setting tells the ListControl what property of your object should be displayed in the list. The other is ValueMember, which is the property of our object that we want to return as the value. For example, if we were to use a `Country` object that contains two properties, `CountryName` and `CountryAbbreviation`, we would set the `DisplayMember` to the `CountryName` property and the `ValueMember` property to `CountryAbbreviation`. Now when the list is displayed, we would see a list of country names, and when the `SelectedValue` property is used the control will return the abbreviation for the selected country in the list.

If we access the Items property we can get the Country object. The Items property is implemented on the controls themselves. On the ListBox control, the Items property returns `ListBox.ObjectCollection`. This is a collection of objects that can be referenced through an indexer. So to get the object (not the ValueMember, but the object itself) we could use the following code:

```
obj = listBox1.Items[listBox1.SelectedIndex];
```

The Items property of the ComboBox returns `ComboBox.ObjectCollection`. A ComboBox is a combination of an edit control and a list box. You set the style of the ComboBox by passing a DropDownStyle enumeration value to the DropDownStyle property. The following table lists the various DropDownStyle values.

Value	Description
DropDown	The text portion of the combo box is editable and users can enter a value. They also must click the arrow button to show the list.
DropDownList	The text portion is not editable. Users must make a selection from the list.
Simple	This is similar to DropDown except that the list is always visible.

If the values in the list are wide you can change the width of the drop-down portion of the control with the DropDownWidth property. The MaxDropDownItems property sets the number of items to show when the drop-down portion of the list is displayed.

The FindString and FindStringExact methods are two other useful methods of the list controls. FindString finds the first string in the list that starts with the passed-in string. FindStringExact finds the first string that matches the passed-in string. Both return the index of the value that is found or -1 if the value is not found. They can also take an integer that is the starting index to search from.

The most commonly used events from a list control are the SelectedIndexChanged and SelectedValueChanged events. These events occur if the user selects a new item in the list. When a new item is selected in the list, you can alter other aspects of the form to match the new selected item. Using the Country list, for example, if the user selects a new country from the list, you can then display an image of a map of that country.

DateTimePicker

The DateTimePicker allows users to select a date or time value (or both) in a number of different formats. You can display the DateTime-based value in any of the standard time and date formats. The Format property takes a DateTimePickerFormat enumeration that sets the format to Long, Short, Time, or Custom. If the Format property is set to `DateTiemePickerFormat.Custom` then you can set the CustomFormat property to a string that represents the format.

There is both a Text property and a Value property. The Text property returns a text representation of the DateTime value where the Value property returns the DateTime object. You can also set the maximum and minimum allowable date values with the MinDate and MaxDate properties.

When users click the down arrow a calendar is displayed, allowing the users to select the date a date in the calendar. There are properties that allow you to change the appearance of the calendar by setting the title and month background colors as well as the foreground colors.

The ShowUpDown property determines whether an UpDown arrow is displayed on the control. The currently highlighted value can be changed by clicking on the up or down arrow.

ErrorProvider

ErrorProvider is actually not a control but a component. When you drag a component to the designer, it shows in the component tray under the designer. What the ErrorProvider does is flash an icon next to a control when an error condition exists. Let's say that you have a TextBox entry for an age. Your business rules say that the age value cannot be greater then 100. If the user tries to enter an age greater then that you must inform the user that the age is greater then the allowable value and that they need to change the entered value. The check for a valid value takes place in the Validated event of the text box. If the validation fails, you call the `SetError` method, passing in the control that caused the error and a string that informs the user what the error is. An icon starts flashing indicating that an error has occurred and when the user hovers over the icon the error text is displayed. Figure 19-4 shows the icon that is displayed when an invalid entry is made in the text box.

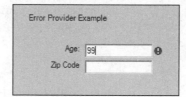

Figure 19-4

You can create an ErrorProvider for each control that produces errors on a form, but if you have a large number of controls this can become unwieldy. Another option is to use one error provider and in the validate event call the `IconLocation` method with the control that is causing the validation and one of the ErrorIconAlignment enumeration values. This value sets where the icon is aligned near the control. Then you call the `SetError` method. If no error condition exists you can clear the ErrorProvider by calling `SetError` with an empty string as the error string. The following example shows how this works:

```
      private void txtAge_Validating(object sender,
                                               System.ComponentModel.CancelEventArgs e)
    {
      if(txtAge.TextLength > 0 && Convert.ToInt32(txtAge.Text) > 65)
      {
        errMain.SetIconAlignment((Control)sender,
                                          ErrorIconAlignment.MiddleRight);
        errMain.SetError((Control)sender, "Value must be less then 65.");
        e.Cancel = true;
      }
      else
      {
        errMain.SetError((Control)sender, "");
      }
    }

    private void txtZipCode_Validating(object sender,
                                               System.ComponentModel.CancelEventArgs e)
    {
      if(txtZipCode.TextLength > 0 && txtZipCode.Text.Length != 5)
      {
        errMain.SetIconAlignment((Control)sender,
                                          ErrorIconAlignment.MiddleRight);
        errMain.SetError((Control)sender, "Must be 5 charactors..");
        e.Cancel = true;

      }
      else
      {
        errMain.SetError((Control)sender, "");
      }
    }
```

If the validation fails (the age is over 65 in txtAge, for example), then the SetIcon method of the ErrorProvider errMain is called. It will set the icon next to the control that failed validation. The error is set next so that when users hover over the icon, the message informs them of what is responsible for the failed validation.

HelpProvider

HelpProvider, like ErrorProvider, is a component and not a control. HelpProvider allows you to hook up controls to help topics. To associate a control with the help provider you call the SetShowHelp method passing the control and a Boolean value that determines whether help will be shown. The HelpNamespace property allows you to set a help file. When the HelpNamespace property is set, the help file is displayed anytime you select F1 and a control that you have registered with the HelpProvider is in focus. You can set a keyword to the help file with the SetHelpKeyword method. SetHelpNavigator takes a HelpNavigator enumeration value to determine which element in the help file should be displayed. You can set it for a specific topic, the index, the table of contents, or the search page. The SetHelpString associates a string value of help-related text to a control. If the HelpNamespace property has not been set, pressing F1 will show this text in a pop-up window. Let's add a HelpProvider to our previous example.

```
helpProvider1.SetHelpString(txtAge,"Enter an age that is less then 65");
helpProvider1.SetHelpString(txtZipCode,"Enter a 5 digit zip code");
```

ImageList

An ImageList component is exactly what the name implies—a list of images. Typically this property is used for holding a collection of images that are used as toolbar icons, or icons in a TreeView control. Many controls have an ImageList property. The ImageList property typically comes with an ImageIndex property. The ImageList property is set to an instance of the ImageList component, the ImageIndex property is set to the index in the ImageList that represents the image that should be displayed on the control. You add images to the ImageList component by using the Add method of the ImageList.Images property. The Images property returns an ImageCollection.

The two most commonly used properties are ImageSize and ColorDepth. ImageSize uses a Size structure as its value. The default value is 16×16 but it can be any value from 1 to 256. The ColorDepth uses a ColorDepth enumeration as its value. The color depth values go from 4 bit to 32 bit. For .NET Framework 1.1 the default is ColorDepth.Depth8Bit.

Label

Labels are generally used to provide descriptive text to the user. The text might be related to other controls or the current system state. You usually see a label together with a text box. The label provides the user with a description of the type of data to be entered in the text box. The Label control is always read-only—the user cannot change the string value of the Text property. However, you can change the Text property in your code. The UseMnemonic property allows you to enable access key functionality. When you precede a character in the Text property with the ampersand (&), that letter will appear underlined in the label control. Pressing the Alt key in combination with the underlined letter puts the focus on the next control in the tab order. If the Text property contains an ampersand in the text, add a second one and it will not underline the next letter. For example, if the label text is "Nuts & Bolts" set the property to "Nuts && Bolts." Since the Label control is read-only, it cannot gain focus; that's why focus is sent to the next control. Because of this it is important to remember: If you enable mnemonics, then you must be certain to set the tab order properly on your form.

The AutoSize property is a Boolean value that specifies whether the Label will resize itself based on the contents of the Label. This can be useful for multilanguage applications where the length of the Text property can change based on the current language.

ListView

The ListView control allows you to display items in one of four different ways. You can display text with an optional large icon, text with an optional small icon, or text and small icons in a vertical list or in detail view, which allows you to display the item text plus any subitems in columns. If this sounds familiar it should, because this is what the right side of File Explorer uses to display the contents of folders. ListView contains a collection of ListViewItems. ListViewItems allows you to set a Text property that is used for the display. ListViewItem has a property called SubItems that contains the text that appears in detail view.

The following example demonstrates how you might useListView. This example includes a short list of countries. Each CountryList object contains a property for the country name, country abbreviation, and currency. Here is the code for the CountryList class:

```
using System;

namespace SimpleListView
{

  public class CountryItem  : System.Windows.Forms.ListViewItem
  {
    string _cntryName = "";
    string _cntryAbbrev = "";

    public CountryItem(string countryName,
                          string countryAbbreviation, string currency)
    {
      _cntryName = countryName;
      _cntryAbbrev = countryAbbreviation;
      base.Text = _cntryName;
      base.SubItems.Add(currency);
    }

    public string CountryName
    {
      get {return _cntryName;}
    }

    public string CountryAbbreviation
    {
      get {return _cntryAbbrev;}
    }
  }
}
```

Notice that we are deriving the CountryList class from ListViewItem. This is because we can add only ListViewItem-based objects to the ListView control. In the constructor we pass the country name to the base.Text property and add the currency value to the base.SubItems property. This displays the country name in the list and the currency in a separate column when in Details view.

Next, we need to add a couple of the CountryItem objects to the ListView control in the code of the form:

```
lvCountries.Items.Add(new CountryItem("United States","US","Dollar"));
lvCountries.Items[0].ImageIndex = 0;
lvCountries.Items.Add(new CountryItem("Great Britain", "GB", "Pound"));
lvCountries.Items[1].ImageIndex = 1;
lvCountries.Items.Add(new CountryItem("Canada", "CA", "Dollar"));
lvCountries.Items[2].ImageIndex = 2;
lvCountries.Items.Add(new CountryItem("Japan", "JP", "Yen"));
lvCountries.Items[3].ImageIndex = 3;
lvCountries.Items.Add(new CountryItem("Germany", "GM", "Deutch Mark"));
lvCountries.Items[4].ImageIndex = 4;
```

Here we add a new CountryItem to the Items collection of the ListView control (lvCountries). Notice that we set the ImageIndex property of the item after we add it to the control. There are two ImageIndex objects, one for large icons and one for small icons (SmallImageList and LargeImageList properties). The trick with having two ImageLists with differing image sizes is to make sure you add the items to the

ImageList in the same order. This way the index of each ImageList represents the same image, just different sizes. In our example, the ImageLists contain icons of the flags for each country we added.

On the top of the form there is a ComboBox (cbView) that lists the four different View enumeration values. We added the items to the cbView like this:

```
cbView.Items.Add(View.LargeIcon);
cbView.Items.Add(View.SmallIcon);
cbView.Items.Add(View.List);
cbView.Items.Add(View.Details);
cbView.SelectedIndex = 0;
```

In the SelectedIndexChanged event of cbView we add the single line of code:

```
lvCountries.View = (View)cbView.SelectedItem;
```

This sets the View property of lvCountries to the new value selected in the ComboBox control. Notice that we need to cast to the View type since object is returned from the SelectedItem property of the cbView.

Last, but hardly least, we have to add columns to the Columns collection. The columns are for Details view. In this case we are adding two columns, Country Name and Currency. The order of the columns is: the Text of the ListViewItem, then each item in the ListViewItem.SubItem collection, in the order it appears in the collection. You can add columns either by creating a `ColumnHeader` object and setting the Text property and optionally the Width and Alignment properties. After creating the ColumnHeader object you can add it to the Columns property. The other way to add columns is to use an override of the Columns.Add method. It allows you to pass in the Text, Width, and Alignment values. Here is an example:

```
lvCountries.Columns.Add("Country",100, HorizontalAlignment.Left);
lvCountries.Columns.Add("Currency",100, HorizontalAlignment.Left);
```

If you set the AllowColumnReorder property to true, then the user can drag the column headers around and rearrange the column order.

The CheckBoxes property on the ListView shows check boxes next to the items in the ListView. This allows the user to easily select multiple items in the ListView control. You can check which items are selected by checking the CheckedItems collection.

The Alignment property sets the alignment of icons in Large and Small icon view. The value can be any of the ListViewAlignment enumeration values. They are Default, Left, Top, SnapToGrid. The Default value allows the user to arrange the icons in any position that they want. When choosing Left or Top the items are aligned with the left or top of the ListView control. When choosing SnapToGrid, the items snap to an invisible grid on the ListView control. The AutoArrange property can be set to a Boolean value and will automatically align the icons based on the Alignment property.

Panel

A Panel is simply a control that contains other controls. By grouping controls together and placing them in a panel, it is a little easier to manage the controls. For example, you can disable all of the controls in the panel by disabling the panel. Since the Panel control is derived from `ScrollableControl`, you also can get the advantage of the AutoScroll property. If you have too many controls to display in the available area, place them in a Panel and set AutoScroll to true—now you can scroll through all of the controls.

Panels do not show a border by default, but by setting the BorderStyle property to something other then none, you can use the Panel to visually group related controls. This makes the user interface more user-friendly.

PictureBox

The PictureBox control is used to display an image. The image can be a BMP, JPEG, GIF, PNG, metafile or icon. The SizeMode property uses the PictureBoxSizeMode enumeration to determine how the image is sized and positioned in the control. The SizeMode property can be AutoSize, CenterImage, Normal, and StretchImage

You can change the size of the display of the PictureBox by setting the ClientSize property. You load the PictureBox by first creating an Image-based object. For example, to load a JPEG file into a PictureBox you would do the following:

```
Bitmap myJpeg = new Bitmap("mypic.jpg");
pictureBox1.Image = (Image)myJpeg;
```

Notice that you will need to cast back to an Image type since that is what the Image property expects.

ProgressBar

The ProgressBar control is a visual clue to the status of a lengthy operation. It indicates to users that there is something going on and that they should wait. The ProgressBar control works by setting the Minimum and Maximum properties. These properties correspond to the progress indicator being all the way to the left (Minimum) or all the way to the right (Maximum). You set the Step property to determine the number that the value is incremented each time the `PerformStep` method is called. You can also use the `Increment` method and increment the value by the value passed in the method call. The Value property returns the current value of the ProgressBar.

You can use the Text property to inform the user of the percentage of the operation that has been completed or the number of items left to process. There is also a BackgroundImage property to customize the look of the progress bar.

RadioButton

Radio buttons are generally used as a group. Sometimes referred to as option buttons, radio buttons allow the user to choose one of several options. When you have multiple RadioButtons controls in the same container, only one at a time may be selected. So if you have three options—for example, Red, Green, and Blue—if the Red option is selected and the user clicks the Blue, the Red is automatically deselected.

The Appearance property takes an Appearance enumeration value. This can be either Button or Normal. When choosing Normal, the radio button looks like a small circle with a label beside it. Selecting the button fills the circle, selecting another button deselects the currently selected button and make the circle look empty. When choosing Button, the control looks like a standard button, but it works like a toggle—selected is the in position, deselected is the normal or out position.

The CheckedAlign property determines where the circle is in relation to the label text. It could be on top of the label, on either side, or below.

The CheckedChanged event is raised whenever the value of the Checked property changes. This way you can perform other actions based on the new value of the control.

TextBox and RichTextBox

The TextBox control is one of the most used controls in the Toolbox. The TextBox and RichTextBox controls are both derived from TextBoxBase. TextBoxBase provides properties such as MultiLine and Lines. Multi-Line is a Boolean value that allows the TextBox control to display text in more then one line. Each line in a text box is a part of an array of strings. This array is exposed through the Lines property. The Text property returns the entire text box contents as a single string. TextLength is the total length of the string that text would return. The MaxLength property will limit the length of the text to the specified amount.

SelectedText, SelectionLength, and SelectionStart all deal with the currently selected text in the text box. The selected text is the text that is highlighted when the control has focus.

The TextBox control adds a couple of interesting properties. AcceptsReturn is a Boolean value that will allow the TextBox to accept the Enter key as a new line or whether it activates the default button on the form. When set to true, pressing the Enter key creates a new line in the TextBox. CharactorCasing determines the casing of the text in the text box. The CharactorCasing enumeration contains three values, Lower, Normal, and Upper. Lower lowercases all text regardless of how it is entered; Upper renders all text in uppercase letters, and Normal displays the text as it is entered. PasswordChar property takes a char the represents what is displayed to the user when they type text in the textbox. This is typically used for entering passwords and pin numbers. The text property will return the actual text that was entered; only the display is affected by this property.

The RichTextBox is a text editing control that can handle special formatting features. As the name implies, the RichTextBox control uses Rich Text Format (RTF) to handle the special formatting. You can make formatting changes by using the Selection properties: SelectionFont, SelectionColor, SelectionBullet and paragraph formatting with SelectionIndent, SelectionRightIndent, and SelectonHangingIndent. All of the Selection properties work in the same way. If there is a section of text highlighted, then a change to a Selection property affects the selected text. If no text is selected then the change takes effect with any text that is inserted to the right of the current insertion point.

The text of the control can be retrieved by using the Text property or the Rtf property. The Text property returns just the text of the control while the Rtf property returns the formatted text.

The `LoadFile` method can load text from a file in a couple of different ways. It can use either a string that represents the path and file name or it can use a stream object. You can also specify the RichText BoxStreamType. The following table lists the values of RichTextBoxStreamType.

Value	Description
PlainText	No formatting information. In places that contained OLE objects, spaces are used.
RichNoOleObjs	Rich text formatting, but spaces where the OLE objects would have been.
RichText	Formatted RTF with OLE objects in place.
TextTextOleObjs	Plain text with text replacing the OLE objects.
UnicodePlainText	Same as PlainText but Unicode encoded.

The `SaveFile` method works with the same parameters, saving the data from the control to a specified file. If a file by that name already exists, it will be overwritten.

Splitter

The Splitter control is used to resize other controls that are docked to it. The classic example of the Splitter control is the bar in between the List View on the right side and the Tree View on the left side of Windows Explorer. When the mouse pointer moves over the splitter, the cursor changes and the user is able to click and drag the splitter either right and left or up and down.

You can set the MinSize and MinExtra properties to limit how much the Splitter can move. The difference is that the MinSize property specifies the minimum distance in pixels that must remain between the splitter and the edge of the container that the splitter is docked to. The MinExtra is the distance in pixels that must remain between the opposite edge of the container and the splitter.

You can set the initial position with the Position property. If the Splitter is not docked to a container control, this value is -1.

The Splitter control raises two events that relate to moving, the SplitterMoving event and the SplitterMoved event. One takes place during the move and the other after the move has happened. They both receive a SplitterEventArgs. The SplitterEventArgs contains properties for the X and Y coordinates of the upper-left corner of the Splitter (SplitX and SplitY) and the X and Y coordinates of the mouse point (X and Y).

StatusBar

The status bar usually sits at the bottom of the form and contains a series of panels that display information about the current status of the application. StatusBarPanel objects are added to the Panels property. A StatusBarPanel can contain text or an icon. You can also handle the DrawItem event and do your own graphics drawing.

The StatusBar control also has properties for sizing grips. If the form that the StatusBar is on is resizable, then this property presents a grip in the bottom-right corner for resizing.

Initially the StatusBar control displays the value of the Text property. Even if you add panels, you must call the ShowPanels method to display them.

TabControl and TabPages

TabControl allows you to group related controls onto a series of tab pages. TabControl manages the collection of TabPages. There are several properties that control the appearance of TabControl. The Appearance property uses the TabAppearance enumeration to determine what the tabs look like. The values are FlatButtons, Buttons, or Normal. The Multiline property is a Boolean that determines if more then one row of tabs are shown. If the Multiline property is set to false and there are more tabs then can fit in the display, a set of arrows appears that allow the user to scroll and see the rest of the tabs.

The TabPage Text property is what is displayed on the tab. The Text property is a parameter in a constructor override as well.

Once you create a TabPage control, it is basically a container control for you to place other controls. The designer in Visual Studio .NET makes it easy to add TabPage controls to a TabControl control by using the collection editor. You can set the various properties as you add each page. Then you can drag the other child controls to each TabPage control.

You can determine the current tab by looking at the SelectedTab property. The SelectedIndex event is raised each time a new tab is selected. By listening to the SelectedIndex property, and then confirming which is the current tab with SelectedTab you can then do special processing based on each tab.

Menu

There are actually three components that are derived from the Menu class: MainMenu, ContextMenu, and MenuItem. The Menu class is abstract, hence you will never use it directly. The Menu class defines a property called MenuItems. MenuItems is a collection of MenuItems. This is how the nesting of menus is created. When you refer to a MenuItem you could be referring to a complete menu structure if there are items in the MenuItems MenuItem collection.

When you drag one of the Menu-based components to a form, it is shown in the component tray under the form in the designer. The component can be selected and then the various properties can be set. The menu also appears in the designer on top of the form. There you can define the menu structure and how the menus are navigated. The menu designer makes it much easier to see what the menu structure will look like after it has been defined. Figure 19-5 shows the ControlSample project open with the Menu Editor enabled.

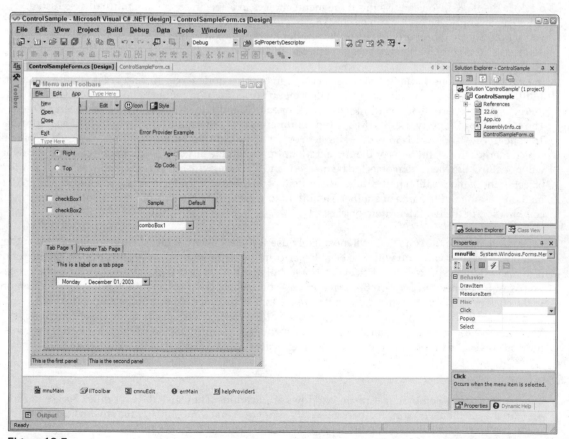

Figure 19-5

MainMenu is used to provide a menu bar on the top of your application forms. It is a container of MenuItem objects that make up the structure of your menu system. The easiest way to create a menu system is in the designer. Add a new MainMenu component to your form. When you activate the component you will see the menu designer become active at the top of your form. Start entering menu text and the appropriate MenuItem objects are created. You can nest menus but you should not go more then 3 levels deep, otherwise it becomes difficult for the user to find menu items. If you precede a character in the menu text it will be underlined and the user can access the menu choice by pressing the Alt key and the underlined letter. This only works if the menu is visible and active.

ContextMenu is another container for MenuItems. The difference between this container and MainMenu is that ContextMenu is the shortcut menu that is displayed when the user clicks the right mouse button on a control or form. Typically the menu contains choices that were relevant to the control or form that the user right-clicked. Each control has a ContextMenu property that you set to the proper ContextMenu. ContextMenu has a property called SourceControl that returns the control that activated the menu.

The MenuItem class defines the menu choices. It has several properties that define how the menu item appears. The Checked property shows a check mark next to the menu text. This is a Boolean value so it can be toggled on or off. If the RadioButton property is set to true, then a radio button (instead of a check mark) is displayed. You can use this if the menu choices in a specific menu are mutually exclusive, which means only one option can be checked at a time. In order to define a shortcut key combination you set the Shortcut property to one of the Shortcut enumeration values. The Shortcut enumeration defines various combinations of keys to assign to the menu.

In larger applications defining a menu structure can become quite large. To help break up the complexity a little you are able to generate several smaller menu structures and merge them together. There is a MergeOrder property that determines the order of each MenuItem structure after it has been merged. The MergeType property uses the MergeType enumeration to determine how merging will be performed. The options are Add, which adds the MenuItem object to the collection of existing MenuItems; MergeItems, which merges the MenuItems of the current MenuItem with the target MenuItem object; Remove, which will not allow the MenuItem object to be merged; and Replace, which will replace the existing MenuItem object in the same position in the target MenuItem object. To perform the merge you call the MergeMenu method passing in the name of another MenuItem to merge with. The current menu will then be the combination of the two MenuItem objects.

In order to execute the code you will most likely use the Click event of the MenuItem object. When the user clicks on the menu you will then be able perform the required process. A good design rule to follow is to never define a process the click event, but to call another method that actually performs the process. This way, if you need to perform the same process somewhere else you can. If the process is defined only in the click event it makes it more difficult to reuse that same functionality. For example, take a button on a toolbar. It is common to have a toolbar button and a menu choice perform the same functionality. You can't use the same event handlers since the event args are different, so having each call the same method solves the problem without having to replicate code.

Toolbar

Toolbars are a very common feature on Windows applications. They give the user quick access to functionality by clicking a button. Toolbars generally share the same functionality that menus do in that a menu choice and a toolbar button often perform the same task when selected.

Toolbar class is a container for ToolbarButtons. The ToolBar control is generally located at the top of the form under the menu structure. The Appearance property uses the ToolBarAppearance enumeration to define whether the toolbar is displayed Flat or Normal. Normal means that each toolbar button looks like a button. When you choose Flat, you can see the text and the icon on the button, but the outline of the button does not become visible until the mouse is hovering over the button. Since ToolBarButton controls can have an icon on them, there is an ImageList property that you would use to manage the toolbar icons.

To create a toolbar, drag the ToolBar control from the Toolbox to the form in the designer. After the Toolbar is on the form, select the ellipse in the property window on the Buttons property. This allows you to add ToolBarButton controls to the ToolBar control. Figure 19-6 shows the ToolBarButton Collection Editor.

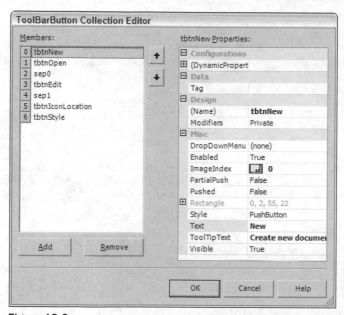

Figure 19-6

The ToolBarButtons are added to the ToolBarButtonCollection of the ToolBar control. To determine the type of button, you set the Style property to one of the ToolBarButtonStyle enumeration values. Your Style options are DropDownButton, PushButton, Separator, or ToggleButton. The PushButton is the standard button. The DropDownButton displays a ContextMenu of options when selected. The ToggleButton is a two-state button that is either in (Pushed property set to true) or out (Pushed property set to false).

To set the icon that should show on the button you set the ImageIndex to the index of the ImageList that is used on the ToolBar control. The Text property defines the text that is displayed on the button. The ToolTip text, when set, is displayed as a ToolTip when the mouse hovers over the button.

In order to perform a task when the ToolBarButton is clicked, you would think there would be a click event in the buttons themselves. That is not the case. There is a ButtonCLick event on the ToolBar control. It receives a ToolBarButtonClickEventArgs object. This object has a Button property that returns the

ToolBarButton that was clicked. Typically in the ButtonClick event there will be a switch statement that interrogates the Button property of the ToolBarButtonClickEventArgs object passed in. Based on which button was pressed, the switch statement executes the proper code. For example, let's assume we have a ToolBar control named tbMain. It has three ToolBar buttons in the ToolBarButtonCollection. We are going to use the Text property of the ToolBarButton to determine what code to execute in the tbMain_ButtonCLick event.

```csharp
private void tbMain_ButtonClick(object sender,
System.Windows.Forms.ToolBarButtonClickEventArgs e)
{

  switch(e.Button.Text)
  {

    case "Button 1"  :
    {
      MessageBox.Show("The Button 1 toolbar button was selected.");
      break;
    }


    case "Button 2" :
    {
      if(e.Button.Pushed)
        MessageBox.Show("The Button 2 toolbar button is pushed.");
      else
        MessageBox.Show("The Button 1 toolbar button is not pushed.");

      break;
    }

    case "Button 3"  :
    {
      MessageBox.Show("The Button 3 toolbar button was selected.");
      break;
    }
  }

}
```

In this simple example we are just showing a MessageBox to the user stating which button was pushed. For the button with Button 2 as the text value, we are also interrogating the Pushed property. This is relevant only if the Style property is set to ToolBarButtonStyle.ToggleButton.

Forms

Earlier in this chapter we discussed how to create a simple Windows application. The example contained one class derived from the System.Windows.Forms.Form class. According to the .NET Framework documentation, "a Form is a representation of any window in your application." If you come from a Visual Basic background, the term form will seem familiar. If your background is C++ using MFC, then you're probably used to calling a form a window, dialog box, or maybe a frame. Regardless, the form is the basic means of interacting with the user. We covered some of the more common and useful properties, methods, and events of the `Control` class, and since the `Form` class is a descendent of the `Control` class, all of the same properties, methods and events exist in the `Form` class. The `Form` class adds considerable functionality to what the `Control` class provides, and that's what we will look at in this section.

Form Class

A Windows client application can contain one form or hundreds of forms. They can be an SDI-based (Single Document Interface) or MDI-based (Multiple Document Interface) application. Regardless, the `System.Windows.Forms.Form` class is the heart of the Windows client. The Form class is derived from ContainerControl, which is derived from ScrollableControl, which is derived from Control. Because of this we can assume that a form is capable of being a container for other controls, capable of scrolling when the contained controls do not fit the client area and has many of the same properties, methods, and events that other controls have. Because of this it also makes the Form class rather complex. This section will try and look at much of that functionality.

Form instantiation and destruction

The process of form creation is important to understand. What you want to do depends on where you write the initialization code. For instantiation, the events occur in the following order:

- ❑ Constructor
- ❑ Load
- ❑ Activated
- ❑ Closing
- ❑ Closed
- ❑ Deactivate

The first three events are of concern during initialization. Depending on what type of initialization you want to do could determine which event you would hook into. The constructor of a class occurs during the object instantiation. The Load event occurs after object instantiation, but just before the form becomes visible. The difference between this and the constructor is the viability of the form. When the Load event is raised, the form exists, but isn't visible. During constructor execution, the form is in the process of existing. The Activated event occurs when the form becomes visible and current.

There is a situation where this order can be altered slightly. If during the constructor execution of the form the Visible property is set to true or the Show method is called (which sets the Visible property to true), the Load event fires immediately. Since this also makes the form visible and current, the Activate event is also raised. If there is code after the Visible property has been set, it will execute. So the startup event might look something like this:

- ❑ Constructor, up to Visible = true
- ❑ Load
- ❑ Activate
- ❑ Constructor, after Visible = true

This could potentially lead to some unexpected results. From a best practices standpoint, it would seem that doing as much initialization as possible in the constructor might be a good idea.

Now what happens when the form is closed? The Closing event gives you the opportunity to cancel the process. The Closing event receives the CancelEventArgs as a parameter. This has a Cancel property that if set to true cancels the event and the form remains open. The Closing event happens as the form is being closed, whereas the Closed event happens after the form has been closed. Both allow you to do any clean-up that might have to be done. Notice that the Deactivate event occurs after the form has been closed. This is another potential source of difficult-to-find bugs. Be sure that you don't have anything in Deactivate that could keep the form from being properly garbage collected.

If you should call the `Application.Exit()` method and you have one or more forms currently open, the Closing and Closed events will not be raised. This is an important consideration if you have open files or database connections that you were going to clean up. The Dispose method is called, so perhaps another best practice would be to put most of your clean-up code in the Dispose method.

Some properties that relate to the start-up of a form are StartPosition, ShowInTaskbar, and TopMost. StartPosition can be any of the FormStartPosition enumeration values. They are:

❑ CenterParent—Form is centered in the client area of the parent form.

❑ CenterScreen—The form is centered in the current display.

❑ Manual—The form's location is based on the values in the Location property.

❑ WindowsDefaultBounds—The form is located at the default Windows position and uses the default size.

❑ WindowsDefaultLocation—The Windows default location is used, but the size is based on the Size property.

The ShowInTaskbar property determines if the form should be available in the taskbar. This is only relevant if the form is a child form and you only want the parent form to show in the taskbar. The TopMost property tells the form to start in the top-most position in the Z-order of the application. This is true even of the form does not immediately have focus.

In order for users to interact with the application, they must be able to see the form. The Show and ShowDialog methods accomplish this. The Show method just makes the form visible to the user. The following code segment demonstrates how to create a form and show it to the user. Assume that the form you want to display is called MyFormClass.

```
MyFormClass myForm = new MyFormClass();
myForm.Show();
```

That's the simple way. The one drawback to this is that there isn't any notification back to the calling code that myForm is finished and has been exited. Sometimes this isn't a big deal and the Show method will work fine. If you do need some type of notification, the ShowDialog is a better option.

When the Show method is called, the code that follows the Show method is executed immediately. When ShowDialog is called, the calling code is blocked and will wait until the form that ShowDialog called is closed. Not only will the calling code be blocked, the form will optionally return a DialogResult value. The DialogResult enumeration is a list of identifiers that describe the reason for the dialog being closed. These include OK, Cancel, Yes, No, and several others. In order for the form to return a DialogResult, the form's DialogResult property must be set or the DialogResult property on one of the form's buttons must be set.

For example, let's say that part of application asks for the phone number of a client. The form has a text box for the phone number and two buttons, one is labeled OK and the other is labeled Cancel. If you set the DialogResult of the OK button to DialogResult.OK and the DialogResult property on the Cancel button to DialogResult.Cancel, then when either of these buttons is selected, the form will become invisible and returns to the calling form the appropriate DialogResult value. Now notice that the form does not get destroyed; only the Visible property is set to false. That's because you still must get values from the form. In the case of this example, we need to phone number. By creating a property on the form for the phone number, the parent form can now get the value and call the Close method on the form. This is what the code for the child form looks like:

```csharp
using System;
using System.Drawing;
using System.Collections;
using System.ComponentModel;
using System.Windows.Forms;

namespace SimpleWinApp
{
  /// <summary>
  /// Summary description for Phone.
  /// </summary>
  public class Phone : System.Windows.Forms.Form
  {
    private System.Windows.Forms.TextBox txtPhone;
    private System.Windows.Forms.Button btnOK;
    private System.Windows.Forms.Button btnCancel;
    private System.Windows.Forms.Label label1;
    /// <summary>
    /// Required designer variable.
    /// </summary>
    private System.ComponentModel.Container components = null;

    public Phone()
    {
      //
      // Required for Windows Form Designer support
      //
      InitializeComponent();

      //
      // TODO: Add any constructor code after InitializeComponent call
      //
    }

    /// <summary>
    /// Clean up any resources being used.
    /// </summary>
    protected override void Dispose( bool disposing )
    {
```

```
    if( disposing )
    {
      if(components != null)
      {
        components.Dispose();
      }
    }
    base.Dispose( disposing );
}

#region Windows Form Designer generated code
/// <summary>
/// Required method for Designer support - do not modify
/// the contents of this method with the code editor.
/// </summary>
private void InitializeComponent()
{
    this.txtPhone = new System.Windows.Forms.TextBox();
    this.btnOK = new System.Windows.Forms.Button();
    this.btnCancel = new System.Windows.Forms.Button();
    this.label1 = new System.Windows.Forms.Label();
    this.SuspendLayout();
    //
    // txtPhone
    //
    this.txtPhone.Location = new System.Drawing.Point(112, 32);
    this.txtPhone.Name = "txtPhone";
    this.txtPhone.TabIndex = 0;
    this.txtPhone.Text = "";
    //
    // btnOK
    //
    this.btnOK.DialogResult = System.Windows.Forms.DialogResult.OK;
    this.btnOK.Location = new System.Drawing.Point(48, 88);
    this.btnOK.Name = "btnOK";
    this.btnOK.TabIndex = 1;
    this.btnOK.Text = "OK";
    //
    // btnCancel
    //
    this.btnCancel.DialogResult =
                      System.Windows.Forms.DialogResult.Cancel;
    this.btnCancel.Location = new System.Drawing.Point(152, 88);
    this.btnCancel.Name = "btnCancel";
    this.btnCancel.TabIndex = 2;
    this.btnCancel.Text = "Cancel";
    //
    // label1
    //
    this.label1.Location = new System.Drawing.Point(8, 32);
    this.label1.Name = "label1";
    this.label1.TabIndex = 3;
    this.label1.Text = "Enter Phone #:";
    this.label1.TextAlign =
                      System.Drawing.ContentAlignment.MiddleRight;
```

```
        //
        // Phone
        //
        this.AutoScaleBaseSize = new System.Drawing.Size(5, 13);
        this.ClientSize = new System.Drawing.Size(264, 155);
        this.ControlBox = false;
        this.Controls.Add(this.label1);
        this.Controls.Add(this.btnCancel);
        this.Controls.Add(this.btnOK);
        this.Controls.Add(this.txtPhone);
        this.HelpButton = true;
        this.MaximizeBox = false;
        this.MinimizeBox = false;
        this.Name = "Phone";
        this.ShowInTaskbar = false;
        this.Text = "Phone";
        this.ResumeLayout(false);

    }
    #endregion

    public string PhoneNumber
    {
      get {return txtPhone.Text;}
      set {txtPhone.Text = value;}
    }

  }
}
```

Now we are looking at the complete code for the Phone form. The first thing to notice is the fact that there isn't code to handle the click events of the buttons. Since we set the DialogResult property for each of the buttons, the form disappears after either the OK or Cancel button is clicked. The only property we have added is the PhoneNumber property. The following code shows the method in the parent form that calls the Phone dialog:

```
Phone frm = new Phone();
frm.ShowDialog();
if(frm.DialogResult == DialogResult.OK)
{
  MessageBox.Show("Phone number is " + frm.PhoneNumber);
}
else if(frm.DialogResult == DialogResult.Cancel)
{
  MessageBox.Show("Form was canceled.");
}
frm.Close();
```

This looks simple enough. Create the new Phone object (frm). When the `frm.ShowDialog()` method is called, the code in this method will stop and wait for the Phone form to return. We can then check the DialogResult property of the Phone form. Since it has not been destroyed yet, just made invisible, we can still access the public properties, one of them being the PhoneNumber property. Once we get the data we need, then we can call the Close method on the form.

This works well, but what if the returned phone number is not formatted correctly. If we put the ShowDialog inside of the loop, then we can just recall it and have the user re-enter the value. This way we get a proper value or handle user who click Cancel.

```
while(true)
{
  frm.ShowDialog();
  if(frm.DialogResult == DialogResult.OK)
  {
    MessageBox.Show("Phone number is " + frm.PhoneNumber);
    if(frm.PhoneNumber.Length == 8 | frm.PhoneNumber.Length == 12)
    {
      break;
    }
    else
    {
      MessageBox.Show("Phone number was not formatted correctly.");
    }
  }
  else if(frm.DialogResult == DialogResult.Cancel)
  {
    MessageBox.Show("Form was canceled.");
    break;
  }
}
frm.Close();
```

Now if the phone number does not pass a simple test for length, the Phone form appears so the user can correct the error. The ShowDialog box does not create a new instance of the form. Any text that is entered on the form will still be there, so if the form has to be reset, it will be up to you to do that.

Appearance

The first thing that the user sees is the form for the application. It should be first and foremost functional. If the application doesn't solve a business problem, then it really doesn't matter how it looks. This is not to say that the form's and application's overall GUI design should not be pleasing to the eye. Simple things like color combinations, font sizing, and window sizing can make an application much easier for the user.

Sometimes you don't want the user to have access to the system menu. This is the menu that appears when you click the icon on the top-left corner of a window. Generally it has items such as Restore, Minimize, Maximize, and Close on it. The ControlBox property allows you to set the visibility of the system menu. You can also set the visibility of the Maximize and Minimize buttons with the MaximizeBox and MinimizeBox properties. If you remove all of the buttons and then set the Text property to an empty string (""), then the title bar disappears completely.

If you set the Icon property of a form and you don't set the ControlBox property to false, the icon will appear in the top-left corner of the form. It's common to set this to the app.ico. This makes each form's icon the same as the application icon.

The FormBorderStyle property sets the type of border that appears around the form. This uses the FormBorderStyle enumeration. The values can be:

- ❑ Fixed3D
- ❑ FixedDialog
- ❑ FixedSingle
- ❑ FixedToolWindow
- ❑ None
- ❑ Sizable
- ❑ SizableToolWindow

Most of these are self-explanatory with the exception of the two tool window borders. A tool window will not appear in the taskbar, regardless of how ShowInTaskBar is set. Also a Tool window will not show in the list of windows when the user presses Alt-Tab. The default setting is Sizable.

Unless a requirement dictates otherwise, colors for most GUI elements should be set to system colors, and not to specific colors. This way if some users like to have all of their buttons green with purple text, then the application will follow along with the same colors. In order to set a control to use a specific system color, you must call the FromKnownColor method of the System.Drawing.Color class. The FromKnownColor method takes a KnownColor enumeration value. There are many colors defined in the enumeration, as well as the various GUI element colors, such as Control, ActiveBorder and Desktop. So, for example, if the Background color of the form should always match the Desktop color, the code would look like this:

```
myForm.BackColor = Color.FromKnownColor(KnownColor.Desktop);
```

Now if users change the color of their desktops, the background of the form changes as well. This is a nice friendly touch to add to an application. Users might pick out some strange color combinations for their desktops, but it is their choice.

Windows XP introduced a feature called visual styles. Visual styles change the way buttons, text boxes, menus, and other controls look and react when the mouse pointer is either hovering or clicking. You can enable visual styles for your application by calling the Application.EnableVisualStyles method. This method has to be called before any type of GUI is instantiated. Because of this it is generally called in the Main method, as demonstrated in this example:

```
[STAThread]
static void Main()
{
  Application.EnableVisualStyles();
  Application.Run(new Form1());
}
```

This code allows the various controls that support visual styles to take advantage of them. Because of an issue with the EnableVisualStyles method, you might have to add an Application.DoEvents() method right after the call to EnableVisualStyles. This should resolve the problem if icons on toolbars begin to disappear at runtime. Also EnableVisualStyles is available only in.NET Framework 1.1.

There is one more task pertaining to the controls that you have to accomplish. There is a FlatStyle property that most controls expose. It takes a FlatStyle enumeration as its value. This property can take one of four different values:

❑ Flat—Similar to flat, except that when the mouse pointer hovers over the control, it appears in 3D.

❑ Standard—The control appears in 3D.

❑ System—The look of the control is controlled by the operating system.

In order to enable visual styles the controls FlatStyle property should be set to `FlatStyle.System`. The application will now take on the XP look and feel. Figures 19-7 and 19-8 demonstrate the difference in the look of a simple application. Figure 19-7 shows the application with EnableVisualStyles set to on; Figure 19-8 shows the same application with EnableVisualStyles set to off.

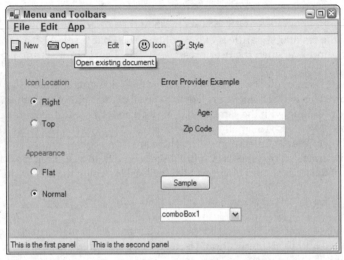

Figure 19-7

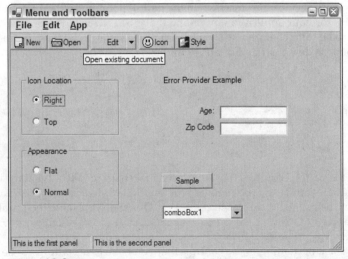

Figure 19-8

Multiple Document Interface (MDI)

MDI-type applications are used when you have an application that can show either multiple instances of the same type of form or different forms that must be contained in some way. An example of multiple instances of the same type of form is a text editor that can show multiple edit windows at the same time. An example of the second type of application is Microsoft Access. You can have query windows, design windows, and table windows all open at the same time. The windows never leave the boundaries of the main Access application.

To create a MDI application you must have at least two forms in your project. One is the MdiParent and the other is the MdiChild. Let's look at an example of how MDI applications work. Create a new C# Windows Application project. Instead of allowing a form to be the start-up class, add a new class and call it StartUp. In the Startup class add a Main method. Be sure to set the StartUp object property in the Project Properties dialog box to the StartUp class. After adding the Main method your Startup class looks like this:

```
using System;
using System.Windows.Forms;

namespace SimpleMDIApp
{
    /// <summary>
    /// Summary description for StartUp.
    /// </summary>
    public class StartUp
    {

        [STAThread]
        static void Main()
        {
            Application.Run(new ParentForm());
        }

    }
}
```

Next you must either add a new Form class and name it ParentForm or rename the class Form1 to ParentForm. If you rename Form1 be sure to delete the Main method from it since you will be starting the application from the StartUp class. You have to tell ParentForm that it is indeed a parent form for MDI children forms. Setting IsMdiContainer to true will do this. If you have the form in the designer you'll notice that the background turns a dark gray color. This is to let you know that this is a MDI parent form. You can still add controls to the form, but it is generally not recommended.

Next you must create child forms. Add a new form to the project and call it ChildForm. You can add a couple of controls to it if want. Add another new form and call it AnotherChildForm. You can also add controls to this form if you want. Currently these are standard forms that might appear in any project. There is nothing at design time that determines that these forms are children of a MDI parent form. This is done at runtime by setting the MdiParent property of the form.

To see how this works you must add a MainMenu control to the ParentForm. Add a File menu at the top level and below it add a New menu option. In the New Click event handler you can instantiate a new ChildForm and show it. Here is the code:

```
private void mnuFileNew_Click(object sender, System.EventArgs e)
{
  ChildForm frm = new ChildForm();
  frm.Name = string.Concat("MDIChildForm",
                                    this.MdiChildren.Length.ToString());
  frm.Text = frm.Name;
  frm.MdiParent = this;
  frm.Show();
}
```

A new ChildForm is created. Assign it to the object variable frm, and then assign a name to the new form by concatenating the string MDIChildForm with the length of the MdiChildren property of the parent form. The MdiChildren property is an Array of the current open MDI children form in the parent. Next, set the form Text equal to the new Name you generated. This is what will show in the caption bar of the form. The next line is where you set the MdiParent property of the child form to the parent form. Now the ChildForm is truly a MDI child. And the last thing you do is show the form.

If you click the New menu choice three times, you should end up with a screen that resembles Figure 19-9.

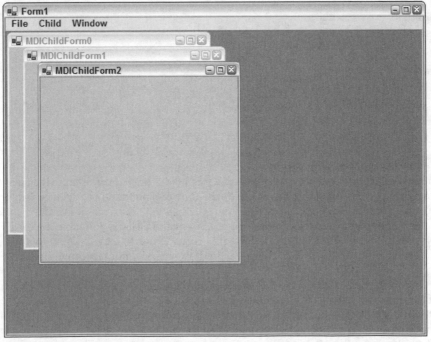

Figure 19-9

The Mdi child forms do not all have to be the same form. If you add another menu item and call it Another New, you can add similar code to its click event. The only difference would be to create a new AnotherChildForm instead of ChildForm. Now if you click the New menu choice a couple of times and the Another New menu choice a couple of times, the item you see should resemble Figure 19-10.

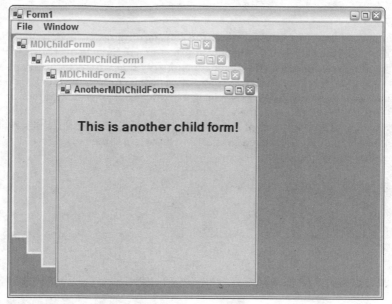

Figure 19-10

Notice that the number keeps incrementing regardless of the child form. The MdiChildren property only keeps one Array object. Any type of form that is created as a MdiChild will be added to the array.

One problem that you have is that the only way to close the child forms is to click the Close icon in the top-right corner of the form. You must add a Menu to the child forms so that you can gracefully close the child forms. Add a new MainMenu to your ChildForm. Now typically the first item in a menu set is File. The next item is Edit and so on. On the child menu you don't want to do that, however. When the child form is shown, its menu structure will automatically be merged with the parent's menu. If the parent's menu already has File, Edit, and so on, what happens is that you will have two File menus, and two Edit menus—not a desirable feature. So on the ChildForm, create the menu structure that just relates to the form. For this example, add a Child menu as the top-level menu. Under it will be the Close menu choice. Now when you run the example and show a child form with a menu, the new menu appears merged with the parent form, not the child form.

One other MDI menu item is the MdiList property. This property shows a list of currently open child windows. Add a new menu choice with the menu text of Window to the parent. Set the MergeOrder order to 3 and the MdiList property to true. Now when you open a couple of child windows, the Window menu always stays to the farthest right, because the MergeOrder is higher then the others, and it contains a list of currently open windows. The text in the menu is the same text that is in the caption of the child window (Text property of the child form).

Custom Controls

Using controls and components is a big part of what makes developing with a forms package such as Windows Forms so productive. The ability to create your own controls, components, and user controls makes it even more productive. By creating controls, functionality can be encapsulated into packages that can be reused over and over.

There are a number of ways to create a control. You can start from scratch, deriving your class from either Control, ScrollableControl, or ContainerControl. You will have to override the Paint event and do all of your drawing, not to mention adding the functionality that your control is supposed to provide. If the control is supposed to be an enhanced version of a current control, the thing to do is to derive from the control that is being enhanced. For example, if a TextBox control is needed that changes background color of the ReadOnly property is set, then creating a completely new TextBox control would be a waste of time. Derive from the TextBox control and override the ReadOnly property. Since the ReadOnly property of the TextBox control is not marked override we have to use the new clause. The following code shows the new ReadOnly property:

```
public new bool ReadOnly
{
  get   { return base.ReadOnly;}
  set   {
    if(value)
      this.BackgroundColor = Color.Red;
    else
      this.BackgroundColor = Color.FromKnowColor(KnownColor.Window);

      base.ReadOnly = value;
  }
}
```

For the property get, you return what the base object is set to. The way that the property handles the process of making a text box read-only is not relevant here, so you just pass that functionality to the base object. In the property set, check to if the passed in value is true or false. If it is true, then change the color to the read-only color (Red in this case); if it is false, then set the BackgroundColor to the default. Finally, pass the value down to the base object so that the text box actually does become read-only. As you can see, by overriding one simple property, you can add new functionality to a control.

Control attributes

You can add attributes to the custom control that will enhance the design time capabilities of the control. The following table describes some the more useful attributes.

Attribute Name	Description
BindableAttribute	Used at design time to determine of the property supports two-way data binding.
BrowsableAttribute	Determines if the property is shown in the visual designer.
CategoryAttribute	Determines under what category the property is displayed in the property window. Use on predefined categories or create new ones. Default is Misc.

Attribute Name	Description
DefaultEventAttribute	Specifies the default event for a class.
DefaultPropertyAttribute	Specifies the default property for a class.
DefaultValueAttribute	Specifies the default value for a property. Typically, this is the initial value.
DecriptionAttribute	This is the text that appears at the bottom of the designer window when the property is selected.
DesignOnlyAttribute	This marks the property as being editable in design mode only.

There are other attributes that relate to the editor that the property uses in design time and other advanced design time capabilities. The Category and Description attributes should almost always be added. This helps other developers who use the control to better understand the properties purpose. In order to add Intellisence support you should add XML comments for each property, method, and event. When the control is compiled with the /doc option, the XML file of comments that is generated will provide intellisence for the control.

TreeView-based custom control

In this section we show you how to develop a custom control based on the TreeView control. This control displays the file structure of a drive. We'll add properties that set the base or root folder and determine whether files and folders will be displayed. We will also use the various attributes that we discussed in the previous section.

As with any new project, requirements for the control have to be defined. Here is a list of basic requirements that have to be implemented:

❑ Read folders and files and display to user.

❑ Display folder structure in a tree-like hierarchical view.

❑ Optionally hide files from view.

❑ Define what folder should be the base or root folder.

❑ Return the currently selected folder.

❑ Provide the ability to delay loading of the file structure.

This should be a good starting point. One requirement has been satisfied by the fact the TreeView control will be the base of the new control.

The TreeView control displays data in a hierarchical format. It displays text describing the object in the list and optionally an icon. This list can be expanded and contracted by clicking an object or using the arrows keys.

Create a new Windows Control Library project in Visual Studio .NET named FolderTree, and delete the class UserControl1. Add a new class and call it `FolderTree`. Since FolderTree will be derived from TreeView, change the class declaration from

```
public class FolderTree
```

to

```
public class FolderTree  :  System.Windows.Forms.TreeView
```

At this point we actually have a fully functional and working FolderTree control. It will do everything that the TreeView can do, and nothing more.

The TreeView control maintains a collection of TreeNode objects. We can't load files and folders directly into the control. There are a couple of ways we can map the TreeNode that is loaded into the Nodes collection of the TreeView and the file or folder that it represents.

For example, when each folder is processed, a new TreeNode object is created, and the text property is set to the name of the file or folder. If at some point additional information about the file or folder is needed, we have to make another trip to the disk to gather that information or store additional data regarding the file or folder in the Tag property.

Another method is to create a new class that is derived from `TreeNode`. New properties and methods can be added and the base functionality of the TreeNode is still there. This is the path that we use in this example. It allows for a more flexible design. If we need new properties, we can add them easily and without breaking the existing code.

There are two types of objects that we must load into the control: folders and files. Each has its own characteristics. For example, folders have a DirectoryInfo object that contains additional information, files have a FileInfo object. Because of these differences there we use two separate classes to load the TreeView control: FileNode and FolderNode. We add these two classes to the project, each is derived from TreeNode. This is the listing for FileNode:

```
using System;
using System.Windows.Forms;
using System.IO;

namespace FolderTree
{
  /// <summary>
  /// Summary description for FileNode.
  /// </summary>
  public class FileNode : System.Windows.Forms.TreeNode
  {

    string _fileName = "";
    FileInfo _info;

    public FileNode(string fileName)
    {
      _fileName = fileName;
      _info = new FileInfo(_fileName);
      base.Text = _info.Name;
    }

    public string FileName
```

```
      {
        get {return _fileName;}
        set {_fileName = value;}
      }

      public FileInfo FileNodeInfo
      {
        get {return _info;}
      }
    }
  }
```

The name of the file that is being processed is passed into the constructor of FileNode. In the constructor the FileInfo object for the file is created and set to the member variable _info. The base.Text property is set to the name of the file. Since we are deriving from TreeNode this sets the TreeNodes Text property. This is the text that is displayed in the TreeView control.

There are two properties added to retrieve the data. FileName returns the name of the file and FileNodeInfo returns the FileInfo object for the file.

Here is the code for the FolderNode class. It is very similar to the FileNode class in structure. The differences are that we have a DirectoryInfo property instead of FileInfo, and instead of FileName we have FolderPath.

```
using System;
using System.Windows.Forms;
using System.IO;

namespace FolderTree
{
  /// <summary>
  /// Summary description for DiskObject.
  /// </summary>
  public class FolderNode : System.Windows.Forms.TreeNode
  {
    string _folderPath = "";
    DirectoryInfo _info;

    public FolderNode(string folderPath)
    {
      _folderPath = folderPath;
      _info = new DirectoryInfo(folderPath);
      this.Text = _info.Name;
    }


    public string FolderPath
    {
      get {return _folderPath;}
      set {_folderPath = value;}
    }
    public DirectoryInfo FolderNodeInfo
    {
```

```
        get {return _info;}
    }
  }
}
```

Now we can construct the FolderTree control. Based on the requirements, we need a property to read and set the RootFolder. We also need a ShowFiles property for determining if files should be shown in the tree. A `SelectedFolder` property returns the currently highlighted folder in the tree. This is what the code looks like so far for the `FolderTree` control:

```
using System;
using System.Windows.Forms;
using System.IO;
using System.ComponentModel;

namespace FolderTree
{
  /// <summary>
  /// Summary description for FolderTreeCtrl.
  /// </summary>
  public class FolderTree :  System.Windows.Forms.TreeView
  {

    string _rootFolder = "";
    bool _showFiles = true;
    bool _inInit = false;

    public FolderTree()
    {
      //
      // TODO: Add constructor logic here
      //
    }

    [Category("Behavior"),
      Description("Gets or sets the base or root folder of the tree"),
      DefaultValue("C:\\")]
    public string RootFolder
    {
      get {return _rootFolder;}
      set
      {
        _rootFolder = value;
        if(!_inInit)
          InitializeTree();

      }
    }


    [Category("Behavior"),
```

```
        Description("Indicates whether files will be seen in the list."),
        DefaultValue(true)]
    public bool ShowFiles
    {
      get {return _showFiles;}
      set {_showFiles = value;}
    }


    [Browsable(false)]
    public string SelectedFolder
    {
      get
      {
        if(this.SelectedNode is FolderNode)
          return ((FolderNode)this.SelectedNode).FolderPath;

        return "";
      }
    }
  }
}
```

We added three properties: ShowFiles, SelectedFolder, and RootFolder. Notice the attributes that have been added. We set Category, Description, and DefaultValues for the ShowFiles and RootFolder. These two properties will appear in the property browser in design mode. The SelectedFolder really has no meaning at design time, so we select the Browsable=false attribute. SelectedFolder does not appear in the property browser. However, since it is a public property, it will appear in Intellisense and is accessible in code.

Next, we have to initialize the loading of the file system. Initializing a control can be tricky. Both design time and runtime initializing must be well thought-out. When a control is sitting on a designer, it is actually running. If there is a call to a database in the constructor, for example, this call will execute when you drop the control on the designer. In the case of the FolderTree control this can be an issue.

Let's take a look at the method that is actually going to load the files:

```
private void LoadTree(FolderNode folder)
{
  string[] dirs = Directory.GetDirectories(folder.FolderPath);
  foreach(string dir in dirs)
  {
    FolderNode tmpfolder = new FolderNode(dir);
    folder.Nodes.Add(tmpfolder);
    LoadTree(tmpfolder);
  }
  if(_showFiles)
  {

    string[] files = Directory.GetFiles(folder.FolderPath);
    foreach(string file in files)
    {
```

```
        FileNode fnode = new FileNode(file);
        folder.Nodes.Add(fnode);
    }


  }
}
```

_showFiles is a Boolean member variable that is set from the ShowFiles property. If true, then files are also shown in the tree. The only question now is when should LoadTree be called. We have several options. It can be called when the RootFolder property is set. That is desirable in some situations, but not at design time. Remember that the control is "live" on the designer so when the RootNode property is set, the control will attempt to load the files system.

What we can do to solve this is to check the DesignMode property. This returns true if the control is in the designer. Now we can write the code to initialize the control:

```
private void InitializeTree()
{
  if(!this.DesignMode && _rootFolder != "")
  {
    FolderNode rootNode = new FolderNode(_rootFolder);
    LoadTree(rootNode);
    this.Nodes.Clear();
    this.Nodes.Add(rootNode);
  }
}
```

If the control is not in design mode and _rootFolder is not an empty string, then the loading of the tree will begin. The Root node is created first and this is passed into the LoadTree method.

Another option is to implement a public Init method. In the Init method the call to LoadTree can happen. The problem with this option is that the developer who uses your control is required to make the Init call. Depending on the situation this might be an acceptable solution.

For added flexibility the ISupportInitialize interface can be implemented. ISupportInitialize has two methods, BeginInit and EndInit. When a control implements ISupportInitialize the BeginInit and EndInit methods are called automatically in the generated code in InitilizeComponent. This allows the initialization process to be delayed until all of the properties are set. ISupportInitialize allows the code in the parent form to delay initialization as well. If the RootNode property is being set in code, a call to BeginInit first will allow the RootNode property as well as other properties to be set or actions to be performed before the control loads the files system. When EndInit is called, the control initializes. This is what BeginInit and EndInit look like:

```
#region ISupportInitialize Members

void ISupportInitialize.BeginInit()
{
  _inInit = true;
}
```

```
void ISupportInitialize.EndInit()
{

  if(_rootFolder != "")
  {
    InitializeTree();
  }

  _inInit = false;
}

#endregion
```

In the `BeginInit` method all that is done is a member variable `_inInit` is set to `true`. This flag is used to determine if the control is in the initialization process and is used in the `RootFolder` property. If the `RootFolder` property is set outside of the `InitilizeComponent` class then the tree will need to be reinitialized. In the `RootFolder` property we check to see if `_inInit` is `true` or `false`. If it is true then we don't want to go through the initialization process. If `_inInit` is false then we call `InitializeTree`. We could also have a public `Init` method and accomplish the same task.

In the `EndInit` method we check to see if the control is in design mode and if `_rootFolder` has a valid path assigned to it. Only then is `InitializeTree` called.

In order to add a final professional-looking touch, we have to add a bitmap image. This is the icon that shows up in the toolbox when the control is added to a project. The bitmap image should be 16 × 16 pixels and 16 colors. You can create this image file with any graphics editor as long as the size and color depth are set properly. You can even create this file in Visual Studio .NET: Right-click the project and select Add New Item. From the list select Bitmap File to open the graphics editor. After you have created the bitmap file, add it to the project, making sure it is in the same namespace and has the same name as the control. Finally, set the Build Action of the bitmap to Embedded Resource: Right-click the bitmap file in the Solution Explorer and select Properties. Select Embedded Resource form the Build Action property.

To test the control, create a TestHarness project in the same solution. The TestHarness is a simple Windows Forms application with a single form. In the references section add a reference to the FolderTreeCtl project. In the Toolbox windows add a reference to the FolderTreeCtl.DLL. FolderTreeCtl should now show up in the toolbox with the bitmap added as the icon. Click the icon and drag it to the TestHarness form. Set the RootFolder to an available folder and run the solution.

This is by no means a complete control. There are several things that could be enhanced to make this a full featured, production-ready control. For example, we could add:

❑ **Exceptions**—If the control tries to load a folder that the user does not have access to an exception is raised.

❑ **Background loading**—Loading a large folder tree can take a long time. Enhancing the initialization process to take advantage of a background thread for loading is a good idea.

❑ **Color codes**—We can make the text of certain file types a different color.

❑ **Icons**—We can add an `ImageList` control and add an icon to each file or folder as it is loaded.

User control

User controls are one of the more powerful features of Windows Forms. They allow encapsulating user interface designs into nice reusable packages that can be plugged into project after project. It is not uncommon for an organization to have a couple of libraries of frequently used user controls. Not only can user interface functionality be contained in user controls but common data validation can be incorporated in them as well. Things like formatting phone numbers or id numbers. A predefined list of items can be in the user control for fast loading of a list box or combo box. State codes or country codes fit into this category. Incorporating as much functionality that does not depend on the current application as possible into a user control makes the control that much more useful in the organization.

In this section we create a simple address user control. We also will add the various events that make the control ready for data binding. The address control will have text entry for two address lines, city, state and zip code.

To create a user control in a current project, just right-click the project in Solution Explorer and select Add and then select Add New User Control. You can also create a new Control Library project and add user controls to it. After a new user control has been started, you will see a form without any borders on the designer. This is where you drop the controls that make up the user control. Remember that a user control is actually one or more controls added to a container control. So it is somewhat like creating a form. For the address control there are five TextBox controls and three Label controls. The controls can be arranged any way that seems appropriate (see Figure 19-11).

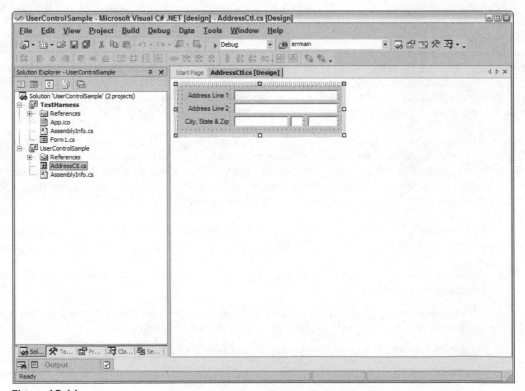

Figure 19-11

The TextBox controls in this example are named as follows:

- ❑ txtAddress1
- ❑ txtAddress2
- ❑ txtCity
- ❑ txtState
- ❑ txtZip

After the TextBox controls are in place and have valid names, add the public properties. You might be tempted to set the visibility of the TextBox controls to public instead of private. However, this is not a good idea, because it defeats the purpose of encapsulating the functionality that you might want to add to the properties. Here is a listing of the properties that must be added:

```
public string AddressLine1
{
  get{return txtAddress1.Text;}
  set{
    if(txtAddress1.Text != value)
    {
      txtAddress1.Text = value;
      if(AddressLine1Changed != null)
        AddressLine1Changed(this, PropertyChangedEventArgs.Empty);
    }
  }
}


public string AddressLine2
{
  get{return txtAddress2.Text;}
  set{
    if(txtAddress2.Text != value)
    {
      txtAddress2.Text = value;
      if(AddressLine2Changed != null)
        AddressLine2Changed(this, PropertyChangedEventArgs.Empty);
    }
  }
}

public string City
{
  get{return txtCity.Text;}
  set{
    if(txtCity.Text != value)
    {
      txtCity.Text = value;
      if(CityChanged != null)
        CityChanged(this, PropertyChangedEventArgs.Empty);
    }
```

```
    }
  }


  public string State
  {
    get{return txtState.Text;}
    set{
      if(txtState.Text != value)
      {
        txtState.Text = value;
        if(StateChanged != null)
          StateChanged(this, PropertyChangedEventArgs.Empty);
      }
    }
  }


  public string Zip
  {
    get{return txtZip.Text;}
    set{
      if(txtZip.Text != value)
      {
        txtZip.Text = value;
        if(ZipChanged != null)
          ZipChanged(this, PropertyChangedEventArgs.Empty);
      }
    }
  }
```

The property gets are fairly straightforward. The property returns the value of the corresponding TextBox controls text property. The property sets, however, are doing a bit more work. All of the property sets work the same way. A check is made to see if the value of the property is actually changing or not. If the new value is the same as the current value, then a quick escape can be made. If there is a new value sent in, then set the text property of the TextBox to the new value and test to see if an event has been instantiated. The event to look for is the changed event for the property. It has a specific naming format, *propertyname*Changed where *propertyname* is the name of the property. In the case of the AddressLine1 property, this event is called AddressLine1Changed. The properties are declared as follows:

```
public event EventHandler AddressLine1Changed;
public event EventHandler AddressLine2Changed;
public event EventHandler CityChanged;
public event EventHandler StateChanged;
public event EventHandler ZipChanged;
```

The purpose of the events is to notify binding that the property has changed. Once validation occurs, binding will make sure that the new value makes its way back to the object that the control is bound to. There is one other step that should be done to support binding. A change to the text box by the user will not set the property directly. So the propertynameChanged event must be raised when the text box changes as well. The easiest way to do this is to monitor the TexhChanged event of the TextBox control.

This example has only one `TextChanged` event handler and all of the text boxes use it. The control name is checked to see which control raised the event and the appropriate `propertynameChanged` event is raised. Here is the code for the event handler:

```
private void TextBoxControls_TextChanged(
                                    object sender, System.EventArgs e)
{
  switch(((TextBox)sender).Name)
  {
    case "txtAddress1" :
      if(AddressLine1Changed != null)
        AddressLine1Changed(this, EventArgs.Empty);

      break;

    case "txtAddress2" :
      if(AddressLine2Changed != null)
        AddressLine2Changed(this, EventArgs.Empty);

      break;

    case "txtCity" :
      if(CityChanged != null)
        CityChanged(this, EventArgs.Empty);

      break;

    case "txtState" :
        if(StateChanged != null)
          StateChanged(this, EventArgs.Empty);

      break;

    case "txtZip" :
        if(ZipChanged != null)
          ZipChanged(this, EventArgs.Empty);

      break;

  }
}
```

This example uses a simple `switch` statement to determine which text box raised the `TextChanged` event. Then a check is made to verify that the event is valid and not equal to null. Then Changed event is raised. One thing to note is that an empty EventArgs is sent (`EventArgs.Empty`). Because these events have been added to the properties to support data binding does not mean that the only way to use the control is with data binding. The properties can be set in and read from code without using data binding. They have been added so that the user control is able to use binding if it is available. This is just one way of making the user control as flexible as possible so that it might be used in as many situations as possible.

Remembering that a user control is essentially a control with some added features, all of the design time issues that we discussed in the previous section apply here as well. Initializing user controls can bring on the same issues that we saw in the FolderTree example. Care must be taken in the design of user controls so that access to data stores that might not be available to other developers using your control is avoided.

The other thing that is similar to the control creation is the attributes that can be applied to user controls. The public properties and methods of the user control are displayed in the Properties Window when the control is placed on the designer. In the example of the address user control it is a good idea to add Category, Description, and DefaultValue attributes to the address properties. A new AddressData category can be created and the default values would all be "". Here is an example of these attributes applied to the `AddressLine1` property:

```
[Category("AddressData"),
    Description("Gets or sets the AddressLine1 value"),
    DefaultValue("")]
public string AddressLine1
{
  get{return txtAddress1.Text;}
  set{
    if(txtAddress1.Text != value)
    {
      txtAddress1.Text = value;
      if(AddressLine1Changed != null)
        AddressLine1Changed(this, EventArgs.Empty);
    }
  }
}
```

As you can see, all that needs to be done to add a new category is set the text in the `Category` attribute. The new category is automatically added.

There still is a lot of room for improvement. For example, we could include a list of state names and abbreviations in the control. Instead of just the state property, the user control could expose both the state name and state abbreviation properties. Exception handling should also be added. We could also add validation for the address lines. Making sure the casing is correct, we might ask ourselves whether AddressLine1 could be optional, or whether apartment and suite numbers should be entered on AddressLine2 and not on AddressLine1.

Summary

This chapter has given you the basics for building Windows client-based applications. We explained each of the basic control by discussing the hierarchy of the Windows.Forms namespace and examining the various properties and methods of the controls.

We also showed you how to create a basic custom control as well as a basic user control. The power and flexibility of creating your own controls cannot be emphasized enough. By creating your own toolbox of custom controls, Windows-based client application will become easier to develop and to test since you will be reusing the same tested components over and over again.

20

Graphics with GDI+

This is the second of the three chapters that deal with user interaction and .NET Framework. In Chapter 19 we focus on Windows Forms, discussing how to display a dialog box or SDI or MDI window, and how to place various controls such as buttons, text boxes, and list boxes.

Although these standard controls are powerful and, by themselves, quite adequate for the complete user interface for many applications, there are situations in which you need more flexibility. For example, you might want to draw text in a given font in a precise position in a window, display images without using a picture box control, or draw simple shapes or other graphics. None of this can be done with the controls discussed in Chapter 19. To display that kind of output, the application must instruct the operating system what to display and where in its window to display it.

Therefore, in this chapter we're going to show you how to draw a variety of items including:

- ❑ Lines and simple shapes
- ❑ .BMP images and other image files
- ❑ Text

In the process, we'll need to use a variety of helper objects, including pens (to define the characteristics of lines), brushes (to define how areas are filled in), and fonts (to define the shape of the characters of text). We'll also go into some detail on how devices interpret and display different colors.

We'll start, however, by discussing a technology called *GDI+*. GDI+ consists of the set of .NET base classes that are available to control custom drawing on the screen. These classes arrange for the appropriate instructions to be sent to graphics device drivers to ensure the correct output is placed on the screen (or printed to a hard copy).

Understanding Drawing Principles

In this section, we'll examine the basic principles that we need to understand in order to start drawing to the screen. We'll start by giving an overview of GDI, the underlying technology on which GDI+ is based, and see how GDI and GDI+ are related. Then we'll move on to a couple of simple examples.

GDI and GDI+

In general, one of the strengths of Windows—and indeed of modern operating systems in general—lies in its ability to abstract the details of particular devices without input from the developer. For example, you don't need to understand anything about your hard drive device driver in order to programmatically read and write files to disk; you simply call the appropriate methods in the relevant .NET classes (or in pre-.NET days, the equivalent Windows API functions). This principle is also true when it comes to drawing. When the computer draws anything to the screen, it does so by sending instructions to the video card. However, there are many hundreds of different video cards on the market, most of which have different instruction sets and capabilities. If you had to take that into account, and write specific code for each video driver, writing any such application would be an almost impossible task. This is why the Windows *graphical device interface* (*GDI*) has been around since the earliest versions of Windows.

GDI provides a layer of abstraction, hiding the differences between the different video cards. You simply call the Windows API function to do the specific task, and internally the GDI figures out how to get your particular video card to do whatever it is you want. Not only this, but if you have several display devices—for example, monitors and printers—GDI achieves the remarkable feat of making your printer look the same as your screen as far as your application is concerned. If you want to print something instead of displaying it, you simply inform the system that the output device is the printer and then call the same API functions in exactly the same way.

As you can see, the device-context object (DC) is a very powerful object and you won't be surprised to learn that under GDI *all* drawing had to be done through a device context. The DC was even used for operations that don't involve drawing to the screen or to any hardware device, such as modifying images in memory.

Although GDI exposes a relatively high-level API to developers, it is still an API that is based on the old Windows API, with C-style functions. *GDI+* to a large extent sits as a layer between GDI and your application, providing a more intuitive, inheritance-based object model. Although GDI+ is basically a wrapper around GDI, Microsoft has been able through GDI+ to provide new features and claims to have made some performance improvements.

The GDI+ part of the .NET base class library is huge, and we will scarcely scratch the surface of its features in this chapter. That's a deliberate decision, because trying to cover more than a tiny fraction of the library would have turned this chapter into a huge reference guide that simply listed classes and methods. It's more important to understand the fundamental principles involved in drawing, so that you are in a good position to explore the available classes. Full lists of all the classes and methods available in GDI+ are of course available in the SDK documentation.

> *Visual Basic developers are likely to find the concepts involved in drawing quite unfamiliar, since Visual Basic focuses on controls that handle their own painting. C++/MFC developers are likely to be in more familiar territory since MFC does require developers to take control of more of the drawing process, using GDI. However, even if you have a strong background in GDI, you'll find a lot of the material presented in this chapter is new.*

GDI+ namespaces

The following table provides an overview of the main namespaces you'll need to explore to find the GDI+ base classes.

Namespace	Description
System.Drawing	Contains most of the classes, structs, enums, and delegates concerned with the basic functionality of drawing
System.Drawing.Drawing2D	Provides most of the support for advanced 2D and vector drawing, including anti-aliasing, geometric transformations, and graphics paths
System.Drawing.Imaging	Contains various classes that assist in the manipulation of images (bitmaps, GIF files, and so on)
System.Drawing.Printing	Contains classes to assist when specifically targeting a printer or print preview window as the "output device"
System.Drawing.Design	Contains some predefined dialog boxes, property sheets, and other user interface elements concerned with extending the design-time user interface
System.Drawing.Text	Contains classes to perform more advanced manipulation of fonts and font families

You should note that almost all of the classes and structs that we use in this chapter are taken from the System.Drawing namespace.

Device contexts and the Graphics object

In GDI, the way that you identify which device you want your output to go to is through an object known as the *device context (DC)*. The DC stores information about a particular device and is able to translate calls to the GDI API functions into whatever instructions need to be sent to that device. You can also query the device context to find out what the capabilities of the corresponding device are (for example, whether a printer prints in color or only in black and white), so the output can be adjusted accordingly. If you ask the device to do something it's not capable of, the DC will normally detect this, and take appropriate action (which, depending on the situation, might mean throwing an error or modifying the request to get the closest match that the device is actually capable of using).

However, the DC doesn't only deal with the hardware device. It acts as a bridge to Windows and is able to take account of any requirements or restrictions placed on the drawing by Windows. For example, if Windows knows that only a portion of your application's window needs to be redrawn, the DC can trap and nullify attempts to draw outside that area. Due to the DC's relationship with Windows, working through the device context can simplify your code in other ways.

For example, hardware devices need to be told where to draw objects, and they usually want coordinates relative to the top-left corner of the screen (or output device). Usually, however, your application will be thinking of drawing something at a certain position within the client area (the area reserved for drawing) of its own window, possibly using its own coordinate system. Since the window might be positioned anywhere on the screen, and a user might move it at any time, translating between the two coordinate systems is potentially a difficult task. However, the DC always knows where your window is and is able to perform this translation automatically.

With GDI+, the device context is wrapped up in the .NET base class System.Drawing.Graphics. Most drawing is done by calling methods on an instance of Graphics. In fact, since the Graphics class is the class that is responsible for handling most drawing operations, very little gets done in GDI+ that doesn't involve a Graphics instance somewhere, so understanding how to manipulate this object is the key to understanding how to draw to display devices with GDI+.

Drawing Shapes

To show this at work, we're going to start off with a short example, DisplayAtStartup, to illustrate drawing to an application's main window. The examples in this chapter are all created in Visual Studio .NET as C# Windows applications. Recall that for this type of project the code wizard gives us a class called Form1, derived from System.Windows.Form, which represents the application's main window. Unless otherwise stated, in all code samples, new or modified code means code that we've added to the wizard-generated code. (You can download the sample code from the Wrox Web site at www.wrox.com.)

> *In .NET usage, when we are talking about applications that display various controls, the terminology form has largely replaced window to represent the rectangular object that occupies an area of the screen on behalf of an application. In this chapter, we've tended to stick to the term window, since in the context of manually drawing items it's rather more meaningful. We'll also talk about the form when we're referring to the .NET class used to instantiate the form/window. Finally, we'll use the terms drawing and painting interchangeably to describe the process of displaying some item on the screen or other display device.*

The first example will simply create a form and draw to it in the constructor, when the form starts up. Note that this is not actually the best or the correct way to draw to the screen—we'll quickly find that this example has a problem in that it is unable to redraw anything after starting up. However this sample illustrates quite a few points about drawing without our having to do very much work.

For this sample, we start Visual Studio .NET and create a Windows application. We first set the background color of the form to white. We've put this line in the InitializeComponent() method so that Visual Studio .NET recognizes the line and is able to alter the design view appearance of the form. We could have used the design view to set the background color, but this would have resulted in pretty much the same line being added automatically:

```
private void InitializeComponent()
{
    this.AutoScaleBaseSize = new System.Drawing.Size(5, 13);
    this.ClientSize = new System.Drawing.Size(292, 266);
    this.Name = "Form1";
    this.Text = "DrawShapesSample";

    this.BackColor = Color.White;
```

Then we add code to the Form1 constructor. We create a Graphics object using the form's Create Graphics() method. This Graphics object contains the Windows DC we need to draw with. The device context created is associated with the display device, and also with this window:

```
public Form1()
{
    InitializeComponent();

    Graphics dc = this.CreateGraphics();
    this.Show();
    Pen bluePen = new Pen(Color.Blue, 3);
    dc.DrawRectangle(bluePen, 0,0,50,50);
    Pen redPen = new Pen(Color.Red, 2);
    dc.DrawEllipse(redPen, 0, 50, 80, 60);
}
```

As you can see, we then call the Show() method to display the window. This is really done to force the window to display immediately, because we can't actually do any drawing until the window has been displayed. If the window isn't displayed then there's nothing for us to draw onto.

Finally, we display a rectangle at coordinates (0,0) and with width and height 50, and an ellipse with coordinates (0,50) and with width 80 and height 50. Note that coordinates (x,y) translates to x pixels to the right and y pixels down from the top-left corner of the client area of the window—and these coordinates start from the top-left corner of the shape to be displayed.

The overloads that we are using of the DrawRectangle() and DrawEllipse() methods each take five parameters. The first parameter of each is an instance of the class System.Drawing.Pen. A Pen is one of a number of supporting objects to help with drawing—it contains information about how lines are to be drawn. Our first pen instructs that lines should be the color blue with a width of 3 pixels; the second pen instructs that lines should be red and have a width of 2 pixels. The final four parameters are coordinates and size. For the rectangle, they represent the (x,y) coordinates of the top left-hand corner of the rectangle in addition to its width and height. For the ellipse these numbers represent the same thing, except that we are talking about a hypothetical rectangle that the ellipse just fits into, rather than the ellipse itself. Figure 20-1 shows the result of running this code. Of course, since this is not a color book, you cannot see the colors.

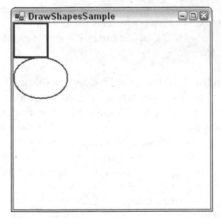

Figure 20-1

Figure 20-1 demonstrates a couple of points. First, you can see clearly where the client area of the window is located. It's the white area—the area that has been affected by our setting the BackColor property. And notice that the rectangle nestles up in the corner of this area, as you'd expect when we specified coordinates of (0,0) for it. Second, notice that the top of the ellipse overlaps the rectangle slightly, which you wouldn't expect from the coordinates we gave in the code. The culprit here is Windows and where it places the lines that border the rectangle and ellipse. By default, Windows will try to center the line on the border of the shape—that's not always possible to do exactly, because the line has to be drawn on pixels (obviously), but normally the border of each shape theoretically lies between two pixels. The result is that lines that are 1 pixel thick will get drawn just *inside* the top and left sides of a shape, but just *outside* the bottom and right sides—which means that shapes that strictly speaking are next to each other will have their borders overlap by one pixel. We've specified wider lines; therefore the overlap is greater. It is possible to change the default behavior by setting the Pen.Alignment property, as detailed in the SDK documentation, but for these purposes the default behavior is adequate.

Unfortunately, if you actually run the sample you'll notice the form behaves a bit strangely. It's fine if you just leave it there, and it's fine if you drag it around the screen with the mouse. If you try minimizing the window and then restoring it, then our carefully drawn shapes just vanish! The same thing happens if you drag another window across the sample. If you drag another window across it so that it only obscures a portion of our shapes, then drag the other window away again, you'll find the temporarily obscured portion has disappeared and you're left with half an ellipse or half a rectangle!

So what's going on? The problem arises when part of a window is hidden, because Windows usually discards immediately all the information concerning exactly what has been displayed. This is something Windows has to do or else the memory usage for storing screen data would be astronomical. A typical computer might be running with the video card set to display 1024×768 pixels, perhaps in a 24-bit color mode, which implies that each pixel on the screen occupies 3 bytes—2.25MB to display the screen. (We'll cover what 24-bit color means later in this chapter.) However, it's not uncommon for a user to work with 10 or 20 minimized windows in the taskbar. In a worst-case scenario, we might have 20 windows, each of which would occupy the whole screen if it wasn't minimized. If Windows actually stored the visual information those windows contained, ready for when the user restores them, that would amount to some 45MB! These days, a good graphics card might have 64MB of memory and be able to cope with that, but it was only a couple of years ago that 4MB was considered generous in a graphics card—and the excess would need to be stored in the computer's main memory. A lot of people still have old machines, some of them with only 4MB graphic cards. Clearly it wouldn't be practical for Windows to manage its user interface like that.

The moment any part of a window is hidden, the "hidden" pixels get lost, because Windows frees the memory that was holding those pixels. It does, however, note that a portion of the window is hidden, and when it detects that it is no longer hidden, it asks the application that owns the window to redraw its contents. There are a couple of exceptions to this rule—generally for cases in which a small portion of a window is hidden very temporarily (a good example is when you select an item from the main menu and that menu item drops down, temporarily obscuring part of the window below). In general, however, you can expect that if part of your window is hidden, your application will need to redraw it later.

That's the source of the problem for our sample application. We placed our drawing code in the Form1 constructor, which is called just once when the application starts up, and you can't call the constructor again to redraw the shapes when required later on.

When working with Windows Forms server controls, there is no need to know anything about how to accomplish this task. This is because the standard controls are pretty sophisticated and they are able to redraw themselves correctly whenever Windows asks them to. That's one reason why when programming controls you don't need to worry about the actual drawing process at all. If we are taking responsibility for drawing to the screen in our application then we also need to make sure our application will respond correctly whenever Windows asks it to redraw all or part of its window. In the next section, we will modify our sample to do just that.

Painting Shapes Using OnPaint()

If the above explanation has made you worried that drawing your own user interface is going to be terribly complicated, don't worry. Getting your application to redraw itself when necessary is actually quite easy.

Windows notifies an application that some repainting needs to be done by raising a Paint event. Interestingly, the Form class has already implemented a handler for this event so you don't need to add one yourself. The Form1 handler for the Paint event will at some point in its processing call up a virtual method, OnPaint(), passing to it a single PaintEventArgs parameter. This means that all we need to do is override OnPaint() to perform our painting.

Although we've chosen to work by overriding OnPaint(), it's equally possible to achieve the same results by simply adding our own event handler for the Paint event (a Form1_Paint() method, say)—in much the same way as you would for any other Windows Forms event. This other approach is arguably more convenient, since you can add a new event handler through the Visual Studio .NET properties window, saving yourself from typing some code. However, our approach, of overriding OnPaint(), is slightly more flexible in terms of letting us control when the call to the base class window processing occurs, and is the approach recommended in the documentation. We suggest you use this approach for consistency.

We'll create a new Windows Application called DrawShapes to do this. As before, we set the background color to white using the Properties Window. We'll also change the form's text to DrawShapes sample. Then we add the following code to the generated code for the Form1 class:

```
protected override void OnPaint( PaintEventArgs e )
{
   base.OnPaint(e);
   Graphics dc = e.Graphics;
   Pen bluePen = new Pen(Color.Blue, 3);
   dc.DrawRectangle(bluePen, 0,0,50,50);
   Pen redPen = new Pen(Color.Red, 2);
   dc.DrawEllipse(redPen, 0, 50, 80, 60);
}
```

Notice that OnPaint() is declared as protected, because it is normally used internally within the class, so there's no reason for any other code outside the class to know about its existence.

PaintEventArgs is a class that is derived from the EventArgs class normally used to pass in information about events. PaintEventArgs has two additional properties, of which the more important one is a Graphics instance, already primed and optimized to paint the required portion of the window. This means that you don't have to call CreateGraphics() to get a DC in the OnPaint() method—you've already been provided with one. We'll look at the other additional property soon; it contains more detailed information about which area of the window actually needs repainting.

In our implementation of OnPaint(), we first get a reference to the Graphics object from PaintEvent-Args, then we draw our shapes exactly as we did before. At the end we call the base class's OnPaint() method. This step is important. We've overridden OnPaint() to do our own painting, but it's possible that Windows may have some additional work of its own to do in the painting process—any such work will be dealt with in an OnPaint() method in one of the .NET base classes.

For this example, you'll find that removing the call to base.OnPaint() doesn't seem to have any effect, but don't ever be tempted to leave this call out. You might be stopping Windows from doing its work properly and the results could be unpredictable.

OnPaint() will also be called when the application first starts up and our window is displayed for the first time, so there is no need to duplicate the drawing code in the constructor.

Running this code gives the same results initially as for our previous example, except that now our application behaves itself properly when you minimize it or hide parts of the window.

Using the Clipping Region

Our DrawShapes sample from the previous section illustrates the main principles involved with drawing to a window, although it's not very efficient. The reason is that it attempts to draw everything in the window, irrespective of how much needs to be drawn. Figure 20-2 shows the result of running the DrawShapes example and opening another window and moving it over the DrawShapes form so part of it is hidden.

Figure 20-2

So far, so good. However, when we move the overlapping window so that the DrawShapes window is fully visible again, Windows will as usual send a Paint event to the form, asking it to repaint itself. The rectangle and ellipse both lie in the top-left corner of the client area, and so were visible all the time; therefore, there's actually nothing that needs to be done in this case apart from repaint the white background area. However, Windows doesn't know that, so it thinks it should raise the Paint event, resulting in our OnPaint() implementation being called. OnPaint() will then unnecessarily attempt to redraw the rectangle and ellipse.

Actually, in this case, the shapes will not get repainted because of the device context. Windows has pre-initialized the device context with information concerning what area actually needed repainting. In the days of GDI, the region that is marked for repainting used to be known as the *invalidated region*, but with GDI+ the terminology has largely changed to *clipping region*. The device context knows what this region is; therefore, it will intercept any attempts to draw outside this region and not pass the relevant drawing commands on to the graphics card. That sounds good, but there's still a potential performance hit here. We don't know how much processing the device context had to do before it figured out that the drawing was outside the invalidated region. In some cases it might be quite a lot, since calculating which pixels need to be changed to what color can be very processor-intensive (although a good graphics card will provide hardware acceleration to help with some of this).

The bottom line to this is that asking the Graphics instance to do some drawing outside the invalidated region is almost certainly wasting processor time and slowing your application down. In a well-designed application, your code will help out the device context by carrying out a few simple checks, to see if the proposed drawing work is likely to be needed before it calls the relevant Graphics instance methods. In this section we're going to code a new example. DrawShapesWithClipping, by modifying the DisplayShapes example to do just that. In our OnPaint() code, we'll do a simple test to see whether the invalidated region intersects the area we need to draw in, and only call the drawing methods if it does.

First, we need to obtain the details of the clipping region. This is where an extra property, ClipRectangle, on PaintEventArgs comes in. ClipRectangle contains the coordinates of the region to be repainted, wrapped up in an instance of a struct, System.Drawing.Rectangle. Rectangle is quite a simple struct—it contains four properties of interest: Top, Bottom, Left, and Right. These respectively contain the vertical coordinates of the top and bottom of the rectangle, and the horizontal coordinates of the left and right edges.

Next, we need to decide what test we'll use to determine whether drawing should take place. We'll go for a simple test here. Notice, that in our drawing, the rectangle and ellipse are both entirely contained within the rectangle that stretches from point (0,0) to point (80,130) of the client area; actually, point (82,132) to be on the safe side, since we know that the lines might stray a pixel or so outside this area. So we'll check whether the top-left corner of the clipping region is inside this rectangle. If it is, we'll go ahead and redraw. If it isn't, we won't bother.

Here is the code to do this:

```
protected override void OnPaint( PaintEventArgs e )
{
    base.OnPaint(e);
    Graphics dc = e.Graphics;

    if (e.ClipRectangle.Top < 132 && e.ClipRectangle.Left < 82)
    {
        Pen bluePen = new Pen(Color.Blue, 3);
        dc.DrawRectangle(bluePen, 0,0,50,50);
        Pen redPen = new Pen(Color.Red, 2);
        dc.DrawEllipse(redPen, 0, 50, 80, 60);
    }
}
```

Note that what gets displayed is exactly the same as before. However, performance is improved now by the early detection of some cases in which nothing needs to be drawn. Notice also that we've chosen a fairly crude test of whether to proceed with the drawing. A more refined test might be to check separately, whether the rectangle or the ellipse needs to be redrawn. However, there's a balance here. You can make your tests in `OnPaint()` more sophisticated, improving performance, but you'll also make your own `OnPaint()` code more complex. It's almost always worth putting some test in, because you've written the code so you understand far more about what is being drawn than the `Graphics` instance, which just blindly follows drawing commands.

Measuring Coordinates and Areas

In our last example, we encountered the base struct, `Rectangle,` which is used to represent the coordinates of a rectangle. GDI+ actually uses several similar structures to represent coordinates or areas. The following table lists the structs that are defined in the `System.Drawing` namespace.

Struct	Main Public Properties
struct Point	X, Y
struct PointF	
struct Size	Width, Height
struct SizeF	
struct Rectangle	Left, Right, Top, Bottom, Width, Height, X, Y, Location, Size
struct RectangleF	

Note that many of these objects have a number of other properties, methods, or operator overloads not listed here. In this section we'll just discuss some of the most important ones.

Point and PointF

We'll look at `Point` first. `Point` is conceptually the simplest of these structs. Mathematically, it's completely equivalent to a 2D vector. It contains two public integer properties, which represent how far you move horizontally and vertically from a particular location (perhaps on the screen), as shown in Figure 20-3.

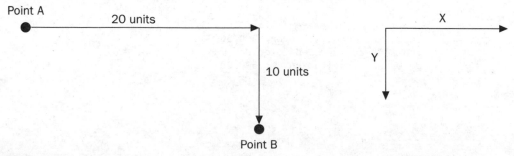

Point A — 20 units — 10 units — Point B

X, Y

Figure 20-3

In order to get from point A to point B, you move 20 units across and 10 units down, marked as x and y on the diagram as this is how they are commonly referred to. The following Point struct would represent that line:

```
Point ab = new Point(20, 10);
Console.WriteLine("Moved {0} across, {1} down", ab.X, ab.Y);
```

X and Y are read-write properties, which means you can also set the values in a Point like this:

```
Point ab = new Point();
ab.X = 20;
ab.Y = 10;
Console.WriteLine("Moved {0} across, {1} down", ab.X, ab.Y);
```

Note that although conventionally horizontal and vertical coordinates are referred to as x and y coordinates (lowercase), the corresponding Point properties are X and Y (uppercase) because the usual convention in C# is for public properties to have names that start with an uppercase letter.

PointF is essentially identical to Point, except that X and Y are of type float instead of int. PointF is used when the coordinates are not necessarily integer values. A cast has been defined so that you can implicitly convert from Point to PointF. (Note that because Point and PointF are structs, this cast involves actually making a copy of the data.) There is no corresponding reverse case—to convert from PointF to Point you have to copy the values across, or use one of three conversion methods, Round(), Truncate(), and Ceiling():

```
PointF abFloat = new PointF(20.5F, 10.9F);
// converting to Point
Point ab = new Point();
ab.X = (int)abFloat.X;
ab.Y = (int)abFloat.Y;
Point ab1 = Point.Round(abFloat);
Point ab2 = Point.Truncate(abFloat);
Point ab3 = Point.Ceiling(abFloat);

// but conversion back to PointF is implicit
PointF abFloat2 = ab;
```

You might be wondering what a unit is measured in. By default, GDI+ interprets units as pixels along the screen (or printer, whatever the graphics device is); that's how the Graphics object methods will view any coordinates that they get passed as parameters. For example, the point new Point(20,10) represents 20 pixels across the screen and 10 pixels down. Usually these pixels are measured from the top left corner of the client area of the window, as has been the case in our examples up to now. However, that won't always be the case. For example, on some occasions you might want to draw relative to the top-left corner of the whole window (including its border), or even to the top-left corner of the screen. In most cases, however, unless the documentation tells you otherwise, you can assume you're talking pixels relative to the top-left corner of the client area.

We'll have more to say on this subject later on, after we've examined scrolling, when we mention the three different coordinate systems in use—world , page, and device coordinates.

Size and SizeF

Like `Point` and `PointF`, sizes come in two varieties. The `Size` struct is for when you are using `int` types; `SizeF` is available if you need to use `float` types. Otherwise `Size` and `SizeF` are identical. We'll focus on the `Size` struct here.

In many ways the `Size` struct is identical to the `Point` struct. It has two integer properties that represent a distance horizontally and a distance vertically. The main difference is that instead of `X` and `Y`, these properties are named `Width` and `Height`. We can represent our earlier diagram using this code:

```
Size ab = new Size(20,10);
Console.WriteLine("Moved {0} across, {1} down", ab.Width, ab.Height);
```

Although strictly speaking, `Size` mathematically represents exactly the same thing as `Point`; conceptually it is intended to be used in a slightly different way. `Point` is used when we are talking about where something is, and `Size` is used when we are talking about how big it is. However, because `Size` and `Point` are so closely related, there are even supported conversions between these two:

```
Point point = new Point(20, 10);
Size size = (Size) point;
Point anotherPoint = (Point) size;
```

As an example, think about the rectangle we drew earlier, with top-left coordinate (0,0) and size (50,50). The size of this rectangle is (50,50) and might be represented by a `Size` instance. The bottom-right corner is also at (50,50), but that would be represented by a `Point` instance. To see the difference, suppose we draw the rectangle in a different location, so its top left coordinate is at (10,10):

```
dc.DrawRectangle(bluePen, 10,10,50,50);
```

Now the bottom-right corner is at coordinate (60,60), but the size is unchanged at (50,50).

The addition operator has been overloaded for `Point` and `Size` structs, so that it is possible to add a `Size` to a `Point` struct, resulting in another `Point` struct:

```
static void Main(string[] args)
{
    Point topLeft = new Point(10,10);
    Size rectangleSize = new Size(50,50);
    Point bottomRight = topLeft + rectangleSize;
    Console.WriteLine("topLeft = " + topLeft);
    Console.WriteLine("bottomRight = " + bottomRight);
    Console.WriteLine("Size = " + rectangleSize);
}
```

This code, running as a simple console application, called `PointsAndSizes`, produces the output shown in Figure 20-4.

Note that this output also shows how the `ToString()` method has been overridden in both `Point` and `Size` to display the value in {X, Y} format.

Figure 20-4

It is also possible to subtract a `Size` from a `Point` struct to give a `Point` struct, and you can add two `Size` structs together, giving another `Size`. It is not possible, however, to add a `Point` struct to another `Point`. Microsoft decided that adding `Point` structs doesn't conceptually make sense, and so chose not supply any overload to the + operator that would have allowed that.

You can also explicitly cast a `Point` to a `Size` struct and vice versa:

```
Point topLeft = new Point(10,10);
Size s1 = (Size)topLeft;
Point p1 = (Point)s1;
```

With this cast `s1.Width` is assigned the value of `topLeft.X`, and `s1.Height` is assigned the value of `topLeft.Y`. Hence, `s1` contains (10,10). `p1` will end up storing the same values as `topLeft`.

Rectangle and RectangleF

These structures represent a rectangular region (usually of the screen). Just as with `Point` and `Size`, we'll only consider the `Rectangle` struct here. `RectangleF` is basically identical except that those of its properties that represent dimensions all use `float`, whereas those of `Rectangle` use `int`.

A `Rectangle` struct can be thought of as composed of a point, representing the top-left corner of the rectangle, and a `Size` struct, which represents how large it is. One of its constructors actually takes a `Point` struct and a `Size` struct as its parameters. We can see this by rewriting our earlier code from the DrawShapes sample that draws a rectangle:

```
Graphics dc = e.Graphics;
Pen bluePen = new Pen(Color.Blue, 3);
Point topLeft = new Point(0,0);
Size howBig = new Size(50,50);
Rectangle rectangleArea = new Rectangle(topLeft, howBig);
dc.DrawRectangle(bluePen, rectangleArea);
```

This code also uses an alternative override of `Graphics.DrawRectangle()`, which takes a `Pen` and a `Rectangle` struct as its parameters.

You can also construct a `Rectangle` struct by supplying the top-left horizontal coordinate, top-left vertical coordinate, width, and height separately, and in that order, as individual numbers:

```
Rectangle rectangleArea = new Rectangle(0, 0, 50, 50);
```

`Rectangle` makes quite a few read-write properties available to set or extract its dimensions in different combinations. See the following table for details.

Property	Description
`int Left`	x-coordinate of left-hand edge
`int Right`	x-coordinate of right-hand edge
`int Top`	y-coordinate of top
`int Bottom`	y-coordinate of bottom
`int X`	Same as `Left`
`int Y`	Same as `Top`
`int Width`	Width of rectangle
`int Height`	Height of rectangle
`Point Location`	Top-left corner
`Size Size`	Size of rectangle

Note that these properties are not all independent. For example, setting `Width` also affects the value of `Right`.

Region

`Region` represents an area of the screen that has some complex shape. For example the shaded area in Figure 20-5 could be represented by `Region`.

Figure 20-5

As you can imagine, the process of initializing a `Region` instance is itself quite complex. Broadly speaking, you can do it by indicating either what component simple shapes make up the region or what path you take as you trace round the edge of the region. If you do need to start working with areas like this, then it's worth looking up the `Region` class in the SDK documentation.

A Note about Debugging

We're just about ready to do some more advanced types of drawing now. First, however, I just want to say a few things about debugging. If you have tried setting break points in the examples of this chapter you will have noticed that debugging drawing routines isn't quite as simple as debugging other parts of your program. This is because entering and leaving the debugger often causes Paint messages to be sent to your application. The result can be that setting a break point in your OnPaint() override simply causes your application to keep painting itself over and over again, so it's basically unable to do anything else.

A typical scenario is as follows. You want to find out why your application is displaying something incorrectly, so you set a break point within the OnPaint() event. As expected, the application hits your break point and the debugger comes in, at which point your developer environment MDI window comes to the foreground. If you're anything like me, you probably have the developer environments set to full screen display so you can more easily view all the debugging information, which means it always completely hides the application you are debugging.

Moving on, you examine the values of some variables and hopefully find out something useful. Then you press F5 to tell the application to continue, so that you can go on to see what happens when the application displays something else after some processing. Unfortunately, the first thing that happens is that the application comes to the foreground and Windows efficiently detects that the form is visible again and promptly sends it a Paint event. This means, of course, that your break point is hit again. If that's what you want, fine. More commonly what you really want is to hit the break point *later,* when the application is drawing something more interesting, perhaps after you've selected some menu option to read in a file or in some other way changed what gets displayed. It looks like you're stuck. Either you don't have a break point in OnPaint() at all, or your application can never get beyond the point where it's displaying its initial startup window.

There is a workaround to this problem.

If you have a big screen the easiest way is simply to keep your developer environment window tiled rather than maximized and keep it well away from your application window, so your application never is hidden in the first place. Unfortunately, in most cases that is not a practical solution, because that would make your developer environment window too small. An alternative that uses the same principle is to have your application declare itself as the topmost application while you are debugging. You do this by setting a property in the Form class, TopMost, which you can easily do in the InitializeComponent() method:

```
private void InitializeComponent()
{
    this.TopMost = true;
```

You can also set this property through the Properties window in Visual Studio .NET.

Being a TopMost window means your application can never be hidden by other windows (except other topmost windows). It always remains above other windows even when another application has the focus. This is how the Task Manager behaves.

Even with this technique you have to be careful, because you can never be certain when Windows might decide for some reason to raise a Paint event. If you really want to trap some problem that occurs in

`OnPaint()` in some specific circumstance (for example, the application draws something after you select a certain menu option, and something goes wrong at that point), then the best way to do this is to place some dummy code in `OnPaint()` that tests some condition, which will only be `true` in the specified circumstances—and then place the break point inside the `if` block, like this:

```
protected override void OnPaint( PaintEventArgs e )
{
    // Condition() evaluates to true when we want to break
    if ( Condition() == true)
    {
        int ii = 0;    // <-- SET BREAKPOINT HERE!!!
    }
}
```

This is a quick-and-easy way of setting a conditional break point.

Drawing Scrollable Windows

Our earlier DrawShapes sample worked very well, because everything we needed to draw fit into the initial window size. In this section we're going to look at what we need to do if that's not the case.

We expand our DrawShapes sample to demonstrate scrolling. To make things a bit more realistic, we'll start by creating an example, BigShapes, in which we make the rectangle and ellipse a bit bigger. Also, while we're at it, we'll demonstrate how to use the `Point`, `Size`, and `Rectangle` structs by using them to assist in defining the drawing areas. With these changes, the relevant part of the `Form1` class looks like this:

```
// member fields
private Point rectangleTopLeft = new Point(0, 0);
private Size rectangleSize = new Size(200,200);
private Point ellipseTopLeft = new Point(50, 200);
private Size ellipseSize = new Size(200, 150);
private Pen bluePen = new Pen(Color.Blue, 3);
private Pen redPen = new Pen(Color.Red, 2);

protected override void OnPaint( PaintEventArgs e )
{
    base.OnPaint(e);
    Graphics dc = e.Graphics;

    if (e.ClipRectangle.Top < 350 || e.ClipRectangle.Left < 250)
    {
        Rectangle rectangleArea =
            new Rectangle (rectangleTopLeft, rectangleSize);
        Rectangle ellipseArea =
            new Rectangle (ellipseTopLeft, ellipseSize);
        dc.DrawRectangle(bluePen, rectangleArea);
        dc.DrawEllipse(redPen, ellipseArea);
    }
}
```

Note that we've also turned the `Pen`, `Size`, and `Point` objects into member fields—this is more efficient than creating a new `Pen` every time we need to draw anything, as we have been doing up to now.

The result of running this example looks like Figure 20-6.

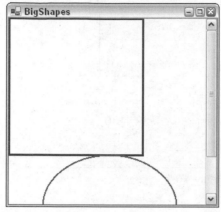

Figure 20-6

We can see a problem instantly. The shapes don't fit in our 300×300 pixel drawing area.

Normally, if a document is too large to display, an application will add scroll bars to let you scroll the window and look at a chosen part of it. This is another area in which if we were building Windows Forms using standard controls, then we'd just let the .NET runtime and the base classes handle everything for us. If your form has various controls attached to it, then the `Form` instance will normally know where these controls are and it will therefore know if its window becomes so small that scroll bars are necessary. The `Form` instance also automatically adds the scroll bars for you, and it is also able to draw correctly whichever portion of the screen you've scrolled to. In that case there is nothing you need to do in your code. In this chapter, however, we're taking responsibility for drawing to the screen; therefore, we're going to have to help the `Form` instance out when it comes to scrolling.

Getting the scroll bars added is actually very easy. The `Form` can still handle all that for us, because it doesn't know how big an area we will want to draw in. (The reason it hasn't in the earlier BigShapes sample is that Windows doesn't know they are needed.) What we need to figure out is the size of a rectangle that stretches from the top-left corner of the document (or equivalently, the top-left corner of the client area before we've done any scrolling), and which is just big enough to contain the entire document. In this chapter, we'll refer to this area as the document area. As shown in Figure 20-7, for this example the document area is (250, 350) pixels.

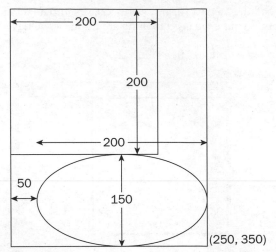

Figure 20-7

It is easy to tell the form how big the document is. We use the relevant property, `Form.AutoScrollMinSize`. Therefore we can add this code to either the `InitializeComponent()` method or the `Form1` constructor:

```
private void InitializeComponent()
{
    this.AutoScaleBaseSize = new System.Drawing.Size(5, 13);
    this.ClientSize = new System.Drawing.Size(292, 266);
    this.Name = "Form1";
    this.Text = "BigShapes";
    this.BackColor = Color.White;
    this.AutoScrollMinSize = new Size(250, 350);
}
```

Alternatively the `AutoScrollMinSize` property can be set using the Visual Studio .NET Properties window.

Setting the minimum size at application startup and leaving it thereafter is fine in this particular example, because we know that is how big the screen area will always be. Our document never changes size while this particular application is running. Keep in mind, however, that if your application does things like display contents of files or something else for which the area of the screen might change, you will need to set this property at other times (and in that case you'll have to sort out the code manually—the Visual Studio .NET Properties window can only help you with the initial value that a property has when the form is constructed).

Setting `AutoScrollMinSize` is a start, but it's not yet quite enough. Figure 20-8 shows what our sample application looks like now—initially we get the screen that correctly displays the shapes.

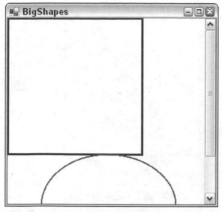

Figure 20-8

Notice that not only has the form correctly set the scroll bars; it has also correctly sized them to indicate what proportion of the document is currently displayed. You can try resizing the window while the sample is running—you'll find the scroll bars respond properly, and even disappear if we make the window big enough so that they are no longer needed.

However, look at what happens when we actually use one of the scrollbars and scroll down a bit (see in Figure 20-9). Clearly, something has gone wrong!

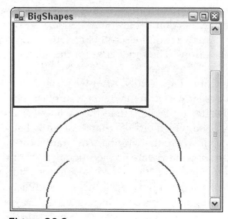

Figure 20-9

What's wrong is that we haven't taken into account the position of the scrollbars in the code in our OnPaint() override. We can see this very clearly if we force the window to repaint itself completely by minimizing and restoring it (see Figure 20-10).

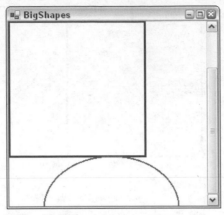

Figure 20-10

The shapes have been painted, just as before, with the top-left corner of the rectangle nestled into the top-left corner of the client area—just as if we hadn't moved the scroll bars at all.

Before we explain how to correct this problem, let's take a closer look at precisely what is happening in these screenshots.

We'll start with the BigShapes sample, shown in Figure 20-8. In this example, the entire window has just been repainted. Reviewing our code we learn that it instructs the graphics instance to draw a rectangle with top-left coordinates (0,0)—relative to the top-left corner of the client area of the window—which is what has been drawn. The problem is that the graphics instance by default interprets coordinates as relative to the client window—it is unaware of the scroll bars. Our code as yet does not attempt to adjust the coordinates for the scroll bar positions. The same goes for the ellipse.

Now, we can tackle the screenshot in Figure 20-9. After we scroll down, we notice that the top half of the window looks fine. That's because it was drawn when the application first started up. When you scroll windows, Windows doesn't ask the application to redraw what was already on the screen. Windows is smart enough to figure out for itself which bits of what's currently being displayed on the screen can be smoothly moved around to match where the scrollbars now are located. That's a much more efficient process, since it may be able to use some hardware acceleration to do that too. The bit in this screenshot that's wrong is the bottom third of the window. This part of the window didn't get drawn when the application first appeared, since before we started scrolling it was outside the client area. This means that Windows asks our BigShapes application to draw this area. It'll raise a Paint event passing in just this area as the clipping rectangle. And that's exactly what our OnPaint() override has done.

One way of looking at the problem is that we are at the moment expressing our coordinates relative to the top-left corner of the start of the document—we need to convert them to express them relative to the top-left corner of the client area instead (see Figure 20-11).

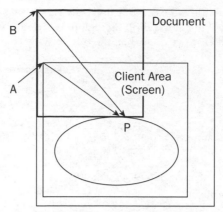

Figure 20-11

To make the diagram clearer we've actually extended the document further downward and to the right, beyond the boundaries of the screen, but this doesn't change our reasoning. We've also assumed a small horizontal scroll as well as a vertical one.

In Figure 20-11 the thin rectangles mark the borders of the screen area and of the entire document. The thick lines mark the rectangle and ellipse that we are trying to draw. P marks some arbitrary point that we are drawing and which we are using as an example. When calling the drawing methods we've supplied the graphics instance with the vector from point B to (say) point P, expressed as a `Point` instance. We actually need to give it the vector from point A to point P.

The problem is that we don't know what the vector from A to P is. We know what B to P is—that's just the coordinates of P relative to the top-left corner of the document—the position where we want to draw point P in the document. We also know the vector from B to A is just the amount we've scrolled by; this is stored in a property of the `Form` class called `AutoScrollPosition`. However, we don't know the vector from A to P.

Now, if you remember your high school math, you will know how to solve this problem—you subtract the one vector from the other. Say, for example, to get from B to P you move 150 pixels across and 200 pixels down, while to get from B to A you have to move 10 pixels across and 57 pixels down. That means to get from A to P you have to move 140 (=150 minus 10) pixels across and 143 (=200 minus 57) pixels down. To make it even simpler, the `Graphics` class actually implements a method that will do these calculations for us. It's called `TranslateTransform()`. You pass it the horizontal and vertical coordinates that say where the top left of the client area is relative to the top-left corner of the document (our `AutoScrollPosition` property, that is the vector from B to A in the diagram). The `Graphics` device will now work out all its coordinates, taking into account where the client area is relative to the document.

Translating this long explanation into code, all we typically need to do is add this line to our drawing code:

```
dc.TranslateTransform(this.AutoScrollPosition.X, this.AutoScrollPosition.Y);
```

Though in our example, it's a little more complicated because we are also separately testing whether we need to do any drawing by looking at the clipping region. We need to adjust this test to take the scroll position into account too. When we've done that, the full drawing code for the sample looks like this:

```
protected override void OnPaint( PaintEventArgs e )
{
   base.OnPaint(e);
 Graphics dc = e.Graphics;
  Size scrollOffset = new Size(this.AutoScrollPosition);
  if (e.ClipRectangle.Top+scrollOffset.Width < 350 ||
     e.ClipRectangle.Left+scrollOffset.Height < 250)
  {
     Rectangle rectangleArea = new Rectangle
        (rectangleTopLeft+scrollOffset, rectangleSize);
     Rectangle ellipseArea = new Rectangle
        (ellipseTopLeft+scrollOffset, ellipseSize);
     dc.DrawRectangle(bluePen, rectangleArea);
     dc.DrawEllipse(redPen, ellipseArea);
  }
}
```

Now we have our scroll code working perfectly; we can at last obtain a correctly scrolled screenshot (see Figure 20-12).

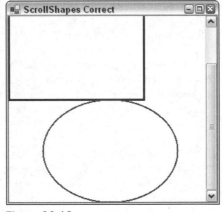

Figure 20-12

World, Page, and Device Coordinates

The distinction between measuring position relative to the top-left corner of the document and measuring it relative to the top-left corner of the screen (desktop) is so important that GDI+ has special names for these coordinate systems:

❑ **World coordinates** specify the position of a point measured in pixels from the top-left corner of the document.

❑ **Page coordinates** specify the position of a point measured in pixels from the top-left corner of the client area.

Developers familiar with GDI will note that world coordinates correspond to what in GDI were known as logical coordinates. Page coordinates correspond to what used to be known as device coordinates. As a developer familiar with GDI you should also note that the way you code conversion between logical and device coordinates has changed in GDI+. In GDI, conversions took place via the device context, using the LPtoDP() *and* DPtoLP() *Windows API functions. In GDI+, it's the* Control *class, from which both* Form *and all the various Windows Forms controls derive, that maintains the information needed to carry out the conversion.*

GDI+ also distinguishes a third coordinate system, which is now known as *device coordinates*. Device coordinates are similar to page coordinates, except that we do not use pixels as the unit of measurement. Instead we use some other unit that can be specified by the user by calling the Graphics.PageUnit property. Possible units, besides the default of pixels, include inches and millimeters. Although we won't use the PageUnit property in this chapter, you might find it useful as a way of getting around the different pixel densities of devices. For example, 100 pixels on most monitors will occupy something like an inch. However, laser printers can have 1,200 or more dpi (dots per inch), which means that a shape specified to be 100 pixels wide will look a lot smaller when printed on it. By setting the units to, say, inches and specifying that the shape should be 1 inch wide, you can ensure that the shape will look the same size on the different devices.

Colors

In this section, we discuss the ways that you can specify what color you want something to be drawn in.

Colors in GDI+ are represented by instances of the System.Drawing.Color struct. Generally, once you've instantiated this struct, you won't do much with the corresponding Color instance—you just pass it to whatever other method you are calling that requires a Color. We've encountered this struct before, when we set the background color of the client area of the window in each of our samples, as well as when we set the colors of the various shapes we were displaying. The Form.BackColor property actually returns a Color instance. In this section, we'll look at this struct in more detail. In particular, we'll examine several different ways that you can construct a Color.

Red-Green-Blue (RGB) Values

The total number of colors that can be displayed by a monitor is huge—over 16 million. To be exact the number is 2 to the power 24, which works out to 16,777,216. Obviously we need some way of indexing those colors so we can indicate which of these is the color we want to display at any given pixel.

The most common way of indexing colors is by dividing them into the red, green, and blue components. This idea is based on the theory that any color that the human eye can distinguish can be constructed from a certain amount of red light, a certain amount of the green light, and a certain amount of blue light. These colors are known as *components*. In practice, it's found that if we divide the amount of each component light into 256 possible intensities, then that gives a sufficiently fine gradation to be able to display images that are perceived by the human eye to be of photographic quality. We therefore specify colors by giving the amounts of these components on a scale of 0 to 255 where 0 means that the component is not present and 255 means that it is at its maximum intensity.

We can now see where are quoted figure of 16,777,216 colors comes from, since that number is just 256 cubed.

This gives us our first way of telling GDI+ about a color. You can indicate a color's red, green, and blue values by calling the static function `Color.FromArgb()`. Microsoft has chosen not to supply a constructor to do this task. The reason is that there are other ways, besides the usual RGB components, to indicate a color. Because of this, Microsoft felt that the meaning of parameters passed to any constructor they defined would be open to misinterpretation:

```
Color redColor = Color.FromArgb(255,0,0);
Color funnyOrangyBrownColor = Color.FromArgb(255,155,100);
Color blackColor = Color.FromArgb(0,0,0);
Color whiteColor = Color.FromArgb(255,255,255);
```

The three parameters are, respectively, the quantities of red, green, and blue. There are a number of other overloads to this function, some of which also allow you to specify something called an alpha-blend (that's the A in the name of the method, `FromArgb()`). Alpha blending is beyond the scope of this chapter, but it allows you to paint a color semitransparently by combining it with whatever color was already on the screen. This can give some beautiful effects and is often used in games.

The Named Colors

Constructing a `Color` using `FromArgb()` is the most flexible technique, since it literally means you can specify any color that the human eye can see. However, if you want a simple, standard, well-known color such as red or blue, it's a lot easier to just be able to name the color you want. Hence Microsoft has also provided a large number of static properties in `Color`, each of which returns a named color. It was one of these properties that we used when we set the background color of our windows to white in our samples:

```
this.BackColor = Color.White;

// has the same effect as:
// this.BackColor = Color.FromArgb(255, 255 , 255);
```

There are several hundred such colors. The full list is given in the SDK documentation. They include all the simple colors: Red, White, Blue, Green, Black, and so on, as well as such delights as MediumAquamarine, LightCoral, and DarkOrchid. There is also a KnownColor enumeration, which lists the named colors.

Incidentally, although it might look that way, these named colors have not been chosen at random. Each one represents a precise set of RGB values, and they were originally chosen many years ago for use on the Internet. The idea was to provide a useful set of colors right across the spectrum whose names would be recognized by Web browsers, thus saving you from having to write explicit RGB values in your HTML code. A few years ago these colors were also important because early browsers couldn't necessarily display very many colors accurately, and the named colors were supposed to provide a set of colors that would be displayed correctly by most browsers. These days that aspect is less important since modern web browsers are quite capable of displaying any RGB value correctly. There are also Web-safe color palettes available that provide developers with a comprehensive list of colors that work with most browsers.

Graphics Display Modes and the Safety Palette

Although we've said that in principle monitors can display any of the over 16 million RGB colors, in practice this depends on how you've set the display properties on your computer. In Windows, there are traditionally three main color options (although some machines might provide other options depending on the hardware): true color (24-bit), high color (16-bit), and 256 colors. (On some graphics cards these days, true color is actually marked as 32-bit. This has to do with optimizing the hardware, though in that case only 24 bits of the 32 bits are used for the color itself.)

Only true-color mode allows you to display all of the RGB colors simultaneously. This sounds like the best option, but it comes at a cost: 3 bytes are needed to hold a full RGB value, which means 3 bytes of graphics card memory are needed to hold each pixel that is displayed. If graphics card memory is at a premium (a restriction that's less common now than it used to be) you might want to choose one of the other modes. High color mode gives you 2 bytes per pixel. That's enough to give 5 bits for each RGB component. So instead of 256 gradations of red intensity you just get 32 gradations; the same for blue and green, which gives a total of 65,536 colors. That is just about enough to give apparent photographic quality on a casual inspection, though areas of subtle shading tend to be broken up a bit.

The 256-color mode gives you even fewer colors. However, in this mode, you get to choose which colors. What happens is that the system sets up something known as a *palette*. This is a list of 256 colors chosen from the 16 million RGB colors. Once you've specified the colors in the palette, the graphics device will be able to display just those colors. The palette can be changed at any time, but the graphics device can only display 256 different colors on the screen at any one time. The 256-color mode is only used when high performance and video memory is at a premium. Most computer games will use this mode, and they can still achieve decent-looking graphics because of a very careful choice of palette.

In general, if a display device is in high-color or 256-color mode and a particular RGB color is requested, it will pick the nearest mathematical match from the pool of colors that it is able to display. It's for this reason that it's important to be aware of the color modes. If you are drawing something that involves subtle shading or photographic quality images, and the user does not have 24-bit color mode selected, she might not see the image the same way you intended it. So if you're doing that kind of work with GDI+, you should test your application in different color modes. (It is also possible for your application to programmatically set a given color mode, though we won't discuss this in this chapter for lack of space.)

The Safety Palette

For reference, we'll quickly mention the safety palette, which is a very commonly used default palette. The way it works is that we set six equally spaced possible values for each color component: 0, 51, 102, 153, 204, and 255. In other words, the red component can have any of these values. So can the green component. So can the blue component. So possible colors from the safety palette include (0,0,0), black; (153,0,0), a fairly dark shade of red; (0, 255,102), green with a smattering of blue added; and so on. This gives us a total of 6 cubed = 216 colors. The idea is that this gives us an easy way of having a palette that contains colors from right across the spectrum and of all degrees of brightness, although in practice this doesn't actually work that well because equal mathematical spacing of color components doesn't mean equal perception of color differences by the human eye. Because the safety palette used to be widely used, however, you'll still find a fair number of applications and images exclusively use colors from the safety palette.

If you set Windows to 256-color mode, you'll find the default palette you get is the safety palette, with 20 Windows standard colors added to it, and 20 spare colors.

Pens and Brushes

In this section, we'll review two helper classes that are needed in order to draw shapes. We've already encountered the Pen class, which we used to instruct the graphics instance how to draw lines. A related class is System.Drawing.Brush, which instructs the graphics instance how to fill regions. For example, the Pen is needed to draw the outlines of the rectangle and ellipse in our previous examples. If we had needed to draw these shapes as solid, we would have used a brush to specify how to fill them in. One aspect of both of these classes is that you will hardly ever call any methods on them. You simply construct a Pen or Brush instance with the required color and other properties, and then pass it to drawing methods that require a Pen or Brush.

We discuss brushes first, then pens.

If you've programmed using GDI before, you have noticed from the first couple of examples that pens are used in a different way in GDI+. In GDI the normal practice was to call a Windows API function, SelectObject(), which actually associated a pen with the device context. That pen was then used in all drawing operations that required a pen until you informed the device context otherwise, by calling SelectObject() again. The same principle held for brushes and other objects such as fonts or bitmaps. With GDI+ Microsoft has opted for a stateless model in which there is no default pen or other helper object. Rather, you simply specify with each method call the appropriate helper object to be used for that particular method.

Brushes

GDI+ has several different kinds of brush—more than we have space to go into in this chapter, so we'll just explain the simpler ones to give you an idea of the principles. Each type of brush is represented by an instance of a class derived from the abstract class System.Drawing.Brush. The simplest brush, System.Drawing.SolidBrush, indicates that a region is to be filled with solid color:

```
Brush solidBeigeBrush = new SolidBrush(Color.Beige);
Brush solidFunnyOrangyBrownBrush =
                        new SolidBrush(Color.FromArgb(255,155,100));
```

Alternatively, if the brush is one of the Web-safe colors you can construct the brush using another class, System.Drawing.Brushes. Brushes is one of those classes that you never actually instantiate (it has a private constructor to stop you from doing that). It simply has a large number of static properties, each of which returns a brush of a specified color. You can use Brushes like this:

```
Brush solidAzureBrush = Brushes.Azure;
Brush solidChocolateBrush = Brushes.Chocolate;
```

The next level of complexity is a hatch brush, which fills a region by drawing a pattern. This type of brush is considered more advanced, so it's in the Drawing2D namespace, represented by the class System.Drawing.Drawing2D.HatchBrush. The Brushes class can't help you with hatch brushes—you'll need to construct one explicitly by supplying the hatch style and two colors, the foreground color followed by the background color (you can omit the background color, in which case it defaults to black). The hatch style comes from an enumeration, System.Drawing.Drawing2D.HatchStyle. You can choose from a large number of HatchStyle values (see the SDK documentation for the full list). To give you an idea, typical styles include ForwardDiagonal, Cross, DiagonalCross, SmallConfetti, and ZigZag. Examples of constructing a hatch brush include:

```
Brush crossBrush = new HatchBrush(HatchStyle.Cross, Color.Azure);

// background color of CrossBrush is black

Brush brickBrush = new HatchBrush(HatchStyle.DiagonalBrick,
                                  Color.DarkGoldenrod, Color.Cyan);
```

Solid and hatch brushes are the only brushes available under GDI. GDI+ has added a couple of new styles of brush:

- ❏ `System.Drawing.Drawing2D.LinearGradientBrush` fills in an area with a color that varies across the screen.

- ❏ `System.Drawing.Drawing2D.PathGradientBrush` is similar, but in this case the color varies along a path around the region to be filled.

Note that both brushes can render some spectacular effects if used carefully.

Pens

Unlike brushes, pens are represented by just one class: `System.Drawing.Pen`. However, the pen is slightly more complex than the brush, because it needs to indicate how thick lines should be (how many pixels wide) and, for a wide line, how to fill the area inside the line. Pens can also specify a number of other properties, which are beyond the scope of this chapter, but which include the `Alignment` property that we mentioned earlier. This property indicates where in relation to the border of a shape a line should be drawn, as well as what shape to draw at the end of a line (whether to round off the shape).

The area inside a thick line can be filled with solid color, or it can be filled using a brush. Hence, a `Pen` instance might contain a reference to a `Brush` instance. This is quite powerful, as it means you can draw lines that are colored in by using, say, hatching or linear shading. There are four different ways that you can construct a `Pen` instance that you have designed yourself. You can do it by passing a color, or you can do it by passing in a brush. Both of these constructors will produce a pen with a width of one pixel. Alternatively, you can pass in a color or a brush, and additionally a `float`, which represents the width of the pen. (It needs to be a `float` in case we are using non-default units such as millimeters or inches for the `Graphics` object that will do the drawing, so we can, for example, specify fractions of an inch.) For example, you can construct pens like this:

```
Brush brickBrush = new HatchBrush(HatchStyle.DiagonalBrick,
                                  Color.DarkGoldenrod, Color.Cyan);
```

```
Pen solidBluePen = new Pen(Color.FromArgb(0,0,255));
Pen solidWideBluePen = new Pen(Color.Blue, 4);
Pen brickPen = new Pen(brickBrush);
Pen brickWidePen = new Pen(brickBrush, 10);
```

Additionally, for the quick construction of pens, you can use the class `System.Drawing.Pens`, which, like the `Brushes` class, contains a number of stock pens. These pens all have one-pixel width and come in the usual sets of Web-safe colors. This allows you to construct pens in this way:

```
Pen solidYellowPen = Pens.Yellow;
```

Drawing Shapes and Lines

We've almost finished the first part of the chapter, in which we've covered all the basic classes and objects required in order to draw specified shapes and so on to the screen. We'll round off by reviewing some of the drawing methods the `Graphics` class makes available and presenting a short example that illustrates the use of several brushes and pens.

`System.Drawing.Graphics` has a large number of methods that allow you to draw various lines, outline shapes, and solid shapes. Once again there are too many to provide a comprehensive list here, but the following table lists the main ones and should give you some idea of the variety of shapes you can draw.

Method	Typical Parameters	What it Draws
DrawLine	Pen, start and end points	A single straight line
DrawRectangle	Pen, position, and size	Outline of a rectangle
DrawEllipse	Pen, position, and size	Outline of an ellipse
FillRectangle	Brush, position, and size	Solid rectangle
FillEllipse	Brush, position, and size	Solid ellipse
DrawLines	Pen, array of points	Series of lines, connecting each point to the next one in the array
DrawBezier	Pen, 4 points	A smooth curve through the two end points, with the remaining two points used to control the shape of the curve
DrawCurve	Pen, array of points	A smooth curve through the points
DrawArc	Pen, rectangle, two angles	Portion of circle within the rectangle defined by the angles
DrawClosedCurve	Pen, array of points	Like DrawCurve but also draws a straight line to close the curve
DrawPie	Pen, rectangle, two angles	Wedge-shaped outline within the rectangle
FillPie	Brush, rectangle, two angles	Solid wedge-shaped area within the rectangle
DrawPolygon	Pen, array of points	Like DrawLines but also connects first and last points to close the figure drawn

Before we leave the subject of drawing simple objects, we'll round off with a simple example that demonstrates the kinds of visual effect you can achieve using brushes. The example is called ScrollMoreShapes, and it's essentially a revision of ScrollShapes. Besides the rectangle and ellipse, we'll add a thick line and fill in the shapes with various custom brushes. We've already explained the principles of drawing so we let the code speak for itself. First, because of our new brushes, we need to indicate we are using the `System.Drawing.Drawing2D` namespace:

```
using System;
using System.Drawing;
using System.Drawing.Drawing2D;
using System.Collections;
using System.ComponentModel;
using System.Windows.Forms;
using System.Data;
```

Next are some extra fields in our Form1 class, which contain details of the locations where the shapes are to be drawn, as well as various pens and brushes we will use:

```
private Rectangle rectangleBounds = new Rectangle(new Point(0,0),
                                                  new Size(200,200));
private Rectangle ellipseBounds = new Rectangle(new Point(50,200),
                                                new Size(200,150));
private Pen bluePen = new Pen(Color.Blue, 3);
private Pen redPen = new Pen(Color.Red, 2);
private Brush solidAzureBrush = Brushes.Azure;
private Brush solidYellowBrush = new SolidBrush(Color.Yellow);
static private Brush brickBrush = new HatchBrush(HatchStyle.DiagonalBrick,
                                         Color.DarkGoldenrod, Color.Cyan);
private Pen brickWidePen = new Pen(brickBrush, 10);
```

The brickBrush field has been declared as static, so that we can use its value to initialize the brickWidePen field. C# won't let us use one instance field to initialize another instance field, because it's not defined which one will be initialized first. However, declaring the field as static solves the problem. Since only one instance of the Form1 class will be instantiated, it is immaterial whether the fields are static or instance fields.

Here is the OnPaint() override:

```
protected override void OnPaint( PaintEventArgs e )
{
   base.OnPaint(e);
   Graphics dc = e.Graphics;
   Point scrollOffset = this.AutoScrollPosition;
   dc.TranslateTransform(scrollOffset.X, scrollOffset.Y);
   if (e.ClipRectangle.Top+scrollOffset.X < 350 ||
       e.ClipRectangle.Left+scrollOffset.Y < 250)
   {
      dc.DrawRectangle(bluePen, rectangleBounds);
      dc.FillRectangle(solidYellowBrush, rectangleBounds);
      dc.DrawEllipse(redPen, ellipseBounds);
      dc.FillEllipse(solidAzureBrush, ellipseBounds);
      dc.DrawLine(brickWidePen, rectangleBounds.Location,
                         ellipseBounds.Location+ellipseBounds.Size);
   }
}
```

As before we also set the AutoScrollMinSize to (250,350). Figure 20-13 shows the new results.

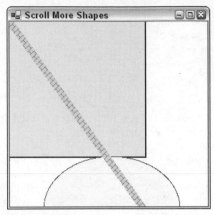

Figure 20-13

Notice that the thick diagonal line has been drawn on top of the rectangle and ellipse, because it was the last item to be painted.

Displaying Images

One of the most common things you might want to do with GDI+ is display an image that already exists in a file. This is actually a lot simpler than drawing your own user interface, because the image is already pre-drawn. Effectively, all you have to do is load the file and instruct GDI+ to display it. The image can be a simple line drawing, an icon, or a complex image such as a photograph. You can also manipulate the image by stretching or rotating it, or simply displaying only a portion of it.

In this section, just for a change, we'll present the sample first. Then we'll discuss some of the issues you need to be aware of when displaying images. We can do this, because the code needed to display an image is so simple.

The class we need is the .NET base class, System.Drawing.Image. An instance of Image represents one image. Reading in an image simply takes one line of code:

```
Image myImage = Image.FromFile("FileName");
```

FromFile() is a static member of Image and is the usual way of instantiating an image. The file can be any of the commonly supported graphics file formats, including .bmp, .jpg, .gif, and .png.

Displaying an image is also very simple, assuming you have a suitable Graphics instance at hand—a call to either Graphics.DrawImageUnscaled() or Graphics.DrawImage() suffices. There are quite a few overloads of these methods, allowing you a lot of flexibility in the information you supply in terms of where the image is located and how big it is to be drawn. But we will use DrawImage(), like this:

```
dc.DrawImage(myImage, points);
```

In this line of code, dc is assumed to be a Graphics instance, while myImage is the Image to be displayed. points is an array of Point structs, where points[0], points[1], and points[2] are the coordinates of top-left, top-right, and bottom-left corner of the image.

Images are probably the area in which developers familiar with GDI will notice the biggest difference between GDI and GDI+. In GDI, displaying an image involved several nontrivial steps. If the image was a bitmap, loading it was reasonably simple. But if it was any other file type, loading it would involve a sequence of calls to OLE objects. Actually getting a loaded image onto the screen involved getting a handle to it, selecting it into a memory device context, then performing a block transfer between device contexts. Although the device contexts and handles are still there behind the scenes, and will be needed if you want to start doing sophisticated editing of the images from your code, simple tasks have now been extremely well wrapped up in the GDI+ object model.

We'll illustrate the process of displaying an image with an example called DisplayImage. The example simply displays a .jpg file in the application's main window. To keep things simple, the path of the .jpg file is hard-coded into the application (so if you run the example you'll need to change it to reflect the location of the file in your system). The .jpg file we'll display is a sunset picture in London.

As with the other examples, the DisplayImage project is a standard C# Visual Studio .NET 2003-generated Windows application. We add the following fields to our Form1 class:

```
Image piccy;
private Point [] piccyBounds;
```

We then load the file in the Form1() constructor:

```
public Form1()
{
   InitializeComponent();

   piccy =
      Image.FromFile(@"C:\ProCSharp\GdiPlus\Images\CF4Group.bmp");
   this.AutoScrollMinSize = piccy.Size;
   piccyBounds = new Point[3];
   piccyBounds[0] = new Point(0,0);          // top left
   piccyBounds[1] = new Point(piccy.Width,0);   // top right
   piccyBounds[2] = new Point(0,piccy.Height);  // bottom left
}
```

Note that the size in pixels of the image is obtained as its Size property, which we use to set the document area. We also set up the piccyBounds array, which is used to identify the position of the image on the screen. We have chosen the coordinates of the three corners to draw the image in its actual size and shape here, but if we'd wanted the image to be resized, stretched, or even sheared into a non-rectangular parallelogram, we could do so simply by changing the values of the Points in the piccyBounds array.

The image is displayed in the OnPaint() override:

```
protected override void OnPaint(PaintEventArgs e)
{
   base.OnPaint(e);
   Graphics dc = e.Graphics;
```

```
        dc.ScaleTransform(1.0f, 1.0f);
        dc.TranslateTransform(this.AutoScrollPosition.X, this.AutoScrollPosition.Y);
        dc.DrawImage(piccy, piccyBounds);
}
```

Finally, note the modification made to the code wizard-generated `Form1.Dispose()` method:

```
    protected override void Dispose(bool disposing)
    {
        piccy.Dispose();
        if( disposing )
        {
            if (components != null)
            {
                components.Dispose();
            }
        }
        base.Dispose( disposing );
    }
```

Disposing of the image as soon as possible when it's no longer needed is important, because images generally take up a lot of memory while in use. After `Image.Dispose()` has been called, the `Image` instance no longer refers to any actual image, and so it can no longer be displayed (unless you load a new image).

Figure 20-14 shows the result of running this code.

Figure 20-14

Issues When Manipulating Images

Although displaying images is very simple, it still pays to have some understanding what's going on behind the scenes.

The most important point to understand about images is that they are always rectangular. That's not just a convenience, but because of the underlying technology. It's because all modern graphics cards have hardware built in that can efficiently copy blocks of pixels from one area of memory to another area of memory, provided that the block of pixels represents a rectangular region. This hardware-accelerated operation can occur virtually as one single operation, and as such is extremely fast. Indeed, it is the key to modern high-performance graphics. This operation is known as a *bitmap block transfer* (or *BitBlt*). `Graphics.DrawImageUnscaled()` internally uses a `BitBlt`, which is why you can see a huge image, perhaps containing as many as a million pixels, appearing almost instantly. If the computer had to copy the image to the screen pixel by pixel, you'd see the image gradually being drawn over a period of up to several seconds.

`BitBlt`s are very efficient; therefore almost all drawing and manipulation of images is carried out using them. Even some editing of images will be done by manipulating portions of images with `BitBlt`s between DCs that represent areas of memory. In the days of GDI, the Windows 32 API function `BitBlt()` was arguably the most important and widely used function for image manipulation, though with GDI+ the `BitBlt` operations are largely hidden by the GDI+ object model.

It's not possible to `BitBlt` areas of images that are not rectangular, although similar effects can be easily simulated. One way is to mark a certain color as transparent for the purposes of a `BitBlt`, so that areas of that color in the source image will not overwrite the existing color of the corresponding pixel in the destination device. It is also possible to specify that in the process of a `BitBlt`, each pixel of the resultant image will be formed by some logical operation (such as a bitwise AND) on the colors of that pixel in the source image and in the destination device before the `BitBlt`. Such operations are supported by hardware acceleration and can be used to give a variety of subtle effects. Note that the `Graphics` object implements another method, `DrawImage()`. This is similar to `DrawImageUnscaled()` but comes in a large number of overloads that allow you to specify more complex forms of `BitBlt` to be used in the drawing process. `DrawImage()` also allows you to draw (using `BitBlt`) only a specified part of the image, or to perform certain other operations on it such as scaling it (expanding or reducing it in size) as it is drawn.

Drawing Text

We've left the very important topic of displaying text until this late in the chapter because drawing text to the screen is (in general) more complex than drawing simple graphics. Although displaying a line or two of text when you're not that bothered about the appearance is extremely easy—it takes one single call to the `Graphics.DrawString()` method, if you are trying to display a document that has a fair amount of text in it, you rapidly find that things become a lot more complex. This is for two reasons:

❑   If you're concerned about getting the appearance just right, you must understand fonts. Where shape drawing requires brushes and pens as helper objects, the process of drawing text requires fonts as helper objects. And understanding fonts is not a trivial task.

❑ Text needs to be very carefully laid out in the window. Users generally expect words to follow naturally from one word to another and to be lined up with clear spaces in between. Doing that is harder than you might think. For starters, you don't usually know in advance how much space on the screen a word is going to take up. That has to be calculated (using the `Graphics.MeasureString()` method). Also, the space a word occupies on the screen affects where in the document every subsequent word is placed. If your application does any line wrapping then it'll need to assess word sizes carefully before deciding where to place the line break. The next time you run Microsoft Word, look carefully at the way Word is continually repositioning text as you do your work: there's a lot of complex processing going on there. Chances are that any GDI+ application you work on won't be nearly as complex as Word. However, if you need to display any text, then many of the same considerations apply.

In short, good quality text processing is tricky to get right. However, putting a line of text on the screen, assuming you know the font and where you want it to go, is actually very simple. Therefore, the next thing we'll do is present a quick example that shows how to display some text, followed by a short review of the principles of fonts and font families and a more realistic (and involved) text-processing example, CapsEditor.

Simple Text Example

This example, DisplayText, is our usual Windows Forms effort. This time we override `OnPaint()` and added member fields as follows:

```
private System.ComponentModel.Container components = null;
private Brush blackBrush = Brushes.Black;
private Brush blueBrush = Brushes.Blue;
private Font haettenschweilerFont = new Font("Haettenschweiler", 12);
private Font boldTimesFont = new Font("Times New Roman", 10, FontStyle.Bold);
private Font italicCourierFont = new Font("Courier", 11, FontStyle.Italic |
    FontStyle.Underline);

protected override void OnPaint(PaintEventArgs e)
{
    base.OnPaint(e);
    Graphics dc = e.Graphics;
    dc.DrawString("This is a groovy string", haettenschweilerFont, blackBrush,
                  10, 10);
    dc.DrawString("This is a groovy string " +
                  "with some very long text that will never fit in the box",
                  boldTimesFont, blueBrush,
                  new Rectangle(new Point(10, 40), new Size(100, 40)));
    dc.DrawString("This is a groovy string", italicCourierFont, blackBrush,
                  new Point(10, 100));
}
```

Figure 20-15 shows the result of running this example.

The example demonstrates the use of the `Graphics.DrawString()` method to draw items of text. The method `DrawString()` comes in a number of overloads, of which we demonstrate three. The different overloads require parameters that indicate the text to be displayed, the font that the string should be drawn in, and the brush that should be used to construct the various lines and curves that make up each character of text. There are a couple of alternatives for the remaining parameters. In general, however, it is possible to specify either a `Point` (or equivalently, two numbers) or a `Rectangle`.

Figure 20-15

If you specify a `Point`, the text will start with its top-left corner at that `Point` and simply stretch out to the right. If you specify a `Rectangle`, then the `Graphics` instance will lay out the string inside that rectangle. If the text doesn't fit within the boundaries of the rectangle, then it'll be cut off (see the fourth line of text in Figure 20-15). Passing a rectangle to `DrawString()` means that the drawing process will take longer, as `DrawString()` will need to figure out where to put line breaks, but the result may look nicer, provided the string fits in the rectangle!

This example also shows a couple of ways of constructing fonts. You always need to include the name of the font, and its size (height). You can also optionally pass in various styles that modify how the text is to be drawn (bold, underline, and so on).

Fonts and Font Families

We all think intuitively that we have a fairly good understanding of fonts; after all we look at them almost all the time. A font describes exactly how each letter should be displayed. Selection of the appropriate font and providing a reasonable variety of fonts within a document are important factors in improving readability.

Oddly, our intuitive understanding usually isn't quite correct. Most people, if asked to name a font, might mention Arial or Times New Roman (if they are Windows users) or Times or Helvetica (if they are Mac OS users). In fact, these are not fonts at all—they are *font families*. The font family tells you in generic terms the visual style of the text and is a key factor in the overall appearance of your application. Most of us will have become used to recognizing the styles of the most common font families, even if we're not consciously aware of it.

An actual *font* would be something like Arial 9-point italic. In other words, the size and other modifications to the text are specified as well as the font family. These modifications might include whether it is **bold**, *italic*, underlined, or displayed in SMALL CAPS or as a $_{subscript}$; this is technically referred to as the *style*, though in some ways the term is misleading, since the visual appearance is determined as much by the font family.

The way the size of the text is measured is by specifying its height. The height is measured in *points*—a traditional unit that represents 1/72 of an inch (0.351 mm). So letters in a 10-point font are roughly 1/7" or 3.5 mm high. However, you won't get seven lines of 10-point text into one inch of vertical screen or paper space, because you need to allow for the spacing between the lines as well.

Strictly speaking, measuring the height isn't quite as simple as that, since there are several different heights that you must consider. For example, there is the height of tall letters like the A or F (this is the measurement that we are referring to when we talk about the height), the additional height occupied by any accents on letters like Å or Ñ (the internal leading), and the extra height below the baseline needed for the tails of letters like y and g (the descent). However, for this chapter we won't worry about that. Once you specify the font family and the main height, these subsidiary heights are determined automatically.

When you're dealing with fonts you might also encounter some other terms that are commonly used to describe certain font families.

❑ **Serif** font families have little tick marks at the ends of many of the lines that make up the characters (these ticks are known as serifs). Times New Roman is a classic example of this.

❑ **Sans serif** font families, by contrast, don't have these ticks. Good examples of sans serif fonts are Arial and Verdana. The lack of tick marks often gives text a blunt, in-your-face appearance, so sans serif fonts are often used for important text.

❑ A **True Type** font family is one that is defined by expressing the shapes of the curves that make up the characters in a precise mathematical manner. This means that that the same definition can be used to calculate how to draw fonts of any size within the family. These days, virtually all the fonts you might use are true type fonts. Some older font families from the days of Windows 3.1 were defined by individually specifying the bitmap for each character separately for each font size, but the use of these fonts is now discouraged.

Microsoft has provided two main classes that we need to deal with when selecting or manipulating fonts. These are:

❑ `System.Drawing.Font`
❑ `System.Drawing.FontFamily`

We have already seen the main use of the `Font` class. When we want to draw text we instantiate an instance of `Font` and pass it to the `DrawString()` method to indicate how the text should be drawn. A `FontFamily` instance is used to represent a family of fonts.

One use of the `FontFamily` class is if you know you want a font of a particular type (Serif, Sans Serif or Monospace), but don't mind which font. The static properties `GenericSerif`, `GenericSansSerif`, and `GenericMonospace` return default fonts that satisfy these criteria:

```
FontFamily sansSerifFont = FontFamily.GenericSansSerif;
```

Generally speaking, however, if you're writing a professional application, you will want to choose your font in a more sophisticated way. Most likely, you will implement your drawing code so that it checks the font families available and selects the appropriate one, perhaps by taking the first available one on a list of preferred fonts. And if you want your application to be very user-friendly, the first choice on the list will probably be the one that the user selected the last time they ran your software. Usually, if you're dealing with the most popular font families, such as Arial and Times New Roman, you'll be safe. However, if you do try to display text using a font that doesn't exist, then the results aren't always predictable and you're quite likely to find that Windows just substitutes the standard system font, which is very easy for the system to draw but it doesn't look very pleasant—and if it does appear in your document it's likely to give the impression of software that is of poor quality.

You can find out what fonts are available on your system using a class called `InstalledFontCollection`, which is in the `System.Drawing.Text` namespace. This class implements a property, `Families`, which is an array of all the fonts that are available to use on your system:

```
InstalledFontCollection insFont = new InstalledFontCollection();
FontFamily [] families = insFont.Families;
foreach (FontFamily family in families)
{

    // do processing with this font family

}
```

Example: Enumerating Font Families

In this section, we will work through a quick example, EnumFontFamilies, which lists all the font families available on the system and illustrates them by displaying the name of each family using an appropriate font (the 10-point regular version of that font family). Figure 20-16 shows the result of running EnumFontFamilies.

Figure 20-16

Of course, the results that you get will depend on the fonts you have installed on your computer.

For this sample we have as usual created a standard C# Windows Application, EnumFontFamilies. We start off by adding an extra namespace to be searched. We will be using the InstalledFontCollection class, which is defined in System.Drawing.Text.

```
using System;
using System.Drawing;
using System.Drawing.Text;
```

We then add the following constant to the Form1 class:

```
private const int margin = 10;
```

margin is the size of the left and top margin between the text and the edge of the document—it stops the text from appearing right at the edge of the client area.

This is designed as a quick-and-easy way of showing off font families; therefore the code is crude and in many instances doesn't do things the way you ought to in a real application. For example, here we hard-code an estimated value for the document size of (200,1500) and set the AutoScrollMinSize property to this value using the Visual Studio .NET Properties window. Normally you would have to examine the text to be displayed to work out the document size. We do that in the next section.

Here is the OnPaint() method:

```
protected override void OnPaint(PaintEventArgs e)
{
    base.OnPaint(e);
    int verticalCoordinate = margin;
    Point topLeftCorner;
    InstalledFontCollection insFont = new InstalledFontCollection();
    FontFamily [] families = insFont.Families;
    e.Graphics.TranslateTransform(AutoScrollPosition.X,
                                  AutoScrollPosition.Y);
    foreach (FontFamily family in families)
    {
        if (family.IsStyleAvailable(FontStyle.Regular))
        {
            Font f = new Font(family.Name, 12);
            topLeftCorner = new Point(margin, verticalCoordinate);
            verticalCoordinate += f.Height;
            e.Graphics.DrawString (family.Name, f,
                                   Brushes.Black, topLeftCorner);
            f.Dispose();
        }
    }
}
```

In this code we start off by using an InstalledFontCollection object to obtain an array that contains details of all the available font families. For each family, we instantiate a 12-point Font. We use a simple constructor for Font—there are many more that allow additional options to be specified. The constructor we've picked takes two parameters, the name of the family and the size of the font:

```
Font f = new Font(family.Name, 12);
```

This constructor builds a font that has the regular style. To be on the safe side, however, we first check that this style is available for each font family before attempting to display anything using that font. This is done using the `FontFamily.IsStyleAvailable()` method. This check is important, because not all fonts are available in all styles:

```
if (family.IsStyleAvailable(FontStyle.Regular))
```

`FontFamily.IsStyleAvailable()` takes one parameter, a `FontStyle` enumeration. This enumeration contains a number of flags that might be combined with the bitwise OR operator. The possible flags are `Bold`, `Italic`, `Regular`, `Strikeout`, and `Underline`.

Finally, note that we use a property of the `Font` class, `Height`, which returns the height needed to display text of that font, in order to work out the line spacing:

```
Font f = new Font(family.Name, 12);
topLeftCorner = new Point(margin, verticalCoordinate);
verticalCoordinate += f.Height;
```

Again, to keep things simple, our version of `OnPaint()` reveals some bad programming practices. For a start, we haven't bothered to check what area of the document actually needs drawing—we just try to display everything. Also, instantiating a `Font` is, as remarked earlier, a computationally intensive process, so we really ought to save the fonts rather than instantiating new copies every time `OnPaint()` is called. As a result of the way the code has been designed, you might note that this example actually takes a noticeable time to paint itself. In order to try to conserve memory and help the garbage collector out we do, however, call `Dispose()` on each font instance after we have finished with it. If we didn't, then after 10 or 20 paint operations, there'd be a lot of wasted memory storing fonts that are no longer needed.

Editing a Text Document: The CapsEditor Sample

We now come to the extended example in this chapter. The CapsEditor example is designed to demonstrate how the principles of drawing that we've learned so far have to be applied in a more realistic context. The CapsEditor example does not require any new material, apart from responding to user input via the mouse, but it shows how to manage the drawing of text so that the application maintains performance while ensuring that the contents of the client area of the main window are always kept up to date.

The CapsEditor program is functionally quite simple. It allows the user to read in a text file, which is then displayed line by line in the client area. If the user double-clicks any line, that line will be changed to all uppercase. That's literally all the sample does. Even with this limited set of features, we'll find that the work involved in making sure everything is displayed in the right place while considering performance issues is quite complex. In particular, we have a new element here: the contents of the document can change—either when the user selects the menu option to read a new file, or when she double-clicks to capitalize a line. In the first case we need to update the document size so the scroll bars still work correctly, and we have to redisplay everything. In the second case, we need to check carefully whether the document size has changed, and what text needs to be redisplayed.

We'll start by reviewing the appearance of CapsEditor. When the application is first run, it has no document loaded and resembles Figure 20-17.

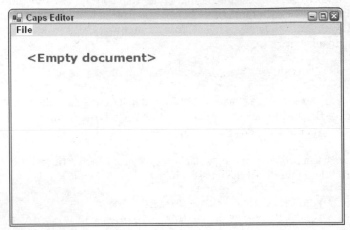

Figure 20-17

The File menu has two options: Open, which evokes `OpenFileDialog` when selected and reads in whatever file the user clicks, and Exit, which closes the application when clicked. Figure 20-18 shows CapsEditor displaying its own source file, Form1.cs. (We've also double-clicked a couple of lines to convert them to uppercase.)

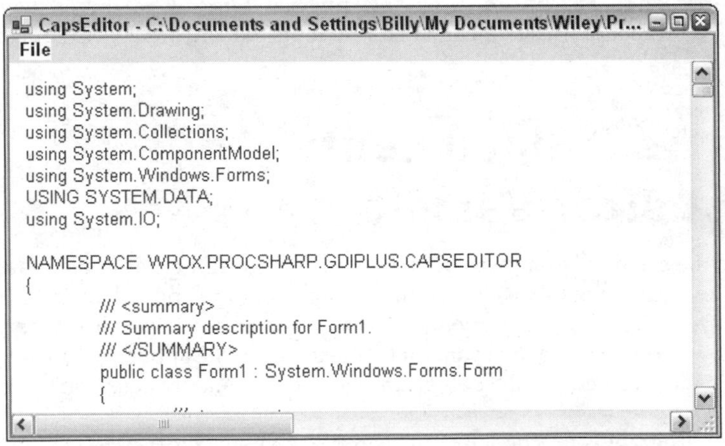

Figure 20-18

The sizes of the horizontal and vertical scrollbars are correct. The client area will scroll just enough to view the entire document. CapsEditor doesn't try to wrap lines of text—the example is already complicated enough as is. It just displays each line of the file exactly as it is read in. There are no limits to the size of the file, but we are assuming it is a text file and doesn't contain any non-printable characters.

Let's begin by adding a `using` command:

```
using System;
using System.Drawing;
using System.Collections;
using System.ComponentModel;
using System.Windows.Forms;
using System.Data;
using System.IO;
```

This is because we'll be using the `StreamReader` class, which is in the `System.IO` namespace. Next we'll add some fields to the `Form1` class:

```
#region Constant fields
private const string standardTitle = "CapsEditor";
                                        // default text in titlebar
private const uint margin = 10;
                        // horizontal and vertical margin in client area
#endregion


#region Member fields
private ArrayList documentLines = new ArrayList();   // the 'document'
private uint lineHeight;        // height in pixels of one line
private Size documentSize;      // how big a client area is needed to
                                // display document
private uint nLines;            // number of lines in document
private Font mainFont;          // font used to display all lines
private Font emptyDocumentFont; // font used to display empty message
private Brush mainBrush = Brushes.Blue;
                                // brush used to display document text
private Brush emptyDocumentBrush = Brushes.Red;
                // brush used to display empty document message
private Point mouseDoubleClickPosition;
        // location mouse is pointing to when double-clicked
private OpenFileDialog fileOpenDialog = new OpenFileDialog();
        // standard open file dialog
private bool documentHasData = false;
        // set to true if document has some data in it
#endregion
```

Most of these fields should be self-explanatory. The `documentLines` field is an `ArrayList` that contains the actual text of the file that has been read in. In a real sense, this is the field that contains the data in the document" Each element of `documentLines` contains information for one line of text that has been read in. Since it's an `ArrayList`, rather than a plain array, we can dynamically add elements to it as we read in a file. Note also that we've used #region preprocessor directives to block bits of the program to make it easier to edit.

As previously mentioned, each `documentLines` element contains information about a line of text. This information is actually an instance of another class, `TextLineInformation`:

```
class TextLineInformation
{
    public string Text;
    public uint Width;
}
```

`TextLineInformation` looks like a classic case where you'd normally use a struct rather than a class since it's just there to group a couple of fields. However, its instances are always accessed as elements of an `ArrayList`, which expects its elements to be stored as reference types, so declaring `TextLineInformation` as a class makes things more efficient by saving a lot of boxing and unboxing operations.

Each `TextLineInformation` instance stores a line of text—and that can be thought of as the smallest item that is displayed as a single item. In general, for each similar item in a GDI+ application, you'd probably want to store the text of the item, as well as the world coordinates of where it should be displayed and its size (the page coordinates will change frequently, whenever the user scrolls, whereas world coordinates will normally only change when other parts of the document are modified in some way). In this case we've only stored the `Width` of the item. The reason is because the height in this case is just the height of whatever our selected font is. It's the same for all lines of text so there's no point storing it separately for each one; we store it once, in the `Form1.lineHeight` field. As for the position... well in this case the x coordinate is just equal to the margin, and the y coordinate is easily calculated as:

```
margin + lineHeight*(however many lines are above this one)
```

If we'd been trying to display and manipulate, say, individual words instead of complete lines, then the x position of each word would have to be calculated using the widths of all the previous words on that line of text, but I wanted to keep it simple here, which is why we're treating each line of text as one single item.

Let's turn to the main menu now. This part of the application is more the realm of Windows Forms (see Chapter 19) than of GDI+. Add the menu options using the design view in Visual Studio .NET, but rename them as `menuFile`, `menuFileOpen`, and `menuFileExit`. Next add event handlers for the File Open and File Exit menu options using the Visual Studio .NET Properties window. The event handlers have their Visual Studio .NET–generated names of `menuFileOpen_Click()` and `menuFileExit_Click()`.

Add some extra initialization code in the `Form1()` constructor:

```
public Form1()
{
    InitializeComponent();

    CreateFonts();
    fileOpenDialog.FileOk += new
        System.ComponentModel.CancelEventHandler(
        this.OpenFileDialog_FileOk);
    fileOpenDialog.Filter =
        "Text files (*.txt)|*.txt|C# source files (*.cs)|*.cs";

}
```

The event handler added here is for when the user clicks OK in the File Open dialog box. We have also set the filter for the Open File dialog box, so that we can only load text files—we've opted for .txt files as well as C# source files, so we can use the application to examine the source code for our samples.

`CreateFonts()` is a helper method that sorts out the fonts we intend to use:

```
private void CreateFonts()
{
   mainFont = new Font("Arial", 10);
   lineHeight = (uint)mainFont.Height;
   emptyDocumentFont = new Font("Verdana", 13, FontStyle.Bold);
}
```

The actual definitions of the handlers are pretty standard stuff:

```
protected void OpenFileDialog_FileOk(object Sender, CancelEventArgs e)
{
   this.LoadFile(fileOpenDialog.FileName);
}

protected void menuFileOpen_Click(object sender, EventArgs e)
{
   fileOpenDialog.ShowDialog();
}

protected void menuFileExit_Click(object sender, EventArgs e)
{
   this.Close();
}
```

Next, we'll examine the `LoadFile()` method. It's the method that handles the opening and reading of a file (as well as ensuring a `Paint` event is raised to force a repaint with the new file):

```
private void LoadFile(string FileName)
{
   StreamReader sr = new StreamReader(FileName);
   string nextLine;
   documentLines.Clear();
   nLines = 0;
   TextLineInformation nextLineInfo;
   while ( (nextLine = sr.ReadLine()) != null)
   {
      nextLineInfo = new TextLineInformation();
      nextLineInfo.Text = nextLine;
      documentLines.Add(nextLineInfo);
      ++nLines;
   }
   sr.Close();
   documentHasData = (nLines>0) ? true : false;

   CalculateLineWidths();
   CalculateDocumentSize();

   this.Text = standardTitle + " - " + FileName;
   this.Invalidate();
}
```

Most of this function is just standard file-reading stuff (see Chapter 30). Note that as the file is read, we progressively add lines to `documentLines ArrayList`, so this array ends up containing information for each of the lines in order. After we've read in the file, we set the `documentHasData` flag, which indicates whether there is actually anything to display. Our next task is to work out where everything is to be displayed, and, having done that, how much client area we need to display the file—the document size that will be used to set the scroll bars. Finally, we set the title bar text and call `Invalidate()`. `Invalidate()` is an important method supplied by Microsoft, so we'll discuss its use first, before we examine the code for the `CalculateLineWidths()` and `CalculateDocumentSize()` methods.

The Invalidate() Method

`Invalidate()` is a member of `System.Windows.Forms.Form`. It marks an area of the client window as invalid and, therefore, in need of repainting, and then makes sure a `Paint` event is raised. There are a couple of overrides to `Invalidate()`: you can pass it a rectangle that specifies (in page coordinates) precisely which area of the window needs repainting, or if you don't pass any parameters it'll just mark the entire client area as invalid.

You might wonder why we are doing it this way. If we know that something needs painting, why don't we just call `OnPaint()` or some other method to do the painting directly? The answer is that in general, calling painting routines directly is regarded as bad programming practice—if your code decides it wants some painting done, you should call `Invalidate()`. Here's why:

❑   Drawing is almost always the most processor-intensive task a GDI+ application will carry out, so doing it in the middle of other work holds up the other work. With our example, if we'd directly called a method to do the drawing from the `LoadFile()` method, then the `LoadFile()` method wouldn't return until that drawing task was complete. During that time, our application can't respond to any other events. On the other hand, by calling `Invalidate()` we are simply getting Windows to raise a `Paint` event before immediately returning from `LoadFile()`. Windows is then free to examine the events that are in line to be handled. How this works internally is that the events sit as what are known as *messages* in a *message queue*. Windows periodically examines the queue, and if there are events in it, it picks one and calls the corresponding event handler. Although the `Paint` event might be the only one sitting in the queue (so `OnPaint()` gets called immediately anyway), in a more complex application there might be other events that ought to get priority over our `Paint` event. In particular, if the user has decided to quit the application, this will be marked by a message known as `WM_QUIT`.

❑   Related to the previous point, if you have a more complicated, multithreaded, application, you'll probably want just one thread to handle all the drawing. Using `Invalidate()` to route all drawing through the message queue provides a good way of ensuring that the same thread (whatever thread is responsible for the message queue, this will be the thread that called `Application.Run()`) does all the drawing, no matter what other thread requested the drawing operation.

❑   There's an additional performance-related reason. Suppose at about the same time a couple of different requests to draw part of the screen come in. Maybe your code has just modified the document and wants to ensure the updated document is displayed, while at the same time the user has just moved another window that was covering part of the client area out of the way. By calling `Invalidate()`, you are giving windows a chance to notice that this has occurred. Windows can then merge the `Paint` events if appropriate, combining the invalidated areas, so that the painting is only done once.

❑ Finally, the code to do the painting is probably going to be one of the most complex parts of the code in your application, especially if you have a very sophisticated user interface. The guys who have to maintain your code in a couple of years time will thank you for having kept your painting code all in one place and as simple as you reasonably can—something that's easier to do if you don't have too many pathways into it from other parts of the program.

The bottom line from all this is that it is good practice to keep all your painting in the OnPaint() routine, or in other methods called from that method. However, you have to strike a balance; if you want to replace just one character on the screen and you know perfectly well that it won't affect anything else that you've drawn, then you might decide that it's not worth the overhead of going through Invalidate(), and just write a separate drawing routine.

In a very complicated application, you might even write a full class that takes responsibility for drawing to the screen. A few years ago when MFC was the standard technology for GDI-intensive applications, MFC followed this model, with a C++ class, C<ApplicationName>View that was responsible for painting. However, even in this case, this class had one member function, OnDraw(), which was designed to be the entry point for most drawing requests.

Calculating Item Sizes and Document Size

We'll return to the CapsEditor example now and examine the CalculateLineWidths() and CalculateDocumentSize() methods that are called from LoadFile():

```
private void CalculateLineWidths()
{
    Graphics dc = this.CreateGraphics();
    foreach (TextLineInformation nextLine in documentLines)
    {
        nextLine.Width = (uint)dc.MeasureString(nextLine.Text,
                                                mainFont).Width;
    }
}
```

This method simply runs through each line that has been read in and uses the Graphics.MeasureString() method to work out and store how much horizontal screen space the string requires. We store the value, because MeasureString() is computationally intensive. If we hadn't made the CapsEditor sample so simple that we can easily work out the height and location of each item, this method would almost certainly have needed to be implemented in such a way as to compute all those quantities too.

Now we know how big each item on the screen is, and we can calculate where each item goes, we are in a position to work out the actual document size. The height is basically the number of lines multiplied by the height of each line. The width will need to be worked out by iterating through the lines to find the longest. For both height and width, we will also want to make an allowance for a small margin around the displayed document, to make the application look more attractive.

Here's the method that calculates the document size:

```
private void CalculateDocumentSize()
{
    if (!documentHasData)
```

```
         {
            documentSize = new Size(100, 200);
         }
         else
         {
            documentSize.Height = (int)(nLines*lineHeight) + 2*(int)margin;
            uint maxLineLength = 0;
            foreach (TextLineInformation nextWord in documentLines)
            {
               uint tempLineLength = nextWord.Width + 2*margin;
               if (tempLineLength > maxLineLength)
                  maxLineLength = tempLineLength;
            }
            documentSize.Width = (int)maxLineLength;
         }
         this.AutoScrollMinSize = documentSize;
      }
```

This method first checks whether there is any data to be displayed. If there isn't we cheat a bit and use a hard-coded document size, which is big enough to display the big red <Empty Document> warning. If we'd wanted to really do it properly, we'd have used MeasureString() to check how big that warning actually is.

Once we've worked out the document size, we tell the Form instance what the size is by setting the Form.AutoScrollMinSize property. When we do this, something interesting happens behind the scenes. In the process of setting this property, the client area is invalidated and a Paint event is raised, for the very sensible reason that changing the size of the document means scroll bars will need to be added or modified and the entire client area will almost certainly be repainted. Why is that interesting? If you look back at the code for LoadFile() you'll realize that our call to Invalidate() in that method is actually redundant. The client area will be invalidated anyway when we set the document size. I left the explicit call to Invalidate() in the LoadFile() implementation to illustrate how in general you should normally do things. In fact in this case, all calling Invalidate() again will do is needlessly request a duplicate Paint event. However, this in turn illustrates what I was saying about how Invalidate() gives Windows the chance to optimize performance. The second Paint event won't in fact get raised: Windows will see that there's a Paint event already sitting in the queue and will compare the requested invalidated regions to see if it needs to do anything to merge them. In this case, both Paint events will specify the entire client area, so nothing needs to be done, and Windows will quietly drop the second Paint request. Of course, going through that process will take up a little bit of processor time, but it'll be a negligible amount of time compared to how long it takes to actually do some painting.

OnPaint()

Now we've seen how CapsEditor loads the file, it's time to look at how the painting is done:

```
      protected override void OnPaint(PaintEventArgs e)
      {
         base.OnPaint(e);
         Graphics dc = e.Graphics;
         int scrollPositionX = this.AutoScrollPosition.X;
         int scrollPositionY = this.AutoScrollPosition.Y;
         dc.TranslateTransform(scrollPositionX, scrollPositionY);
```

```
        if (!documentHasData)
        {
            dc.DrawString("<Empty document>", emptyDocumentFont,
                emptyDocumentBrush, new Point(20,20));
            base.OnPaint(e);
            return;
        }

        // work out which lines are in clipping rectangle
        int minLineInClipRegion =
                    WorldYCoordinateToLineIndex(e.ClipRectangle.Top -
                                            scrollPositionY);
        if (minLineInClipRegion == -1)
            minLineInClipRegion = 0;
        int maxLineInClipRegion =
                    WorldYCoordinateToLineIndex(e.ClipRectangle.Bottom -
                                            scrollPositionY);
        if (maxLineInClipRegion >= this.documentLines.Count ||
            maxLineInClipRegion == -1)
        maxLineInClipRegion = this.documentLines.Count-1;

        TextLineInformation nextLine;
        for (int i=minLineInClipRegion; i<=maxLineInClipRegion ; i++)
        {
            nextLine = (TextLineInformation)documentLines[i];
            dc.DrawString(nextLine.Text, mainFont, mainBrush,
                            this.LineIndexToWorldCoordinates(i));
        }
    }
}
```

At the heart of this `OnPaint()` override is a loop that goes through each line of the document, calling `Graphics.DrawString()` to paint each one. The rest of this code is mostly to do with optimizing the painting—the usual stuff about figuring out what exactly needs painting instead of rushing in and telling the graphics instance to redraw everything.

We begin by checking if there is any data in the document. If there isn't, we draw a quick message saying so, call the base class's `OnPaint()` implementation, and exit. If there is data, then we start looking at the clipping rectangle. The way we do this is by calling another method that we've written, `WorldYCoordinateToLineIndex()`. We'll examine this method next, but essentially it takes a given y position relative to the top of the document, and works out what line of the document is being displayed at that point.

The first time we call the `WorldYCoordinateToLineIndex()` method, we pass it the coordinate value `(e.ClipRectangle.Top - scrollPositionY)`. This is just the top of the clipping region, converted to world coordinates. If the return value is –1, then we'll play safe and assume we need to start at the beginning of the document (this is the case if the top of the clipping region is within the top margin).

Once we've done all that, we essentially repeat the same process for the bottom of the clipping rectangle, in order to find the last line of the document that is inside the clipping region. The indices of the first and last lines are respectively stored in `minLineInClipRegion` and `maxLineInClipRegion`, so then we can just run a `for` loop between these values to do our painting. Inside the painting loop, we actually need to do roughly the reverse transformation to the one performed by `WorldYCoordinateToLineIndex()`. We are given the index of a line of text, and we need to check where it should be drawn. This calculation is actually quite simple, but we've wrapped it up in another method, `LineIndexToWorldCoordinates()`, which returns the required coordinates of the top left corner of the item. The returned coordinates are world coordinates, but that's fine, because we have already called `TranslateTransform()` on the `Graphics` object so that we need to pass it world, rather than page, coordinates when asking it to display items.

Coordinate Transforms

In this section, we'll examine the implementation of the helper methods that we've written in the CapsEditor sample to help us with coordinate transforms. These are the `WorldYCoordinateToLineIndex()` and `LineIndexToWorldCoordinates()` methods that we referred to in the previous section, as well as a couple of other methods.

First, `LineIndexToWorldCoordinates()` takes a given line index, and works out the world coordinates of the top left corner of that line, using the known margin and line height:

```
private Point LineIndexToWorldCoordinates(int index)
{
    Point TopLeftCorner = new Point(
        (int)margin, (int)(lineHeight*index + margin));
    return TopLeftCorner;
}
```

We also use a method that roughly does the reverse transform in `OnPaint()`. `WorldYCoordinateToLineIndex()` works out the line index, but it only takes into account a vertical world coordinate. This is because it is used to work out the line index corresponding to the top and bottom of the clip region.

```
private int WorldYCoordinateToLineIndex(int y)
{
    if (y < margin)
        return -1;
    return (int)((y-margin)/lineHeight);
}
```

There are three more methods, which will be called from the handler routine that responds to the user double-clicking the mouse. First, we have a method that works out the index of the line being displayed at given world coordinates. Unlike `WorldYCoordinateToLineIndex()`, this method takes into account the x and y positions of the coordinates. It returns –1 if there is no line of text covering the coordinates passed in:

```
private int WorldCoordinatesToLineIndex(Point position)
{
    if (!documentHasData)
        return -1;
    if (position.Y < margin || position.X < margin)
        return -1;
    int index = (int)(position.Y-margin)/(int)this.lineHeight;
    // check position isn't below document
    if (index >= documentLines.Count)
        return -1;
```

```
                  // now check that horizontal position is within this line
                  TextLineInformation theLine =
                                      (TextLineInformation)documentLines[index];
                  if (position.X > margin + theLine.Width)
                     return -1;

                  // all is OK. We can return answer
                  return index;
               }
```

Finally, on occasions we also need to convert between line index and page, rather than world, coordinates. The following methods achieve this:

```
               private Point LineIndexToPageCoordinates(int index)
               {
                  return LineIndexToWorldCoordinates(index) +
                                              new Size(AutoScrollPosition);
               }

               private int PageCoordinatesToLineIndex(Point position)
               {
                  return WorldCoordinatesToLineIndex(position - new
                                              Size(AutoScrollPosition));
               }
```

Note that when converting *to* page coordinates, we add the AutoScrollPosition, which is negative.

Although these methods by themselves don't look particularly interesting, they do illustrate a general technique that you'll probably need to use often. With GDI+, we'll often find ourselves in a situation where we have been given specific coordinates (for example the coordinates of where the user has clicked the mouse) and we'll need to figure out what item is being displayed at that point. Or it could happen the other way round—given a particular display item, whereabouts should it be displayed? Hence, if you are writing a GDI+ application, you'll probably find it useful to write methods that do the equivalent of the coordinate transformation methods illustrated here.

Responding to User Input

So far, with the exception of the File menu in the CapsEditor sample, everything we've done in this chapter has been one way: the application has talked to the user, by displaying information on the screen. Almost all software of course works both ways: the user can talk to the software as well. We're now going to add that facility to CapsEditor.

Getting a GDI+ application to respond to user input is actually a lot simpler than writing the code to draw to the screen (we have already covered how to handle user input in Chapter 19). Essentially, you override methods from the Form class that get called from the relevant event handler, in much the same way that OnPaint() is called when a Paint event is raised.

The following table lists the methods you might want to override when the user clicks or moves the mouse.

Method	Called when...
OnClick(EventArgs e)	Mouse is clicked.
OnDoubleClick(EventArgs e)	Mouse is double-clicked.
OnMouseDown(MouseEventArgs e)	Left mouse button pressed.
OnMouseHover(MouseEventArgs e)	Mouse stays still somewhere after moving.
OnMouseMove(MouseEventArgs e)	Mouse is moved.
OnMouseUp(MouseEventArgs e)	Left mouse button is released.

If you want to detect when the user types in any text, then you'll probably want to override the methods listed in the following table.

Method	Called When...
OnKeyDown(KeyEventArgs e)	A key is pressed.
OnKeyPress(KeyPressEventArgs e)	A key is pressed and released.
OnKeyUp(KeyEventArgs e)	A pressed key is released.

Note that some of these events overlap. For example, if the user presses a mouse button this will raise the MouseDown event. If the button is immediately released again, this will raise the MouseUp event and the Click event. Also, some of these methods take an argument that is derived from EventArgs rather than an instance of EventArgs itself. These instances of derived classes can be used to give more information about a particular event. MouseEventArgs has two properties X and Y, which give the device coordinates of the mouse at the time it was pressed. Both KeyEventArgs and KeyPressEventArgs have properties that indicate which key or keys the event concerns.

That's all there is to it. It's up to you to think about the logic of precisely what you want to do. The only point to note is that you'll probably find yourself doing a bit more logic work with a GDI+ application than you would have with a Windows.Forms application. That's because in a Windows.Forms application you are typically responding to high-level events (TextChanged for a text box, for example). By contrast with GDI+, the events tend to be more elementary—user clicks the mouse or presses the H key. The action your application takes is likely to depend on a sequence of events rather than a single event. For example, say your application works like Word for Windows, where in order to select some text the user clicks the left mouse button, then moves the mouse and releases the left mouse button. Your application receives the MouseDown event, but there's not much you can do with this event except record that the mouse was clicked with the cursor in a certain position. Then, when the MouseMove event is received, you'll want to check from the record whether the left button is currently down, and if so highlight text as the user selects it. When the user releases the left mouse button, your corresponding action (in the OnMouseUp() method) will need to check whether any dragging took place while the mouse button was down, and act accordingly. Only at this point is the sequence complete.

Another point to consider is that, because certain events overlap, you will often have a choice of which event you want your code to respond to.

The golden rule really is to think carefully about the logic of every combination of mouse movement or click and keyboard event that the user might initiate, and ensure that your application responds in a way that is intuitive and in accordance with the expected behavior of applications in *every* case. Most of your work here will be in thinking rather than in coding, though the coding you do will be tricky, because you might need to take into account a lot of combinations of user input. For example, what should your application do if the user starts typing in text while one of the mouse buttons is held down? It might sound like an improbable combination, but sooner or later some user is going to try it!

For the CapsEditor example, we are keeping things very simple, so we don't really have any combinations to think about. The only thing we are going to respond to is when the user double-clicks, in which case we capitalize whatever line of text the mouse pointer is hovering over.

This should be a fairly simple task, but there is one snag. We need to trap the DoubleClick event, but the previous table shows that this event takes an EventArgs parameter, not a MouseEventArgs parameter. The trouble is that we'll need to know where the mouse is when the user double-clicks, if we are to identify correctly the line of text to be capitalized—and you need a MouseEventArgs parameter to do that. There are two workarounds. One is to use a static method that is implemented by the Form1 object, Control.MousePosition, to find out the mouse position:

```
protected override void OnDoubleClick(EventArgs e)
{
    Point MouseLocation = Control.MousePosition;
    // handle double click
}
```

In most cases this will work. However, there could be a problem if your application (or even some other application with a high priority) is doing some computationally intensive work at the moment the user double-clicks. It just might happen in that case that the OnDoubleClick() event handler doesn't get called until perhaps half a second or so *after* the user has double-clicked. You don't really want delays like that, because they usually annoy users intensely, but even so, occasionally it does happen, and sometimes for reasons beyond the control of your app (a slow computer, for instance). Trouble is, half a second is easily enough time for the mouse to get moved halfway across the screen, in which case your call to Control.MousePosition will return the completely wrong location!

A better way here is to rely on one of the many overlaps between mouse-event meanings. The first part of double-clicking a mouse involves pressing the left button down. This means that if OnDoubleClick() is called then we know that OnMouseDown() has also just been called, with the mouse at the same location. We can use the OnMouseDown() override to record the position of the mouse, ready for OnDoubleClick(). This is the approach we take in CapsEditor:

```
protected override void OnMouseDown(MouseEventArgs e)
{
    base.OnMouseDown(e);
    this.mouseDoubleClickPosition = new Point(e.X, e.Y);
}
```

Now let's look at our OnDoubleClick() override. There's quite a bit more work to do here:

```
protected override void OnDoubleClick(EventArgs e)
{
    int i = PageCoordinatesToLineIndex(this.mouseDoubleClickPosition);
```

```
              if (i >= 0)
              {
                  TextLineInformation lineToBeChanged =
                                    (TextLineInformation)documentLines[i];
                  lineToBeChanged.Text = lineToBeChanged.Text.ToUpper();
                  Graphics dc = this.CreateGraphics();
                  uint newWidth =(uint)dc.MeasureString(lineToBeChanged.Text,
                                                  mainFont).Width;
                  if (newWidth > lineToBeChanged.Width)
                      lineToBeChanged.Width = newWidth;
                  if (newWidth+2*margin > this.documentSize.Width)
                  {
                      this.documentSize.Width = (int)newWidth;
                      this.AutoScrollMinSize = this.documentSize;
                  }
                  Rectangle changedRectangle = new Rectangle(
                                          LineIndexToPageCoordinates(i),
                                          new Size((int)newWidth,
                                          (int)this.lineHeight));
                  this.Invalidate(changedRectangle);
              }
              base.OnDoubleClick(e);
      }
```

We start off by calling `PageCoordinatesToLineIndex()` to work out which line of text the mouse pointer was hovering over when the user double-clicked. If this call returns –1 then we weren't over any text, so there's nothing to do; except, of course, call the base class version of `OnDoubleClick()` to let Windows do any default processing.

Assuming we've identified a line of text, we can use the `string.ToUpper()` method to convert it to uppercase. That was the easy part. The hard part is figuring out what needs to be redrawn where. Fortunately, because we kept this example simple, there aren't too many combinations. We can assume for a start, that converting to uppercase will always either leave the width of the line on the screen unchanged or increase it. Capital letters are bigger than lowercase letters; therefore, the width will never go down. We also know that since we are not wrapping lines, our line of text won't overflow to the next line and push out other text below. Our action of converting the line to uppercase won't, therefore, actually change the locations of any of the other items being displayed. That's a big simplification!

The next thing the code does is use `Graphics.MeasureString()` to work out the new width of the text. There are now just two possibilities:

❏   The new width might make our line the longest line, and cause the width of the entire document to increase. If that's the case then we'll need to set `AutoScrollMinSize` to the new size so that the scrollbars are correctly placed.

❏   The size of the document might be unchanged.

In either case, we need to get the screen redrawn, by calling `Invalidate()`. Only one line has changed; therefore, we don't want to have the entire document repainted. Rather, we need to work out the bounds of a rectangle that contains just the modified line, so that we can pass this rectangle to `Invalidate()`, ensuring that just that line of text will be repainted. That's precisely what the previous code does. Our call to `Invalidate()` initiates a call to `OnPaint()` when the mouse event handler finally returns.

Keeping in mind our earlier comments about the difficulty in setting a break point in OnPaint(), if you run the sample and set a break point in OnPaint() to trap the resultant painting action, you'll find that the PaintEventArgs parameter to OnPaint() does indeed contain a clipping region that matches the specified rectangle. And since we've overloaded OnPaint() to take careful account of the clipping region, only the one required line of text will be repainted.

Printing

So far we've focused exclusively on drawing to the screen. However, at some point you will probably also want to be able to produce a hard copy of the data. That's the topic of this section. We're going to extend the CapsEditor sample so that it is able to print preview and print the document that is being edited.

Unfortunately, we don't have enough space to go into too much detail about printing here, so the printing functionality we will implement is very basic. Usually, if you are implementing the ability for an application to print data, you will need to add three items to the application's main File menu:

❑ Page Setup, which allows the user to choose options such as which pages to print, which printer to use and so on.

❑ Print Preview, which opens a new Form that displays a mock-up of what the printed copy should look like.

❑ Print, which prints the document.

In our case, to keep things simple, we won't implement a Page Setup menu option. Printing will only be possible using default settings. Note, however, that, if you do want to implement Page Setup, Microsoft has already written a page setup dialog class for you to use: System.Windows.Forms.PrintDialog. You will normally want to write an event handler that displays this form, and saves the settings chosen by the user.

In many ways printing is just the same as displaying to a screen. You will be supplied with a device context (Graphics instance) and call all the usual display commands against that instance. Microsoft has written a number of classes to assist you in doing this; the two main ones that we need to use are System.Drawing.Printing.PrintDocument and System.Drawing.Printing.PrintPreview-Dialog. These two classes handle the process of making sure that drawing instructions passed to a device context are handled appropriately for printing, leaving you to think about the logic of what to print where.

There are some important differences between printing or print previewing on the one hand, and displaying to the screen on the other hand. Printers cannot scroll; instead they turn out pages. So you'll need to make sure you find a sensible way of dividing your document into pages, and draw each page as requested. Among other things that means calculating how much of your document will fit onto a single page, and therefore how many pages you'll need, and which page each part of the document needs to be written to.

Despite the above complications, the process of printing is quite simple. Programmatically, the steps you need to go through look roughly like this:

❑ **Printing**. You instantiate a `PrintDocument` object, and call its `Print()` method. This method signals the `PrintPage` eventto print the first page. `PrintPage` takes a `PrintPageEventArgs` parameter, which supplies information concerning paper size and setup, as well as a `Graphics` object used for the drawing commands. You should therefore have written an event handler for this event, and have implemented this handler to print a page. This event handler should also set a Boolean property of the `PrintPageEventArgs`, `HasMorePages`, to either `true` or `false` to indicate whether there are more pages to be printed. The `PrintDocument.Print()` method will repeatedly raise the `PrintPage` event until it sees that `HasMorePages` has been set to `false`.

❑ **Print Previewing**. In this case, you instantiate both a `PrintDocument` object and a `Print-PreviewDialog` object. You attach the `PrintDocument` to the `PrintPreviewDialog` (using the property `PrintPreviewDialog.Document`) and then call the dialog's `ShowDialog()` method. This method modally displays the dialog, which turns out to be a standard Windows print preview form, and which displays pages of the document. Internally, the pages are displayed once again by repeatedly raising the `PrintPage` event until the `HasMorePages` property is `false`. There's no need to write a separate event handler for this; you can use the same event handler as used for printing each page since the drawing code ought to be identical in both cases. (After all, whatever is print previewed ought to look identical to the printed version!)

Implementing Print and Print Preview

Now that we've outlined this process in broad strokes, let's see how this works in code terms. You can download the code as the PrintingCapsEdit project at www.wrox.com; it consists of the CapsEditor project, with the changes highlighted in the following snippet.

We begin by using the Visual Studio .NET design view to add two new items to the `File` menu: Print and Print Preview. We also use the properties window to name these items `menuFilePrint` and `menuFilePrintPreview`, and to set them to be disabled when the application starts up (we can't print anything until a document has been opened!). We arrange for these menu items to be enabled by adding the following code to the main form's `LoadFile()` method, which is responsible for loading a file into the CapsEditor application:

```
private void LoadFile(string FileName)
{
    StreamReader sr = new StreamReader(FileName);
    string nextLine;
    documentLines.Clear();
    nLines = 0;
    TextLineInformation nextLineInfo;
    while ( (nextLine = sr.ReadLine()) != null)
    {
        nextLineInfo = new TextLineInformation();
        nextLineInfo.Text = nextLine;
        documentLines.Add(nextLineInfo);
        ++nLines;
    }
    sr.Close();
    if (nLines > 0)
    {
        documentHasData = true;
        menuFilePrint.Enabled = true;
        menuFilePrintPreview.Enabled = true;
```

```
      }
      else
      {
         documentHasData = false;
         menuFilePrint.Enabled = false;
         menuFilePrintPreview.Enabled = false;
      }

   CalculateLineWidths();
   CalculateDocumentSize();

   this.Text = standardTitle + " - " + FileName;
   this.Invalidate();
}
```

The highlighted code above is the new code we have added to this method. Next we add a member field to the Form1 class:

```
public class Form1 : System.Windows.Forms.Form
{
   private int pagesPrinted = 0;
```

This field will be used to indicate which page we are currently printing. We are making it a member field, since we will need to remember this information between calls to the PrintPage event handler.

Next, the event handlers that handle the selection of the Print or Print Preview menu options:

```
private void menuFilePrintPreview_Click(object sender, System.EventArgs e)
{
   this.pagesPrinted = 0;
   PrintPreviewDialog ppd = new PrintPreviewDialog();
   PrintDocument pd = new PrintDocument();
   pd.PrintPage += new PrintPageEventHandler
      (this.pd_PrintPage);
   ppd.Document = pd;
   ppd.ShowDialog();
}

private void menuFilePrint_Click(object sender, System.EventArgs e)
{
   this.pagesPrinted = 0;
   PrintDocument pd = new PrintDocument();
   pd.PrintPage += new PrintPageEventHandler
      (this.pd_PrintPage);
   pd.Print();
}
```

We've already outlined the steps involved in printing, and we can see that these event handlers are simply implementing that procedure. In both cases we are instantiating a PrintDocument object and attaching an event handler to its PrintPage event. In the case of printing, we call PrintDocument.Print(), while for print previewing, we attach the PrintDocument object to a PrintPreviewDialog and call the preview dialog box object's ShowDialog() method. The real work to the PrintPage event is done in the event handler. Here is what this handler looks like:

```csharp
private void pd_PrintPage(object sender, PrintPageEventArgs e)
{
   float yPos = 0;
   float leftMargin = e.MarginBounds.Left;
   float topMargin = e.MarginBounds.Top;
   string line = null;

   // Calculate the number of lines per page.
   int linesPerPage = (int)(e.MarginBounds.Height /
      mainFont.GetHeight(e.Graphics));
   int lineNo = this.pagesPrinted * linesPerPage;

   // Print each line of the file.
   int count = 0;
   while(count < linesPerPage && lineNo < this.nLines)
   {
      line = ((TextLineInformation)this.documentLines[lineNo]).Text;
      yPos = topMargin + (count * mainFont.GetHeight(e.Graphics));
      e.Graphics.DrawString(line, mainFont, Brushes.Blue,
         leftMargin, yPos, new StringFormat());
      lineNo++;
      count++;
   }

   // If more lines exist, print another page.
   if(this.nLines > lineNo)
      e.HasMorePages = true;
   else
      e.HasMorePages = false;
   pagesPrinted++;
}
```

After declaring a couple of local variables, the first thing we do is work out how many lines of text can be displayed on one page, which will be the height of a page divided by the height of a line and rounded down. The height of the page can be obtained from the PrintPageEventArgs.MarginBounds property. This property is a RectangleF struct that has been initialized to give the bounds of the page. The height of a line is obtained from the Form1.mainFont field, which is the font used for displaying the text. There is no reason here for not using the same font for printing too. Note that for the PrintingCapsEditor sample, the number of lines per page is always the same, so we arguably could have cached the value the first time we calculated it. However, the calculation isn't too hard, and in a more sophisticated application the value might change, so it's not bad practice to recalculate it every time we print a page.

We also initialize a variable called lineNo. This gives the zero-based index of the line of the document that will be the first line of this page. This information is important because in principle, the pd_PrintPage() method could have been called to print any page, not just the first page. lineNo is computed as the number of lines per page times the number of pages that have so far been printed.

Next we run through a loop, printing each line. This loop will terminate either when we find that we have printed all the lines of text in the document, or when we find that we have printed all the lines that will fit on this page, whichever condition occurs first. Finally, we check whether there is any more of the document to be printed, and set the `HasMorePages` property of our `PrintPageEventArgs` accordingly, and also increment the `pagesPrinted` field, so that we know to print the correct page the next time the `PrintPage` event handler is invoked.

One point to note about this event handler is that we do not worry about where the drawing commands are being sent. We simply use the `Graphics` object that was supplied with the `PrintPageEventArgs`. The `PrintDocument` class that Microsoft has written will internally take care of making sure that, if we are printing, the `Graphics` object will have been hooked up to the printer; if we are print previewing, then the `Graphics` object will have been hooked up to the print preview form on the screen.

Finally, we need to ensure the `System.Drawing.Printing` namespace is searched for type definitions:

```
using System;
using System.Drawing;
using System.Drawing.Printing;
using System.Collections;
using System.ComponentModel;
using System.Windows.Forms;
using System.Data;
using System.IO;
```

All that remains is to compile the project and check that the code works. Figure 20-19 shows what happens when you run CapsEdit, load a text document (as before, we've picked the C# source file for the project), and select Print Preview.

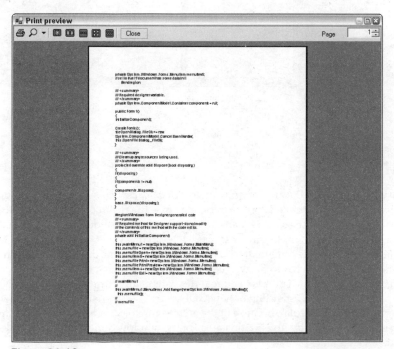

Figure 20-19

In Figure 20-19, we have scrolled to page 5 of the document, and set the preview to display normal size. The `PrintPreviewDialog` has supplied quite a lot of features for us, as you can see by looking at the toolbar at the top of the form. The options available include printing the document, zooming in or out, and displaying two, three, four, or six pages together. These options are all fully functional, without our having to do any work. Figure 20-20 shows the result of changing the zoom to auto and clicking to display four pages (third toolbar button from the right).

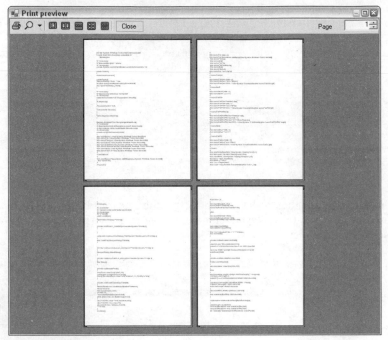

Figure 20-20

Summary

In this chapter, we've covered the area of drawing to a display device, where the drawing is done by your code rather than by some predefined control or dialog box—the realm of GDI+. GDI+ is a powerful tool, and there are many .NET base classes available to help you draw to a device. We've seen that the process of drawing is actually relatively simple—in most cases you can draw text or sophisticated figures or display images with just a couple of C# statements. However, managing your drawing—the behind-the-scenes work involving working out what to draw, where to draw it, and what does or doesn't need repainting in any given situation—is far more complex and requires careful algorithm design. For this reason, it is also important to have a good understanding of how GDI+ works, and what actions Windows takes in order to get something drawn. In particular, because of the architecture of Windows, it is important that where possible drawing should be done by invalidating areas of the window and relying on Windows to respond by issuing a `Paint` event.

There are many more .NET classes for drawing than we've had space to cover in this chapter. However, if you've worked through it and understood the principles involved in drawing, you'll be in an excellent position to explore them by looking at their lists of methods in the SDK documentation and instantiating instances of them to see what they do. In the end, drawing, like almost any other aspect of programming, requires logic, careful thought, and clear algorithms if you want to go beyond the standard controls. Your software will benefit in both user-friendliness and visual appearance if it is well thought out. There are many applications out there that rely entirely on controls for their user interface. While this can be effective, such applications very quickly end up resembling each other. By adding some GDI+ code to do some custom drawing you can mark out your software as distinct and make it appear more original, which can only help increase your sales!

Part IV: Data

21

Data Access with .NET

This chapter discusses how to get at data from your C# programs using ADO.NET and covers the following details:

- ❑ Connecting to the database—We explain how to use the new `SqlConnection` and `OleDbConnection` classes to connect to and disconnect from the database.

- ❑ Executing commands—ADO.NET has command objects, which can execute SQL commands or issue a stored procedure with return values. We discuss the various command object options and show how commands can be used for each of the options presented by the `Sql` and `OleDB` classes.

- ❑ Stored procedures—We detail how to call stored procedures with command objects, and how the results of those stored procedures can be integrated into the data cached on the client.

- ❑ The ADO.NET object model—This is significantly different from the objects available with ADO, and we discuss the `DataSet`, `DataTable`, `DataRow`, and `DataColumn` classes as well as the relationships between tables and constraints that are part of `DataSet`.

- ❑ Using XML and XML schemas—We examine the XML framework on which ADO.NET is built.

As is the case with the other chapters, you can download the code for the examples used in this chapter from the Wrox Web site at www.wrox.com. Let's begin with a brief tour of ADO.NET.

ADO.NET Overview

ADO.NET is more than just a thin veneer over some existing API. The similarity to ADO is fairly minimal—the classes and methods of accessing data are completely different.

ADO (ActiveX Data Objects) is a library of COM components that has had many incarnations over the last few years. Currently at version 2.7, ADO consists primarily of the Connection, Command, Recordset, and Field objects. Using ADO, a connection is opened to the database, some data is selected into a record set consisting of fields, that data is then manipulated and updated on the server, and the connection isclosed. ADO also introduced a so-called disconnected record set, which is used when keeping the connection open for long periods of time is not desirable.

There were several problems that ADO did not address satisfactorily, most notably the unwieldiness (in physical size) of a disconnected recordset. This support was more necessary than ever with the evolution of Web-centric computing, so a fresh approach was required. There are a number of similarities between ADO.NET programming and ADO (not only the name), so upgrading from ADO shouldn't be too difficult. What's more, if you're using SQL Server, there's a fantastic new set of managed classes that are tuned to squeeze maximum performance out of the database. This alone should be reason enough to migrate to ADO.NET.

ADO.NET ships with four database client namespaces: one for SQL Server, another for Oracle, the third for ODBC datasources, and the fourth for any database exposed through OLEDB. If your database of choice is not SQL Server or Oracle then the OLEDB route should be taken unless you have no other choice than to use ODBC.

Namespaces

All of the examples in this chapter access data in one way or another. The following namespaces expose the classes and interfaces used in .NET data access:

❑   System.Data—All generic data access classes

❑   System.Data.Common—Classes shared (or overridden) by individual data providers

❑   System.Data.Odbc—ODBC provider classes

❑   System.Data.OleDb—OLE DB provider classes

❑   System.Data.Oracle—Oracle provider classes

❑   System.Data.SqlClient—SQL Server provider classes

❑   System.Data.SqlTypes—SQL Server data types

The main classes in ADO.NET are listed in the following subsections.

Shared Classes

ADO.NET contains a number of classes that are used regardless of whether you are using the SQL Server classes or the OLE DB classes.

The following classes are contained in the System.Data namespace:

❑   DataSet—This object is designed for disconnected use and can contain a set of DataTables and include relationships between these tables.

❑   DataTable—A container of data that consists of one or more DataColumns and, when populated, will have one or more DataRows containing data.

❑   DataRow—A number of values, akin to a row from a database table, or a row from a spreadsheet.

❑   DataColumn—This object contains the definition of a column, such as the name and data type.

❑   DataRelation—A link between two DataTable classes within a DataSet class. Used for foreign key and master/detail relationships.

❑   Constraint—This class defines a rule for a DataColumn class (or set of data columns), such as unique values.

The following classes can be found in the System.Data.Common namespace:

❑   DataColumnMapping—Maps the name of a column from the database with the name of a column within a DataTable.

❑   DataTableMapping—Maps a table name from the database to a DataTable within a DataSet.

Database-Specific Classes

In addition to the shared classes introduced in the previous section, ADO.NET contains a number of database-specific classes. These classes implement a set of standard interfaces defined within the System.Data namespace, allowing the classes to be used in a generic manner if necessary. For example, both the SqlConnection and OleDbConnection classes implement the IDbConnection interface.

❑   SqlCommand, OleDbCommand, OracleCommand, and ODBCCommand—Used as wrappers for SQL statements or stored procedure calls.

❑   SqlCommandBuilder, OleDbCommandBuilder, OracleCommandBuilder, and ODBCCommandBuilder—Used to generate SQL commands (such as INSERT, UPDATE, and DELETE statements) from a SELECT statement.

❑   SqlConnection, OleDbConnection, OracleConnection, ODBCConnection—Used to connect to the database. Similar to an ADO Connection.

❑   SqlDataAdapter, OleDbDataAdapter, OracleDataAdapter, ODBCDataAdapter—Used to hold select, insert, update, and delete commands, which are then used to populate a DataSet and update the Database.

❑   SqlDataReader, OleDbDataReader, OracleDataReader, ODBCDataReader—Used as a forward only, connected data reader.

❑   SqlParameter, OleDbParameter, OracleParameter, ODBCParameter—Used to define a parameter to a stored procedure.

❑   SqlTransaction, OleDbTransaction, OracleTransaction, ODBCTransaction—Used for a database transaction, wrapped in an object.

As can be seen from the previous list, there are four classes for each type of object—one for each of the providers that are part of .NET version 1.1. In the rest of this chapter, unless otherwise stated, the prefix <provider> is used to indicate that the particular class used is dependant on the database provider in use.

The most important new feature of the ADO.NET classes is that they are designed to work in a disconnected manner, which is important in today's highly Web-centric world. It is now common practice to architect a service (such as an online bookshop) to connect to a server, retrieve some data, and then work on that data on the client before reconnecting and passing the data back for processing. The disconnected nature of ADO.NET enables this type of behavior.

ADO 2.1 introduced the disconnected record set, which would permit data to be retrieved from a database, passed to the client for processing, and then reattached to the server. This used to be cumbersome to use, because disconnected behavior was not part of the original design. The ADO.NET classes are different—in all but one case (the <provider>`DataReader`) they are designed for use offline from the database.

The classes and interfaces used for data access in.NET Framework are introduced in the course of this chapter. The focus is mainly on the SQL classes when connecting to the database, because the Framework SDK samples install an MSDE database (SQL Server). In most cases the OleDb, Oracle and ODBC classes mimic exactly the SQL code.

Using Database Connections

In order to access the database, you need to provide connection parameters, such as the machine that the database is running on, and possibly your login credentials. Anyone who has worked with ADO will be familiar with the .NET connection classes, `OleDbConnection` and `SqlConnection`. Figure 21-1 shows the connection classes and the interfaces they support.

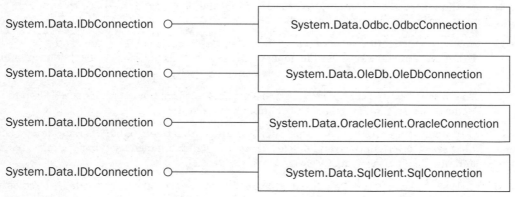

Figure 21-1

The examples in this chapter use the Northwind database, which is installed with the .NET Framework SDK samples. The following code snippet illustrates how to create, open, and close a connection to the Northwind database:

```
using System.Data.SqlClient;

string source = "server=(local)\\NetSDK;" +
                "integrated security=SSPI;" +
                "database=Northwind";
SqlConnection conn = new SqlConnection(source);
conn.Open();
```

```
    // Do something useful

    conn.Close();
```

The connection string should be very familiar to you if you've used ADO or OLE DB before—indeed, you should be able to cut and paste from your old code if you use the `OleDb` provider. In the example connection string, the parameters used are as follows (the parameters are delimited by a semicolon in the connection string):

❑ `server=(local)\\NetSDK`—This denotes the database server to connect to. SQL Server permits a number of separate database server processes to be running on the same machine, so here we're connecting to the `NetSDK` processes on the local machine.

❑ `integrated security=SSPI`—This uses Windows Authentication to connect to the database, which is highly recommended over using a username and password within the source code.

❑ `database=Northwind`—This describes the database instance to connect to; each SQL Server process can expose several database instances.

The example opens a database connection using the defined connection string and then closes that connection. Once the connection has been opened, you can issue commands against the data source, and when you're finished, the connection can be closed.

SQL Server has another mode of authentication—it can use Windows-integrated security, so that the credentials supplied at logon are passed to SQL Server. This is accomplished by removing the `uid` and `pwd` portions of the connection string, and adding in `Integrated Security=SSPI`.

In the download code available for this chapter, you will find the file Login.cs that simplifies the examples in this chapter. It is linked to all the example code, and includes database connection information used for the examples; you can alter this to supply your own server name, user, and password as appropriate. This by default uses Windows-integrated security; however, you can change the username and password as appropriate.

The following subsections provide some best practices using ADO.NET.

Using Connections Efficiently

In general, when using *scarce* resources in .NET, such as database connections, windows, or graphics objects, it is good practice to ensure that each resource is closed after use. Although the designers of .NET have implemented automatic garbage collection, which will tidy up eventually, it is necessary to release resources as early as possible to avoid starvation of resources.

This is all too apparent when writing code that accesses a database, bcause keeping a connection open for slightly longer than necessary can affect other sessions. In extreme circumstances, not closing a connection can lock other users out of an entire set of tables, considerably hurting application performance. Closing database connections should be considered mandatory, so this section shows how to structure your code so as to minimize the risk of leaving a resource open.

There are two main ways to ensure that database connections and the like are released after use.

Option One: try...catch...finally

The first option to ensure that resources are cleaned up is to use `try...catch...finally` blocks, and ensure that you close any open connections within the finally block. Here's a short example:

```
try
{
    // Open the connection
    conn.Open();
    // Do something useful
}
catch ( Exception ex )
{
    // Do something about the exception
}
finally
{
    // Ensure that the connection is freed
    conn.Close ( ) ;
}
```

Within the `finally` block you can release any resources you have used. The only trouble with this method is that you have to ensure that you close the connection—it is all too easy to forget to add in the `finally` clause, so something less prone to vagaries in coding style might be worthwhile.

Also, you might find that you open a number of resources (say two database connections and a file) within a given method, so the cascading of `try...catch...finally` blocks can sometimes become less easy to read. There is however another way to guarantee resource cleanup—the `using` statement.

Option Two: The using block statement

During development of C#, the debate on how .NET uses nondeterministic destruction became very heated.

In C++, as soon as an object went out of scope, its destructor would be automatically called. This was great news for designers of resource-based classes, because the destructor was the ideal place to close the resource if the user had forgotten to do so. A C++ destructor is called whenever an object goes out of scope—so for instance if an exception was raised and not caught, all destructors would be called.

With C# and the other managed languages, there is no concept of automatic, deterministic destruction. Instead there is the garbage collector, which disposes of resources at some point in the future. What makes this nondeterministic is that you have little say over when this process actually happens. Forgetting to close a database connection could cause all sorts of problems for a .NET executable. Luckily, help is at hand. The following code demonstrates how to use the `using` clause to ensure that objects that implement the `IDisposable` interface (see Chapter 4) are cleared up immediately after the block exits.

```
string source = "server=(local)\\NetSDK;" +
                "integrated security=SSPI;" +
                "database=Northwind";
```

```
using ( SqlConnection conn = new SqlConnection ( source ) )
{
    // Open the connection
    conn.Open ( ) ;

    // Do something useful
}
```

In this instance, the using clause ensures that the database connection is closed, regardless of how the block is exited.

Looking at the IL code for the Dispose() method of the connection classes, all of them check the current state of the connection object, and if open will call the Close() method. A great tool for browsing .NET assemblies is Reflector (available at /www.aisto.com/roeder/dotnet/). This tool permits you to view the IL code for any .NET method, and will also reverse-engineer the IL into source code so you can easily see what a given method is doing.

When programming, you should use at least one of these methods, and probably both. Wherever you acquire resources it is good practice to use the using statement; even though we all mean to write the Close() statement, sometimes we forget, and in the face of exceptions the using clause does the right thing. There is no substitute for good exception handling either, so in most instances I would suggest you use both methods together as in the following example:

```
try
{
    using (SqlConnection conn = new SqlConnection ( source ))
    {
        // Open the connection
        conn.Open ( ) ;

        // Do something useful

        // Close it myself
        conn.Close ( ) ;
    }
}
catch (Exception e)
{
    // Do something with the exception here...
}
```

Note that we called Close() which isn't strictly necessary, because the using clause will ensure that this is done anyway. However, you should ensure that any resources such as this are released as soon as possible—you might have more code in the rest of the block and there's no point locking a resource unnecessarily.

In addition, if an exception is raised within the using block, the IDisposable.Dispose method will be called on the resource guarded by the using clause, which in this example ensures that the database connection is always closed. This produces easier to read code than having to ensure you close a connection within an exception clause.

In conclusion, if you are writing a class that wraps a resource, whatever that resource may be, always implement the IDisposable interface to close the resource. That way anyone coding with your class can use the using() statement and guarantee that the resource will be cleared up.

Transactions

Often when there is more than one update to be made to the database, these updates must be performed within the scope of a transaction. A transaction in ADO.NET is initiated by calling one of the BeginTransaction() methods on the database connection object. These methods return an object that implements the IDbTransaction interface, defined within System.Data.

The following sequence of code initiates a transaction on a SQL Server connection:

```
string source = "server=(local)\\NetSDK;" +
                "integrated security=SSPI;" +
                "database=Northwind";
SqlConnection conn = new SqlConnection(source);
conn.Open();
SqlTransaction tx = conn.BeginTransaction();

// Execute some commands, then commit the transaction

tx.Commit();
conn.Close();
```

When you begin a transaction, you can choose the isolation level for commands executed within that transaction. The level determines how changes made in one database session are viewed by another. Not all database engines support all of the four levels presented in the following table.

Isolation Level	Description
ReadCommitted	The default for SQL Server. This level ensures that data written by one transaction will only be accessible in a second transaction after the first transaction commits.
ReadUncommitted	This permits your transaction to read data within the database, even data that has not yet been committed by another transaction. For example, if two users were accessing the same database, and the first inserted some data without concluding their transaction (by means of a Commit or Rollback), then the second user with their isolation level set to ReadUncommitted could read the data.
RepeatableRead	This level, which extends the ReadCommitted level, ensures that if the same statement is issued within the transaction, regardless of other potential updates made to the database, the same data will always be returned. This level does require extra locks to be held on the data, which could adversely affect performance.
	This level guarantees that, for each row in the initial query, no changes can be made to that data. It does, however, permit "phantom" rows to show up—these are completely new rows that another transaction might have inserted while your transaction is running.

Isolation Level	Description
Serializable	This is the most "exclusive" transaction level, which in effect serializes access to data within the database. With this isolation level, phantom rows can never show up, so a SQL statement issued within a serializable transaction will always retrieve the same data. The negative performance impact of a Serializable transaction should not be underestimated—if you don't absolutely need to use this level of isolation, stay away from it.

The SQL Server default isolation level, ReadCommitted, is a good compromise between data coherence and data availability, because fewer locks are required on data than in RepeatableRead or Serializable modes. However, there are situations where the isolation level should be increased, and so within .NET you can simply begin a transaction with a different level from the default. There are no hard-and-fast rules as to which levels to pick—that comes with experience.

If you are currently using a database that does not support transactions, it is well worth changing to a database that does. Once I was working as a trusted employee, and had been given complete access to the bug database. I typed in what I thought was delete from bug where id=99999, but in fact had typed a < rather than an =. I deleted the entire database of bugs (except the one I wanted to!). Luckily for me our I.S. team backed up the database on a nightly basis and we could restore this, but a rollback command would have been much easier.

Commands

We briefly touched on the idea of issuing commands against a database in the "Using Database Connections" section. A command is, in its simplest form, a string of text containing SQL statements that is to be issued to the database. A command could also be a stored procedure, or the name of a table that will return all columns and all rows from that table (in other words, a SELECT *-style clause).

A command can be constructed by passing the SQL clause as a parameter to the constructor of the Command class, as shown in this example:

```
string source = "server=(local)\\NetSDK;" +
                "integrated security=SSPI;" +
                "database=Northwind";
string select = "SELECT ContactName,CompanyName FROM Customers";
SqlConnection conn = new SqlConnection(source);
conn.Open();

SqlCommand cmd = new SqlCommand(select, conn);
```

The <provider>Command classes have a property called CommandType, which is used to define whether the command is a SQL clause, a call to a stored procedure, or a full table statement (which simply selects all columns and rows from a given table). The following table summarizes the CommandType enumeration:

CommandType	Example
Text (default)	String select = "SELECT ContactName FROM Customers";
	SqlCommand cmd = new SqlCommand(select , conn);
StoredProcedure	SqlCommand cmd = new SqlCommand("CustOrderHist", conn);
	cmd.CommandType = CommandType.StoredProcedure;
	cmd.Parameters.Add("@CustomerID", "QUICK");
TableDirect	OleDbCommand cmd = new OleDbCommand("Categories", conn);
	cmd.CommandType = CommandType.TableDirect;

When executing a stored procedure, it might be necessary to pass parameters to that procedure. The previous example sets the @CustomerID parameter directly, although there are other ways of setting the parameter value, which we will look at later in the chapter.

The TableDirect command type is only valid for the OleDb provider; other providers will throw an exception if you attempt to use this command type with them.

Executing Commands

After you have defined the command, you need to execute it. There are a number of ways to issue the statement, depending on what you expect to be returned (if anything) from that command. The <provider>Command classes provide the following execute methods:

❑   ExecuteNonQuery()—Executes the command but does not return any output

❑   ExecuteReader()—Executes the command and returns a typed IDataReader

❑   ExecuteScalar()—Executes the command and returns a single value

In addition to these methods, the SqlCommand class also exposes the following method

❑   ExecuteXmlReader()—Executes the command and returns an XmlReader object, which can be used to traverse the XML fragment returned from the database.

As with the other chapters, you can download the sample code from the Wrox Web site at www.wrox.com.

ExecuteNonQuery()

This method is commonly used for UPDATE, INSERT, or DELETE statements, where the only returned value is the number of records affected. This method can, however, return results if you call a stored procedure that has output parameters.

```
using System;
using System.Data.SqlClient;
public class ExecuteNonQueryExample
```

```
{
   public static void Main(string[] args)
   {
      string source = "server=(local)\\NetSDK;" +
                      "integrated security=SSPI;" +
                      "database=Northwind";
      string select = "UPDATE Customers " +
                      "SET ContactName = 'Bob' " +
                      "WHERE ContactName = 'Bill'";
      SqlConnection  conn = new SqlConnection(source);
      conn.Open();
      SqlCommand cmd = new SqlCommand(select, conn);
      int rowsReturned = cmd.ExecuteNonQuery();
      Console.WriteLine("{0} rows returned.", rowsReturned);
      conn.Close();
   }
}
```

`ExecuteNonQuery()` returns the number of rows affected by the command as an `int`.

ExecuteReader()

This method executes the command and returns a typed data reader object, depending on the provider in use. The object returned can be used to iterate through the record(s) returned, as shown in the following code:

```
using System;
using System.Data.SqlClient;
public class ExecuteReaderExample
{
   public static void Main(string[] args)
   {
      string source = "server=(local)\\NetSDK;" +
                      "integrated security=SSPI;" +
                      "database=Northwind";
      string select = "SELECT ContactName,CompanyName FROM Customers";
      SqlConnection conn = new SqlConnection(source);
      conn.Open();
      SqlCommand cmd = new SqlCommand(select, conn);
      SqlDataReader reader = cmd.ExecuteReader();
      while(reader.Read())
      {
         Console.WriteLine("Contact : {0,-20} Company : {1}" ,
                           reader[0] , reader[1]);
      }
   }
}
```

Figure 21-2 shows the output of this code.

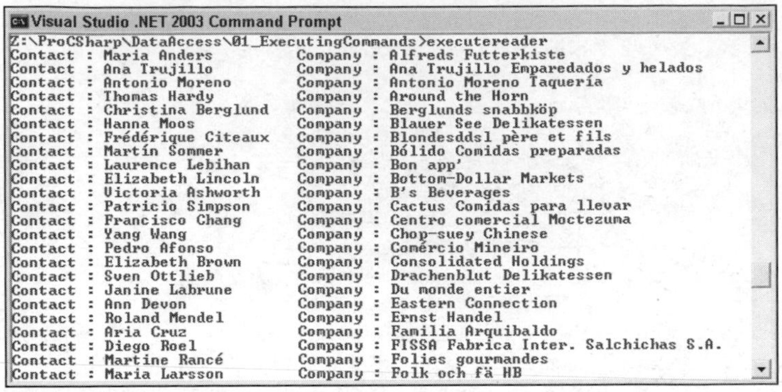

Figure 21-2

The `<provider>DataReader` objects are discussed later in this chapter.

ExecuteScalar()

On many occasions it is necessary to return a single result from a SQL statement, such as the count of records in a given table, or the current date/time on the server. The `ExecuteScalar` method can be used in such situations:

```
using System;
using System.Data.SqlClient;
public class ExecuteScalarExample
{
    public static void Main(string[] args)
    {
        string source = "server=(local)\\NetSDK;" +
                        "integrated security=SSPI;" +
                        "database=Northwind";
        string select = "SELECT COUNT(*) FROM Customers";
        SqlConnection conn = new SqlConnection(source);
        conn.Open();
        SqlCommand cmd = new SqlCommand(select, conn);
        object o = cmd.ExecuteScalar();
        Console.WriteLine ( o ) ;
    }
}
```

The method returns an object, which you can cast in the appropriate type if required.

ExecuteXmlReader() (SqlClient Provider Only)

As its name implies, this method executes the command and returns an `XmlReader` object to the caller. SQL Server permits a SQL `SELECT` statement to be extended with a `FOR XML` clause. This clause can take one of three options:

❑   `FOR XML AUTO`—Builds a tree based on the tables in the `FROM` clause

❑   `FOR XML RAW`—Maps result set rows to elements, with columns mapped to attributes

❑   `FOR XML EXPLICIT`—Requires that you specify the shape of the XML tree to be returned

Professional SQL Server 2000 XML (Wrox Press, ISBN 1-861005-46-6) includes a complete description of these options. For this example use AUTO:

```
using System;
using System.Data.SqlClient;
using System.Xml;
public class ExecuteXmlReaderExample
{
    public static void Main(string[] args)
    {
        string source = "server=(local)\\NetSDK;" +
                        "integrated security=SSPI;" +
                        "database=Northwind";
        string select = "SELECT ContactName,CompanyName " +
                        "FROM Customers FOR XML AUTO";
        SqlConnection conn = new SqlConnection(source);
        conn.Open();
        SqlCommand cmd = new SqlCommand(select, conn);
        XmlReader xr = cmd.ExecuteXmlReader();
        xr.Read();
        string s;
        do
        {
            s = xr.ReadOuterXml();
            if (s!="")
                Console.WriteLine(s);
        } while (s!= "");
        conn.Close();
    }
}
```

Note that we have to import the System.Xml namespace in order to output the returned XML. This namespace and further XML capabilities of .NET Framework are explored in more detail in Chapter 24.

Here we include the FOR XML AUTO clause in the SQL statement, then call the ExecuteXmlReader() method. Figure 21-3 shows the output of this code.

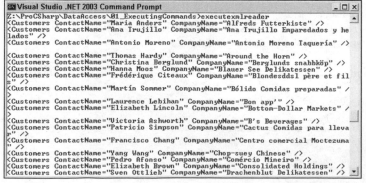

Figure 21-3

In the SQL clause, we specified FROM Customers, so an element of type Customers is shown in the output. To this are added attributes, one for each column selected from the database. This builds up an XML fragment for each row selected from the database.

Calling Stored Procedures

Calling a stored procedure with a command object is just a matter of defining the name of the stored procedure, adding a definition for each parameter of the procedure, then executing the command with one of the methods presented in the previous section.

In order to make the examples in this section more useful, a set of stored procedures has been defined that can be used to insert, update, and delete records from the Region table in the Northwind sample database. Despite its small size this is a good candidate to choose for the example, as it can be used to define examples for each of the types of stored procedures you will commonly write.

Calling a stored procedure that returns nothing

The simplest example of calling a stored procedure is one that returns nothing to the caller. There are two such procedures defined in the following two subsections: one for updating a pre-existing Region record and one for deleting a given Region record.

Record Update

Updating a Region record is fairly trivial, as there is only one column that can be modified (assuming primary keys cannot be updated). You can type these examples directly into the SQL Server Query Analyzer, or run the StoredProcs.sql file that is part of the downloadable code for this chapter. This file installs each of the stored procedures in this section:

```
CREATE PROCEDURE RegionUpdate (@RegionID INTEGER,
                               @RegionDescription NCHAR(50)) AS
   SET NOCOUNT OFF
   UPDATE Region
       SET RegionDescription = @RegionDescription
       WHERE RegionID = @RegionID
GO
```

An update command on a more real-world table might need to re-select and return the updated record in its entirety. This stored procedure takes two input parameters (@RegionID and @RegionDescription), and issues an UPDATE statement against the database.

To run this stored procedure from within .NET code, you need to define a SQL command and execute it:

```
SqlCommand aCommand = new SqlCommand("RegionUpdate", conn);

aCommand.CommandType = CommandType.StoredProcedure;
aCommand.Parameters.Add(new SqlParameter ("@RegionID",
                                          SqlDbType.Int,
                                          0,
                                          "RegionID"));
aCommand.Parameters.Add(new SqlParameter("@RegionDescription",
                                          SqlDbType.NChar,
```

```
                                        50,
                                        "RegionDescription"));
        aCommand.UpdatedRowSource = UpdateRowSource.None;
```

This code creates a new `SqlCommand` object named `aCommand`, and defines it as a stored procedure. We then add each parameter in turn, and finally set the expected output from the stored procedure to one of the values in the `UpdateRowSource` enumeration, which is discussed later in this chapter.

The stored procedure takes two parameters: the unique primary key of the Region record being updated, and the new description to be given to this record. After the command has been created, it can be executed by issuing the following commands:

```
        aCommand.Parameters[0].Value = 999;
        aCommand.Parameters[1].Value = "South Western England";
        aCommand.ExecuteNonQuery();
```

Here the value of each parameter is set, then the stored procedure is executed. Because the procedure returns nothing, `ExecuteNonQuery()` will suffice. Command parameters may be set by ordinal numbers (as shown in the previous example) or by name.

Record Deletion

The next stored procedure required is one that can be used to delete a Region record from the database:

```
        CREATE PROCEDURE RegionDelete (@RegionID INTEGER) AS
            SET NOCOUNT OFF
            DELETE FROM Region
            WHERE       RegionID = @RegionID
        GO
```

This procedure only requires the primary key value of the record. The code uses a `SqlCommand` object to call this stored procedure as follows:

```
        SqlCommand aCommand = new SqlCommand("RegionDelete" , conn);
        aCommand.CommandType = CommandType.StoredProcedure;
        aCommand.Parameters.Add(new SqlParameter("@RegionID" , SqlDbType.Int , 0 ,
                                        "RegionID"));
        aCommand.UpdatedRowSource = UpdateRowSource.None;
```

This command only accepts a single parameter as shown in the following code, which will execute the `RegionDelete` stored procedure; here we see an example of setting the parameter by name:

```
        aCommand.Parameters["@RegionID"].Value= 999;
        aCommand.ExecuteNonQuery();
```

Calling a stored procedure that returns output parameters

Both of the previous examples execute stored procedures that return nothing. If a stored procedure includes output parameters, then these need to be defined within the .NET client so that they can be filled when the procedure returns. The following example shows how to insert a record into the database, and return the primary key of that record to the caller.

Record insertion

The Region table only consists of a primary key (RegionID) and description field (RegionDescription). To insert a record, this numeric primary key needs to be generated, and then a new row needs to be inserted into the database. The primary key generation in this example has been simplified by creating one within the stored procedure. The method used is exceedingly crude, which is why we have a section on key generation later in this chapter. For now this primitive example suffices:

```
CREATE PROCEDURE RegionInsert(@RegionDescription NCHAR(50),
                              @RegionID INTEGER OUTPUT)AS
    SET NOCOUNT OFF
    SELECT @RegionID = MAX(RegionID)+ 1
    FROM Region
    INSERT INTO Region(RegionID, RegionDescription)
    VALUES(@RegionID, @RegionDescription)
GO
```

The insert procedure creates a new Region record. As the primary key value is generated by the database itself, this value is returned as an output parameter from the procedure (@RegionID). This is sufficient for this simple example, but for a more complex table (especially one with default values), it is more common not to utilize output parameters, and instead select the entire inserted row and return this to the caller. The .NET classes can cope with either scenario.

```
SqlCommand  aCommand = new SqlCommand("RegionInsert" , conn);
aCommand.CommandType = CommandType.StoredProcedure;
aCommand.Parameters.Add(new SqlParameter("@RegionDescription" ,
                                         SqlDbType.NChar ,
                                         50 ,
                                         "RegionDescription"));
aCommand.Parameters.Add(new SqlParameter("@RegionID" ,
                                         SqlDbType.Int,
                                         0 ,
                                         ParameterDirection.Output ,
                                         false ,
                                         0 ,
                                         0 ,
                                         "RegionID" ,
                                         DataRowVersion.Default ,
                                         null));
aCommand.UpdatedRowSource = UpdateRowSource.OutputParameters;
```

Here, the definition of the parameters is much more complex. The second parameter, @RegionID, is defined to include its parameter direction, which in this example is Output. In addition to this flag, on the last line of the code, the UpdateRowSource enumeration is used to indicate that data will be returned from this stored procedure via output parameters. This flag is mainly used when issuing stored procedure calls from a DataTable (which is discussed later in this chapter).

Calling this stored procedure is similar to the previous examples, except in this instance the output parameter is read after executing the procedure:

```
aCommand.Parameters["@RegionDescription"].Value = "South West";
aCommand.ExecuteNonQuery();
int newRegionID = (int) aCommand.Parameters["@RegionID"].Value;
```

After executing the command, the value of the @RegionID parameter is read and cast to an integer.

You might be wondering what to do if the stored procedure you call returns output parameters and a set of rows. In this instance, define the parameters as appropriate, and rather than calling ExecuteNonQuery(), call one of the other methods (such as ExecuteReader()) that will permit you to traverse any record(s) returned.

Fast Data Access: The Data Reader

A data reader is the simplest and fastest way of selecting some data from a data source, but also the least capable. You cannot directly instantiate a data reader object—an instance is returned from the appropriate database's command object (such as SqlCommand) after having called the ExecuteReader() method.

The following code demonstrates how to select data from the Customers table in the Northwind database. The example connects to the database, selects a number of records, loops through these selected records, and outputs them to the console.

This example utilizes the OLE DB provider as a brief respite from the SQL provider. In most cases the classes have a one-to-one correspondence with their SqlClient cousins; for example, there is the OleDbConnection object, which is similar to the SqlConnection object used in the previous examples.

To execute commands against an OLE DB data source, the OleDbCommand class is used. The following code shows an example of executing a simple SQL statement and reading the records by returning an OleDbDataReader object.

Note the second using directive below that makes available the OleDb classes:

```
using System;
using System.Data.OleDb;
```

All the data providers currently available are shipped within the same DLL, so it is only necessary to reference the System.Data.dll assembly to import all classes used in this section:

```
public class DataReaderExample
{
   public static void Main(string[] args)
   {
      string source = "Provider=SQLOLEDB;" +
                      "server=(local)\\NetSDK;" +
                      "integrated security=SSPI;" +
                      "database=northwind";
      string select = "SELECT ContactName,CompanyName FROM Customers";
      OleDbConnection conn = new OleDbConnection(source);
      conn.Open();
      OleDbCommand cmd = new OleDbCommand(select , conn);
      OleDbDataReader aReader = cmd.ExecuteReader();
      while(aReader.Read())
         Console.WriteLine("'{0}' from {1}" ,
                           aReader.GetString(0) , aReader.GetString(1));
```

```
        aReader.Close();
        conn.Close();
    }
}
```

The preceding code includes many familiar aspects of C# already covered in this chapter. To compile the example, issue the following command:

```
csc /t:exe /debug+ DataReaderExample.cs /r:System.Data.dll
```

The following code from the previous example creates a new OLE DB .NET database connection, based on the source connection string:

```
OleDbConnection conn = new OleDbConnection(source);
conn.Open();
OleDbCommand cmd = new OleDbCommand(select, conn);
```

The third line creates a new `OleDbCommand` object, based on a particular SELECT statement, and the database connection to be used when the command is executed. When you have a valid command, you need to execute it, which returns an initialized `OleDbDataReader`:

```
OleDbDataReader aReader = cmd.ExecuteReader();
```

An `OleDbDataReader` is a forward-only "connected" cursor. In other words, you can only traverse through the records returned in one direction, and the database connection used is kept open until the data reader has been closed.

> **An OleDbDataReader keeps the database connection open until explicitly closed.**

The `OleDbDataReader` class cannot be instantiated directly—it is always returned by a call to the `ExecuteReader()` method of the `OleDbCommand` class. Once you have an open data reader, there are various ways to access the data contained within the reader.

When the `OleDbDataReader` object is closed (via an explicit call to `Close()`, or the object being garbage collected), the underlying connection may also be closed, depending on which of the `ExecuteReader()` methods is called. If you call `ExecuteReader()` and pass `CommandBehavior.CloseConnection`, you can force the connection to be closed when the reader is closed.

The `OleDbDataReader` class has an indexer that permits access (although not type-safe access) to any field using the familiar array style syntax:

```
object o = aReader[0];
object o = aReader["CategoryID"];
```

Assuming that the `CategoryID` field was the first in the SELECT statement used to populate the reader, these two lines are functionally equivalent, although the second is slower than the first; to verify this a test application was written that performed a million iterations of accessing the same column from an open data reader, just to get some numbers that were big enough to read. You probably don't read the same column a million times in a tight loop, but every (micro) second counts, and you might as well write code that is as close to optimal as possible.

As an aside, the numeric indexer took on average 0.09 seconds for the million accesses, and the textual one 0.63 seconds. The reason for this difference is that the textual method looks up the column number internally from the schema and then accesses it using its ordinal. If you know this information beforehand you can do a better job of accessing the data.

So should you use the numeric indexer? Maybe, but there is a better way.

In addition to the indexers presented above, OleDbDataReader has a set of type-safe methods that can be used to read columns. These are fairly self-explanatory, and all begin with Get. There are methods to read most types of data, such as GetInt32, GetFloat, GetGuid, and so on.

The million iterations using GetInt32 took 0.06 seconds. The overhead in the numeric indexer is incurred while getting the data type, calling the same code as GetInt32, then boxing (and in this instance unboxing) an integer. So, if you know the schema beforehand, are willing to use cryptic numbers instead of column names, and you can be bothered to use a type-safe function for each and every column access, you stand to gain somewhere in the region of a ten-fold speed increase over using a textual column name (when selecting those million copies of the same column).

Needless to say, there is a tradeoff between maintainability and speed. If you must use numeric indexers, define constants within class scope for each of the columns that you will be accessing. The code above can be used to select data from any OLE DB database; however, there are a number of SQL Server–specific classes that can be used with the obvious portability tradeoff.

The following example is the same as the above, except in this instance the OLE DB provider and all references to OLE DB classes have been replaced with the SQL counterparts. The changes in the code from the previous example have been highlighted. The example is in the 04_DataReaderSql directory:

```
using System;
using System.Data.SqlClient;
public class DataReaderSql
{
    public static int Main(string[] args)
    {
        string source = "server=(local)\\NetSDK;" +
                        "integrated security=SSPI;" +
                        "database=northwind";
        string select = "SELECT ContactName,CompanyName FROM Customers";
        SqlConnection conn = new SqlConnection(source);
        conn.Open();
        SqlCommand cmd = new SqlCommand(select , conn);
        SqlDataReader aReader = cmd.ExecuteReader();
        while(aReader.Read())
            Console.WriteLine("'{0}' from {1}" , aReader.GetString(0) ,
                                aReader.GetString(1));
        aReader.Close();
        conn.Close();
        return 0;
    }
}
```

Notice the difference? If you're typing this in, then do a global replace on OleDb with Sql, change the data source string and recompile. It's that easy!

The same performance tests were run on the indexers for the SQL provider, and this time the numeric indexers were both exactly the same at 0.13 seconds for the million accesses, and the string-based indexer ran at about 0.65 seconds. You would expect the native SQL Server provider to be faster than going through OleDb, which up until this was tested under the release version of .NET it was. This might be an anomaly due to the simplistic test approach we've been using (selecting the same value 1,000,000 times); a real-world test should show better performance from the managed SQL provider.

Managing Data and Relationships: The DataSet Class

The DataSet class has been designed as an offline container of data. It has no notion of database connections. In fact, the data held within a DataSet doesn't necessarily need to have come from a database—it could just as easily be records from a CSV file, or points read from a measuring device.

A DataSet class consists of a set of data tables, each of which will have a set of data columns and data rows (see Figure 21-4). In addition to defining the data, you can also define *links* between tables within the DataSet class. One common scenario would be when defining a parent-child relationship (commonly known as master/detail). One record in a table (say Order) links to many records in another table (say Order_Details). This relationship can be defined and navigated within the DataSet.

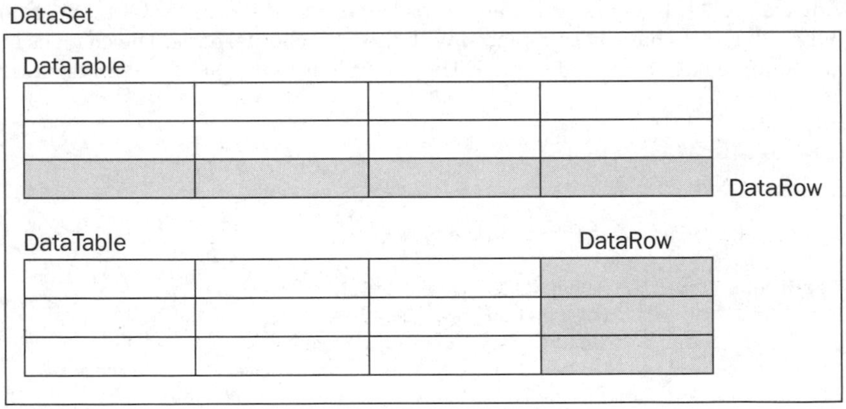

Figure 21-4

The following sections describe the classes that are used with a DataSet class.

Data Tables

A data table is very similar to a physical database table—it consists of a set of columns with particular properties, and might have zero or more rows of data. A data table might also define a primary key, which can be one or more columns, and might also contain constraints on columns. The generic term for this information used throughout the rest of the chapter is *schema*.

There are several ways to define the schema for a particular data table (and indeed the `DataSet` class as a whole). These are discussed after we introduce data columns and data rows. Figure 21-5 shows some of the objects that are accessible through the data table:

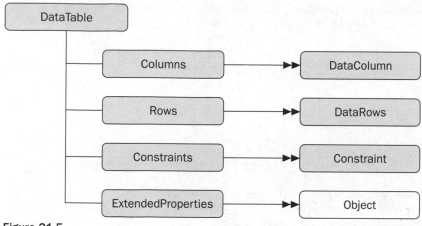

Figure 21-5

A `DataTable` object (and also a `DataColumn`) can have an arbitrary number of extended properties associated with it. This collection can be populated with any user-defined information pertaining to the object. For example, a given column might have an input mask used to validate the contents of that column—a typical example is the U.S. social security number. Extended properties are especially useful when the data is constructed within a middle tier and returned to the client for some processing. You could, for example, store validation criteria (such as `min` and `max`) for numeric columns in extended properties and use this in the UI tier when validating user input.

When a data table has been populated—by selecting data from a database, reading data from a file, or manually populating within code—the `Rows` collection will contain this retrieved data.

The `Columns` collection contains `DataColumn` instances that have been added to this table. These define the schema of the data, such as the data type, nullability, default values, and so on. The `Constraints` collection can be populated with either unique or primary key constraints.

One example of where the schema information for a data table is used is when displaying that data in a `DataGrid` (which is discussed in Chapter 22). The `DataGrid` control uses properties such as the data type of the column to decide what control to use for that column. A bit field within the database will be displayed as a check box within the `DataGrid`. If a column is defined within the database schema as NOT NULL, then this fact will be stored within the `DataColumn` so that it can be tested when the user attempts to move off a row.

Data Columns

A `DataColumn` object defines properties of a column within the `DataTable`, such as the data type of that column, whether the column is read-only, and various other facts. A column can be created in code, or it can be automatically generated by the runtime.

When creating a column, it is also useful to give it a name; otherwise the runtime will generate a name for you in the form Column*n* where *n* is an incrementing number.

The data type of the column can be set either by supplying it in the constructor, or by setting the DataType property. Once you have loaded data into a data table you cannot alter the type of a colum—you'll just receive an ArgumentException.

Data columns can be created to hold the following .NET Framework data types:

Boolean	Decimal	Int64	TimeSpan
Byte	Double	Sbyte	UInt16
Char	Int16	Single	UInt32
DateTime	Int32	String	UInt64

Once created, the next thing to do with a DataColumn object is to set up other properties, such as the nullability of the column or the default value. The following code fragment shows a few of the more common options to set on a DataColumn object:

```
DataColumn customerID = new DataColumn("CustomerID" , typeof(int));
customerID.AllowDBNull = false;
customerID.ReadOnly = false;
customerID.AutoIncrement = true;
customerID.AutoIncrementSeed = 1000;
DataColumn name = new DataColumn("Name" , typeof(string));
name.AllowDBNull = false;
name.Unique = true;
```

The following tbale shows the properties that can be set on a DataColumn object:

Property	Description
AllowDBNull	If true, permits the column to be set to DBNull.
AutoIncrement	Defines that this column value is automatically generated as an incrementing number.
AutoIncrementSeed	Defines the initial seed value for an AutoIncrement column.
AutoIncrementStep	Defines the step between automatically generated column values, with a default of one.
Caption	Can be used for displaying the name of the column on screen.
ColumnMapping	Defines how a column is mapped into XML when a DataSet class is saved by calling DataSet.WriteXml.
ColumnName	The name of the column. This is auto-generated by the runtime if not set in the constructor.
DataType	Defines the System.Type value of the column.

Property	Description
DefaultValue	Can define a default value for a column.
Expression	Defines the expression to be used in a computed column.

Data rows

This class makes up the other part of the DataTable class. The column within a data table are defined in terms of the DataColumn class. The actual data within the table is accessed using the DataRow object. The following example shows how to access rows within a data table. First, the connection details:

```
string source = "server=(local)\\NetSDK;" +
                "uid=QSUser;pwd=QSPassword;" +
                "database=northwind";
string select = "SELECT ContactName,CompanyName FROM Customers";
SqlConnection  conn = new SqlConnection(source);
```

The following code introduces the SqlDataAdapter class, which is used to place data into a DataSet class. SqlDataAdapter issues the SQL clause and fills a table in the DataSet class called Customers with the output of the following query. (For more details on the SqlDataAdapter class see the section "Populating a DataSet".)

```
SqlDataAdapter da = new SqlDataAdapter(select, conn);
DataSet ds = new DataSet();
da.Fill(ds , "Customers");
```

In the code below, you might notice the use of the DataRow indexer to access values from within that row. The value for a given column can be retrieved using one of the several overloaded indexers. These permit you to retrieve a value knowing the column number, name, or DataColumn:

```
foreach(DataRow row in ds.Tables["Customers"].Rows)
    Console.WriteLine("'{0}' from {1}" , row[0] ,row[1]);
```

One of the most appealing aspects of DataRow is that it is versioned. This permits you to receive various values for a given column in a particular row. The versions are described in the following table:

DataRow Version Value	Description
Current	The value existing at present within the column. If no edit has occurred, this will be the same as the original value. If an edit (or edits) have occurred, the value will be the last valid value entered.
Default	The default value (in other words, any default set up for the column).
Original	The value of the column when originally selected from the database. If the DataRow's AcceptChanges method is called, then this value will update to the Current value.
Proposed	When changes are in progress for a row, it is possible to retrieve this modified value. If you call BeginEdit() on the row and make changes, each column will have a proposed value until either EndEdit() or CancelEdit() is called.

The version of a given column could be used in many ways. One example is when updating rows within the database, in which instance it is common to issue a SQL statement such as the following:

```
UPDATE  Products
SET     Name = Column.Current
WHERE   ProductID = xxx
AND     Name = Column.Original;
```

Obviously this code would never compile, but it shows one use for original and current values of a column within a row.

To retrieve a versioned value from the `DataRow` indexer, use one of the indexer methods that accept a `DataRowVersion` value as a parameter. The following snippet shows how to obtain all values of each column in a `DataTable` object:

```
foreach (DataRow row in ds.Tables["Customers"].Rows )
{
  foreach ( DataColumn dc in ds.Tables["Customers"].Columns )
  {
    Console.WriteLine ("{0} Current  = {1}" , dc.ColumnName ,
                                              row[dc,DataRowVersion.Current]);
    Console.WriteLine ("    Default = {0}" , row[dc,DataRowVersion.Default]);
    Console.WriteLine ("    Original = {0}" , row[dc,DataRowVersion.Original]);
  }
}
```

The whole row has a state flag called `RowState`, which can be used to determine what operation is needed on the row when it is persisted back to the database. The `RowState` property is set to keep track of all the changes made to the `DataTable`, such as adding new rows, deleting existing rows, and changing columns within the table. When the data is reconciled with the database, the row state flag is used to determine what SQL operations should occur. The following table provides an overview of the flags that are defined by the `DataRowState` enumeration.

DataRowState Value	Description
Added	Indicates that the row has been newly added to a `DataTable`'s `Rows` collection. All rows created on the client are set to this value, and will ultimately issue SQL INSERT statements when reconciled with the database.
Deleted	Indicates that the row has been marked as deleted from the `DataTable` by means of the `DataRow.Delete()` method. The row still exists within the `DataTable`, but will not normally be viewable on screen (unless a `DataView` has been explicitly set up). `DataViews` will be discussed in the next chapter. Rows marked as deleted in the `DataTable` will be deleted from the database when reconciled.
Detached	Indicates that a row is in this state immediately after it is created, and can also be returned to this state by calling `DataRow.Remove()`. A detached row is not considered to be part of any data table, and as such no SQL for rows in this state will be issued.

DataRowState Value	Description
Modified	Indicates that a row will be Modified if the value in any column has been changed.
Unchanged	Indicates that the row has not been changed since the last call to AcceptChanges().

The state of the row depends also on what methods have been called on the row. The AcceptChanges() method is generally called after successfully updating the data source (that is, after persisting changes to the database).

The most common way to alter data in a DataRow is to use the indexer; however, if you have a number of changes to make you also need to consider the BeginEdit() and EndEdit() methods.

When an alteration is made to a column within a DataRow, the ColumnChanging event is raised on the row's DataTable. This permits you to override the ProposedValue property of the DataColumn-ChangeEventArgs class, and change it as required. This is one way of performing some data validation on column values. If you call BeginEdit() before making changes, the ColumnChanging event will not be raised. This permits you to make multiple changes and then call EndEdit() to persist these changes. If you want to revert to the original values, call CancelEdit().

A DataRow can be linked in some way to other rows of data. This permits the creation of navigable links between rows, which is common in master/detail scenarios. The DataRow contains a GetChildRows() method that will return an array of associated rows from another table in the same DataSet as the current row. These are discussed in the "Data Relationships" section later in this chapter.

Schema generation

There are three ways to create the schema for a DataTable:

❑ Let the runtime do it for you.

❑ Write code to create the table(s).

❑ Use the XML schema generator.

Runtime schema generation

The DataRow example shown earlier presented the following code for selecting data from a database and populating a DataSet class:

```
SqlDataAdapter da = new SqlDataAdapter(select , conn);
DataSet ds = new DataSet();
da.Fill(ds , "Customers");
```

This is obviously easy to use, but it has a few drawbacks as well. For example, you have to make do with the default column names, which might work for you, but in certain instances you might want to rename a physical database column (say PKID) to something more user-friendly.

You could naturally alias columns within your SQL clause, as in SELECT PID AS PersonID FROM PersonTable; I would always recommend not renaming columns within SQL, because a column only really needs to have a "pretty" name onscreen.

Another potential problem with automated DataTable/DataColumn generation is that you have no control over the column types that the runtime chooses for your data. It does a fairly good job of deciding the correct data type for you, but as usual there are instances where you need more control. For example, you might have defined an enumerated type for a given column, so as to simplify user code written against your class. If you accept the default column types that the runtime generates, the column will likely be an integer with a 32-bit range, as opposed to an enum with your predefined options.

Lastly, and probably most problematic, is that when using automated table generation, you have no type-safe access to the data within the DataTable—you are at the mercy of indexers, which return instances of object rather than derived data types. If you like sprinkling your code with typecast expressions then skip the following sections.

Hand-coded schema

Generating the code to create a DataTable, replete with associated DataColumns is fairly easy. The examples within this section access the Products table from the Northwind database shown in Figure 21-6.

Products

	Column Name	Data Type	Length	Allow Nulls
🔑	ProductID	int	4	
	ProductName	nvarchar	40	
	SupplierID	int	4	✓
	CategoryID	int	4	✓
	QuantityPerUnit	nvarchar	20	✓
	UnitPrice	money	8	✓
	UnitsInStock	smallint	2	✓
	UnitsOnOrder	smallint	2	✓
	ReorderLevel	smallint	2	✓
	Discontinued	bit	1	

Figure 21-6

The following code manufactures a DataTable, which corresponds to the above schema (but doesn't cover the nullability of columns).

```
public static void ManufactureProductDataTable(DataSet ds)
{
    DataTable   products = new DataTable("Products");
    products.Columns.Add(new DataColumn("ProductID", typeof(int)));
    products.Columns.Add(new DataColumn("ProductName", typeof(string)));
    products.Columns.Add(new DataColumn("SupplierID", typeof(int)));
    products.Columns.Add(new DataColumn("CategoryID", typeof(int)));
    products.Columns.Add(new DataColumn("QuantityPerUnit", typeof(string)));
    products.Columns.Add(new DataColumn("UnitPrice", typeof(decimal)));
    products.Columns.Add(new DataColumn("UnitsInStock", typeof(short)));
    products.Columns.Add(new DataColumn("UnitsOnOrder", typeof(short)));
    products.Columns.Add(new DataColumn("ReorderLevel", typeof(short)));
    products.Columns.Add(new DataColumn("Discontinued", typeof(bool)));
    ds.Tables.Add(products);
}
```

You can alter the code in the `DataRow` example to utilize this newly generated table definition as follows:

```
string source = "server=(local)\\NetSDK;" +
                "integrated security=sspi;" +
                "database=Northwind";
string select = "SELECT * FROM Products";
SqlConnection conn = new SqlConnection(source);
SqlDataAdapter cmd = new SqlDataAdapter(select, conn);
DataSet ds = new DataSet();
ManufactureProductDataTable(ds);
cmd.Fill(ds, "Products");
foreach(DataRow row in ds.Tables["Products"].Rows)
    Console.WriteLine("'{0}' from {1}", row[0], row[1]);
```

The `ManufactureProductDataTable()` method creates a new `DataTable`, adds each column in turn, and finally appends this to the list of tables within the `DataSet`. The `DataSet` has an indexer that takes the name of the table and returns that `DataTable` to the caller.

The previous example is still not really type-safe, as indexers are being used on columns to retrieve the data. What would be better is a class (or set of classes) derived from `DataSet`, `DataTable`, and `DataRow` that define type-safe accessors for tables, rows, and columns. You can generate this code yourself; t's not particularly tedious and you end up with truly type-safe data access classes.

If you don't like generating these type-safe classes yourself then help is at hand. .NET Framework includes support for using XML schemas to define a `DataSet` class, a `DataTable` class, and the other classes that have been described in this section. (For more details on this method see the section "XML Schemas" later in this chapter.)

Data Relationships

When writing an application, it is often necessary to obtain and cache various tables of information. The `DataSet` class is the container for this information. With regular OLE DB it was necessary to provide a strange SQL dialect to enforce hierarchical data relationships, and the provider itself was not without its own subtle quirks.

The `DataSet` class on the other hand has been designed from the start to establish relationships between data tables with ease. The code in this section shows how to generate manually and populate two tables with data. So, if you don't have access to SQL Server or the NorthWind database, you can run this example anyway.

```
DataSet ds = new DataSet("Relationships");
ds.Tables.Add(CreateBuildingTable());
ds.Tables.Add(CreateRoomTable());
ds.Relations.Add("Rooms",
                 ds.Tables["Building"].Columns["BuildingID"],
                 ds.Tables["Room"].Columns["BuildingID"]);
```

The tables used in this example are shown in Figure 21-7. They contain a primary key and name field, with the `Room` table having `BuildingID` as a foreign key.

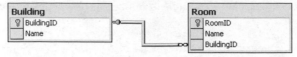

Figure 21-7

These tables have been kept deliberately simple. The following code shows how to iterate through the rows in the Building table, and traverse the relationship to list all of the child rows from the room table.

```
foreach(DataRow theBuilding in ds.Tables["Building"].Rows)
{
   DataRow[] children = theBuilding.GetChildRows("Rooms");
   int roomCount = children.Length;
   Console.WriteLine("Building {0} contains {1} room{2}",
                     theBuilding["Name"],
                     roomCount,
                     roomCount > 1 ? "s" : "");
   // Loop through the rooms
   foreach(DataRow theRoom in children)
      Console.WriteLine("Room: {0}", theRoom["Name"]);
}
```

The key difference between the `DataSet` class and the old-style hierarchical `Recordset` object is in the way the relationship is presented. In a hierarchical `Recordset` object, the relationship was presented as a pseudo-column within the row. This column itself was a `Recordset` object that could be iterated through. Under ADO.NET, however, a relationship is traversed simply by calling the `GetChildRows()` method:

```
DataRow[] children = theBuilding.GetChildRows("Rooms");
```

This method has a number of forms, but the simple example shown above just uses the name of the relationship to traverse between parent and child rows. It returns an array of rows that can be updated as appropriate by using the indexers as shown in earlier examples.

What's more interesting with data relationships is that they can be traversed both ways. Not only can you go from a parent to the child rows, but you can also find a parent row (or rows) from a child record simply by using the `ParentRelations` property on the `DataTable` class. This property returns a `Data-RelationCollection`, which can be indexed using the `[]` array syntax (for example, `ParentRelations-["Rooms"]`), or as an alternative the `GetParentRows()` method can be called as shown below:

```
foreach(DataRow theRoom in ds.Tables["Room"].Rows)
{
   DataRow[] parents = theRoom.GetParentRows("Rooms");
   foreach(DataRow theBuilding in parents)
      Console.WriteLine("Room {0} is contained in building {1}",
                     theRoom["Name"],
                     theBuilding["Name"]);
}
```

There are two methods with various overrides available for retrieving the parent row(s): `GetParentRows()` (which returns an array of zero or more rows) and `GetParentRow()` (which retrieves a single parent row given a relationship).

Data Constraints

Changing the data type of columns created on the client is not the only thing a DataTable is good for. ADO.NET permits you to create a set of constraints on a column (or columns), which are then used to enforce rules within the data.

The following table lists the constraint types that are currently supported by the runtime, embodied as classes in the System.Data namespace.

Constraint	Description
ForeignKeyConstraint	Enforces a link between two DataTables within a DataSet
UniqueConstraint	Ensures that entries in a given column are unique

Setting a primary key

As is common for a table in a relational database, you can supply a primary key, which can be based on one or more columns from the DataTable.

The following code creates a primary key for the Products table, whose schema we constructed by hand earlier.

Note that a primary key on a table is just one form of constraint. When a primary key is added to a DataTable, the runtime also generates a unique constraint over the key column(s). This is because there isn't actually a constraint type of PrimaryKey—a primary key is simply a unique constraint over one or more columns.

```
public static void ManufacturePrimaryKey(DataTable dt)
{
    DataColumn[] pk = new DataColumn[1];
    pk[0] = dt.Columns["ProductID"];
    dt.PrimaryKey = pk;
}
```

Because a primary key can contain several columns, it is typed as an array of DataColumns. A table's primary key can be set to those columns simply by assigning an array of columns to the property.

To check the constraints for a table, you can iterate through the ConstraintCollection. For the auto-generated constraint produced by the above code, the name of the constraint is Constraint1. That's not a very useful name, so to avoid this problem it is always best to create the constraint in code first, then define which column(s) make up the primary key.

The following code names the constraint before creating the primary key:

```
DataColumn[] pk = new DataColumn[1];
pk[0] = dt.Columns["ProductID"];
dt.Constraints.Add(new UniqueConstraint("PK_Products", pk[0]));
dt.PrimaryKey = pk;
```

Unique constraints can be applied to as many columns as you want.

Setting a foreign key

In addition to unique constraints, a `DataTable` class can also contain foreign key constraints. These are primarily used to enforce master/detail relationships, but can also be used to replicate columns between tables if you set the constraint up correctly. A master/detail relationship is one where there is commonly one parent record (say an order) and many child records (order lines), linked by the primary key of the parent record.

A foreign key constraint can only operate over tables within the same `DataSet`, so the following example uses the Categories table from the Northwind database (shown in Figure 21-8), and assigns a constraint between it and the Products table.

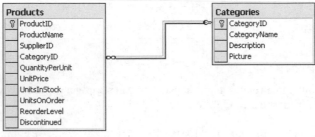

Figure 21-8

The first step is to generate a new data table for the Categories table.

```
DataTable categories = new DataTable("Categories");
categories.Columns.Add(new DataColumn("CategoryID", typeof(int)));
categories.Columns.Add(new DataColumn("CategoryName", typeof(string)));
categories.Columns.Add(new DataColumn("Description", typeof(string)));
categories.Constraints.Add(new UniqueConstraint("PK_Categories",
                            categories.Columns["CategoryID"]));
categories.PrimaryKey = new DataColumn[1]
                        {categories.Columns["CategoryID"]};
```

The last line of the previous code creates the primary key for the Categories table. The primary key in this instance is a single column; however, it is possible to generate a key over multiple columns using the array syntax shown.

Then the constraint can be created between the two tables:

```
DataColumn parent = ds.Tables["Categories"].Columns["CategoryID"];
DataColumn child = ds.Tables["Products"].Columns["CategoryID"];
ForeignKeyConstraint fk =
    new ForeignKeyConstraint("FK_Product_CategoryID", parent, child);
fk.UpdateRule = Rule.Cascade;
fk.DeleteRule = Rule.SetNull;
ds.Tables["Products"].Constraints.Add(fk);
```

This constraint applies to the link between `Categories.CategoryID` and `Products.CategoryID`. There are four different `ForeignKeyConstraint`—use those that permit you to name the constraint.

Setting Update and Delete constraints

In addition to defining the fact that there is some type of constraint between parent and child tables, you can define what should happen when a column in the constraint is updated.

The previous example sets the update rule and the delete rule. These rules are used when an action occurs to a column (or row) within the parent table, and the rule is used to decide what should happen to row(s) within the child table that could be affected. There are four different rules that can be applied through the `Rule` enumeration:

❑   `Cascade`—If the parent key has been updated, then copy the new key value to all child records. If the parent record has been deleted, delete the child records also. This is the default option.

❑   `None`—No action whatsoever. This option leaves orphaned rows within the child data table.

❑   `SetDefault`—Each child record affected has the foreign key column(s) set to its default value, if one has been defined.

❑   `SetNull`—All child rows have the key column(s) set to `DBNull`. (Following the naming convention that Microsoft uses, this should really be `SetDBNull`).

> Constraints are only enforced within a **DataSet** class if the **EnforceConstraints** property of the **DataSet** is true.

This covers the main classes that make up the constituent parts of the `DataSet` class, and has shown how to generate manually each of these classes in code. You can also define a `DataTable`, `DataRow`, `DataColumn`, `DataRelation`, and `Constraint` using the XML schema file(s) and the XSD tool that ships with .NET. The following section describes how to set up a simple schema and generate type-safe classes to access your data.

XML Schemas

XML is firmly entrenched in ADO.NET—indeed, the remoting format for passing data between objects is now XML. With the .NET runtime, it is possible to describe a `DataTable` class within an XML schema definition file (XSD). What's more, you can define an entire `DataSet` class, with a number of `DataTable` classes, a set of relationships between these tables, and include various other details to fully describe the data.

When you have defined an XSD file, there is a new tool in the runtime that will convert this schema to the corresponding data access class(es), such as the type-safe product `DataTable` class shown above. Let's start with a simple XSD file (`Products.xsd`) that describes the same information as the Products sample discussed earlier, and then extend it to include some extra functionality.

```
<?xml version="1.0" encoding="utf-8" ?>
<xs:schema id="Products" targetNamespace="http://tempuri.org/XMLSchema1.xsd"
  xmlns:mstns="http://tempuri.org/XMLSchema1.xsd"
    xmlns:xs="http://www.w3.org/2001/XMLSchema"
    xmlns:msdata="urn:schemas-microsoft-com:xml-msdata">
```

```
      <xs:element name="Product">
        <xs:complexType>
          <xs:sequence>
            <xs:element name="ProductID" msdata:ReadOnly="true"
              msdata:AutoIncrement="true" type="xs:int" />
            <xs:element name="ProductName" type="xs:string" />
            <xs:element name="SupplierID" type="xs:int" minOccurs="0" />
            <xs:element name="CategoryID" type="xs:int" minOccurs="0" />
            <xs:element name="QuantityPerUnit" type="xs:string" minOccurs="0" />
            <xs:element name="UnitPrice" type="xs:decimal" minOccurs="0" />
            <xs:element name="UnitsInStock" type="xs:short" minOccurs="0" />
            <xs:element name="UnitsOnOrder" type="xs:short" minOccurs="0" />
            <xs:element name="ReorderLevel" type="xs:short" minOccurs="0" />
            <xs:element name="Discontinued" type="xs:boolean" />
          </xs:sequence>
        </xs:complexType>
      </xs:element>
    </xs:schema>
```

These options are covered in detail in Chapter 24; for now, this file basically defines a schema with the id attribute set to Products. A complex type called Product is defined, which contains a number of elements, one for each of the fields within the Products table.

These items map to data classes as follows. The Products schema maps to a class derived from DataSet. The Product complex type maps to a class derived from DataTable. Each subelement maps to a class derived from DataColumn. The collection of all columns maps to a class derived from DataRow.

Thankfully there is a tool within .NET Framework that produces the code for these classes with the help of the input XSD file. Because its sole job in life is to perform various functions on XSD files, the tool itself is called XSD.EXE.

Generating Code with XSD

Assuming you save the above file as Product.xsd, you would convert the file into code by issuing the following command in a command prompt:

```
xsd Product.xsd /d
```

This creates the file Product.cs.

There are various switches that can be used with XSD to alter the output generated. Some of the more commonly used are shown in the following table.

Switch	Description
/dataset (/d)	Enables you to generate classes derived from DataSet, Data-Table, and DataRow.
/language:<language>	Permits you to choose which language the output file will be written in. C# is the default, but you can choose VB for a Visual Basic .NET file.

Switch	Description
`/namespace:<namespace>`	Enables you to define the namespace that the generated code should reside within. The default is no namespace.

An abridged version of the output from XSD for the Products schema is shown below. The output has been altered slightly to fit into a format appropriate for the book. To see the complete output, run XSD.EXE on the Products schema (or one of your own making) and take a look at the .cs file generated. The example includes the entire source code plus the Product.xsd file. (Note this output is part of the downloadable code file at `www.wrox.xom`)

```
//-----------------------------------------------------------------------------
// <autogenerated>
//      This code was generated by a tool.
//      Runtime Version: 1.1.4322.573
//
//      Changes to this file may cause incorrect behavior and will be lost if
//      the code is regenerated.
// </autogenerated>
//-----------------------------------------------------------------------------

//
// This source code was auto-generated by xsd, Version=1.1.4322.573.
//
using System;
using System.Data;
using System.Xml;
using System.Runtime.Serialization;

[Serializable()]
[System.ComponentModel.DesignerCategoryAttribute("code")]
[System.Diagnostics.DebuggerStepThrough()]
[System.ComponentModel.ToolboxItem(true)]
public class Products : DataSet
{
    private ProductDataTable tableProduct;
    public Products()
    public ProductDataTable Product
    public override DataSet Clone()
    public delegate void ProductRowChangeEventHandler ( object sender,
                                               ProductRowChangeEvent e);

    [System.Diagnostics.DebuggerStepThrough()]
    public class ProductDataTable : DataTable, System.Collections.IEnumerable

    [System.Diagnostics.DebuggerStepThrough()]
    public class ProductRow : DataRow
}
```

All private and protected members have been removed from the above so as to concentrate on the public interface. The emboldened `ProductDataTable` and `ProductRow` definitions show the positions of two nested classes, which will be implemented next. We review the code for these classes after a brief explanation of the `DataSet`-derived class.

The Products() constructor calls a private method, InitClass(), which constructs an instance of the DataTable-derived class ProductDataTable, and adds the table to the Tables collection of the DataSet class. The Products data table can be accessed by the following code:

```
DataSet ds = new Products();
DataTable products = ds.Tables["Products"];
```

Or, more simply by using the property Product, available on the derived DataSet object:

```
DataTable products = ds.Product;
```

As the Product property is strongly typed, you could naturally use ProductDataTable rather than the DataTable reference shown above.

The ProductDataTable class includes far more code:

```
[System.Diagnostics.DebuggerStepThrough()]
public class ProductDataTable : DataTable, System.Collections.IEnumerable
{
    private DataColumn columnProductID;
    private DataColumn columnProductName;
    private DataColumn columnSupplierID;
    private DataColumn columnCategoryID;
    private DataColumn columnQuantityPerUnit;
    private DataColumn columnUnitPrice;
    private DataColumn columnUnitsInStock;
    private DataColumn columnUnitsOnOrder;
    private DataColumn columnReorderLevel;
    private DataColumn columnDiscontinued;

    internal ProductDataTable() : base("Product")
    {
        this.InitClass();
    }
```

The ProductDataTable class, derived from DataTable and implementing the IEnumerable interface, defines a private DataColumn instance for each of the columns within the table. These are initialized again from the constructor by calling the private InitClass() member. Each column is given an internal accessor, which is used by the DataRow class (which we describe shortly).

```
[System.ComponentModel.Browsable(false)]
public int Count
{
    get { return this.Rows.Count; }
}
internal DataColumn ProductIDColumn
{
    get { return this.columnProductID; }
}
// Other row accessors removed for clarity -- there is one for each of the columns
```

Adding rows to the table is taken care of by the two overloaded (and significantly different) AddProductRow() methods. The first takes an already constructed DataRow and returns a void.

The second takes a set of values, one for each of the columns in the `DataTable`, constructs a new row, sets the values within this new row, adds the row to the `DataTable` object and returns the row to the caller. Such widely different functions shouldn't really have the same name!

```
public void AddProductRow(ProductRow row)
{
    this.Rows.Add(row);
}

public ProductRow AddProductRow ( string ProductName , int SupplierID ,
                                   int CategoryID , string QuantityPerUnit ,
                                   System.Decimal UnitPrice , short UnitsInStock ,
                                   short UnitsOnOrder , short ReorderLevel ,
                                   bool Discontinued )
{
    ProductRow rowProductRow = ((ProductRow)(this.NewRow()));
    rowProductRow.ItemArray = new object[]
    {
        null,
        ProductName,
        SupplierID,
        CategoryID,
        QuantityPerUnit,
        UnitPrice,
        UnitsInStock,
        UnitsOnOrder,
        ReorderLevel,
        Discontinued
    };
    this.Rows.Add(rowProductRow);
    return rowProductRow;
}
```

Just like the `InitClass()` member in the `DataSet`-derived class, which added the table into the `DataSet` class, the `InitClass()` member in `ProductDataTable` adds columns to the `DataTable` class. Each column's properties are set as appropriate, and the column is then appended to the columns collection.

```
private void InitClass()
{
    this.columnProductID = new DataColumn ( "ProductID",
                                            typeof(int),
                                            null,
                                            System.Data.MappingType.Element);
    this.Columns.Add(this.columnProductID);
    // Other columns removed for clarity

    this.columnProductID.AutoIncrement = true;
    this.columnProductID.AllowDBNull = false;
    this.columnProductID.ReadOnly = true;
    this.columnProductName.AllowDBNull = false;
    this.columnDiscontinued.AllowDBNull = false;
}

public ProductRow NewProductRow()
```

```
    {
        return ((ProductRow)(this.NewRow()));
    }
```

NewRowFromBuilder() is called internally from the DataTableclass's NewRow() method. Here it cre-ates a new strongly typed row. The DataRowBuilder instance is created by the DataTable class, and its members are only accessible within the System.Data assembly.

```
protected override DataRow NewRowFromBuilder(DataRowBuilder builder)
{
    return new ProductRow(builder);
}
```

The last class to discuss is the ProductRow class, derived from DataRow. This class is used to provide type-safe access to all fields in the data table. It wraps the storage for a particular row, and provides members to read (and write) each of the fields in the table.

In addition, for each nullable field, there are functions to set the field to null, and check if the field is null. The following example shows the functions for the SupplierID column:

```
[System.Diagnostics.DebuggerStepThrough()]
public class ProductRow : DataRow
{
    private ProductDataTable tableProduct;

    internal ProductRow(DataRowBuilder rb) : base(rb)
    {
        this.tableProduct = ((ProductDataTable)(this.Table));
    }

    public int ProductID
    {
        get { return ((int)(this[this.tableProduct.ProductIDColumn])); }
        set { this[this.tableProduct.ProductIDColumn] = value; }
    }
 // Other column accessors/mutators removed for clarity

    public bool IsSupplierIDNull()
    {
        return this.IsNull(this.tableProduct.SupplierIDColumn);
    }

    public void SetSupplierIDNull()
    {
        this[this.tableProduct.SupplierIDColumn] = System.Convert.DBNull;
    }
}
```

The following code utilizes the class' ouptut from the XSD tool to retrieve data from the Products table and display that data to the console:

```
using System;
using System.Data;
using System.Data.SqlClient;

public class XSD_DataSet
{
    public static void Main()
    {
        string source = "server=(local)\\NetSDK;" +
                        "uid=QSUser;pwd=QSPassword;" +
                        "database=northwind";
        string select = "SELECT * FROM Products";
        SqlConnection conn = new SqlConnection(source);
        SqlDataAdapter da = new SqlDataAdapter(select , conn);
        Products ds = new Products();
        da.Fill(ds , "Product");
        foreach(Products.ProductRow row in ds.Product )
        Console.WriteLine("'{0}' from {1}" ,
                          row.ProductID ,
                          row.ProductName);
    }
}
```

The main areas of interest are highlighted. The output of the XSD file contains a class derived from `DataSet`, `Products`, which is created and then filled by the use of the data adapter. The `foreach` statement uses the strongly typed `ProductRow` and also the `Product` property, which returns the `Product` data table.

To compile this example, issue the following commands:

xsd product.xsd /d

and

csc /recurse:*.cs

The first generates the Products.cs file from the Products.XSD schema, and then the csc command utilizes the /recurse:*.cs parameter to go through all files with the extension .cs and add these to the resulting assembly.

Populating a DataSet

After you have defined the schema of your data set, replete with `DataTable`, `DataColumn`, and `Constraint` classes, and whatever else is necessary, you need to be able to populate the `DataSet` class with some information. There are two main ways to read data from an external source and insert it into the `DataSet` class:

- ❑ Use a data adapter.
- ❑ Read XML into the `DataSet` class.

Populating a DataSet Class with a Data Adapter

The section on data rows briefly introduced the `SqlDataAdapter` class, as shown in the following code:

```
string select = "SELECT ContactName,CompanyName FROM Customers";
SqlConnection conn = new SqlConnection(source);
SqlDataAdapter da = new SqlDataAdapter(select , conn);
DataSet ds = new DataSet();
da.Fill(ds , "Customers");
```

The two highlighted lines show the `SqlDataAdapter` class in use; the other data adapter classes are again virtually identical in functionality to the `Sql` equivalent.

The adapter classes are all derived from a common base class rather than a set of interfaces, as are most of the other database-specific classes. Here is the inheritance hierarchy:

```
System.Data.Common.DataAdapter
    System.Data.Common.DbDataAdapter
        System.Data.Odbc.OdbcDataAdapter
        System.Data.OleDb.OleDbDataAdapter
        System.Data.OracleClient.OracleDataAdapter
        System.Data.SqlClient.SqlDataAdapter
```

In order to retrieve data into a `DataSet`, it is necessary to have some form of command that is executed to select that data. The command in question could be a SQL `SELECT` statement, a call to a stored procedure, or for the OLE DB provider, a `TableDirect` command. The previous example uses one of the constructors available on `SqlDataAdapter` that converts the passed SQL `SELECT` statement into a `SqlCommand`, and issues this when the `Fill()` method is called on the adapter.

In the stored procedures example earlier in this chapter, the INSERT, UPDATE and DELETE procedures were defined but the SELECT procedure was not. That gap is filled in the next section, which also shows how to call a stored procedure from a `SqlDataAdapter` class to populate data in a `DataSet` class.

Using a stored procedure in a data adapter

The first step in this example is to define the stored procedure. The stored procedure to `SELECT` data is as follows:

```
CREATE PROCEDURE RegionSelect AS
  SET NOCOUNT OFF
  SELECT * FROM Region
GO
```

This stored procedure can be typed directly into the SQL Server Query Analyzer, or you can run the StoredProc.sql file that is provided for use by this example.

Next, the `SqlCommand` that executes this stored procedure needs to be defined. Again the code is very simple, and most of it was already presented in the earlier section on issuing commands:

```
private static SqlCommand GenerateSelectCommand(SqlConnection conn )
{
    SqlCommand  aCommand = new SqlCommand("RegionSelect" , conn);
```

```
        aCommand.CommandType = CommandType.StoredProcedure;
        aCommand.UpdatedRowSource = UpdateRowSource.None;
        return aCommand;
    }
```

This method generates the `SqlCommand` that calls the `RegionSelect` procedure when executed. All that remains is to hook up this command to a `SqlDataAdapter` class, and call the `Fill()` method:

```
DataSet ds = new DataSet();
// Create a data adapter to fill the DataSet
SqlDataAdapter da = new SqlDataAdapter();
// Set the data adapter's select command
da.SelectCommand = GenerateSelectCommand (conn);
da.Fill(ds , "Region");
```

Here the `SqlDataAdapter` class, is created, and the generated `SqlCommand` is then assigned to the `SelectCommand` property of the data adapter. Subsequently `Fill()` is called, which will execute the stored procedure and insert all rows returned into the Region `DataTable` (which in this instance is generated by the runtime).

There's more to a data adapter than just selecting data by issuing a command, as discussed in the section "Persisting DataSet Changes".

Populating a DataSet from XML

In addition to generating the schema for a given `DataSet` and associated tables and so on, a `DataSet` class can read and write data in native XML, such as a file on disk, a stream, or a text reader.

To load XML into a `DataSet` class, simply call one of the `ReadXML()` methods to read data from a disk file, as shown in this example:

```
DataSet ds = new DataSet();
ds.ReadXml(".\\MyData.xml");
```

The `ReadXml()` method attempts to load any inline schema information from the input XML, and if found, uses this schema in the validation of any data loaded from that file. If no inline schema is found then the `DataSet` will extend its internal structure as data is loaded. This is similar to the behavior of `Fill()` in the previous example, which retrieves the data and constructs a `DataTable` based on the data selected.

Persisting DataSet Changes

After editing data within a `DataSet`, it is usually necessary to persist these changes. The most common example would be selecting data from a database, displaying it to the user, and returning those updates to the database.

In a less "connected" application, changes might be persisted to an XML file, transported to a middle-tier application server, and then processed to update several data sources.

A `DataSet` class can be used for either of these examples, and what's more it's really easy to do.

Updating with Data Adapters

In addition to the `SelectCommand` that an `SqlDataAdapter` most likely includes, you can also define an `InsertCommand`, `UpdateCommand`, and `DeleteCommand`. As these names imply, these objects are instances of the command object appropriate for your provider such as `SqlCommand` and `OleDbCommand`).

With this level of flexibility, you are free to tune the application by judicious use of stored procedures for frequently used commands (say `SELECT` and `INSERT`), and use straight SQL for less commonly used commands such as `DELETE`. In general it is recommended to provide stored procedures for all database interaction, because it is faster and easier to tune.

This example uses the stored procedure code from the "Calling Stored Procedures" section for inserting, updating, and deleting `Region` records, coupled with the `RegionSelect` procedure written above, which produces an example that utilizes each of these commands to retrieve and update data in a `DataSet` class. The main body of code is shown in the following section.

Inserting a new row

There are two ways to add a new row to a `DataTable`. The first way is to call the `NewRow()` method, which returns a blank row that you then populate and add to the `Rows` collection, as follows:

```
DataRow r = ds.Tables["Region"].NewRow();
r["RegionID"]=999;
r["RegionDescription"]="North West";
ds.Tables["Region"].Rows.Add(r);
```

The second way to add a new row would be to pass an array of data to the `Rows.Add()` method as shown in the following code:

```
DataRow r = ds.Tables["Region"].Rows.Add
            (new object [] { 999 , "North West" });
```

Each new row within the `DataTable` will have its `RowState` set to `Added`. The example dumps out the records before each change is made to the database, so after adding the following row (either way) to the `DataTable`, the rows will look something like the following. Note that the right-hand column shows the row state.

```
New row pending inserting into database
    1    Eastern                                  Unchanged
    2    Western                                  Unchanged
    3    Northern                                 Unchanged
    4    Southern                                 Unchanged
    999  North West                               Added
```

To update the database from the `DataAdapter`, call one of the `Update()` methods as shown below:

```
da.Update(ds , "Region");
```

For the new row within the `DataTable`, this executes the stored procedure (in this instance `RegionInsert`). The example then dumps the state of the data so you can see that changes have been made to the database.

```
New row updated and new RegionID assigned by database
   1    Eastern                                           Unchanged
   2    Western                                           Unchanged
   3    Northern                                          Unchanged
   4    Southern                                          Unchanged
   5    North West                                        Unchanged
```

Look at the last row in the `DataTable`. The `RegionID` had been set in code to 999, but after executing the `RegionInsert` stored procedure the value has been changed to 5. This is intentional—the database will often generate primary keys for you, and the updated data in the `DataTable` is due to the fact that the `SqlCommand` definition within our source code has the `UpdatedRowSource` property set to `UpdateRowSource.OutputParameters`:

```
SqlCommand aCommand = new SqlCommand("RegionInsert" , conn);

aCommand.CommandType = CommandType.StoredProcedure;
aCommand.Parameters.Add(new SqlParameter("@RegionDescription" ,
                        SqlDbType.NChar ,
                        50 ,
                        "RegionDescription"));
aCommand.Parameters.Add(new SqlParameter("@RegionID" ,
                        SqlDbType.Int,
                        0 ,
                        ParameterDirection.Output ,
                        false ,
                        0 ,
                        0 ,
                        "RegionID" ,   // Defines the SOURCE column
                        DataRowVersion.Default ,
                        null));
aCommand.UpdatedRowSource = UpdateRowSource.OutputParameters;
```

What this means is that whenever a data adapter issues this command, the output parameters should be mapped to the source of the row, which in this instance was a row in a `DataTable`. The flag states what data should be updated—the stored procedure has an output parameter that is mapped to the `DataRow`. The column it applies to is `RegionID`, as this is defined within the command definition.

The following table shows the values for `UpdateRowSource`.

UpdateRowSource Value	Description
Both	A stored procedure might return output parameters and also a complete database record. Both of these data sources are used to update the source row.

Table continued on following page

UpdateRowSource Value	Description
FirstReturnedRecord	This infers that the command returns a single record, and that the contents of that record should be merged into the original source DataRow. This is useful where a given table has a number of default (or computed) columns, as after an INSERT statement these need to be synchronized with the DataRow on the client. An example might be 'INSERT (columns) INTO (table) WITH (primarykey)', then 'SELECT (columns) FROM (table) WHERE (primarykey)'. The returned record would then be merged into the original row.
None	All data returned from the command is discarded.
OutputParameters	Any output parameters from the command are mapped onto the appropriate column(s) in the DataRow.

Updating an existing row

Updating an existing row within the DataTable is just a case of utilizing the DataRow class's indexer with either a column name or column number, as shown in the following code:

```
r["RegionDescription"]="North West England";
r[1] = "North East England";
```

Both of these statements are equivalent (in this example):

```
Changed RegionID 5 description
    1   Eastern                                      Unchanged
    2   Western                                      Unchanged
    3   Northern                                     Unchanged
    4   Southern                                     Unchanged
    5   North West England                           Modified
```

Prior to updating the database, the row updated has its state set to Modified as shown above.

Deleting a row

Deleting a row is a matter of calling the Delete() method:

```
r.Delete();
```

A deleted row has its row state set to Deleted, but you cannot read columns from the deleted DataRow, because they are no longer valid. When the adaptor's Update() method is called, all deleted rows will use the DeleteCommand, which in this instance executes the RegionDelete stored procedure.

Writing XML Output

As you have seen already, the DataSet class has great support for defining its schema in XML, and just like you can read data from an XML document, you can also write data to an XML document.

The `DataSet.WriteXml()` method enables you to output various parts of the data stored within the `DataSet`. You can elect to output just the data, or the data and the schema. The following code shows an example of both for the Region example shown above:

```
ds.WriteXml(".\\WithoutSchema.xml");
ds.WriteXml(".\\WithSchema.xml" , XmlWriteMode.WriteSchema);
```

The first file, WithoutSchema.xml is shown below:

```
<?xml version="1.0" standalone="yes"?>
<NewDataSet>
  <Region>
    <RegionID>1</RegionID>
    <RegionDescription>Eastern                              </RegionDescription>
  </Region>
  <Region>
    <RegionID>2</RegionID>
    <RegionDescription>Western                              </RegionDescription>
  </Region>
  <Region>
    <RegionID>3</RegionID>
    <RegionDescription>Northern                             </RegionDescription>
  </Region>
  <Region>
    <RegionID>4</RegionID>
    <RegionDescription>Southern                             </RegionDescription>
  </Region>
</NewDataSet>
```

The closing tag on `RegionDescription` is over to the right of the page, because the database column is defined as `NCHAR(50)`, which is a 50 character string padded with spaces.

The output produced in the WithSchema.xml file includes the XML schema for the `DataSet` as well as the data itself:

```
<?xml version="1.0" standalone="yes"?>
<NewDataSet>
  <xs:schema id="NewDataSet" xmlns=""
             xmlns:xs="http://www.w3.org/2001/XMLSchema"
             xmlns:msdata="urn:schemas-microsoft-com:xml-msdata">
    <xs:element name="NewDataSet" msdata:IsDataSet="true">
      <xs:complexType>
        <xs:choice maxOccurs="unbounded">
          <xs:element name="Region">
            <xs:complexType>
              <xs:sequence>
                <xs:element name="RegionID"
                            msdata:AutoIncrement="true"
                            msdata:AutoIncrementSeed="1"
                            type="xs:int" />
                <xs:element name="RegionDescription"
                            type="xs:string" />
              </xs:sequence>
```

```
                            </xs:complexType>
                        </xs:element>
                    </xs:choice>
                </xs:complexType>
            </xs:element>
        </xs:schema>
        <Region>
            <RegionID>1</RegionID>
            <RegionDescription>Eastern                        </RegionDescription>
        </Region>
        <Region>
            <RegionID>2</RegionID>
            <RegionDescription>Western                        </RegionDescription>
        </Region>
        <Region>
            <RegionID>3</RegionID>
            <RegionDescription>Northern                       </RegionDescription>
        </Region>
        <Region>
            <RegionID>4</RegionID>
            <RegionDescription>Southern                       </RegionDescription>
        </Region>
    </NewDataSet>
```

Note the use in this file of the `msdata` schema, which defines extra attributes for columns within a `DataSet`, such as `AutoIncrement` and `AutoIncrementSeed`—these attributes correspond directly with the properties definable on a `DataColumn` class.

Working with ADO.NET

In this section we address some common scenarios when developing data access applications with ADO.NET.

Tiered Development

Producing an application that interacts with data is often done by splitting up the application into tiers. A common model is to have an application tier (the front end), a data services tier, and the database itself.

One of the difficulties with this model is deciding what data to transport between tiers, and the format that it should be transported in. With ADO.NET you'll be pleased to learn that these wrinkles have been ironed out, and support for this style of architecture is part of the design.

Copying and merging data

Ever tried copying an entire OLE DB record set? In .NET it's easy to copy a `DataSet`:

```
DataSet source = {some dataset};
DataSet dest = source.Copy();
```

This creates an exact copy of the source DataSet—each DataTable, DataColumn, DataRow, and Relation will be copied, and all data will be in exactly the same state as it was in the source. If all you want to copy is the schema of the DataSet, you can use the following code:

```
DataSet source = {some dataset};
DataSet dest = source.Clone();
```

This again copies all tables, relations, and so on. However, each copied DataTable will be empty. This process really couldn't be more straightforward.

A common requirement when writing a tiered system, whether based on Win32 or the Web, is to be able to ship as little data as possible between tiers. This reduces the amount of resources consumed.

To cope with this requirement, the DataSet class has the GetChanges() method. This simple method performs a huge amount of work, and returns a DataSet with only the changed rows from the source data set. This is ideal for passing data between tiers, because only a minimal set of data has to be passed along.

The following example shows how to generate a "changes" DataSet:

```
DataSet source = {some dataset};
DataSet dest = source.GetChanges();
```

Again, this is trivial. Under the hood, things are a little more interesting. There are two overloads of the GetChanges() method. One overload takes a value of the DataRowState enumeration, and returns only rows that correspond to that state (or states). GetChanges() simply calls GetChanges(Deleted | Modified | Added), and first checks to ensure that there are some changes by calling HasChanges(). If no changes have been made, then null is returned to the caller immediately.

The next operation is to clone the current DataSet. Once done, the new DataSet is set up to ignore constraint violations (EnforceConstraints = false), and then each changed row for every table is copied into the new DataSet.

When you have a DataSet that just contains changes, you can then move these off to the data services tier for processing. After the data has been updated in the database, the "changes" DataSet can be returned to the caller (for example, there might be some output parameters from the stored procedures that have updated values in the columns). These changes can then be merged into the original DataSet using the Merge() method. Figure 21-9 depicts this sequence of operations.

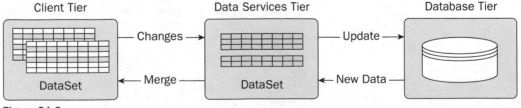

Figure 21-9

Key Generation with SQL Server

The `RegionInsert` stored procedure presented earlier in this chapter is one example of generating a primary key value on insertion into the database. The method for generating the key in this particular example is fairly crude and wouldn't scale well, so for a real application you should use some other strategy for generating keys.

Your first instinct might be to define an identity column, and return the `@@IDENTITY` value from the stored procedure. The following stored procedure shows how this might be defined for the Categories table in the Northwind example database. Type this stored procedure into SQL Query Analyzer, or run the StoredProcs.sql file that is part of the code download.

```
CREATE PROCEDURE CategoryInsert(@CategoryName NVARCHAR(15),
                                @Description NTEXT,
                                @CategoryID INTEGER OUTPUT) AS
    SET NOCOUNT OFF
    INSERT INTO Categories (CategoryName, Description)
        VALUES(@CategoryName, @Description)
    SELECT @CategoryID = @@IDENTITY
GO
```

This inserts a new row into the `Category` table, and returns the generated primary key to the caller (the value of the CategoryID column). You can test the procedure by typing in the following SQL in Query Analyzer:

```
DECLARE @CatID int;
EXECUTE CategoryInsert 'Pasties' , 'Heaven Sent Food' , @CatID OUTPUT;
PRINT @CatID;
```

When executed as a batch of commands, this inserts a new row into the Categories table, and returns the identity of the new record, which is then displayed to the user.

Let's say that some months down the line, someone decides to add a simple audit trail, which will record all insertions and modifications made to the category name. In that case, you define a table similar to the one shown in Figure 21-10, which will record the old and new value of the category.

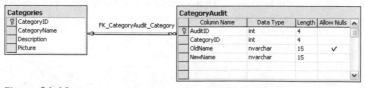

Figure 21-10

The script for this table is included in the StoredProcs.sql file. The AuditID column is defined as an IDENTITY column. You then construct a couple of database triggers that will record changes to the CategoryName field:

```
CREATE TRIGGER CategoryInsertTrigger
    ON Categories
    AFTER UPDATE
AS
    INSERT INTO CategoryAudit(CategoryID , OldName , NewName )
        SELECT old.CategoryID, old.CategoryName, new.CategoryName
        FROM Deleted AS old,
            Categories AS new
        WHERE old.CategoryID = new.CategoryID;
GO
```

For those of you used to Oracle stored procedures, SQL Server doesn't exactly have the concept of OLD and NEW rows, instead for an insert trigger there is an in memory table called Inserted, and for deletes and updates the old rows are available within the Deleted table.

This trigger retrieves the CategoryID of the record(s) affected, and stores this together with the old and new value of the CategoryName column.

Now, when you call your original stored procedure to insert a new CategoryID, you receive an identity value; however, this is no longer the identity value from the row inserted into the Categories table, it is now the new value generated for the row in the CategoryAudit table. Ouch!

To view the problem first hand, open a copy of SQL Server Enterprise manager, and view the contents of the Categories table (see Figure 21-11).

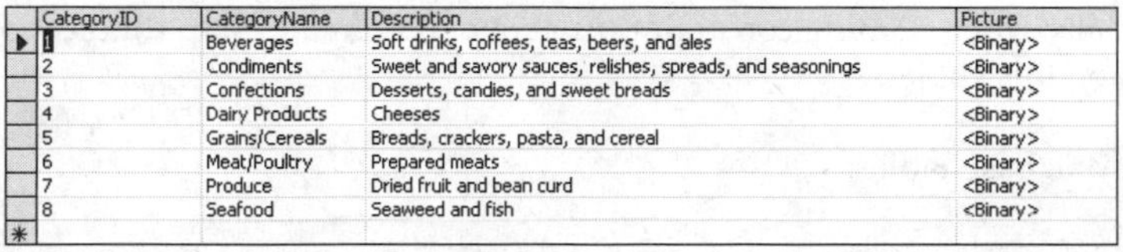

CategoryID	CategoryName	Description	Picture
1	Beverages	Soft drinks, coffees, teas, beers, and ales	<Binary>
2	Condiments	Sweet and savory sauces, relishes, spreads, and seasonings	<Binary>
3	Confections	Desserts, candies, and sweet breads	<Binary>
4	Dairy Products	Cheeses	<Binary>
5	Grains/Cereals	Breads, crackers, pasta, and cereal	<Binary>
6	Meat/Poultry	Prepared meats	<Binary>
7	Produce	Dried fruit and bean curd	<Binary>
8	Seafood	Seaweed and fish	<Binary>

Figure 21-11

This lists all the categories in the Northwind database.

The next identity value for the Categories table should be 9, so a new row can be inserted by executing the code shown below, to see what ID is returned:

```
DECLARE @CatID int;
EXECUTE CategoryInsert 'Pasties' , 'Heaven Sent Food' , @CatID OUTPUT;
PRINT @CatID;
```

The output value of this on a test PC was 1. If you look at the CategoryAudit table shown in Figure 21-12, you will find that this is the identity of the newly inserted audit record, not that of the category record created.

	AuditID	CategoryID	OldName	NewName
▶	1	9	\<NULL\>	Pasties
*				

Figure 21-12

The problem lies in the way that @@IDENTITY actually works. It returns the LAST identity value created by your session, so as shown in Figure 21-12 it isn't completely reliable.

There are two other identity functions that you can use instead of @@IDENTITY, but neither are free from possible problems. The first, SCOPE_IDENTITY(), returns the last identity value created within the current *scope*. SQL Server defines scope as a stored procedure, trigger, or function. This may work most of the time, but if for some reason someone adds another INSERT statement into the stored procedure, then you can receive this value rather than the one you expected.

The other identity function, IDENT_CURRENT(), returns the last identity value generated for a given table in any scope. For example, if two users were accessing SQL Server at exactly the same time, it might be possible to receive the other user's generated identity value.

As you might imagine, tracking down a problem of this nature isn't easy. The moral of the story is to beware when utilizing IDENTITY columns in SQL Server.

Naming Conventions

The following tips and conventions are not directly .NET related. However, they are worth sharing and following, especially when naming constraints as above. Feel free to skip this section if you already have your own views on this subject.

Conventions for database tables:

❑ Always use singular names—Product rather than Products. This one is largely due to having to explain to customers a database schema; it's much better grammatically to say "The Product table contains products" than "The Products table contains products". Check out the Northwind database to see an example of how not to do this.

❑ Adopt some form of naming convention for the fields that go into a table—Ours is \<Table\>_ID for the primary key of a table (assuming that the primary key is a single column), Name for the field considered to be the user-friendly name of the record, and Description for any textual information about the record itself. Having a good table convention means you can look at virtually any table in the database and instinctively know what the fields are used for.

Conventions for database columns:

❑ Use singular rather than plural names.

❑ Any columns that link to another table should be named the same as the primary key of that table. For example, a link to the Product table would be Product_ID, and to the Sample table Sample_ID. This isn't always possible, especially if one table has multiple references to another. In that case use your own judgment.

❑ Date fields should have a suffix of _On, as in Modified_On, Created_On. Then it's easy to read some SQL output and infer what a column means just by its name.

❑ Fields that record the user should be suffixed with _By, as in Modified_By and Created_By. Again, this aids legibility.

Conventions for constraints:

❑ If possible, include in the name of the constraint the table and column name, as in CK_<Table>_<Field>. For example, CK_PERSON_SEX for a check constraint on the SEX column of the PERSON table. A foreign key example would be FK_Product_Supplier_ID, for the foreign key relationship between product and supplier.

❑ Show the type of constraint with a prefix, such as CK for a check constraint and FK for a foreign key constraint. Feel free to be more specific, as in CK_PERSON_AGE_GT0 for a constraint on the age column indicating that the age should be greater than zero.

❑ If you have to trim the length of the constraint, do it on the table name part rather than the column name. When you get a constraint violation, it's usually easy to infer which table was in error, but sometimes not so easy to check which column caused the problem. Oracle has a 30-character limit on names, which is easy to surpass.

Stored procedures

Just like the obsession many have fallen into over the past few years of putting a C in front of each and every class they have declared (you know you have!), many SQL Server developers feel compelled to prefix every stored procedure with sp_ or something similar. This is not a good idea.

SQL Server uses the sp_ prefix for all (well, most) system stored procedures. So, on the one hand, you risk confusing your users into thinking that 'sp_widget' is something that comes as standard with SQL Server. In addition, when looking for a stored procedure, SQL Server will treat procedures with the sp_ prefix differently from those without.

If you use this prefix, and do not qualify the database/owner of the stored procedure, then SQL Server will look in the current scope and then jump into the master database and look up the stored procedure there. Without the sp_ prefix your users would get an error a little earlier. What's worse, and also possible to do, is to create a local stored procedure (one within your database) that has the same name and parameters as a system stored procedure. Avoid this at all costs—if in doubt, don't prefix.

When calling stored procedures, always prefix with the owner of the procedure, as in dbo.selectWidgets. This is slightly faster than not using the prefix as SQL Server has less work to do to find the stored proc. Something like this is not likely to have a huge impact on the execution speed of your application, but it is a tuning trick that is essentially available for free.

Above all, when naming entities, whether within the database or within code, *be consistent*.

Summary

The subject of data access is a large one, especially in .NET, because there is an abundance of new material to cover. This chapter has provided an outline of the main classes in the ADO.NET namespaces, and shown how to use the classes when manipulating data from a data source.

Firstly, the `Connection` object was explored, through the use of both the `SqlConnection` (SQL Server specific) and `OleDbConnection` (for any OLE DB data sources). The programming model for these two classes is so similar that one can normally be substituted for the other and the code will continue to run. With the advent of .NET version 1.1, you can now use an Oracle provider and also an ODBC provider.

We also discussed how to use connections properly, so that these scarce resources could be closed as early as possible. All of the connection classes implement the `IDisposable` interface, called when the object is placed within a `using` clause. If there's one thing you should take away from this chapter, it is the importance of closing database connections as early as possible.

Furthermore we discussed database commands by way of examples that executed with no returned data to calling stored procedures with input and output parameters. We described various execute methods, including the `ExecuteXmlReader` method available only on the SQL Server provider. This vastly simplifies the selection and manipulation of XML-based data.

The generic classes within the `System.Data` namespace were all described in detail, from the `DataSet` class through `DataTable`, `DataColumn`, `DataRow` and on to relationships and constraints. The `DataSet` class is an excellent container of data, and various methods make it ideal for cross-tier data flow. The data within a `DataSet` is represented in XML for transport, and in addition, methods are available that pass a minimal amount of data between tiers. The ability of having many tables of data within a single `DataSet` can greatly increase its usability; being able to maintain relationships automatically between master/details rows will be expanded upon in the next chapter.

Having the schema stored within a `DataSet` is one thing, but .NET also includes the data adapter that, next to various `Command` objects, can be used to select data into a `DataSet` and subsequently update data in the data store. One of the beneficial aspects of a data adapter is that a distinct command can be defined for each of the four actions: `SELECT`, `INSERT`, `UPDATE` and `DELETE`. The system can create a default set of commands based on database schema information and a `SELECT` statement, but for the best performance, a set of stored procedures can be used, with the `DataAdapter`'s commands defined appropriately to pass only the necessary information to these stored procedures.

We also co vered the XSD tool (XSD.EXE) was described, using an example that shows how to work with classes based on an XML schema from within .NET. The classes produced are ready to be used within an application, and their automatic generation can save many hours of laborious typing.

Finally, we discussed some best practices and naming conventions for database development.

Armed with this knowledge, you're now in a good position to move on to Chapter 22, which explores the use of Visual Studio and the .NET Windows Forms data controls.

Viewing .NET Data

This chapter builds on the content of Chapter 21, which covers various ways of selecting and changing data, showing you how to present data to the user by binding to various Windows controls. More specifically, this chapter discusses:

❏ The most revolutionary aspect of the .NET data access model, the new DataGrid control, the most

❏ The .NET data-binding capabilities and how they work

❏ How to use the Server Explorer to create a connection and generate a DataSet class (all without writing a line of code)

❏ How to use hit testing and reflection on rows in the DataGrid

You can download the source code for the examples in this chapter from the Wrox Web site at www.wrox.com.

The DataGrid Control

One of the best features of the new DataGrid control is its flexibility—the data source can be an Array, DataTable, DataView, DataSet class, or a component that implements either the IListSource or IList interface. The DataGrid control gives you a variety of views of the same data. In its simplest guise, data can be displayed (as in a DataSet class) by calling the SetDataBinding() method. This new control also provides more complex capabilities, which we discuss in this chapter in the course of this chapter.

Displaying Tabular Data

Chapter 21 introduces numerous ways of selecting data and reading it into a data table, although the data is displayed in a very basic fashion using Console.WriteLine().

In the following example, we demonstrate how to retrieve some data and display it in a `DataGrid` control. For this purpose, we build a new application, DisplayTabularData, shown in Figure 22-1.

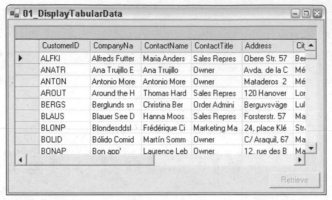

Figure 22-1

This simple application selects every record from the customer table in the Northwind database, and displays these records to the user in the `DataGrid` control. The following snippet shows the the code for this example:

```
using System;
using System.Windows.Forms;
using System.Data;
using System.Data.SqlClient;

public class DisplayTabularData : System.Windows.Forms.Form
{
    private System.Windows.Forms.Button retrieveButton;
    private System.Windows.Forms.DataGrid dataGrid;
    public DisplayTabularData()
    {
        this.AutoScaleBaseSize = new System.Drawing.Size(5, 13);
        this.ClientSize = new System.Drawing.Size(464, 253);
        this.Text = "01_DisplayTabularData";
```

This initial section of code creates the main window class and defines the instance variables for that class. It also specifies some properties of the window. Next comes the code that creates the `DataGrid` control.

```
        this.dataGrid = new System.Windows.Forms.DataGrid();
        dataGrid.BeginInit();
        dataGrid.Location = new System.Drawing.Point(8, 8);
        dataGrid.Size = new System.Drawing.Size(448, 208);
        dataGrid.TabIndex = 0;
        dataGrid.Anchor = AnchorStyles.Bottom | AnchorStyles.Top |
                          AnchorStyles.Left | AnchorStyles.Right;
        this.Controls.Add(this.dataGrid);
        dataGrid.EndInit();
```

The second line: `dataGrid.BeginInit();` disables the firing of events on the grid, which is useful when making many modifications to the control. If events are not inhibited, each change to the grid could force a redraw on screen. The location and size of the control are then defined, as is the tab index, and the control is set to anchor to both the top left and bottom right corners of the window, so that its proportions track those of the main application window.

Next we create the button. We follow the same basic steps as in the previous snippet to initialize the button:

```
        this.retrieveButton = new System.Windows.Forms.Button();
        retrieveButton.Location = new System.Drawing.Point(384, 224);
        retrieveButton.Size = new System.Drawing.Size(75, 23);
        retrieveButton.TabIndex = 1;
        retrieveButton.Anchor = AnchorStyles.Bottom | AnchorStyles.Right;
        retrieveButton.Text = "Retrieve";
        retrieveButton.Click += new System.EventHandler
                                    (this.retrieveButton_Click);
        this.Controls.Add(this.retrieveButton);
    }
```

The button raises the `Click` event, so a handler for this event (`retrieveButton_Click`) is also defined:

```
    protected void retrieveButton_Click(object sender, System.EventArgs e)
    {
        retrieveButton.Enabled = false;
        string source = "server=(local)\\NetSDK;" +
                        "uid=QSUser;pwd=QSPassword;" +
                        "database=Northwind";
```

After selecting the data from the Customers table and filling the data set, the data is bound to the grid by calling the `SetDataBinding` method. The data set and name of the table within that data set are passed to this method. A grid can only display the data from one `DataTable` at a time, even if the `DataSet` contains multiple tables. Further on in the chapter, there is an example of displaying data from a `DataSet` with multiple `DataTables`. Of course, the data within the `DataSet` class could come from many actual database tables (or a view over many tables):

```
        string select = "SELECT * FROM Customers" ;
        SqlConnection conn = new SqlConnection(source);
        SqlDataAdapter da = new SqlDataAdapter( select , conn);
        DataSet ds = new DataSet();
        da.Fill(ds , "Customers");
        dataGrid.SetDataBinding(ds , "Customers");
    }
    static void Main()
    {
        Application.Run(new DisplayTabularData());
    }
}
```

To compile this example, type the following at a command prompt:

```
csc /t:winexe /debug+ /r:System.dll /r:System.Data.dll /r:system.windows.forms.dll
    /recurse:*.cs
```

The /recurse:*.cs parameter will compile all .cs files in the current directory and all subdirectories. Here it is used to ensure that all associated code files are included into the executable.

Data Sources

The DataGrid control provides a flexible way to display data; in addition to calling SetDataBinding() with a DataSet and the name of the table to display, this method can be called with any of the following data sources:

- ❑ An array (the grid can bind to any one dimensional array)
- ❑ DataTable
- ❑ DataView
- ❑ DataSet or DataViewManager
- ❑ Components that implement the IListSource interface
- ❑ Components that implement the IList interface

The following sections will give an example of each of these data sources.

Displaying data from an array

At first glance this seems to be easy. Create an array, fill it with some data, and call SetDataBinding (array, null) on the DataGrid control. Here's some example code:

```
string[] stuff = new string[] {"One", "Two", "Three"};
dataGrid.SetDataBinding(stuff, null);
```

SetDataBinding accepts two parameters. The first is the data source, which is the array in this instance. The second parameter should be null unless the data source is a DataSet or DataViewManager class, in which case it should be the name of the table to be displayed.

You could replace the code in the previous example's retrieveButton_Click event handler with the array code above. The problem with this code is the resulting display (see Figure 22-2).

Figure 22-2

Instead of displaying the strings defined within the array, the grid is displays the length of those strings. The reason for this is that when using an array as the source of data for a `DataGrid` control, the grid looks for the first public property of the object within the array, and displays this value rather than the string value. The first (and only) public property of a string is its length, so that is what is displayed.

One way to rectify this is to create a wrapper class for strings:

```
protected class Item
{
    public Item(string text)
    {
        _text = text;
    }
    public string Text
    {
        get{return _text;}
    }
    private string _text;
}
```

Figure 22-3 shows the output when an array of this `Item` class (which could as well be a `struct` for all the processing that it does) is added to our data source array code.

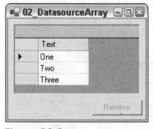

Figure 22-3

DataTable

There are two ways to display a `DataTable` within a `DataGrid` control:

❑   If your `DataTable` is standalone, call `SetDataBinding(DataTable, null)`

❑   If your `DataTable` is contained within a `DataSet`, call `SetDataBinding(DataSet, "<Table Name>")`

Figure 22-4 shows the result of running the Datasourcedatatable sample code.

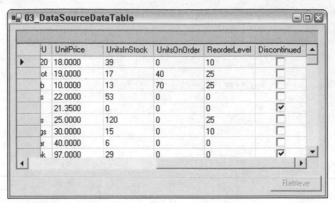

Figure 22-4

Note the display of the last column; it shows a check box instead of the more common edit control. The `DataGrid` control, in the absence of any other information, will read the schema from the data source (which in this case is the Products table), and infer from the column types what control is to be displayed. Don't get too excited, though—the only two types that are currently supported are text boxes and check boxes—any other sort of mapping has to be done manually.

The data in the database does not change when fields are altered in the data grid, because the data is only stored locally on the client computer—there is no active connection to the database. Updating data in the database is discussed later in this chapter.

Displaying data from a DataView

A `DataView` provides a means to filter and sort data within a `DataTable`. When data has been selected from the database, it is common to permit the user to sort that data, such as by clicking on column headings. In addition, the user might want to filter the data to show only certain rows, such as all those that have been altered. A `DataView` can be filtered so that only selected rows are shown to the user; however, it does not limit the columns from the `DataTable`.

> **A DataView does not permit filtering of columns only rows**

An example of how to limit the columns shown is provided in the section "DataGridTableStyle and DataGridColumnStyle" later in this chapter.

To create a `DataView` based on an existing `DataTable` use the following code:

```
DataView dv = new DataView(dataTable);
```

Once created, further settings can be altered on the `DataView`, which affect the data and operations permitted on that data when it is displayed within the data grid. For example:

- ❑ Setting `AllowEdit = false` disables all column edit functionality for rows
- ❑ Setting `AllowNew = false` disables the new row functionality
- ❑ Setting `AllowDelete = false` disables the delete row capability

❑   Setting the `RowStateFilter` displays only rows of a given state

❑   Setting the `RowFilter` enables you to filter rows

❑   Sorting the rows by certain columns

The next section explains how to use the `RowStateFilter` setting; the other options are fairly self-explanatory.

Filtering rows by data

After the `DataView` has been created, the data displayed by that view can be altered by setting the `RowFilter` property. This property, typed as a string, is used as a means of filtering based on certain criteria defined by the value of the string. Its syntax is similar to a `WHERE` clause in regular SQL, but it is issued against data already selected from the database.

The following table shows some examples of filter clauses.

Clause	Description
`UnitsInStock > 50`	Show only those rows where the UnitsInStock column is greater than 50.
`Client = 'Smith'`	Return only the records for a given client.
`County LIKE 'C*'`	Return all records where the `County` field begins with a C—in this example, the rows for Cornwall, Cumbria, Cheshire, and Cambridgeshire would be returned. The `%` character can be used as a single character wildcard, whereas the `*` denotes a general wildcard that will match zero or more characters.

The runtime will do its best to coerce the data types used within the filter expression into the appropriate types for the source columns. As an example, it is perfectly legal to write `"UnitsInStock > '50'"` in the earlier example, even though the column is an integer. If an invalid filter string is provided, then an `EvaluateException` will be thrown.

Filtering rows on state

Each row within a `DataView` has a defined row state, which has one of the values shown in the following table. This state can also be used to filter the rows viewed by the user.

DataViewRowState	Description
`Added`	Lists all rows that have been newly created.
`CurrentRows`	Lists all rows except those that have been deleted.
`Deleted`	Lists all rows that were originally selected and have been deleted; does not show newly created rows that have been deleted.
`ModifiedCurrent`	Lists all rows that have been modified, and shows the current value of each column.

Table continued on following page

DataViewRowState	Description
ModifiedOriginal	Lists all rows that have been modified, but shows the original value of the column and not the current value.
OriginalRows	Lists all rows which were originally selected from a data source. Does not include new rows. Shows the original values of the columns (that is, not the current values if changes have been made).
Unchanged	Lists all rows that have not changed in any way.

Figure 22-5 shows a data grid that can have rows added, deleted, or amended, and a second data grid that lists rows in one of the above states.

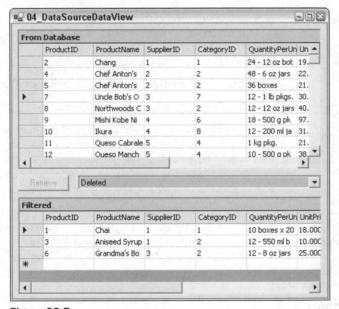

Figure 22-5

The filter not only applies to the rows that are visible, but also to the state of the columns within those rows. This is evident when choosing the ModifiedOriginal or ModifiedCurrent selections. These states are described in Chapter 21, and are based on the DataRowVersion enumeration. For example, when the user has updated a column in the row, then the row will be displayed when either ModifiedOriginal or ModifiedCurrent are chosen; however, the actual value will either be the Original value selected from the database (if ModifiedOriginal is choosen), or the current value in the DataColumn (if ModifiedCurrent is choosen).

Sorting rows

as Apart from filtering data, you might also have to sort the data within a DataView. To sort data in ascending or descending order, simply click the column header in the DataGrid control (see Figure 22-6). The only trouble is that the control can only sort by one column, whereas the underlying DataView control can sort by multiple columns.

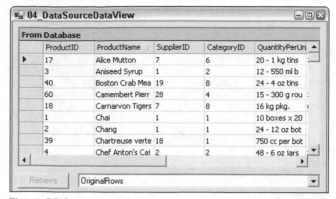

Figure 22-6

When a column is sorted, either by clicking on the header (as shown on the ProductName column) or in code, the `DataGrid` displays an arrow bitmap to indicate which column the sort has been applied to.

To set the sort order on a column programmatically, use the `Sort` property of the `DataView`:

```
dataView.Sort = "ProductName";
dataView.Sort = "ProductName ASC, ProductID DESC";
```

The first line sorts the data based on the ProductName column, as shown in Figure 22-6. The second line sorts the data in ascending order, based on the ProductName column, then in descending order of ProductID.

The `DataView` supports both ascending (default) and descending sort orders on columns. If more than one column is sorted in code in the `DataView`, the `DataGrid` will cease to display any sort arrows.

Each column in the grid can be strongly typed, so its sort order is not based on the string representation of the column but instead is based on the data within that column. The upshot is that if there is a date column in the `DataGrid`, then the user can sort numerically on date rather than on the date string representation.

Displaying data from a DataSet class

The `DataGrid` comes in to its own when displaying data from a `DataSet`. As with the preceding examples, the `DataGrid` can only display a single `DataTable` at a time. However, as shown in the following example, DataSourceDataSet, it is possible to navigate relationships within the `DataSet` on screen. The following code can be used to generate such a `DataSet` based on the Customers and Orders tables in the Northwind database. This example loads data from these two `DataTables`, and then creates a relationship between these tables called `CustomerOrders`:

```
string source = "server=(local)\\NetSDK;" +
                "uid=QSUser;pwd=QSPassword;" +
                "database=northwind";
string orders = "SELECT * FROM Orders";
string customers = "SELECT * FROM Customers";
SqlConnection conn = new SqlConnection(source);
```

```
SqlDataAdapter da = new SqlDataAdapter(orders, conn);
DataSet ds = new DataSet();
da.Fill(ds, "Orders");
da = new SqlDataAdapter(customers , conn);
da.Fill(ds, "Customers");
ds.Relations.Add("CustomerOrders",
                 ds.Tables["Customers"].Columns["CustomerID"],
                 ds.Tables["Orders"].Columns["CustomerID"]);
```

Once created, the data in the `DataSet` is bound to the `DataGrid` simply by calling `SetDataBinding()`:

```
dataGrid1.SetDataBinding(ds, "Customers");
```

This produce output shown in Figure 22-7.

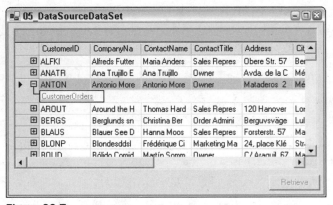

Figure 22-7

Unlike the other `DataGrids` shown in this chapter, there is now a + sign to the left of each record. This reflects the fact that the `DataSet` has a navigable relationship, between customers and orders. Any number of such relationships can defined in code.

When the user clicks the + sign, the list of relationships is shown (or hidden if already visible). Clicking the name of the relationship enables you to navigate to the linked records (see Figure 22-8), in this example listing all orders placed by the selected customer.

The `DataGrid` control also includes a couple of new icons in the top right corner. The arrow permits the user to navigate to the parent row, and will change the display to that on the previous page. The header row showing details of the parent record can be shown or hidden by clicking on the other button.

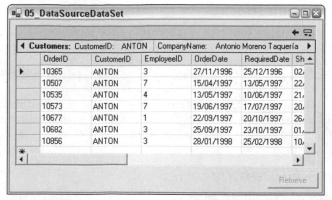

Figure 22-8

Displaying data in a data view manager

The display of data in a `DataViewManager` is the same as that for the `DataSet` shown in the previous section. However, when a `DataViewManager` is created for a `DataSet`, an individual `DataView` is created for each `DataTable`, which then permits the code to alter the displayed rows, based on a filter or the row state as shown in the `DataView` example. Even if the code doesn't need to filter data, it is good practice to wrap the `DataSet` in a `DataViewManager` for display, as it provides more options when revising the source code.

The following creates a `DataViewManager` based on the `DataSet` from the previous example, and then alters the `DataView` for the `Customers` table to show only customers from the United Kingdom:

```
DataViewManager dvm = new DataViewManager(ds);
dvm.DataViewSettings["Customers"].RowFilter = "Country='UK'";
dataGrid.SetDataBinding(dvm, "Customers");
```

Figure 22-9 shows the output of the DataSourceDataViewManager sample code.

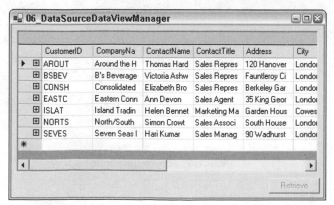

Figure 22-9

745

IListSource and IList interfaces

The DataGrid also supports any object that exposes one of the interfaces IListSource or IList. IListSource only has one method, GetList(), which returns an IList interface. IList on the other hand is somewhat more interesting, and is implemented by a large number of classes in the runtime. Some of the classes that implement this interface are Array, ArrayList, and StringCollection.

When using IList, the same caveat for the object within the collection holds true as for the Array implementation shown earlier—if a StringCollection is used as the data source for the DataGrid, the length of the strings is displayed within the grid, not the text of the item as expected.

DataGrid Class Hierarchy

The class hierarchy for the main parts of the DataGrid is shown in Figure 22-10.

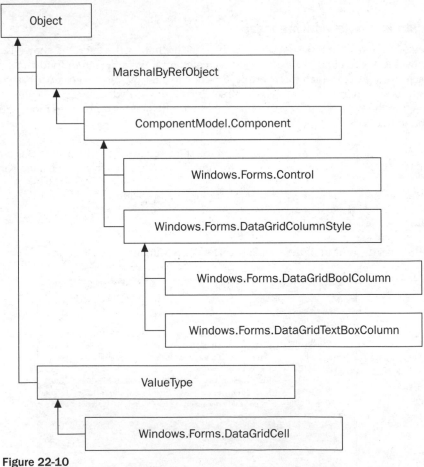

Figure 22-10

The `DataGrid` consists of zero or more `DataGridTableStyles`. These styles consist of zero or more `DataGridColumnStyles`. A given cell in the grid can be accessed by means of the `DataGridCell` struct.

However, there's more to `DataGridTableStyle` and `DataGridColumnStyle` than simply letting the runtime create them for you. The following sections discuss these and the other main classes shown in Figure 22-10.

DataGridTableStyle and DataGridColumnStyle

A `DataGridTableStyle` contains the visual representation of a `DataTable`. The `DataGrid` contains a collection of these styles, accessible by the `TableStyles` property. When a `DataTable` is displayed, a check is made through all `DataGridTableStyle` objects to find one with its `MappingName` property equal to the `TableName` property of the `DataTable`. On finding a match, that style will be used in the display of the table.

The `DataGridTableStyle` permits the definition of the visual parameters for the `DataGrid`, such as the background and foreground color, the font used in the column header, and various other properties. The `DataGridColumnStyle` can be used to refine the display options on a column-by-column basis, such as setting the alignment for the data in the column, the text that is displayed for a `null` value, and the width of the column on screen.

When the `DataGrid` displays a `DataTable` with a defined `DataGridTableStyle`, the only columns displayed are those for which a `DataGridColumnStyle` has been constructed. Only columns that have a defined style will be displayed, which can be useful for hiding columns such as primary key values that are not normally displayed. Column styles can also be defined as `ReadOnly`. This hiding of columns is not as simple as if there were a method to filter columns similar to that of filtering rows, however it's not too difficult to use.

The following code shows an example of creating a `DataGridTableStyle`. The code creates a `DataGridTableStyle` object, adds two `DataGridColumnStyle` objects, and then displays all of the data in the Customers table. The code is shown in its entirety, because it is the basis for several examples in this section. The first part of the code should be familiar from the earlier example:

```
using System;
using System.Windows.Forms;
using System.Data;
using System.Data.SqlClient;
public class CustomDataGridTableStyle : System.Windows.Forms.Form
{
    private System.Windows.Forms.Button retrieveButton;
    private System.Windows.Forms.DataGrid dataGrid;
    public CustomDataGridTableStyle()
    {
        this.AutoScaleBaseSize = new System.Drawing.Size(5, 13);
        this.ClientSize = new System.Drawing.Size(464, 253);
        this.Text = "07_CustomDataGridTableStyle";
        this.dataGrid = new System.Windows.Forms.DataGrid();
        dataGrid.BeginInit();
        dataGrid.Location = new System.Drawing.Point(8, 8);
        dataGrid.Size = new System.Drawing.Size(448, 208);
        dataGrid.TabIndex = 0;
```

```
                dataGrid.Anchor = AnchorStyles.Bottom | AnchorStyles.Top |
                              AnchorStyles.Left | AnchorStyles.Right;
            this.Controls.Add(this.dataGrid);
            dataGrid.EndInit();
            this.retrieveButton = new System.Windows.Forms.Button();
            retrieveButton.Location = new System.Drawing.Point(384, 224);
            retrieveButton.Size = new System.Drawing.Size(75, 23);
            retrieveButton.TabIndex = 1;
            retrieveButton.Anchor = AnchorStyles.Bottom | AnchorStyles.Right;
            retrieveButton.Text = "Retrieve";
            retrieveButton.Click += new
                              System.EventHandler(this.retrieveButton_Click);
            this.Controls.Add(this.retrieveButton);
        }
        protected void retrieveButton_Click(object sender, System.EventArgs e)
        {
            retrieveButton.Enabled = false;
```

This generates the `DataSet` that will be used, then creates the `DataGridTableStyles` for use in the example, and finally binds the `DataGrid` to the `DataSet`. The `CreateDataSet` method is nothing particularly new as you will see shortly; it simply retrieves all rows from the `Customers` table:

```
            DataSet ds = CreateDataSet();
            CreateStyles(dataGrid);
            dataGrid.SetDataBinding(ds, "Customers");
        }
```

The `CreateStyles()` method, however, is more interesting. The first few lines create the new `DataGridTableStyle` object, and set its `MappingName` property. This property is used when the `DataGrid` displays a given `DataTable`. The `DataGrid` can display rows in alternating colors. The code here also defines the color for every second row (to get a glimpse of the output, look ahead to Figure 22-11)

```
        private void CreateStyles(DataGrid dg)
        {
            DataGridTableStyle style = new DataGridTableStyle();
            style.MappingName = "Customers";
            style.AlternatingBackColor = System.Drawing.Color.Bisque;
            DataGridTextBoxColumn customerID = new DataGridTextBoxColumn();
            customerID.HeaderText = "Customer ID";
            customerID.MappingName = "CustomerID";
            customerID.Width = 200;
            DataGridTextBoxColumn name = new DataGridTextBoxColumn();
            name.HeaderText = "Name";
            name.MappingName = "CompanyName";
            name.Width = 300;
```

After the columns have been defined, they are added to the `GridColumnStyles` collection of the `DataGridTableStyle` object, which is then added to the `TableStyles` property of the `DataGrid`:

```
        style.GridColumnStyles.AddRange
                (new DataGridColumnStyle[]{customerID , name});
        dg.TableStyles.Add(style);
    }
    private DataSet CreateDataSet()
    {
        string source = "server=(local)\\NetSDK;" +
                        "uid=QSUser;pwd=QSPassword;" +
                        "database=northwind";
        string customers = "SELECT * FROM Customers";
        SqlConnection con = new SqlConnection(source);
        SqlDataAdapter da = new SqlDataAdapter(customers , con);
        DataSet ds = new DataSet();
        da.Fill(ds, "Customers");
        return ds;
    }
    static void Main()
    {
        Application.Run(new CustomDataGridTableStyle());
    }
}
```

After creating the `DataGridTableStyle` object, two objects derived from `DataGridColumnStyle` are created—in this instance they are text boxes. Each column has a number of defined properties. The following table lists some of the key properties.

Property	Description
Alignment	One of the `HorizontalAlignment` enumerated values: `Left`, `Center`, or `Right`. This indicates how data in the column is justified.
FontHeight	The size of the font in pixels. This defaults to the font size of the `DataGrid` if no value is set. This property is `protected`, so can only be modified by creating a subclass.
HeaderText	The text displayed in the column heading.
MappingName	The column in the `DataTable` represented by the displayed column.
NullText	The text displayed within the column if the underlying data value is `DBNull`.
PropertyDescriptor	This is discussed later in this chapter.
ReadOnly	A flag indicating whether the column is read-write or read-only.
Width	The width of the column in pixels.

The display resulting from this CustomDataGridTableStyle sample code is shown in Figure 22-11.

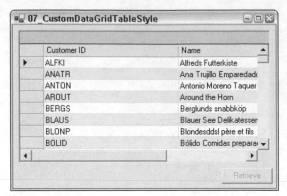

Figure 22-11

Data Binding

The previous examples have all used the `DataGrid` control, which is only one of the controls in the .NET runtime that can be used to display data. The process of linking a control to a data source is called *data binding*.

In MFC the process of linking data from class variables to a set of controls was termed *Dialog Data Exchange* (*DDX*). The facilities available within .NET for binding data to controls is substantially easier to use and also more capable. For example, in .NET you can bind data to most properties of a control, not just the text property. You can also bind data in a similar manner to ASP.NET controls (see Chapter 25).

Simple Binding

A control that supports single binding typically displays only a single value at once, such as a text box or radio button. The following example shows how to bind a column from a `DataTable` to a `TextBox`:

```
DataSet ds = CreateDataSet();
textBox1.DataBindings.Add("Text", ds , "Products.ProductName");
```

After retrieving some data from the Products table and storing it in the returned `DataSet` with the `CreateDataSet()` method as above, the second line then binds the `Text` property of the control (`textBox1`) to the `Products.ProductName` column. Figure 22-12 shows the result of this type of data binding.

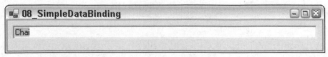

Figure 22-12

The text box displays a string from the database. Figure 22-13 shows how the SQL Server Query Analyzer tool could be used to verify the contents of the Products table to verify that it is the right column and value.

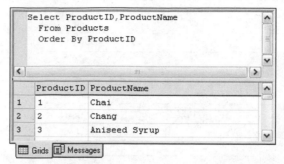

Figure 22-13

Having a single text box on screen with no way to scroll to the next or the previous record and no way to update the database is not very useful, so the following section shows a more realistic example, and introduces the other objects that are necessary for data binding to work.

Data-Binding Objects

Figure 22-14 shows a class hierarchy for the objects that are used in data binding. In this section we discuss the BindingContext, CurrencyManager, and PropertyManager classes of the System .Windows.Forms namespace, and show how they interact when data is bound to one or more controls on a form. The shaded objects are those that are used in binding.

In the previous example, the DataBindings property of the TextBox control was used to bind a column from a DataSet to the Text property of the control. The DataBindings property is an instance of the ControlBindingsCollection shown above:

```
textBox1.DataBindings.Add("Text", ds, "Products.ProductName");
```

This line adds a Binding object to the ControlBindingsCollection.

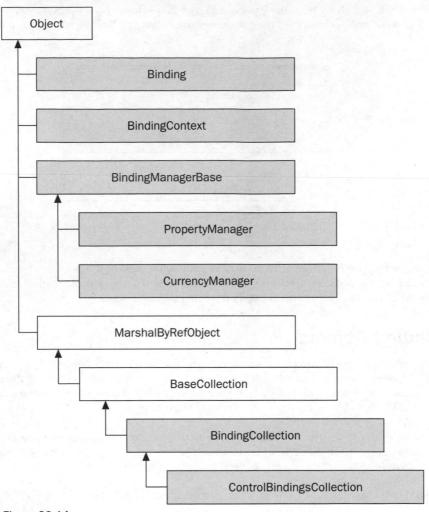

Figure 22-14

BindingContext

Each Windows form has a BindingContext property. Incidentally, Form is derived from Control, which is where this property is actually defined, so most controls have this property. A BindingContext object has a collection of BindingManagerBase instances (see Figure 22-15). These instances are created and added to the binding manager object when a control is data bound.

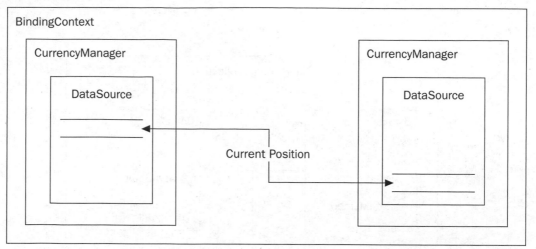

Figure 22-15

The `BindingContext` might contain several data sources, wrapped in either a `CurrencyManager` or a `PropertyManager`. The decision on which class is used is based on the data source itself.

If the data source contains a list of items, such as a `DataTable`, `DataView`, or any object that implements the `IList` interface, then a `CurrencyManager` will be used. A `CurrencyManager` can maintain the current position within that data source. If the data source returns only a single value then a `PropertyManager` will be stored within the `BindingContext`.

A `CurrencyManager` or `PropertyManager` is only created once for a given data source. If two text boxes are bound to a row from a `DataTable`, only one `CurrencyManager` will be created within the binding context.

Each control added to a form is linked to the form's binding manager, so all controls share the same instance. When a control is initially created, its `BindingContext` property is `null`. When the control is added to the `Controls` collection of the form, the `BindingContext` is set to that of the form.

To bind a control to a form, an entry needs to be added to its `DataBindings` property, which is an instance of `ControlBindingsCollection`. The following code shown creates a new binding:

```
textBox1.DataBindings.Add("Text", ds, "Products.ProductName");
```

Internally, the `Add()` method of `ControlBindingsCollection` creates a new instance of a `Binding` object from the parameters passed to this method, and adds this to the bindings collection represented in Figure 22-16.

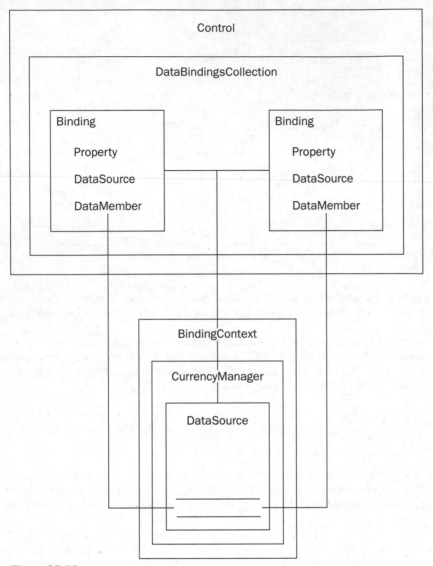

Figure 22-16

Figure 22-16 illustrates roughly what is going on when a `Binding` object is added to a `Control`. The binding links the control to a data source, which is maintained within the `BindingContext` of the `Form` (or control itself). Changes within the data source are reflected into the control, as are changes in the control.

Binding

This class links a property of the control to a member of the data source. When that member changes, the control's property is updated to reflect this change. The opposite is also true—if the text in the text box is updated, this change is reflected in the data source.

Bindings can be set up from any column to any property of the control. For example, you can not only bind the text of a text box, but also the color of that text box. It is possible to bind properties of a control to completely different data sources; for example, the color of the cell might be defined in a colors table, and the actual data might be defined in another table.

CurrencyManager and PropertyManager

When a `Binding` object is created, a corresponding `CurrencyManager` or `PropertyManager` object is also created, provided this is the first time that data from the given source has been bound. The purpose of this class is to define the position of the current record within the data source, and to coordinate all list bindings when this current record is changed. Figure 22-17 displays two fields from the Products table, and includes a way to move between records by means of a `TrackBar` control.

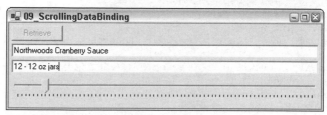

Figure 22-17

The following example shows the ScrollingDataBinding sample code in its entirety:

```
using System;
using System.Windows.Forms;
using System.Data;
using System.Data.SqlClient;

public class ScrollingDataBinding : System.Windows.Forms.Form
{
    private Button retrieveButton;
    private TextBox textName;
    private TextBox textQuan;
    private TrackBar trackBar;
    private DataSet ds;
```

The application creates the window, including its controls, in the `ScrollingDataBinding` constructor:

```
public ScrollingDataBinding()
{
    this.AutoScaleBaseSize = new System.Drawing.Size(5, 13);
    this.ClientSize = new System.Drawing.Size(464, 253);
    this.Text = "09_ScrollingDataBinding";
```

```
         this.retrieveButton = new Button();
         retrieveButton.Location = new System.Drawing.Point(4, 4);
         retrieveButton.Size = new System.Drawing.Size(75, 23);
         retrieveButton.TabIndex = 1;
         retrieveButton.Anchor = AnchorStyles.Top | AnchorStyles.Left;
         retrieveButton.Text = "Retrieve";
         retrieveButton.Click += new System.EventHandler
                                   (this.retrieveButton_Click);
         this.Controls.Add(this.retrieveButton);
         this.textName = new TextBox();
         textName.Location = new System.Drawing.Point(4, 31);
         textName.Text = "Please click retrieve...";
         textName.TabIndex = 2;
         textName.Anchor = AnchorStyles.Top | AnchorStyles.Left |
                     AnchorStyles.Right ;
         textName.Size = new System.Drawing.Size(456, 20);
         textName.Enabled = false;
         this.Controls.Add(this.textName);
         this.textQuan = new TextBox();
         textQuan.Location = new System.Drawing.Point(4, 55);
         textQuan.Text = "";
         textQuan.TabIndex = 3;
         textQuan.Anchor = AnchorStyles.Top | AnchorStyles.Left |
                     AnchorStyles.Top;
         textQuan.Size = new System.Drawing.Size(456, 20);
         textQuan.Enabled = false;
         this.Controls.Add(this.textQuan);
         this.trackBar = new TrackBar();
         trackBar.BeginInit();
         trackBar.Dock = DockStyle.Bottom ;
         trackBar.Location = new System.Drawing.Point(0, 275);
         trackBar.TabIndex = 4;
         trackBar.Size = new System.Drawing.Size(504, 42);
         trackBar.Scroll += new System.EventHandler(this.trackBar_Scroll);
         trackBar.Enabled = false;
         this.Controls.Add(this.trackBar);
      }
```

When the Retrieve button is clicked, the event handler selects all records from the Products table, and stores this data in the private data set ds:

```
   protected void retrieveButton_Click(object sender, System.EventArgs e)
   {
      retrieveButton.Enabled = false ;
      ds = CreateDataSet();
```

Next, the two text controls are bound:

```
      textName.DataBindings.Add("Text" , ds ,
                          "Products.ProductName");
      textQuan.DataBindings.Add("Text" , ds ,
                          "Products.QuantityPerUnit");
      trackBar.Minimum = 0 ;
```

```
        trackBar.Maximum = this.BindingContext[ds,"Products"].Count -- 1;
        textName.Enabled = true;
        textQuan.Enabled = true;
        trackBar.Enabled = true;
    }
```

Here is a trivial record scrolling mechanism, which responds to movements of the `TrackBar` thumb:

```
    protected void trackBar_Scroll(object sender , System.EventArgs e)
    {
        this.BindingContext[ds,"Products"].Position = trackBar.Value;
    }
    private DataSet CreateDataSet()
    {
        string source = "server=(local)\\NetSDK;" +
                        "uid=QSUser;pwd=QSPassword;" +
                        "database=northwind";
        string customers = "SELECT * FROM Products";
        SqlConnection con = new SqlConnection(source);
        SqlDataAdapter da = new SqlDataAdapter(customers , con);
        DataSet ds = new DataSet();
        da.Fill(ds , "Products");
        return ds;
    }
    static void Main()
    {
        Application.Run(new ScrollingDataBinding());
    }
}
```

When the data is originally retrieved, the maximum position on the track bar is set to be the number of records. Then, in the scroll method above, the position of the `BindingContext` for the products `DataTable` is set to the position of the scroll bar thumb. This changes the current record from the `DataTable`, so all controls bound to the current row (in this example, the two text boxes) are updated.

Now that you know how to bind to various data sources, such as arrays, data tables, data views, and various other containers of data and sort and filter that data, we can discuss how Visual Studio has been extended to permit data access to be better integrated with the application.

Visual Studio.NET and Data Access

This section discusses some of the new ways that Visual Studio allows data to be integrated into the GUI. More specifically, we discuss how to create a connection, select some data, generate a `DataSet`, and use all of the generated objects to produce a simple application. The available tools enable you to create a database connection with the `OleDbConnection` or `SqlConnection` classes. The class you use depends on the type of database you are using. After a connection has been defined, you can create a `DataSet` and populate it from within Visual Studio .NET. This generates an XSD file for the `DataSet` (similar to the file that we created manually in Chapter 21) and the .cs code. The result is a type-safe `DataSet`.

Creating a Connection

First, create a new Windows application, then create a new database connection. Using the Server Explorer (see Figure 22-18), you can manage various aspects of data access.

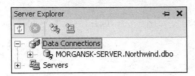

Figure 22-18

For this example, create a connection to the Northwind database. Select the Add Connection option from the context menu available on the Data Connections item to launch a wizard that enables you to choose a database provider. Select Microsoft OLE DB Provider for SQL Server. Figure 22-19 shows the second page of the Data Link Properties dialog box.

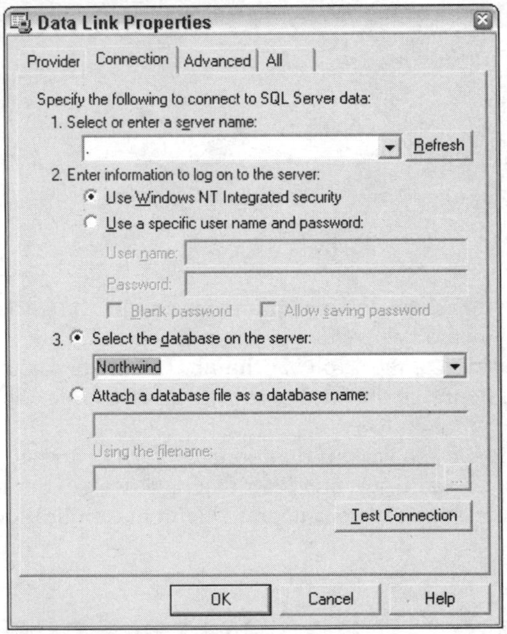

Figure 22-19

Depending on your .NET Framework installation, the samples databases might be located in SQL Server, MSDE (Microsoft SQL Server Data Engine), or both.

To connect to the local MSDE database, if it exists, type **(local)\\NETSDK** for the name of the server. To connect to a regular SQL Server instance, type **(local)** to select a database on the current machine, or the name of the desired server on the network. You may need to enter a username and password to access the database.

Select the Northwind database from the drop-down list of databases, and to ensure everything is set up correctly, click the Test Connection button. If everything is set up properly, you should see a message box with a confirmation message.

To create a connection object, click and drag the newly added server to the main application window. This creates a member variable of the appropriate connection type. Then add the following code to the `InitializeComponent` method of the main form:

```
this.sqlConnection = new System.Data.SqlClient.SqlConnection();

//
// sqlConnection
//

this.sqlConnection.ConnectionString = "data source=(local)\\NETSDK;" +
                                       "initial catalog=Northwind;" +
                                       "user id=QSUser;password=QSPassword;" +
                                       "persist security info=True;" +
                                       "workstation id=BILBO;" +
                                       "packet size=4096";
```

As you can see, the connection string information is persisted directly in code.

When you add this object to the project, the `sqlConnection1` object is displayed in the tray area at the bottom of the Visual Studio window (see Figure 22-20).

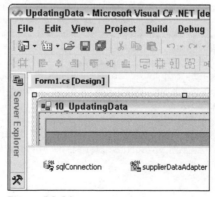

Figure 22-20

The properties of this object can be altered by selecting it and showing the Properties dialog box (press F4).

Selecting Data

When the data connection has been defined, you can select a table (or view) from the available list, and drag it to an active project form (see Figure 22-21),

Figure 22-21

For this example, we have chosen the Customers table. When this object is dragged to the project (it can be droped on the form or the server controls palette), it adds an object to the form derived from `SqlDataAdapter`, or `OleDbDataAdapter` if you're not using SQL Server.

The data adapter generated contains commands for SELECT, INSERT, UPDATE, and DELETE. Needless to say, these can (and probably should) be tailored to call stored procedures rather than using straight SQL. The wizard-generated code will do for now, however. Visual Studio .NET adds the following code to the .cs file:

```
private System.Data.SqlClient.SqlCommand sqlSelectCommand1;
private System.Data.SqlClient.SqlCommand sqlInsertCommand1;
private System.Data.SqlClient.SqlCommand sqlUpdateCommand1;
private System.Data.SqlClient.SqlCommand sqlDeleteCommand1;
private System.Data.SqlClient.SqlDataAdapter sqlDataAdapter1;
```

There is an object defined for each of the SQL commands, and a `SqlDataAdapter`. Further down the file, in the `InitializeComponent()` method, the wizard has generated code to create each one of these commands as well as the data adapter.

There are two aspects of the code generated by Visual Studio .NET that are worth looking at: the `UpdateCommand` and `InsertCommand` properties. Here is an abridged version showing the pertinent information:

```
//
// sqlInsertCommand1
//
this.sqlInsertCommand1.CommandText = @"INSERT INTO Customers
    (CustomerID, CompanyName, ContactName, ContactTitle, Address, City,
     Region, PostalCode, Country, Phone, Fax)
  VALUES (@CustomerID, @CompanyName, @ContactName, @ContactTitle, @Address, @City,
          @Region, @PostalCode, @Country, @Phone, @Fax);
  SELECT CustomerID, CompanyName, ContactName, ContactTitle, Address, City,
         Region, PostalCode, Country, Phone, Fax
    FROM Customers
    WHERE (CustomerID = @CustomerID)";
```

```
    this.sqlInsertCommand2.Connection = this.sqlConnection1;

    this.sqlInsertCommand2.Parameters.Add(
      new System.Data.SqlClient.SqlParameter("@CustomerID",
        System.Data.SqlDbType.NVarChar, 5, "CustomerID"));

    // Other Parameters omitted for clarity

    //
    // sqlUpdateCommand1
    //

    this.sqlUpdateCommand2.CommandText = @"UPDATE Customers
      SET CustomerID = @CustomerID, CompanyName = @CompanyName,
        ContactName = @ContactName, ContactTitle = @ContactTitle,
        Address = @Address, City = @City, Region = @Region,
        PostalCode = @PostalCode, Country = @Country, Phone = @Phone, Fax = @Fax
      WHERE (CustomerID = @Original_CustomerID)
        AND (Address = @Original_Address OR @Original_Address IS NULL
            AND Address IS NULL)
        AND (City = @Original_City OR @Original_City IS NULL AND City IS NULL)
        AND (CompanyName = @Original_CompanyName)
        AND (ContactName = @Original_ContactName OR @Original_ContactName IS NULL
            AND ContactName IS NULL)
        AND (ContactTitle = @Original_ContactTitle OR @Original_ContactTitle IS NULL
            AND ContactTitle IS NULL)
        AND (Country = @Original_Country OR @Original_Country IS NULL
            AND Country IS NULL)
        AND (Fax = @Original_Fax OR @Original_Fax IS NULL AND Fax IS NULL)
        AND (Phone = @Original_Phone OR @Original_Phone IS NULL AND Phone IS NULL)
        AND (PostalCode = @Original_PostalCode OR @Original_PostalCode IS NULL
            AND PostalCode IS NULL)
        AND (Region = @Original_Region OR @Original_Region IS NULL
            AND Region IS NULL);
      SELECT CustomerID, CompanyName, ContactName, ContactTitle, Address, City, Region,
          PostalCode, Country, Phone, Fax
        FROM Customers
        WHERE (CustomerID = @CustomerID)";

    this.sqlUpdateCommand2.Connection = this.sqlConnection1;
    this.sqlUpdateCommand2.Parameters.Add(
      new System.Data.SqlClient.SqlParameter("@CustomerID",
          System.Data.SqlDbType.NVarChar, 5, "CustomerID"));
    // Other parameters omitted for clarity
```

The main area of interest in these commands are the SQL statements that have been generated. For both the INSERT and UPDATE commands there are actually two SQL statements: one for inserting or updating data, and the other to reselect the row from the database.

These seemingly redundant clauses are used as a way to re-synchronize the data on the client machine with that on the server. There might be defaults applied to columns when inserted, or database triggers that fire to update some of the columns in the inserted/updated record, so re-syncing the data has some benefit. The @Select2_CustomerID parameter used to reselect the data is the same value passed into the INSERT/UPDATE statement for the primary key; the name has been generated by the wizard.

For tables that include an IDENTITY column, the SQL generated uses the @@IDENTITY value after the INSERT statement. As discussed in Chapter 21, relying on @@IDENTITY to produce primary keys can result in some annoying bugs, so that's one area of the SQL that you might have to change manually. Similarly, if there are no calculated columns it seems a little wasteful to re-select all columns from the original table just in case something has been updated.

The wizard-generated code works, but is less than optimal. For a production system, all the generated SQL should probably be replaced with calls to stored procedures. If the INSERT or UPDATE clauses didn't have to re-synchronize the data, then the removal of the redundant SQL clause would speed up the application a little.

Generating a DataSet

Now that the data adapter has been defined, you can use it to create a DataSet. To generate the DataSet, select the data adapter and display its properties (press F4). Towards the bottom of the property sheet there are three options: Configure Data Adapter, Generate Dataset, and Preview Data.

Select Generate DataSet. You will be prompted to provide a name for the new DataSet object before you can choose the tables that you want to add to the data set. If you have dragged multiple tables from Server Explorer and dropped them onto the form, you can link them from inside the dialog box to a single DataSet.

What is actually created is an XSD schema, defining the DataSet and each table that was included in the DataSet. This is similar to the hand-crafted example in Chapter 21, but in this instance the XSD file has been created automatically:

In addition to the XSD file there is a (hidden) .cs file that defines various type-safe classes. To view this file, click the Show All Files toolbar button (see Figure 22-22), and then expand the XSD file.

Figure 22-22

Visual Studio .NET creates a .cs file with the same name as the XSD file. The classes defined are as follows:

❑　A class derived from DataSet

❑　A class derived from DataTable for the data adapter chosen

❑ A class derived from `DataRow`, defining the columns accessible within the `DataTable`

❑ A class derived from `EventArgs`, used when a row changes

The tool used to generate this file is the same as in the previous chapter: xsd.exe.

The XSD file can be updated once the wizards have done their thing, but don't be tempted to edit the .cs file to tweak it in some way, because it will be regenerated when the project is recompiled, and all your changes would be lost.

Updating the Data Source

So far our applications have selected data from the database. In this section, we discuss how to persist changes to the database. If you followed the steps in the previous section, you should have an application that contains a connection, data adapter and `DataSet` objects. All that is left to do is connect the `DataSet` to a `DataGrid`, add some logic to retrieve data from the database, display it, and then simply persist any changes back to the database.

Figure 22-23 shows the form for this example; the form is based on the UpdatingData sample code.

Figure 22-23

The form consists of a `DataGrid` control and two buttons. When the user clicks the Retrieve button, the following code is executed:

```
private void retrieveButton_Click(object sender, System.EventArgs e)
{
  // Fill the data adapter from the database
  supplierDataAdapter.Fill ( supplierDataSet , "Supplier" ) ;

  // And display the data in the data grid...
  dataGrid1.SetDataBinding ( supplierDataSet , "Supplier" ) ;

  // And disable the retrieve button...
  retrieveButton.Enabled = false ;
}
```

This code uses the data adapter created earlier (by dragging a database table from the Server Explorer) to fill a `DataSet`. The `Customer` data table is filled with all records from the table of the same name in the database. The call to `SetDataBinding()` then displays these records on screen.

After navigating through the data and making some changes, the user can click the Update button. This action executes the following code:

```
private void updateButton_Click(object sender, System.EventArgs e)
{
   // Update the database
   int modified = supplierDataAdapter.Update ( supplierDataSet , "Supplier" ) ;

   if ( modified > 0 )
     MessageBox.Show ( string.Format ( "Modified {0} rows" , modified ) ) ;
}
```

This code is simple, because the data adapter is doing most of the work for you. The `Update()` method loops through the data in the selected table of the `DataSet`, and for each change executes the appropriate SQL statement against the database. Note that this method returns an `int` type, which is the number of rows modified by the update. This number is used in this example to display the number of modified rows.

Chapter 21 discusses in detail the use of the data adapter. In brief, it represents SQL statements for `SELECT`, `INSERT`, `UPDATE`, and `DELETE` operations. Calling the `Update()` method executes the appropriate statement for each modified row. This causes all modified rows to execute an `UPDATE` statement, all deleted rows to issue a `DELETE` statement, and so on. The commands issued are by default simple SQL statements. However, you can substitute stored procedures by creating the appropriate command objects and assigning these to properties on the data adapter.

To reap all the benefits of using stored procedures without having to write them, use the Visual Studio .NET wizards. Choose the Configure Data Adapter item from the data adapter's context menu to show the Configuration Wizard, which enables you to choose the source of data for the adapter (see Figure 22-24).

Select Create new stored procedures and click Next to step through the wizard and instruct it to generate new stored procedures for `SELECT`, `INSERT`, `UPDATE`, and `DELETE` statements, and ultimately modify the code generated within the project to add calls to these stored procedures instead of the calls to straight SQL statements.

In addition to generating new stored procedures, existing stored procedures can be used to populate the four SQL commands on the adapter. This might be useful when hand-crafted stored procedures are already available, or when some other function is performed by a procedure, such as auditing changes or updating linked records.

Building a Schema

Chapter 21 shows you how to define an XSD schema. Visual Studio .NET includes an editor for creating XSD schemas. You can access this editor by choosing Add New Item from the Proejct menu and then selecting the XML Schema item from the Data category (see Figure 22-25). Name your schema TestSchema.xsd.

Figure 22-24

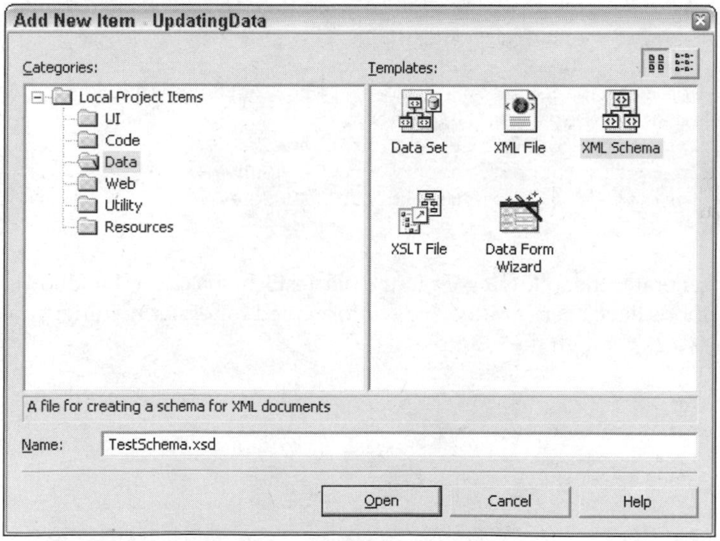

Figure 22-25

This adds two new files to the project: an .xsd file and a corresponding .xsx file (which is used by the designer to store layout information for the schema elements that are designed). To create a corresponding set of code for the schema, choose the Generate Dataset option from the Schema menu (see Figure 22-26).

Figure 22-26

Choosing this option adds an extra C# file to the project, which is displayed below the XSD file in Solution Explorer. This file is automatically generated whenever changes are made to the XSD schema, and so should not be edited manually; it is generated with the xsd.exe tool.

The Visual Studio .NET editor has two views of an XSD file: Schema view and XML view. Clicking the XML tab displays the raw schema template.

```xml
<?xml version="1.0" encoding="utf-8" ?>
<xs:schema id="TestSchema"
        targetNamespace="http://tempuri.org/TestSchema.xsd"
        elementFormDefault="qualified"
        xmlns="http://tempuri.org/TestSchema.xsd"
        xmlns:mstns="http://tempuri.org/TestSchema.xsd"
        xmlns:xs="http://www.w3.org/2001/XMLSchema">
</xs:schema>
```

This XSD script generates the following C# in the file TestSchema.cs. In the following code some of the bodies of the methods have been omitted and/or formatted for easier reading; you can inspect the code generated as you work through the example.

```csharp
using System;
using System.Data;
using System.Xml;
using System.Runtime.Serialization;

[Serializable()]
[System.ComponentModel.DesignerCategoryAttribute("code")]
[System.Diagnostics.DebuggerStepThrough()]
[System.ComponentModel.ToolboxItem(true)]
public class TestSchema : DataSet
{
    public TestSchema() { ... }

    protected TestSchema(SerializationInfo info, StreamingContext context)
```

```
   { ... }
   public override DataSet Clone() { ... }
   protected override bool ShouldSerializeTables() { ... }
   protected override bool ShouldSerializeRelations() { ... }
   protected override void ReadXmlSerializable(XmlReader reader) { ... }
   protected override System.Xml.Schema.XmlSchema GetSchemaSerializable()
   { ... }
   internal void InitVars() { ... }
   private void InitClass() { ... }
   private void SchemaChanged(object sender,
                System.ComponentModel.CollectionChangeEventArgs e)
   { ... }
}
```

This code provides the starting point for this section, so that the code changes can be described as items are added into the XSD schema. The two main things to note are that an XSD schema is mapped to a `DataSet`, and that this `DataSet` is serializable—note the protected constructor that can be used by an `ISerializable` implementation. Serialization is covered in greater depth in Chapter 11.

Adding an element

To add a new top-level element, right-click inside your workspace and choose Add⇨New Element from the context menu. This displays in a new, unnamed element. Figure 22-27 shows the attributes for this example's product element.

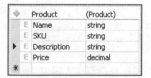

Figure 22-27

When the XSD file is saved, the C# file is modified and a number of new classes is generated, as shown in the following code. The most pertinent aspects of the code generated in the file TestSchema.cs are discussed in the next section.

```
public class TestSchema : DataSet
{
   private ProductDataTable tableProduct;
   [System.ComponentModel.DesignerSerializationVisibilityAttribute
          (System.ComponentModel.DesignerSerializationVisibility.Content)]
   public ProductDataTable Product
   {
      get
      {
         return this.tableProduct;
      }
   }
}
```

A new member variable of the class `ProductDataTable` is created. This object is returned by the `Product` property, and is constructed within the updated `InitClass()` method. From this small section of code, it's evident that the user of these classes can construct a `DataSet` from the class in this file, and use `DataSet.Products` to return the products `DataTable`.

Generated DataTable

The following code is generated for the `DataTable` (`Product`) that was added to the schema template:

```
public delegate void ProductRowChangeEventHandler
                   (object sender, ProductRowChangeEvent e);
public class ProductDataTable : DataTable, System.Collections.IEnumerable
{
   internal ProductDataTable() : base("Product")
   {
      this.InitClass();
   }
   [System.ComponentModel.Browsable(false)]
   public int Count
   {
      get { return this.Rows.Count;}
   }
   public ProductRow this[int index]
   {
      get { return ((ProductRow)(this.Rows[index]));}
   }
   public event ProductRowChangeEventHandler ProductRowChanged;
   public event ProductRowChangeEventHandler ProductRowChanging;
   public event ProductRowChangeEventHandler ProductRowDeleted;
   public event ProductRowChangeEventHandler ProductRowDeleting;
```

The generated `ProductDataTable` class is derived from `DataTable`, and includes an implementation of the `IEnumerable` interface. Four events are defined that use the delegate defined above the class when raised. This delegate is passed an instance of the `ProductRowChangeEvent` class, again defined by Visual Studio .NET.

The generated code includes a class derived from `DataRow`, which permits type-safe access to columns within the table. A new row can be created in one of two ways:

❑ Call the `NewRow()` (or generated `NewProductRow()`) method to return a new instance of the row class. Pass this new row to the `Rows.Add()` method (or the type-safe `AddProductRow()`).

❑ Call the `Rows.Add()` (or generated `AddProductRow()`) method, and pass an array of objects, one for each column in the table.

The following code demonstrates the `AddProductRow()` methods:

```
public void AddProductRow(ProductRow row)
{
   this.Rows.Add(row);
}
public ProductRow AddProductRow ( ... )
```

```
    {
      ProductRow rowProductRow = ((ProductRow)(this.NewRow()));
      rowProductRow.ItemArray = new Object[0];
      this.Rows.Add(rowProductRow);
      return rowProductRow;
    }
```

As you can see, the second method creates a new row, inserts that row in the Rows collection of the DataTable, and then returns this object to the caller. The bulk of the other methods on the DataTable are for raising events.

Generated DataRow

The following code shows the ProductRow class:

```
public class ProductRow : DataRow
{
    private ProductDataTable tableProduct;
    internal ProductRow(DataRowBuilder rb) : base(rb)
    {
        this.tableProduct = ((ProductDataTable)(this.Table));
    }
    public string Name { ... }
    public bool IsNameNull { ... }
    public void SetNameNull { ... }
    // Other accessors/mutators omitted for clarity
}
```

When attributes are added to an element, a property is added to the generated DataRow class as shown above. The property has the same name as the attribute; in this example, for the Product row, we have properties for Name, SKU, Description, and Price.

For each attribute added, several changes are made to the .cs file. In the following example, suppose there is an attribute called ProductId of type int.

At first a private member is added to the ProductDataTable class (derived from DataTable), which is the new DataColumn:

```
private DataColumn columnProductId;
```

This is joined by a property named ProductIDColumn. This property is defined as internal:

```
internal DataColumn ProductIdColumn
{
    get { return this.columnProductId; }
}
```

The AddProductRow() method shown above is also modified; it now takes an integer ProductID, and stores the value entered in the newly created column:

```
public ProductRow AddProductRow ( ... , int ProductId)
{
    ProductRow rowProductRow = ((ProductRow)(this.NewRow()));
    rowProductRow.ItemArray = new Object[] { ... , ProductId};
    this.Rows.Add(rowProductRow);
    return rowProductRow;
}
```

Finally, in the `ProductDataTable`, there is a modification to the `InitClass()` method:

```
private void InitClass()
{
    ...
    this.columnProductID = new DataColumn("ProductID", typeof(int), null,
                                System.Data.MappingType.Attribute);
    this.Columns.Add(this.columnProductID);
    this.columnProductID.Namespace = "";
}
```

This creates the new `DataColumn` and adds it to the `Columns` collection of the `DataTable`. The final parameter to the `DataColumn` constructor defines how this column is mapped to XML; this is of use when the `DataSet` is saved to an XML file, for example.

The `ProductRow` class is updated to add an accessor for this column:

```
public int ProductId
{
    get { return ((int)(this[this.tableProduct.ProductIdColumn])); }
    set { this[this.tableProduct.ProductIdColumn] = value; }
}
```

Generated EventArgs

The final class that is added to the source code is a derivation of `EventArgs`, which provides methods for directly accessing the row that has changed (or is changing), and for the action that is applied to that row. This code has been omitted for brevity.

Other Common Requirements

A common requirement when displaying data is to provide a pop-up menu for a given row. There are numerous ways of doing this. In this example, we focus on one approach that can simplify the code required, especially if the display context is a `DataGrid`, where a `DataSet` with some relations is displayed. The problem here is that the context menu depends on the row that is selected, and that row could be part of any source `DataTable` in the `DataSet`.

As the context menu functionality is likely to be general purpose in nature, the implementation here uses a base class (`ContextDataRow`) that supports the menu-building code, and each data row class that supports a pop-up menu derives from this base class.

When the user right-clicks on any part of a row in the `DataGrid`, the row is looked up to check if it derives from `ContextDataRow`, and if so, `PopupMenu()` can be called. This could be implemented using an interface; however, in this instance a base class provides a simpler solution.

This example demonstrates how to generate `DataRow` and `DataTable` classes that can be used to provide type-safe access to data in much the same way as the previous XSD sample. However, this time we write the code ourselves to show how to use custom attributes and reflection in this context.

Figure 22-28 illustrates the class hierarchy for this example.

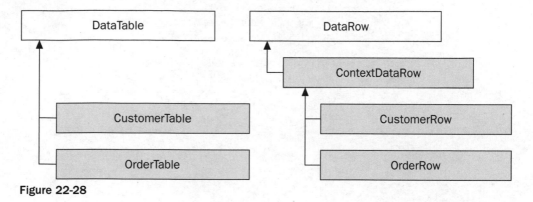

Figure 22-28

Here is the code for this example:

```
using System;
using System.Windows.Forms;
using System.Data;
using System.Data.SqlClient;
using System.Reflection;

public class ContextDataRow : DataRow
{
    public ContextDataRow(DataRowBuilder builder) : base(builder)
    {
    }
    public void PopupMenu(System.Windows.Forms.Control parent, int x, int y)
    {

        // Use reflection to get the list of popup menu commands
        MemberInfo[] members = this.GetType().FindMembers (MemberTypes.Method,
                          BindingFlags.Public | BindingFlags.Instance ,
                          new System.Reflection.MemberFilter(Filter),
                          null);
        if (members.Length > 0)
        {

            // Create a context menu

            ContextMenu menu = new ContextMenu();

            // Now loop through those members and generate the popup menu
            // Note the cast to MethodInfo in the foreach
            foreach (MethodInfo meth in members)
```

```
        {
            // Get the caption for the operation from the
            // ContextMenuAttribute

            ContextMenuAttribute[] ctx = (ContextMenuAttribute[])
                meth.GetCustomAttributes(typeof(ContextMenuAttribute), true);
            MenuCommand callback = new MenuCommand(this, meth);
            MenuItem item = new MenuItem(ctx[0].Caption, new
                                    EventHandler(callback.Execute));
            item.DefaultItem = ctx[0].Default;
            menu.MenuItems.Add(item);
        }
        System.Drawing.Point pt = new System.Drawing.Point(x,y);
        menu.Show(parent, pt);
    }
}

private bool Filter(MemberInfo member, object criteria)
{
    bool bInclude = false;

    // Cast MemberInfo to MethodInfo

    MethodInfo meth = member as MethodInfo;
    if (meth != null)
        if (meth.ReturnType == typeof(void))
        {
            ParameterInfo[] parms = meth.GetParameters();
            if (parms.Length == 0)
            {

                // Lastly check if there is a ContextMenuAttribute on the
                // method...

                object[] atts = meth.GetCustomAttributes
                            (typeof(ContextMenuAttribute), true);
                bInclude = (atts.Length == 1);

            }
        }
    return bInclude;
}
```

The ContextDataRow class is derived from DataRow, and contains just two member functions:
PopupMenu and Filter(). PopupMenu uses reflection to look for methods that correspond to a particular signature, and it displays a pop-up menu of these options to the user. Filter() is used as a delegate by PopupMenu when enumerating methods. It simply returns true if the member function does correspond to the appropriate calling convention:

```
MemberInfo[] members = this.GetType().FindMembers(MemberTypes.Method,
            BindingFlags.Public | BindingFlags.Instance,
            new System.Reflection.MemberFilter(Filter),
            null);
```

This single statement is used to filter all methods on the current object, and return only those that match the following criteria:

- ❏ The member must be a method
- ❏ The member must be a public instance method
- ❏ The member must return `void`
- ❏ The member must accept zero parameters
- ❏ The member must include the `ContextMenuAttribute`

The last of these criteria refers to a custom attribute, written specifically for this example. (We discuss it after discussing the `PopupMenu` method.)

```
ContextMenu menu = new ContextMenu();
foreach (MethodInfo meth in members)
{
   // ... Add the menu item
}
System.Drawing.Point pt = new System.Drawing.Point(x,y);
menu.Show(parent, pt);
```

A context menu instance is created, and a popup menu item is added for each method that matches the above criteria. The menu is subsequently displayed as shown in Figure 22-29.

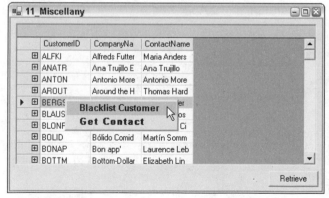

Figure 22-29

The main area of difficulty with this example is the following section of code, repeated once for each member function that is to be displayed on the pop-up menu:

```
System.Type ctxtype = typeof(ContextMenuAttribute);
ContextMenuAttribute[] ctx = (ContextMenuAttribute[])
                          meth.GetCustomAttributes(ctxtype, true);
MenuCommand callback = new MenuCommand(this, meth);
MenuItem item = new MenuItem(ctx[0].Caption,
                new EventHandler(callback.Execute));
item.DefaultItem = ctx[0].Default;
menu.MenuItems.Add(item);
```

Each method that should be displayed on the context menu is attributed with the `ContextMenu Attribute`. This defines a user-friendly name for the menu option, as a C# method name cannot include spaces, and it's wise to use real English on pop-up menus rather than some internal code. The attribute is retrieved from the method, and a new menu item created and added to the menu items collection of the pop-up menu.

This sample code also shows the use of a simplified Command class (a common design pattern). The `MenuCommand` class used in this instance is triggered by the user choosing an item on the context menu, and it forwards the call to the receiver of the method—in this case the object and method that was attributed. This also helps keep the code in the receiver object more isolated from the user interface code. We explain this code in the following sections.

Manufactured tables and rows

The XSD example earlier in the chapter showed the code produced when the Visual Studio .NET editor is used to generate a set of data access classes. The following class shows the required methods for a `DataTable`, which are fairly minimal (and they all have been generated manually):

```csharp
public class CustomerTable : DataTable
{
    public CustomerTable() : base("Customers")
    {
        this.Columns.Add("CustomerID", typeof(string));
        this.Columns.Add("CompanyName", typeof(string));
        this.Columns.Add("ContactName", typeof(string));
    }
    protected override System.Type GetRowType()
    {
        return typeof(CustomerRow);
    }
    protected override DataRow NewRowFromBuilder(DataRowBuilder builder)
    {
        return(DataRow) new CustomerRow(builder);
    }
}
```

The first prerequisite of a `DataTable` is to override the `GetRowType()` method. This is used by the .NET internals when generating new rows for the table. The type used to represent each row should be returned from this method.

The next prerequisite is to implement `NewRowFromBuilder()`, which is called by the runtime when creating new rows for the table. That's enough for a minimal implementation. This implementation includes adding columns to the `DataTable`. Since we know the list of columns in this example, these can add them accordingly. The corresponding `CustomerRow` class is fairly simple. It implements properties for each of the columns within the row, and then implements the methods that ultimately are displayed on the context menu:

```csharp
public class CustomerRow : ContextDataRow
{
    public CustomerRow(DataRowBuilder builder) : base(builder)
    {
    }
```

```
    public string CustomerID
    {
       get { return (string)this["CustomerID"];}
       set { this["CustomerID"] = value;}
    }

    // Other properties omitted for clarity

    [ContextMenu("Blacklist Customer")]
    public void Blacklist()
    {
       // Do something
    }
    [ContextMenu("Get Contact",Default=true)]
    public void GetContact()
    {
       // Do something else
    }
}
```

The class simply derives from ContextDataRow, including the appropriate getter/setter methods on properties which are named the same as each field, and then a set of methods may be added that are used when reflecting on the class:

```
    [ContextMenu("Blacklist Customer")]
    public void Blacklist()
    {

       // Do something
    }
```

Each method that is to be displayed on the context menu has the same signature, and includes the custom ContextMenu attribute.

Using an attribute

The idea behind writing the ContextMenu attribute is to be able to supply a free text name for a given menu option. The following example also adds a Default flag, which is used to indicate the default menu choice. The entire attribute class is presented here:

```
[AttributeUsage(AttributeTargets.Method,AllowMultiple=false,Inherited=true)]
public class ContextMenuAttribute : System.Attribute
{
    public ContextMenuAttribute(string caption)
    {
       Caption = caption;
       Default = false;
    }
    public readonly string Caption;
    public bool Default;
}
```

The `AttributeUsage` attribute on the class marks `ContextMenuAttribute` as only being usable on a method, and it also defines that there can only be one instance of this object on any given method. The `Inherited=true` clause defines whether the attribute can be placed on a superclass method, and still reflected on by a subclass.

There are a number of other members that could be added to this attribute, including:

❑   A hotkey for the menu option

❑   An image to be displayed

❑   Some text to be displayed in the toolbar as the mouse pointer rolls over the menu option

❑   A help context ID

Dispatching methods

When a menu is displayed in .NET, each menu option is linked to the processing code for that option by means of a delegate. In implementing the mechanism for connecting menu choices to code, you have two options:

❑   Implement a method with the same signature as the `System.EventHandler`. This is defined as shown in this snippet:

```
public delegate void EventHandler(object sender, EventArgs e);
```

❑   Define a proxy class, which implements the above delegate, and forwards calls to the received class. This is known as the Command pattern, and is what has been chosen for this example.

The Command pattern separates the sender and the receiver of the call by means of a simple intermediate class. This may be overkill for such an example, but it makes the methods on each `DataRow` simpler (because they don't need the parameters passed to the delegate), and it is more extensible:

```
public class MenuCommand
{
    public MenuCommand(object receiver, MethodInfo method)
    {
        Receiver = receiver;
        Method = method;
    }
    public void Execute(object sender, EventArgs e)
    {
        Method.Invoke(Receiver, new object[] {} );
    }
    public readonly object Receiver;
    public readonly MethodInfo Method;
}
```

The class simply provides an `EventHandler` delegate (the `Execute` method), which invokes the desired method on the receiver object. This example handles two different types of row: rows from the `Customers` table and rows from the `Orders` table. Naturally, the processing options for each of these types of data are likely to differ. Figure 22-29 shows the operations available for a `Customer` row, whereas Figure 22-30 shows the options available for an `Order` row:

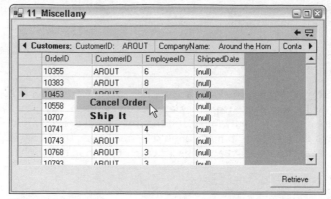

Figure 22-30

Getting the selected row

The last piece of the puzzle for this example is how to work out which row within the `DataSet` the user has selected. You might think that it must be a property on the `DataGrid`. However, this control is not available in this context. The hit test information obtained from within the `MouseUp()` event handler might also be a likely candidate to look at, but that only helps if the data displayed is from a single `DataTable`.

Remember how the grid is filled:

```
dataGrid.SetDataBinding(ds,"Customers");
```

This method adds a new `CurrencyManager` to the `BindingContext`, which represents the current `DataTable` and the `DataSet`. Now, the `DataGrid` has two properties, `DataSource` and `DataMember`, which are set when the `SetDataBinding()` is called. `DataSource` in this instance refers to a `DataSet`, and `DataMember` are `Customers`.

Given the data source, a data member, and the binding context of the form, the current row can be located with the following code:

```
protected void dataGrid_MouseUp(object sender, MouseEventArgs e)
{
    // Perform a hit test
    if(e.Button == MouseButtons.Right)
    {
        // Find which row the user clicked on, if any
        DataGrid.HitTestInfo hti = dataGrid.HitTest(e.X, e.Y);

        // Check if the user hit a cell
        if(hti.Type == DataGrid.HitTestType.Cell)
        {
            // Find the DataRow that corresponds to the cell
            //the user has clicked upon
```

After calling `dataGrid.HitTest()` to calculate where the user has clicked the mouse, the `BindingManagerBase` instance for the data grid is retrieved:

```
BindingManagerBase bmb = this.BindingContext[ dataGrid.DataSource,
                                              dataGrid.DataMember];
```

This uses the `DataGrid`'s `DataSource` and `DataMember` to name the object to be returned. All that is left now is to find the row the user clicked and display the context menu. With a right-click on a row, the current row indicator doesn't normally move, but that's not good enough for us. The row indicator should be moved and then the pop-up menu should be displayed. The `HitTestInfo` object includes the row number, so the `BindingManagerBase` object's current position can be changed as follows:

```
bmb.Position = hti.Row;
```

This changes the cell indicator, and at the same time means that when a call is made into the class to get the `Row`, then the current row is returned and not the previous one selected:

```
DataRowView drv = bmb.Current as DataRowView;
if(drv != null)
{
    ContextDataRow ctx = drv.Row as ContextDataRow;
    if(ctx != null) ctx.PopupMenu(dataGrid,e.X,e.Y);
}
}
}
}
```

As the `DataGrid` is displaying items from a `DataSet`, the `Current` object within the `BindingManagerBase` collection is a `DataRowView`, which is tested by an explicit cast in the previous code. If this succeeds, the actual row that the `DataRowView` wraps can be retrieved by performing another cast to check if it is indeed a `ContextDataRow`, and finally pop up a menu.

In this example, you'll notice that two data tables, `Customers` and `Orders`, have been created, and a relationship has been defined between these tables, so that when the user clicks `CustomerOrders` they see a filtered list of orders. When the user clicks, the `DataGrid` changes the `DataMember` from `Customers` to `Customers.CustomerOrders`, which just so happens to be the correct object that the `BindingContext` indexer uses to retrieve the data being shown.

Summary

This chapter has introduced some of the methods of displaying data under .NET. There are a large number of classes to be explored in `System.Windows.Forms`, and the `DataGrid` has been used to display data from many different data sources, such as an `Array`, `DataTable`, or `DataSet`.

The `DataGrid` control provides many innovative features, including the ability to navigate parent-child relationships defined within a `DataSet`, while being highly customizable.

Because it is not always appropriate to display data in a grid, we also dicussed how to link a column of data to a single control in the user interface. The binding capabilities of .NET make this type of user interface very easy to support, because it's generally just a case of binding a control to a column and letting .NET do the rest of the work.

Furthermore we explored the integration of Visual Studio .NET and XML schemas. We discussed XSD and automatic code generation, and presented a minimal implementation of XSD using a hand-crafted example. Using an XSD schema to generate `DataSet` code can save you a lot of time (and typing), because this tool takes care of all of the underlying code.

The following chapter explores in more detail how you can use XML in Visual Studio .NET, and how well it has been integrated into .NET Framework.

23

Manipulating XML

XML plays a significant role in .NET Framework. Not only does .NET Framework allow you to use XML in your application; .NET Framework itself uses XML for configuration files and source code documentation, as well as SOAP, Web services, and ADO.NET just to name a few.

To accommodate this extensive use of XML, .NET Framework includes the `System.Xml` namespace. This namespace is loaded with classes that can be used for the processing of XML, and many of these classes are discussed in this chapter.

We explain how to use the `XmlDocument` class, which is the implementation of the document object model (DOM), as well as what .NET offers as a replacement for SAX (the `XmlReader` and `XmlWriter` classes). We also discuss the class implementations of XPath and XSLT and demonstrate how XML and ADO.NET work together, and how easy it is to transform one to the other. We also discuss how you can serialize your objects to XML and create an object from (or deserialize) an XML document using classes in the `System.Xml.Serialization` namespace. More to the point, we look at how you can incorporate XML into your C# applications.

You should note that the XML namespace allows you to get similar results in a number of different ways. It is impossible to include all these variations in one chapter, so while exploring one possible way of doing things we'll try our best to mention in passing alternative routes that will yield the same or similar results.

Since we don't have the space to teach you XML from scratch, we are assuming that you are already somewhat familiar with XML technology. For example, you should be familiar what elements, attributes, and nodes, and you should also know what is meant by a well-formed document. You should also be familiar with SAX and DOM. If you want to find out more about XML, Wrox's *Beginning XML* (ISBN 1-861003-41-2) and *Professional XML* (ISBN 1-861003-11-0) are great places to start.

Let's begin our discussion with a brief overview of the current status of XML standards.

XML Standards Support in .NET

The World Wide Web Consortium (W3C) has developed a set of standards that give XML its power and potential. Without these standards, XML would not have the impact on the development world that it does. The W3C Web site (www.w3.org) is a valuable source of all things XML.

As of August 2003, .NET Framework supports the following W3C standards:

- ❑ XML 1.0 (www.w3.org/TR/1998/REC-xml-19980210), including DTD support
- ❑ XML Namespaces (www.w3.org/TR/REC-xml-names), both stream-level and DOM
- ❑ XML Schemas (www.w3.org/2001/XMLSchema)
- ❑ XPath expressions (www.w3.org/TR/xpath)
- ❑ XSLT transformations (www.w3.org/TR/xslt)
- ❑ DOM Level 1 Core (www.w3.org/TR/REC-DOM-Level-1/)
- ❑ DOM Level 2 Core (www.w3.org/TR/DOM-Level-2-Core/)
- ❑ SOAP 1.1 (www.w3.org/TR/SOAP)

The level of standards support will be changing as the Framework matures and the W3C updates the recommended standards. Because of this, you will always need to make sure you stay up-to-date with the standards and the level of support provided by Microsoft.

Introducing the System.Xml Namespace

Support for processing XML is provided by the classes in the System.Xml namespace in .NET. Let's take a look (in no particular order) at some of the more important classes that the System.Xml namespace provides. The following table lists the main XML reader and writer classes.

Class Name	Description
XmlReader	An abstract reader class that provides fast, non-cached XML data. Xml-Reader is forward only, like the SAX parser.
XmlWriter	An abstract writer class that provides fast, non-cached XML data in stream or file format.
XmlTextReader	Extends XmlReader. Provides fast forward-only stream access to XML data.
XmlTextWriter	Extends XmlWriter. Fast forward-only generation of XML streams.

The following table lists some other useful classes for handling XML.

Class Name	Description
XmlNode	An abstract class that represents a single node in an XML document. Base class for several classes in the XML namespace.
XmlDocument	Extends XmlNode. This is the W3C DOM implementation. It provides a tree representation in memory of an XML document, enabling navigation and editing.
XmlDataDocument	Extends XmlDocument. This is a document that can be loaded from XML data or from relational data in an ADO.NET DataSet. Allows the mixing of XML and relational data in the same view.
XmlResolver	An abstract class that resolves external XML-based resources such as DTD and schema references. Also used to process <xsl:include> and <xsl:import> elements.
XmlUrlResolver	Extends XmlResolver. Resolves external resources named by a uniform resource identifier (URI).

Many of the classes in the System.Xml namespace provide a means to manage XML documents and streams, while others (such as the XmlDataDocument class) provide a bridge between XML data stores and the relational data stored in DataSets.

> It is worth noting that the XML namespace is available to any language that is part of the .NET family. This means that all of the examples in this chapter could also be written in Visual Basic .NET, managed C++, and so on.

Using MSXML in .NET

What if you have a ton of code developed using the latest Microsoft parser (currently MSXML 4.0)? Do you have to toss it away and start over if you want to use it with .NET? What if you are comfortable using the MSXML 4.0 DOM? Do you have to switch to .NET right away?

The answer is no. XML 4.0, 3.0, or 2.0 can be used directly in your applications. When you add a reference to msxml4.DLL to your solution, you can start writing some code.

The following examples use books.xml as the source of data. This file can be downloaded from the Wrox Web site (www.wrox.com), but it is also included in several examples in the .NET SDK. The books.xml file is a book catalog for an imaginary bookstore. It includes book information such as genre, author name, price, and ISBN number. As with the other chapters, you can download all code examples in this chapter from the Wrox Web site. In order to run the examples, the XML data files will need to be in a path structure that looks something like this:

```
/XMLChapter/Sample1
/XMLChapter/Sample2
/XMLChapter/Sample3
...
```

You can call the directories anything you want, as long as the individual directories maintain their relative positions to each other. You can also modify the examples to point to anywhere you want. The example code is commented to show which line(s) to change if you want to do this.

This is what the books.xml file looks like:

```xml
<?xml version='1.0'?>
<!-- This file represents a fragment of a book store inventory database -->
<bookstore>
    <book genre="autobiography" publicationdate="1981" ISBN="1-861003-11-0">
        <title>The Autobiography of Benjamin Franklin</title>
        <author>
            <first-name>Benjamin</first-name>
            <last-name>Franklin</last-name>
        </author>
        <price>8.99</price>
    </book>
    <book genre="novel" publicationdate="1967" ISBN="0-201-63361-2">
        <title>The Confidence Man</title>
        <author>
            <first-name>Herman</first-name>
            <last-name>Melville</last-name>
        </author>
        <price>11.99</price>
    </book>
    <book genre="philosophy" publicationdate="1991" ISBN="1-861001-57-6">
        <title>The Gorgias</title>
        <author>
            <name>Plato</name>
        </author>
        <price>9.99</price>
    </book>
</bookstore>
```

Let's look at some code that uses MSXML 4.0 to load a list box with the ISBNs from books.xml. You'll find the full code in the MSXML_Sample folder of the download. You can copy this code into the Visual Studio IDE or create a new Windows Form from scratch. This form contains a list box and a button. Both use the default names of listBox1 and button1, with the Text property of button1 set to Load XML.

One thing that should be pointed out is that since MSXML 4 is a COM-based component, we will need to create the interop assembly. The easiest way is to select Add Reference from the Project menu in the Visual Studio IDE. Go to the COM tab and select Microsoft XML, v4.0 (or v3.0, v2.6). You will see MSXML2 as the added namespace in Solution Explorer. Why is it MSXML2? When you import a COM component the namespace that is given to the new assembly is the typelib name for the COM component. In this case it is MSXML2. If you use TLBIMP you can change the namespace to something else if you wish to.

Next we take a closer look at the most important lines from the MSXML_sample example code.

Since we now have the reference, we add the line:

```
using MSXML2;
```

We also need a class-level variable.

```
private DOMDocument40 doc;
```

Now we are ready to use MSXML in our application.

We want to take the ISBN from the list box, and, using a simple XPath search, find the book node that it matches and display the node text (the book title and book price) in a message box XML Path Language (XPath) is an XML notation that can be used for querying and filtering text in an XML document. We will look more closely at how to use XPath in .NET later in the chapter.

Here is the event handler code for selecting an entry in the list box:

```
protected void listBox1_SelectedIndexChanged (
                        object sender, System.EventArgs e)
{
    string srch=listBox1.SelectedItem.ToString();
    IXMLDOMNode nd=doc.selectSingleNode(
                        "bookstore/book[@ISBN='" + srch + "']");
    MessageBox.Show(nd.text);
}
```

Now we'll look at the event handler for clicking the button. First, we load the books.xml file—note that if you're running the executable from somewhere that isn't the bin/debug or bin/release folder, you'll need to adjust the path appropriately:

```
protected void button1_Click (object sender, System.EventArgs e)
{
    doc=new DOMDocument40 ();
    doc.load("..\\..\\..\\books.xml");
```

The next lines declare that nodes is a NodeList of book nodes. In this case there are three book nodes:

```
IXMLDOMNodeList nodes;
nodes = doc.selectNodes("bookstore/book");
IXMLDOMNode node=nodes.nextNode();
```

Then we loop through the nodes, and add the text value of the ISBN attribute to listBox1:

```
while(node!=null)
{
    listBox1.Items.Add(node.attributes.getNamedItem("ISBN").text);
        node=nodes.nextNode ();
}
}
```

Figure 23-1 shows the example executing. First the button was clicked to load the data into the list box. Then an item in the list box was selected.

Figure 23-1

Using System.Xml Classes

If you have done any work with MSXML 3.0 or 4.0, the previous code above will look pretty familiar. So why would you want to do this if .NET Framework is supposed to have all of these wonderful XML classes to use?

While the `System.Xml` namespace is powerful and relatively easy to use, it is different from the MSXML 3.0 model. If you are comfortable using MSXML 3.0, then use it until you become familiar with the `System.Xml` namespace.

However, `System.Xml` classes have several advantages over MSXML classes. First, `System.Xml` is managed code, so by using it you will gain all of the code security and type safety of using managed code. Also, using COM interop incurs some overhead. Most importantly, however, the `System.Xml` namespace is easy to use and offers a great deal of flexibility. By the end of this chapter this will have become very evident to you.

You should note that we will be using the books.xml file for several examples in this chapter, and the code sample we just looked at will be the basis for many examples too.

Reading and Writing Streamed XML

Now that we have seen how things can be done today, let's take a look at what .NET will allow us to do. We start by looking at how to read and write XML.

The `XmlReader` and `XmlWriter` classes will feel familiar to anyone who has ever used SAX. `XmlReader`-based classes provide a very fast, forward-only, read-only cursor that streams the XML data for processing. Since it is a streaming model, the memory requirements are not very demanding. However, you don't have the navigation flexibility and the read or write capabilities that would be available from a DOM-based model. `XmlWriter`-based classes produce an XML document that conforms to the W3C's XML 1.0 Namespace Recommendations.

`XmlReader` and `XmlWriter` are both abstract classes. Figure 23-2 shows the classes that are derived from `XmlReader` and `XmlWriter`.

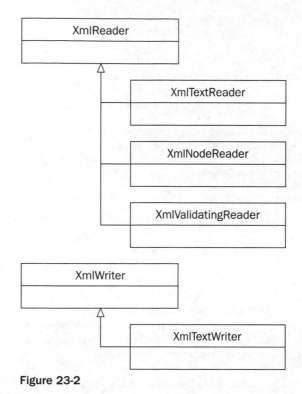

Figure 23-2

`XmlTextReader` and `XmlTextWriter` work with either a stream-based object or `TextReader`/ `TextWriter` objects from the `System.IO` namespace. `XmlNodeReader` uses an `XmlNode` as its source instead of a stream. The `XmlValidatingReader` adds DTD and schema validation and therefore offers data validation. We'll look at these a bit more closely later in this chapter.

Using the XmlTextReader Class

As mentioned previously, `XmlTextReader` is a lot like SAX. One of the biggest differences, however, is that while SAX is a *push* type of model (that is, it pushes data out to the application, and the developer has to be ready to accept it), the `XmlTextReader` has a *pull* model, where data is pulled into an application requesting it. This provides an easier and more intuitive programming model. Another advantage to this is that a pull model can be selective about the data that is sent to the application: if you don't want all of the data, then you don't need to process it. In a push model, all of the XML data has to be processed by the application, whether it is needed or not.

Let's take a look at a very simple example of reading XML data, and then we can take a closer look at the XmlTextReader class. You'll find the code in the XmlReaderSample1 folder. Instead of using the namespace MSXML2 as in the previous example, we now use the following:

```
using System.Xml;
```

We also need to remove the following line from the module-level code:

```
private DOMDocument40 doc;
```

This is what our button click event handler looks like now:

```
protected void button1_Click (object sender, System.EventArgs e)
{
    //Modify this path to find books.xml
    string fileName = "..\\..\\..\\books.xml";
    //Create the new TextReader Object
    XmlTextReader tr = new XmlTextReader(fileName);
    //Read in a node at a time
    while(tr.Read())
    {
      if(tr.NodeType == XmlNodeType.Text)
        listBox1.Items.Add(tr.Value);
    }
}
```

This is XmlTextReader at its simplest. First we create a string object with the name of the XML file. We then create a new XmlTextReader object passing in the fileName string. XmlTextReader has thirteen different constructor overloads. We can pass in various combinations of strings (file names and URLs), streams, and NameTables (when an element or attribute name occurs several times, it can be stored in a NameTable, which allows for faster comparisons).

Just after an XmlTextReader object has been initialized, no node is selected. This is the only time that a node isn't current. When we go into the tr.Read() loop, the first Read() will move us to the first node in the document. This would typically be the XML declaration node. In this sample, as we move to each node we compare tr.NodeType against the XmlNodeType enumeration, and when we find a text node, we add the text value to the list box. Figure 23-3 shows the result.

Read methods

There are several ways to move through the document. As shown in the previous example, Read() takes us to the next node. We can then verify whether the node has a value (HasValue()) or, as you will see shortly, whether the node has any attributes (HasAttributes()). We can also use the ReadStartElement() method, which verifies whether the current node is the start element, and then position you on to the next node. If you are not on the start element, an XmlException is raised. Calling this method is the same as calling the IsStartElement() method, followed by a Read() method.

The ReadString() and ReadChars() methods both read in the text data from an element. ReadString() returns a string object containing the data, while ReadChars() reads the data into an array of chars.

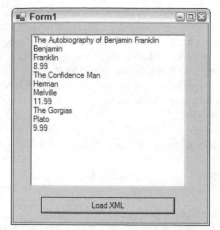

Figure 23-3

ReadElementString() is similar to ReadString(), except that you can optionally pass in the name of an element. If the next content node is not a start tag, or if the Name parameter does not match the current node Name, then an exception is raised.

Here is an example of how ReadElementString() can be used (you'll find the code in the XmlReaderSample2 folder). Notice that this example uses FileStreams, so you will need to make sure that you include the System.IO namespace via a using statement.

```
protected void button1_Click (object sender, System.EventArgs e)
{
    //use a filestream to get the data
    FileStream fs = new FileStream("..\\..\\..\\books.xml",FileMode.Open);
    XmlTextReader tr = new XmlTextReader(fs);
    while(!tr.EOF)
    {
        //if we hit an element type, try and load it in the listbox
        if(tr.MoveToContent() == XmlNodeType.Element && tr.Name=="title")
        {
            listBox1.Items.Add(tr.ReadElementString());
        }
        else
        {
            //otherwise move on
            tr.Read();
        }
    }
}
```

In the while loop we use MoveToContent() to find each node of type XmlNodeType.Element with the name title. We use the EOF property of the XmlTextReader as the loop condition. If the node is not of type Element or not named title, the else clause will issue a Read() method to move to the next node. When we find a node that matches the criteria, we add the result of a ReadElementString() to the list box. This should leave us with just the book titles in the list box. Note that we don't have to issue a Read() call after a successful ReadElementString(). This is because ReadElementString() consumes the entire Element, and positions you on the next node.

If you remove `&& tr.Name=="title"` from the `if` clause, you will have to catch the `XmlException` exception when it is thrown. If you look at the data file, you will see that the first element that `MoveTo Content()` will find is the `<bookstore>` element. Since it is an element, it will pass the check in the `if` statement. However, since it does not contain a simple text type, it will cause `ReadElementString()` to raise an `XmlException`. One way to work around this is to put the `ReadElementString()` call in a function of its own. Then, if the call to `ReadElementString()` fails inside this function, we can deal with the error and return to the calling function.

Let's do this; we'll call this new method `LoadList()`, and pass in the `XmlTextReader` as a parameter. This is what the sample code looks like with these changes (you'll find the code in the XmlReaderSample3 folder):

```
protected void button1_Click (object sender, System.EventArgs e)
{
    //use a filestream to get the data
    FileStream fs = new FileStream("..\\..\\..\\books.xml",FileMode.Open);
    XmlTextReader tr = new XmlTextReader(fs);
    while(!tr.EOF)
    {
        //if we hit an element type, try and load it in the listbox
        if(tr.MoveToContent() == XmlNodeType.Element)
        {
            LoadList(tr);
        }
        else
        {
            //otherwise move on
            tr.Read();
        }
    }
}
private void LoadList(XmlReader reader)
{
    try
    {
        listBox1.Items.Add(reader.ReadElementString());
    }
    // if an XmlException is raised, ignore it.
    catch(XmlException er){}
}
```

After running this example the results should be the same as before. What we are seeing is that there is more then one way to accomplish the same goal. This is where the flexibility of the classes in the `System.Xml` namespace starts to become apparent.

Retrieving attribute data

As you play with the sample code, you might notice that when the nodes are read in, you don't see any attributes. This is because attributes are not considered part of a document's structure. When you are on an element node, you can check for the existence of attributes, and optionally retrieve the attribute values.

For example, the `HasAttributes` property returns `true` if there are any attributes; otherwise it returns `false`. The `AttributeCount` property will tell you how many attributes there are, and the `Get Attribute()` method gets an attribute by name or by index. If you want to iterate through the attributes one at a time, there are also `MoveToFirstAttribute()` and `MoveToNextAttribute()` methods.

Here is an example of iterating through the attributes from `XmlReaderSample4`:

```csharp
protected void button1_Click (object sender, System.EventArgs e)
{
    //set this path to match your data path structure
    string fileName = "..\\..\\..\\books.xml";
    //Create the new TextReader Object
    XmlTextReader tr = new XmlTextReader(fileName);
    //Read in node at a time
    while(tr.Read())
    {
        //check to see if it's a NodeType element
        if(tr.NodeType == XmlNodeType.Element)
        {
            //if it's an element, then let's look at the attributes.
            for(int i = 0; i < tr.AttributeCount; i++) {
                listBox1.Items.Add(tr.GetAttribute(i));
            }
        }
    }
}
```

This time we are looking for element nodes. When we find one, we loop through all of the attributes and, using the `GetAttribute()` method, we load the value of the attribute into the list box. In this example those attributes would be `genre`, `publicationdate`, and `ISBN`.

Using the XmlValidatingReader Class

If you want to validate an XML document, you'll need to use the `XmlValidatingReader` class. It contains the same functionality as `XmlTextReader` (both classes extend `XmlReader`), with the exception that `XmlValidatingReader` adds a `ValidationType` property, a `Schemas` property, and a `SchemaType` property.

You set the `ValidationType` property to the type of validation that you want to do. The following table lists the valid values for this property.

Property Value	Description
Auto	If a DTD is declared in a `<!DOCTYPE...>` declaration, that DTD will be loaded and processed. Default attributes and general entities defined in the DTD will be made available.
	If an XSD `schemalocation` attribute is found, the XSD is loaded and processed, and will return any default attributes defined in the schema.
	If a namespace with the MSXML `x-schema:` prefix is found, it will load and process the XDR schema and return any default attributes defined.

Table continued on following page

791

Property Value	Description
DTD	Validates according to DTD rules.
Schema	Validates according to XSD schema.
XDR	Validates according to XDR schema.
None	No validation is performed.

After this property is set, a `ValidationEventHandler` will need to be assigned. This is an event that gets raised when a validation error occurs. You can then react to the error in any way you see fit.

Let's look at an example of how this works. First we add an XDR (XM-Data Reduced) schema namespace to our books.xml file, and rename this file booksVal.xml. It now looks like this:

```
<?xml version='1.0'?>
<!-- This file represents a fragment of a book store inventory database -->
<bookstore xmlns="x-schema:books.xdr">
    <book genre="autobiography" publicationdate="1981" ISBN="1-861003-11-0">
        <title>The Autobiography of Benjamin Franklin</title>
        <author>
            <first-name>Benjamin</first-name>
            <list-name>Franklin</list-name>
        </author>
        <price>8.99</price>
    </book>
    ...
</bookstore>
```

Note that the bookstore element now has the attribute `xmlns="x-schema:books.xdr"`. This will point to the following XDR schema, called books.xdr:

```
<?xml version="1.0"?>
<Schema xmlns="urn:schemas-microsoft-com:xml-data"
        xmlns:dt="urn:schemas-microsoft-com:datatypes">
    <ElementType name="first-name" content="textOnly"/>
    <ElementType name="last-name" content="textOnly"/>
    <ElementType name="name" content="textOnly"/>
    <ElementType name="price" content="textOnly" dt:type="fixed.14.4"/>
    <ElementType name="author" content="eltOnly" order="one">
        <group order="seq">
            <element type="name"/>
        </group>
        <group order="seq">
            <element type="first-name"/>
            <element type="last-name"/>
        </group>
    </ElementType>
    <ElementType name="title" content="textOnly"/>
    <AttributeType name="genre" dt:type="string"/>
    <ElementType name="book" content="eltOnly">
        <attribute type="genre" required="yes"/>
```

```
            <element type="title"/>
            <element type="author"/>
            <element type="price"/>
        </ElementType>
        <ElementType name="bookstore" content="eltOnly">
            <element type="book"/>
        </ElementType>
    </Schema>
```

Now everything looks good except for the fact that we have a couple of attributes in the XML file that are not defined in the schema (publicationdate and ISBN from the book element). We have added these in order to show that validation is really taking place by raising a validation error. We can use the following code (from XmlReaderSample5) to verify this.

First, you will also need to add the following line to your class:

```
using System.Xml.Schema;
```

Then add the following code to the button event handler:

```
protected void button1_Click (object sender, System.EventArgs e)
{
    //change this to match your path structure.
    string fileName = "..\\..\\..\\booksVal.xml";
    XmlTextReader tr=new XmlTextReader(fileName);
    XmlValidatingReader trv = new XmlValidatingReader(tr);
    //Set validation type
    trv.ValidationType=ValidationType.XDR;
    //Add in the Validation eventhandler
    trv.ValidationEventHandler +=
                    new ValidationEventHandler(this.ValidationEvent);
    //Read in node at a time
    while(trv.Read())
    {
        if(trv.NodeType == XmlNodeType.Text)
        listBox1.Items.Add(trv.Value);
    }
}
public void ValidationEvent (object sender, ValidationEventArgs args)
{
    MessageBox.Show(args.Message);
}
```

Here we create an XmlTextReader to pass to the XmlValidatingReader. Once the XmlValidating Reader (trv) is created, we can use it in much the same way that we used XmlTextReader in the previous examples. The differences are that we specify the ValidationType, and add a ValidationEvent Handler. You can handle the validation error any way that you see fit; in this example we are showing a message box with the error. Figure 23-4 shows what the message box looks like when the ValidationEvent is raised.

Unlike some parsers, once a validation error occurs, XmlValidatingReader will keep on reading. It's up to you to stop the reading and deal with the errors accordingly if you believe that the error is serious enough.

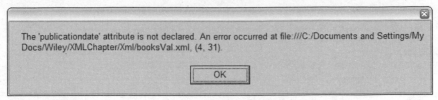

The 'publicationdate' attribute is not declared. An error occurred at file:///C:/Documents and Settings/My Docs/Wiley/XMLChapter/Xml/booksVal.xml, (4, 31).

OK

Figure 23-4

Using the Schemas property

The `Schemas` property of `XmlValidatingReader` holds an `XmlSchemaCollection`, which is found in the `System.Xml.Schema` namespace. This collection holds pre-loaded XSD and XDR schemas. This allows for very fast validation, especially if you need to validate several documents, since the schema will not have to be reloaded on each validation. In order to make use of this performance gain, you create an `XmlSchemaCollection` object. The `Add()` method, used to populate an `XmlSchemaCollection`, has four overloads. You can pass in an `XmlSchema`-based object, an `XmlSchemaCollection`-based object, a `string` with the `namespace` along with a `string` with the URI of the schema file, and finally a string with the `namespace` and an `XmlReader`-based object that contains the schema.

Using the XmlTextWriter Class

The `XmlTextWriter` class allows you write XML to a stream, a file, or a `TextWriter` object. Like `XmlTextReader`, it does so in a forward-only, non-cached manner. `XmlTextWriter` is highly configurable, allowing you to specify such things as whether or not to indent content, the amount to indent, what quote character to use in attribute values, and whether namespaces are supported.

Let's look at a simple example to see how the `XmlTextWriter` class can be used. You can find this example in the `XmlWriterSample1` folder:

```
private void button1_Click(object sender, System.EventArgs e)
{
    // change to match your path structure
    string fileName="..\\..\\..\\booknew.xml";
    // create the XmlTextWriter
    XmlTextWriter tw=new XmlTextWriter(fileName,null);
    // set the formatting to indented
    tw.Formatting=Formatting.Indented;
    tw.WriteStartDocument();
    // Start creating elements and attributes
    tw.WriteStartElement("book");
    tw.WriteAttributeString("genre","Mystery");
    tw.WriteAttributeString("publicationdate","2001");
    tw.WriteAttributeString("ISBN","123456789");
    tw.WriteElementString("title","The Case of the Missing Cookie");
    tw.WriteStartElement("author");
    tw.WriteElementString("name","Cookie Monster");
    tw.WriteEndElement();
    tw.WriteElementString("price","9.99");
    tw.WriteEndElement();
    tw.WriteEndDocument();
```

```
        //clean up
        tw.Flush();
        tw.Close();
    }
```

Here we are writing to a new XML file called booknew.xml, adding the data for a new book. Note that `XmlTextWriter` will overwrite an existing file with a new one. We will look at inserting a new element or node into an existing document later in this chapter. We are instantiating the `XmlTextWriter` object using a `FileStream` object as a parameter. We could also pass in a string with a file name and path, or a `TextWriter`-based object. The next thing that we do is set the `Indenting` property. After this is set, child nodes are automatically indented from the parent. `WriteStartDocument()` adds the document declaration. Now we start writing data. First comes the `book` element, and then we add the `genre`, `publicationdate`, and `ISBN` attributes, and then we write the `title`, `author`, and `price` elements. Note that the `author` element has a child element name.

When we click the button, we produce the booknew.xml file, which looks like this:

```xml
<?xml version="1.0"?>
<book genre="Mystery" publicationdate="2001" ISBN="123456789">
  <title>The Case of the Missing Cookie</title>
  <author>
    <name>Cookie Monster</name>
  </author>
  <price>9.99</price>
</book>
```

The nesting of elements is controlled by paying attention to when you start and finish writing elements and attributes. You can see this when we add the `name` child element to the `authors` element. Note how the `WriteStartElement()` and `WriteEndElement()` method calls are arranged, and how that arrangement produces the nested elements in the output file.

To go along with the `WriteElementString()` and `WriteAttributeString()` methods, there are several other specialized write methods. `WriteCData()` outputs a CData section (`<!CDATA[...]]>`), writing out the text it takes as a parameter. `WriteComment()` writes out a comment in proper XML format. `WriteChars()` writes out the contents of a char buffer. This works in a similar fashion to the `ReadChars()` method that we looked at earlier; they both use the same type of parameters. `WriteChars()` needs a buffer (an array of characters), the starting position for writing (an integer) and the number of characters to write (an integer).

Reading and writing XML using the `XmlReader` and `XmlWriter`-based classes is surprisingly flexible and simple to use. Next, we explain how the DOM is implemented in the `System.Xml` namespace, through the `XmlDocument` and `XmlNode` classes.

Using the DOM in .NET

The DOM implementation in .NET supports the W3C DOM Level 1 and Core DOM Level 2 specifications. The DOM is implemented through the `XmlNode` class, which is an abstract class that represents a node of an XML document.

There is also an XmlNodeList class, which is an ordered list of nodes. This is a live list of nodes, and any changes to any node are immediately reflected in the list. XmlNodeList supports indexed access or iterative access. There is another abstract class, XmlCharacterData, that extends XmlLinkedNode, and provides text manipulation methods for other classes.

The XmlNode and XmlNodeList classes make up the core of the DOM implementation in.NET Framework. The following table lists some of the classes that are based on XmlNode.

Class Name	Description
XmlLinkedNode	Returns the node immediately before or after the current node. Adds NextSibling and PreviousSibling properties to XmlNode.
XmlDocument	Represents the entire document. Implements the DOM Level 1 and Level 2 specifications.
XmlDocumentFragment	Represents a fragment of the document tree.
XmlAttribute	Represents an attribute object of an XmlElement object.
XmlEntity	Represents a parsed or unparsed entity node.
XmlNotation	Contains a notation declared in a DTD or schema.

The following table list classes that extend XmlCharacterData.

Class Name	Description
XmlCDataSection	Represents a CData section of a document.
XmlComment	Represents an XML comment object.
XmlSignificantWhitespace	Represents a node with whitespace. Nodes created only if the PreserveWhiteSpace flag is true.
XmlWhitespace	Represents whitespace in element content. Nodes are created only if the PreserveWhiteSpace flag is true.
XmlText	Represents the textual content of an element or attribute.

The following table lists classes that extend the XmlLinkedNode.

Class Name	Description
XmlDeclaration	Represents the declaration node (<?xml version='1.0'...>).
XmlDocumentType	Represents data relating to the document type declaration.
XmlElement	Represents an XML element object.
XmlEntityReferenceNode	Represents an entity reference node.
XmlProcessingInstruction	Contains an XML processing instruction.

As you can see, .NET makes available a class to fit just about any XML type that you might encounter. Because of this, you end up with a very flexible and powerful tool set. We won't look at every class in detail, but we will use several examples to give you an idea of what you can accomplish. Figure 23-5 illustrates what the inheritance diagram looks like.

Using the XmlDocument Class

XmlDocument and its derived class XmlDataDocument (discussed later in this chapter) are the classes that you will be using to represent the DOM in .NET. Unlike XmlReader and XmlWriter, XmlDocument gives you read and write capabilities as well as random access to the DOM tree. XmlDocument resembles the DOM implementation in MSXML. If you have experience programming with MSXML, then you will feel comfortable using XmlDocument.

Let's introduce an example that creates an XmlDocument object, loads a document from disk and loads a list box with data from the title elements. This is similar to one of the examples that we constructed in the XmlReader section. The difference here is that we will be selecting the nodes we want to work with, instead of going through the entire document as in the XmlReader-based example.

Here is our code. Look at how simple it looks in comparison to the XmlReader example (the file can be found in the DOMSample1 folder of the download):

```
private void button1_Click(object sender, System.EventArgs e)
{
    // doc is declared at the module level
    // change path to match your path structure
    doc.Load("..\\..\\..\\books.xml");
    // get only the nodes that we want
    XmlNodeList nodeLst=doc.GetElementsByTagName("title");
    // iterate through the XmlNodeList
    foreach(XmlNode node in nodeLst) listBox1.Items.Add(node.InnerText);
}
```

Note that we also add the following declaration at the module level for the examples in this section:

```
private XmlDocument doc=new XmlDocument();
```

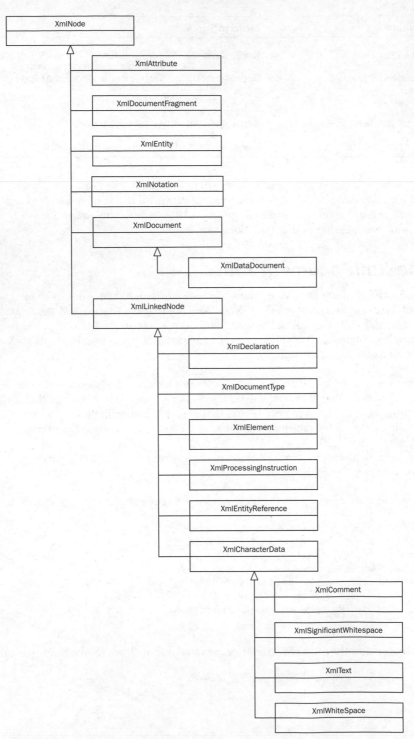

Figure 23-5

If this is all that we wanted to do, using the XmlReader would have been a much more efficient way to load the list box, because we just go through the document once, and then we are finished with it. This is exactly the type of work that XmlReader was designed for. However, if we wanted to revisit a node, then using XmlDocument is a better way. Let's extend the previous example by adding another event handler (this is DOMSample2):

```csharp
private void listBox1_SelectedIndexChanged(object sender, System.EventArgs e)
{
    //create XPath search string
    string srch="bookstore/book[title='" + listBox1.SelectedItem.ToString()
                                  + "']";
    //look for the extra data
    XmlNode foundNode = doc.SelectSingleNode(srch);
    if(foundNode != null)
        MessageBox.Show(foundNode.InnerText);
    else
        MessageBox.Show("Not found");
}
```

In this example, we load the list box with the titles from the books.xml document, as in the previous example. When we click on the list box, it triggers the SelectedIndexChanged() event handler. In this case, we take the text of the selected item in the list box (the book title) create an XPath statement and pass it to the SelectSingleNode() method of the doc object. This returns the book element that the title is part of (foundNode). Then we display the InnerText of the node in a message box. We can keep clicking on items in the list box as many times as we want, since the document is loaded and stays loaded until we release it.

A quick comment regarding the SelectSingleNode() method. This is an XPath implementation in the XmlDocument class. There are the methods SelectSingleNode() and SelectNodes(). Both of these methods are defined in XmlNode, which XmlDocument in based on. SelectSingleNode() returns an XmlNode and SelectNodes() returns an XmlNodeList. However, the System.Xml.XPath namespace contains a richer XPath implementation, and we will be looking at that in a later section.

Inserting nodes

Earlier we looked at an example using XmlTextWriter that created a new document. The limitation was that it would not insert a node into a current document. With the XmlDocument class we can do just that. Change the button1_Click() event handler from the last example to the following (DOMSample3 in the download code):

```csharp
private void button1_Click(object sender, System.EventArgs e)
{
    //change path to match your structure
    doc.Load("..\\..\\..\\books.xml");
    //create a new 'book' element
    XmlElement newBook=doc.CreateElement("book");
    //set some attributes
    newBook.SetAttribute("genre","Mystery");
    newBook.SetAttribute("publicationdate","2001");
    newBook.SetAttribute("ISBN","123456789");
    //create a new 'title' element
    XmlElement newTitle=doc.CreateElement("title");
```

```
    newTitle.InnerText="The Case of the Missing Cookie";
    newBook.AppendChild(newTitle);
    //create new author element
    XmlElement newAuthor=doc.CreateElement("author");
    newBook.AppendChild(newAuthor);
    //create new name element
    XmlElement newName=doc.CreateElement("name");
    newName.InnerText="C. Monster";
    newAuthor.AppendChild(newName);
    //create new price element
    XmlElement newPrice=doc.CreateElement("price");
    newPrice.InnerText="9.95";
    newBook.AppendChild(newPrice);
    //add to the current document
    doc.DocumentElement.AppendChild(newBook);
    //write out the doc to disk
    XmlTextWriter tr=new XmlTextWriter("..\\..\\..\\booksEdit.xml",null);
    tr.Formatting=Formatting.Indented;
    doc.WriteContentTo(tr);
    tr.Close();
    //load listBox1 with all of the titles, including new one
    XmlNodeList nodeLst=doc.GetElementsByTagName("title");
    foreach(XmlNode node in nodeLst)
        listBox1.Items.Add(node.InnerText);
}
```

After executing this code, you end up with the same functionality as in the previous example, but there is one additional book in the list box, *The Case of the Missing Cookie* (a soon-to-be classic). Clicking on the cookie caper title will show all of the same info as the other titles. Breaking down the code, we can see that this is actually a fairly simple process. The first thing that we do is create a new book element:

```
XmlElement newBook = doc.CreateElement("book");
```

CreateElement() has three overloads that allow you to specify:

❑   The element name

❑   The name and namespace URI

❑   The prefix, localname, and namespace

Once the element is created we need to add attributes:

```
newBook.SetAttribute("genre","Mystery");
newBook.SetAttribute("publicationdate","2001");
newBook.SetAttribute("ISBN","123456789");
```

Now that we have the attributes created, we need to add the other elements of a book:

```
XmlElement newTitle = doc.CreateElement("title");
newTitle.InnerText = "The Case of the Missing Cookie";
newBook.AppendChild(newTitle);
```

Once again we create a new `XmlElement`-based object (`newTitle`). Then we set the `InnerText` property to the title of our new classic, and append the element as a child to the `book` element. We repeat this for the rest of the elements in this `book` element. Note that we add the `name` element as a child to the `author` element. This will give us the proper nesting relationship as in the other `book` elements.

Finally, we append the `newBook` element to the `doc.DocumentElement` node. This is the same level as all of the other `book` elements. We have now updated an existing document with a new element.

The last thing to do is to write the new XML document to disk. In this example we create a new `XmlTextWriter`, and pass it to the `WriteContentTo()` method. `WriteContentTo()` and `WriteTo()` both take an `XmlTextWriter` as a parameter. `WriteContentTo()` saves the current node and all of its children to the `XmlTextWriter`, whereas `WriteTo()` just saves the current node. Because `doc` is an `XmlDocument`-based object, it represents the entire document and so that is what is saved. We could also use the `Save()` method. It will always save the entire document. `Save()` has four overloads. You can specify a string with the file name and path, a `Stream`-based object, a `TextWriter`-based object, or an `XmlWriter`-based object.

We also call the `Close()` method on `XmlTextWriter` to flush the internal buffers and close the file.

Figure 23-6 shows what we get when we run this example. Notice the new entry at the bottom of the list:

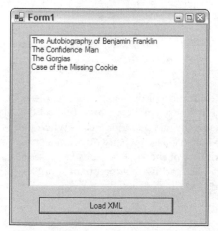

Figure 23-6

If we wanted to create a document from scratch, we could use the `XmlTextWriter`, which we saw in action earlier in the chapter. We can also use `XmlDocument`. Why would you use one in preference to the other? If the data that you want streamed to XML is available and ready to write, then the `XmlTextWriter` class would be the best choice. However, if you need to build the XML document a little at a time, inserting nodes into various places, then creating the document with `XmlDocument` might be the better choice. We can accomplish this by changing the following line:

```
doc.Load("..\\..\\..\\books.xml");
```

to this code (example `DOMSample4`):

```
      //create the declaration section
      XmlDeclaration newDec = doc.CreateXmlDeclaration("1.0",null,null);
      doc.AppendChild(newDec);
      //create the new root element
      XmlElement newRoot = doc.CreateElement("newBookstore");
      doc.AppendChild(newRoot);
```

First, we create a new `XmlDeclaration`. The parameters are the version (always `1.0` for now), the encoding, and the standalone flag. The encoding parameter should be set to a string that is part of the `System.Text.Encoding` class if `null` isn't used. (`null` defaults to UTF-8). The standalone flag can be either `yes`, `no`, or `null`. If it is `null` then the attribute is not used and will not be included in the document.

The next element that is created will become the `DocumentElement`. In this case, we called it `newBookstore` so that you can see the difference. The rest of the code is the same as in the previous example and works in the same way. This is booksEdit.xml, which is generated from the code:

```
<?xml version="1.0"?>
<newBookstore>
   <book genre="Mystery" publicationdate="2001" ISBN="123456789">
      <title>The Case of the Missing Cookie</title>
      <author>
         <name>C. Monster</name>
      </author>
      <price>9.95</price>
   </book>
</newBookstore>
```

We have not exhausted our exploration of the `XmlDocument` class, or of the other classes that help to create the DOM model in .NET. However, you how powerful and flexible the DOM implementation in .NET offers. You will want to use the `XmlDocument` class when you want to have random access to the document, or the `XmlReader`-based classes when you want a streaming type model instead. Remember that there is a cost for the flexibility of the `XmlNode`-based `XmlDocument` class—memory requirements are higher and the performance of reading the document is not as good as using `XmlReader`. So think carefully about which method best fits your needs.

Using XPath and XSLT in .NET

In this section, we discuss support for XPath and XSL Transforms (XSLT) in.NET Framework. XPath support is provided through the `System.Xml.XPath` namespace, and `XSLT` through the `System.Xml.Xsl` namespace. The reason that we are looking at them together is that the `XPathNavigator` class of the `System.Xml.XPath` namespace provides a very performance-oriented way of performing XSL Transforms in .NET.

XPath is the query language for XML. You would use XPath to select a subset of elements based on element text values or perhaps based on attribute values. XSLT is used to transform a base document into another document of different structure or type.

We will first look at `System.Xml.XPath` and then discuss how it is used to feed the `System.Xml.Xsl` classes.

The System.Xml.XPath Namespace

The System.Xml.XPath namespace is built for speed. It provides a read-only view of your XML documents, so there are no editing capabilities. Classes in this namespace are built to do fast iteration and selections on the XML document in a cursor fashion.

Here is a table that lists the key classes in System.Xml.XPath, and gives a short description of the purpose of each class:

Class Name	Description
XPathDocument	Provides a view of the entire XML document. Read-only.
XPathNavigator	Provides the navigation capabilities to an XPathDocument.
XPathNodeIterator	Provides iteration capabilities to a node set. XPath equivalent to a nodeset in Xpath.
XPathExpression	Represents a compiled XPath expression. Used by SelectNodes, SelectSingleNodes, Evaluate, and Matches.
XPathException	Is an XPath exception class.

XPathDocument

XPathDocument doesn't offer any of the functionality of the XmlDocument class. If you need editing capabilities, then XmlDocument is the way to go; if you're using ADO.NET, go with XmlDataDocument (discussed later in this chapter). However, if speed is of concern, then use XPathDocument as your store. It has four overloads allowing you to open an XML document from a file and path string, a TextReader object, an XmlReader object, or a Stream-based object.

XPathNavigator

XPathNavigator contains all of the methods for moving and selecting elements that you need. The following table lists some of the "move" methods defined in this class.

Method Name	Description
MoveTo()	Takes XPathNavigator as a parameter. Moves the current position to be the same as that passed in to XPathNavigator.
MoveToAttribute()	Moves to the named attribute. Takes the attribute name and namespace as parameters.
MoveToFirstAttribute()	Moves to the first attribute in the current element. Returns true if successful.
MoveToNextAttribute()	Moves to the next attribute in the current element. Returns true if successful.
MoveToFirst()	Moves to the first sibling in the current node. Returns true if successful; otherwise it returns false.

Table continued on following page

Method Name	Description
MoveToLast()	Moves to the last sibling in the current node. Returns true if successful.
MoveToNext()	Moves to the next sibling in the current node. Returns true if successful.
MoveToPrevious()	Moves to the previous sibling in the current node. Returns true if successful.
MoveToFirstChild()	Moves to the first child of the current element. Returns true if successful.
MoveToId()	Moves to the element with the ID supplied as a parameter. There needs to be a schema for the document, and the data type for the element must be of type ID.
MoveToParent()	Moves to the parent of the current node. Returns true if successful.
MoveToRoot()	Moves to the root node of the document.

There are several Select() methods for selecting a subset of nodes to work with. All of these Select() methods return an XPathNodeIterator object.

There are also SelectAncestors() and SelectChildren() methods that you can use. Both return an XPathNodeIterator object. While Select() takes an XPath expression as a parameter, the other select methods take XPathNodeType as a parameter.

You can extend XPathNavigator to use such things as the file system or registry as the store instead of XPathDocument.

XPathNodeIterator

XPathNodeIterator can be thought of as the equivalent of a NodeList or a NodeSet in XPath. This object has three properties and two methods:

- ❑ Clone—Creates a new copy of itself
- ❑ Count—Number of nodes in the XPathNodeIterator object
- ❑ Current—Returns an XPathNavigator pointing to the current node
- ❑ CurrentPosition()—Returns an integer with the current position
- ❑ MoveNext()—Moves to the next node that matches the XPath expression that created the XpathNodeIterator

Using classes from the XPath namespace

The best way to see how these classes are used is to look at some code that iterates through the books.xml document. This will allow you to see how the navigation works. In order to use the examples, we first add a reference to the System.Xml.Xsl and System.Xml.XPath namespaces:

```
using System.Xml.XPath;
using System.Xml.Xsl;
```

For this example we are using the file booksxpath.xml. It is similar to the books.xml that we have been using previously, except there are a couple of extra books added. Here's the form code, which can be found in the XPathXSLSample1 folder:

```
private void button1_Click(object sender, System.EventArgs e)
{
    //modify to match your path structure
    XPathDocument doc=new XPathDocument("..\\..\\..\\booksxpath.xml");
    //create the XPath navigator
    XPathNavigator nav=doc.CreateNavigator();
    //create the XPathNodeIterator of book nodes
    // that have genre attribute value of novel
    XPathNodeIterator iter=nav.Select("/bookstore/book[@genre='novel']");

    while(iter.MoveNext())
    {
        LoadBook(iter.Current);
    }
}
private void LoadBook(XPathNavigator lstNav)
{
    //We are passed an XPathNavigator of a particular book node
    //we will select all of the descendents and
    //load the list box with the names and values
    XPathNodeIterator iterBook=lstNav.SelectDescendants
                            (XPathNodeType.Element,false);
    while(iterBook.MoveNext())
        listBox1.Items.Add(iterBook.Current.Name + ": "
                                    + iterBook.Current.Value);
}
```

The first thing we do in the button1_Click() method is to create the XPathDocument (called doc), passing in the file and path string of the document we want opened. The next line is where the XPathNavigator is created:

```
XPathNavigator nav = doc.CreateNavigator();
```

In the example you can see that we use the Select() method to retrieve a set of nodes that all have novel as the value of the genre attribute. We then use the MoveNext() method to iterate through all of the novels in the book list.

To load the data into the list box, we use the XPathNodeIterator.Current property. This creates a new XPathNavigator object based on just the node that the XPathNodeIterator is pointing to. In this case, we are creating an XPathNavigator for one book node in the document.

The LoadBook() method takes this XPathNavigator and creates another XPathNodeIterator by issuing another type of select method, the SelectDescendants() method. This gives us an XPathNodeIterator of all of the child nodes and children of the child nodes of the book node that we passed to the LoadBook() method.

Then we do another `MoveNext()` loop on the `XPathNodeIterator` and load the list box with the element names and element values.

Figure 23-7 shows what the screen looks like after running the code. Note that novels are the only books listed now.

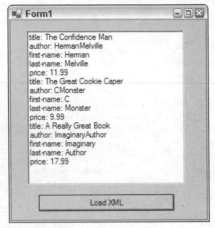

```
title: The Confidence Man
author: HermanMelville
first-name: Herman
last-name: Melville
price: 11.99
title: The Great Cookie Caper
author: CMonster
first-name: C
last-name: Monster
price: 9.99
title: A Really Great Book
author: ImaginaryAuthor
first-name: Imaginary
last-name: Author
price: 17.99
```

Load XML

Figure 23-7

What if we wanted to add up the cost of these books? `XPathNavigator` includes the `Evaluate()` method for just this reason. `Evaluate()` has three overloads. The first one contains a string that is the XPath function call. The second overload uses the `XPathExpression` object as a parameter, and the third uses `XPathExpression` and an `XPathNodeIterator` as parameters. The changes are highlighted below (this version of the code can be found in XPathXSLSample2):

```csharp
private void button1_Click(object sender, System.EventArgs e)
{
    //modify to match your path structure
    XPathDocument doc = new XPathDocument("..\\..\\..\\booksxpath.XML");
    //create the XPath navigator
    XPathNavigator nav = doc.CreateNavigator();
    //create the XPathNodeIterator of book nodes
    // that have genre attribute value of novel
    XPathNodeIterator iter = nav.Select("/bookstore/book[@genre='novel']");
    while(iter.MoveNext())
    {
        LoadBook(iter.Current.Clone());
    }
    //add a break line and calculate the sum
    listBox1.Items.Add("=========================");
    listBox1.Items.Add("Total Cost = "
            + nav.Evaluate("sum(/bookstore/book[@genre='novel']/price)"));
}
```

This time, we see the total cost of the books evaluated in the list box (see Figure 23-8).

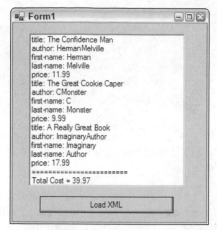

Figure 23-8

The System.Xml.Xsl Namespace

The `System.Xml.Xsl` namespace contains the classes that .NET Framework uses to support XSL Transforms. The contents of this namespace are available to any store whose classes implement the `IXPathNavigable` interface. In.NET Framework that would currently include `XmlDocument`, `XmlDataDocument`, and `XPathDocument`. Again, just as with `XPath`, use the store that makes the most sense. If you plan to create a custom store, such as one using the file system, and you want to be able to do transforms, be sure to implement the `IXPathNavigable` interface in your class.

XSLT is based on a streaming pull model. Because of this, you can chain several transforms together. You could even apply a custom reader between transforms if needed. This allows a great deal of flexibility in design.

Transforming XML

The first example we will look at takes the books.xml document and transforms it into a simple HTML document for display using the XSLT file books.xsl. (This code can be found in the XPathXSLSample3 folder.) We will need to add the following `using` statements:

```
using System.IO;
using System.Xml.Xsl;
using System.Xml.XPath;
```

Here is the code to perform the transform:

```
private void button1_Click(object sender, System.EventArgs e)
{
    //create the new XPathDocument
    XPathDocument doc = new XPathDocument("..\\..\\..\\booksxpath.xml");
    //create a new XslTransForm
    XslTransform transForm = new XslTransform();
    transForm.Load("..\\..\\..\\books.xsl");
```

```
        //this FileStream will be our output
        FileStream fs=new FileStream("..\\..\\..\\booklist.html",
                                FileMode.Create);
        //Create the navigator
        XPathNavigator nav = doc.CreateNavigator();
        //Do the transform. The output file is created here
        transForm.Transform(nav, null, fs, null);
}
```

A transform doesn't get any simpler than this. We create an XPathDocument-based object and an XslTransform-based object. We load the booksxpath.xml file into the XPathDocument object, and books.xsl file into XslTransform.

In this example, we also create a FileStream object to write the new HTML document to disk. If this were an ASP.NET application, we would have used a TextWriter object and passed it to the HttpResponse object instead. If we were transforming to another XML document we would have used an XmlWriter-based object.

After the XPathDocument and XslTransform objects are ready, we create the XPathNavigator on the XPathDocument, and pass the XPathNavigator and the FileStream into the Transform() method of the XslTransform object. Transform() has several overloads, passing in combinations of navigators, XsltArgumentList (more on this shortly), IO streams and XmlResolvers. The navigator parameter can be XPathNavigator, or anything that implements the IXPathNavigable interface. The IO streams can be a TextWriter, Stream, or XmlWriter-based object. The XmlResolver is used to manage the process of getting a resource from an external source. The XmlResolver handles the security, opening the data source and returning the data or stream. In .Net Framework 1.0 the XmlResolver parameter was not a requirement. All of those versions of the Transform method have been deprecated and now the XmlResolver parameter is required, however you can pass null if the features of an XmlResolver, namely security and credential management are not needed.

The books.xsl document is a fairly straightforward style sheet. The document looks like this:

```
<xsl:stylesheet version="1.0"
                    xmlns:xsl="http://www.w3.org/1999/XSL/Transform">
<xsl:template match="/">
    <html>
        <head>
            <title>Price List</title>
        </head>
        <body>
            <table>
                <xsl:apply-templates/>
            </table>
        </body>
    </html>
    </xsl:template>
<xsl:template match="bookstore">
    <xsl:apply-templates select="book"/>
</xsl:template>
<xsl:template match="book">
    <tr><td>
        <xsl:value-of select="title"/>
```

```
        </td><td>
          <xsl:value-of select="price"/>
        </td></tr>
    </xsl:template>
</xsl:stylesheet>
```

Using XsltArgumentList

Earlier we mentioned `XsltArgumentList`. This is a way that you can bind an object with methods to a namespace. Once this is done, you can invoke the methods during the transform. Let's look at an example to see how this works (located in XPathXSLSample4). Add the highlighted code to your sample code:

```
private void button1_Click(object sender, System.EventArgs e)
{
    //new XPathDocument
    XPathDocument doc=new XPathDocument("..\\..\\..\\booksxpath.xml");
    //new XslTransform
    XslTransform transForm=new XslTransform();
    transForm.Load("..\\..\\..\\booksarg.xsl");
    //new XmlTextWriter since we are creating a new XML document
    XmlWriter xw=new XmlTextWriter("..\\..\\..\\argSample.xml",null);
    //create the XsltArgumentList and new BookUtils object
    XsltArgumentList argBook=new XsltArgumentList();
    BookUtils bu=new BookUtils();
    //this tells the argumentlist about BookUtils
    argBook.AddExtensionObject("urn:ProCSharp",bu);
    //new XPathNavigator
    XPathNavigator nav=doc.CreateNavigator();
    //do the transform
    transForm.Transform(nav,argBook,xw,null);
    xw.Close();
}
//simple test class
public class BookUtils
{
    public BookUtils(){}

    public string ShowText()
    {
        return "This came from the ShowText method!";
    }
}
```

This is what the output of the transform looks like; we've formatted the output for easier viewing (argSample.xml):

```
<books>
    <discbook>
        <booktitle>The Autobiography of Benjamin Franklin</booktitle>
        <showtext>This came from the ShowText method!</showtext>
    </discbook>
    <discbook>
        <booktitle>The Confidence Man</booktitle>
```

```
      <showtext>This came from the ShowText method!</showtext>
   </discbook>
   <discbook>
      <booktitle>The Gorgias</booktitle>
      <showtext>This came from the ShowText method!</showtext>
   </discbook>
   <discbook>
      <booktitle>The Great Cookie Caper</booktitle>
      <showtext>This came from the ShowText method!</showtext>
   </discbook>
   <discbook>
      <booktitle>A Really Great Book</booktitle>
      <showtext>This came from the ShowText method!</showtext>
   </discbook>
</books>
```

In this example, we define a new class, BookUtils. In this class we have one rather useless method that returns the string "This came from the ShowText method!" In the button1_Click() event, we create the XPathDocument and XslTransform objects just as we did before, with one exception. This time we are going to create an XML document, so we use the XmlWriter instead of the FileStream that we used before. The next change is here:

```
XsltArgumentList argBook=new XsltArgumentList();
BookUtils bu=new BookUtils();
argBook.AddExtensionObject("urn:ProCSharp",bu);
```

This is where we create the XsltArgumentList object. We create an instance of our BookUtils object, and when we call the AddExtensionObject() method, we pass in a namespace for our extension, and the object that we want to be able to call methods from. When we make the Transform() call, we pass in the XsltArgumentList (argBook) along with the XPathNavigator and the XmlWriter object we made.

Here is the booksarg.xsl document (based on books.xsl):

```
<xsl:stylesheet version="1.0" xmlns:xsl="http://www.w3.org/1999/XSL/Transform"
                             xmlns:bookUtil="urn:ProCSharp">
   <xsl:output method="xml" indent="yes"/>

   <xsl:template match="/">
      <xsl:element name="books">
         <xsl:apply-templates/>
      </xsl:element>
   </xsl:template>
   <xsl:template match="bookstore">
      <xsl:apply-templates select="book"/>
   </xsl:template>
   <xsl:template match="book">
      <xsl:element name="discbook">
         <xsl:element name="booktitle">
            <xsl:value-of select="title"/>
         </xsl:element>
         <xsl:element name="showtext">
            <xsl:value-of select="bookUtil:ShowText()"/>
```

```
          </xsl:element>
        </xsl:element>
      </xsl:template>
   </xsl:stylesheet>
```

The two important new lines are highlighted. First we add the namespace that we created when we added the object to `XsltArgumentList`. Then when we want to make the method call, we use standard XSLT namespace prefixing syntax and make the method call.

Another way we could have accomplished this is with XSLT scripting. You can include C#, Visual Basic, and JavaScript code in the style sheet. The great thing about this is that unlike current non-.NET implementations the script is compiled at the `XslTransform.Load()` call; this way you are executing already compiled scripts, much the same way that ASP.NET works.

Let's modify the previous XSLT file in this way. First we add the script to the style sheet. You can see the following changes in booksscript.xsl:

```
<xsl:stylesheet version="1.0" xmlns:xsl="http://www.w3.org/1999/XSL/Transform"
                              xmlns:msxsl="urn:schemas-microsoft-com:xslt"
                              xmlns:user="http://wrox.com">

   <msxsl:script language="C#" implements-prefix="user">

      string ShowText()
         {
            return "This came from the ShowText method!";

         }
   </msxsl:script>

   <xsl:output method="xml" indent="yes"/>
      <xsl:template match="/">
   <xsl:element name="books">
      <xsl:apply-templates/>
   </xsl:element>
      </xsl:template>
   <xsl:template match="bookstore">
      <xsl:apply-templates select="book"/>
   </xsl:template>
      <xsl:template match="book">
      <xsl:element name="discbook">
      <xsl:element name="booktitle">
         <xsl:value-of select="title"/>
      </xsl:element>
      <xsl:element name="showtext">
         <xsl:value-of select="user:ShowText()"/>
      </xsl:element>
    </xsl:element>
   </xsl:template>
</xsl:stylesheet>
```

Once again the changes are highlighted. We set the scripting namespace, add the code (which was copied and pasted in from the Visual Studio .NET IDE), and make the call in the style sheet. The output looks the same as that of the previous example.

To summarize, the key thing to keep in mind when performing transforms is to remember to use the proper XML data store. Use XPathDocument if you don't need edit capabilities, XmlDataDocument if you're getting your data from ADO.NET, and XmlDocument if you need to be able to edit the data. In each case you are dealing with the same process.

XML and ADO.NET

XML is the glue that binds ADO.NET to the rest of the world. ADO.NET was designed from the ground up to work within the XML environment. XML is used to transfer the data to and from the data store and the application or Web page. Since ADO.NET uses XML as the transport in remoting scenarios, data can be exchanged with applications and systems that are not even aware of ADO.NET. Because of the importance of XML in ADO.NET, there are some powerful features in ADO.NET that allow the reading and writing of XML documents. The System.Xml namespace also contains classes that can consume or utilize ADO.NET relational data.

Converting ADO.NET Data to XML

The first example that we are going to look at uses ADO.NET, streams, and XML to pull some data from the Northwind database into a DataSet, load an XmlDocument object with the XML from the DataSet, and load the XML into a list box. In order to run the next few examples, you need to add the following using statements:

```
using System.Data;
using System.Xml;
using System.Data.SqlClient;
using System.IO;
```

Since we will be using XmlDocument, we also need to add the following at the module level:

```
private XmlDocument doc = new XmlDocument();
```

Also, for the ADO.NET samples we have added a DataGrid object to the forms. This will allow us to see the data in the ADO.NET DataSet since it is bound to the grid, as well as the data from the generated XML documents that we load in the list box. Here is the code for the first example (which can be found in the ADOSample1 folder):

```
private void button1_Click(object sender, System.EventArgs e)
{
    //create a dataset
    DataSet ds = new DataSet("XMLProducts");
    //connect to the northwind database and
    //select all of the rows from products table
    //make sure your login matches your version of SqlServer
    SqlConnection conn = new SqlConnection
                (@"server=GLYNNJ_CS\NetSDK;uid=sa;pwd=;database=northwind");
    SqlDataAdapter da = new SqlDataAdapter("SELECT * FROM Products",conn);
```

After we create the `SqlDataAdapter`, `da`, and the `DataSet`, `ds`, we instantiate a `MemoryStream` object, a `StreamReader` object, and a `StreamWriter` object. The `StreamReader` and `StreamWriter` objects will use the `MemoryStream` to move the XML around:

```
MemoryStream memStrm=new MemoryStream();
StreamReader strmRead=new StreamReader(memStrm);
StreamWriter strmWrite=new StreamWriter(memStrm);
```

We will use a `MemoryStream` so that we don't have to write anything to disk, however, we could have used any object that was based on the `Stream` class such as `FileStream`. Next, we fill the `DataSet` and bind it to the `DataGrid`. The data in the `DataSet` will now be displayed in the `DataGrid`:

```
da.Fill(ds,"products");
//load data into DataGrid
dataGrid1.DataSource=ds;
dataGrid1.DataMember="products";
```

This next step is where the XML is generated. We call the `WriteXml()` method from the `DataSet` class. This method generates an XML document. There are two overloads to `WriteXml()`: one takes a string with the file path and name, and the other adds a mode parameter. This mode is an `XmlWriteMode` enumeration, with possible values:

❑ `IgnoreSchema`

❑ `WriteSchema`

❑ `DiffGram`

`IgnoreSchema` is used if you don't want `WriteXml()` to write an inline schema at the start of your XML file; use the `WriteSchema` parameter if you do want one. We will look at `DiffGrams` later in this section.

```
    ds.WriteXml(strmWrite,XmlWriteMode.IgnoreSchema);
    memStrm.Seek(0,SeekOrigin.Begin);
    //read from the memory stream to an XmlDocument object
    doc.Load(strmRead);
    //get all of the products elements
    XmlNodeList nodeLst=doc.GetElementsByTagName("ProductName");
    //load them into the list box
    foreach(XmlNode nd in nodeLst)
      listBox1.Items.Add(nd.InnerText);
}
private void listBox1_SelectedIndexChanged(object sender,
                                           System.EventArgs e)
{
    //when you click on the listbox,
    //a message box appears with the unit price
    string srch="XMLProducts/products[ProductName=" +
                    '"'+ listBox1.SelectedItem.ToString() + '"' + "]";
    XmlNode foundNode=doc.SelectSingleNode(srch);
    if(foundNode!=null)
      MessageBox.Show(foundNode.SelectSingleNode("UnitPrice").InnerText);
    else
      MessageBox.Show("Not found");
}
```

Figure 23-9 shows the data in the list as well as the bound data grid.

Figure 23-9

If we had only wanted the schema, we could have called `WriteXmlSchema()` instead of `WriteXml()`. This method has four overloads. One takes a string, which is the path and file name of where to write the XML document. The second overload uses an object that is based on the `XmlWriter` class. The third overload uses an object that is based on the `TextWriter` class. The fourth overload is derived from the `Stream` class.

Also, if we wanted to persist the XML document to disk, we would have used something like this:

```
string file = "c:\\test\\product.xml";
ds.WriteXml(file);
```

This would give us a well-formed XML document on disk that could be read in by another stream, or by `DataSet`, or used by another application or Web site. Since no `XmlMode` parameter is specified, this `XmlDocument` would have the schema included. In our example, we use the stream as a parameter to the `XmlDocument.Load()` method.

Once the `XmlDocument` is prepared, we load the list box using the same XPath statement that we used before. If you look closely, you'll see that we changed the `listBox1_SelectedIndexChanged()` event slightly. Instead of showing the `InnerText` of the element, we do another XPath search using `SelectSingleNode()` to get the `UnitPrice` element. So now every time you select a product in the list box, a `MessageBox` pops up with the `UnitPrice`. We now have two views of the data, but more importantly, we can manipulate the data using two different models. We can use the `System.Data` namespace to use the data or we can use the `System.Xml` namespace on the data. This can lead to some very flexible designs in your applications, because now you are not tied to just one object model to program with. This is the real power to the ADO.NET and `System.Xml` combination. You have multiple views of the same data and multiple ways to access the data.

In the following example we will simplify the process by eliminating the three streams and by using some of the ADO capabilities built into the `System.Xml` namespace. We will need to change the module-level line of code:

```
private XmlDocument doc = new XmlDocument();
```

to:

```
private XmlDataDocument doc;
```

We need this because we are now using the `XmlDataDocument`. Here is the code (which can be found in the ADOSample2 folder):

```
private void button1_Click(object sender, System.EventArgs e)
{
    //create a dataset
    DataSet ds=new DataSet("XMLProducts");
    //connect to the northwind database and
    //select all of the rows from products table
    //make changes to connect string to match your login and server name
    SqlConnection conn=new SqlConnection
               (@"server=GLYNNJ_CS\NetSDK;uid=sa;pwd=;database=northwind");
    SqlDataAdapter da=new SqlDataAdapter("SELECT * FROM products",conn);
    //fill the dataset
    da.Fill(ds,"products");
    //load data into grid
    dataGrid1.DataSource=ds;
    dataGrid1.DataMember="products";
    doc=new XmlDataDocument(ds);
    //get all of the products elements
    XmlNodeList nodeLst=doc.GetElementsByTagName("ProductName");
    //load them into the list box
    //we'll use a for loop this time
    for(int ctr=0;ctr<nodeLst.Count;ctr++)
        listBox1.Items.Add(nodeLst[ctr].InnerText);
}
```

As you can see, the code to load the `DataSet` object into the XML document has been simplified. Instead of using the `XmlDocument` class, we are using the `XmlDataDocument` class. This class was built specifically for using data with a `DataSet` object.

The `XmlDataDocument` is based on the `XmlDocument` class, so it has all of the functionality that the `XmlDocument` class has. One of the main differences is the overloaded constructor that the `XmlData Document` has. Note the line of code that instantiates `XmlDataDocument` (doc):

```
doc = new XmlDataDocument(ds);
```

815

It passes in the `DataSet` object that we created, `ds`, as a parameter. This creates the XML document from the `DataSet`, and we don't have to use the `Load()` method. In fact, if you instantiate a new `XmlDataDocument` object without passing in a `DataSet` as the parameter, it will contain a `DataSet` with the name `NewDataSet` that has no `DataTables` in the `tables` collection. There is also a `DataSet` property that you can set after an `XmlDataDocument`-based object is created.

Suppose we add the following line of code after the `DataSet.Fill()` call:

```
ds.WriteXml("c:\\test\\sample.xml", XmlWriteMode.WriteSchema);
```

In this case, the following XML file, sample.xml, is produced in the folder c:\test:

```
<?xml version="1.0" standalone="yes"?>
<XMLProducts>
    <xs:schema id="XMLProducts" xmlns=""
               xmlns:xs="http://www.w3.org/2001/XMLSchema"
               xmlns:msdata="urn:schemas-microsoft-com:xml-msdata">
        <xs:element name="XMLProducts" msdata:IsDataSet="true">
            <xs:complexType>
                <xs:choice maxOccurs="unbounded">
                    <xs:element name="products">
                        <xs:complexType>
                            <xs:sequence>
                                <xs:element name="ProductID" type="xs:int"
                                            minOccurs="0" />
                                <xs:element name="ProductName" type="xs:string"
                                            minOccurs="0" />
                                <xs:element name="SupplierID" type="xs:int"
                                            minOccurs="0" />
                                <xs:element name="CategoryID" type="xs:int"
                                            minOccurs="0" />
                                <xs:element name="QuantityPerUnit" type="xs:string"
                                            minOccurs="0" />
                                <xs:element name="UnitPrice" type="xs:decimal"
                                            minOccurs="0" />
                                <xs:element name="UnitsInStock" type="xs:short"
                                            minOccurs="0" />
                                <xs:element name="UnitsOnOrder" type="xs:short"
                                            minOccurs="0" />
                                <xs:element name="ReorderLevel" type="xs:short"
                                            minOccurs="0" />
                                <xs:element name="Discontinued" type="xs:boolean"
                                            minOccurs="0" />
                            </xs:sequence>
                        </xs:complexType>
                    </xs:element>
                </xs:choice>
            </xs:complexType>
        </xs:element>
    </xs:schema>
    <products>
        <ProductID>1</ProductID>
        <ProductName>Chai</ProductName>
```

```
        <SupplierID>1</SupplierID>
         <CategoryID>1</CategoryID>
        <QuantityPerUnit>10 boxes x 20 bags</QuantityPerUnit>
        <UnitPrice>18</UnitPrice>
        <UnitsInStock>39</UnitsInStock>
        <UnitsOnOrder>0</UnitsOnOrder>
        <ReorderLevel>10</ReorderLevel>
        <Discontinued>false</Discontinued>
    </products>
</XMLProducts>
```

Only the first `products` element is shown. The actual XML file would contain all of the products in the Products table of Northwind database.

Converting relational data

This looks simple enough for a single table, but what about relational data, such as multiple `DataTables` and `Relations` in the `DataSet`? It all still works the same way. Let's make the following changes to the code that we've been using (this version can be found in ADOSample3):

```
private void button1_Click(object sender, System.EventArgs e)
{
    //create a dataset
    DataSet ds=new DataSet("XMLProducts");
    //connect to the northwind database and
    //select all of the rows from products table and from suppliers table
    //make sure your connect string matches your server configuration
    SqlConnection conn=new SqlConnection
             (@"server=GLYNNJ_CS\NetSDK;uid=sa;pwd=;database=northwind");
    SqlDataAdapter daProd=new SqlDataAdapter("SELECT * FROM products",conn);
    SqlDataAdapter daSup=new SqlDataAdapter("SELECT * FROM suppliers",conn);
    //Fill DataSet from both SqlAdapters
    daProd.Fill(ds,"products");
    daSup.Fill(ds,"suppliers");
    //Add the relation
    ds.Relations.Add(ds.Tables["suppliers"].Columns["SupplierId"],
                     ds.Tables["products"].Columns["SupplierId"]);
    //Write the XML to a file so we can look at it later
    ds.WriteXml("..\\..\\..\\SuppProd.xml",XmlWriteMode.WriteSchema);
    //load data into grid
    dataGrid1.DataSource=ds;
    dataGrid1.DataMember="suppliers";
    //create the XmlDataDocument
    doc=new XmlDataDocument(ds);
    //Select the productname elements and load them in the grid
    XmlNodeList nodeLst=doc.SelectNodes("//ProductName");
    foreach(XmlNode nd in nodeLst)
        listBox1.Items.Add(nd.InnerXml);
}
```

In this sample we are creating two `DataTables` in the `XMLProducts` `DataSet`: Products and Suppliers. The relation is that `Suppliers` supply `Products`. We create a new relation on the column SupplierId in both tables. This is what the `DataSet` looks like:

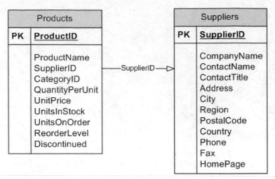

Figure 23-10

By making the same `WriteXml()` method call that we did in the previous example, we will get the following XML file (SuppProd.xml):

```
<?xml version="1.0" standalone="yes"?>
<XMLProducts>
    <xs:schema id="XMLProducts" xmlns=""
               xmlns:xs="http://www.w3.org/2001/XMLSchema"
               xmlns:msdata="urn:schemas-microsoft-com:xml-msdata">
      <xs:element name="XMLProducts" msdata:IsDataSet="true">
        <xs:complexType>
          <xs:choice maxOccurs="unbounded">
            <xs:element name="products">
              <xs:complexType>
                <xs:sequence>
                  <xs:element name="ProductID" type="xs:int"
                              minOccurs="0" />
                  <xs:element name="ProductName" type="xs:string"
                              minOccurs="0" />
                  <xs:element name="SupplierID" type="xs:int"
                              minOccurs="0" />
                  <xs:element name="CategoryID" type="xs:int"
                              minOccurs="0" />
                  <xs:element name="QuantityPerUnit" type="xs:string"
                              minOccurs="0" />
                  <xs:element name="UnitPrice" type="xs:decimal"
                              minOccurs="0" />
                  <xs:element name="UnitsInStock" type="xs:short"
                              minOccurs="0" />
                  <xs:element name="UnitsOnOrder" type="xs:short"
                              minOccurs="0" />
                  <xs:element name="ReorderLevel" type="xs:short"
                              minOccurs="0" />
                  <xs:element name="Discontinued" type="xs:boolean"
                              minOccurs="0" />
                </xs:sequence>
              </xs:complexType>
            </xs:element>
            <xs:element name="suppliers">
              <xs:complexType>
```

```
                              <xs:sequence>
                                  <xs:element name="SupplierID" type="xs:int"
                                              minOccurs="0" />
                                  <xs:element name="CompanyName" type="xs:string"
                                              minOccurs="0" />
                                  <xs:element name="ContactName" type="xs:string"
                                              minOccurs="0" />
                                  <xs:element name="ContactTitle" type="xs:string"
                                              minOccurs="0" />
                                  <xs:element name="Address" type="xs:string"
                                              minOccurs="0" />
                                  <xs:element name="City" type="xs:string"
                                              minOccurs="0" />
                                  <xs:element name="Region" type="xs:string"
                                              minOccurs="0" />
                                  <xs:element name="PostalCode" type="xs:string"
                                              minOccurs="0" />
                                  <xs:element name="Country" type="xs:string"
                                              minOccurs="0" />
                                  <xs:element name="Phone" type="xs:string"
                                              minOccurs="0" />
                                  <xs:element name="Fax" type="xs:string"
                                              minOccurs="0" />
                                  <xs:element name="HomePage" type="xs:string"
                                              minOccurs="0" />
                              </xs:sequence>
                          </xs:complexType>
                      </xs:element>
                  </xs:choice>
              </xs:complexType>
              <xs:unique name="Constraint1">
                  <xs:selector xpath=".//suppliers" />
                  <xs:field xpath="SupplierID" />
              </xs:unique>
              <xs:keyref name="Relation1" refer="Constraint1">
                  <xs:selector xpath=".//products" />
                  <xs:field xpath="SupplierID" />
              </xs:keyref>
          </xs:element>
      </xs:schema>
      <products>
          <ProductID>1</ProductID>
          <ProductName>Chai</ProductName>
          <SupplierID>1</SupplierID>
          <CategoryID>1</CategoryID>
          <QuantityPerUnit>10 boxes x 20 bags</QuantityPerUnit>
          <UnitPrice>18</UnitPrice>
          <UnitsInStock>39</UnitsInStock>
          <UnitsOnOrder>0</UnitsOnOrder>
          <ReorderLevel>10</ReorderLevel>
          <Discontinued>false</Discontinued>
      </products>
  <suppliers>
      <SupplierID>1</SupplierID>
      <CompanyName>Exotic Liquids</CompanyName>
```

```
        <ContactName>Charlotte Cooper</ContactName>
        <ContactTitle>Purchasing Manager</ContactTitle>
        <Address>49 Gilbert St.</Address>
        <City>London</City>
        <PostalCode>EC1 4SD</PostalCode>
        <Country>UK</Country>
        <Phone>(171) 555-2222</Phone>
      </suppliers>
   </XMLProducts>
```

The schema includes both DataTables that were in the DataSet. In addition, the data includes all of the data from both tables. For the sake of brevity, we only show the first suppliers and products records here. As before, we could have saved just the schema or just the data by passing in the correct XmlWriteMode parameter.

Converting XML to ADO.NET Data

Let's say that you have an XML document that you would like to get into an ADO.NET DataSet. You would want to do this so you could load the XML into a database, or perhaps bind the data to a .NET data control such as DataGrid. This way you could actually use the XML document as your data store and could eliminate the overhead of the database altogether. If your data is reasonably small in size, then this is an attractive possibility. Here is some code to get you started (ADOSample5):

```
private void button1_Click(object sender, System.EventArgs e)
{
    //create a new DataSet
    DataSet ds=new DataSet("XMLProducts");
    //read in the XML document to the Dataset
    ds.ReadXml("..\\..\\..\\prod.xml");
    //load data into grid
    dataGrid1.DataSource=ds;
    dataGrid1.DataMember="products";
    //create the new XmlDataDocument
    doc=new XmlDataDocument(ds);
    //load the product names into the listbox
    XmlNodeList nodeLst=doc.SelectNodes("//ProductName");
    foreach(XmlNode nd in nodeLst)
       listBox1.Items.Add(nd.InnerXml);
}
```

It is that easy. We instantiate a new DataSet object. Then we call the ReadXml() method, and you have XML in a DataTable in your DataSet. As with the WriteXml() methods, ReadXml() has an XmlReadMode parameter. ReadXml() has a couple more options in the XmlReadMode, as shown in the following table.

There is also the ReadXmlSchema() method. This reads in a standalone schema and creates the tables, columns, and relations. You would use this if your schema is not inline with your data. ReadXmlSchema() has the same four overloads: string with file and path name, Stream-based object, TextReader-based object and an XmlReader-based object.

Value	Description
Auto	Sets the XmlReadMode to the most appropriate setting. If data is in DiffGram format, DiffGram is selected. If a schema has already been read, or an inline schema is detected, then ReadSchema is selected. If no schema has been assigned to the DataSet, and none is detected inline, then IgnoreSchema is selected.
DiffGram	Reads in the DiffGram and applies the changes to the DataSet. DiffGrams are described later in the chapter.
Fragment	Reads documents that contain XDR schema fragments, such as the type created by SQL Server.
IgnoreSchema	Ignores any inline schema that may be found. Reads data into the current DataSet schema. If data does not match DataSet schema it is discarded.
InferSchema	Ignores any inline schema. Creates the schema based on data in the XML document. If a schema exists in the DataSet, that schema is used, and extended with additional columns and tables if needed. An exception is thrown if a column exists, but is of a different data type.
ReadSchema	Reads the inline schema and loads the data. Will not overwrite a schema in the DataSet, but will throw an exception if a table in the inline schema already exists in the DataSet.

To show that the data tables are getting created properly, let's load the XML document that contains the Products and Suppliers tables that we used in an earlier example. This time, however, let's load the list box with the DataTable names and the DataColumn names and data types. We can look at this and compare it to the original Northwind database to see that all is well. Here is the code for this example (ADOSample5):

```
private void button1_Click(object sender, System.EventArgs e)
{
    //create the DataSet
    DataSet ds=new DataSet("XMLProducts");
    //read in the XML document
    ds.ReadXml("..\\..\\..\\SuppProd.xml");
    //load data into grid
    dataGrid1.DataSource=ds;
    dataGrid1.DataMember="products";
    //load the listbox with table, column and datatype info
    foreach(DataTable dt in ds.Tables)
    {
        listBox1.Items.Add(dt.TableName);
        foreach(DataColumn col in dt.Columns)
        {
            listBox1.Items.Add(
                        '\t' + col.ColumnName + " - " + col.DataType.FullName);
        }
    }
}
```

Note the addition of the two `foreach` loops. The first loop gets the table name from each table in the `Tables` collection of the `DataSet`. Inside the inner `foreach` loop we get the name and data type of each column in the `DataTable`. We load this data into the list box, allowing us to display it. Figure 23-11 shows the output.

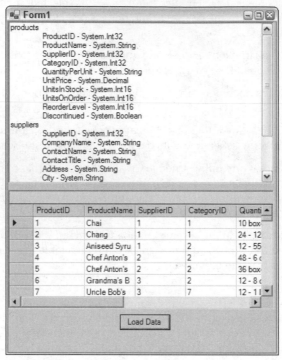

Figure 23-11

Looking at the list box you can check that the data tables were created with the columns all having the correct names and data types.

Something else you might want to note is that since the previous two examples didn't transfer any data to or from a database, no `SqlDataAdapter` or `SqlConnection` was defined. This shows the real flexibility of both the `System.Xml` namespace and ADO.NET: you can look at the same data in multiple formats. If you need to do a transform and show the data in HTML format, or if you need to bind the data to a grid, you can take the same data, and with just a method call, have it in the required format.

Reading and Writing a DiffGram

A DiffGram is an XML document that contains the before and after data of an edit session. This can include any combination of data changes, additions, and deletions. A DiffGram can be used as an audit trail or for a commit/rollback process. Most DBMS systems today have this built in, but if you happen to be working with a DBMS that does not have these features or if XML is your data store and you do not have a DBMS, you can implement commit or rollback features yourself.

Let's see some code that shows how a DiffGram is created and how a DataSet can be created from a DiffGram (this code can be found in the ADOSample6 folder).

The beginning part of this code should look familiar. We define and set up a new DataSet, ds, a new SqlConnection, conn, and a new SqlDataAdapter, da. We connect to the database, select all of the rows from the Products table, create a new DataTable named products, and load the data from the database into the DataSet:

```
private void button1_Click(object sender, System.EventArgs e)
{
    //new DataSet
    DataSet ds=new DataSet("XMLProducts");
    //Make connection and load products rows
    SqlConnection conn=new SqlConnection
                (@"server=GLYNNJ_CS\NetSDK;uid=sa;pwd=;database=northwind");
    SqlDataAdapter da=new SqlDataAdapter("SELECT * FROM products",conn);
    //fill the DataSet
    da.Fill(ds,"products");
    //edit first row
    ds.Tables["products"].Rows[0]["ProductName"]="NewProdName";
```

In this next code block we do two things. First, we modify the ProductName column in the first row to NewProdName. Second, we create a new row in the DataTable, set the column values, and finally add the new data row to the DataTable.

```
    //add new row
    DataRow dr=ds.Tables["products"].NewRow();;
    dr["ProductId"]=100;
    dr["CategoryId"]=2;
    dr["Discontinued"]=false;
    dr["ProductName"]="This is the new product";
    dr["QuantityPerUnit"]=12;
    dr["ReorderLevel"]=1;
    dr["SupplierId"]=12;
    dr["UnitPrice"]=23;
    dr["UnitsInStock"]=5;
    dr["UnitsOnOrder"]=0;
    ds.Tables["products"].Rows.Add(dr);
```

The next block is the interesting part of the code. First, we write out the schema with WriteXmlSchema(). This is important because you cannot read back in a DiffGram without the schema. WriteXml() with the XmlWriteMode.DiffGram parameter passed to it actually creates the DiffGram. The next line accepts the changes that we made. It is important that the DiffGram is created before calling AcceptChanges(), otherwise there would not appear to be any modifications to the data.

```
    //Write the Schema
    ds.WriteXmlSchema("..\\..\\..\\diffgram.xsd");
    //generate the DiffGram
    ds.WriteXml("..\\..\\..\\diffgram.xml",XmlWriteMode.DiffGram);
    ds.AcceptChanges();
    //load data into grid
    dataGrid1.DataSource=ds;
    dataGrid1.DataMember="products";
```

```
      //new XmlDataDocument
      doc=new XmlDataDocument(ds);
      //load the productnames in the list
      XmlNodeList nodeLst=doc.SelectNodes("//ProductName");
      foreach(XmlNode nd in nodeLst)
          listBox1.Items.Add(nd.InnerXml);
}
```

In order to get the data back into a `DataSet`, we can do the following:

```
      DataSet dsNew=new DataSet();
      dsNew.ReadXmlSchema("..\\..\\..\\diffgram.xsd");
      dsNew.XmlRead("..\\..\\..\\diffgram.xml",XmlReadMode.DiffGram);
```

Here we are creating a new `DataSet`, dsNew. The call to the `ReadXmlSchema()` method creates a new `DataTable` based on the schema information. In this case it would be a clone of the `products` `DataTable`. Now we can read in the DiffGram. The DiffGram does not contain schema information, so it is important that the `DataTable` be created and ready before you call the `ReadXml()` method.

Here is a sample of what the DiffGram (diffgram.xml) looks like:

```
<?xml version="1.0" standalone="yes"?>
<diffgr:diffgram xmlns:msdata="urn:schemas-microsoft-com:xml-msdata"
                 xmlns:diffgr="urn:schemas-microsoft-com:xml-diffgram-v1">
  <XMLProducts>
    <products diffgr:id="products1" msdata:rowOrder="0"
              diffgr:hasChanges="modified">
      <ProductID>1</ProductID>
      <ProductName>NewProdName</ProductName>
      <SupplierID>1</SupplierID>
      <CategoryID>1</CategoryID>
      <QuantityPerUnit>10 boxes x 20 bags</QuantityPerUnit>
      <UnitPrice>18</UnitPrice>
      <UnitsInStock>39</UnitsInStock>
      <UnitsOnOrder>0</UnitsOnOrder>
      <ReorderLevel>10</ReorderLevel>
      <Discontinued>false</Discontinued>
    </products>
    ...
    <products diffgr:id="products78" msdata:rowOrder="77"
              diffgr:hasChanges="inserted">
      <ProductID>100</ProductID>
      <ProductName>This is the new product</ProductName>
      <SupplierID>12</SupplierID>
      <CategoryID>2</CategoryID>
      <QuantityPerUnit>12</QuantityPerUnit>
      <UnitPrice>23</UnitPrice>
      <UnitsInStock>5</UnitsInStock>
      <UnitsOnOrder>0</UnitsOnOrder>
      <ReorderLevel>1</ReorderLevel>
      <Discontinued>false</Discontinued>
    </products>
  </XMLProducts>
```

```
   <diffgr:before>
     <products diffgr:id="products1" msdata:rowOrder="0">
       <ProductID>1</ProductID>
       <ProductName>Chai</ProductName>
       <SupplierID>1</SupplierID>
       <CategoryID>1</CategoryID>
       <QuantityPerUnit>10 boxes x 20 bags</QuantityPerUnit>
       <UnitPrice>18</UnitPrice>
       <UnitsInStock>39</UnitsInStock>
       <UnitsOnOrder>0</UnitsOnOrder>
       <ReorderLevel>10</ReorderLevel>
       <Discontinued>false</Discontinued>
     </products>
   </diffgr:before>
 </diffgr:diffgram>
```

Note that each `DataTable` row is repeated, and that there is a `diffgr:id` attribute for each `<products>` element (we've only shown the first and last of the `<products>` elements in order to save space). `diffgr` is the namespace prefix for `urn:schemas-microsoft-com:xml-diffgram-v1`. For rows that were modified or inserted, ADO.NET adds a `diffgr:hasChanges` attribute. There's also a `<diffgr:before>` element after the `<XMLProducts>` element, which contains a `<products>` element indicating the previous contents of any modified rows. Obviously the inserted row didn't have any previous contents, so this doesn't have an element in `<diffgr:before>`.

After the DiffGram has been read into the `DataTable`, it is in the state that it would be in after changes were made to the data but before `AcceptChanges()` is called. At this point you can actually roll back changes by calling the `RejectChanges()` method. By looking at the `DataRow.Item` property and passing in either `DataRowVersion.Original` or `DataRowVersion.Current`, we can see the before and after values in the `DataTable`.

If you keep a series of `DiffGrams` it is important that you are able to reapply them in the proper order. You probably would not want to try to roll back changes for more then a couple of iterations. You could, however use the DiffGrams as a form of logging or for auditing purposes if the DBMS that is being used does not offer these facilities.

Serializing Objects in XML

Serializing is the process of persisting an object to disk. Another part of your application, or even a separate application, can deserialize the object and it will be in the same state it was in prior to serialization. .NET Framework includes a couple of ways to do this.

In this section, we look at the `System.Xml.Serialization` namespace, which contains classes used to serialize objects into XML documents or streams. This means that an object's public properties and public fields are converted into XML elements or attributes or both.

The most important class in the `System.Xml.Serialization` namespace is `XmlSerializer`. To serialize an object, we first need to instantiate an `XmlSerializer` object, specifying the type of the object to serialize. Then we need to instantiate a stream/writer object to write the file to a stream/document. The final step is to call the `Serialize()` method on the `XMLSerializer`, passing it the stream/writer object, and the object to serialize.

Data that can be serialized can be primitive types, fields, arrays, and embedded XML in the form of `XmlElement` and `XmlAttribute` objects.

To deserialize an object from an XML document, we reverse the process in the previous example. We create a stream/reader and an `XmlSerializer` object, and then pass the stream/reader to the `Deserialize()` method. This method returns the deserialized object, although it needs to be cast to the correct type.

> **The XML serializer cannot convert private data, only public data, and it cannot serialize object graphs.**

However, these should not be serious limitations; by carefully designing your classes, they should be easily avoided. If you do need to be able to serialize public and private data as well as an object graph containing many nested objects, then you will want to use the `System.Runtime.Serialization.Formatters.Binary` namespace.

Some of the other tasks that you can accomplish with `System.Xml.Serialization` classes are:

- ❑ Determine if the data should be an attribute or element
- ❑ Specify the namespace
- ❑ Change the attribute or element name

The links between your object and the XML document are the custom C# attributes that annotate your classes. These attributes are what are used to inform the serializer how to write out the data. There is a tool, xsd.exe, that is included with.NET Framework that can help you create these attributes for you; xsd.exe can do the following:

- ❑ Generate an XML schema from an XDR schema file
- ❑ Generate an XML schema from an XML file
- ❑ Generate `DataSet` classes from an XSD schema file
- ❑ Generate runtime classes that have the custom attributes for `XmlSerialization`
- ❑ Generate an XSD file from classes that you have already developed
- ❑ Limit which elements are created in code
- ❑ Determine which programming language the generated code should be in (C#, Visual Basic .NET, or JScript .NET)
- ❑ Create schemas from types in compiled assemblies

You should refer to the Framework documentation for details of command-line options for xsd.exe.

Despite these capabilities, you don't *have* to use xsd.exe to create the classes for serialization. The process is quite simple. Let's take a look at a simple application that serializes a class that reads in the Products data we saved earlier in the chapter. This can be found in the SerialSample1 folder. At the beginning of the example we have very simple code that creates a new `Product` object, pd, and fills it with some data:

```
private void button1_Click(object sender, System.EventArgs e)
{
    //new products object
    Products pd=new Products();
    //set some properties
    pd.ProductID=200;
    pd.CategoryID=100;
    pd.Discontinued=false;
    pd.ProductName="Serialize Objects";
    pd.QuantityPerUnit="6";
    pd.ReorderLevel=1;
    pd.SupplierID=1;
    pd.UnitPrice=1000;
    pd.UnitsInStock=10;
    pd.UnitsOnOrder=0;
```

Serialize() method of the XmlSerializer class actually performs the serialization, and it has six overloads. One of the parameters required is a stream to write the data to. It can be a Stream, TextWriter, or an XmlWriter parameter. In our example we create a TextWriter-based object, tr. The next thing to do is to create the XmlSerializer-based object sr. The XmlSerializer needs to know type information for the object that it is serializing, so we use the typeof keyword with the type that is to be serialized. After the sr object is created, we call the Serialize() method, passing in the tr (Stream-based object), and the object that you want serialized, in this case pd. Be sure to close the stream when you are finished with it.

```
    //new TextWriter and XmlSerializer
    TextWriter tr=new StreamWriter("..\\..\\..\\serialprod.xml");
    XmlSerializer sr=new XmlSerializer(typeof(Products));
    //serialize object
    sr.Serialize(tr,pd);
    tr.Close();
}
```

Now let's examine the Products class, the class that is to be serialized. The only differences between this and any other class that you may write are the C# attributes that have been added. The XmlRootAttribute and XmlElementAttribute classes in the attributes inherit from the System.Attribute class. Don't confuse these attributes with the attributes in an XML document. A C# attribute is simply some declarative information that can be retrieved at runtime by the CLR (see Chapter 6 for more details). In this case, the attributes describe how the object should be serialized:

```
    //class that will be serialized.
    //attributes determine how object is serialized
    [System.Xml.Serialization.XmlRootAttribute(Namespace="", IsNullable=false)]
    public class Products
    {
        [System.Xml.Serialization.XmlElementAttribute(IsNullable=false)]
        public int ProductID;
        [System.Xml.Serialization.XmlElementAttribute(IsNullable=false)]
        public string ProductName;
        [System.Xml.Serialization.XmlElementAttribute()]
        public int SupplierID;
        [System.Xml.Serialization.XmlElementAttribute()]
```

```
      public int CategoryID;
      [System.Xml.Serialization.XmlElementAttribute()]
      public string QuantityPerUnit;
      [System.Xml.Serialization.XmlElementAttribute()]
      public System.Decimal UnitPrice;
      [System.Xml.Serialization.XmlElementAttribute()]
      public short UnitsInStock;
      [System.Xml.Serialization.XmlElementAttribute()]
      public short UnitsOnOrder;
      [System.Xml.Serialization.XmlElementAttribute()]
      public short ReorderLevel;
      [System.Xml.Serialization.XmlElementAttribute()]
      public bool Discontinued;
}
```

The `XmlRootAttribute()` invocation in the attribute above the `Products` class definition identifies this class as a root element (in the XML file produced upon serialization). The attribute containing `XmlElementAttribute()` identifies that the member below the attribute represents an XML element.

If we take a look at the XML document that is created during serialization, you will see that it looks like any other XML document that we might have created, which is the point of the exercise. Let's take a look at the document:

```
<?xml version="1.0" encoding="utf-8"?>
<Products xmlns:xsd="http://www.w3.org/2001/XMLSchema"
          xmlns:xsi="http://www.w3.org/2001/XMLSchema-instance">
    <ProductID>200</ProductID>
    <ProductName>Serialize Objects</ProductName>
    <SupplierID>1</SupplierID>
    <CategoryID>100</CategoryID>
    <QuantityPerUnit>6</QuantityPerUnit>
    <UnitPrice>1000</UnitPrice>
    <UnitsInStock>10</UnitsInStock>
    <UnitsOnOrder>0</UnitsOnOrder>
    <ReorderLevel>1</ReorderLevel>
    <Discontinued>false</Discontinued>
</Products>
```

There is nothing out of the ordinary here. You could use this any way that you would use an XML document. You could transform it and display it as HTML, load into a `DataSet` using ADO.NET, load an `XmlDocument` with it, or, as you can see in the example, deserialize it and create an object in the same state that `pd` was in prior to serializing it (which is exactly what we're doing with our second button).

Next we add another button event handler to deserialize a new `Products`-based object `newPd`. This time we use a `FileStream` object to read in the XML:

```
private void button2_Click(object sender, System.EventArgs e)
{
    //create a reference to products type
    Products newPd;
    //new filestream to open serialized object
    FileStream f=new FileStream("..\\..\\..\\serialprod.xml",FileMode.Open);
```

Once again, we create a new `XmlSerializer`, passing in the type information of `Product`. We can then make the call to the `Deserialize()` method. Note that we still need to do an explicit cast when we create the `newPd` object. At this point `newPd` is in exactly the same state as `pd` was:

```
    //new serializer
    XmlSerializer newSr=new XmlSerializer(typeof(Products));
    //deserialize the object
    newPd=(Products)newSr.Deserialize(f);
    //load it in the list box.
    listBox1.Items.Add(newPd.ProductName);
    f.Close();
}
```

The example that we just looked at is very simple; let's look at a more complex example using the `XmlSerializer` class. We'll make each field `private`, accessible only via `get` and `set` properties in the `Products` class. We will also add a `Discount` attribute to the XML file, to demonstrate that attributes can be serialized too.

This example can be found in the SerialSample2 folder; here's what our new `Products` class looks like:

```
    [System.Xml.Serialization.XmlRootAttribute()]
public class Products
{
    private int prodId;
    private string prodName;
    private int suppId;
    private int catId;
    private string qtyPerUnit;
    private Decimal unitPrice;
    private short unitsInStock;
    private short unitsOnOrder;
    private short reorderLvl;
    private bool discont;
    private int disc;
    //add the Discount attribute
    [XmlAttributeAttribute(AttributeName="Discount")]
    public int Discount
    {
        get {return disc;}
        set {disc=value;}
    }
    [XmlElementAttribute()]
    public int ProductID
    {
        get {return prodId;}
        set {prodId=value;}
    }
    ...
    // properties for most of the fields are not shown for sake of brevity
    ...
    [XmlElementAttribute()]
    public bool Discontinued
    {
```

```
        get {return discont;}
        set {discont=value;}
    }
}
```

You also need to make the following modifications to the button click event handlers:

```
private void button1_Click(object sender, System.EventArgs e)
{
    //new products object
    Products pd=new Products();
    //set some properties
    pd.ProductID=200;
    pd.CategoryID=100;
    pd.Discontinued=false;
    pd.ProductName="Serialize Objects";
    pd.QuantityPerUnit="6";
    pd.ReorderLevel=1;
    pd.SupplierID=1;
    pd.UnitPrice=1000;
    pd.UnitsInStock=10;
    pd.UnitsOnOrder=0;
    pd.Discount=2;
    //new TextWriter and XmlSerializer
    TextWriter tr=new StreamWriter("..\\..\\..\\serialprod1.xml");
    XmlSerializer sr=new XmlSerializer(typeof(Products));
    //serialize object
    sr.Serialize(tr,pd);
    tr.Close();
}
private void button2_Click(object sender, System.EventArgs e)
{
    //create a reference to products type
    Products newPd;
    //new filestream to open serialized object
    FileStream f=new FileStream("..\\..\\..\\serialprod1.xml",FileMode.Open);
    //new serializer
    XmlSerializer newSr=new XmlSerializer(typeof(Products));
    //deserialize the object
    newPd=(Products)newSr.Deserialize(f);
    //load it in the list box.
    listBox1.Items.Add(newPd.ProductName);
    f.Close();
}
```

Running this code yields the same results as the earlier example—with one difference. The output (serialprod1.xml) looks like this:

```
<?xml version="1.0" encoding="utf-8"?>
<Products xmlns:xsd="http://www.w3.org/2001/XMLSchema"
          xmlns:xsi="http://www.w3.org/2001/XMLSchema-instance"
          Discount="2">
    <ProductID>200</ProductID>
    <ProductName>Serialize Objects</ProductName>
```

```
      <SupplierID>1</SupplierID>
      <CategoryID>100</CategoryID>
      <QuantityPerUnit>6</QuantityPerUnit>
      <UnitPrice>1000</UnitPrice>
      <UnitsInStock>10</UnitsInStock>
      <UnitsOnOrder>0</UnitsOnOrder>
      <ReorderLevel>1</ReorderLevel>
      <Discontinued>false</Discontinued>
   </Products>
```

Note that the `Discount` attribute on the `Products` element. So, now that you have property accessors defined, you can add more complex validation code in the properties.

What about situations where we have derived classes, and possibly properties that return an array? `XmlSerializer` has that covered as well. Let's look at a slightly more complex example that deals with these issues.

First we define three new classes, `Product`, `BookProduct` (derived from `Product`), and `Inventory` (which contains both of the other classes):

```csharp
public class Product
{
   private int prodId;
   private string prodName;
   private int suppId;
   public Product() {}
   public int  ProductID
   {
      get {return prodId;}
      set {prodId=value;}
   }
   public string ProductName
   {
      get {return prodName;}
      set {prodName=value;}
   }
   public int SupplierID
   {
      get {return suppId;}
      set {suppId=value;}
   }
}
public class BookProduct : Product
{
   private string isbnNum;
   public BookProduct() {}
   public string ISBN
   {
      get {return isbnNum;}
      set {isbnNum=value;}
   }
}
public class Inventory
{
```

```
        private Product[] stuff;
        public Inventory() {}
        //need to have an attribute entry for each data type
        [XmlArrayItem("Prod",typeof(Product)),
        XmlArrayItem("Book",typeof(BookProduct))]
        public Product[] InventoryItems
        {
           get {return stuff;}
           set {stuff=value;}
        }
    }
```

The `Inventory` class is the one of interest to us here. If we are to serialize this class, we need to insert an attribute containing `XmlArrayItem` constructors for each type that can be added to the array. You should note that `XmlArrayItem` is the name of the .NET attribute represented by the `XmlArrayItemAttribute` class.

The first parameter supplied to these constructors is what we would like the element name to be in the XML document that is created during serialization. If we leave off the `ElementName` parameter, the elements will be given the same name as the object type (`Product` and `BookProduct` in this case). The second parameter that must be specified is the type of the object.

There is also an `XmlArrayAttribute` class that you would use if the property were returning an array of objects or primitive type. Since we are returning different types in the array, we use `XmlArrayItemAttribute`, which allows the higher level of control.

In the `button1_Click()` event handler, we create a new `Product` object and a new `BookProduct` object (`newProd` and `newBook`). We add data to the various properties of each object, and add the objects to a `Product` array. We then create a new `Inventory` object and pass in the array as a parameter. We can then serialize the `Inventory` object to recreate it at a later time:

```
    private void button1_Click(object sender, System.EventArgs e)
    {
        //create new book and bookproducts objects
        Product newProd=new Product();
        BookProduct newBook=new BookProduct();
        //set some properties
        newProd.ProductID=100;
        newProd.ProductName="Product Thing";
        newProd.SupplierID=10;
        newBook.ProductID=101;
        newBook.ProductName="How to Use Your New Product Thing";
        newBook.SupplierID=10;
        newBook.ISBN="123456789";
        //add the items to an array
        Product[] addProd={newProd,newBook};
        //new inventory object using the addProd array
        Inventory inv=new Inventory();
        inv.InventoryItems=addProd;
        //serialize the Inventory object
        TextWriter tr=new StreamWriter("..\\..\\..\\order.xml");
        XmlSerializer sr=new XmlSerializer(typeof(Inventory));
```

```
        sr.Serialize(tr,inv);
        tr.Close();
    }
```

This is what the XML document looks like (the code can be found in the SerialSample3 folder):

```
<?xml version="1.0" encoding="utf-8"?>
<Inventory xmlns:xsd="http://www.w3.org/2001/XMLSchema">
          xmlns:xsi="http://www.w3.org/2001/XMLSchema-instance">
    <InventoryItems>
        <Prod>
            <ProductID>100</ProductID>
            <ProductName>Product Thing</ProductName>
            <SupplierID>10</SupplierID>
        </Prod>
        <Book>
            <ProductID>101</ProductID>
            <ProductName>How to Use Your New Product Thing</ProductName>
            <SupplierID>10</SupplierID>
            <ISBN>123456789</ISBN>
        </Book>
    </InventoryItems>
</Inventory>
```

The `button2_Click()` event handler implements deserialization of the `Inventory` object. Note that we iterate through the array in the newly created `newInv` object to show that it is the same data:

```
private void button2_Click(object sender, System.EventArgs e)
{
    Inventory newInv;
    FileStream f=new FileStream("..\\..\\..\\order.xml",FileMode.Open);
    XmlSerializer newSr=new XmlSerializer(typeof(Inventory));
    newInv=(Inventory)newSr.Deserialize(f);
    foreach(Product prod in newInv.InventoryItems)
        listBox1.Items.Add(prod.ProductName);
    f.Close();
}
```

Serialization without Source Code Access

Well this all works great, but what if you don't have access to the source code for the types that are being serialized? You can't add the attribute if you don't have the source. There is another way. You can use the `XmlAttributes` class and the `XmlAttributeOverrides` class. Together these classes enable you to accomplish exactly what we have just done, but without adding the attributes. Let's look at an example of how this works (the code is in the SerialSample4 folder).

For this example, imagine that the `Inventory`, `Product`, and the derived `BookProduct` classes are in a separate DLL, and that we don't have the source. The `Product` and `BookProduct` classes are the same as in the previous example, but you should note that there are now no attributes added to the `Inventory` class:

```
public class Inventory
{
   private Product[] stuff;
   public Inventory() {}
   public Product[] InventoryItems
   {
      get {return stuff;}
      set {stuff=value;}
   }
}
```

Next, we deal with the serialization in the `button1_Click()` event handler:

```
private void button1_Click(object sender, System.EventArgs e)
{
```

The first step in the serialization process is to create an `XmlAttributes` object, and an `XmlElementAttribute` object for each data type that you will be overriding:

```
XmlAttributes attrs=new XmlAttributes();
attrs.XmlElements.Add(new XmlElementAttribute("Book",typeof(BookProduct)));
attrs.XmlElements.Add(new XmlElementAttribute("Product",typeof(Product)));
```

Here you can see that we are adding new `XmlElementAttribute` objects to the `XmlElements` collection of the `XmlAttributes` class. The `XmlAttributes` class has properties that correspond to the attributes that can be applied; `XmlArray` and `XmlArrayItems`, which we looked at in the previous example, are just a few of these. We now have an `XmlAttributes` object with two `XmlElementAttribute`-based objects added to the `XmlElements` collection.

The next thing we have to do is create an `XmlAttributeOverrides` object:

```
XmlAttributeOverrides attrOver=new XmlAttributeOverrides();
attrOver.Add(typeof(Inventory),"InventoryItems",attrs);
```

The `Add()` method of this class has two overloads. The first one takes the type information of the object to override and the `XmlAttributes` object that we created earlier. The other overload, which is the one we are using, also takes a string value that is the member in the overridden object. In our case we want to override the `InventoryItems` member in the `Inventory` class.

When we create the `XmlSerializer` object, we add the `XmlAttributeOverrides` object as a parameter. Now the `XmlSerializer` knows which types we want to override and what we need to return for those types.

```
//create the Product and Book objects
Product newProd=new Product();
BookProduct newBook=new BookProduct();
newProd.ProductID=100;
newProd.ProductName="Product Thing";
newProd.SupplierID=10;
newBook.ProductID=101;
newBook.ProductName="How to Use Your New Product Thing";
newBook.SupplierID=10;
```

```
        newBook.ISBN="123456789";
        Product[] addProd={newProd,newBook};

        Inventory inv=new Inventory();
        inv.InventoryItems=addProd;
        TextWriter tr=new StreamWriter("..\\..\\..\\inventory.xml");
        XmlSerializer sr=new XmlSerializer(typeof(Inventory),attrOver);
        sr.Serialize(tr,inv);
        tr.Close();
}
```

If we execute the `Serialize()` method we get this XML output:

```
<?xml version="1.0" encoding="utf-8"?>
<Inventory xmlns:xsd="http://www.w3.org/2001/XMLSchema">
          xmlns:xsi="http://www.w3.org/2001/XMLSchema-instance">
    <Product>
        <ProductID>100</ProductID>
        <ProductName>Product Thing</ProductName>
        <SupplierID>10</SupplierID>
    </Product>
    <Book>
        <ProductID>101</ProductID>
        <ProductName>How to Use Your New Product Thing</ProductName>
        <SupplierID>10</SupplierID>
        <ISBN>123456789</ISBN>
    </Book>
</Inventory>
```

As you can see, we get the same XML as we did with the earlier example. In order to deserialize this object and recreate the `Inventory`-based object that we started out with, we need to create all of the same `XmlAttributes`, `XmlElementAttribute`, and `XmlAttributeOverrides` objects that we created when we serialized the object. Once we do that we can read in the XML and recreate the `Inventory` object just as we did before. Here is the code to deserialize the `Inventory` object:

```
private void button2_Click(object sender, System.EventArgs e)
{
    //create the new XmlAttributes collection
    XmlAttributes attrs=new XmlAttributes();
    //add the type information to the elements collection
    attrs.XmlElements.Add(new XmlElementAttribute("Book",typeof(BookProduct)));
    attrs.XmlElements.Add(new XmlElementAttribute("Product",typeof(Product)));
    XmlAttributeOverrides attrOver=new XmlAttributeOverrides();
    //add to the Attributes collection
    attrOver.Add(typeof(Inventory),"InventoryItems",attrs);
    //need a new Inventory object to deserialize to
    Inventory newInv;
    //deserialize and load data into the listbox from deserialized object
    FileStream f=new FileStream("..\\..\\..\\inventory.xml",FileMode.Open);
    XmlSerializer newSr=new XmlSerializer(typeof(Inventory),attrOver);
    newInv=(Inventory)newSr.Deserialize(f);
    if(newInv!=null)
    {
```

```
        foreach(Product prod in newInv.InventoryItems)
            listBox1.Items.Add(prod.ProductName);
    }
    f.Close();
}
```

Note that the first few lines of code are identical to the code we used to serialize the object.

The `System.Xml.XmlSerialization` namespace provides a very powerful tool set for serializing objects to XML. By serializing and deserializing objects to XML instead of to binary format, you are given the option of doing something else with this XML, greatly adding to the flexibility of your designs.

Summary

In this chapter we explored many of the corners of the `System.Xml` namespace of .NET Framework. We looked at how to read and write XML documents using the very fast `XmlReader`- and `XmlWriter`-based classes. We looked at how the DOM is implemented in .NET, and how to use the power of DOM. We saw that XML and ADO.NET are indeed very closely related. A `DataSet` and an XML document are just two different views of the same underlying architecture. And, of course, we visited XPath and XSL Transforms.

Finally, we serialized objects to XML, and were able to bring them back with just a couple of method calls.

XML will be an important part of your application development for years to come. .NET Framework has made available a very rich and powerful tool set for working with XML. For more information on XML and C#, with emphasis on XPath and XSLT, see *Data-Centric .NET Programming with C#* (Wrox Press, ISBN 1-861005-92-x).

In the next chapter we look at how to handle files and the registry using C# classes.

24

Working with Active Directory

A major (maybe the most important) feature that was introduced with Windows 2000 is *Active Directory*. Active Directory is a *directory service* that provides a central, hierarchical store for user information, network resources, services, and so on. It is also possible to extend the information in this directory service to store custom data that is of interest for the enterprise.

For example, Microsoft Exchange Server 2000 and 2003 use Active Directory intensively to store public folders and other items.

Before the release of Active Directory, Exchange Server used its own private store for its objects. It was necessary for a system administrator to configure two user IDs for a single person: a user account in the Windows NT domain so that a logon was possible, and a user in Exchange Directory. This was necessary because additional information for users was needed (such as e-mail addresses, phone numbers, and so on), and the user information for the NT domain was not extensible to put the required information in there. Now the system administrator only needs to configure a single user for a person in Active Directory; the information for a `user` object can be extended so that it fits the requirements of Exchange Server. You can also extend this information.

User information is stored in Active Directory. Suppose information is extended with a skills list. This way, it would easily be possible to track down a C# developer by searching for the required C# skill.

In this chapter, we look at how we can use .NET Framework to access and manipulate the data in a directory service using classes from the `System.DirectoryServices` namespace.

> *In this chapter we have used Windows Server 2003 with Active Directory configured. You can also use Windows 2000 Server. The classes of the `System.DirectoryServices` namespace can also be used for Novell Directory Services and Windows NT 4, with small modifications to the code presented here.*

In this chapter we cover:

❑ The architecture of Active Directory, including features and basic concepts

❑ Some of the tools available for administration of Active Directory, and their benefit to programming

❑ How to read and modify data in Active Directory

❑ Searching for objects in Active Directory

After discussing the architecture and how to program Active Directory we create a Windows application where you can specify properties and a filter to search for user objects. As is the case with the other chapters, you can download the code for the examples in this chapter from the Wrox Web site at www.wrox.com.

The Architecture of Active Directory

Before starting to program Active Directory, you have to know how Active Directory works, what it is used for, and what data can be stored there.

Features

The features of Active Directory can be summarized as follows:

❑ The data in Active Directory is grouped *hierarchically*. Objects can be stored inside other container objects. Instead of having a single, large list of users, the users can be grouped inside organizational units. An organizational unit can contain other organizational units, so you can build a tree.

❑ Active Directory uses a *multimaster replication*. In Windows NT 4 domains the *primary domain controller* (PDC) was the master. In Windows 2000 with Active Directory every *domain controller* (DC) is a master. If the PDC in a Windows NT 4 domain is down, users cannot change their passwords; the system administrator can only update users when the PDC is up and running. With Active Directory, updates can be applied to any DC. This model is much more scalable, because updates can be made to different servers concurrently. The disadvantage of this model is a more complex replication. Replication issues will be discussed later in this chapter.

❑ The *replication topology* is flexible, to support replications across slow links in WANs. How often data should be replicated is configurable by the domain administrators.

❑ Active Directory supports *open standards*. The *Lightweight Directory Access Protocol*(LDAP), is one of the standards that can be used to access the data in Active Directory. LDAP is an Internet standard that can be used to access a lot of different directory services. With LDAP a programming interface, LDAP API, is also defined. The LDAP API can be used to access the Active Directory with the C language. Microsoft's preferred programming interface to directory services is the *Active Directory Service Interface* (ADSI). This, of course, is not an open standard. In contrast to the LDAP API, ADSI makes it possible to access all features of Active Directory.

Another standard that's used within Active Directory is *Kerberos*, which is used for authentication. The Windows 2000 Kerberos service can also be used to authenticate UNIX clients.

❑ With Active Directory a *fine-grained security* is available. Every object stored in Active Directory can have an associated access-control list that defines who can do what with that object.

The objects in the directory are *strongly typed*, which means that the type of an object is exactly defined; no attributes that are not specified may be added to an object. In the *Schema*, the object types as well as the parts of an object (attributes) are defined. Attributes can be mandatory or optional.

Active Directory Concepts

Before programming Active Directory, we need to begin with some basic terms and definitions.

Objects

Active Directory stores objects. An object refers to something concrete such as a user, a printer, or a network share. Objects have mandatory and optional attributes that describe them. Some examples of the attributes of a `user` object are the first name, last name, e-mail address, phone number, and so on.

Figure 24-1 shows a container object called `Wrox Press` that contains some other objects; two user objects, a contact object, a printer object, and a user group object.

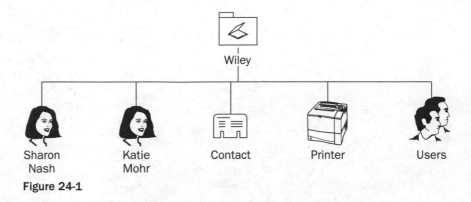

Figure 24-1

Schema

Every object is an instance of a class that is defined in the *schema*. The schema *defines the types*, and is itself stored in objects in Active Directory. You have to differentiate between `classSchema` and `attributeSchema`. The types of objects are defined in `classSchema`, as well as detailing what mandatory and optional attributes an object has. `attributeSchema` defines what an attribute looks like, and what the allowed syntax for a specific attribute is.

You can define custom types and attributes, and add these to the schema. Be aware, however, that a new schema type cannot be removed from Active Directory. You can mark it as inactive, so that new objects cannot be created any more, but there can be existing objects of that type, so it's not possible to remove classes or attributes that are defined in the schema.

The user group `Administrator` doesn't have enough rights to create new schema entries; the group `Domain Enterprise Administrator` is needed here.

Configuration

Besides objects and class definitions that are stored as objects, the configuration of Active Directory itself is stored in Active Directory. The configuration of Active Directory stores the information about all sites, such as the replication intervals, that is set up by the system administrator. Since the configuration itself is stored in Active Directory, we can access the configuration information like all other objects in Active Directory.

The Active Directory domain

A domain is a security boundary of a Windows network. In the Active Directory domain, the objects are stored in a hierarchical order. Active Directory itself is made up of one or more domains. Figure 24-2 shows the hierarchical order of objects in a domain; the domain is represented by a triangle. Container objects such as `Users`, `Computers`, and `Books` can store other objects. Each oval in the picture represents an object, with the lines between the objects representing parent-child relationships. For example, `Books` is the parent of `.NET` and `Java`, and `Pro C#`, `Beg C#`, and `ASP.NET` are child objects of the `.NET` object.

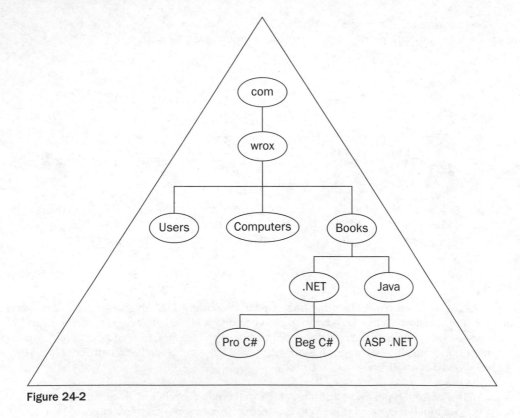

Figure 24-2

Domain controller

A single domain can have multiple domain controllers, each of which stores all of the objects in the domain. There is no master server, and all DCs are treated equally; we have a multimaster model. The objects are replicated across the servers inside the domain.

Site

A *site* is a location in the network that holds at least one DC. If we have multiple locations in the enterprise, which are connected with slow network links, we can use multiple sites for a single domain. For backup or scalability reasons, each site can have one or more DCs running. Replication between servers in a site can happen at shorter intervals due to the faster network connection. Replication is configured to occur at larger time intervals between servers across sites, depending on the speed of the network. Of course, the domain administrator can configure this.

Domain tree

Multiple domains can be connected by trust relationships. These domains share a *common schema*, a *common configuration*, and a *global catalog* (more on global catalogs shortly). A common schema and a common configuration mean that this data is replicated across domains. Domain trees share the same class and attribute schema. The objects themselves are not replicated across domains.

Domains connected in such a way form a Domain Tree. Domains in a domain tree have a *contiguous, hierarchical namespace*. This means that the domain name of the child domain is the name of that child domain appended to the name of the parent domain. Between domains, trusts that use the Kerberos protocol are established.

For example, we have the root domain `wrox.com`, which is the *parent domain* of the *child domains* `india.wrox.com` and `uk.wrox.com`. A trust is set up between the parent and the child domains, so that accounts from one domain can be authenticated by another domain.

Forest

Multiple domain trees that are connected by using a common schema, a common configuration, and a global catalog without a contiguous namespace, are called a forest. A forest is a set of domain trees. A forest can be used if the company has a subcompany where a different domain name should be used. Let's say that `wrox.com` should be relatively independent of the domain `wiley.com`, but it should be possible to have a common management, and be possible for users from `wrox.com` to access resources from the `wiley.com` domain, and vice versa. With a forest we can have trusts between multiple domain trees.

Global catalog

A search for an object can span multiple domains. If we look for a specific `user` object with some attributes we have to search every domain. Starting with `wrox.com`, the search continues to `uk.wrox.com` and `india.wrox.com`; across slow links such a search could take a while.

To make searches faster, all objects are copied to the *global catalog* (GC). The GC is replicated in every domain of a forest. There's at least one server in every domain holding a GC. For performance and scalability reasons, we can have more than one GC server in a domain. Using a GC, a search through all the objects can happen on a single server.

The GC is a *read-only cache* of all the objects that can only be used for searches; the domain controllers must be used to do updates.

Not all attributes of an object are stored in the GC. We can define whether or not an attribute should be stored with an object. The decision whether to store an attribute in the GC depends on the frequency of the attribute use in searches. A picture of a user isn't useful in the GC, because you would never search for a picture. Conversely, the phone number would be a useful addition to the store. You can also define that an attribute should be indexed so that a query for it is faster.

Replication

As programmers we are unlikely to ever configure replication, but because it affects the data we store in Active Directory, we have to know how it works. Active Directory uses a *multimaster* server architecture. Updates happen to every domain controller in the domain. The *replication latency* defines how long it takes until an update happens.

❑ The configurable *change notification* happens, by default, every 5 minutes inside a site if some attributes change. The DC where a change occurred informs one server after the other with 30-second intervals, so the fourth DC can get the change notification after 7 minutes. The default change notification across sites is set to 180 minutes. Intra- and intersite replication can each be configured to other values.

❑ If no changes occurred, the *scheduled replication* occurs every 60 minutes inside a site. This is to ensure that a change notification wasn't missed.

❑ For security-sensitive information such as account lockout *immediate notification* can occur.

With a replication, only the changes are copied to the DCs. With every change of an attribute a version number (update sequence number or USN) and a time stamp are recorded. These are used to help resolve conflicts if updates happened to the same attribute on different servers.

Let's look at one example. The mobile phone attribute of the user John Doe has the USN number 47. This value is already replicated to all DCs. One system administrator changes the phone number. The change occurs on the server DC1; the new USN of this attribute on the server DC1 is now 48, whereas the other DCs still have the USN 47. For someone still reading the attribute, the old value can be read until the replication to all domain controllers has occurred.

Now the rare case can happen that another administrator changes the phone number attribute, and here a different DC was selected because this administrator received a faster response from the server DC2. The USN of this attribute on the server DC2 is also changed to 48.

At the notification intervals, notification happens because the USN for the attribute changed, and the last time replication occurred was with a USN value 47. With the replication mechanism it is now detected that the servers DC1 and DC2 both have a USN of 48 for the phone number attribute. What server is the winner is not really important, but one server must win. To resolve this conflict the time stamp of the change is used. Because the change happened later on DC2 the value stored in the DC2 domain controller gets replicated.

> When reading objects, we have to be aware that the data is not necessarily current. The currency of the data depends on replication latencies. When updating objects, another user can still read some old values after the update. It's also possible that different updates can happen at the same time.

Characteristics of Active Directory Data

Active Directory doesn't replace a relational database or the registry; so what kind of data would you store in it?

❑ With Active Directory you get *hierarchical data*. You can have containers that store further containers, and also objects. Containers themselves are objects, too.

❑ The data should be used for *read-mostly*. Because of replication occurring at certain time-intervals, we cannot be sure that we will read up-to-date data. You must be aware that in applications the information you read is possibly not the current up-to-date information.

❑ Data should be of global interest to the enterprise; this is because adding a new data type to the schema replicates to it all the servers in the enterprise. For data types that are only of interest to a small number of users, the domain enterprise administrator normally wouldn't install new schema types.

❑ The data stored should be of *reasonable size* because of replication issues. If the data size is 100K, it is fine to store this data in the directory if the data changes only once a week. However, if the data changes once per hour, then the data of this size is too large. Always think about replicating the data to different servers: where the data gets transferred to, and at what intervals. If you have larger data it's possible to put a link into Active Directory and store the data itself in a different place.

To summarize, the data we store in Active Directory should be hierarchically organized, of reasonable size, and important to the enterprise.

Schema

Active Directory objects are strongly typed. The schema defines the types of the objects, mandatory and optional attributes, and the syntaxes and constraints of these attributes. In the schema it is necessary to differentiate between class-schema and attribute-schema objects. A class is a collection of attributes. With the classes, single inheritance is supported. As you can see in Figure 24-3, the `user` class derives from the `organizationalPerson` class, `organizationalPerson` is a subclass of `person`, and the base class is `top`. The `classSchema` that defines a class describes the attributes with the `systemMayContain` attribute.

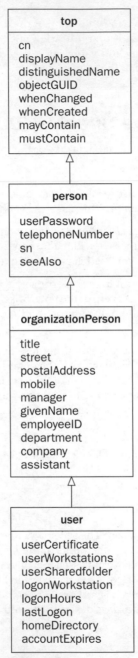

Figure 24-3

Figure 24-3 only shows a few of all the systemMayContain values. Using the ADSI Edit tool, you can easily see all the values; we will look at this in the next section.

In the root class `top` you can see that every object can have common name (`cn`), `displayName`, `objectGUID`, `whenChanged`, and `whenCreated` attributes. The `person` class derives from `top`. A person object also has a `userPassword` and a `telephoneNumber`. `OrganizationalPerson` derives from `person`. In addition to the attributes of `person` it has a `manager`, `department`, and `company`; and a `user` has extra attributes needed to log on to a system.

Administration Tools for Active Directory

Looking into some of the Active Directory administration tools can help to give you an idea of Active Directory, what data is in there, and what can be done programmatically.

The system administrator has a lot of tools to enter new data, update data, and configure Active Directory:

❑ The **Active Directory Users and Computers** MMC snap-in is used to enter new users and update user data.

❑ The **Active Directory Sites and Services** MMC snap-in is used to configure sites in a domain and replication between these sites.

❑ The **Active Directory Domains and Trusts** MMC snap-in can be used to build up a trust relationship between domains in a tree.

❑ **ADSI Edit** is the editor of Active Directory, where every object can be viewed and edited.

Active Directory Users and Computers

The Active Directory Users and Computers snap-in is the tool that system administrators use to manage users. Select Start ➪ Programs ➪ Administrative Tools➪Active Directory Users and Computers to start this program (see Figure 24-4).

Figure 24-4

With this tool you can add new users, groups, contacts, organizational units, printers, shared folders, or computers, and modify existing ones. Figure 24-5 shows the attributes that can be entered for a `user` object: office, phone numbers, e-mail addresses, Web pages, organization information, addresses, groups, and so on. This is much more information than was ever possible in an NT 4 domain.

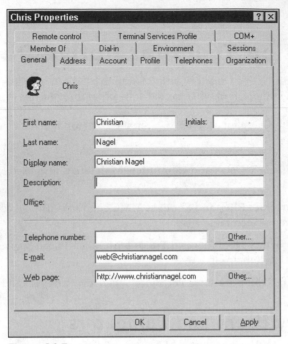

Figure 24-5

Active Directory Users and Computers can also be used in big enterprises with millions of objects. It's not necessary to look through a list with a thousand objects, because we can select a custom filter so that only some of the objects are displayed. We can also perform an LDAP query to search for the objects in the enterprise. We explore these possibilities later in this chapter.

ADSI Edit

ADSI Edit is the editor of Active Directory. This tool is not installed automatically; on the Windows 2000 Server or Windows Server 2003 CD you can find a directory named Supporting Tools. When the supporting tools are installed you can access ADSI Edit by selecting Start⇨Programs⇨Windows 2000 Support Tools⇨Tools⇨ADSI Edit.

ADSI Edit offers greater control than the Active Directory Users and Computers tool (see Figure 24-6); with ADSI Edit everything can be configured, and we can also look at the schema and the configuration. This tool is not very intuitive to use, however, and it is very easy to enter wrong data.

By opening the Properties window of an object, we can view and change every attribute of an object in Active Directory. With this tool you can see mandatory and optional attributes, with their types and values (see Figure 24-7).

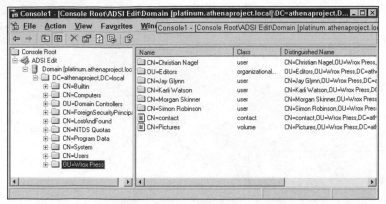

Figure 24-6

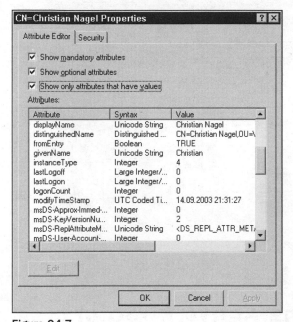

Figure 24-7

Active Directory Service Interfaces (ADSI)

Active Directory Service Interfaces (ADSI) is a programmatic interface to directory services. ADSI defines some COM interfaces that are implemented by ADSI providers. This means that the client can use different directory services with the same programmatic interfaces. The .NET Framework classes in the `System.DirectoryServices` namespace make use of ADSI.

Figure 24-8 shows some ADSI Providers (LDAP, WinNT, and NDS) that implement COM interfaces such as IADs and IUnknown. The assembly System.DirectoryServices makes use of the ADSI providers.

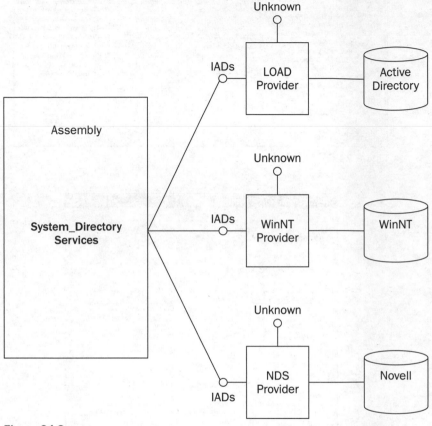

Figure 24-8

Programming Active Directory

To develop programs for Active Directory, you have to import the System.DirectoryServices namespace and you have to reference the System.DirectoryServices assembly. With the classes in this assembly you can query objects, view and update properties, search for objects, and move objects to other container objects. In the following code segments we use a simple C# console application to demonstrate the functionality of the classes in the System.DirectoryServices namespace.

In this section, we'll cover:

❑ Classes in the System.DirectoryServices namespace

❑ The process of connecting to the Active Directory (binding)

❑   Getting directory entries and creating new objects and updating existing entries

❑   Searching Active Directory

Classes in System.DirectoryServices

The following table shows the major classes in the `System.DirectoryServices` namespace.

Class	Description
DirectoryEntry	This class is the main class of the `System.DirectoryServices` namespace. An object of this class represents an object in the Active Directory store. This class is used to bind to an object, and to view and to update properties. The properties of the object are represented in a `PropertyCollection`. Every item in the `PropertyCollection` has a `PropertyValueCollection`.
DirectoryEntries	`DirectoryEntries` is a collection of `DirectoryEntry` objects. The `Children` property of a `DirectoryEntry` object returns a list of objects in a `DirectoryEntries` collection.
DirectorySearcher	This class is the main class used for searching for objects with specific attributes. To define the search the `SortOption` class and the enumerations `SearchScope`, `SortDirection`, and `ReferalChasingOption` can be used. The search results in a `SearchResult` or a `SearchResultCollection`. You also get `ResultPropertyCollection` and `ResultPropertyValueCollection` objects.

Binding

To get the values of an object in Active Directory, you have to connect to the Active Directory service. This connecting process is called *binding*. The binding path can look like this:

```
LDAP://dc01.athenaproject.com/OU=Development, DC=AthenaProject, DC=Com
```

With the binding process we can specify these items:

❑   The **protocol** specifies the provider to be used

❑   The **server name** of the domain controller

❑   The **port number** of the server process

❑   The **distinguished name** of the object; this identifies the object we want to access

❑   The **username and password** if a user that's different to the account running the current process is needed for accessing the Active Directory

❑   An **authentication** type can also be specified if encryption is needed

The following subsections discuss these options in more detail.

Protocol

The first part of a binding path specifies the ADSI provider. The provider is implemented as a COM server; for identification a progID can be found in the registry directly under HKEY_CLASSES_ROOT. The providers that are available with Windows XP are listed in the following table.

Provider	Description
LDAP	LDAP Server, such as the Exchange directory and Windows 2000 Server or Windows Server 2003 Active Directory Server.
GC	GC is used to access the global catalog in Active Directory. It can be used for fast queries.
IIS	With the ADSI provider for IIS it's possible to create new Web sites and to administer them in the IIS catalog.
WinNT	To access the user database of old Windows NT 4 domains you can use the ADSI provider for WinNT. The fact that NT 4 users only have a few attributes remains unchanged. It is also possible to use this protocol to bind to a Windows 2000 domain, but here you are also restricted to the attributes that are available with NT 4.
NDS	This progid is used to communicate with Novell Directory Services.
NWCOMPAT	With NWCOMPAT you can access old Novell directories, such as Novell Netware 3.x.

Server name

The *server name* follows the protocol in the binding path. The server name is optional if you are logged on to an Active Directory domain. Without a server name *serverless binding* occurs; this means that Windows Server 2003 tries to get the "best" domain controller in the domain that's associated with the user doing the bind. If there's no server inside a site, the first domain controller that can be found will be used.

A serverless binding might look like this: LDAP://OU=Sales, DC=AthenaProject, DC=Local.

Port number

After the server name you can specify the *port number* of the server process, by using the syntax :xxx. The default port number for the LDAP server is port 389: LDAP://dc01.sentinel.net:389. The Exchange server uses the same port number as the LDAP server. If the Exchange server is installed on the same system—for example, as a domain controller of Active Directory—a different port can be configured.

Distinguished name

The fourth part that we can specify in the path is the *distinguished name* (DN). The distinguished name is a unique name that identifies the object we want to access. With Active Directory you can use LDAP syntax that is based on X.500 to specify the name of the object.

This is an example of a distinguished name:

```
CN=Christian Nagel, OU=Consultants, DC=AthenaProject, DC=local
```

This distinguished name specifies the common name (CN) of Christian Nagel in the organizational unit (OU) called Consultants in the domain component (DC) called AthenaProject of the domain AthenaProject.local. The part that is specified to the right is the root object of the domain. The name has to follow the hierarchy in the object tree.

The LDAP specification for the string representation of distinguished names can be found in RFC 2253 at www.ietf.org/rfc/rfc2253.txt.

Relative distinguished name

A *relative distinguished name* (RDN) is used to reference objects within a container object. With an RDN the specification of OU and DC is not needed, as a common name is enough. CN=Christian Nagel is the relative distinguished name inside the organizational unit. A relative distinguished name can be used, if you already have a reference to a container object and if you want to access child objects.

Default naming context

If a distinguished name is not specified in the path, the binding process will be made to the default naming context. We can read the default naming context with the help of rootDSE. LDAP 3.0 defines rootDSE as the root of a directory tree on a directory server. For example:

```
LDAP://rootDSE
```

or:

```
LDAP://servername/rootDSE
```

By enumerating all properties of the rootDSE you can get the information about the defaultNamingContext that will be used when no name is specified. schemaNamingContext and configurationNamingContext specify the required names to be used to access the schema and the configuration in the Active Directory store.

The following code is used to get all properties of rootDSE:

```
using (DirectoryEntry de = new DirectoryEntry())
{
   de.Path = "LDAP://platinum/rootDSE";
   de.Username = @"platinum\christian";
   de.Password = "password";

   PropertyCollection props = de.Properties;
   foreach (string prop in props.PropertyNames)
   {
      PropertyValueCollection values = props[prop];
      foreach (string val in values)
      {
         Console.Write(prop + ": ");
```

```
                Console.WriteLine(val);
        }
    }
}
```

This program shows the default naming context (`defaultNamingContext DC=athenaproject, DC=local`), the context that can be used to access the schema (`CN=Schema, CN=Configuration, DC=athenaproject, DC=local`), and the naming context of the configuration (`CN=Configuration, DC=athenaproject, DC=local`), as shown in Figure 24-9.

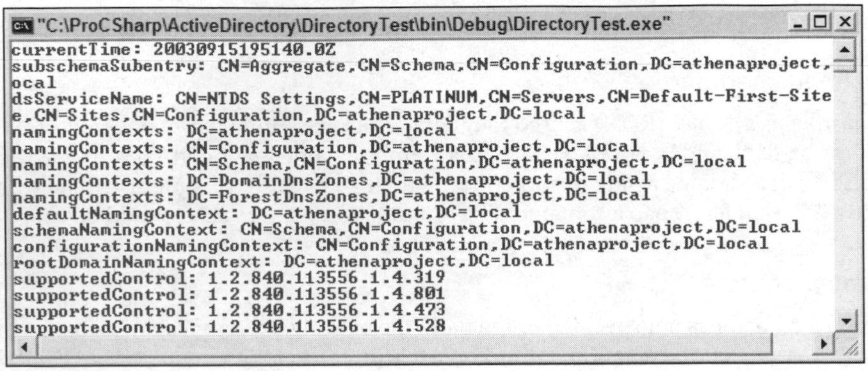

Figure 24-9

Object identifier

Every object has a *globally unique identifier* (GUID). A GUID is a unique 128-bit number as you may already know from COM development. We can bind to an object using the GUID. This way we always get to the same object, regardless of whether the object was moved to a different container. The GUID is generated at object creation and always remains the same.

You can get to a GUID string representation with `DirectoryEntry.NativeGuid`. This string representation can then be used to bind to the object.

This example shows the path name for a serverless binding to bind to a specific object represented by a GUID:

```
LDAP://<GUID=14abbd652aae1a47abc60782dcfc78ea>
```

Object names in Windows NT domains

The WinNT provider doesn't allow LDAP syntax in the name part of the binding string. With this provider the object is specified using `ObjectName, ClassName`. Valid binding strings for a Windows NT domain are:

```
WinNT:
WinNT://DomainName
WinNT://DomainName/UserName, user
WinNT://DomainName/ServerName/MyGroup, group
```

The `user` and `group` postfixes specify that objects of type `user` or `group` are accessed.

User name

If a user other than the user of the current process must be used for accessing the directory (maybe this user doesn't have the required permissions to access Active Directory), explicit *user credentials* must be specified for the binding process. With Active Directory there are multiple ways to specify the user name.

Downlevel logon

With a downlevel logon the user name can be specified with the pre-Windows 2000 domain name:

```
domain\username
```

Distinguished name

The user can also be specified by a distinguished name of a `user` object, for example:

```
CN=Administrator, CN=Users, DC=athenaproject, DC=local
```

User Principal Name (UPN)

The *user principal name* (*UPN*) of an object is defined with the `userPrincipalName` attribute. The system administrator specifies this with the logon information in the Account tab of the User properties with the Active Directory Users and Computers tool. Note that this is not the e-mail address of the user.

This information also uniquely identifies a user, and can be used for a logon:

```
Nagel@athenaproject.local
```

Authentication

For secure encrypted authentication the *authentication* type can also be specified. The authentication can be set with the `AuthenticationType` property of the `DirectoryEntry` class. The value that can be assigned is one of the `AuthenticationTypes` enumeration values. Because the enumeration is marked with the `[Flags]` attribute, multiple values can be specified. Some of the possible values are where the data sent is encrypted, `ReadonlyServer`, where we specify that we need only read access, and `Secure` for secure authentication.

Binding with the DirectoryEntry class

The `System.DirectoryServices.DirectoryEntry` class can be used to specify all the binding information. We can use the default constructor and define the binding information with the properties `Path`, `Username`, `Password`, and `AuthenticationType`, or pass all the information in the constructor:

```
DirectoryEntry de = new DirectoryEntry();
de.Path = "LDAP://platinum/DC=athenaproject, DC=local";
de.Username = "nagel@athenaproject.local";
de.Password = "password";

// use the current user credentials
DirectoryEntry de2 = new DirectoryEntry(
                        "LDAP://DC=athenaproject, DC=local");
```

Even if constructing the `DirectoryEntry` object is successful, this doesn't mean that the binding was a success. Binding will happen the first time a property is read to avoid unnecessary network traffic. At the first access of the object, it can be seen if the object exists and if the specified user credentials are correct.

Getting Directory Entries

Now that we know how to specify the binding attributes to an object in Active Directory, let's read the attributes of an object. In the following example, we read the properties of user objects.

The `DirectoryEntry` class has some properties to get information about the object: the `Name`, `Guid`, and `SchemaClassName` properties. The first time a property of the `DirectoryEntry` object is accessed, the binding occurs and the cache of the underlying ADSI object is filled. (We discuss this in more detail shortly.) Additional properties are read from the cache, and communication with the server isn't necessary for data from the same object.

In the following example the `user` object with the common name `Christian Nagel` in the organizational unit `Wrox Press` is accessed:

```
using (DirectoryEntry de = new DirectoryEntry())
{
    de.Path = "LDAP://platinum/CN=Christian Nagel, " +
              "OU=Wrox Press, DC=athenaproject, DC=local";

    Console.WriteLine("Name: " + de.Name);
    Console.WriteLine("GUID: " + de.Guid);
    Console.WriteLine("Type: " + de.SchemaClassName);
    Console.WriteLine();

    //...
}
```

An Active Directory object holds much more information, with the information available depending on the type of the object; the `Properties` property returns a `PropertyCollection`. Each property is itself a collection, because a single property can have multiple values, for example, the `user` object can have multiple phone numbers. In this example, we go through the values with an inner `foreach` loop. The collection that is returned from `properties[name]` is an `object` array. The attribute values can be strings, numbers, or other types. Here just the `ToString()` method is used to display the values.

```
Console.WriteLine("Properties: ");
PropertyCollection properties = de.Properties;
foreach (string name in properties.PropertyNames)
{
    foreach (object o in properties[name])
    {
        Console.WriteLine(name + ": " + o.ToString());
    }
}
```

In the resulting output you can see all attributes of the `user` object `Christian Nagel` (see Figure 24-10). `otherTelephone` is a multivalue property that has many phone numbers. Some of the property values just display the type of the object, System.__ComObject; for example lastLogoff, lastLogon, and nTSecurityDescriptor. To get the values of these attributes you have to use the ADSI COM interfaces directly from the classes in the System.DirectoryServices namespace.

Chapter 28 explains how to work with COM objects and interfaces.

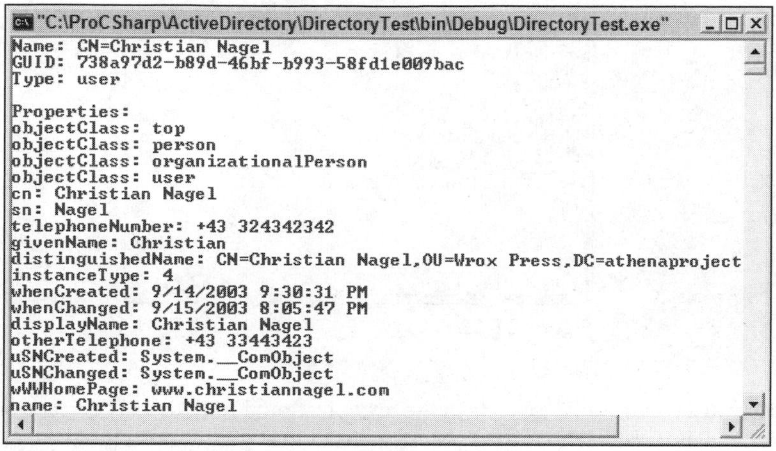

```
"C:\ProCSharp\ActiveDirectory\DirectoryTest\bin\Debug\DirectoryTest.exe"        _ □ X
Name: CN=Christian Nagel
GUID: 738a97d2-b89d-46bf-b993-58fd1e009bac
Type: user

Properties:
objectClass: top
objectClass: person
objectClass: organizationalPerson
objectClass: user
cn: Christian Nagel
sn: Nagel
telephoneNumber: +43 324342342
givenName: Christian
distinguishedName: CN=Christian Nagel,OU=Wrox Press,DC=athenaproject
instanceType: 4
whenCreated: 9/14/2003 9:30:31 PM
whenChanged: 9/15/2003 8:05:47 PM
displayName: Christian Nagel
otherTelephone: +43 33443423
uSNCreated: System.__ComObject
uSNChanged: System.__ComObject
wWWHomePage: www.christiannagel.com
name: Christian Nagel
```

Figure 24-10

Access a property directly by name

With DirectoryEntry.Properties you can access all properties. If a property name is known you can access the values directly:

```
foreach (string homePage in de.Properties["wWWHomePage"])
    Console.WriteLine("Home page: " + homePage);
```

Object Collections

Objects are stored hierarchically in the Active Directory. Container objects contain children. You can enumerate these child objects with the Children property of the class DirectoryEntry. In the other direction, you can get the container of an object with the Parent property.

A user object doesn't have children, so we use an organizational unit in the following example (see Figure 24-11). Non-container objects return an empty collection with the Children property. Let's get all user objects from the organizational unit Wrox Press in the domain athenaproject.local. The Children property returns a DirectoryEntries collection that collects DirectoryEntry objects. We iterate through all DirectoryEntry objects to display the name of the child objects:

```
using (DirectoryEntry de = new DirectoryEntry())
{
    de.Path = "LDAP://platinum/OU=Wrox Press, " +
            "DC=athenaproject, DC=local";

    Console.WriteLine("Children of " + de.Name);
```

```
    foreach (DirectoryEntry obj in de.Children)
    {
        Console.WriteLine(obj.Name);
    }
}
```

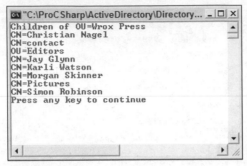

Figure 24-11

In this example you've seen all the objects in the organizational unit: `users`, `contacts`, `printers`, `shares`, and others. If you want to see only some object types you can use the `SchemaFilter` property of the `DirectoryEntries` class. The `SchemaFilter` property returns a `SchemaNameCollection`. With this `SchemaNameCollection` you can use the `Add()` method to define the object types you want to see. Here we are just interested in seeing the `user` objects, so `user` is added to this collection:

```
using (DirectoryEntry de = new DirectoryEntry())
{
    de.Path = "LDAP://platinum/OU=Wrox Press, " +
            "DC=athenaproject, DC=local";

    Console.WriteLine("Children of " + de.Name);
    de.Children.SchemaFilter.Add("user");
    foreach (DirectoryEntry obj in de.Children)
    {
        Console.WriteLine(obj.Name);
    }
}
```

As a result you only see the `user` objects in the organizational unit in Figure 24-12.

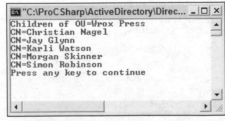

Figure 24-12

Cache

To reduce the network transfers, ADSI uses a cache for the object properties. As we mentioned earlier, the server isn't accessed when a `DirectoryEntry` object is created; instead with the first read of a value from the directory store all the properties are written into the cache, so that a round trip to the server isn't necessary when the next property is accessed.

Writing any changes to objects only changes the cached object; setting properties doesn't generate network traffic. You must use `DirectoryEntry.CommitChanges()` to flush the cache and to transfer any changed data to the server. To get the newly written data from the directory store, you can use `DirectoryEntry.RefreshCache()` to read the properties. Of course, if you change some properties without calling `CommitChanges()` and do a `RefreshCache()`, all your changes will be lost, because we read the values from the directory service again using `RefreshCache()`.

It is possible to turn off this property cache by setting the `DirectoryEntry.UsePropertyCache` property to `false`. However, unless you are debugging your code, it's better not to turn off the cache because of the extra round trips to the server that will be generated.

Creating New Objects

When you want to create new Active Directory objects—such as users, computers, printers, contacts, and so on—you can do this programmatically with the `DirectoryEntries` class.

To add new objects to the directory you first have to bind to a container object, such as an organizational unit, where new objects can be inserted—you cannot use objects that cannot contain other objects. The following example uses the container object with the distinguished name `CN=Users, DC=athenaproject, DC=local`:

```
DirectoryEntry de = new DirectoryEntry();
de.Path = "LDAP://platinum/CN=Users, DC=athenaproject, DC=local";
```

You can get to the `DirectoryEntries` object with the `Children` property of a `DirectoryEntry`:

```
DirectoryEntries users = de.Children;
```

The class `DirectoryEntries` offers methods to add, remove, and find objects in the collection. Here a new `user` object is created. With the `Add()` method, the name of the object and a type name are required. You can get to the type names directly using ADSI Edit.

```
DirectoryEntry user = users.Add("CN=John Doe", "user");
```

The object now has the default property values. To assign specific property values you can add properties with the `Add()` method of the `Properties` property. Of course, all of the properties must exist in the schema for the `user` object. If a specified property doesn't exist you'll get a `COMException`, "The specified directory service attribute or value doesn't exist":

```
user.Properties["company"].Add("Some Company");
user.Properties["department"].Add("Sales");
user.Properties["employeeID"].Add("4711");
user.Properties["samAccountName"].Add("JDoe");
```

```
user.Properties["userPrincipalName"].Add("JDoe@athenaproject.local");
user.Properties["givenName"].Add("John");
user.Properties["sn"].Add("Doe");
user.Properties["userPassword"].Add("someSecret");
```

Finally, to write the data to Active Directory, you have to flush the cache:

```
user.CommitChanges();
```

Updating Directory Entries

Objects in the Active Directory service can be updated as easily as they can be read. After reading the object, you can change the values. To remove all values of a single property, you can call the method PropertyValueCollection.Clear(). You can add new values to a property with Add(). Remove() and RemoveAt() remove specific values from a property collection.

You can change a value simply by setting it to the specified value. The following example uses an indexer for PropertyValueCollection to set the mobile phone number to a new value. With the indexer a value can only be changed if it exists. Therefore, you should always check with DirectoryEntry.Properties.Contains() if the attribute is available:

```
using (DirectoryEntry de = new DirectoryEntry())
{
    de.Path = "LDAP://platinum/CN=Christian Nagel, " +
              "OU=Wrox Press, DC=athenaproject, DC=local";

    if (de.Properties.Contains("mobile"))
    {
        de.Properties["mobile"][0] = "+43(664)3434343434";
    }
    else
    {
        de.Properties["mobile"].Add("+43(664)3434343434");
    }

    de.CommitChanges();
}
```

The else part in this example uses the method PropertyValueCollection.Add() to add a new property for the mobile phone number, if it doesn't exist already. If you used the Add() method with already existing properties, the resulting effect would depend on the type of the property (single-value or multi-value property). Using the Add() method with a single-value property that already exists, you get a COMException: "A constraint violation occurred." Using Add() with a multivalue property, however, succeeds, and an additional value is added to the property.

The property mobile for a user object is defined as a single-value property, so additional mobile phone numbers cannot be added. However a user can have more than one mobile phone number. For multiple mobile phone numbers the property otherMobile is available. otherMobile is a multivalue property that allows setting multiple phone numbers, and so calling `Add()` multiple times. Note that multivalue properties are checked for uniqueness. In case the second phone number is added to the same `user` object again, we get a `COMException`: "The specified directory service attribute or value already exists."

> Remember to call **`DirectoryEntry.CommitChanges()`** after creating or updating new directory objects. Otherwise only the cache gets updated, and the changes are not sent to the directory service.

Accessing Native ADSI Objects

Often it is a lot easier to call methods of predefined ADSI interfaces instead of searching for the names of object properties. Some ADSI objects also support methods that cannot be used directly from the `DirectoryEntry` class. One example of a practical use is the `IADsServiceOperations` interface that has methods to start and stop Windows services. (For more details on Windows Services see Chapter 32.)

The classes of the `System.DirectoryServices` namespace use the underlying ADSI COM objects as mentioned earlier. The `DirectoryEntry` class supports calling methods of the underlying objects directly by using the `Invoke()` method.

The first parameter of `Invoke()` requires the method name that should be called in the ADSI object; the `params` keyword of the second parameter allows a flexible number of additional arguments that can be passed to the ADSI method:

```
public object Invoke(string methodName, params object[] args);
```

You can find the methods that can be called with the `Invoke()` method in the ADSI documentation. Every object in the domain supports the methods of the `IADs` interface. The `user` object that we created previously also supports the methods of the `IADsUser` interface.

In the following example, the method `IADsUser.SetPassword()` changes the password of the previously created `user` object:

```
using (DirectoryEntry de = new DirectoryEntry())
{
    de.Path = "LDAP://platinum/CN=John Doe, " +
              "CN=Users, DC=athenaproject, DC=local";

    de.Invoke("SetPassword", "anotherSecret");
    de.CommitChanges();
}
```

Instead of using `Invoke()` it is also possible to use the underlying ADSI object directly. To use these objects choose Project⇨Add Reference to add a reference to the Active DS Type Library (see Figure 24-13). This creates a wrapper class where we can access these objects in the namespace `ActiveDs`.

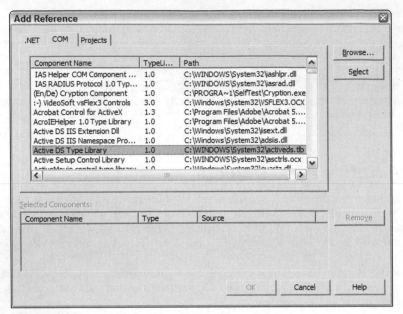

Figure 24-13

The native object can be accessed with the `NativeObject` property of the `DirectoryEntry` class. In the following example, the object `de` is a `user` object, so it can be cast to `ActiveDs.IADsUser`. `SetPassword()` is a method that is documented in the `IADsUser` interface, so you can call it directly instead of using the `Invoke()` method. By setting the `AccountDisabled` property of `IADsUser` to `false`, you can enable the account. As in the previous examples the changes are written to the directory service by calling `CommitChanges()` with the `DirectoryEntry` object:

```
ActiveDs.IADsUser user = (ActiveDs.IADsUser)de.NativeObject;
user.SetPassword("someSecret");
user.AccountDisabled = false;
de.CommitChanges();
```

Searching in Active Directory

Since Active Directory is a data store that is optimized for *read-mostly* access, you will generally be searching it for values. To search in Active Directory, .NET Framework provides the `DirectorySearcher` class.

> *You can only use `DirectorySearcher` with the LDAP provider; it doesn't work with the other providers such as NDS or IIS.*

In the constructor of the `DirectorySearcher` class you can define four important parts for the search. You can also use a default constructor and define the search options with properties.

SearchRoot

The search root specifies where the search should start. The default of `SearchRoot` is the root of the domain you're currently using. `SearchRoot` is specified with the `Path` of a `DirectoryEntry` object.

Filter

The filter defines the values where you want to get hits. The filter is a string that must be enclosed in parentheses.

Relational operators such as <=, =, and >= are allowed in expressions. `(objectClass=contact)` searches all objects of type `contact`; `(lastName>=Nagel)` searches all objects alphabetically where the `lastName` property is equal to or larger than `Nagel`.

Expressions can be combined with the & and | prefix operators. For example, `(&(objectClass=user) (description=Auth*))` searches all objects of type user where the property description starts with the string `Auth`. Because the & and | operators are at the beginning of the expressions, it's possible to combine more than two expressions with a single prefix operator.

The default filter is `(objectClass=*)` so all objects are valid.

> *The filter syntax is defined in RFC 2254, "The String Representation of LDAP Search Filters." This RFC can be found at www.ietf.org/rfc/rfc2254.txt.*

PropertiesToLoad

With `PropertiesToLoad` you can define a `StringCollection` of all the properties that you are interested in. Objects can have a lot of properties, most of which will not be important for our search request. We define the properties that should be loaded into the cache. The default properties that are returned if nothing is specified are the path and the name of the object.

SearchScope

`SearchScope` is an enumeration that defines how deep the search should extend:

❑ `SearchScope.Base` only searches the attributes in the object where the search started, so at most one object is found.

❑ With `SearchScope.OneLevel` the search continues in the child collection of the base object. The base object itself is not searched for a hit.

❑ `SearchScope.Subtree` defines that the search should go down the complete tree.

The default value of the `SearchScope` property is `SearchScope.Subtree`.

Search Limits

A search for specific objects in a directory service can span multiple domains. To limit the search to the number of objects or the time taken we have some additional properties to define, as shown in the following table.

Property	Description
ClientTimeout	The maximum time the client waits for the server to return a result. If the server does not respond, no records are returned.
PageSize	With a *paged search* the server returns a number of objects defined with the PageSize instead of the complete result. This reduces the time for the client to get a first answer and the memory needed. The server sends a cookie to the client, which is sent back to the server with the next search request, so that the search can continue at the point where it finished.
ServerPageTimeLimit	For paged searches this value defines the time a search should continue to return a number of objects that's defined with the Page-Size value. If the time is reached before the PageSize value, the objects that were found up to that point are returned to the client. The default value is -1, which means infinite.
ServerTimeLimit	Defines the maximum time the server will search for objects. When this time is reached all objects that are found up to this point are returned to the client. The default is 120 seconds, and you cannot set the search to a higher value.
ReferalChasing	A search can cross multiple domains. If the root that's specified with SearchRoot is a parent domain or no root was specified, the search can continue to child domains. With this property we can specify if the search should continue on different servers.

ReferalChasingOption.None means that the search does not continue on other servers.

The value ReferalChasingOption.Subordinate specifies that the search should go on to child domains. When the search starts at DC=Wrox, DC=COM the server can return a result set and the referral to DC=France, DC=Wrox, DC=COM. The client can continue the search in the subdomain.

ReferalChasingOption.External means that the server can refer the client to an independent server that is not in the subdomain. This is the default option.

With ReferalChasingOption.All both external and subordinate referrals are returned. |

In our search example all user objects with a property description value of Author are searched in the organizational unit Wrox Press.

First, bind to the organizational unit Wrox Press. This is where the search should start. Create a DirectorySearcher object where the SearchRoot is set. The filter is defined as (&(objectClass=user)(description=Auth*)), so that the search spans all objects of type user with a description of Auth following by something else. The scope of the search should be a subtree, so that child organizational units within Wrox Press are searched, too:

```
using (DirectoryEntry de =
    new DirectoryEntry("LDAP://OU=Wrox Press, DC=athenaproject, DC=local"))
using (DirectorySearcher searcher = new DirectorySearcher())
{
    searcher.SearchRoot = de;
    searcher.Filter = "(&(objectClass=user)(description=Auth*))";
    searcher.SearchScope = SearchScope.Subtree;
```

The properties that should be in the result of the search are `name`, `description`, `givenName`, and `wWWHomePage`:

```
    searcher.PropertiesToLoad.Add("name");
    searcher.PropertiesToLoad.Add("description");
    searcher.PropertiesToLoad.Add("givenName");
    searcher.PropertiesToLoad.Add("wWWHomePage");
```

You are ready to do the search. However, the result should also be sorted. `DirectorySearcher` has a property `Sort`, where we can set a `SortOption`. The first argument in the constructor of the `SortOption` class defines the property that will be used for a sort; the second argument defines the direction of the sort. The `SortDirection` enumeration has values `Ascending` and `Descending`.

To start the search you can use the method `FindOne()` to find the first object, or `FindAll()`. `FindOne()` returns a simple `SearchResult`, whereas `FindAll()` returns a `SearchResultCollection`. Here all authors should be returned, so `FindAll()` is used here:

```
    searcher.Sort = new SortOption("givenName", SortDirection.Ascending);

    SearchResultCollection results = searcher.FindAll();
```

With a `foreach` loop every `SearchResult` in the `SearchResultCollection` is accessed. A `SearchResult` represents a single object in the search cache. The `Properties` property returns a `ResultPropertyCollection`, where we access all properties and values with the property name and the indexer:

```
    SearchResultCollection results = searcher.FindAll();

    foreach (SearchResult result in results)
    {
        ResultPropertyCollection props = result.Properties;
        foreach (string propName in props.PropertyNames)
        {
            Console.Write(propName + ": ");
            Console.WriteLine(props[propName][0]);
        }
        Console.WriteLine();
    }
}
```

If you would like to get to the complete object after a search that's also possible: `SearchResult` has a method `GetDirectoryEntry()` that returns the corresponding `DirectoryEntry` of the found object.

The resulting output shows the beginning of the list of all authors of Professional C# with the properties that have been chosen (see Figure 24-14).

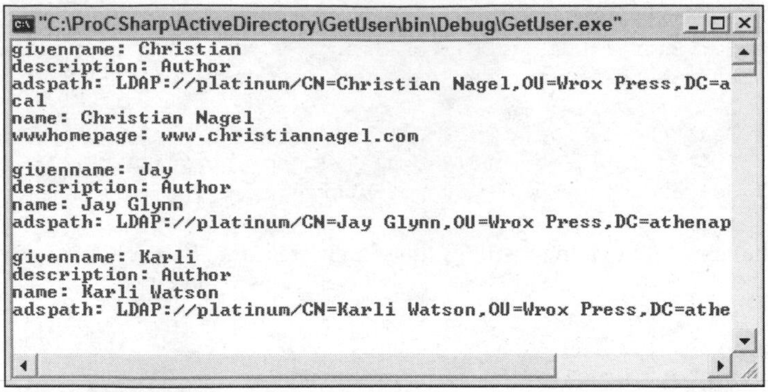

Figure 24-14

Searching for User Objects

In the final section of this chapter we will build a Windows Forms application called UserSearch. This application is flexible in so far as a specific domain controller, username, and password to access the Active Directory can be entered; otherwise the user of the running process is used. In this application we access the schema of the Active Directory service to get the properties of a `user` object. The user can enter a filter string to search all `user` objects of a domain. It's also possible to set the properties of the `user` objects that should be displayed.

User Interface

The user interface shows numbered steps to indicate how to use the application (see Figure 24-15):

1. In the first step `Username`, `Password`, and the `Domain Controller` can be entered. All this information is optional. If no domain controller is entered the connection works with serverless binding. If the user name is missing the security context of the current user is taken.

2. A button allows all the property names of the `user` object to be loaded dynamically in the `listBoxProperties` list box.

3. After the property names are loaded, the properties that should be displayed can be selected. The `SelectionMode` of the list box is set to `MultiSimple`.

4. The filter to limit the search can be entered. The default value that's set in this dialog box searches for all `user` objects: `(objectClass=user)`.

5. Now the search can start.

Get the Schema Naming Context

This application has only two handler methods: one method for the button to load the properties, and one to start the search in the domain. First, we read the properties of the `user` class dynamically from the schema to display it in the user interface.

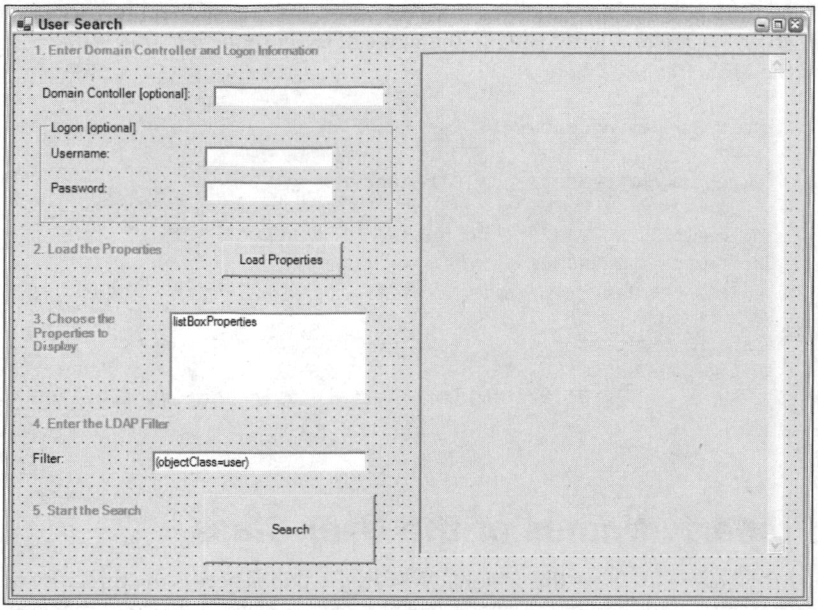

Figure 24-15

In the handler `buttonLoadProperties_Click()` method, `SetLogonInformation()` reads the user name, password, and host name from the dialog box and stores them in members of the class. Next the method `SetNamingContext()` sets the LDAP name of the schema and the LDAP name of the default context. This schema LDAP name is used in the call to set the properties in the list box: `SetUserProperties()`:

```
private void buttonLoadProperties_Click(object sender, System.EventArgs e)
{
    try
    {
        SetLogonInformation();
        SetNamingContext();

        SetUserProperties(schemaNamingContext);
    }
    catch (Exception ex)
    {
        MessageBox.Show("Check your inputs! " + ex.Message);
    }
}
protected void SetLogonInformation()
{
    username = (textBoxUsername.Text == "" ? null : textBoxUsername.Text);
    password = (textBoxPassword.Text == "" ? null : textBoxPassword.Text);
    hostname = textBoxHostname.Text;
    if (hostname != "") hostname += "/";
}
```

In the helper method `SetNamingContext()`, we are using the root of the directory tree to get the properties of the server. We are only interested in the value of two properties: `schemaNamingContext` and `defaultNamingContext`:

```
protected void SetNamingContext()
{
   using (DirectoryEntry de = new DirectoryEntry())
   {
      string path = "LDAP://" + hostname + "rootDSE";
      de.Username = username;
      de.Password = password;
      de.Path = path;
      schemaNamingContext = de.Properties["schemaNamingContext"][0].ToString();
      defaultNamingContext =
                      de.Properties["defaultNamingContext"][0].ToString();
   }
}
```

Get the Property Names of the User Class

We have the LDAP name to access the schema. We can use this to access the directory and read the properties. We are not only interested in the properties of the `user` class, but also of the base classes of `user`: `Organizational-Person`, `Person`, and `Top`. In this program, the names of the base classes are hard-coded. We could also read the base class dynamically with the `subClassOf` attribute. `GetSchemaProperties()` returns a string array with all property names of the specific object type. All the property names are collected in the `StringCollection` properties:

```
protected void SetUserProperties(string schemaNamingContext)
{
   StringCollection properties = new StringCollection();
   string[] data = GetSchemaProperties(schemaNamingContext, "User");
   properties.AddRange(GetSchemaProperties(schemaNamingContext,
                     "Organizational-Person"));
   properties.AddRange(GetSchemaProperties(schemaNamingContext, "Person"));
   properties.AddRange(GetSchemaProperties(schemaNamingContext, "Top"));
   listBoxProperties.Items.Clear();
   foreach (string s in properties)
   {
      listBoxProperties.Items.Add(s);
   }
}
```

In `GetSchemaProperties()` we are accessing the Active Directory service again. This time `rootDSE` is not used, rather the LDAP name to the schema that we discovered earlier. The property `systemMayContain` holds a collection of all attributes that are allowed in the class `objectType`:

```
protected string[] GetSchemaProperties(string schemaNamingContext,
                                   string objectType)
{
   string[] data;
   using (DirectoryEntry de = new DirectoryEntry())
   {
      de.Username = username;
      de.Password = password;
```

```
       de.Path = "LDAP://" + hostname + "CN=" + objectType + "," +
               schemaNamingContext;

       DS.PropertyCollection properties = de.Properties;
       DS.PropertyValueCollection values = properties["systemMayContain"];

       data = new String[values.Count];
       values.CopyTo(data, 0);
    }
    return data;
}
```

Note the presence of DS.PropertyCollection in the above code; this is because in a Windows Forms application, the PropertyCollection class of the System.DirectoryServices namespace has a naming conflict with System.Data.PropertyCollection, and to avoid long names like System .DirectoryServices.PropertyCollection, the namespace name can be shortened as follows:

```
using DS = System.DirectoryServices;
```

Step 2 in the application is completed. The listbox control has all the property names of the user objects.

Search for User Objects

The handler for the search button calls only the helper method FillResult():

```
private void buttonSearch_Click(object sender, System.EventArgs e)
{
   try
   {
      FillResult();
   }
   catch (Exception ex)
   {
      MessageBox.Show("Check your input: " + ex.Message);
   }
}
```

In FillResult() we are doing a normal search in the complete Active Directory Domain as we've seen earlier. SearchScope is set to Subtree, the Filter to the string we get from a TextBox object, and the properties that should be loaded into the cache are set by the values the user selected in the list box. The method GetProperties() that is used to pass an array of properties to the method searcher. PropertiesToLoad.AddRange() is a helper method that reads the selected properties from the list box into an array. After setting the properties of the DirectorySearcher object, the properties are searched by calling the SearchAll() method. The result of the search inside the SearchResultCollection is used to generate summary information that is written to the text box textBoxResults.

```
protected void FillResult()
{
   using (DirectoryEntry root = new DirectoryEntry())
   {
      root.Username = username;
```

```
        root.Password = password;
        root.Path = "LDAP://" + hostname + defaultNamingContext;

        using (DirectorySearcher searcher = new DirectorySearcher())
        {
            searcher.SearchRoot = root;
            searcher.SearchScope = SearchScope.Subtree;
            searcher.Filter = textBoxFilter.Text;
            searcher.PropertiesToLoad.AddRange(GetProperties());

            SearchResultCollection results = searcher.FindAll();
            StringBuilder summary = new StringBuilder();
            foreach (SearchResult result in results)
            {
                foreach (string propName in
                result.Properties.PropertyNames)
                {
                    foreach (string s in result.Properties[propName])
                    {
                        summary.Append(" " + propName + ": " + s + "\r\n");
                    }
                }
                summary.Append("\r\n");
            }
            textBoxResults.Text = summary.ToString();
        }
    }
}
```

Starting the application we get a list of all objects where the filter is valid (see Figure 24-16).

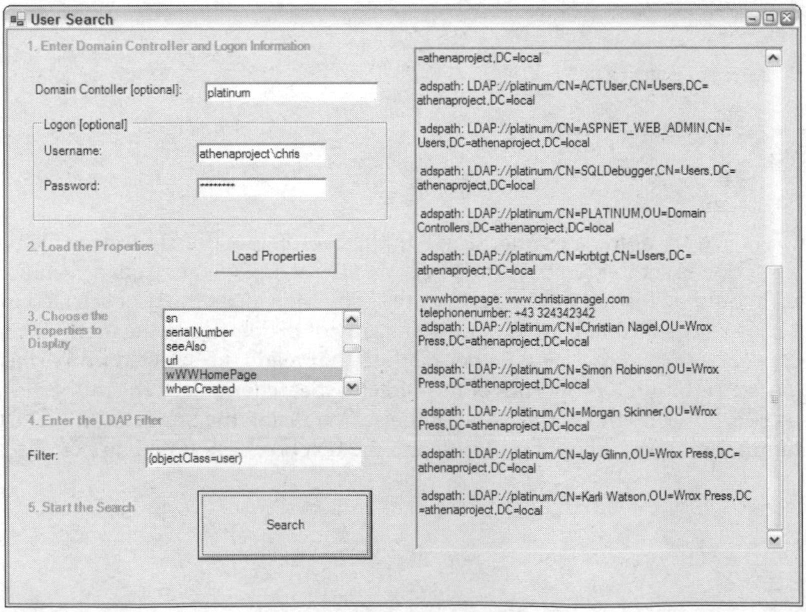

Figure 24-16

Summary

In this chapter we've seen the architecture of Active Directory: the important concepts of domains, trees, and forests. We can access information in the complete enterprise. When writing applications that access Active Directory services, we have to be aware that the data we read might not be up-to-date because of the replication latency.

The classes in the `System.DirectoryServices` namespaces give us easy ways to access Active Directory services by wrapping to the ADSI providers. The `DirectoryEntry` class makes it possible to read and write objects directly in the data store.

With the `DirectorySearcher` class we can do complex searches and define filters, timeouts, properties to load, and a scope. Using the global catalog we can speed up the search for objects in the complete enterprise, because it stores a read-only version of all objects in the forest.

Part V: Web Programming

25

ASP.NET Pages

If you are new to the world of C# and .NET you might wonder why a chapter on ASP.NET has been included in this book. It's a whole new language, right? Well, not really. In fact, as you will see, you can use C# to create ASP.NET pages.

ASP.NET is part of .NET Framework and is a technology that allows for the dynamic creation of documents on a Web server when they are requested via HTTP. This mostly means HTML documents, although it is equally possible to create WML documents for consumption on WAP browsers, or anything else that supports the MIME type.

In some ways ASP.NET is similar to many other technologies—such as PHP, ASP, or ColdFusion. There is, however, one key difference: ASP.NET, as its name suggests, has been designed to be fully integrated with the .NET Framework, part of which includes support for C#.

Perhaps you are familiar with Active Server Pages (ASP) technology, which enables you to create dynamic content. If this is the case then you will probably know that programming in this technology used scripting languages such as VBScript or JScript. The result was not always perfect, at least not for those of us who are used to "proper," compiled programming languages, and it certainly resulted in a loss of performance.

One major difference, related to the use of more advanced programming languages, is the provision of a complete server-side object model for use at runtime. ASP.NET provides access to all of the controls on a page as objects, in a rich environment. On the server side we also have access to other .NET classes, allowing for the integration of many useful services. Controls used on a page expose a lot of functionality; in fact we can do almost as much as with Windows Forms classes, which provides plenty of flexibility. For this reason, ASP.NET pages that generate HTML content are often called *Web Forms*.

In this chapter we will take a more detailed look at ASP.NET, including how it works, what we can do with it, and how C# fits in.

ASP.NET Introduction

ASP.NET works with Internet Information Server (IIS) to deliver content in response to HTTP requests. ASP.NET pages are found in .aspx files; Figure 25-1 illustrates the technology's basic architecture.

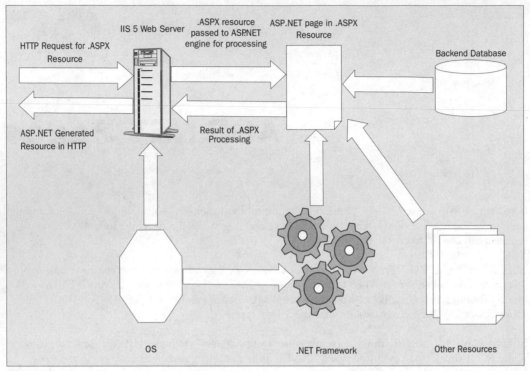

Figure 25-1

During ASP.NET processing we have access to all .NET classes, custom components created in C# or other languages, databases, and so on. In fact, we have as much power as we would have running a C# application; using C# in ASP.NET is in effect running a C# application.

An ASP.NET file can contain any of the following:

❑ Processing instructions for the server

❑ Code in C#, Visual Basic .NET, JScript .NET, or any other language that the .NET Framework supports

❑ Content in whatever form is appropriate for the generated resource, such as HTML

❑ Client-side script code

❑ Embedded ASP.NET server controls

So, in fact we could have an ASP.NET file as simple as this:

```
Hello!
```

This would simply result in an HTML page being returned (as HTML is the default output of ASP.NET pages) containing just this text.

As we will see later in this chapter, it is also possible to split certain portions of the code into other files, which can provide a more logical structure.

State Management in ASP.NET

One of the key properties of ASP.NET pages is that they are effectively stateless. By default, no information is stored on the server between user requests (although there are methods for doing this as we'll see later in this chapter). At first glance this seems a little strange, because state management is something that seems essential for user-friendly interactive sessions. However, ASP.NET provides a work-around to this problem, such that session management becomes almost transparent.

In short, information such as the state of controls on a Web Form (including data entered in text boxes or selections from drop-down lists) is stored in a hidden *viewstate* field that is part of the page generated by the server and passed to the user. Subsequent actions, such as triggering events that require server-side processing like submitting form data, result in this information being sent back to the server, known as *postback*. On the server this information is used to repopulate the page object model allowing us to operate on it as if the changes had been made locally.

We'll see this in action shortly and point out the details.

ASP.NET Web Forms

As mentioned earlier, much of the functionality in ASP.NET is achieved using Web Forms. Before long we'll dive in and create a simple Web Form to give us a starting point to explore this technology. First, however, we'd like to review some key points pertinent to Web Form design. It should be noted that many ASP.NET developers simply use a text editor such as Notepad to create files. This enables us to combine all code in one file. We achieve this by enclosing code in <script> elements, using two attributes on the opening <script> tag:

```
<script language="c#" runat="server">
    // Server-side code goes here.
</script>
```

The runat="server" attribute here is crucial, because it instructs the ASP.NET engine to execute this code on the server rather than sending it to the client, thus giving us access to the rich environment hinted at earlier. We can place our functions, event handlers, and so on, in server-side script blocks.

If we omit the runat="server" attribute, we are effectively providing client-side code, which will fail if it uses any of the server-side style coding we discuss in this chapter. However, there might be times when we want to provide client-side code (indeed, ASP.NET generates some itself sometimes, depending on browser capabilities and what Web Form code is used). Unfortunately we can't use C# here; to do so would require the .NET Framework to be installed on the client, which might not always be the case. JScript is probably the next best option, because it is supported on the widest variety of client browsers. To change the language we simply change the value of the `language` attribute as follows:

```
<script language="jscript">
    // Client-side code goes here; we can also use "vbscript".
</script>
```

It is equally possible to create ASP.NET files in Visual Studio .NET, which is great for us as we are already familiar with this environment for C# programming. However, the default project setup for Web applications in this environment has a slightly more complex structure than a single .aspx file. This isn't a problem for us though, and does make things a bit more logical (read: more programmer-like and less Web developer-like). For this reason, we'll use Visual Studio .NET throughout this chapter for our ASP.NET programming (instead of Notepad).

The .aspx files can also include code in blocks enclosed by `<%` and `%>` tags. However, function definitions and variable declarations can not go here. Instead we can insert code that is executed as soon as the block is reached, which is useful when outputting simple HTML content. This behavior is similar to that of old-style ASP pages, with one important difference: the code is compiled, not interpreted. This results in far better performance.

Now it's time for an example. Create a new project of type ASP.NET Web Application called PCSWebApp1 as shown in Figure 25-2.

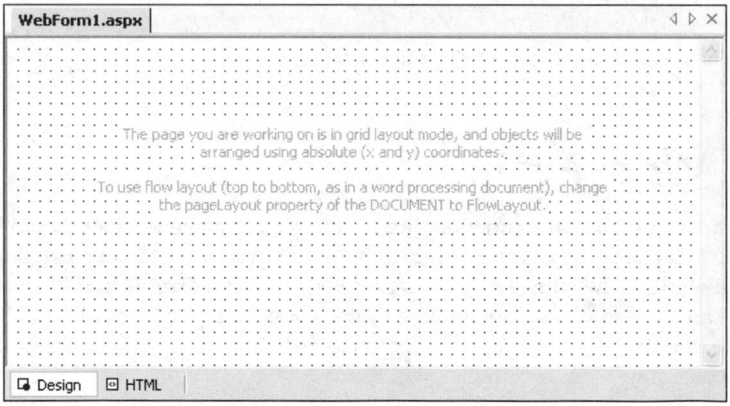

Figure 25-2

By default, Visual Studio .NET uses FrontPage extensions to set up a Web application at the required location, which may be remote if your Web server is on a different machine. However, it also provides an alternative (and slightly faster) method for doing this, using the file system over a LAN (which is of course impossible if your remote Web server isn't on the same LAN as your development server). If the first method fails then Visual Studio .NET will try the second.

Regardless of which method is used, Visual Studio .NET keeps a local cache of all project files, and keeps these in sync with the files on the Web server.

After a few moments Visual Studio .NET should have set up the following:

- ❑ PCSWebApp1, a new solution containing the C# Web Application PCSWebApp1
- ❑ AssemblyInfo.cs, the standard Visual Studio .NET file describing the assembly
- ❑ Global.asax, the application global information and events file (see later in this chapter)
- ❑ Web.config, the configuration information file for the application (see later in this chapter)
- ❑ WebForm1.aspx, the first ASP.NET page in the Web application

We'll cover all of the generated files over the course of this and the next two chapters; for now concentrate on the meat of the application, which is the .aspx file that Visual Studio .NET has generated for us.

We can view .aspx files in design or code view (as well as the HTML view in the designer). This is the same as for Windows Forms (as discussed in Part III). The initial view in Visual Studio .NET is the design view, shown in Figure 25-3.

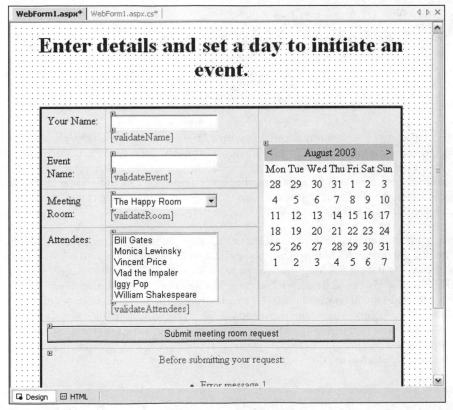

Figure 25-3

The text shown in this view by default isn't text that we'll see in our application, it's just a note from Visual Studio .NET to say what layout mode is in use. Here we are using the *GridLayout* mode, which allows extra flexibility in control positioning, but we can change this to *FlowLayout* if we require a more traditional HTML-type positioning scheme.

If we select the HTML view from the buttons below the layout display we'll see the code generated inside the .aspx file:

```
<%@ Page language="c#"
        Codebehind="WebForm1.aspx.cs"
        AutoEventWireup="false"
        Inherits="PCSWebApp1.WebForm1" %>
<!DOCTYPE HTML PUBLIC "-//W3C//DTD HTML 4.0 Transitional//EN" >
```

```
<html>
  <head>
    <title>WebForm1</title>
    <meta name="GENERATOR" Content="Microsoft Visual Studio .NET 7.1">
    <meta name="CODE_LANGUAGE" Content="C#">
    <meta name=vs_defaultClientScript content="JavaScript">
    <meta name=vs_targetSchema
          content="http://schemas.microsoft.com/intellisense/ie5">
  </head>
  <body MS_POSITIONING="GridLayout">

    <form id="Form1" method="post" runat="server">

    </form>

  </body>
</html>
```

The <html> element here has been populated with a little metadata that doesn't really concern us, and a <form> element to contain ASP.NET code. The most important element here is the runat attribute. Just as with the server-side code blocks we saw at the start of this section this is set to server, meaning that the processing of the form will take place on the server. If we don't include this reference, then no server-side processing will be performed and the form won't do anything. There can only be one server-side <form> element in an ASP.NET page.

The other interesting thing about this code is the <%@ Page %> tag at the top. This tag defines page characteristics that are important to us as C# Web application developers. There is a language attribute that specifies that we will use C# throughout our page, as we saw earlier with <script> blocks (the default for Web applications is Visual Basic .NET, although this can be changed using the Web.config file). The next three attributes are necessary, because the code driving the page has been set up by Visual Studio .NET to reside in a separate file, WebForm1.aspx.cs. This file, which we'll look at shortly, contains a class definition that is used as the base class for the Web Forms page. Now we start to see how ASP.NET ties in with a rich object model! This base class is used in conjunction with code in this file to generate the HTML output that reaches the user.

Note that not all .aspx files require this multi-layer model; you can use the base .NET Web Form class as the base class for the page, which is the default. In this case the .aspx file would include all of our C# code in **<script>** *blocks as mentioned earlier.*

Since we are providing a customized base class for the page we might also have customized events. To ensure that the ASP.NET engine is aware of this we use the AutoEventWireup attribute, which signifies whether the Page_Load() event handler (called on loading the page) is automatically wired up to the

`OnPageLoad` event. By setting this attribute to `false` we must provide our own code to do this if required, but this gives us a bit more freedom in what we do.

Next we'll look at the "code-behind" code generated for this file. To do this, right-click the WebForm1 .aspx file in the Solution Explorer and select View Code. This loads the code in WebForm1.aspx.cs into the text editor. First, we see the default set of namespace references required for basic usage:

```
using System;
using System.Collections;
using System.ComponentModel;
using System.Data;
using System.Drawing;
using System.Web;
using System.Web.SessionState;
using System.Web.UI;
using System.Web.UI.WebControls;
using System.Web.UI.HtmlControls;
```

Below these references we see a namespace declaration for our Web application, followed by the definition of `WebForm1`, the base class used for the .aspx page. This class inherits from `System.Web.UI.Page`, the base class for Web Forms:

```
namespace PCSWebApp1
{
    /// <summary>
    /// Summary description for WebForm1.
    /// </summary>
    public class WebForm1 : System.Web.UI.Page
    {
```

The rest of the code in this form performs various initialization tasks and includes the code required to design Web Forms in Visual Studio .NET. No constructor is included (the .NET default one is used), but there is an event handler called `Page_Load()` that we can use to add any code that is required when the page is loaded:

```
private void Page_Load(object sender, System.EventArgs e)
{
    // Put user code to initialize the page here
}
```

The rest of the code is enclosed in a `#region` block, so to view it we need to expand it:

```
#region Web Form Designer generated code
override protected void OnInit(EventArgs e)
{
    //
    // CODEGEN: This call is required by the ASP.NET Web Form Designer.
    //
    InitializeComponent();
    base.OnInit(e);
}

/// <summary>
/// Required method for Designer support - do not modify
```

```
    /// the contents of this method with the code editor.
    /// </summary>
    private void InitializeComponent()
    {
        this.Load += new System.EventHandler(this.Page_Load);
    }
    #endregion
```

Here the `OnInit()` event handler inherited from `System.Web.UI.Control` is overridden. This event handler is executed when the page initializes, and results in `InitializeComponent()` being called before the base implementation of `OnInit()` is processed. `InitializeComponent()` simply wires up the `Page_Load()` event handler to the `Load` event of the page, necessary as `AutoEventWireup` was set to `false`.

Strictly speaking, this is more code than is required for a simple ASP.NET Web Form page, which can be as simple as we saw right at the start of the chapter (albeit as a trivial example). However, the structure created does lend itself to reusability and expansion using C# techniques, without causing a noticeable amount of overhead, so we'll run with it.

ASP.NET Server Controls

Our generated code doesn't do very much as yet, so next we need to add some content. We can do this in Visual Studio .NET using the Web Form designer, which supports drag-and-drop in just the same way as the Windows Forms designer.

There are four types of control that we can add to our ASP.NET pages:

❑ **HTML server controls**—These controls mimic HTML elements, which will be familiar to HTML developers.

❑ **Web server controls**—This is a new set of controls, some of which have the same functionality as HTML controls. These controls have a common naming scheme for properties and other elements to ease development, and provide consistency with analogous Windows Forms controls. There are also some completely new and very powerful controls as we will see later.

❑ **Validation controls**—This is a set of controls capable of performing validation of user input in a simple way.

❑ **Custom and user controls**—These controls are defined by the developer, which can be created in a number of ways as discussed in Chapter 27.

The next section provides a complete list of Web server and validation controls, along with usage notes. HTML controls will not be covered in this chapter. These controls don't do anything more than the Web server controls, and the Web server controls provide a richer environment for developers more familiar with programming than HTML design. Learning how to use the Web server controls provides enough knowledge to use HTML server controls. For more information, check out Professional ASP.NET 1.1 (ISBN 0-7645-5890-0, Wiley).

Let's add a couple of Web server controls to our project. All Web server and validation controls are used in the following XML element-type form:

```
<asp:X runat="server" attribute="value">Contents</asp:X>
```

X is the name of the ASP.NET server control, *attribute="value"* is one or more attribute specifications, and *Contents* specifies the control content, if any. Some controls allow properties to be set using attributes and control element content, such as `Label` (used for simple text display), where `Text` can be specified in either way. Other controls might use an element containment scheme to define their hierarchy, for example `Table` (which defines a table) that can contain `TableRow` elements in order to specify table rows declaratively.

Because the syntax for controls is based on XML (although the controls may be used embedded in non-XML code such as HTML), it is an error to omit the closing tags and `/>` for empty elements, or overlap controls.

Finally, we once again see the `runat="server"` attribute on the Web server controls. It is just as essential here as it is elsewhere, and it is a common mistake to miss this attribute, resulting in Web Forms that don't function.

We'll keep things simple for this first example. Change the HTML design view for WebForm1.aspx as follows:

```
<%@ Page language="c#"
         Codebehind="WebForm1.aspx.cs"
         AutoEventWireup="false"
         Inherits="PCSWebApp1.WebForm1" %>
<!DOCTYPE HTML PUBLIC "-//W3C//DTD HTML 4.0 Transitional//EN" >

<html>
  <head>
    <title>WebForm1</title>
    <meta name="GENERATOR" Content="Microsoft Visual Studio .NET 7.1">
    <meta name="CODE_LANGUAGE" Content="C#">
    <meta name=vs_defaultClientScript content="JavaScript">
    <meta name=vs_targetSchema
          content="http://schemas.microsoft.com/intellisense/ie5">
  </head>
  <body MS_POSITIONING="GridLayout">

    <form id="Form1" method="post" runat="server">
      <asp:Label Runat="server" ID="resultLabel"/><br>
      <asp:Button Runat="server" ID="triggerButton" Text="Click Me"/>
    </form>

  </body>
</html>
```

Here we have added two Web Form controls, a label and a button.

> *Note that as you do this, Visual Studio .NET IntelliSense predicts your code entry just like in the C# code editor.*

Going back to the design screen we can see that our controls have been added, and named using their `ID` attributes. As with Windows Forms we have full access to properties, events, and so on through the Properties window, and get instant feedback in code or design whenever we make changes.

Next, have another look at WebForm1.aspx.cs. The following two members have been added to our `WebForm1` class:

```
protected System.Web.UI.WebControls.Button triggerButton;
protected System.Web.UI.WebControls.Label resultLabel;
```

Any server controls we add will automatically become part of the object model for our form that we are building in this code-behind file. This is an instant bonus for Windows Forms developers—the similarities are beginning to emerge!

To make this application do something, let's add an event handler for clicking the button. Here we can either enter a method name in the Properties window for the button or just double-click the button to get the default event handler. If we double-click the button we'll automatically add an event-handling method as follows:

```
private void triggerButton_Click(object sender,
                                   System.EventArgs e)
{
}
```

This is hooked up to the button by some code added to `InitializeComponent()`:

```
private void InitializeComponent()
{
    this.triggerButton.Click +=
        new System.EventHandler(this.triggerButton_Click);
    this.Load += new System.EventHandler(this.Page_Load);
}
```

Modify the code in `triggerButton_Click()` as follows:

```
protected void triggerButton_Click(object sender,
                                     System.EventArgs e)
{
    resultLabel.Text = "Button clicked!";
}
```

Now we're ready to make it go. Build the application from Visual Studio .NET in the normal way and all the files will be compiled and/or placed on the Web server ready for use. To test the Web application we can either run the application (which will give us full use of the Visual Studio .NET debugging facilities), or just point a browser at `http://localhost/PCSWebApp1/WebForm1.aspx`. Either way you should see the Click Me button on a Web page. Before pressing the button, take a quick look at the code received by the browser using View⇨Source (in IE). The `<form>` section should look like this:

```
<form name="Form1" method="post" action="WebForm1.aspx"
    id="Form1">
<input type="hidden" name="__VIEWSTATE"
        value="dDwtOTk1MjE0NDA4Ozs+" />
<span id="resultLabel"></span><br>
<input type="submit" name="triggerButton" value="Click Me"
        id="triggerButton" />
</form>
```

The Web server controls have generated straight HTML, `<span>` and `<input>` for `<asp:Label>` and `<asp:Button>`, respectively. There is also a `<input type="hidden">` field with the name `__VIEWSTATE`. This encapsulates the state of the form as mentioned earlier. This information is used when the form is posted back to the server to recreate the user interface, keeping track of changes and so on. Note that the `<form>` element has been configured for this; it will post data back to `WebForm1.aspx` (specified in `action`) via an HTTP POST operation (specified in `method`). It has also been assigned the name `Form1`.

After clicking the button and seeing the text appear, check out the source HTML again (we added spacing for clarity):

```
<form name="Form1" method="post" action="WebForm1.aspx"
      id="Form1">
   <input type="hidden" name="__VIEWSTATE"
          value="dDwtOTk1MjE0NDA4O3Q8O2w8aTwxPjs+O2w8dDw7bDxpPDE
                 +Oz47bDx0PHA8cDxsPFRleHQ7O7jtsPEJ1dHRvbiBjbGlja2
                 VkITs+Pjs+Ozs+Oz4+Oz4+Oz4=" />
   <span id="resultLabel">Button clicked!</span><br>
   <input type="submit" name="triggerButton" value="Click Me"
          id="triggerButton" />
</form>
```

This time the value of the view state contains more information, because the HTML result relies on more than the default output from the ASP.NET page. In complex forms this can be a very long string indeed, but we shouldn't complain, as so much is done for us behind the scenes. We can almost forget about state management, keeping field values between posts, and so on.

The control palette

In this section we'll take a quick look at the available controls before we put more of them together into a full, and more interesting, application. We'll divide this section into Web server controls and validation controls. Note that we refer to properties in the control descriptions—in all cases the corresponding attribute for use in ASP.NET code is identically named. We haven't attempted to provide a complete reference here, so we've omitted many properties and included only the most frequently used ones.

Web server controls

Almost all the Web server controls inherit from `System.Web.UI.WebControls.WebControl`, which in turn inherits from `System.Web.UI.Control`. Those that don't use this inheritance instead derive either directly from `Control` or from a more specialized base class that derives (eventually) from `Control`. As such the Web server controls have many common properties and events that we can use if required. There are quite a few of these, so we won't attempt to cover them all, just as with the properties and events of the Web server controls themselves.

Many of the frequently used inherited properties are those that deal with display style. This can be controlled simply, using properties such as `ForeColor`, `BackColor`, `Font`, and so on, but can also be controlled using cascading style sheet (CSS) classes. This is achieved by setting the string property `CssClass` to the name of a CSS class in a separate file. Other notable properties include `Width` and `Height` to size a control, `AccessKey` and `TabIndex` to ease user interaction, and `Enabled` to set whether the control's functionality is activated in the Web Form.

We are likely to use the inherited `Load` event most often, to perform initialization on a control, and `PreRender`, to perform last-minute modifications before HTML is output by the control.

There are plenty more events and properties for us to use, and we'll see many of these in more detail in Chapter 27. The following table describes the Web server controls in detail.

Control	Description
PlaceHolder	This control doesn't render any output, but can be handy for grouping other controls together, or for adding controls programmatically to a given location. Contained controls can be accessed using the Controls property.
Label	Simple text display; use the Text property to set and programmatically modify displayed text.
Literal	Performs the same function as Label, but has no styling properties, just a Text one.
Xml	A more complicated text display control, used for displaying XML content, which may be transformed using an XSLT style sheet. The XML content is set using one of the Document, DocumentContent, or DocumentSource properties (depending on the format of the original XML), and the XSLT style sheet (optional) using either Transform or TransformSource.
TextBox	Provides a text box that users can edit. Use the Text property to access the entered data, and the TextChanged event to act on selection changes on postback. If automatic postback is required (as opposed to using a button) set the AutoPostBack property to true.
DropDownList	Allows the user to select one of a list of choices, either by choosing it directly from a list or typing the first letter or two. Use the Items property to set the item list (this is a ListItemCollection class containing ListItem objects) and the SelectedItem and SelectedIndex properties to determine what is selected. The SelectedIndexChanged event can be used to determine whether the selection has changed, and this control also has an AutoPostBack property so that this selection change will trigger a postback operation.
ListBox	Allows the user to make one or more selections from a list. Set SelectionMode to Multiple or Single to specify how many items can be selected at once, and Rows to determine how many items to display. Other properties and events as for DropDownList.
Image	Displays an image. Use ImageUrl for the image reference, and AlternateText to provide text if the image fails to load.
AdRotator	Displays several images in succession, with a different one displayed after each server round trip. Use the AdvertisementFile property to specify the XML file describing the possible images and the AdCreated event to perform processing before each image is sent back. You can also use the Target property to name a window to open when an image is clicked.
CheckBox	Displays a box that can be checked or unchecked. The state is stored in the Boolean property Checked, and the text associated with the check box in Text. The AutoPostBack property can be used to initiate automatic postback and the CheckedChanged event to act on changes.

Control	Description
CheckBoxList	Creates a group of check boxes. Properties and events are identical to other list controls, such as DropDownList.
RadioButton	Displays a button that can be turned on or off. Generally these are grouped such that only one in the group is active at any time. Use the GroupName property to link RadioButton controls into a group. Other properties and events are as per CheckBox.
RadioButtonList	Creates a group of radio buttons where only one button in the group can be selected at a time. Properties and events are as per other list controls.
Calendar	Allows the user to select a date from a graphical calendar display. This control has many style-related properties, but essential functionality can be achieved using the SelectedDate and VisibleDate properties (of type System.DateTime) to get access to the date selected by the user and the month to display (which will always contain VisibleDate). The key event to hook up to is SelectionChanged. Postback from this control is automatic.
Button	Adds a standard button for the user to click. Use the Text property for text on the button, and the Click event to respond to clicks (server postback is automatic). You can also use the Command event to respond to clicks, which gives access to additional CommandName and CommandArgument properties on receipt.
LinkButton	Is identical to Button, but displays button as a hyperlink.
ImageButton	Displays an image that doubles as a clickable button. Properties and events are inherited from Button and Image.
HyperLink	Adds an HTML hyperlink. Set the destination with NavigateUrl and the text to display with Text. You can also use ImageUrl to specify an image for the link and Target to specify the browser window to use. This control has no non-standard events, so use a LinkButton instead if additional processing is required when the link is followed.
Table	Specifies a table. Use this in conjunction with TableRow and TableCell at design time or programmatically assign rows using the Rows property of type TableRowCollection. You can also use this property for runtime modifications. This control has several styling properties unique to tables, as do TableRow and TableCell.
TableRow	Specifies a row within a Table. The key property is Cells, which is a TableCellCollection class containing TableCell objects.
TableCell	Specifies an individual cell within a TableRow. Use Text to set the text to display, Wrap to determine whether to wrap text, and RowSpan and ColumnSpan to set how much of the table is covered by the cell.
Panel	Adds a container for other controls. You can use HorizontalAlign and Wrap to specify how the contents are arranged.

Table continued on following page

Control	Description
Repeater	Used to output data from a data query. Allows greater flexibility when using templates. We'll look at this control in detail later in this chapter.
DataList	Similar to the Repeater control, but provides more flexibility when it comes to arranging data and formatting. Can automatically render a table, which may be editable, for example. We'll discuss this control later in this chapter.
DataGrid	Similar to Repeater and DataList with a few extra facilities, such as sorting.

Validation controls

Validation controls provide a method of validating user input without (in most cases) writing any code at all. Whenever postback is initiated each validation control checks the control it is validating and changes its IsValid property accordingly. If this property is false then the user input for the validated control has failed validation. The page containing all the controls also has an IsValid property—if any of the validation controls has its version of this property set to false then this will be false also. We can check this property from our server-side code and act on it.

Validation controls also have another function. Not only do they validate controls at runtime, they can also output helpful hints to users. Simply setting the ErrorMessage property to the text you want means users will see it when they attempt to post back invalid data.

The text stored in ErrorMessage may be output at the point where the validation control is located, or at a separate point, along with the messages from all other validation controls on a page. This latter behavior is achieved using the ValidationSummary control, which displays all error messages along with additional text as required.

On browsers that support it, these controls even generate client-side JavaScript functions to streamline their validation behavior. This means that in some cases postback won't even occur, because the validation controls can prevent this under certain circumstances and output error messages without involving the server.

All validation controls inherit from BaseValidator, and thus share several important properties. Perhaps the most important is the ErrorMessage property discussed earlier, the ControlToValidate property coming in a close second. This property specifies the programmatic ID of the control that is being validated. Another important property is Display, which determines whether to place text at the validation summary position (if set to none), or at the validator position. We also have the choice to make space for the error message even when it's not being displayed (set Display to Static) or to dynamically allocate space when required, which might shift page contents around slightly (set Display to Dynamic). The following table describes the validation controls.

Server control example

In this example we create the framework for a Web application, a meeting room booking tool. (As with the other examples in this book, you can download the sample application and code from the Wrox Web site at www.wrox.com.) At first we include only the front end and simple event processing; later we will extend this example with ADO.NET and data binding to include server-side business logic.

Control	Description
RequiredFieldValidator	Used to check if the user has entered data in a control such as TextBox.
CompareValidator	Used to check that data entered fulfils simple requirements, by use of an operator set using the Operator property and a ValueToCompare property to validate against. Operator can be Equal, GreaterThan, GreaterThanEqual, LessThan, LessThanEqual, NotEqual, and DataTypeCheck. DataTypeCheck simply compares the data type of ValueToCompare with the data in the control to be validated. ValueToCompare is a string property, but is interpreted as different data types based on its contents.
RangeValidator	Validates that data in the control falls between MaximumValue and MinimumValue property values.
RegularExpressionValidator	Validates the contents of a field based on a regular expression stored in ValidationExpression. This can be useful for known sequences such as zip codes, phone numbers, IP numbers, and so on.
CustomValidator	Used to validate data in a control using a custom function. ClientValidationFunction is used to specify a client-side function used to validate a control (which means, unfortunately, that we can't use C#). This function should return a Boolean value indicating whether validation was successful. Alternatively, we can use the ServerValidate event to specify a server-side function to use for validation. This function is a bool type event handler that receives a string containing the data to validate instead of an EventArgs parameter. Return true if validation succeeds, otherwise false.
ValidationSummary	Displays validation errors for all validation controls that have an ErrorMessage set. The display can be formatted by setting the DisplayMode (BulletList, List, or SingleParagraph) and HeaderText properties. The display can be disabled by setting ShowSummary to false, and displayed in a pop-up message box by setting ShowMessageBox to true.

The Web Form we are going to create contains fields for user name, event name, meeting room, and attendees, along with a calendar to select a date (we're assuming for the purposes of this example that we are dealing with all-day events). We will include validation controls for all fields except the calendar, which we will validate on the server side, and provide a default date in case none has been entered.

For user interface (UI) testing we will also have a Label control on the form that we can use to display submission results.

For starters, create a new Web application project in Visual Studio .NET and call it PCSWebApp2. Next, design the form, which is generated using the following code in WebForm1.aspx (with auto-generated code not highlighted):

```
<%@ Page language="c#"
        Codebehind="WebForm1.aspx.cs"
        AutoEventWireup="false"
        Inherits="PCSWebApp2.WebForm1" %>
<!DOCTYPE HTML PUBLIC "-//W3C//DTD HTML 4.0 Transitional//EN" >

<html>
  <head>
    <title>WebForm1</title>
    <meta name="GENERATOR" Content="Microsoft Visual Studio .NET 7.1">
    <meta name="CODE_LANGUAGE" Content="C#">
    <meta name=vs_defaultClientScript content="JavaScript">
    <meta name=vs_targetSchema
          content="http://schemas.microsoft.com/intellisense/ie5">
  </head>
  <body MS_POSITIONING="GridLayout">

    <form id="Form1" method="post" runat="server">
      <h1 align="center">
        Enter details and set a day to initiate an event.
      </h1>
      <br>
```

After the title of the page (which is enclosed in HTML `<h1>` tags to get large, title-style text), the main body of the form is enclosed in an HTML `<table>`. We could use a Web server control table, but this introduces unnecessary complexity as we are using a table purely for formatting the display, not to be a dynamic UI element (an important point to bear in mind when designing Web Forms—don't add Web server controls unnecessarily). The table is divided into three columns: the first column holds simple text labels; the second column holds UI fields corresponding to the text labels (along with validation controls for these); and the third column contains a calendar control for date selection, which spans four rows. The fifth row contains a submission button spanning all columns, and the sixth row contains a `ValidationSummary` control to display error messages when required (all the other validation controls have `Display="None"`, since they will use this summary for display). Beneath the table is a simple label that we can use to display results for now, before we add database access later.

```
      <table bordercolor="#000000" cellspacing="0" cellpadding="8"
        rules="none" align="center" bgcolor="#fff99e" border="2"
        width="540">
        <tr>
          <td valign="top">Your Name:</td>
          <td valign="top">
            <asp:TextBox ID="nameBox" Runat="server" Width="160px" />
            <asp:RequiredFieldValidator ID="validateName"
              Runat="server" ErrorMessage="You must enter a name."
              ControlToValidate="nameBox" Display="None" />
          </td>
          <td valign="middle" rowspan="4">
            <asp:Calendar ID="calendar" Runat="server"
              BackColor="White" />
```

```
          </td>
      </tr>
      <tr>
        <td valign="top">Event Name:</td>
        <td valign="top">
          <asp:TextBox ID="eventBox" Runat="server" Width="160px" />
          <asp:RequiredFieldValidator ID="validateEvent"
              Runat="server"
              ErrorMessage="You must enter an event name."
              ControlToValidate="eventBox" Display="None" />
        </td>
      </tr>
      <tr>
```

Most of the ASP.NET code in this file is remarkably simple, and much can be learned simply by reading through it. Of particular note in this code is the way in which list items are attached to the controls for selecting a meeting room and multiple attendees for the event:

```
        <td valign="top">Meeting Room:</td>
        <td valign="top">
          <asp:DropDownList ID="roomList" Runat="server"
              Width="160px">
            <asp:ListItem Value="1">The Happy Room</asp:ListItem>
            <asp:ListItem Value="2">The Angry Room</asp:ListItem>
            <asp:ListItem Value="3">The Depressing
            Room</asp:ListItem>
            <asp:ListItem Value="4">The Funked Out
            Room</asp:ListItem>
          </asp:DropDownList>
          <asp:RequiredFieldValidator ID="validateRoom"
              Runat="server" ErrorMessage="You must select a room."
              ControlToValidate="roomList" Display="None" />
        </td>
      </tr>
      <tr>
        <td valign="top">Attendees:</td>
        <td valign="top">
          <asp:ListBox ID="attendeeList" Runat="server" Width="160px"
              SelectionMode="Multiple" Rows="6">
            <asp:ListItem Value="1">Bill Gates</asp:ListItem>
            <asp:ListItem Value="2">Monica Lewinsky</asp:ListItem>
            <asp:ListItem Value="3">Vincent Price</asp:ListItem>
            <asp:ListItem Value="4">Vlad the Impaler</asp:ListItem>
            <asp:ListItem Value="5">Iggy Pop</asp:ListItem>
            <asp:ListItem Value="6">William
            Shakespeare</asp:ListItem>
          </asp:ListBox>
```

Here we are associating `ListItem` objects with the two Web server controls. These objects are not Web server controls in their own right (they simply inherit from `System.Object`), which is why we don't need to use `Runat="server"` on them. When the page is processed the `<asp:ListItem>` entries are used to create `ListItem` objects, which are added to the `Items` collection of their parent list control. This makes it easier for us to initialize lists than having to write code for this ourselves (we'd have to create a

`ListItemCollection` object, add `ListItem` objects, and then pass the collection to the list control). Of course, we can still do all of this programmatically if we want.

```
            <asp:RequiredFieldValidator ID="validateAttendees"
                Runat="server"
                ErrorMessage="You must have at least one attendee."
                ControlToValidate="attendeeList" Display="None" />
        </td>
    </tr>
    <tr>
        <td align="center" colspan="3">
            <asp:Button ID="submitButton" Runat="server" Width="100%"
                Text="Submit meeting room request" />
        </td>
    </tr>
    <tr>
        <td align="center" colspan="3">
            <asp:ValidationSummary ID="validationSummary"
                Runat="server"
                HeaderText="Before submitting your request:" />
        </td>
    </tr>
    </table>
    <br>
    Results:
    <asp:Label Runat="server" ID="resultLabel" Text="None." />
    </form>
</body>
</html>
```

In Design view the form we have created looks like Figure 25-4. This is a fully functioning UI, which maintains its own state between server requests, and validates user input. Considering the brevity of the above code this is quite something. In fact, it leaves us with very little to do, at least for this example; we just have to specify the button click event for the submission button.

Actually, that's not quite true. So far we have no validation for the calendar control. All we have to do is give it an initial value. We can do this in the `Page_Load()` event handler for our page in the code-behind file:

```
    private void Page_Load(object sender, System.EventArgs e)
    {
        if (!this.IsPostBack)
        {
            calendar.SelectedDate = System.DateTime.Now;
        }
    }
```

Here we just select today's date as a starting point. Note that we first check to see if `Page_Load()` is being called as the result of a postback operation by checking the `IsPostBack` property of the page. If a postback is in progress this property will be `true` and we leave the selected date alone (we don't want to lose the user's selection, after all).

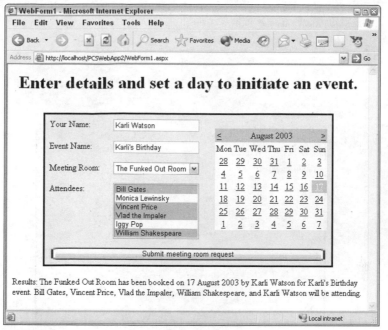

Figure 25-4

To add the button click handler simply double-click the button and add the following code:

```
private void submitButton_Click(object sender,
                                System.EventArgs e)
{
    if (this.IsValid)
    {
        resultLabel.Text = roomList.SelectedItem.Text +
            " has been booked on " +
            calendar.SelectedDate.ToLongDateString() +
            " by " + nameBox.Text + " for " +
            eventBox.Text + " event. ";
        foreach (ListItem attendee in attendeeList.Items)
        {
            if (attendee.Selected)
            {
                resultLabel.Text += attendee.Text + ", ";
            }
        }
        resultLabel.Text += " and " + nameBox.Text +
            " will be attending.";
    }
}
```

Here we just set the `resultLabel` control `Text` property to a result string, which will then appear below the main table. In IE the result of such a submission might look something like Figure 25-4, unless there are errors, in which case the `ValidationSummary` will activate instead, as shown in Figure 25-5.

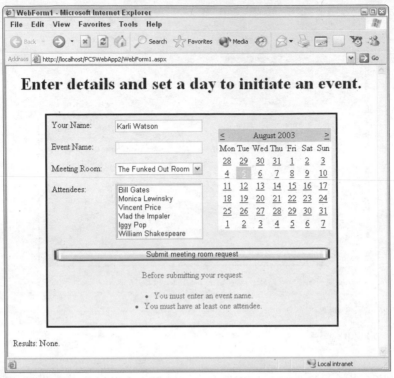

Figure 25-5

ADO.NET and Data Binding

The Web Form application we created in the previous section is perfectly functional, but only contains static data. In addition, the event booking process does not include persisting event data. In order to solve both of these problems we can make use of ADO.NET to access data stored in a database, such that we can store and retrieve event data along with the lists of rooms and attendees.

Data binding makes the process of retrieving data even easier. Controls such as list boxes (and some of the more specialized controls we'll look at a bit later) come enabled for this technique. They can be bound to any object that exposes an IEnumerable, ICollection, or IListSource interface, which includes DataTable objects.

In this section we will start by updating our event-booking application to be data-aware, and then move on to take a look at some of the other results we can achieve with data binding, using some of the other data-aware Web controls.

Updating the Event-Booking Application

To keep things separate from the last example, create a new Web application project called PCSWebApp3 and copy the code from the PCSWebApp2 application created earlier into the new application. Before we start on our new code, let's look at the database we will be accessing.

The database

For the purposes of this example we will use a Microsoft Access database called PCSWebApp3.mdb, which is part of the downloadable code for this book. For an enterprise-scale application it would make more sense to use a SQL Server database, but the techniques involved are practically identical and MS Access makes life a bit easier for testing. We will point out the differences in code as they occur.

The database provided contains three tables:

❑   Attendees, which contains a list of possible event attendees

❑   Rooms, which contains a list of possible rooms for events

❑   Events, which contains a list of booked events

Attendees

The Attendees table contains the following columns:

Column	Type	Notes
ID	AutoNumber, primary key	Attendee identification number
Name	Text, required, 50 chars	Name of attendee
Email	Text, optional, 50 chars	E-mail address of attendee

The supplied database includes entries for 20 attendees, all with their own (fictional) e-mail addresses. It is envisioned that in a more developed application e-mails could automatically be sent to attendees when a booking is made, but this is left to the reader as an optional exercise using techniques found elsewhere in this book.

Rooms

The Rooms table contains the following columns:

Column	Type	Notes
ID	AutoNumber, primary key	Room identification number
Room	Text, required, 50 chars	Name of room

20 records are supplied in the database.

Events

The Events table contains the following columns:

Column	Type	Notes
ID	AutoNumber, primary key	Event identification number
Name	Text, required, 255 chars	Name of event
Room	Number, required	ID of room for event
AttendeeList	Memo, required	List of attendee names
EventDate	Date/Time, required	Date of event

A few events are supplied in the downloadable database.

Binding to the database

The two controls we'd like to bind to data are attendeeList and roomList. To do this we have to set the DataSource properties of these controls to tables containing our data. Our code must load data into these tables and perform this binding at runtime. Both of these controls also have DataTextField and DataValueField properties that specify what columns to use for displaying list items and setting value properties, respectively. In both cases we can set these properties at design time and they will be used as soon as the DataSource property is set to populate the list items in the control.

Remove the existing entries from the ASP.NET code for these controls so that the declarations read as follows:

```
...
<asp:DropDownList ID="roomList" Runat="server"
    Width="160px" DataTextField="Room"
    DataValueField="ID"></asp:DropDownList>
...
<asp:ListBox ID="attendeeList" Runat="server" Width="160px"
    SelectionMode="Multiple" Rows="6"
    DataTextField="Name" DataValueField="ID"></asp:ListBox>
...
```

The next task is to create a connection to the database. There are several ways to do this (as discussed in Chapter 9). We'll hand-code it to keep things simple. Since we are using an Access database the provider type for this connection is the Microsoft Jet 4.0 OLE DB Provider, so we need to add a System.Data.OleDb.OleDbConnection object to our form called oleDbConnection1:

```
public class WebForm1 : System.Web.UI.Page
{
    ...
    protected System.Data.OleDb.OleDbConnection oleDbConnection1;
```

For a SQL Server connection we would add a SqlClient.SqlConnection object.

Next we add some code to `InitializeComponent()` to set the `ConnectionString` property of `oleDbConnection1` so it is all ready for us to use:

```
private void InitializeComponent()
{
    this.oleDbConnection1 = new System.Data.OleDb.OleDbConnection();
    ...
    this.oleDbConnection1.ConnectionString =
        @"Provider=Microsoft.Jet.OLEDB.4.0;Password="""";User ID=" +
        @"Admin;Data Source=" +
        @"C:\Inetpub\wwwroot\PCSWebApp3\PCSWebApp3.mdb";
```

We want to perform our data binding in the `Page_Load()` event handler, so that the controls are fully populated when we want to use them in other parts of our code. We will read data from the database regardless of whether a postback operation is in progress (even though the list controls will persist their contents via the viewstate) to ensure that we have access to all the data we might need, although we don't need to perform the data binding itself in a postback. This might seem slightly wasteful, but you can practice later adding additional logic to the code to optimize this behavior. Here we are concentrating on how to get things working, without going into too much detail.

All of our code will be placed in-between calling the `Open()` and `Close()` methods of our connection object:

```
private void Page_Load(object sender, System.EventArgs e)
{
    oleDbConnection1.Open();
    if (!this.IsPostBack)
    {
        calendar.SelectedDate = System.DateTime.Now;
    }
    oleDbConnection1.Close();
}
```

We'll see why the calendar date setting is left inside this postback-checking code shortly.

For our data exchange we need to use several objects in which to store our data. We can declare these at the class level so that we have access to them from other functions. We need a `DataSet` object to store the database information, three `OleDb.OleDbDataAdapter` objects to execute queries on the dataset, and a `DataTable` object to store our events for later access. Declare these as follows:

```
public class WebForm1 : System.Web.UI.Page
{
    ...
    protected System.Data.DataSet ds;
    protected System.Data.DataTable eventTable;
    protected System.Data.OleDb.OleDbDataAdapter daAttendees;
    protected System.Data.OleDb.OleDbDataAdapter daRooms;
    protected System.Data.OleDb.OleDbDataAdapter daEvents;
```

SQL Server versions of all the OLE DB objects exist, and their usage is identical.

Page_Load() now needs to create the DataSet object:

```
private void Page_Load(object sender, System.EventArgs e)
{
    oleDbConnection1.Open();
    ds = new DataSet();
```

Then we must assign the OleDbDataAdapter objects with queries and a link to the connection object:

```
    ds = new DataSet();
    daAttendees = new System.Data.OleDb.OleDbDataAdapter(
                    "SELECT * FROM Attendees",
                    oleDbConnection1);
    daRooms = new System.Data.OleDb.OleDbDataAdapter(
                    "SELECT * FROM Rooms", oleDbConnection1);
    daEvents = new System.Data.OleDb.OleDbDataAdapter(
                    "SELECT * FROM Events", oleDbConnection1);
```

Next we execute the queries using calls to Fill():

```
    daEvents = new System.Data.OleDb.OleDbDataAdapter(
                    "SELECT * FROM Events", oleDbConnection1);
    daAttendees.Fill(ds, "Attendees");
    daRooms.Fill(ds, "Rooms");
    daEvents.Fill(ds, "Events");
```

Now we come to the data binding itself. As mentioned earlier, this simply involves setting the DataSource property on our bound controls to the tables we want to bind to:

```
    daEvents.Fill(ds, "Events");
    attendeeList.DataSource = ds.Tables["Attendees"];
    roomList.DataSource = ds.Tables["Rooms"];
```

This sets the properties, but data binding itself won't occur until we call the DataBind() method of the form, which we'll do shortly. Before we do this we'll populate the DataTable object with the event table data:

```
    roomList.DataSource = ds.Tables["Rooms"];
    eventTable = ds.Tables["Events"];
```

We will only data bind if a postback is not in progress; otherwise, we will simply be refreshing data (which we're assuming is static in the database for the duration of an event-booking request). Data binding in a postback would also wipe the selections in the roomList and attendeeList controls. We could make a note of these before binding and then renew them, but it is simpler to call DataBind() in our existing if statement (this is the reason that this statement is kept in the region of code where the data connection is open):

```
    eventTable = ds.Tables["Events"];
    if (!this.IsPostBack)
    {
        calendar.SelectedDate = System.DateTime.Now;
        this.DataBind();
```

```
      }
   oleDbConnection1.Close();
}
```

Running the application now will result in the full attendee and room data being available from our data bound controls.

> Please note that in order for the code to run you might have to close any open connections to the database, either in Access or in Server Explorer. To do this simply right-click the data source in Server Explorer and choose Close.

Customizing the calendar control

Before we discuss adding events to the database let's modify our calendar display. It would be nice to display any day where a booking has previously been made in a different color, and prevent such days from being selectable. This requires modifying the way we set dates in the calendar, and the way day cells are displayed.

We'll start with date selection. There are three places where we need to check for dates where events are booked and modify the selection accordingly: when we set the initial date in Page_Load(), when the user attempts to select a date from the calendar, and when an event is booked and we wish to set a new date to prevent the user booking two events on the same day before selecting a new date. As this is going to be a common feature we might as well create a private method to perform this calculation. This method should accept a trial date as a parameter and return the date to use, which will either be the same date as the trial date, or the next available day after the trial date.

Add this method, getFreeDate(), to the code-behind file:

```
private System.DateTime getFreeDate(System.DateTime trialDate)
{
   if (eventTable.Rows.Count > 0)
   {
      System.DateTime testDate;
      bool trialDateOK = false;
      while (!trialDateOK)
      {
         trialDateOK = true;
         foreach (System.Data.DataRow testRow in eventTable.Rows)
         {
            testDate = (System.DateTime)testRow["EventDate"];
            if (testDate.Date == trialDate.Date)
            {
               trialDateOK = false;
               trialDate = trialDate.AddDays(1);
            }
         }
      }
   }
   return trialDate;
}
```

This simple code uses the `eventTable` object that we populated in `Page_Load()` to extract event data. First we check for the trivial case where no events have been booked, in which case we can just confirm the trial date by returning it. Next we iterate through the dates in the `Event` table comparing them with the trial date. If we find a match we add one day to the trial date and perform another search.

Extracting the date from the `DataTable` is remarkably simple:

```
testDate = (System.DateTime)testRow["EventDate"];
```

Casting the column data into `System.DateTime` works fine.

The first place we will use `getFreeDate()`, then, is back in `Page_Load()`. This simply means making a minor modification to the code that sets the calendar `SelectedDate` property:

```
if (!this.IsPostBack)
{
    System.DateTime trialDate = System.DateTime.Now;
    calendar.SelectedDate = getFreeDate(trialDate);
    this.DataBind();
}
```

Next we need to respond to date selection on the calendar. To do this we simply add an event handler for the `SelectionChanged` event of the calendar, and force the date to be checked against existing events. Double-click the calendar in the Designer and add this code:

```
private void calendar_SelectionChanged(object sender,
                                       System.EventArgs e)
{
    System.DateTime trialDate = calendar.SelectedDate;
    calendar.SelectedDate = getFreeDate(trialDate);
}
```

The code here is identical to that in `Page_Load()`.

The third place that we must perform this check is in response to the pressed booking button. We'll come back to this shortly, since we have several changes to make here.

Next we want to color the day cells of the calendar to signify existing events. To do this we add an event handler for the `DayRender` event of the calendar object. This event is raised each time an individual day is rendered, and gives us access to the cell object being displayed and the date of this cell through the `Cell` and `Date` properties of the `DayRenderEventArgs` parameter we receive in the handler function. We simply compare the date of the cell being rendered to the dates in our `eventTable` object, and color the cell using the `Cell.BackColor` property if there is a match:

```
protected void calendar_DayRender(object sender,
                System.Web.UI.WebControls.DayRenderEventArgs e)
{
    if (eventTable.Rows.Count > 0)
    {
        System.DateTime testDate;
        foreach (System.Data.DataRow testRow in eventTable.Rows)
```

```
        {
            testDate = (System.DateTime)testRow["EventDate"];
            if (testDate.Date == e.Day.Date)
            {
                e.Cell.BackColor = Color.Red;
            }
        }
    }
}
```

Here we are using red, which will give us a display along the lines of Figure 25-6, where March 15, 27, 28, 29, and 30 all contain events, and the user has selected March 17.

Figure 25-6

With the addition of the date-selection logic it is now impossible to select a day that is shown in red; if an attempt is made then a later date is selected instead. For example, selecting March 28 results in the selection of March 31.

Adding events to the database

The `submitButton_Click()` event handler currently assembles a string from the event characteristics and displays it in the `resultLabel` control. To add an event to the database we simply reformat the string created into a SQL `INSERT` query and execute it.

> *Note that in order to write to an Access database, the "ASPNET" user (which is the account that ASP.NET processes run under by default) must be explicitly given write permission to the file, which we can do using Windows Explorer. In more advanced situations you might want to access resources using other accounts, for example a domain account used to access a SQL Server instance elsewhere on a network. The capability to do this (via impersonation, COM+ Services, or other means) exists in ASP.NET, but is beyond the scope of this book.*

Much of the following code will therefore look familiar:

```
protected void submitButton_Click(object sender, System.EventArgs e)
{
    if (this.IsValid)
    {
        String attendees = "";
        foreach (ListItem attendee in attendeeList.Items)
        {
```

```
            if (attendee.Selected)
            {
                attendees += attendee.Text + " (" + attendee.Value
                            + "), ";
            }
        }
        attendees += " and " + nameBox.Text;
        String dateString =
            calendar.SelectedDate.Date.Date.ToShortDateString();
        String oleDbCommand = "INSERT INTO Events (Name, Room, " +
                            "AttendeeList, EventDate) VALUES ('" +
                            eventBox.Text + "', '" +
                            roomList.SelectedItem.Value + "', '" +
                            attendees + "', '" + dateString +
                            "')";
```

After we have created our SQL query string, we can use it to build an `OleDb.OleDbCommand` object:

```
        System.Data.OleDb.OleDbCommand insertCommand =
            new System.Data.OleDb.OleDbCommand(oleDbCommand,
                                            oleDbConnection1);
```

Next we reopen the connection that was closed in `Page_Load()` (again, this is perhaps not the most efficient way of doing things, but it works fine for demonstration purposes), and execute the query:

```
        oleDbConnection1.Open();
        int queryResult = insertCommand.ExecuteNonQuery();
```

`ExecuteNonQuery()` returns an integer representing how many table rows were affected by the query. If this is equal to 1 then we know that our insertion was successful. If so then we put a success message in `resultLabel`, execute a new query to repopulate `eventTable` and our dataset with our new list of events (we clear the dataset first, otherwise events will be duplicated), and change the calendar selection to a new, free, date:

```
        if (queryResult == 1)
        {
            resultLabel.Text = "Event Added.";
            daEvents = new System.Data.OleDb.OleDbDataAdapter(
                "SELECT * FROM Events", oleDbConnection1);
            ds.Clear();
            daEvents.Fill(ds, "Events");
            eventTable = ds.Tables["Events"];
            calendar.SelectedDate =
                getFreeDate(calendar.SelectedDate.AddDays(1));
        }
```

If `ExecuteNonQuery()` returns a number other than 1, we know that there has been a problem. For this example we won't worry too much about this, and simply display a failure notification in `resultLabel`:

```
        else
        {
            resultLabel.Text = "Event not added due to DB access "
                            + "problem.";
        }
```

Finally, we close the connection again and our data-aware version of the event booking application is complete:

```
            oleDbConnection1.Close();
        }
    }
```

Note that due to the syntax of the SQL INSERT query we must avoid using certain characters in the event name, such as apostrophes ("'"), because they will cause an error. It would be relatively easy to enforce a custom validation rule that prevented the user from using such characters, or to perform some type of character escaping before inserting data and after reading data, but the code for this is beyond the scope of this chapter.

More on Data Binding

As mentioned earlier in this chapter, the available Server Controls have three controls that deal with data display: `DataGrid`, `Repeater`, and `DataList`. These are all extremely useful when it comes to outputting data to a Web page, since they perform many tasks automatically that would otherwise require a fair amount of coding.

For starters, let's look at the easiest of these, `DataGrid`. Let's add an event-detail display to the bottom of the display of PCSWebApp3. This enables us to ignore database connections for now, since we have already configured our application for this access.

Add the following code to the bottom of the WebForm1.aspx in the PCSWebApp3 project:

```
        <br>Results:
        <asp:Label  ID=resultLabel Runat="server"
                Text="None."></asp:label>
        <br>
        <br>
        <asp:DataGrid Runat="server" ID="eventDetails1" />
        </form>
    </body>
</HTML>
```

Also, add the following to `Page_Load()` in WebForm1.aspx.cs:

```
        attendeeList.DataSource = ds.Tables["Attendees"];
        roomList.DataSource = ds.Tables["Rooms"];
        eventTable = ds.Tables["Events"];
        eventDetails1.DataSource = eventTable;
        if (!this.IsPostBack)
        {
            System.DateTime trialDate = System.DateTime.Now;
            calendar.SelectedDate = getFreeDate(trialDate);
            this.DataBind();
        }
        else
        {
            eventDetails1.DataBind();
        }
        oleDbConnection1.Close();
    }
```

Note that the event list may have changed between requests if another user has added an event, so we need to call `DataBind()` on the `DataGrid` to reflect these changes. Remember that calling `DataBind()` on the whole form will result in room and attendee selections being lost, so this is a fair compromise.

If you load the application in your Web browser you should see a list underneath the booking details section containing the full list of events, as shown in Figure 25-7.

ID	Name	Room	AttendeeList	EventDate
1	My Birthday	4	Iggy Pop (5), Sean Connery (7), Albert Einstein (10), George Clooney (14), Jules Verne (18), Robin Hood (20), and Karli Watson	17/09/2002 00:00:00
2	Dinner	1	Bill Gates (1), Monika Lewinsky (2), and Bruce Lee	05/08/2002 00:00:00
5	Discussion of darkness	6	Vlad the Impaler (4), Myra Hindley (13), and Beelzebub	29/10/2002 00:00:00
6	Christmas with Pals	9	Dr Frank N Furter (11), Bobby Davro (15), John F Kennedy (16), Stephen King (19), and Karli Watson	25/12/2002 00:00:00
7	Escape	17	Monika Lewinsky (2), Stephen King (19), and Spartacus	10/05/2002 00:00:00
8	Planetary Conquest	14	Bill Gates (1), Albert Einstein (10), Dr Frank N Furter (11), Bobby Davro (15), and Darth Vader	15/06/2002 00:00:00
9	Homecoming Celebration	7	William Shakespeare (6), Christopher Columbus (12), Robin Hood (20), and Ulysses	22/06/2002 00:00:00
10	Dalek Reunion Ball	12	Roger Moore (8), George Clooney (14), Bobby Davro (15), and Davros	12/06/2002 00:00:00
11	Romantic meal for two	13	George Clooney (14), and Donna Watson	29/03/2002 00:00:00
50	Book Launch	3	Bill Gates (1), William Shakespeare (6), Jules Verne (18), and Julian Skinner	06/04/2002 00:00:00
53	Tree Hugging	1	Vlad the Impaler (4), and Gary	16/05/2002 00:00:00

Figure 25-7

We can also make one further modification in `submitButton_Click()` to ensure that this data is updated when new records are added:

```
if (queryResult == 1)
{
    resultLabel.Text = "Event Added.";
    daEvents = new System.Data.OleDb.OleDbDataAdapter(
        "SELECT * FROM Events", oleDbConnection1);
    ds.Clear();
    daEvents.Fill(ds, "Events");
    eventTable = ds.Tables["Events"];
    calendar.SelectedDate =
        getFreeDate(calendar.SelectedDate.AddDays(1));
    eventDetails1.DataBind();
}
```

Note that we call `DataBind()` on `DataGrid`, not on `this`. This prevents all data-bound controls from being refreshed, which is unnecessary. All data-bindable controls support this method, which is normally called by the form if we call the top-level (`this`) `DataBind()` method.

As you might expect, the `DataGrid` control contains many properties that we can use to format the displayed data in a more user-friendly way, but we'll leave these for you to discover.

Data display with templates

The other two data display controls, Repeater and DataList, require you to use templates to format data for display. Templates, in an ASP.NET sense, are parameterized sections of HTML that are used as elements of output in certain controls. They enable us to customize exactly how data is output to the browser, and can result in professional-looking displays without too much effort.

There are several templates available to customize various aspects of list behavior, but the one template that is essential for both Repeater and DataList is <ItemTemplate>, which is used in the display of each data item. We declare this template (and all the others) inside the control declaration, for example:

```
<asp:DataList Runat="server" ... >
   <ItemTemplate>
      ...
   </ItemTemplate>
</asp:DataList>
```

Within template declarations we will normally want to output sections of HTML along with parameters from the data that is bound to the control. There is a special syntax that we can use to output such parameters:

```
<%# expression %>
```

The *expression* placeholder might be simply an expression binding the parameter to a page or control property, but is more likely to consist of a DataBinder.Eval() expression. This function can be used to output data from a table bound to a control simply by specifying the column, using the following syntax:

```
<%# DataBinder.Eval(Container.DataItem, "ColumnName") %>
```

There is also an optional third parameter that allows us to format the data returned, which has identical syntax to string formatting expressions used elsewhere. The following tables provide a list of available templates and when they are used.

Template	Description
<ItemTemplate>	Used for list items.
<HeaderTemplate>	Used for output before the list.
<FooterTemplate>	Used for output after the list.
<SeparatorTemplate>	Used between items in list.
<AlternatingItemTemplate>	Used for alternate items; can aid visibility.
<SelectedItemTemplate>	(DataList only) Used for selected items in the list.
<EditItemTemplate>	(DataList only) Used for list items that are edited.

The easiest way to understand how to use these is by way of an example, and we can use our existing data query in PCSWebApp3 to achieve this.

Using templates

We'll extend the table at the top of the page to contain a `DataList` displaying each of the events stored in the database. We'll make these events selectable such that details of any event can be displayed by clicking on its name.

The changes to the code in WebForm1.aspx in the PCSWebApp3 project are shown in the shaded area:

```
<tr>
  <td align="center" colspan="3">
    <asp:ValidationSummary ID="validationSummary"
     Runat="server"
     HeaderText="Before submitting your request:" />
  </td>
</tr>
<tr>
  <td align="left" colSpan="3" width="100%">
    <table cellspacing="4">
      <tr>
        <td width="40%" bgcolor="#ccffcc">
          <asp:DataList Runat="server" ID="eventDetails2"
           OnSelectedIndexChanged=
           "eventDetails2_SelectedIndexChanged">
            <ItemTemplate>
              <asp:LinkButton Runat="server"
               CommandName="Select" ForeColor="#0000ff"
               ID="Linkbutton1" CausesValidation="false">
                <%# DataBinder.Eval(Container.DataItem,
                                     "Name")%>
              </asp:LinkButton>
              <br>
            </ItemTemplate>
            <SelectedItemTemplate>
              <b>
                <%# DataBinder.Eval(Container.DataItem,
                                     "Name") %>
              </b>
              <br>
            </SelectedItemTemplate>
          </asp:DataList>
        </td>
        <td valign="top">
          <asp:Label Runat="server" ID="edName"
           Font-Name="Arial" Font-Bold="True"
           Font-Italic="True" Font-Size="14">
            Select an event to view details.
          </asp:Label>
          <br>
          <asp:Label Runat="server" ID="edDate" />
          <br>
          <asp:Label Runat="server" ID="edRoom" />
          <br>
          <asp:Label Runat="server" ID="edAttendees" />
        </td>
```

```
            </tr>
          </table>
        </td>
      </tr>
    </table>
```

Here we have added a new table row containing a table with a `DataList` control in one column and a detail view in the other. The detail view is simply four labels for event properties, one of which contains the text "Select an event to view details" when no event is selected (the situation when the form is first loaded).

The `DataList` uses `<ItemTemplate>` and `<SelectedItemTemplate>` to display event details. To facilitate selection we raise a `Select` command from the event name link rendered in `<ItemTemplate>`, which automatically changes the selection. We also use the `OnSelectedIndexChanged` event, triggered when the `Select` command changes the selection, to populate the event detail labels. The event handler we get when we double-click `eventDetails2` in the Designer is shown in the following code. You'll need to change the protection level of the method from `private` to `protected`. (Note that we need to `DataBind()` first to update the selection.)

```
protected void eventDetails2_SelectedIndexChanged(object sender,
                                        System.EventArgs e)
{
    eventDetails2.DataBind();
    DataRow selectedEventRow =
        eventTable.Rows[eventDetails2.SelectedIndex];
    edName.Text = (string)selectedEventRow["Name"];
    edDate.Text = "<b>Date:</b> " +
      ((DateTime)selectedEventRow["EventDate"]).ToLongDateString();
    edAttendees.Text = "<b>Attendees:</b> " +
        (string)selectedEventRow["AttendeeList"];
    DataRow selectedEventRoomRow =
        ds.Tables["Rooms"].Rows[(int)selectedEventRow["Room"] - 1];
    edRoom.Text = "<b>Room:</b> " + selectedEventRoomRow["Room"];
}
```

This uses data in `ds` and `eventTable` to populate the details.

As with the `DataGrid` control we used earlier, we need to set the data for `eventDetails2` and bind in `Page_Load()`:

```
eventDetails1.DataSource = eventTable;
eventDetails2.DataSource = eventTable;
...
    eventDetails1.DataBind();
    eventDetails2.DataBind();
```

and re-bind in `submitButton_Click()`:

```
    eventDetails1.DataBind();
    eventDetails2.DataBind();
```

Now event details are available in the table, as shown in Figure 25-8.

Figure 25-8

There is *much* more that we can do with templates and data-bound controls in general, enough in fact to fill a whole book. However, this should be enough to get you started with your experimentation.

Application Configuration

One thing that we alluded to throughout this chapter is the existence of a conceptual application containing Web pages and configuration settings. This is an important concept to grasp, especially when configuring your Web site for multiple concurrent users.

A few notes on terminology and application lifetime are necessary here. An *application* is defined as all files in your project, and is configured by the Web.config file. An Application object is created when an application is started for the first time, which will be when the first HTTP request arrives. Also at this time the Application_Start event is triggered and a pool of HttpApplication instances is created. Each incoming request receives one of these instances, which performs request processing. Note that this means HttpApplication objects do not need to cope with concurrent access, unlike the global

Application object. When all HttpApplication instances finish their work the Application_End event fires and the application terminates, destroying the Application object.

The event handlers for the events mentioned earlier (along with handlers for all other events discussed in this chapter) must be defined in the Global.asax file, which contains blanks for you to fill in; for example:

```
protected void Application_Start(Object sender, EventArgs e)
{
}
```

When an individual user accesses the Web application a *session* is started. Similar to the application, this involves the creation of a user-specific Session object, along with the triggering of a Session_Start event. Within a session individual *requests* trigger Application_BeginRequest and Application_EndRequest events. These can occur several times over the scope of a session as different resources within the application are accessed. Individual sessions can be terminated manually, or will time out if no further requests are received. Session termination triggers a Session_End event and the destruction of the Session object.

Against the background of this process, there are several things we can do to streamline our application. Consider our sample application in this chapter. Every time our .aspx page is accessed a recordset is populated with the contents of PCSWebApp3.mdb. This recordset is only ever used for reading data, as the method of inserting events into the database is different. In cases like this we could populate the recordset in the Application_Start event handler and make it available to all users. The only time we would need to refresh the recordset would be if an event were added. This will drastically improve performance with multiple users, as in most requests no database access will be required.

Another technique we can use is to store session-level information for use by individual users across requests. This might include user-specific information extracted from a data store when the user first connects, and available until the user ceases to submit requests or logs out.

These techniques are beyond the scope of this book (and you might want to consult *Professional ASP.NET 1.1* [ISBN 0-7645-5890-0] for details), but it helps to have a broad understanding of the processes. In the next chapter, dealing with Web Services, we will see some of these techniques in action.

Summary

This chapter has provided an overview of Web application creation with ASP.NET. We have seen how we can use C# in combination with Web server controls to provide a truly rich development environment. We have developed an event booking sample application to illustrate many of the techniques available, such as the variety of server controls that exist, and data binding with ADO.NET.

In the next two chapters we will cover two more important Web topics: Web services and Custom Controls. We will continue to develop our sample application, taking it in radically different directions to illustrate the tools at our disposal.

26

Web Services

Web services are a new way of performing remote method calls over HTTP that can make use of *SOAP* (*Simple Object Access Protocol*). In the past this issue has been fraught with difficulty, as anyone who has any DCOM (Distributed COM) experience knows. The act of instantiating an object on a remote server, calling a method, and obtaining the result was far from simple—and the necessary configuration was even trickier.

SOAP simplifies matters immensely. This technology is an XML-based standard that details how method calls may be made over HTTP in a reproducible manner. A remote SOAP server is capable of understanding these calls and performing all the hard work for us, such as instantiating the required object, making the call, and returning a SOAP-formatted response to the client.

.NET Framework makes it very easy for us to make use of all this. As with ASP.NET, we are able to use the full array of C# and .NET techniques on the server, but (perhaps more importantly) the simple consumption of Web services can be achieved from any platform with HTTP access to the server. In other words, it is conceivable that Linux code could, for example, use .NET Web Services, or even Internet-enabled fridges.

In addition, Web services can be completely described using *WSDL* (*Web Service Description Language*), allowing dynamic discovery of Web services at runtime. WSDL provides descriptions of all methods (along with the types required to call them) using XML with XML schemas. There are a wide variety of types available to Web services, which range from simple primitive types to full `DataSet` objects, such that full in-memory databases can be marshaled to a client, which can result in a dramatic reduction in load on a database server.

In this chapter we will:

❑ Look at the syntax of SOAP and WSDL, then move on to see how they are used by Web services.

❑ Discuss how to expose and consume Web services.

❑ Work through a complete example building on the event-booking application from Chapter 25 to illustrate the use of Web services.

❑ Discuss how to exchange data using SOAP Headers.

SOAP

As mentioned above, one method used to exchange data with Web services is SOAP. This technology has had a lot of press, especially since Microsoft decided to adopt it for use in the .NET Framework. Now, though, the excitement seems to be dying down a bit as the SOAP specification is finalized. When you think about it, finding out exactly how SOAP works is a bit like finding out about how HTTP works— interesting, but not essential. Most of the time we never have to worry about the format of the exchanges made with Web services; they just happen, we get the results we want, and everyone is happy.

For this reason we won't go into a huge amount of depth in this section, but we will see some simple SOAP requests and responses so you can get a feel for what is going on under the hood.

Let's imagine that we want to call a method in a Web service with the following signature:

```
int DoSomething(string stringParam, int intParam)
```

The SOAP headers and body required for this are shown in the following code, with the address of the Web service (more on this later) at the top:

```
POST /SomeLocation/myWebService.asmx HTTP/1.1
Host: karlivaio
Content-Type: text/xml; charset=utf-8
Content-Length: length
SOAPAction: "http://tempuri.org/DoSomething"
<?xml version="1.0" encoding="utf-8"?>
<soap:Envelope xmlns:xsi="http://www.w3.org/2001/XMLSchema-instance"
               xmlns:xsd="http://www.w3.org/2001/XMLSchema"
               xmlns:soap="http://schemas.xmlsoap.org/soap/envelope/">
   <soap:Body>
      <DoSomething xmlns="http://tempuri.org/">
         <stringParam>string</stringParam>
         <intParam>int</intParam>
      </DoSomething>
   </soap:Body>
</soap:Envelope>
```

The `length` parameter here specifies the total byte size of the content, and will vary depending on the values sent in the `string` and `int` parameters.

The `soap` namespace referenced here defines various elements that we use to build our message. When we send this over HTTP the actual data sent is slightly different (but related). For example, we could call the above method using the simple GET method:

```
GET /PCSWebSrv1/Service1.asmx/DoSomething?stringParam=string&intParam=int HTTP/1.1
Host: hostname
```

The SOAP response of this method is as follows:

```
HTTP/1.1 200 OK
Content-Type: text/xml; charset=utf-8
Content-Length: length
<?xml version="1.0" encoding="utf-8"?>
<soap:Envelope xmlns:xsi="http://www.w3.org/2001/XMLSchema-instance"
               xmlns:xsd="http://www.w3.org/2001/XMLSchema"
               xmlns:soap="http://schemas.xmlsoap.org/soap/envelope/">
  <soap:Body>
    <DoSomethingResponse xmlns="http://tempuri.org/">
      <DoSomethingResult>int</DoSomethingResult>
    </DoSomethingResponse>
  </soap:Body>
</soap:Envelope>
```

where `length` varies depending on to the contents, in this case `int`.

The actual response over HTTP is simpler, as shown in this example:

```
HTTP/1.1 200 OK
Content-Type: text/xml; charset=utf-8
Content-Length: length
<?xml version="1.0"?>
<int xmlns="http://tempuri.org/">int</int>
```

This is a far simpler XML format.

As discussed at the start of this section, the beauty of all this is that we can ignore it completely. It is only if we want to do something really odd that the exact syntax becomes important.

WSDL

WSDL completely describes Web services, the methods available, and the various ways of calling these methods. The exact details of this process won't really benefit us that much, but a general understanding is useful.

WSDL is another fully XML-compliant syntax, and specifies Web services by the methods available, the types used by these methods, the formats of request and response messages sent to and from methods via various protocols (pure SOAP, HTTP GET, and so on), and various bindings between the above.

Perhaps the most important part of a WSDL file is the type-definition section. This section uses XML schemas to describe the format for data exchange with the XML elements that can be used, and their relationships.

For example, the Web service method used as an example in the last section:

```
int DoSomething(string stringParam, int intParam)
```

would have types declared for the request as follows:

```xml
<?xml version="1.0" ?>
<definitions xmlns:http="http://schemas.xmlsoap.org/wsdl/http/"
             xmlns:soap="http://schemas.xmlsoap.org/wsdl/soap/"
             xmlns:s="http://www.w3.org/2001/XMLSchema"
             ...other namespaces...>
   <types>
      <s:schema elementFormDefault="qualified"
                targetNamespace="http://tempuri.org/">
         <s:element name="DoSomething">
            <s:complexType>
               <s:sequence>
                  <s:element minOccurs="0" maxOccurs="1" name="stringParam"
                             type="s:string" />
                  <s:element minOccurs="1" maxOccurs="1" name="intParam"
                             type="s:int" />
               </s:sequence>
            </s:complexType>
         </s:element>
         <s:element name="DoSomethingResponse">
            <s:complexType>
               <s:sequence>
                  <s:element minOccurs="1" maxOccurs="1" name="DoSomethingResult"
                             type="s:int" />
               </s:sequence>
            </s:complexType>
         </s:element>
         <s:element name="int" type="s:int" />
      </s:schema>
   </types>
   ...other definitions...
</definitions>
```

These types are all that are required for the SOAP and HTTP requests and responses we saw earlier, and are bound to these operations later in the file. All the types are specified using standard XML schema syntax, for example:

```xml
<s:element name="DoSomethingResponse">
   <s:complexType>
      <s:sequence>
         <s:element minOccurs="1" maxOccurs="1" name="DoSomethingResult"
                    type="s:int" />
      </s:sequence>
   </s:complexType>
</s:element>
```

This specifies that an element called DoSomethingResponse has a child element called DoSomething Result that contains an integer. This integer must occur 0 or 1 times, meaning that it can be omitted.

If we have access to the WSDL for a Web service then we can use it. As we will see shortly, this isn't that difficult to do.

After this brief look at SOAP and WSDL it's time to move on to discuss how we create and consume Web services.

Web Services

Our discussion of Web services is divided into two subsections:

- ❑ "Exposing Web Services," which concerns writing Web services and placing them on Web servers.
- ❑ "Consuming Web Services," which concerns using the services you design on a client.

Exposing Web Services

Web services are exposed by placing code either directly into .asmx files or by referencing Web service classes from these files. As with ASP.NET pages, creating a Web service in Visual Studio .NET uses the latter method, and we will too for demonstration purposes.

Create a Web service project and call it PCSWebSrv1 (see Figure 26-1). Creating a Web service project generates a similar set of files as creating a Web application project. In fact, the only difference is that instead of a file called WebForm1.aspx, a file called Service1.asmx is created.

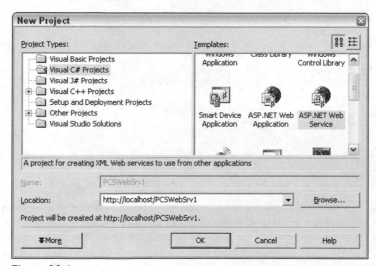

Figure 26-1

The code in Service1.asmx isn't directly accessible through Visual Studio .NET, but inspection with Notepad reveals the following single line of code:

```
<%@ WebService Language="c#" Codebehind="Service1.asmx.cs"
    Class="PCSWebSrv1.Service1" %>
```

This references the code file that we can see in Visual Studio .NET, Service1.asmx.cs, accessible by right-clicking on Service1.asmx in the Solution Explorer and selecting View Code. The following listing shows the generated code, with comments removed for brevity:

```
using System;
using System.Collections;
using System.ComponentModel;
using System.Data;
using System.Diagnostics;
using System.Web;
using System.Web.Services;

namespace PCSWebSrv1
{
    public class Service1 : System.Web.Services.WebService
    {
        public Service1()
        {
            InitializeComponent();
        }
        #region Component Designer generated code
        private IContainer components = null;

        private void InitializeComponent()
        {
        }

        protected override void Dispose(bool disposing)
        {
            if (disposing && components != null)
            {
                components.Dispose();
            }
            base.Dispose(disposing);
        }
        #endregion
    }
}
```

This code contains several standard namespace references, and defines the `PCSWebSrv1` namespace. The namespace contains the definition of the Web service class `Service1` (which is referenced in Service1.asmx), descended from `System.Web.Services.WebService`. It also contains similar code to that found in the ASP.NET page code-behind file, which is discussed in Chapter 25. This code is required in order to design Web services in Visual Studio .NET, part of which is a private member that will contain any components that can be added to the Web service. In order for the Web service class to free resources properly there is also a `Dispose()` method, which cleans up any components in this collection. It is now up to us to provide additional methods on this Web service class.

Adding a method accessible through the Web service simply requires defining the method as `public` and giving it the `WebMethod` attribute. This attribute simply labels the methods we want to be accessible. We'll look at the types we can use for the return type and parameters shortly, but for now add the following method:

```
[WebMethod]
public String CanWeFixIt()
{
    return "Yes we can!";
}
```

Now compile the project.

To see whether everything works, point your Web browser at Service1.asmx (if you run the project you'll be taken directly to this page), as shown in Figure 26-2.

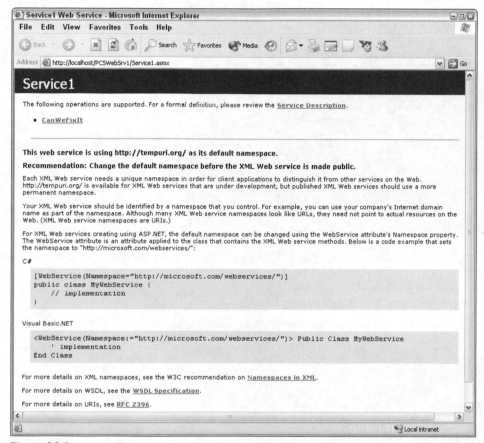

Figure 26-2

Most of the text shown in the browser concerns the fact that the Web service namespace is set to `http://tempuri.org/`. This isn't a problem during development, although (as the text says) it should be changed later on. This can be done using the `WebService` attribute as shown. For now, though, we'll leave things as they are.

Clicking the method name gives us information about the SOAP request and response, as well as examples of how the request and response will look using the HTTP GET and HTTP POST methods. We can also test the method by clicking the Invoke button. If the method requires simple parameters we can enter these on this form as well. If we do this we will see the XML returned by the method call:

```
<?xml version="1.0" encoding="utf-8"?>
<string xmlns="http://tempuri.org/">Yes we can!</string>
```

This demonstrates that our method is working perfectly.

Following the Service Description link from the browser screen shown in Figure 26-2 allows us to view the WSDL description of the Web service. The most important part is the description of the element types for requests and responses:

```
<types>
    <s:schema elementFormDefault="qualified"
              targetNamespace="http://tempuri.org/">
        <s:element name="CanWeFixIt">
            <s:complexType />
        </s:element>
        <s:element name="CanWeFixItResponse">
            <s:complexType>
                <s:sequence>
                    <s:element minOccurs="0" maxOccurs="1" name="CanWeFixItResult"
                               type="s:string" />
                </s:sequence>
            </s:complexType>
        </s:element>
    </s:schema>
</types>
```

The description also contains descriptions of the types required for requests and responses, as well as various bindings for the service, making it quite a long file.

Types available for Web services

Web services can be used to exchange any of the following types:

String	Char	Byte
Boolean	Int16	Int32
Int64	UInt16	UInt32
UInt64	Single	Double
Guid	Decimal	DateTime
XmlQualifiedName	Class	struct
XmlNode	DataSet	enum

Arrays of all these types are also allowed. Note also that only public properties and fields of Class and struct types are marshaled.

Consuming Web Services

Now that we know how to create Web services, we'll look at how to use them. To do this we need to generate a proxy class in our code that knows how to communicate with a given Web service. Any calls from our code to the Web service will go through this proxy, which looks identical to the Web service, giving our code the illusion that we have a local copy of it. In actual fact there is a lot of HTTP communication going on, but we are shielded from the details. There are two ways of doing this. We can either use the WSDL.exe command line tool or the Add Web Reference menu option in Visual Studio .NET.

Using WSDL.exe from the command line generates a .cs file containing a proxy class, based on the WSDL description of the Web service. We specify this using the URL of the Web service, for example:

```
WSDL http://localhost/PCSWebSrv1/Service1.asmx?WSDL
```

This generates a proxy class for the example from the last section in a file called Service1.cs. The class will be named after the Web service, in this case `Service1`, and contain methods that call identically named methods of the service. To use this class we simply add the .cs file generated to a project and use code along the lines of:

```
Service1 myService = new Service1();
String result = myService.CanWeFixIt();
```

By default the class generated is placed in the root namespace, so no `using` statement is necessary, but we can specify a different namespace to use with the `/n:<namespace>` command-line option of WSDL.exe.

This technique works fine but can be annoying to continually redo if the service is being developed and changing continuously. Of course, it could be executed in the build options for a project in order to automatically update the generated proxy before each compile, but there is a better way.

We'll illustrate this better way by creating a client for the example in the last section, in a new Web application called PCSWebClient1. Create this project now and replace the existing `form` declaration in the .aspx page generated with the following code:

```
<form method="post" runat="server">
   <asp:Label Runat="server" ID="resultLabel"/><br>
   <asp:Button Runat="server" ID="triggerButton"
               Text="Invoke CanWeFixIt()"/>
</form>
```

We'll bind the button-click event handler to the Web service shortly. First we must add a reference to the Web service to our project. To do this, right-click on the new client project in the Solution Explorer and select the Add Web Reference option. In the window that appears type in the URL of the Web service Service1.asmx file, or use the Web services on the local machine link to find it automatically, as shown in Figure 26-3.

From here we can add a reference with the Add Reference button. First, though, change the default entry for Web reference name from `localhost` to `myWebService`. Pressing the Add Reference button now adds `myWebService` to the Web References section of the project in Solution Explorer. When showing hidden files in Solution Explorer, we can see that the files Reference.map, Reference.cs, Service1.disco, and Service1.wsdl have been added to the project.

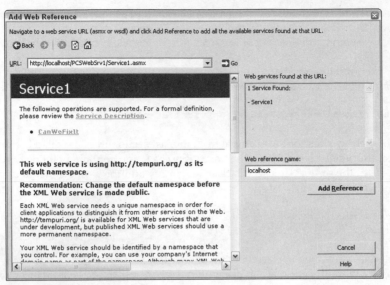

Figure 26-3

The Web Reference name, `myWebService`, is also the namespace we need to reference to use the proxy class that has been created for us. Add the following `using` statement to our code in WebForm1.aspx.cs:

```
using PCSWebClient1.myWebService;
```

Now we can use the service in our class without fully qualifying its name.

Add an event handler to the button on the form (double-click the button) with the following code:

```
private void triggerButton_Click(object sender, System.EventArgs e)
{
    Service1 myService = new Service1();
    resultLabel.Text = myService.CanWeFixIt();
}
```

Running the application and clicking the button displays `CanWeFixIt()` in the browser window.

This Web service might change later, but with this method we can simply right-click on the Web reference folder in the Server Explorer and select Update Web Reference. This generates a new proxy class for us to use.

Extending the Event-Booking Example

Now that we know the basics of creating and consuming Web services, let's apply our knowledge to extending the event-booking application from Chapter 25. Specifically, we extract the database access aspects from the application and place them into a Web service. This Web service has two methods:

❑ GetData(), which returns a DataSet class containing all three tables in the PCSWebApp3.mdb database.

❑ AddEvent(), which adds an event and returns an updated version of DataSet that includes the change.

In addition, we'll design the Web service with some of the load-reducing techniques from Chapter 25 in mind. Specifically, we store DataSet at the application level in the Web service application. This means that multiple requests for the data won't require additional database requests. The data in this application-level DataSet class will only be refreshed when new data is added to the database. This means that changes made to the database by other means, such as manual editing, will *not* be reflected in DataSet. Still, as long as we know that our Web service is the only application with direct access to the data we have nothing to worry about.

The Event-Booking Web Service

Create a new Web service project in Visual Studio .NET and call it PCSWebSrv2. First we add to this project some code in the Application_Start() handler in Global.asax.cs. We want to load all the data in PCSWebApp3.mdb into a dataset and store it. This mostly involves code that we've already seen, since getting the database into a DataSet is something we've already done. In fact, we can copy all the code we need from WebForm1.aspx.cs in PCSWebApp3 from Chapter 25—including the database connection string in InitializeComponent() (which we won't show here because yours is likely to be different)— with only a few modifications:

```
protected void Application_Start(Object sender, EventArgs e)
{
    System.Data.DataSet ds;
    System.Data.OleDb.OleDbConnection oleDbConnection1;
    System.Data.OleDb.OleDbDataAdapter daAttendees;
    System.Data.OleDb.OleDbDataAdapter daRooms;
    System.Data.OleDb.OleDbDataAdapter daEvents;
    oleDbConnection1 = new System.Data.OleDb.OleDbConnection();
    oleDbConnection1.ConnectionString = @" ... ";
    oleDbConnection1.Open();
    ds = new DataSet();
    daAttendees = new System.Data.OleDb.OleDbDataAdapter(
                    "SELECT * FROM Attendees", oleDbConnection1);
    daRooms = new System.Data.OleDb.OleDbDataAdapter(
                    "SELECT * FROM Rooms", oleDbConnection1);
    daEvents = new System.Data.OleDb.OleDbDataAdapter(
                    "SELECT * FROM Events", oleDbConnection1);
    daAttendees.Fill(ds, "Attendees");
    daRooms.Fill(ds, "Rooms");
    daEvents.Fill(ds, "Events");
    oleDbConnection1.Close();
    Application["ds"] = ds;
}
```

The important code to note here is in the last line. Application (and Session) objects have a collection of name-value pairs that we can use to store data. Here we are creating a name in the Application store called ds, which takes the serialized value of ds DataSet containing the Attendees, Rooms, and Events tables from our database. This value will be accessible to all instances of the Web service at any time.

919

In order for the previous code to work we also need to add a reference to the `System.Data` namespace to Global.asax.cs:

```
...
using System.Data;
```

This technique is very useful for read-only data since multiple threads will be able to access it, reducing the load on our database. Note, however, that the `Events` table is likely to change, and we'll have to update the application-level `DataSet` class when this happens. We'll look at this shortly.

Next we must add the `GetData()` method to our service in Service1.asmx.cs:

```
[WebMethod]
public DataSet GetData()
{
    return (DataSet) Application["ds"];
}
```

This uses the same syntax as `Application_Load()` to access `DataSet`, which we simply cast to the correct type and return.

The `AddEvent()` method is slightly more complicated. Conceptually, we need to do the following:

❑   Accept event data from the client.

❑   Create a SQL `INSERT` statement using this data.

❑   Connect to the database and execute the SQL statement.

❑   Refresh the data in `Application["ds"]` if the addition is successful.

❑   Return a success or failure notification to the client (we'll leave it up to the client to refresh its `DataSet` if required).

Starting from the top, we'll accept all fields as strings:

```
[WebMethod]
public int AddEvent(String eventName, String eventRoom,
                    String eventAttendees, String eventDate)
{
}
```

Next we declare the objects we'll need for database access, connect to the database, and execute our query, all using similar code to that in PCSWebApp3 (remember, we need the connection string here, but we won't show it):

```
[WebMethod]
public int AddEvent(String eventName, String eventRoom,
                    String eventAttendees, String eventDate)
{
    System.Data.OleDb.OleDbConnection oleDbConnection1;
    System.Data.OleDb.OleDbDataAdapter daEvents;
    DataSet ds;
    oleDbConnection1 = new System.Data.OleDb.OleDbConnection();
```

```
oleDbConnection1.ConnectionString = @" ... ";
String oleDbCommand = "INSERT INTO Events (Name, Room, AttendeeList," +
                       " EventDate) VALUES ('" + eventName + "', '" +
                       eventRoom + "', '" + eventAttendees + "', '" +
                       eventDate + "')";
System.Data.OleDb.OleDbCommand insertCommand =
        new System.Data.OleDb.OleDbCommand(oleDbCommand,
                                            oleDbConnection1);
oleDbConnection1.Open();
int queryResult = insertCommand.ExecuteNonQuery();
}
```

We use `queryResult` to store the number of rows affected by the query as before. We can check this to see whether it is 1 to gauge our success. If we are successful then we execute a new query on the database to refresh the `Events` table in our `DataSet`. It is vital to lock the application data while we perform our updates, to ensure that no other threads can access `Application["ds"]` while we update it. We can do this using the `Lock()` and `UnLock()` methods of the `Application` object:

```
[WebMethod]
public int AddEvent(String eventName, String eventRoom,
                    String eventAttendees, String eventDate)
{
    ...
    int queryResult = insertCommand.ExecuteNonQuery();
    if (queryResult == 1)
    {
        daEvents = new System.Data.OleDb.OleDbDataAdapter(
                        "SELECT * FROM Events", oleDbConnection1);
        ds = (DataSet)Application["ds"];
        ds.Tables["Events"].Clear();
        daEvents.Fill(ds, "Events");
        Application.Lock();
        Application["ds"] = ds;
        Application.UnLock();
        oleDbConnection1.Close();
    }
}
```

Finally, we return `queryResult`, allowing the client to know if the query was successful:

```
[WebMethod]
public int AddEvent(String eventName, String eventRoom,
                    String eventAttendees, String eventDate)
{
    ...
    return queryResult;
}
```

And with that, we have completed our Web service. As before, we can test this service out simply by pointing a Web browser at the .asmx file, so we can add records and look at the XML representation of the `DataSet` returned by `GetData()` without writing any client code.

Before moving on it's worth discussing the use of `DataSet` objects with Web Services. At first glance this seems like a fantastic way of exchanging data, and indeed it is an extremely powerful technique.

However, the fact that the `DataSet` class is so versatile does have implications. If you examine the WSDL generated for the `GetData()` method you'll see the following:

```
<s:element name="GetDataResponse">
  <s:complexType>
    <s:sequence>
      <s:element minOccurs="0" maxOccurs="1" name="GetDataResult">
        <s:complexType>
          <s:sequence>
            <s:element ref="s:schema" />
            <s:any />
          </s:sequence>
        </s:complexType>
      </s:element>
    </s:sequence>
  </s:complexType>
</s:element>
```

As you can see, this is very generic code, which allows the `DataSet` object passed to contain any data specified with an inline schema. Unfortunately, this does mean that the WSDL is not completely describing the Web service. For .NET clients this isn't a problem, and things progress as naturally as they did when passing a simple string in our earlier example, the only difference being that we exchange a `DataSet` object. However, non-.NET clients must have prior knowledge of the data that will be passed, or some equivalent of a `DataSet` class in order to access the data.

A work-around to this requirement is to repackage the data into a different format, an array of structs, for example. However, for our purposes using a `DataSet` object is not a problem, and greatly simplifies other code.

The Event-Booking Client

The client we'll use is a development of the PCSWebApp3 Web application from Chapter 25. We'll call this application PCSWebApp4, and use the code from PCSWebApp3 as a starting point.

We'll make two major modifications to the project. Firstly, we'll remove all direct database access from this application and use the Web service instead. Secondly, we'll introduce an application-level store of the `DataSet` object returned from the Web service that is only updated when necessary, meaning that even less of a load is placed on the database.

The first thing to do to our new Web application is to add a Web reference to the `PCSWebSrv2/ Service1.asmx` service. We can do this in the same way we discussed earlier in this chapter through right-clicking on the project in Server Explorer, locating the .asmx file, calling the Web reference `eventDataService`, and clicking Add Reference.

Next we add code to Global.asax.cs in much the same way as we did for our Web service. This code, though, is a lot simpler. First we reference the Web service and the `System.Data` namespace:

```
...
using System.Data;
using PCSWebApp4.eventDataService;
```

Next we fill a `DataSet` object and place it into an application-level data store called `ds`:

```
protected void Application_Start(Object sender, EventArgs e)
{
    Service1 dataService = new Service1();
    DataSet ds = dataService.GetData();
    Application["ds"] = ds;
}
```

This `DataSet` object is now available to all instances of PCSWebApp4, meaning that multiple users can read data without any calls to the Web service, or indeed to the database.

Next we must modify the WebForm1.aspx.cs file so we can use it. We start by removing the declarations of `oleDbConnection1`, `daAttendees`, `daRooms`, and `daEvents`, since we won't be accessing any database. We can also remove the initialization code for `oleDbConnection1`, found in `InitializeComponent()`. Next we must add a `using` statement for `PCSWebApp4.eventDataService`, as we did for Global.asax.cs, and change `Page_Load()` as follows:

```
private void Page_Load(object sender, System.EventArgs e)
{
    ds = (DataSet)Application["ds"];
    attendeeList.DataSource = ds.Tables["Attendees"];
    roomList.DataSource = ds.Tables["Rooms"];
    eventTable = ds.Tables["Events"];
    eventDetails1.DataSource = eventTable;
    eventDetails2.DataSource = eventTable;
    if (!this.IsPostBack)
    {
        System.DateTime trialDate = System.DateTime.Now;
        calendar.SelectedDate = getFreeDate(trialDate);
        this.DataBind();
    }
    else
    {
        eventDetails1.DataBind();
        eventDetails2.DataBind();
    }
}
```

Most of the code remains the same, all we need to do is to use `Application["ds"]` instead of getting the `DataSet` object ourselves.

We also must change `submitButton_Click()` to use the Web service `AddData()` method. Again, much of the code remains unchanged:

```
private void submitButton_Click(object sender, System.EventArgs e)
{
    if (this.IsValid)
    {
        String attendees = "";
        foreach (ListItem attendee in attendeeList.Items)
        {
```

```
            if (attendee.Selected)
            {
                attendees += attendee.Text + " (" + attendee.Value + "), ";
            }
        }
        attendees += " and " + nameBox.Text;
        String dateString =
                calendar.SelectedDate.Date.Date.ToShortDateString();
        Service1 dataService = new Service1();
        int queryResult = dataService.AddEvent(eventBox.Text,
                                        roomList.SelectedItem.Value,
                                        attendees,
                                        dateString);
        if (queryResult == 1)
        {
            resultLabel.Text = "Event Added.";
            ds = dataService.GetData();
            Application.Lock();
            Application["ds"] = ds;
            Application.UnLock();
            eventTable = ds.Tables["Events"];
            calendar.SelectedDate =
                        getFreeDate(calendar.SelectedDate.AddDays(1));
            eventDetails1.DataSource = eventTable;
            eventDetails1.DataBind();
            eventDetails2.DataSource = eventTable;
            eventDetails2.DataBind();
        }
        else
        {
            resultLabel.Text = "Event not added due to DB access problem.";
        }
    }
}
```

In fact, all we've really done is simplify things a great deal. This is often the case when using well-designed Web services—we can forget about much of the workings and instead concentrate on the user experience.

There isn't a huge amount to comment on in this code. Continuing to make use of `queryResult` is a bonus, and locking the application is essential as already noted.

The PCSWebApp4 Web application should look and function exactly like PCSWebApp3, but perform substantially better. We can also use the same Web service very easily for other applications—simply displaying events on a page, for example, or even editing events, attendee names, and rooms if we add some more methods. Doing this won't break PCSWebApp4 since it will simply ignore any new methods created.

Exchanging Data Using SOAP Headers

One final topic to look at in this chapter is using SOAP headers to exchange information, rather than including information in method parameters. The reason for covering it is that it is a very nice system to use for maintaining a user login. We won't go into detail about setting up your server for SSL connections, or the various methods of authentication that can be configured using IIS, since these do not affect the Web service code we need to get this behavior.

Let's say we have a service that contains a simple authentication method with a signature as follows:

```
AuthenticationToken AuthenticateUser(string userName, string password);
```

Where `AuthenticationToken` is a type we define that can be used by the user in later method calls, for example:

```
void DoSomething(AuthenticationToken token, OtherParamType param);
```

After logging in, the user has access to other methods using the token received from `AuthenticateUser()`. This technique is typical of secure Web systems, although it can be implemented in a far more complex way.

We can simplify this process further by using a SOAP header to exchange tokens (or any other data). We can restrict methods so that they can only be called if a specified SOAP header is included in the method call. This simplifies their structure as follows:

```
void DoSomething(OtherParamType param);
```

The advantage here is that, after we have set the header on the client, it persists. So after an initial bit of setting up we can ignore authentication tokens in all further Web method calls.

To see this in action create a new Web service project called PCSWebSrv3, and add a new class called `AuthenticationToken.cs` as follows:

```
using System;
using System.Web.Services.Protocols;

namespace PCSWebSrv3
{
   public class AuthenticationToken : SoapHeader
   {
      public Guid InnerToken;
   }
}
```

We'll use a GUID to identify the token, a common procedure, since we can be sure that it is unique.

To declare that the Web service can have a custom SOAP header we simply add a public member to the service class, of our new type:

```
public class Service1 : System.Web.Services.WebService
{
      public AuthenticationToken AuthenticationTokenHeader;
```

We also need a `using` statement for `System.Web.Services.Protocols` in the Service1.asmx.cs file. This namespace contains an attribute called `SoapHeaderAttribute`, which we can use to mark those Web methods that require the extra SOAP header in order work.

However, before we add such a method, let's add a very simple `Login()` method that clients can use to obtain an authentication token:

```
[WebMethod]
public Guid Login(string userName, string password)
{
    if ((userName == "Karli") && (password == "Cheese"))
    {
        Guid currentUser = Guid.NewGuid();
        Application["currentUser"] = currentUser;
        return currentUser;
    }
    else
    {
        Application["currentUser"] = null;
        return Guid.Empty;
    }
}
```

If the correct username and password are used then a new `Guid` object is generated, stored in an application-level variable, and returned to the user. If authentication fails then an empty `Guid` instance is returned and stored at the application level.

Next we have a method that accepts the header, as specified by the `SoapHeaderAttribute` attribute:

```
[WebMethod]
[SoapHeaderAttribute("AuthenticationTokenHeader",
                     Direction = SoapHeaderDirection.In)]
public string DoSomething()
{
    if (Application["currentUser"] != null &&
        AuthenticationTokenHeader != null &&
        AuthenticationTokenHeader.InnerToken
        == (Guid)Application["currentUser"])
    {
        return "Authentication OK.";
    }
    else
    {
        return "Authentication failed.";
    }
}
```

This returns one of two strings, depending on whether the `AuthenticationTokenHeader` header exists, isn't an empty `Guid`, and matches the one stored in `Application["currentUser"]` (if this `Application` variable exists).

In order to use the code as shown above we need to add the following `using` statement to Service1.asmx.cs:

```
using System.Web.Services.Protocols;
```

This is the same `using` statement we added to AuthenticationToken.cs.

Next we must create a quick client to test this service. Create a new Web application called PCSWebClient3, with the following simple code for the user interface:

```
<form id="Form1" method="post" runat="server">
   User Name:
   <asp:TextBox Runat="server" ID="userNameBox" /><br>
   Password:
   <asp:TextBox Runat="server" ID="passwordBox" /><br>
   <asp:Button Runat="server" ID="loginButton" Text="Log in" /><br>
   <asp:Label Runat="server" ID="tokenLabel" /><br>
   <asp:Button Runat="server" ID="invokeButton" Text="Invoke DoSomething()" /><br>
   <asp:Label Runat="server" ID="resultLabel" /><br>
</form>
```

Add the PCSWebSrv3 service as a Web reference with the name authenticateService, and add the following using statement to WebForm1.aspx.cs:

```
using PCSWebClient3.authenticateService;
```

We use a protected member to store the Web reference proxy, and another to store a Boolean value indicating whether the user is authenticated or not:

```
public class WebForm1 : System.Web.UI.Page
{
   protected System.Web.UI.WebControls.TextBox userNameBox;
   protected System.Web.UI.WebControls.TextBox passwordBox;
   protected System.Web.UI.WebControls.Button loginButton;
   protected System.Web.UI.WebControls.Label tokenLabel;
   protected System.Web.UI.WebControls.Button invokeButton;
   protected System.Web.UI.WebControls.Label resultLabel;
   protected Service1 myService;
   protected bool authenticated;
```

We initialize this member in Page_Load(). After we have a header to use with this Web service we'll store it in the ViewState collection of the form (a useful way to persist information between postbacks, which works in a similar way to storing information at the application or session level). Page_Load() looks to see if there is a stored header and assigns the header to the proxy accordingly (assigning the header in this way is the only step we must take for the data to be sent as a SOAP header). This way any event handlers that are being called (such as the one for the Web method–invoking button) don't have to assign a header—that step has already been taken:

```
private void Page_Load(object sender, System.EventArgs e)
{
   myService = new Service1();
   AuthenticationToken header = new AuthenticationToken();
   if (ViewState["AuthenticationTokenHeader"] != null)
   {
      header.InnerToken = (Guid)ViewState["AuthenticationTokenHeader"];
   }
   else
   {
      header.InnerToken = Guid.Empty;
   }
   myService.AuthenticationTokenValue = header;
}
```

Next we add an event handler for the Log in button by double-clicking it in the Designer:

```
private void loginButton_Click(object sender, System.EventArgs e)
{
    Guid authenticationTokenHeader = myService.Login(userNameBox.Text,
                                             passwordBox.Text);
    tokenLabel.Text = authenticationTokenHeader.ToString();
    ViewState.Add("AuthenticationTokenHeader", authenticationTokenHeader);
}
```

This handler uses any data entered in the two text boxes to call Login(), displays the Guid returned, and stores the Guid in the ViewState collection.

Finally, we have to add a handler in the same way for the Invoke DoSomething() button:

```
private void invokeButton_Click(object sender, System.EventArgs e)
{
    resultLabel.Text = myService.DoSomething();
}
```

This handler simply outputs the text returned by DoSomething().

When we run this application we can press the Invoke DoSomething() button directly, since Page_Load() has assigned the correct header (if we haven't assigned a header then an exception will be thrown, because we have specified that the header is required for this method). This results in a failure message, returned from DoSomething(), as shown in Figure 26-4.

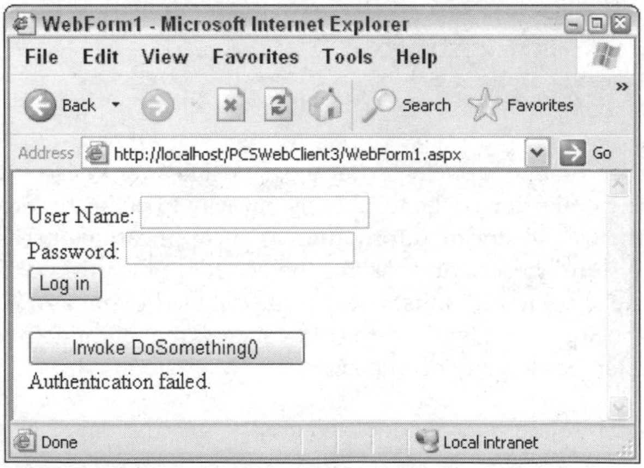

Figure 26-4

If we try to log in with any user name and password except "Karli" and "Cheese" we will get the same result. If, on the other hand, we log in using these credentials and then call DoSomething() we get the success message:

We can also see a string representation of the Guid used for validation.

Of course, applications that use this technique of exchanging data via SOAP headers are likely to be far more complicated. They will need to store login tokens in a more sensible way than just one application-level variable, perhaps in a database. For completeness we can also expire these tokens when a certain amount of time has passed, and provide the option for users to log out, which would simply mean removing the token. We could even validate the token against the IP address used by the user for further security. The key points here though are that the username and password of the user are only sent once, and that using a SOAP header simplifies later method calls.

Summary

In this chapter we have seen how to create and consume Web services using C# and the Visual Studio .NET development platform. Doing this is perhaps surprisingly simple, but is instantly recognizable as something that could prove to be incredibly useful. Already we are seeing many announcements about new Web services, and I suspect that they will be everywhere before long.

It has also been pointed out that Web services may be accessed from any platform. This is due to the SOAP protocol, which doesn't limit us to .NET.

The main example developed in this chapter illustrates how we can create .NET-distributed applications with ease. We have assumed here that you are using a single server to test things out, but there is no reason why the Web service shouldn't be completely separate from the client. It may even be on a separate server from the database if an additional data tier is required.

The use of data caching throughout is another important technique to master for use in large-scale applications, which might have thousands of users connecting simultaneously. Naturally, using Microsoft Access as a data source under such circumstances might not necessarily be the best idea!

Exchanging data via SOAP headers, introduced in the last example, is another useful technique that can be worked into your applications. The example uses the exchange of a login token, but there is no reason why more complex data shouldn't be exchanged in this way. Perhaps this could be used for simple password protection of Web Services, without having to resort to imposing more complex security.

Finally, remember that Web service consumers don't necessarily have to be Web applications. There is no reason why we can't use Web services from Windows Forms applications—which certainly seems like an attractive option for a corporate intranet.

All in all, the potential of Web services certainly astounds me, and I hope you're impressed too!

27

User Controls and Custom Controls

It has often been the case with Web development that the tools available, however powerful, don't quite match up with your requirements for a specific project. Perhaps a given control doesn't quite work as you'd like it to, or perhaps one section of code, intended for reuse on several pages, is too complex in the hands of multiple developers. In cases such as these there is a strong argument for building your own controls. Such controls can, at their simplest, wrap multiple existing controls together, perhaps with additional properties specifying layout. They can also be completely unlike any existing control. Using a control you have built yourself can be as simple as using any other control in ASP.NET (if you have written them well), which can certainly ease Web site coding.

In the past it has been tricky to implement such custom-built controls, especially on large-scale systems where complex registration procedures might be required in order to use them. Even on simple systems, the coding required to create a custom control could become a very involved process. The scripting capabilities of older Web languages also suffered by not giving the perfect access to your cunningly crafted object models, and resulted in poor performance all around.

.NET Framework provides an ideal setting for the creation of custom controls, using simple programming techniques. Every aspect of ASP.NET server controls is exposed for you to customize, including such capabilities as templating, client-side scripting, and so on. However, there is no need to write code for all of these eventualities; simpler controls can be a lot easier to create.

In addition, the dynamic discovery of assemblies that is inherent in a .NET system makes installation of Web applications on a new Web server as simple as copying the directory structure containing your code. To make use of the controls you have created you simply copy the assemblies containing those controls along with the rest of the code. You can even place frequently used controls in an assembly located in the global assembly cache (GAC) on the Web server, so that all Web applications on the server have access to them.

In this chapter we discuss two different kinds of controls:

❑ User controls (and how to convert existing ASP.NET pages into controls)

❑ Custom controls (and how to group the functionality of several controls, extending existing controls, and creating new controls from scratch)

We'll illustrate user controls by creating a simple control that displays a card suit (club, diamond, heart, or spade), so that we can embed it in other ASP.NET pages with ease. In the case of custom controls, we'll create a straw poll control allowing the user to vote for a candidate in a list and see how the vote is progressing.

User Controls

User controls are controls that you create using ASP.NET code, just as you would in standard ASP.NET Web pages. The difference is that after you have created a user control you can reuse it in multiple ASP.NET pages with a minimum of difficulty.

For example, let's say that you have created a page that displays some information from a database, perhaps information about an order. Instead of creating a fixed page that does this, it is possible to place the relevant code into a user control, and then insert that control into as many different Web pages as you want.

In addition, it is possible to define properties and methods for user controls. For example, you can specify a property for the background color for displaying your database table in a Web page, or a method to re-run a database query to check for changes.

Let's dive in and create a simple user control. As is the case with the other chapters, you can download the code for the sample projects in this chapter from the Wrox Web site at www.wrox.com.

A Simple User Control

In Visual Studio .NET, create a new Web application called PCSUserCWebApp1. After the standard files have been generated, select the Project➪Add New Item menu option, and add a Web User Control called PCSUserC1.ascx as shown in Figure 27-1.

The files added to our project, with the extensions .ascx and .ascx.cs, work in a very similar way to the .aspx files we've seen already. The .ascx file contains our ASP.NET code and looks very similar to a normal .aspx file. The .ascx.cs file is our code-behind file, which defines the user control, much in the same way that forms are defined in .aspx.cs files.

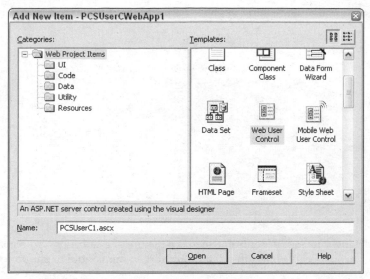

Figure 27-1

.ascx files can be viewed in Design or HTML view just like .aspx files. Looking at the file in HTML view reveals an important difference: there is no HTML code present, and in particular no `<form>` element. This is because user controls are inserted inside ASP.NET forms in other files and so don't need a `<form>` tag of their own. The generated code is as follows:

```
<%@ Control Language="c#" AutoEventWireup="false"
    Codebehind="PCSUserC1.ascx.cs"
    Inherits="PCSUserCWebApp1.PCSUserC1"
    TargetSchema="http://schemas.microsoft.com/intellisense/ie5"%>
```

This is very similar to the `<%@ Page %>` directive generated in .aspx files, except that `Control` is specified rather than `Page`, and a `TargetSchema` attribute is included. This attribute specifies what browser the control is designed for (in this case Internet Explorer 5), which affects what items are available to add from the Visual Studio .NET Toolbox.

Looking at the generated code in the .ascx.cs file reveals another important difference to ASP.NET pages: the class generated inherits from `System.Web.UI.UserControl`. Again, this is because the control is used inside a form; it isn't a form itself.

Our simple control will be one that displays a graphic corresponding to one of the four standard suits in cards (club, diamond, heart, spade). The graphics required for this are shipped as part of Visual Studio .NET; you can find them in the directory C:\Program Files\Microsoft Visual Studio.NET 2003\Common7\ Graphics\bitmaps\assorted, with the filenames CLUB.BMP, DIAMOND.BMP, HEART.BMP, and SPADE.BMP. Copy these files into your project's directory so that you can use them in a moment.

Let's add some code to our new control. In the HTML view of PCSUserC1.ascx add the following:

```
<%@ Control Language="c#" AutoEventWireup="false"
    Codebehind="PCSUserC1.ascx.cs"
    Inherits="PCSUserCWebApp1.PCSUserC1"
    TargetSchema="http://schemas.microsoft.com/intellisense/ie5"%>
<table cellspacing=4>
  <tr valign="middle">
    <td>
       <asp:Image Runat="server" ID="suitPic" ImageURL="club.bmp"/>
    </td>
    <td>
       <asp:Label Runat="server" ID="suitLabel">Club</asp:Label>
    </td>
  </tr>
</table>
```

This defines a default state for our control, which is a picture of a club along with a label. Before we add any additional functionality we'll test this default by adding this control to our project Web page WebForm1.aspx.

In order to use a custom control in an .aspx file, we first need to specify how we will refer to it, that is, the name of the tag that will represent the control in our HTML. To do this we use the `<%@ Register %>` directive at the top of the code as follows:

```
<%@ Register TagPrefix="PCS" TagName="UserC1" Src="PCSUserC1.ascx" %>
```

The `TagPrefix` and `TagName` attributes specify the tag name to use (in the form `<TagPrefix: TagName>`), and we use the `Src` attribute to point to the file containing our user control. Now we can use our control by adding the following element:

```
<form id="Form1" method="post" runat="server">
   <PCS:UserC1 Runat="server" ID="myUserControl"/>
</form>
```

User controls aren't declared by default in the code behind our form, so we also need to add the following declaration to WebForm1.aspx.cs:

```
public class WebForm1 : System.Web.UI.Page
{
   protected PCSUserC1 myUserControl;
   ...
```

This is all we need to do to test our user control. Figure 27-2 shows the results of running this code.

As it stands this control groups two existing controls, an image and a label, in a table layout. As such it falls into the category of a composite control.

Figure 27-2

To gain control over the displayed suit, we can use an attribute on the `<PCS:UserC1>` element. Attributes on user control elements are automatically mapped to properties on user controls, so all we have to do to make this work is add a property to the code behind our control, PCSUserC1.ascx.cs. We'll call this property `Suit`, and let it take any suit value. To make it easier for us to represent the state of the control, we'll define an enumeration to hold the four suit names, inside the PCSUserCWebApp1 namespace in the PCSUserC1.ascx.cs file:

```
namespace PCSUserCWebApp1
{
    ...
    public enum suit
    {
        club, diamond, heart, spade
    }
    ...
}
```

The `PCSUserC1` class needs a member variable to hold the suit type, `currentSuit`:

```
public class PCSUserC1 : System.Web.UI.UserControl
{
    protected System.Web.UI.WebControls.Image suitPic;
    protected System.Web.UI.WebControls.Label suitLabel;
    protected suit currentSuit;
```

And a property to access this member variable, `Suit`:

```
public suit Suit
{
    get
    {
        return currentSuit;
    }
    set
    {
        currentSuit = value;
        suitPic.ImageUrl = currentSuit.ToString() + ".bmp";
        suitLabel.Text = currentSuit.ToString();
    }
}
```

The set accessor here sets the URL of the image to one of the files we copied earlier, and the text displayed to the suit name.

Next we must add code to WebForm1.aspx so we can access this new property. We could simply specify the suit using the property we have just added:

```
<PCS:UserC1 Runat="server" id="myUserControl" Suit="diamond"/>
```

The ASP.NET processor is intelligent enough to get the correct enumeration item from the string provided. To make things a bit more interesting and interactive, though, we'll use a radio button list to select a suit:

```
<form id="Form1" method="post" runat="server">
    <PCS:UserC1 Runat="server" ID="myUserControl"/>
    <asp:RadioButtonList Runat="server" ID="suitList"
                         AutoPostBack="True">
        <asp:ListItem Value="club" Selected="True">Club</asp:ListItem>
        <asp:ListItem Value="diamond">Diamond</asp:ListItem>
        <asp:ListItem Value="heart">Heart</asp:ListItem>
        <asp:ListItem Value="spade">Spade</asp:ListItem>
    </asp:RadioButtonList>
</form>
```

We also need to add an event handler for the SelectedIndexChanged event of the list, which we can do simply by double-clicking the radio button list control in Design view.

> Note that we have set the AutoPostBack property of this list to True, as the suitList_
> SelectedIndexChanged() event handler won't be executed on the server unless a postback is in
> operation, and this control doesn't trigger a post back by default.

The suitList_SelectedIndexChanged() method requires the following code in WebForm1.aspx.cs:

```
protected void suitList_SelectedIndexChanged(object sender,
                                             System.EventArgs e)
{
    myUserControl.Suit = (suit)Enum.Parse(typeof(suit),
                                          suitList.SelectedItem.Value);
}
```

We know that the Value attributes on the <ListItem> elements represent valid values for the suit enumeration we defined earlier, so we simply parse these as enumeration types and use them as values of the Suit property of our user control. We cast the returned object type to suit using simple casing syntax, as this can't be achieved implicitly.

Now we can change the suit when we run our Web application (see Figure 27-3).

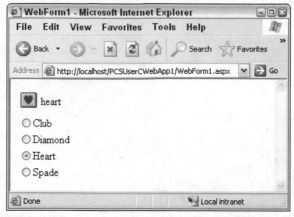

Figure 27-3

Next we'll give our control some methods. Again, this is very simple; we just add methods to our PCSUserC1 class:

```
public void Club()
{
    Suit = suit.club;
}
public void Diamond()
{
    Suit = suit.diamond;
}
public void Heart()
{
    Suit = suit.heart;
}
public void Spade()
{
    Suit = suit.spade;
}
```

These four methods—Club(), Diamond(), Heart(), and Spade()—change the suit displayed on the screen to the respective suit clicked.

We'll call these functions from four ImageButton controls in our .aspx page:

```
</asp:RadioButtonList>
<asp:ImageButton Runat="server" ID="clubButton"
             ImageUrl="CLUB.BMP"
             OnClick="clubButton_Click"/>
<asp:ImageButton Runat="server" ID="diamondButton"
             ImageUrl="DIAMOND.BMP"
             OnClick="diamondButton_Click"/>
```

```
        <asp:ImageButton Runat="server" ID="heartButton"
                         ImageUrl="HEART.BMP"
                         OnClick="heartButton_Click"/>
        <asp:ImageButton Runat="server" ID="spadeButton"
                         ImageUrl="SPADE.BMP"
                         OnClick="spadeButton_Click"/>
</form>
```

We'll use the following event handlers:

```
protected void clubButton_Click(object sender,
                                System.Web.UI.ImageClickEventArgs e)
{
   myUserControl.Club();
   suitList.SelectedIndex = 0;
}

protected void diamondButton_Click(object sender,
                                   System.Web.UI.ImageClickEventArgs e)
{
   myUserControl.Diamond();
   suitList.SelectedIndex = 1;
}

protected void heartButton_Click(object sender,
                                 System.Web.UI.ImageClickEventArgs e)
{
   myUserControl.Heart();
   suitList.SelectedIndex = 2;
}

protected void spadeButton_Click(object sender,
                                 System.Web.UI.ImageClickEventArgs e)
{
   myUserControl.Spade();
   suitList.SelectedIndex = 3;
}
```

Now we have four new buttons we can use to change the suit, as shown in Figure 27-4.

Now that we've created our user control we can use it in any other Web page simply by using the <%@ Register %> directive and the two source code files (PCSUserC1.ascx and PCSUserC1.ascx.cs) we have created for the control.

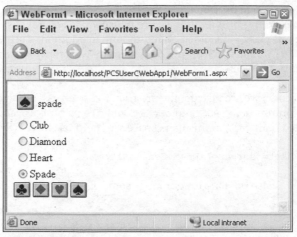

Figure 27-4

Custom Controls

Custom controls go a step beyond user controls in that they are entirely self-contained in C# assemblies, requiring no separate ASP.NET code. This means that we don't need to go through the process of assembling a user interface (UI) in an .ascx file. Instead, we have complete control over what is written to the output stream, that is, the exact HTML generated by our control.

In general, it will take longer to develop custom controls than user controls, because the syntax is more complex and we often have to write significantly more code to get results. A user control may be as simple as a few other controls grouped together as we've seen, whereas a custom control can do just about anything short of making you a cup of coffee.

To get the most customizable behavior for our custom controls we can derive a class from `System.Web.UI.WebControls.WebControl`. If we do this then we are creating a full custom control. Alternatively, we can extend the functionality of an existing control, creating a derived custom control. Finally, we can group existing controls together, much like we did in the last section but with a more logical structure, to create a composite custom control.

Whatever we create can be used in ASP.NET pages in pretty much the same way. All we need to do is to place the generated assembly in a location where the Web application that will use it can find it, and register the element names to use with the `<%@ Register %>` directive. For this location, you have we have two options: we can either put the assembly in the bin directory of the Web application, or place it in the GAC if we want all Web applications on the server to have access to it.

The `<%@ Register %>` directive takes a slightly different syntax for custom controls:

```
<%@ Register TagPrefix="PCS" Namespace="PCSCustomWebControls"
             Assembly="PCSCustomWebControls"%>
```

We use the `TagPrefix` option in the same way as before, but we don't use the `TagName` or `Src` attributes. This is because the custom control assembly we use may contain several custom controls, and each of these will be named by its class, so `TagName` is redundant. In addition, since we can use the dynamic discovery capabilities of.NET Framework to find our assembly we simply have to name it and the namespace in it that contains our controls.

In the previous line of code, we are instruct the program to use an assembly called `PCSCustomWeb Controls.dll` with controls in the `PCSCustomWebControls` namespace, and use the tag prefix `PCS`. If we have a control called `Control1` in this namespace we could use it with the ASP.NET code:

```
<PCS:Control1 Runat="server" ID="MyControl1"/>
```

With custom controls it is also possible to reproduce some of the control nesting behavior that exists in list controls:

```
<asp:DropDownList ID="roomList" Runat="server" Width="160px">
    <asp:ListItem Value="1">The Happy Room</asp:ListItem>
    <asp:ListItem Value="2">The Angry Room</asp:ListItem>
    <asp:ListItem Value="3">The Depressing Room</asp:ListItem>
    <asp:ListItem Value="4">The Funked Out Room</asp:ListItem>
</asp:DropDownList>
```

We can create controls that should be interpreted as being children of other controls in a very similar way to this. We'll discuss how to do this later in this chapter.

Custom Control Project Configuration

Let's start putting some of this theory into practice. We'll use a single assembly to hold all of the example custom controls in this chapter for simplicity, which we can create in Visual Studio .NET by choosing a new project of type Web Control Library. We'll call our library PCSCustomWebControls, as shown in Figure 27-5.

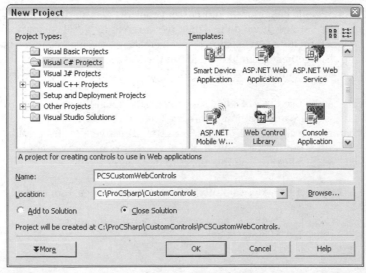

Figure 27-5

Here I have created the project in C:\ProCSharp\CustomControls. There is no need for the project to be created on the Web server as with Web applications, since it doesn't need to be externally accessible in the same way. Of course, we can create Web control libraries anywhere, as long as we remember to copy the generated assembly somewhere where the Web application that uses it can find it!

One technique we can use to facilitate testing is to add a Web application project to the same solution. We'll call this application PCSCustomWebControlsTestApp. For now, this is the only application that will use our custom control library, so to speed things up a little we can make the output assembly for our library be created in the correct bin directory (this means that we don't have to copy the file across every time we recompile). We can do this through the property pages for the PCSCustomWebControls project (see Figure 27-6).

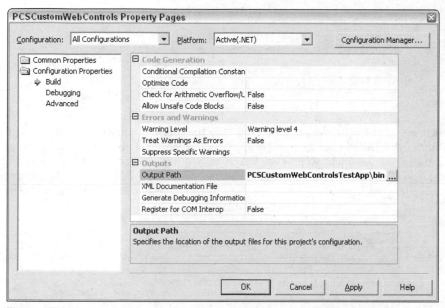

Figure 27-6

Note that we have changed the Configuration dropdown to All Configurations, debug and release build outputs will be placed in the same place. The Output Path has been changed to C:\Inetpub\wwwroot\ PCSCustomWebControlsTestApp\bin. To make debugging easier we can also change the Debug Mode option on the Debugging property page to URL and the Start URL to, `http://localhost/ PCSCustomWebControlsTestApp/WebForm1.aspx` so we can just execute our project in debug mode to see our results.

We can make sure that this is all working by testing the control that is supplied by default in the .cs file of our custom control library, WebCustomControl1.cs. We just need to make the following changes to the code in WebForm1.aspx, which simply references the newly created control library and embeds the default control in this library into the page body:

```
<%@ Page language="c#" Codebehind="WebForm1.aspx.cs" AutoEventWireup="false"
        Inherits="PCSCustomWebControlsTestApp.WebForm1" %>
<%@ Register TagPrefix="PCS" Namespace="PCSCustomWebControls"
            Assembly="PCSCustomWebControls"%>
<!DOCTYPE HTML PUBLIC "-//W3C//DTD HTML 4.0 Transitional//EN" >
<HTML>
    <HEAD>
        <title>WebForm1</title>
        <meta name="GENERATOR"content="Microsoft Visual Studio 7.0" >
        <meta name="CODE_LANGUAGE"content="C#" >
        <meta name="vs_defaultClientScript"content="JavaScript" >
        <meta name="vs_targetSchema"
              content="http://schemas.microsoft.com/intellisense/ie5" >
    </HEAD>
    <body MS_POSITIONING="GridLayout">
        <form id="Form1" method="post" runat="server">
            <PCS:WebCustomControl1 ID="testControl" Runat="server"
                                   Text="Testing again..."/>
        </form>
    </body>
</html>
```

In fact, there is an even better way of doing this after the control library project has been compiled. The Visual Studio .NET Toolbox has a tab called My User Controls that you can use to add your own controls (or you can add your own tab). Right-click the tab to which you want to add your new control and choose the Add/Remove Items menu option. Next, from the .NET Framework Components tab browse to the PCSCustomWebControls.dll assembly, load it, and then choose controls from the list, as shown in Figure 27-7.

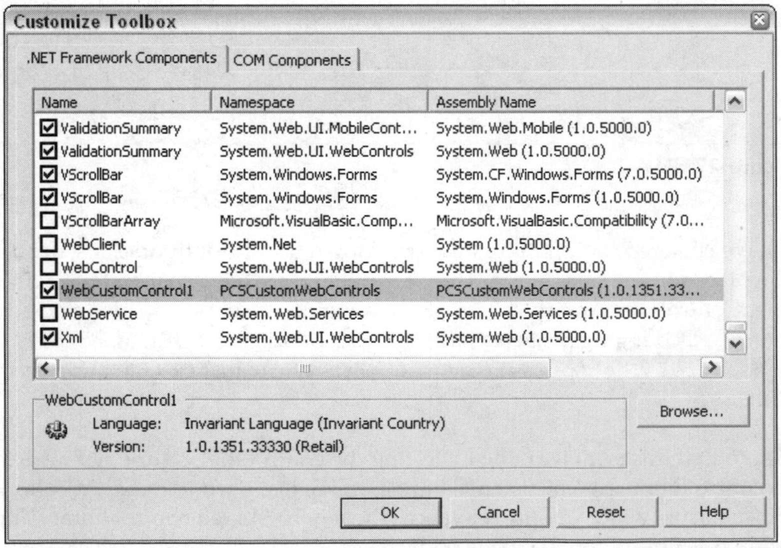

Figure 27-7

Select WebCustomControl1 as shown in Figure 27-7 to display the new control in the Toolbox, ready for adding to our form (see Figure 27-8).

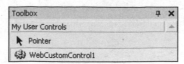

Figure 27-8

The nice thing about this is that if we add the control from the Toolbox both a project reference to PCSCustomWebControls and the `<%@ Register %>` directive are added automatically to the control. The tag prefix for the control library is also assigned automatically (in our example: `cc1`). This is fine, although doing this ourselves gives us greater flexibility that could improve code readability. In the rest of the code in this chapter we'll assume that the prefix PCS is used for controls from PCSCustomWebControls.

> *Note that the prefix used for Toolbox items can be controlled in the code for the control, by adding the following attribute to the code for the control:*

```
[assembly: TagPrefix("WebCustomControl1", "PCS")]
```

One thing that isn't added for us is a `using` statement to our `PCSCustomWebControlsTestApp` namespace in WebForm1.aspx.cs. Rather than use fully qualified names for our controls we can add the `using` statement ourselves:

```
using PCSCustomWebControls;
```

This will enable us to use our custom controls from the code behind the form without full name qualification.

Now, as long as we have the PCSCustomWebControls library configured as our startup application we can click the Debug button to see our results. Try changing the `Text` property of the newly added control to Testing again and run the application. The result is shown in Figure 27-9.

Figure 27-9

Basic Custom Controls

As can be inferred from the results in the previous section, the sample control generated by default is simply a version of the standard <asp:Label> control. The code generated in the .cs file for the project, WebCustomControl1.cs, is as follows (omitting the standard and XML documentation comments):

```csharp
using System;
using System.Web.UI;
using System.Web.UI.WebControls;
using System.ComponentModel;

namespace PCSCustomWebControls
{
   [DefaultProperty("Text"),
    ToolboxData("<{0}:WebCustomControl1 runat=server></{0}:WebCustomControl1>")]
   public class WebCustomControl1 : System.Web.UI.WebControls.WebControl
   {
      private string text;

      [Bindable(true), Category("Appearance"), DefaultValue("")]
      public string Text
      {
         get
         {
            return text;
         }
         set
         {
            text = value;
         }
      }

      protected override void Render(HtmlTextWriter output)
      {
         output.Write(Text);
      }
   }
}
```

The single class defined here is the WebCustomControl1 class (note how the class name mapped directly to an ASP.NET element in the simple example we saw before), which is derived from the WebControl class as discussed earlier. Two attributes are provided for this class: DefaultProperty and ToolboxData. The DefaultProperty attribute specifies what the default property for the control will be if used in languages that support this functionality. The ToolboxData attribute specifies exactly what HTML will be added to an .aspx page if this control is added using the Toolbox (as we discussed earlier, once the project is compiled we can add the control to the toolbox by configuring the toolbox to use the assembly created). Note that a {0} placeholder is used to specify where the tag prefix will be placed.

The class contains one property: Text. This is a very simple text property much like those we've seen before. The only point to note here is the three attributes:

❑ `Bindable`, which specifies whether the property can be bound to data.

❑ `Category`, which specifies where the property will be displayed in the property pages.

❑ `DefaultValue`, which specifies the default value for the property.

Exposing properties in this way works in exactly the same way as it did for custom controls, and is definitely preferable to exposing public fields.

The remainder of the class consists of the `Render()` method. This is the single most important method to implement when designing custom controls, as it is where we have access to the output stream to display our control content. There are only two cases where we don't need to implement this method:

❑ When we are designing a control that has no visual representation (usually known as a component).

❑ When we are deriving from an existing control and don't need to change its display characteristics.

Custom controls can also expose custom methods, raise custom events, and respond to child controls (if any). In the remainder of this chapter, where we discuss how to:

❑ Create a derived control.

❑ Create a composite control.

❑ Create a more advanced control.

The final example is a straw poll control, capable of allowing the user to vote for one of several candidates, and displaying voting progress graphically. Options are defined using nested child controls, in the manner described earlier.

We'll start with a simple derived control.

The RainbowLabel derived control

For this first example we'll derive a control from a `Label` control and override its `Render()` method to output multicolored text. To keep the code for the sample controls in this chapter separate, we'll create new source files as necessary, so for this control add a new .cs code file called RainbowLabel.cs to the PCSCustomWebControls project and add the following code:

```
using System;
using System.Web.UI;
using System.Web.UI.WebControls;
using System.ComponentModel;
using System.Drawing;

namespace PCSCustomWebControls
{
    public class RainbowLabel : System.Web.UI.WebControls.Label
    {
```

```
        private Color[] colors = new Color[] {Color.Red, Color.Orange,
                                              Color.Yellow,
                                              Color.GreenYellow,
                                              Color.Blue, Color.Indigo,
                                              Color.Violet};

        protected override void Render(HtmlTextWriter output)
        {
            string text = Text;
            for (int pos=0; pos < text.Length; pos++)
            {
                int rgb = colors[pos % colors.Length].ToArgb() & 0xFFFFFF;
                output.Write("<font color='#" + rgb.ToString("X6") + "'>"
                            + text[pos] + "</font>");
            }
        }
    }
}
```

This class derives from the existing Label control (System.Web.UI.WebControls.Label) and doesn't require any additional properties, because the inherited Text one will do fine. We have added a new private field, colors[], which contains an array of colors that we'll cycle through when we output text.

The main functionality of the control is in Render(), which we have overridden, because we want to change the HTML output. Here we get the string to display from the Text property and display each character in a color from the colors[] array.

To test this control we add it to the form in PCSCustomWebControlsTestApp:

```
<form method="post" runat="server" ID="Form1">
    <PCS:RainbowLabel Runat="server" Text="Multicolored label!"
                      ID="rainbowLabel1"/>
</form>
```

Figure 27-10

Maintaining state in custom controls

Each time a control is created on the server in response to a server request it is created from scratch. This means that any simple field of the control will be reinitialized. In order for controls to maintain state between requests they must use the ViewState maintained on the client, which means we need to write controls with this in mind.

To illustrate this, we'll add an additional capability to the RainbowLabel control. We'll add a method called Cycle() that cycles through the colors available, which will make use of a stored offset field to determine which color should be used for the first letter in the string displayed. This field must use the ViewState of the control in order to be persisted between requests.

We'll show the code for both with and without ViewState storage cases to demonstrate how easy it is to make an error that results in a non-persistent control.. First we'll look at code that fails to make use of the ViewState:

```csharp
public class RainbowLabel : System.Web.UI.WebControls.Label
{
    private Color[] colors = new Color[] {Color.Red, Color.Orange,
                                          Color.Yellow,
                                          Color.GreenYellow,
                                          Color.Blue, Color.Indigo,
                                          Color.Violet};
    private int offset = 0;

    protected override void Render(HtmlTextWriter output)
    {
        string text = Text;
        for (int pos=0; pos < text.Length; pos++)
        {
            int rgb = colors[(pos + offset) % colors.Length].ToArgb()
                                                     & 0xFFFFFF;
            output.Write("<font color='#" + rgb.ToString("X6") + "'>"
                         + text[pos] + "</font>");
        }
    }

    public void Cycle()
    {
        offset = ++offset;
    }
}
```

Here we initialize the offset field to zero, then allow the Cycle() method to increment it, using the % operator to ensure that it wraps round to 0 if it reaches 7 (the number of colors in the colors array).

To test this we need a way of calling Cycle(), and the simplest way to do that is to add a button to our form:

```html
<form method="post" runat="server" ID="Form1">
    <PCS:RainbowLabel Runat="server" Text="Multicolored label!"
                      ID="rainbowLabel1"/>
        <asp:Button Runat="server" ID="cycleButton"
                                    Text="Cycle colors"/>
</form>
```

Add an event handler by double-clicking on the button in design view and add the following code (you'll need to change the protection level to protected):

```
        protected void cycleButton_Click(object sender, System.EventArgs e)
        {
            this.rainbowLabel1.Cycle();
        }
```

If you run this code you'll find that the colors change the first time you click the button, but further clicks will leave the colors as they are.

If this control persisted itself on the server between requests then it would work adequately, because the offset field would maintain its state without us having to worry about it. However, this technique wouldn't make sense for a Web application, with thousands of users potentially using it at the same time. Creating a separate instance for each user would be counterproductive.

In any case, the solution is quite simple. We have to use the ViewState property bag of our control to store and retrieve data. We don't have to worry about how this is serialized, recreated, or anything else. We just put things in and take things out, safe in the knowledge that state will be maintained between requests in the standard ASP.NET way.

To place the offset field into ViewState we simply use:

```
    ViewState["_offset"] = offset;
```

ViewState consists of name-value pairs, and here we are using one called _offset. We don't have to declare this anywhere; it will be created the first time this code is used.

Similarly, to retrieve state we use:

```
    offset = (int)ViewState["_offset"];
```

If we do this when nothing is stored in the ViewState under that name we will get a null value. Casting a null value in this code will throw an exception, so we can either test for this or check whether the object type retrieved from ViewState is null before we cast it, which is what we'll do in our code.

In fact, we can update our code in a very simple way by replacing the existing offset member with a private offset property that makes use of ViewState, with code as follows:

```
        public class RainbowLabel : System.Web.UI.WebControls.Label
        {
            ...
            private int offset
            {
                get
                {
                    object rawOffset = ViewState["_offset"];
                    if (rawOffset != null)
                    {
                        return (int)rawOffset;
                    }
                    else
                    {
```

```
                    ViewState["_offset"] = 0;
                    return 0;
                }
            }
        set
        {
            ViewState["_offset"] = value;
        }
    }
    ...
}
```

This time, the control allows the `Cycle()` method to work each time.

In general, we might see `ViewState` being used for simple public properties, for example:

```
public string Name
{
    get
    {
        return (string)ViewState["_name"];
    }
    set
    {
        ViewState["_name"] = value;
    }
}
```

One further point about using `ViewState` concerns child controls. If our control has children and is used more than once on a page, then we have the problem that the children will share their `ViewState` by default. In almost every case this isn't the behavior we'd like to see, and luckily we have a simple solution. By implementing `INamingContainer` on the parent control we force child controls to use qualified storage in `ViewState`, such that child controls will not share their `ViewState` with similar child controls with a different parent.

Using this interface doesn't require any property or method implementation, we just have to use it, as if it were simply a marker for interpretation by the ASP.NET server, as discussed in the following sections.

Creating a Composite Custom Control

As a simple example of a composite custom control, we can combine the control from the previous section with the cycle button we have in the test form.

We'll call this composite control RainbowLabel2, and place it in a new file, RainbowLabel2.cs. This control needs to:

❑   Inherit from `WebControl` (not `Label`).

❑   Support `INamingContainer`.

❑   Possess two fields to hold its child controls.

To fulfill these three requirements, we must modify the code obtained by generating a new class file:

```
using System;
using System.Web.UI;
using System.Web.UI.WebControls;
using System.ComponentModel;

namespace PCSCustomWebControls
{
    public class RainbowLabel2 : System.Web.UI.WebControls.WebControl,
                                 INamingContainer
    {
        private RainbowLabel rainbowLabel = new RainbowLabel();
        private Button cycleButton = new Button();
        ...
```

In order to configure a composite control we have to ensure that any child controls are added to the `Controls` collection and properly initialized. We do this by overriding the `CreateChildControls()` method and placing the required code there (here we should call the base `CreateChildControls()` implementation, which won't affect our class but may prevent unexpected surprises):

```
        protected override void CreateChildControls()
        {
            cycleButton.Text = "Cycle colors.";
            cycleButton.Click += new System.EventHandler(cycleButton_Click);
            Controls.Add(cycleButton);
            Controls.Add(rainbowLabel);
            base.CreateChildControls();
        }
```

Here we just use the `Add()` method of `Controls` to get things set up correctly. We've also added an event handler for the button so that we can make it cycle colors. The handler is the now familiar:

```
        protected void cycleButton_Click(object sender, System.EventArgs e)
        {
            rainbowLabel.Cycle();
        }
```

This call makes the label colors cycle.

To give users of our composite control access to the text in the `rainbowLabel` child we can add a property that maps to the `Text` property of the child:

```
        public string Text
        {
            get
            {
                return rainbowLabel.Text;
            }
            set
            {
                rainbowLabel.Text = value;
            }
        }
```

The last thing to do is to implement `Render()`. The base implementation of this method takes each control in the `Controls` collection of the class and tells it to render itself. Since `Render()` is a protected method, it doesn't call `Render()` for each of these controls; instead it calls the public method `RenderControl()`. This has the same effect, because `RenderControl()` calls `Render()`, so we don't have to change any more code in the `RainbowLabel` class. To get more control over this rendering (for example in composite controls that output HTML around that generated by child controls) we can call this method ourselves:

```
protected override void Render(HtmlTextWriter output)
{
    rainbowLabel.RenderControl(output);
    cycleButton.RenderControl(output);
}
```

We just pass the `HtmlTextWriter` instance we receive to the `RenderControl()` method for a child, and the HTML normally generated by that child will be rendered.

We can use this control in much the same way as `RainbowLabel`:

```
<form method="post" runat="server" ID="Form1">
    <PCS:RainbowLabel2 Runat="server"
                       Text="Multicolored label composite"
                       ID="rainbowLabel2"/>
</form>
```

This time a button to cycle the colors is included.

A Straw Poll Control

Next we'll use and build on the techniques we've covered so far to make a more involved custom control. The end result of this will enable the following ASP.NET code to give us the result shown in Figure 27-11:

```
<form method="post" runat="server" ID="Form1">
    <PCS:StrawPoll Runat="server" ID="strawPoll1"
                   PollStyle="voteonly"
                   Title="Who is your favorite James Bond?">
        <PCS:Candidate Name="Sean Connery" Votes="101"/>
        <PCS:Candidate Name="Roger Moore" Votes="83"/>
        <PCS:Candidate Name="George Lazenby" Votes="32"/>
        <PCS:Candidate Name="Timothy Dalton" Votes="28"/>
        <PCS:Candidate Name="Pierce Brosnan" Votes="95"/>
    </PCS:StrawPoll>
</form>
```

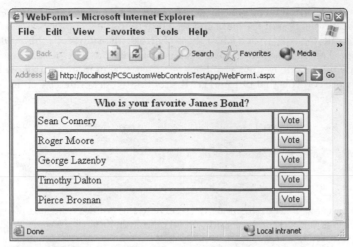

Figure 27-11

And when we click a vote button the display changes to a straw poll control, as shown in Figure 27-12.

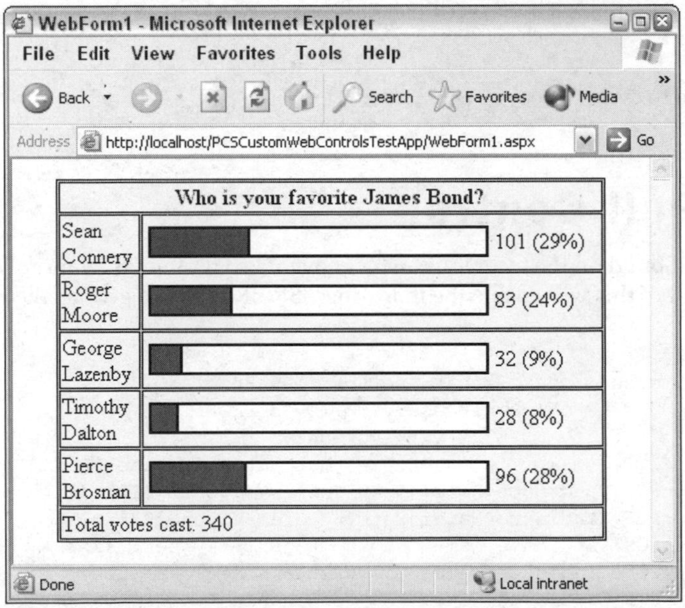

Figure 27-12

Alternatively, we can view results and voting buttons at the same time, and allow multiple votes, mainly for testing purposes.

The ASP.NET code sets the Name and Votes property for each Candidate. This is fine for this example, although it is foreseeable that a more advanced version of this control might be data-bound to get these results. However, we won't cover this in this chapter, because that could get quite involved.

When the ASP.NET code is parsed, structures such as this one are interpreted in a consistent way: each child element is interpreted in the way that we specify in a control builder class associated with the parent control. This control builder, for which we'll see the code shortly, handles anything nested inside the control it is associated with, including literal text.

The two controls we need to create are `Candidate` to hold individual candidates, and `StrawPoll`, which will contain and render the straw poll control. Both of these are placed in new source files: Candidate.cs and StrawPoll.cs.

The Candidate Controls

To start with, we'll create our `Candidate` controls, each of which will store a name and the number of votes cast for that candidate. In addition, these controls will maintain a voting button, and handle any clicks of this button.

For this project, we need:

❑ Code for the `Name` and `Votes` properties (stored in the `ViewState`).

❑ Initialization code in `CreateChildControls()`.

❑ Code for our button click handler.

We'll also include a utility method, `Increment()`, which will add a vote to the current vote count for the Candidate instance. This utility method will be called by the button click handler.

We'll also need to support `INamingContainer`, because we'll have multiple instances of these controls with their own children.

The code for the `Candidate` class goes in Candidate.cs, which we should add to our project along with the standard `namespace` and `using` statements as per the `RainbowLabel` controls we saw earlier. The code is as follows:

```
public class Candidate : System.Web.UI.WebControls.WebControl,
                         INamingContainer
{
  public string Name
  {
    get
    {
      object rawName = ViewState["_name"];
      if (rawName != null)
      {
        return (string)rawName;
      }
      else
      {
        ViewState["_name"] = "Candidate";
        return "Candidate";
      }
    }
    set
    {
```

```
                ViewState["_name"] = value;
        }
    }
    public long Votes
    {
        get
        {
            object rawVotes = ViewState["_votes"];
            if (rawVotes != null)
            {
                return (long)rawVotes;
            }
            else
            {
                ViewState["_votes"] = (long)0;
                return 0;
            }
        }
        set
        {
            ViewState["_votes"] = value;
        }
    }
    public void Increment()
    {
        Votes += 1;
    }
    public void Reset()
    {
        Votes = 0;
    }
    protected override void CreateChildControls()
    {
        Button btnVote = new Button();
        btnVote.Text = "Vote";
        btnVote.Click += new System.EventHandler(btnVote_Click);
        Controls.Add(btnVote);
        base.CreateChildControls();
    }
    protected void btnVote_Click(object sender, System.EventArgs e)
    {
        Increment();
    }
}
```

Note that `Render()` hasn't been overridden here. This is because this control has a single child, the voting button, and no other information to display. So, we can just go with the default, which will simply be a rendering of the button.

The StrawPoll Control Builder

Next we'll discuss how we can translate the ASP.NET code for each option into a control that is a child of our `StrawPoll` control. To do this we associate a control builder with the `StrawPoll` class (defined in

StrawPoll.cs), using the `ControlBuilderAttribute` attribute. We also need to specify that child controls should not be parsed as properties of the `StrawPoll` class by setting the `ParseChildren` attribute to false:

```
[ControlBuilderAttribute(typeof(StrawPollControlBuilder))]
[ParseChildren(false)]
public class StrawPoll : System.Web.UI.WebControls.WebControl,
                         INamingContainer
{
}
```

Here we are using a class called `StrawPollControlBuilder`, defined in StrawPollControlBuilder.cs, as follows:

```
internal class StrawPollControlBuilder : ControlBuilder
{
    public override Type GetChildControlType(string tagName,
                                             IDictionary attribs)
    {
        if (tagName.ToLower().EndsWith("candidate"))
            return typeof(Candidate);
        return null;
    }

    public override void AppendLiteralString(string s)
    {
        // Do nothing, to avoid embedded text being added to control
    }
}
```

In this example we override the `GetChildControlType()` method of the base `ControlBuilder` class to return the type of our `Candidate` class in response to a tag named `<Candidate>`. In fact, to make sure things work smoothly in as many situations as possible, we just look for any tag name that ends with the string `"candidate"`, with letters in upper- or lowercase.

We also override the `AppendLiteralString()` method so that any intervening text, including whitespace, is ignored and won't cause us any problems.

After this is set up, and assuming we don't place any other controls in `StrawPoll`, we will have all `Candidate` controls contained in the `Controls` collection of `StrawPoll`. This collection won't contain any other controls.

Note that the control builder makes use of a collection of attributes. In order to support this we need to add the following using statement to our namespace:

```
using System.Collections;
```

Straw Poll Style

Before we look at the `StrawPoll` class itself, there is one more design consideration. The straw poll should be able to display itself in one of three forms:

Chapter 27

❑ Voting buttons only

❑ Results only

❑ Voting buttons and results

We can define an enumeration for this that we can use as a property of our StrawPoll control (putting this in StrawPoll.cs is fine):

```
public enum pollStyle
{
    voteonly,
    valuesonly,
    voteandvalues
}
```

As we discussed earlier, properties that are enumerations are easy to use—we can simply use the text names as attribute values in ASP.NET.

The Straw Poll Control

Now we can start putting things together. First we define two properties, Title for the title to display for the control, and PollStyle to hold the enumerated display type. Both of these properties use the ViewState for persistence:

```
[ControlBuilderAttribute(typeof(StrawPollControlBuilder))]
[ParseChildren(false)]
public class StrawPoll : System.Web.UI.WebControls.WebControl,
                         INamingContainer
{
    public string Title
    {
        get
        {
            object rawTitle = ViewState["_title"];
            if (rawTitle != null)
            {
                return (string)rawTitle;
            }
            else
            {
                ViewState["_title"] = "Straw Poll";
                return "Straw Poll";
            }
        }
        set
        {
            ViewState["_title"] = value;
        }
    }

    public pollStyle PollStyle
    {
        get
```

```
        {
            object rawPollStyle = ViewState["_pollStyle"];
            if (rawPollStyle != null)
            {
                return (pollStyle)rawPollStyle;
            }
            else
            {
                ViewState["_pollStyle"] = pollStyle.voteandvalues;
                return pollStyle.voteandvalues;
            }
        }
        set
        {
            ViewState["_pollStyle"] = value;
        }
    }
}
```

The remainder of this class is taken up with the Render() method. This displays the entire straw poll control along with any options, taking into account the poll style to use. We'll display voting buttons by calling the RenderControl() method of child Candidate controls, and display the votes cast graphically and numerically using the Votes properties of child Candidate controls to generate simple HTML.

The code is as follows (commented for clarity):

```
protected override void Render(HtmlTextWriter output)
{
    Candidate currentCandidate;
    long iTotalVotes = 0;
    long iPercentage = 0;
    int iColumns = 2;
    // Start table, display title
    if (PollStyle == pollStyle.voteandvalues)
    {
        iColumns = 3;
    }
    output.Write("<TABLE border='1' bordercolor='black'"
                + " bgcolor='#DDDDBB'"
                + " width='90%' cellpadding='1' cellspacing='1'"
                + " align='center'>");
    output.Write("<TR><TD colspan='" + iColumns
                                    + "' align='center'"
                + " bgcolor='#FFFFDD'>");
    output.Write("<B>" + Title + "</B></TD></TR>");
    if (Controls.Count == 0)
    {
        // Default text when no options contained
        output.Write("<TR><TD bgcolor='#FFFFDD'>No options to"
                    + " display.</TR></TD>");
    }
    else
    {
```

```csharp
            // Get total votes
            for (int iLoop = 0; iLoop < Controls.Count; iLoop++)
            {
               // Get option
               currentCandidate = (Candidate)Controls[iLoop];
               // Sum votes cast
               iTotalVotes += currentCandidate.Votes;
            }
            // Render each option
            for (int iLoop = 0; iLoop < Controls.Count; iLoop++)
            {
               // Get option
               currentCandidate = (Candidate)Controls[iLoop];
               // Place option name in first column
               output.Write("<TR><TD bgcolor='#FFFFDD' width='15%'> "
                            + currentCandidate.Name + " </TD>");
               // Add voting option to second column if required
               if (PollStyle != pollStyle.valuesonly)
               {
                  output.Write("<TD width='1%' bgcolor='#FFFFDD'>"
                               + "<FONT color='#FFFFDD'>.</FONT>");
                  currentCandidate.RenderControl(output);
                  output.Write("<FONT color='#FFFFDD'>.</FONT></TD>");
               }
               // Place graph, value, and percentage in third
               // column if required
               if (PollStyle != pollStyle.voteonly)
               {
                  if (iTotalVotes > 0)
                  {
                     iPercentage = (currentCandidate.Votes * 100) /
                                   iTotalVotes;
                  }
                  else
                  {
                     iPercentage = 0;
                  }
                  output.Write("<TD bgcolor='#FFFFDD'>"
                     + "<TABLE width='100%'>"
                     + "<TR><TD><TABLE border='1' bordercolor='black'"
                               + " width='100%' cellpadding='0'"
                               + " cellspacing='0'>");
                  output.Write("<TR><TD bgcolor='red' width='"
                               + iPercentage
                               + "%'><FONT color='red'>.</FONT></TD>");
                  output.Write("<TD bgcolor='white' width='"
                               + (100-iPercentage)
                               + "%'><FONT color='white'>."
                               + "</FONT></TD></TR></TABLE></TD>");
                  output.Write("<TD width='75'>"
                               + currentCandidate.Votes + " ("
                               + iPercentage
                               + "%)</TD></TR></TABLE></TD>");
               }
               // End row
```

```
                    output.Write("</TR>");
                }
                // Show total votes cast if values displayed
                if (PollStyle != pollStyle.voteonly)
                {
                    output.Write("<TR><TD bgcolor='#FFFFDD' colspan='"
                                + iColumns
                                + "'>Total votes cast: " + iTotalVotes
                                + "</TD></TR>");
                }
            }
            // Finish table
            output.Write("</TABLE>");
        }
```

There is one more thing we have to do. If the straw poll is displayed in voteonly mode then voting should trigger a change of display to valuesonly mode. To do this we must modify in the voting button handler in our Candidate class:

```
        protected void btnVote_Click(object sender, System.EventArgs e)
        {
            Increment();
            StrawPoll parent = (StrawPoll)Parent;
            if (parent.PollStyle == pollStyle.voteonly)
            {
                parent.PollStyle = pollStyle.valuesonly;
            }
        }
```

Now you are free to use the ASP.NET code shown at the start of this section to vote for your favorite James Bond to your heart's content!

Adding an event handler

It is often the case with custom controls that you want to raise custom events, and allow users of the control to act on them. This can be used to excellent effect, as is immediately apparent if you look at the existing server controls that ASP.NET supplies. For example, the Calendar control is nothing more than a well-formatted selection of hyperlinks. We could build something like that ourselves using the techniques built up in the previous sections. However, it has the useful function that when you click a date other than the selected one it raises a SelectionChanged event. We can act on this event, either ignoring it if the selection is OK to change, or performing some processing, which we did in Chapter 26 when we checked to see if the selected date was already booked. In a similar vein, it would be nice if our straw poll control had a Voted event, which will notify the form that a vote has been made, and supply it with all the information needed to act on this.

To register a custom event we have to add the following code to a control:

```
        public event EventHandler Voted;

        protected void OnVoted(EventArgs e)
        {
            if (Voted != null)
```

```
        {
            Voted(this, e);
        }
    }
```

Then, whenever we want to raise the event, we simply call `OnVoted()`, passing the event arguments.

Whenever we call `OnVoted()` an event is raised that the user of the control can act on. To do this the user has to register an event handler for this event:

```
strawPoll1.Voted += new EventHandler(this.strawPoll1_Voted);
```

The user also has to provide the handler code, `strawPoll1_Voted()`.

We'll extend this slightly by having custom arguments for our event, in order to make the `Candidate` that triggers the event available. We'll call our custom argument object `CandidateEventArgs`, defined in a new class, `CandidateEventArgs.cs`, as follows:

```
public class CandidateEventArgs : EventArgs
{
    public Candidate OriginatingCandidate;
    public CandidateEventArgs(Candidate originator)
    {
        OriginatingCandidate = originator;
    }
}
```

We've simply added an additional public field to the existing `EventArgs` class. As we've changed the arguments we're using, we also need a specialized version of the `EventHandler` delegate that can be declared in the `PCSCustomWebControls` namespace as follows:

```
public delegate void CandidateEventHandler(object sender,
                                           CandidateEventArgs e);
```

We can use these examples in `StrawPoll` as follows:

```
public class StrawPoll : System.Web.UI.WebControls.WebControl,
                         INamingContainer
{
    public event CandidateEventHandler Voted;

    protected void OnVoted(CandidateEventArgs e)
    {
        if (Voted != null)
        {
            Voted(this, e);
        }
    }
    ...
```

We'll also have a method to raise the event, called from child `Candidate` controls when voting buttons are clicked:

```
        internal void ChildVote(CandidateEventArgs e)
        {
            OnVoted(e);
        }
```

We also have to modify the button click handler in `Candidate` to call this method, supplying it with the correct parameters:

```
        protected void btnVote_Click(object sender, System.EventArgs e)
        {
            Increment();
            StrawPoll parent = (StrawPoll)Parent;
            if (parent.PollStyle == pollStyle.voteonly)
            {
                parent.PollStyle = pollStyle.valuesonly;
            }
            CandidateEventArgs eCandidate = new CandidateEventArgs(this);
            parent.ChildVote(eCandidate);
        }
```

Now we're ready to implement the handler on the page using the control. We simply have to specify it in our ASP.NET page, adding a label to use in the handler:

```
    <form id=Form1 method=post runat="server">
        <PCS:StrawPoll Runat="server" ID=strawPoll1 PollStyle="voteonly"
                        Title="Who is your favorite James Bond?"
                        Voted="strawPoll1_Voted">
            <PCS:Option Name="Sean Connery" Votes="101"/>
            <PCS:Option Name="Roger Moore" Votes="83"/>
            <PCS:Option Name="George Lazenby" Votes="32"/>
            <PCS:Option Name="Timothy Dalton" Votes="27"/>
            <PCS:Option Name="Pierce Brosnan" Votes="95"/>
        </PCS:StrawPoll>
        <br>
        <br>
        <asp:Label Runat="server" ID="resultLabel" Text="No vote cast."/>
    </form>
```

Then we add the event handler itself:

```
        protected void strawPoll1_Voted(object sender, CandidateEventArgs e)
        {
            resultLabel.Text = "You voted for "
                                + e.OriginatingCandidate.Name + ".";
        }
```

We also have to register this event handler in `InitializeComponent()` (we'll need a `using` statement for `PCSCustomWebControls` to do this):

```
        this.strawPoll1.Voted +=
            new PCSCustomWebControls.CandidateEventHandler(this.strawPoll1_Voted);
```

Now when we vote we receive feedback on our vote, as shown in Figure 27-13.

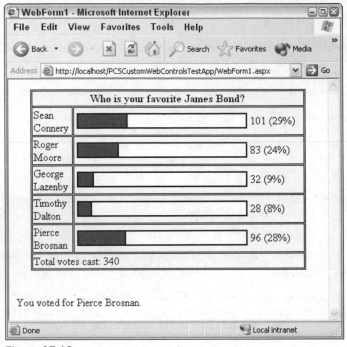

Figure 27-13

Summary

In this chapter we have looked at the various ways we can create reusable ASP.NET server controls using C#. We have discussed how to create simple user controls from existing ASP.NET pages, as well as how to create custom controls from scratch.

There is a lot we can do with custom controls; unfortunately, we cannot possibly cover every detail in this book. (For example, it would have been interesting to discuss data-binding, and how to create controls with data-binding in mind.) However, with the information in this chapter you should be able to start building (and experiment with) your own custom controls. For more details on this subject, check out *Professional ASP.NET 1.1* (ISBN: 0-7645-5890-0).

Part VI: Interop

28

COM Interoperability

If you had written Windows programs before learning .NET, usually there is not the time and resources available to rewrite everything with .NET. Existing functional code will not be rewritten just because a new technology is available. You might have thousands of lines of existing, running code, which would mean too much effort to rewrite this code just to move it into the managed environment.

The same applies to Microsoft. With the namespace System.DirectoryServices, Microsoft hasn't rewritten the COM objects accessing the hierarchical data store; the classes inside this namespace are wrappers accessing the ADSI COM Objects instead. The same thing happens with System.Data.OleDb where the OLE DB providers that are used by classes from this namespace do have quiet complex COM interfaces.

The same issue may apply for your own solutions. If you have existing COM objects that should be used from .NET applications, or the other way around if you want to write .NET components that should be used in old COM clients, this chapter will be a starter for using COM interoperability.

In this chapter we are going to:

❑   Compare COM and .NET technologies

❑   Use COM objects from within .NET applications

❑   Use .NET components from within COM clients

As is the case with the other chapters, you can download the sample code for this chapter from the Wrox Web site at www.wrox.com.

.NET and COM

The major issues using COM interoperability with .NET are to know COM. Offering .NET components for COM clients or using COM objects with .NET, that is all problems we had in the last year with COM are [CKS1]coming back. So first we discuss how COM compares to .NET

If you already have a good grasp of COM technologies, this section may be a refresher to your COM knowledge. Otherwise it introduces you to the concepts of COM that—now using .NET—we can be happy not to deal with it anymore in our daily business. However, all the problems we had with COM still apply when COM technology is integrated in .NET applications.

COM and .NET do have many similar concepts with very different solutions. Here we will discuss:

❑   Metadata

❑   Freeing memory

❑   Interfaces

❑   Method binding

❑   Data types

❑   Registration

❑   Threading

❑   Error handling

❑   Event handling

Metadata

With COM all information about the component is stored inside the type library. The type library includes information such as names and ids of interfaces, methods, and arguments. With .NET all this information can be found inside the assembly itself as we have seen in Chapters 10 and 13. The problem we had with COM is that the type library is not extensible. With C++ IDL (interface definition language) files have been used to describe the interfaces and methods. Some of the IDL modifiers cannot be found inside the type library, because Visual Basic (and the Visual Basic team was responsible for the type library) couldn't use these IDL modifiers. With .NET this problem doesn't exist because the .NET metadata is extensible using custom attributes.

As a result of this behavior, some COM components have a type library, and others don't. Where no type library is available, a C++ header file can be used that describes the interfaces and methods. With .NET it is easier using COM components that do have a type library, but it is also possible to use COM components without a type library. In that case it is necessary to redefine the COM interface by using C# code.

Freeing Memory

With .NET, memory is released by the garbage collector. This is completely different with COM. COM relies on reference counts.

The interface IUnknown which is the interface that is required to be implement by every COM object, offers three methods. Two of these methods are related to reference counts. The method AddRef() must be called by the client, if another interface pointer is needed; this method increments the reference count. The method Release() decrements the reference count, and if the resulting reference count is 0, the object destroys itself to free memory.

Interfaces

Interfaces are the heart of COM to differ between a contract that is used between the client and the object, and the implementation. The interface (the contract) defines the methods that are offered by the component, and that can be used by the client. With .NET interfaces play an important part, too.

COM distinguishes between three interface types: *custom*, *dispatch*, and *dual* interfaces.

Custom interfaces

Custom interfaces derive from the interface IUnknown. A custom interface defines the order of the methods in a virtual table (vtable), so that the client can access the methods of the interface directly. This also means that the client needs to know the vtable during development time, as binding to the methods happen by using memory addresses. As a conclusion, custom interfaces cannot be used by scripting clients. Figure 28-1 shows the vtable of the custom interface IMath that offers the methods Add() and Sub() in addition to the methods of the IUnknown interface.

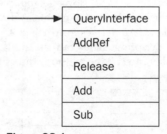

Figure 28-1

Dispatch interfaces

Because a scripting client (and earlier Visual Basic clients) doesn't support custom interfaces, a different interface type is needed. With dispatch interfaces, the interface that is available for the client is always the IDispatch interface. IDispatch derives from IUnknown and offers four methods in addition to the IUnknown methods. The two most important methods are GetIDsOfNames() and Invoke(). As shown in Figure 28-2, with a dispatch interface two tables are needed. The first one maps the method or property name to a dispatch id; the second one maps the dispatch-id to the implementation of the method or property.

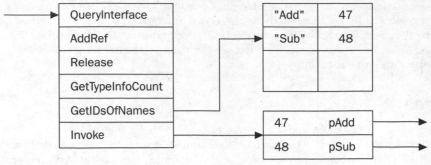

Figure 28-2

When the client invokes a method in the component, at first it calls the method `GetIDsOfNames()` passing the name of the method it wants to call. `GetIDsOfNames()` makes a lookup into the name-to-id table to return the dispatch id. This id is used by the client to call the method `Invoke()`.

> *Usually, the two tables for the **IDispatch** interface are stored inside the type library, but this is not a requirement, and some components have the tables on other places.*

Dual interfaces

As you can imagine, dispatch interfaces are a lot slower compared to custom interfaces. On the other hand, custom interfaces cannot be used by scripting clients. A dual interface can solve this dilemma. As can be seen in Figure 28-3, a dual interface derives from `IDispatch`, but offers the additional methods of the interface directly in the vtable. Scripting clients can use the `IDispatch` interface to invoke the methods, while clients aware of the vtable can call the methods directly.

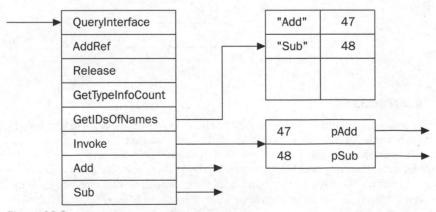

Figure 28-3

Casting and QueryInterface

If a .NET class implements multiple interfaces, casts can be done to get one interface or another. With COM, the interface `IUnknown` offers a similar mechanism with the method `QueryInterface()`. As discussed in the previous section, the interface `IUnknown` is the base interface of every interface, so `QueryInterface()` is available anyway.

Method Binding

How a client maps to a method is defined with the terms early and late binding. Late binding means that the method to invoke is looked for during runtime. .NET uses the `System.Reflection` namespace to make this possible (see Chapter 10).

COM uses the `IDispatch` interface that has been discussed earlier for late binding. Late binding is possible with dispatch and dual interfaces.

With COM early binding has two different options. One way of early binding that is also known as vtable binding is using the vtable directly—this is possible with custom and dual interfaces. The second option of early binding is also known as id binding. Here the dispatch id is stored inside the client code, so during runtime only a call to `Invoke()` is necessary. `GetIdsOfNames()` is done during design time. With such clients it is important to remember that the dispatch id must not be changed.

Data Types

For dual and dispatch interfaces the data types that can be used with COM are restricted to a list of automation-compatible data types. The `Invoke()` method of the `IDispatch` interface accepts an array of `VARIANT` data types. The `VARIANT` is a union of many different data types such as `BYTE`, `SHORT`, `LONG`, `FLOAT`, `DOUBLE`, `BSTR`, `IUnknown*`, `IDispatch*`... `VARIANT`s have been easy to use from Visual Basic, but it was complex to use them from C++. With .NET we have the `Object` class instead of `VARIANT`s.

With custom interfaces, all data types that are available with C++, can be used with COM. However, this also restricts the clients that can use this component to certain programming languages.

Registration

.NET distinguishes between private and shared assemblies as discussed in Chapter 13. With COM, all components are globally available by a registry configuration.

All COM objects do have a unique identifier that consists of a 128-bit number, and that is also known as class id (CLSID). Creating a COM object, the COM API call `CoCreateInstance()` just looks into the registry to find the CLSID and the path to the DLL or EXE to load the DLL or launch the EXE and instantiate the component.

Because such a 128-bit number cannot be easily remembered, many COM objects also do have a prog id. The prog id is an easy-to-remember name such as `Excel.Application` that just maps to the CLSID.

Besides the CLSID, COM objects also do have a unique identifier for each interface (IID), and for the type library (typelib id).

Later in this chapter we will discuss information in the registry with more detail.

Threading

COM uses apartment models to relieve the programmer from threading issues. However, this also adds some more complexity. Different apartment types have been added with different releases of the operating system. We have to discuss the single-threaded apartment and the multi-threaded apartment.

Single-threaded apartment

The single-threaded apartment (STA) was introduced with Windows NT 3.51. With an STA only one thread (the thread that created the instance) is allowed to access the component. However, it is legal having multiple STAs inside one process (see Figure 28-4).

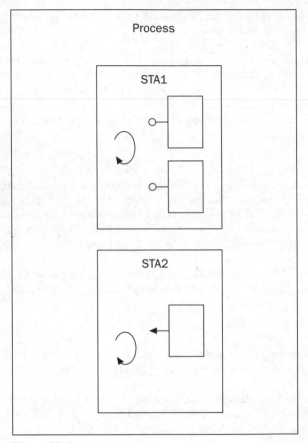

Figure 28-4

With STAs there's no need to protect instance variables from multiple thread access, as this protection is done by a COM facility, and only one thread accesses the component.

A COM object that is not programmed with thread safety, it marks the requirements for a STA in the registry with the registry key `ThreadingModel` set to `Apartment`.

Multi-threaded apartment

Windows NT 4.0 introduced the concept of a multi-threaded apartment (MTA). With an MTA, multiple threads can access the component simultaneously. Figure 28-5 shows a process with one MTA and two STAs.

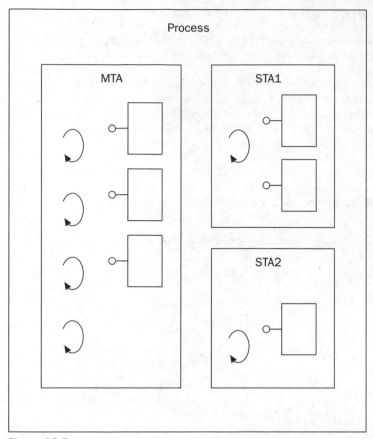

Figure 28-5

A COM object programmed with thread-safety in mind marks the requirement for an MTA in the registry with the key `ThreadingModel` set to `Free`. The value `Both` is used for thread-safe COM objects that don't mind about the apartment type.

Visual Basic 6.0 didn't offer support for multi-threaded apartments.

Error Handling

With .NET, errors are generated by throwing exceptions. With the older technology COM, errors are defined by returning `HRESULT` values with the methods. A `HRESULT` value of `S_OK` means that the method was successful.

If a more detailed error message is offered by the COM component, the COM component implements the interface `ISupportErrorInfo` where not only an error message, but also a link to a help file, and the source of the error, and returns an error information object with the method return. Objects that implement `ISupportErrorInfo` are automatically mapped to more detailed error information with an exception in .NET.

Event Handling

.NET offers an event-handling mechanism with the C# keywords `event` and `delegate` (see Chapter 6). In Chapter 16 we discuss that the same mechanism is also available with .NET Remoting.

Figure 28-6 shows the COM event-handling architecture. With COM events, the component has to implement the interface `IConnectionPointContainer`, and one more connection point objects (CPO) that implement the interface `IConnectionPoint`. The component also defines an outgoing interface—`ICompletedEvents` in Figure 28-6—that is invoked by the CPO. The client must implement this outgoing interface in the sink object, that itself is a COM object. During runtime, the client queries the server for the interface `IConnectionPointContainer`. With the help of this interface the client asks for a CPO with the method `FindConnectionPoint()`, to get a pointer to `IConnectionPoint` returned. This interface pointer is used by the client to call the `Advise()` method where a pointer to the sink object is passed to the server. In turn, the component can invoke methods inside the sink object of the client.

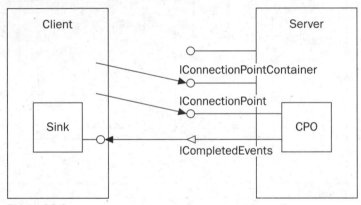

Figure 28-6

Later in this chapter we discuss how the .NET events and the COM events can be mapped, so that COM events can be handled by a .NET client and vice versa.

Marshaling

Data that is passed from .NET to the COM component and the other way around must be converted to the corresponding representation. This mechanism is also known as *marshaling*. What happens here depends on the data type of the data that is passed. Here we have to differentiate between *blittable* and *non-blittable* data types.

Blittable data types have a common representation with both .NET and COM, and no conversion is needed. Simple data types such as `byte`, `short`, `int`, `long`, and classes and arrays that only contain these simple data types belong to the blittable data types. Arrays must be one-dimensional to be blittable.

With non-blittable data types a conversion is needed. The following table lists some of the non-blittable COM data types with their .NET-related data type. Non-blittable types do need more performance because of the conversion.

COM Data Type	.NET Data Type
SAFEARRAY	Array
VARIANT	Object
BSTR	String
IUnknown*, IDispatch*	Object

Using a COM Component from a .NET Client

To see how a .NET application can use a COM component we first have to create a COM component. Creating COM components is not possible with C# or Visual Basic .NET; we need either Visual Basic 6 or C++ (or any other language that supports COM). In this chapter we use the Active Template Library (ATL) and C++.

Because this is not a COM book, we will not discuss all aspects of the code. We discuss only what we need to build the sample.

Creating a COM Component

To create a COM component with ATL and C++, create a new ATL Project. You can find the ATL Project Wizard within the Visual C++ Projects group when you select File | New | Project. Set the name to COMServer. With the Application Settings, select Attributed and Dynamic Link Library, and press Finish.

Since Visual Studio .NET 2002, the ATL offers attributes that make it easier to build COM server. These attributes have nothing in common with the .NET attributes; instead they are only used with ATL. Instead of writing a separate IDL file and a C++ file defining the interface, only a C++ file is needed that also has attributes that are required by COM.

The ATL Project Wizard just created the foundation for the server. A COM object is still needed. Add a class in Solution Explorer, and select ATL Simple Object. With the dialog that starts up, enter **COMDemo** in the field for the Short name. The other fields will be filled automatically, but change the interface name to **IWelcome** (see Figure 28-7).

The COM component will offer two interfaces, so that you can see how QueryInterface() is mapped from .NET, and just three simple methods, so that you can see how the interaction takes place. In the Class View, select the interface IWelcome, and add the method Greeting() (see Figure 28-7), with these parameters:

```
HRESULT Greeting([in] BSTR name, [out, retval] BSTR* message);
```

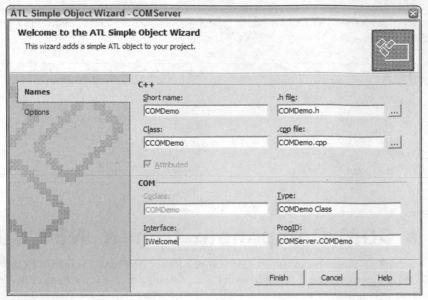

Figure 28-7

Your wizard-generated code from the file COMDemo.h should look similar to the following code. The unique identifiers (uuids) will differ. The interface IWelcome defines the methods Greeting(). The brackets before the keyword __interface define some attributes for the interface. uuid defines the interface id, and dual marks the type of the interface.

```
// COMDemo.h : Declaration of the CCOMDemo

#pragma once
#include "resource.h"        // main symbols

// IWelcome
[
  object,
  uuid("015ED275-3DE6-4716-A6FA-4EBC71E4A8EA"),
  dual, helpstring("IWelcome Interface"),
  pointer_default(unique)
]
__interface IWelcome : IDispatch
{
  [id(1), helpstring("method Greeting")] HRESULT Greeting([in] BSTR name, [out,
retval] BSTR* message);
};
```

The class CCOMDemo is also in the file COMDemo.h. The attribute uuid() in the header section of the class defines the CLSID. The attributes vi_progid and progid name the prog id that will be written into the registry.

```
// CCOMDemo

[
coclass,
threading("apartment"),
vi_progid("COMServer.COMDemo"),
progid("COMServer.COMDemo.1"),
version(1.0),
uuid("2388AAA8-AD72-4022-948D-555316F708E8"),
helpstring("COMDemo Class")
]
class ATL_NO_VTABLE CCOMDemo :
  public IWelcome
{
public:
  CCOMDemo()
  {
  }


  DECLARE_PROTECT_FINAL_CONSTRUCT()

  HRESULT FinalConstruct()
  {
    return S_OK;
  }

  void FinalRelease()
  {
  }

public:

  STDMETHOD(Greeting)(BSTR name, BSTR* message);
};
```

> With custom attributes it is possible to change the name of the class and interfaces
> that are generated by a .NET wrapper class. You just have to add the attribute
> custom with the identifier 0F21F359-AB84-41e8-9A78-36D110E6D2F9, and the
> name how it should appear within .NET.

Add the custom attribute with the same identifier and the name Wrox.ProCSharp.COMInterop.
Server.IWelcome to the header section of the IWelcome interface. Add the same attribute with a
corresponding name to the class CCOMDemo.

```
// IWelcome
[
  object,
  uuid("015ED275-3DE6-4716-A6FA-4EBC71E4A8EA"),
  dual, helpstring("ICOMDemo Interface"),
  pointer_default(unique),
```

```
   custom(0F21F359-AB84-41e8-9A78-36D110E6D2F9,
     "Wrox.ProCSharp.COMInterop.Server.IWelcome")
]
__interface IWelcome : IDispatch
{
    [id(1)] HRESULT Greeting([in] BSTR name, [out, retval] BSTR* message);
};
```

Now add a second interface to the file COMDemo.h. You can copy the header section of the IWelcome interface to the header section of the new IMath interface, but be sure to change the unique identifier that is defined with the uuid keyword. You can generate such an id with the utility guidgen. The interface IMath offers the methods Add() and Sub().

```
// IMath
[
  object,
  uuid("2158751B-896E-461d-9012-EF1680BE0628"),
  dual,
  helpstring("IMath Interface"),
  pointer_default(unique),
  custom(0F21F359-AB84-41e8-9A78-36D110E6D2F9,
    "Wrox.ProCSharp.COMInterop.Server.IMath")
]
__interface IMath : IDispatch
{
    [id(1)] HRESULT Add([in] LONG val1, [in] LONG val2, [out, retval] LONG* result);
    [id(2)] HRESULT Sub([in] LONG val1, [in] LONG val2, [out, retval] LONG* result);
};
```

The class CCOMDemo must also be changed, so that it implements both interfaces IWelcome and IMath:

```
[
  coclass,
  threading("apartment"),
  vi_progid("COMServer.COMDemo"),
  progid("COMServer.COMDemo.1"),
  version(1.0),
  custom(0F21F359-AB84-41e8-9A78-36D110E6D2F9,
    "Wrox.ProCSharp.COMInterop.Server.COMDemo"),
  uuid("2388AAA8-AD72-4022-948D-555316F708E8"),
  helpstring("COMDemo Class")
]
class ATL_NO_VTABLE CCOMDemo :
    public IWelcome, public IMath
{
```

Now you can implement the three methods in the file COMDemo.cpp with the following code. The CComBSTR is an ATL class that makes it easier to deal with BSTRs. In the Greeting() method just a welcome message is returned that adds the name passed in the first argument to the message that is returned. The Add() method just does a simple addition of two values, while the Sub() method does a subtraction, and returns the result.

```
STDMETHODIMP CCOMDemo::Greeting(BSTR name, BSTR* message)
{
    CComBSTR tmp("Welcome, ");
    tmp.Append(name);
    *message = tmp;
    return S_OK;
}


STDMETHODIMP CCOMDemo::Add(LONG val1, LONG val2, LONG* result)
{
    *result = val1 + val2;
    return S_OK;
}


STDMETHODIMP CCOMDemo::Sub(LONG val1, LONG val2, LONG* result)
{
    *result = val1 -- val2;
    return S_OK;
}
```

Now you can build the component. The build process also configures the component in the registry.

Creating a Runtime Callable Wrapper

You can now use the COM component from within .NET. To make this possible, you must create a runtime callable wrapper (RCW). Using the RCW the .NET client sees a .NET object instead of the COM component, there is no need to deal with the COM characteristics as this is done by the wrapper. A RCW hides IUnknown and IDispatch interfaces (see Figure 28-8) and deals itself with the reference counts of the COM object.

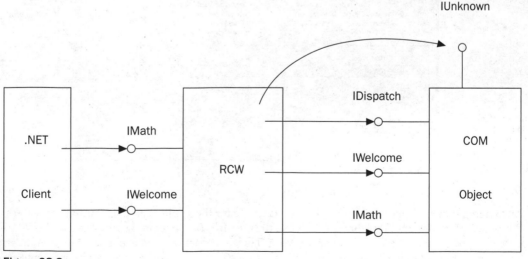

Figure 28-8

The RCW can be created by using the command-line utility tlbimp, or by using Visual Studio .NET. Starting the command

```
tlbimp COMServer.dll /out: Interop.COMServer.dll
```

creates the file Interop.COMServer.dll including a .NET assembly with the wrapper class. In this generated assembly we can find the namespace COMWrapper with the class CCOMDemoClass and the interfaces CCOMDemo, IMath, and IWelcome. The name of the namespace can be changed by using options of the tlbimp utility. The option /namespace allows us to specify a different namespace, with /asmversion the version number of the assembly can be defined.

> *Another important option of this command-line utility is /keyfile for assigning a strong name to the generated assembly. Strong names are discussed in Chapter 13.*

An RCW can also be created by using Visual Studio .NET. To create a simple sample application, create a C# console project. In Solution Explorer, add a reference to the COM server by selecting the COM tab and scroll down to the entry COMServer 1.0 Type Library (see Figure 28-9). Here all COM objects are listed that are configured in the registry. Selecting a COM component from the list creates an assembly with an RCW class.

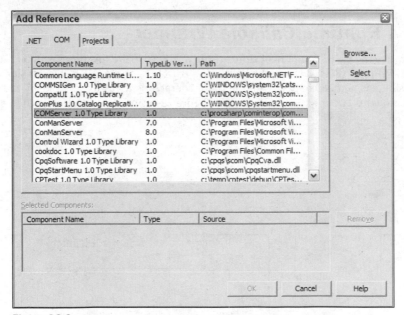

Figure 28-9

After creating the wrapper class you can write the code for the application to instantiate and access the component. Because of the custom attributes in the C++ file, the generated namespace of the RCW class is Wrox.ProCSharp.COMInterop.Server. Add this namespace as well as the namespace System. Runtime.InteropServices to the declarations. From the namespace System.Runtime.Interop Services the Marshal class will be used to release the COM object.

```
using System;
using System.Runtime.InteropServices;
using Wrox.ProCSharp.COMInteorp.Server

namespace Wrox.ProCSharp.COMInterop.Client
{
    class Class1
    {
        [STAThread]
        static void Main(string[] args)
        {
```

Now the COM component can be used similar to a .NET class. `obj` is a variable of type COMDemo. COMDemo is a .NET interface that offers the methods of both the IWelcome and the IMath interfaces. However, it is also possible to cast to a specific interface such as IWelcome. With a variable that is a declared of type IWelcome, the method Greeting() can be called.

```
COMDemo obj = new COMDemoClass();
IWelcome welcome = (IWelcome)obj;
Console.WriteLine(obj.Greeting("Christian"));
```

If the object—as in our case—offers multiple interfaces, a variable of the other interface can be declared, and by using a simple assignment with the cast operator, the wrapper class does a QueryInterface() with the COM object to return the second interface pointer. With the math variable the methods of the IMath interface can be called.

```
IMath math;
math = (IMath)obj;
int x = math.Add(4, 5);
Console.WriteLine(x);
```

If the COM object should be released before the garbage collector cleans up the object, the static method Marshal.ReleaseComObject() invokes the Release() method of the component, so that the component can destroy itself and free memory.

```
Marshal.ReleaseComObject(math);
        }
    }
}
```

As can be seen, with a runtime callable wrapper, a COM component can be used similar to a .NET object.

A special case of a runtime callable wrapper is a primary interop assembly.

Primary interop assemblies

A *primary interop assembly* is an assembly that is already prepared by the vendor of the COM component. This makes it easier to use the COM component. A primary interop assembly is a runtime-callable wrapper that might differ from an automatically generated RCW.

You can find primary interop assemblies in the directory <program files>\Microsoft .NET\Primary Interop Assemblies. A primary interop assembly already exists for the use of ADO from within .NET. If you add a reference to the COM library Microsoft ActiveX Data Objects 2.7 Library, no wrapper class is created because a primary interop assembly already exists; instead the primary interop assembly is referenced.

Threading Issues

As discussed earlier in this chapter, a COM components marks the apartment (STA or MTA) it wants to live in, based on whether it is implemented thread-safe or not. However, the thread has to join an apartment. You have already seen the attribute [STAThread] that is applied to the Main() method by Visual Studio .NET with every Windows or console application. This attribute means that the thread joins an STA. The opposite is the attribute [MTAThread], which means the thread joins an MTA. Joining an MTA is the default if no attribute is applied.

It is also possible to set the apartment state programmatically with the ApartmentState property of the Thread class. The ApartmentState property allows you to set a value from the ApartmentState enumeration. ApartmentState has the possible values STA and MTA. (and Unknown if it wasn't set). Be aware that the apartment state of a thread can only be set once. If it is set for a second time, the second setting is ignored.

> **What happens if the thread chooses a different apartment from the apartments that are supported by the component? The correct apartment for the COM component is created automatically by the COM runtime. However, the performance decreases if the apartment boundaries are crossed while calling the methods of a component.**

Adding Connection Points

To see how COM events can be handled in a .NET application, at first the COM component must be extended. Implementing a COM event in an ATL class using attributes looks very similar to the events in .NET although the functionality is different.

First you have to add another interface to the header file COMDemo.h. The interface _ICompletedEvents is implemented by the client, which is the .NET application, and called by the component. In this example the method Completed() is called by the component when the calculation is ready. Such an interface is also known as an outgoing interface. An outgoing interface must be either a dispatch or a custom interface. Dispatch interfaces are supported by all clients. The custom attribute with the id 0F21F359-AB84-41e8-9A78-36D110E6D2F9 defines the name of this interface that will be created in the RCW.

```
// _ICompletedEvents
[
  dispinterface,
  uuid("B2CBBCD3-2993-4148-8EF4-356EACFD834B"),
  custom(0F21F359-AB84-41e8-9A78-36D110E6D2F9,
    "Wrox.ProCSharp.COMInterop.Server.ICompletedEvents"),
  helpstring("_ICompletedEvents Interface")
]
```

```
__interface _ICompletedEvents
{
 [id(1)] void Completed(void);
};
```

Apply the attribute `event_source("com")` to the class `CCOMDemo` to create a connection point object, and add the `__event` keyword to the public section of this class as shown in the following code. This keyword `__event` creates a helper class for all methods of the defined interface that fires events to the client. The event is fired using the `__raise` keyword inside the method `FireCompleted()`.

```
[
  coclass,
  threading("apartment"),
  vi_progid("COMServer.COMDemo"),
  progid("COMServer.COMDemo.1"),
  version(1.0),
  custom(0F21F359-AB84-41e8-9A78-36D110E6D2F9,
    "Wrox.ProCSharp.COMInterop.Server.COMDemo"),
  uuid("2388AAA8-AD72-4022-948D-555316F708E8"),
  event_source("com"),
  helpstring("COMDemo Class")
]
class ATL_NO_VTABLE CCOMDemo :
   public IWelcome, public IMath
{
public:
   CCOMDemo()
   {
   }

   __event __interface _ICompletedEvents;
   void FireCompleted()
   {
      __raise Completed();
   }
```

Finally, the method `FireCompleted()` can be called inside the methods `Add()` and `Sub()` in the file `COMDemo.cpp`.

```
STDMETHODIMP CCOMDemo::Add(LONG val1, LONG val2, LONG* result)
{
   *result = val1 + val2;
   FireCompleted();
   return S_OK;
}

STDMETHODIMP CCOMDemo::Sub(LONG val1, LONG val2, LONG* result)
{
   *result = val1 - val2;
   FireCompleted();
   return S_OK;
}
```

After rebuilding the COM DLL, you can change the .NET client to use these COM events.

```
static void Main(string[] args)
{
    COMDemo obj = new COMDemoClass();

    IWelcome welcome = (IWelcome)obj;
    Console.WriteLine(welcome.Greeting("Christian"));

    obj.Completed +=
        new ICompletedEvents_CompletedEventHandler(Completed);

    IMath math = (IMath)welcome;
    int result = math.Add(3, 5);
    Console.WriteLine(result);

    Marshal.ReleaseComObject(math);
}

private static void Completed()
{
    Console.WriteLine("Calculation completed");
}
```

As you can see, the RCW offers automatic mapping from COM events to .NET events. COM events can be used similar to .NET events in a .NET client.

Using ActiveX Controls in Windows Forms

ActiveX controls are COM objects with a user interface and many optional COM interfaces to deal with the user interface and the interaction with the container. ActiveX controls can be used by many different containers such as Internet Explorer, Word, Excel, applications written using Visual Basic 6, MFC (Microsoft Foundation Classes), or ATL (Active Template Library). A Windows Forms application is another container that can manage ActiveX controls. ActiveX controls can be used similar to Windows Forms controls as we discuss shortly.

ActiveX Control Importer

Similar to runtime callable wrappers, you can also create a wrapper for ActiveX controls. A wrapper for an ActiveX controls is created by using the command-line utility *Windows Forms ActiveX Control Importer* aximp.exe. This utility creates a class that derives from the base class System.Windows.Forms.AxHost that acts as a wrapper to use the ActiveX control.

You can enter this command to create a wrapper class from the Web Forms Control:

aximp c:\windows\system32\shdocvw.dll

Creating a Windows Forms application

To see ActiveX controls running inside a Windows Forms application, create a simple Windows Forms application project. With this application we will build a simple Internet browser that uses the Web Browser control that comes as part of the operating system.

Create a form as shown in Figure 28-10. The form should include a text box that is used to enter a URL with the name `textUrl`, three buttons with the names `buttonNavigate`, `buttonBack` and `buttonForward` to navigate Web pages, and a status bar with the name `statusBar`.

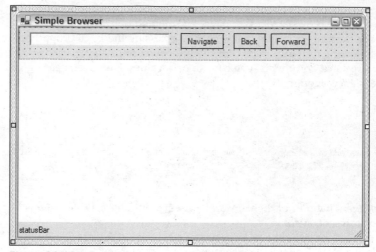

Figure 28-10

Using Visual Studio .NET, you can add ActiveX controls to the toolbar to use it in the same way as a Windows Forms control. In the Customize Toolbox context menu, select the menu entry Add/Remove Items..., and select the Microsoft Web Browser control in the category COM Components (see Figure 28-11).

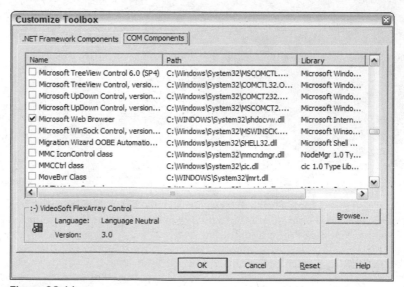

Figure 28-11

This way an icon will show up in the toolbox. Similar to other Windows controls, you can drag and drop this icon to the Windows Forms designer to create (with the aximp utility) a wrapper assembly hosting the ActiveX control. You can see the wrapper assemblies with the references in the project: AxSHDocVw and SHDocVw. Now you can invoke methods of the control by using the generated variable axWeb Browser1 as shown in the following code. Add a Click event handler to the button buttonNavigate in order to navigate the browser to a Web page. The method Navigate() used for this purpose requires a URL string with the first argument that we get by accessing the Text property of the text field textUrl. The following four arguments are all optional with the Navigate() method. Because C# doesn't support optional arguments, you have to pass values. However, passing null values with the noArg variable is good enough.

```
private void OnNavigate(object sender, System.EventArgs e)
{
    object noArg = null;
    axWebBrowser1.Navigate(textUrl.Text, ref noArg, ref noArg, ref noArg,
                           ref noArg);
}
```

With the Click event handler of the Back and Forward buttons, call the GoBack() and GoForward() methods of the browser control:

```
private void OnBack(object sender, System.EventArgs e)
{
    try
    {
        axWebBrowser1.GoBack();
    }
    catch
    {
    }
}

private void OnForward(object sender, System.EventArgs e)
{
    try
    {
        axWebBrowser1.GoForward();
    }
    catch
    {
    }
}
```

The Web control also offers some events that can be used just like a .NET event. Add the event handler OnStatusChange() to the event StatusTextChange to set the status that is returned by the control to the status bar in the Windows Forms application.

```
private void OnStatusChange(object sender,
                AxSHDocVw.DWebBrowserEvents2_StatusTextChangeEvent e)
{
    statusBar.Text = e.text;
}
```

Now you have a simple browser that you can use to navigate to Web pages (see Figure 28-12).

Figure 28-12

Using COM Objects from within ASP.NET

COM objects can be used in a similar way we have seen before from within ASP.NET. However, there is one important distinction. The ASP.NET runtime by default runs in a MTA. If the COM object is configured with the threading model value Apartment (as all COM object that have been written with Visual Basic 6), an exception is thrown. Because of performance and scalability reasons, it is best to avoid STA objects within ASP.NET. If you really want to use an STA object with ASP.NET, you can set the AspCompat attribute with the Page directive as shown in the following snippet. Be aware that the Web site performance might suffer when you are using this option.

```
<%@ Page AspCompat="true" Language="C#" %>
```

Using a .NET Component from a COM Client

So far we have discussed how to access a COM component from a .NET client. Equally interesting is to find a solution for accessing .NET components in an old COM client that is using Visual Basic 6, MFC, or ATL.

COM Callable Wrapper

If you want to access a COM component with a .NET client, you have to work with a RCW. To access a .NET component from a COM client application, you must use a COM Callable Wrapper (CCW). Figure 28-13 shows a CCW that wraps a .NET class, and offers COM interfaces that a COM client expects to use. The CCW offers interfaces such as `IUnknown`, `IDispatch`, `ISupportErrorInfo`, and others. It also offers interfaces such as `IConnectionPointContainer` and `IConnectionPoint` for events. A COM client gets what it expects from a COM object—although a .NET component is behind the scenes. The wrapper deals with methods such as `AddRef()`, `Release()`, `QueryInterface()` from the `IUnknown` interface, while in the .NET object we can count on the garbage collector without the need to deal with reference counts.

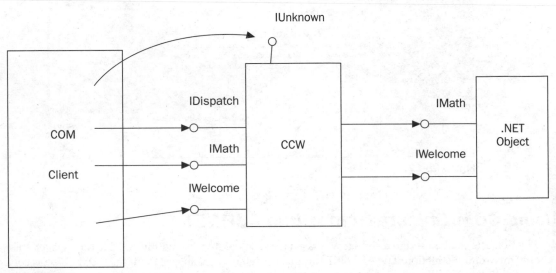

Figure 28-13

Creating a .NET Component

In the following example, we built the same functionality that we built previously into a COM component into a .NET class. Start by creating a C# class library, and name it `DotNetComponent`. Then add the interfaces `IWelcome` and `IMath`, and the class `NetComponent` that implements these interfaces.

```csharp
using System;

namespace Wrox.ProCSharp.COMInterop.Server
{
    public interface IWelcome
    {
        string Greeting(string name);
    }

    public interface IMath
    {
```

```
      int Add(int val1, int val2);
      int Sub(int val1, int val2);
   }

   public class DotnetComponent : IWelcome, IMath
   {
      public DotnetComponent()
      {
      }

      public string Greeting(string name)
      {
         return "Hello " + name;
      }

      public int Add(int val1, int val2)
      {
         return val1 + val2;
      }

      public int Sub(int val1, int val2)
      {
         return val1 - val2;
      }
   }
}
```

After building the project, you can create a type library.

Creating a Type Library

A type library can be created by using the command-line utility tlbexp. The command

```
tlbexp DotnetComponent.dll
```

creates the type library `DotnetComponent.tlb`. You can view the type library with the utiltiy
OLE/COM Object Viewer. To access this utility in Visual Studio .NET select Tools⇨OLE/COM Object
Viewer. Next, select File⇨View TypeLib to open the type library. You can now view the interface defini-
tion shown in the following code. The unique ids will differ.

The name of the type library is created from the name of the assembly. The header of the type library
also defines the full name of the assembly in a custom attribute, and all the interfaces are forward
declared before they are defined.

```
// Generated .IDL file (by the OLE/COM Object Viewer)
//
// typelib filename: <could not determine filename>

[
  uuid(0AA0953A-B2A0-32CB-A5AC-5DA0DF698EB8),
  version(1.0),
  custom(90883F05-3D28-11D2-8F17-00A0C9A6186D, DotNetComponent,
```

```
            Version=1.0.1321.19165, Culture=neutral, PublicKeyToken=null)
]
library DotnetComponent
{
    // TLib : Common Language Runtime Library :
    // {BED7F4EA-1A96-11D2-8F08-00A0C9A6186D}
    importlib("mscorlib.tlb");
    // TLib : OLE Automation : {00020430-0000-0000-C000-000000000046}
    importlib("stdole2.tlb");

    // Forward declare all types defined in this typelib
    interface IWelcome;
    interface IMath;
    interface _DotnetComponent;
```

In the following generated code you can see that the interfaces IWelcome and IMath are defined as COM dual interfaces. You can see all methods that have been declared in the C# code are here listed in the type library definition. The parameters changed: the .NET types are mapped to COM types (such as the String class to the BSTR type), and the signature is changed, so that a HRESULT is returned. Because the interfaces are dual interfaces, dispatch ids are also generated.

```
[
  odl,
  uuid(F39A4143-F88D-321E-9A33-8208E256A2DF),
  version(1.0),
  dual,
  oleautomation,
  custom(0F21F359-AB84-41E8-9A78-36D110E6D2F9,
         Wrox.ProCSharp.COMInterop.Server.IWelcome)
]
interface IWelcome : IDispatch {
    [id(0x60020000)]
    HRESULT Greeting([in] BSTR name, [out, retval] BSTR* pRetVal);
};


[
  odl,
  uuid(EF596F3F-B69B-3657-9D48-C906CBF12565),
  version(1.0),
  dual,
  oleautomation,
  custom(0F21F359-AB84-41E8-9A78-36D110E6D2F9,
         Wrox.ProCSharp.COMInterop.Server.IMath)
]
interface IMath : IDispatch {
    [id(0x60020000)] HRESULT Add([in] long val1, [in] long val2,
                                 [out, retval] long* pRetVal);
    [id(0x60020001)] HRESULT Sub([in] long val1, [in] long val2,
                                 [out, retval] long* pRetVal);
};
```

The `coclass` section marks the COM object itself. The `uuid` in the header is the CLSID that is used to instantiate the object. The class `DotnetComponent` supports the interfaces `_DotnetComonent`, `_Object`, `IWelcome`, and `IMath`. `_Object` is defined in the file mscorlib.tlb that is included in an earlier code section, and offers the methods of the base class `Object`. The default interface of the component is `_DotnetComponent` that is defined after the `coclass` section as a dispatch interface. In the interface declaration it is marked as dual, but because no methods are included, it is a dispatch interface. With this interface it is possible to access all methods of the component using late binding.

```
[
  uuid(5BCD9C26-D68D-38C2-92E3-DA0C1741A8CD),
  version(1.0),
  custom(0F21F359-AB84-41E8-9A78-36D110E6D2F9,
        Wrox.ProCSharp.COMInterop.Server.DotnetComponent)
]
coclass DotnetComponent {
  [default] interface _DotnetComponent;
  interface _Object;
  interface IWelcome;
  interface IMath;
};

[
  odl,
  uuid(884C59C6-B3C2-3455-BB74-52753C409097),
  hidden,
  dual,
  oleautomation,
  custom(0F21F359-AB84-41E8-9A78-36D110E6D2F9,
        Wrox.ProCSharp.COMInterop.Server.DotnetComponent)
]
interface _DotnetComponent : IDispatch {
};
};
```

There are quite a few defaults for generating the type library. However, often it is advantageous to change some of the default .NET to COM mappings. This can be done with several attributes in the `System.Runtime.InteropServices` namespaces.

COM Interop Attributes

Applying attributes from the namespace `System.Runtime.InteropServices` to classes, interfaces, or methods allows us to change the implementation of the CCW.

Attribute	Description
Guid	This attribute can be assigned to the assembly, interfaces, and classes. Using the Guid as an assembly attribute defines the type-library id, applying it to interfaces defines the interface id (IID), and setting the attribute to a class defines the class id (CLSID). The unique ids needed to be defined with this attribute can be created with the utility guidgen. Automatically the CLSID and type-library ids are changed with every build. If you don't want to change it with every build, you can fix it by using this attribute. The IID is only changed if the signature of the interface changes, for example, a method is added or removed, or some parameters changed. Because with COM the IID should change with every new version of this interface, this is a very good default behavior, and usually there's no need to apply the IID with the Guid attribute. The only reason when you want to apply a fixed IID for an interface is when the .NET interface is an exact representation of an existing COM interface, and the COM client already expects this identifier.
ProgId	This attribute can be applied to a class to specify what name should be used when the object is configured into the registry.
ComVisible	This attribute enables you to hide classes, interfaces, delegates from COM when set to false. This prevents a COM representation from being created.
InterfaceType	This attribute, if set to a ComInterfaceType enumeration value, enables you to modify the default dual interface type that is created for .NET interfaces. ComInterfaceType has the values InterfaceIsDual, InterfaceIsIDispatch, and InterfaceIsIUnknown. If you want to apply a custom interface type to a .NET interface, set the attribute like this: [InterfaceType(ComInterfaceType.InterfaceIsIUnkwnown)]
ClassInterface	This attribute enables you to modify the default dispatch interface that is created for a class. ClassInterface accepts an argument of a ClassInterfaceType enumeration. The possible values are AutoDispatch, AutoDual, and None. In the previous example we have seen that the default is AutoDispatch, since a dispatch interface is created. If the class should only be accessible by the defined interfaces, apply the attribute [ClassInterface(ClassInterfaceType.None)] to the class.
DispId	This attribute can be used with dual and dispatch interfaces to define the dispid of methods and properties.
In	COM allows specifying attributes to parameter types if the parameter should be sent to the component [In], from the component to the client [Out], or in both directions [In, Out].
Out	
Optional	Parameters of COM methods may be optional. Parameters that should be optional can be marked with the Optional attribute.

Now you can change the C# code to specify a dual interface type for the `IWelcome` interface, a custom interface type for the `IMath` interface, and with the class `DotnetCompnent` the attribute `ClassInterface` with the argument `ClassInterfaceType.None` so that no separate COM interface will be generated, a prog id and a guid:

```
[InterfaceType(ComInterfaceType.InterfaceIsDual)]
public interface IWelcome
{
    [DispId(60040)] string Greeting(string name);
}

[InterfaceType(ComInterfaceType.InterfaceIsIUnknown)]
public interface IMath
{
  int Add(int val1, int val2);
  int Sub(int val1, int val2);
}

[ClassInterface(ClassInterfaceType.None)]
[ProgId("Wrox.DotnetComponent")]
[Guid("77839717-40DD-4876-8297-35B98A8402C7")]
public class DotnetComponent : IWelcome, IMath
{
    public DotnetComponent()
    {
    }
}
```

Rebuilding the class library and the type library changes the interface definition. You can verify this with OleView.exe. As you can see in the following IDL code, the interface `IWelcome` is still a dual interface, while the `IMath` interface now is a custom interface that derives from `IUnknown` instead of `IDispatch`. In the `coclass` section, the interface `_DotnetComponent` is removed, and now the `IWelcome` is the new default interface, because it was the first interface in the inheritance list of the class `DotnetComponent`.

```
// Generated .IDL file (by the OLE/COM Object Viewer)
//
// typelib filename: <could not determine filename>

[
 uuid(11E86506-EA54-3611-A55C-6830C48A554B),
 version(1.0),
 custom(90883F05-3D28-11D2-8F17-00A0C9A6186D, DotNetComponent,
        Version=1.0.1321.28677, Culture=neutral, PublicKeyToken=null)
]
library DotnetComponent
{
    // TLib : Common Language Runtime Library :
    // {BED7F4EA-1A96-11D2-8F08-00A0C9A6186D}
    importlib("mscorlib.tlb");
    // TLib : OLE Automation : {00020430-0000-0000-C000-000000000046}
    importlib("stdole2.tlb");

    // Forward declare all types defined in this typelib
    interface IWelcome;
    interface IMath;
```

```
  [
    odl,
    uuid(F39A4143-F88D-321E-9A33-8208E256A2DF),
    version(1.0),
    dual,
    oleautomation,
    custom(0F21F359-AB84-41E8-9A78-36D110E6D2F9,
            Wrox.ProCSharp.COMInterop.Server.IWelcome)
  ]
  interface IWelcome : IDispatch {
      [id(0x0000ea88)]
      HRESULT Greeting([in] BSTR name, [out, retval] BSTR* pRetVal);
  };


  [
    odl,
    uuid(EF596F3F-B69B-3657-9D48-C906CBF12565),
    version(1.0),
    oleautomation,
    custom(0F21F359-AB84-41E8-9A78-36D110E6D2F9,
            Wrox.ProCSharp.COMInterop.Server.IMath)
  ]
  interface IMath : IUnknown {
      HRESULT _stdcall Add([in] long val1, [in] long val2,
                           [out, retval] long* pRetVal);
      HRESULT _stdcall Sub([in] long val1, [in] long val2,
                           [out, retval] long* pRetVal);
  };


  [
    uuid(77839717-40DD-4876-8297-35B98A8402C7),
    version(1.0),
    custom(0F21F359-AB84-41E8-9A78-36D110E6D2F9,
            Wrox.ProCSharp.COMInterop.Server.DotnetComponent)
  ]
  coclass DotnetComponent {
      interface _Object;
      [default] interface IWelcome;
      interface IMath;
  };
};
```

COM Registration

Before the .NET component can be used as a COM object, it is necessary to configure it in the registry. Also, if you don't want to copy the assembly into the same directory as the client application, it is necessary to install the assembly in the global assembly cache. The global assembly cache was discussed in Chapter 13.

For installing the assembly into the global assembly cache you have to create a key pair with the strong name utility:

```
sn -k mykey.snk
```

Add the key file to the `AssemblyKeyFile` attribute in the file AssemblyInfo.cs:

```
[assembly: AssemblyKeyFile("../../mykey.snk")]
```

And register the assembly in the global assembly cache:

```
gacutil -i dotnetcomponent.dll
```

Now you can use the regasm utility to configure the component inside the registry. The option /tlb extracts the type library, and also configures the type library in the registry.

```
regasm dotnetcomponent.dll /tlb
```

The information for the .NET component that is written to the registry is as follows. All COM configuration is in the hive HKEY_CLASSES_ROOT (HKCR). Directly to this hive the key of the prog id (in the case of this example, it is `Wrox.DotnetComponent`) is written, along with the CLSID.

The key HKCR\CLSID\{CLSID}\InProcServer32 has the following entries:

❑   **mscoree.dll**: mscoree.dll represents the CCW. This is a real COM object that is responsible for hosting the .NET component. This COM object accesses the .NET component to offer COM behavior for the client. The file `mscoree.dll` is loaded and instantiated from the client via the normal COM instantiation mechanism.

❑   **ThreadingModel=Both**: This is an attribute of the mscoree.dll COM object. This component is programmed in a way to offer support both for STA and MTA.

❑   **Assembly=DotnetComponent, Version=1.0.1321.33886, Culture=neutral, PublicKeyToken=5cd57c93b4d9c41a**: The value of the Assembly stores the assembly full name including the version number and the public key token, so that the assembly can be uniquely identified. The assembly registered here will be loaded by mscoree.dll.

❑   **Class=Wrox.ProCSharp.COMInterop.Server.DotnetComponent**: The name of the class will also be used by mscoree.dll. This is the class that will be instantiated.

❑   **RuntimeVersion=v1.1.4322**: The registry entry RuntimeVersion specifies the version of the .NET runtime that will be used to host the .NET assembly.

In addition to the configurations shown here, all the interfaces and the type-library are configured with their identifiers, too.

Creating a COM Client

Now it's time to create a COM client. Start by creating a simple C++ Win32 Console Project, and name it COMClient. You can leave the default options selected, and press Finish with the project wizard.

In the beginning of the file COMClient.cpp add a preprocessor command to include the <iostream> header file and to import the type library that you created for the .NET component. The import statement creates a "smart pointer" class that makes it easier dealing with COM objects. During a build process, the import statement creates .tlh and .tli files that you can find in the debug directory of your project, which includes the smart pointer class. Then add using namespace directives to open the namespace std that will be used for writing output messages to the console, and the namespace DotnetComponent that is created inside the smart pointer class.

```cpp
// COMClient.cpp : Defines the entry point for the console application.
//

#include "stdafx.h"
#include <iostream>
#import "../DotNetComponent/bin/debug/DotnetComponent.tlb"

using namespace std;
using namespace DotnetComponent;
```

In the _tmain() method, the first thing to do before any other COM call, is initialization of COM with the API call CoInitialize(). CoIntialize() creates and enters an STA for the thread. The variable spWelcome is of type IWelcomePtr that is a smart pointer. The smart pointer method CreateInstance() accepts the prog id as an argument to create the COM object by using the COM API CoCreateInstance(). The operator -> is overridden with the smart pointer, so that you can invoke the methods of the COM object such as Greeting().

```cpp
int _tmain(int argc, _TCHAR* argv[])
{
  HRESULT hr;
  hr = CoInitialize(NULL);

  try
  {
    IWelcomePtr spWelcome;
    hr = spWelcome.CreateInstance("Wrox.DotnetComponent");   // CoCreateInstance()

    cout << spWelcome->Greeting("Bill") << endl;
```

The second interface that is supported by our .NET component is IMath, and there is also a smart pointer that wraps the COM interface: IMathPtr. You can directly assign one smart pointer to another as in spMath = spWelcome; in the implementation of the smart pointer (the = operator is overridden), a QueryInterface() is done. With the IMath interface you can call the Add() method.

```cpp
    IMathPtr spMath;
    spMath = spWelcome; // QueryInterface()

    long result = spMath->Add(4, 5);
    cout << "result:" << result << endl;
  }
```

In case a HRESULT error value is returned by the COM object (this is done by the CCW that returns HRESULT errors if the .NET component generates exceptions), the smart pointer wraps the HRESULT errors, and generates _com_error exceptions instead. Errors are handled in the catch block. At the end of the program, the COM DLL's are closed and unloaded using CoUninitialize().

```cpp
  catch (_com_error& e)
  {
    cout << e.ErrorMessage() << endl;
```

```
    }

    CoUninitialize();
    return 0;
}
```

Now you can run the application, and you will get outputs from the Greeting() and the Add() methods to the console. You can also try to debug into the smart pointer class, where you can see the COM API calls directly.

> **In case you get an exception that the component cannot be found, check if the same version of the assembly that is configured in the registry, is installed in the global assembly cache.**

Adding Connection Points

Adding support for COM events to the .NET components requires some changes to the implementation of your .NET class. Offering COM events is not a simple usage of the event and delegate keywords, it is necessary to add some more COM interop attributes.

First you have to add an additional interface to the .NET project: IMathEvents. This interface is the source or outgoing interface for the component, and will be implemented by the sink object in the client. A source interface must be either a dispatch or a custom interface. Just a scripting client only supports dispatch interfaces. Dispatch interfaces are usually preferred as source interfaces.

```
[InterfaceType(ComInterfaceType.InterfaceIsIDispatch)]
public interface IMathEvents
{
    [DispId(46200)] void CalculationCompleted();
}
```

Next you have to add a delegate. The delegate must have the same signature and return type as the method in the outgoing interface. If you have multiple methods in your source interface, for each that differs with the arguments, you have to specify a separate delegate. Because the COM client does not have to access this delegate directly, the delegate can be marked with the attribute [ComVisible(false)].

```
[ComVisible(false)]
public delegate void CalculationCompletedDelegate();
```

With the class DotnetComponent, a source interface must be specified. This can be done with the attribute [ComSourceInterfaces]. Add the attribute [ComSourceInterfaces], and specify the outgoing interface declared earlier. You can add more than one source interface with different constructors of the attribute class; however, the only client language that supports more than one source interface is C++. Visual Basic 6 clients only support one source interface.

```
[ClassInterface(ClassInterfaceType.None)]
[ProgId("Wrox.DotnetComponent")]
[Guid("77839717-40DD-4876-8297-35B98A8402C7")]
```

```
[ComSourceInterfaces(typeof(IMathEvents))]
public class DotnetComponent : IWelcome, IMath
{
    public DotnetComponent()
    {
    }
```

Inside the class `DotnetComponent` you have to declare an event for every method of the source interface. The type of the method must be the name of the delegate, and the name of the event must be exactly the name of the method inside the source interface. You can add the event calls to the `Add()` and `Sub()` methods. This step is the normal .NET way to invoke events as discussed in Chapter 6.

```
    public event CalculationCompletedDelegate CalculationCompleted;

    public int Add(int val1, int val2)
    {
        int result = val1 + val2;
        if (CalculationCompleted != null)
            CalculationCompleted();
        return result;
    }

    public int Sub(int val1, int val2)
    {
        int result = val1 - val2;
        if (CalculationCompleted != null)
            CalculationCompleted();
        return result;
    }
}
```

> **The name of the event must be the same as the name of the method inside the source interface. Otherwise, the events cannot be mapped for COM clients.**

Creating a Client with a Sink Object

After you've build and registered the .NET assembly, and installed it into the global assembly cache, you can build a client application by using the event sources. This time we will use Visual Basic 6 to write a client that uses the events.

Start Visual Basic 6 and create a Standard EXE file. Select Project⇨References, browse for the type library of the .NET component, and add the type library. Next add a button to the form, and add the following code. Using Visual Basic 6, the `WithEvents` keyword automatically creates a sink object implementing the default source interface of the component. With this example, the source interface is `IMathEvents`. The handler method that is invoked when the event is fired from the component, is `obj_Calcuation Completed()`, which consists of the variable name of the object, and the name of the method that is defined with the source interface. You can start the application, and you will see that the event gets fired.

```
Dim WithEvents obj As DotnetComponent.DotnetComponent
Dim math As DotnetComponent.IMath

Private Sub Command1_Click()
   Dim greeting As String
   Set obj = New DotnetComponent.DotnetComponent
   greeting = obj.greeting("Bill")
   MsgBox (greeting)

   Set math = obj
   Dim result As Integer
   result = math.Add(4, 5)
   MsgBox (result)
End Sub

Private Sub obj_CalculationCompleted()
   MsgBox "calculation ready"
End Sub
```

Running Windows Forms Controls in Internet Explorer

Windows Forms controls can be hosted in Internet Explorer as ActiveX controls. Because there are many different ActiveX control containers, and all these containers do have different requirements on the ActiveX controls. Hosting Windows Forms controls in any container is not supported by Microsoft. Visual Studio .NET 2003 adds one more supported container with MFC applications. However, you have to manually change the code to host ActiveX controls from an MFC application.

For hosting a Windows Forms control inside Internet Explorer, you have to copy the assembly file to your Web server, and add some information about the control inside the HTML page. For the support of Windows Forms controls, the syntax of the <object> tag has been extended. With the attribute classid, you can add the assembly file and the name of the class separated by a # sign: classid="<assembly file>#class name".

With the assembly file ControlDemo.dll and the class UserControl1 in the namespace Wrox.ProCSharp.COMInterop, the syntax looks like this:

```
<object id="myControl"
  classid="ControlDemo.dll#Wrox.ProCSharp.COMInterop.UserControl1"
  height="400" width="400">
</object>
```

As soon as a user opens the HTML page, the assembly is downloaded to the client system. The assembly is stored in the download assembly cache, and every time the user accesses the page, the version numbers are rechecked. In case the version number didn't change, the assembly will be used from the local cache.

As a requirement to use Windows Forms control in a Web page, the client must have the .NET runtime installed, Internet Explorer 5.5 or higher must be used, and the security setting must allow downloading assemblies. The default security setting with .NET 1.1 doesn't allow downloading assemblies from the Internet.

Summary

In this chapter we have seen how the different generations of COM and .NET applications can interact. Instead of rewriting applications and components, a COM component can be used from a .NET application just like a .NET class. The tool that makes this possible is tlbimp, which creates a runtime callable wrapper (RCW) that hides the COM object behind a .NET façade.

Likewise, tlbexp creates a type-library from a .NET component that is used by the COM callable wrapper (CCW). The CCW hides the .NET component behind a COM façade. Using .NET classes as COM components makes it necessary to use some attributes from the namespace System.Runtime.InteropServices, to define specific COM characteristics that are needed by the COM client.

In the next chapter we look at Enterprise Services, where .NET components can be installed next to COM components to use features such as automatic transactions, object pooling, and loosely coupled events in distributed solutions.

Enterprise Services

Enterprise Services is the name of the Microsoft application server technology that offers services for distributed solutions. Enterprise Services is based on the COM+ technology that has already been in use for many years. However, instead of wrapping .NET objects as COM objects so that they can use these services, .NET offers extensions so that the .NET components can take direct advantage of these services. With .NET you get easy access of the COM+ services for .NET components.

In this chapter you learn:

- ❑ When to use Enterprise Services
- ❑ What services you get with this technology
- ❑ How to create a serviced component to use Enterprise Services
- ❑ How to deploy COM+ applications
- ❑ How to use transactions with Enterprise Services

Overview

We'll start with a short introduction to Enterprise Services and their benefits.

History

Enterprise Services can be traced back to Microsoft Transaction Server (MTS) that was released as a Windows NT 4.0 option pack. MTS extended COM by offering services such as transactions for COM objects. Because MTS extended COM in ways that were incompatible with COM, workarounds such as special MTS API calls to invoke COM objects from within MTS applications were necessary.

One of the most important new features of Windows 2000 was the integration of MTS and COM in COM+. With Windows 2000, COM+ base services are aware of the context that is needed by COM+ services (previously MTS services) such as distributed transactions. COM+ also added some more services.

COM+ 1.5 is available with Windows XP and Windows Server 2003. COM+ 1.5 adds some more features to increase scalability and availability, including application pooling and recycling, and configurable isolation levels.

.NET Enterprise Services enables us to use COM+ services from within .NET components. Support is offered for Windows 2000 and later. Running .NET components within COM+ applications, no COM callable wrapper is used (see Chapter 28); instead it runs as a .NET component. When you install the .NET runtime on an operating system, with the runtime some extensions are added to COM+ Services. If two .NET components are installed with Enterprise Services, and component A is using component B, COM marshaling is not used; instead the .NET components can invoke each other directly.

Where to Use Enterprise Services?

Business applications can be logically separated into presentation, business, and data service layers. The *presentation service layer* is responsible for user interaction. Here the user can interact with the application to enter and view data. Technologies used with this layer are Windows Forms and ASP.NET Web Forms. The *business service layer* consists of business rules and data rules. The *data service layer* interacts with persistent storage. Here we can use components that make use of ADO.NET. Enterprise Services fits both to the business service layer as well as to the data service layer.

Figure 29-1 shows two typical application scenarios. Enterprise Services can be used directly from a rich client that is using Windows Forms, or from a Web application that is running ASP.NET.

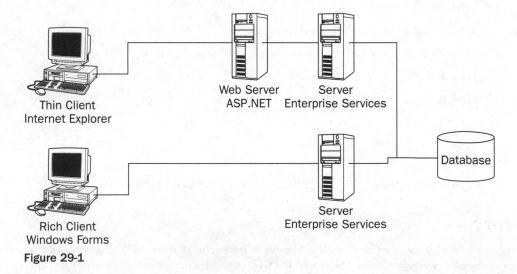

Thin Client
Internet Explorer

Web Server
ASP.NET

Server
Enterprise Services

Database

Rich Client
Windows Forms

Server
Enterprise Services

Figure 29-1

Enterprise Services is also a scalable technology. Using *component load balancing* it is possible to distribute the load of the clients across different systems.

You can also use Enterprise Services on the client system, because this technology is included in Windows XP.

Contexts

The base functionality behind the services offered by Enterprise Services is the context. The context makes it possible that during a method call the method call can be intercepted, and some service functionality can be carried out before the expected method call is invoked.

Contexts are discussed in Chapter 16 with .NET Remoting contexts. .NET Remoting contexts also play an important role with Enterprise Services, because these contexts are used for intercepting .NET objects configured with Enterprise Services. However, because COM components can be configured with Enterprise Services in a similar way to .NET components, the COM+ context exists in conjunction with the .NET Remoting context. This way a COM component and a .NET component can participate in the same transaction.

Automatic Transactions

The most commonly used feature of Enterprise Services is *automatic transactions*. With automatic transactions, there is no need to start and commit a transaction in the code. Instead, an attribute can be applied to a class. Using the [Transaction] attribute with the options Required, Supported, RequiresNew, NotSupported, you can mark a class with the requirements it has regarding transactions. If you mark the class with the option Required, a transaction is created automatically when a method starts, and committed to or aborted when the root component of the transaction is finished.

Such a declarative way to program is of particular advantage when developing a complex object model and programming transactions manually. For example, suppose you have a Person object with multiple Address and Document objects that are associated with the Person. Now you want to store the Person object together with all associated objects in a single transaction. Doing transactions programmatically would mean passing a transaction object to all the related objects, so that they can participate in the same transaction. Using transactions declaratively, there is no need to pass the transaction object, because this happens behind the scenes using the context.

Distributed Transactions

Enterprise Services not only offers automatic transactions, but the transactions can also be distributed across multiple databases. Enterprise Services transactions are enlisted with the *Distributed Transaction Coordinator* (DTC). The DTC supports databases that make use of the XA protocol, which is a two-phase commit protocol, and is supported by SQL Server and Oracle. A single transaction can span writing data to both a SQL Server and an Oracle database.

Distributed transactions are not only useful with databases, but a single transaction can also span writing data to a database, and writing data to a message queue. If one of these two actions fails, a rollback is done with the other action.

Object Pooling

Pooling is another feature offered by Enterprise Services. These services use a pool of threads to answer requests from clients. Object pooling can be used for objects with a long initialization time. With object pooling, objects are created in advance, so that clients don't have to wait until the object is initialized.

Role-based Security

Using *role-based security* you can define roles declaratively, and define what methods or components can be used from what roles. The system administrator assigns users or user groups to these roles. In the program there is no need to deal with access control lists, instead roles that are simple strings can be used.

Queued Components

Queued components is an abstraction layer to message queuing. Instead of sending messages to a message queue, the client can invoke methods with a recorder that offers the same methods as a .NET class configured in Enterprise Services. The recorder in turn creates messages that are transferred via a message queue to the server application.

Queued components and message queuing is useful if the client application is running in a disconnected environment (for example, on a laptop that not always has a connection to the server), or if the request that is send to the server should be cached before it is forwarded to a different server (for example, to a server of a partner company).

Loosely Coupled Events

Chapter 16 discussed how to use events with .NET Remoting. Chapter 28 discusses how to use events in a COM environment. With both of these event mechanisms, the client and the server do have a tight connection. This is different with *loosely coupled events* (LCE). With LCE the COM+ facility is inserted between client and server (see Figure 29-2). The publisher registers the events it will offer with COM+ by defining an event class. Instead of sending the events directly to the client, the publisher sends events to the event class that is registered with the LCE service. The LCE service forwards the events to the subscriber, which is the client application that registered a subscription for the event.

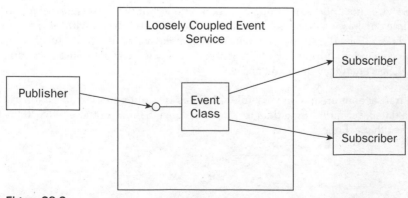

Figure 29-2

Creating a Simple COM+ Application

Creating a .NET class that can be configured with Enterprise Services, you have to reference the assembly System.EnterpriseServices, and add the namespace `System.EnterpriseServices` to the using declarations. The most important class to use is the class `ServicedComponent`.

The first example just shows the basic requirements to create a serviced component. Start with creating a C# library application. All COM+ applications must be written as library application—regardless whether they will run in their own process or in the process of the client. Name the library SimpleServer. Reference the assembly System.EnterpriseServices, and add the declaration `using System.EnterpriseServices;` to the assmblyinfo.cs and class1.cs files.

Class *ServicedComponent*

Every serviced component class must derive from the base class `ServicedComponent`. `ServicedComponent` itself derives from the class `ContextBoundObject`, so an instance is bound to a .NET Remoting context.

The class `ServicedComponent` has some protected methods that can be overridden:

Protected Method	Description
`Activate()` `Deactivate()`	The `Activate()` and `Deactivate()` methods are called if the object is configured to use object pooling. When the object is taken from the pool, the `Activate()` method is called. Before the object is put back into the pool, `Deactivate()` is called.
`CanBePooled()`	This is another method for object pooling. If the object is in an inconsistent state, you can return `false` in your overridden implementation of `CanBePooled()`. This way the object is not put back into the pool, but destroyed instead. For the pool a new object will be created.
`Construct()`	This method is called at instantiation time, where a construction string can be passed to the object. The construction string can be modified by the system administrator. Later in this chapter we use the construction string to define the database connection string.

Application Attributes

Libraries that are configured with Enterprise Services need a strong name. For some Enterprise Services features it is also necessary to install the assembly in the global assembly cache. Strong names and the global assembly cache are discussed in Chapter 13.

Create a key pair to sign the assembly by using the strong name utility:

```
sn -k mykey.snk
```

To the file assemblyinfo.cs add the attribute `AssemblyKeyFile` with the reference to the key file created.

```
[assembly: AssemblyKeyFile("../../../mykey.snk")]
```

Some Enterprise Services attributes are also needed. The attribute `ApplicationName` defines the name of the application how it will be seen in the Component Services administrative tool. The value of the `Description` attribute shows up as description within the application configuration tool.

`ApplicationActivation` allows defining if the application should be configured as a library application or a server application, using the options `ActivationOption.Library` or `ActivationOption.Server`. With a library application, the application is loaded inside the process of the client. In that case the client might be the ASP.NET runtime. With a server application, a process for the application is started. The name of the process is dllhost.exe. With the attribute `ApplicationAccessControl` you can turn off security, so that every user is allowed to use the component.

```
[assembly: ApplicationName("Wrox EnterpriseDemo")]
[assembly: Description("Wrox Sample Application for Professional C#")]
[assembly: ApplicationActivation(ActivationOption.Server)]
[assembly: ApplicationAccessControl(false)]
```

With the attribute `ApplicationAccessControl`, the default values have changed from .NET 1.0 to .NET 1.1. Without setting the attribute, .NET 1.0 by default turns off security checking for the COM+ application. With .NET 1.1 by default security checking is turned on. So it is always best to set the attribute.

Creating the Component

In the file class1.cs you can create your serviced component class. With serviced components it is best to define interfaces that are used as the contract between the client and the component. This is not a strict requirement, but some of the Enterprise Services features (such as setting role-based security on a method or interface level) do require interfaces. Create the interface `IGreeting` with the method `Welcome()`.

```csharp
using System;
using System.EnterpriseServices;

namespace Wrox.ProCSharp.EnterpriseServices
{
    public interface IGreeting
    {
        string Welcome(string name);
    }
```

The class `SimpleComponent` derives from the base class `ServicedComponent` and implements the interface `IGreeting`. The class `ServicedComponent` acts as a base class of all serviced component classes, and offers some methods for the activation and construction phases. Applying the attribute `[EventTrackingEnabled]` to this class makes it possible to monitor the objects with the administrative tool. By default monitoring is disabled, because using this feature reduces performance. The attribute `[Description]` only specifies text that shows up in the admin tool.

```
    [EventTrackingEnabled(true)]
    [Description("Simple Serviced Component Sample")]
    public class SimpleComponent : ServicedComponent, IGreeting
    {
        public SimpleComponent()
        {
        }
```

The method `Welcome()` only returns `"Hello, "` with the name that is passed to the argument. To see the component run in the administrative tool, `Thread.Sleep()` simulates some processing time.

```
        public string Welcome(string name)
        {
            // simulate some processing time
            System.Threading.Thread.Sleep(1000);
            return "Hello, " + name;
        }
    }
}
```

Other than applying some attributes and deriving the class from `ServicedComponent` there's nothing special to do with classes that should use Enterprises Services features. All that is left to do is building and deploying a client application.

Deployment

Assemblies with serviced components must be configured with COM+. This configuration can be done automatically or by registering the assembly manually.

Automatic Deployment

If a .NET client application that uses the serviced component is started, the COM+ application is configured automatically. This is true for all classes that derive from the class `ServicedComponent`. Application and class attributes such as `[EventTrackingEnabled]` define the characteristics of the configuration.

However, with automatic deployment the client application must be a .NET application and needs administrative rights. If the client application is ASP.NET, the ASP.NET runtime usually doesn't have administrative rights. So, automatic deployment is only useful during development time. However, here it is an extremely advantageous feature. During development time it is not necessary to do manual deployment after every build.

Manual Deployment

Deploying the assembly manually can be done with the command line utility *.NET Services Installation Tool* regsvcs.exe. Starting the command

```
regsvcs SimpleServer.dll
```

registers the assembly SimpleServer as a COM+ application and configures the included components according to their attributes, and also creates a type library that can be used by COM clients accessing the .NET component.

After you've configured the assembly, you can start the Component Services administrative tool by selecting Administrative Tools⇨Component Services from the Windows menu. In the left tree view of this application you can select Component Services⇨Computers⇨My Computer⇨COM+ Applications to verify that the application was configured.

Component Services Admin Tool

After a successful configuration you can see Wrox EnterpriseDemo as an application name in the tree view. This name was set by the attribute [ApplicationName]. Selecting the Action⇨Properties opens the dialog box shown in Figure 29-3. Both the name and the description have been configured by using attributes. When you select the Activation tab, you can see that the application is configured as a server application because this has been defined with the [ApplicationActivation] attribute, and selecting the Security tab shows that the Enforce access checks for this application option is not selected because the attribute [ApplicationAccessControl] was set to false.

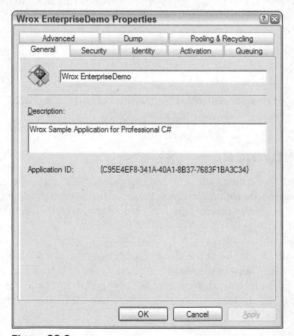

Figure 29-3

There are some more options that can be set with this application:

❑ **Security.** With the security configuration, you can enable or disable access checks. If security is enabled, you can set access checks to either the application level, or also the component, to the interface, and to the method level. It is also possible to encrypt messages that are sent across the network using packet privacy as an authentication level for calls. Of course, this also reduces performance.

❑ **Identity.** With server applications you can use the Identity tab to configure the user account that will be used for the process that hosts the application. By default this is the interactive user. This setting is very useful while debugging the application, but cannot be used on a production system if the application is running on a server, because nobody might be logged on. The configuration can be changed for a specific user.

❑ **Activation.** The Activation tab allows configuring the application either as a library or as a server application. Two new options with COM+ 1.5 are the option to run the application as a Windows Service and to use SOAP to access the application. We discuss Windows Services in Chapter 33. Selecting the option SOAP uses .NET Remoting configured within Internet Information Server to access the component. .NET Remoting is discussed in Chapter 16.

❑ **Queuing.** The Queuing configuration is required for service components that make use of Message Queuing.

❑ **Advanced.** With the Advanced tab you can specify whether the application should be shut down after a certain period of client inactivity. You can also specify whether to lock a certain configuration, so no one can change it accidentally.

❑ **Dump.** If the application crashes, you can specify where in the directory the dumps should be stored. This is useful for components developed with C++.

❑ **Pooling & Recycling.** Pooling and recycling is a new option with COM+ 1.5. With this option you can configure if the application should be restarted (recycled) depending on application lifetime, memory needs, number of calls, and so on.

With the Component Services administrative tool you can also view and configure the component itself. When opening child elements of the application, you can view the component `Wrox.ProCSharp.EnterpriseServices.SimpleComponent`. Selecting Action ➪ Properties opens the dialog box shown in Figure 29-4.

Using this dialog box, you can configure these options:

❑ **Transactions.** With the Transactions tab you can specify whether the component requires transactions. We will use this feature in our next sample.

❑ **Security.** If security is enabled with the application, with this configuration you can define what roles are allowed to use the component.

❑ **Activation.** The Activation configuration enables you to set object pooling and to assign a construction string.

❑ **Concurrency.** If the component is not thread-safe, concurrency can be set to Required or Requires New. This way the COM+ runtime only allows one thread at a time to access the component.

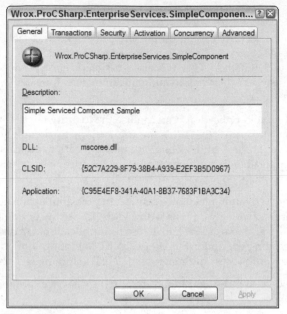

Figure 29-4

Client Application

After building the serviced component library, you can create a client application. This can be as simple as a C# console application. After you've created the project for the client, you have to reference both the assembly from the serviced component, SimpleServer, as well as the assembly System.EnterpriseServices. Then you can write the code to instantiate a new `SimpleComponent` instance, and invoke the method `Welcome()`. In the following code calling the method `Welcome()` is repeated for 10 times. The `using` statement helps to release the resources allocated with the instance before the garbage collector takes action. With the `using` statement, the `Dispose()` method of the serviced component is called with the end of the `using` statement.

```
using System;

namespace Wrox.ProCSharp.EnterpriseServices
{
    class Class1
    {
        static void Main(string[] args)
        {
            using (SimpleComponent obj = new SimpleComponent())
            {
                for (int i = 0; i < 10; i++)
                {
                    Console.WriteLine(obj.Welcome("Sharon"));
                }
```

```
              }
          }
      }
  }
```

If you start the client application before configuring the server, the server will be configured automatically. The automatic configuration of the server is done with the values that you've specified using attributes. For a test you can unregister the serviced component and start the client again. If the serviced component is configured during the start of the client application, the startup needs more time. Remember that this feature is only useful during development time.

While the application is running, you can monitor the serviced component with the Component Services administrative tool. Selecting Components in the tree view, and choosing View➪Detail, you can view the number of instantiated objects if the attribute [EventTrackingEnabled] is set.

As you've seen, creating serviced components is just a matter of deriving the class from the base class ServicedCompoonent, and by setting some attributes to configure the application. Next you will see how transactions can be used with serviced components.

Transactions

Automatic transactions is the mostly used feature of Enterprise Services. What are transactions? Think about ordering a book from a Web site. The book order process removes the book you want to buy from the stock and puts it in your order box, and the cost of your book is charged to your credit card. With these two actions, either both actions should complete successfully, or none of these actions should happen. This is the role of a transaction.

ACID Properties

Transactions can be described by using ACID properties. ACID is the short form for *atomicity*, *consistency*, *isolation*, and *durability*.

❑   **Atomicity.** Atomicity represents one unit of work. With a transaction either the complete unit of work succeeds, or nothing is changed.

❑   **Consistency.** The state of the database must be a valid, consistent state after the transaction committed.

❑   **Isolation.** Isolation means that transactions that happen concurrently are isolated from state that is changed during a transaction. Transaction A can not see the changed state of transaction B while the transaction is not completed.

❑   **Durability.** After the transaction is completed, it must be stored in a durable way. This means that if the power goes down or the server crashes, the state must be recovered at reboot.

Transaction Attributes

Serviced components can be marked with the [Transaction] attribute to define if and how transactions are required with the component.

TransactionOption Value	Description
Required	Setting the [Transaction] attribute to Transaction Option.Required means that the component runs inside a transaction. If a transaction has been created already, then the component will run in the same transaction. If no transaction exists, a transaction will be created.
RequiresNew	TransactionOption.RequiresNew always results in a newly created transaction. The component never participates in the same transaction as the caller.
Supported	With TransactionOption.Supported, the component doesn't need transactions itself. However, the transaction will span the caller and the called component, if these components require transactions.
NotSupported	The option TransactionOption.NotSupported means that the component never runs in a transaction, regardless whether the caller has a transaction.
Disabled	TransactionOption.Disabled means that a possible transaction of the current context is ignored.

Figure 29-5 shows multiple components with different transactional configurations. The client invokes component A. Because component A is configured with *Transaction Required* and no transaction existed previously, the new transaction 1 is created. Component A invokes component B which in turn invokes component C. Because component B is configured with *Transaction Supported*, and the configuration of component C is set to *Transaction Required*, all three components A, B, and C do use the same transaction context. If component B were configured with the transaction setting *NotSupported*, component C would get a new transaction. Component D is configured with the setting *New Transaction Required*, so a new transaction is created when it is called by component A.

Transaction Results

A transaction can be influenced by setting the *consistent* and the *done* bit of the context. If the consistent bit is set to true means that the component is happy with the outcome of the transaction. The transaction can be committed if all components participating with the transaction are similar successful. If the consistent bit is set to false, the component is not happy with the outcome of the transaction, and the transaction will be aborted when the root object that started the transaction is finished. If the done bit is set, the object can be deactivated after the method call ended. A new instance will be created with the next method call.

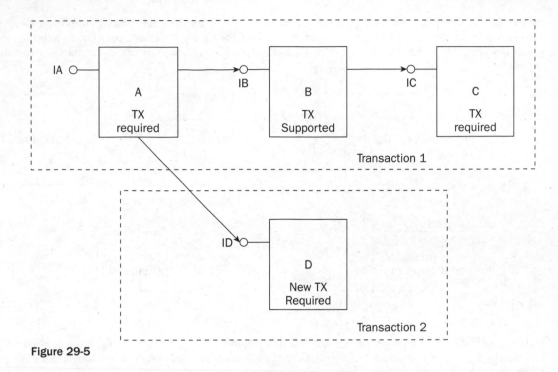

Figure 29-5

The consistent and done bits can be set using four methods of the ContextUtil class with the results that you can see in the table below.

ContextUtil Method	Consistent Bit	Done Bit
SetComplete	true	true
SetAbort	false	true
EnableCommit	true	false
DisableCommit	false	false

With .NET it is also possible to set the consistent and done bit by applying the attribute [AutoComplete] to the method instead of calling the ContextUtil methods. With this attribute the method ContextUtil.SetComplete() will be called automatically if the method is successful. If the method fails and an exception is thrown, with [AutoComplete], the method ContextUtil.SetAbort() will be called.

Sample Application

With this sample application we simulate a simplified scenario that writes new orders to the Northwind sample database. As shown in Figure 29-6, multiple components are used with the COM+ application. The class OderControl is called from the client application to create new orders. OrderControl uses the `OrderData` component. `OrderData` has the responsibility to create a new entry in the Order table of the Northwind database. The `OrderData` component uses the `OrderLineData` component to write Order Detail entries to the database. Both `OrderData` and `OrderLineData` must participate in the same transaction.

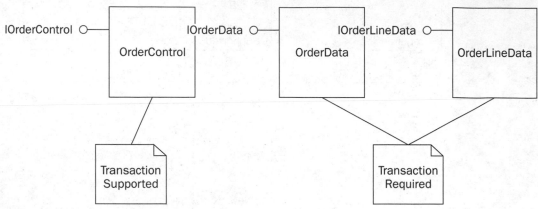

Figure 29-6

Start by creating a C# Component library with the name NorthwindComponent. In the file assemblyinfo.cs add the key file with the attribute `[AssemblyKeyFile]`, and define the Enterprise Services application attributes as shown in the following code:

```
[assembly: AssemblyKeyFile("../../../mykey.snk")]

[assembly: ApplicationName("Wrox.NorthwindDemo")]
[assembly: ApplicationActivation(ActivationOption.Library)]
[assembly: ApplicationAccessControl(false)]
```

Entity classes

Next add some entity classes that represent the columns in the Northwind database tables Order and Order Details. The class `Order` has a static method `Create()` that creates and returns a new instance of the class `Order`, and initializes this instance with the arguments passed to this methods. Also, the class Order has some read-only properties to access the fields `oderId`, `customerId`, `orderData`, `shipAddress`, `shipCity`, and `shipCountry`. `OrderId` is not known at creation time of the class `Order`, but because the Order table in the Northwind database has an auto-increment attribute, `OrderId` is just known after the order is written to the database. The method `SetOrderId()` is used to set the corresponding id after the order has been written to the database. Because this method is called by a class inside the same assembly, the access level of this method is set to `internal`. The method `AddOrderLine()` adds order details to the order.

```csharp
using System;
using System.Collections;

namespace Wrox.ProCSharp.EnterpriseServices
{
    public class Order
    {
```

```
public static Order Create(string customerId, DateTime orderDate,
            string shipAddress, string shipCity, string shipCountry)
{
   Order o = new Order();
   o.customerId = customerId;
   o.orderDate = orderDate;
   o.shipAddress = shipAddress;
   o.shipCity = shipCity;
   o.shipCountry = shipCountry;
   return o;
}

public Order()
{
}

internal void SetOrderId(int orderId)
{
   this.orderId = orderId;
}

public void AddOrderLine(OrderLine orderLine)
{
   orderLines.Add(orderLine);
}

private int orderId;
private string customerId;
private DateTime orderDate;
private string shipAddress;
private string shipCity;
private string shipCountry;
private ArrayList orderLines = new ArrayList();

public int OrderId
{
   get
   {
      return orderId;
   }
}
public string CustomerId
{
   get
   {
      return customerId;
   }
}
public DateTime OrderDate
{
   get
   {
      return orderDate;
   }
}
public string ShipAddress
```

```
        {
          get
          {
            return shipAddress;
          }
        }
        public string ShipCity
        {
          get
          {
            return shipCity;
          }
        }
        public string ShipCountry
        {
          get
          {
            return shipCountry;
          }
        }
        public OrderLine[] OrderLines
        {
          get
          {
            OrderLine[] ol = new OrderLine[orderLines.Count];
            orderLines.CopyTo(ol);
            return ol;
          }
        }
    }
}
```

The second entity class is `OrderLine`. `OrderLine` has a static `Create()` method similar to the one of the `Order` class. Other than that, the class only has some properties for the fields `productId`, `unitPrice`, and `quantity`.

```
using System;

namespace Wrox.ProCSharp.EnterpriseServices
{
    [Serializable]
    public class OrderLine
    {
        public static OrderLine Create(int productId, float unitPrice, int quantity)
        {
            OrderLine detail = new OrderLine();
            detail.productId = productId;
            detail.unitPrice = unitPrice;
            detail.quantity = quantity;
            return detail;
        }
        public OrderLine()
        {
        }
```

```
      private int productId;
      private float unitPrice;
      private int quantity;

      public int ProductId
      {
         get
         {
            return productId;
         }
         set
         {
            productId = value;
         }
      }
      public float UnitPrice
      {
         get
         {
            return unitPrice;
         }
         set
         {
            unitPrice = value;
         }
      }
      public int Quantity
      {
         get
         {
            return quantity;
         }
         set
         {
            quantity = value;
         }
      }
   }
}
```

The OrderControl component

The class OrderControl represents a simple business services component. In this example just one method, NewOrder(), is defined in the interface IOrderControl. The implementation of NewOrder() does nothing more than instantiating a new instance of the data services component OrderData, and calling the method Insert() to write an Order object to the database. In a more complex scenario, this method could be extended to write a log entry to a database, or to invoke a queued component to send the Order object to a message queue.

```
using System;
using System.EnterpriseServices;
using System.Data;
using System.Data.SqlClient;
using System.Collections;
```

```
namespace Wrox.ProCSharp.EnterpriseServices
{
    public interface IOrderControl
    {
        void NewOrder(Order order);
    }

    [Transaction(TransactionOption.Supported)]
    [EventTrackingEnabled(true)]
    public class OrderControl : ServicedComponent, IOrderControl
    {
        [AutoComplete()]
        public void NewOrder(Order order)
        {
            OrderData data = new OrderData();
            data.Insert(order);
        }
    }
}
```

The OrderData component

The OrderData class is responsible to write the values of Order objects to the database. The interface IOrderUpdate defines the Insert() method. You can extend this interface to also support an Update() method where an existing entry in the database gets updated.

```
using System;
using System.EnterpriseServices;
using System.Data;
using System.Data.SqlClient;

namespace Wrox.ProCSharp.EnterpriseServices
{
    public interface IOrderUpdate
    {
        void Insert(Order order);
    }
```

The class OrderData has the attribute [Transaction] with the value TransactionOption.Required applied. This means that the component will run in a transaction in any case. Either a transaction is created by the caller, and OrderData uses the same transaction, or a new transaction is created. Here a new transaction will be created because the calling component OrderControl doesn't have a transaction.

With serviced components you can only use default constructors. However, you can use the component services administrative tool to configure a construction string that is send to a component (see Figure 29-7). Selecting the Activation tab of the component configuration enables you to change the construction string. The option Enable object construction is turned on when the attribute [Construction Enabled] is set, as it is with the class OrderData. The Default property of the [ConstructionEnabled] attribute defines the default connection string that is shown in the Activation settings after registration of the assembly. Setting this attribute also requires to overload the method Construct() from the base class ServicedComponent. This method is called by the COM+ runtime at object instantiation, and the construction string is passed as an argument. The construction string is set to the variable connectionString that is used later to connect to the database.

```
[Transaction(TransactionOption.Required)]
[EventTrackingEnabled(true)]
[ConstructionEnabled(true, Default="server=localhost;
                     database=northwind;trusted_connection=true")]
public class OrderData : ServicedComponent, IOrderUpdate
{
    private string connectionString = null;

    protected override void Construct(string s)
    {
        connectionString = s;
    }
}
```

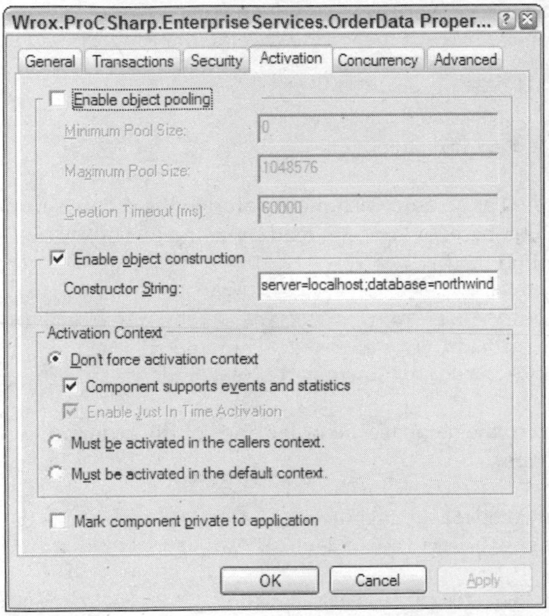

Figure 29-7

The method Insert() is at the heart of the component. Here we use ADO.NET to write the Order object to the database. (ADO.NET is discussed in more detail in Chapter 22.) For this example, we create a SqlConnection object where the connection string that was set with the Construct() method is used to initialize the object.

The attribute [AutoComplete()] is applied to the method to get automatic transaction handling as discussed earlier.

```
[AutoComplete()]
public void Insert(Order order)
{
    SqlConnection connection = new SqlConnection(connectionString);
```

The method `connection.CreateCommand()` creates a `SqlCommand` object where the `CommandText` property is set to an SQL INSERT statement to add a new record to the Orders table. The method `ExecuteNonQuery()` executes the SQL statement.

```
try
{
    SqlCommand command = connection.CreateCommand();
    command.CommandText = "INSERT INTO Orders (CustomerId, OrderDate, " +
        "ShipAddress, ShipCity, ShipCountry)" +
        "VALUES(@CustomerId, @OrderDate, @ShipAddress, @ShipCity, " +
        "@ShipCountry)";
    command.Parameters.Add("@CustomerId", order.CustomerId);
    command.Parameters.Add("@OrderDate", order.OrderDate);
    command.Parameters.Add("@ShipAddress", order.ShipAddress);
    command.Parameters.Add("@ShipCity", order.ShipCity);
    command.Parameters.Add("@ShipCountry", order.ShipCountry);

    connection.Open();

    command.ExecuteNonQuery();
```

Because `OrderId` is defined as an auto-increment value in the database, and this id is needed for writing the Order Details to the database, `OrderId` is read by using `@@IDENTITY`. Then it is set to the `Order` object by calling the method `SetOrderId()`.

```
    command.CommandText = "SELECT @@IDENTITY AS 'Identity'";
    object identity = command.ExecuteScalar();
    order.SetOrderId(Convert.ToInt32(identity));
```

After the order is written to the database, all order lines of the order are written using the `OrderLineData` component.

```
    OrderLineData updateOrderLine = new OrderLineData();
    foreach (OrderLine orderLine in order.OrderLines)
    {
        updateOrderLine.Insert(order.OrderId, orderLine);
    }
}
```

Finally, regardless whether the code in the `try` block was successful, or an exception occurred, the connection is closed.

```
finally
{
    connection.Close();
}
        }
    }
}
```

The OrderLineData component

The OrderLineData component is implemented similar to the OrderData component. You use the
attribute [ConstructionEnabled] to define the database connection string:

```csharp
using System;
using System.EnterpriseServices;
using System.Data;
using System.Data.SqlClient;

namespace Wrox.ProCSharp.EnterpriseServices
{
    public interface IOrderLineUpdate
    {
        void Insert(int orderId, OrderLine orderDetail);
    }

    [Transaction(TransactionOption.Required)]
    [EventTrackingEnabled(true)]
    [ConstructionEnabled(true, Default="server=localhost;database=northwind;" +
        "trusted_connection=true")]
    public class OrderLineData : ServicedComponent, IOrderLineUpdate
    {
        private string connectionString = null;

        protected override void Construct(string s)
        {
            connectionString = s;
        }
```

With the Insert() method of the OrderLineData class the [AutoComplete] attribute isn't used to
demonstrate a different way to define the transaction outcome. It shows how to set the *consistent* and
done bit with the ContextUtil class instead. The method SetComplete() is called at the end of the
method, depending on whether inserting the data in the database was successful. In case there was an
error and an exception is thrown, the method SetAbort() sets the consistent bit to false instead, so
that the transaction is undone with all components participating in the transaction.

```csharp
public void Insert(int orderId, OrderLine orderDetail)
{
    SqlConnection connection = new SqlConnection(connectionString);
    try
    {
        SqlCommand command = connection.CreateCommand();
        command.CommandText = "INSERT INTO [Order Details] (OrderId, " +
            "ProductId, UnitPrice, Quantity)" +
            "VALUES(@OrderId, @ProductId, @UnitPrice, @Quantity)";
        command.Parameters.Add("@OrderId", orderId);
        command.Parameters.Add("@ProductId", orderDetail.ProductId);
        command.Parameters.Add("@UnitPrice", orderDetail.UnitPrice);
        command.Parameters.Add("@Quantity", orderDetail.Quantity);

        connection.Open();
```

```
            command.ExecuteNonQuery();
        }
        catch (Exception ex)
        {
            ContextUtil.SetAbort();
            throw;
        }
        finally
        {
            connection.Close();
        }
        ContextUtil.SetComplete();
    }
}
}
```

Client application

Having built the component, you can create a client application. For testing purposes, a console application serves the purpose. After referencing the assembly NorthwindComponent and the assembly System.EnterpriseServices, you can create a new Order with the static method `Order.Create()`. `order.AddOrderLine()` adds an order line to the order. `OrderLine.Create()` accepts product ids, the price, and quantity to create an order line. With a real application it would be useful to add a `Product` class instead of using product ids, but for the purpose of our example, we only want to demonstrate transactions in general.

Finally, the serviced component class `OrderControl` is created to invoke the method `NewOrder()`.

```
Order order = Order.Create("PICCO", DateTime.Today, "Georg Pipps",
                           "Salzburg", "Austria");
order.AddOrderLine(OrderLine.Create(16, 17.45F, 2));
order.AddOrderLine(OrderLine.Create(67, 14, 1));

OrderControl orderControl = new OrderControl();
orderControl.NewOrder(order);
```

You can try to write products that don't exist to the OrderLine (using a product id that is not listed in the table Products). In this case, the transaction will be aborted, and no data will be written to the database.

While a transaction is active you can see the transaction in the Component Services administrative tool by selecting Distributed Transaction Coordinator in the tree view (see Figure 29-8).

Figure 29-8

If you are debugging the serviced component while it is running inside a transaction be aware that the default transaction timeout is 60 seconds for serviced components. You can change the default for the complete system by selecting Options in the properties of My Computer in the Component Services administrative tool, or on a component-by-component level with the Transaction options of the component.

Summary

In this chapter we have discussed the rich features that are offered by Enterprise Services, such as automatic transactions, object pooling, queued components and loosely coupled events.

For creating serviced components, you have to reference the assembly System.EnterpriseServices. The base class of all serviced components is `ServicedComponent`. With this class the context makes it possible to intercept method calls. You can use attributes to specify the interception that will be used. You've also learned how to configure an application and its components using attributes, as well as how to manage transactions and specify transactional requirements of components using the `[Transaction]` attribute.

Part VII: Windows Base Services

30

File and Registry Operations

In this chapter, we examine how to perform tasks involving reading from and writing to files and the system registry in C#. In particular, we are going to cover:

- ❑ Exploring the directory structure, finding out what files and folders are present, and checking their properties
- ❑ Moving, copying, and deleting files and folders
- ❑ Reading and writing text in files
- ❑ Reading and writing keys in the registry

Microsoft has provided very intuitive object models covering these areas, and during this chapter we will show you how to use .NET base classes to perform the tasks mentioned above. In the case of file system operations, the relevant classes are almost all found in the `System.IO` namespace, while registry operations are dealt with by a classes in the `Microsoft.Win32` namespace.

> *The .NET base classes also include a number of classes and interfaces in the* `System.Runtime.Serialization` *namespace that are concerned with serialization—that is, the process of converting data (for example, the contents of a document) into a stream of bytes for storage. We won't be focusing on these classes in this chapter; we will be focusing on the classes that give you direct access to files.*

Note that security is particularly important when modifying files or registry entries. The whole area of security is covered separately in Chapter 14. In this chapter, however, we will simply assume that you have sufficient access rights to run all the examples that modify files or registry entries, which should be the case if you are running from an account with administrator privileges.

Managing the File System

The classes that are used to browse around the file system and perform operations, such as moving, copying, and deleting files, are shown in Figure 30-1. The namespace of each class is shown in brackets beneath the class name.

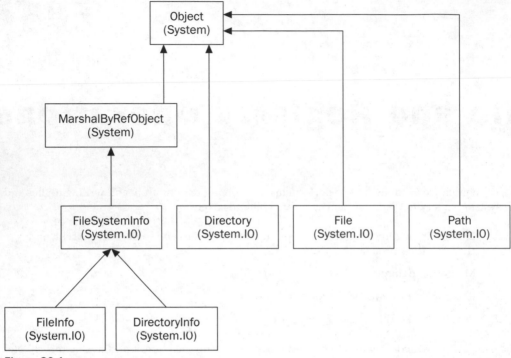

Figure 30-1

The following list explains the function of these classes:

❑   `System.MarshalByRefObject`—Base object class for .NET classes that are remotable; permits marshaling of data between application domains.

❑   `FileSystemInfo`—Base class that represents any file system object.

❑   `FileInfo` and `File`—These classes represent a file on the file system.

❑   `DirectoryInfo` and `Directory`—These classes represent a folder on the file system.

❑   `Path`—This class contains static members that you can use to manipulate pathnames.

On Windows, the objects that contain files and are used to organize the file system are termed folders. For example, in the path C:\My Documents\ReadMe.txt, ReadMe.txt is a file and My Documents is a folder. Folder is a very Windows-specific term: On virtually every other operating system the term directory is used in place of folder, and in accordance with Microsoft's goal to design .NET as a platform-independent technology, the corresponding .NET base classes are called `Directory` *and* `Directory Info`*. However, due to the potential for confusion with LDAP directories (as discussed in Chapter 24), and because this is a Windows book, we'll stick to the term folder in this discussion.*

.NET Classes That Represent Files and Folders

You will notice from the previous list that there are two classes used to represent a folder and two classes for a file. Which one of these classes you use depends largely on how many times you need to access that folder or file:

❑   `Directory` and `File` contain only static methods and are never instantiated. You use these classes by supplying the path to the appropriate file system object whenever you call a member method. If you only want to do one operation on a folder or file then using these classes is more efficient, because it saves the overhead of instantiating a .NET class.

❑   `DirectoryInfo` and `FileInfo` implement roughly the same public methods as `Directory` and `File`, as well as some public properties and constructors, but they are stateful and the members of these classes are not static. You need to instantiate these classes before each instance is associated with a particular folder or file. This means that these classes are more efficient if you're performing multiple operations using the same object, because they read in the authentication and other information for the appropriate file system object on construction, and then do not need to read that information again, no matter how many methods and so on you call against each object (class instance). In comparison, the corresponding stateless classes need to check the details of the file or folder again with every method you call.

In this section, we will be mostly using the `FileInfo` and `DirectoryInfo` classes, but it so happens that many (though not all) of the methods we call are also implemented by `File` and `Directory` (although in those cases these methods require an extra parameter—the pathname of the file system object, and a couple of the methods have slightly different names). For example:

```
FileInfo myFile = new FileInfo(@"C:\Program Files\My Program\ReadMe.txt");
myFile.CopyTo(@"D:\Copies\ReadMe.txt");
```

Has the same effect as:

```
File.Copy(@"C:\Program Files\My Program\ReadMe.txt", @"D:\Copies\ReadMe.txt");
```

The first code snippet above will take slightly longer to execute, because of the need to instantiate a `FileInfo` object, `myFile`, but it leaves `myFile` ready for you to perform further actions on the same file. By using the second example, there is no need to instantiate an object to copy the file.

You can instantiate a `FileInfo` or `DirectoryInfo` class by passing to the constructor a string containing the path to the corresponding file system. We've just illustrated the process for a file. For a folder the code looks similar:

```
DirectoryInfo myFolder = new DirectoryInfo(@"C:\Program Files");
```

If the path represents an object that does not exist, then an exception will not be thrown at construction, but will instead be thrown the first time that you call a method that actually requires the corresponding file system object to be there. You can find out whether the object exists and is of the appropriate type by checking the `Exists` property, which is implemented by both of these classes:

```
FileInfo test = new FileInfo(@"C:\Windows");
Console.WriteLine(test.Exists.ToString());
```

Note that for this property to return `true`, the corresponding file system object must be of the appropriate type. In other words, if you instantiate a `FileInfo` object supplying the path of a folder, or you instantiate a `DirectoryInfo` object, giving it the path of a file, `Exists` will have the value `false`. On the other hand, most of the properties and methods of these objects will return a value if at all possible— they won't necessarily throw an exception just because the wrong type of object has been called, unless they are asked to do something that really is impossible. For example, the above code snippet might first display `false` (because C:\Windows is a folder). However it still displays the time the folder was created, because a folder still has that information. But if we tried to open the folder as if it were a file, using the `FileInfo.Open()` method, we'd get an exception.

After you have established whether the corresponding file system object exists, you can (if you are using the `FileInfo` or `DirectoryInfo` class) find out information about it using of the properties in the following table.

Name	Description
CreationTime	Time file or folder was created
DirectoryName (FileInfo only)	Full pathname of the containing folder
Parent (DirectoryInfo only)	The parent directory of a specified subdirectory
Exists	Whether file or folder exists
Extension	Extension of the file; returns blank for folders
FullName	Full pathname of the file or folder
LastAccessTime	Time file or folder was last accessed
LastWriteTime	Time file or folder was last modified
Name	Name of the file or folder
Root (DirectoryInfo only)	The root portion of the path
Length (FileInfo only)	The size of the file in bytes

You can also perform actions on the file system object using the methods in the following table.

Name	Purpose
Create()	Creates a folder or empty file of the given name. For a `FileInfo` this also returns a stream object to let you write to the file. (We cover streams later in the chapter.)
Delete()	Deletes the file or folder. For folders there is an option for the `Delete` to be recursive.
MoveTo()	Moves and/or renames the file or folder.
CopyTo()	(`FileInfo` only) Copies the file. Note that there is no copy method for folders. If copying complete directory trees you'll need to individually copy each file and create new folders corresponding to the old folders.

Name	Purpose
GetDirectories()	(DirectoryInfo only) Returns an array of DirectoryInfo objects representing all folders contained in this folder.
GetFiles()	(DirectoryInfo only) Returns an array of FileInfo objects representing all files contained in this folder.
GetFileSystemInfos()	(DirectoryInfo only) Returns FileInfo and DirectoryInfo objects representing all objects contained in this folder, as an array of FileSystemInfo references.

Note that the above tables list the main properties and methods, and are not intended to be exhaustive.

In the above tables we've not listed most of the properties or methods that allow you to write to or read the data in files. This is actually done using stream objects, which we'll cover later in this chapter. FileInfo also implements a number of methods Open(), OpenRead(), OpenText(), OpenWrite(), Create(), and CreateText() that return stream objects for this purpose.

Interestingly, the creation time, last access time, and last write time are all writable:

```
// displays the creation time of a file, then changes it and displays it
// again
FileInfo test = new FileInfo(@"C:\My Documents\MyFile.txt");
Console.WriteLine(test.Exists.ToString());
Console.WriteLine(test.CreationTime.ToString());
test.CreationTime = new DateTime(2001, 1, 1, 7, 30, 0);
Console.WriteLine(test.CreationTime.ToString());
```

Being able to manually modify these properties might seem strange at first, but it can be quite useful. For example, if you have a program that effectively modifies a file by simply reading it in, then deleting it and creating a new file with the new contents, then you'd probably want to modify the creation date to match the original creation date of the old file.

The Path Class

The Path class is not a class that you would instantiate. Rather, it exposes some static methods that make operations on path names easier. For example, suppose you want to display the full path name for a file, ReadMe.txt in the folder C:\My Documents. You could find the path to the file using the following code:

```
Console.WriteLine(Path.Combine(@"C:\My Documents", "ReadMe.txt"));
```

Using the Path class is a lot easier than trying to fiddle about with separation symbols manually, especially because the Path class is aware of different formats for pathnames on different operating systems. At the time of writing, Windows is the only operating system supported by .NET. However, if .NET were later ported to Unix, Path would be able to cope with Unix paths, in which /, rather than \, is used as a separator in pathnames. Path.Combine() is the method of this class that you are likely to use most often, but Path also implements other methods that supply information about the path or the required format for it.

In the following section we present an example that illustrates how to browse directories and view the properties of files.

Example: A File Browser

In this section we'll present a sample C# application called FileProperties that presents a simple user interface that allows you to browse around the file system, and view the creation time, last access time, last write time, and size of files. (You can download the sample code for this application from the Wrox Web site at www.wrox.com.)

The FileProperties application works like this. You type in the name of a folder or file in the main text box at the top of the window and click the Display button. If you type in the path to a folder, its contents are listed in the list boxes. If you type in the path to a file, its details are displayed in the text boxes at the bottom of the form and the contents of its parent folder are displayed in the list boxes. Figure 30-2 shows the FileProperties sample application in action.

Figure 30-2

The user can very easily navigate around the file system by clicking any folder in the right-hand list box to move down to that folder, or by clicking the Up button to move up to the parent folder. Figure 30-2 shows the contents of the My Documents folder. The user can also select a file by clicking its name in the list box. This displays the file's properties in the text boxes at the bottom of the application (see Figure 30-3).

Figure 30-3

Note that if we'd wanted, we could also display the creation time, last access time, and last modification time for folders using the `DirectoryInfo` property. We are going to display these properties only for a selected file to keep things simple.

We create the project as a standard C# Windows application in Visual Studio .NET, and add the various text boxes and the list box from the Windows Forms area of the toolbox. We've also renamed the controls with the more intuitive names of `textBoxInput`, `textBoxFolder`, `buttonDisplay`, `buttonUp`, `listBoxFiles`, `listBoxFolders`, `textBoxFileName`, `textBoxCreationTime`, `textBoxLastAccessTime`, `textBoxLastWriteTime`, and `textBoxFileSize`.

Next, we need to indicate that we will be using the `System.IO` namespace:

```
using System;
using System.Drawing;
using System.Collections;
using System.ComponentModel;
using System.Windows.Forms;
using System.Data;
using System.IO;
```

We need to do this for all the file system-related examples in this chapter, but we won't explicitly show this part of the code in the remaining examples. We then add a member field to the main form:

```
public class Form1 : System.Windows.Forms.Form
{
    private string currentFolderPath;
```

`currentFolderPath` stores the path of the folder whose contents are displayed in the list boxes.

Next we need to add event handlers for the user-generated events. The possible user inputs are:

❑ **User clicks the Display button.** In this case we need to figure out whether what the user has typed in the main text box is the path to a file or folder. If it's a folder we list the files and sub-folders of this folder in the list boxes. If it is a file, we still do this for the folder containing that file, but we also display the file properties in the lower text boxes.

❑ **User clicks on a file name in the Files list box.** In this case we display the properties of this file in the lower text boxes.

❑ **User clicks on a folder name in the Folders list box.** In this case we clear all the controls and then display the contents of this subfolder in the list boxes.

❑ **User clicks on the Up button.** In this case we clear all the controls and then display the contents of the parent currently selected folder.

Before we show the code for the event handlers, we'll list the code for the methods that do all the work. First, we need to clear the contents of all the controls. This method is fairly self-explanatory:

```
protected void ClearAllFields()
{
    listBoxFolders.Items.Clear();
    listBoxFiles.Items.Clear();
    textBoxFolder.Text = "";
    textBoxFileName.Text = "";
    textBoxCreationTime.Text = "";
    textBoxLastAccessTime.Text = "";
    textBoxLastWriteTime.Text = "";
    textBoxFileSize.Text = "";
}
```

Next we define a method, `DisplayFileInfo()`, that handles the process of displaying the information for a given file in the text boxes. This method takes one parameter, the full pathname of the file as a `String`, and it works by creating a `FileInfo` object based on this path:

```
protected void DisplayFileInfo(string fileFullName)
{
    FileInfo theFile = new FileInfo(fileFullName);
    if (!theFile.Exists)
        throw new FileNotFoundException("File not found: " + fileFullName);
    textBoxFileName.Text = theFile.Name;
    textBoxCreationTime.Text = theFile.CreationTime.ToLongTimeString();
    textBoxLastAccessTime.Text = theFile.LastAccessTime.ToLongDateString();
    textBoxLastWriteTime.Text = theFile.LastWriteTime.ToLongDateString();
    textBoxFileSize.Text = theFile.Length.ToString() + " bytes";
}
```

Note that we take the precaution of throwing an exception if there are any problems locating a file at the specified location. The exception itself will be handled in the calling routine (one of the event handlers). Finally, we define a method, `DisplayFolderList()`, which displays the contents of a given folder in the two list boxes. The full pathname of the folder is passed in as a parameter to this method:

```
protected void DisplayFolderList(string folderFullName)
{
   DirectoryInfo theFolder = new DirectoryInfo(folderFullName);
   if (!theFolder.Exists)
      throw new DirectoryNotFoundException("Folder not found: "
                                        + folderFullName);
   ClearAllFields();
   textBoxFolder.Text = theFolder.FullName;
   currentFolderPath = theFolder.FullName;

   // list all subfolders in folder
   foreach(DirectoryInfo nextFolder in theFolder.GetDirectories())
      listBoxFolders.Items.Add(nextFolder.Name);

   // list all files in folder
   foreach(FileInfo nextFile in theFolder.GetFiles())
      listBoxFiles.Items.Add(nextFile.Name);
}
```

Next we examine the event handlers. The event handler that manages the event that is triggered when the user clicks the Display button is the most complex, since it needs to handle three different possibilities for the text the user enters in the text box. For instance, it could be the path name of a folder, the path name of a file, or neither of these:

```
protected void OnDisplayButtonClick(object sender, EventArgs e)
{
   try
   {
      string folderPath = textBoxInput.Text;
      DirectoryInfo theFolder = new DirectoryInfo(folderPath);
      if (theFolder.Exists)
      {
         DisplayFolderList(theFolder.FullName);
         return;
      }
      FileInfo theFile = new FileInfo(folderPath);
      if (theFile.Exists)
      {
         DisplayFolderList(theFile.Directory.FullName);
         int index = listBoxFiles.Items.IndexOf(theFile.Name);
         listBoxFiles.SetSelected(index, true);
         return;
      }
      throw new FileNotFoundException("There is no file or folder with "
                                   + "this name: " + textBoxInput.Text);
   }
   catch(Exception ex)
```

```
        {
            MessageBox.Show(ex.Message);
        }
    }
```

In the above code, we establish if the supplied text represents a folder or file by instantiating `DirectoryInfo` and `FileInfo` instances and examining the `Exists` property of each object. If neither exists, then we throw an exception. If it's a folder, we call `DisplayFolderList()` to populate the list boxes. If it's a file, we need to populate the list boxes and sort out the text boxes that display the file properties. We handle this case by first populating the list boxes. We then programmatically select the appropriate file name in the Files list box. This has exactly the same effect as if the user had selected that item—it raises the item-selected event. We can then simply exit the current event handler, knowing that the selected item event handler will immediately be called to display the file properties.

The following code is the event handler that is called when an item in the Files list box is selected, either by the user or, as indicated above, programmatically. It simply constructs the full path name of the selected file, and passes this to the `DisplayFileInfo()` method that we presented earlier:

```
protected void OnListBoxFilesSelected(object sender, EventArgs e)
{
    try
    {
        string selectedString = listBoxFiles.SelectedItem.ToString();
        string fullFileName = Path.Combine(currentFolderPath, selectedString);
        DisplayFileInfo(fullFileName);
    }
    catch(Exception ex)
    {
        MessageBox.Show(ex.Message);
    }
}
```

The event handler for the selection of a folder in the Folders list box is implemented in a very similar way, except that in this case we call `DisplayFolderList()` to update the contents of the list boxes:

```
protected void OnListBoxFoldersSelected(object sender, EventArgs e)
{
    try
    {
        string selectedString = listBoxFolders.SelectedItem.ToString();
        string fullPathName = Path.Combine(currentFolderPath, selectedString);
        DisplayFolderList(fullPathName);
    }
    catch(Exception ex)
    {
        MessageBox.Show(ex.Message);
    }
}
```

Finally, when the Up button is clicked, `DisplayFolderList()` must also be called, except that this time we need to obtain the path of the parent of the folder currently being displayed. This is done with the `FileInfo.DirectoryName` property, which returns the parent folder path:

```
protected void OnUpButtonClick(object sender, EventArgs e)
{
    try
    {
        string folderPath = new FileInfo(currentFolderPath).DirectoryName;
        DisplayFolderList(folderPath);
    }
    catch(Exception ex)
    {
        MessageBox.Show(ex.Message);
    }
}
```

Moving, Copying, and Deleting Files

We have already mentioned that moving and deleting files or folders is done by the `MoveTo()` and `Delete()` methods of the `FileInfo` and `DirectoryInfo` classes. The equivalent methods on the `File` and `Directory` classes are `Move()` and `Delete()`. The `FileInfo` and `File` classes also implement the methods `CopyTo()` and `Copy()`, respectively. However, no methods exist to copy complete folders—you need to do that by copying each file in the folder.

Use of all these methods is quite intuitive—you can find detailed descriptions in the SDK documentation. In this section we are going to illustrate their use for the particular cases of calling the static `Move()`, `Copy()`, and `Delete()` methods on the `File` class. To do this we will build on our previous FileProperties example and call its iteration FilePropertiesAndMovement. This example will have the extra feature that whenever the properties of a file are displayed, the application gives us the option of deleting that file, or moving or copying the file to another location.

Example: FilePropertiesAndMovement

Figure 30-4 shows the user interface of our new sample application.

As you can see, FilePropertiesAndMovement is similar in appearance FileProperties, except for the group of three buttons and a text box at the bottom of the window. These controls are only enabled when the example is actually displaying the properties of a file; at all other times, they are disabled. We've also squashed the existing controls up a bit to stop the main form from getting too big. When the properties of a selected file are displayed, FilePropertiesAndMovement automatically places the full pathname of that file in the bottom textbox for the user to edit. The user can then click any of the buttons to perform the appropriate operation. When they do, a message box is displayed that confirms the action taken by the user (see Figure 30-5).

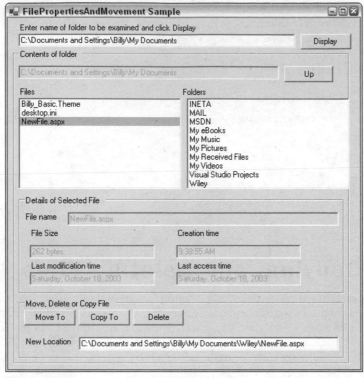

Figure 30-4

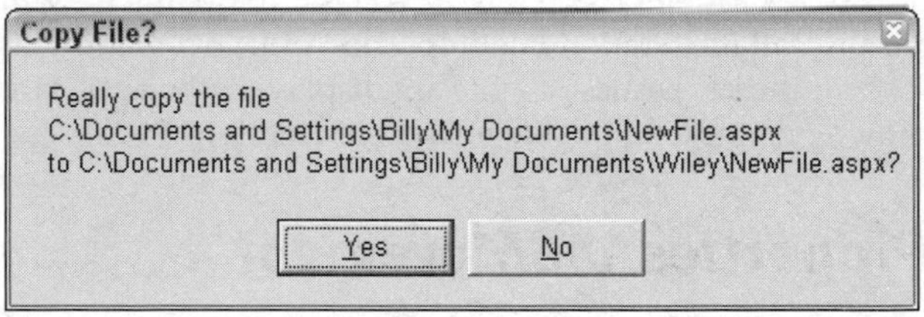

Figure 30-5

When the user clicks the Yes button, the action will be initiated. There are some actions in the form that the user can take that will then cause the display to be incorrect. For instance, if the user moves or deletes a file, we obviously can not continue to display the contents of that file in the same location. Also if we change the name of a file in the same folder, our display will also be out of date. In these cases, FilePropertiesAndMovement resets its controls to display only the folder where the file resides after the file operation.

To code this process, we need to add the relevant controls, as well as their event handlers to the code for the FileProperties example. We have given the new controls the names `buttonDelete`, `buttonCopyTo`, `buttonMoveTo`, and `textBoxNewPath`.

We'll look first at the event handler that gets called when the user clicks the Delete button.

```
protected void OnDeleteButtonClick(object sender, EventArgs e)
{
   try
   {
      string filePath = Path.Combine(currentFolderPath,
                                     textBoxFileName.Text);
      string query = "Really delete the file\n" + filePath + "?";
      if (MessageBox.Show(query,
         "Delete File?", MessageBoxButtons.YesNo) == DialogResult.Yes)
      {
         File.Delete(filePath);
         DisplayFolderList(currentFolderPath);
      }
   }
   catch(Exception ex)
   {
      MessageBox.Show("Unable to delete file. The following exception"
                      + " occurred:\n" + ex.Message, "Failed");
   }
}
```

The code for this method is contained in a `try` block because of the obvious risk of an exception being thrown if, for example, we don't have permission to delete the file, or the file is moved by another process after it has been displayed but before the user presses the Delete button. We construct the path of the file to be deleted from the `CurrentParentPath` field, which contains the path of the parent folder, and the text in the `textBoxFileName` text box, which contains the name of the file.

The methods to move and copy the file are structured in a very similar manner:

```
protected void OnMoveButtonClick(object sender, EventArgs e)
{
   try
   {
      string filePath = Path.Combine(currentFolderPath,
                                     textBoxFileName.Text);
      string query = "Really move the file\n" + filePath + "\nto "
                     + textBoxNewPath.Text + "?";
      if (MessageBox.Show(query,
         "Move File?", MessageBoxButtons.YesNo) == DialogResult.Yes)
      {
         File.Move(filePath, textBoxNewPath.Text);
         DisplayFolderList(currentFolderPath);
      }
   }
   catch(Exception ex)
   {
      MessageBox.Show("Unable to move file. The following exception"
                      + " occurred:\n" + ex.Message, "Failed");
   }
}

protected void OnCopyButtonClick(object sender, EventArgs e)
{
```

```
    try
    {
        string filePath = Path.Combine(currentFolderPath,
                                        textBoxFileName.Text);
        string query = "Really copy the file\n" + filePath + "\nto "
                       + textBoxNewPath.Text + "?";
        if (MessageBox.Show(query,
            "Copy File?", MessageBoxButtons.YesNo) == DialogResult.Yes)
        {
            File.Copy(filePath, textBoxNewPath.Text);
            DisplayFolderList(currentFolderPath);
        }
    }
    catch(Exception ex)
    {
        MessageBox.Show("Unable to copy file. The following exception"
                        + " occurred:\n" + ex.Message, "Failed");
    }
}
```

We're not quite done yet. We also need to make sure the new buttons and text box are enabled and disabled at the appropriate times. To enable them when we are displaying the contents of a file, we add the following code to `DisplayFileInfo()`:

```
protected void DisplayFileInfo(string fileFullName)
{
    FileInfo theFile = new FileInfo(fileFullName);
    if (!theFile.Exists)
        throw new FileNotFoundException("File not found: " + fileFullName);

    textBoxFileName.Text = theFile.Name;
    textBoxCreationTime.Text = theFile.CreationTime.ToLongTimeString();
    textBoxLastAccessTime.Text = theFile.LastAccessTime.ToLongDateString();
    textBoxLastWriteTime.Text = theFile.LastWriteTime.ToLongDateString();
    textBoxFileSize.Text = theFile.Length.ToString() + " bytes";

    // enable move, copy, delete buttons
    textBoxNewPath.Text = theFile.FullName;
    textBoxNewPath.Enabled = true;
    buttonCopyTo.Enabled = true;
    buttonDelete.Enabled = true;
    buttonMoveTo.Enabled = true;
}
```

We also need to make one change to `DisplayFolderList`:

```
protected void DisplayFolderList(string folderFullName)
{
    DirectoryInfo theFolder = new DirectoryInfo(folderFullName);
    if (!theFolder.Exists)
        throw new DirectoryNotFoundException("Folder not found: " + folderFullName);

    ClearAllFields();
```

```
        DisableMoveFeatures();
        textBoxFolder.Text = theFolder.FullName;
        currentFolderPath = theFolder.FullName;

        // list all subfolders in folder
        foreach(DirectoryInfo nextFolder in theFolder.GetDirectories())
            listBoxFolders.Items.Add(NextFolder.Name);

        // list all files in folder
        foreach(FileInfo nextFile in theFolder.GetFiles())
            listBoxFiles.Items.Add(NextFile.Name);
    }
```

DisableMoveFeatures is a small utility function that disables the new controls:

```
        void DisableMoveFeatures()
        {
            textBoxNewPath.Text = "";
            textBoxNewPath.Enabled = false;
            buttonCopyTo.Enabled = false;
            buttonDelete.Enabled = false;
            buttonMoveTo.Enabled = false;
        }
```

We also need to add extra code to ClearAllFields() to clear the extra textbox:

```
        protected void ClearAllFields()
        {
            listBoxFolders.Items.Clear();
            listBoxFiles.Items.Clear();
            textBoxFolder.Text = "";
            textBoxFileName.Text = "";
            textBoxCreationTime.Text = "";
            textBoxLastAccessTime.Text = "";
            textBoxLastWriteTime.Text = "";
            textBoxFileSize.Text = "";
            textBoxNewPath.Text = "";
        }
```

With that, the code is complete.

Reading and Writing to Files

Reading and writing to files is in principle very simple; however, it is not done through the DirectoryInfo or FileInfo objects. Instead, it is done through a number of classes that represent a generic concept called a *stream*.

Streams

The idea of a stream has been around for a very long time. A stream is an object used to transfer data. The data can be transferred in one of two directions:

❑ If the data is being transferred from some outside source into your program, then we talk about *reading* from the stream.

❑ If the data is being transferred from your program to some outside source, then we talk about *writing* to the stream.

Very often, the outside source will be a file, but that is not necessarily the case. Other possibilities include:

❑ Reading or writing data on the network using some network protocol, where the intention is for this data to be picked up by or sent from another computer

❑ Reading or writing to a named pipe

❑ Reading or writing to an area of memory

Of these examples, Microsoft has supplied a .NET base class for writing to or reading from memory, `System.IO.MemoryStream`, while `System.Net.Sockets.NetworkStream` handles network data. There are no base stream classes for writing to or reading from pipes, but there is a generic stream class, `System.IO.Stream`, from which you would inherit if you wanted to write such a class. `Stream` does not make any assumptions about the nature of the external data source.

The outside source might even be a variable within your own code. This might sound paradoxical, but the technique of using streams to transmit data between variables can be a useful trick for converting data between data types. The C language used something like this to convert between integer data types and strings or to format strings using a function, `sprintf`.

The advantage of having a separate object for the transfer of data, rather than using the `FileInfo` or `DirectoryInfo` classes to do this, is that by separating the concept of transferring data from the particular data source, it makes it easier to swap data sources. Stream objects themselves contain a lot of generic code that concerns the movement of data between outside sources and variables in your code, and by keeping this code separate from any concept of a particular data source, we make it easier for this code to be reused (through inheritance) in different circumstances. For example, the `StringReader` and `StringWriter` classes mentioned above are part of the same inheritance tree as two classes that we will be using later on to read and write text files, `StreamReader` and `StreamWriter`. The classes will almost certainly share a substantial amount of code behind the scenes.

Figure 30-6 illustrates the actual hierarchy of stream-related classes in the `System.IO` namespace.

As far as reading and writing files is concerned, the classes that concern us most are:

❑ `FileStream`—This class is intended for reading and writing binary data in a binary file. However, you can also use it to read from or write to any file.

❑ `StreamReader` and `StreamWriter`—These classes are designed specifically for reading from and writing to text files.

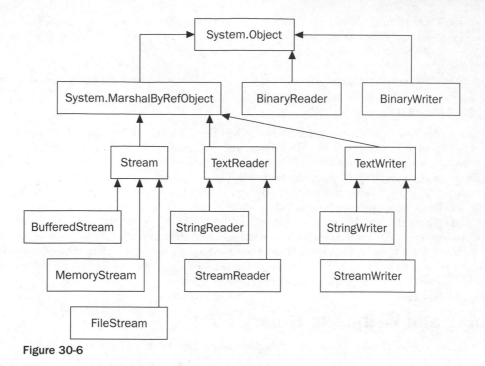

Figure 30-6

Although we won't be using them in our examples, you might also find useful `BinaryReader` and `BinaryWriter`. These classes do not actually implement streams themselves, but they are able to provide wrappers around other stream objects. `BinaryReader` and `BinaryWriter` provide extra formatting of binary data, which allows you to directly read or write the contents of C# variables to the relevant stream. Think of the `BinaryReader` and `BinaryWriter` as sitting between the stream and your code, providing extra formatting (see Figure 30-7).

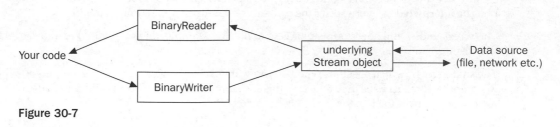

Figure 30-7

The difference between using these classes and directly using the underlying stream objects is that a basic stream works in bytes. For example, suppose as part of the process of saving some document you want to write the contents of a variable of type `long` to a binary file. Each `long` occupies 8 bytes, and if you used an ordinary binary stream you would have to explicitly write each of those 8 bytes of memory. In C# code that would mean you'd have to perform some bitwise operations to extract each of those 8 bytes from the `long` value. Using a `BinaryWriter` instance, you can encapsulate the entire operation in an overload of the `BinaryWriter.Write()` method that takes a `long` as a parameter, and which will place those 8 bytes into the stream (and hence if the stream is directed to a file, in the file). A corresponding `BinaryReader.Read()` method will extract 8 bytes from the stream and recover the value of the `long`.

For more information on the `BinaryReader` and `BinaryWriter` classes refer to the SDK documentation.

Buffered streams

For performance reasons, when you read or write to a file, the output is buffered. This means that if your program asks for the next 2 bytes of a file stream, and the stream passes the request on to Windows, then Windows will not go through the trouble of connecting to the file system and then locating and reading the file off the disk, just to get 2 bytes. Instead, Windows will retrieve a large block of the file in one go, and store this block in an area of memory known as a *buffer*. Subsequent requests for data from the stream will be satisfied from the buffer until the buffer runs out, at which point Windows grabs another block of data from the file. Writing to files works in the same way. For files this is done automatically by the operating system, but you might have to write a stream class to read from some other device that isn't buffered. If so, you can derive your class from `BufferedStream`, which implements a buffer itself. (Note, however, that `BufferedStream` is not designed for the situation in which an application frequently alternates between reading and writing data.)

Reading and Writing to Binary Files

Reading and writing to binary files is usually done using the `FileStream` class.

The FileStream class

A `FileStream` instance is used to read or write data to or from a file. In order to construct a `FileStream`, you need four pieces of information:

- ❑ The **file** you want to access.
- ❑ The **mode**, which indicates how you want to open the file. For example, are you intending to create a new file or open an existing file, and if opening an existing file, should any write operations be interpreted as overwriting the contents of the file or appending to the file?
- ❑ The **access**, indicating how you want access to file; for example, do you want to read or write to the file or do both?
- ❑ The **share** access, which specifies whether you want exclusive access to the file, or are you willing for other streams to be able to access this file simultaneously? If so, should other streams have access to read the file, to write to it, or to do both?

The first of these pieces of information is usually represented by a string that contains the full pathname of the file, and in this chapter we will only consider those constructors that require a string here. Besides those constructors, however, there are some additional ones that take an old Windows-API-style Windows handle to a file instead. The remaining three pieces of information are represented by three .NET enumerations called `FileMode`, `FileAccess`, and `FileShare`. The values of these enumerations are listed in the following table; they should be self-explanatory.

Enumeration	Values
FileMode	Append, Create, CreateNew, Open, OpenOrCreate, or Truncate
FileAccess	Read, ReadWrite, or Write
FileShare	Inheritable, None, Read, ReadWrite, or Write

Note that in the case of `FileMode`, exceptions can be thrown if you request a mode that is inconsistent with the existing status of the file. `Append`, `Open`, and `Truncate` will throw an exception if the file does not already exist, and `CreateNew` will throw an exception if it does. `Create` and `OpenOrCreate` will cope with either scenario, but `Create` will delete any existing file to replace it with a new, initially empty, one. The `FileAccess` and `FileShare` enumerations are bitwise flags, so values can be combined with the C# bitwise `OR` operator, `|`.

There are a large number of constructors for the `FileStream`. The three simplest ones work as follows:

```
// creates file with read-write access and allows other streams read access
FileStream fs = new FileStream(@"C:\C# Projects\Project.doc",
                   FileMode.Create);
// as above, but we only get write access to the file
FileStream fs2 = new FileStream(@"C:\C# Projects\Project2.doc",
                   FileMode.Create, FileAccess.Write);
// as above but other streams don't get access to the file while
// fs3 is open
FileStream fs3 = new FileStream(@"C:\C# Projects\Project3.doc",
                   FileMode.Create, FileAccess.Write, FileShare.None);
```

As this code reveals, the overloads of these constructors have the effect of providing default values of `FileAccess.ReadWrite` and `FileShare.Read` to the third and fourth parameters. It is also possible to create a file stream from a `FileInfo` instance in various ways:

```
FileInfo myFile4 = new FileInfo(@"C:\C# Projects\Project4.doc");
FileStream fs4 = myFile4.OpenRead();
FileInfo myFile5= new FileInfo(@"C:\C# Projects\Project5doc");
FileStream fs5 = myFile5.OpenWrite();
FileInfo myFile6= new FileInfo(@"C:\C# Projects\Project6doc");
FileStream fs6 = myFile6.Open(FileMode.Append, FileAccess.Write,
                   FileShare.None);
FileInfo myFile7 = new FileInfo(@"C:\C# Projects\Project7.doc");
FileStream fs7 = myFile7.Create();
```

`FileInfo.OpenRead()` supplies a stream that gives you read-only access to an existing file, while `FileInfo.OpenWrite()` gives you read-write access. `FileInfo.Open()` allows you to specify the mode, access, and file share parameters explicitly.

Of course, after you've finished with a stream, you should close it:

```
fs.Close();
```

Closing the stream frees up the resources associated with it, and allows other applications to set up streams to the same file. In between opening and closing the stream, you'll want to read data from it and/or write data to it. `FileStream` implements a number of methods to do this.

`ReadByte()` is the simplest way of reading data. It grabs one byte from the stream, and casts the result to an `int` having a value between 0 and 255. If we have reached the end of the stream, it returns -1:

```
int NextByte = fs.ReadByte();
```

If you prefer to read a number of bytes at a time, you can call the `Read()` method, which reads a specified number of bytes into an array. `Read()` returns the number of bytes actually read—if this value is zero then you know you're at the end of the stream. Here's an example where we read into a `Byte` array `ByteArray`:

```
int nBytesRead = fs.Read(ByteArray, 0, nBytes);
```

The second parameter to `Read()` is an offset, which you can use to request that the `Read` operation starts populating the array at some element other than the first, and the third parameter is the number of bytes to read into the array.

If you want to write data to a file, then there are two parallel methods available, `WriteByte()` and `Write()`. `WriteByte()` writes a single byte to the stream:

```
byte NextByte = 100;
fs.WriteByte(NextByte);
```

`Write()`, on the other hand, writes out an array of bytes. For instance, if we initialized the `ByteArray` we mentioned before with some values, we could use the following code to write out the first `nBytes` of the array:

```
fs.Write(ByteArray, 0, nBytes);
```

As with `Read()`, the second parameter allows you to start writing from some point other than the beginning of the array. Both `WriteByte()` and `Write()` return `void`.

Besides these methods, `FileStream` implements various other methods and properties to do with book-keeping tasks like determining how many bytes are in the stream, locking the stream, or flushing the buffer. These other methods aren't usually required for basic reading and writing, and if you need them, full details are in the SDK documentation.

Example: BinaryFileReader

We'll illustrate the use of the `FileStream` class by writing an example, BinaryFileReader, which reads in and displays any file. Create the project in Visual Studio .NET as a Windows application. We've added one menu item, which brings up a standard `OpenFileDialog` asking what file to read in, then displays the file as binary code. As we are reading in binary files, we need to be able to display non-printable characters. The way we will do this is by displaying each byte of the file individually, showing 16 bytes on each line of a multi-line text box. If the byte represents a printable ASCII character we'll display that character, otherwise we'll display the value of the byte in a hexadecimal format. In either case, we pad out the displayed text with spaces so that each byte displayed occupies four columns so the bytes line up nicely under each other.

Figure 30-8 shows what the BinaryFileReader application looks like when viewing a text file (since BinaryFileReader can view any file, it's quite possible to use it on text files as well as binary ones). In this case, the application has read in a basic ASP.NET page (.aspx).

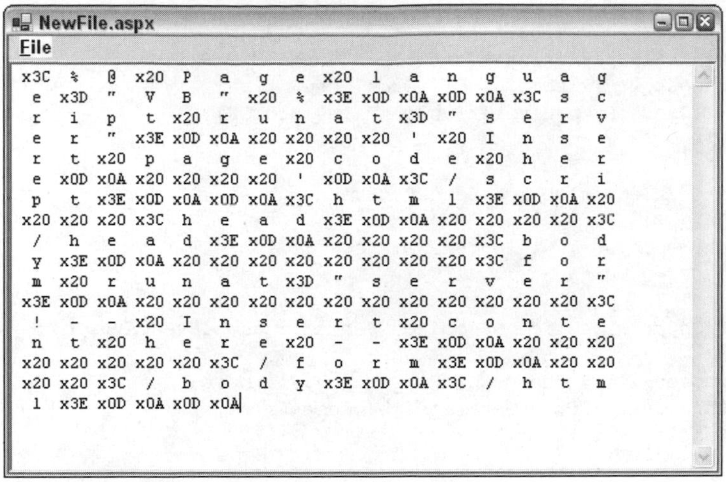

Figure 30-8

Clearly this format is more suited to looking at the values of individual bytes rather than displaying text! Later in this chapter, we'll develop an example that is specifically designed to read text files; then we will be able to see what this file really says. On the other hand, the advantage of this example is that we can look at the contents of any file.

For this example, we won't demonstrate writing to files. That's because we don't want to get bogged down in the complexities of trying to translate the contents of a text box like the one above into a binary stream! We will demonstrate writing to files later on when we develop an example that can read or write, but only to text files.

Let's look at the code used to get these results. First, we need an extra using statement, since apart from System.IO, this example is going to use the StringBuilder class from the System.Text namespace to construct the strings in the textbox:

```
using System.IO;
using System.Text;
```

Next, we add a couple of fields to the main form class—one representing the file dialog, and a string that gives the path of the file currently being viewed:

```
public class Form1 : System.Windows.Forms.Form
{
    private OpenFileDialog chooseOpenFileDialog = new OpenFileDialog();
    private string chosenFile;
```

We also need to add some standard Windows Forms code to deal with the handlers for the menu and the file dialog:

```
public Form1()
{
    InitializeComponent();
    menuFileOpen.Click += new EventHandler(OnFileOpen);
    chooseOpenFileDialog.FileOk += new
        CancelEventHandler(OnOpenFileDialogOK);
}

void OnFileOpen(object Sender, EventArgs e)
{
    chooseOpenFileDialog.ShowDialog();
}

void OnOpenFileDialogOK(object Sender, CancelEventArgs e)
{
    chosenFile = chooseOpenFileDialog.FileName;
    this.Text = Path.GetFileName(chosenFile);
    DisplayFile();
}
```

As this code demonstrates, when the user clicks OK to select a file in the file dialog, we call the `DisplayFile()` method, which does the work of reading in the selected file:

```
void DisplayFile()
{
    int nCols = 16;
    FileStream inStream = new FileStream(chosenFile, FileMode.Open,
                                            FileAccess.Read);

    long nBytesToRead = inStream.Length;
    if (nBytesToRead > 65536/4)
        nBytesToRead = 65536/4;

    int nLines = (int)(nBytesToRead/nCols) + 1;
    string [] lines = new string[nLines];
    int nBytesRead = 0;

    for (int i=0 ; i<nLines ; i++)
    {
        StringBuilder nextLine = new StringBuilder();
        nextLine.Capacity = 4*nCols;

        for (int j = 0 ; j<nCols ; j++)
        {
            int nextByte = inStream.ReadByte();
            nBytesRead++;
            if (nextByte < 0 || nBytesRead > 65536)
                break;
            char nextChar = (char)nextByte;
            if (nextChar < 16)
                nextLine.Append(" x0" + string.Format("{0,1:X}",
                                                (int)nextChar));
```

```
        else if
          (char.IsLetterOrDigit(nextChar) ||
                             char.IsPunctuation(nextChar))
          nextLine.Append("  " + nextChar + " ");
        else
          nextLine.Append(" x" + string.Format("{0,2:X}",
                            (int)nextChar));
      }
      lines[i] = nextLine.ToString();
    }
    inStream.Close();
    this.textBoxContents.Lines = lines;
}
```

There's quite a lot going on in this method, so we'll break it down. We instantiate a `FileStream` object for the selected file, which specifies that we want to open an existing file for reading. We then work out how many bytes there are to read in and how many lines should be displayed. The number of bytes will normally be the number of bytes in the file. However, textboxes can only display a maximum of 65,536 characters and with our chosen display format, we are displaying 4 characters for every byte in the file, so we will need to cap the number of bytes shown in the text box if the selected file is longer than 65,536/4 = 16,384 bytes.

> If you want to display longer files in this sort of environment, you might want to look up the `RichTextBox` class in the `System.Windows.Forms` namespace. `RichTextBox` is similar to a text box, but has many more advanced formatting facilities and does not have a limit on how much text it can display. We are using `TextBox` here to keep the example simple and focused on the process of reading in files.

The bulk of the method is given over to two nested `for` loops that construct each line of text to be displayed. We use a `StringBuilder` class to construct each line for performance reasons: We are appending suitable text for each byte to the string that represents each line 16 times. If on each occasion we allocate a new string and take a copy of the half-constructed line, we are not only going to be spending a lot of time allocating strings, but will be wasting a lot of memory on the heap. Notice that our definition of *printable* characters is anything that is a letter, digit, or punctuation, as indicated by the relevant static `System.Char` methods. We've excluded any character with a value less than 16 from the printable list, however, which means we'll trap the carriage return (13) and line feed (10) as binary characters (a multi-line text box isn't able to display these characters properly if they occur individually within a line).

Furthermore, using the Properties Window, we changed the Font property for the textbox to a fixed width font. In this case, we chose `Courier New 9pt regular`, and also set the textbox to have vertical and horizontal scroll bars.

Upon completion, we close the stream and set the contents of the text box to the array of strings that we've built up.

Reading and Writing to Text Files

Theoretically, it's perfectly possible to use the `FileStream` class to read in and display text files. We have, after all, just demonstrated doing that. The format in which we displayed the NewFile.aspx file above wasn't particularly user-friendly, but that has nothing to do with any intrinsic problem with the `FileStream` class, only with how we chose to display the results in the text box.

Having said that, if you know that a particular file contains text, you will usually find it more convenient to read and write it using the StreamReader and StreamWriter classes. That's because these classes work at a slightly higher level and are specifically geared to reading and writing text. The methods that they implement are able to automatically detect where convenient points to stop reading text are, based on the contents of the stream. In particular:

❑ These classes implement methods to read or write one line of text at a time, StreamReader.ReadLine() and StreamWriter.WriteLine(). In the case of reading, this means that the stream will automatically figure out for you where the next carriage return is, and stop reading at that point. In the case of writing, it means that the stream will automatically append the carriage return-line feed combination to the text that it writes out.

❑ By using the StreamReader and StreamWriter classes you don't need to worry about the encoding (the text format) used in the file. Possible encodings include ASCII (1 byte for each character), or any or the Unicode-based formats, UNICODE, UTF7, and UTF8. Text files on Windows 9x systems are always in ASCII, because Windows 9x doesn't support Unicode, but Windows NT, 2000, XP, and 2003 all do support Unicode, and so text files might theoretically contain Unicode, UTF7, or UTF8 data instead of ASCII data. The convention is that if the file is in ASCII format, it will simply contain the text. If it is in any Unicode format, this will be indicated by the first two or three bytes of the file, which are set to particular combinations of values to indicate the format used in the file.

These bytes are known as the *byte code markers*. When you open a file using any of the standard Windows applications, such as Notepad or WordPad, you don't need to worry about this because these applications are aware of the different encoding methods and will automatically read the file correctly. This is also the case for the StreamReader class, which will correctly read in a file in any of these formats, while the StreamWriter class is capable of formatting the text it writes out using whatever encoding technique you request. On the other hand, if you wanted to read in and display a text file using the FileStream class, you would have to handle all this yourself.

The StreamReader class

StreamReader is used to read text files. Constructing a StreamReader is in some ways easier than constructing a FileStream instance, because some of the FileStream options are not required when using StreamReader. In particular, the mode and access types are not relevant to StreamReader, because the only thing you can do with a StreamReader is read! Furthermore, there is no direct option to specify the sharing permissions. However, there are a couple of new options:

❑ We need to specify what to do about the different encoding methods. We can instruct the StreamReader to examine the byte code markers in the beginning of the file to determine the encoding method, or we can simply tell the StreamReader to assume that the file uses a specified encoding method.

❑ Instead of supplying a file name to be read from, we can supply a reference to another stream.

This last option deserves a bit more discussion, because it illustrates another advantage of basing our model for reading and writing data on the concept of streams. Because the StreamReader works at a relatively high level, you might find it useful if you are in the situation in which you have another stream that is there to read data from some other source, but you would like to use the facilities provided by StreamReader to process that other stream as if it contained text. You can do so by simply passing the output from this stream to a StreamReader. In this way, StreamReader can be used to read

File and Registry Operations

and process data from any data source—not only files. This is essentially the situation we discussed earlier with regard to the `BinaryReader` class. However, in this book we will only use `StreamReader` to connect directly to files.

The result of these possibilities is that `StreamReader` has a large number of constructors. Not only that, but there are a couple of `FileInfo` methods that return `StreamReader` references too: `OpenText()` and `CreateText()`. Here we will just illustrate some of the constructors.

The simplest constructor takes just a file name. This `StreamReader` will examine the byte order marks to determine the encoding:

```
StreamReader sr = new StreamReader(@"C:\My Documents\ReadMe.txt");
```

Alternatively, if you prefer to specify that UTF8 encoding should be assumed:

```
StreamReader sr = new StreamReader(@"C:\My Documents\ReadMe.txt",
                                   Encoding.UTF8);
```

We specify the encoding by using one of several properties on a class, `System.Text.Encoding`. This class is an abstract base class, from which a number of classes are derived and which implements methods that actually perform the text encoding. Each property returns an instance of the appropriate class, and the possible properties we can use here are:

❑   `ASCII`

❑   `Unicode`

❑   `UTF7`

❑   `UTF8`

❑   `BigEndianUnicode`

The following example demonstrates hooking up a `StreamReader` to a `FileStream`. The advantage of this is that we can specify whether to create the file and the share permissions, which we cannot do if we directly attach a `StreamReader` to the file:

```
FileStream fs = new FileStream(@"C:\My Documents\ReadMe.txt",
                      FileMode.Open, FileAccess.Read, FileShare.None);
StreamReader sr = new StreamReader(fs);
```

For this example, we specify that the `StreamReader` will look for byte code markers to determine the encoding method used, as it will do in the following examples, in which the `StreamReader` is obtained from a `FileInfo` instance:

```
FileInfo myFile = new FileInfo(@"C:\My Documents\ReadMe.txt");
StreamReader sr = myFile.OpenText();
```

Just as with a `FileStream`, you should always close a `StreamReader` after use. Failure to do so will result in the file remaining locked to other processes (unless you used a `FileStream` to construct the `StreamReader` and specified `FileShare.ShareReadWrite`):

```
sr.Close();
```

1049

Now that we've gone to the trouble of instantiating a `StreamReader`, we can do something with it. As with the `FileStream`, we'll simply point out the various ways to read data, and leave the other, less commonly used, `StreamReader` methods to the SDK documentation.

Possibly the easiest method to use is `ReadLine()`, which keeps reading until it gets to the end of a line. It does not include the carriage return–line feed combination that marks the end of the line in the returned string:

```
string nextLine = sr.ReadLine();
```

Alternatively, you can grab the entire remainder of the file (or strictly, the remainder of the stream) in one string:

```
string restOfStream = sr.ReadToEnd();
```

You can read a single character:

```
int nextChar = sr.Read();
```

This overload of `Read()` casts the returned character to an `int`. This is so that it has the option of returning a value of -1 if the end of the stream has been reached.

Finally, you can read a given number of characters into an array, with an offset:

```
// to read 100 characters in.

int nChars = 100;
char [] charArray = new char[nChars];
int nCharsRead = sr.Read(charArray, 0, nChars);
```

`nCharsRead` will be less than `nChars` if we have requested to read more characters than are left in the file.

The StreamWriter class

This works in basically the same way as the `StreamReader`, except that you can only use `StreamWriter` to write to a file (or to another stream). Possibilities for constructing a `StreamWriter` include:

```
StreamWriter sw = new StreamWriter(@"C:\My Documents\ReadMe.txt");
```

The above code will use UTF8 Encoding, which is regarded by .NET as the default encoding method. If you want, you can specify an alternative encoding:

```
StreamWriter sw = new StreamWriter(@"C:\My Documents\ReadMe.txt", true,
    Encoding.ASCII);
```

In this constructor, the second parameter is a `Boolean` that indicates whether the file should be opened for appending. There is, oddly, no constructor that takes only a file name and an encoding class.

Of course, you may want to hook up `StreamWriter` to a file stream to give you more control over the options for opening the file:

```
FileStream fs = new FileStream(@"C:\My Documents\ReadMe.txt",
    FileMode.CreateNew, FileAccess.Write, FileShare.Read);
StreamWriter sw = new StreamWriter(fs);
```

`FileStream` does not implement any methods that return a `StreamWriter` class.

Alternatively, if you want to create a new file and start writing data to it, you'll find this sequence useful:

```
FileInfo myFile = new FileInfo(@"C:\My Documents\NewFile.txt");
StreamWriter sw = myFile.CreateText();
```

Just as with all other stream classes it is important to close a `StreamWriter` class when you have finished with it:

```
sw.Close();
```

Writing to the stream is done using any of four overloads of `StreamWriter.Write()`. The simplest writes out a string, and appends it with a carriage return-line feed combination:

```
string nextLine = "Groovy Line";
sw.Write(nextLine);
```

It is also possible to write out a single character:

```
char nextChar = 'a';
sw.Write(nextChar);
```

An array of characters is also possible:

```
char [] charArray = new char[100];

// initialize these characters

sw.Write(charArray);
```

It is even possible to write out a portion of an array of characters:

```
int nCharsToWrite = 50;
int startAtLocation = 25;
char [] charArray = new char[100];

// initialize these characters

sw.Write(charArray, startAtLocation, nCharsToWrite);
```

Example: ReadWriteText

The ReadWriteText example displays the use of the `StreamReader` and `StreamWriter` classes. It is similar to the earlier ReadBinaryFile example, but it assumes the file to be read in is a text file and displays it as such. It is also capable of saving the file (with any modifications you've made to the text in the textbox). It will save any file in Unicode format.

The screenshot in Figure 30-9 shows ReadWriteText displaying the same NewFile.aspx file that we used earlier. This time, however, we are able to read the contents a bit more easily!

Figure 30-9

We won't go over the details of adding the event handlers for the Open File dialog box, because they are basically the same as with the earlier BinaryFileReader example. As with that example, opening a new file causes the DisplayFile() method to be called. The only real difference between this example and the previous one is the implementation of DisplayFile as well as that we now have the option to save a file. This is represented by another menu option, Save. The handler for this option calls another method we've added to the code, SaveFile(). (Note that the new file always overwrites the original file; this example does not have an option to write to a different file.)

We'll look at SaveFile() first, since that is the simplest function. We simply write each line of the text box, in turn, to a StreamWriter stream, relying on the StreamReader.WriteLine() method to append the trailing carriage return and line feed at the end of each line:

```csharp
void SaveFile()
{
    StreamWriter sw = new StreamWriter(chosenFile, false, Encoding.Unicode);

    foreach (string line in textBoxContents.Lines)
        sw.WriteLine(line);
    sw.Close();
}
```

chosenFile is a string field of the main form, which contains the name of the file we have read in (just as for the previous example). Notice that we specify Unicode encoding when we open the stream. If we'd wanted to write files in some other format then we'd simply need to change the value of this parameter. The second parameter to this constructor would be set to true if we wanted to append to a file, but we don't in this case. The encoding must be set at construction time for a StreamWriter. It is subsequently available as a read-only property, Encoding.

Now we'll examine how files are read in. The process of reading in is complicated by the fact that we don't know until we've read in the file how many lines it is going to contain (in other words, how many `(char)13(char)10` sequences are in the file) since `char(13)char(10)` is the carriage return-line feed combination that occurs at the end of a line). We solve this problem by initially reading the file into an instance of the `StringCollection` class, which is in the `System.Collections.Specialized` namespace. This class is designed to hold a set of strings that can be dynamically expanded. It implements two methods that we will be interested in: `Add()`, which adds a string to the collection, and `CopyTo()`, which copies the string collection into a normal array (a `System.Array` instance). Each element of the `StringCollection` object will hold one line of the file.

The `DisplayFile()` method calls another method, `ReadFileIntoStringCollection()`, which actually reads in the file. After doing this, we now know how many lines there are, so we are in a position to copy the `StringCollection` into a normal, fixed-size array and feed this array into the text box. Since only the references to the strings that are copied when we make the copy, not the strings themselves, the process is reasonably efficient:

```
void DisplayFile()
{
    StringCollection linesCollection = ReadFileIntoStringCollection();
    string [] linesArray = new string[linesCollection.Count];
    linesCollection.CopyTo(linesArray, 0);
    this.textBoxContents.Lines = linesArray;
}
```

The second parameter of `StringCollection.CopyTo()` indicates the index within the destination array of where we want the collection to start.

Now we will examine the `ReadFileIntoStringCollection()` method. We use a `StreamReader` to read in each line. The main complication here is the need to count the characters read in to make sure we don't exceed the capacity of the text box:

```
StringCollection ReadFileIntoStringCollection()
{
    const int MaxBytes = 65536;
    StreamReader sr = new StreamReader(chosenFile);
    StringCollection result = new StringCollection();
    int nBytesRead = 0;
    string nextLine;
    while ( (nextLine = sr.ReadLine()) != null)
    {
        nBytesRead += nextLine.Length;
        if (nBytesRead > MaxBytes)
            break;
        result.Add(nextLine);
    }
    sr.Close();
    return result;
}
```

That completes the code for this example.

If we run ReadWriteText, read in the NewFile.aspx file, and then save it, the file will be in Unicode format. We wouldn't be able to tell this from any of the usual Windows applications: Notepad, WordPad, and even our own `ReadWriteText` example, will still read the file in and display it correctly under Windows NT/2000/XP/2003, although because Windows 9x doesn't support Unicode, applications like Notepad won't be able to understand the Unicode file on those platforms. (If you download the example from the Wrox Press Web site at www.wrox.com, you can try this!) However, if we try to display the file again using our earlier BinaryFileReader example, we can see the difference immediately, as shown in Figure 30-10. The two initial bytes that indicate the file is in Unicode format are visible, and thereafter we see that every character is represented by two bytes. This last fact is very obvious, because the high-order byte of every character in this particular file is zero, so every second byte in this file now displays x00.

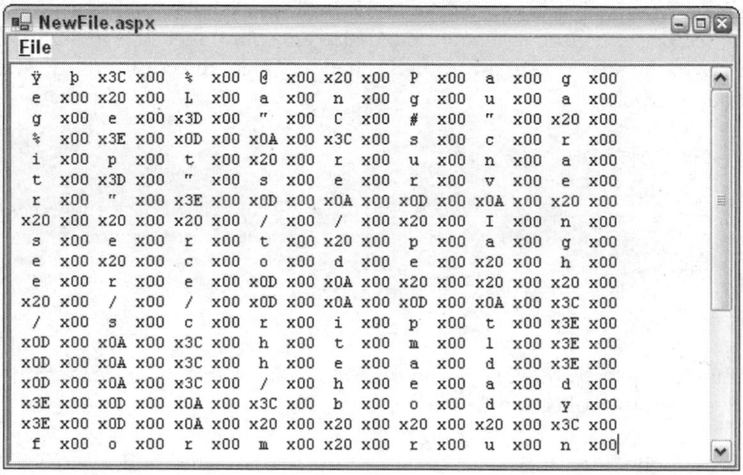

Figure 30-10

Reading and Writing to the Registry

In all versions of Windows since Windows 95, the registry has been the central repository for all configuration information relating to Windows setup, user preferences, and installed software and devices. Almost all commercial software these days uses the registry to store information about itself, and COM components must place information about themselves in the registry in order to be called by clients. .NET Framework and its accompanying concept of zero-impact installation has slightly reduced the significance of the registry for applications in the sense that assemblies are entirely self-contained, so no information about particular assemblies needs to be placed in the registry, even for shared assemblies. In addition, .NET Framework has brought the concept of isolated storage, by which applications can store information that is particular to each user in files, with .NET Framework taking care of making sure that data is stored separately for each user registered on a machine. (Isolated storage is beyond the scope of this book, but if you are interested, you can find the relevant .NET base classes in the `System.IO.IsolatedStorage` namespace.)

The fact that applications can now be installed using the Windows Installer also frees developers from some of the direct manipulation of the registry that used to be involved in installing applications.

However, despite this, the possibility exists that if you distribute any complete application, your application will use the registry to store information about its configuration. For instance, if you want your application to show up in the Add/Remove Programs dialog box in the Control Panel, then this will involve appropriate registry entries. You may also need to use the registry for backward compatibility with legacy code.

As you'd expect from a library as comprehensive as the .NET library, it includes classes that give you access to the registry. There are two classes concerned with the registry, and both are in the `Microsoft.Win32` namespace. The classes are `Registry` and `RegistryKey`. Before we examine these classes, we will briefly review the structure of the registry itself.

The Registry

The registry has a hierarchical structure much like that of the file system. The usual way to view or modify the contents of the registry is with one of two utilities: regedit or regedt32. Of these, regedit comes with all versions of Windows, since Windows 95 as standard. regedt32 comes with Windows NT and Windows 2000; it is less user-friendly than regedit, but allows access to security information that regedit is unable to view. Windows Server 2003 has merged regedit and regedt32 into a single new editor simply called regedit. For our discussion here, we'll use regedit from Windows XP Professional, which you can launch by typing in regedit at the Run dialog or command prompt.

Figure 30-11 shows what you get when you launch regedit for the first time.

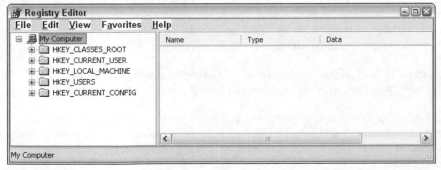

Figure 30-11

`regedit` has a similar tree view/list view style user interface to Windows Explorer, which matches the hierarchical structure of the registry itself. However, there are some key differences that we'll discuss shortly.

In a file system, the topmost level nodes can be thought of as being the partitions on your disks, C:\, D:\, and so on. In the registry, the equivalent to a partition is the *registry hive*. It is not possible to change the existing hives—they are fixed, and there are seven of them, although only five are actually visible through regedit:

❑   HKEY_CLASSES_ROOT (HKCR) contains details of types of files on the system (.txt, .doc, and so on), and which applications are able to open files of each type. It also contains registration information for all COM components (this latter area is usually the largest single area of the registry, since Windows these days comes with a huge number of COM components).

❑ HKEY_CURRENT_USER (HKCU) contains details of user preferences for the user currently logged on to the machine locally. These settings include desktop settings, environment variables, network and printer connections, and other settings that define the user operating environment of the user.

❑ HKEY_LOCAL_MACHINE (HKLM) is a huge hive that contains details of all software and hardware installed on the machine. These settings are not user-specific, but are for all users that log onto the machine. This hive also includes the HKCR hive: HKCR is actually not really an independent hive in its own right, but is simply a convenient mapping onto the registry key HKLM/SOFTWARE/Classes.

❑ HKEY_USERS (HKUSR) contains details of user preferences for all users. As you might guess, it also contains the HKCU hive, which is simply a mapping onto one of the keys in HKEY_USERS.

❑ HKEY_CURRENT_CONFIG (HKCF) contains details of hardware on the machine.

The remaining two keys contain information that is of a temporary nature, and which changes frequently:

❑ HKEY_DYN_DATA is a general container for any volatile data that needs to be stored somewhere in the registry.

❑ HKEY_PERFORMANCE_DATA contains information concerning the performance of running applications.

Within the hives is a tree structure of registry *keys*. Each key is in many ways analogous to a folder or file on the file system. However, there is one very important difference. The file system distinguishes between files (which are there to contain data), and folders (which are primarily there to contain other files or folders), but in the registry there are only keys. A key may contain both data and other keys.

If a key contains data, then this will be presented as a series of values. Each value will have an associated name, data type, and data. In addition, a key can have a default value, which is unnamed.

We can see this structure by using regedit to examine registry keys. Figure 30-12 shows the contents of the key HKCU\Control Panel\Appearance, which contains the details of the chosen color scheme of the currently logged in user. regedit shows which key is being examined by displaying it with an open folder icon in the tree view.

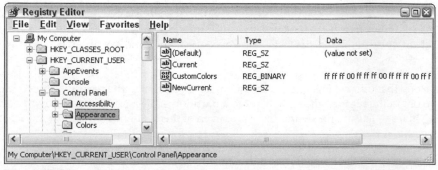

Figure 30-12

The HKCU\Control Panel\Appearance key has three named values set, although the default value does not contain any data. The column in the screenshot marked Type details the data type of each value. Registry entries can be formatted as one of three data types:

❑ REG_SZ (which roughly corresponds to a .NET string instance; the matching is not exact because the registry data types are not .NET data types)

❑ REG_DWORD (corresponds roughly to `uint`)

❑ REG_BINARY (array of bytes)

An application that stores data in the registry will do so by creating a number of registry keys, usually under the key HKLM\Software\<CompanyName>. Note that it is not necessary for these keys to contain any data. Sometimes the very fact of whether a key exists provides the data that an application needs.

The .NET Registry Classes

Access to the registry is available through two classes in the `Microsoft.Win32` namespace, `Registry` and `RegistryKey`. A `RegistryKey` instance represents a registry key. This class implements methods to browse child keys, to create new keys, or to read or modify the values in the key. In other words, to do everything you would normally want to do with a registry key (except set security levels for the key). `RegistryKey` will be the class you use for almost all your work with the registry. `Registry`, by contrast, is a class that you will never instantiate. Its role is simply to provide you with `RegistryKey` instances that represent the top-level keys, the different hives, in order to enable you to navigate the registry. `Registry` provides these instances through static properties, and there are seven of them, called respectively `ClassesRoot`, `CurrentConfig`, `CurrentUser`, `DynData`, `LocalMachine`, `PerformanceData`, and `Users`. It should be obvious which property corresponds to which hive.

So, for example, to obtain a `RegistryKey` instance that represents the HKLM key, you would write:

```
RegistryKey hklm = Registry.LocalMachine;
```

The process of obtaining a reference to a `RegistryKey` object is known as opening the key.

Although you might expect that the methods exposed by `RegistryKey` would be similar to those implemented by `DirectoryInfo`, given that the registry has a similar hierarchical structure to the file system, this actually isn't the case. Often, the way that you access the registry is different from the way that you would use files and folders, and `RegistryKey` implements methods that reflect this.

The most obvious difference is in how you open a registry key at a given location in the registry. The `Registry` class does not have any public constructor that you can use, nor does it have any methods that let you go directly to a key, given its name. Instead, you are expected to browse down to that key from the top of the relevant hive. If you want to instantiate a `RegistryKey` object, the only way is to start off with the appropriate static property of `Registry`, and work down from there. So, for example, if you want to read some data in the HKLM/Software/Microsoft key, you'd get a reference to it like this:

```
RegistryKey hklm = Registry.LocalMachine;
RegistryKey hkSoftware = hklm.OpenSubKey("Software");
RegistryKey hkMicrosoft = hkSoftware.OpenSubKey("Microsoft");
```

A registry key accessed in this way will give you read-only access. If you want to be able to write to the key (that includes writing to its values or creating or deleting direct children of it), you need to use another override to `OpenSubKey`, which takes a second parameter, of type `bool`, that indicates whether you want read-write access to the key. So for example, if you want to be able to modify the `Microsoft` key (and assuming you are a systems administrator with permission to do this) you would write this:

```
RegistryKey hklm = Registry.LocalMachine;
RegistryKey hkSoftware = hklm.OpenSubKey("Software");
RegistryKey hkMicrosoft = hkSoftware.OpenSubKey("Microsoft", true);
```

Incidentally, since this key contains information used by Microsoft's applications, in most cases you probably shouldn't be modifying this particular key.

The `OpenSubKey()` method is the one you will call if you are expecting the key to be present. If the key isn't there, it will return a `null` reference. If you want to create a key, then you should use the `CreateSubKey()` method (which automatically gives you read-write access to the key through the reference returned):

```
RegistryKey hklm = Registry.LocalMachine;
RegistryKey hkSoftware = hklm.OpenSubKey("Software");
RegistryKey hkMine = hkSoftware.CreateSubKey("MyOwnSoftware");
```

The way that `CreateSubKey()` works is quite interesting. It will create the key if it doesn't already exist, but if it does already exist, then it will quietly return a `RegistryKey` instance that represents the existing key. The reason for the method behaving in this manner has to do with how you will normally use the registry. The registry, on the whole, contains long-term data such as configuration information for Windows and for various applications. It's not very common, therefore, that you find yourself in a situation where you need to explicitly create a key.

What is much more common is that your application needs to make sure that some data is present in the Registry—in other words create the relevant keys if they don't already exist, but do nothing if they do. `CreateSubKey()` fills that need perfectly. Unlike the situation with `FileInfo.Open()`, for example, there is no chance with `CreateSubKey()` of accidentally removing any data. If deleting registry keys is your intention, then you'll need to call the `RegistryKey.DeleteSubKey()` method. This makes sense given the importance of the registry to Windows. The last thing you want is to completely break Windows accidentally by deleting a couple of important keys while you're debugging your C# registry calls!

Once you've located the registry key you want to read or modify, you can use the `SetValue()` or `GetValue()` methods to set or get at the data in it. Both of these methods take a string giving the name of the value as a parameter, and `SetValue()` requires an additional object reference containing details of the value. Since the parameter is defined as an object reference, it can actually be a reference to any class you want. `SetValue()` will decide from the type of class actually supplied whether to set the value as a `REG_SZ`, `REG_DWORD`, or `REG_BINARY` value. For example:

```
RegistryKey hkMine = HkSoftware.CreateSubKey("MyOwnSoftware");
hkMine.SetValue("MyStringValue", "Hello World");
hkMine.SetValue("MyIntValue", 20);
```

This code will set the key to have two values: `MyStringValue` will be of type `REG_SZ`, while `MyIntValue` will be of type `REG_DWORD`. These are the only two types we will consider here, and use in the example that we present later.

`RegistryKey.GetValue()` works in much the same way. It is defined to return an object reference, which means it is free to actually return a `string` reference if it detects the value is of type REG_SZ, and an `int` if that value is of type REG_DWORD:

```
string stringValue = (string)hkMine.GetValue("MyStringValue");
int intValue = (int)hkMine.GetValue("MyIntValue");
```

Finally, after you've finished reading or modifying the data, close the key:

```
hkMine.Close();
```

`RegistryKey` implements a large number of methods and properties. The following tables list the most useful properties.

Property Name	Description
Name	Name of the key (read-only)
SubKeyCount	The number of children of this key
ValueCount	How many values the key contains

The following table lists the most useful methods.

Method Name	Purpose
Close()	Closes the key
CreateSubKey()	Creates a subkey of a given name (or opens it if it already exists)
DeleteSubKey()	Deletes a given subkey
DeleteSubKeyTree()	Recursively deletes a subkey and all its children
DeleteValue()	Removes a named value from a key
GetSubKeyNames()	Returns an array of strings containing the names of the subkeys
GetValue()	Returns a named value
GetValueNames()	Returns an array of strings containing the names of all the values of the key
OpenSubKey()	Returns a reference to a `RegistryKey` instance that represents a given subkey
SetValue()	Sets a named value

Example: SelfPlacingWindow

We will illustrate the use of the registry classes with an application, which we call SelfPlacingWindow. This example is a simple C# Windows application that has almost no features. The only thing you can do with it is click a button, which brings up a standard Windows color dialog box (represented by the `System.Windows.Forms.ColorDialog` class), to let you choose a color, which will become the background color of the form.

Despite this lack of features, the self-placing window scores over just about every other application that we have developed in this book in one important and very user-friendly way. If you drag the window around the screen, change its size, or maximize or minimize it before you exit the application, it will remember the new position, as well as the background color, so that the next time it is launched it can automatically resume the way you chose last time. It remembers this information, because it writes it to the registry whenever it shuts down. In this way, we get to demonstrate not only the .NET registry classes themselves, but also a very typical use for them, which you'll almost certainly want to replicate in any serious commercial Windows Forms application you write.

The location in which SelfPlacingWindow stores its information in the registry is the key HKLM\Software\WroxPress\SelfPlacingWindow. HKLM is the usual place for application configuration information, but note that it is not user-specific. If you wanted to be more sophisticated in a real application, you'd probably want to replicate the information inside the HK_Users hive as well, so that each user can have his or her own profile.

It's also worth noting that, if you are implementing this in a real .NET application, you may want to consider using isolated storage instead of the Registry to store this information. On the other hand, since isolated storage is only available in .NET, you'll need to use the Registry if you need any interoperability with non-.NET apps.

The very first time that you run the example, it will look for this key and not find it (obviously). Therefore it is forced to use a default size, color, and position that we set in the developer environment. The example also features a list box in which it displays any information read in from the registry. On its first run, it will look similar to Figure 30-13.

Figure 30-13

If we now modify the background color and resize SelfPlacingWindow or move it around on the screen a bit before exiting, it will create the HKLM\Software\WroxPress\SelfPlacingWindow key and write its new configuration information into it. We can examine the information using regedit. The details are shown in Figure 30-14.

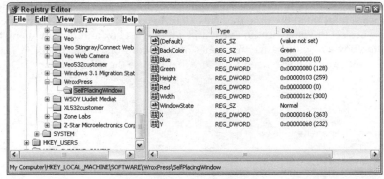

Figure 30-14

As this figure shows SelfPlacingWindow has placed a number of values in the registry key.

The values Red, Green, and Blue give the color components that make up the selected background color (see Chapter 20). For now, just take it that any color display on the system can be completely described by these three components, which are each represented by a number between 0 and 255 (or 0x00 and 0xff in hexadecimal). The values given here make up a bright green color. There are also four more REG_DWORD values, which represent the position and size of the window: X and Y are the coordinates of top left of the window on the desktop—that is to say the numbers of pixels across from the top left of the screen and the numbers of pixels down. Width and Height give the size of the window. WindowsState is the only value for which we have used a string data type (REG_SZ), and it can contain one of the strings Normal, Maximized, or Minimized, depending on the final state of the window when we exited the application.

When we launch SelfPlacingWindow again, it will read this registry key, and automatically position itself accordingly (see Figure 30-15).

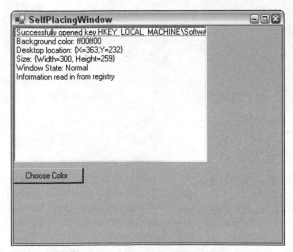

Figure 30-15

This time when we exit SelfPlacingWindow, it will overwrite the previous registry settings with whatever new values are relevant at the time that we exit it. To code the example, we create the usual Windows Forms project in Visual Studio .NET, and add the list box and button, using the developer environment's toolbox. We will change the names of these controls, respectively, to `listBoxMessages` and `buttonChooseColor`. We also need to ensure that we use the `Microsoft.Win32` namespace:

```
using System;
using System.Drawing;
using System.Collections;
using System.ComponentModel;
using System.Windows.Forms;
using System.Data;
using Microsoft.Win32;
```

We need to add one field (`chooseColorDialog`) to the main `Form1` class, which will represent the color dialog box:

```
public class Form1 : System.Windows.Forms.Form
{
    private System.Windows.Forms.ListBox listBoxMessages;
    private System.Windows.Forms.Button buttonChooseColor;
    private ColorDialog chooseColorDialog = new ColorDialog();
```

Quite a lot of action takes place in the `Form1` constructor:

```
public Form1()
{
    InitializeComponent();
    buttonChooseColor.Click += new EventHandler(OnClickChooseColor);
    try
    {
        if (ReadSettings() == false)
            listBoxMessages.Items.Add("No information in registry");
        else
            listBoxMessages.Items.Add("Information read in from registry");
            StartPosition = FormStartPosition.Manual;
    }
    catch (Exception e)
    {
        listBoxMessages.Items.Add("A problem occurred reading in data
                                    from registry:");
        listBoxMessages.Items.Add(e.Message);
    }
}
```

In this constructor, we begin by setting up the event handler for when the user clicks the button. The handler is a method called `OnClickChooseColor`, which we will cover shortly. Reading in the configuration information is done using another method that we have to write, called `ReadSettings()`. `ReadSettings()` returns `true` if it finds the information in the registry, and `false` if it doesn't (which it should be since this is the first time we have run the application). We place this part of the constructor in a `try` block, just in case any exceptions are generated while reading in the registry values (this might happen if some user has come in and played around with the registry using regedit).

The `StartPosition = FormStartPosition.Manual;` statement tells the form to take its initial starting position from the `DeskTopLocation` property instead of using the Windows default location (the default behavior). Possible values are taken from the `FormStartPosition` enumeration.

`SelfPlacingWindow` is also one of the few applications in this book in which we have a serious use for adding code to the `Dispose()` method. Remember that `Dispose()` is called whenever the application terminates normally, so this is the ideal place from which to save the configuration information to the registry. This is done using another method that we have to write, `SaveSettings()`:

```
protected override void Dispose( bool disposing )
{
    if( disposing )
    {
        if (components != null)
        {
            components.Dispose();
        }
    }
    SaveSettings();
    base.Dispose( disposing );
}
```

The `SaveSettings()` and `ReadSettings()` methods are the ones that contain the registry code we are interested in, but before we examine them we have one more piece of housekeeping to do: to handle the event of the user clicking that button. This involves displaying the color dialog and setting the background color to whatever color the user chose:

```
void OnClickChooseColor(object Sender, EventArgs e)
{
    if(chooseColorDialog.ShowDialog() == DialogResult.OK)
        BackColor = chooseColorDialog.Color;
}
```

Now let's look at how we save the settings:

```
void SaveSettings()
{
    RegistryKey softwareKey =
                Registry.LocalMachine.OpenSubKey("Software", true);
    RegistryKey wroxKey = softwareKey.CreateSubKey("WroxPress");
    RegistryKey selfPlacingWindowKey =
                wroxKey.CreateSubKey("SelfPlacingWindow");
    selfPlacingWindowKey.SetValue("BackColor",
                (object)BackColor.ToKnownColor());
    selfPlacingWindowKey.SetValue("Red", (object)(int)BackColor.R);
    selfPlacingWindowKey.SetValue("Green", (object)(int)BackColor.G);
    selfPlacingWindowKey.SetValue("Blue", (object)(int)BackColor.B);
    selfPlacingWindowKey.SetValue("Width", (object)Width);
    selfPlacingWindowKey.SetValue("Height", (object)Height);
    selfPlacingWindowKey.SetValue("X", (object)DesktopLocation.X);
    selfPlacingWindowKey.SetValue("Y", (object)DesktopLocation.Y);
    selfPlacingWindowKey.SetValue("WindowState",
                (object)WindowState.ToString());
}
```

There's quite a lot going on here. We start off by navigating through the registry to get to the HKLM\Software\WroxPress\SelfPlacingWindow registry key using the technique we demonstrated earlier, starting with the `Registry.LocalMachine` static property that represents the HKLM hive.

Then we use the `RegistryKey.OpenSubKey()` method, rather than `RegistryKey.CreateSubKey()` to get to the HKLM/Software key. That's because we can be very confident this key already exists; if it doesn't then there's something very seriously wrong with our computer, as this key contains settings for a lot of system software! We also indicate that we need write access to this key. That's because if the `WroxPress` key doesn't already exist we will need to create it, which involves writing to the parent key.

The next key to navigate to is HKLM\Software\WroxPress—and here we are not certain whether the key already exists, so we use `CreateSubKey()` to automatically create it if it doesn't. Note that `CreateSubKey()` automatically gives us write access to the key in question. Once we have reached HKLM\Software\WroxPress\SelfPlacingWindow, it is simply a matter of calling the `RegistryKey.SetValue()` method a number of times to either create or set the appropriate values. There are, however, a couple of complications.

Firstly, you might notice that we are using a couple of classes that we've not encountered before. The `DeskTopLocation` property of the `Form` class indicates the position of the top-left corner of the screen, and is of type `Point`. (We discuss the `Point` in Chapter 20.) What we need to know here is that it contains two `int` values, `X` and `Y`, which represent the horizontal and vertical position on the screen. We also look up three member properties of the `Form.BackColor` property, which is an instance of the `Color` class: `R`, `G`, and `B`: `Color` which represents a color, and these properties on it give the red, green, and blue components that make up the color and are all of type `byte`. We also use the `Form.WindowState` property, which contains an enumeration that gives the current state of the window: `Minimized`, `Maximized`, or `Normal`.

The other complication here is that we need to be a little careful about our casts: `SetValue()` takes two parameters: a `string` that gives the name of the key and a `System.Object` instance, which contains the value. `SetValue()` has a choice of format for storing the value—it can store it as REG_SZ, REG_BINARY, or REG_DWORD—and it is actually pretty intelligent about making a sensible choice depending on the data type that has been given. Hence for the `WindowState`, we pass it a `string` and `SetValue()` determines that this should be translated to REG_SZ. Similarly, for the various positions and dimensions we supply ints, which will be converted into REG_DWORD. However, the color components are more complicated as we want these to be stored as REG_DWORD too because they are numeric types. However, if `SetValue()` sees that the data is of type `byte`, it will store it as a string—as REG_SZ in the Registry. In order to prevent this, we cast the color components to `ints`.

We've also explicitly cast all the values to the type `object`. We don't really need to do this as the cast from any other data type to `object` is implicit, but we are doing so in order to make it clear what's going on and remind ourselves that `SetValue()` is defined to take just an object reference as its second parameter.

The `ReadSettings()` method is a little longer because for each value read in, we also need to interpret it, display the value in the list box, and make the appropriate adjustments to the relevant property of the main form. `ReadSettings()` looks like this:

```
bool ReadSettings()
{
    RegistryKey softwareKey =
```

```
                  Registry.LocalMachine.OpenSubKey("Software");
   RegistryKey wroxKey = softwareKey.OpenSubKey("WroxPress");
   if (wroxKey == null)
      return false;
   RegistryKey selfPlacingWindowKey =
               wroxKey.OpenSubKey("SelfPlacingWindow");
   if (selfPlacingWindowKey == null)
      return false;
   else
      listBoxMessages.Items.Add("Successfully opened key " +
               selfPlacingWindowKey.ToString());
   int redComponent = (int)selfPlacingWindowKey.GetValue("Red");
   int greenComponent = (int)selfPlacingWindowKey.GetValue("Green");
   int blueComponent = (int)selfPlacingWindowKey.GetValue("Blue");
   this.BackColor = Color.FromArgb(redComponent, greenComponent,
               blueComponent);
   listBoxMessages.Items.Add("Background color: " + BackColor.Name);
   int X = (int)selfPlacingWindowKey.GetValue("X");
   int Y = (int)selfPlacingWindowKey.GetValue("Y");
   this.DesktopLocation = new Point(X, Y);
   listBoxMessages.Items.Add("Desktop location: " +
               DesktopLocation.ToString());
   this.Height = (int)selfPlacingWindowKey.GetValue("Height");
   this.Width = (int)selfPlacingWindowKey.GetValue("Width");
   listBoxMessages.Items.Add("Size: " + new
               Size(Width,Height).ToString());
   string initialWindowState =
               (string)selfPlacingWindowKey.GetValue("WindowState");
   listBoxMessages.Items.Add("Window State: " + initialWindowState);
   this.WindowState = (FormWindowState)FormWindowState.Parse
               (WindowState.GetType(), initialWindowState);
   return true;
}
```

In `ReadSettings()` we first have to navigate to the HKLM/Software/WroxPress/SelfPlacingWindow registry key. In this case, however, we are hoping to find the key there so that we can read it. If it's not there, then it's probably the first time we have run the example. In this case, we just want to abort reading the keys, and we certainly don't want to create any keys. Now we use the `RegistryKey.OpenSubKey()` method all the way down. If at any stage `OpenSubkey()` returns a `null` reference then we know that the registry key isn't there and we can simply return the value `false` back to the calling code.

When it comes to actually reading the keys, we use the `RegistryKey.GetValue()` method, which is defined as returning an object reference (which means this method can actually return an instance of literally any class it chooses). Like `SetValue()`, it will return a class of object appropriate to the type of data it found in the key. Hence, we can usually assume that the REG_SZ keys will give us a string and the other keys will give us an `int`. We also cast the return reference from `SetValue()` accordingly. If there is an exception, say someone has fiddled with the registry and mangled the value types, then our cast will cause an exception to be thrown—which will be caught by the handler in the `Form1` constructor.

The rest of this code uses one more data type, the `Size` structure. This is similar to a `Point` structure, but is used to represent sizes rather than coordinates. It has two member properties, `Width` and `Height`, and we use the `Size` structure here simply as a convenient way of packaging up the size of the form for displaying in the list box.

Summary

In this chapter, we have examined how to use the .NET base classes to access the file system and registry from your C# code. We've seen that in both cases the base classes expose simple, but powerful, object models that make it very simple to perform almost any kind of action in these areas. In the case of the file system, these are copying files; moving, creating, and deleting files and folders; and reading and writing both binary and text files; and in the case of the registry, these are creating, modifying, or reading keys.

In this chapter we have assumed that you are running your code from an account that has sufficient access rights to do whatever the code needs to do. Obviously, the question of security is an important one, and it is discussed in Chapter 14.

Accessing the Internet

Chapters 25 through 27 discuss how you can use C# to write powerful, efficient, and dynamic Web pages using ASP.NET and XML Web services. For the most part, the clients accessing ASP.NET pages will be users running Internet Explorer or other Web browsers. However, you might want to add Web-browsing features to your own application, or need your applications to programmatically obtain information from a Web site. In this latter case, it is usually better for the site to implement a Web service. However, if you are accessing public Internet sites you might not have any control over how the site is implemented.

In this chapter, we will cover facilities provided through the .NET base classes for using various network protocols, particularly HTTP and TCP, to access networks and the Internet as a client. In particular, we will cover:

❑   Downloading files from the World Wide Web

❑   Using Internet Explorer as an ActiveX control

❑   Manipulating IP addresses and performing DNS lookups

❑   Socket programming with TCP, UDP, and socket classes

The two namespaces we are most interested in for networking are the `System.Net` and the `System.Net.Sockets` namespaces. The `System.Net` namespace is generally concerned with higher-level operations, for example, downloading and uploading files, and making Web requests using HTTP and other protocols, while `System.Net.Sockets` contains classes to perform lower-level operations. You will find these classes more useful when you want to work directly with sockets or protocols such as TCP/IP. The methods in these classes closely mimic the Windows socket (Winsock) API functions derived from the Berkeley sockets interface.

We are going to take a fairly practical approach in this chapter, mixing examples with a discussion of the relevant theory and networking concepts as appropriate. This chapter is not a guide to computer networking, but an introduction to using .NET Framework for network communication.

We will start with the simplest case of sending a request to a server and storing the information sent back in the response. (As is the case with the other chapters, you can download the sample code for this chapter from the Wrox Web site at www.wrox.com.)

The WebClient Class

If you only want to request a file from a particular URI, then you will find that the easiest .NET class to use is System.Net.WebClient. This class is an extremely high-level class designed to perform basic operations with only one or two commands. .NET Framework currently supports URIs beginning with http:, https:, and file: identifiers.

> *It is worth noting that the term URL (uniform resource locator) is no longer in use in new technical specifications, and URI (uniform resource identifier) is now preferred. URI has roughly the same meaning as URL, but is a bit more general since URI does not imply we are using one of the familiar protocols, such as HTTP or FTP.*

Downloading Files

There are two methods available for downloading a file using WebClient. The method we choose depends on how we want to process the file contents. If we simply want to save the file to disk we use the DownloadFile() method. This method takes two parameters: the URI of the file, and a location (path and file name) to save the requested data.

```
WebClient Client = new WebClient();
Client.DownloadFile("http://www.Wrox.com/index.asp", "index.htm");
```

More commonly, your application will want to process the data retrieved from the Web site. In order to do this you use the OpenRead() method. OpenRead() returns a Stream reference you can then use to retrieve the data into memory.

```
WebClient Client = new WebClient();
Stream strm = Client.OpenRead("http://www.Wrox.com/default.asp");
```

Basic Web Client Example

Our first example will demonstrate the WebClient.OpenRead() method. We will display the contents of the downloaded page in a ListBox control. To begin, create a new project as a standard C# Windows Application, add a ListBox called listBox1 with the docking property set to DockStyle.Fill. At the beginning of the file, we will need to add the System.Net and System.IO namespaces references to our list of using directives. We then make the following changes to the constructor of the main form

```
public Form1()
{
    InitializeComponent();
    System.Net.WebClient Client = new WebClient();
    Stream strm = Client.OpenRead("http://www.wrox.com");
    StreamReader sr = new StreamReader(strm);
    string line;
    while ( (line=sr.ReadLine()) != null )
    {
        listBox1.Items.Add(line);
    }

    strm.Close();
}
```

In this example, we connect a `StreamReader` class from the `System.IO` namespace to the network stream. This allows us to obtain data from the stream as text through the use of higher-level methods, such as `ReadLine()`. This is an excellent example of the point made in Chapter 30 about the benefits of abstracting data movement into the concept of a stream.

Figure 31-1 shows the results of running this sample code.

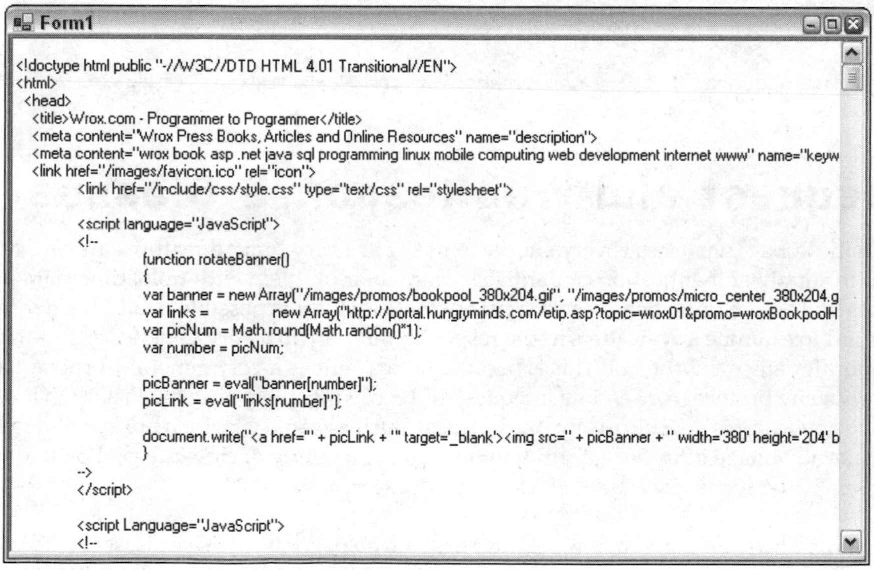

Figure 31-1

There is also an `OpenWrite()` method in the `WebClient` class. This method returns a writeable stream for you to send data to a URI. You can also specify the method used to send the data to the host; the default method is POST. The following code snippet assumes a writeable directory named `accept` on the local machine. The code will create a file in the directory with the name newfile.txt and the contents "Hello World".

```
WebClient webClient = new WebClient();

Stream stream = webClient.OpenWrite("http://localhost/accept/newfile.txt", "PUT");

StreamWriter streamWriter = new StreamWriter(stream);
streamWriter.WriteLine("Hello World");
streamWriter.Close();
```

Uploading Files

The WebClient class also features UploadFile() and UploadData() methods. UploadFile() uploads a file to a specified location given the local file name, while UploadData() uploads binary data supplied as an array of bytes to the specified URI (there is also a DownloadData() method for retrieving an array of bytes from a URI).

```
WebClient client = new WebClient();
client.UploadFile("http://www.ourwebsite.com/NewFile.htm",
                  "C:\\WebSiteFiles\\NewFile.htm");
byte[] image;
// code to initialise image so it contains all the binary data for
// some jpg file
client.UploadData("http://www.ourwebsite.com/NewFile.jpg", image);
```

WebRequest and WebResponse Classes

Although the WebClient class is very simple to use, it has very limited features. In particular, you cannot use it to supply authentication credentials— particular problem with uploading data is that not many sites will accept uploaded files without authentication! It is possible to add header information to requests and to examine any headers in the response, but only in a very generic sense—there is no specific support for any one protocol. This is because WebClient is a very general-purpose class designed to work with any protocol for sending a request and receiving a response (such as HTTP, or FTP). It cannot handle any features specific to any one protocol, such as cookies, which are specific to HTTP. If you want to take advantage of these features you need to use a family of classes based on two other classes in the System.Net namespace: WebRequest and WebResponse.

We will start off by showing you how to download a web page using these classes. This is the same example as before, but using WebRequest and WebResponse. In the process we will uncover the class hierarchy involved, and then see how to take advantage of extra HTTP features supported by this hierarchy.

The following code shows the modifications we need to make to the BasicWebClient sample to use the WebRequest and WebResponse classes.

```
public Form1()
{
   InitializeComponent();

   WebRequest wrq = WebRequest.Create("http://www.wrox.com");
   WebResponse wrs = wrq.GetResponse();
   Stream strm = wrs.GetResponseStream();
   StreamReader sr = new StreamReader(strm);
   string line;
   while ( (line = sr.ReadLine()) != null)
   {
      listBox1.Items.Add(line);
   }
   strm.Close();
}
```

In the code we start by instantiating an object representing a Web request. We don't do this using a constructor, but instead call the static method WebRequest.Create(). As we will explain in more detail later in this chapter, the WebRequest class is part of a hierarchy of classes supporting different network protocols. In order to receive a reference to the correct object for the request type, a factory mechanism is in place. The WebRequest.Create() method will create the appropriate object for the given protocol.

The WebRequest class represents the request for information to send to a particular URI. The URI is passed as a parameter to the Create() method. A WebResponse represents the data we retrieve from the server. By calling the WebRequest.GetResponse() method, we actually send the request to the Web server and create a WebResponse object to examine the return data. As with the WebClient object, we can obtain a stream to represent the data, but in this case we use the WebResponse.GetResponseStream() method.

Other WebRequest and WebResponse Features

In this section, we briefly discuss a couple of the other areas supported by WebRequest, WebResponse, and other related classes.

HTTP header information

An important part of the HTTP protocol is the ability to send extensive header information with both request and response streams. This information can include cookies, and the details of the particular browser sending the request (the user agent). As you would expect,.NET Framework provides full support for accessing the most significant data. The WebRequest and WebResponse classes provide some support for reading the header information. However, two derived classes provide additional HTTP-specific information: HttpWebRequest and HttpWebResponse. As we will explain in more detail later, creating a WebRequest with an HTTP URI results in an HttpWebRequest object instance. Since HttpWebRequest is derived from WebRequest, you can use the new instance whenever a WebRequest is required. In addition, you can cast the instance to an HttpWebRequest reference and access properties specific to the HTTP protocol. Likewise, the GetResponse() method call will actually return an HttpWebResponse instance as a WebResponse reference when dealing with HTTP. Again, you can perform a simple cast to access the HTTP-specific features.

We can examine a couple of the header properties by adding the following code before the `GetResponse()` method call.

```
WebRequest wrq = WebRequest.Create("http://www.wrox.com");
HttpWebRequest hwrq = (HttpWebRequest)wrq;

listBox1.Items.Add("Request Timeout (ms) = " + wrq.Timeout);
listBox1.Items.Add("Request Keep Alive = " + hwrq.KeepAlive);
listBox1.Items.Add("Request AllowAutoRedirect = " + hwrq.AllowAutoRedirect);
```

The `Timeout` property is specified in milliseconds, and the default value is 100,000. You can set the time-out property to control how long the `WebRequest` object will wait on the response before throwing a `WebException`. You can check the `WebException.Status` property to view the reason for an exception. This enumeration includes status codes for timeouts, connection failures, protocol errors, and more.

The `KeepAlive` property is a specific extension to the HTTP protocol, so we access this property through an `HttpWebRequest` reference. `KeepAlive` allows multiple requests to use the same connection, saving time in closing and reopening connections on subsequent requests. The default value for this property is `true`.

The `AllowAutoRedirect` property is also specific to the `HttpWebRequest` class. Use this property to control if the Web request should automatically follow redirection responses from the Web server. Again, the default value is `true`. If you want to allow only a limited number of redirections, set the `MaximumAutomaticRedirections` property of the `HttpWebRequest` to the desired number.

While the request and response classes expose most of the important headers as properties, you can also use the `Headers` property itself to view the entire collection of headers. Add the following code after the `GetResponse()` method call to place all of the headers in the `ListBox` control:

```
WebRequest wrq = WebRequest.Create("http://www.wrox.com");
WebResponse wrs = wrq.GetResponse();
WebHeaderCollection whc = wrs.Headers;
for(int i = 0; i < whc.Count; i++)
{
    listBox1.Items.Add("Header " + whc.GetKey(i) + " : " + whc[i]);
}
```

This example code produces the list of headers shown in Figure 31-2.

Figure 31-2

Authentication

A further property in the WebRequest class is the Credentials property. If you needed authentication credentials to accompany our request, you could create an instance of the NetworkCredential class (also from the System.Net namespace) with a username and password. You could place the following code *before* the call to GetResponse().

```
NetworkCredential myCred = new NetworkCredential("myusername", "mypassword");
wrq.Credentials = myCred;
```

Asynchronous page requests

An additional feature of the WebRequest class is the ability to request pages asynchronously. This feature is significant since there can be quite a long delay between sending a request off to a host and receiving the response. Methods such as WebClient.DownloadData() and WebRequest.GetResponse() will not return until the response from the server is complete. You might not want your application frozen due to a long period of inactivity, and in such scenarios it is better to use the BeginGetResponse() and EndGetResponse() methods. BeginGetResponse() works asynchronously and returns almost immediately. Under the covers, the runtime will asynchronously manage a background thread to retrieve the response from the server. Instead of returning a WebResponse object, BeginGetResponse() returns an object implementing the IAsyncResult interface. With this interface you can poll or wait for the response to become available, and then invoke EndGetResponse() to gather the results.

You can also pass a callback delegate into the BeginGetResponse() method. The target of a callback delegate is a method returning void and accepting an IAsyncResult reference as a parameter. When the worker thread is finished gathering the response, the runtime invokes the callback delegate to inform you of the completed work. As shown in the following code, calling EndGetResponse() in the callback method allows you to retrieve the WebResponse object.

```
public Form1()
{
    InitializeComponent();

    WebRequest wrq = WebRequest.Create("http://www.wrox.com");
    wrq.BeginGetResponse(new AsyncCallback(OnResponse), wrq);
}

protected void OnResponse(IAsyncResult ar)
{
    WebRequest wrq = (WebRequest)ar.AsyncState;
    WebResponse wrs = wrq.EndGetResponse(ar);

    // read the response ...
}
```

Notice that you can retrieve the original WebRequest object by passing the object as the second parameter to BeginGetResponse(). The third parameter is an object reference known as the state parameter. During the callback method you can retrieve the same state object using the AsyncState property of IAsyncResult.

Displaying Output as an HTML Page

Our examples show how the .NET base classes make it very easy to download and process data from the Internet. However, so far we have only displayed files as plain text. Quite often you will want to view an HTML file in an Internet Explorer–style interface where the rendered HTML allows you to see what the Web document actually looks like. Unfortunately, the .NET base classes don't include any intrinsic support for a control with an Internet Explorer–style interface. You will need to either programmatically call up Internet Explorer, or host the Web browser as an ActiveX control.

You can programmatically start an Internet Explorer process and navigate to a Web page using the `Process` class in the `System.Diagnostics` namespace.

```
Process myProcess = new Process();
myProcess.StartInfo.FileName = "iexplore.exe";
myProcess.StartInfo.Arguments = "http://www.wrox.com";
myProcess.Start();
```

However, the previous code launches Internet Explorer as a separate window. Your application has no connection to the new window and therefore cannot control the browser.

On the other hand, using the browser as an ActiveX control allows you to display and control the browser as an integrated part of your application. The Web browser control is quite sophisticated, featuring a large number of methods, properties, and events.

The easiest way to incorporate this control, using Visual Studio .NET, is to add the control to the toolbox (see Figure 31-3). To do this, right-click on the toolbox in Visual Studio .NET and select Add/Remove Items from the context menu to bring up the Customize Toolbox dialog box. Select the COM Components tab, and check Microsoft Web Browser.

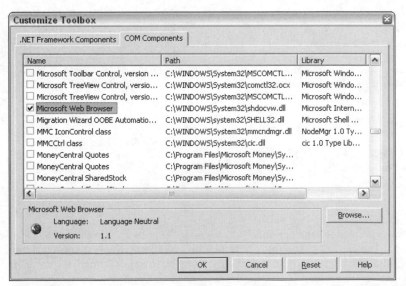

Figure 31-3

The Web Browser control now appears in the toolbox. You can drag and drop the control onto your forms in the same manner as you drag and drop native .NET controls from the toolbox. Visual Studio .NET automatically generates all the COM interoperability code required to host the Web Browser control in your application's form. We will demonstrate this technique with another example, DisplayWebPage, which will display a Web page retrieved from the Internet in a typical Windows form.

We create DisplayWebPage as a standard C# Windows Application, and drop the Web Browser ActiveX control onto the form. By default, Visual Studio .NET names the control axWebBrowser1. We then add the following code to the Form1 constructor:

```csharp
public Form1()
{
    // Required for Windows Form Designer support
    InitializeComponent();
    int zero = 0;
    object oZero = zero;
    string emptyString = "";
    object oEmptyString = emptyString;
    axWebBrowser1.Navigate("http://www.wrox.com",
                            ref oZero,
                            ref oEmptyString,
                            ref oEmptyString,
                            ref oEmptyString);
}
```

In this code we use the Navigate() method of the WebBrowser control, which actually sends an HTTP request and displays the output from a given URI. The first parameter to this method is a string containing the URI to navigate to. The second parameter accepts a number of flags to modify the navigation behavior, for example, if the browser adds the new URI to the history list or not. The third parameter contains the name of the target frame (if any) used to display the resource. The fourth parameter contains POST data to send with the request, and the final parameter allows you to pass additional HTTP header information. For our purposes, we can pass the default values for zero and the empty string into the last four parameters. These parameters are defined as optional parameters, but C# does not support optional parameters so we supply them explicitly. We also explicitly declare object references for these variables to pass them by reference.

Calling Navigate() with the parameters shown above is the same as typing the URL into the Internet Explorer address bar. This code is the only code we need to add to the DisplayWebPage project. If we run the example we get the results shown in Figure 31-4.

The Web Request and Web Response Hierarchy

In this section we take a closer look at the underlying architecture of the WebRequest and WebResponse classes.

Figure 31-5 illustrates the inheritance hierarchy of the classes involved.

Figure 31-4

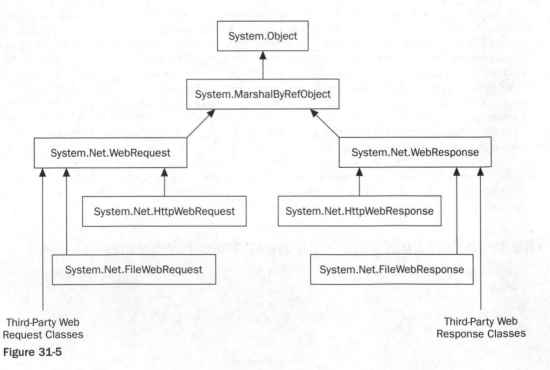

Third-Party Web
Request Classes

Third-Party Web
Response Classes

Figure 31-5

The hierarchy contains more than just the two classes we have used in our code. We also should point out that the `WebRequest` and `WebResponse` classes are both abstract and cannot be instantiated. These base classes provide general functionality for dealing with Web requests and responses independent of the protocol used for a given operation. Requests are made using a particular protocol (HTTP, FTP, SMTP, and so on) and a derived class written for the given protocol will handle the request. Microsoft refers to this scheme as *pluggable protocols*. Remember in the code we examined earlier, our variables are defined as references to the base classes; however, `WebRequest.Create()` actually gives us an `HttpWebRequest` object, and the `GetResponse()` method actually returns an `HttpWebResponse` object. This factory-based mechanism hides many of the details from the client code, allowing support for a wide variety of protocols from the same code base.

The fact that we need an object specifically capable of dealing with the HTTP protocol is clear from the URI that we supply to `WebRequest.Create()`. `WebRequest.Create()` examines the protocol specifier in the URI to instantiate and return an object of the appropriate class. This keeps your code free from having to know anything about the derived classes or specific protocol used. When you need to access specific features of a protocol, you might need the properties and methods of the derived class, in which case you can cast your `WebRequest` or `WebResponse` reference to the derived class.

With this architecture we should be able to send requests using any of the common protocols. However, Microsoft currently only provides derived classes to cover the HTTP, HTTPS, and FILE protocols. If you want to utilize other protocols, for example, FTP or SMTP, then you will need to either fall back on the Windows API, write your own classes, or wait for an independent software vendor to write some of the suitable .NET classes. The .NET Framework version 2.0, when released, will then be able to work with FTP.

Utility Classes

In this section we cover a couple of utility classes to make Web programming easier when dealing with URIs and IP addresses.

URIs

`Uri` and `UriBuilder` are two classes in the `System` (not `System.Net`) namespace, and they are both intended to represent a URI. `UriBuilder` allows you to build a URI given the strings for the component parts, while the `Uri` class allows you to parse, combine, and compare URIs.

For the `Uri` class, the constructor requires a completed URI string.

```
Uri MSPage = new
        Uri("http://www.Microsoft.com/SomeFolder/SomeFile.htm?Order=true");
```

The class exposes a large number of read-only properties. A `Uri` object is not intended to be modified once it has been constructed.

```
string Query = MSPage.Query;                      // Order=true;
string AbsolutePath = MSPage.AbsolutePath;        // SomeFolder/SomeFile.htm
string Scheme = MSPage.Scheme;                    // http
int Port = MSPage.Port;                           // 80 (the default for http)
string Host = MSPage.Host;                        // www.Microsoft.com
bool IsDefaultPort = MSPage.IsDefaultPort;        // true since 80 is default
```

URIBuilder, on the other hand, implements fewer properties; just enough to allow you to build up a complete URI. These properties are read-write.

You can supply the components to build up a URI to the constructor:

```
Uri MSPage = new
    UriBuilder("http", "www.Microsoft.com", 80, "SomeFolder/SomeFile.htm");
```

Or you can build the components by assigning values to the properties:

```
UriBuilder MSPage = new UriBuilder();
MSPage.Scheme ="http";
MSPage.Host = "www.Microsoft.com";
MSPage.Port = 80;
MSPage.Path = "SomeFolder/SomeFile.htm";
```

Once you have completed initializing the UriBuilder, you can obtain the corresponding Uri object with the Uri property:

```
Uri CompletedUri = MSPage.Uri;
```

The DisplayPage example

We will illustrate the use of UriBuilder along with creating an Internet Explorer process with an example: DisplayPage. This example allows the user to type in the component parts of a URL (not URI), since this is an HTTP request. The user can then click a button marked View Page and the application will display both the completed URL in a text box and the page using the Web browser ActiveX control. The example is a standard C# Windows application (see Figure 31-6).

Figure 31-6

The textbox names are txtBoxServer, txtBoxPath, txtBoxPort, and txtBoxURI respectively. The code to add to the example is entirely in the ViewPage button event handler:

```
private void ViewPage_Click (object sender, System.EventArgs e)
{
   UriBuilder Address = new UriBuilder();
   Address.Host = txtBoxServer.Text;
   Address.Port = int.Parse(txtBoxPort.Text);
   Address.Scheme = Uri.UriSchemeHttp;
   Address.Path = txtBoxPath.Text;

   Uri AddressUri = Address.Uri;

   Process myProcess = new Process();
   myProcess.StartInfo.FileName = "iexplore.exe";
   txtBoxURI.Text = AddressUri.ToString();
   myProcess.StartInfo.Arguments = AddressUri.ToString();
   myProcess.Start();
}
```

IP Addresses and DNS Names

On the Internet we identify servers as well as clients by IP address or host name (also referred to as a DNS name). Generally speaking, the host name is the human-friendly name that you type in a Web browser window, such as www.wrox.com or www.microsoft.com. An IP address, on the other hand, is the identifier computers use to identify each other. IP addresses are the identifiers used to ensure Web requests and responses reach the appropriate machines. It is even possible for a computer to have more than one IP address.

For host names to work, we must first send a network request to translate the host name into an IP address, a task carried out by one or more DNS servers.

A DNS server stores a table mapping host names to IP addresses for all the computers it knows about, as well as the IP addresses of other DNS servers to look up the host names it does not know about. Your local computer should always know about at least one DNS server. Network administrators configure this information when a computer is set up.

Before sending out a request, your computer will first ask the DNS server to tell it the IP address corresponding to the host name you have typed in. Once armed with the correct IP address, the computer can address the request and send it over the network. All of this work normally happens behind the scenes while the user is browsing the Web.

.NET Classes for IP Addresses

.NET Framework supplies a number of classes that are able to assist with the process of looking up IP addresses and finding out information about host computers.

IPAddress

IPAddress represents an IP address. The address itself is available as the Address property, and may be converted to a dotted decimal format with the ToString() method. IPAddress also implements a static Parse() method, which effectively performs the reverse conversion of ToString()—converting from a dotted decimal string to an IPAddress.

```
IPAddress ipAddress = IPAddress.Parse("234.56.78.9");
long address = ipAddress.Address;
string ipString = ipAddress.ToString();
```

In the previous example, the long integer address is assigned 156121322, and the string ipString is assigned the text "234.56.78.9".

IPAddress also provides a number of constant static fields to return special addresses. For example, the Loopback address allows a machine to send messages to itself, while the Broadcast address allows multicasting to the local network.

```
// The following line will set loopback to "127.0.0.1".
// the loopback address indicates the local host.
string loopback = IPAddress.Loopback.ToString();

// The following line will set broadcast address to "255.255.255.255".
// the broadcast address is used to send a message to all machines on
// the local network.
string broadcast = IPAddress.Broadcast.ToString();
```

IPHostEntry

The IPHostEntry class encapsulates information relating to a particular host computer. This class makes the host name available via the HostName property (which returns a string), and the AddressList property returns an array of IPAddress objects. We are going to use the IPHostEntry class in the in next example: DNSLookupResolver.

Dns

The Dns class is able to communicate with your default DNS server in order to retrieve IP addresses. The two important (static) methods are Resolve(), which uses the DNS server to obtain the details of a host with a given host name, and GetHostByAddress(), which also returns details of the host, but this time using the IP address. Both methods return an IPHostEntry object.

```
IPHostEntry wroxHost = Dns.Resolve("www.wrox.com");
IPHostEntry wroxHostCopy = Dns.GetHostByAddress("168.215.86.81");
```

In this code both IPHostEntry objects will contain details of the Wrox.com servers.

The Dns class differs from the IPAddress and IPHostEntry classes since it has the ability to actually communicate with servers to obtain information. In contrast, IPAddress and IPHostEntry are more along the lines of simple data structures with convenient properties to allow access to the underlying data.

The DnsLookup example

We will illustrate the DNS and IP-related classes with an example that looks up DNS names: DnsLookup (see Figure 31-7).

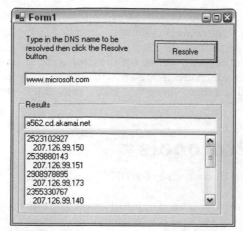

Figure 31-7

This sample application simply invites the user to type in a DNS name using the main text box. When the user clicks the Resolve button, the sample uses the Dns.Resolve() method to retrieve an IPHostEntry reference and display the host name and IP addresses. Note how the host name displayed may be different from the name typed in. This can occur if one DNS name (www.microsoft.com) simply acts as a proxy for another DNS name (a562.cd.akamai.net).

The DnsLookup application is a standard C# Windows application. The controls are added as shown in Figure 31-7, giving them the names txtBoxInput, btnResolve, txtBoxHostName, and listBoxIPs respectively. Then we simply add the following method to the Form1 class as the event handler for the buttonResolve click event.

```
void btnResolve_Click (object sender, EventArgs e)
{
    try
    {
        IPHostEntry iphost = Dns.Resolve(txtBoxInput.Text);
        foreach (IPAddress ip in iphost.AddressList)
        {
            string ipaddress = ip.AddressFamily.ToString();
            listBoxIPs.Items.Add(ipaddress);
            listBoxIPs.Items.Add("    " + ip.ToString());
        }
        txtBoxHostName.Text = iphost.HostName;
    }
    catch(Exception ex)
    {
        MessageBox.Show("Unable to process the request because " +
```

```
            "the following problem occurred:\n" +
            ex.Message, "Exception occurred");
    }
}
```

Notice that in this code we are careful to trap any exceptions. An exception might occur if the user types in an invalid DNS name, or if the network is down.

After retrieving the `IPHostEntry` instance, we use the `AddressList` property to obtain an array containing the IP addresses, which we then iterate through with a `foreach` loop. For each entry we display the IP address as an integer and as a string, using the `IPAddress.AddressFamily.ToString()` method.

Lower-Level Protocols

In this section we will briefly discuss some of the .NET classes used to communicate at a lower level.

Network communications work on several different levels. The classes we have covered in this chapter so far work at the highest level: the level at which specific commands are processed. It is probably easiest to understand this concept if you think of file transfer using FTP. Although today's GUI applications hide many of the FTP details, it was not so long ago when we executed FTP from a command-line prompt. In this environment we explicitly typed commands to send to the server for downloading, uploading, and listing files.

FTP is not the only high-level protocol relying on textual commands. HTTP, SMTP, POP, and other protocols are based on a similar type of behavior. Again, many of the modern graphical tools hide the transmission of commands from the user, so you are generally not aware of them. For example, when you type a URL into a Web browser, and the Web request goes off to a server, the browser is actually sending a (plain text) GET command to the server, which fulfills a similar purpose as the FTP `get` command. It can also send a POST command, which indicates that the browser has attached other data to the request.

However, these protocols are not sufficient by themselves to achieve communication between computers. Even if both the client and the server understand, for example, the HTTP protocol, it will still not be possible for them to understand each other unless there is also agreement on exactly how to transmit the characters: what binary format will be used, and getting down to the lowest level, what voltages will be used to represent 0s and 1s in the binary data? Since there are so many items to configure and agree upon, developers and hardware engineers in the networking field often refer to a protocol stack. When you list all of the various protocols and mechanisms required for communication between two hosts, you create a protocol stack with high-level protocols on the top and low-level protocols on the bottom. This approach results in a modular and layered approach to achieving efficient communication.

Luckily, for most development work, we don't need to go far down the stack or work with voltage levels, but if you are writing code that requires efficient communication between computers, it's not unusual to write code that works directly at the level of sending binary data packets between computers. This is the realm of protocols such as TCP, and Microsoft has supplied a number of classes that allow you to conveniently work with binary data at this level.

Lower-Level Classes

The `System.Net.Sockets` namespace contains the relevant classes. These classes, for example, allow you to directly send out TCP network requests or to listen to TCP network requests on a particular port. The following table explains the main classes.

Class	Purpose
Socket	Low-level class that deals with managing connections. Classes such as `WebRequest`, `TcpClient`, and `UdpClient` use this class internally.
NetworkStream	Derived from `Stream`. Represents a stream of data from the network.
TcpClient	Enables you to create and use TCP connections.
TcpListener	Enables you to listen for incoming TCP connection requests.
UdpClient	Enables you to create connections for UDP clients. (UDP is an alternative protocol to TCP, but is much less widely used, mostly on local networks.)

Using the TCP classes

The transmission control protocol (TCP) classes offer simple methods for connecting and sending data between two endpoints. An endpoint is the combination of an IP address and a port number. Existing protocols have well defined port numbers, for example, HTTP uses port 80, while SMTP uses port 25. The Internet Assigned Number Authority, IANA, (`http://www.iana.org/`) assigns port numbers to these well-known services. Unless you are implementing a well-known service, you will want to select a port number above 1,024.

TCP traffic makes up the majority of traffic on the Internet today. TCP is often the protocol of choice because it offers guaranteed delivery, error correction, and buffering. The `TcpClient` class encapsulates a TCP connection and provides a number of properties to regulate the connection, including buffering, buffer size, and timeouts. Reading and writing is accomplished by requesting a `NetworkStream` object via the `GetStream()` method.

The `TcpListener` class listens for incoming TCP connections with the `Start()` method. When a connection request arrives you can use the `AcceptSocket()` method to return a socket for communication with the remote machine, or use the `AcceptTcpClient()` method to use a higher-level `TcpClient` object for communication. The easiest way to demonstrate the `TcpListener` and `TcpClient` classes working together is to work through an example.

The TcpSend and TcpReceive examples

To demonstrate how these classes work we need to build two applications. Figure 31-8 shows the first application, TcpSend. This application opens a TCP connection to a server and sends the C# source code for itself.

Figure 31-8

Once again we create a C# Windows application. The form consists of two text boxes (txtHost and txtPort) for the host name and port, respectively, as well as a button (btnSend) to click and start a connection. First, we ensure that we include the relevant namespaces:

```
using System.Net;
using System.Net.Sockets;
using System.IO;
```

The following code shows the event handler for the button's click event:

```
private void btnSend_Click(object sender, System.EventArgs e)
{
    TcpClient tcpClient = new TcpClient(txtHost.Text, Int32.Parse(txtPort.Text));
    NetworkStream ns = tcpClient.GetStream();
    FileStream fs = File.Open("..\\..\\form1.cs", FileMode.Open);

    int data = fs.ReadByte();
    while(data != -1)
    {
        ns.WriteByte((byte)data);
        data = fs.ReadByte();
    }

    fs.Close();
    ns.Close();
    tcpClient.Close();
}
```

This example creates the TcpClient using a host name and a port number. Alternatively, if you have an instance of the IPEndPoint class, you can pass the instance to the TcpClient constructor. After retrieving an instance of the NetworkStream class we open the source code file and begin to read bytes. Like many of the binary streams, we need to check for the end of the stream by comparing the return value of the ReadByte() method to -1. After our loop has read all of the bytes and sent them along to the network stream, we make sure to close all of the open files, connections, and streams.

On the other side of the connection, the TcpReceive application displays the received file after the transmission is finished (see Figure 31-9).

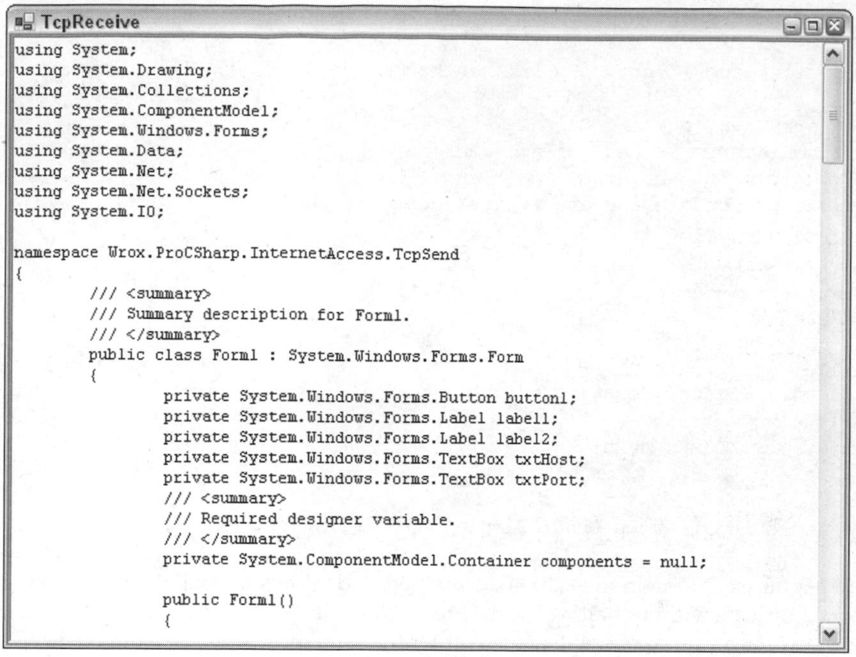
TcpReceive

```
using System;
using System.Drawing;
using System.Collections;
using System.ComponentModel;
using System.Windows.Forms;
using System.Data;
using System.Net;
using System.Net.Sockets;
using System.IO;

namespace Wrox.ProCSharp.InternetAccess.TcpSend
{
        /// <summary>
        /// Summary description for Form1.
        /// </summary>
        public class Form1 : System.Windows.Forms.Form
        {
                private System.Windows.Forms.Button button1;
                private System.Windows.Forms.Label label1;
                private System.Windows.Forms.Label label2;
                private System.Windows.Forms.TextBox txtHost;
                private System.Windows.Forms.TextBox txtPort;
                /// <summary>
                /// Required designer variable.
                /// </summary>
                private System.ComponentModel.Container components = null;

                public Form1()
                {
```

Figure 31-9

The form consists of a single RichTextBox control, named `txtDisplay`. The `TcpReceive` application uses a `TcpListener` to wait for the incoming connection. In order to avoid freezing the application interface, we use a background thread to wait for and then read from the connection. Thus we need to include the `System.Threading` namespace as well:

```
using System.Net;
using System.Net.Sockets;
using System.IO;
using System.Threading;
```

Inside the form's constructor we spin up a background thread:

```
public Form1()
{
   InitializeComponent();

   Thread thread = new Thread(new ThreadStart(Listen));
   thread.Start();
}
```

The remaining important code is this:

```
public void Listen()
{
   TcpListener tcpListener = new TcpListener(2112);
```

```
    tcpListener.Start();

    TcpClient tcpClient = tcpListener.AcceptTcpClient();

    NetworkStream ns = tcpClient.GetStream();
    StreamReader sr = new StreamReader(ns);
    string result = sr.ReadToEnd();
    Invoke(new UpdateDisplayDelegate(UpdateDisplay),
            new object[] {result} );

    tcpClient.Close();
    tcpListener.Stop();
}

public void UpdateDisplay(string text)
{
    txtDisplay.Text= text;
}

protected delegate void UpdateDisplayDelegate(string text);
```

The thread begins execution in the Listen() method and allows us to make the blocking call to AcceptTcpClient() without halting the interface. Notice that we have hard-coded the port number 2112 into the application, so you will need to enter the same port number from the client application.

We use the TcpClient object returned by AccepTcpClient() to open a new stream for reading. Similar to the earlier example, we create a StreamReader to convert the incoming network data into a string. Before we close the client and stop the listener, we update the form's text box. We do not want to access the text box directly from our background thread, so we use the form's Invoke() method with a delegate, and pass the result string as the first element in an array of object parameters. Invoke() ensures our call is correctly marshaled into the thread owning the control handles in the user interface.

TCP versus UDP

The other protocol to cover in this section is UDP (user datagram protocol). UDP is a simple protocol with few features but also little overhead. Developers often use UDP in applications where the speed and performance requirements outweigh the reliability needs, for example, video streaming. In contrast, TCP offers a number of features to confirm the delivery of data. TCP provides error correction and retransmission in the case of lost or corrupted packets. Last, but hardly least, TCP buffers incoming and outgoing data and also guarantees a sequence of packets scrambled in transmission are reassembled before delivery to the application. Even with the extra overhead, TCP is the most widely used protocol across the Internet because of the higher reliability.

The UDP class

As you might expect, the UdpClient class features a smaller and simpler interface compared to TcpClient. This reflects the relatively simpler nature of the protocol in comparison to TCP. While both TCP and UDP classes use a socket underneath the covers, the UdpClient client does not contain a method to return a network stream for reading and writing. Instead, the member function Send() accepts an array of bytes as a parameter, while the Receive() function returns an array of bytes. Also, since UDP is a connectionless protocol, you can wait to specify the endpoint for the communication as a parameter to the `Send()` and `Receive()` methods, instead of earlier in a constructor or `Connect()` method. You can also change the endpoint on each subsequent send or receive.

The following code fragment uses the `UdpClient` class to send a message to an echo service. A server with an echo service running accepts TCP or UDP connections on port 7. The echo service simply echoes any data sent to the server back to the client. This service is useful for diagnostics and testing, although many system administrators disable echo services for security reasons.

```csharp
using System;
using System.Text;
using System.Net;
using System.Net.Sockets;


namespace Wrox.ProCSharp.InternetAccess.UdpExample
{

    class Class1
    {
        [STAThread]
        static void Main(string[] args)
        {
            UdpClient udpClient = new UdpClient();

            string sendMsg = "Hello Echo Server";
            byte [] sendBytes = Encoding.ASCII.GetBytes(sendMsg);

            udpClient.Send(sendBytes, sendBytes.Length, "SomeEchoServer.net", 7);

            IPEndPoint endPoint = new IPEndPoint(0,0);
            byte [] rcvBytes = udpClient.Receive(ref endPoint);
            string rcvMessage = Encoding.ASCII.GetString(rcvBytes,
                                                         0,
                                                         rcvBytes.Length);

            // should print out "Hello Echo Server"
            Console.WriteLine(rcvMessage);
        }
    }
}
```

We make heavy use of the `Encoding.ASCII` class to translate strings into arrays of `byte` and vice versa. Also note that we pass an `IPEndPoint` by reference into the `Receive()` method. Since UDP is not a connection-oriented protocol, each call to `Receive()` might pick up data from a different endpoint, so `Receive()` populates this parameter with the IP address and port of the sending host.

Both `UdpClient` and `TcpClient` offer a layer of abstraction over the lowest of the low-level classes: the `Socket`.

The Socket class

The Socket class offers the highest level of control in network programming. One of the easiest ways to demonstrate the class is to rewrite the TcpReceive application with the Socket class. The updated Listen() method is listed in this example:

```
public void Listen()
{
    Socket listener = new Socket(AddressFamily.InterNetwork,
                                 SocketType.Stream,
                                 ProtocolType.Tcp);
    listener.Bind(new IPEndPoint(IPAddress.Any, 2112));
    listener.Listen(0);

    Socket socket = listener.Accept();
    Stream netStream = new NetworkStream(socket);
    StreamReader reader = new StreamReader(netStream);

    string result = reader.ReadToEnd();

    Invoke(new UpdateDisplayDelegate(UpdateDisplay),
           new object[] {result} );
    socket.Close();
    listener.Close();
}
```

The Socket class requires a few more lines of code to complete the same task. For starters, the constructor arguments need to specify an IP addressing scheme for a streaming socket with the TCP protocol. These arguments are just one of the many combinations available to the Socket class, and the TcpClient class configured these settings for you. We then bind the listener socket to a port and begin to listen for incoming connections. When an incoming request arrives we can use the Accept() method to create a new socket for handling the connection. We ultimately attach a StreamReader instance to the socket to read the incoming data, in much the same fashion as before.

The Socket class also contains a number of methods for asynchronously accepting, connecting, sending, and receiving. You can use these methods with callback delegates in the same way we used the asynchronous page requests with the WebRequest class. If you really need to dig into the internals of the socket, the GetSocketOption() and SetSocketOption() methods are available. These methods allow you to see and configure options, including timeout, time-to-live, and other low-level options.

Summary

In this chapter we have reviewed the .NET Framework classes available in the System.Net namespace for communication across networks. We have seen some of the .NET base classes that deal with opening client connections on the network and Internet, and how to send requests to and receive responses from servers; the most obvious use of this being to receive HTML pages. By taking advantage of COM interoperability in .NET, you can easily make use of Internet Explorer from your desktop applications.

As a rule of thumb, when programming with classes in the `System.Net` namespace, you should always try to use the most generic class possible. For instance, using the `TCPClient` class instead of the `Socket` class isolates your code from many of the lower-level socket details. Moving one step higher, the `WebRequest` class allows you to take advantage of the pluggable protocol architecture of .NET Framework. Your code will be ready to take advantage of new application-level protocols as Microsoft and other third-party developers introduce new functionality.

Finally, we discussed the use of the asynchronous capabilities in the networking classes, which give a Windows Forms application the professional touch of a responsive user interface.

32

Windows Services

Windows Services are programs that can be started automatically at boot-time without the need of anyone to log on to the machine After reading this chapter you can modify the server processes we discuss in Chapters 16 and 31 to be started automatically.

In this chapter we explore:

❑ The architecture of Windows Services; the functionality of a service program, service control program, and service configuration program.

❑ How to implement a Windows Service with the classes found in the `System .ServiceProcess` namespace.

❑ Installation programs to configure the Windows Service in the registry.

❑ Writing a program to control the Windows Service using the `ServiceController` class.

❑ How to implement event handling.

❑ Adding event logging to other application types.

❑ Implementing performance monitoring for a Windows Service.

First, we'll define what a Windows Service is. (You can download the code for this chapter from the Wrox Web site at `www.wrox.com`.)

What Is a Windows Service?

Windows Services are applications that can be automatically started when the operating system boots. They can run without having an interactive user logged on to the system. You can configure a Windows Service to be run from a specially configured user account; or from the system user account—a user account that has even more privileges than that of the system administrator.

> Windows Services don't run on Windows 95, 98, or ME; the NT kernel is a require-
> ment. Windows Services do run on Windows NT 4, Windows 2000, Windows XP,
> and Windows Server 2003.

Unless otherwise noted, when we are referring to a service, we are referring to a Windows Service.

Here are few examples of services:

❑ Simple TCP/IP Services is a service program that hosts some small TCP/IP servers: echo, day-
time, quote, and others

❑ World Wide Publishing Service is the service of the Internet Information Server (IIS)

❑ Event Log is a service to log messages to the event log system

❑ Microsoft Search is a service that creates indexes of data on the disk

You can use the Services administration tool, shown in Figure 32-1, to see all of the services on a system.
On a Windows 2000 Server this program can be accessed be selecting Start⇨Programs⇨Administrative
Tools⇨Services; on Windows 2000 Professional and Windows XP the program is accessible through
Settings⇨Control Panel⇨Administrative Tools⇨Services.

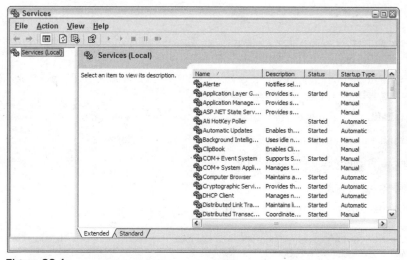

Figure 32-1

Windows Services Architecture

Three program types are necessary to operate a Windows Service:

- ❏ A service program
- ❏ A service control program
- ❏ A service configuration program

The *service program* itself provides the actual functionality we are looking for. With a *service control* program, it's possible to send control requests to a service, such as start, stop, pause, and continue. With a *service configuration* program, a service can be installed; it's copied to the file system, written into the registry, and configured as a service. While .NET components can be installed simply with an xcopy because they don't need the use of the registry, installation for services does require registry configuration. A service configuration program can also be used to change the configuration of that service at a later point.

In the following subsections, we discuss these three ingredients of a Windows Service.

Service Program

Before looking at the .NET implementation of a service, let's look at it from an independent point of view and discover what the Windows architecture of services looks like, and what the inner functionality of a service is.

The service program implements the functionality of the service. It needs three parts:

- ❏ A main function
- ❏ A service-main function
- ❏ A handler

Before we can discuss these parts, we must introduce the *Service Control Manager* (*SCM*) . The SCM plays an important role for services, sending requests to our service to start and to stop it.

Service Control Manager

The SCM is the part of the operating system that communicates with the service. Figure 32-2 illustrates how this communication works with a UML sequence diagram.

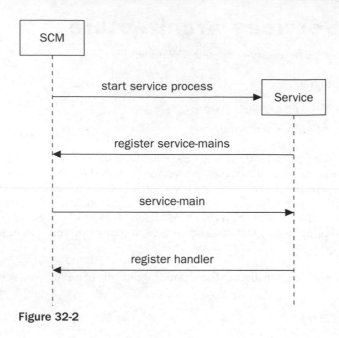

Figure 32-2

> At boot time, each process for which a service is set to start automatically is started, and so the main function of this process gets called. The service has the responsibility to register the service-main function for each of its services. The main function is the entry point of the service program, and in here, the entry points for the service-main functions must be registered with the SCM.

Main function, service-main, and handlers

The main function of the service might register more than one service-main function. The service must register a service-main function for each service it provides. A service program can provide a lot of services in a single program; for example, <windows>\system32\services.exe is the service program that includes Alerter, Application Management, Computer Browser, and DHCP Client, among others.

The SCM now calls the service-main function for each service that should be started. The *service-main* function contains the actual functionality of the service. One important task of the service-main function is to register a handler with the SCM.

The *handler* function is the third part of service program. The handler must respond to events from the SCM. Services can be stopped, suspended, and resumed, and the handler must react to these events.

Once a handler has been registered with the SCM, the service control program can post requests to the SCM to stop, suspend, and resume the service. The service control program is independent of the SCM and the service itself. We get many service control programs with the operating system; one is the MMC Services snap-in that we've seen earlier. You can also write our own service control program; a good example of this is the SQL Server Service Manager shown in Figure 32-3.

Figure 32-3

Service Control Program

As the name suggests, with a service control program we can control the service. For stopping, suspending, and resuming the service, you can send control codes to the service, and the handler should react to these events. It's also possible to ask the service about the actual status, and to implement a custom handler that responds to custom control codes.

Service Configuration Program

You can't use xcopy installation with services, since services must be configured in the registry. You can set the startup type to automatic, manual, or disabled. You have to configure the user of the service program, and dependencies of the service—for example, the services that must be started before this one can start. All these configurations are made within a service configuration program. The installation program can use the service configuration program to configure the service, but this program can also be used at a later time to change service configuration parameters.

System.ServiceProcess Namespace

In .NET Framework, you can find service classes in the System.ServiceProcess namespace that implement the three parts of a service:

❑ You have to inherit from the ServiceBase class to implement a service. The ServiceBase class is used to register the service and to answer start and stop requests.

❑ The ServiceController class is used to implement a service control program. With this class you can send requests to services.

❑ The ServiceProcessInstaller and ServiceInstaller classes are, as their names suggest, classes to install and configure service programs.

Now we are ready to create a new service.

Creating a Windows Service

The service that we create will host a quote server. With every request that is made from a client the quote server returns a random quote from a quote file. The first part of the solution uses three assemblies, one for the client and two for the server. Figure 32-4 shows an overview of the solution. The assembly QuoteServer holds the actual functionality. The service reads the quote file in a memory cache, and answers requests for quotes with the help of a socket server. The QuoteClient is a Windows Forms rich-client application. This application creates a client socket to communicate with the QuoteServer. The third assembly is the actual service. The QuoteService starts and stops the QuoteServer; the service controls the server:

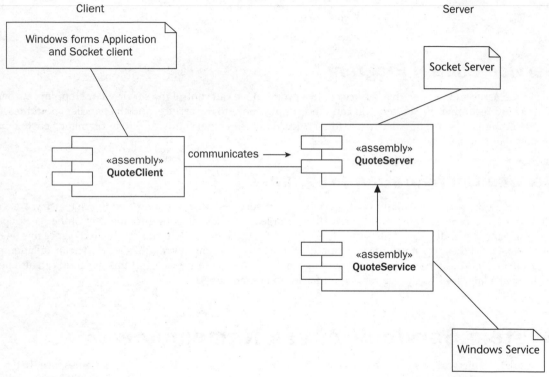

Figure 32-4

Before creating the service part of our program, we create a simple socket server in an extra C# class library that will be used from our service process.

A Class Library Using Sockets

You could build any functionality in the service such as scanning for files to do a backup or a virus check, or starting a .NET Remoting server, for example. However, all service programs share some similarities. The program must be able to start (and to return to the caller), stop, and suspend. We will look at such an implementation using a socket server.

With Windows 2000 or Windows XP, the Simple TCP/IP Services can be installed as part of the Windows components. Part of the Simple TCP/IP Services is a "quote of the day," or qotd, TCP/IP server. This simple service listens to port 17 and answers every request with a random message from the file <windir>\system32\drivers\etc\quotes. With the sample service a similar server will be built. The sample server returns a Unicode string, in contrast to the good old qotd server that returns an ASCII string.

First create a Class Library called `QuoteServer` and implement the code for the server. Let's step through the source code of our `QuoteServer` class in the file QuoteServer.cs:

```
using System;
using System.IO;
using System.Threading;
using System.Net;
using System.Net.Sockets;
using System.Text;
using System.Collections.Specialized;

namespace Wrox.ProCSharp.WinServices
{
    public class QuoteServer
    {
        private TcpListener listener;
        private int port;
        private string filename;
        private StringCollection quotes;
        private Random random;
        private Thread listenerThread;
```

The constructor `QuoteServer()` is overloaded, so that a file name and a port can be passed to the call. The constructor where just the file name is passed uses the default port 7890 for the server. The default constructor defines the default file name for the quotes as quotes.txt:

```
        public QuoteServer() : this ("quotes.txt")
        {
        }
        public QuoteServer(string filename) : this(filename, 7890)
        {
        }
        public QuoteServer(string filename, int port)
        {
            this.filename = filename;
            this.port = port;
        }
```

`ReadQuotes()` is a helper method that reads all the quotes from a file that was specified in the constructor. All the quotes are added to the `StringCollection` quotes. In addition, we are creating an instance of the `Random` class that will be used to return random quotes:

```
        protected void ReadQuotes()
        {
            quotes = new StringCollection();
            Stream stream = File.OpenRead(filename);
```

```
        StreamReader streamReader = new StreamReader(stream);
        string quote;
        while ((quote = streamReader.ReadLine()) != null)
        {
            quotes.Add(quote);
        }
        streamReader.Close();
        stream.Close();
        random = new Random();
    }
```

Another helper method is GetRandomQuoteOfTheDay(). This method returns a random quote from the
StringCollection quotes:

```
    protected string GetRandomQuoteOfTheDay()
    {
        int index = random.Next(0, quotes.Count);
        return quotes[index];
    }
```

In the Start() method, the complete file containing the quotes is read in the StringCollection
quotes by using the helper method ReadQuotes(). After this, a new thread is started, which immediately calls the Listener() method—similar to the TcpReceive example in Chapter 31.

Here a thread is used because the Start() method can not block and wait for a client; it must return
immediately to the caller (SCM). The SCM would assume the start failed if the method didn't return to
the caller in a timely fashion (30 seconds):

```
    public void Start()
    {
        ReadQuotes();
        listenerThread = new Thread(
            new ThreadStart(this.Listener));
        listenerThread.Start();
    }
```

The thread function Listener() creates a TcpListener instance. The AcceptSocket() method waits
for a client to connect. As soon as a client connects, AcceptSocket() returns with a socket associated
with the client. Next GetRandomQuoteOfTheDay() is called to send the returned random quote to the
client using socket.Send():

```
    protected void Listener()
    {
        try
        {
            IPAddress ipAddress = Dns.Resolve("localhost").AddressList[0];
            listener = new TcpListener(ipAddress, port);
            listener.Start();
            while (true)
            {
```

```
                Socket socket = listener.AcceptSocket();
                string message = GetRandomQuoteOfTheDay();
                UnicodeEncoding encoder = new UnicodeEncoding();
                byte[] buffer = encoder.GetBytes(message);
                socket.Send(buffer, buffer.Length, 0);
                socket.Close();
            }
        }
        catch (SocketException e)
        {
            Console.WriteLine(e.Message);
        }
    }
```

In addition to the `Start()` method, the following methods are needed to control the service: `Stop()`, `Suspend()`, and `Resume()`:

```
    public void Stop()
    {
        listener.Stop();
    }
    public void Suspend()
    {
        listenerThread.Suspend();
    }
    public void Resume()
    {
        listenerThread.Resume();
    }
```

Another method that will be publicly available is `RefreshQuotes()`. If the file containing the quotes changes, then the fire is re-read with this method:

```
    public void RefreshQuotes()
    {
        ReadQuotes();
    }
    }
}
```

Before building a service around the server, it is useful to build a test program that just creates an instance of the `QuoteServer` and calls `Start()`. This way, you can test the functionality without the need to handle service-specific issues. This test server must be started manually, and you can easily walk through the code with a debugger.

The test program is a C# console application, TestQuoteServer. You have to reference the assembly of the `QuoteServer` class. The file containing the quotes must be copied to the directory c:\ProCSharp\Services (or you have to change the argument in the constructor to specify where you have copied the file). After calling the constructor, the `Start()` method of the `QuoteServer` instance is called. `Start()` returns immediately after having created a thread, so the console application keeps running until `Return` is pressed:

```
static void Main(string[] args)
{
    QuoteServer qs = new QuoteServer(@"c:\ProCSharp\Services\quotes.txt",
                                     4567);
    qs.Start();
    Console.WriteLine("Hit return to exit");
    Console.ReadLine();
    qs.Stop();
}
```

Note that QuoteServer will be running on port 4567 on localhost using this program—you will have to use these settings in the client later.

TcpClient Example

The client is a simple Windows application where you can enter the host name and the port number of the server. This application uses the TcpClient class to connect to the running server, and receives the returned message, displaying it in a multiline text box. There's also a status bar at the bottom of the form (see Figure 32-5).

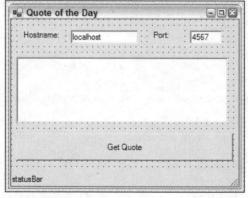

Figure 32-5

You have to add the following using directives to our code:

```
using System;
using System.Drawing;
using System.Collections;
using System.ComponentModel;
using System.Windows.Forms;
using System.Data;
using System.Net;
using System.Net.Sockets;
using System.Text;
```

The remainder of the code is automatically generated by the IDE, so we won't go into detail here. The major functionality of the client lies in the handler for the click event of the Get Quote button:

```
protected void buttonQuote_Click (object sender, System.EventArgs e)
{
    statusBar.Text = "";
    string server = textHostname.Text;
    try
    {
        int port = Convert.ToInt32(textPortNumber.Text);
    }
    catch (FormatException ex)
    {
        statusBar.Text = ex.Message;
        return;
    }
    TcpClient client = new TcpClient();
    try
    {
        client.Connect(textHostname.Text,
                       Convert.ToInt32(textPortNumber.Text));
        NetworkStream stream = client.GetStream();
        byte[] buffer = new Byte[1024];
        int received = stream.Read(buffer, 0, 1024);
        if (received <= 0)
        {
            statusBar.Text = "Read failed";
            return;
        }
        textQuote.Text = Encoding.Unicode.GetString(buffer);
    }
    catch (SocketException ex)
    {
        statusBar.Text = ex.Message;
    }
    finally
    {
        client.Close();
    }
}
```

After starting the test server and this Windows application client, you can test the functionality. Figure 32-6 shows a successful run of this application.

Next we implement the service functionality in the server. The program is already running, so what more do we need? Well, the server program should be automatically started at boot-time without anyone logged on to the system, and we want to control it by using service control programs.

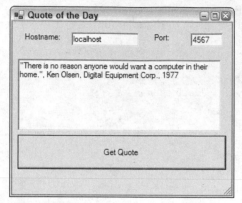

Figure 32-6

Windows Service Project

Using the new project wizard for C# Windows Services, you can now start to create a Windows Service. For the new service use the name QuoteService. Pay careful not to select a Web Service project (see Figure 32-7).

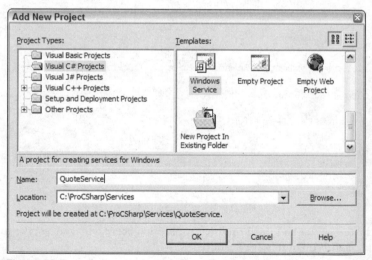

Figure 32-7

After you press the OK button to create the Windows Service application, you will see the Designer surface (just like with Windows Forms applications). However you can't insert any Windows Forms components, because the application can not directly display anything on the screen. The Designer surface is used later in this chapter to add other components, such as performance counters and event logging.

Selecting the properties of this service opens up the Properties editor window (see Figure 32-8).

Figure 32-8

With the service properties, you can configure the following values:

❑ `AutoLog` specifies that events are automatically written to the event log for starting and stopping the service.

❑ `CanPauseAndContinue`, `CanShutdown`, and `CanStop` specify pause, continue, shutdown, and stop requests.

❑ `ServiceName` is the name of the service that's written to the Registry and is used to control the service.

❑ `CanHandlePowerEvent` is a very useful option for services running on a laptop. If this option is enabled, the service can react to low power events, and change the behavior of the service accordingly.

> The default service name is **WinService1**, regardless of what the project is called. You can install only one WinService1 service. If you get installation errors during your testing process, you might already have installed one WinService1 service. Therefore, make sure that you change the name of the service with the Properties editor to a more suitable name at the beginning of the service development.

Changing these properties with the Properties editor sets the values of our `ServiceBase`-derived class in the `InitalizeComponent()` method. You already know this method from Windows Forms applications. With services it's used in a similar way.

A wizard generates the code, but change the file name to QuoteService.cs, the name of the namespace to `Wrox.ProCSharp.WinServices`, and the class name to `QuoteService`. We discuss the code of the service in detail shortly..

The ServiceBase Class

The `ServiceBase` class is the base class for all .NET services. The class `QuoteService` derives from `ServiceBase`; this class communicates with the SCM using an undocumented helper class, `System.ServiceProcess.NativeMethods`, which is just a wrapper class to the Win32 API calls. The class is private, so it can not be used in your code.

The sequence diagram in Figure 32-9 shows the interaction of the SCM, the class `QuoteService`, and the classes from the `System.ServiceProcess` namespace. In the sequence diagram you can see the life-lines of objects vertically and the communication going on in the horizontal direction. The communication is time-ordered from top to bottom.

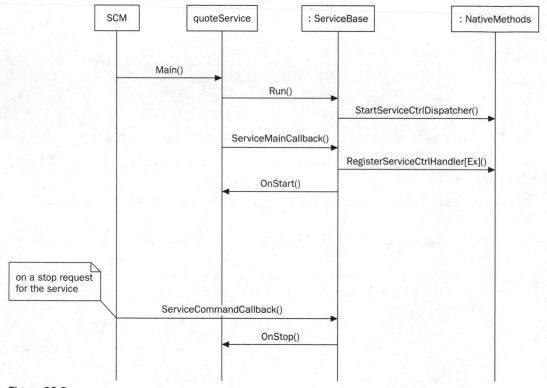

Figure 32-9

The SCM starts the process of a service that should be started. At startup, the `Main()` method is called. In the `Main()` method of the sample service the `Run()` method of the base class `ServiceBase` is called. `Run()` registers the method `ServiceMainCallback()` using `NativeMethods.StartServiceCtrl Dispatcher()` in the SCM and writes an entry to the event log.

Next, the SCM calls the registered method `ServiceMainCallback()` in the service program. `Service MainCallback()` itself registers the handler in the SCM using `NativeMethods.RegisterService CtrlHandler[Ex]()` and sets the status of the service in the SCM. Then the `OnStart()` method is called. In `OnStart()` you have to implement the startup code. If `OnStart()` is successful, the string "Service started successfully" is written to the event log.

The handler is implemented in the `ServiceCommandCallback()` method. The SCM calls this method when changes are requested from the service. The `ServiceCommandCallback()` method routes the requests further to `OnPause()`, `OnContinue()`, `OnStop()`, `OnCustomCommand()`, and `OnPowerEvent()`.

Main function

Let's look into the application wizard–generated main function of the service process. In the main function, an array of `ServiceBase` classes, `ServicesToRun` is declared. One instance of the `QuoteService` class is created and passed as the first element to the `ServicesToRun` array. If more than one service should run inside this service process, it is necessary to add more instances of the specific service classes to the array. This array is then passed to the static `Run()` method of the `ServiceBase` class. With the `Run()` method of `ServiceBase`, we are giving the SCM references to the entry points of our services. The main thread of our service process is now blocked and waits for the service to terminate.

Here's the automatically generated code:

```
// The main entry point for the process
static void Main()
{
    System.ServiceProcess.ServiceBase[] ServicesToRun;

    // More than one user Service may run within the same process. To
    // add another service to this process, change the following line
    // to create a second service object. For example,
    //
    //    ServicesToRun = New System.ServiceProcess.ServiceBase[]
    //    {
    //        new WinService1(), new MySecondUserService()
    //    };
    //

    ServicesToRun = new System.ServiceProcess.ServiceBase[]
    {
        new QuoteService()
    };
    System.ServiceProcess.ServiceBase.Run(ServicesToRun);
}
```

If there's only a single service in the process the array can be removed; the `Run()` method accepts a single object derived from the class `ServiceBase`, so the `Main()` method can be reduced to this:

```
System.ServiceProcess.ServiceBase.Run(new QuoteService());
```

If there is more than one service, like the Windows program Services.exe that includes multiple services, and you need some shared initialization for the services, then this shared initialization must be done before the `Run()` method, because the main thread is blocked until the service process is stopped, and any following instructions would not be reached before the end of the service.

The initialization shouldn't take longer than 30 seconds. If the initialization code were to take longer than this, then the service control manager would assume that the service startup failed. You have to take into account the slowest machines where this service should run within the 30-second limit. If the initialization takes longer, we could start the initialization in a different thread so that the main thread calls `Run()` in time. An event object can then be used to signal that the thread has completed its work.

Service start

At service start the OnStart() method is called. In this method you can start the previously created socket server. You must reference the QuoteServer assembly for the use of the QuoteService. The thread calling OnStart() can not be blocked; this method must return to the caller, which is the ServiceMainCallback() method of the ServiceBase class. The ServiceBase class registers the handler and informs the SCM that the service started successfully after calling OnStart():

```
protected override void OnStart(string[] args)
{
    quoteServer = new QuoteServer(@"c:\ProCSharp\Services\quotes.txt",
                                  5678);
    quoteServer.Start();
}
```

The quoteServer variable is declared as a private member in the class:

```
namespace Wrox.ProCSharp.WinServices
{
    public class QuoteService : System.ServiceProcess.ServiceBase
    {
        private System.ComponentModel.Container components = null;
        private QuoteServer quoteServer;
```

Handler methods

When the service is stopped, the OnStop() method is called. You should stop the service functionality in this method:

```
protected override void OnStop()
{
    quoteServer.Stop();
}
```

In addition to OnStart() and OnStop(), you can override the following handlers in the service class:

❑   OnPause() is called when the service should be paused.

❑   OnContinue() is called when the service should return to normal operation after being paused. To make it possible for the overridden methods OnPause() and OnContinue() to be called, the CanPauseAndContinue property must be set to true.

❑   OnShutdown() is called when Windows is undergoing system shutdown. Normally, the behavior of this method should be similar to the OnStop() implementation; if more time were needed for a shutdown, you can request additional time. Similar to OnPause() and OnContinue(), a property must be set to enable this behavior: CanShutdown must be set to true.

❑   OnCustomCommand() is a handler that can serve custom commands which are sent by a service control program. The method signature of OnCustomCommand() has an int argument where we get the custom command number. The value can be in the range from 128 to 256; values below 128 are system-reserved values. In our service we are re-reading the quotes file with the custom command 128:

```
        protected override void OnPause()
        {
            quoteServer.Suspend();
        }
        protected override void OnContinue()
        {
            quoteServer.Resume();
        }
        protected override void OnShutdown()
        {
            OnStop();
        }
        public const int commandRefresh = 128;
        protected override void OnCustomCommand(int command)
        {
            switch (command)
            {
                case commandRefresh:
                    quoteServer.RefreshQuotes();
                    break;
                default:
                    break;
            }
        }
```

Threading and Services

With services, we have to deal with threads. As stated earlier, the SCM will assume that the service failed if the initialization takes too long. To deal with this, you have to create a thread.

The OnStart() method in our service class must return in time. If you call a blocking method like AcceptSocket() from the TcpListener class, you have to start a thread for doing this. With a networking server that deals with multiple clients, a thread pool is also very useful. AcceptSocket() should receive the call and hand the processing off to another thread from the pool. This way, no one waits for the execution of code and the system seems responsive.

Service Installation

A service must be configured in the registry. All services can be found in HKEY_LOCAL_MACHINE \System\CurrentControlSet\Services. You can view the registry entries using regedit. The type of the service, display name, path to the executable, startup configuration, and so on, are all found here. Figure 32-10 shows the registry configuration of the Alerter service.

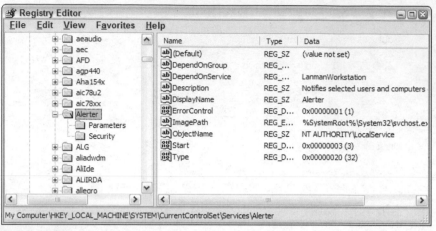

Figure 32-10

This configuration can be done by using the installer classes from the `System.ServiceProcess` namespace, as discussed in the following section..

Installation Program

You can add an installation program to the service by switching to the design view with Visual Studio .NET and then selecting the Add Installer option from the context menu. With this option a new `ProjectInstaller` class is created, and a `ServiceInstaller` and a `ServiceProcessInstaller` instance are created.

Figure 32-11 shows the class diagram of the installer classes for services.

With this diagram in mind, let's go through the sourcecode in the file ProjectInstaller.cs that was created with the Add Installer option.

The Installer class

The class `ProjectInstaller` is derived from `System.Configuration.Install.Installer`. This is the base class for all custom installers. With the `Installer` class, it's possible to build transaction-based installations. With a transaction-based installation, it's possible to roll back to the previous state if the installation fails, and any changes made by this installation up to that point will be undone. As you can see in Figure 32-11, the `Installer` class has `Install()`, `Commit()`, `Rollback()`, and `Uninstall()` methods, and they are called from installation programs.

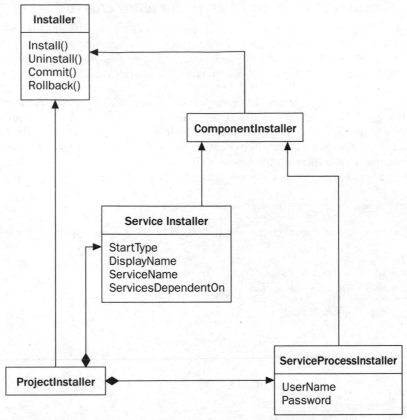

Figure 32-11

The attribute `[RunInstaller(true)]` means that the class `ProjectInstaller` should be invoked when installing an assembly. Custom action installers as well as installutil.exe (which will be used later) check for this attribute:

```
using System;
using System.Collections;
using System.ComponentModel;
using System.Configuration.Install;

namespace Wrox.ProCSharp.WinServices
{
/// <summary>
    ///     Summary description for ProjectInstaller.
    /// </summary>

    [RunInstaller(true)]
    public class ProjectInstaller : System.Configuration.Install.Installer
    {
```

The ServiceProcessInstaller and ServiceInstaller classes

Similar to Windows Forms applications, `InitializeComponent()` is called inside the constructor of the `ProjectInstaller` class. In `InitializeComponent()`, instances of the `ServiceProcessInstaller` class and the `ServiceInstaller` class are created. Both of these classes derive from the `ComponentInstaller` class, which itself derives from `Installer`.

Classes derived from `ComponentInstaller` can be used as part within an installation process. Remember that a service process can include more than one service. The `ServiceProcessInstaller` class is used for the configuration of the process that defines values for all services in this process, and the `ServiceInstaller` class is for the configuration of the service, so one instance of `ServiceInstaller` is required for each service. If there are three services inside the process, you have to add additional `ServiceInstaller` objects—three `ServiceInstaller` instances are needed in that case.

```
private System.ServiceProcess.ServiceProcessInstaller
            serviceProcessInstaller1;
private System.ServiceProcess.ServiceInstaller serviceInstaller1;

/// <summary>
///     Required designer variable.
/// </summary>
private System.ComponentModel.Container components = null;
public ProjectInstaller()
{
   // This call is required by the Designer.
   InitializeComponent();

   // TODO: Add any initialization after the InitComponent call
}
/// <summary>
///     Required method for Designer support - do not modify
///     the contents of this method with the code editor.
/// </summary>
private void InitializeComponent()
{
   this.serviceProcessInstaller1 =
            new System.ServiceProcess.ServiceProcessInstaller();
   this.serviceInstaller1 =
            new System.ServiceProcess.ServiceInstaller();
   //
   // serviceProcessInstaller1
   //
   this.serviceProcessInstaller1.Password = null;
   this.serviceProcessInstaller1.Username = null;
   //
   // serviceInstaller1
   //
   this.serviceInstaller1.ServiceName = "QuoteService";
   //
   // ProjectInstaller
```

```
            //
        this.Installers.AddRange(
            new System.Configuration.Install.Installer[]
                {this.serviceProcessInstaller1,
                 this.serviceInstaller1});
        }
    }
}
```

`ServiceProcessInstaller` installs an executable that implements the class `ServiceBase`. `ServiceProcessInstaller` has properties for the complete process. The following table explains the properties shared by all the services inside the process.

Property	Description
Username, Password	Indicates the user account under which the service runs if the `Account` property is set to `ServiceAccount.User`.
Account	With this property we can specify the account type of the service.
HelpText	`HelpText` is a read-only property that returns the help text for setting the user name and password.

The process that is used to run the service can be specified with the `Account` property of the `ServiceProcessInstaller` class using the `ServiceAccount` enumeration. The following table explains the different values of the `Account` property.

Value	Meaning
LocalSystem	Setting this value specifies that the service uses a highly privileged user account on the local system, but this account presents an anonymous user to the network. Thus it doesn't have rights on the network.
LocalService	This account type presents the computer's credentials to any remote server.
NetworkService	Similar to `LocalService`, this value specifies that the computer's credentials are passed to remote servers, but unlike `LocalService` such a service acts as a non-privileged user on the local system. As the name implies, this account should be used only for services that need resources from the network.
User	Setting the `Account` property to `ServiceAccount.User` means that we can define the account that should be used from the service.

`ServiceInstaller` is the class needed for every service; it has the following properties for each service inside a process: `StartType`, `DisplayName`, `ServiceName`, and `ServicesDependedOn`.

Property	Description
StartType	The StartType property indicates if the service is manually or automatically started. Possible values are ServiceStartMode. Automatic, ServiceStartMode.Manual, ServiceStartMode. Disabled. With ServiceStartMode.Disabled the service cannot be started. This option is useful for services that shouldn't be started on a system. You might want to set the option to Disabled if for example a required hardware controller is not available.
DisplayName	DisplayName is the friendly name of the service that is displayed to the user. This name is also used by management tools that control and monitor the service.
ServiceName	ServiceName is the name of the service. This value must be identical to the ServiceName property of the ServiceBase class in the service program. This name associates the configuration of the ServiceInstaller to the required service program.
ServicesDependentOn	Specifies an array of services that must be started before this service can be started. When the service is started, all these dependent services are started automatically, and then our service will start.

> **If you change the name of the service in the ServiceBase-derived class, also change the ServiceName property in the ServiceInstaller object!**

In the testing phases set StartType to Manual. This way, if you can't stop the service (for example, when it has a bug), then you still have the possibility to reboot the system. But if you have StartType set to Automatic, the service would be started automatically with the reboot! You can change this configuration at a later time when you're sure that it works.

The ServiceInstallerDialog class

Another installer class in the System.ServiceProcess.Design namespace is the ServiceInstaller Dialog. This class can be used if we want the System Administrator to enter the username and password during the installation.

If you set the Account property of the class ServiceProcessInstaller to ServiceAccount.User, and the Username and Password properties to null, then you will see the Set Service Login dialog box at installation time (see Figure 32-12). You can also cancel the installation at this point.

installutil

After adding the installer classes to the project you can use the installutil.exe utility to install and uninstall the service. This utility can be used to install any assembly that has an Installer class. The installutil.exe utility calls the method Install() of the class that derives from the Installer class for installation, and Uninstall() for the *deinstallation*.

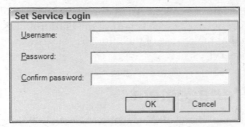

Figure 32-12

The command line inputs for the installation and deinstallation of our service are:

```
installutil quoteservice.exe

installutil /u quoteservice.exe
```

> If the installation fails be sure to check the installation log files InstallUtil.InstallLog
> and <servicename>.InstallLog. Often you can find very useful information, such as
> "The specified service already exists".

Client

After the service has been successfully installed, you can start the service manually from the Services
MMC (see next section for further details), and then you can start the client application. Figure 32-13
shows the client accessing the service.

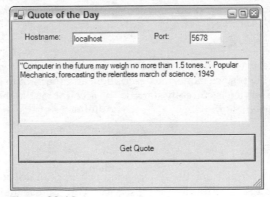

Figure 32-13

Monitoring and Controlling the Service

To monitor and control services you can use the Services MMC snap-in that is part of the Computer
Management administration tool. With every Windows system you also get a command line utility,

net.exe, which allows you to control services. Another command line utility is sc.exe. This utility has much more functionality than net.exe, which is part of the Platform SDK. In this section we create a small Windows application that makes use of the `System.ServiceProcess.ServiceController` class to monitor and control services.

MMC Computer Management

Using the Services snap-in to the Microsoft Management Console (MMC), you can view the status of all services (see Figure 32-14). It's also possible to send control requests to services to stop, enable, or disable them, as well as to change their configuration. The Services snap-in is a service control program as well as a service configuration program.

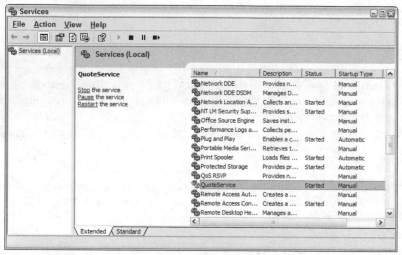

Figure 32-14

If you double-click QuoteService, you'll get the Properties dialog box shown in Figure 32-15. This dialog box enables you to view the service name, the description, and the path to the executable, the startup type, and the status. The service is currently started. The account for the service process can be changed with the Log On tab in this dialog.

net.exe

The Services snap-in is easy to use, but the system administrator can not automate it, because it's not usable within an administrative script. To control services, you can use the command line utility net.exe: net start shows all running services, net start servicename starts a service, net stop servicename sends a stop request to the service. It's also possible to pause and to continue a service with net pause and net continue (only if the service allows it, of course).

Figure 32-16 shows the result of net start in the console window.

Figure 32-15

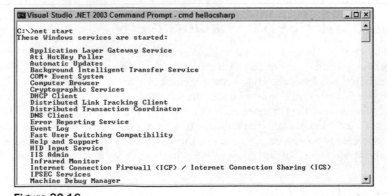

Figure 32-16

sc.exe

There's a little known utility that's delivered with Visual Studio .NET, but starting with Windows XP is also part of the operating system: sc.exe.

sc.exe is a great tool to play with services. A lot more can be done with sc.exe compared to the net.exe utility. With sc.exe, it's possible to check the actual status of a service, or configure, remove, and add services. This tool also faciliates the de-installation of the service, if it fails to function correctly.

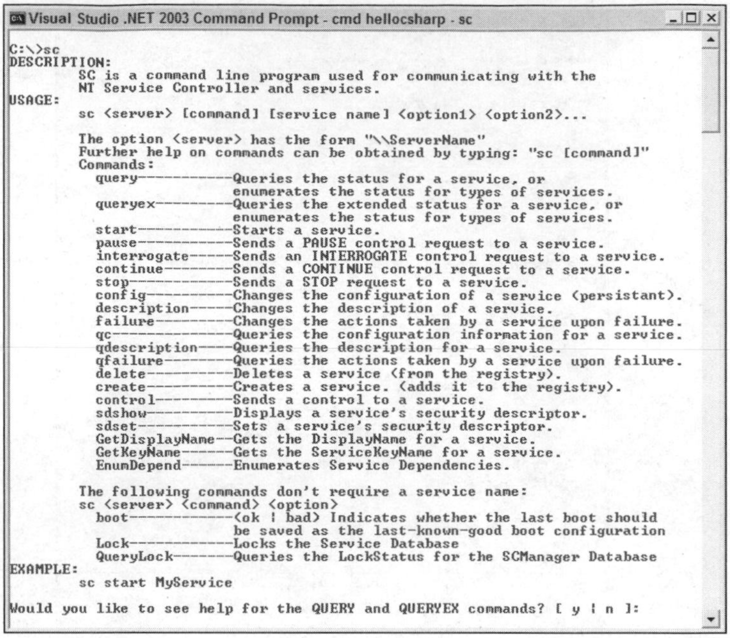

Figure 32-17

Visual Studio .NET Server Explorer

It is also possible to control services using the Server Explorer within Visual Studio .NET; Services is below Servers and the name of your computer. By selecting a service and opening the context menu a service can be started and stopped. This context menu can also be used to add a `ServiceController` class to the project. If you want to control a specific service in your application, drag and drop a service from the Server Explorer to the Designer: a `ServiceController` instance is added to the application. The properties of this object are automatically set to access the selected service, and the assembly System.ServiceProcess is referenced. You can use this instance to control a service in the same way as you can with the application that will be developed in the next section.

ServiceController Class

In this section, we create a small Windows application that uses the `ServiceController` class to monitor and control Windows Services.

Create a windows forms application with a user interface (see Figure 32-18). The user interface of this application has a list box to show all services, four text boxes to display the display name, status, type, and name of the service, and four buttons to send control events.

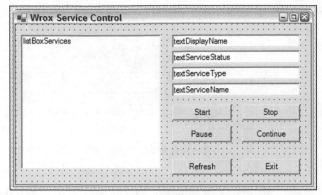

Figure 32-18

Because the class System.ServiceProcess.ServiceController is used, you must reference the assembly System.ServiceProcess.

Create and implement the method RefreshServiceList() that lists all services in the list box with the following code. This method is called within the constructor of the class ServiceControlForm. In the implementation this method fills a ListBox control with the display names of all services. GetServices() is a static method of the ServiceController class, and it returns a ServiceController array representing all Windows Services. The ServiceController class also has the static method GetDevices() that returns a ServiceController array representing all device drivers.

The ListBox is filled by simply binding ServiceController.GetServices() to the ListBox.

```
private System.ServiceProcess.ServiceController[] services;

public ServiceControlForm()
{
    //
    // Required for Windows Form Designer support
    //

    InitializeComponent();
    RefreshServiceList();
}
protected void RefreshServiceList()
{
    services = ServiceController.GetServices();
    listBoxServices.DisplayMember = "DisplayName";
    listBoxServices.DataSource = services;
}
```

Now, all Windows Services are displayed in the list box. Next, you must get the information about a service that is displayed in the text boxes.

Monitoring the service

Using the `ServiceController` class, you can get the information about each service. The following tables shows the properties of the `ServiceController` class.

Property	Description
CanPauseAndContinue	If pause and continue requests can be sent to the service, `true` is returned.
CanShutdown	Returns `true` if the service has a handler for a system shutdown.
CanStop	Returns `true` if the service is stoppable.
DependentServices	Returns a collection of dependent services. If the service is stopped all dependent services are stopped beforehand.
ServicesDependentOn	Returns a collection of the services that this service depends on.
DisplayName	Specifies the name that should be displayed for this service.
MachineName	Specifies the name of the machine that the service runs on.
ServiceName	Specifies the name of the service.
ServiceType	Specifies the type of the service. The service can be run inside a shared process where more than one service uses the same process (`Win32ShareProcess`), or run in that way that there's just one service in a process (`Win32OwnProcess`). If the service can interact with the desktop the type is `InteractiveProcess`.
Status	Specifies the status of the service. The status can be running, stopped, paused, or in some intermediate mode like start pending, stop pending, and so on. The status values are defined in the enumeration `ServiceControllerStatus`.

In the sample application, the properties `DisplayName`, `ServiceName`, `ServiceType`, and `Status` are used to display the service information. Also, `CanPauseAndContinue` and `CanStop` are used to enable or disable the Pause, Continue, and Stop buttons.

The status and type of the service can not be set that easily, because a string should be displayed instead of a number, which is what the `ServiceController` class returns. To get a string for the status and type two helper functions are implemented: `SetServiceStatus()` and `GetServiceTypeName()`.

The method `GetServiceTypeName()` returns a string that represents the type of the service. Depending on the type that is passed with the `ServiceType` argument, a string is returned. The `ServiceType` you get from the property `ServiceController.ServiceType` represents a set of flags that can be combined by using the bitwise `OR` operator. The `InteractiveProcess` bit can be set together with `Win32OwnProcess` and `Win32ShareProcess`. So at first it is checked if the `InteractiveProcess` bit is set before continuing to check for the other values. With services the string returned will be "Win32 Service Process", or "Win32 Shared Process".

```
protected string GetServiceTypeName(ServiceType type)
{
   string serviceType = "";
   if ((type & ServiceType.InteractiveProcess) != 0)
   {
      serviceType = "Interactive ";
      type -= ServiceType.InteractiveProcess;
   }
   switch (type)
   {
      case ServiceType.Adapter:
          serviceType += "Adapter";
          break;
      case ServiceType.FileSystemDriver:
      case ServiceType.KernelDriver:
      case ServiceType.RecognizerDriver:
          serviceType += "Driver";
          break;
      case ServiceType.Win32OwnProcess:
          serviceType += "Win32 Service Process";
          break;
      case ServiceType.Win32ShareProcess:
          serviceType += "Win32 Shared Process";
          break;
      default:
          serviceType += "unknown type " + type.ToString();
          break;
   }
   return serviceType;
}
```

The method `SetServiceStatus()` sets the current status of the service in the text box `textServiceStatus`. Also, the start/stop/pause/continue buttons will be enabled or disabled depending on the status of the service.

```
protected void SetServiceStatus(ServiceController controller)
{
   buttonStart.Enabled = true;
   buttonStop.Enabled = true;
   buttonPause.Enabled = true;
   buttonContinue.Enabled = true;
   if (!controller.CanPauseAndContinue)
   {
      buttonPause.Enabled = false;
      buttonContinue.Enabled = false;
   }
   if (!controller.CanStop)
   {
      buttonStop.Enabled = false;
   }
   ServiceControllerStatus status = controller.Status;
   switch (status)
   {
      case ServiceControllerStatus.ContinuePending:
```

```
                    textServiceStatus.Text = "Continue Pending";
                    buttonContinue.Enabled = false;
                    break;
            case ServiceControllerStatus.Paused:
                    textServiceStatus.Text = "Paused";
                    buttonPause.Enabled = false;
                    buttonStart.Enabled = false;
                    break;
            case ServiceControllerStatus.PausePending:
                    textServiceStatus.Text = "Pause Pending";
                    buttonPause.Enabled = false;
                    buttonStart.Enabled = false;
                    break;
            case ServiceControllerStatus.StartPending:
                    textServiceStatus.Text = "Start Pending";
                    buttonStart.Enabled = false;
                    break;
            case ServiceControllerStatus.Running:
                    textServiceStatus.Text = "Running";
                    buttonStart.Enabled = false;
                    buttonContinue.Enabled = false;
                    break;
            case ServiceControllerStatus.Stopped:
                    textServiceStatus.Text = "Stopped";
                    buttonStop.Enabled = false;
                    break;
            case ServiceControllerStatus.StopPending:
                    textServiceStatus.Text = "Stop Pending";
                    buttonStop.Enabled = false;
                    break;
            default:
                    textServiceStatus.Text = "Unknown status";
                    break;
    }
```

OnSelectedIndexChanged() is the handler for the ListBox event SelectedIndexChanged. This handler is called when the user selects a service in the ListBox event. In OnSelectedIndexChanged() the display and the service name is set directly with properties of the ServiceController class. The service type is set by calling the helper method GetServiceTypeName().

```
        protected void OnSelectedIndexChanged (object sender,
                        System.EventArgs e)
        {
            ServiceController controller =
                        (ServiceController)listBoxServices.SelectedItem;
            textDisplayName.Text = controller.DisplayName;
            textServiceType.Text = GetServiceTypeName(controller.ServiceType);
            textServiceName.Text = controller.ServiceName;
            SetServiceStatus(controller);
        }
```

Controlling the service

With the `ServiceController` class you can also send control requests to the service. The following table explains the methods you can use.

Method	Description
Start()	Start() tells the SCM that the service should be started. In our service program OnStart() is called.
Stop()	Stop() calls OnStop() in our service program with the help of the SCM if the property CanStop is true in the service class.
Pause()	Pause() calls OnPause() if the property CanPauseAndContinue is true.
Continue()	Continue calls OnContinue() if the property CanPauseAndContinue is true.
ExecuteCommand()	With ExecuteCommand() it's possible to send a custom command to the service.

The following code controls the services. Because the code for starting, stopping, suspending, and pausing is similar, only one handler is used for the four buttons:

```csharp
protected void buttonCommand_Click(object sender, System.EventArgs e)
{
    Cursor.Current = Cursors.WaitCursor;
    ServiceController controller =
                    (ServiceController)listBoxServices.SelectedItem;
    if (sender == this.buttonStart)
    {
        controller.Start();
        controller.WaitForStatus(ServiceControllerStatus.Running);
    }
    else if (sender == this.buttonStop)
    {
        controller.Stop();
        controller.WaitForStatus(ServiceControllerStatus.Stopped);
    }
    else if (sender == this.buttonPause)
    {
        controller.Pause();
        controller.WaitForStatus(ServiceControllerStatus.Paused);
    }
    else if (sender == this.buttonContinue)
    {
        controller.Continue();
        controller.WaitForStatus(ServiceControllerStatus.Running);
    }
    int index =listBoxServices.SelectedIndex;
    RefreshServiceList();
    listBoxServices.SelectedIndex = index;
```

```
        Cursor.Current = Cursors.Default;
    }

    protected void buttonExit_Click(object sender, System.EventArgs e)
    {
        Application.Exit();
    }
    protected void buttonRefresh_Click(object sender, System.EventArgs e)
    {
        RefreshServiceList();
    }
```

As the action of controlling the services can take some time, the cursor is switched to the wait cursor in the first statement. Then, a `ServiceController` method is called depending on the pressed button. With the `WaitForStatus()` method, we are waiting to check that the service changes the status to the requested value, but we only wait a maximum of 10 seconds. After this time, the information in the `ListBox` is refreshed; and the same service as before is selected, and the new status of this service is displayed.

Figure 32-19 shows the completed, running application.

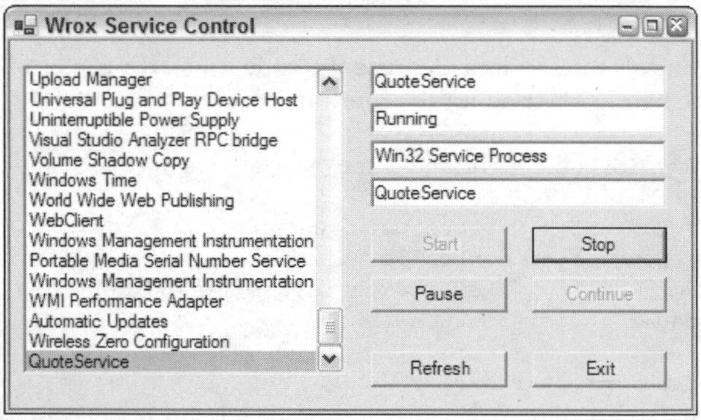

Figure 32-19

Troubleshooting

Troubleshooting services is different from troubleshooting normal applications. In this section, we cover the following troubleshooting topics:

❑   The problems of interactive services

❑   Event logging

❑   Performance monitoring

The best way to begin building a service is to create an assembly with the functionality you want and a test client, before the service is actually created. Here you can do normal debugging and error handling.

As soon as the application is running you can build a service by using this assembly. Of course, there still might be problems with the service:

❑ Don't display errors in a message box from the service (except for interactive services that are running on the client system). Instead, use the event logging service to write errors to the event log. Of course, you can display a message box to inform the user about errors in the client application that uses the service.

❑ The service can't be started from within a debugger, but a debugger can be attached to the running service process. Open the solution with the sourcecode of the service and set breakpoints. From the Visual Studio .NET Debug menu select Processes and attach the running process of the service.

❑ The Windows 2000 Performance Monitor can be used to monitor the activity of services. You can add our own performance objects to the service. This can add some useful information for debugging. For example, with the Quote service, you could set up an object to give the total number of quotes returned, the time it takes to initialize, and so on.

Interactive Services

If an interactive service runs with a logged-on user it can be helpful to display message boxes to the user. If the service should run on a server that is locked inside a computer room, the service should never display a message box. When you open a message box, to wait for some user input, the user input probably won't happen for some days as nobody is looking at the server in the computer room; but it can get even worse than that: if the service isn't configured as an interactive service, the message box opens up on a different, hidden, window station. In this case, no one can answer that message box because it is hidden, and the service is blocked.

> **Never open dialog boxes for services running on a server system. Nobody will answer them.**

In those cases where you really want to interact with the user, an interactive service can be configured. Some examples of such interactive services are the Print Spooler that displays paper-out messages to the user, and the NetMeeting Remote Desktop Sharing service.

To configure an interactive service, you must set the option Allow service to interact with desktop in the Services configuration tool (see Figure 32-20). This changes the type of the service by adding the `SERVICE_INTERACTIVE_PROCESS` flag to the type.

Event Logging

Services can report errors and other information by adding events to the event log. A service class derived from `ServiceBase` automatically logs events when the `AutoLog` property is set to `true`. The `ServiceBase` class checks this property and writes a log entry at start, stop, pause, and continue requests.

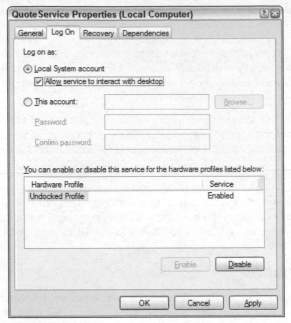

Figure 32-20

In this section, we explore:

❑　Error-logging architecture

❑　Classes for event logging from the `System.Diagnostics` namespace

❑　Adding event logging to services and to other application types

❑　Creating an event-log listener with the `EnableRaisingEvents` property of the `EventLog` class

Figure 32-21 shows an example of a log entry from a service.

For custom event logging, you can use classes from the `System.Diagnostics` namespace.

Event Logging architecture

By default, the event log is stored in three log files: Application, Security, and System. Looking at the registry configuration of the event log service, you'll notice three entries under HKEY_LOCAL_MACHINE \System\CurrentControlSet\Services\Eventlog with configurations pointing to the specific files. The System log file is used from the system and device drivers. Applications and services write to the Application log. The Security log is a read-only log for applications. The auditing feature of the operating system uses the Security log.

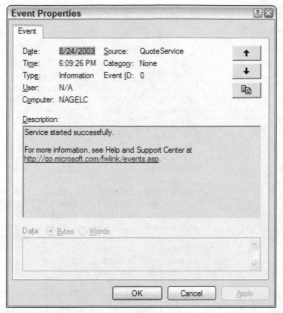

Figure 32-21

You can read these events by using the administrative tool Event Viewer. The Event Viewer can be started directly from the Server Explorer of Visual Studio .NET by right-clicking on the Event Logs item, and selecting the Launch Event Viewer entry from the context menu. The Event Viewer is shown in Figure 32-22.

In the event log you can see this information:

- ❏ The type can be Information, Warning, or Error. Information is an infrequent successful operation, Warning a problem that's not immediately significant, and Error a major problem. Additional types are FailureAudit and SuccessAudit, but these types are only used for the Security log.

- ❏ Date and Time show the time when the event occurred.

- ❏ The Source is the name of the software that logs the event. The source for the Application log is configured in:

      HKEY_LOCAL_MACHINE\System\CurrentControlSet\Services\
          Eventlog\Application\[ApplicationName]

- ❏ Below this key the value EventMessageFile is configured to point to a resource DLL that holds error messages.

- ❏ A Category can be defined so that event logs can be filtered when using the Event Viewer. Categories can be defined by an event source.

- ❏ The Event identifier specifies a particular event message.

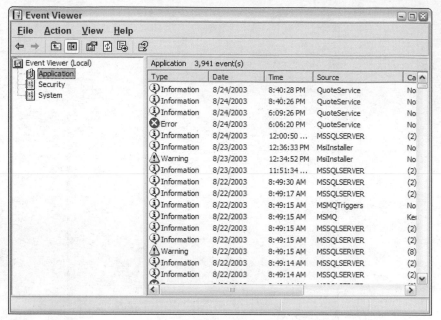

Figure 32-22

Event Logging classes

The System.Diagnostics namespace has some classes for event logging:

❑ With the EventLog class you can read and write entries in the event log, and establish applications as event sources.

❑ The EventLogEntry class represents a single entry in the event log. With the EventLogEntryCollection you can iterate through EventLogEntry items.

❑ The EventLogInstaller class is the installer for an EventLog component. EventLogInstaller calls EventLog.CreateEventSource() to create an event source.

❑ With the help of the EventLogTraceListener traces can be written to the event log. This class implements the abstract class TraceListener.

Adding event logging

If the AutoLog property of the ServiceBase class is set to true, event logging is automatically turned on. The ServiceBase class logs an informational event at startup, stop, pause, and continue requests of the service. In the ServiceInstaller class an EventLogInstaller instance is created so that an event log source is configured. This event log source has the same name as the service. If you want to write events you can use the WriteEntry() method of the EventLog class. The Source property was already set in the ServiceBase class:

```
eventLog.WriteEntry("event log message");
```

This method logs an informational event. If warning or error events should be created, an overloaded method of `WriteEvent()` can be used to specify the type:

```
eventLog.WriteEntry("event log message", EventLogEntryType.Warning);
eventLog.WriteEntry("event log message", EventLogEntryType.Error);
```

Adding event logging to other application types

With services the `ServiceBase` class automatically adds event-logging features. If you would like to use event logging within other application types, it can easily be done by using Visual Studio .NET.

❑ Use the Toolbox to add an EventLog component to the Designer.

❑ Set the Log property of the EventLog component to Application and the Source property to a name of your choice. This name is typically the name of the application that shows up in the Event Viewer.

❑ Logs can now be written with the `WriteEntry()` method of the `EventLog` instance.

❑ An installer can be added from the Add Installer context menu item of the EventLog component. This creates the `ProjectInstaller` class that configures the event source in the registry.

❑ The application can now be registered with the `installutil` command. `installutil` calls the `ProjectInstaller` class and registers the event source.

If you do an xcopy-installation the last two steps are not really necessary. If the `Source` property of the `EventLog` instance is set, this source is automatically registered when an event log is written the first time. That's really easy to do. However, for a real application you are better off adding the installer. With `installutil /u` the event log configuration is unregistered. If the application is just deleted, this registry key remains unless `EventLog.DeleteEventSource()` is called.

Adding event logging to the QuoteServer

The library QuoteServer that is used from the QuoteService currently doesn't have event logging included. This can be changed easily. In order to use the Visual Studio .NET Designer to drag and drop the EventLog component to the class, you have to add designer support to the class.

To add designer support to the class you have to derive the class from the base class System .ComponentModel.Component, and invoke the method InitializeComponent() inside the constructor of the class. The method InitializeComponent() that will be used from the Designer to set the properties of the components will be added automatically as soon as the first component is dropped onto the Designer surface, but you have to invoke this method yourself.

After you change the code of the `QuoteServer` class in the library `QuoteServer` with a derivation from the base class `System.ComponentModel.Component`, you can switch Visual Studio .NET to the design view.

```
public class QuoteServer : System.ComponentModel.Component
{
    //...

    public QuoteServer() : this ("quotes.txt")
```

```
        {
        }

        public QuoteServer(string filename) : this(filename, 7890)
        {
        }

        public QuoteServer(string filename, int port)
        {
            this.filename = filename;
            this.port = port;

            InitializeComponent();
        }
```

After this change you can drag and drop the EventLog component from the toolbox to the design view, where an instance of the EventLog class is created. Change the Log property of the object to Application, and the Source property to QuoteService.

Then you can change the implementation of the method Listener() in the class QuoteServer, so that an event log entry is written in case an exception is generated:

```
        protected void Listener()
        {
            try
            {
                IPAddress ipAddress = Dns.Resolve("localhost").AddressList[0];
                listener = new TcpListener(ipAddress, port);
                listener.Start();
                while (true)
                {
                    Socket socket = listener.AcceptSocket();
                    string message = GetRandomQuoteOfTheDay();
                    UnicodeEncoding encoder = new UnicodeEncoding();
                    byte[] buffer = encoder.GetBytes(message);
                    socket.Send(buffer, buffer.Length, 0);
                    socket.Close();
                }
            }
            catch (SocketException e)
            {
                string message = "Quote Server failed in Listener: "
                                 + e.Message;
                eventLog.WriteEntry(message, EventLogEntryType.Error);
            }
        }
```

Trace

It's also possible that all your trace messages are redirected to the event log. You shouldn't really do this, because on a normal running system the event log gets overblown with trace messages, and the system administrator could miss the really important logs, if this happens. Turning on trace messages to the event log can be useful when testing features for problematic services. Tracing is possible with debug as well as with release code.

To send trace messages to the event log you must create an `EventLogTraceListener` object and add it to the listener's list of the `Trace` class:

```
EventLogTraceListener listener = new EventLogTraceListener(eventLog1);
Trace.Listeners.Add(listener);
```

Now, all trace messages are sent to the event log:

```
Trace.WriteLine("trace message");
```

Creating an event log listener

Next we write an application that receives an event when a service encounters a problem. Create a simple Windows application that monitors the events of our `Quote` service. This Windows application consists only of a list box and an Exit button as shown in Figure 32-23.

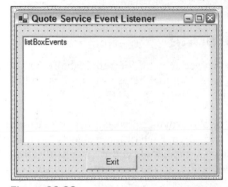

Figure 32-23

Add an `EventLog` component to the design view by dragging and dropping it from the Toolbox. Set the `Log` property to `Application`, and the `Source` to the source of our service, `QuoteService`. The `EventLog` class also has a property, `EnableRaisingEvents`. The default value is `false`; setting it to `true` means that an event is generated each time this event occurs, and you can add an event handler for the `EntryWritten` event of the `EventLog` class. Add a handler with the name `OnEntryWritten()` to this event.

The `OnEntryWritten()` handler receives an `EntryWrittenEventArgs` object as argument, from which you can get the complete information about an event. With the `Entry` property an `EventLogEntry` object with information about the time, event source, type, category, and so on is returned.

```
protected void OnEntryWritten (object sender,
    System.Diagnostics.EntryWrittenEventArgs e)
{
    DateTime time = e.Entry.TimeGenerated;
    string message = e.Entry.Message;
    listBoxEvents.Items.Add(time + " " + message);
}
```

The running application displays all events for the QuoteService as shown in Figure 32-24.

Figure 32-24

Performance Monitoring

Performance monitoring can be used to get information about the normal running of the service. Performance monitoring is a great tool that helps us to understand the workload of the system, and to observe changes and trends.

Microsoft Windows has a lot of performance objects, such as System, Memory, Objects, Process, Processor, Thread, Cache, and so on. Each of these objects has many counts to monitor. For example, with the Process object the user time, handle count, page faults, thread count, and so on, can be monitored for all processes, or for specific process instances. Some applications, such as SQL Server, also add application-specific objects.

For the quote service sample application it might be interesting to get information about the number of client requests, the size of the data that is sent over the wire, and so on.

Performance monitoring classes

The System.Diagnostics namespace provides these classes for performance monitoring:

❑ PerformanceCounter can be used both to monitor counts and to write counts. New performance categories can also be created with this class.

❑ PerformanceCounterCategory enables you to step through all existing categories as well as create new ones. You can programmatically get all the counters of a category.

❑ PerformanceCounterInstaller is used for the installation of performance counters. The use is similar to the EventLogInstaller we discussed previously.

Performance Counter Builder

You can create a new performance counter category by selecting the performance counters in the Server Explorer and by selecting the menu entry Create New Category on the context menu. This launches the Performance Counter Builder (see Figure 32-25).

Figure 32-25

Set name of the performance counter category to `Quote Service`. The following table shows all performance counters of the quote service.

Name	Description	Type
# of Bytes sent	Total # of bytes sent to the client	`NumberOfItems32`
# of Bytes sent / sec	# of bytes sent to the client in one second	`RateOfCountsPerSecond32`
# of Requests	Total # of requests	`NumberOfItems32`
# of Requests / sec	# of requests in one second	`RateOfCountsPerSecond32`

The Performance Counter Builder writes the configuration to the performance database. This can also be done dynamically by using the `Create()` method of the `PerformanceCounterCategory` class in the `System.Diagnostics` namespace. An installer for other systems can easily be added later using Visual Studio .NET.

Adding PerformanceCounter Components

Now you can add PerformanceCounter components from the Toolbox. Instead of using the components from the toolbox category Components, you can directly drag and drop the previously created performance counts from the Server explorer to the design view. This way the instances are configured automatically: the `CategoryName` property is set to "Quote Service Count" for all objects, and the `CounterName` property is set to one of the values available in the selected category. Because with this application the performance counts will not be read but written, you have to set the `ReadOnly` property to `false`.

Here is part of the code that is generated into `InitializeComponent()` by adding the PerformanceCounter components to the Designer and by setting the properties as indicated above:

```
private void InitializeComponent()
{
  //...
  // performanceCounterRequestsPerSec
  //
  this.performanceCounterRequestsPerSec.CategoryName =
    "Quote Service Counts";
  this.performanceCounterRequestsPerSec.CounterName = "# of Requests / sec";
  this.performanceCounterRequestsPerSec.MachineName = "NAGELC";
  this.performanceCounterReqeustsPerSec.ReadOnly = false;
  //
  // performanceCounterBytesSentTotal
  //
  this.performanceCounterBytesSentTotal.CategoryName =
    "Quote Service Counts";
  this.performanceCounterBytesSentTotal.CounterName = "# of Bytes sent";
  this.performanceCounterBytesSentTotal.MachineName = "NAGELC";
  this.performanceCounterBytesSentTotal.ReadOnly = false;
  //
  // performanceCounterBytesSentPerSec
  //
  this.performanceCounterBytesSentPerSec.CategoryName =
    "Quote Service Counts";
  this.performanceCounterBytesSentPerSec.CounterName =
    "# of Bytes sent / sec";
  this.performanceCounterBytesSentPerSec.MachineName = "NAGELC";
  this.performanceCounterBytesSentPerSec.ReadOnly = false;
  //
  // performanceCounterRequestsTotal
  //
  this.performanceCounterRequestsTotal.CategoryName =
    "Quote Service Counts";
  this.performanceCounterRequestsTotal.CounterName = "# of Requests";
  this.performanceCounterRequestsTotal.MachineName = "NAGELC";
  this.performanceCoutnerRequestsTotal.ReadOnly = false;
  //...
}
```

For the calculation of the performance values you have to add the fields `requestsPerSec` and `bytesPerSec` to the class `QuoteServer`:

```
public class QuoteServer : System.ComponentModel.Component
{
  private int requestsPerSec;
  private int bytesPerSec;
```

The performance counts that show the total values are incremented directly in the `Listener()` method (shown below) of the `QuoteServer` class. You can use `PerformanceCounter.Increment()` to count the number of total requests, and `IncrementBy()` to count the number of bytes sent.

For the performance counts that show the value by seconds, just the two variables, `requestsPerSec` and `bytesPerSec`, are updated in the `Listener()` method:

```
protected void Listener()
{
    try
    {
        listener = new TCPListener(port);
        listener.Start();
        while (true)
        {
            Socket socket = listener.Accept();
            string message = GetRandomQuoteOfTheDay();
            UnicodeEncoding encoder = new UnicodeEncoding();
            byte[] buffer = encoder.GetBytes(message);
            socket.Send(buffer, buffer.Length, 0);
            socket.Close();

            performanceCounterRequestsTotal.Increment();
            performanceCounterBytesSentTotal.IncrementBy(buffer.Length);

            requestsPerSec++;
            bytesPerSec += buffer.Length;
        }
    }
    catch (Exception e)
    {
        string message = "Quote Server failed in Listener: "
                            + e.Message;
        eventLog.WriteEntry(message, EventLogEntryType.Error);
    }
}
```

In order to show updated values every second, add a Timer component. Set the `OnTimer()` method to the `Elapsed` event of this component. The `OnTimer()` method is called once per second, if you set the Interval property to 1000. In the implementation of this method set the performance counts by using the `RawValue` property of the `PerformanceCounter` class:

```
protected void OnTimer (object sender, System.Timers.ElapsedEventArgs e)
{
    performanceCounterBytesSentPerSec.RawValue = bytesPerSec;
    performanceCounterRequestsPerSec.RawValue = requestsPerSec;
    bytesPerSec = 0;
    requestsPerSec = 0;
}
```

perfmon.exe

Now you can monitor the service. You can start the Performance tool by selecting Administrative Tools⇨Performance. Pressing the + button in the toolbar, you can add performance counts. The Quote

Service shows up as a performance object. All the counters that have been configured show up in the counter list as shown in Figure 32-26.

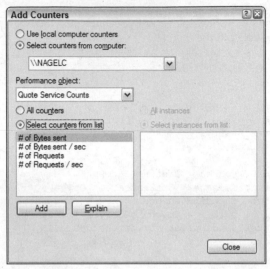

Figure 32-26

After you've added the counters to the performance monitor, you can see the actual values of the service over time (see Figure 32-27). Using this performance tool, you can also create log files to analyze the performance at a later time.

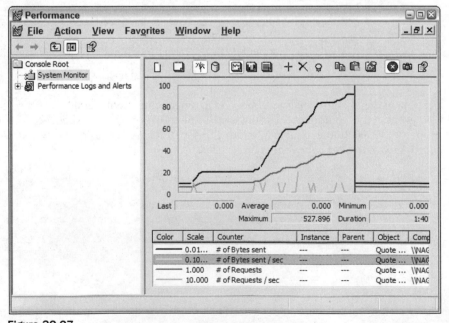

Figure 32-27

Power Events

Starting with Windows 2000, services can also react to power changes. There's support to hibernate the system—the memory is written to disk, so a faster boot is possible. It's also possible to suspend the system in order to reduce the power consumption, but it can be awakened automatically when needed.

For all power events, the service can receive the control code SERVICE_CONTROL_POWEREVENT with additional parameters. The reason for the event is passed through these parameters. The reason could be low battery power, or the system is going to a suspended state, or a power status change. Depending on the circumstance the service should slow down, suspend background threads, close network connections, close files, and so on.

The classes in the `System.ServiceProcess` namespace have support for power events. In the same way as you can configure a service so that it reacts to pause and continue events with the `CanPauseAndContinue` property, you can also set a property for power management: `CanHandlePowerEvent`. Windows 2000 services that handle power events are registered in the SCM with the Win32 API method `RegisterServiceCtrlHandlerEx()`.

If you set the property `CanHandlePowerEvent` to `true` the method `OnPowerEvent()` of the class `ServiceBase` is called. You can override this method to receive power events, and to react with your service implementation accordingly. The reason for the power event is passed in an argument of type `PowerBroadcastStatus`. The possible values of this enumeration are listed in this table:

Value	Description
BatteryLow	The battery power is low. We should reduce the functionality of the service to a minimum.
PowerStatusChange	A switch from battery power to A/C happened, or the battery power slips below a threshold, and so on.
QuerySuspend	The system requests permissions to go into a suspended mode. We could deny the permissions, or prepare to go into the suspended mode by closing files, disconnecting network connections, and so on.
QuerySuspendFailed	Change into the suspended mode was denied for the system. We can go on with the functionality as before.
Suspend	Nobody denied the request to go into the suspended mode. The system will be suspended soon.

Summary

In this chapter, you have seen what Windows Services are and how you can create them with .NET Framework. Applications can start automatically at boot-time with Windows Services, and you can use a privileged system account as the user of the service.

.NET Framework has great support for Windows Services. All the plumbing code that's necessary for building, controlling, and installing services is built into the .NET Framework classes in the `System.ServiceProcess` namespace. By deriving a class from `ServiceBase` you can override methods that are invoked when the service is paused, resumed, or stopped. For installation of services, the classes `ServiceProcessInstaller` and `ServiceInstaller` deal with all registry configurations needed for services.

Support technologies such as event logging and performance monitoring can easily be used with .NET applications with classes in the `System.Diagnostics` namespace: `EventLog` and `PerformanceCounter`.

Index

Page numbers in italic refer to the appendixes, which are posted on www.wrox.com.

J